Nineteenth-Century Literature Criticism

Topics Volume

Guide to Gale Literary Criticism Series

For criticism on	You need these Gale series
Authors now living or who died after December 31, 1959	*CONTEMPORARY LITERARY CRITICISM (CLC)*
Authors who died between 1900 and 1959	*TWENTIETH-CENTURY LITERARY CRITICISM (TCLC)*
Authors who died between 1800 and 1899	*NINETEENTH-CENTURY LITERATURE CRITICISM (NCLC)*
Authors who died between 1400 and 1799	*LITERATURE CRITICISM FROM 1400 TO 1800 (LC)* *SHAKESPEAREAN CRITICISM (SC)*
Authors who died before 1400	*CLASSICAL AND MEDIEVAL LITERATURE CRITICISM (CMLC)*
Authors of books for children and young adults	*CHILDREN'S LITERATURE REVIEW (CLR)*
Black writers of the past two hundred years	*BLACK LITERATURE CRITICISM (BLC)*
Short story writers	*SHORT STORY CRITICISM (SSC)*
Poets	*POETRY CRITICISM (PC)*
Dramatists	*DRAMA CRITICISM (DC)*
Major authors from the Renaissance to the present	*WORLD LITERATURE CRITICISM, 1500 TO THE PRESENT (WLC)*

For criticism on visual artists since 1850, see

MODERN ARTS CRITICISM (MAC)

R

ISSN 0732-1864

Volume 40

Nineteenth-Century Literature Criticism

Topics Volume

Excerpts from Criticism of Various Topics in Nineteenth-Century Literature, including Literary and Critical Movements, Prominent Themes and Genres, Anniversary Celebrations, and Surveys of National Literatures

Joann Cerrito
Editor

Judith Galens
Alan Hedblad
Jelena O. Krstović
Zoran Minderović
Lawrence J. Trudeau
Associate Editors

Gale Research Inc. • DETROIT • WASHINGTON, D.C. • LONDON

STAFF

Joann Cerrito, *Editor*

Judith Galens, Alan Hedblad, Jelena O. Krstović, Lawrence J. Trudeau, *Associate Editors*

Patrick Bruch, Jim Edwards, Kathryn Horste, Michael Magoulias, *Assistant Editors*

Jeanne A. Gough, *Permissions & Production Manager*
Linda M. Pugliese, *Production Supervisor*
Donna Craft, Paul Lewon, Maureen Puhl, Camille P. Robinson, Sheila Walencewicz, *Editorial Associates*

Sandra C. Davis, *Permissions Supervisor (Text)*
Maria L. Franklin, Josephine M. Keene, Michele M. Lonoconus, Shalice Shah, Denise Singleton, Kimberly F. Smilay, *Permissions Associates*
Jennifer A. Arnold, Brandy C. Merritt, *Permissions Assistants*

Margaret A. Chamberlain, *Permissions Supervisor (Pictures)*
Pamela A. Hayes, Keith Reed, *Permissions Associates*
Susan Brohman, Arlene Johnson, Barbara Wallace, *Permissions Assistants*

Victoria B. Cariappa, *Research Manager*
Maureen Richards, *Research Supervisor*
Robert S. Lazich, Mary Beth McElmeel, Donna Melnychenko, Tamara C. Nott, *Editorial Associates*
Karen Farrelly, Kelly Hill, Julie Leonard, Stefanie Scarlett, *Editorial Assistants*

Mary Beth Trimper, *Production Manager*
Catherine Kemp, *Production Assistant*

Cynthia Baldwin, *Art Director*
C. J. Jonik, *Desktop Publisher/Typesetter*
Wille F. Mathis, *Camera Operator*

Library of Congress Catalog Card Number 84-643008
ISBN 0-8103-7979-1
ISSN 0732-1864

Printed in the United States of America
Published simultaneously in the United Kingdom
by Gale Research International Limited
(An affiliated company of Gale Research Inc.)
10 9 8 7 6 5 4 3 2 1

I(T)P™

The trademark **ITP** is used under license.

Contents

Preface

Since its inception in 1981, *Nineteenth-Century Literature Criticism* has been a valuable resource for students and librarians seeking critical commentary on writers of this transitional period in world history. Designated an "Outstanding Reference Source" by the American Library Association with the publication of its first volume, *NCLC* has since been purchased by over 6,000 school, public, and university libraries. The series has covered more than 300 authors representing 26 nationalities and over 15,000 titles. No other reference source has surveyed the critical reaction to nineteenth-century authors and literature as thoroughly as *NCLC.*

Scope of the Series

NCLC is designed to introduce students and advanced readers to the authors of the nineteenth century, and to the most significant interpretations of these authors' works. The great poets, novelists, short story writers, dramatists, and philosophers of this period are frequently studied in high school and college literature courses. By organizing and reprinting commentary written on these authors, *NCLC* helps students develop valuable insight into literary history, promotes a better understanding of the texts, and sparks ideas for papers and assignments. Each entry in *NCLC* presents a comprehensive survey of an author's career or an individual work of literature and provides the user with a multiplicity of interpretations and assessments. Such variety allows students to pursue their own interests; furthermore, it fosters an awareness that literature is dynamic and responsive to many different opinions.

Every fourth volume of *NCLC* is devoted to literary topics that cannot be covered under the author approach used in the rest of the series. Such topics include literary movements, prominent themes in nineteenth-century literature, literary reaction to political and historical events, significant eras in literary history, prominent literary anniversaries, and the literatures of cultures that are often overlooked by English-speaking readers.

NCLC continues the survey of criticism of world literature begun by Gale's *Contemporary Literary Criticism (CLC)* and *Twentieth-Century Literary Criticism (TCLC),* both of which excerpt and reprint commentary on authors of the twentieth century. For additional information about *TCLC, CLC,* and Gale's other criticism series, users should consult the Guide to Gale Literary Criticism Series preceding the title page in this volume.

Coverage

Each volume of *NCLC* is carefully compiled to present:

- criticism of authors, or literary topics, representing a variety of genres and nationalities
- both major and lesser-known writers and literary works of the period
- 7-10 authors or 4-6 topics per volume
- individual entries that survey critical response to an author's work or a topic in literary history, including early criticism to reflect initial reactions; later criticism to represent any rise or decline in reputation; and current retrospective analyses.

Organization

An author entry consists of the following elements: author heading, biographical and critical introduction, list of principal works, excerpts of criticism (each preceded by an annotation and followed by a bibliographic citation), and a bibliography of further reading.

- The **Author Heading** consists of the name under which the author most commonly wrote, followed by birth and death dates. If an author wrote consistently under a pseudonym, the pseudonym will be listed in the author heading and the real name given in parentheses on the first line of the biographical and critical introduction. Also located at the beginning of the introduction to the author entry are any name variations under which an author wrote, including transliterated forms for an author whose language uses a nonroman alphabet.

- The **Biographical and Critical Introduction** outlines the author's life and career, as well as the critical issues surrounding his or her work. References are provided to past volumes of *NCLC* in which further information about the author may be found.

- Most *NCLC* entries include a **Portrait** of the author. Many entries also contain reproductions of materials pertinent to an author's career, including manuscript pages, title pages, dust jackets, letters, and drawings, as well as photographs of important people, places, and events in an author's life.

- The list of **Principal Works** is chronological by date of first publication and identifies the genre of each work. In the case of foreign authors with both foreign-language publications and English translations, the title and date of the first English-language edition are given in brackets. Unless otherwise indicated, dramas are dated by first performance, not first publication.

- **Criticism** in each author entry is arranged chronologically to provide a perspective on changes in critical evaluation over the years. All titles of works by the author featured in the entry are printed in boldface type to enable the user to easily locate discussion of particular works. Also for purposes of easier identification, the critic's name and the publication date of the essay are given at the beginning of each piece of criticism. Unsigned criticism is preceded by the title of the journal in which it appeared. Publication information (such as publisher names and book prices) and parenthetical numerical references (such as footnotes or page and line references to specific editions of works) have been deleted at the editors' discretion to provide smoother reading of the text.

- Critical excerpts are prefaced by **Annotations** providing the reader with information about both the critic and the criticism that follows. Included are the critic's reputation, individual approach to literary criticism, and particular expertise in an author's works. Also noted are the relative importance of a work of criticism, the scope of the excerpt, and the growth of critical controversy or changes in critical trends regarding an author. In some cases, these annotations cross-reference excerpts by critics who discuss each other's commentary.

- A complete **Bibliographic Citation** designed to facilitate location of the original essay or book follows each piece of criticism.

- An annotated list of **Further Reading** appearing at the end of each entry suggests secondary sources on the author. In some cases it includes essays for which the editors could not obtain reprint rights.

Cumulative Indexes

- Each volume of *NCLC* contains a cumulative **Author Index** listing all authors who have appeared in Gale's Literary Criticism Series, along with cross-references to such biographical series as *Contemporary Authors* and *Dictionary of Literary Biography.* Useful for locating authors within the various series, this index is particularly valuable for those authors who are identified with a certain period but who, because of their death dates, are placed in another, or for those authors whose careers span two periods. For example, Fyodor Dostoevsky is found in *NCLC,* yet Leo Tolstoy, another major nineteenth-century Russian novelist, is found in *TCLC* because he died after 1899.

- Each *NCLC* volume includes a cumulative **Nationality Index** which lists all authors who have appeared in *NCLC,* arranged alphabetically under their respective nationalities, as well as Topics volume entries devoted to particular national literatures.

- Each new volume in Gale's Literary Criticism Series includes a cumulative **Topic Index**, which lists all literary topics treated in *NCLC, TCLC, LC 1400-1800*, and the *CLC* Yearbook.

- Each new volume of *NCLC*, with the exception of the Topics volumes, contains a **Title Index** listing the titles of all literary works discussed in the volume. In response to numerous suggestions from librarians, Gale has also produced a **Special Paperbound Edition** of the *NCLC* title index. This annual cumulation lists all titles discussed in the series since its inception and is issued with the first volume of *NCLC* published each year. Additional copies of the index are available on request. Librarians and patrons have welcomed this separate index: it saves shelf space, is easy to use, and is recyclable upon receipt of the following year's cumulation. Titles discussed in the Topics volume entries are not included in the *NCLC* cumulative index.

Citing *Nineteenth-Century Literature Criticism*

When writing papers, students who quote directly from any volume in Gale's Literary Criticism Series may use the following general forms to footnote reprinted criticism. The first example pertains to material drawn from periodicals, the second to material reprinted from books:

[1]T.S. Eliot, "John Donne," *The Nation and Athenaeum*, 33 (9 June 1923), 321-32; excerpted and reprinted in *Literature Criticism from 1400-1800,* Vol. 10, ed. James E. Person, Jr. (Detroit: Gale Research, 1989), pp. 28-9.

[2]Clara G. Stillman, *Samuel Butler: A Mid-Victorian Modern* (Viking Press, 1932); excerpted and reprinted in *Twentieth-Century Literary Criticism,* Vol. 33, ed. Paula Kepos (Detroit: Gale Research, 1989), pp. 43-5.

Suggestions Are Welcome

In response to suggestions, several features have been added to *NCLC* since the series began, including annotations to excerpted criticism, a cumulative index to authors in all Gale literary criticism series, entries devoted to criticism on a single work by a major author, more extensive illustrations, and a title index listing all literary works discussed in the series.

Readers who wish to suggest authors or topics to appear in future volumes, or who have other suggestions, are cordially invited to write the editors.

Acknowledgments

The editors wish to thank the copyright holders of the excerpted criticism included in this volume, the permissions managers of many book and magazine publishing companies for assisting us in securing reprint rights, and Anthony Bogucki for assistance with copyright research. We are also grateful to the staffs of the Detroit Public Library, the Library of Congress, the University of Detroit Library, Wayne State University Purdy/Kresge Library Complex, and the University of Michigan Libraries for making their resources available to us. Following is a list of the copyright holders who have granted us permission to reprint material in this volume of *NCLC*. Every effort has been made to trace copyright, but if omissions have been made, please let us know.

COPYRIGHTED EXCERPTS IN *NCLC* VOLUME 40, WERE REPRINTED FROM THE FOLLOWING PERIODICALS:

Biography, v. 5, December, 1982. © 1982 by the Biographical Research Center. All rights reserved. Reprinted by permission of the publisher.—***Children's Literature Association Quarterly,*** v. 14, Winter, 1989. © 1989 Children's Literature Association. Reprinted by permission of the publisher.—***Eighteenth-Century Life,*** v. 15, November, 1991. © copyright, 1991 University Center for International Studies, University of Pittsburgh. Reprinted by permission of the publisher.—***ELH,*** v. 48, Fall, 1981. Copyright © 1981 by The Johns Hopkins University Press. All rights reserved. Reprinted by permission of the publisher.—***Modern Philology,*** v. LI, February, 1954 for "Ruskin and the Poets: Alterations in Autobiography" by Elizabeth K. Helsinger. Copyright 1954, renewed 1982 by The University of Chicago. Reprinted by permission of the University of Chicago Press and the author./ v. 74, November, 1976 for "The Victorian Approach to Autobiography" by Keith Rinehart. © 1976 by The University of Chicago. Reprinted by permission of the University of Chicago Press and the Literary Estate of Keith Rinehart.—***Nineteenth-Century Fiction,*** v. 33, December, 1978 for " 'The Last Man': Anatomy of Failed Revolutions" by Lee Sterrenburg. © 1978 by The Regents of the University of California Reprinted by permission of The Regents and the author.—***Nineteenth-Century Literature,*** v. 45, March, 1991 for " 'The Shield of Human Nature': Wordsworth's Reflections on the Revolution in France" by Eugene L. Stelzig. © 1991 by The Regents of the University of California. Reprinted by permission of The Regents and the author.—***Prose Studies,*** v. 9, December, 1986. © Frank Cass & Co. Ltd. 1986. Reprinted by permission of Frank Cass & Co. Ltd., 11 Gainsborough Road, London E11, England.—***Studies in Romanticism,*** v. 28, Fall, 1989. Copyright 1989 by the Trustees of Boston University. Reprinted by permission of the publisher.—***Studies in the Novel,*** v. 8, Spring, 1976. © 1976 by North Texas State University. Reprinted by permission of the publisher.—***The Times Literary Supplement,*** n. 4360, October 24, 1986 for "Playing Host to the Doppelgänger" by Robert Alter. © The Times Literary Supplements Limited 1986. Reprinted by permission of the author.—***University of Toronto Quarterly,*** v. L, Winter, 1980-81. © University of Toronto Press 1981. Reprinted by permission of Toronto Press, Inc.—***Wascana Review,*** v. 12, Spring, 1977. Copyright, 1977 by The University of Regina. Reprinted by permission of the publisher.—***Women's Studies: An Interdisciplinary Journal,*** v. 18, 1990. © Gordon and Breach Science Publishers. Reprinted by permission of the publisher.

COPYRIGHTED EXCERPTS IN *NCLC* VOLUME 40, WERE REPRINTED FROM THE FOLLOWING BOOKS:

Apter, T.E. From ***Fantasy Literature: An Approach to Reality.*** Indiana University Press, 1982, Macmillan Press, 1982. Copyright © 1982 by T.E. Apter. All rights reserved. Reprinted by permission of Macmillan, London and Basingstoke.—Borges, Jorge Luis. From ***The Book of Imaginary Beings.*** Translated by Norman Thomas di Giovanni. Revised edition. E.P. Dutton, 1969. Copyright © 1969 by Jorge Luis Borges and Norman Thomas di Giovanni. All rights reserved.—Brooke, Stopford A. From ***Naturalism in English Poetry.*** Dutton 1920. Dent, 1920. Copyright 1920 by E.P. Dutton. Renewed 1948 by Sybil D. Brooke. All rights reserved. Reprinted by permission of J.M. Dent & Sons Ltd.—Brooks, Peter. From "The Opening of the Depths," in ***The French Revolution, 1789-***

1989: Two Hundred Years of Rethinking. Edited by Sandy Petry. Texas Tech University Press, 1989. Copyright 1989 Texas Tech University Press. All rights reserved. Reprinted by permission of the publisher and the author.—Clubbe, John. From "Epic Heroes in 'The French Revolution'," in ***Thomas Carlyle 1981: Papers Given at the International Thomas Carlyle Centenary Symposium.*** Edited by Horst W. Drescher. Peter Lang, 1983. © Verlag Peter Lang GmbH, Frankfurt am Main 1983. Reprinted by permission of Horst W. Drescher.—Cox, Jeffrey N. From "The French Revolution in the English Theater," in ***History & Myth: Essays on English Romantic Literature.*** Edited by Stephen C. Behrendt. Wayne State University Press, 1990. Copyright © 1990 by Wayne State University Press. All rights reserved. Reprinted by permission of the publisher and the author.—Doody, Margaret A. From "English Women Novelists and the French Revolution," in ***Le Femme en Angleterre et dans les colonies américaines aux XVIIe et XVIIIe siècles: acte du Colloque tenu à Paris les 24 et 25 octobre 1975.*** Publications de l'Université de Lille III, 1976. Reprinted by permission of the publisher.—Fleishman, Avrom. From ***Figures of Autobiography: The Language of Self-Writing in Victorian and Modern England.*** University of California Press, 1983. © 1983 by The Regents of the University of California. Reprinted by permission of the publisher.—Gelpi, Barbara Charlesworth. From "The Innocent I: Dickens' Influence on Victorian Autobiography," in ***The Worlds of Victorian Fiction.*** Edited by Jerome H. Buckley. Harvard English Studies Series Vol. 6. Cambridge, Mass.: Harvard University Press, 1975. Copyright © 1975 by the President and Fellows of Harvard College. All rights reserved. Excerpted by permission of the publisher.—Hawthorn, Jeremy. From ***Multiple Personality and the Disintegration of Literary Character: From Oliver Goldsmith to Sylvia Plath.*** Edward Arnold, 1983. © Jeremy Hawthorn 1983. All rights reserved. Reprinted by permission of the publisher.—Helsinger, Howard. From "Credence and Credibility: The Concern for Honesty in Victorian Autobiography," in ***Approaches to Victorian Autobiography.*** Edited by George P. Landow. Ohio University Press, 1979. Copyright © 1979 by Ohio University Press. All rights reserved. Reprinted by permission of the publisher.—Herdman, John. From ***The Double in Nineteenth-Century Fiction.*** The Macmillan Press Ltd., 1990. Published in the U.S. as ***The Double in Nineteenth-Century Fiction: The Shadow Life.*** St. Martin's Press, 1991. © John Herdman 1990. All rights reserved. Reprinted by permission of Macmillan, London and Basingstoke. In the U.S. by St. Martin's Press, Inc.—Keppler, C.F. From ***The Literature of the Second Self.*** University of Arizona Press, 1972. Copyright © 1972 The Arizona Board of Regents. All rights reserved. Reprinted by permission of the publisher.—Kohlschmidt, Werner. From ***A History of German Literature, 1760-1805.*** Translated by Ian Hilton. Macmillan Press Ltd., 1975. All rights reserved. Reprinted by permission of Macmillan, London and Basingstoke.—Kohlschmidt, Werner. From " 'Sturm und Drang'," in ***German Literature: A Critical Survey.*** Edited by Bruno Boesch, translated by Ronald Taylor. Methuen, 1971. © 1971 Methuen & Co. Ltd. Reprinted by permission of the publisher.—Lamport, F.J. From ***German Classical Drama: Theatre, Humanity and Nation, 1750-1870.*** Cambridge University Press, 1990. © Cambridge University Press 1990. Reprinted by permission of the publisher and the author.—Lange, Victor. From ***The Classical Age of German Literature 1740-1815.*** Holmes & Meier Publishers, Inc., 1982. Copyright © Victor Lange 1982. All rights reserved. Reprinted by permission of the publisher.—Massey, Irving. From ***The Gaping Pig: Literature and Metamorphosis.*** University of California Press, 1976. Copyright © 1976 by The Regents of the University. Reprinted by permission of the publisher.—Menhennet, Alan. From " 'Sturm und Drang': The Struggle for Freedom," in ***Order and Freedom: Literature and Society in Germany from 1720 to 1805.*** Weidenfeld and Nicolson, 1973, Basic Books, 1974. © Alan Menhennet 1973. All rights reserved. Reprinted by permission of George Weidenfeld & Nicolson Limited. In the U.S. by Basic Books, a division of HarperCollins Publishers, Inc.—Paulson, Ronald. From ***Representations of Revolution: 1789-1820.*** Yale University Press, 1983. Copyright © 1983 by Yale University. All rights reserved. Reprinted by permission of the publisher.—Radant, Friedhelm. From ***From Baroque to Storm and Stress.*** Croom Helm, 1977. © 1977 Friedhelm Radant. Reprinted by permission of the publisher.—Rank, Otto. From ***The Double: A Psychoanalytic Study.*** Edited and translated by Harry Tucker. The University of North Carolina Press, 1971. Copyright © 1971 by The University of North Carolina Press. All rights reserved. Reprinted by permission of the publisher and the translator.—Roe, Nicholas. From an introduction to ***Wordsworth and Coleridge: The Radical Years.*** Oxford at the Clarendon Press, 1988. © Nicholas Roe 1988. All rights reserved. Reprinted by permission of Oxford University Press.—Rogers, Robert. From ***A Psychoanalytic Study of the Double in Literature.*** Wayne State University Press, 1970. Copyright © 1970 by Wayne State University Press. All rights reserved. Reprinted by permission of the publisher and the author.—Stahl, E.L., and W.E. Yuill. From " 'Sturm und Drang'," in ***German Literature of the Eighteenth and Nineteenth Centuries.***

Barnes & Noble, Inc., 1970, Cressett Press, 1970. —Walther, LuAnn. From "The Invention of Childhood in Victorian Autobiography," in ***Approaches to Victorian Autobiography.*** Edited by George P. Landow. Ohio University Press, 1979.

PHOTOGRAPHS AND ILLUSTRATIONS APPEARING IN *NCLC*, VOLUME 40, WERE RECEIVED FROM THE FOLLOWING SOURCES:

Illustration by W. Stein: **p. 25**; Kevin Brownlow Collection: **p. 171**.

The Double in Nineteenth-Century Literature

INTRODUCTION

The theme of the double, or "second self," is prominent in nineteenth-century literature, from stories by E. T. A. Hoffmann in Germany and Fyodor Dostoevsky in Russia, to works of Robert Louis Stevenson in Great Britain, Edgar Allan Poe in the United States, and countless others. Although stories as ancient as the Greek myth of Narcissus feature characters' fascination with their mirror images, and numerous folk tales center on the mysterious relation between a person and his or her shadow, the double as a dominant element in an artistic work was the creation of the German Romantics. Critics commonly identify the German writer Jean-Paul as the progenitor of the literary double. In his novel *Siebenkäs* Jean-Paul developed the theme of the dual nature of humanity—exemplified in such earlier works as Johann Wolfgang von Goethe's drama *Faust* (1808-32)—presenting in Siebenkäs and his friend Leibgeber two intimately connected figures who are clearly meant to be taken as aspects of a single personality. Subsequently the German fantasist and musician Hoffmann imaginatively and forcefully exploited the artistic potential of doubling in numerous short stories, and, particularly, in the novel *The Devil's Elixir,* which explores the power of demonic forces over a person's existence. While Jean-Paul imagined the double Liebgeber as a counterpart to the main character, Hoffmann conjured up the doppelgänger: a tangible and wholly independent embodiment of sinister powers. Hoffmann's doubles draw from both human psychology and belief in the supernatural, reflecting nineteenth-century interest in scientific psychology but also retaining a link to occult traditions. As writers strove to explain duality according to the laws of reason and common sense, the double became an important metaphor of humankind's struggle to reconcile opposing inner forces, such as destructiveness and creativity. Moreover, as the consequences of the industrial revolution became apparent, writers increasingly began to express in their works the idea of the divided self as a reaction to unnatural pressures exerted on the individual by an alienating society.

While many works, for example Guy de Maupassant's "Le Horla," Stevenson's *The Strange Case of Dr. Jekyll and Mr. Hyde* and Oscar Wilde's *The Picture of Dorian Gray,* feature doubles, the theme attained its highest point in the work of Dostoevsky, who succeeded in synthesizing the various avatars of the double in nineteenth-century literature into a psychologically convincing, profoundly suggestive fictional creation in his 1846 novel *The Double.* Perceiving the rise of industrial capitalism as a threat to human individuality, Dostoevsky absorbed the psychological knowledge of his times but sought answers to the mysteries of human duality in religion. In his view, human duality is more than a sociological or psychological problem: it is the symptom of a profound spiritual malaise which can only be healed by submission to God. Dostoevsky thus utilized the theme of the double to implicitly criticize the dominant intellectual standpoint of the age—rationalism. As Dmitry Chizhevsky wrote, "Dostoevsky's raising of the problem of the double appears as one of the most significant milestones in the nineteenth-century philosophical struggle against ethical rationalism, a struggle which has not by any means been concluded and which may even have barely begun." Indeed, some modern critics argue that the main intellectual legacy of the nineteenth-century double theme is in the realm of philosophy. At the same time, the double remains a potent literary image that effectively symbolizes the problematic duality of the modern individual.

REPRESENTATIVE WORKS

Brown, Charles Brockden
Wieland; or, the Transformation (novel) 1798
Chamisso, Adalbert von
Peter Schlemihls wundersame Geschichte (novella) 1814
[*The Shadowless Man; or, The Wonderful Story of Peter Schlemihl,* 1845]
Collins, Wilkie
The Woman in White (novel) 1859-60
Conrad, Joseph
"The Secret Sharer" (short story) 1912
Dostoevsky, Fyodor Mikhaylovich
Dvoynik (novel) 1846
[*The Double,* 1917]
Hoffman, E. T. A.
"Die Abenteuer der Sylvester-Nacht" (short story) 1814-15
["The Lost Reflection," 1855]
Die Elixire des Teufels (novel) 1815-16
[*The Devil's Elixir,* 1824]
"Der Sandmann" 1817 (short story)
["Coppelius, the Sandman," 1855]
Hogg, James
The Private Memoirs and Confessions of a Justified Sinner (novel) 1824
Jean-Paul (pseudonym of Johann Paul Friedrich Richter)
Blumen-, Frucht- und Dornenstücke, oder Ehestand, Tod und Hochzeit des Armenadvokaten Fr. St. Siebenkäs im Reichsmarktflecken Kuhschappel (novel) 1796-97
[*Flower, Fruit, and Thorn Pieces; or, the Wedded Life, Death, and Wedding of the Advocate of the Poor, Firmian Stanislaus Siebenkas,* 1845]
Maturin, Charles Robert
Melmoth the Wanderer (novel) 1820

Maupassant, Guy de
"Le Horla" (short story) 1887
["The Horla," 1910]
Nerval, Gérard de
Aurélia (novel) 1855
[*Aurelia,* 1932]
Poe, Edgar Allan
"William Wilson" (short story) 1839
Shelley, Mary Wollstonecraft
Frankenstein; or, the Modern Prometheus (novel) 1818
Stevenson, Robert Louis
The Strange Case of Dr. Jekyll and Mr. Hyde (novel) 1886
Wilde, Oscar
The Picture of Dorian Gray (novel) 1891

GENESIS AND DEVELOPMENT OF THE THEME

John Herdman

[*In the following excerpt, Herdman traces the genesis and development of the double theme in literature; he further comments on the specific varieties of the double in nineteenth-century Russian literature, with particular emphasis on Gogol and Dostoevsky.*]

The Romantic obsession with the arbitrary and the irrational found its most characteristic symbolisation in the idea of Fate. No concept is more central to the theme of the double. Again and again protagonists, confronted with an embodiment of the dark forces from within their own natures, attribute their possession to the inscrutable workings of a destiny which they are powerless to evade. The notion of Fate as understood in the pagan classical world now attaches itself to the Augustinian and Calvinist theology of predestination, which carries with it . . . the attendant questions of the status of free will and the possibility of repentance and redemption. Philosophy added its voice to those which spoke of a threat from within to the rule of reason and goodness in the heart and mind, and hence in the society, of man. Kant subscribed to the view that good and evil were equally real and equally at home in the human soul, and spoke of a struggle between reason and the evil and irrational, in which reason must prevail if the good is to survive and flourish.

In the Romantic consciousness, then, a strong rationalist and realistic element persisted which sought to control and order the emergent extravagances of fantasy and imagination. The psychological impulse appealed to both of these conflicting tendencies. While it offered ample scope for the exploration of the vague longings and affective aspirations of the individual soul, it also provided the opportunity to learn more about the constitution of the human mind through close and realistic observation. Such observation, however, was no longer confined to the rational, conscious layers of the psyche. The investigations and theories of such influential figures as Mesmer and, later, G. H. Schubert, were providing access to the night-side of the mind where a second, shadowy self might be discovered.

As it happens, St Augustine . . . had been there before. In Book x of the *Confessions* he asks how it is that in sleep the urges of the flesh imprinted on his memory by his former habits return to him so strongly as almost to amount to acquiescence in the acts that are imaged: 'The power which these illusory images have over my soul and body is so great that what is no more than a vision can influence me in sleep in a way that the reality cannot do when I am awake. Surely it cannot be that when I am asleep I am not myself, O Lord my God?'

To dream and religious vision were now added, for the early Romantics, the more startling and disturbing divisions and dissociations within and of the mind occasioned by mesmeric trance and—witness the experience of Coleridge and De Quincey—opium. The second selves thus suggested or revealed interacted with the old Platonic and occultist yearning for the unification of the severed twin souls of man in the work of the early German Romantics. It was in Germany, in the thrills and terrors and sensations of the *Schauerroman* and the Romantic drama, that the supernatural double, the mainstream of the device which was to be employed with such psychological power and depth by Hoffmann, Hogg and Dostoevsky, had its humble fictional source.

The term *'Doppelgänger'* was invented by Jean-Paul Richter (who used the *nom-de-plume* 'Jean Paul'), but Ralph Tymms, the first chronicler of the psychological provenance of the double as a literary device, rightly asserts [in *Doubles in Literary Psychology,* 1949] that 'Jean Paul's conception of the double is never profound, and sometimes it is quite trivial.' In such works as *Siebenkäs,* Richter presents us with 'pairs of friends (in the original sense of "fellows, two of a pair"), who together form a unit, but individually appear as a "half", dependent on the *alter ego*'. Richter's main importance lies in the strong influence which he exerted upon E. T. A. Hoffmann, who was to exploit the potentialities of the *Doppelgänger* much more profoundly and with a far surer imaginative and psychological grasp.

Goethe was similarly interested in contrasting and complementary pairs of characters who may be taken as the divided parts of a single personality. Early works such as *Wilhelm Meister* prepare the way for the relationship between Faust and Mephisto, who in embodying respectively emotional and rational qualities of personality suggest the sundered elements of an ideal whole: 'Two souls, alas, are housed within my breast.' Yet in spite of the immense and pervasive influence of Goethe's *Faust* it cannot be said that his treatment of the archetypal Faust theme advances specifically the development of the double as a literary device greatly beyond the point attained in Marlowe's drama. Far more influential in terms of dualistic fashion was Schiller's drama *Die Räuber,* with its brother-doubles Franz and Karl Moor, a play whose shock-waves were still registering in 1880 when Dostoevsky made Fyodor Karamazov ironically compare his sons Dmitry and Ivan to the dual heroes of the drama. (pp. 12-13)

We have seen that the double proper had its birth, as a fictional device, in Germany. It is necessary to be clear about the nature of the true double, or *Doppelgänger.* The *Doppelgänger* is a second self, or *alter ego,* which appears as a distinct and separate being apprehensible by the physical senses (or at least, by *some* of them), but exists in a dependent relation to the original. By 'dependent' we do not mean 'subordinate', for often the double comes to dominate, control, and usurp the functions of the subject; but rather that, *qua* double, it has its *raison d'être* in its *relation* to the original. Often, but not always, the subject and his double are physically similar, often to the point of absolute identity. Brothers (sisters are a rarity in this literature), and especially twins, may be doubles, but where this is the case there is always an element, whether overtly supernatural, numinous or otherwise extraordinary, which goes beyond the merely natural relationship. The most characteristic *Doppelgänger* always have a supernatural or subjective *aspect,* which does not imply that, within the scheme of the fictions they inhabit, they have no objective existence. On the contrary, the psychological power of the device lies in its ambiguity, in the projection of the subject's subjectivity upon a being whose reality the structure of the novel or story obliges the reader to accept. It was above all E. T. A. Hoffmann who brought this procedure to maturity.

A second kind of double is that which, in relation to some of the characters of Dostoevsky, has been called by Joseph Frank the 'quasi-double' [*Dostoevsky: The Seeds of Revolt 1821-1849,* 1977]. Quasi-doubles come in various forms, but always have an unambiguously independent existence within the fictional scheme. Frank cites 'characters who exist in their own right, but reflect some internal aspect of another character in a strengthened form'. In the work of Dostoevsky (whose novels furnish examples of almost every kind of double), Smerdyakov in *The Brothers Karamazov* has such an intensive relation to Ivan. Quasi-doubles may also, however, be complementary opposites, whether Platonic soul-mates or, more often, characters whose unlikenesses and contradictions reflect hostility and conflict, yet at the same time mutual dependence and interlocked destinies. Such a pair are Myshkin and Rogozhin in *The Idiot,* who represent a bifurcation and division of an originally conceived single character. Such characters are sometimes inaccurately referred to as 'mirror-images', which implies an identical likeness, though an inverted one; they should rather be thought of as the interlocking pieces of a two-piece jigsaw puzzle, whose oppositeness and complementarity imply a fractured or severed unity.

It is clear that such quasi-doubles may be hard to distinguish from the merely opposite (or congruent) characters who are bound to crop up in the work of even the most naturalistic novelists, since all characterisation involves an element of dialectic; that is, characters may testify to duality without in the least being doubles. We must then ask whether the likeness, opposition or complementarity in question is sufficiently marked to have a clear symbolic function. Dostoevsky, once again, affords an example of the distinction. In *The Brothers Karamazov* Ivan and Alyosha both have their origins in a single character in the original plan for *The Life of A Great Sinner,* whose attributes came to be divided between them; they are brothers and they stand for opposite values, but they are in no sense doubles—Ivan has two doubles, and neither of them is Alyosha. With Myshkin and Rogozhin the case is quite different In their relation there is a consistently developed numinous dimension, something that goes beyond any natural or realistic correspondence: Rogozhin *haunts* Myshkin, and the haunting is clearly developed in such a way as to point to their interwoven destinies and their underlying identity.

Divided, split or schizophrenic characters are, again, not in themselves doubles or *Doppelgänger,* though these terms may become appropriate if and when their division gives rise to a second, sensibly apprehensible personality (even if apprehensible only to the subject), which can occur for instance in the case of a hallucination fictionally presented as a distinct personage. The loose use of the term *'Doppelgänger'* to refer to split personalities, fictional or otherwise (Eigner persistently uses the word in such a sense [Edwin M. Eigner, *Robert Louis Stevenson and Romantic Tradition,* 1966]) is to be avoided, since it blurs important distinctions. Clearly, however, the phenomenon of the double life is closely *related* to the device of the double, and several dualistically inclined writers deal in both types. Often the one can throw revealing light on the other, and we shall have occasion to refer in passing to several stories involving dramatically divided personalities.

The diverse variants of the double flourished unevenly on different national soils. The central stream of the supernatural double was developed by Hoffmann to the point at which the device became a precision tool of psychological penetration, and it quickly became naturalised in Scotland and Russia. That such a small country as Scotland should have contributed, in James Hogg and R. L. Stevenson, two of the foremost masters of the double is a remarkable fact, but though the ultimate reasons for the heightened Scottish awareness of duality may lie deep in the national psyche and history, a proximate causation in the schematic polarities of Calvinist theology can scarcely be in doubt. In Russia dualism became something of a literary fashion through the immense influence of Hoffmann; the Hoffmannisers were selective in what they borrowed from the German romancer, but the double was high on their list of priorities. Dostoevsky took up the theme in the late 1840s at a time when many others, whose concern with it was primarily fashionable, were dropping it; thenceforth it remained central to his apprehension of reality, and in his later work the various strands of the tradition come together and find their culmination.

In England the supernatural double was never truly at home. It is remarkable that Gothic romances such as M. G. Lewis's *The Monk* and Mrs Radcliffe's *The Italian* employ almost every supernatural device except that of the double. The English Gothic novel is none the less important for the development of the theme, because so many of its characteristic preoccupations and motifs are taken up by later works which harness them to the device of the double. *The Monk,* for instance, is a crucial model for Hoffmann's *The Devil's Elixirs.* Some of the earliest examples of quasi-doubles occur in English works, although here there is no clear line of transmission or development. William Godwin's *Caleb Williams,* a work at once affected by and critical of the 'Italian' tale of terror, provides two types of double: a complementary opposite whose character after his death is taken on by his rival, and an externalised embodiment of conscience. Charles Maturin's *Melmoth the Wanderer* (of Irish Protestant provenance, but clearly in the tradition of *The Monk,* though with more considerable claims to literary distinction) features a shadowy doubling between brothers and also an evil second self who is however a clearly independent character.

In America a characteristically materialist and rationalist cast of mind exists in tension with a strong consciousness of the 'other', and a heightened sensitivity to the power of unconscious forces, which is connected with the proximity of the wilderness and the closeness of the irrational and the untamed. Charles Brockden Brown was an enlightened admirer of Godwin but his novels are set on the frontier between civilisation and savagery, and his doubles reflect this dichotomy, in that while they are susceptible of rational explanation, they evoke and coax into activity dark and sinister unconscious powers. Hawthorne and Melville are dualists, but true doubles are not prominent in their work. Poe was obsessively concerned with the mysterious, the eccentric, the other-worldly and the horrible, but he strives to assimilate these preoccupations to an ultimately materialist perspective. His mental temper is profoundly dualistic, and gave rise to at least one classic of the double, 'William Wilson'.

The first *floreat* of the double achieves its consummation by the end of the first quarter of the nineteenth century. *The Devil's Elixirs* appeared in 1814, as did Chamisso's *Peter Schlemihl,* which initiated the sub-genre of 'shadow' romances. *Melmoth,* the last major work of the Gothic tradition, appeared in 1820; Hogg's *Private Memoirs and Confessions of a Justified Sinner* followed in 1824. To 1818 belongs Mary Shelley's *Frankenstein,* one of the great mythic constructs of the century, which, though not a novel about a double in the usual sense, contains strong intimations of a quasi-doubling relationship between creator and monster to which attention has been vividly drawn by Muriel Spark [in *Mary Shelley,* 1988] and Masao Miyoshi [in *The Divided Self: A Perspective on the Literature of the Victorians,* 1969]. To Frankenstein the 'daemon' he has introduced into the world appears 'nearly in the light of my own vampire, my own spirit let loose from the grave'. Spark examines these two characters as 'both complementary and antithetical beings' who are 'bound together by the nature of their relationship', ultimately 'facets of the same personality'. In this they anticipate the symbiotic relationship between the later monster-maker Dr Jekyll and his stunted shadow-self Mr Hyde, the originator locked in symbolic conflict with the sinister power he has unleashed from within his own being.

In the 1830s the double was kept alive by Poe in America and by Gogol and the minor Hoffmannists in Russia, but in Western Europe the theme goes more or less into abeyance as a serious fictional concern for nearly fifty years. Dickens, it is true, sometimes hovers on the verge of creating characters who are at least quasi-doubles. Jonas Chuzzlewit, and Jasper in *Edwin Drood,* are certainly split personalities, murderers with double lives in the tradition of Hoffmann's Cardillac in 'Mademoiselle de Scudéry', but their inner division is not dramatised in terms of the appearance of a fully embodied second self. Various pairs of Dickensian opposites who have been proposed as doubles are scarcely developed in ways which justify the description; the only true exception lies in the dual heroes of *A Tale of Two Cities.* John Gross, writing of this novel, remarks that 'the theme of the double has such obvious attractions for a writer preoccupied with disguises, rival impulses, and hidden affinities that it is surprising that Dickens didn't make more use of it elsewhere' [John Gross and Gabriel Pearson, eds., *Dickens in the Twentieth Century,* 1962]. But, as Gross observes, the device is not very satisfactorily handled here. Charles Darnay and Sidney Carton are, however, doubles in a real sense: strikingly alike in appearance but divergent in character, they symbolically appear together in reflection in the mirror above the dock after Darnay's acquittal at the trial at the Old Bailey; Carton's mingled attraction and dislike for Darnay reflect his own self-hatred and self-love. Henceforth their destinies are inseparable, and it will be Carton's fate to give up his life for the other to whom he is so ambiguously related.

The mid-century decline in the literary double was almost certainly connected with the loss of intellectual respectability of the Romantic psychology on which it was founded. The ideas of Mesmer and Schubert had been taken with great seriousness both by creative artists and by the educated general public, and had found their philosophical counterpart in the idealist metaphysics represented most notably by Schelling; much later they were to regain a measure of recognition as foreshadowings of psychoanalysis and Jungian psychology. But in the middle of the nineteenth century mesmerism and its associated systems of psychological understanding seemed decidedly dated and cranky. It is perhaps significant that Dostoevsky, who alone of major writers carried the techniques of the double forward into the third quarter of the century with renewed vitality and power, had discovered for himself a satisfying intellectual foundation in the psychology of C. G. Carus, who advanced ideas very consistent with those of G. H. Schubert, and who, while enjoying the highest scientific repute as a physiologist, remained devoted to Schelling's idealist understanding of the world. . . . (pp. 14-18)

During these decades of comparative neglect of the double theme by novelists writing with a 'serious' intent—writers, that is, who would use it to shed light on the inner workings of the human mind and soul—it was enthusiastically taken up by other novelists who exploited it for sensational effects. This tradition, in fact, goes all the way back to Jean-Paul Richter and other practitioners of the *Schauerroman.* G. W. M. Reynolds, for instance, in his *Mysteries of London* (1847) describes the protracted haunting by a bad brother of a good brother; Wilkie Collins put the double to sensationalist use in *The Woman in White* (1859-60) and especially in *Armadale* (1864-6); and by the end of the century the theme and other motifs related to it had percolated deeply into the hinterland of popular fiction, as witness the work of the renowned Marie Corelli, who in *The Sorrows of Satan* (1895) paints an engaging devil who haunts the hero and is seen through only by a beautiful popular novelist. No hard-and-fast line, however, can be drawn between serious and sensationalist use of the theme. Stevenson, for example, adopted both approaches in different stories, and we may feel that there was on occasion a significant overlap.

In the last quarter of the century the work of the new French psychologists, led by the radically materialist Taine, reinstated the concept of double personality in the world of scientific psychology. The clinical work in mental institutions of [Pierre Janet and Paul Janet], of Charcot and Binet, largely endorsed the theories of the Romantic psychologists in revealing, as they believed, a second personality (activated, for instance, in somnambulism) eternally at war with the first, and liable to usurp and take possession of the entire life of the subject. But the crucial difference between the Romantic psychologists and their successors the 'nerve doctors' lay, as Eigner observes, 'in the connections or lack of connections which they made between psychology and theology. The psychologists at the end of the century, as one might expect, fought shy of making moral value judgments'. This disjunction was to prove fatal to the central tradition of the supernatural double, which was preeminently a device at the service of a *moral* psychology, essentially anti-determinist in spirit, though usually concerned with protagonists who see their own history deterministically as a product of Fate. To put it at its crudest, the anti-heroes of this tradition go mad because they are bad (usually proud), rather than behaving badly because they are mad.

The dilemma faced by a writer contemplating a work in the tradition of the supernatural double in the new cultural climate is typified by the case of Stevenson. He was a profound admirer of the new psychology and actively interested in psychic research, yet his mind was cast in the ineradicable mould of a morally conceived dualism. If he were to develop the theme of the supernatural double in terms of the new clinical understanding of the divided personality he would be obliged, if he were to remain intellectually respectable, to eschew the moral dimension. Yet it was precisely the moral dimension which—and most unequivocally in *Dr Jekyll and Mr Hyde*—he aimed at. In order to attain his end he must, therefore, approach his theme allegorically, thus making it clear that his viewpoint was different from (though not necessarily opposed to) the scientific one; and this is the path which in fact he chose. Yet the allegorical approach was not capable of the subtlety of penetration which was available to the mode of the supernatural double as practised by Hoffmann and Hogg, and supremely by Dostoevsky, with its unique blend of psychological realism and supernatural, or at least numinous, symbolism, an approach committed to a moral-spiritual understanding of the mind and soul of man.

The alternative route involved bowing to the spirit of the age and dissociating the double from any application to a morally or spiritually based view of the world. This course was chosen by Chekhov when he pointedly described his story 'The Black Monk' as 'the case history of a disease', the disease in question being megalomania. Thus at the close of the nineteenth century we can observe a bifurcation of the broad river of the supernatural double into two streams, the allegorical and what may be called the 'clinical', neither of them capable of the artistic centrality available to the undivided tradition. (pp. 18-20)

. . . . .

The age of Hoffmann and Hogg might be called the 'high noon' of the double in Western Europe; in the middle years of the century . . . the theme fell somewhat into abeyance as a serious literary preoccupation, to experience a new resurgence in the last years of the century, a fresh access of vitality which was related to a revival of the Gothic mode and to new scientific developments which cast a beguiling light on matters of duality and psychic division. In Russia, however, the hiatus was bridged, for the influence of Hoffmann and the 'Russian Hoffmannists' bore new fruit in the 1840s in the early work of Dostoevsky, who throughout his career continued pertinaciously to revert to the preoccupation with duality and self-division which had so fascinated him in his youth. In his last book, *The Brothers Karamazov,* the double proper was to surface again as a crucial dramatic motif.

By far the most influential Russian prose writer of the 1830s and early 1840s was Gogol. The inimitable mixture of social satire, fantastic humour and aberrant psychology which characterises his writing was a rich spawning-ground of dualistic obsession, and in some of his stories he verges on adopting the device of the double to carry these preoccupations. In his most famous story 'The Overcoat' (1842), the prized coat of the wretched clerk Akaky Akakievich becomes his 'companion', a kind of extension of his self, and hence a rudimentary double. In 'The Nose' (1836), Gogol had created a gruesome and evocative image of dissociation: Collegiate Assessor Kovalyov, an aspiring social climber, wakes up one morning to find that his nose has vanished, and when he later sees it in uniform and confronts it, it claims, 'I am a person in my own right!'

[In *The Russian Hoffmannists,* 1963] Charles E. Passage has seen this story as a 'bitter parody' of Hoffmann, a '*reductio ad absurdum*' of the habits of the writer whom Gogol had at first so unreservedly admired: the loss of Kovalyov's nose is absurdly analogous to Spikher's loss of his mirror-image in 'Die Abenteuer der Sylvesternacht', and its adventures are a burlesque of Hoffmann's *Doppelgänger* themes. The nose travels all over St Petersburg in the guise of a State Councillor, cutting a figure to which Kovalyov cannot attain; there are satirical references to the popularity of magnetism in the capital at that date. Eventually, the nose returns to the Collegiate Assessor's face as mysteriously as it had parted from it. Still earlier, in the farcical tale 'The Story of the Quarrel between Ivan Ivanovich and Ivan Nikiforovich' (1834), Gogol had used to great comic effect the motif of complementary opposites. The two absurd characters are 'friends the like of whom the world had never seen', of whom it was said that 'the devil himself tied Ivan Nikiforovich and Ivan Ivanovich together with a rope'; but they become mortal enemies when, in the course of a crazy altercation, one of them calls the other a goose.

These essays on the theme of the double are fairly vestigial; the importance of Gogol in the present context lies in the immense influence which he exercised on Dostoevsky, who was to become one of the great masters of the double. Gogol's characters are typically viewed from without, sometimes, as in the case of Akaky Akakievich, with real compassion, but always with the detached, microscopic eye of a scientist examining a specimen. The reader is encouraged to deduce, as it were, the obscure movements of their souls from the very exact information which Gogol provides about their externals.

Dostoevsky, by nature a writer of passionate psychological inwardness, is also deeply interested in the clues provided by behaviour and appearance to the inner psychology of his characters. His early work inhabits the world of Gogol, the world of seedy, depressed, tyrannised government clerks and minor civil servants looked down upon as insects by the lofty superiors to whose altitude they hopelessly aspire. But from the start Dostoevsky was instinctively involved with the great passions of the human soul, though not, in his pre-Siberian days, from any consciously developed or deeply committed position. In his attempts to harness the style and tone of Gogol to the demands of a more emotional and inward-directed art he turned to the tale of terror, and drew on what he had imbided from the example of writers such as Mrs Radcliffe, Eugene Sue and, above all, Hoffmann.

Yet if *The Double* (1846) was born of a marriage between Hoffmann and Gogol, Dostoevsky himself was very much more than just the midwife. His distinctive tone of voice and way of seeing things is already unmistakably present in this, his second novel. Greatly shaken in his high hopes for the book, and his confidence in its excellence, by the quite hostile response it provoked after the rapturous reception of *Poor Folk* by Belinsky and his circle, Dostoevsky continued to believe that the idea itself was first-rate and seminal, and that there were elements in it that were of great and permanent value. During the 1860s he planned to recast it in a radically new form to do the concept greater justice and to reflect his new ideological preoccupations; but this was never done. The revision which he undertook in 1866, resulting in the version with which we are familiar, was much less far-reaching: he cut out the original mock-heroic framework, simplified the plot, and strengthened the ending by making Golyadkin's ultimate fate more explicit. As Joseph Frank observes, 'Golyadkin is the ancestor of all Dostoevsky's great split personalities, who are always confronted with their doubles or quasi-doubles (whether in the form of other "real" characters, or as hallucinations) in the memorable scenes of the great novels.'

Dostoevsky's story introduces to the literature of the double the element of humour, which had earlier, if present at all, been merely marginal or incidental. The humorous tone derives from Gogol, though its particular *timbre* is already very much Dostoevsky's own: according to Passage, the idea for *The Double* had its origin in an attempt to amalgamate the spirit of Gogol's 'Diary of a Madman' with the framework of Hoffmann's 'Sylvesternacht', whence the important role of the mirror-image in *The Double.* It is a very funny book, combining the mock-heroic, the absurd, sometimes almost the grotesque, with an inspired inwardness which imparts to the comic vision an underlying realism. The horror of the tale is entirely internalised: its hero, Mr Golyadkin, does nothing outwardly wicked or outrageous, yet his humiliated soul is fertile in monstrous growths.

Dostoevsky's perception of his protagonist's weakness and vanity is relentless, and the narrative tone may seem cruel in its detachment, the mocking, parodic distance of its viewpoint, yet his power of entering imaginatively into the minute obscurities, hesitances and dubieties of the psyche involves a counterbalancing sympathy and understanding. The novel is also more 'psychological' in a modern scientific sense than anything we have yet encountered: we are now closer to the world of the neurosis, the complex and the case history. With Dostoevsky, though, psychology is never divorced from the moral consciousness. Mr Golyadkin does go mad, but his madness has its roots not only in the restrictions, frustrations and oppressions of his social situation, but in vanity, ambition, envy and wounded pride. Dostoevsky's *feuilleton* for the novel says that Golyadkin 'goes mad out of *ambition,* while at the same time despising ambition and even suffering from the fact that he happens to suffer from such nonsense as ambition'.

On the morning on which we first make the acquaintance of Mr Golyadkin, his first action on rising from his bed is to look in the mirror, and we are told that he is 'evidently quite satisfied with all that he saw there'. The world is smiling on him, and he responds with a 'complacent smile'. The first emotion he exhibits on contact with another human being, his servant, Petrushka, is 'righteous indignation'; riding in a carriage he assumes a 'sedate and decorous air' when he thinks he is being looked at. It is quickly apparent that Mr Golyadkin's dominant characteristics are extreme self-consciousness, morbid suspiciousness and complacent vanity. When the head of the section of his Department passes in a droshky, he is utterly overcome with confusion, with 'indescribable anguish', for Mr Golyadkin does not usually ride in a carriage. Shall he acknowledge their acquaintance? he asks himself. 'Or shall I pretend it's not me but somebody else strikingly like me, and look as if nothing's the matter?' He raises his hat to Andrey Philippovich, but at the same time whispers to himself, 'It's quite all right; this is not me at all, Andrey Philippovich, it's not me at all, not me, and that's all about it'. The psychic dissociation has already begun, and his flight from himself will become complete with the appearance of the double whom, by these words, he in a sense conjures up.

Mr Golyadkin's consciousness is riven by inner conflict and he swings constantly from arrogance and self-assertion to utter self-doubt, collapse of confidence and self-depreciation. He has two mechanisms of defence to which he recurrently resorts: 'a terrible challenging stare . . . a stare calculated to reduce all his enemies to dust', and an inner voice which, however sorry his plight, seeks to reassure him that in spite of everything he is really 'all right'. He believes that he has been invited to a very important dinner party, but on the way he feels suddenly impelled to visit his physician, Dr Rutenspitz, an impressive elderly gentleman 'with an expressive glittering eye'. The description of Golyadkin's excruciating indecision and self-consciousness at the start of their interview—and even his paranoia—cannot fail to remind one of Dostoevsky's own sufferings in this respect during his tormented youth—for the novelist's crippling social gaucherie and sense of persecution apparently disappeared during his Siberian exile. (pp. 99-103)

Dostoevsky's masterly treatment of the theme of the double in this early novel . . . combines a more clinically searching and carefully elaborated psychological realism than anything attempted by his predecessors (enhanced by a wonderful exploitation of the previously untapped comic potentiality of the motif), with the retention of essential traditional elements. The place of supernatural and fantastic causation in earlier double romances is here entirely supplied by the subjective and hallucinatory emanations of the protagonist's psyche (a development initiated by Hoffmann and Hogg, but in their work still ambiguously intertwined with the supernatural); but the independent existence of the double is safeguarded by a narrative structure which requires our acceptance of his objective presence, at least at some points in the story.

In later writers . . . this subjective-objective balance will be lost, largely due to changes in sensibility connected with scientific and psychological advance and altered attitudes to religious belief, changes which make it more difficult to render convincing such an interpenetration of the moral-spiritual and the physical worlds. Tales of the double then tend to divide off, on the one hand into pure moral allegory, which depends once more on the frankly fantastic, or on a scientism that is really glorified magic; and on the other into a merely clinical interpretation which lacks any spiritual dimension.

It is Dostoevsky's strength that his innovating development and extension of the psychological-realistic strand is securely based on traditional moral foundations. This is underlined by the pointed diablerie of the closing scenes, but the source of Golyadkin's troubles in his exclusive preoccupation with self is reverted to throughout the novel. He is not just an unfortunate victim of mental disorder, nor yet simply of social injustice, though that element is undoubtedly contributory. In spite of his being partly at the mercy of his social circumstances, of the autocratic, hierarchically repressive Russian society of his day, his character is relentlessly depicted by Dostoevsky as that of a man in whom vanity, pride, paltry ambition and envy have been allowed to develop monstrously and unchecked. The psychic disintegration which overtakes him is thus the fruit of what is traditionally called sin, and particularly of a variety of the sin of pride, which we have repeatedly observed to be the precondition for the appearance of a double.

Mr Golyadkin himself mutely acknowledges the connection between his mental collapse and his transgressions when, in the penultimate sentence of the book, he perceives the doctor as judge. Because *The Double* is a comic novel, this view may at first sight appear to be overstated, but the analogy of Dostoevsky's later work may persuade us otherwise. In his last novel he resorts once again to the device of the double to express one of the most important thematic ingredients of his narrative, and here, as in *The Double,* the appearance of the second self is associated with mental breakdown, this time quite explicitly arising from the dark, evil side of the subject's psyche, and specifically from the sin of pride.

Joseph Frank has expressed the view that Dostoevsky's final dissatisfaction with the form of his novel refers to its 'uncertain oscillation between the psychic and the supernatural', the fear that the objective aspect of Golyadkin's double was too troubling and mysterious for the reader. Feeling this as a weakness, Dostoevsky makes sure that this ambivalence in the status of the double does not recur in his later work: 'his doubles will either be clear-cut hallucinations, or what may be called "quasi-doubles"—characters who exist in their own right, but reflect some internal aspect of another character in a strengthened form'. This supposition is highly plausible, but it may well be that adverse criticism had caused Dostoevsky to question a procedure which his original artistic instinct had assured him could be both valid and effective. The ambivalence referred to is an inherent characteristic of the supernatural double, and to realise that it can constitute its essential strength, indeed its *raison d'être,* we need look no further than Hoffmann's Coppelius or the *Justified Sinner.* In *The Double* it is partly this ambiguity which makes possible an analysis that is, as Chizhevsky puts it, both 'realistically' and 'transcendentally psychological', a successful interpenetration of naturalistic and fantastic modes. [René Wellek, ed., *Dostoevsky,* 1962]. But Dostoevsky did move in the direction Frank indicates, and the results certainly cannot be any cause for regret.

The split personality and the divided will are such pervasive and important themes in the work of Dostoevsky that a full treatment of them would be almost equivalent to a comprehensive study of the novelist's *oeuvre.* During his years in the prison-camp and his subsequent exile in Siberia, Dostoevsky's attitudes underwent a profound transformation. The social-psychological frame of reference of his early work is transcended by a moral and metaphysical world-view in which suffering becomes the precondition for spiritual advance and understanding, the Russian people appear as the central symbol of his hope for the salvation of society, and their orthodox faith, centred on the Russian conception of Christ, is seen as the road to individual redemption and freedom.

In 1854, shortly after his release from *katorga,* Dostoevsky formed a project, never carried out, of translating C. G. Carus's notable work, *Psyche, zur Entwicklungsgeschichte der Seele,* which had been published in 1846, the same year as *The Double.* Carus, a highly distinguished physiologist and a man of very wide culture, inherited the psychological tradition of G. H. Schubert, and exercised an influence on the later work of Dostoevsky comparable to that of Schubert on the Romantic generation. While Carus subscribed to the most advanced biological and physiological theories, he remained committed to Schelling's idealist conception of the universe, with which the young Dostoevsky was permeated, and entertained what we would now call a 'holistic' view of nature. The universe, for Carus, had its origin in a Divine Idea, and the human soul was immortal because it shared in the Divine creative principle. 'The law of love' should be the animating principle of human conduct, moral evil is comparable to a state of physical illness, and conscience acts as a regulator to correct moral and psychic imbalance and restore the equilibrium of the soul.

Carus believed that 'The key to the understanding of the essence of the conscious life of the soul lies in the region of the unconscious.' It is not surprising, then, that he has been regarded as an important forerunner of psychoanalysis, but his world-view is much closer to Jung's than to that of Freud. Dostoevsky's distinctive artistic province, the area in which his genius was most characteristically at home, was that of describing the emergence into consciousness of obscure, complex and half-submerged movements of the soul, and here the ideas of Carus provided him with an invaluable theoretical framework to facilitate the articulation of his intuitive insights.

Dostoevsky used a rich variety of approaches to dramatise internal division. Among these is the shadowy doubling of one character by another quite separate one, in whom are evoked and embodied latent or hidden or half-developed elements of the psyche of the first character, or even elements which the novelist has excluded purposely from the character. Many years ago Harry Levin, in [*The Overreacher: A Study of Christopher Marlowe,* 1954], likened the dialogues between Faustus and Mephistophilis to 'those cat-and-mouse interrogations, in which Porfiry [the examining magistrate in *Crime and Punishment*] teaches the would-be criminal, Raskolnikov, to accuse and convict himself'; that is, he is Raskolnikov's buried conscience, externalised and challenging him in the form of another. The figure of Svidrigailov, in the same novel, reflects in a heightened form the tendencies which have turned Raskolnikov into a murderer, and confronts him with the embodied moral implications of the nihilistic philosophy which has inspired him.

In *The Idiot,* Myshkin and Rogozhin were in Dostoevsky's original conception one single, complex and ambivalent figure, akin to Stavrogin in *The Devils,* a figure who in successive drafts separates off into two opposite, contradictory characters who are also of necessity complementary. George Steiner describes their relationship incisively [in *Tolstoy or Dostoevsky,* 1967]:

> Rogojin is Muishkin's original sin. To the extent that the Prince is human, and thus heir to the Fall, the two men must remain inseparable companions. They enter the novel together and leave it to a common doom. . . . Their inextricable nearness is a Dostoevskyan parable on the necessary presence of evil at the gates of knowledge. . . . Without darkness, how should we apprehend the nature of light?

Nowhere is their identity more apparent than in the scenes in which Rogozhin mysteriously shadows Myshkin before the latter succumbs to the renewed onset of his epilepsy, the Prince's disturbed state of consciousness lending a phantasmagoric quality to his perception of the appearances of his rival for the love of the possessed Nastasya Philippovna. On his arrival at the station that morning he had seen 'two strange, burning eyes' staring at him out of the crowd, but believes that he has imagined it. Later he goes to see Rogozhin and realises that the eyes were his, though Rogozhin effectively denies it. Myshkin notices a new knife on his table. He and Rogozhin exchange crosses, Myshkin asserts their brotherhood and Rogozhin renounces his claim to Nastasya. But when they part the Prince becomes conscious that he is being followed, and is repeatedly aware of Rogozhin's fiery eyes fixed upon him. He experiences his suspicion of the other as a potential murderer as almost a 'temptation', a 'demon' which has taken possession of him and which he cannot shake off.

He goes to Nastasya's house, but she is not there; he realises that he has gone because he expected to see 'those eyes' there, and indeed he does see them: Rogozhin stands opposite, 'like an accuser and a judge—in full view'. Unbearably ashamed of his suspicions yet aware that they have grown to conviction, Myshkin returns to his hotel and sees Rogozhin lurking inside the gates by the stairs. He follows him up, and is confronted by his rival's two eyes staring at him from a niche. A knife flashes in Rogozhin's hand, as it did in the hand of Medardus, but before he can strike the Prince falls to the ground with the terrible scream of an epileptic fit. It is the scream which saves the Prince, for the attacker is paralysed by its 'unbearable' and 'mystical' horror, the sense that the victim is alienated from himself: 'One gets the impression that it is someone inside the man who is screaming'.

These scenes are eerie with the sense of shifting and shared identity. The two characters acknowledge their kinship, the almost mystical cords that bind them together, yet this finds expression in fear on the one hand and murderous antagonism on the other. Myshkin's perception of Rogozhin as accuser and judge strikes the reader as a kind of acknowledgement on the Prince's part of the impossibility of his Christ-like goodness, a recognition that Rogozhin, as his blood-brother, is a separated part of himself which is necessary to his wholeness; it is the lack of his Rogozhin–part which is the focus of his ineffectuality, of the failure to bring into reality the ideal which he represents. It is this, too, which is symbolised in the self-alienation expressed by his epileptic cry.

Versilov, in *A Raw Youth,* is conscious of a mental split which he likens to the presence beside one of his double; consulting a medical book, he finds that this experience is said to be the first sign of a serious mental derangement which may end fatally. Something of the sort is the case with Stavrogin, who in passages excised when *The Devils* appeared in book form, tells Dasha about visitations he has received from a 'demon' who is 'stupid and impudent' and wishes to make himself out to be independent, whereas Stavrogin knows that 'it is I myself divided in different ways and that I speak with myself'. In his 'Confession' he relates to the monk Tikhon how these hallucinations came to him, mostly at night, when he 'saw or felt beside him the presence of some kind of malignant creature, mocking and "rational", in all sorts of guises and in different characters, but it is the same, and it always makes me angry. . . . It is myself, different aspects of myself. Nothing more. You don't think, do you, that because I've just added that—er—phrase I'm still doubtful and not sure that it's me and not in fact the devil.' Tikhon is aware of his perplexity, and tells him that it is 'most probably' an illness, though he confirms that devils most certainly exist. Stavrogin himself then makes a point of asserting that he believes canonically 'in a personal devil, not an allegory'; so the purely hallucinatory status of his demon remains somewhat in doubt.

Stavrogin is the ultimate in protean personalities. Chizhevsky has argued that he does not really live himself, but others live for him and through him, so that he dwells 'among the emanations of his spirit, in a world of phantoms, of "demons" '. Thus Shatov and Kirilov, themselves utterly opposing characters in their ideologies and views of life, both live in his shadow, as his disciples, in a sense his creations, acting out the potentialities that lie latent and unrealised in Stavrogin's rich but also finally barren soul. Pyotr Verkhovensky is his 'ape', Fedka the convict his 'little devil'. All look to him for leadership, see in him either an idol and a prophet or else a great criminal; but he cannot carry his spiritual potential into reality because he is 'divided from living reality by his pride, his limitless presumption, his scornful relation to life, his contempt for his concrete neighbours'—ultimately by his complete lack of love. Fundamentally unrelated, he is unable to act in the real world, hc knows 'only negation', and this negation finds its final expression in his suicide. His fruitless spiritual power is known only through his multifarious emanations, his doubles, and in their actions it is seem to be a power mostly for evil.

Stavrogin's hallucinatory double remains a shadowy creation, alluded to but not active in the dramatic structure of *The Devils.* The major characters who function as 'emanations' of his soul, on the other hand, carry the idea of the double into a dimension very far removed from its roots, and one that goes beyond the scope of the present study. In *The Brothers Karamazov* (1880), however, Dostoevsky returns to the theme in a way that is more traditional and delimited, though closely related to the approach developed in the earlier work. Ivan, the most inwardly riven of the brothers, attracts both types of double. In the character of Smerdyakov he is confronted with an embodiment of his half-conscious wicked desires, of everything in himself that is vulgar, inferior and evilly disposed. Like the second Mr Golyadkin, but in a far more sinister way, Smerdyakov acts out what in the primary character are impulses that are not fully formed, which are desired but have not received the full consent of the will. But Ivan also spawns another kind of double: as he succumbs to mental breakdown he projects a hallucinatory embodiment of his intellectual pride, his destructive negativity, and this figure is explicitly identified by Ivan as his Devil.

The Devils and *The Brothers Karamazov* were both in origin fragments of a huge projected work to be called *The Life of a Great Sinner,* and it is certain that Ivan's Devil brings to fruition the idea of hallucinatory phantoms emanating from a morbidly divided psyche which is adumbrated in Stavrogin's 'Confession'. The unrealised project was to trace the life history of a would-be saint who struggles to true sainthood by way of the expurgation of demonic pride. In *The Brothers Karamazov* both Ivan and Alyosha fall heir to different attributes of this single character as originally conceived.

The Brothers Karamazov treats of three brothers, and also a fourth. C. G. Jung has written a good deal of what he has called 'the dilemma of 3 + 1'. He describes how in alchemy 'There are always four elements, but often three of them are grouped together, with the fourth in a special position [*Psychology and Alchemy,* 1968]. Similarly the Christian Trinity can become a quaternity by the addition of the Devil (or of the Virgin Mary). This 'uncertainty as to three or four amounts', according to Jung, [points] 'to a wavering between the spiritual and the physical'. Psychologically, in the context of the self, three is a 'defective quaternity', the complement of quaternity being unity. In the *complexio oppositorum* which is the self, the quaternity is contrasted with the 3 + 1 motif, 'and the positive, good, admirable and lovable human being with a daemonic, misbegotten creature who is negative, ugly, despicable and an object of fear'.

In *The Brothers Karamazov,* the first half of this contrast exactly describes the saintly Alyosha, the second half the bastard Smerdyakov. In Jung's psychology of the functions there are three relatively differentiated functions and one undifferentiated, 'inferior' function. In Dostoevsky's novel the 3 + 1 motif is exemplified in the three legitimate Karamazov brothers and the illegitimate fourth, who bears every mark of inferiority—the bastard offspring of Fyodor Karamazov's intercourse with an idiot girl, a 'lackey', epileptic and morally despicable.

Of the three legitimate brothers, Dmitry, the eldest, represents the earthly, the physical, the unrestrainedly sensual. Alyosha, as we have seen, is almost entirely spiritual, the nearly impossible incarnation of a soaring religious ideal. Midway between them stands Ivan, divided between his sensual Karamazov nature and his higher aspirations. It is because he is divided that he attracts to himself a double in the form of Smerdyakov, who is his inferior nature separated off and personified. Smerdyakov is his admirer, his ape and his parody. Ivan's intellectual prowess finds its distorted reflection in the servant's cleverness and animal cunning. One of the first things we are told about Ivan is that very early in his life he began to show 'quite an extraordinarily brilliant aptitude for learning'. Of Alyosha, by contrast, we are told that though he was always one of the best pupils 'he was never singled out as the top boy of the form'. The very first opinion about Ivan expressed by another character is, 'He's proud.' Intellectual pride is Ivan's leading characteristic and the root of his inner conflict.

Passage has argued forcefully that the ground-plan of *The Life of a Great Sinner* is based on the structure of *The*

Devil's Elixirs, and that *The Brothers Karamazov* inherits this schema. Certainly the relation of Ivan to Smerdyakov echoes that of Medardus to Count Victor, and it is plausible that Ivan's Devil owes something to Peter Schönfeld/Pietro Belcampo. It is true also that Father Zossima's sending of Alyosha into the world can be related to the similar action of Prior Leonardus with respect to Medardus; but Passage is surely on less firm ground when he claims that Alyosha, undergoing a similar temptation, fails and falls. The fact is that Alyosha does not fall, unless to be subject to temptation is in itself to fall, which, of course, it is not.

The argument is based on the assumption that *The Brothers Karamazov* is simply the first part of *The Life of a Great Sinner,* and that Dostoevsky's references to Alyosha as the hero of a future novel indicate that he is the great sinner whose history was to be developed in the manner originally intended. It is far more likely, however, that the primary conception of this character became split into the two separate figures of Ivan and Alyosha, which was precisely the fate of the earlier projected protagonist whose personality came to be divided in *The Idiot* between Myshkin and Rogozhin; and that Dostoevsky decided to develop his theme in terms of a dialectical dramatic encounter between the opposing values represented by these two brothers. If this is the case, spiritual pride inheres solely in Ivan, and indeed all the internal evidence points to such a conclusion.

The activating theme of *The Brothers Karamazov,* that which propels into motion the great metaphysical issues which the novel confronts, is parricide. In the last years of his life Dostoevsky was perhaps reliving and re-enacting his tangled emotions respecting the death of his own father, who was murdered by his serfs when Dostoevsky was seventeen. It is the naïvely outspoken and impetuous Dmitry who first articulates the longing to kill the hateful and hated father (hateful and hated to all but Alyosha): 'Why does such a man live?' he snarls; and old Karamazov cries out to the witnesses of the outburst, 'Listen, listen, monks, to the parricide!' Yet Dmitry, though accused and convicted of murdering his father, is not the parricide. Dmitry wants and threatens to kill his father, but does not do so; Smerdyakov actually does so; but it is Ivan who, desiring it, passively and half-consciously colludes in the murder and thus makes it possible, and at last comes to believe himself the true parricide.

From the time of Ivan's arrival in 'our town' Smerdyakov, his father's cook, shows an admiration for him and a desire to imitate him. His atheistic and reductive arguments, superficial and sometimes illogical but always tortuously cunning, reflect in a horrible distorted fashion the nihilistic blankness at the heart of Ivan's brilliantly articulated and passionately expressed discourses on God, the world and the Devil. Old Karamazov shrewdly divines that the servant's speeches are for Ivan's benefit and mischievously encourages the latter to praise him. Ivan for his part exhibits a fascinated, though often repelled, interest in Smerdyakov, who becomes in a sense his protégé. The servant is repeatedly described as shrivelled and 'eunuch-like'; the idea which we are encouraged to form of him is of one who is unproductive, barren, sterile and malicious. Yet it is just these qualities in him which make Ivan see in him 'First-class material . . . when the time comes'. Ivan means the time of revolution; and it is Smerdyakov's essential heartlessness, his empty but envious negativity, which will make him 'first-class material'.

Ivan too has a cold and heartless side to his character. When Dmitry, overwhelmed by fury, resentment and jealousy, rushes into his father's house and attacks him, kicking him viciously on the head, Ivan whispers, 'with a malicious grin, "One reptile will devour another reptile, and serve them both right!" ' It is a phrase which will later repeatedly return to haunt him. Alyosha shudders, and Ivan adds, 'I won't of course let him be murdered as I didn't just now'. But in the event Ivan does let him be murdered, though the murderer is not Dmitry but Smerdyakov. Ivan is not, however a whited sepulchre, but a man in real conflict. There is a passionate side to his nature, and even an impulsively sensual one. When he talks to Alyosha about his love for children, about their suffering and about how the doctrine of inherited sin is 'incomprehensible to the human heart here on earth', he is speaking with full and passionate conviction. He believes it, too, when he says that 'if the devil doesn't exist and, therefore, man has created him, he has created him in his own image and likeness'. (pp. 110-19)

The theme of moral responsibility has been insistently emphasised throughout the novel. Ivan knows very well that he *did* collude with Smerdyakov in order to fulfil his desire for his father's death, yet if he can believe that Smerdyakov is not the actual killer then he can push further from him the sense of responsibility. He is too honest, however, to allow the voice of his conscience to be stilled. Almost masochistically he three times goes to visit the servant to try to assure himself, one way or the other, of the truth. (p. 121)

[After his last meeting with Smerdyakov], Ivan's further instruction in self-knowledge will be acquired in his confrontation with his second, phantasmal double. We have already learned that he receives visits from a hallucinatory second self. When Alyosha sought to assure him that he was not the murderer, Ivan at once believed that his brother must have been in the room when 'he' came, that it was 'he' who had told Alyosha of Ivan's thoughts. Now the reader is to make the acquaintance of this visitor, who as it were 'takes over' from Smerdyakov, raising Ivan's quarrel with himself to a higher level of consciousness.

We must be clear, however, that the 'Devil', as Ivan thinks of him and as he characterises himself, is entirely a hallucination. The narrator emphasises that his appearances are pathological, symptomatic of the severe nervous breakdown to which Ivan is soon to succumb. The cup which he hurls at his double is still intact on the table when Alyosha enters the room. Ivan knows this; the question which torments him is whether the apparition is a mere emanation of his psyche and nothing more, or *corresponds* to a non-physical but real entity in the spiritual world. He is an embodiment of the evil within Ivan; but is he also an embodiment of an evil that exists *in itself,* and independent of any individual? The question is not answered, but on it hinges the dialectic of Ivan's argument with his double.

The visitor comes in the guise of a sponger, 'a well-bred gentleman who was rather hard-up . . . ready to assume any amiable expression that occasion should demand'. Ivan is clear enough about the relationship between them: '*it is I,* I myself who am talking and not you!' To begin with he denies his reality with fury: 'You're the embodiment of myself, but only of one side of me—of my thoughts and feelings, but only the most vile and stupid.' He addresses him as a 'flunkey', the epithet with which he has frequently insulted Smerdyakov, and regards him, too, as 'stupid and vulgar'. Yet he knows that he is insulting himself, for the phantom is only himself with a different face, one who put his own thoughts into words.

The Devil propounds his own position. He is a fallen angel who sometimes assumes a human form, 'and yet I'm only your nightmare and nothing more'. But this is only his 'special method' of convincing Ivan of his reality. When the latter protests again that his visitant is not an independent entity but 'I and nothing more', the Devil makes the essential point: 'Well, if you like, I have the same philosophy as you. That would be fair.' In his unwelcome guest's flippant, sceptical, nihilistic rationalism Ivan is forced to see, more unavoidably than in the distorting mirror of Smerdyakov's tortured logic, the moral emptiness on which his own more high-flown and poetic arguments are really founded. Confronted by this reflection, Ivan changes his ground: he still does not believe in the Devil's real existence, but he would like to, for otherwise he must acknowledge this horror as existing only in himself, and consequently must accept responsibility for it.

The Devil now has Ivan at his mercy. 'Leave me, please, you are hammering on my brain like an excruciating nightmare', the sick man pleads, in words which echo the experience of Mr Golyadkin when confronted by *his* double. The visitor, however, is relentless. He tells Ivan that he is hurt in his aesthetic feelings and, more importantly, in his pride: 'how could such a vulgar devil come to visit such a great man?' Ivan is in torment: all that is 'stupid' in him, all that he believes he has rejected and flung out 'like carrion' is being thrown back in his face. He is deeply and furiously ashamed: 'Why should my soul have begotten such a flunkey as you?' he cries in anguish as he recognises the Smerdyakov in himself. The Devil now rams his message home: Ivan has seen that in order to overturn society all that must be done is to destroy 'the idea of God in mankind'. Then man will become divinised and the man-god will appear, and then 'everything is permitted'. Dostoevsky here offers his deepest critique of the philosophy of Nietzsche, which he hated and feared so much because he was in many ways so close to it himself and recognised its attraction. So the Devil leaves his cruellest thrust to the last: 'All this is very charming; only, if you want to lead a life of crime, what do you want the sanction of truth for?'

This is too much for Ivan and he hurls his cup at his visitor. And here, with the sense of timing of which he is such a master, Dostoevsky switches his attack from the realm of philosophical argument to that of dramatic enactment. Alyosha arrives with a piece of news, and the Devil vanishes. Smerdyakov, the Judas within Ivan, has hanged himself. Ivan seems to know it: 'it was *he* who told me that'. For Smerdyakov had not sought the sanction of truth in order to lead a life of crime. His crime has been committed in the true spirit of the philosophy of his teacher, Ivan, taken to the conclusion from which Ivan shrank.

He has commited the murder for no real reason, but only because 'everything is permitted'. At their last interview, before they parted, Smerdyakov asked Ivan to let him look at the money once more and stared at it for ten seconds, as if to say, 'Was it for this? He knew that it was not for this; and, unable to live with his own nullity, his own lack of meaning, he hanged himself. The life and death of Smerdyakov constitute perhaps the most powerful expression in literature of Augustine's theology of evil, that evil is not a thing in itself, but only the privation of the good. At the centre of Smerdyakov is nullity, non-entity, and Ivan has been forced to see that he, too, has the seed of this negativity, this evil, in his heart.

Ivan has one more struggle of conscience to endure. He has told Alyosha that the Devil is himself, 'All that is base, rotten and contemptible in me!' He is also 'stupid', but 'cunning, cunning like an animal'. 'Still, he told me a great deal about myself that was true', he adds, and one of the things is that he intends to give evidence at the trial out of pride: he wishes to perform a great act of virtue without believing in virtue, so his true motivation must be the desire to be praised for his generous feelings.

He is now in a terrible dilemma: his first double, Smerdyakov, has assured him that he will *not* tell the truth because of his pride, and now his second, the Devil, has told him that he *will* do so, also out of pride. Alyosha understands his torment. Ivan does not yet believe in God or the truth, yet they have gained a hold on his heart. He will give evidence, because in spite of everything his conscience is still deep-seated and alive; and he will do so knowing that he will not be believed, because Smerdyakov is dead. So he must either acknowledge to himself that he does believe, must 'rise up in the light of truth', or he must 'perish in hate' because he has served the truth in which he does not believe.

Ivan tells the truth at the trial, but he does so in hatred. He leaves the witness-box without having spoken up, but then returns and says his piece with casual directness, in the process rather strikingly anticipating one of Freud's more deathless insights: 'It was he and not my brother who murdered my father. He murdered him, and I told him to do it. Who doesn't wish his father dead?' His struggle of conscience, 'the agony of a proud decision', has been too much for him to withstand, and he breaks down in the courtroom in madness and delirium. Whether he is destined to rise up again from hell, Dostoevsky does not tell us.

In the story of Ivan the theme of the double reaches the apogee of its development, giving access to recesses of the soul and subtleties of inner division never before opened up and laid bare, and charting what Ralph Tymms has well described as 'the emergence of half-formed emotional reactions into the conscious mind' [*Doubles in Literary Psychology,* 1949]. Using successively the devices of the external, independent shadow-figure and the hallucinatory projection to embody the dark and deformed second self, Dostoevsky brings to his psychological–realist approach a passionate inwardness which allows him to depict the terrors of the soul with a sharpness and vividness beyond the reach of even the greatest of his Gothic-inspired predecessors. But Dostoevsky's psychology is never merely clinical or diagnostic; he knows that *psyche* means soul, and that madness is born of the conflicts of the soul, of its quarrel with its own evil tendencies. (pp. 122-26)

John Herdman, "The Emergence and Development of the Double Theme" and "The Russian Double," in his The Double in Nineteenth-Century Fiction, *The Macmillan Press Ltd., 1990, pp. 11-20, 99-126.*

Ralph Tymms

[*Tymms is a specialist in the area of Germanic studies whose writings include* Doubles in Literary Psychology *(1949) and* German Romantic Literature *(1955). In the following excerpt from the former work, he comments on the evolution of the doppelgänger theme in nineteenth-century European literature, uncovering two distinct interpretations of the double: the realistic or psychological and the allegorical.*]

Those periods of modern literature in which the double appears as a vehicle for psychological analysis are seen to coincide with the recurrence of 'subjective realism'—the paradoxical attitude that insists on the faithful and realistic reproduction of mental processes, even when they seem to have a purely subjective validity; such fantasies as hallucinations or derangement may suggest to the imagination are then treated with the objectivity of a psychiater's case-book. In this way the impulses of the subconscious mind are given the same attention as that which pre-romantic writers reserved for the rational consciousness; and the incalculable forces of personal emotion are shown to exert influence over the personality as a whole, though at times in direct opposition to the voluntary principles of the reason.

Subjective realism takes then as its true hero this part of the mind inaccessible to the conscious personality—the subconscious self, which may at times emerge from its latent state to dominate the whole mind and determine a man's actions. Hoffmann represents characters as being vaguely aware, even in their normal consciousness, of the existence of this secondary, non-conscious self; in the *Elixiere* these characters then imagine that the subconscious self is freed from its hiding-place, and projected into the outside world, in the visible form of a physical double. This delusion is recorded with every sign of realistic detail; it finds a place in the midst of the narrative of objectively valid circumstances that are observed and corroborated by independent witnesses. Further realism is shown in the description of the states of mind in which this secondary self becomes dominant: they are those in which the conscious mind is in abeyance.

Because of the realism of their subjective descriptions, Hoffmann and Kleist have frequently been reproached with morbidity; for they seem obsessed with somnambulism, magnetic trances, drunkenness, madness and maniacal crises; Dostoevsky in turn inherits the reputation of creating a literary 'charnel-house' of apoplectic pathology. Yet contemporary psycho-therapists appear to confirm that such pictures of madness may have a general application for sane and insane alike; and do not relegate them to the category of freaks, without relevance to normal humanity.

Kaiser's indifference to the rules of 'normality' is based, on the other hand, not on the romantic belief in the universal significance of the eccentricities of the subconscious mind, but on the personal irresponsibility of the expressionist artist, whose symbolism has a higher realism that automatically raises it beyond the reach of workaday standards of truth. Yet he has much the same general purpose as the romantics; he, too, probes into the innermost recesses of the mind, often freeing the incongruous denizens from the bonds of the unconscious by means of the 'psychological hammer-blow' that disintegrates the personality.

In the intervening periods between the occurrences of this ruthless analysis of the mind—between the hey-days of Hoffmann, of Dostoevsky, and of Kaiser—the double does not disappear from the pages of fiction, though it loses its distinctively realistic role. Instead it is assigned a place in the symbolical literature that constantly reappears, to explain by means of a venerable ethical system of dualism the complex and disharmonious nature of man; though even this allegorical version of the theme, depending on the conception of a struggle between good and evil principles within the soul (and frequently reverting to an age-old belief in the existence of a soul-double, or genius, in the likeness of man), is frequently coloured by the romantic device of projecting the secondary self in the guise of an external, and possibly phantom, *Doppelgänger.*

On the whole, it may be said that the *Doppelgänger,* in its psychologically realistic form, is a predominantly romantic theme, for it finds its first and most striking expression in Hoffmann's works; and there embodies the conception of the unconscious self which is first explicitly formulated by the romantic psychologist Schubert, combining the characteristically romantic extremes of exact self-analysis and exuberant imaginativeness. Nor does the *Doppelgänger* lose this romantic character when it reappears in Dostoevsky's works, later in the nineteenth century; for his use of the theme only corroborates Hoffmann's half-intuitive understanding of the obscurest processes of the mind, and his realism creates a new 'horror-romanticism', the *Schauerromantik* of psycho-pathology. But in expressionist drama the *Doppelgänger* is separated from the idea of the evil secondary self; for Kaiser even reverses the process by showing the *Doppelgänger* as a desirable alternative to the habitual personality, and one into which the unhappy hero hopes to transfer himself; yet again the theme is treated with confidence in the validity of subjective realism.

In the evolution of the theme, the alternation between realistic and allegorical interpretations reproduces the interaction of those two approaches to literature in the history of the last hundred and fifty years. The essentially romantic nature of the psychological interpretation is a forceful reminder of the origin of so much modern psychological doctrine in the bizarre medley of fact and fancy forming the German romantic science of the mind. The allegorical treatment of the double, though the product of a contrasting attitude to literature, does in effect supplement the psychological interpretation by a corroborative theory of dualism, yet one based on preconceived ethical values. These two aspects, then, together determine the evolution of the double; the one a product of the unconscious, and the other of the conscious mind, they appropriately present the twin faces of its Janus-head. (pp. 119-21)

Ralph Tymms, in a conclusion to his Doubles in Literary Psychology, *Bowes & Bowes, 1949, pp. 119-21.*

Irving Massey

[*Massey's writings include* The Gaping Pig: Literature and Metamorphosis *(1976) and* Find You the Virtue: Ethics, Image and Desire in Literature *(1987). In the following excerpt from the first-named work, he interprets the doppelgänger—in his opinion a subspecies of metamorphosis—as a manifestation of the subject's rejection of public language in favor of inner speech.*]

[I view] metamorphosis as a critique of public language. Gregor Samsa as bug [in Franz Kafka's "The Metamorphosis"] may be merely the fulfillment of a figure of speech; but he no longer uses the idiom which yielded the phrase that he illustrates. Lucius, in [Apuleius's] *The Golden Ass,* will never come to understand life as long as he participates in the exchange of ignorance that passes for human communication; in his silent existence as ass he can begin to know the limits of knowledge, the realities of experience, and glimpse the contours of the fate that suits him. Akaki Akakievich, in Gogol's "Overcoat," is happy as long as words have no meaning for him; the moment he emerges into the world where language has a purpose, he is doomed. Major Kovalyov, in "The Nose," is the victim of a synecdoche. [Lewis Carroll's] Alice, of course, is almost entirely wrapped up in words, though her attitude towards language is more active, manipulative, and domineering than that of most characters involved in metamorphic processes; perhaps because she is a child, she does not have such a grim and final view of its influence. She is a sort of impresario of language-imbricated metamorphoses. These appear safe some of the time: the Snap-dragonfly is robust enough to cause us no worry, with its body of plum-pudding, its wings of holly-leaves, and its head a raisin burning in brandy. On the other hand, the Bread-and-butter-fly, which lives entirely on weak tea, threatens subtly to draw us into its fate, for what happens to it sounds as though it might happen to us too—must, eventually, in fact, happen to everybody.

> "Supposing it couldn't find any?" she suggested.
>
> "Then it would die, of course."
>
> "But that must happen very often," Alice remarked thoughtfully.
>
> "It always happens," said the Gnat.

My reading of Flaubert's "Legend of St. Julian the Hospitaler" may be idiosyncratic in stressing the animal element, the crudities of style, and Flaubert's refusal to communicate a subjective dimension to the events of the story on either his own behalf or Julien's. But it is a fact that the redeemed Julien is no more expressive or articulate than the savage hunter of the first chapters. Similarly, [Adalbert von Chamisso's] Peter Schlemihl, in his altered state at the end of his story, finds himself as remote from the exchange values of social communication as he is from

An excerpt from *The Book of Imaginary Beings*

Suggested or stimulated by reflections in mirrors and in water and by twins, the idea of the Double is common to many countries. It is likely that sentences such as *A friend is another self* by Pythagoras or the Platonic *Know thyself* were inspired by it. In Germany this Double is called *Doppelgänger,* which means "double walker." In Scotland there is the *fetch,* which comes to fetch a man to bring him to his death; there is also the Scottish word *wraith* for an apparition thought to be seen by a person in his exact image just before death. To meet oneself is, therefore, ominous. The tragic ballad "Ticonderoga" by Robert Louis Stevenson tells of a legend on this theme. There is also the strange picture by Rossetti ("How They Met Themselves") in which two lovers come upon themselves in the dusky gloom of a woods. We may also cite examples from Hawthorne ("Howe's Masquerade"), Dostoyevsky, Alfred de Musset, James ("The Jolly Corner"), Kleist, Chesterton ("The Mirror of Madmen"), and Hearn *(Some Chinese Ghosts).*

The ancient Egyptians believed that the Double, the *ka,* was a man's exact counterpart, having his same walk and his same dress. Not only men, but gods and beasts, stones and trees, chairs and knives had their *ka,* which was invisible except to certain priests who could see the Doubles of the gods and were granted by them a knowledge of things past and things to come.

To the Jews the appearance of one's Double was not an omen of imminent death. On the contrary, it was proof of having attained prophetic powers. This is how it is explained by Gershom Scholem. A legend recorded in the Talmud tells the story of a man who, in search of God, met himself.

In the story "William Wilson" by Poe, the Double is the hero's conscience. He kills it and dies. In a similar way, Dorian Gray in Wilde's novel stabs his portrait and meets his death. In Yeats's poems the Double is our other side, our opposite, the one who complements us, the one we are not nor will ever become.

Plutarch writes that the Greeks gave the name *other self* to a king's ambassador.

Jorge Luis Borges, in his Book of Imaginary Beings, *E. P. Dutton, 1969.*

gold, that other medium of exchange, the pursuit of which had led to his predicament.

In narratives that deal with doubling—an important subspecies of metamorphosis—the suspicion of public language is hardly less consistent. Perhaps in some instances—for example, in [Mary Shelley's] *Frankenstein*—the dialogue never becomes genuinely public because it is really the obsessive answer and counter-answer of the same mind, rather like Rousseau judging Jean-Jacques. When the monster is finally detached from the abstract structure provided by Frankenstein, he has no one left to communicate with, and the garrulity can have a stop. But in any case, from the beginning, by far the most effective means of reaching others that the monster has known is not speech but violence, an option which several other doubles and metamorphic heroes take, as we shall see. In Hoffmann one thinks first of "Mademoiselle de Scudéry" as an instance. But on the whole, for both Hoffmann and Kleist (say, in Kleist's essay on the puppet theater) language is more inadequate than oppressive or petrifying. The mechanical musician or musical instrument, the puppet, the dueling bear, are all closer to God or to nature than we are, partly because language does not clog the avenues of their experience and response, slowing the mind with the syntax or logic which is our usual apparatus for thought. With the instantaneousness of perception that we call inspiration, when the mind can flash back and forth with unlimited speed, as it is natural for it to do, and as it does in dreams; foreseeing their goal and constituting their means in the same moment, these beings can run around the end of words, free in the fields of inarticulacy. Paradoxically, music itself comes closer to the divine message than Hoffmann's own words can possibly do. At the same time, some disquiet is undeniably aroused by the dancing puppet or the mechanical flautist, animated by a spirit over which we have no jurisdiction. They remind us of our bodies, and of our death, because they are mere bodies, as we will be. As such, they are passive, as helpless and out of control as the abject victims of Ovid's *Metamorphoses.* It is difficult to invoke the apparatus of metamorphosis, even in as playful a virtuoso piece as Donne's "The Flea," without creating some sense of uneasiness in the reader, as if the bounds of psychological propriety had been violated.

This horror is most intensely experienced in Hoffmann's "The Sandman," where the beloved, Olimpia, is a puppet. She remains a puppet because her lover Nathanael is unable to see her with enough belief in the ideal to transform her into the living body of the imagination. When she is finally dismembered, Nathanael's eyes, the animating eyes that were supposed to give life to her but failed to do so, are thrown unceremoniously back at him, and the rest of Olimpia's body reverts to its natural state as a wooden doll. The story is full of detached members, always in danger of becoming mere objects: above all, eyes, which must either become the instruments of ideal vision (at one point opera glasses are used to help), or fall into the grip of that archpuppeteer, Coppelius, who makes men into the frenzied executors of his will. But to return to the matter of language: Olimpia can say only five words; it is not for her gift of tongues that Nathanael falls in love with her. Presumably, if he had been able to fulfill her potential in the way that Coppelius had in mind for her, he and she would have shared another language; not the public language of which literary language is a tormented analogue, but the primal language of Atlantis of which Hoffmann, his mentor Schubert, Novalis, and many others had dreamt.

The problem of the double recurs in Gérard de Nerval. In *Aurélia,* for instance, the speaker does not always seem sure of who is dominant at any given moment; he or his double. Often the narrator also seems quite remote from the former self whom he is describing. What appears to happen is that Nerval throws off a series of masks to represent him in the successive contacts with the world which life necessitates. (Jean-Pierre Richard, in *Poésie et profondeur,* emphasizes this aspect of Nerval's psychology.) But Nerval keeps sending out doubles that do not have full credentials, that have not been totally committed to the outside world. In truth, none of his personae has ever gotten outside himself. Nerval presents himself, during *Aurélia,* in a succession of trancelike states, dreams, or alienated fantasies. In spite of his assurances to Alexandre Dumas that he has really awakened and is writing with a clear and reasoning mind, it is evident that reasonableness is only one more mask for Nerval's dream. "Le rêve est une second vie," ("Dream is another life,") begins *Aurélia:* but one would rather ask, with "Artémis," "La première ou dernière?" ("the first or the last?"). The question is, what is Nerval protecting by insisting on returning each time to the "abîme" of unconsciousness, insanity, or paganism? For the truth is that Nerval never allowed himself to surface completely: his writing, even in a highly wrought, intricate work like *Sylvie,* operates at a level just below full rational consciousness. Nerval's most natural *persona* is the catatonic soldier at the end of Aurélia, with whom he sympathizes so deeply. For him, as for Nerval, every awakening is another falling asleep; when Nerval finally brings him to speech, he asks the soldier: " 'Porquoi,' lui dis-je, 'ne veux-tu pas manger et boire comme les autres?'—'c'est que je suis mort', dit-il; 'j'ai été enterré dans tel cimetière, à telle place . . . ' " (" 'Why,' I asked him, 'don't you want to eat and drink like the others?'—'it's because I'm dead,' he said; 'I've been buried in such and such a cemetery, at such and such a place . . .' "). (pp. 26-30)

[In] dream we speak our own language, when we wake, the language of others. Surrendering our sleep is difficult not so much because it requires us to interrupt our fantasies as because it forces us to assume the language of others, to begin to talk, as even a baby must eventually begin to talk. The catatonic soldier is fortunate because his thinking is "sans le mélange de la pensée d'un autre" ("without the admixture of someone else's thought"). This is the burden and the strain of consciousness: that we must speak a borrowed language. If it be true that the structure of the unconscious is the structure of language (Lacan), then it is the structure of some kind of language other than the public language that we are required to speak when we address others. Perhaps it is the basic language of some essential or universal man. According to my view, there would almost have to be a transposition of the ideas of "parole" [private language] and "langue" [universal language] (Saussure) if we were to attempt a description of the internal language. It is private, though it may also be universal; it need not find itself in conflict with "deep structure." On the other hand, the external language that we attempt to speak consciously, no matter how idiosyncratic our treatment of it may be, is always a public language, never a genuine "parole," never really ours. Perhaps it is easier to understand the situation in terms of a quadruple rather than a dual pattern. There is the universal language, which exists alive in dreams, and, also, as an abstract set of possibilities in consciousness. Then, third, there is the private language, our own language, which exists *only* in dreams, and is somehow at one with the living universal language. Fourth, there is the individual speech of consciousness, which is external, nonpersonal, despite our extremest efforts to make it so. Perhaps the artist is the only one who can contend successfully with the demand for public and private speech at once, who can say something to others without having had to relinquish his state of dream. (Nerval may only be somewhat more explicit about this procedure than other poets.) In *Jekyll and Hyde,* for instance, I think of the reconciliation of Hyde with Utterson as the reconciliation of two rhythms: of the bare, basic patterns of universal speech with the individual statements that the book is forced to make, with its public existence: so that it may end in silence after having absorbed its own example. A book is a permission to return to silence, something that has earned the right to return to silence.

My interpretation of . . . *Jekyll and Hyde* . . . hinges on the protection of the inner language from the demands of public communication. Hyde seems to destroy people because of his impatience with their demand that he respond to them in their terms, enter into transactions with them, give them directions in the street. [In Prosper Mérimée's story "Lokis"] Lokis (the bear) and the bronze Venus of Ille spread the doctrine of the first, silent language (in one case symbolized by old Lithuanian, in the other by classical Latin) through the example of violence, which, like Hyde's behavior, is a denial of communication. The particular acts of violence in these stories (as in much of Greek drama) are directed against the institution which best represents the easy, optimistic belief in the efficacy of communication within social dimensions, namely, marriage.

The anonymity of Hyde, the hidden, may finally be seen to resemble the anonymity of Akaki Akakievich and the anonymity of Lokis, the bear. All are engaged in protecting themselves from the demands of public communication, from the requirement that they utter, and that they fit into a verbal social order by confessing to a name. This critique of language from the shelter of anonymity or of the animal form represents the principal strain in my interpretation of metamorphosis. If, as Flaubert claims in *Madame Bovary,* language is good only for making bears dance, then we might say that Kleist's bear dances only to his own tune, and Mérimée's bear won't dance at all. Such ideas are, of course, not new. Hinze the cat in Tieck's *Puss in Boots* informs us that cats don't talk only because they have learned contempt for speech through long acquaintance with humans. For animals to persist in "human" styles of behavior leads inevitably toward a kind of absurdity; it is better for them to be as they are. Yeats, in a letter to O'Leary, says of Maud Gonne, "Her pet monkey was making, much of the time, little melancholy cries at the hearthrug—the monkeys are degenerate men, not men's ancestors, hence their look of sadness and old age." Sometimes the claim that beasts are the predecessors of men persuades us of the contrary, and we are left with the feeling that animals alone have retained what was once worthwhile in man. The passage on the exchange of glances with an animal in Buber's *I and Thou* (echoed in the last sentence of Lévi-Strauss's *Tristes Tropiques*) speaks of the hesitant, anxious state of the cat, struggling for fulfillment, but confined below the threshold of consciousness and language: "the stammering of nature at the first touch of spirit . . . " In the gaze of recognition the two levels of consciousness, man's and cat's, communicate; but an instant later the cat has slipped below the threshold of interrogation again. "I myself could continue to think about the matter, but the animal had sunk back out of the stammer of its glance into the disquietude where there is no speech and almost no memory." It has supposedly left man behind it at a higher level, meditating on the I-Thou relationship that can overcome the alienation of the "it." Yet in fact we, Buber's readers, seem to have followed the cat in its plunge back into inarticulacy, into the silence of its anxious state; we are more with the cat than with the man. The cat, with all its anxiety, still seems better able to stream with its glance over the alienation of the "It." In the same way we feel, in Thoreau's description of winter animals, that the foxes, with their ragged, restless barking, are not rudimentary men, awaiting their metamorphosis into articulate beings, as Thoreau tells us they are; but rather (like Cortazar's axolotls), men who have shrunk to a fraction of their stature, standing half in the mouth of their burrow and barking their complaints at the world of full-grown, speech-making men, the world of public pronouncements that they have left behind. The bark of the foxes seems to remain the most compelling, or even the only adequate utterance, despite the fact that it stands at the beginning of a line, twice again broken (at the stages of dog and man), that moves out of the burrow and toward the world of public speech.

> Sometimes I heard the foxes as they ranged over the snow crust, in moonlight nights, in search of a partridge or other game, barking raggedly and demoniacally like forest dogs, as if laboring with some anxiety, or seeking expression, struggling for light and to be dogs outright and run freely in the streets. . . . They seemed to me to be rudimental, burrowing men, still standing on their defense, awaiting their transformation.

As long as they can wait, the language that they harbor is safe. (pp. 30-3)

Irving Massey, in an introduction to his The Gaping Pig: Literature and Metamorphosis, *University of California Press, 1976, pp. 1-33.*

THE DOUBLE AND ROMANTICISM

Georg Brandes

[*Brandes was a prominent Danish literary critic and biographer whose acclaimed* Hovedstrømninger i det 19de aarhundredes europaeiske litteratur *(1872-90;* Main Currents in Nineteenth Century Literature, *1901-05) examines literary movements in the broad context of European literature. In the following excerpt from the second volume of that work, he defines the doppelgänger theme as emblematic of Romanticism's essentially dualistic conception of the human psyche.*]

Those among my readers who have stood in a room lined with mirrors, and seen themselves and everything else reflected *ad infinitum,* above, below, on every side, have some idea of the vertigo which the study of Romantic art at times produces.

Every one who has read Holberg's *Ulysses von Ithacia* remembers how droll the effect is when the characters, as they are perpetually doing, make fun of themselves and what they represent—when, for example, Ulysses exhibits the long beard which has grown during the ten years' campaign, or when we read upon a screen, "This is Troy," or when, at the close, the Jews rush in and tear off the actor's back the clothes which he had borrowed to play Ulysses in. Histrionic art, as every one knows, depends for its effect upon illusion. And illusion is an aim common to many of the arts. A statue and a painting deceive quite as much as a play, the illusion being contingent upon our momentarily taking the stone for a human being, and the painted flat surface for receding reality, in exactly the same way as we forget the actor in his rôle. This illusion, however, is only complete for a moment. . . . The effect of the work of art is, as it were, focussed in this illusion. The illusion is the reflection of the work of art in the spectator's mind—the appearance, the play, by means of which the unreal becomes reality to the spectator.

In the simple, straightforward work of art no special attention is devoted to illusion; it is not aimed at; nothing is done to strengthen it or to give it piquancy; but still less is anything done to destroy it.

It is not difficult, however, to understand how a certain piquant quality may be communicated to the illusion produced by any art. When, for instance, a Hermes, or any idol, is represented on a bas-relief, when a picture represents a studio or a room with pictures hanging on the walls, a strong indication is hereby conveyed that the bas-relief itself is not intended to affect us as statuary, nor the pictures as painting. And the same sort of effect is produced when one or other of the characters in a comedy cries: "Do you take me for a stage-uncle?"

The theatrical illusion is still further heightened, or, to be quite correct, is still more entirely forgotten, when some of the characters in a play themselves perform a play, as in *Hamlet* or *A Midsummer Night's Dream.* It seems extraordinary or impossible that the spectators of this second play should also be acting. The illusion here is artificially strengthened, and yet at the same time weakened, by attention being drawn to it. It is plain that this play with illusions had an immense attraction for Tieck; it was inevitable that it should have. Since it is illusion which makes art serious reality to the spectator, it is by the destroying of the illusion that he is made to feel strongly that art is free, fanciful play. (pp. 152-53)

In a different department of literature, in the writings of our Danish philosopher, Kierkegaard, we come upon the mirror chamber with its repeated reflections psychologically applied. As the German Romanticist ironically hovers above his own play, with its Chinese puzzle-box scenes and figures, so the Danish psychologist draws further and further away from his subject by putting one author, as it were, inside another. Listen to his explanation in the *Afsluttende Efterskrift* (*Concluding Postscript*).

> My position is even a more external one than that of any author whose characters are imaginary, but who appears personally in his preface. A prompter, impersonal, or personal in the third degree, I have created authors whose prefaces, nay, whose very names are their own production. In the pseudonymous books there is not a word of my own; I judge them as an uninterested third party, have no knowledge of their meaning except that of the ordinary reader, and not the most remote private connection with them, as is indeed impossible in the case of a doubly reflected communication. A single word from me personally, in my own name, would be a piece of presumptuous self-forgetfulness, and would, from the dialectical point of view, destroy the pseudonymous character of the work. I am no more the publisher, Victor Eremita, than I am the Seducer or the Assessor in *Enten-Eller;* Eremita is the poetically real subjective thinker, whom we meet again in *In Vino Veritas.* In *Frygt og Bœven* (*Fear and Trembling*) I am no more Johannes de Silentio than I am the Knight of Faith whom he depicts; and just as little am I the author of the preface to the book, it being a characteristic utterance of a poetically-real subjective thinker. In that tale of woe, *Skyldig?—Ikke Skyldig?* (*Guilty or not Guilty?*), I am no more the experimenter than I am the subject of the experiment, since the experimenter is a poetically-real subjective thinker, and the being he experiments on is his psychologically inevitable production. I am a negligible quantity, *i.e.* it is immaterial what I am. . . . I have all along been sensible that my personality was an obstruction which the Pseudonymi must involuntarily and inevitably long to be rid of, or to have made as insignificant as possible, yet which they at the same time, regarding the matter from the ironical and reflective standpoint, must desire to retain as repellant opposition; for I stand to them in the ironically combined relation of secretary and dialectically reduplicated author of the author or authors.

However different the causes of the reduplication may be in this case, the phenomenon itself is of near kin to the foregoing one. To keep the general public at a distance, to avoid laying bare his heart, and, most important of all, to avoid the tiresome responsibility entailed by speaking in his own name, Kierkegaard places as many authors between himself and the public as possible. Even taking his reasons into consideration, I confess that to me the proceeding seems super-subtle, a sort of reminiscence of the Romantic irony. For although Kierkegaard, as regards his matter, is in many ways ahead of Romanticism, he is still connected with it by his style. It is natural enough that he cannot, or will not, bear the responsibility for what his imaginary characters, the Assessor and the Seducer, say; but it is pure imagination on his part to suppose himself capable of producing his authors at second hand, to suppose, for instance, that he has created the hero in the Engagement Story exactly as Frater Taciturnus would have created him. Several of his would-be authors, Constantin Constantius and Frater Taciturnus, for example, are scarcely to be distinguished from one another, and there is nothing peculiarly characteristic about their productions. (pp. 156-58)

Along with all this duplication and reduplication we have in the case of the Romanticists the wildest caprices in the matter of the order of presentation. *The Topsy-turvy World* begins with the epilogue and ends with the prologue; by such pranks imagination proclaims its independence of all law. Frater Taciturnus records what happened to him last year along with what is happening to him this year; every day at noon he notes down what happened that day a year ago (What a memory!), and at midnight what has occurred during the day. Naturally, it is almost impossible to separate the two threads of event. In Hoffmann's *Kater Murr,* the cat writes its memoirs on sheets of paper which have its master's, Kapellmeister Kreisler's, memoranda on the other side. Both sides of the sheets are printed, the one following the other, so that we read two utterly unconnected manuscripts mixed up with each other, often with interruptions in the middle of sentences or words. Wilfulness, caprice, play with one's own production could scarcely be carried farther. Yet the dissolution of established form did go further, much further. The Romanticists did not rest content with having shattered the conventions of art; they proceeded to decompose the human personality, and that in many different manners.

It was Novalis who led the way. In *Heinrich von Ofterdingen* the hero seems to have a foreknowledge of everything that happens to him. "Each new thing that he saw and heard seemed only to shove back bolts, to open secret doors in his soul." But the strangest impression of all is produced on him by his discovery of a mysterious book in the cave of the hermit Count of Hohenzollern, a book in which, although he is as yet unable to interpret it, he finds the enigma of his existence, an existence beginning before his birth and stretching into the future after his death. Novalis's romance being an allegory and myth, his design being to make a single individual represent the whole eternal story of the soul, he turns to his purpose one of the oldest hypotheses of humanity, the idea that the individual reappears generation after generation. Thus the past and the future take part in the present, in the shape of memory and prophetic intuition. He does not actually believe in the transmigration of souls, but to him, the Romanticist who lives in the contemplation of the eternal, time is of such subordinate significance that, just as he recognises no difference between a natural and a supernatural event, so he sees none between past, present, and future. In this way the individual existence is extended throughout an unlimited period of history.

In Danish literature we find this Romantic use of the idea of a previous existence in Heiberg's *De Nygifte.* The mother is telling her adopted son about the death of her real son:—

"Den Morgen, da han led sin skrækkelige Dom,
Endnu var det neppe daget—
Traadte Slutteren ind og sagde: "Kom!
Klokken er nu paa Slaget."

Da sank han for sidste Gang til mit Bryst
Og udbröd: "Et Ord du mig give,
Et kraftigt Ord, som kan være min Tröst
Paa min sidste Gang i Live!"

Og jeg sagde . . .
  Men, Fredrik, du skræmmer mig! sig . . .
Du rejser dig . . . hvad har du i Sinde?
Du stirrer paa mig saa bleg som et Lig . . .

Fredrik.
O Moder! Moder! hold inde!

Du sagde: "Naar du for din Frelser staar,
Da sig: Min Gud og min Broder,
Tilgiv mig for dine Martyrsaar,
For min Anger og for min Moder."

Gertrud.
Ha! hvoraf ved du det?

Fredrik.
Mig det var,
Förste nu mig selv jeg fatter.
Det er din virkelige Sön, du har,
Og nu lever han Livet atter.

[The morning he suffered his terrible sentence, ere yet it was day, the warder entered and said: 'Come! the hour is about to strike.' Then he fell on my breast for the last time, crying: 'Say a word, a word of power, to strengthen me for the last steps I am to take on earth!' And I said . . . But, Fredrik, you frighten me. What is it? Why do you rise and gaze on me thus, pale as a corpse? *Fredrik*—O mother! mother! stop! You said: 'When you stand before your Creator, say: My God and my Brother, forgive me for the sake of Thy passion, of my repentance, and of my mother!' *Gertrud*—Oh, tell how you know this? *Fredrik*—Because it was to me you spoke; not till this moment have I understood myself; I am your own son, now living life over again.]

Heiberg here makes a beautiful and ingenious use of the idea. But the Romanticists are not content with this. It is not enough for them to transpose the personality into the past, or to deck it with the bright peacock's tail of future existences. They split the Ego into strips, they resolve it into its elements. They scatter it abroad through space, as they stretch it out through time. For the laws of space and time affect them not.

Self-consciousness is self-duplication. But it is an unhealthy self which cannot overcome and master this self-duplication. . . . There is no greater misery than morbid self-contemplation. He who indulges in it separates himself from himself, observes himself from the point of view of a spectator, and ere long experiences the horrible feeling of the prisoner who, when he looks up, sees the eye of the warder at the little glass pane in the door of his cell. His own eye has become quite as terrible to him as another man's. What tends to make this condition permanent is partly the religious and moral feeling that one ought never to lose sight of, but to be always labouring at and improving one's self, and partly natural curiosity regarding the unknown; one looks upon one's self as a country, the coast of which is known, but the interior of which is still to be explored.

In the case of the man who is healthy in mind and body, this exploration goes on slowly, almost imperceptibly. One fine day the poor prisoner, looking up from his work, finds that the eye has disappeared from the peep-hole. Only now does he begin to breathe, to live. Whether his work be important or unimportant, divine or merely useful, whether he be a Michael Angelo or a cork-cutter, from that moment there is a feeling of balance and unity in his mind; he feels that he is an entire being. In the case of sickly, inactive natures, the eye is never removed from the peep-hole, and a long continuation of this condition leads the individual to the verge of madness. But it is to this very condition that the Romanticists cling. It is this which gives birth to the Romantic idea of the "Doppelgänger," an idea which finds its first expression in Jean Paul's *Leibgeber-Schoppe* (in the meditation on Fichte's Ego), and is to be found in almost all Hoffmann's tales, reaching its climax in his chief work, *Die Elixire des Teufels.* It crops up in the writings of all the Romanticists; we have it in Kleist's *Amphitryon,* in Achim von Arnim's *Die beiden Waldemar,* in Chamisso's poem, *Erscheinung,* and Brentano treats it comically in *Die mehreren Wehmüller.* To Hoffmann the Ego is simply a disguise worn on the top of another disguise, and he amuses himself by peeling off these disguises one by one. (pp. 158-62)

It was a settled conviction with Hoffmann that when anything good befalls a man, an evil power is always lurking in the background to paralyse the action of the good power. As he expresses it: "The devil thrusts his tail into everything." He was haunted, says his biographer, Hitzig, by a fear of mysterious horrors, of "Doppelgänger" and spectral apparitions of every kind. He used to look anxiously round while writing about them; and if it was at night, he would often wake his wife and beg her to keep him company till he had finished. He imparted his own fear of ghosts to the characters he created; he drew them "as he himself was drawn in the great book of creation." It does not surprise us to learn that of his own works, he preferred those which contain the most gruesome pictures of madness or the weirdest caricatures—*Brambilla,* for instance.

He relies for effect, in a manner which soon becomes mannerism, upon the sharp contrasts with which he ushers in his terrific or comical scenes. From the commonest, most prosaic every-day life we are suddenly transported into a perfectly distorted world, where miracles and juggling tricks of every kind so bewilder us that in the end no relation, no species of life, no personality, seems definite and certain. We are always in doubt as to whether we are dealing with a real person, with his spectre, with his essence in another form or other power, or with his fantastic "Doppelgänger."

In one of the lighter tales of Hoffmann's last period, *Der Doppelgänger,* the two principal characters resemble each other so closely that one is constantly being taken for the other; the one is wounded instead of the other; the betrothed of the one cannot distinguish him from the other, &c., &c. All kinds of absurd mistakes are made possible, and the dread of "Doppelgängerei" is turned to good account. The common-sense explanation of the matter is insisted on (much as it is in Brentano's *Die mehreren Wehmüller*), simply because Hoffmann for once, by way of a change, fancied making some attempt at explanation. The explanation, as a matter of fact, explains nothing. All Hoffmann really cared for was the fantastically gruesome effect, just as all Brentano cared for was the fantastically comical one. *Der Doppelgänger* possesses no artistic merit.

There is wittier and more audacious invention in the tale, *The Latest Adventures of the Dog Berganza.* In the first place, we are left uncertain whether the dog is a metamorphosed human being or not; he himself says: "It is possible that I am really Montiel, who was punished by being compelled to assume the shape of a dog; if so, the punishment has been a source of pleasure and amusement." In the second place, even the dog, as dog, sees himself duplicated, and is conscious of the dissolution of the unity of his being. "Sometimes I actually saw myself lying in front of myself like another Berganza, another which yet was myself; and I, Berganza, saw another Berganza maltreated by the witches, and growled and barked at him."

Still greater is the audacity, still more extravagant the whimsicality in the tale of *The Golden Jar.* In it an ugly old Dresden applewoman is at the same time the beautiful bronze knocker on Registrar Lindhorst's door. The metal face of the door-knocker occasionally wrinkles itself up into the old crone's crabbed smile. In addition to this, she is the odious fortune-teller, Frau Rauerin, and good old Lise, the fond nurse of the young heroine of the tale. She can (like the fortune-teller in *Der Doppelgänger*) suddenly change dress, shape, and features. When the matter of her parentage is cleared up, we learn that her papa was a "shabby feather broom," made of feathers from a dragon's wing, while her mamma was a "miserable beetroot."

Lindhorst, the stolid Registrar, who never seems to feel at home except when sitting in his library in his flowered dressing-gown, surrounded by old manuscripts, is also a great magician, who, in the middle of an ordinary conversation, suddenly begins to relate the most insane occurrences as if they were the most natural in the world. He tells, for instance, that he was once invisibly present at a party—quite a simple matter—he was in the punch-bowl. On another occasion he takes off his dressing-gown, steps without more ado into a bowl of blazing arrack, vanishes in the flames, and allows himself to be drunk.

In creating these doubled and trebled existences, the character, for instance, of the Archive Keeper, who is a Registrar by day and a salamander at night, Hoffmann obviously had in his mind the strange contrast between his own official life, as the conscientious criminal judge, severly rejecting all considerations of sentiment or æstheticism, and his free night life as king of the boundless realm of imagination—a life in which reality, as such, had no part.

But of all Hoffmann's tales, it is *Die Elixire des Teufels* (*The Elixir of Satan*) which makes the most powerful impression. Let us dwell for a moment on the hero of this romance, Brother Medardus; for he is a typical character. It is impossible in a brief summary to convey any idea of the mysterious, weird horror of the book; to feel this one must read it. A work more saturated with voluptuousness and horrors the Romantic School, with all its long practice in the style, never produced.—In a certain monastery is preserved a flask of Satanic elixir, which had belonged to St. Anthony. This elixir is believed to possess magic properties. A monk who has tasted it becomes so eloquent that ere long he is the most famous preacher of the monastery. But his eloquence is not of a pious or healthy, but of a carnal, strangely exciting, dæmonic description. Brother Medardus drinks from the flask. A charming woman, his penitent, falls in love with him, and a longing for the pleasures and delights of the world impels him to leave the monastery. He finds a young man, Count Viktorin, asleep in the forest on the edge of a precipice, and half accidentally pushes him over. From this time onwards every one takes him for the Count.

"My own Ego, the sport of a cruel accident, was dissolved into strange forms, and floated helplessly away upon the sea of circumstances. I could not find myself again. Viktorin is undoubtedly pushed over the precipice by the accident which directed my hand, not my will—I step into his place." And as though this were not marvellous enough, he adds: "But Reinhold knows Father Medardus, the preacher of the Capuchin Monastery; and thus to him I am what I really am. Nevertheless, I am obliged to take Viktorin's place with the Baroness, for I am Viktorin. I am that which I appear to be, and I do not appear to be that which I am. At strife with my own Ego, I am an unanswerable riddle to myself."

Medardus, in his own form, now enters into relations with Viktorin's mistress, the Baroness, who has no idea that he is not Viktorin. He is possessed by carnal desires; women fall in love with him; he gives himself up to sensual pleasures, and in order to attain the fulfilment of his wishes, commits crimes of every kind, including murder. Horrible visions haunt him and drive him from place to place. In the end he is denounced and imprisoned. In prison the confusion of individualities reaches a climax. "I could not sleep; in the strange reflections cast by the dull, wavering light of the lamp upon the walls and ceiling, I saw all kinds of distorted faces grinning at me. I put out the lamp and buried my head in my pillow of straw, only to be still more horribly tormented by the hollow groans of the prisoners and the rattling of their chains." It seems to him that he is listening to the death-rattle of his victims. And now he plainly hears a gentle, measured knocking beneath him. "I listened, the knocking continued, and sounds of strange laughter came up through the floor. I sprang up and flung myself upon the straw mattress, but the knocking went on, accompanied by laughter and groans. Presently, an ugly, hoarse, stammering voice began calling gently but persistently: 'Me-dar-dus, Me-dar-dus!' An icy shiver ran through my veins, but I took courage and shouted: 'Who is there? Who is there?' " Then the knocking and stammering begins directly beneath his feet: "He, he, he! He, he, he! Lit-tle brother, lit-tle brother Me-dar-dus . . . I am here, am here . . . le-let me in . . . we will g-g-go into the woo-woo-woods, to the woo-woo-woods." To his horror he seems to recognise his own voice. Some of the flagstones of the floor are pushed up, and his own face, in a monk's cowl, appears. This other Medardus is, like him, imprisoned, has confessed, and is condemned to death. Now everything happens as if in a dream. He no longer knows whether he is really the hero of the events which he believes to have happened, or whether the whole is a vivid dream. "I feel as if I had been listening in a dream to the story of an unfortunate wretch, the plaything of evil powers, who have driven him hither and thither, and urged him on from crime to crime."

He is acquitted; the happiest moment of his life is at hand; he is to be united to the woman he loves. It is their wedding day.

> At that very moment a dull sound rose from the street below; we heard the shouting of hollow voices and the slow rumbling of a heavy vehicle. I ran to the window. In front of the palace, a cart, driven by the headsman's apprentice, was stopping; in it sat the Monk and a Capuchin friar who was praying loudly and fervently with him. Though the Monk was disfigured by fear and by a bristly beard, the features of my terrible Doppelgänger were only too easily recognisable. Just as the cart, which had been stopped for the moment by the throng, rolled on again, he suddenly glared up at me with his horrible glistening eyes, and laughed loud, and yelled: "Bridegroom! Bridegroom! Come up on to the housetop! There we will wrestle with one another, and he who throws the other down is king and has the right to drink blood!" I cried: "You monster! What have I to do with you?" Aurelia flung her arms round me and drew me forcibly away from the window, crying: "For God and the Holy Virgin's sake! . . . It is Medardus, my brother Leonard's murderer, whom they are taking to execution." . . . Leonard! Leonard! The spirits of hell awoke within me, and exerted all the power they possess over the wicked, abandoned sinner. I seized Aurelia with such fury that she shook with fear: "Ha, ha, ha! mad, foolish woman! I, I, your lover, your bridegroom, am Medardus, am your brother's murderer. You, the Monk's bride, would call down vengeance upon him? Ho, ho, ho! I am king—I will drink your blood."

He strikes her to the earth. His hands are covered with her blood. He rushes out into the street, frees the Monk, deals blows right and left with knife and fist, and escapes into the forest.

> I had but one thought left, the hunted animal's thought of escape. I rose, but had not taken

> many steps before a man sprang upon my back and flung his arms round my neck. In vain I tried to shake him off; I flung myself down; I rubbed myself against the trees—all to no purpose—the man only chuckled scornfully. Suddenly the moon shone clear through the dark firs, and the horrible, deathly pale face of the Monk, the supposed Medardus, the Doppelgänger, glared at me with the same appalling glance he had shot at me from the cart. "He, he, he! little brother! I am w-w-with you still; I'll n-n-never let you go. I can't r-r-run like you. Y-you must carry me. They were go-go-going to break me on the wh-wh-wheel, but I got away."

This situation is spun out *ad infinitum,* but I forbear. To the end of the book one is uncertain of the real significance of the events, of the ethical tendency of the actions, so completely in this case has imagination disintegrated personality.

The Scandinavian author, Ingemann, has followed Hoffmann in this path. He turns to account, for instance, the eeriness in the idea of loudly calling one's own name in a churchyard at midnight; see his tale, *The Sphinx,* and others in the so-called Callot-Hoffmann style.

But, as already observed, Romanticism is not content with stretching out and splitting up the Ego, with spreading it throughout time and space. It dissolves it into its elements, takes from it here, adds to it there, makes it the plaything of free fancy. Here, if anywhere, Romanticism is profound; its psychology is correct, but one-sided; it is always on the night side or on the inevitability of things that it dwells; there is nothing emancipating or elevating about it.

In the old days the Ego, the soul, the personality, was regarded as a being whose attributes were its so-called capacities and powers. The words "capacity" and "power," however, only signify that there is in me the possibility of certain events, of my seeing, reading, &c. My true being does not consist of possibilities, but of these events themselves, of my actual condition. My real being is a sequence of inward events. For me, my Ego is composed of a long series of mental pictures and ideas. Of this Ego, I constantly, daily, lose some part. Forgetfulness swallows up gigantic pieces of it. Of all the faces I saw on the street yesterday and the day before, of all the sensations which were mine, only one or two remain in my memory. If I go still farther back, only an exceptionally powerful sensation or thought here and there emerges, like a solitary rocky island, from the ocean of forgetfulness. We only keep together the ideas and pictures that remain to us from our past lives by means of the association of these ideas, that is to say, by the aid of the peculiar power they have, in virtue of certain laws, of recalling each other. If we had no numerical system, no dates, no almanacs, wherewith to give some coherence to our different memories, we should have an extremely slight and indistinct idea of our Ego. But however substantial the long inward chain may seem (and it is strengthened, it gains in tenacity, every time we run over its links in our memory), it happens that we at times introduce into it a link which does not belong to it, at times take a link from it and place it in another chain.

The first of these actions, the introducing of new, incongruous links into the chain of memory, happens in dreams. We dream we have done many things which we have never done. It also happens when we have a false recollection. He who has seen a white sheet blowing about in the dark, and believes he has seen a ghost, has such a false recollection. Most myths and legends, especially religious legends, come into existence in this way.

It frequently happens, however, that, instead of adding links to the chain of the Ego, we withdraw them. Thus the sick man, when his mind is wandering, supposes that the words he hears are spoken by a strange voice, or endows his inward visions with an outward reality, as Luther did when he saw the devil in his room in the Wartburg; and the madman not only partly, but entirely confuses himself with some one else.

In a state of reason, then, the Ego is an artificial production, the result of association of ideas. I am certain of my own identity—in the first place, because I associate my name, that sound which I call my name, with the chain of my inward experiences, and secondly, because I keep all the links of this chain connected by the association of ideas, by virtue of which they produce each other. But, since the Ego is thus not an innate but an acquired conception, founded upon an association of ideas which has to maintain itself against the constant attacks of sleep, dreams, imaginations, hallucinations, and mental derangement, it is by its nature exposed to manifold dangers. Just as disease is ever lying in wait for our bodies, so madness lies in wait at the threshold of the Ego, and every now and again we hear it knock.

It is of this correct psychological theory, originally propounded by Hume, that the Romanticists, though they do not define it scientifically, nevertheless have a presentiment. Dreams, dipsomania, hallucinations, madness, all the powers which disintegrate the Ego, which disconnect its links, are their familiar friends. Read, for instance, Hoffmann's tale, *The Golden Jar,* and you will hear voices issue from the apple-baskets, and the leaves and flowers of the elder-tree sing; you will see the door-knocker make faces, &c., &c. The strange, striking effect is here specially due to the way in which the apparitions suddenly emerge from a background of the most humdrum, ordinary description, from piles of legal documents, or from tureens and goblets. All Hoffmann's characters (like Andersen's Councillor in *The Galoshes of Fortune,* which is an imitation of Hoffmann) are considered by their neighbours to be either drunk or mad, because they always treat their dreams and visions as realities.

Hoffmann created most of his principal characters in his own image. His whole life resolved itself into moods. We see from his diary how anxiously and minutely he observed these. We come on such entries as:

> Romantically religious mood; excitedly humorous mood, leading finally to those thoughts of madness which so often force themselves upon me; humorously discontented, highly-wrought musical, romantic moods; extremely irritable mood, romantic and capricious in the highest degree; strange, excited, but poetic gloominess;

> very comfortable, brusque, ironical, overstrained, morose, perfectly weak moods; extraordinary, but miserable moods; moods in which I felt deep veneration for myself and praised myself immoderately; *senza entusiasmo, senza esaltazione,* every-day moods, &c., &c.

We seem to see the man's spiritual life spread and split itself up fan-wise into musical high and low spirits. It is easy to guess from this register of moods that Hoffmann, genuine lover of night as he was, was in the habit of going to bed towards morning, after having spent the evening and night in a tavern.

Romanticism having thus dissolved the Ego, proceeds to form fantastic Egos, adding here, taking away there.

Take, for an example, Hoffmann's *Klein Zaches,* the little monster who has been endowed by a fairy with the peculiarity "that everything good that others think, say, or do in his presence is attributed to him; the result being that in the society of handsome, refined, intelligent persons he also is taken to be handsome, refined, and cultured—is taken, in short, for a model of every species of perfection with which he comes in contact." When the student reads aloud his charming poems, it is Zaches who is credited with them; when the musician plays or the professor performs his experiments, it is Zaches who gets the honour and the praise. He grows in greatness, becomes an important man, is made Prime Minister, but ends his days by drowning in a toilet-basin. Without overlooking the satiric symbolism of the story, I draw attention to the fact that the author has here amused himself by endowing one personality with qualities properly belonging to others, in other words, by dissolving individuality and disregarding its limits. With the same satirical intention, the same idea is worked out more ingeniously, though more roughly, by Hostrup, the Dane, in his comedy, *En Spurv i Tranedans* (*A Sparrow among the Cranes*—a dwarf among the giants), in which each one of the other characters attributes to the comical young journeyman tailor the qualities which he himself values most.

Here we have Romanticism amusing itself by adding qualities to human nature; but it found subtracting them an equally attractive amusement. It deprives the individual of attributes which would seem to form an organic part of it; and by taking these away it divides the human being as lower organisms, worms, for example, are divided into greater and smaller parts, both of which live. It deprives the individual, for instance, of his shadow. In Chamisso's *Peter Schlemihl,* the man in the grey coat kneels down before Peter, and, with admirable dexterity, strips the shadow off him and off the grass, rolls it up and pockets it—and the story shows us the misfortunes which are certain to befall the man who has lost his shadow.

This same tale of *Peter Schlemihl* shows how Romanticism, as a spiritual force, succeeded in impressing a uniform stamp on the most heterogeneous talents. It would be difficult to imagine two natures more unlike than Chamisso's and Hoffmann's; hence the plot of Chamisso's tale is as simple and readily comprehensible as the plots of Hoffmann's are morbidly extraordinary.

Adalbert von Chamisso was a Frenchman born, who acquired the German character remarkably quickly and completely, to the extent even of developing more than one quality which we are accustomed to consider essentially German. The son of a French nobleman, he was born in 1781 in the castle of Boncourt, in Champagne. Driven from France as a boy during the Reign of Terror, he became one of Queen Louisa of Prussia's pages, and later, at the age of twenty, a lieutenant in the Prussian army. He was a serious, almost painfully earnest, but absolutely healthy-minded man of sterling worth, brave and honourable, with a little of the heaviness of the German about him and much of the liveliness of the Frenchman.

The reverse of Hoffmann, he was no lover of social pleasures, but all the more ardent a lover of nature. He longed on hot summer days to be able to go about naked in his garden with his pipe in his mouth. Modern dress, modern domestic life and social formalities he regarded in the light of burdensome fetters. His love of nature led him to circumnavigate the globe, enamoured him of the South Sea Islands, and is expressed in much of his poetry.

Nevertheless, the imperceptible intellectual compulsion exercised by the age caused him, as author, to adopt Romantic theories and write in the Romantic style. It is characteristic, however, that when in such a poem as "Erscheinung" ("The Apparition") he treats the Romantic idea of the "Doppelgänger," he does it with a certain moral force which leaves on the reader's mind the impression of genuine despair. The narrator comes home at night and sees himself sitting at his desk. "Who are you?" he asks. "Who disturbs me thus?" returns the "Doppelgänger":—

> Und er: "So lass uns, wer du seist, erfahren!"
> Und ich: "Ein solcher bin ich, der getrachtet
> Nur einzig nach dem Schönen, Guten, Wahren;
> Der Opfer nie dem Götzendienst geschlachtet,
> Und nie gefröhnt dem weltlich-eitlen Brauch,
> Verkannt, verhöhnt, der Schmerzen nie geachtet:
> Der irrend zwar und träumend oft den Rauch
> Für Flamme hielt, doch mutig beim Erwachen
> Das Rechte nur verfocht:—bist du das auch?"
> Und er mit wildem kreischend-lautem Lachen:
> "Der du dich rühmst zu sein, der bin ich nicht.
> Gar anders ist's bestellt um meine Sachen.
> Ich bin ein feiger, lügenhafter Wicht,
> Ein Heuchler mir und andern, tief im Herzen
> Nur Eigennutz, und Trug im Angesicht.
> Verkannter Edler du mit deinen Schmerzen,
> Wer kennt sich nun? wer gab das rechte Zeichen?
> Wer soll, ich oder du, sein Selbst verscherzen?
> Tritt her, so du es wagst, ich will dir weichen!"
> Drauf mit Entsetzen ich zu jenem Graus:
> "Du bist es, bleib und lass hinweg mich schleichen!"
> Und schlich zu weinen, in die Nacht hinaus.
>
> [*He.* Then tell who you are!
>
> *I.* I am a man whose one and only aim has been

> the beautiful, the good, the true. I have never sacrificed to idols, never pandered to the foolish requirements of fashion; the pain caused by misunderstanding and scorn I have disregarded. In my wanderings, in my dreams, I have indeed often taken smoke for flame, but the moment I awoke I upheld what I knew to be the right. Can you say the same?
>
> *He* (with a wild, loud, grating laugh). *I* am not the man that *you* boast yourself to be, but one of a very different character. I am a cowardly, untruthful wretch, a hypocrite to myself and others; my heart is the home of selfishness, deceit is on my tongue. You misunderstood hero of the many sufferings, which of us is it that knows himself? which of us has given the true description? which is the real man? Come here and take my place if you dare? I am ready to make way for you.
>
> *I* (with horrible conviction). You are the man! Stay here and let me slink away!—And out into the night I went, to weep.]

The painful moral self-recognition endows the ghost story with marvellous significance.

Chamisso's double nationality was a source of much unhappiness to him in his younger days, when there was violent enmity between the land of the birth and his adopted country. In one of his letters to Varnhagen (December 1805) he writes: " 'No country, no people—each man for himself!' These words of yours seemed to come straight from my own heart. They almost startled me; I had to wipe away the tears that rolled down my cheeks. Oh! the same sentiment must have made itself felt in all my letters, every one!" (pp. 165-76)

The year 1813, the year of Prussia's declaration of war against France, was the most trying of all for the unfortunate young Franco-German. His heart was divided; he desired the fall of Napoleon because he hated despotism, but at the same time he felt every humiliation which befell the French troops during their retreat from Russia, and every insulting word spoken of the Emperor, as if the misfortune had happened, the insult been offered, to himself. And with this very natural feeling his German associates showed no forbearance. He often cried despairingly: "No, the times have no sword for me." "Action and inaction," he writes in May 1813, "are equally painful to me."

This was the mood which produced his most notable work, *Peter Schlemihl.* The great historical events which harrowed his feelings made him intellectually productive; the summer of 1813 was a turning-point in his life. "I had no longer a country," he says, "or as yet no country." And so the man without a country writes the tale of the man without a shadow. In spite of its intangibility, a man's shadow is, like his country, like his home, one of his natural possessions, a thing which belongs to him from his birth, which is, as it were, part of him. In ordinary circumstances it is regarded as so entirely natural that a man should have a country, that it is hardly reckoned as a special possession, but is, like his shadow, taken as a matter of course. Chamisso gave expression to all his sadness, to the great sorrow of his life, in his daringly imagined fable. And strangely enough, he not only figuratively gave in it the essence of all his past experiences, but also prophetically imaged his future, his voyage round the world and his scientific labours. After Schlemihl has escaped from the temptations of the devil, he accidentally comes into possession of the seven-leagued boots, which take him to every country in the world, and enable him to pursue his favourite study to the greatest advantage. Schlemihl himself says: "My future suddenly showed itself clearly to the eyes of my soul. Banished from human society by the misdemeanours of my youth, I was thrown into the arms of Nature, whom I had always loved. The earth was given to me as a rich garden, study as the directing influence and strength of my life, knowledge as its aim."

The originality of its plot and the remarkable clearness of its style (this last a characteristic of all Chamisso's writing, and evidently his intellectual inheritance as a Frenchman) made *Peter Schlemihl* an extraordinary success. It was translated into nearly every language. Ten years after its publication a new kind of lamp, which cast no shadow, was named the Schlemihl lamp.

Chamisso's success naturally roused Hoffmann to emulation. In the clever little *Story of the Lost Reflection,* the hero leaves his reflection in Italy with the entrancing Giulietta, who has bewitched him, and returns home to his wife without it. His little son, discovering suddenly one day that his father has no reflection, drops the mirror he is holding, and runs weeping from the room. The mother comes in with astonishment and fright written on every feature. "What is this Rasmus has been telling me about you?" she asks. "That I have no reflection, I suppose, my dear," answers Spikher with a forced laugh, and proceeds to try to prove that it is foolish to believe that a man can lose his reflection, but that even if the thing be possible, it is a matter of no importance, seeing that a reflection is simply an illusion. Self-contemplation only leads to vanity, and, moreover, such an image splits up one's personality into truth and imagination.

Here we have the mirror chamber developed to such a point that the reflections move about independently, instead of following their originals. It is very amusing, very original and fantastic, and, as one is at liberty to understand by the reflection whatever one chooses, it may even be said to be very profound. I express no opinion, but simply draw attention to fact.

We have seen that the Romanticist is instinctively, inevitably, the enemy of clearly defined form in art. We have seen Hoffmann mixing up the different parts of his book to the extent of having part of one story on the front, part of quite a different one on the back of the same leaf; have seen Tieck composing dramas like so many puzzle balls one within the other, to prevent the reader taking them too *seriously,* and Kierkegaard fitting one author inside another in the Chinese box fashion, on the strength of the theory that truth can only be imparted indirectly, a theory which he ended by treating with scorn—we have seen, in a word, that the artistic standpoint of Romanticism is the exact opposite of the artistic standpoint of the ancients. And when, with their learning to the supernatural, the Romanticists extend the personality of the individual throughout several successive generations, representing him as living before his birth and after his death, or represent him as a day-dreamer, half visionary and half madman, or humorously endow him with other men's attributes and despoil him of his own, fantastically filching now a shadow, now a reflection, they show by all this fantastic duplication and imagination that their psychological standpoint too, is an absolutely different one; for in the days of old both the work of art and the personality were whole, were of one piece. The movement is a perfectly consistent one, regarded as the antipodes of classicism, in short, as Romanticism.

But, granted that man is of necessity, by his very nature, a divided, complex being, he is nevertheless, as the healthy, vigorous personality, one. Aim, will, resolve, make him a complete unit. If, as a natural product, the human being is only a group held more or less firmly together by association of ideas, as a mind he is a complete whole; in his will all the elements of the mind are united. Romanticism only understood and depicted human nature with genius from the natural, from the night side. It made no closer approach in this than in any other of its endeavours to intellectual collectedness, unity, and liberty. (pp. 177-80)

Georg Brandes, "Romantic Duplication and Psychology," in his Main Currents in Nineteenth Century Literature: The Romantic School in Germany, Vol. II, *translated by Diana White and Mary Morison, The Macmillan Company 1902, pp. 152-80.*

Marianne Wain

[In the following excerpt, Wain focuses on the role of the double in Romantic literature, suggesting that while writers used the theme of the split ego to illustrate a general malaise, they also searched for remedies.]

In the romantic predilection for the symbol of the Doppelgänger we are confronted with one of the central problems of the movement. It is crucial, because it represents at once the excellences and the weaknesses of the Romantic search for means of expression through a new mythology. How important this search was is shown not only by F. Schlegel's *Athenäum* piece—the *Gespräch über die Poesie*—but by numerous other writings of the period, from Novalis' fragmentary jottings to G. H. Schubert's collections of legendary *curiosa.* This in itself should make us reconsider the too facile current denigrations of the Romantic addiction to the fairy-tale as a serious literary genre. There are, it is true, grave errors of taste, an undeniable coyness and, perhaps worst of all, a sense of strain wherever this basically simple and dramatic form is made to carry unduly philosophical or lyrical matter. Nevertheless, it would be equally biased to deny the Romantic achievements in this genre, if only because they have left their traces on contemporary habits of expression. By renewing and exploring the possibilities of ancient myths, the Romantics handed down to our day the instruments for venturing into the depths of human consciousness, a fact to which the works of Freud and C. G. Jung bear ample witness. Tieck's *Der blonde Eckbert* is a telling example of such pioneer work; for while it is, superficially, a random account of unrealistic happenings, the proper meaning and cohesion of the story cannot be grasped until one takes into account the distortions of reality which guilt and its "projection" mechanisms force upon the presentation of the events. Here, the acceptance of irrational "sequences" of events which is the basic assumption of the fairy-tale is adapted to the irrational functionings of the human mind, thereby bringing to light subtle reactions which would normally pass unobserved. There is no attempt to force an explanation or analysis on these movements of the soul, no schematization by established patterns of syndromes or "complexes," and thus the integrity of the story as a work of art is preserved. But it is not merely entertaining, it is, in its miniature way, a contribution to the understanding of acute moral consciousness and of a sensitiveness peculiarly modern.

In common with the rest of *Märchendichtung,* the symbol of the Double cannot escape the criticism of excessive and disingenuous naivety. Also, it has a tendency to crop up in the works of periods of decadence. For this reason alone it would seem safe to claim that its appeal and the psychological reactions it evokes are not immediate or valid at all times. There are, evidently, problems within the hierarchy of symbols which are outside the scope of this essay but which ought to be stated briefly and borne in mind nevertheless. These distinctions appear to be due partly to the nature of the image itself and partly to the handling which the image receives. It is not always easy to distinguish between the two, more especially so because modern man does not seem to be a spontaneous symbol-maker, but has to rely on the artists to make him conscious of their power and their value. There should be no reason, on the face of it, for the symbol of the Siren, of the Vampire-woman to receive greater credence and popularity than the Double: it can hardly be claimed that anyone literally believes in either. Yet, to take a most obvious example, there is the lasting popularity of Heine's *Lorelei.* The continuing popularity of this poem, while Brentano's handling of the identical motif has fallen into neglect, cannot be explained entirely by the musical setting, nor yet, entirely, by arguments based on literary quality. In both cases, that human love for danger (which Valéry strikingly defined as the "soif de désastre" in "La Jeune Parque"), is made concrete. It is embodied in the sinister maiden and she appears as the central figure in both poems. But in Heine's, the woman's attributes of danger and indifference to the sufferings she causes are echoed by the natural setting of which she is part: she is a mirage born of the treacherous twilight and the melancholy mood it induces. Although we are told nothing of her feelings, be they triumph and "Schadenfreude" or commiseration, she has a reality which is on a level with that of the sunset, the rock, and the water. The sunset and the water are both inconstant and deluding, the rock is hard, unfeeling, and a death trap for the mariner: they underline and reflect these qualities in the Lorelei, while she resumes and crystallizes *their* attributes. In contrast to this multiplicity of dimensions, the version of the story that Brentano gives us seems not much more than an enumeration of the manifold disasters wrought by the unfortunate girl, who appears as much worried by her unwelcome powers as do her victims. On the face of it, there is no reason why this treatment of the legend should not be equally interesting; in fact, there seems plenty of scope here for translating the somewhat primitive and externalized image into psychologically and emotionally more human terms. It seems true, however, that to be fully effective a symbol should have around it a context of subordinate images which reflect its main significance and enhance it by resonances and fine gradations.

Now the Double image in its heyday had precisely something of this contextual background, both by implication and by overt references, even though we have here the creation, not of an immemorial folklore, but of a set of highly sophisticated writers. (We shall find that some of their presentations of the image are quite frankly literary.) I have used the word "heyday" deliberately, because a study of the image will show that it enjoyed a period of flourishing and that it also suffered a decline. The curve is not strictly chronological, but rather a process which can be traced through different authors. I shall, in the main, be concerned with those who seem to me to have made the most interesting and mature use of the image and, therefore, leave out of account Chamisso's *Peter Schlemihl,* even though this may seem perverse, since it is Chamisso's story which first springs to mind when mention is made of the Double. I believe that we have in Schlemihl a trivialized use of the symbol and if Chamisso's story rather than the others is still read, this is due as much as anything to its relative brevity: a certain prolixity was a besetting sin of the Romantics, and it was also a fashion with which we are no longer in sympathy.

One of the echo-dimensions of the Double is the figure of Hamlet. The *Stürmer und Dränger* had discovered Shakespeare, in whom they appreciated the extrovert master-creator of the histories and lighter comedies. The revelation of Shakespeare as a decadent and a sensitive was reserved for the Romantics. Whatever Goethe's part in setting them on the track with his discussion of the play in *Wilhelm Meister,* they soon emancipated themselves from such mild suggestions of "mal du siècle." From their own studies emerge infinitely more contemporary—and sinister—features of the Prince of Denmark. It is instructive to watch F. Schlegel appropriating Hamlet for his contemporaries with something of the exasperation of a jealous lover, disputing the older man's right to claim any sympathetic understanding of the afflicted Prince. The technical and textual problems raised by the play, as well as the character of the Prince, had interested Goethe. For Schlegel, nothing exists but the central character, who becomes the embodiment of "heroic hopelessness." For him, as for the other Romantics, Hamlet was a fellow-sufferer from that cancerous proliferation of the intellect with which Fichte was infecting them and, like themselves, had undergone a degeneration of the more human qualities in consequence. . . . By 1798, in the essay on Goethe's *Meister,* Schlegel had not moved from this position; the essay is too well-known for me to quote at length here, but we may take the following remark about the "fürchterliche Trauerspiel" as the keynote of the whole tone: its moral climate, according to this essay, is one of hesitation between crime and madness ("zwischen Verbrechen und Wahnsinn schwankend").

Now the moral uncertainty in Hamlet is due, of course, chiefly to excess of intellectual development without parallel culture of the heart, and one of the symptoms of this barbarization of the feelings is the absence of any kind of faith. (pp. 257-60)

These critical remarks are by no means isolated chance sayings, brought together to support my argument. It is in fact astonishing, when one goes through Romantic writing generally, whether criticism, biography, or fiction, to see how this preoccupation with the lost centre of personality is a veritable obsession. In the lectures on dramatic art, for instance, A. W. Schlegel seems to see this quality of "doubleness" as the essential fact about modern man: an interesting development, it would appear, of Schiller's idea of the conflict within the post-classical consciousness. But more than that, he brings this thought into so many of his detailed analyses of plays, and in particular of those of Shakespeare, that it is hardly too much to say that it is the "Leitmotif" of his critical approach at this stage. It is particularly striking that when he comes to discuss comedy he quotes with approval a passage in *Phantasus* where Tieck had said that " . . . die Basis der komischen Bühne . . . ruht . . . auf der Zweiheit, der Doppelheit des menschlichen Geistes, dem wunderbaren Widerspruch in uns . . . "

This unifying concept of the irony of opposites which brings together comedy and tragedy is echoed—unconsciously—in Solger's Hamlet criticism. He had evidently been struck by the absence here of one of Shakespeare's favorite devices for pointing up the darkness of the tragic picture, his use of the convention of the Fool. He suggests that the reason for the Fool's absence in *Hamlet* is the fact that he has been incorporated into the hero: "Er braucht keinen parodirenden Narren, er hat ihn (wie denn freilich jeder Mensch auch) selbst in sich . . . " This irony, poised halfway between laughter and tears, between heaven and hell, is the realization of the disproportion between human ideal aspirations and the shoddy but overwhelming realities of bread-and-butter. It can, on the one hand, be a sign of awareness of failure, but it can, on the other, be no more than inactive realization, leading through discouragement and acceptance of things as they are, to despair. Of this process, too, Hamlet is the prime example, as [E. T. A. Hoffmann asserts]. . . . (pp. 260-61)

As will not appear surprising after this, another of the chords which the Double cannot fail to strike is that of madness. This is true even in such late manifestations as R. L. Stevenson's *Dr. Jekyll and Mr. Hyde* and Dostoevsky's *The Double.* It is all the more marked with the Romantics, whose affinity with this state of consciousness always dangerously bordered on identification with it. Again, it has a double aspect: that of the *furor poeticus,* of divine inspiration; and also that of punishment for those whose intellect usurps the power reserved to the Godhead alone. . . . This view of madness as a state of moral inspiredness is [furnished] by Bonaventura in several passages of the *Nachtwachen.* The other attitude to madness has already been hinted at through the reference to *Ham-*

let in the 1798 essay by Schlegel. The more overt and explicit statements about this negative valuation, however, have to be looked for mainly in the artistic, rather than the theoretical, productions of the Romantic school.

It is generally known that Jean-Paul coined the expression "Doppeltgänger," but he is rarely given credit for his treatment of this discovery in some of his most important works. Yet it is he who gave the most significant version of this symbol. Beside him, only E. T. A. Hoffmann seems as fully aware of the range of meaning contained in it. From what has gone before it can be appreciated that there was more than a superficial coincidence in the fact that a study of the solipsistic philosophy of J. G. Fichte, as expressed in his *Grundlage der gesammten Wissenschaftslehre* of 1794, led Jean-Paul to the elaboration of this figure. *Hesperus,* and more particularly *Siebenkäs, Titan,* and *Dr. Katzenbergers Badereise* represent the stages by which he worked out, and finally liberated himself from, the most fearful implications of Fichte's system, as it appeared to him. These are, chiefly, the glorification of the human intellect as the only creator of "reality" and the consequent imprisonment of each individual within his own mental creation. All possibilities of communication are denied, since all "other" individuals are of necessity mere projections of the self; all feelings, all standards are therefore equally *subjective,* in this most sinister interpretation of the term. Jean-Paul formulates this in an image of utter desolation: "Rund um mich eine weite versteinerte Menschheit—ich so ganz allein, nirgends ein Pulsschlag, kein Leben, nichts um mich und ohne mich nichts als nichts."

Frontispiece to Dr. Jekyll and Mr. Hyde.

The novel *Hesperus* presents the Double theme for the first time. In 1795, however, it had not yet fully crystalized under the impact of Fichte's thought. It represents, rather, the fear of the automatism of the life-processes, of the "homme-machine," as the rationalistic determinism of the eighteenth century had already known it. But even now the hero, Victor, fears the annihilation of reason by very reasoning in the abyss of madness, as he contemplates his wax-effigy: "Ich! Ich! du Abgrund der im Spiegel des Gedankens tief ins Dunkel zurückläuft—Ich! du Spiegel im Spiegel—du Schauder im Schauder!" He too seeks deliverance through love, through a reaching-out, that is, to others and a confirmation of himself through others, but finds himself inadequate to this task. He is actually recalled from the depths by the loving embrace of his friends, but his own part in this remains passive, and the description of the healing is far less convincing than that of his suffering, no doubt because it is never fully lived. His problem, then, is not resolved in an intrinsic manner and duly crops up again in *Blumen-, Frucht- und Dornenstücke, oder Ehestand, Leben und Tod Siebenkäs* (1796–1797), where it becomes the central theme of discussion. It is, in essence, the story of the failure of a man to adjust himself to the conditions of a bourgeois marriage. Admittedly, Jean-Paul's attitude to this failure is ambiguous, and he rescues his hero by making him enter upon an ideal union with a very grand soul, but the impression it leaves on the reader is again one of a lack of reality. The trouble is caused here no longer by a mere wax-image, but by a fully-fledged *Doppelgänger,* the hero's best friend, Leibgeber, with whom Siebenkäs has exchanged names. Although their physical lives are individualized and separate, neither is complete without the other and Siebenkäs' marriage is clearly regarded as an act of unfaithfulness on his part. It seems no more than poetic justice, for instance, that Leibgeber should appear at the wedding-ceremony to disturb the proceedings. He does not limit his protests to this and is finally responsible for the break-up of the marriage; beside his untrammelled irresponsibility, the solid virtues of Lenette come to look more and more stifling, and Siebenkäs becomes aware, to the point of agony, of her "geistige Provinzialismen." Perhaps the most significant scene in the whole novel is the passage where, after the wedding-ceremony, the young couple are left alone and Siebenkäs is on the point at last of breaking through his isolation of self-doubt and self-denigration by kissing his bride; but Leibgeber suddenly materializes behind his friend's chair, clears his throat and pronounces (in desperate *fear,* as Jean-Paul tells us): "Unser Abend war ganz schön." This puts an effective end to any further proceedings. Siebenkäs' relationship with Lenette deteriorates: "Ihn drückte in derselben Minute der Wunsch und das Unvermögen, sie zu lieben, die Einsicht ihrer Mängel und die Gewißheit ihrer Kälte." His exchange of names with Leibgeber also debars him from claiming his inheritance; he founders in a sea of depression and is saved only by a change of scene, though Jean-Paul seems aware of the makeshift nature of such a solution: "Wir vertauschen die Bühnen, aber wir verlassen sie nicht." Towards the end, it is the figure of Leibgeber which becomes predominant: Siebenkäs is pushed out of the picture with his ideal marriage, but Leibgeber is left with nothing to do except haunting his friend's creditor. His problems are, quite literally, quadruplicated when he has a fearful vision of his four selves in the mirror. He fears that one of his selves, whether this be the "I" in the mirror (the soul, or spiritual self), or the "I" without (the emotional, physically-centered self) has died, so that the identity of whichever "I" remains is arbitrary, meaningless, and without anchorage in the dimensions of the objective world. As Siebenkäs and he try to sort out their relationship, they are forced to the conclusion that what gives them reality is that aspect of their personalities by which they differ from one another and not, as might be imagined, those by which they are made as one. This provides an excellent motivation for allowing them to go on their several ways, a course that is smoother for the supposedly less complicated Siebenkäs. Nevertheless, one of the results is that Leibgeber now seems to take over and carry the burden of inner disunity of both of them—a clear indication that Jean-Paul could not rest content with the patchy solution he had worked out: Siebenkäs is cured, long suffer Leibgeber! He does, in fact, suffer right in to *Titan* (1800–1803). Here he appears under the guise of Schoppe, tutor to Albano, the hero of this *Erziehungsroman,* a character who has drunk too deeply at the spring of Fichtean wisdom. As such he represents one of the possible directions of development which the main character might have taken and which is fruitful only because it is explored, exploited, and finally transcended. Regretfully and at last, Jean-Paul now settles Schoppe/Leibgeber's account: Siebenkäs reappears briefly, but long enough for Leibgeber to imagine he has come face to face with his Double and to die of shock and horror in consequence. Although he had appeared throughout *Titan* as a devoted and loving man, this love remained tortured and restricted in scope: it was mostly directed towards Albano, whose Double relationship to him is hinted at and which therefore remained another case, so to speak, of "amitié particulière." In the last analysis, such limitations upon the feeling must invalidate its latent possibilities, because they prevent it from exercising its full power on that which is different, other, objective, and outside oneself, and by extension on that within one's personality which differs from one's ideal conception of it. For this reason, a confrontation of the kind reserved for Leibgeber must prove the ultimate horror. With his reaction to it, Jean-Paul passes judgment on this much-loved and in many ways admirable figure. The condemnation proves Jean-Paul's own maturing awareness and in the novel helps to liberate Siebenkäs, and more particularly, Albano, from the most private danger of their completeness and integrity as human beings. (I have purposely left the Roquairol/Albano problem out of the discussion for the sake of unity, but it would be interesting to delve into the precise nature of the relationship between it and the one under examination.) All that was now left for Jean-Paul was to assert his independence from this recurrent theme by lifting it to the plane of comedy, and this he did with *Dr. Katzenbergers Badereise* in 1804, so that the wheel came full circle. The protagonists in this novel have strongly marked allegorical features, though these are not unduly stressed. A scurrilous poetaster here usurps the name of an honest military engineer and nearly succeeds in winning the affections of a trustful and affectionate maiden. An almost Kleistian situation is precipitated in due course, in which the innocent Heart struggles towards true insight and finally makes the right choice in favour of Practical Life and against the calculating and useless Aesthetic Intellect. Here too, Jean-Paul arranges a confrontation between the supposed friends, but the two halves are no longer dangerously complementary and, in fact, the honest hero is totally unaware of the existence of the man who claims his friendship.

If we turn to E. T. A. Hoffmann we can distinguish a strikingly similar pattern. I cannot hope to give an exhaustive, or even a moderately complete analysis of his *Doppelgängerdichtung* in this essay, but I shall confine my remarks to the *Elixiere des Teufels* (1815–16) and to *Prinzessin Brambilla* (1820) which best illustrate my point and carry on the chronology in a satisfactory manner. The *Elixiere* are a species of "gothic horror-thriller," with all the mysterious accidents and complicated relationships proper to that genre. In this work, Hoffmann, as it were, plays a virtuoso cadenza on the variations possible on the Double theme, much as Jean-Paul had done in *Siebenkäs.* He presents his hero as a man brought up in a pious, scholarly atmosphere, whose origins may be shrouded in mystery, but whose earthly future at least seems clear, inasmuch as he intends to enter a monastery. In late adolescence, the adumbration of erotic experience shatters his peace for a while, though he is careful to wipe all trace of this from his mind. From then on, however, his state of being becomes clouded: in the train of excessive intellectual culture and attainments come disasterous repercussions on his personal character and even his career. Brilliant though this career may be outwardly, it is in constant jeopardy from fits of absent-mindedness and from hallucinations which overcome him at unpredictable moments. He reaches the crossroads of his development with the surrender of his mad desire for a "fair penitent" and the sacrilegious tasting of a magic potion which is in the safe-keeping of the monastery. This latter obviously has a function similar to that of the Apple of Knowledge and here, as in the Biblical story, the connection between one-sided intellectualism and ravening sensuality is hinted at constantly. Sent into the world for a time by his Superior, Medardus commits near-incestuous adultery and, he imagines, murder. From then on he is dogged by his "victim" whose personalia he has assumed. When he is finally apprehended by worldly justice and would dearly love to rid himself by confession of all the confusions in which he is involved, this proves impossible, first in a "rehearsal" dream where he finds his lips will not obey his will, and then in the real court of law, where circumstances have once more outdistanced him, and he finds he is officially innocent. A more meaningful, inner expiation is required of him, and this is brought about by the murder of his beloved Aurelie at the hands of his mad Double. Aurelie's forgiveness at the hour of death and Medardus' acceptance of all that has happened at last bring about an inner illumination which, if it does not make the remainder of his life a haven of bliss, does at least bring wisdom, peace, and unity. The Double disappears after the crime has been committed, presumably having played out his self-centered depravity and by this vicarious action apparently curing Medardus, whose feeling for Aurelie undergoes a spiritual transformation thereafter. It might seem that Hoffmann is here being deeply pessimistic about the conditions of earthly life, as if he held out no hope of anything beyond total renunciation of temporal vanities. In actual fact, the picture is not quite so unrelievedly black: Medardus labors under the special disadvantage of four generations of criminal ancestors (unless this be taken as an image of the fallen condition of man generally), and there are minor figures in the story who appear to make a success of life without too great an ascetic sacrifice. These either live close to nature, like the forester (and are thus an instance of a well-worn literary convention), or like the Prior Leonardus, they have discovered the secret of *Heiterkeit,* that serenity and gaiety produced by a sense of proportion, and it is to Hoffmann's credit that he has drawn a convincing picture of this attitude, even if he could not make his hero partake of it at this stage.

The case of *Prinzessin Brambilla* (1820) is altogether different. No longer is the imagination the playground merely of sinful phantasies: the hero is an actor by profession and this does put strange and potentially destructive ideas into his head. Thus, he considers he is too good for his fiancée, the sempstress Giacinta and she, in turn, is led by the magic of *her* art to think of herself as the bride of the Prince of Bergamo. A kindly impresario suggests that they act out their phantasies on a real stage where they improvise under the inspiration of their hallucinatory state. At least, these fancies now have a real audience: the world of makebelieve is no longer a threat to reality and the actors have ceased to be their "eigner spielender Kasperl und . . . Frontloge . . . zugleich," as Jean-Paul remarks of Siebenkäs and Leibgeber. Before estrangement and heartbreak can come to Giglio and Giacinta they regain their senses, and all ends in joyful recognition and in a humility which makes them accept their mediocre station in real life as a matter of course: they know that in the innermost depths of their hearts they are indeed prince and princess, and this casts a glorious reflection on their day-to-day life without depriving it of its vital reality. The impresario adds an explanatory note to this tale when he enlightens Giacinta in the following words: ". . . ich könnte sagen, du seist die Fantasie, deren Flügel erst der Humor bedurfte, um sich emporzuschwingen, aber ohne den Körper des Humors wärst du nichts, als Flügel, und verschwebtest, ein Spiel der Winde, in den Lüften."

With this statement, oblique as it may be, we reach the core of the matter: phantasy, the unbridled imagination which derives its destructive dynamism from the deficiencies of the personality, is recognized as such and condemned by the Romantics. Although it frequently masquerades as an immortal aspiration after a richer and more rewarding form of existence, it gives itself away by leaving the individual it possesses a poorer and more negative creature, one spiritually "disinherited," as Siebenkäs was in symbolic fact. The chafing at the disproportion between man's wish for ultimate fulfillment, and the opportunities given him on earth may all too easily come under the sway of his self-regarding instincts and degenerate into pride and discontent. This contempt for the order of creation leads to a further blurring of man's vision, to a state akin to the unreality of drunkenness, where things may indeed be seen as "double" or by the improperly focussed eye. In the spiritual realm such maladjustment induces the anxiety we have met in the figures of *Doppelgängerdichtung* and which in a more orthodox context would be called the sin of despair. If this line of argument is accepted, the intentions of other writers within the convention become much clearer and the purpose and force of lighter and more fanciful creations—such as Chamisso's Schlemihl and Brentano's "Wondrous Tales" of Bogs the Watchmaker and Wehmüller the Painter—acquire additional meaning.

Finally, it should not be forgotten that the Romantics were not content with mere diagnosis: in all the narratives where the Double theme is treated with seriousness some form of remedy is suggested. We have already seen an instance of this in the case of Hoffmann's *Elixiere,* and his conclusions reappear, materially identical, in all these works. The first rule appears to be to trust the world around us and the evidence of our senses and, above all, to keep these in good working order by preserving a balance in all things. That such a rule of life need not lead to dull uniformity is shown by the variety of guises in which it is presented to us: whether in the monastery under the rule of the Prior Leonardus or the homely maccaroni suppers of Giacinta, the Kingdom of Hohenfließ, or the bourgeois domesticity of Theoda, née Katzenberger. The evidence of things as they are must be the starting-point of a truly human life, not the measure of the "überweise Narrheit" of the intellect, or, as Jean-Paul expressed this truth in a very idiosyncratic and "contemporary" form: "Je älter man wird, desto demütiger glaubt man an die Allmacht der Objektivität; Gott ist das einzige Subjekt." (pp. 261-68)

Marianne Wain, "The Double in Romantic Narrative: A Preliminary Study," in The Germanic Review, *Vol. XXXVI, No. 4, December, 1961, pp. 257-68.*

SOCIOLOGICAL VIEWS

Robert Alter

[*Alter is a highly respected American scholar whose writings include* Rogue's Progress: Studies in the Picaresque Novel *(1965),* Partial Magic: The Novel as a Self-Conscious Genre *(1975), and* Defenses of the Imagination *(1978). In the following excerpt, he comments on the double in nineteenth-century literature, arguing that the theme was a literary response to the specif-*

ic pressures and limitations that nineteenth-century society imposed on the individual.]

[To a large extent] fictional doubles are creatures of the nineteenth century. Doubles, of course, have long been part of the paraphernalia of folklore—arguably, as far back as the Akkadians—but it is chiefly in the nineteenth century, from the third decade onward, that the double is frequently adopted by fiction aspiring to psychological realism. This tradition is capped by Joseph Conrad's story "The Secret Sharer" (1912). It may be that in our own time this convention has come to seem too schematic a division of the self; in recent decades, it has been invoked chiefly by way of parody—perhaps most prominently in the fiction of Vladimir Nabokov, who coyly played with doubles from *Despair* (1932) to *Lolita* (1954). Not surprisingly, Nabokov was an admirer of *Dr Jekyll and Mr Hyde.*

The term *Doppelgänger,* which has been applied to a variety of literary works, actually brackets together two different figures, allied in nature but distinct in origin. We may conveniently call them splits and doubles. In the case of the former, the self is divided inwardly in a kind of moral meiosis, its mixed properties separated and polarized; Stevenson's tale of "polar twins" is the supreme expression of this version of the *Doppelgänger.* For the splits, it is ghastly difference rather than resemblance that is the key. In the more common case of the double proper, the self encounters a disturbing mirror-image in the external world. In the supernatural versions, this doubling of the self is affected by capricious fate or infernal powers; in the more psychological versions, it is a projection of the self, and as such begins to converge with the split. The double draws on a background of folktales about confrontations with demonic figures who exercise a maddening ability to mime the self, generally as part of a scheme to destroy it. The split, on the other hand, may ultimately derive from the tales of opposed twins, or at any rate siblings, like Jacob and Esau, Cain and Abel. Fratricide is very often on the mind of at least one of the members of the split or double pair, including Stevenson's. The convention of the *Doppelgänger,* then, seems to bring to the fore a masked element of internal violence.

A good many of these elements come together in the remarkable Scottish antecedent to *Dr Jekyll and Mr Hyde,* James Hogg's *The Private Memoirs and Confessions of a Justified Sinner* (1824). Some have claimed that Hogg was influenced by E. T. A. Hoffmann; Hoffmann's melodramatic story, *Die Doppelgänger,* published two years earlier, represents the lower end of the spectrum of doubles fiction: sheer contrivance. I think it more likely that the two writers simply breathed the same *Zeitgeist.* In any case, Hogg anticipates later developments in combining the supernatural with the psychological. Indeed, his novel has both splits and doubles, first an allusion to Cain and Abel in the lethal pursuit of one brother by another, then the devil as seductive mirror-image or split-off externalization of the self—presented, to be sure, with supernatural trappings but in the end figuring persuasively as an extrapolation, an enlarged and frightening reflection, of the potential for evil latent in the self. Hogg himself makes elaborate connections between the plot of doom through the sinister double and the grim theological vistas of Scottish Calvinism. Six decades later, that theological background is still palpable in Stevenson's novel, for all the secularity of its London setting: "in the law of God", the attorney Utterson reflects gloomily on his friend Dr Hyde, "there is no statute of limitations".

In any event, Calvinism may reinforce the imagining of doubles and splits but it could hardly be their ultimate source, since they appear at such disparate points on the European cultural map. Dostoevsky's bizarre novel *The Double* (1846) is an instructive case in point by virtue of its thoroughgoing secularity and its representation of the mocking, subversive double as a reflex of social self-consciousness. Mr Golyadkin, the hapless protagonist, is one of those familiar superfluous men of nineteenth-century Russian literature, a low-level civil servant doing meaningless work who is acutely anxious about his position in the bureaucratic hierarchy, about the social and professional role he is expected to play *vis-à-vis* peers and superiors. The terrific strain of maintaining propriety in the virtual isolation of urban *anomie* leads to a kind of explosion of the self: in this regard, Mr Golyadkin's Petersburg and Dr Jekyll's London are rather similar, both cities shrouded with fogs that blur perception and visually cut off the individual from whatever there may be in the way of community. Dostoevsky shrewdly suggests that to possess a unitary self is a kind of social obligation, or more radically, that modern urban societies need a myth of the unitary self in order to function, cannot countenance the possibility that their members may be inwardly divided, fragmented, multiple in nature, something other than cogs in the social machine. As Mr Golyadkin's insolent servant says to him at a point when the mischievous double has already disrupted his life, "Nice people don't live falsely and don't have doubles."

It may be instructive to sketch the social profile of the figure who becomes host to the *Doppelgänger.* He is almost invariably male, perhaps because the idea of holding a place in society through the exercise of a profession is paramount. He has no friends, or few (Dr Jekyll's don't see him for months on end), and usually no visible relatives (the parents of Hogg's justified sinner, who exert a baleful influence on him, are a limited exception). He is educated, intelligent, and has modest to ample financial means. Perhaps most crucially, he is always a bachelor. Sterility, disconnection, the displacement of personal by professional life, a developed mind with the leisure to exercise it, are the general fate of the *Doppelgänger* host.

Now, some of these figures are mainly distraught and victimized, like Mr Golyadkin; and in one instance, Poe's "William Wilson" (1839), the *Doppelgänger* is actually not satanic but, on the contrary, the embodiment of conscience, whom the dissolute protagonist will eventually destroy. But the convention as a rule is associated with the irruption or revelation of evil in lives of seeming probity, and the most basic question to be asked about these sundry secret sharers is the nature of the evil they represent. Readers of *Dr Jekyll and Mr Hyde* have puzzled for a century over precisely what it is that the repulsive Mr Hyde does in his nocturnal expeditions. Since Dr Jekyll tells us explicitly that he has devised this second self to serve his pleasure, it would seem plausible to think of sex. Given what we do know about Hyde, it is easy enough to imagine that this would involve visits to brothels provided with whips, manacles, and similar appurtenances. But Stevenson's absolute silence on these activities is not, as is often said, simply a matter of Victorian *pudeur;* there is something intrinsically, and weirdly, sexless about both Jekyll and Hyde as there is about most of the arid *Doppelgänger* bachelors. Hogg's Robert Wringhim is, quite properly, scandalized when sexual promiscuity is attributed to him, and heartily affirms his general loathing of women; though his satanic double has in fact seduced an innocent girl in his name, the vicarious sexual conquest remains purely an off-stage event. Aggression is the true name of the *Doppelgänger* game, its consummation not in the touch of flesh against flesh, however sadistic, but in murder. Robert Wringhim's tutor in evil sets him on the path to perdition by persuading him to commit murder, trusting that from the seed of one killing many others will blossom. Our first vision of Hyde is trampling a little girl with whom he collides on the sidewalk "like some damned Juggernaut". Disturbingly—this is a detail that should not be neglected—the reaction of the crowd of onlookers is in the same key of violence: an apothecary turns "sick and white with the desire to kill him"; a circle of hateful-faced women are "wild as harpies". The initial incident, then, is an introduction to the psychological ambience of the metropolis as well as to Hyde's evil nature, which is fully revealed when he clubs and stamps to death Sir Danvers Carew, not merely murdering him but "audibly" shattering his bones.

The psychological power of the *Doppelgänger,* whether projection or split, is as an incarnation of the suppressed rage and frustration of the self. Hemmed in, isolated, deprived of friends, family, wife or mistress, the *Doppelgänger* host dreams of turning himself into an unfeeling instrument of sheer destructive force. Towards the end of Stevenson's narrative, Dr Jekyll describes Mr Hyde "drinking pleasure with bestial avidity from any degree of torture to another; relentless like a man of stone". The progression is itself instructive: from drinking pleasure, still implicitly a human activity, however orgiastic, to bestiality, to the man of stone.

This exercise of destructive power is a fantasy of terrible freedom, beyond all social and moral restraints. Appropriately, it is a fantasy entertained by what Michel Foucault would call "the carceral subject". Images of imprisonment are very frequently associated with the *Doppelgänger.* In Hogg's novel, there is a growing sense that the protagonist is chained to his secret sharer, who by stages becomes his jailer and executioner. William Wilson's native home and then his school are both explicitly represented as prisons. And Dr Jekyll's bachelor quarters are like a condemned man's cell, "that house of voluntary bondage" in which he sits "like some disconsolate prisoner", having become the abject slave of the creature through whom he thought to act out a dream of pure, immoral freedom. The emotional climax of the novel is not the revelation of the secret itself but that horrendous moment when the servant Poole, directed by Utterson, smashes his axe five times against the locked, unyielding door of Jekyll's surgical theatre, and they can hear "a dismal screech, as of mere animal terror", from the expiring prisoner within.

Whatever the continuities between the societies of the previous century and our own, this vision of modern life as incarceration seems to have lost its old potency, and that may explain in part why writers are less often drawn to the *Doppelgänger.* At one point in his "Statement of the Case", Dr Jekyll, having affirmed that "man is . . . truly two", conjures up a still more vertiginous possibility:

> I say two, because the state of my own knowledge does not pass beyond that point. Others will follow, others will outstrip me on the same lines; and I hazard the guess that man will be ultimately known for a mere polity of multifarious, incongruous and independent denizens.

It is a moment of haunting prescience. Those multifarious denizens look forward to versions of the protean or serial self in the fiction of Thomas Pynchon, John Barth, Gabriel García Márquez or in Joyce Carey's *The Horse's Mouth* (1944) and Saul Bellow's *The Adventures of Augie March* (1953), as Stevenson's two become many.

Robert Alter, "Playing Host to the Doppelgänger," in The Times Literary Supplement, *No. 4360, October 24, 1986, p. 1190.*

Jeremy Hawthorn

[*Hawthorn is a literary scholar whose books include* Multiple Personality and the Disintegration of Literary Character *(1983),* A Glossary of Contemporary Literary Theory *(1992) and* Studying the Novel: An Introduction *(1993). In the following excerpt from the first-named work, he interprets the double in nineteenth-century literature as a metaphor for human alienation caused by the anomie of industrial society.*]

It is clear, . . . that an increased interest in the portrayal of doubles on the part of a significant number of writers in a given period bespeaks some sort of concern with the issue of individual identity, and this in turn suggests that something is making this issue more problematic for these writers than it was, perhaps, for writers of a different period. Introducing his [1979] translation of Otto Rank's classic work *The Double,* Harry Tucker Jr comments upon the striking tripartite conjunction of interest in the theme of the literary double, major upheavals of society, and the development of psychology in its recognizably modern form. We might add to this list the medical profession's discovery of—and increasing concern with—multiple personality.

Tucker points out that there have been periods of social upheaval (he refers to the Thirty Year's War) during which the theme of the double either did not appear in literature or was insignificant, and so we should avoid positing any mechanical relationship between social upheaval and literary convention or subject matter. Clearly fashion may play some element in the popularity of the double theme in certain historical periods—as Arnold M. Ludwig and others suggest [in "The Objective Study of a Multiple Personality," *Archives of General Psychology,* 1972] is also true of the diagnosis of multiple personality. But 'fashion' is itself a problematic concept; what is fashionable may be partly a matter of accident, but it is hard to believe that no isolable causal factors enter into the determination of the fashion that dominates an art form at a particular time.

Ralph Tymms, in his important *Doubles in Literary Psychology* (1949), sees the roots of the theme of the double in the ordinary phenomenon of family likeness and chance resemblance, but he adds that these roots 'will also be seen to be firmly embedded in magic and in the earliest speculations on the nature of the soul'. He further suggests that there is a complex relationship between the development of modern psychology, the 'Mesmerist's observation of hitherto unsuspected traits of character', and the great development of interest in doubles in the literature of the Romantic period. Like Tucker, then, he perceives a family of traits, including the development of psychology, literary romanticism and social change, to be involved in the eruption of interest in the portrayal of literary doubles. It would seem that the development of psychology can be seen both as effect and as cause; a feeling that human consciousness was complex and concealed enough to merit analysis perhaps contributes to the development of the discipline, but the findings of psychological inquiry react back on to people's conception of the nature of human consciousness and individual identity.

Tymms quotes some interesting links between psychological writings of the Romantic period and literary figures, which indicate that in some cases a direct influence seems to be traceable from psychological inquiry to literary creation:

> In *Die Symbolik des Traumes,* G. H. Schubert (whose lectures Kleist attended in Dresden) quotes from the standard works on magnetism available to him—not all of which would be accessible to Kleist, but which correspond to the theories of magnetic phenomena in vogue at the period. Schubert mentions women whose lives were divided into separate, alternating parts, with completely different characteristics [. . .].

Claims involving such direct 'influences' have to be treated with some circumspection; whatever they offer, it is not any sort of final answer to the significance of the double in Romantic—or other—literature. We have to ask what led the Mesmerists to conduct their experiments in the first place, and why writers were willing to be influenced by the published results of such experiments.

Both C. F. Keppler in his book *The Literature of the Second Self* (1972), and Robert Rogers in his book *The Double in Literature* (1970), have considered the varying ways in which different writers have utilized the double or second self in their work. Many of their individual analyses are extremely illuminating, but in both works I feel the need for more stress on the historical determinants at work in the literary portrayal of the double. To this end I would like now to turn to the portrayals of doubles, split-identities, and 'secret lives' in the works of five major nineteenth-century novelists. Dostoyevsky's *The Double* is a very obvious starting-point, as in it the Russian author focuses attention on the theme that is to dominate all of his writing: the divided nature of human consciousness, split between the 'public' and the 'underground'. A number of critics have referred to a passage in *A Raw Youth* in which Dostoyevsky specifically refers to clinical cases of dissociation:

> What then precisely is the 'double'? The 'double', at any rate according to a medical work by an expert which I afterwards read for the purpose, is nothing but the first stage in some serious mental derangement which may lead to a pretty bad conclusion.

Dostoyevsky, then, at some stage in his writing career clearly knew something of the existence of clinical dissociation. But it is important to stress that his whole life's work is concerned with the question of opposing elements in human individuals, and that he *uses* information from clinical case-histories to illuminate what is presented in his works as a far more widespread duplicity in the characters he portrays. Even when he presents his readers with a character who is undivided, honest and 'good', like the Prince in his *The Idiot,* the underlying literary aim is to explore the impossibility of such a person in his contemporary world.

We need, then, to see *The Double* as a novel which uses information perhaps partly gained from clinical case-histories to explore more socially representative forms of duplicity and contradiction, rather than as a novel which sets out to investigate a particular neurotic or disturbed condition. Dostoyevsky appears to use the knowledge of such clinical cases of dissociation as were available to him to make Golyadkin's character psychologically convincing, however. [As Joseph Frank has written in his *Dostoyevsky: The Seeds of Revolt,* 1977]

> the novel originally contained a passage that explicitly motivates Golyadkin as engaging in ego-enhancing daydreams. Mr Golyadkin, Dostoevsky wrote, 'very much loved occasionally to make certain romantic assumptions touching his person; he liked to promote himself now and then into the hero of the most ingenious novel, to imagine himself entangled in various intrigues and difficulties, and, at last, to emerge with honor from all the unpleasantnesses, triumphing over all obstacles, vanquishing difficulties and magnanimously forgiving his enemies'.

Golyadkin is, then, just the sort of nervous, introverted character who we have seen to be vulnerable to personality dissociation. He also, incidentally, resembles Conrad's Lord Jim, who as a youth indulges in fantasies of heroic deeds, and as an adult speaks of his fatal jump as of the action of another person—almost a double.

It also emerges, in the later text of the novel (which is the one available in English translation), that Golyadkin has been under considerable strain for some time at work and in his relationships, real or imagined, with one or more women. The actual appearance of the double is also preceded by a profound crisis in his life which, again, is as we have seen typical of the nonliterary cases of multiple personality we have looked at:

> Mr Golyadkin, seeing that Andrey Philippovich had recognized him beyond doubt and was staring with all his might, so that he could not hope to remain concealed, blushed to the roots of his hair. 'Ought I to bow? Should I speak to him or not? Ought I to acknowledge our acquaintance?' our hero wondered in indescribable anguish. 'Or shall I pretend it's not me but somebody else strikingly like me, and look as if nothing's the matter?' said Mr Golyadkin, lifting his hat to Andrey Philippovich and not taking his eyes off him. 'I. . . . It's all right', he whispered, hardly able to speak, 'It's quite all right; this is not me at all, Andrey Philippovich, it's not me at all, not me, and that's all about it.'

According to Ralph Tymms, Dostoyevsky's principle source of psychological data was 'an old-fashioned work on romantic lines, *Psyche, zur Entwicklungsgeschichte der Seele,* by Carl Gustav Carus', which was published in 1846, and which was based on the theories of animal magnetism popularized by G. H. Schubert. But as he began work on *The Double* in 1845 (according to Jessie Coulson, translator of the work), such an influence can only have been operative after the germ of the story had begun to mature in his mind.

Moreover, as Dmitri Chizhevsky points out in his 'The Theme of the Double in Dostoyevsky' [in René Wellek, ed., *Dostoyevsky: A Collection of Critical Essays,* 1962], in 1859 Dostoyevsky, talking about the theme of the double, remarked: 'Why should I abandon an excellent idea, a type of great social importance, which I was the first to discover and of which I was the first prophet?' To seek for wider social meaning in the theme of the double in Dostoyevsky's work is, then, not to impose on it critical theories or assumptions which Dostoyevsky would have seen to be irrelevant. If accounts of multiple personality influenced Dostoyevsky, then they did so after he had become interested in the theme of the double, and they were part of a family of ideas concerning the complexity of human personality which for Dostoyevsky, at least later on in his life, had a social significance. Joseph Frank points out that in *Poor Folk,* written prior to *The Double,* at the point where Devushkin in complete despair is summoned for his interview with the General, his feelings are described as follows:

> 'My heart began shuddering within me, and I don't know myself why I was so frightened; I only know that I was panic-stricken as I had never been before in all my life. I sat rooted to my chair—as though there were nothing the matter, as though it were not I' [. . .] Here is exactly the reaction of terror that leads to the splitting of Golyadkin's personality and the appearance of the double [. . .].

This passage was certainly written before Dostoyevsky had read Carus's book.

In both cases the experience of terror that ushers in a sense of personality loss or estrangement is given a clear social setting: it is in the presence of a superior who has a particular social authority with regard to the 'split' individual. This links up with Golyadkin's subsequent fear, immediately after meeting the double for the first time, that

> It would be terrible going into the office again. He had a strong foreboding that it was precisely there that something was wrong.

Golyadkin is an individual who is torn between conflicting demands: the demands of subservience to an arrogant, mechanical and unfeeling authority, and the demands of the truly human. As Dmitri Chizhevsky points out

> The appearance of the double and his success in squeezing out Golyadkin from his place only shows that Golyadkin's place was completely illusory to begin with. For even the double can keep all his 'places'—from the office to his Excellency's cabinet—only through the purely external traits of his character: by the flattery and servility which the older Golyadkin would have liked to master himself but which are no less superficial, unessential, and inhuman and incapable of ensuring him a 'place' in life.

It is the impossibility of uniting these contradictory demands in a single, consistent, integrated personality that we see personified in an exaggerated form in the two Golyadkins.

In her undergraduate study of the theme of the double in *The Double* and *The Brothers Karamazov* [*The Magic Mirror: A Study of the Double in Two of Dostoevsky's Novels,* 1955] Sylvia Plath points out that Golyadkin's immediate response to the double is paradoxical. In spite of his anxiety, she notes, he himself admits that it is as if a hundred tons had been lifted from his chest. She suggests that the reason for this relief is that his hitherto repressed and starved desires may now be satisfied. But this relief is temporary and partial:

> By creating a Double, the schizophrenic no longer needs to castigate himself or to feel guilty for harboring these corrupt urges; at least he can blame someone else for transgressions which he once felt were his.
>
> However, the advantages of this radical division involve danger as well as distinct relief. The double alleviation of tension, which frees the victim from responsibility for his repressed desires and yet satisfies those desires, is countered by a new fear of attack from the outside.

Plath's view of Golyadkin's double as the 'return of the repressed', in Freudian terminology, is echoed by Robert Rogers who argues that

> It is clear that Golyadkin Sr, who entertains a romantic, idealistic attitude toward women, represses his instinctual impulses; he sees his double as a lecher.

There is certainly some textual authority for such views. After reading Vakhrameyev's letter accusing him of having mistreated Karolina Ivanovna, Golyadkin, we are told,

> remained for a considerable time sitting motionless on the sofa. A new light was breaking

> through the cloud of obscurity and mystery that had enveloped him for the past two days. It was partly that our hero was beginning to remember. . . .

The mental process here depicted does strongly suggest the return to consciousness of sexually motivated behaviour the memory of which has been repressed by Golyadkin, and the eccentric behaviour associated with Clara Olsufyevna is also strongly suggestive of a sexual fantasy which has overcome its originator. The medical advice given to Golyadkin at the start of the story, that he should not 'stay at home all the time' also suggests that, like the hero of *White Nights,* he has replaced a real life in the outside world with a fantasy life that has, eventually, destroyed his hold upon normality. But although these elements of repressed sexuality clearly enter into Golyadkin's dissociation, there is more to the latter than the return of unacknowledged lust.

Erik Krag, in his *Dostoyevsky The Literary Artist* (1976) has indicated how much Dostoyevsky owed to Gogol in *The Double,* and notes that the parallels between *The Double* and, in particular, Gogol's *The Nose* and *The Overcoat* were such that a contemporary Russian reader would have easily recognized them (and was meant to do so). In the translated version of *The Double,* based on Dostoyevsky's revised text, many references to noses have been deleted, as if Dostoyevsky wished to play down the debt he owed to Gogol. It seems apparent, however, that ideas from *The Nose* set Dostoyevsky's imagination working: the idea that part of a man could leave him and lead an independent life, interfering with his social and, particularly, sexual relationships, must have struck important chords in Dostoyevsky's mind. The nose, of course, has always had important sexual connotations; not only is it often (as in *Tristram Shandy*) used as an analogue for the penis, but 'losing one's nose' is the result of syphilis, and thus serves as a public and visible sign that private and perhaps illicit sexual behaviour has been indulged in.

In his interesting book on literature and metamorphosis, *The Gaping Pig,* Irving Massey makes a couple of points concerning *The Nose* which it is perhaps worth pondering with regard to *The Double.* Firstly he suggests that the nose is a byword for status in a host of expressions, and that its separation from its owner in Gogol's story represents the gaining of a desired status which then leaves the self behind in an uncomfortable superfluity, without any role. Secondly, that the detachment of Kovalyov's nose 'is a kind of protective imitation', in which 'one takes on the deadness of the meaningless thing or situation with which one is confronted and meets its threat by becoming it'. As I have suggested, these comments are peculiarly apt with regard to Golyadkin, for once he gains the status he clearly desires so much, in the shape of his double, his remaining self is rendered superfluous and with no role in life at all. And there is also a case for seeing the madness which his dissociation represents as a form of protective reaction to a life with which he can no longer cope; the end of the tale is the end of all his hopes, true, but it is also the end of all his problems.

But in some ways Gogol's *The Overcoat* seems to represent an even more significant source for certain elements in *The Double* than does *The Nose.* Aikeky Aikeyevitch is, like Golyadkin, persecuted at the office, and has to assert his essential humanity to stop the young clerks from cruelly teasing him. There is an important parallel scene in *The Double* in which Golyadkin's encounter with two junior colleagues away from the office startles Golyadkin into acting a part foreign to his actual feelings:

> 'Yakov Petrovich, Yakov Petrovich,' twittered the two young clerks, 'you here? What has . . . ?'
>
> 'Ah, it's you, gentlemen!' Mr Golyadkin hurriedly interrupted them, somewhat disconcerted and scandalized by the clerks' amazement and at the same time by the familiarity of their address, but involuntarily acting the free-and-easy good fellow all the same.

Golyadkin's disconcertment, it becomes clear, arises from his revealing aspects of himself to his colleagues that he normally conceals at work. Dostoyevsky, then, uses this encounter with the two clerks in a rather different way from the scene Gogol gives us of Aikeky Aikeyevitch being teased by his fellow-workers. Here the encounter, like a later encounter in Dickens's *Great Expectations* between Wemmick and Jaggers, which I will look at later, revolves around the unintended display of 'human' characteristics to 'work' colleagues; the latter ask Golyadkin how he comes to be 'scented and pomaded like this, and all dressed up', and Golyadkin, significantly, has to admit to 'another side'.

> 'You all know me, gentlemen, but up till now you have only known one side of me. Nobody is to blame for that, and I admit it is partly my own fault.'

Golyadkin's earlier claims to openness and a lack of duplicity, then, have to be taken with a pinch of salt.

The scene in *The Double* which most directly parallels Gogol's description of the teasing of Aikeky Aikeyevitch involves not an encounter between Golyadkin and his colleagues, however, but one between Golyadkin and himself—his double.

> The man now sitting opposite Mr Golyadkin was Mr Golyadkin's horror, he was Mr Golyadkin's shame, he was Mr Golyadkin's nightmare of the previous day; in short, he was Mr Golyadkin himself—not the Mr Golyadkin who now sat in his chair with his mouth gaping and the pen frozen in his grasp; not the one who liked to keep in the background and bury himself in the crowd; not, finally, the one whose demeanour said so clearly, 'Leave me alone and I'll leave you alone,' or, 'Leave me alone; I'm not interfering with you, am I?'

The phrases in inverted commas are almost identical to those uttered by the hero of *The Overcoat* to his tormentors, and it seems apparent that Dostoyevsky wanted his readers to recognize this—and that it was now a dissociated part of himself that torments the hero. The conflict has been internalized, has gone underground. (pp. 47-53)

Stanley M. Coleman, noting [in "The Phantom Double," *British Journal of Medical Psychology,* 1934] that *The Double* is the first of Dostoyevsky's novels to explore the subject of the mind in conflict with itself, argues that for Dostoyevsky the divided mind is never alternating personality—repression with amnesia—but is always the simultaneous presentation of conflicting feelings and impulses. It is true that the only mention of possible amnesia concerns the mental stirrings that Vakhrameyev's letter causes Golyadkin. But this apart I think that in general Coleman is without any doubt correct to insist upon the fact that Golyadkin suffers from simultaneous contradictory feelings and impulses which oppress him. One sign of this is that—as a cursory glance at the novel will reveal—he talks to himself, argues with himself, continuously. On one level this is a sign of his isolation (he has hardly anyone else *to* talk to), but on another level it represents an internalization of external conflicts; he talks about problems concerning his behaviour in the external world. We talk to ourselves, normally, to solve problems; without problems our cerebration is rarely consciously verbal. But talking to oneself is not for nothing referred to in popular myth as 'the first sign of madness'. Golyadkin's inner speech serves, paradoxically, further to bifurcate his life: it divides him up into a seething inner mass of problems, and a halting, inarticulate public persona. This, of course, is not an accurate picture of the double, who represents a possible solution to all Mr Golyadkin's problems so far as his public behaviour is concerned, but which Golyadkin's honesty and humanity will not allow him consciously to adopt. This, if one likes, is the parallel to the force of repression that we [see operating in] case-histories. Paradoxically, it is Golyadkin's attempted refusal to be double that makes him double; because he would rather not dissemble and operate according to double standards, he breaks apart.

> '[. . .] I am not an intriguer—and I am proud of that, too. I don't do things on the sly, but openly, without guile, and although I might do harm, like other people, [. . .]'

Golyadkin seems to be torn between a desire to shine in society in a way hitherto foreign to his nature, or his apparent nature, and a wish to present himself as simple, uncomplicated, of-a-piece. In his early interview with his doctor these opposing elements are clearly apparent:

> '[. . .] There, Christian Ivanovich, in society, I say you must learn how to polish the parquet with your shoes . . . ' (here Mr Golyadkin scraped his foot lightly over the floor); it's expected of you, sir, and you're expected to make puns, too . . . you have to be able to produce a well-turned compliment . . . that's what's expected of you. And I've not learnt to do all that, Christian Ivanovich, I've never studied all those clever tricks; I had no time. I am a simple, uncomplicated person, and it isn't in me to shine in society. [. . .]'

As Golyadkin's later, assumed, finery reveals, in one sense this wish to shine in society clearly *is* 'in' him, however, and is demanding to be let out. This inner conflict is revealed in a number of different ways in this early interview with the doctor, and it is clear from these that Robert Rogers's assertion that decomposition in literature, like dissociation and autoscopy in clinical practice, 'always reflect[s] psychosexual conflict, however obliquely', is not the case. As I have argued earlier, sexual repression seems to enter into Golyadkin's fragmentation, but this is not the whole story. Take the following complex piece of duplicity on Golyadkin's part: he is talking again to the doctor.

> 'Yes, somebody I know very well congratulated somebody else whom I also know very well, and who is, moreover, a friend, as it is termed, of the object of my affections, on being promoted, receiving the rank of Assessor. This is how he put it. "I feel really glad," he said, "of this opportunity to offer you my congratulations, my *sincerest* congratulations, Vladimir Semyonovich, on your promotion. And I am all the more delighted because nowadays, as all the world knows, a lot of maundering old women have been getting promotion." ' Here Mr Golyadkin nodded his head slyly and looked at Christian Ivanovich with a frown.

As is apparent from a later slip of Golyadkin's, the 'somebody' is in fact himself, and the comment about maundering old women is meant to be a hit against his sexual rival. But sexual jealousy is mixed up with other things here; professional competition and duplicity to a business superior.

In Golyadkin's *telling* this anecdote to his doctor, however, we can surely see a desire to re-establish his integrity, to bring the different parts of his life together. Talking, later on in the novel, to Anton Antonovich, Golyadkin puts forward 'the notion' that 'people wearing masks have ceased to be a rarity, sir, and that it is difficult nowadays to recognize the man under the mask'. This statement seems to relate both to a realization that he himself masks some of his impulses and characteristics and also to a genuine desire that such double standards as necessitate the wearing of masks should be ended. (pp. 54-5)

Golyadkin's case suggests that it may, indeed, be a more effective way of handling a particular sort of reality. Golyadkin's collapse is precipitated, after all, not by his having divided himself into two, but by his inability to keep these separate parts of himself distinct. It is his meeting, early on, with Andrey Philippovich, which causes him to wish to be someone else. Although his life is already divided between his 'office self' and his 'private self'—the person he thinks of himself as in his imagination—he is also possessed of a strong impulse to achieve some sort of consistency and unity, an impulse evidenced, it would seem, by his visit to the doctor. [In *The Gaping Pig: Literature and Metamorphosis,* 1976] Irving Massey makes a very similar point to this when, referring to such stories as *Dracula, Dr Jekyll and Mr Hyde,* and Mérimée's 'Lokis,' he suggests that he would like

> to shift the emphasis from the familiar areas of discussion of the double (such as split personality, or the suppressed natural man) to what one might rather call the discussion of the single. In other words, I would suggest that the problems

> in these situations arise from the unity rather than from the duality of character.

As I have already indicated, Dostoyevsky wrote that he saw the double as a 'type of great social significance;' and the social and historical context of Golyadkin's bifurcation is immediately relevant to its full understanding. [In his *Activity, Consciousness and Personality,* 1978, discussing] another of Dostoyevsky's stories—*White Nights*—A. N. Leont'ev argues that

> a historically arising separation of internal theoretical activity not only gives rise to a one-sided development of personality but may lead to psychological disorders, to splitting of personality into two spheres strange to each other—the sphere of its appearance in real life and the sphere of its appearance in the life that exists only as an illusion, only in autistic thought. It is impossible to describe such a psychological disturbance more penetratingly than did Dostoyevsky; from a wretched existence filled with senseless matters, his hero escapes into a life of the imagination, into dreams; before us there are as if two personalities, one, the personality of a man who is humiliatingly cowardly, an eccentric who shuts himself off in his den, the other, a romantic and even a heroic personality open to all the joys of life.

From other writings of Dostoyevsky it seems clear that the phenomenon of talking to oneself was seen by him to have a social rather than a purely individual significance; it is not simply that the hero of *White Nights,* or Golyadkin, escape from society in their dreams and inner conversations, but rather that society pursues them in these activities. In *Crime and Punishment,* in which Raskolnikov leads a life cut off from social intercourse not dissimilar to that led by the hero of *White Nights,* the activity of talking to oneself is given a specifically social significance: talking to Raskolnikov, Svidrigaylov tells him:

> And another thing. I'm convinced there are lots of people in Petersburg who talk to themselves while they walk. It's a city of semi-lunatics. If we had been a scientific nation, our doctors, lawyers, and philosophers could have made valuable investigations, each in his own field, in Petersburg. You won't often find a place like Petersburg where so many strange, harsh and gloomy things exert an influence on a man's mind. Think what the influence of the climate alone is worth. And in addition, it is the administrative centre of Russia, and its character must be reflected in everything.

Svidrigaylov goes on to describe Raskolnikov's behaviour when he leaves the house and walks in the street. His head drops, he starts to notice less and less, begins to talk to himself, and finally stops in the middle of the street. The anonymity of the street, in spite of its many passers-by, allows Raskolnikov to indulge his flight from the realities of actual human contact.

Thus references to Dostoyevsky's personal situation as the root of his concern with doubles are not enough: as he has Svidrigaylov say, the streets of the administrative capital of Russia (a telling detail) are full of people talking to themselves. It is true that Dostoyevsky referred to *The Double* as a confession, and Stanley M. Coleman suggests that Golyadkin can be seen as a self-portrait:

> There can be no doubt that the sudden change in [Dostoyevsky's] circumstances, resulting from instantaneous popularity, had turned the young author's head. *The Double* represents in an exaggerated manner his own bitter reflections at the foolish way in which he had behaved at that time.

But, . . . if this were all Golyadkin and his double stood for then there would be little of interest for the reader with no curiosity about the author's personal experiences.

The theme of the double in Dostoyevsky's work always seems to raise large *social* issues for consideration. In his masterpiece, *The Brothers Karamazov,* the long monologues both of the Elder Zossima and of the Public Prosecutor make this palpably clear. As the former argues:

> in our age all men are separated into self-contained units, everyone crawls away into his own hole, everyone separates himself from his neighbour, hides himself away and hides away everything he possesses, and ends up by keeping himself at a distance from people and keeping other people at a distance from him. He accumulates riches by himself and thinks how strong he is now and how secure, and does not realize, madman that he is, that the more he accumulates the more deeply does he sink into self-destroying impotence. For he is used to relying on himself alone and has separated himself as a self-contained unit from the whole. He has trained his mind not to believe in the help of other people, in men and mankind, and is in constant fear of losing his money and the rights he has won for himself. Everywhere today the mind of man has ceased, ironically, to understand that true security of the individual does not lie in isolated personal efforts but in general human solidarity.
>
> (pp. 56-8)

[Here we see two systems of values]: the perspectives of exchange and those of solidarity. Golyadkin, ironically, is in one sense not a madman; he does not want to accumulate riches, he does not want to rely on himself alone, hiding himself away from others. He wishes to be respected and loved for himself as a real person, without a mask, without hypocrisy, and he does seek help from others. But he lives in a society in which it is only those who behave in the artificial manner of the double who are accepted, who do succeed.

If Dostoyevsky's entire *oeuvre* is permeated by a fascination with the complexities and contradictions of personality, his literary techniques for exploring this fascination change. Except on rare, dramatic occasions doubles are not introduced directly in his fiction after *The Double* (an example of such dramatic exceptions would be Ivan's hallucinated image of aspects of himself, personified as the devil, in *The Brothers Karamazov*). He uses, more often, characters who are either unusually revealing of their inner thoughts—eccentrics—or unusually reticent, to bring out into the open those conflicts which are often hidden within the 'normal' individual. Thus in his address to the reader in book one of *The Brothers Karamazov* he denies that an eccentric is an exception, and claims that sometimes, on the contrary, he 'expresses the very sum and substance of a certain period'. A few pages later, we are told of old Karamazov that he 'liked to dissemble, to play some unexpected part before you, sometimes moreover, without the slightest need for it'. Such characters are, as Dostoyevsky claims, unusual not so much because they are different from ordinary people, but because they reveal what is hidden in ordinary people. The artistic effect of *The Idiot* is dependent upon the veil-stripping effects of an individual who acts always in an open, human way, unmotivated by desire for personal gain.

In *Crime and Punishment* it is Mr Luzhin who expresses this dilemma that the individual hesitating between self-interest and solidarity is imprisoned in—although, of course, the whole novel explores the inability of man to live by pure self-interest alone.

> '[. . .] If, say, I've been told in the past, "Love thy neighbour as thyself," and I did, what was the result of it? [. . .] The result of it was that I tore my coat in half to share it with my neighbour, and both of us were left half naked. As the Russian proverb has it, "If you run after two hares, you won't catch one." But science tells us, "Love yourself before everyone else, for everything in the world is based on self-interest. If you love only yourself, you'll transact your business as it ought to be transacted, and your coat will remain whole." And economic truth adds that the more successfully private business is run, and the more whole coats, as it were, there are, the more solid are the foundations of our social life and the greater is the general well-being of the people. [. . .]'

Milton Friedman's theories are, we may note in passing, hardly modern. Their implementation has led to about as much human happiness in the present day as it did in Dostoyevsky's time. Moreover, Dostoyevsky's work shows, time and time again, how impossible and contradictory an aim total self-interest is. The hero of *Notes from the Underground* is as incapable of maintaining his initial posture of universal selfishness in that work as is Raskolnikov. And again it is worth noting that his contradictory modes of behaviour to Liza coincide with contradictory social attitudes concerning human relationships and, in particular, the treatment of women. The brothel and the loving family circle are used to exemplify and symbolize these contradictory attitudes, but as the story reveals very tellingly, the contradictions exist within the consciousness and beliefs of the underground man as much as outside in society in institutions as different as the house of prostitution and the respectable private home. The long monologue which Golyadkin delivers while standing behind the pile of logs late on in *The Double* oscillates between the same two views of womanhood and male–female relationships as does the account of the underground man. Although he is ostensibly waiting for Clara Olsufyevna in order to elope with her, he is also conducting an imaginary conversation with her in which he pours scorn on the romantic illusions spread by French novels, and counsels obedience to parental authority.

Georg Lukács is perhaps best known today for the uncompromising nature of his critique of modernism, and to the extent that Dostoyevsky's work is prophetic of certain modernist developments it might be thought that Lukács would be critical of the Russian novelist. In fact Lukács deals with Dostoyevsky very sympathetically, and discusses his work in terms of its containing symptomatic evidence of the corrupting power of modern society. In particular, he sees in Dostoyevsky's work an element that Brecht was later to detect in the work of Kafka: a response to the alienating pressures of contemporary urban life. As he says [in his contribution to Wellek's 1962 book],

> Dostoyevsky was the first—and is still unsurpassed—in drawing the mental deformations that are brought about as a social necessity by life in a modern city.

The city is, for the first century or so of its modern existence as an accumulation of millions of people, a specifically capitalist phenomenon, and aspects of city life are, for most of the nineteenth century, inseparable from the particular nature of capitalist social relations. This is an important point, and needs to be remembered when we consider the treatment of the city in literature. Writers' fascination with the odd mixture of cooperation and privacy, of the social and the individualist, that is found in the city has to be seen in the context of their belonging to societies in which the relationship of the public with the private was generally problematic.

The city becomes increasingly crucial as context for the portrayal of shattered or divided personality in literature as the nineteenth century unfolds. The anonymity its paradoxically crowded streets provide gives the writer a suitable objective correlative for the depiction of that hidden, 'personal' side of his or her characters' personalities. At the same time, as we have already seen, that ability to indulge one's private fantasies and impulses in secret which the city provides, allows individuals to re-project their repressed selves back into the social world. That classic of Victorian pornography with its revealing title—*My Secret Life*— is set mainly in the towns and cities of late Victorian England, and especially London. (pp. 58-60)

[Pertinent to this discussion is] the 'Strange Case of Silas Pronge', as Robert Howland Chase's title has it, who disappeared from his home at the age of 60 and was found in another town suffering from amnesia and running a shop under another name. In his account of the case Chase makes reference to Stevenson's *Dr Jekyll and Mr Hyde,* and it is true that Pronge's story does have a Jekyll and Hyde aspect to it. But it bears a much closer resemblance to another work of Victorian literature—Nathaniel Hawthorne's short story *Wakefield.* As does Pronge's case, *Wakefield* serves to illuminate for us the complex relationship between the anonymity provided by modern society, and the divisions and contradictions that its members internalize. In the case of Silas Pronge the size of the United States, and the existence of an efficient transport system are crucial factors. In the fictional account it is the anonymity provided within the modern, mass-population city that is central.

Hawthorne claimed that he had based the story on a newspaper report of a man living in London who absented himself for a long while from his wife.

> The man, under pretence of going a journey, took lodgings in the next street to his own house, and there, unheard of by his wife or friends, and without the shadow of a reason for such self-banishment, dwelt upwards of 20 years. During that period, he beheld his home every day, and frequently the forlorn Mrs Wakefield [*his wife*]. And after so great a gap in his matrimonial felicity—when his death was reckoned certain, his estate settled, his name dismissed from memory, and his wife, long, long ago, resigned to her autumnal widowhood—he entered the door one evening, quietly, as from a day's absence, and became a loving spouse till death.

The story has the quality of myth, and like all myths it tells us something of the lives of those to whom the myth appeals. In part this is seen in the mixture of the familiar and the unfamiliar in the tale. There is nothing odd, in London, in knowing nothing about the person who lives a street away from you—indeed, many people know nothing of the person who lives next door to them. I say that there is nothing odd, by which I mean that there is nothing unusual; but of course there is something odd about this; millions of people, whose survival depends upon their mutual cooperation, are locked up in separate, non-communicating compartments.

Again, there is nothing odd in the simple sense about a wife not knowing too much about her husband's life outside the home. Many wives in modern societies hardly know what work their husbands do; it is important to note that the myth only works in the tale because it is the husband, not the wife, who extends that area of freedom and privacy he enjoys but which his wife does not to nearly the same extent.

Hawthorne suggests a link between the secret thoughts and selfish ideas of Wakefield and his mysterious absence. He notes of Wakefield's wife that without her

> having analyzed his character, [she] was partly aware of a quiet selfishness, that had rusted into his inactive mind; of a peculiar sort of vanity, the most uneasy attribute about him; of a disposition to craft which had seldom produced more positive effects than the keeping of petty secrets [. . .]

The mythical quality of the story comes from this bringing together of the anonymity of London's streets with the private, secret lives of its inhabitants—especially its male inhabitants.

But there are other suggestive elements in the story. Soon after his departure, Wakefield contents himself with the thought that his wife is, after all, only in the next street; but an authorial interjection denies this: 'Fool! it is in another world.' The similarity of this passage to one in De Quincey's *The Confessions of an English Opium Eater,* written some 20 years before *Wakefield,* is instructive. De Quincey had, revealingly, travelled from countryside to town prior to indulging himself with the altered states of consciousness achieved by means of opium (taken innocently at first, if we are to believe him). During poverty-stricken wandering through the streets of London he met a young prostitute, Ann, who was kind to him but with whom he lost contact. De Quincey claims to have searched for her, but without success.

> If she lived, doubtless we must have been sometimes in search of each other, at the very same moment, through the mighty labyrinths of London; perhaps even within a few feet of each other—a barrier no wider, in a London street, often amounting in the end to a separation for eternity!

What interests me here, in particular, is the repetitive idea of a search for human contact and solidarity which is frustrated by the anonymity of London. It is as if the geographical peculiarities and complexities of the city are made to stand for something deeper, some inability of this vast commercial network to satisfy its members' human needs and aspirations. Hawthorne tells of Wakefield that 'It was [his] unprecedented fate to retain his original share of human sympathies, and to be still involved in human interests, while he had lost his reciprocal influence on them.' It does not seem too wayward an interpretation of the fascination this situation has for Hawthorne to see it as something not limited to such extreme situations as Wakefield's. In his extraordinary absence we see objectified a more common absence from controlling or reciprocal influence on 'human interests' suffered by millions of Wakefield's contemporaries in their daily lives.

To strike a more sombre note, it can be noted that the roots of the myth are still well-fed. Lukács, in his *The Meaning of Contemporary Realism,* took great exception to a comment in Musil's *The Man Without Qualities* in which Musil, referring to Moosbrugger, 'a mentally-retarded sexual pervert with homicidal tendencies,' suggested that if humanity were able to dream collectively it would dream Moosbrugger. In one sense, of course, Lukács is correct to object to the negative and reactionary aspects of this statement. It universalizes a particular social decadence and—in the manner of much modernism—ignores its social and historical roots. Yet when this necessary context is added the statement is thought-provoking. During the year in which I am writing the trial of the so-called 'Yorkshire Ripper' has taken place in Britain. What has dominated much media coverage of this case—particularly in the time prior to an arrest having been made—has been the shocking idea that the man responsible might be leading a perfectly ordinary domestic life, surrounded by a loving family who knew nothing of his horrific exploits. 'It might be your next-door neighbour.' The fascination that such a case evokes seems to be related to the extent to which it is capable of revealing certain odd things about 'ordinary' life that habit and custom blind us to. One of these things is the wider issue of male violence to women, and an aspect of this is the relationship between the secrecies of male fantasy lives and the scope that the modern city gives for their indulgence.

If this seems rather a forced interpretation, consider the

implications of the following case from 'real life', reported upon by Morton Prince in an essay which has recently been republished [in *Psychotherapy and Multiple Personality: Selected Essays,* 1975]. The subject of the report was a young man of 22 years old, who according to Prince was 'essentially normal and responsible, of robust character and of decided intellectual ability'. Under hypnosis this young man revealed at least four distinct phases or moods, which Prince categorizes as follows: firstly the ordinary or quiet mood, very similar to his waking mood; secondly a 'gay mood' in which the man became hilarious and absurd, played practical jokes and was generally 'obstreperous and fantastic;' thirdly a 'malicious' mood in which he became 'a sort of "Jack the Ripper" ', exhibited a strong desire to inflict pain, asked permission to stab the experimenter and attempted surreptitiously so to do, and confessed to a wish to vivisect or, failing that, to strangle; and fourthly—not altogether surprisingly—a 'depressed mood'. I do not refer to this case to suggest that we are all Jack-the-Rippers manqué. On the other hand, as a reading of so many of Dostoyevsky's novels reveals, Prince's subject is not the only young man who is outwardly normal and responsible, of robust character and decided intellectual ability, who contains within himself violent and anti-social impulses.

One of the essential components of the mythic quality that the original Victorian Jack-the-Ripper's case possessed was the fact that he remained uncaught and anonymous, and it is significant that interest in his twentieth-century emulator lessened after his capture. When all was public, then the ability of the case to symbolize that underworld of repressed violence in society at large and in reflected form in the individual psyche was reduced.

If Silas Pronge's case leads us to think of Hawthorne's *Wakefield,* the horrific murders of a Jack-the-Ripper figure lead our thoughts back to *Dr Jekyll and Mr Hyde,* a story which Morton Prince suggests, literary exaggeration apart, 'is so true a picture of what is actually observed in cases of double personality that it can be used almost as well as an actual case from life'. Prince finds much significance too in the fact that Stevenson claimed to have based his story on a dream; according to Prince the dream was probably an allegorical working out of previous thoughts originating in personal mental conflicts. In support of this view Stevenson's own statement, quoted by Masao Myoshi in his [1969 book *The Divided Self: A Perspective on the Literature of the Victorians*], that he had long been trying to write a story on this subject, 'to find a body, a vehicle, for that strong sense of man's double being which must at times come in upon and overwhelm the mind of every thinking creature' is highly relevant. Myoshi, however, also makes some interesting comments on the text of *Dr Jekyll and Mr Hyde* itself:

> The important men of the book, then, are all unmarried, intellectually barren, emotionally stifled, joyless. Nor are things much different in the city as a whole. The more prosperous business people fix up their homes and shops, but in a fashion without chic. Houses give an appearance of 'coquetry', and store fronts invite one like 'rows of smiling saleswomen' (Chapter 1). The rather handsome town houses in the back streets of Dr Jekyll's neighborhood are rented out to all sorts—'map-engravers, architects, shady lawyers, and the agents of obscure enterprises' (Chapter 2). Everywhere the fog of the dismal city is inescapable, even creeping under the doors and through the window jambs (Chapter 5). The setting hides a wasteland behind that secure and relatively comfortable respectability of its inhabitants.

As Myoshi's commentary suggests, Stevenson's classic study of dual consciousness can only be fully understood if it is seen not as a statement of the universal dualism of humankind, torn between good and evil (which is, admittedly, how Stevenson may have seen it), but as a work which arises out of the particular tensions and contradictions of Victorian society. Stevenson has Dr Jekyll himself talk of his recognition of 'the thorough and primitive duality of man', but an attentive reading of the book takes us not into the heart of an eternal truth about all human beings, but deeper and deeper into the specific contradictions of Victorian Britain.

The alternation of Jekyll and Hyde has much in common with the details of cases of multiple personality we have already looked at. The division serves, after its emergence, to solve problematic tensions for Jekyll:

> [. . .] I saw that, of the two natures that contended in the field of my consciousness, even if I could rightly be said to be either, it was only because I was radically both; and from an early date, even before the course of my scientific discoveries had begun to suggest the most naked possibility of such a miracle, I had learned to dwell with pleasure, as a beloved daydream, on the thought of the separation of these elements. If each, I told myself, could but be housed in separate identities, life would be relieved of all that was unbearable; the unjust might go his way, delivered from the aspirations and remorse of his more upright twin; and the just could walk steadfastly and securely on his upward path, doing the good things in which he found his pleasure, and no longer exposed to disgrace and penitence by the hands of this extraneous evil.

It is, surely, only in the context of a society in which the claims of self-interest and common humanity are in conflict that such a passage could be written.

In her undergraduate study of the theme of the double in Dostoyevsky's *The Double* and *The Brothers Karamazov* Sylvia Plath compares Smerdyakov and Ivan, from the latter work, with Hyde and Jekyll. She points out that Smerdyakov's growing confidence in Ivan's presence—like Hyde's increasing physical stature and strength—reflects the gradually maturing power of the evil Smerdyakov and the moral collapse of Ivan. She also draws attention to the fact that the crime of parricide, actually committed by Smerdyakov, with Ivan's tacit compliance, is symbolically attached to Hyde, who plays 'apelike tricks' on Jekyll, 'scrawling in my own hand blasphemies on the pages of my books, burning the letters and destroying the portrait of my father'. (pp. 60-4)

Hyde's name, of course, suggests the 'hidden' nature of the impulses he represents, and it is appropriate that the murder he commits should take place in the streets of London. London is the natural setting for *Dr Jekyll and Mr Hyde,* both because of its physical extensiveness and complexity and also because of the ethical and moral ambivalences which its Victorian expansion revealed and enacted. We cannot imagine this tale set in a quiet country village, or in a pre-industrial society; its links with nineteenth-century London are radical. Consider the resemblances between the following passage, and those quoted earlier from both Hawthorne and De Quincey:

> I was the first that could thus plod in the public eye with a load of genial respectability, and in a moment, like a schoolboy, strip off these lendings and spring headlong into the sea of liberty. But for me, in my inpenetrable mantle, the safety was complete. Think of it—I did not even exist!

We are also, I think, given here some indication of the source of the fascination—morbid and horrific though it be—that the Jack-the-Ripper myth exercises upon the contemporary imagination.

The complex symbolism of the contemporary city, with its secrecies and compartmentalizations alongside its collectivities and its thronging 'public', needs to be remembered when we turn to consider the work of Dickens. For Dickens, the city—especially London—is no mere backdrop for his characters. It is the stuff from which they are constructed and from which they inherit their inner tensions and contradictions. Like Conrad, Virginia Woolf and Kafka—very different novelists admittedly, but with something in common with him—Dickens perceives necessary links between the nature of the contemporary city and the nature of the characters he depicts inhabiting it. . . . Dickens, like Kafka, uses the city as a sort of metaphor for modern man. Its complexity is set against its compartmentalization; everything is connected, and everything is concealed. Indeed, we might say that for Dickens the *plot* of one of his novels is strikingly similar to the city in which it often unfolds; everything is, again, linked by iron laws of causal connection, but at the same time everything seems so unique, autonomous, free-standing: character, experience, personality.

I want now to spend some time talking about one novel of Dickens's—*Great Expectations.* There is a case to be made for *Great Expectations* as Dickens's finest novel: more tightly structured than many of its predecessors, more profound in its analysis of Victorian realities, less willing to escape into sentimentality or whimsy. Crucial to the novel is, again, the movement from country to city. Pip moves from a life in the countryside where experiences are above all direct and sensory rather than conceptual—the tickler, the fire, eating with Joe—to a life where such experiences are mediated through more complex sets of social relations, through more involved systems of value and significance. A fair example of this is the treatment of eating in the novel. Early on this represents one of Pip's central pleasures; eating silently, with Joe, each holding up their piece of bread to indicate, without the necessity for words, how ingestion was proceeding. Newly in London, Pip is schooled in the need to improve his table manners by the tolerant Herbert Pocket; the sensual is being overlaid by the conventional. Finally, when Magwitch returns and is given food in Pip's London rooms, Pip is disgusted by the animality of his eating. Pip is, at this stage, noticeably less tolerant of Magwitch than was Herbert of him.

Another sign of the increasing importance of *mediation* as Pip moves from the countryside to the town is the very acquisition of literacy. When we meet Pip on the first page of the novel he cannot pronounce his own name properly, and he reads more into the shape of the letters on his parents' tombstone than into their meaning. Even during the period of his greatest degeneracy in London, we learn that he sticks to his books, and while he is learning to speak correctly both Biddy and Joe are developing their command of language as well. Whereas Joe, early on in the novel, when asked by Pip how he spells 'Gargery' responds that he doesn't spell it at all, by the end of the novel both he and Biddy have acquired a certain level of literacy that makes both of them into more complex characters.

But this acquisition of literacy is two-sided. When Magwitch returns to see the 'gentleman' he has created—and the distorted echoes of *Frankenstein* are strong here—he insists on Pip's reading in a foreign tongue which he does not comprehend. Pleased with what he finds in Pip he exclaims

> '[. . .] I says to myself, "If I ain't a gentleman, nor yet ain't got no learning, I'm the owner of such. All on you owns stocks and land; which on you owns a brought-up London gentleman?" [. . .]'

It is this corruption of a genuine extension of human ability—literacy—with the values of commercialism, that represents a central item of concern in *Great Expectations.* The fundamental paradox, surely, with which Dickens is battling in the novel is that the more an individual improves himself, the more he separates himself from others. It is a paradox for Dickens because he knows that history cannot be reversed and that the communality of pre-industrial, pre-urban society cannot be recaptured. And indeed, he knew from his own life that Pip's expectations were not contemptible: he had no desire to return to the blacking factory. But he perceives, too, the loss involved.

It is perhaps in the character of Wemmick that these tensions are presented most clearly, although I would argue that they are implicit through the book in Pip's own progress: the very ambiguity of the title of the work, with its hinting at the intertwining of commercial and human expectations indicates the direction of Dickens's concern. Wemmick's divisions are not at all arbitrary; the opposition between country and town is important here, but so too is that between the worlds of work and of leisure, of commercial relationships and family ones. When Pip visits Wemmick's home in the country—built like a castle—he asks him:

> 'Is it your own, Mr Wemmick?'
>
> 'O yes,' said Wemmick, 'I have got hold of it, a bit at a time. It's a free-hold, by George!'

> 'Is it, indeed? I hope Mr Jaggers [*his employer*] admires it?'
>
> 'Never seen it,' said Wemmick. 'Never heard of it. Never seen the Aged. Never heard of him. No; the office is one thing, and private life is another. When I go into the office, I leave the Castle behind me, and when I come into the Castle, I leave the office behind me. If it's not in any way disagreeable to you, you'll oblige me by doing the same. I don't wish it professionally spoken about.'

Wemmick is a man living by two opposed value-systems; his advice to Pip in London is based on the assumption that self-interest should predominate, but advising him on the same matter in the countryside he bases his response on the assumption that Magwitch is to be helped. Even so, there is, be it noted, a paradox in his London behaviour, for were it completely self-interested the invitation to Pip to seek further advice in the country would not be given. Even with Wemmick's geographical separation of solidarity and exchange, the former intrudes into the realm of the latter.

It seems clear that the conflict between enlightened self-interest and unselfish mutuality was inescapable for the Victorian writer trying to portray accurately the contending elements of single characters. In Mrs Gaskell's *North and South* Margaret Hale is struck by this same Wemmick-like contradiction in Thornton, the manufacturer, who is extremely kind to her and to her mother, but who defends a system which Margaret sees to be unfeeling and inhumane. We are told by Mrs Gaskell that 'Margaret's whole soul rose up against' Thornton while he reasoned 'as if commerce were everything and humanity nothing', and at this point she can hardly thank him for the individual kindness which he has just displayed to her and her mother. Margaret perceives that he is aware that her mother is incurably ill;

> She saw it in his pitying eyes. She heard it in his grave and tremulous voice. How reconcile those eyes, that voice, with the hard, reasoning, dry, merciless way in which he laid down axioms of trade, and serenely followed them out to their full consequences? The discord jarred upon her inexpressibly.

Margaret's solution to this jarring discord—and the solution is also, we feel, Elizabeth Gaskell's—is for there to be more direct personal contact between the social classes. She longs for Thornton and Higgins—the union leader—to speak together, 'as man to man', and for the latter to forget that Mr Thornton is a master, while the former listens with his human heart and not his master's ears. This urge for human reconciliation, symbolized at one point in the novel by the praying together of Higgins, Margaret and her father, is not so different from the later solution to social division advanced by E. M. Forster: 'only connect'. After his bankruptcy, and his consequent humbling, Thornton adopts this viewpoint, seeking to 'have the opportunity of cultivating some intercourse with the hands beyond the mere "cash nexus",' and arguing the need to 'bring the individuals of the different classes into actual personal contact'. The provision of money by Margaret allows this ideologically attractive compromise actually to take place.

In tension with this very unconvincing solution to class struggle in *North and South,* however, are a number of powerful passages in the novel which take a far more sombre view of the contradictions involved. Consider the following passage, which opens chapter 50 of the novel:

> Meanwhile at Milton the chimneys smoked, the ceaseless roar and mighty beat, and dizzying whirl of machinery, struggled and strove perpetually. Senseless and purposeless were wood and iron and steam in their endless labours; but the persistence of their monotonous work was rivalled in tireless endurance by the strong crowds, who, with sense and with purpose, were busy and restless in seeking after—What? In the streets there were few loiterers,—none walking for mere pleasure; every man's face was set in lines of eagerness or anxiety; news was sought for with fierce avidity; and men jostled each other aside in the Mart and in the Exchange, as they did in life, in the deep selfishness of competition. There was gloom over the town. Few came to buy, and those who did were looked at suspiciously by the sellers; for credit was insecure [. . .].

It seems clear that the tensions here are not going to be solved by personal contact between masters and men; quite apart from anything else, such contact is not going to bring new orders into the town.

In passages such as this I think that Mrs Gaskell avoids the fudging and blurring brought about by the ideological pressure for compromise. She sees here that there is no reconciliation to be found between the 'deep selfishness of competition' and the human needs of those enmeshed by the senselessness of the system. It is interesting that she fixes upon the behaviour of people in the street to symbolize their profounder social relationships, and her commentary upon their individualistic and selfish jostling of one another is prophetic of the view of the crowded street to be taken by so many modernist writers later on (and, at the same time, reminiscent of the same view of the street and its inhabitants in Blake's remarkable poem 'London').

In *Great Expectations* the anonymity of London is crucial to the divisions and complexities of individual characters. As Wemmick tells Pip when the latter wishes to conceal Magwitch, 'Under existing circumstances there is no place like a great city when you are once in it.' Wemmick's office—as important an element in his double life as Golyadkin's is to his—is in the heart of the city, and it deals with the most heartrending human problems in a purely business-like, cash-nexus manner. But Wemmick is not a bad man, and neither is Jaggers.

Waiting for Estella in London, having passed by the grim jail, Pip is struck by what he takes to be the utter contrast between her and the prison:

> While my mind was thus engaged, I thought of the beautiful young Estella, proud and refined, coming towards me, and I thought with absolute

> abhorrence of the contrast between the jail and her.

But the reader learns, in due course, that the proud and refined Estella is the daughter of the convict Magwitch, and this concealed connection between what appear to Pip to be two polar opposites is an apt reminder of the fact that Victorian society is a network of concealed connections, a mass of mediations joining—often very indirectly—people and institutions with apparently nothing in common. In one of the neatest illustrations of this Herbert Pocket tells Pip that although a gentleman may not keep a public house, a public house may keep a gentleman. Private property is an institution that gives the individual owner a double relationship to that owned; he or she is connected with the thing owned on one level, but separate from it on another.

One of the most oddly moving scenes in *Great Expectations* takes place late on in the book when Jaggers and Wemmick find out about each other's hidden selves.

> 'What's all this?' said Mr Jaggers. 'You with an old father, and you with pleasant and playful ways?'
>
> 'Well!' returned Wemmick. 'If I don't bring 'em here, what does it matter?'
>
> 'Pip,' said Mr Jaggers, laying his hand upon my arm, and smiling openly, 'this man must be the most cunning imposter in all London.'
>
> 'Not a bit of it,' returned Wemmick, growing bolder and bolder. 'I think you're another.'
>
> Again they exchanged their former odd looks, each apparently still distrustful that the other was taking him in.

Jaggers, for once, is doing something 'openly'; behaving like a human being rather than a legal robot. But this genuine mutual pleasure at the discovery of each other's humanity soon gives way to suspicion and concern. The 'odd looks' are repeated several times,

> with this difference now, that each of them seemed suspicious, not to say conscious, of having shown himself in a weak and unprofessional light to the other.

To re-establish their professional credentials they are unnecessarily unkind to Mike, who makes the mistake of bringing his personal sorrows to their attention. Business etiquette is thus made the mode of their office relationship once more.

In *Dr Jekyll and Mr Hyde* Stevenson has Jekyll utter a remark that links his use of Hyde with the idea of a commercial relationship, by comparing the way he summoned up Hyde with the behaviour of those who hire others to do their dirty work for them:

> Men have before hired bravos to transact their crimes, while their own person and reputation sat under shelter. I was the first that ever did so for his pleasures.

The suggestion, surely, is that the Jekyll-Hyde division is no more marked than the concealed contradictions allowed for by commercial relationships. That outwardly respectable, upright citizen may be associated with some very dubious goings-on through a financial interest, and were this association to come to light—as it does in the case of Bulstrode, in George Eliot's *Middlemarch*—then it is as if Dr Jekyll's door is burst open to reveal Mr Hyde. Stevenson's mention of 'bravos' in the above quotation suggests another interesting literary parallel, with the early nineteenth-century tale *The Bravo of Venice,* which 'Monk' Lewis claimed to have translated from the German. In this particular tale the theme of hiring someone else to do your dirty work—a 'bravo'—is linked to a typical double-identity theme. The novel is a poor one, full of clichés and predictabilities, but it is interesting how at this early date (1804) the double-identity theme whereby the 'respectable' Abellino becomes the 'bravo' Flodoardo to expose the corruption of Venetian society, is linked with the concealments and hypocrisies made possible by money and commercial interest.

I have spoken as if the double-identity theme in *Great Expectations* were associated only with commerce and with the city of London. But as a number of critics have pointed out, Pip possesses a shadowy double in the figure of Orlick before he sets off for London. Masao Myoshi suggests that

> Pip and Orlick are the symbolic representation of a personality divided in the classical Freudian sense. In fact, Pip's sexual passivity can only be adequately explained by Orlick's lecherous interest in Biddy and by his successor's (Drummle's) brutal beatings of Estella. In this use of doubling there is at least the tacit assumption that the psychological reality can no longer be contained within a single character but requires two or more for any adequate expression.

Another possible explanation is that Dickens was unhappy in the portrayal of inner tensions and contradictions, and preferred to objectify these in the form of separate, opposed, but internally integrated characters. Even Wemmick, it may be noted, although divided is divided in a remarkably clean and uncluttered way. This predilection on Dickens's part may represent a tension in his own mind between his perception that human beings were divided by forces powerful in his society, and a desire to see these divisions overcome. Alternatively, we may note that objectifying human divisions in opposed but separate individuals rather than portraying them as internal tensions makes it easier to expose them in detail and to explore their ramifications.

Orlick represents Pip's darker impulses, perhaps, in ways other than are suggested by Myoshi. Almost everything he does can be seen as an expression of suppressed desires on the part of Pip. He strikes down Mrs Joe—after having verbally insulted her—he lusts after Biddy, he is drawn in apparent curiosity and fascination to Miss Havisham's place of self-imposed incarceration, and he stuffs Pumblechook's mouth full of bulbs! The nearest Dickens comes to any overt suggestion that the two represent forces in conflict within the individual rather than between individuals is in the final, rather unsuccessful melodramatic scene where Orlick announces that he is going to kill Pip. Thus what *Great Expectations* lacks is what

Dostoyevsky portrays so well in his work: the revealed existence of contradictory impulses in the same individual struggling for mastery. The displacement of Pip's darker self into the figure of Orlick may have the effect of objectifying it and making it more apparent, but it tends to preclude a concern with more internalized individual conflict.

The treatment of Herbert Pocket in *Great Expectations* gives some evidence that Dickens shied away from the ultimate implications of certain of the contradictions he depicts in the novel. Early on in the text Pocket is presented in a way that suggests clearly that Dickens detected a clear incompatibility between his humanity and his chances of material and social success.

> Herbert Pocket had a frank and easy way with him that was very taking. I had never seen anyone then, and have never seen anyone since, who more strongly expressed to me, in every look and tone, a natural incapacity to do anything secret and mean. There was something wonderfully hopeful about his general air, and something that at the same time whispered to me he would never be very successful or rich.

The thrust of this passage is towards a recognition of the incompatibility of openness and honesty, and success in Victorian Britain. But by the end of the novel Herbert—without being *very* successful or rich—is a successful enough businessman to undercut the force of this earlier description. It is not insignificant that his and Pip's success comes from work abroad, the implications of which in human terms—unlike the work of Jaggers and Wemmick—are never displayed. Here, as so often in the Victorian novel, we see the ideological retreat from the implications of what has been discovered. Just as Dickens qualifies his creative insight into the doomed nature of the 'old-fashioned' qualities of goodness portrayed early on in *Dombey and Son,* so too Mrs Gaskell retreats from the full implications of her insights in *North and South,* implying that perhaps a union of 'Southern' capital and 'Northern' business acumen, along with personal contacts between masters and hands, will resolve the incompatibilities between the human and the commercial that have previously been exposed. (pp. 65-72)

Jeremy Hawthorn, "Double Lives: Dostoyevsky, Hawthorne, Stevenson, Dickens and Gaskell," in his Multiple Personality and the Disintegration of Literary Character: From Oliver Goldsmith to Sylvia Plath, *Edward Arnold, 1983, pp. 47-72.*

C. F. Keppler

[*In the excerpt below, Keppler focuses on examples in nineteenth-century fiction in which the double is presented as a beneficent force.*]

Often we welcome novelty, but we are still too near the forest primeval to be much at ease with genuine strangeness. The unknown, for most of us, tends to be automatically the sinister, and we use the word "dark" for both. This is doubtless why the second self, being the uncanny self, is in the majority of cases the evil self; actively evil as Pursuer and Tempter, more or less passively evil as Vision of Horror.

But the second self is not always evil. (p. 99)

In [this essay] we turn to that rarer but very important type of second self who is genuinely good, *un homme de bonne volonté.* There is nothing contradictory in such an idea. Often, if we have patience and courage, we may find that the strange does not menace us after all, and that the hand which approaches us out of the shadows holds a boon that we need, and offers it to us for our well-being. It is possible, as Thoreau realized in the solitude of Walden, to "be beside ourselves in a sane sense," and in a beneficial and healing sense as well.

This aspect of our subject is the second self as Saviour. Naturally I do not mean the most famous of Saviours, for, though Christ has sometimes been thought of as the counterpart of Satan or Judas-Satan, his stature would make it scarcely possible for him to serve as the second self of a human hero. Nevertheless I use the word "saviour" purposely, in order to suggest the Christ-like in man, which is always the essential characteristic of the good second self, just as the Antichrist-like is always that of the evil second-self. The former is sometimes referred to as the *Schützgeist,* or protective spirit, but such a name does justice neither to his role as sharer of identity with the first self nor to the quality of his goodness, which may be anything but protective in the usual sense of the word.

Early and primitive versions of the good second self (and there are very few) do tend to concentrate on physical protection: the Twin Brother of Amerindian legend, for example, who must come to the aid of his counterpart in the latter's hour of need, who must save his life or, finding him dead, bring him back to life. The function of Enkidu, on the other hand, is much more sophisticated. He does not save Gilgamesh physically, but awakens dormant possibilities within Gilgamesh; by the friendship and later the grief that he brings he opens the eyes of Gilgamesh to the fact of death, and sends the first self on his lonely quest through the underworld, the endless quest of man's soul. This comes far closer than any physical saving to the function of the good second self in recent and modern literature. As the evil second self carries the force of Death for the first self, especially internal Death, deathful contraction of the spirit, so the good second self carries the force of Life, especially in the sense of spiritual growth, even though to be internally effective the latter force may be externally fatal.

With this reversal in nature and function of the second self, there must be a corresponding reversal in the first self. As in rotating a sphere on its axis, we cannot alter the position of one side without equally altering that of the other. Therefore when the second self becomes good the first self necessarily becomes evil. But this does not mean that he becomes simply interchangeable with the evil second self. In all cases the first self is the one nearer to us, whose viewpoint we tend to share and to find the comparatively reasonable one, the "daylight" one. When he proves or becomes evil, even when he is [a despicable creature] . . . , we feel him to be less absolutely vicious than benighted, someone like ourselves who has been corrupted, temporarily or permanently. . . . And one manifestation of this mystery further distinguishes the second self, good or evil, from the first: the fact that in all relationships between them it is he who, from a never quite understandable motive, possibly one that not even he can understand, works upon the character and life of the first self, rather than the other way around. The first self may strongly affect the second in an emotional way because of the bond between them (though this is often hard to be sure of since we know so little about the internal workings of the latter), but the result of this effect is to make the second self act on the first, who always remains essentially the recipient rather than the initiator in any important exchange of influence.

It is the mystery of the second self, then, that differentiates him from the first. But the mystery of the evil second self . . . pales a little beside the mystery of the good one. For what we are dealing with in this category is a paradox within a paradox. The evil second self is at least all of one piece in that he is a dark figure in both senses of the word, both mysterious and malicious. The good second self is dark in the former sense, but the contrary of dark in the latter. What we must look for, therefore, is the backward-foremost situation in which it is the Power of Evil that is presented to us as the more familiar and at least more immediately plausible half of the twofold being, while the Power of Good appears as the uncanny and suspect counterpart, the alien intruder from the shadows.

This fact makes it difficult for us to recognize the second self as good, but of course the writer of a work in which such a second self appears would fail in his intention if we did not ultimately do so. The one for whom such recognition becomes almost insuperably difficult is the first self. Since the moral attributes of the selves are reversed, moral valuations are also reversed. From the viewpoint of the first self his own evil is the reasonable and justified, whether or not conventional, way of life, with which the influence for good exerted on him by the second self is bound to seem unwarranted, injurious, and sometimes immoral interference. As a result, the goodness of the second self means no less oppositeness between the selves than we have seen thus far, and certainly no less opposition.

The ways in which the second self as Saviour prosecutes the cause of goodness on behalf of the first self are interestingly akin to the ways in which the three aspects of the second self . . . prosecute the cause of evil. The first way . . . is comparatively obvious and direct, and the second self who uses it corresponds, though for purposes of salvation rather than of destruction, to the second self as Pursuer. (pp. 100-02)

In a . . . famous example of the pursuing Saviour, Poe's "William Wilson" [a cure for evil] is conceivable in the early stages of the relationship, but gradually is made impossible by the hero's development. This development is one of increasing self-dedication to the cause of evil, which, like Milton's Satan, the first self embraces as his good. The result is a "transvaluation of values" in the first self 's mind, causing the effort to save him to become for him a monstrous persecution, and arousing such resistance that in the end he murders both his Pursuer and himself.

The hero and first self of this story, William Wilson, meets at school only one rival to his dominance over all other boys in both studies and sports. The boy, as it happens, possesses the same name, not in itself a very remarkable coincidence since the name is such an everyday one, but becoming remarkable as the first William Wilson begins to discover other things they have in common: height, general stature and facial appearance, even date of birth. An intense rivalry springs up between the two boys, intense at least on the first self 's part, though the second self so easily maintains equality with him in their various competitions that one might well suspect it to be really superiority. Not only does the second William Wilson cross the first in this way; he has an impertinent though very unobtrusive way of interfering with the other's purposes, and he makes this all the more galling by an unwelcome *affectionateness* of manner, which the first self ascribes to conceit. At the same time, for all the first self 's resentment and growing hostility toward his rival, he finds things in his own attitude that he cannot altogether understand. There is something at times strangely familiar about this second William Wilson, as though recalling memories so early that they antedate memory. There is furthermore an unexpected congeniality in their tempers which results in a confusingly heterogeneous mixture of emotions in the first self 's feeling toward the second: with animosity a certain grudging esteem, with fear a real respect, and "a world of uneasy curiosity." They are inseparable companions, and under normal conditions they might have become fast friends.

But they do not, and for this fact the first William Wilson holds the second to blame. When the former makes fun of the latter's speech, which by some vocal weakness is restricted to a low whisper, the latter retaliates by mimicking the former in dress, words, actions, gait, manner, even voice; for though he cannot imitate the louder tones, his whisper becomes the very echo of the hero's own. And still more offensive is increased interference in the hero's affairs, often presumptuously becoming advice, advice later recognized by the hero to have been sound, but resented at the time as intolerable arrogance.

The climax of their rivalry comes when the first William Wilson goes at night to play a practical joke on the second, while the latter is asleep. Looking down at the other boy he is suddenly chilled to the heart at his sense of not only a resemblance but some much closer and stranger tie between them which he does not dare to name. Stealing out of the other's chamber, he leaves the school at once. His flight has begun, but . . . the second self who would be his Saviour is not to be eluded or shaken off. As the first William Wilson, having largely freed himself from the influence of the second, sinks steadily deeper into dissipation, depravity, and crime, the second pursues, appearing in critical moments in his counterpart's career; at Eton checks him in the midst of a wild orgy by the mere stern whisper of his name; at Oxford exposes him publicly as a cheater at cards and forces him to leave in disguise. At last, at the Carnival in Rome, when the first William Wilson is planning the seduction of an elderly nobleman's young and pretty wife, a hand is laid on his arm and the familiar whisper sounds in his ear. Furiously dragging his tormenter into an adjoining chamber the hero stabs him through the bosom and, after his glance is distracted for an instant by someone's trying the door, turns back to see what appears to be a large mirror facing him, with his reflection in it, blood-stained and tottering. But then he realizes that it is no mirror. It is the second self, now unmistakable in his identity with the first; it is the pursuing Saviour who has failed, and whose failure, as he points out with his last breath, means equally destruction for them both.

The allegorical element in this story is obvious, but should not be overemphasized. To be sure the second William Wilson is the first one's "better self," but so, if not always this clearly, the second self as Saviour is bound to be, just as the second self in any of his evil aspects is bound to be the "worse self." But if he is a genuine second self, as I take the second William Wilson to be, he can never be simply translated into an abstraction, as "conscience" on the one hand or "innate depravity" on the other. What makes ["William Wilson" and similar stories about the double] works of creative literature rather than fictionalized moral tracts is the fact that they are first of all alive, living records of imaginative experience, of a relationship given a peculiar electrical excitement by the simultaneous separateness and sameness, attraction and repulsion, of the two beings involved in it. (pp. 105-06)

[The good second self can also resemble] in technique the second self as Tempter; he is a more subtle Saviour than the ones we have thus far considered, realizing that the major task of salvation must be done by the person being saved, and enticing him by one means or another toward the inward state with which such self-salvation is synonymous. Naturally, as the second self who pursues in order to save is bound to seem objectionable and menacing to the first self who stands in need of salvation, so the second self who tempts for the same purpose is bound to seem devious, suspect, allied with the Devil or perhaps the Devil himself. It is for the latter that the unnamed intruder of Stevenson's *Markheim* is mistaken by the first self, though he proves [to be an unusual Devil]. Similar in plan to Dostoyevsky's *Crime and Punishment,* this story begins with a murder, and again it is the murder of an old pawnbroker by an impoverished young man; again, also, the murder is merely the prelude to the real story, the story of its consequences in the mind of the murderer-protagonist. Markheim's need differs from Raskolnikov's in that he has brought it upon himself by a life of dissipation, but he justifies himself no less than the young Russian, not by the philosophy of Might Makes Right but by assuring himself that God, being just, will surely forgive him. Like Macbeth before the murder of Duncan, he is conscious only of the fear of earthly retribution, and he looks down with no stirring of conscience on the crumpled, blood-stained body that a moment ago was a living man.

But Markheim, in realms of his being of which he has not taken account, is no more immune to the monstrousness of his deed than is Raskolnikov. He has looked upon his victim, before plunging his dagger into the latter's heart, with infinite pity and a touch of horror; he has, for all the danger of doing so, delayed the stroke, trying to converse with the flint-hard old dealer, trying to penetrate the mask of everyday to some vestige of humanity within, trying as Raskolnikov tries to find some excuse for *not* doing the act to which his sense of duty to himself has brought him. And once the crime is committed, and he is alone and free to search for the pawnbroker's money, he discovers that he is neither alone nor free; on every side there are companions, there are watchers, there are reminders and compellers. As he moves about with a candle, the mirrors on all sides catch his reflection: once more the old device of the mirror, placing the self outside the self, as though independent of its original . . . , in this case not only inimical but manifold, "as it were an army of spies." The silence is vexed by sounds other than clocks: his own stealthy footsteps—or is he positive they are his own? In the drawing room upstairs, going through the dealer's keys, he hears them again, and now in horror he knows they are *not* his own; they are mounting the stairs from below. Suddenly the knob turns, and, as Markheim cries out hoarsely, a visitor, apparently taking this for an invitation, enters and shuts the door behind him. The outlines of the newcomer seem to waver slightly, to Markheim's terrified gaze, like those of idols in candlelight. Markheim has no doubt of the other's reality, but he has increasing doubt of the other's humanity; "and at times he thought he knew him; and at times he thought he bore a likeness to himself; and always, like a lump of living terror, there lay in his bosom the conviction that this thing was not of the earth and not of God."

In other words Markheim, like Ivan Karamazov and Faust in their hours of extreme vulnerability, appears to be playing host to the Devil. And like those other diabolical visitants, Markheim's is no gloomy fallen Archangel but a poised, polite, cynical man of the world, precisely the sort of man Markheim ought to have been in order to carry out his plans with full success. At once he seems to take Markheim's side, gives him sound advice on how to proceed, urges him to hurry before the maidservant returns, offers to tell him where the money is hidden ("for a Christmas gift," as he sweetly puts it), and suggests that Markheim be content with the kind of scoundrel he is and act accordingly. All this is much the sort of thing we have seen other Devils doing, tempting to evil with plausible diabolical arguments that are articulations of thoughts already present in the first self 's mind. But Markheim's visitor differs from the others in that he tempts in just the reverse direction from theirs, toward good instead of evil. By affecting to take the side of Markheim's viciousness he forces Markheim to face the fact of this viciousness, to stop deluding himself with notions of his justification or of good intentions to reform, and to see that the course he has taken can lead him only where it has always led him, steadily deeper into degradation and hopeless damnation. Nor is this done, as . . . done by Svidrigaïlov, out of malice; for as Markheim at last defies the diabolical counsel (the maidservant has returned, and the "Devil" suggests that Markheim murder her as well) and chooses the one door of freedom left open to him, that of self-renunciation, the features of the visitor "brightened and softened with a tender triumph." Markheim walks down the stairs and opens the house door.

> He confronted the maid upon the threshold with something like a smile. "You had better go for the police," he said. "I have killed your master."

To be sure there is a certain allegorical flavor about the tempter of Markheim, just as there is about the pursuer of the first William Wilson. Nevertheless, the former is no more a mere personified idea than the latter, but from his first appearance, for all his mystery, he is a living, breathing, flesh-and-blood character in the story, perhaps even more vivid than his counterpart. It is true that he is perceived only by Markheim, as the Devil of *The Brothers Karamazov* is perceived only by Ivan. But it should be noted how careful Stevenson is to avoid stamping his visitant as "nothing but" a mental content; just as careful as Dostoyevsky is to do the opposite. The fact that the features of the visitor "faded and dislimned" as Markheim turns away to give himself up is not the same thing as his disappearance before Markheim's eyes. Indeed Markheim does not watch the transformation, even though we are told that the transformation takes place, and have it described for us. In other words, we are made aware of something (whether or not a supernatural something) happening to the visitor of which Markheim is not aware, something that must therefore take place outside the range of Markheim's experience, in the realm of objective reality.

In *Markheim,* then, we find the second self as Saviour assuming the guise of the Devil and apparently tempting *as* the Devil, but using the process of pseudo-temptation to accomplish his real temptation, which leads Markheim from the lostness of self-love to the triumph of self-conquest. (pp. 106-09)

Dostoevsky.

The examples of the second self as Saviour that we have covered thus far are analogous to the evil second self in his active aspects. A third group is reminiscent rather of the second self as Vision of Horror. Like the latter, these second selves have no conscious intention of influencing the first self as they do, and the kind of influence they exert could probably not be brought about by plan, for it is the result in each case simply of the impact of the second self 's personality on the mind of the first self, as a vision of something in the latter's own personality as yet unknown or unacknowledged. Indeed the parallel goes further, for since the first self in these cases is the evil or at least limited self, the vision that he gets of his identity with the second self *is* for him a vision of horror, either mildly, as in the first example we shall consider, or catastrophically, as in the last.

The first example is [one] of Conrad's stories, *The Secret Sharer,* the clearest instance of Conrad's treatment of the relationship between the selves, making frequent use of the terms "double," "other self," and "second self." At first glance it would appear to be the first self of this narrative, the young captain, who saves the second, but the counter-salvation that goes on at a deeper level is far more important. At the outset the young captain, unexpectedly, has just been given his command; he feels himself a stranger to his ship and something of a stranger to himself. While waiting for a wind that will let him sail he takes a night watch by himself, and while walking alone on deck notices a rope ladder that has been left hanging over the side. He is about to haul it in when he sees at the foot of it, floating in the water and flickering with phosphorescence, the naked body of a man. The man proves to be one Leggatt, formerly chief mate of a ship anchored in the same harbor. Without hesitation he explains that he has killed someone, an insolent sailor who goaded him to fury during the setting of a reefed foresail in a storm. He has no regrets; the man was a vicious troublemaker who deserved to die. He has therefore taken his chance to escape; has entrusted himself to the black, measureless ocean; and finally has made his way here (just as the captain has made his way), to the ladder that "happens" to have been left over the side.

The difference between the two men is immediately established. For all his desperate situation, this naked derelict from out of the sea is really far more determined, far less subject to self-doubt and hesitation, than the captain who receives him; in this sense, the inward sense, he is more "in command" than the captain is. It is such qualities that have brought him here, confronting his host with a test no less critical than that with which the pseudo-diabolical visitor confronts Markheim. Here, however, it is not the killer who is being tested but the one who has found the killer; here too, in view of the nature of the crime, the motive for turning the killer over would be less that of serving justice than that of serving convention.

The captain-narrator does not make the "proper" choice, and for the reason we must look to the peculiar effect which Leggatt exerts on him from the moment of their meeting at either end of the rope ladder. Something about this stranger, even before anything more is visible than the flickering phosphorescence of his body in the water, unaccountably appeals to the captain: the calm and resolute voice that comes up from below, the deliberateness with which Leggatt weighs the alternatives, whether to go on swimming until he sinks or to trust himself on board. The captain waits, and in the silence "a mysterious communication was established already between us two—in the face of that silent, darkened tropical sea." And this mysterious communication continues, even after Leggatt is on board, and they resume their low-voiced conspiratorial exchange; for the most important part of what is communicated goes far beyond the words that are spoken. Above all what is communicated, for the captain, is the increasingly weird but inescapable message that the man who has just risen to him out of the sea is not a stranger, but himself.

In part this is conveyed by physical appearance and juxtaposition. Leggatt is about the same age as the captain, the same height, the same build; the sleeping suit with which the captain clothes him, an exact duplicate of the captain's own, exactly fits him. So dressed, with their shadowy dark heads together as they whisper, they are like mirrored reflections of each other. And not only does the captain dress Leggatt in his own clothes; he also lets Leggatt sleep in his bed while he, supposedly in bed, sleeps on the couch; he lets Leggatt drink the early-morning coffee that he is supposedly drinking; and so forth, frequently with the confused sensation of being in two places at once.

But of course this is not a story about mistaken identity, but about the discovery of a shared identity. The physical parallels are simply the external manifestations of the really significant process that is going on in their relationship. The moment the captain makes his first move on the criminal's behalf, and after the fashion of Saint Francis and Fidelman clothes the naked man in his own garment, his sense of the true parallel between them is awakened and grows rapidly to a sense of continuity, even an uncertainty from time to time as to which is the captain and which is the criminal; and with this growth comes an increasing conviction of the rightness of Leggatt's cause, and increasing determination to do for the other what he can.

This is true sympathy: a "feeling with" to the extent of becoming one with, of being beside oneself in a sane sense. But for the average person, accustomed to our neat, orderly system of divisions, such sympathy puts a severe strain upon the kind of sanity to which he is used. The captain sits at his desk in the daytime, his double sitting exactly behind him out of sight, not in mockery as Golyadkin junior might have done, but because there is nowhere else to sit; and there Leggatt must remain, hour after hour, like a carbon copy. Often the captain has the feeling, so familiar among the symptoms of psychic disease, of looking at himself from outside. His strangeness to his ship increases, for just like a psychic disorder this experience isolates him even further from his men.

There is no way to put Leggatt ashore. The only chance is to let him slip off at night into the sea and make for the islands off the Cambodian coast. But first he must be taken near enough. Under the pretense of seeking the land breeze the captain changes course and sails toward the inhabited island of Koh-ring. Aware of the risk he is running, aware that his whole future as seaman is at stake, he presses on through the darkness, disregarding the fears of the helmsman, overruling the hysterical protests of his mate, on until "the black southern hill of Koh-ring seemed to hang right over the ship like a towering fragment of the everlasting night," on until he is sure that Leggatt has had his chance; and only then, with the fate of the ship balanced on a hair, does he she swing away. For a moment he cannot tell whether the ship will respond or not. Then he catches a glimpse of white on the black water below him, his own floppy straw hat which he has put on Leggatt's head to protect the latter from the tropic sun, and which has apparently slid off when Leggatt struck the sea. "It had been meant to save his homeless head from the dangers of the sun. And now—behold—it was saving the ship, by serving me for a mark to help out the ignorance of my strangeness."

Thus Leggatt, saved by the captain, has in turn saved the captain. But the episode of the hat, again, is only an external manifestation of the real saving. The story has begun with the statement of the captain's problem. Young, inexperienced in his new post, untrusted by his subordinates, unsure of himself, he knows that as yet he is captain in name only; he must win the respect of the men he commands before he can truly command them; he must "get the feel" of the ship before he can truly sail her. And it is the solution to this problem which Leggatt, rising out of the dark sea like a force from his own unconscious depths, has brought him; it is his supreme effort to meet the demands laid upon him by his relationship with Leggatt which solves not only Leggatt's problem but his own as well.

> Already the ship was drawing ahead. And I was alone with her. Nothing! no one in the world should stand now between us, throwing a shadow on the way of silent knowledge and mute affection, the perfect communion of a seaman with his first command.

The Secret Sharer is an exception to the general rule of second-self literature in that there is at no time any real opposition between the two main characters. The only thing that approaches it is the captain's appalled astonishment at the way in which, under Leggatt's influence, he is risking his ship, his men, and himself for the sake of a naked, derelict murderer he has never laid eyes on before. But we should not infer that there is necessarily less of such opposition in situations where the second self as Saviour works nonpurposively, through the impact of his character, than in those where he saves or tries to save as a matter of conscious intent. To the contrary, such influencing through personality often involves an opposition that may be literally carried to the death. Such is the case in the last two examples we shall consider in this [essay].

One of these is Melville's story, *Bartleby, the Scrivener,* to which in the original version was added the subtitle (the significance of which will become apparent), *A Story of Wall Street.* The first self and narrator of this story is a far cry from the doubt-troubled young captain of *The Secret Sharer.* He is an elderly lawyer who never addresses a jury or pleads a case or does anything else that might invade his peace, but devotes himself to taking care of bonds and mortgages and title-deeds for the wealthy. He is not a brilliant man, or a dynamic man, but an eminently *safe* man, and his outstanding qualities are prudence and method. Even his chambers on Wall Street are adequate, prudently unexciting, and safely circumscribed, at one end looking out on the white wall of the interior of a skylight shaft, at the other looking out on a brick wall black with age and everlasting shade, so close that the interval between looks a little like a huge square cistern.

Our hero, then, is a dull old mole who has spent his life digging about in other people's titles and conveyances, and, far from objecting to the dullness of his existence, he is complacently contented with it, has grown sleekly fat on it. Even a shade duller than his own life is that of his two clerks, or scriveners, who spend their days copying out by hand the numerous documents with which the lawyer must deal. From sunrise to sunset, while the earth turns and the winds blow and men love and die, they sit at their high tables and copy. Unlike their employer, they show certain symptoms of rebellion against this reduction of man to a machine as the price of allowing him to live. Turkey, the elder of the two, is a model of industry until the lunch hour, at which time he not only dines, but wines, and through the afternoon works with a "strange, inflamed, flurried, flighty recklessness of activity," becoming guilty of numerous blots and errors. Nippers, the younger, is temperate, but suffers from indigestion and a general irritability, as well as a specific discontent with the table at which he works, which he can never adjust to suit him. Conveniently, Nippers is difficult only during the morning hours, so that his symptoms of rebellion alternate with Turkey's, like the changing of the guard. It is a sorry sort of rebellion in both cases, a mere impotent gesture of eccentricity, as empty and mechanical as the way of life it seeks to rebel against.

But another type of rebellion is soon to make its appearance. So many are the documents waiting to be copied that an additional scrivener is needed, and in answer to the lawyer's advertisement a young man named Bartleby comes one morning to the office and is engaged. A few words are exchanged concerning his qualifications, but none concerning himself. . . . He surrounds himself with an air of pallid and austere reserve; in his wholly undramatic way he is perhaps the most mysterious of all the second selves we have met, and the lack of drama is of the essence of the mystery.

There are two parts of the process by which Bartleby comes to fill the narrator's horizon, and they go on simultaneously. One is the way in which he installs himself physically, as a permanent fixture, in the narrator's office. In this installation the narrator, like the traditional witch's victim, takes the initiative. Not only does he "invite" Bartleby by the advertisement, and then by hiring him, but he goes further. Though the other scriveners are kept in a room separated from the lawyer's by ground-glass folding doors, he places Bartleby's desk in his own room, next to a little window looking out on a wall, and enclosed in a high green folding screen. Bartleby's presence therefore, if not in his person, is always within the lawyer's vision. And by degrees it becomes apparent that this presence is not restricted to ordinary working hours. Bartleby never goes out to meals; he never goes anywhere. "He was a perpetual sentry in the corner," comments the narrator, though not realizing at this point quite how perpetual and faithful a sentry Bartleby is. One Sunday morning, however, when he stops in at his chambers, he discovers that Bartleby, who has somehow got hold of the extra key to the door, is living there. In [fact] . . . Bartleby takes possession of the lawyer's office. At first the narrator ascribes the situation to Bartleby's poverty, but in Bartleby's desk he finds money, tied up in an old bandanna handkerchief.

The other part of the process by which Bartleby becomes a preoccupation crowding out all others from the narrator's mind is his opposition to the narrator's will. It is a rebellion which, though far quieter than that of Turkey and Nippers, is no mere gesture like theirs, but an absolute and inflexible defiance. A scrivener must not only copy, but also verify the accuracy of his copy, word by word; and it is this that even the narrator admits is dull, the quintessential dullness of the scrivener's dull existence. When called on for this part of his service Bartleby, to the thunderstruck surprise of his employer, simply refuses. He refuses in an interesting way, saying instead of "I will not," "I would prefer not to"; thus both emphasizing the bleak mildness of his manner and underscoring the monstrous fact of a scrivener's having such a thing as a preference at all.

The reaction of the narrator, for all his equable temperament, is strangely intense and ambivalent. On the other hand he is outraged, and as Bartleby persists he finds himself giving way to an impulse which he knows to be evil, renewing his first request and making new ones, attempting to goad Bartleby into even more outrageous rebellion. On the other hand, though he intimates that terrible retribution will follow, he finds " . . . something about Bartleby that not only strangely disarmed me, but, in a wonderful manner, touched and disconcerted me." What especially disconcerts him is the way Bartleby seems carefully to consider everything the narrator says to him, tacitly to grant the logic of it, but, because of "some paramount consideration" that takes precedence over logic, to persist in his refusal. The narrator's faith in the rightness of his cause is actually shaken a little, and for the time Bartleby wins, being exempted from any duties but copying. What is more, instead of being roused to fury at his discovery that Bartleby has taken over the office for living quarters, the narrator is struck with the thought of the other's friendlessness and loneliness. This is an emotion such as the elderly lawyer has never before known. "For the first time in my life a feeling of overpowering stinging melancholy seized me. Before, I had never experienced aught but a not unpleasing sadness. The bond of a common humanity now drew me irresistibly to gloom."

But soon the habit of prudential common sense reasserts itself, and the sympathy with which Bartleby has "infected" the narrator gives way to fear and even repulsion. There is something morbid about Bartleby, and safety requires getting him much farther out of sight than behind his folding screen. This decision is strengthened by the narrator's discovery of a further infection; he has commenced using, involuntarily and not appropriately, Bartleby's word "prefer." "And I trembled to think that my contact with the scrivener had already and seriously affected me in a mental way." When Bartleby ceases even to do any copying, will do nothing but stand at his little window staring out with dead eyes at the dead wall facing him, the narrator summons up his resolution and gives the scrivener notice. But on the morning after what was supposed to be Bartleby's last day the recalcitrant scrivener is still there. Professional visitors begin to stare at this extraordinary creature who stands "like the last column of some ruined temple"; a whisper of wonder about him begins to go around; and the narrator, never a man of much moral courage, fears that his reputation is being damaged by this taint of strangeness. Seeing no way to persuade Bartleby to quit him, he quits Bartleby, removing to new offices. The last thing to go is the folding screen, and there still stands Bartleby, motionless in the stripped room, staring at the blank wall outside the little window.

Yet even left behind, Bartleby is not entirely got rid of. He makes no move to follow, but remains in the old office, and when ejected he remains in the building, sitting on the banisters by day and sleeping in the entry by night. Notified of the fact the narrator goes to him and for the last time tries to reason with him, even offers to take Bartleby to his home; but Bartleby would prefer not to make any change. The narrator washes his hands of all responsibility, and the police remove Bartleby to the Tombs. There he stands in the courtyard as he has done in the office, facing a high wall, refusing now to speak to the narrator, refusing to eat when the narrator pays the "grub-man" to feed him. A few days later the narrator visits the prison again, and finds the wasted Bartleby lying at the base of the wall, apparently asleep. He touches Bartleby, and realizes what sort of sleep it is, the sleep from which there will be no waking.

The effect that the narrator has on Bartleby is given us in far less detail, as we should expect, than the effect that Bartleby has on the narrator. But quietly and pallidly though it may be shown there *is* such an effect, and to notice the signs of what is going on in the second self is most important, in this story, to a full understanding of what is going on in the first. Toward everyone else who appears Bartleby is completely indifferent, but he is not indifferent to the narrator. For example, after the narrator has discovered that Bartleby is living in the office, and through this discovery has got some sense of the man's isolation from all the rest of humanity, he tries in a friendly manner to question Bartleby about himself. This friendliness, however, is chiefly in manner, for the narrator's initial sympathy has already begun to give way to fear, fear really of the sympathy itself, and the questioning is designed as a prelude to getting rid of Bartleby. Bartleby as usual prefers not to comply, but for the first time there is a sign of emotion on the cadaverous face, "the faintest conceivable tremor of the white attenuated mouth." When Bartleby announces that he will do no more copying and is asked for his reason, he does not give his formula-reply, that he would prefer not to, but for the only time in the story puts a question of his own to the narrator. "Do you not see the reason for yourself?" The narrator, noticing that Bartleby's eyes look dull and glazed, concludes that he must be suffering from eyestrain. But we have long since been told of the dimness of Bartleby's eyes, and even when the eyes have had full time to recover, Bartleby persists in his refusal; apparently, in other words, the narrator has failed to see the reason for himself, and when, taken to the Tombs from the deserted office, Bartleby is visited by the narrator, he declines even to look at him, and stands facing the wall at the foot of which he is to fall into his last sleep. " 'I know you,' he said, without looking around—'and I want nothing to say to you'."

Why should Bartleby feel such resentment against the man who has shown him such consideration, made every effort to help him? Resentment against a mechanized society for having crushed his spirit is no adequate explanation, for Bartleby's spirit is not crushed, and in any case his resentment is not against society but against the narrator. In fact it is the very pinpointing of this emotion, when seen against the background of the other writings we have considered in this chapter, that will enable us to find once more the same basic pattern of relationship. It is the pattern of a certain claim made by the second self upon the first, the demand that the latter not do something or that he do something or that he become something he is not but has within him the capacity to be; and of the struggle by the first self either to meet the demand or to resist it sometimes both. The demand in this story is never put into words, but it is the thing of paramount importance for both selves from the beginning of their relationship to the end. Obviously Bartleby's demand is not for consideration or pity; he receives these. It seems to be rather for sympathy in the most complete sense of the word, sympathy which (like that of Conrad's young captain) follows through in active commitment, sympathy which *gives itself,* and which in this case by giving itself would complement and realize itself. He is not asking condonement of his rebellion; he is, doubtless quite unconsciously, demanding allegiance in it, and he is making this demand of the man, diametrically Bartleby's opposite, who has compromised with the soul-squashing monotony of the life of getting and spending to the point where he no longer knows it to be monotonous; who has faded almost indistinguishably into the dull gray landscape of profits and losses, desks and documents.

What is demanded of the narrator is, to put it into the simplest terms, that he save his soul; and this demand is made by Bartleby not as dispassionate observer but as co-owner of the soul to be saved. He rises out of the unknown to protest the grievous wrong that is being done to their shared being, rises both before the narrator and within the narrator to install himself at the heart of just those activities which have made the narrator what he is, and remains fixed there as a pale, silent ghost of reproach, the banner of passive insurrection planted at the center of the enemy's bastions. And under his influence the narrator's shell of comfortable complacency fits somewhat less comfortably; he is shaken a little in his confidence that his is the reasonable way; the long winter ice of conformity begins to thaw slightly; for the first time in his life he is touched with gloom at the thought of what such a life can do to a man, is moved to sympathy for a victim of it. But no sooner do the sympathy, and the insight that accompanies it, arise in him than, frightened and repelled by such painful things, he hurriedly enshells himself again, and resolves (a resolution embroidered with all sorts of altruistic sentiments) to put this Satan of salvation once and for all behind him. With even keener insight Bartleby seems to know exactly what has been going on; it is at this point that he shows his first sign of resentment; and it is shortly after this that, refusing even the limited concession he has made so far, he turns his face to the wall.

In an epilogue the narrator mentions a rumor he has heard, that Bartleby was once a subordinate clerk in the Dead Letter Office; and he conjectures that the dreariness of this business has produced or heightened Bartleby's own natural dreariness, and that the continual handling of dead letters, striking their dead chill through skin and into blood, has produced a dead man. But this is the narrator's comment, not Melville's, and if read in the light of the story that precedes it it becomes, not an explanation of Bartleby, but an attempt at self-justification by the man whom Bartleby has tried to save. For the essential irony of this novella is that Bartleby, who moves through the story like a walking corpse, is in fact the only living person in it, the only person capable of genuine "preferring." He is not a dead man, but a death's head, a memento mori to the dead of soul who surround him, only one of whom (the narrator) is capable of being stirred by the reminder; and even this stirring is only an intimation that flickers for an instant and then goes out. *Bartleby, the Scrivener* is light in tone, but is probably the bitterest story Melville ever wrote, all the more bitter for the fact that there is no anger in it; no blackness, only grayness, that in the end like gray dust settles back placidly over all.

The other example of a work in which the second self 's influence for good is exerted on the first self chiefly through the impact of his personality, and in which the first self 's resistance to this personality is carried to the point of death (though in this case his own rather than the second self 's), occurs in Victor Hugo's gigantic novel, *Les Misérables.* The relationship between the hero, Jean Valjean, and his nemesis, the police inspector Javert, might be thought to belong with those we have discussed as examples of the second self as Pursuer, with Javert as the pursuing and evil second self. But in this novel, so far as the relationship between the selves is concerned, a most peculiar thing happens. Through the book as a whole Jean Valjean is the protagonist and more than any other one person the viewpoint character. But in his relationship with Javert, though we are given neither viewpoint consistently, we know far more about and are far more involved in Javert's reaction to Jean Valjean than we are in the latter's reaction to Javert, and this becomes increasingly true as we approach the climax of their relationship. Our general sympathy is with Jean Valjean, but throughout his long persecution it is the man who persecutes him to whom we are always closer, whose attitude is presented to us as the human and understandable and to this extent reasonable one. Jean Valjean's attitude toward Javert, on the other hand, we must infer as something far less familiar to our experience, and in this respect he is almost as much of a mystery to us as he is to Javert.

Les Misérables is an immensely complicated work, of which the relationship with which we are dealing constitutes only one among many strands. But it is necessary that we study this relationship in the context of the novel as a whole, and to do so we must begin at a point considerably before the paths of the two men involved in it cross, indeed before either of them even appears. The whole first book, "A Just Man," is devoted to a character who, so far as participation in the plot is concerned, might seem a very minor personage indeed. Nevertheless the personality of this man, long after he is dead, reverberates through the entire work, becoming the main single influence in the life of Jean Valjean, and through him in the life of Javert as well.

The "just man" is the elderly Charles Myriel, the Bishop of D—. He is a genuine bishop, but his episcopal palace, his handsome income, and all his personal energies he has long since dedicated to the succor, both physical and spiritual, of the miserable.

The bishop is not literally the second self of the relationship we are studying. But in a very broad sense, which it is vitally important that we understand, he is. Long before the relationship between Jean Valjean and Javert begins, it is prepared for by a much briefer relationship between Jean Valjean and the bishop. What we have here, in other words, is something that structurally at least resembles the plan of Hogg's *Private Memoirs and Confessions of a Justified Sinner.* There, however, the central character shifts from the role of second self to that of first; here the reverse happens, with results far more remarkable and moving. In the earlier relationship of *Les Misérables,* Jean Valjean is the first self, showing qualities to be unmistakably paralleled by Javert, the first self of the later relationship; just as there are equally unmistakable parallels between the Bishop of D—, who in this earlier episode is Jean Valjean's second self, and the later Jean Valjean, who becomes the second self of Javert. It is a complicated plan, but not really an obscure one. We are still dealing with only two halves, the old division between the Light Twin and the Dark. This time the two extremes are represented by the diametrically contrasted figures of the saintly bishop and the "dog son of a wolf" Javert. But in their own persons the bishop and Javert never meet. Midway between them stands the figure of Jean Valjean, who possesses qualities of both, and who in the early part of the story shows his Javert-side in his encounter with the bishop, but who then, "infected" by the bishop, shows his bishop-side throughout his relationship with Javert. If this sounds mechanical, it is only because I am giving the skeleton without the flesh and blood that clothe it. Let us now briefly trace the way in which this change takes place.

To the home of the bishop, "Monseigneur Bienvenu" (My Lord Welcome), there comes one night a ragged wanderer, fierce-looking and harsh of voice, whose name is Jean Valjean. He is a recently discharged convict who has served nineteen years as a galley slave at Toulon; five years for stealing bread to feed his sister's starving children, fourteen years for trying to escape. Because of his yellow passport, which brands him as a dangerous exconvict, he has been refused admittance at all inns, refused by everyone, ejected even from a dog's house in which he has sought shelter. But by the bishop he is not refused. To Jean Valjean's astonishment the old man whom he accosts with hostile defiance treats him in return with every kindness and courtesy, has a place laid for him at his own poor table, has a bed made for him in the alcove next to his own room. For Jean Valjean the change is too abrupt, and the darkness of mind, the surly resentment that has been hardening within him for nineteen years, is too strong. In the middle of the night he steals into the bishop's room, takes the bishop's silver plate, and flees. He is captured by the police and brought before the bishop. But the bishop presses no charges. To the contrary, he insists that he gave the plate to his guest, and that he also gave him the two heavy silver candlesticks, which he now presents to Jean Valjean. As the officers leave he says in a low voice, "Jean Valjean, my brother, you no longer belong to evil, but to good. I have bought your soul of you. I withdraw it from black thoughts and the spirit of perdition, and give it to God."

Like Judas, Jean Valjean has sold his soul for silver, but to the Power of Light rather than the Power of Darkness. The true transaction, however, has barely begun; and it is at this point that the Bishop of D—, dropping out of the story in his own person, makes his real entrance into the moral life of Jean Valjean. Utterly bewildered, torn by sensations he cannot comprehend, the exconvict wanders about the neighborhood, and at sunset he finds himself sitting in the midst of a large, deserted plain. A little ragged chimney sweep named Gervais comes past, tossing a coin in the air; it drops to the ground, and Jean Valjean, placing his foot on it, drives the child away. When he comes to himself, he is horrified; he searches the countryside for half the night, calling vainly "Little Gervais! Little Gervais!" At last he falls in exhaustion, and for the first time in nineteen years he begins to weep.

This weeping marks the climax and resolution of a struggle such as this man has never known: the struggle, on the part of the Jean Valjean who has been, to choke off the birth of the Jean Valjean who is to be. But it is already too late. The robbing of Little Gervais is not only an automatic gesture, but also an anachronistic one. "It was a curious phenomenon, and one only possible in his present situation, that, in robbing the boy of that money, he committed a deed of which he was no longer capable." It is an act which has damned him (it pursues him all the rest of his life), but which, in the sense of damnation that it forces upon him, also has saved him.

> When he exclaimed, "I am a wretch!" he saw himself as he really was, and was already so separated from himself that he fancied himself merely a phantom, and that he had there before him, in flesh and blood, cudgel in hand, his blouse on his back, his knapsack full of stolen objects, the frightful galley-slave, Jean Valjean, with his resolute and gloomy face, and his mind full of hideous schemes. . . . He contemplated himself, so to speak, face to face; and at the same time he saw through this hallucination, in a mysterious depth, a light which at first he took for a torch. On looking more attentively at this light which appeared to his conscience, he perceived that it had a human shape, and that the torch was the bishop. His conscience examined in turn the two men standing before him,—the bishop and Jean Valjean. By one of those singular effects peculiar to an ecstasy of this nature, the more his revery was prolonged, the taller and more brilliant the bishop appeared, while Jean Valjean grew less, and faded out of sight. At length he disappeared and the bishop alone remained, filling the wretched man's soul with magnificent radiance.

This bishop is, of course, a vision only, purely subjective, and so recognized by both Jean Valjean and the reader. But behind this vision is its objective original, the gently relentless Monseigneur Bienvenu, who not by any mere conversion but by an actual invasion of Jean Valjean's being with his own, and an awakening to predominance of the latent bishop-force present there, becomes the Saviour of Jean Valjean's soul.

Only after a considerable lapse of time do we again meet Jean Valjean. By now his situation, his personality, his appearance, his direction in life, are all completely changed. Even the name is different; it is now "Father" Madeleine, originator of a new process of bead manufacture, owner-operator of a large factory from which flows the lifeblood of the town of M. sur M., and, after several times declining the office, made mayor by the king. This success is of no importance except for what it enables him to do for others, for the bishop-self that has been brought to birth during the labor pains of self-division and self-confrontation has grown now to maturity. Like the bishop the new Jean Valjean lives simply and frugally and with but one aim—to give such help as he can to those who need help, especially that lowest substratum of the needy from which he has so recently risen, the miserable of the earth.

But Jean Valjean is not the only one who has risen from the depths. In the same town, as it "happens," is another man who has done so, though in a very different way. Not a galley slave himself but the son of one, born in prison of a fortune-teller, he has grown up with an inexpressible loathing for the class of people to which by birth he belongs, and motivated by this loathing he has found employment with the police, becoming in time an inspector and performing the useful duty of spy. His name is Javert. Years of pain and disgrace have made Jean Valjean at first resentful against his oppressors, later deeply sympathetic with the oppressed. But the same factors have had the reverse effect on Javert. As though to divorce himself as completely as possible from the dregs of society out of which he has come, he has developed into the fanatical supporter of established authority, the inflexible enemy of the slightest disrespect toward it. In persecuting transgressors he is absolutely without mercy, and just in this mercilessness he finds "his connecting link with humanity."

Such is Javert, not a sadistic man but a dedicated man, and in what he is dedicated to surely no one could be more the opposite of the sadly gentle, the tolerant and forgiving Father Madeleine. We must remember, however, that Father Madeleine is only the present version of Jean Valjean. And just as, earlier, the old Jean Valjean met his opposite, the bishop, who confronted him with the latent decency of his own nature, so now the new Jean Valjean meets *his* opposite, Javert, who confronts him with the former savagery of soul that Jean Valjean has put behind him. Each—the bishop and the police inspector—is the opposite of Jean Valjean, but since in the interval between the two encounters Jean Valjean has reversed his character, they are opposites in opposite ways, that is, opposites of each other. Each, finally, in his oppositeness to the Jean Valjean whom he meets, is linked to him by a bond of identity with the part of Jean Valjean's own nature which at that point is buried deep inside him. The bishop anticipates the "Father Madeleine" of the future. Javert recalls the Jean Valjean of the past.

Hints of such a complicated linkage are given us, at this point in the story, by means of certain quasi-musical devices resembling those by which Dostoyevsky suggests the linkage between Raskolnikov and Svidrigaïlov. Thus the name of Javert, in its two dominant consonantal sounds, echoes in the same sequence the initials of the name which M. Madeleine has sought to leave behind him: Jean Valjean. Thus the three main changes in the appearance of Jean Valjean, now that he has become M. Madeleine, are the fact that he is clean-shaven instead of wearing the long beard in which we first saw him, the fact that he has discarded the leather cap that was pulled low over his eyes, and the fact that he no longer carries a cudgel. It is just these changes that are underscored for us by three main items in the appearance of Javert: the enormous whiskers that cover most of his face, the hat with a turned-down brim that hides his entire forehead, and the cudgel that he conceals beneath his coat. But of course the important parallels lie deeper. Though Javert is no exconvict but the pursuer of convicts, though he has become the watchdog of respectable society instead of its outcast enemy, his fundamental traits of character are in exaggerated form the same as those of the man who, on that fateful night, ate of the bishop's bread and stole the bishop's silver. There is the same resentment, except that it is directed downward rather than upward; there is the same hardness, except that encouraged by opportunities for exercise which Jean Valjean's never knew it has become even harder; there is the same gloomy habit of thought, the same animallike ferocity of temper, the same self-justification, which has become in Javert an almost maniacal self-righteousness.

Quite naturally, in view of these parallels, it is the Javert-side of Jean Valjean that Javert senses even before he knows the other man's true identity; and once he has learned this it is only the exconvict, the old Jean Valjean, that he can ever think of; all the rest is to him sheer hypocrisy. But ironically it is not the old Jean Valjean but only the new one, the one whose existence he refuses to acknowledge, that he can ever respond to. His initial response is not at all what we should expect of him, for it is explainable as a reaction neither to the mayor of M. sur M. that Jean Valjean nominally is, nor to the criminal he really is. Toward the former, Javert as worshipper of authority would normally feel the utmost respect; toward the latter he would feel the contemptuous severity he feels for all violators of the law. But in this case what he feels is an immediate and instinctive antipathy which he cannot understand, which is like that of certain animals to certain other animals, " 'refractory to all the counsels of intelligence and all the solvents of reason, and which, whatever the way in which destinies are made, surely warns the man-dog of the man-cat, and the man-fox of the presence of the man-lion." Mixed with (though not the cause of) this antipathy is a kind of fascinated suspicion, the feeling that he has seen this man before—as he has, since in his early years with the police he has served in the southern galleys.

Yet it is not this suspicion of a criminal past (criminal pasts are an old story to the police inspector), but M. Madeleine's humanity, his selflessness, his gentleness toward the helpless and especially the errant, that most outrage Javert; just as the humanity of the bishop so outraged the old Jean Valjean. And as we later learn, the reason for the former's outrage is the same as was the reason for the latter's: the fact that there is something in this narrow, implacable man susceptible of being touched by the bishop-spirit, and that the whole self to which he is used and with which he is so satisfied cries out in protest against the possibility. For all his rigid self-possession under all other circumstances, Javert is stirred to the depths by the mild, quiet M. Madeleine; he displays a personal hatred that gnaws him from within and rises to almost hysterical proportions. When the mayor refuses to let him send a prostitute to prison, Javert, most uncharacteristically losing his head, denounces the other with no evidence to support him, and puts himself in a most uncharacteristically humiliating position. When the mayor, in order to save someone who has been wrongly accused in his place, confesses that he *is* Jean Valjean, and Javert is appointed to make the arrest, the unholy joy of the police inspector, to whom the making of arrests is a routine matter, is so great that it amounts to an "internal earthquake." "Upright, haughty, and dazzling, he flaunted the superhuman bestiality of a ferocious archangel in the azure of heaven."

Nor is Javert without his effect on Jean Valjean, to the extent that we are shown the second self 's side of the relationship. Javert is the only person in the book capable of arousing, in the new Jean Valjean, some of the harshness reminiscent of the old (this in their dispute over the prostitute Fantine). Furthermore it is Javert who, bringing news of the false arrest of someone resembling the exconvict, precipitates an "internal earthquake" in his counterpart: a titanic struggle between self-justification and self-renunciation, the Javert-side of his nature and the bishop-side. For while Javert is a man of probity, he is above all a man of iron hardness, to whom the stability of the social order always takes precedence over the welfare of the individual. This is precisely the hardness which now, as the result of Javert's visit, rises within Jean Valjean, urging on him the view that it is not only his right but his duty to let the worthless old Champmathieu go to the galleys in order that he, M. Madeleine, may in his position of mayor continue to do good for the people of M. sur M. It is the Javert within that presents the argument to foil the Javert without.

> I am saved, and all is settled. There was only one open door through which my past could invade my life; and that door is now walled up forever. That Javert, who has so long annoyed me, whose terrible instinct seemed to have scented me out, and, by heavens! had scented me out, the frightful dog ever making a point at me, is routed, engaged elsewhere, and absolutely thrown out! . . . After all, if some people are made unhappy, it is no fault of mine. Providence has done it all, and apparently decrees it. Have I the right to meddle with the arrangements of Providence?

But this is only a brief spasm of self-assertion by the old Jean Valjean, and the argument of social expediency is soon rejected. Returned to the galleys for life, Jean Valjean falls into the sea beside his ship and is apparently drowned.

So for a time Javert too believes, but the thought of Jean Valjean remains in the back of his mind. Piecing together various scraps of evidence, he follows the trail to the parish of Saint Medard, borrows the rags of a begging ex-beadle (for he is aware of and despises his enemy's charity to the poor), and kneels in an attitude of prayer in the beggar's usual place. As Jean Valjean approaches to put a gift in his hand Javert raises his head, and the two men, each with a violent shock of recognition, look into each other's eyes. Another long pursuit begins, but this time Jean Valjean, who has taken under his protection the daughter of the now-dead prostitute, a child named Cosette, does not give himself up, and for many years evades Javert. It is not until the Revolution of 1832, in the battle of the Rue de la Chanvrerie, that the two men again meet face to face. Javert has come in his capacity of spy for the established order and has been exposed and condemned to death. Jean Valjean has come in the hope of rescuing the young man, Marius, who is Cosette's betrothed. As Javert is being bound to a table, one thing takes his attention: the shadow of a man standing in the doorway. He turns his eyes, and again confronts Jean Valjean. When the time comes for Javert's execution, Jean Valjean asks permission to do the deed himself. He leads the other into a nearby deserted lane, where they are unseen by anyone else, draws out a knife (which Javert assumes to be for his own throat), cuts Javert's bonds, and sets him free. Javert, after a moment of gaping astonishment, rebuttons his frock coat, resumes his military stiffness, folds his arms and walks off. But before he has gone out of sight he wheels about. Jean Valjean is still looking after him. And suddenly Javert shouts: "You annoy me. I would sooner you killed me!"

The famous episode that follows will be familiar to all readers. As the barricade falls, and Marius is wounded, Jean Valjean snatches up the unconscious young man and descends with him into the sewers of Paris. Through the whole system of loathsome subways he makes his way, carrying Cosette's bethrothed on his back, crossing the whole city of Paris, not by its streets but by its unseen under-streets, stifled by the fetid air, wading through the sea of excrement. On the other side of the river he reemerges, and, crouching on the bank, commences to bathe Marius' face. At this moment, in the same instinctive way in which Javert has felt the importance of the shadow cast from the doorway, Jean Valjean becomes aware of being watched from behind; he turns, and there is Javert. He makes no effort to escape. At his request, Javert helps him to convey the unconscious Marius to the home of the latter's grandfather and then, before taking Jean Valjean on to the police station, allows him to enter his own home for a moment, telling the exconvict that he will wait at the door. But when Jean Valjean, who has every intention of returning at once, glances out the window on the landing, he sees to his amazement—the same amazement with which Javert has found himself set free at the barricade—that the police inspector has disappeared.

The street is short, and physically the disappearance has been simple enough to manage, but psychically and morally it is the first act in Javert's life that has not been simple; and in its reverberations throughout his mind it is cataclysmically complex. The reader who wishes to see for himself the skill with which the character and fate of Jean Valjean are intertwined with those of Javert should compare the following section, the effects of his last meeting with Jean Valjean upon Javert, with the early section already discussed, the effects of his meeting with the bishop upon Jean Valjean. Not only are the two experiences of mental turmoil carefully paralleled with each other, but they are related to each other as result to cause, for it is the earlier agony of Jean Valjean that has led directly to the present agony of Javert. Like Jean Valjean, he has been "infected" by the bishop, but in his case it is the bishop in Jean Valjean, grown by now nearly as old as the bishop was then, and nearly as selfless. Like Jean Valjean, he is consumed by his infection as by an inward flame; like Jean Valjean he wrestles with it and vainly tries to throw it off; but unlike Jean Valjean he cannot give in to it. For the first time in his life he sees before him not one road but two, and they run in directions contrary to each other; for the first time in his life he is faced with a major moral choice, and he cannot make it. Here is the way he puts it to himself.

> "What has this convict done, this desperate man, whom I pursued even unto persecution, and who had me under his heel, and could have avenged himself, and owed it, both to his rancour and to his security to do so,—what has he done in leaving me my life, and showing me mercy? His duty? No. Something more. And what have I done in showing him mercy in my turn,—my duty? No. Something more. Is there, then, something higher than duty?"

This is the question, utterly unprecedented in Javert's experience, before which he totters and quails, like a man on the edge of a precipice. Unable to move either forward or backward, and finding only one way to avoid the choice demanded of him, he takes this way. With a firm step he goes to the nearest police station; in a firm hand he writes a series of recommendations for the good of the service (none of them mentioning Jean Valjean); then, walking to the quay over the rapids of the Seine, he plunges into the water to his death.

It may seem a strange salvation that puts a man through intolerable torments of mind and drives him at last to suicide. But we have already seen that the second self as Saviour does not always succeed in saving the first self. Javert is not born anew out of his pain as Jean Valjean was, precisely because he is not Jean Valjean, but the other half of Jean Valjean. Nevertheless, just in the torments that his encounter with his other self has inflicted on him, just in the infection that proves fatal to him, a kind of salvation has been achieved, far more at least than in the case of the narrator of *Bartleby.* Both the relationship in *Bartleby* and that in *Les Misérables* end in death. But in *Bartleby* it is second self who dies, in disgust and despair at his failure ever effectively to touch the first self. "I know you, and I want nothing to say to you." In *Les Misérables* it is the first self who dies, and dies because he *has* been touched, beyond his powers of endurance. Bartleby's employer gets a glimmer of light, but it never really penetrates to anything deep within, because there is no longer anything deep within. Javert gets a blinding, bewildering flash that not only dazzles his eyes but floods through his whole angular, unresilient being, and bursts it asunder. (pp. 111-29)

C. F. Keppler, "The Second Self as Saviour," in his The Literature of the Second Self, *University of Arizona Press, 1972, pp. 99-129.*

PSYCHOLOGICAL INTERPRETATIONS

Otto Rank

[*A member of Sigmund Freud's circle, Rank is widely known for his pioneering efforts to apply psychoanalysis to various aspects of culture, such as mythology and literature. His writings include* Der Doppelgänger: Eine Psychoanalytische Studie *(1925;* The Double: A Psychoanalytic Study, *1971) and* Das Inzest-Motiv in Dichtung und Sage: Grundzüge einer Psychologie des dichterischen Schaffens *(1926;* The Incest Theme in Literature and Legend, *1991). In the following excerpt, he places the doppelgänger theme in the context of general psychology. In addition, Rank explores the connections between psychological doubling and narcissism.*]

There is not much doubt that Ewers, who has been called "the modern E. T. A. Hoffman," gained the inspiration for his film [*The Student of Prague*] mainly from his literary predecessor and master, even though still other sources and influences were effective. Hoffman is the classical creator of the double-projection, which was among the most popular motifs in Romantic literature. Almost none of his numerous works is entirely free of references to this theme, and it predominates in many of his more significant writings. The immediate model for Ewers' treatment is in Section III ("Adventures on New Year's Eve") of the second part of the *Fantastic Tales,* entitled "The Story of the Lost Reflection." In a strange connection with the imagination and dreams of the "traveling enthusiast," we read that one Erasmus Spikher, an honorable German husband and father, gets into the amorous clutches of the irresistible Giulietta during a stay in Florence and, at her request, leaves behind his reflection when he flees after murdering a rival. They were standing in front of the mirror, "which reflected him and Giulietta in a sweet embrace"; she "longingly stretched out her arms toward the mirror. Erasmus saw his image emerging independently of his movements, gliding into Giulietta's arms, and disappearing with her in a strangely sweet odor."

Homeward bound, Erasmus becomes an object of ridicule when people chance to notice his deficiency. Therefore, "wherever he went, he demanded that all mirrors be quickly covered, on the pretext of a natural aversion to any reflections; so people jokingly called him 'General Suvarov,' who behaved similarly." At home his wife spurns him and his son laughs at him. In his despair, Giulietta's mysterious companion, Doctor Dapertutto, comes to him and promises that he can regain her love and his reflection, providing that he sacrifice his wife and son to this end. The apparition of Giulietta causes him to feel love's madness anew. By taking the cloth from the mirror, she shows him how faithfully she has preserved his mirror-image. "With rapture, Erasmus saw his image folding Giulietta in its arms; but independently of himself it did not reflect any of his movements." He is just on the point of concluding the infernal pact, delivering himself and his family to the other-worldly powers, when he is able to exorcise the demonic spirits through the suddenly warning appearance of his wife. Then, on his wife's advice, he goes out into the wide world to seek his reflection. There he encounters the shadowless Peter Schlemihl, who had already appeared in the introduction to Hoffmann's story. This meeting indicates that Hoffmann, in his fantastic narrative, intended to provide a counterpart to the famous "strange story" by Chamisso, the plot of which we can assume he knew.

For the sake of relevance, we will indicate briefly only the essential correspondencies and parallels. Just as with Balduin and Spikher, with Schlemihl's sale of his shadow it is also a case of bargaining with the soul (pact with the devil); and here, too, the main character receives the mockery and contempt of the world. The "gray man's" strange admiration of the shadow is especially evident as an analogy to the admiration of the mirror-image, just as vanity is one of the most prominent traits of Schlemihl ("this is the spot in mankind, where the anchor catches hold most reliably"). Here too, the catastrophe . . . is brought about through the relationship to woman. The beautiful "Fanny" is terrified by Schlemihl's lack of a shadow; and this same deficiency causes him to forfeit his life's happiness with the affectionate Mina. The insanity which became evident in Balduin as a result of his catastrophe is suggested only incidentally in Spikher and Schlemihl, both of whom are finally able to escape evil.

After breaking with Mina, Schlemihl roams through "forests and plains with no goal in mind. A cold sweat dripped from my brow; a hollow groan broke from my breast; madness was raging within me."

This comparison demonstrates the equivalence of the mirror and shadow as images, both of which appear to the ego as its likeness. Later on, we shall confirm this equivalence from another point of view. Of the numerous imitations of *Peter Schlemihl* we mention here only Andersen's excellent fairy tale. "The Shadow," which tells of the scholar whose shadow frees itself of its owner in the torrid zones and some years later meets him personally. At first, the loss of his shadow has no bad results at all for the man—in the manner of Schlemihl's fate—for a new shadow, though of modest proportions, appears behind him. But the first shadow, which has become very wealthy and eminent, gradually succeeds in making use of its original owner. At first, it demands of him silence concerning its earlier existence as a shadow, since it intends a betrothal. Soon, however, it carries boldness to the point of treating its former master as its shadow, thereby attracting the attention of a princess, who finally desires it as a husband. The shadow endeavors to persuade its former master, in return for a large stipend, to play the part of the shadow on all occasions. Since everything in the scholar's nature goes against this proposition, he prepares to betray this usurper of his human rights. But the shadow anticipates him and has him imprisoned. Since it assures its betrothed that its "shadow" has gone mad and believes itself to be a person, the task is easy. The night before the wedding, it effects the secret removal of the man who is dangerous to its love and thus assures itself of happiness in love.

In an intentional contrast to the story of Peter Schlemihl, this tale connects the plot of the serious results of being shadowless with the treatment of the motif as it appears in *The Student of Prague.* For in Andersen's fairy tale too, it is not simply a question of lacking something (as with Chamisso); rather, emphasis is on the pursuit by the double, which has become an independent entity and which always and everywhere balks the self—again, however, with a catastrophic effect in the relationship of love.

The loss of one's shadow, again, is more clearly emphasized in Lenau's poem "Anna," the source of which is the Swedish legend of a pretty girl who fears the loss of her beauty through childbirth. *Her wish to remain always so young and beautiful* drives her, before her wedding, to a mysterious old woman who magically rids her of the seven children she would bear. She passes seven years of marriage in unchanged beauty until, one night by moonlight, her husband notices that she casts no shadow. Asked for an explanation, she confesses her guilt and becomes an outcast. After seven more years of harsh penitence and intense misery, which have left their deep traces, Anna is absolved by a hermit and dies reconciled with God, after the shades of her seven unborn children have appeared to her in a chapel.

We mention briefly the following less explicit occurrences of the shadow-motif. Goethe's "Fairy Tale" describes a giant who lives on the bank of a river. His shadow at noon is ineffectual and weak but is so much the more powerful at sunrise and sunset. If one sits down there on the neck of his shadow, one is carried across the river simultaneously as the shadow moves. In order to avoid this method of transportation, a bridge was built at the spot. But when in the morning the giant rubbed his eyes, the shadow of his fists moved so powerfully over both men and animals that all of them collapsed. Further, in Mörike's poem "The Shadow," a count who travels to the Holy Land exacts a pledge of loyalty from his wife. The oath is false, for his wife takes her pleasure in the company of her lover and sends her husband a poisoned potion that kills him. At the same hour, however, his faithless wife also dies; only her shadow remains, inextinguishable, in the hall. Finally, Richard Dehmel's little poem "The Shadow," modeled after R. L. Stevenson, describes very nicely the puzzling character of the shadow for the child who does not know why it has its small shadow:

> The funniest thing about him is the way he likes
>   to grow—
> Not at all like proper children, which is always
>   very slow;
> For he sometimes shoots up taller like an india-
>   rubber ball,
> And he sometimes gets so little that there's none
>   of him at all.

The modes of treatment of this subject which we have so far considered—in which the uncanny double is clearly an independent and visible cleavage of the ego (shadow, reflection)—are different from those actual figures of the double who confront each other as real and physical persons of unusual external similarity, and whose paths cross. Hoffmann's first novel, *The Devil's Elixirs* (1815), depends for its effect upon a resemblance of the monk Medardus to the Count Viktorin, both of whom are unaware that they are sons of the same father; this similarity leads to the strangest complications. The remarkable destinies of these two people are possible—and comprehensible—only on the basis of this mystical presupposition. Having a pathological inheritance from their father, both men become mentally ill, a condition whose masterful description forms the chief content of the novel. Viktorin, who has become insane after a fall, thinks that he is Medardus and so identifies himself to all. His identification with Medardus goes so far (poetic license, to be sure, must be taken into account) that he utters the latter's thoughts: Medardus believes that he hears himself speaking and that his innermost thoughts are being expressed by a voice outside himself. This paranoiac picture is supplemented by the notions to which he is subject in the monastery, of being watched and pursued; by the erotomania associated with the picture of his beloved which he sees only momentarily; and by his morbidly intensified mistrust and self-esteem. He is also dominated by the tormenting idea of having a double who is ill, a notion confirmed by the appearance of the deranged Capuchin.

The main theme of this novel can be seen in a later development in the tale "The Doubles," in a clear association with rivalry for the beloved woman. Again, it is a case of two youths who are indistinguishable in external appearance and who are closely related through mysterious family circumstances. As a result of this peculiar fate, and through their love for the same girl, they get involved in the most incomprehensible adventures, the solution to which is found only when the two rivals face their beloved and voluntarily renounce all claims to her. In the *Opinions on Life of Tomcat Murr,* the same external resemblance links the fate of Kreisler, who is predisposed to mental illness, with that of the insane painter Ettlinger, whom Kreisler resembles so closely, according to Princess Hedwiga, that they could be brothers. The situation reaches the point that Kreisler believes his reflection in the water to be the insane painter and reprimands it; but immediately thereafter he imagines that he sees his own self and his likeness walking along together. Seized by the most intense horror, he rushes into Master Abraham's room and demands that the latter despatch the troublesome pursuer with a dagger (the completion of such an impulsive act cost the student of Prague his life).

Hoffmann, who treated the problem of the second self in other works ("Princess Brambilla," "The Heart of Stone," "The Choice of a Bride," "The Sandman," and others), doubtless had strong personal motives for this choice of theme; yet one cannot underestimate the influence exercised by Jean Paul, who introduced the motif of the double into Romantic literature and who at this time was at the height of his fame. In Jean Paul's works this theme predominates in all its psychological variants. Leibgeber and Siebenkäs are real doubles: they look exactly alike, and Siebenkäs even exchanges names with his friend. In *Siebenkäs* the constant confusion between these persons—a motif elsewhere frequent with Jean Paul (e.g., in "Katzenberger's Trip to the Spa")—is the central point of interest; in *Titan* it occurs only episodically. In addition to this occurrence of the double as an actual person—which Jean Paul also varies by having someone attempt to seduce the beloved in the shape of the lover (the Amphytrion-motif)—this writer has delineated again and again, and to an extreme, the problem of the splitting and reduplication of the ego as no one has done before or after him. (pp. 8-14)

In *Titan* we [also] come across the tendency toward depersonalization, which is indicated by the name 'Leibgeber.' Roquairol, who is described as a boundless egoist, once does long to have a friend and writes to Albano: "Then I saw you, and wanted to become your You—but that won't work, for I cannot go back; but you can go on ahead, one of these days you will become my Self." "Performing his own tragedy, mimicking his own ego, he kills himself." "Schoppe's notion of being chased by himself becomes a most dreadful torment. For him, blissfulness lies in being eternally rid of his ego. If his glance only by chance falls upon his hands or his legs, that is enough to cause the cold fear to come over him that he could appear to himself and see his ego. The mirror must be veiled, for he shakes with fright before the spectacle of his mirror-orangutan" [F. J. Schneider, *Jean Pauls Jugend und sein Auftreten in der Literatur, 1905*].

There are also mirrors which cause rejuvenation and aging, a motif which seems to have been transferred to Spikher, whose old and distorted face grins at him on one occasion (similarly, there are pictures whose proper lines can be recognized only under one particular lens). We recall here that Spikher too, like Balduin, has all mirrors covered: "but for the contrary reason, that they no longer may reflect his ego" [Johann Czerny, "Jean Pauls Beziehungen zu E. T. A. Hoffmann."]. With Schoppe, this fear goes so far that he even smashes the hated mirrors, since they cause his Self to move toward him. And just as Kreisler and Balduin want to slay their second selves, Schoppe sends his sword-cane to Albano with the demand that the latter do away with the uncanny apparition in Ratto's cellar. "Schoppe finally perishes of his delusion, with the declaration of his identity on his lips" (Schneider).

It is known that Jean Paul in *Titan* expressed his views on Fichte's philosophy and intended to show what would be the ultimate consequence of transcendental idealism. Critics have argued whether the poet merely meant to present his opinions to the philosopher or to lead him *ad absurdum.* However that may be, it seems clear in any case that both tried, each in his own way, to arrive at an understanding of the problem of the ego—a problem which concerned them personally.

From the corporeal figures of the double, we can pass, by way of some individual and original treatments, over to those representations which allow us to recognize the subjective limitation and meaning of the strange attitude. One of them is Ferdinand Raimund's Romantic-comic fable *The King of the Alps and the Misanthropist,* in which the double of the wealthy Rappelkopf is represented by the Spirit of the Alps, objectified with genuine Raimund naïveté. Rappelkopf, who appears disguised as his brother-in-law, sees a performance of his own ridiculous faults and weaknesses by Astralagus, the King of the Alps, who plays the part of Rappelkopf himself. The action brings about the cure of the hero of his hypochondriacal misanthropy and his paranoiac mistrust by having him look at his own self as if in a "mirror of the soul." Through this sight he learns to hate himself and to love the surroundings which he earlier hated so much.

It is noteworthy that some typical motifs of the double-phenomenon seem here to be raised from their unconscious tragedy into the cognitive sphere of humor. In the end, the stubborn Rappelkopf agrees to the exchange of souls as if to a joke; and the confrontation of the two doubles in the main scenes of the play leads to multiple confusions and complications. The hero finally does not know where to look for his self and remarks, "I am afraid of myself." These "damned carryings-on with doubles" finally lead to mutual insults and to duelling.

The impulse to rid oneself of the uncanny opponent in a violent manner belongs, as we saw, to the essential features of the motif; and when one yields to this impulse—as, for example, in *The Student of Prague* and in other treatments which we still have to discuss—it becomes clear that the life of the double is linked quite closely to that of the individual himself. In Raimund's play, this mysterious basis of the problem becomes a conscious requisite of the test. In the last moment before the duel, Rappelkopf recalls this condition: "Both of us have only one life. If I kill him, I will kill myself." He is released from the spell when Astralagus plunges into the water: Rappelkopf, who fears drowning, falls into a swoon and awakes cured. Especially interesting to us is a remnant of the mirror-motif, pointing to the inner significance of the double. At the height of his delusion shortly before his flight from home and family, Rappelkopf catches sight of himself in the tall pier glass in his room. He is unable to endure the sight of his face and "shatters the mirror with his clenched fist." But in a tall pier glass in Rappelkopf 's house, the King of the Alps then becomes visible and later appears as a double.

Raimund has treated the same theme in a different form in *The Spendthrift.* The beggar, who for a year has been following Flottwell everywhere, turns out twenty years later to be his double and saves him from total ruin—in the way of a protective spirit, as is the King of the Alps. Flottwell actually believes that this beggar is the spirit of his father, until, taught by his harsh fate, he recognizes in the warning figure himself at the age of fifty. Here, too, the pursued attempts to kill his burdensome companion but is unable to attack in any way. The relationship of this double to that which appears in *The King of the Alps* is indicated by a common motif, the psychological discussion of which is more relevant elsewhere. Just as the beggar wheedles treasures from Flottwell in order to return them to the completely impoverished man ("I have begged from you for you"), so Rappelkopf, who likewise is apparently poor and in the end becomes rich again, gives a comic turn to this motif of the "jointly-held funds" by picking up the money cast aside by his double with the remark that this joint ownership is a far more convenient arrangement than the undesirable mutual ownership of health and life.

Even though there is an interesting connection here between the theme of aging and the financial complex which is not taken into account here, this or that thread of reference to the problem of the double can be traced. The fact that the beggar appears in the shape of Flottwell twenty years older reminds us of the girl's belief that looking at the King of the Alps makes one forty years older. And when the King appears in the mirror, Lieschen shuts her eyes so that she might not lose her beauty. In this we can note the connection with Jean Paul's mirrors, which can make one old or young, as well as with the distorting mirrors in Hoffmann's works and those of other writers.

This fear of becoming old, as one of the deepest problems of the self, is treated in Oscar Wilde's novel *The Picture of Dorian Gray.* The handsome and vigorous Dorian, when viewing his well-done portrait, expresses the presumptuous desire always to remain so young and handsome and to be able to transfer any traces of age and of sin to the portrait—a wish to be fulfilled in a sinister way. . . . [The portrait] teaches him, who loves himself inordinately, to despise his own soul. He covers and locks up the picture which inspires him with fear and terror, only gazing at it in particular moments of his life and comparing it with his own eternally immutable mirror-image. His former delight in his handsomeness gradually gives way to an abhorrence of his own self. Finally, " . . . he loathed his own beauty, and, flinging the mirror on the floor, crushed it into silver splinters beneath his heel." A definitely neurotic spectrophobia, related with great artistic effect, is the theme of one of Dorian's favorite novels, whose main character, quite in contrast to Dorian, had lost his extraordinary beauty in his early youth. Since then, he had a " . . . grotesque dread of mirrors, and polished metal surfaces, and still water. . . ." (pp. 15-18)

Of other Romanticists who dealt with the double-motif—and in one form or another it was used by almost all of them—Heine may be mentioned briefly. The double, which in the opinion of scholarship is one of his basic motifs, likewise appears not as a corporeal counterpart, but rather in a more subjective form. "In *Ratcliff* he intends to describe the fate of two persons whose lives are filled with meaninglessness through being compelled to exist as doubles—persons who must murder each other although they are in love. Their daily existence is constantly criss-crossed by their ancestral lives, which they are forced to live once again. This compulsion brings about the split in their personalities." Ratcliff obeys an inner voice which admonishes him to murder anyone who approaches Marie.

The motif is found in a different form in *Nights in Florence,* as exemplified by the double existence of Madame Laurencer. Her cheerful life in the daytime alternates with terpsichorean ecstasies at night, and she speaks of them by day calmly as of something long past. A similar narrative is in *Atta Troll* about the dead Laskaro, "whose loving mother every night rubs a magic life into him with [a] most powerful ointment." In *Germany, a Winter's Tale,* a queer fellow always appears to the poet when he is sitting at his desk at night. Upon being questioned, this person acknowledges: "I am the action of your thoughts." There are also similar references in several of Heine's poems.

One can see that these treatments of the motif come close to an extreme which has only a somewhat loose connection with our topic. Up to this point, it has been a question either of a physical double, which takes a more distantly related form in the comedies of mistaken identities, or of a likeness which has been detached from the ego and become an individual being (shadow, reflection, portrait). Now we come upon the representationally opposite form of expression of the same psychic constellation: the representation, by one and the same person, of two distinct beings separated by amnesia. These cases of double-consciousness have also been observed clinically and have been presented quite often in recent literary works, though they need not be an object of our further investigation.

From these marginal cases, we turn again to those subjects more fruitful for our analysis. In them the figure of a double is more or less clearly shaped but, at the same time, appears as the spontaneous subjective creation of a morbidly active imagination. Those cases of double-consciousness which we do not consider here—but which appear psychologically as the basis, and representationally as a kind of preliminary stage, of the fully-developed double-delusion—include Maupassant's impressive tale "The Horla" (1887), which serves as a direct transition over to the classification which is of interest to us.

The main character, whose diary we read, suffers from anxiety-reactions that torment him especially at night, pursue him even in his dreams, and cannot be permanently dispelled by any remedy. One night, he discovers to his terror that his carafe, filled at evening, is completely empty, although no one could enter the locked room. From this moment on, his entire interest concentrates upon that invisible spirit—the Horla—who lives in him, or next to him. He makes attempts to escape it in every way, but in vain; he is only more and more convinced of the independent existence of the mysterious creature. Everywhere he feels that it overhears him, watches him, enters into his thoughts, controls him, pursues him. Often he turns around in a split second, to see it at last, and to grasp it. Often he rushes into the empty darkness of his room, where he thinks the Horla is, in order "to seize it, to throttle it, to kill it."

Finally, this thought of being rid of the invisible tyrant gains the upper hand: he has the windows and doors of his room fitted with iron shutters which can be firmly locked, and he cautiously steals out one evening to imprison the Horla inescapably behind him. Then he sets the house on fire and, from a distance, watches as it is destroyed together with any living creatures inside. But, in the end, he is beset by doubts whether the Horla, for which all this was intended, could actually be destroyed; and he sees no other way to escape from it except by killing himself. Here again, the death which is intended for the ego as a double strikes down instead the person himself. How far his disintegration goes here is shown by a mirror-fantasy which occurs prior to the decisive catastrophe. The hero has brightly illuminated his room in order to lie in wait for the Horla:

> Behind me stands a tall wardrobe with a mirror, which daily assisted me in shaving and getting dressed and in which I looked at myself from head to toe every time I walked past it. I was pretending to write, to deceive him, for he was watching for me also. And suddenly I felt—I knew very well what I was doing—that he was bending over my shoulder and reading, that he was there, and that he brushed against my ear. I stood up, stretched out my hands, and turned around so quickly that I almost fell. What now? One could see as well here as if the sun were shining, and *I did not see myself in my mirror.* The glass was empty, clear, deep, brightly lit, but my reflection was missing, though I was standing where it would be cast. I looked at the large, clear, mirrored surface from top to bottom, looked at it with horrified eyes! I no longer dared to step forward; I dared make no movement; I felt that he was there but that again he would escape me, he whose opaque body prevented my reflecting myself. And—how terrible!—suddenly I saw myself in a mist in the center of the mirror, through a sort of watery veil; and it seemed to me as if this water were slipping from left to right, very slowly, so that my image appeared more sharply outlined from second to second. . . . Finally I could recognize myself as fully as I do every day when glancing into the mirror. I had seen him; and even now I am still trembling with fright.

In a small sketch, "He", which gives the impression of being a draft for "The Horla," Maupassant has caused some features of interest to us to emerge more prominently—for example, a man's relationship to a woman. The entire narrative about the mysterious "he"—who inspires the main character with a dreadful fear of himself—appears as the confession of a man who wants to marry, must marry, against his better judgment, simply because he can no longer endure being alone at night after once, upon coming home, having seen "him" occupying his own accustomed place in the armchair by the fireplace. "He pursues me incessantly. That's madness! Yet it is so. Who, he? I know very well that he does not exist, that he is unreal. He lives only in my misgivings, in my fears, in my anxiety!—But when I am living with someone, I feel clearly, yes, quite clearly, he will no longer exist. For he exists only because I am alone, solely because I am alone!"

This same atmosphere has found moving expression, shaded with melancholy resignation, in Musset's "December Night" (1835). In a dialogue with the "vision," the poet tells us that since his childhood a shadowy double who resembles him like a brother has been following him always and everywhere. In the decisive moments of his life this companion appears, clothed in black. He cannot escape this companion however far he flees, and he is unable to ascertain its nature. And just as once upon a time, as a youth in love, he found himself alone with his double, so now, many years later, he is absorbed one night in sweet memories of that time of love, and the apparition reveals itself again. The poet seeks to fathom its essence. He addresses it as his evil fate, as his good angel, and finally, when he cannot banish love's memories, as his own reflection:

> But all at once I saw, in th' nocturnal gloom,
> A noiseless form glide apace.
> I saw a shadow o'er my curtain loom,
> Upon my bed it took its place.
> Who art thou, countenance so pale and drear,
> Somber likeness of sable hue?
> Sad fleeting bird, why just to me appear?
> Is it an empty dream, *my* image here,
> Which within this mirror comes to view?

In the end, the apparition identifies itself as "Solitude." Even though it may seem strange at first glance that solitude, as with Maupassant, is perceived and represented as the burdensome companionship of a second being, the emphasis lies—as Nietzsche, too, stated—on the sociability with one's own self, objectified as a duplication. A similar monologue with one's own personified self is the foundation of Jean Paul's "The Devil's Confession to an Eminent Official." The same motif takes an interesting psychological turn in the story by J. E. Poritzky entitled "One Night." One evening, "a Doctor Faust in age and wisdom" apparently joins the main character of this fine little sketch for a serious conversation, abundant in recollections. The previous night, so the old man relates, he had the experience at midnight of being seized in front of his mirror by a childhood memory that contained the superstitious fear of gazing into a mirror at midnight.

> I smiled upon remembering this and stepped before the mirror, as though intending to give the lie to the legends of youth and to scorn them. I

> glanced into it, but since my mind was completely filled with thoughts of my boyhood years and I inwardly viewed myself as I had appeared as a boy—I had completely forgotten, as it were, my present existence—I stared fixedly and with distaste into the wrinkled old man's face which gazed at me from the mirror.

This bizarre state of mind reaches the point that the figure before the mirror shouts for help in his former boyish tones. The old man wants to protect the vision which has suddenly disappeared. He tries to justify the experience:

> I am very well aware of the division in our consciousness. Everyone has felt it more or less intensely—that division in which one sees one's own person passing by, like a shadow, in all of the shapes in which he ever existed. . . . But it is also possible for us now and then to catch sight of our future modes of existence. . . . This view of our future self is sometimes so vivid that we think that we see alien persons as independent entities physically detaching themselves from us, as a child at birth. And then, one meets these apparitions of the future, conjured up from one's self, and greets them with a nod. That is my secret discovery. We are indebted to the French psychologist Ribot for some very odd examples of psychic cleavage which cannot be explained away simply as hallucinations. A very intelligent man possessed the ability of conjuring up his double before him. He would always laugh loudly at this vision, and his double responded with the same laughter. This dangerous entertainment amused him for a long time, but it finally came to a bad end. He gradually arrived at the conviction that he *was being pursued by himself;* and since his second self constantly tormented, teased, and annoyed him, he decided one day to put an end to this sad existence.

After citing an additional example, the old man asks his companion whether he had never felt old, despite his thirty-five years. Upon receiving a negative answer, the old man takes his leave. His companion seeks to shake hands, but to his astonishment only air meets his grasp; he sees no one either near or far. "I was alone, and opposite me was a mirror which held me captive. Only now, when it had released my eyes, did I see that the candle had burned down low. . . . Had I spoken with myself ? Had I departed from my body and returned to it only now? Who knows . . . ? Or *had I confronted myself, like Narcissus,* and then had encountered the future shapes of my own self, and greeted them? Who knows . . . ?"

In his short story "William Wilson," Edgar Allan Poe used the theme of the double in a way that has become a model for several later treatments. William Wilson, the main character of this first-person narrative, meets a double in his childhood at school. The double not only has Wilson's own name and birthday, but also resembles him so much in physique, speech, behavior, and gait that both of them are considered to be brothers—indeed, even twins. Soon this strange namesake, who imitates Wilson in everything, becomes his faithful comrade, inseparable companion, and finally his most feared rival. Only by his voice, which cannot rise above a whisper, is the double distinguishable from his original; but this voice is identical in accent and pronunciation, so that ". . . *his singular whisper, it grew the very echo of my own.*"

Despite this uncanny imitation, the main character is incapable of hating his counterpart; nor is he able to reject the "advice not openly given, but hinted or insinuated" which he obeys, but only with repugnance. This tolerance is justified to some extent by the fact that the counterpart is apparently perceived only by the main character himself and attracts no further attention from his companions. One circumstance—the mention of his name—irritated Wilson without exception: "The words were venom in my ears; and when, upon the day of my arrival, a second William Wilson came also to the academy, I felt angry with him for bearing the name and doubly disgusted with the name because a stranger bore it, who would be the cause of its twofold repetition. . . ." One night the hero sneaks into his double's bedroom in order to convince himself that the features of the sleeper cannot be the result of a mere sarcastic imitation.

He flees in terror from the school and, after some months at home, goes to study at Eton, where he begins to lead a life of profligacy. He has long since forgotten the uncanny episode at the academy, but one night at a carousal his double appears to him in the same modish attire as his own, but with indistinct facial features. With only the warningly whispered words "William Wilson," the double disappears. All attempts to discover this person's identity and whereabouts are useless, except for the information that he had disappeared from the academy on the same day as his prototype. (pp. 19-26)

The catastrophe finally comes at a masked ball in Rome after Wilson has determined to rid himself, at any cost, of the unknown's oppressive tyranny. At just the moment when Wilson is trying to approach the charming wife of his aging host, a hand grasps him by the shoulder. He recognizes his double by the identical costume, drags him into an adjoining room, and challenges him to a duel. After a brief passage at arms, he plunges his sword into the double's heart. Someone tries the latch of the door and Wilson turns away momentarily. Suddenly, however, the situation surprisingly changes:

> A large mirror—so at first it seemed to me in my confusion—now stood where none had been perceptible before; and as I stepped up to it in extremity of terror, mine own image, but with features all pale and dabbled in blood, advanced to meet me with a feeble and tottering gait. Thus it appeared, I say, but was not. It was my antagonist—it was Wilson who then stood before me in the agonies of his dissolution. His mask and cloak lay where he had thrown them upon the floor. Not a thread in all his raiment—not a line in all the marked and singular lineaments of his face—which was not, even in the most absolute identity, *mine own!* It was Wilson; but he spoke no longer in a whisper, and I could have fancied that I myself was speaking while he said: "*You have conquered, and I yield. Yet hence-forward art thou also dead—dead to the World, to Heaven, and to Hope! In me didst thou exist; and in*

my death see by this image, which is thine own,
how utterly thou hast murdered thyself!"

The most moving, and psychologically the most profound, treatment of our theme is probably Dostoyevsky's early novel *The Double* (1846). The novel describes the onset of mental illness in a person who is not aware of it, since he is unable to recognize the symptoms in himself, and who paranoiacally views all his painful experiences as the pursuits of his enemies. His gradual transition into a delusional state, and confusion with reality (the real theme of this work otherwise sparse in external events) is depicted with an unsurpassable skill. We recognize the great artistic accomplishment here by the completely objective descriptions; they include not only every feature of the paranoiac clinical picture, but also cause the delusional configurations to have an effect upon the environment of the victim himself. The development of the story until its catastrophe is compressed into a few days and can hardly be reproduced except through reprinting the entire tale. (pp. 26-7)

By no means can psychoanalysis consider it as a mere accident that the death significance of the double appears closely related to its narcissistic meaning—as also noted elsewhere in Greek legend. Our reason for not being satisfied with Frazer's account lies in the fact that his explanation of the Narcissus fable only shifts the problem to the question of the origin and significance of the underlying superstitious ideas. If we accept the basis of Frazer's assumption and look first for an explanation of why the idea of death in the Narcissus legend, associated with the sight of the double, should have been masked especially by the theme of self-love, then we are compelled next to think of the generally effective tendency to exclude with particular stubbornness the idea of death, which is extremely painful to our self-esteem. To this tendency correspond the frequent euphemistic substitute-ideas, which in superstition gradually come to overlie the original death meaning. In the myth of the Fates, in the changed forms of which the goddess of love takes the place of the goddess of death, Freud has shown that this tendency aims at establishing an equivalent as distant and pleasant as possible—the reason being an understandable endeavor to compensate. This development of the motif, however, is not capricious. It only refers to an old, original identity of these two figures. This identity is consciously based upon the conquest of death by a new procreation and finds its deepest foundation in the relationship to the mother.

That the death meaning of the double likewise tends to be replaced by the love meaning can be seen from manifestly late, secondary, and isolated traditions. According to these traditions, girls are able to see their sweethearts in the mirror under the same conditions in which death or misfortune also reveal themselves. And in the exception that this does not apply to vain girls we may recognize a reference to narcissism, which interferes with the choice of a love object. Similarly, in the Narcissus legend there is a late but psychologically valid version which reports that the handsome youth thought he saw his beloved twin sister (his sweetheart) in the water. Besides this plainly narcissistic infatuation, the death meaning too has so much validity that the close association and deep relationship of both complexes are removed from any doubt.

The Narcissus meaning by its nature is not alien to the motif of the double, which exhibits meanings of the spirit and of death in the folklore material. This observation is shown not simply from the cited mythological traditions of creation by self-reflection, but above all by the literary treatments which cause the Narcissus theme to appear in the forefront along with the problem of death, be it directly or in pathological distortion.

Along with fear and hate of the double, the narcissistic infatuation in one's own image and self is most strongly marked in Oscar Wilde's *Dorian Gray.* "The sense of his own beauty came on him like a revelation" at the first view of his portrait, when he "stood gazing at the shadow of his own loveliness." At the same time, the fear seizes him that he could become old and different—a fear closely associated with the idea of death: "When I find that I am growing old, I shall kill myself." Dorian, who is directly characterized as Narcissus, loves his own image and therefore his own body: "Once, in boyish mockery of Narcissus, he had kissed . . . those painted lips that now smiled so cruelly at him. Morning after morning he had sat before the portrait, wondering at its beauty, almost enamoured of it, as it seemed to him at times." "Often . . . he himself would creep upstairs to the locked room . . . and stand with a mirror in front of the portrait . . . looking now at the evil and aging face on the canvas, and now at the fair young face that laughed back at him from the polished glass. . . . He grew more and more enamoured of his own beauty. . . . "

Tied in with this narcissistic attitude is his imposing egoism, his inability to love, and his abnormal sexual life. The intimate friendships with young men, for which Hallward reproaches him, are attempts to realize the erotic infatuation with his own youthful image. From women he is able to obtain only the crudest sensual pleasures, without being capable of a spiritual relationship. Dorian shares this defective capacity for love with almost all double-heroes. He himself says in a significant quotation that this deficiency arises from his narcissistic fixation on his own ego. " 'I wish I could love,' cried Dorian Gray, with a deep note of pathos in his voice. 'But I seem to have lost the passion, and forgotten the desire. *I am too much concentrated on myself* [Rank's emphasis]. My own personality has become a burden to me. I want to escape, to go away, to forget'." In a particularly clear *defensive form, The Student of Prague* shows how the *feared* self obstructs the love for a woman; and in Wilde's novel it becomes clear that fear and hate with respect to the double-self are closely connected with the narcissistic love for it and with the resistance of this love. The more Dorian despises his image, which is becoming old and ugly, the more intensive does his self-love become: "The very sharpness of the contrast used to quicken his sense of pleasure. He grew more and more enamoured of his own beauty. . . . "

This erotic attitude toward one's own self, however, is only possible because along with it the defensive feelings can be discharged by way of the hated and feared double. Narcissus is ambivalent toward his ego for something in him seems to resist exclusive self-love. The form of defense against narcissicism finds expression principally in two ways: in fear and revulsion before one's own image, as seen in Dorian and most of the characters of Jean Paul; or, as in the majority of cases, in the loss of the shadow-image or mirror-image. This loss, however, is no loss at all, as the persecutions show. On the contrary, it is strengthening, a becoming independent and superiorly strong, which in its turn only shows the exceedingly strong interest in one's own self. Thus the apparent contradiction—the loss of the shadow-image or mirror-image represented as pursuit—is understood as a representation of the opposite, the recurrence of what is repressed in that which represses (see the concluding paragraph of this [essay]).

This same mechanism is shown by the dénouement of madness, almost regularly leading to suicide, which is so frequently linked with pursuit by the double, the self. Even when the depiction does not measure up to Dostoyevsky's unsurpassable clinical exactitude, it does become clear that it is a question of paranoid ideas of pursuit and influencing to which the hero is prey by reason of his double. Since Freud's psychoanalytic clarification of paranoia, we know that this illness has as a basis "a fixation in narcissism," to which corresponds typical megalomania, the sexual overrating of oneself. The stage of development from which paranoids regress to their original narcissism is sublimated homosexuality, against the undisguised eruption of which they defend themselves with the characteristic mechanism of projection. On the basis of this insight, it can easily be shown that the pursuit of the ill person regularly proceeds from the originally loved persons (or their surrogates).

The literary representations of the double-motif which describe the persecution complex confirm not only Freud's concept of the narcissistic disposition toward paranoia, but also, in an intuition rarely attained by the mentally ill, they reduce the chief pursuer to the ego itself, the person formerly loved most of all, and now direct their defense against it. This view does not contradict the homosexual etiology of paranoia. We know, as was already mentioned, that the homosexual love object was originally chosen with a narcissistic attitude toward one's own image.

Connected with paranoid pursuit is yet another theme which deserves emphasis. We know that the person of the pursuer frequently represents the father or his substitute (brother, teacher, etc.), and we also find in our material that the double is often identified with the brother. It is clearest in Musset but also appears in Hoffmann (*The Devil's Elixirs, The Doubles*), Poe, Dostoyevsky, and others. The appearance for the most part is as a twin and reminds us of the legend of the womanish Narcissus, for Narcissus thinks that he sees in his image his sister, who resembles him in every respect. That those writers who preferred the theme of the double also had to contend with the male sibling complex follows from the not infrequent treatment of fraternal rivalry in their other works. So Jean Paul, in the famous novel *The Twins,* has treated the theme of twin brothers who compete with each other, as has Maupassant in *Peter and John* and the unfinished novel *The Angelus,* Dostoyevsky in *The Brothers Karamazov,* and so on.

Actually, and considered externally, the double is the rival of his prototype in anything and everything, but primarily in the love for woman—a trait which he may partly owe to the identification with the brother. One author expresses himself about this relationship in another connection: "The younger brother is accustomed, even in ordinary life, to be somehow similar to the elder, at least in external appearance. He is, as it were, a reflection of his fraternal self which has come to life; and on this account he is also a rival in everything that the brother sees, feels, and thinks" [J. B. Schneider, "Das Geschwisterproblem," in *Geschlecht und Gesellschaft,* 1913]. What connection this identification might have with the narcissistic attitude may be shown by another statement by the same author: "The relationship of the older to the younger brother is analogous to that of the masturbator to himself."

From this fraternal attitude of rivalry toward the hated competitor in the love for the mother, the death wish and the impulse toward murder against the double becomes reasonably understandable, even though the significance of the brother in this case does not exhaust our understanding. The theme of the brothers is not precisely the root of the belief in the double, but rather only an interpretation—well-determined, to be sure—of the doubtlessly purely subjective meaning of the double. This meaning is not sufficiently explained by the psychological statement that "the mental conflict creates the double," which corresponds to a "projection of inner turmoil" and the shaping of which brings about an inner liberation, an unburdening, even if at the price of the "fear of encounter." So "fear shapes from the ego-complex the terrifying phantom of the double," which "fulfills the secret, always suppressed wishes of his soul" [Emil Lucka, "Dostojewski und der Teufel," *Literarisches Echo,* 1913]. Only after determining this formal meaning of the double do the real problems arise, for we aim at an understanding of the psychological situation and of the attitude which together create such an inner division and projection.

The most prominent symptom of the forms which the double takes is a powerful consciousness of guilt which forces the hero no longer to accept the responsibility for certain actions of his ego, but to place it upon another ego, a double, who is either personified by the devil himself or is created by making a diabolical pact. This detached personification of instincts and desires which were once felt to be unacceptable, but which can be satisfied without responsibility in this indirect way, appears in other forms of the theme as a beneficent admonitor (e.g., William Wilson) who is directly addressed as the "conscience" of the person (e.g., Dorian Gray, etc.). As Freud has demonstrated, this awareness of guilt, having various sources, measures on the one hand the distance between the ego-ideal and the attained reality; on the other, it is nourished by a powerful fear of death and creates strong tendencies toward self-punishment, which also imply suicide.

After having stressed the narcissistic significance of the double in its positive meaning as well as in its various defensive forms, it still remains for us to understand more about the meaning of death in our material and to demonstrate its relationship to the meaning already gained. What the folkloric representations and several of the literary ones directly reveal is a tremendous thanatophobia, which refers to the defensive symptoms heretofore discussed to the extent that, in these, fear (of the image, of its loss, or of pursuit) formed the most prominent characteristic.

One motif which reveals a certain connection between the fear of death and the narcissistic attitude is the wish to remain forever young. On the one hand, this wish represents the libidinous fixation of the individual onto a definite developmental stage of the ego; and on the other, it expresses the fear of becoming old, a fear which is really the fear of death. Thus Wilde's Dorian says, "When I find that I am growing old, I shall kill myself." Here we are at the significant theme of suicide, at which point a whole series of characters come to their ends while pursued by their doubles. Of this motif, apparently in such contradiction to the asserted fear of death, it can be shown precisely from its special application in this connection that it is closely relevant not only to the theme of thanatophobia, but also with narcissism. For these characters and their creators—as far as they attempted suicide or did carry it out (Raimund, Maupassant)—did not fear death; rather, the *expectation* of the unavoidable destiny of death is unbearable to them. As Dorian Gray expresses it: "I have no terror of Death. It is only *the coming* [Rank's emphasis] of Death that terrifies me." The normally unconscious thought of the approaching destruction of the self—the most general example of the repression of an unendurable certainty—torments these unfortunates with the conscious idea of their eternal . . . inability to return, an idea from which release is only possible in death. Thus we have the strange paradox of the suicide who voluntarily seeks death in order to free himself of the intolerable thanatophobia.

It could be objected that the fear of death is simply the expression of an overly strong instinct for self-preservation, insisting upon fulfillment. Certainly the only too-justified fear of death, seen as one of the fundamental evils of mankind, has its main root in the self-preservation instinct, the greatest threat to which is death. But this motivation is insufficient for pathological thanatophobia, which occasionally leads directly to suicide. In this neurotic constellation—in which the material to be repressed and against which the individual defends himself is finally and actually realized—it is a question of a complicated conflict in which, along with the ego-instincts serving self-preservation, the libidinous tendencies also function, which are merely rationalized in the conscious ideas of fear. Their unconscious participation explains fully the pathological fear arising here, behind which we must expect a portion of repressed libido. This, along with other already-known factors, we believe we have found in that part of narcissism which feels just as intensely threatened by the idea of death as do the pure ego-instincts, and which thereupon reacts with the pathological fear of death and its final consequences.

As proof that the pure ego-interests of self-preservation cannot explain the pathological fear of death satisfactorily to other observers either, we cite the testimony of a researcher who is completely unprejudiced psychologically. Spiess . . . expresses the view that "man's horror of death does not result merely from the natural love of life." He explains this [in Edmund Spiess, *Entwicklungsgeschichte der Vorstellungen vom Zustande nach dem Tode,* 1877] with the following words:

> That, however, is not a dependency upon earthly existence, for man often hates that. . . . No, it is the love for the personality peculiar to him, found in his conscious possession, the love for his self, for the central self of his individuality, which attaches him to life. This *self-love* is an inseparable element of his being. In it is founded and rooted the instinct for self-preservation, and from it emerges the deep and powerful longing to escape death or the submergence into nothingness, and the hope of again awakening to a new life and to a new era of continuing development. The thought of losing oneself is so unbearable for man, and it is this thought which makes death so terrible for him. . . . This hopeful longing may be criticized as childish vanity, foolish megalomania; the fact remains that it lives in our hearts; it influences and rules over our imagination and endeavors.

This relationship is evident in all of its desirable clarity—indeed, downright plasticity—in literary material, although narcissistic self-assertion and self-exaggeration generally prevail there. The frequent slaying of the double, through which the hero seeks to protect himself permanently from the pursuits of his self, is really a suicidal act. It is, to be sure, in the painless form of slaying a different ego: an unconscious illusion of the splitting-off of a bad, culpable ego—a separation which, moreover, appears to be the precondition for every suicide. The suicidal person is unable to eliminate by direct self-destruction the fear of death resulting from the threat to his narcissism. To be sure, he seizes upon the only possible way out, suicide, but he is incapable of carrying it out other than by way of the phantom of a feared and hated double, because he loves and esteems his ego too highly to give it pain or to transform the idea of his destruction into the deed. In this subjective meaning, the double turns out to be a functional expression of the psychological fact that an individual with an attitude of this kind cannot free himself from a certain phase of his narcissistically loved ego-development. He encounters it always and everywhere, and it constrains his actions within a definite direction. Here, the allegorical interpretation of the double as a part of the ineradicable past gets its psychological meaning. What attaches the person to the past becomes clear, and why this assumes the form of the double is evident.

Finally, the significance of the double as an embodiment of the soul—a notion represented in primitive belief and living on in our superstition—has close relevance to the previously discussed factors. It seems that the development of the primitive belief in the soul is largely analogous to the psychological circumstances demonstrated here by the pathological material—an observation which would seem to confirm anew the "agreement in the psychology of aborigines and of neurotics." This circumstance would also explain how the primitive conditions are repeated in the later mythical and artistic representations of the theme, specifically with particular emphasis on the libidinous factors which do not so clearly emerge in the primeval history but which nonetheless allowed us to form a conclusion about the less transparent primal phenomena.

Freud, by pointing out the animistic view of the world based on the power of thoughts, has justified our thinking of primitive man, just as of the child, as being exquisitely narcissistic. Also, the narcissistic theories of the creation of the world which he cites, just like the later philosophical systems based on the ego (e.g., Fichte), indicate that man is able to perceive the reality surrounding him mainly only as a reflection, or as a part, of his ego. Likewise, Freud has pointed out that it is death, ANANKE the implacable, which opposes the primitive man's narcissism and obliges him to turn over a part of his omnipotence to the spirits. Linked to this fact of death, however, which is forced upon man and which he constantly seeks to deny, are the first concepts of the soul, which can be traced in primitive peoples as well as those of advanced cultures.

Among the very first and most primitive concepts of the soul is that of the shadow, which appears as a faithful image of the body but of a lighter substance. It is true that Wundt contends [in his *Völkerpsychologie,* 1912] that the shadow provided an original motif for the concept of the soul. He believes that the "shadow-soul," the *alter ego,* as distinct from that of the body, "as far as we can tell has its sole source in dreams and visions." But other researchers—Tylor, for example—have shown by a wealth of material that among primitive peoples designations of images or shadows predominate; and Heinzelmann, who finds support in the most recent investigations, objects to Wundt on this point by showing in an abundance of examples "that here, too, it is a question of quite constant and extensively recurring views." Just as Spencer justly asserts in the case of the child, primitive man considers his shadow as something real, as a being attached to him, and he is confirmed in his view of it as a soul by the fact that the dead person (who is lying down) simply no longer casts a shadow. From the experience of dreaming, man may have taken the proof for his belief that the viable ego might exist even after death; but only his shadow and his reflected image could have convinced him that he had a mysterious double even while he was alive.

The various taboos, precautions, and evasions which primitive man uses with regard to his shadow show equally well his narcissistic esteem of his ego and his tremendous fear of its being threatened. Primitive narcissism feels itself primarily threatened by the ineluctable destruction of the self. Very clear evidence of the truth of this observation is shown by the choice, as the most primitive concept of the soul, of an image as closely similar as possible to the physical self, hence a true double. The idea of death, therefore, is denied by a duplication of the self incorporated in the shadow or in the reflected image.

We [know] that among primitives the designations for shadow, reflected image, and the like, also serve for the notion "soul," and that the most primitive concept of the soul of the Greeks, Egyptians, and other culturally prominent peoples coincides with a double which is essentially identical with the body. Then, too, the concept of the soul as a reflected image assumes that it resembles an exact copy of the body. Indeed, Negelein speaks directly of a "primitive monism of body and soul," by which he means that the idea of the soul originally coincided completely with that of a second body [J. Negelein, "Ein Beitrag Zum indischen Seelenwanderungs-glauben," 1901]. As proof he cites the fact that the Egyptians made images of the dead in order to protect them from eternal destruction. Such a material origin, then, does the idea of the soul have. Later, it became an immaterial concept with the increasing reality-experience of man, who does not want to admit that death is everlasting annihilation.

Originally, to be sure, the question of a belief in immortality was of no concern; but the complete ignorance of the idea of death arises from primitive narcissism, as it is evidenced even in the child. For the primitive, as for the child, it is self-evident that he will continue to live, and death is conceived of as an unnatural, magically produced event. Only with the acknowledgment of the idea of death, and of the fear of death consequent upon threatened narcissism, does the wish for immortality as such appear. This wish really restores the original naive belief in an eternally continuing existence in partial accommodation to the experience of death gained in the meantime. In this way, therefore, the primitive belief in souls is originally nothing else than a kind of belief in immortality which energetically denies the power of death; and even today the essential content of the belief in the soul—as it subsists in religion, superstition, and modern cults—has not become other, nor much more, than that. The thought of death is rendered supportable by assuring oneself of a second life, after this one, as a double. As in the threat to narcissism by sexual love, so in the threat of death does the idea of death (originally averted by the double) recur in this figure who, according to general superstition, announces death or whose injury harms the individual.

So, then, we see primitive narcissism as that in which the libidinous interests and those serving self-preservation are concentrated upon the ego with equal intensity, and which in the same way protect against a series of threats by reactions directed against the complete annihilation of the ego, or else toward its damage and impairment. These reactions do not result merely from the real fear which, as Visscher says, can be termed the defensive form of an exceedingly strong instinct for self-preservation. They arise also from the fact that the primitive, along with the neurotic, exhibits this "normal" fear, increased to a pathological degree, which "cannot be explained from the actual experiences of terror." We have derived the libidinous component, which plays a part here, from the equally-intensively felt threat to narcissism, which resists the utter immolation of the ego just as much as it resists its dissolution in sexual love. That it is actually primitive narcissism which resists the threat is shown quite clearly by the reactions in which we see the threatened narcissism assert itself with heightened intensity: whether it be in the form of pathological self-love as in Greek legend or in Oscar Wilde, the representative of the modern esthete; or in the defensive form of the pathological fear of one's self, often leading to paranoid insanity and appearing personified in the pursuing shadow, mirror-image, or double. On the other hand, in the same phenomena of defense the threat also recurs, against which the individual wants to protect and assert himself. So it happens that the double, who personifies narcissistic self-love, becomes an unequivocal rival in sexual love; or else, originally created as a wish-defense against a dreaded eternal destruction, he reappears in superstition as the messenger of death. (pp. 69-86)

Otto Rank, "Examples of the Double in Literature" and "Narcissism and the Double," in his The Double: A Psychoanalytic Study, *edited and translated by Harry Tucker, Jr., The University of North Carolina Press, 1971, pp. 8-33, 69-86.*

Lawrence Kohlberg

[*Kohlberg is a psychologist whose writings include* The Development of Modes of Moral Thinking and Choice in the Years 10 to 16 *(1958). In the following excerpt, he classifies, and provides a psychological interpretation of, the varieties of doubles in Dostoevsky's novels.*]

In contrast with its revolutionary impact upon creative writing, psychoanalysis seems of only minor importance to modern literary criticism. The common awareness of psychological sickness and symbol in a literary work is believed to detract, rather than add to, understanding and appreciation of the work. Critics who feel that this awareness can be used constructively, such as Burke, Guerard, Hyman, Kazin, Trilling, and Wilson use psychoanalysis primarily as myth, as one element or world-view among many which sensitize the reader of a work of art to its meaning. The construction and "proof" of a detailed psychoanalytic interpretation seems out of place in such literary criticism.

Critical articles in the professional psychiatric journals present a striking contrast. In these, the literary meaning of the work of art is not considered as central to the analytic task. In contrast with the critical use of psychoanalysis as sensitizing "myth," the professional psychoanalyst attempts to use psychoanalytic theory to provide a comprehensive and true explanation of why a given writer wrote just what he did. He brings to literature the habits of the clinic which require that a decision or diagnosis be made, and the habits of a scientist which require that a hypothesis be judged, not as inspiring, but as true or false.

Of all writers, none has elicited more of this case-study approach than Dostoevsky, that archetype of the psychopathological genius. Some of these studies, diagnosing Dostoevsky on the basis of biographical data, as if he were a case to be committed to a hospital or a course of therapy, have come to such conclusions as, "Dostoevsky was an epileptic, schizophrene, paranoid type, complicated by hysterical overlay" [P. C. Squires, "Fyodor Dostoevsky, A Psychopathological Sketch," in *Psychoanalytic Review,* 1937]. Other studies focus upon Dostoevsky's unconscious conflicts as projected into his novels. The classic example of this type of study is Freud's essay on Dostoevsky ["Dostoevsky and Parricide"], in which he views Dostoevsky as preoccupied by parricidal impulses and resultant guilt, a conflict projected into Dmitri and Ivan Karamazov. Still other studies focus upon the analysis of a specific character in a novel as if he were a real person, coming to such conclusions as that "Raskolnikov was an autistic personality with traces of the manic depressive" [Smith and Isotoff, "Dostoevsky: The Abnormal from Within," in *Psychoanalytic Review,* 1935] or that "Raskolnikov's murder was a result of efforts to appease unconscious guilt due to an incestuous attachment to his sister" [Edna C. Florance, "The Neurosis of Raskolnikov: A Study in Incest and Murder," in *Archives of Criminal Psychodynamics,* 1955].

Both academic psychologist and humanist question this sort of study. In the first place, it is impossible to know whether these interpretations are true. The characters are not real people, the biographical data on the author is inadequate, and a novel is not a psychological projective-test response by an author. Even if the case data were adequate, one could not achieve scientific certainty in the interpretation of a single case. Few would disagree with Kris that "It would seem as well demonstrated as any conclusion in the social sciences that the struggle against incestuous impulses, dependency, guilt, and aggression has remained a recurrent topic of Western literature from Sophocles to Proust" [E. Kris, *Psychoanalytic Exploration in Art,* 1952]. The ubiquity of certain themes in myth and literature, though undeniable, does not, however, contribute to certainty of interpretation of any individual case.

The second reservation is an even more crucial one. What difference does it make to the intelligent reader's understanding of a novel to know that Dostoevsky had parricidal impulses or was an epileptic schizophrene? Even Freud seems to agree with this caveat, since he begins his essay on Dostoevsky as follows:

> Four facets may be distinguished in the rich personality of Dostoevsky—the creative artist, the neurotic, the moralist and the sinner. How is one to find one's way in this bewildering complexity? The creative artist is least doubtful. *The Brothers Karamazov* is the most magnificent novel ever written. . . . Before the problem of the creative artist, analysis must, alas, lay down its arms.

Freud would feel that his analysis of Dostoevsky helps explain the power of Dostoevsky's novel in that "It can scarcely be owing to chance that three of the masterpieces of all literature *Oedipus Rex, Hamlet,* and *The Brothers Karamazov* should all deal with the same subject, parricide." In Freud's view, "parricide is the principal and primal crime of humanity as well as of the individual, and the main source of the sense of guilt"; and in some sense the power of *The Brothers Karamazov* lies in its confrontation of the reader with his own guilt-laden impulses in a situation in which identification with the hero is at a sufficient distance to allow "catharsis through pity and fear." Even if one granted this interpretation, it hardly explains the difference between murder in Dostoevsky and murder in Mickey Spillane.

The present paper is an effort to show that psychoanalysis need not entirely "lay down its arms" before Dostoevsky, the creative artist; it will use a psychological analysis to clarify two literary problems important in the appreciation and understanding of Dostoevsky's novels: the first, his use of Doubles; the second, his particular and unique moral ideology.

In recent years, literary critics have come to believe that an understanding of Dostoevsky's use of Doubles is the key to an understanding of the structure of his novels, a key which radically revises early critical views of Dostoevsky's novels as "badly constructed and unwieldly." An example of such a recent structural or "technique" interpretation of the Doubles is Beebe's analysis of *Crime and Punishment* [J. M. Beebe, "The Three Motives of Raskolnikov," in E. Wasiolek, *Crime and Punishment and the Critics,* 1961]:

> If we approach *Crime and Punishment* with a knowledge of Dostoevsky's character and method of writing, we are likely to be surprised at the disciplined skill the structure of the novel reveals. It meets the test of unity in action; all the parts contribute to the whole and the parts may be fully understood only when the whole is known. One of the ways in which Dostoevsky unified his novel is through his technique of "doubles." The dual nature of his heroes is, of course, a commonplace of criticism. Because his protagonists are usually split personalities, the psychological and philosophical drama in a Dostoevsky novel is expressed in terms of a conflict between opposite poles of sensibility and intelligence, self-sacrifice and self-assertion, God-Man and Man-God, or sometimes "good" and "bad." To dramatize this conflict, Dostoevsky often gives his characters several alter-egos or doubles, each projecting one of the extremes of the split personality. Even when the hero is not present in the scene, he may represent the center of interest because the characters present, represent different facets of his personality. According to most interpretations of *Crime and Punishment,* the struggle within Raskolnikov becomes physical external action as he wavers between Svidrigailov, epitome of self-willed evil, and Sonia, epitome of self-sacrifice and spiritual goodness.

Dostoevsky's Doubles, however, are not mere portrayals of ties between stereotyped representatives of good and evil to be found throughout good and bad fiction. They obviously contain much personal symbolic meaning and are intended to have a psychopathological basis. They not only express ideological values and requirements of plot but enact or express murders of kin, rapes of little girls, spider fantasies, mutilation themes, epileptic attacks, suicide, necrophilia and hallucinations, and were viewed by Dostoevsky himself as forms of psychopathology. The *Raw Youth* says: "What then precisely is the 'double'? The 'double,' at any rate according to a medical work by an expert which I read for the purpose is nothing but the first stage in some serious mental derangement which may lead to a bad conclusion, a dualism between feeling and willing."

Not only does Dostoevsky view his Doubles as "psychopathological," but his preoccupation with Doubles precedes the ideological and structural use he was to make of them in his later novels. This preoccupation on a purely psychological level is expressed in Dostoevsky's second novel, written before his Siberian exile and entitled *The Double,* a novel which he said "contained a great deal of myself."

The hero of this novel, Golyadkin, is one of Dostoevsky's typical, socially isolated petty officials desperately striving to maintain some appearance of respectability in spite of poverty, social incompetence, and deep feelings of inferiority. He awakes in a clouded state, on the verge of a breakdown, believing that something is being got up against him by his colleagues at the office, that there is a conspiracy afloat, that his reputation has been blackened and that his enemies are trying to ruin him.

After consulting his doctor he decides to attend a ball that evening given by his former patron ("who has been a father to him") in honor of his daughter. Golyadkin has not been invited and is under a cloud because of some unspecified recent behavior. He is refused admission by the footman, but enters the house surreptitiously and lurks in the corridor. Suddenly in contradiction to his usual self-effacement, some mysterious brazen impulse "projects" him into the ballroom and leads him to insist on dancing with the daughter. He is ignominiously thrown out on the street.

He then wanders about the streets and contemplates suicide by drowning. He has an uncanny feeling that there is someone near, and in terror recognizes the presence of a Double, a figure exactly like himself, who accompanies him home.

The next day, he finds the Double ensconced at a desk at his office, as if he had always worked there, ingratiating himself with his colleagues and superiors, and ridiculing Golyadkin. All of this Golyadkin II's misconduct is blamed on Golyadkin I, while Golyadkin II gets credit for all of Golyadkin I's efforts. Golyadkin views the Double as an indecent, shameless, malevolent toady but nevertheless attempts to be friendly with him and is insulted and humiliated for his pains.

After agonies of humiliation, rage, fear, and suspicion, Golyadkin believes a solution awaits him. He believes he has received a note from the daughter of his patron asking him to elope with her and arranging a rendezvous. He awaits her at the appointed time in hiding outside her house, just as he had in the episode preceding the emergence of the Double. His Double trots out and hustles him into the house where a crowd is gathered, staring at him. He is suddenly surrounded by an "infinite procession of Golyadkins noisily bursting in at every door of the room." He is carried away to the lunatic asylum by his own cruel doctor while the Double hangs on to the carriage door and pokes his head in the window.

In this tale, Dostoevsky's use of the Double theme of Hoffman and Gogol does not achieve any grand artistic purpose, but it does offer a compelling picture of psychopathology. Accordingly, we shall attempt to settle the purely diagnostic questions about the Double phenomena it presents before considering the literary meanings of the Double themes.

The only serious treatment of *The Double* from a psychopathological view is provided in a monograph written in the early twenties by Otto Rank, Freud's "most gifted follower" [*Der Doppelgänger,* 1925]. Rank proclaims the novel to be a classic portrayal of a paranoid state. There are indeed strong resemblances between the phenomena presented in *The Double* and familiar psychiatric phenomena of paranoid states. Paranoid delusions or hallucinations of persecutory figures emerge from feelings of shame and pathologically low self-esteem. These delusions are presumed to be the result of the defence mechanism of "disowning projection." Shameful impulses and tendencies toward self-accusation are denied as belonging to the self and are projected upon external imagined enemies. Obviously Dostoevsky intended Golyadkin II to be a hallucination representing the assertive, shameless impulses which first "propelled" Golyadkin I into his patron's ballroom, since the novel ends with the double propelling him again into the same ballroom. Golyadkin I's sense of low esteem, his feeling that he is being intrigued against, his life in a world in which he makes and receives veiled threats and innuendoes, are indeed striking portrayals of the paranoid attitude.

It also seems likely that *The Double* may have expressed one of Dostoevsky's states at the time of the writing of the novel, a state of feeling humiliated and "persecuted" in connection with the outbreak of previously unsuspected or unacknowledged qualities in his own personality. Just previous to writing *The Double,* the success of *Poor Folk* had completely turned his head and transformed him from a shy, sensitive, aloof romantic to someone capable of writing such statements as the following to his brother:

> Well brother, I believe my fame is just now in its fullest flower. Everybody looks on me as a wonder of the world. If I but open my mouth the air resounds with what Dostoevsky said, what Dostoevsky means to do. . . . Bielinsky declares Turgenev has quite lost his heart to me. . . . All the Minnas, Claras, Mariannas, etc., have got amazingly pretty, but cost a lot of money.

The reaction of his acquaintances to this sort of bombast was to nickname Dostoevsky "the literary pimple." Indeed, *The Double* commences with Golyadkin saying: "A fine thing if something untoward had happened today and a strange pimple had come up." Presumably his double was the "literary pimple" which erupted that day from within Golyadkin's personality.

In spite of these considerations, *The Double* is not the portrayal of a genuine psychiatric phenomenon of paranoia, as Dostoevsky himself may have believed. While the feelings of persecution and the disowning of part of the self portrayed in *The Double* have psychiatric parallels in paranoid states, the experience of a hallucinatory duplicate of the self is not explained by, or consistent with, a paranoid psychosis. The typical paranoid concept is one of a spotless self being unjustly blamed and tortured by evil others. In contrast, Dostoevsky's hallucinatory or semi-hallucinatory Doubles persecute their creators by asserting their identity with them, and usually their creators are aware that the Double is their "other self." Stavrogin says of his hallucinations (in the suppressed chapter of *The Possessed*):

> It shows different faces and characters yet it is always the same. I know it is different aspects of myself splitting themselves off yet it wants to be an independent devil so an independent devil it must be.

Such self-awareness is quite alien to the paranoid state. If the paranoid persecutors were to be experienced as duplicates of the self, the defensive function of the hallucinations would break down, since they would no longer protect the self against the awareness that it is the possessor of shameful impulses.

Another "popular-psychiatry" concept often used by literary critics, the "split personality," is equally inadequate as an accurate interpretation of the Double phenomenon. This concept is suggested by Versilov in *A Raw Youth* who says:

> I am really split in two mentally, and I am horribly afraid of it. It is just as though one's *second self* were standing beside one; one is sensible and rational oneself, but the other self is compelled to do something perfectly senseless and sometimes very funny; and suddenly you notice you are longing to do that amusing thing, goodness knows why. I once knew a doctor who suddenly began whistling in church, at his father's funeral.

These divided selves of Dostoevsky do not, however, correspond to psychiatric notions of the "split personality." The most common psychiatric conception of the "split personality" refers to the hysterical phenomenon of multiple personalities, the *Three Faces of Eve;* each living a Jekyll and Hyde existence in independence of one another. Unlike such multiple personalities, the "selves" within any of Dostoevsky's figures are simultaneously aware of one another. These "split selves" have equally little to do with schizophrenia, in the sense in which this has been misleadingly mistranslated as "split personality."

Dostoevsky's consciously "split" characters do present classical symptoms of the obsessive-compulsive character, however. The "split" is not a separation of selves, it is an obsessive balancing or undoing of one idea or force with its opposite. Most characteristically, a sacred idea compulsively arouses a degrading idea; the sacredness of the father's funeral compels the impulse to whistle. The hero of *Notes from Underground* says, "At the very moment when I am most capable of feeling every refinement of all that is good and beautiful it would, as though by design, happen to me not only to feel, but to do, such ugly things."

Not only impulse and counter-impulse, but belief and disbelief are opposed and simultaneously felt in a compulsion neurosis. According to [Ivan Karamazov's] devil, "Some can contemplate such depths of belief and disbelief at the same moment that sometimes it really seems as if they are within a hairbreadth of being turned upside down."

Psychoanalysts view these obsessional oppositions as representing conflicts derived from a battle of wills in early childhood, centering around training conflicts. According to [Erik] Erikson's *Childhood and Society,* this conflict is between autonomy and shame or doubt. Shame, Erikson says, "is an emotion, insufficiently studied because in our culture it is so early and easily absorbed by guilt. Shame supposes that one is completely exposed and conscious of being looked at, i.e. self-conscious. It is essentially rage turned against the self."

The "Underground" man tells us:

> With an intense acute pang I was stabbed to the heart by the thought that ten years, twenty years, forty years would pass and even in forty years I would remember with loathing and humiliation those filthiest, most ludicrous, and awful moments of my life. No one could have gone out of his way to degrade himself more shamelessly, and I fully realized it, fully, and yet I went on.

In the self-abasers, feelings of shame are responded to by further self-abasement, since such self-lowering debases and denies the others before whom shame is felt. Fyodor Karamazov says, "I feel when I meet people that I am lower than all and that they all take me for a buffoon, so I say let me play the buffoon for you are, every one of you, lower than I."

The psychoanalytic notion of the obsessional character focused on a conflict between autonomy and shame helps us understand a very puzzling aspect of the literary structure of *Notes from Underground.* The book is composed of two quite different parts: the first an ideological discussion, the second a presentation of some excursions in self-degradation. The ideological portion is an assertion of the need for free will, rational or irrational, against the rational determinism of Western scientific thought. The other half of the work is the expression of the "shame-humiliation syndrome." Some unity in these two parts of the book is provided by the emotional congruity of a personality type in whom the desperate need for freedom from domination or control is linked to the cycle of shame and denial of others.

This analysis of Dostoevsky's "split personalities" as related to obsessional ambivalence and shame does not directly aid us in understanding his Doubles. There is, however, a very direct psychiatric parallel to the kind of hallucination described in *The Double.* This parallel is the "autoscopic syndrome," a syndrome with no relationship to paranoid states. A typical case is that of Mrs. A [quoted in N. Lukianowicz, "Autoscopic Phenomena," in *Archives of Neurology and Psychiatry,* 1958]:

> Mrs. A returned home from her husband's funeral and when she opened the door to her bedroom, she immediately became aware of the presence of somebody else in the room. In the twilight she noticed a lady in front of her. Under the light she noticed that the stranger wore an exact replica of her own coat, hat, and veil. Mrs. A was neither surprised nor afraid and began to undress. The lady in black did exactly the same. Only then looking into the stranger's face, did Mrs. A become aware that it was she herself, as if in a mirror, that it was her 'double,' her 'second self' looking at her. She felt it was more alive and warm than she was herself. Feeling tired and weary, she lay down on her bed. As soon as she closed her eyes, the apparition disappeared. She felt stronger and when she opened her eyes, the apparition was not visible. Since that evening she had been visited almost daily by her 'astral body,' as she called it, mostly at dusk when she was alone. Of the double she says, 'In a detached intellectual way I am fully aware that my double is only a hallucination. Yet I see it; I hear it; I feel it with my senses. Emotionally I feel it as a living part of myself. It is me split and divided. It is all so confusing.'

Almost everything Mrs. A says is echoed by one or another of Dostoevsky's Double-haunted figures. The physical details of the appearance of Dostoevsky's hallucinatory Double are very close to those described by autoscopic patients. Ivan's satanic Double has frozen in his trip through space, and is underdressed in summer clothes, though it is winter; autoscopic Doubles are typically cold, often described as bringing "a breeze of cold air." As in autoscopic experiences, Dostoevsky's Doubles appear at dusk or night, typically when the subject is alone in his bedroom. Like them, Dostoevsky's Doubles tend to be colorless, to be described in shades of grey.

Surprisingly, the likelihood of Dostoevsky's having experienced the autoscopic syndrome has not been mentioned in the extensive psychological literature on Dostoevsky. Nevertheless, there is good reason to believe that he actually had these experiences. While the autoscopic syndrome is rare, it is often linked with severe epilepsy of the sort known to have affected Dostoevsky. The syndrome is extremely puzzling since it is found associated with a variety of conditions, usually organic (epilepsy, parietal brain damage, and severe migraine) but occasionally purely emotional (schizoid personality, depressions).

There is reason to believe that an unusual number of writers have experienced autoscopic hallucinations. Maupassant definitely had hallucinations of a duplicate self in the middle stages of his syphilitic or paretic psychosis, hallucinations quite faithfully described in "Le Horla." Some writers without organic pathology definitely experienced the autoscopic syndrome, including Hoffman, de Musset, Richter and probably Poe. The phenomenon represents a projection of the body-image into space, or a loss of bodily coordinates of the body image. The variations in reported emotional reactions to autoscopic hallucinations are striking: sometimes satisfaction, sometimes sadness, sometimes dread, sometimes indifference. There does not seem to be a single emotional meaning or genesis common to all cases of the autoscopic syndrome. While the psychiatric label provides a basis for understanding Dostoevsky's preoccupation with Doubles, it does not seem to specify their meaning to him or to his novels.

To cast further light on this problem, we must consider the variety of Doubles in Dostoevsky's other novels. (pp. 346-55)

[Six basic types can be identified among Dostoevsky's doubles: (I) Bad Doubles; (II) Christ Figures; (III) Self-Abasers; (IV) Feminines; (V) Will-Murderers; (VI) Impulsives.] The most unique of Dostoevsky's Doubles are hallucinations (Golyadkin II in *The Double* and the devils in *The Possessed* and *The Brothers Karamazov*). These hallucinations persecute their flesh and blood counterparts by insisting on the fundamental identity of the two. These hallucinatory Doubles are all our Type I "bad Doubles," and they are imagined by our Type V "will murderers." Raters assigned high scores to Type I characters on the traits: "A mysterious and sinister affinity to another character," "Is a Double who is an intellectual inferior, a caricature of his alter-ego," "Is a persecuting Double." Type V characters tended to be rated high on the complementary traits, e.g., "Is persecuted by a Double."

A second type of Double is defined by the figures of Smerdyakov in *The Brothers Karamazov* and Pyotr Verkhovensky in *The Possessed.* These flesh and blood characters were distinct from the hallucinatory Doubles on the psychoanalytic traits but not the ideological. They are "psychopathic" figures who carry out murders wished for by the "paranoids" Ivan and Stavrogin, and are mysterious "half-brothers" to them.

Still a third type of Double is represented by the Christ-figures of our Type II. These Christ-figures, with the exception of Sonia in *Crime and Punishment,* have alter-egos among our Type VI impulsives. These relations, like those last mentioned, are described in a terminology of "brother" and "sister," real or spiritual. Prince Myshkin has a mysterious affinity to Rogozhin and to Nastasya in *The Idiot,* both an attraction and a feeling of a linkage of fate. Alyosha Karamazov is, in a somewhat similar sense, an alter-ego to his brother Dmitri who enacts sexual and aggressive impulses which Alyosha somehow shares. Dmitri tells him:

> I want to tell you now about the insects to whom God gave sensual lust. I am that insect, brother, and all we Karamazovs are such insects, and, angel as you are, that insect lives in you, too, and will stir up a tempest in your blood.

Like Myshkin, Alyosha knows his impulsive Double will attempt murder, dreads it, but is strangely paralyzed or passive about preventing it. In some sense, Type VI, the impulsives, seem to represent or enact the impulses of Type II, the Christ-figures, just as Type I figures enact the impulses of Type V, the "paranoid" will-murderers. The relationship between Types I and V is explicit and consciously intended by Dostoevsky, while the relationship between Type II and VI is much more cloudy and undefined. (pp. 357-58)

[There are] many clear-cut and recurring aspects to Dostoevsky's Doubles. These are not the result of the requirements of structure of a particular book since they are repeated from novel to novel. They are also not explained, however, by mere knowledge that Dostoevsky may have experienced the autoscopic phenomenon. The autoscopic Doubles are assigned a definite evil personality constant from book to book and are in some mysterious way part of a world including good-and-evil, flesh-and-blood alter-egos.

To enrich our notion of the meaning of these facts in relation to the autoscopic syndrome, we may turn to Otto Rank's discussion of "The Double as Immortal Self" in his last book, *Beyond Psychology.* No better [illustration of Dostoevsky's claim, in *The Brothers Karamazov,* that] "psychology is a knife which cuts both ways" can be provided than Rank's two writings on the Double. His first treatment is an orthodox psychoanalytic interpretation; his second written thirty years later is part of his own effort to form a theory which is "Beyond Psychology," *i.e.,* beyond psychoanalysis.

Rank's last discussion of literary Doubles is based on his postulation of a universal striving for immortality or rebirth in man's non-instinctual but irrational will. This striving is especially strong in the artist type, says Rank in *Art and the Artist,* since the urge to create is essentially the urge to immortalize the self. While the average individual takes himself as given, the artist (and the neurotic who is essentially an artist manqué) cannot. The artist is continually striving to remold his ego in terms of self-created ideals, in order to perpetuate or immortalize himself. This perpetually recreated or reborn self is projected and justified in the art work.

In *Beyond Psychology,* Rank also postulates the immortalizing tendency as underlying social ideologies and forms of social organization, through which the individual attains collective immortality. Rank believes that one point at which the individual, self-immortalizing needs of the artist intersect with collective ideologies is in the literary use of the Double. This literary use parallels genuine folk-beliefs in many primitive cultures, as well as mythological themes. In these primitive cultures there is an equation of the individual's soul when alive, his ghost after death, and his actual shadow. This shadow-soul survives the individual's death, and may sometimes leave the body in sleep, etc. There may, however, be some differences in appearance and character between the actual self and the ghostly Double.

Rank points out that in modern literature, the Double is usually a symbol of a character's past, his evil tendencies and his death rather than of future immortality, as in naive folk-beliefs. A typical example is E. T. A. Hoffmann's "Story of the Lost Reflection," in which the hero sells his mirror reflection (his "immortal soul") to a devil-figure. This reflection takes on a life of its own and persecutes its former owner until the victim attempts to kill it and so kills himself. (Wilde's *Picture of Dorian Gray* presents a similar theme.) Rank explains the modern negative attitude toward the Double as due to modern man's overrationalistic alienation from life and death and from his own fundamentally irrational will.

Rank sees folk-beliefs and myths of the Double as related to the wide-spread mythology of twins. A common theme of myth is that of twins who have creative powers and who found cities and cultures (e.g., Romulus and Remus). Often in these myths, one twin is killed by the other, or is killed in his place. Rank interprets this as indicating a concept of the twins as Doubles, one of whom becomes immortal and creative through the death of his mortal counterpart. According to Rank, primitive cultures see Doubles and twins as duplicate selves necessary for immortality, just as patriarchal cultures see the son as a duplicate of the father, necessary for immortality.

Rank applies these suggestive ideas to Dostoevsky's Doubles in only a vague, brief and superficial fashion. Their importance, however, is suggested by the clinical literature on the autoscopic syndrome. A number of the cases reported are like those of Mrs. A, cases in which the Double first appears immediately after the death of a significant person. In some sense the Double seems to be a substitute or resurrection of the lost person. In other cases, the Double represents, not a "resurrected self" but the self as dead. De Musset, just after walking through a cemetery, saw a hallucination of "a mysterious stranger which he recognized with terror as *himself,* twenty years older, with features ravaged by debauchery, eyes aghast with fear." [J. Todd and K. Dewhurst, in "The Double: Its Psychopathology and Psychophysiology," *Journal of Mental and Nervous Diseases,* 1955, reported a clinical case] of a woman in great anxiety, about to enter the hospital for surgical completion of a miscarriage, who was suddenly confronted by a realistic vision of herself lying in a coffin. This was the first appearance of a recurring mirror-like hallucination of a Double.

Our discussion suggests a close connection between Double or autoscopic experiences and epilepsy on the one hand, and concern about death and immortality on the other. Dostoevsky's extreme concern with death and immortality was expressed both in ideological and in symptomatic behavior.

On the ideological level, he wrote: "Without a superior idea, there cannot exist either the individual or the nation. But here on earth we have only one superior idea—the *immortality of the soul* because all other superior ideas have their source in this idea" [*The Diary of a Writer*].

On the symptomatic level, his fear of death was associated with his epileptic attacks. An attack was triggered off by passing a chance funeral procession. The association of death and epilepsy led him to fears of being buried alive, of being closed in for eternity. He would leave notes that he should not be buried for five days after an attack. His own Siberian sentence he viewed as a living burial after his near execution: "It is difficult [he wrote in a letter] to express how much I have suffered. These four years I look upon as a time of living burial. I was put in a coffin." These feelings suggest that he feared not only death, but his own ghostly immortality in the face of his apparent death to the world.

Dostoevsky told his friends that his epileptic attacks were associated not only with fear of death and ghostly immortality, but with the joyful experiences of eternal life described by his epileptic figures Myshkin and Kirrilov.

The association we would expect between epilepsy, experiences of immortality, and the Double phenomenon is found in the grouping of these traits in Dostoevsky's characters. A number of both the Type II good Doubles (Myshkin, Kirrilov, Alyosha) and the Type I bad Doubles (Smerdyakov) have epileptic or epileptic-like seizures, while none of the other characters are portrayed as epileptic. In the good Doubles epilepsy is connected with a high rating on the trait, "Joyful experience in which eternal life is collapsed into an instant." All the Type I good Doubles are rated high on the trait, "Lives for and believes in positive immortality." Of Alyosha, Dostoevsky says: "As soon as he reflected seriously, he was convinced of the existence of God and immortality and instinctively said to himself: 'I want to live for immortality and I will accept no compromise.' "

If Dostoevsky's Type II good Doubles express his ideas, concerns and experiences of positive immortality, his Type I bad Doubles express his ideas and experience of negative immortality, of living burial. Svidrigailov says: "We always imagine eternity as something beyond our conception, something vast. But why must it be vast? Instead of all that, what if it is one little room, like a bathhouse in the country, black and grimey and spiders in every corner, and that's all eternity is?"

Dostoevsky intended this to be a reflection of his Siberian "living burial" and wrote [in a letter] of *Crime and Punishment,* "My Dead House was really most interesting. And here again shall be a picture of a hell, of the same kind as that 'Turkish Bath in the Prison' (a chapter in the House of the Dead on the horrors of a multitude of naked, filthy bodies closely packed together in the prisoners' weekly steambath)."

Svidrigailov in *Crime and Punishment* and Stavrogin in *The Possessed* are flesh and blood characters who are sinister alter-egos to others. Both also experience hallucinations which are directly said to represent the ghosts or resurrections of dead or murdered persons. In the passage on eternity just mentioned, Svidrigailov discussed his hallucinations of his dead wife Marfa (whom he has mistreated and probably murdered) and of a servant whom he drove to suicide. These hallucinations are not only experienced but believed in by Svidrigailov, who says, "I agree that ghosts only appear to the sick, but that only proves they are unable to appear except to the sick, not that they don't exist."

Stavrogin also has two related sets of hallucinations (described in the suppressed chapter of *The Possessed*). One is of the devil, the other is of the twelve-year-old girl whom he seduced and led to suicide.

At first sight, hallucinatory Doubles in the novels would seem to be one thing, and flesh and blood alter-egos another. The line of thinking we have pursued suggests, however, that the "living" bad Doubles may have a meaning similar to that of the "hallucinatory" bad Doubles. As in the case of Mrs. A, the Double is both a resurrection of a dead person and is the self. (pp. 358-61)

Lawrence Kohlberg, "Psychological Analysis and Literary Form: A Study of the Doubles in Dostoevsky," in Daedalus: Journal of the American Academy of Arts and Sciences, *Vol. 92, No. 2, Spring, 1963, pp. 345-62.*

Robert Rogers

[In the excerpt below, Rogers analyzes psychological doubling in nineteenth-century literature, emphasizing the narcissistic context of the double's emergence. In addition, he explains the aesthetic limitations of doubling.]

Hallucinations of seeing oneself constitute a special category, one to be distinguished sharply from hallucinations of anything or anyone else because delusions of encountering one's own self betray a morbid preoccupation of the individual with his own essence. These visions of the self can be characterized without exception as narcissistic, and a consideration of such cases must be founded on an understanding of the nature of narcissism.

Narcissism is a kind of love, but it is misleading to translate the concept into what is known commonly as "self-love." Self-love in the everyday sense of "egotism" is a metaphorical expression. In narcissism the self-love is literal. The only difference between this kind of love and the erotic love of another person is in the object. Narcissism paradoxically involves a relationship, a relationship of self to self in which one's self is regarded as though it were another person. [In the *New Introductory Lectures*] Freud stated the paradox in a way which emphasizes the connection between narcissism and decomposition:

> The ego is in its very essence a subject; how can it be made into an object? Well, there is no doubt that it can be. The ego can take itself as an object, can treat itself like other objects, can observe itself, criticize itself, and do Heaven knows what with itself. In this, one part of the ego is setting itself over against the rest. So the ego can be split; it splits itself during a number of its functions—temporarily at least.

Such a taking of the ego as object is a libidinal taking, an erotic process. Elsewhere, in his essay "On Narcissism," Freud emphasizes the libidinal nature of narcissism when it occurs as a component of states which do not, at first glance, seem characterized by self-love, such as physical illness, often marked by regression and withdrawal; sleep, which like illness "implies a narcissistic withdrawal of the libido away from its attachments back to the subject's own person"; dreams, the dreamer himself always being the central figure or observer; and hypochondria, where the body of the patient (specifically, its imagined hurts) receives the attention of the libido. The results of the taking of one's own ego as an object can be seen in their most morbid form in the psychoses, with their radical megalomania and marked withdrawal of interest in the external world. Since narcissism involves an investment of libido in the ego, it is always in some sense pleasurable, though it may not be felt as such. Thus even the paranoid's characteristic sense of being watched or spoken to is considered by Freud to be a delusion of observation which results in a narcissistic gratification for the ego-ideal. Another form of narcissistic gratification is that obtained by the homosexual in seeking out objects more like himself.

In examining a number of literary works displaying manifest doubling of the self, particular stress will be laid upon the presence of narcissistic complications and the esthetic limitations of manifest doubling.

A special genre of the manifest double is the mirror image, the projected self being not merely a similar self but an exact duplicate. A special case of the mirror image can be seen in the celebrated story of Narcissus, whose behavior has given us a name for a basic psychological concept. One sign of morbidity in Narcissus' preoccupation with himself is that he has trouble discriminating between the "me" and the "not-me." "Am I the lover / Or beloved?" he asks (in Ovid's [*Metamorphoses*]). Like the victim of autoscopy, Narcissus is at least partly aware that his vision is not completely real in the sense of being corporally separate from himself. For the most part, however, the myth presents the mirror image in the pool as a symbol of Narcissus' unawareness that what he sees is only a reflection of himself. Another sign of morbidity in the hero is the sexualization of his self-love. In fact, erotic behavior pervades the tale. Not only does Narcissus *love* himself, this child of passion is born of the rape of Liriope by Cephisus. He is loved by the rejected young swain whose curse, "O may he love himself alone . . . yet fail in that great love," is carried out by Nemesis. He is also loved by Echo, whose passion seems undisguisedly sexual: she throws herself in his arms and is described as being like "sulphur / At the tip of torches, leaping to fire / When another flame leans toward it." That the love of Narcissus for himself transcends mere admiration or egotism, that he wants in a literal way to possess himself sexually, is symbolized by his attempt to kiss his image in the pool.

Edgar Allan Poe in 1848.

One facet of his erotomania can be seen in his compulsive flirtatiousness:

> The way Narcissus had betrayed frail Echo,
> Now swift, now shy, so he had played with all:

Girls of the rivers, women of the mountains,
With boys and men.

This passage points to another feature of psychological interest, the homoerotic element. Narcissus flirts with males, loves his own sex in loving himself, and performs a traditionally feminine ritual of grief in beating his breast with his "pale hands," the same action which his sisters perform as they grieve for him. The metamorphosis of Narcissus into a flower confirms the presence of a feminine strain in him, and intimations of his psychosexual impotence are contained in the two references to loss of sight in Ovid's version: we are told that neither food nor sleep can lure him away from the pool as he lies there "until sight failed," and at the end "death shut fast the eyes that shone with light / At their own lustre." Given his psychological makeup, it is not surprising that he rejects the lovely Echo: "May I be dead / Before you throw your fearful chains around me."

One of the most charming tales on the theme of the mirror image is Hawthorne's whimsical "Monsieur du Miroir." The tone of light irony is sounded at the very beginning of the fantasy sketch: "Than the gentleman above named, there is nobody, in the whole circle of my acquaintance, whom I have more attentively studied, yet of whom I have less real knowledge, beneath the surface which it pleases him to present." Hawthorne's easy, punning humor seems at first to belie any awareness of the gravity of his theme. He speaks of his subject as involving "grave reflection" and concludes the sketch by doubting that M. du Miroir is the wiser for all his meditation, though his whole business is "reflection." He jokes about there being reasons for supposing M. du Miroir to be a near relative except for his French name, which obliges him to disclaim all kinship. He chides his mirror double, who moves his lips but makes no sound, for being a "dumb devil." He notes that M. du Miroir shares his own taste in clothes to the last detail and all his moods and feelings, even to the point of simulating a swollen jaw when Hawthorne has a toothache. M. du Miroir, something of a wag, thrusts his head into a bright new warming pan in the hardware store and paddles, in full dress, "from one mud puddle to another . . . plunging into the filthy depths of each."

But beneath the surface levity of Hawthorne's style lurks the troubling theme of narcissism. M. du Miroir shares Narcissus' fondness for water. He is often seen in the ballroom "in my age of vanities." Even his impish omnipresence reflects an exaggerated awareness of the self. At one point Hawthorne says directly, "I loved him well," speaking of his youth when "Monsieur du Miroir had then a most agreeable way of calling me a handsome fellow"—a compliment which Hawthorne is careful to return to the image in the mirror. The intimate connection between the physical image and the image of the artist in his own eyes is sounded when Hawthorne wonders if M. du Miroir will haunt his grave after death, lingering "to remind the neglectful world of one who staked much to win a name."

Though it is couched in light irony, serious notes creep into the sketch again and again. The mirror image is a conjurer, capable of passing through brick walls and bolted oaken doors. Twice the demonic motif appears, once when the image is referred to as a "dumb devil" and once when it is criticized for lacking the common sense to know that Hawthorne "would as willingly exchange a nod with the Old Nick" as greet him in public. It seems ominous, too, when Hawthorne—who did himself away from people for many years—admits that even when isolated in his chamber, with the key turned, withdrawn, and the keyhole stuffed with paper, he cannot escape the haunting presence of his other self. Remarks concerning the speaker's relations with the opposite sex, which occur sporadically in the sketch—seemingly without any important connection—actually form a consistent pattern. "Whenever I have been in love," we are told, "Monsieur du Miroir has looked passionate and tender." At the lady, we wonder, or at his counterpart in front of the mirror? During one tender moment the mischievous imp "stole into the heaven of a young lady's eyes; so that, while I gazed and was dreaming only of herself, I found him also in my dreams." In a similar vein we hear Hawthorne jokingly insist that when the "intrusive intimate" follows him into his bedchamber, "I should prefer—scandal apart—the laughing bloom of a young girl to the dark and bearded gravity of my present companion." In each instance, love of a woman is either blended with or partly obstructed by narcissism, a pattern which bears out Freud's suggestion that a kind of reciprocity exists between ego-libido and object-libido such that "the more that is absorbed by the one, the more impoverished does the other become." In any case, there can be little doubt concerning the profundity of Hawthorne's comparison of the attempt to escape his M. du Miroir with "the hopeless race that men sometimes run with memory, or their own hearts, or their moral selves, which, though burdened with cares enough to crush an elephant, will never be one step behind."

Just such a hopeless race with memory, heart, and moral self is run in Wilde's *The Picture of Dorian Gray*, a tale which implies that the worship of one's own physical beauty is more hazardous for men than for women. The novel presents a young man ravished by a painting of himself (the portrait double being but a variation of the mirror-image double). Dorian Gray's first glance at the canvas teaches him to love his own beauty and to know that "when one loses one's good looks . . . one loses everything." The name of Narcissus is invoked in the text, and the protagonist says of the portrait, "I am in love with it . . . It is part of myself." Sad at the thought that the image in the portrait will remain young and handsome while he grows old and ugly, Dorian Gray expresses the fateful wish that the situation be reversed. And so it happens: the face in the diabolical painting, hidden away, reflects over the years the passions, crimes, and physical age of the subject, while the living Dorian Gray appears untouched by time, at least until the protagonist, hounded by guilt, decides to stab the portrait. This symbolic act magically causes his actual death, whereupon his servants discover him, withered and loathsome beyond recognition, beside the handsome "original." With respect to the dangers of narcissism, the tale speaks for itself. Almost as obvious to the modern eye is the epicene atmosphere of the novel. One need not make any inferences from Oscar Wilde's life to perceive the androgynous nature of Dorian Gray and the homoerotic attraction which he has for his friends, Lord Wotton and the painter of the portrait, Basil Hallward. Given this context, Gray's declaration that he cannot love because "I am too much concentrated on myself" occasions no surprise. What may not be apparent in the novel is that the painter, Basil Hallward, is a latent double of Dorian Gray. "I have put too much of myself into it," Hallward says, to which Lord Wotton replies, "Too much of yourself . . . Basil, I didn't know you were so vain." What seems to have happened in psychological terms is that Hallward, himself perhaps an allegorical artist-surrogate of Oscar Wilde, has projected his narcissistic ideal into the painting; in any case, Hallward's goodness and integrity are complementary to Dorian Gray's corruption and hypocrisy.

The complementarity of personality traits typical of a man and his double obtains in Hans Christian Andersen's "The Shadow," a droll tale about a wise and humble Learned Man who loses his shadow only to have it return to him, sassy and presumptuous, with pretentions of having an independent existence. The shadow proposes that the real man serve as traveling companion and supposed shadow of the shadow. Having visited the abode of Poetry, about which the Learned Man is curious, the shadow claims to know everything and to be privy to all men's secrets. As a result he has become extraordinarily vain, even to the point of insisting that the Learned Man not *tutoyer* him, though when the man becomes the shadow's servant the shadow says "thou" to the man. In a curious variation on the theme of the incompatibility of narcissism with romantic love, the shadow presumes to win the hand of a princess. When the Learned Man threatens to expose the fraud for what he is, a mere shadow, the shadow has the man declared insane and executed, and the story ends with the marriage of the shadow and the princess. The shadow seems to symbolize the narcissistic hazards of too much knowledge, the dangers of a Faustian yearning for worldliness, and the ill fortune that portends when a man sees his shadow.

Alfred de Musset, one of a number of authors who actually saw their own doubles, presents an equally narcissistic version of the mirror image in his "La Nuit de Décembre." In the first part of the poem the speaker describes various mournful crises in his life when, alone, he saw a figure dressed in black which "resembled me like a brother." The shadowy figure always mirrors the poet's current melancholy mood. He is invariably alone at these moments, and it turns out that when the vision speaks at the end of the poem he personifies Solitude:

> Je ne suis ni dieu ni démon,
> Et tu m'as nommé par mon nom
> Quand tu m'as appelé ton frère;
> Où tu vas, j'y serai toujours,
> Jusques au dernier de tes jours,
> Où j'irai m'asseoir sur ta pierre.
>
> Le ciel m'as confié ton coeur.
> Quand tu seras dans la douleur,
> Viens à moi sans inquiétude.
> Je te suivrai sur le chemin;
> Mais je ne puis toucher ta main,
> Ami, je suis la Solitude.

Though Musset presumably did not intend it that way, the vision seems to represent the spirit of sentimental Self-Pity more than Solitude. This is in keeping with the theme of narcissism pervading the work. Since most of the sad moments stem from disappointed love, we are confronted once again with the evidence of the conflict between self-love and love of others.

The proclivity of phantom doubles to show up only when the subject is in solitude can be seen in one of Maupassant's stories: "But if there were two of us in the place, I feel certain that he would not be there any longer, for he is there just because I am alone, simply and solely because I am alone!" So ends "He?"—in which the narrator explains to a friend that though he feels more than ever incapable of loving one woman alone "because I shall always adore all the others too much," he intends to marry, a very ordinary girl as it happens, in order to insure that when he wakes in the middle of the night, he will not be alone and hence subject to a visitation of the unidentified "he." Although the monstrous presence christened "The Horla" in Maupassant's story of that title is never directly identified as a double, passages such as "He is becoming my soul" and the scene in which the maddened narrator fails to perceive his reflection in a mirror just after he has "felt" the Horla reading over his shoulder leave little doubt that he is a double, even though elsewhere he is thought to be a suffocating, soul-sucking vampire. Having failed to kill the visitant by the expedient of burning his chateau to the ground, the victim concludes that to destroy the Horla he must kill himself—as Maupassant tried to do in his final madness. The narrator in "The Horla" appears to live alone except for servants and no love interest is mentioned, but the drift of "He?" when matched with Maupassant's notorious satyriasis leads to the supposition that the Don Juan impulse in him amounted to a defensive reaction-formation against the feeling of being unable to love at all. If so, it would follow that the persecutory double in both stories is a superego projection which hounds the guilty protagonists. Extreme anxiety plagues the heroes of both tales.

One of the most representative superego doubles appears in Poe's "William Wilson." Here the narrator emphasizes his own evil proclivities in contrast to the good advice and cautionary whispers of his "guardian angel" double, who resembles him in name, feature, age, and so forth. Indicative of the burden of unconscious guilt borne by the narrator is the seemingly shameless young decadent's confession that "an intolerable weight of anxiety" is lifted from him when the other William Wilson spoils his attempt to cheat a fellow Oxford student at cards. Except for cheating at cards and excessive drinking, the various "debaucheries" are with one exception unspecified. In this disparity between the relatively innocuous nature of the protagonist's crimes and the extreme baseness by which they are characterized in the story itself, the tyrannical severity of the superego finds expression. Poe's own gambling and wine-bibbing at the University of Virginia, which caused his tightfisted foster father to refuse him further support, despite Poe's success as a student, appear in exaggerated form in the narrative, at least according to Marie Bonaparte, who [in *The Life and Works of Edgar Allan Poe,*

1949] stresses that the double in this story represents, quite in conformity with psychoanalytic theory, "the introjection of the repressive father system" in the son. The only "crime" involving women in the story is the implied but unspecified plan to seduce "the young, the gay, the beautiful wife of the aged and doting Di Broglio." This plot, in which oedipal overtones are obvious, is foiled by the double. Enraged, the protagonist challenges the double to a duel and ends by realizing as he looks into a mirror that he has stabbed himself—a rather stereotyped ending perhaps borrowed from E. T. A. Hoffmann's "Story of the Lost Reflection." No pronounced narcissism appears to possess William Wilson, but Bonaparte suggests that the ambivalence toward the self portrayed in this story may be regarded as a defensive reaction against narcissism.

Perhaps the most famous and certainly the most influential of all double stories concerns the adventures of Peter Schlemihl, who sells his shadow to a remarkable man in a gray coat in exchange for unlimited riches. Chamisso's tale is a feeble variation of the Faust legend, with Peter Schlemihl cast as Faust and the man in the gray coat as Mephistopheles. Despite the inexhaustible riches Schlemihl gets in return, he becomes a pariah, avoided by all who perceive him to be without his soul-shadow. His Helen of Troy is the beautiful Minna, whom he cannot marry if he does not have a shadow.

Several passages in the narrative point to narcissism as the source of Schlemihl's problem. He says concerning his feeling for the lovely Franny, "My vanity was only intent on exciting hers to make a conquest of me; but although the intoxication disturbed my head, it failed to make the least impression on my heart." He is flattered at being mistaken for the King of Prussia. And when he meets Minna, it is significant that he thinks that "she lived but in me, her whole soul being bound up in mine regardless what her own fate might be." Since shadows are invariably gray and since the man in the gray coat leads Schlemihl to "the pleasures of the world," old Graycoat functions as a bad angel or devil double of Schlemihl; that is, he in effect replaces the shadow which Schlemihl sells. That Graycoat can be overcome only by conscience ties in with the protagonist's statement early in the story that he has sacrificed his conscience for riches and his remark elsewhere that he has long been "a rigid censor" of himself and has nourished in his heart "the worm of remorse." Yet Peter Schlemihl, who uses his riches primarily for display and commits no really nefarious acts, cannot be called an evil figure. His real problem seems to be that his narcissism is even more inexhaustible than his riches. That is the true reason why he cannot marry Minna.

Along with Chamisso many other writers in the period of German romantic literature shared a penchant for portraying doppergänger in their works, among them Goethe, Tieck, Fouqué, Heinrich von Kleist, E. T. A. Hoffmann, and Jean Paul Richter, who introduced the term doppelgänger. For the most part, [as Ralph Tymms wrote in his *Double in Literary Psychology,* 1949], "the romantic of the early period used the theme as a straightforward device for humorous, or grisly, misunderstandings in the tradition of the farce of mistaken identity or of folklore." Of all these authors Hoffmann is best known for his portrayal of doubles.

Hoffmann, who experienced autoscopic hallucinations, once rewarded the praise of his hostess in the bitterness of his old age with the sarcastic comment that she mistook him, the Councillor Hoffmann, for Hoffmann the writer, a man of such genius that he could not deem her invitation worthy of notice. This split between artist and practical man, resembling that between fantasy-maker Lewis Carroll and mathematician Lutwidge Dodgson, is the theme of Hoffmann's "The Doubles." The two doubles, alike even in their birthmarks, undergo a series of mysterious experiences in a plot worthy of Plautus or Shakespeare in its variations on mistaken identity. These experiences culminate in Deodatus Schwendy's being recognized as heir to the late prince, while his counterpart, painter George Haberland, dedicates himself anew to the life of the artist. The familiar pattern of frustrated love emerges in the renunciation that both men must make of the beautiful Nathalie, who cannot choose between them. Schwendy, the true prince, is left with the responsibilities of administering a realm, while Haberland has the task of idealizing Nathalie in his art.

[In his "The 'Uncanny',"] Freud provides some important remarks about decomposition in his analysis of another of the many tales by Hoffman which deal in doubles, "The Sandman." The story begins with the student Nathaniel's anxiety about his encounter with an itinerant optician, Coppola. The encounter reminds him of his childhood fears of the Sandman, a bogyman whose function, according to Nathaniel's nurse, was to throw handfuls of sand in the eyes of children when they refused to go to bed, making their eyes jump out of their heads. Coppola resembles the lawyer Coppelius, who used to visit Nathaniel's father after the boy went to bed and whom Nathaniel believed responsible for his father's death in connection with certain alchemical experiments. The rest of the action of the story, in brief, involves Nathaniel's obsessive love for Olympia, an automaton doll fabricated by Professor Spalanzani with the help of Coppola; his rejection of his betrothed, Clara; his madness; his recovery; his ultimate relapse into madness when he attempts to murder Clara; and his eventual suicide. In the sequel Clara eventually marries, finding a domestic happiness which Nathaniel, "with his tempest-tossed soul," could never have given her. Although Nathaniel does not see his double in any direct fashion, Clara suggests—and at one moment of temporary insight Nathaniel accepts—that Coppelius and Coppola exist only in his mind and are phantoms of his own self.

Freud's analysis stresses that the main motif in the story concerns the tearing out of children's eyes by the Sandman. He explains that "morbid anxiety connected with the eyes and with going blind is often enough a substitute for the dread of castration," citing Oedipus' blinding of himself as a parallel. Why, asks Freud, does Hoffmann make such an intimate connection between the father's death and anxiety about eyes, and why does the Sandman interfere with love each time he appears (dividing Nathaniel from Clara and from his best friend, her brother; destroying Olympia; and later driving Nathaniel to suicide just when he has regained Clara)? "Things like these and many more seem arbitrary and meaningless in the story so long as we deny all connection between fears about the eye and castration; but they become intelligible as soon as we replace the Sand-Man by the dreaded father at whose hands castration is awaited." Freud goes on to explain that Nathaniel's father and Coppelius represent a split of the father image generated by the child's ambivalence; one threatens to blind (castrate) him while one intercedes for his sight. The repressed wish for the death of the father is symbolized in the narrative by the father's accidental death. In Nathaniel's student days Professor Spalanzani and Coppola reproduce the split father imago: "Just as before they used to work together over the fire, so now they have jointly created the doll Olympia; the Professor is even called the father of Olympia." Another castration equivalent in the story, the fantasied unscrewing of Nathaniel's arms and legs by Coppelius, helps to explain what Olympia really represents. "She, the automatic doll, can be nothing else than a personification of Nathaniel's feminine attitude towards his father in his infancy." This inference enables us to understand the otherwise mysterious assertion that the optician, Coppola, has stolen Nathaniel's eyes in order to set them in the doll. Olympia is, then, "a dissociated complex of Nathaniel's which confronts him as a person, and Nathaniel's enslavement to this complex is expressed in his senseless obsessive love for Olympia. We may with justice call such love narcissistic." In this connection Freud might well have quoted the reverie Nathaniel has after the ball given by Professor Spalanzani: "Upon me alone did her [Olympia's] loving glances fall, and through my mind and thoughts alone did they radiate; and only in her love can I find my own self again."

Thus the story embodies all of the elements which Freud singles out in his essay as pertaining to uncanny experiences: the revival of repressed infantile complexes by some chance impression; the confirmation of primitive beliefs; animism; magic and witchcraft; the omnipotence of thoughts; repetition-compulsion; man's attitude toward death; and the castration complex. Elsewhere in the same essay Freud emphasizes that the primitive conception of the double as a second self and immortal soul springs from the soil of man's primary narcissism, the unbounded love for himself originating in infancy, and he links the defensive reduplication of the self with the similarly defensive representation of castration anxiety in dream language by multiplication of genital symbols.

These examples of manifest doubling in literature provide a basis for considering what common ground literary versions of decomposition share with actual hallucinations of one's mirror image. The most obvious inference is that case histories of autoscopy confirm the psychological validity of subject doubling in fiction. When an author portrays a protagonist as seeing his double, it is not simply a device or gimmick calculated to arouse the reader's interest by virtue of the strangeness of the episode but is, in fact, a result of his sense of the division to which the human mind in conflict with itself is susceptible.

An equally obvious inference to be drawn is that when an author wishes to depict mental conflict within a single mind a most natural way for him to dramatize it is to represent that mind by two or more characters. Such a technique is a natural one whether the author is aware of what he is doing or not. It must also be insisted that when a man sees an image of himself a few paces away and when an artist doubles or splits up a coherent psychological entity into two or more seemingly autonomous characters, both the neurotic and the artist are "thinking" archaically, that is, their mental operations in this matter are not logical and in accordance with objective reality. This kind of mental activity is what Todd and Dewhurst call "archetypic thinking" in their discussion of autoscopy in life and literature [John Todd and Kenneth Dewhurst, "The Double: Its Psychopathology and Psychophysiology," *Journal of Nervous and Mental Diseases,* CXXII, 1955]. They mean that the mental processes of neurotics and psychotics who see visions of themselves resemble in their content the magical conceptions of "primitive" superstition as seen in myth and folklore. In psychoanalysis such mental processes, occurring characteristically in neurosis, psychosis, narcosis, extreme inebriation, dreams, and in the fantasies of children, are known technically as "primary process thinking." While artistic creation, in literature and other media, may involve critical, ratiocinative, ego-oriented thinking (the secondary process), it should be borne in mind—though the fact cannot be demonstrated here—that id-oriented primary process mentation in the artist is largely responsible for the concreteness of symbolic representation which so distinguishes the literary imagination from that of the analytical, discursive thinker. Where a philosopher might speak of conflicts between body and spirit, for example, a literary artist would be likely to conjure up representative characters: a Sancho Panza and a Don Quixote, let us say. In short, autoscopy and decomposition always involve archaic thinking.

Three other features of autoscopic hallucinations which have counterparts in literature are the double as a conscience figure, as a projected wish-fulfillment, and as a reflection of the subject's narcissism. Mr. G., the patient who succeeded in outpacing the facial expressions of his double by changing his own faster than the alter ego could, spoke of his mirror image as a conscience trying to "put me right" and called it a "copycat" with no original ideas of its own, except when it scolded him [N. Lukianowicz, "Autoscopic Phenomena," *Archives of Neurology and Psychiatry,* LXXX, 1958]. We have already seen in "William Wilson" the conscience or superego double *par excellence* and can discern in Dorian Gray's portrait and the shadow of Peter Schlemihl sections of the self which, when missing, leave the rest without moral control. Wish-fulfillment finds expression in some of the other cases cited by Lukianowicz: Mrs. A. feels her double to be more alive and warm than she is herself; Mr. B., who had lost his right leg, is visited by a double resembling him in all respects except that it wears no prosthesis; Mr. C., apparently a would-be musician, sees himself conducting an orchestra. Correlative examples of wish-fulfillment in stories discussed are numerous. One might single out in particular the patent wish elements in the Narcissus myth, in Dorian Gray's desire for permanent youth and beauty, and in Peter Schlemihl's yearning for riches and beautiful women. The narcissistic aspects of autoscopic phenomena would seem to be self-evident. A curious instance of the narcissism involved in autoscopy can be seen in the comical example of the dream spectacle of a homosexual who "always dreamed of committing mutual masturbation *with a man very similar in appearance* to himself" [Todd and Dewhurst]. As narcissism has been stressed in the stories analyzed, further instances need not be repeated. Still another parallel between art and life is the general apprehension—if not positive fear—which vision of the self excites in the beholder, such as in the stories by Maupassant. As for the love life of patients who experience autoscopic hallucinations, the studies drawn upon do not mention it, but the patients probably experienced marked difficulties in romantic object relations with the opposite sex.

While the mere psychological authenticity of manifest doubling in literature can be confirmed by virtue of its resemblance to the phenomenon of autoscopy, what of the merit of decomposition, of the overt sort, as a vehicle for the imaginative rendering of psychic conflict? Such merit, which may appear to have been assumed all along, hardly seems to be supported by the prevailing quality of the stories so far discussed. And if the quality of stories analyzed are not representative of the best that might have been chosen, what works presenting palpable doubles are? While no one would disparage the artistic might of Ovid and Hawthorne, the Narcissus passage and "Monsieur du Miroir" cannot by themselves bear the full weight of these authors' artistic reputations, and the other authors discussed in this chapter belong to the secondary and tertiary ranks of world writers, however popular they may be as tellers of tales. Thus we are left with the inference which Tymms makes in the first sentence of *Doubles in Literary Psychology:* "Superficially, doubles are among the facile, and less reputable devices in fiction." But by "doubles" Tymms refers solely to manifest doubles. His statement does not hold true for latent doubling.

The reader's response to stories portraying manifest doubles may be presumed to be akin to his reaction to such figures as Virtue and Vice in the old morality plays. As Leslie Fiedler might put it, Archetype becomes Stereotype; that is, the archetypal potential of the demonic in man degenerates all too often into the stereotype of The Diabolical Other Self. Such work possesses all the worst features of melodrama, the author resembling to some extent an amateurish prestidigitator who either moves with clumsy slowness or fails to distract his audience from the bare mechanics of his act with an obfuscating line of patter.

The literary deployment of the manifest double involves several inherent limitations which can be stated in psychological terms. A crucial drawback lies in the reader's awareness that some kind of decomposition is being represented. The lack of esthetic distance resulting from this transparency allows incipient guilt and anxiety feelings in the reader to inhibit deep identification with the characters. Where decomposition is latent, the reader can identify with the protagonist consciously and with the antagonist unconsciously, but where decomposition is manifest, the reader's awareness that the "bad guy" is somehow part of the "good guy" tends to block his identification with both of them. A corresponding factor operates in the mind of the composing artist which deters free and spontaneous play of his fantasy powers. This assumption is based on the concept known in ego psychology as "flexibility of repression." The artist's special talent for temporarily reducing repression in order to dredge up id material and then subsequently manipulate such material in a relatively conscious, critical, ego-oriented fashion without awareness of its unconscious significance is handicapped when he deals in manifest doubles. A third factor, related to the other two but dynamic in its essence, concerns the relative absence of shifts in psychic distance by both reader and writer stemming from an insufficiency of ambiguity in the work. Such works are relatively static and esthetically uninteresting. Only when the work is surcharged with ambiguity, as Hawthorne's sketch, can these limitations inherent in the use of the overt double be partially overcome. The drawbacks may be presumed to operate regardless of the merit of the artist employing the device.

James Hogg's novel-length treatment of the motif in *The Private Memoirs and Confessions of a Justified Sinner* illustrates the esthetic limitations of the mode. In this satire of theological extremism growing out of the Reformation, George Colwan, laird of Dalchastel, marries a religious prude beguiled by the doctrines of her Protestant minister, Robert Wringham, a righteous Calvinist certain that he numbers among the Elect of God. A son, George, is born of the match. He is a generous, warmhearted, aristocratic young man. Another son, privately disowned though publicly acknowledged by the laird, is borne by the mother and is given the name of the minister. When this son, Robert, is eighteen, his minister foster-father (and implied father-in-the-flesh) tells him that he, too, numbers among the Elect. Shortly thereafter the righteous young Robert sees his double, whom we are led to understand is Satan in masquerade, and is tempted to perform certain crimes by this double and duplicitous friend whom Robert idolizes. For practice, as it were, he kills a good minister. Then begin the machinations of haunting and finally murdering his brother George. Later on, after becoming laird of Dalchastel upon the death of the old laird, Robert commits a number of other crimes. They include murdering his mother and his sweetheart, though Robert professes he has no recollection of doing these latter deeds (which seem to have been performed during fugue periods). Finally driven from his lands, Robert commits suicide, believing himself—as he reveals in the memoirs which constitute the second portion of the novel—a "justified" sinner to the last, that is, justified in the dogmatic sense of the term (the doctrine of justification by faith alone as opposed to good works).

The devil-double is an obvious projection of Robert's evil inner impulses, which are released from the bonds of conscience when the minister informs him that he is one of the Elect (and hence beyond good and evil). In a more subtle way, both young Robert and his double function as latent doubles of George in an oedipal matrix, George being the normal, healthy, heterosexually orientated son of a warm, normal, lusty father and Robert being the sick, corrupt, homosexually oriented son of a cold, doctrinaire, and seemingly prudish father. Robert's matricide can be construed as symbolic incest. The murder of his sweetheart is at once consonant with and contradictory to his self-confessed misogyny: he declares that he despises and abhors "the beauty of women," regarding it as "the greatest snare" to which mankind is subject, but he shows himself capable of obtaining narcissistic satisfaction through a woman's devotion to him: "I felt a sort of indefinite pleasure, an ungracious delight in having a beautiful woman solely at my disposal." While the psychology of the work is much more complex than it appears on the surface, Hogg emphasizes the overt relationship between Robert and his clearcut devil-double for satirical purposes—to the neglect of the covert relationship between Robert and George as complementary parts of the composite son. The characterization of the main figures is crude, and melodrama bulks large in the action of the story, so much so that one can only account for André Gide's unrestrained enthusiasm (in the introduction which he wrote for a recent edition of the book he calls the personification of the Devil in the novel "the most ingenious ever invented") by assuming that the author of a work like *Les Faux-Monnayeurs* entertained a special fondness for the theme of the double. Hogg's really choice touches in the novel, such as the wonderful treatment of local color in the dialect and folk wisdom of the servant class, and his shrewd satire of the doctrines of election, predestination, and so forth, bear little relation to his pedestrian management of the psychological elements of the work.

The novel presents us with the paradox of a study which dwells on the subject of evil, largely in psychological terms, yet fails to involve our emotions deeply because of the way in which evil is accentuated and isolated in a diabolical other self. Just as the principal character projects his malevolent impulses onto his double, thereby disclaiming any responsibility for such impulses, so is the reader easily able to shunt off the guilt he unconsciously shares with the evil protagonist. As a result, the novel does not provide that balanced appeal to the principal parts of the human psyche which Simon O. Lesser regards as characteristic of great fiction [*Fiction and the Unconscious,* 1962]. Hogg's *Justified Sinner* circumvents true involvement of the superego by offering the reader a villain to hang in effigy; hence the manifest doubling tends to undercut rather than support the dramatic effect.

Dostoevsky's *The Double,* on the contrary, is a marked exception to the meretricious effects of decomposition nakedly presented. The intricacy of the narrative line, the complexity of the double figure, the richness of psychological detail, and the ambiguity which pervades all features of the novella enable the reader to respond in a less guarded fashion to the piteous spectacle of a petty, weak, rather obnoxious man who clutches at any straws—including nonexistent ones—in his futile attempt to save himself from humiliation and madness. Enhancing the ambiguity of the work is the inability of the reader to know which of the events depicted actually occur and which are only figments of Golyadkin's autistic and diseased imagination. But the most saving ambiguity stems from the fact that Golyadkin Jr., the double, has no simple, easily discernable value.

The "real" Golyadkin is a dreamer given to creating his triumphs out of the whole cloth of fantasy, whereas the double is a man of action, all of it successful. Golyadkin Sr. is a loner, a queer fellow of schizoid tendencies who has no friends, preferring like the Underground Man whom he so much resembles to cut himself off from society (though he simultaneously yearns to be a part of it) in spite of his doctor's advice that he indulge in amusements, visit friends, and cultivate cheerful company. Golyadkin Jr. is a highly sociable creature with a talent for ingratiating himself with other people. Golyadkin Sr. is insecure, anxious, unsuccessful, inarticulate, and awkward, while Golyadkin Jr. is quite the opposite and takes over Golyadkin Sr.'s position in the bureaucracy with ease by showing a preternatural efficiency. Filled with a sense of unworthiness and insignificance, except when in his rages he endeavors to secure what he believes to be his "rights," Golyadkin Sr. imagines his double has unlimited confidence and self-respect. The irascible, truculent, rebellious Golyadkin Sr., who dotes on his imagined independence and straightforwardness, depicts Golyadkin Jr. as a servile toady and lickspittle, though in fact Golyadkin Sr. is always humble in the presence of his superiors and is much given to the guile and innuendo he claims he hates in others, especially in Golyadkin Jr. Golyadkin Sr. constantly feels humiliated by others and writhes in the embarrassment which he experiences at the hands of his shameless double. Nevertheless, Golyadkin Sr. likes to be haughty and cruel, as he is with his servant, Petrushka, and other inferiors in the social and bureaucratic hierarchies. It is clear that Golyadkin Sr., who entertains a romantic, idealistic attitude toward women, represses his instinctual impulses; he sees his double as a lecher. Golyadkin Sr. professes religious orthodoxy and believes his double to be an agent of the devil. Most significant of all, Golyadkin Sr. believes himself subject to all sorts of conspiracies, his double being his principal and most unrelenting persecutor. In general Golyadkin Jr. combines all the traits and accomplishments Golyadkin Sr. desires, and at the same time the double embodies all those Golyadkin fears or claims to despise.

Why, then, does Golyadkin see his mirror image? The first episode of autoscopy follows Golyadkin's presumptuous attempt to crash the birthday party of the beautiful and socially prominent Klara Olsufyevna and his humiliating ejection from the festivities. Seeing his double offers him an escape. He is "fleeing from his foes, from persecution, from a hailstorm of fillips aimed at him," and looks "as though he wanted to hide somewhere from himself, as though he were trying to run away from himself." The appearance of the double amounts to wish-fulfillment. After first seeing the stranger double, Golyadkin fears him but knows he will see him again: "Oddly enough, he positively desired this meeting, considered it inevitable." Once Golyadkin has conjured up his double he has an explanation for all of his problems. His weakened contact with reality and his feeble ego identity provide grounds for the split. After seeing his double he begins "to doubt his own existence" and pinches himself, as he does repeatedly, to see if he is really "there"—just as a schizophrenic will pinch himself for similar reasons. Early in the story Golyadkin's German doctor advises him in faulty syntax,

"You must a radical change of your entire life have, must, in a certain sense, your character break." We are told that special stress is laid on the word "break." The doctor, who means that he must break with his past seclusive way of life, thereby provides Golyadkin with the suggestion for a quite different kind of "break," one widening his split from reality and totally disintegrating his ego. Yet even though it is easy to understand that Golyadkin's double provides him with an excuse to explain his misfortune, various details of the narration seem on the surface not to have any connection, but are undeniably linked and important. Why is the doctor's role so crucial, turning up as he does in the apartments of his Excellency (the chief bureaucrat) and at the house of Berendeyev, Klara Olsufyevna's father and Mr. Golyadkin's "quondam benefactor"? What were Golyadkin's relations with Karolina Ivanovna, the "German woman" at whose lodgings he used to board? How is it that Golyadkin reasons in this fashion concerning Anton Antonovich, the head clerk: "I'm afraid to trust him; his hair's too gray, and he's tottering with old age"?

Freud's study of Dostoevsky ["Dostoevsky and Parricide"] helps give psychological coherence to these puzzles and nonsequiturs. This essay dwells on Dostoevsky's sadism and masochism; on his unconscious guilt for death wishes against his doctor father, a guilt reinforced by the seeming fulfillment of this childhood wish when Dostoevsky *père* is murdered by his serfs; on Dostoevsky's epilepsy (a disease often linked with autoscopy) as a malady combining discharge of libido in seizures and signifying in those deathlike seizures an identification with the dead parent, the disease being at the same time a punishment for death wishes directed toward the father. It considers also the bisexuality of Dostoevsky's disposition, the feminine side resulting from Dostoevsky's attempt to propitiate the father by his passivity and by winning the father's love through identifying with the mother as a love object of the father. It emphasizes the "hard, violent and cruel" superego Dostoevsky developed on the basis of similar traits in the father. Freud also suggests that Dostoevsky's passive acceptance of largely undeserved punishment at the hands of "the Little Father, the Tsar" amounted to acceptance of punishment for his psychological crime against his real father. Freud sees further evidence of this in Dostoevsky's passive acceptance of an authoritarian God. Though Freud confines his discussion of Dostoevsky's work to *The Brothers Karamazov,* his commentary proves equally revealing when applied to *The Double.*

No overt theme of parricide appears in *The Double;* on the contrary, the protagonist makes repeated declarations of loyalty and submissiveness to authoritarian figures, declarations which are often suspiciously out of context. Several times Golyadkin says that he regards his bureaucratic superiors as fathers. To Andrey Filippovich he states, "I regard my beneficent superior as a father and blindly entrust my fate to him" and to his Excellency, the chief bureaucrat, he plans to declare, "Do not destroy me, I look upon you as my father, do not abandon me . . . save my dignity, my honor, my name . . . save me from a miscreant, a vicious man." He blurts out a similarly couched appeal in his Excellency's chambers only to have Golyadkin Jr. (who by this time has won his Excellency's confidence and been given "special assignments") demand with righteous severity, "Allow me to ask you, in whose presence you are making this explanation? Before whom are you standing, in whose study are you?" The answer, in psychoanalytic terms, is The Father. Almost all of the personages in the story, with the exception of Golyadkin's double, his servant, and the women, are father surrogates. They are old men with an authoritarian manner—including even Gerasimych, the old valet of Olsufy Ivanovich who turns Golyadkin out of doors. Of Olsufy Ivanovich, Golyadkin's "benefactor" and Klara Olsufyevna's father, Golyadkin remarks that he "has, in a sense, been a father to me," so that Golyadkin's humiliating expulsion from the birthday party amounts as well to total rejection by the father. Golyadkin Jr. represents the loved and accepted son that Golyadkin wishes to be. It becomes apparent from the letter which Golyadkin imagines he receives from Klara Olsufyevna that Golyadkin's double has merged in his mind with Vladimir Semyonovich, Klara Olsufyevna's successful suitor, whose promotion to the rank of assessor Golyadkin envies, though he denies it. This promotion, in fact, may possibly precipitate Golyadkin's disorder, for he discusses it with his doctor, Krestyan Ivanovich, at the beginning of the novel. Krestyan Ivanovich, of the same profession as Dostoevsky's father, functions as a key father surrogate in the work, and it is he who condemns Golyadkin to hell or the insane-asylum (it is not clear which) at the end of the story: "Krestyan Ivanovich's answer rang out, stern and terrible as a judge's sentence: 'You will get quarters at public expense, viz. firewood, light, and service, which you don't deserve.' "

In continually protesting his submission to authority Golyadkin protests too much. His unconscious hostility becomes clear, for example, when Anton Antonovich berates him for impudence, saying, "I don't allow anyone to be impudent. I've grown gray in the government service, sir, and I don't allow anyone to be impudent to me in my old age." The charge is just, as is Anton Antonovich's annihilating accusation that Golyadkin has damaged the reputation of both "a wellborn maiden," meaning Klara Olsufyevna, and "that other maiden who, though poor, is of honorable foreign extraction," meaning the German woman. Golyadkin's ambivalence toward women, particularly as sexual objects, need not be explored directly, because it will become understandable by implication in terms of his paranoia.

[In an essay in *Daedalus* 92, No. 2, 1963, Lawrence Kohlberg] challenges Rank's claim that *The Double* offers a classic example of the paranoid state [Otto Rank, *Der Doppelgänger,* 1925], particularly because of the mechanism of projection used, on the grounds that the true paranoid always feels himself completely blameless and never has any awareness of a second half. His argument that Golyadkin and other doppelgänger of Dostoevsky manifest the symptoms of an obsessive-compulsive character, whose separation of selves amounts to a defensive "balancing or undoing" of a force or idea by its opposite, is accurate enough and a valuable formulation but one which does not exclude the presence of paranoid elements, obvious in Golyadkin's delusions of persecution. In fact, the complexity of the double in this work is borne out by the fact that no single nosological label of psychiatry applies to him. But recognition of the presence of elements of the paranoia syndrome helps us to comprehend that Golyadkin Jr. is largely a superego double, embodying variously faults that Golyadkin feels guilty about, punishment for that guilt in the form of persecution, and the ego-ideal elements of the good, submissive, loved son. At the same time he embodies the introjected values and characteristics of the father which come to constitute the superego and hence technically serve as a symbol of the internalized father. Since the father is viewed as an implacable tyrant, so is the double. The homosexual disposition invariably underlying paranoia appears in veiled form in *The Double,* especially in the seductive way Golyadkin Jr. behaves toward Golyadkin Sr., pinching, patting, and kissing him and calling him "darling." This behavior also represents the narcissistic self-love which can be expected wherever we encounter subjective decomposition, a narcissism betrayed early in the novel in Golyadkin's case when the bald, unprepossessing man feels "satisfied" with his image in the mirror. More profound implications of the psychotic's characteristic withdrawal of object-libido into the ego can be seen in the form of Golyadkin's delusions of persecution (a man who feels the entire world to be against him cannot fail to appreciate how important he must be to warrant so much attention) and in his delusions of grandeur, symbolized among other ways in the novel by Golyadkin's aspirations for promotion, romantic love, and acceptance by high bourgeois society.

Yet in spite of the fascination which Golyadkin exerts over the reader, he can never long forget that this man who sees his double is mad, mad in a clinical sort of way which we are not aware of when we hear the wild and whirling words of a Hamlet or the tempestuous lamentations of a Lear. The reader, therefore, inevitably disengages himself to some extent from Golyadkin and his double, all of the ambiguities of the work notwithstanding, in a manner which does not occur when Dostoevsky (and other authors) employ the medium of latent decomposition. (pp. 18-39)

Robert Rogers, "The Mirror Image," in his A Psychoanalytic Study of the Double in Literature, *Wayne State University Press, 1970, pp. 18-39.*

Claire Rosenfield

[*In the excerpt below, Rosenfield investigates the conscious and unconscious mechanisms underlying the use of doubles in nineteenth-century fiction.*]

The *symposium* of Plato has amused us with the comic image that each of us has a Double to whom we were once physically attached. Mistaken identity, the birth and later separation of twins, a god assuming the bodily form of an absent husband—indeed, all the absurd and irrational portrayals of Doubles inherent in the comedies of civilized literature from the *Amphitryon* of Plautus to *The Comedy of Errors* by Shakespeare—have provoked our unthinking laughter. To the sophisticated audiences of the Classical World, the Middle Ages, and the Renaissance, Doubles were either facsimiles, bodily duplicates manipulated to divert us, or allegorized opposites to instruct us. Perhaps not until after the development of the novel, have we been made aware of what primitives have always intuitively known: that duality inspires both terror and awe whether that duality be manifested in a twin birth, or in a man and his shadow, or in one's reflection in water or in a mirror, or in the creation of an artifact resembling the exterior self. Not until Freud revealed the importance of the irrational in man have we been willing to admit the possibility that each of us has within us a second or a shadow self dwelling beside the eminently civilized, eminently rational self, a Double who may at any time assert its anti-social tendencies.

By analyzing superstitions, folk beliefs, and modern literature, Otto Rank has attempted to show the evolution of the Double: that "What we really have in common with our remote ancestors is a *spiritual,* not a primitive self" ["The Double as Immortal Self" in *Beyond Psychology,* 1958]. Frightened by the possible destruction of his ego and the loss of his individuality in death, primitive man created a body-soul which he located in his shadow or his reflection, and which he deemed immortal. His very real dreams provided him with the proof that a soul must exist independent of the body, for in his dreams he saw the souls of the absent, of others who had died, of enemies whom he had killed. Motivated by what Freud has called his "primary narcissism," he could not grant life to others and not to himself. Though his body would die and disintegrate—as had the bodies of the dead he had seen—his soul would survive as his shadow or Double.

> How man came to see the soul in his shadow may be explained by the assumption that he first saw his own image in it, inseparable from himself and yet not only changing in its form but also disappearing at night. It seems to me that this observation of the human shadow disappearing with the fertilizing sun to reappear with its return made it a perfect symbol for the idea of an immortal soul. . . . It is then, in my opinion, not so much the resemblance of the shadow to the self as its appearance and disappearance, its regular return to life, as it were, which made the shadow and symbol of the returning soul still surviving in our spiritual belief in immortality. In the original duality of the soul concept, I am inclined to see the root of man's two endeavors to preserve his self and to maintain the belief in its immortality: religion and psychology. From the belief in a soul of the dead in one form or another sprang all religion; from the belief in the soul of the living, psychology eventually developed.

Possessing this belief in an immortal soul, man was able gradually to develop a personality which seemed to have an essential totality. But, Rank points out, modern literature presents the Double as a symbol not of eternal life but of death, a representation which anticipates the division of the personality into two opposing forces, and a subsequent loss of a sense of identity and continuity in time.

Because the Romantic Movement made the inner life of

man—spontaneity of feeling, imagination, spiritual exploration—fashionable if not respectable, nineteenth century audiences generally accepted works which revealed the two opposing selves within the human personality. But they accepted these only on terms which would not destroy communal or personal complacency, either in folk songs and stories which portrayed a primitive self in which they believed they no longer shared, or in fairy tales written down for children, or in fantasies or mystery stories which titillated the senses without disrupting equanimity. In the romance, a *genre* where by definition the imagination was allowed free play, the hero might lose his shadow as in *The Wonderful History of Peter Schlemihl,* or sell his reflection to the devil as in Hoffmann's "Story of a Lost Reflection." When, however, the reader approached a work in which the disintegration of the personality was plausibly presented, he ignored it as completely as he ignored Melville's *Pierre.* Or else he dismissed it as the work of a monster, as De Vogüé, who introduced Russian literature to France, dismissed Dostoevsky. Dickens' terrifying *Edwin Drood* offered no threat to the mind which had created a defense mechanism almost as satisfactory as the dream work, and called the book a mystery story. And Emily Brontë, perhaps unwittingly, made her amoral, passionate fictional world palatable by sifting it through the consciousness of two extraordinarily conventional and imperceptive narrators.

That the motif of the Double should manifest itself so abundantly in the nineteenth century can be explained both culturally and psychologically. The French Revolution betrayed an irrationality in direct proportion to earlier oppression. With the "Rights of Man" came a new emphasis upon the individual. Not only did the Romantic Movement sanction introspection; it also reintroduced into society the collective inheritance of the folk. As I have already noted, the Double or *Doppelgänger* was made initially respectable in romance, fairy tale, and mystery story where repressed fantasies asserted themselves with particular vengeance in extravagant plots. But the novel requires that the opposing selves submit to the canons of plausibility. Therefore, the novelist who consciously or unconsciously exploits psychological Doubles may either juxtapose or duplicate two characters; the one representing the socially acceptable or conventional personality, the other externalizing the free, uninhibited, often criminal self. Conrad's *The Secret Sharer,* Mann's *Doctor Faustus,* Dostoevsky's *The Double* all reveal this pattern. Or he may present two characters who complement each other both physically and psychologically and who together are projections of the crippled or struggling personality of a third character with whom the author is primarily concerned, as in Dostoevsky's *Crime and Punishment* or Melville's *Pierre.* These complementary Doubles may appear in the narrative as simple opposites; what is important is not their contrary natures and descriptions, but the way in which they reveal the loss of identity of the main character. When the passionate, uninhibited self is a woman, she more often than not is dark and the sister or half-sister of the protagonist, thus introducing the suggestion of incest, the most horrific of crimes in Christian culture. Again, the presence of biological Doubles or Twins, in a novel of psychic disintegration can suggest authorial awareness of the problem of inner duality and the subsequent terrors involved.

The first novelist to use duality consciously in order to reveal the mental struggles of his characters was Goethe. Because he was contemplating a Faust play before writing *Wilhelm Meister's Apprenticeship,* the Double motif in the former may illuminate authorial intention in the latter. What Mephistopheles mirrors in the drama is the demonic forces within the titanic Faust himself. This dynamic tension between good and evil does not appear overtly in the novel, where the young Wilhelm seeks harmony through active humanism. Part of his search for personal fulfillment involves the search for a wife. The various women he encounters seem to him but fragmentary parts of himself; many of them—actresses—appear to him first dressed as boys, playing a male role. Even the mysterious Mignon, who refuses to dress like a girl and who reveals a diabolic disorder which he has never experienced, momentarily excites his orderly soul: "He longed to incorporate this forsaken being within his own heart, to take her in his arms, and with a father's love to awaken in her the joy of existence." Finally, he realizes totality in his union with Natalie, the "beautiful soul" with whom he reconciles all contraries. The modern disintegration of the self, on the other hand, is seen in the story of Mignon's parents, Sperata and Augustin, the brother and sister who unknowingly commit incest. Mignon, whose frantic artistry and behavior exist within the realm of madness, duplicates in her gradual decline the previous degradation of her parents. Because Goethe achieved a balance between the classic and romantic aspects of his own life and nature, he could construct both a positive representation of harmony and a negative picture of personality decay; few other novelists, however, were able to do the same.

When the reader confronts a novelist like Emily Brontë, all presuppositions about conscious creation disappear. So intimate was she with the projections of her own unconscious life that she may have been only intuitively aware that Cathy and Heathcliff are themselves exact Doubles differing in sex alone, and that each possesses a complementary self in his choice of a mate. Both are dark; both are accustomed to roam freely over the moors; both are proud and headstrong; both carry into maturity an energy and violence which normally is pushed into the buried self by conventional society. Both realize their similar natures. Cathy, when deciding to marry Edgar Linton, explains why she cannot forsake Heathcliff:

> "My love for Heathcliff resembles the eternal rocks beneath—a source of little visible delight, but necessary. . . . I *am* Heathcliff—he's always, always in my mind—not as a pleasure, any more than I am always a pleasure to myself—but as my own being—so, don't talk of our separation again—it is impracticable; and. . . .

When dying she claims " 'That is not *my* Heathcliff. I shall love mine yet; and take him with me—he's in my soul.' " To Heathcliff Cathy is not merely a second self but also his immortal soul. It is a soul which he has destroyed, yet one which he hopes will return to haunt him.

> The murdered *do* haunt their murderers. I be-

> lieve—I know that ghosts *have* wandered on earth. Be with me always—take any form—drive me mad! only *do* not leave me in this abyss where I cannot find you! Oh God! it is unutterable! I *cannot* live without my life! I *cannot* live without my soul!

Cathy marries the blond and pallid Edgar, hoping to reconcile the refined, conventional, civilized society of the Lintons and the unconscious, passionate, natural world of childhood; she, in other words, "adopt[s] a double character without exactly intending to deceive any one." Heathcliff marries the blond and pallid Isabella not that the two worlds may coexist but rather that the world of the Lintons may be destroyed by his strength. Cathy wills her death when she discovers that she cannot reconcile these divided selves; and yet, alone, she and Heathcliff are incomplete selves. Heathcliff wills his death when he discovers that the biological entity, the child, does combine within itself those qualities which could not join within the psychological Doubles, that young Cathy does possess sweetness to tame her mother's wildness, that Hareton cannot be entirely brutalized. Cathy and Heathcliff can exist only in the world of childhood or death where capacity for freedom is infinite, where the claims of others do not impinge upon the self. The amoral landscape of *Wuthering Heights,* moreover, could only be made *respectable* by being filtered through the sensibilities of two narrators in whom Victorian mores have been so internalized that the outlaw self is completely misunderstood because completely submerged.

That Melville in *Pierre* was aware of the essential oppositions which he establishes between Lucy and Isabel, between the blond, socially sanctioned, spiritual creature and the dark, desirable, sexually forbidden half-sister Isabel, is undeniable. What he probably did not realize is the fact that these apparently conventional opposites are Doubles in the psychological sense: together they externalize the total personality Pierre must experience as an artist; separately, the disintegration he chose as a man. Professor Henry Murray is right in claiming [in his introduction to the 1949 Hendricks House edition of *Pierre*] that only Isabel, for whom Pierre thinks he possesses fraternal compassion but to whom he is really sexually attracted, can rescue him from the narrow maternal paradise which confines him. She alone can provide him with the tragic awareness necessary to manhood. Her mysterious force suggests both madness, a longing for death, and the world of the unconscious with which society has never allowed Pierre to be troubled. In abandoning the acceptable Lucy for the desirable Isabel, he deserts the God of his Puritan fathers and his community. Once his choice is made, however, he is unable to bear the consequences of his incest, of his discovery of the abyss, of the revelation that his new God is his society's devil. When the light, rational world once more collides with his irrational one, when his now avowed "good angel" appears in the form of Lucy, Pierre has already begun to shun Isabel and her potentially tragic self as he had earlier shunned Lucy. Ironically, Lucy wishes to live as a sister with the couple whom she believes are husband and wife; but she cannot be made to live with the anarchy of incest. Finally, Pierre must die, a poor artist for the same reason he is an incomplete man: he is unable to balance the creative and destructive forces within himself.

In 1845, Charles Dickens parodied a "romance" in "Count Ludwig," a comic tale in which the Double theme is disguised by the narrative distortions. Here are no visible threats to the ego. At the end of his career in 1870 he began but never finished *The Mystery of Edwin Drood,* in which the disguised Double is less fantastic, more realistic. Choirmaster Jack Jasper is torn between his genuine devotion to his nephew and his love of that nephew's betrothed, between the respectable boredom of his occupation and his unconscious striving. His antisocial impulses reveal themselves in his predilection for opium, in his habitual appearances in the night world, and in his rambles through the privacy of the graveyard. Since the novel was never finished, we can only conjecture that Jasper's eventual disintegration culminates in the murder (or, at least, the abduction) of that nephew, a "good self." Though on a narrative level Jasper is Edwin's guardian; on a symbolic level, Edwin is the guardian angel whom Jasper dispatches. Henceforth, the forbidden dominates Jasper's behavior: he is described as possessing "destructive power"; he seems "an older devil." Dickens' conscious intention becomes obvious when we see that the novel contains two sets of biological Doubles: the "lovers" Edwin and Rosa who by agreement become like brother and sister, and the strange twins Neville and Helena Landless who are direct opposites. While the former are English and fair, the latter are exceedingly dark, foreign, "land less"; there is "something untamed about them both." When Neville is accused of Edwin's murder, one feels that his situation and physical characteristics alone rather than any intrinsic passion for the demonic mark him as an unconscious, criminal force and that Dickens is yielding to the romantic stereotype. Although these conventionalized Doubles add to the intricacies of the Dickensian plot, the dramatic tensions which exist within the divided soul of Jack Jasper, at once struggling for some balance and sinking deeper and deeper into the underground of the irrational, are the real energizing force of the novel.

Dostoevsky, whatever his own fears might have been, was sufficiently sensible of the tyranny of his unconscious to respond to the motif of the divided self. Throughout his career he consciously wrought variations on this theme. In 1874 in *A Raw Youth* Versilov actually describes his visual hallucination, his apparent perception which possesses no object. Although the narrator, Versilov's illegitimate son Arkady, finally gives the negative clinical diagnosis of madness to his father's disordered state, he himself accepts only the less damning idea of a split between the real man and his ego ideal.

> What is a second self, exactly? The second self, according to a medical book written by an expert that I purposely read afterward, is nothing else than the first stage of serious mental derangement, which may lead to something very bad. And in the scene at my Mother's, Versilov himself had with strange frankness described the "duality" of his will and feelings. But I repeat again, . . . that scene at Mother's and that bro-

ken ikon were undoubtedly partly due to the influence of a real "second self."

In *The Double,* Golyadkin, before the appearance of a Mr. Golyadkin Junior, evidences most of the symptoms of a developing split personality. He acts, as it were, because of a perverse inner compulsion which he cannot control. The appearance of Mr. Golyadkin Junior, who is "a double in every respect," reinforces all the protagonist's insecurities, for the new Mr. Golyadkin is not an "insect" or a "rag"; though physically similar, he possesses all those qualities for advancement—self-possession, wit, the power of decision—which the original Mr. Golyadkin lacks. Persecuted by this Double, Golyadkin Senior grows more indecisive and declines finally into madness. While he is being carried to an asylum by the doctor he had earlier consulted, he imagines that he is confronted in the darkness by this doctor's infernal presence whose eyes glitter in "hellish glee."

In Conrad's *The Secret Sharer* and *Heart of Darkness,* a bodily Double is present whose outlaw freedom is evidence for the narrator and the reader that even the most rational man possesses a dual nature, that no man is above the threat of the irrational. As Albert J. Guerard has pointed out [in his Introduction to the 1961 American Library edition of *Heart of Darkness* and *The Secret Sharer*], both Marlow and the young captain must "come to know themselves . . . , must recognize their own potential criminality and test their own resources, *must travel through Kurtz* and *Leggatt,* before they will be capable of manhood. . . . " In both short novels the actual journeys which the two narrators take "exploit the ancient myth or archetypal experience of the 'night journey,' of the provisional descent into the primitive and unconscious sources of being." The final choice each makes symbolizes the choice between internal division or personal coherence. The young captain hides the murderer Leggatt with whom he identifies himself even though this new allegiance may mean his isolation from a crew and a command which he does not know, may foster irresponsibility to his fellow men. Surely the repeated use of such phrases as "the secret sharer of my cabin," "my secret double" indicates Conrad's intentional pursuit of the *Doppelgänger* motif. Marlow's journey into the Congo for Kurtz is also a journey into the recesses of the mind; the actual jungle and its darkness mirror the intricacies of the internal landscape. When Marlow pursues a crawling Kurtz driven to the last extremity of madness, he describes him as "that Shadow," "the nightmare of my choice," "the shade." Both the captain and Marlow emerge from their visions of criminal freedom. In so far as the hero does return from the underworld of his being and is able to use his new knowledge for the benefit of his fellow men—as do the captain and Marlow—the Double novel reveals not a disintegration of the personality but a reintegration, a recognition of the necessary balance between order and freedom. (pp. 326-33)

Double novels become Devil novels in a social context which places a negative value upon what is free and uninhibited. Freud states that psychologically, the Devil is simply the projection into the external world of man's buried instinctual life ["Neurosis of Demoniacal Possession, *Collected Papers,* 1959]. But Hebraic-Christian mythology, not Freud, assigned the pejorative word "evil" to that projection. Primitive religions made no distinction between gods and devils; the gods were both worshipped and feared. According to Rank, the original Double, when it was insurance against the destruction of the self, was a guardian angel; later it "appears as precisely the opposite, a reminder of the individual's mortality, indeed the announcer of death itself" ["The Double as Immortal Self"]. The Church, which used the belief in immortality as a means of distributing rewards and punishments, created the Devil as we know him today and the destructive concept of the Double. Poe's "William Wilson" is one of the few examples in which the whispering Double appears as a "guardian angel" seeking to annul the evil of the narrator.

In *The Private Memoirs and Confessions of a Justified Sinner,* one of the clearest examples of the Devil Novel, James Hogg has skillfully juxtaposed primitive superstition, diabolism, religious fanaticism, and psychic disintegration in a perilous equilibrium which threatens constantly to dissolve. The bodily Doubles are two brothers: George Colwan, the legitimate heir of the gay laird of Dalcastle who has a fanatic wife; and Robert Wringhim, the son of that wife and her spiritual guide. Usually, the Double-Devil Novel makes the "free" self the evil self. To promote Hogg's religious satire, however, the evil brother is not the gay, spontaneous, fun-loving George, who has instinctive moral goodness, but the son of Wringhim who is obsessed with his belief in absolute predestination, that salvation depends upon the grace of God alone. Moreover, he believes that he is one of God's elect and, in the name of that election but actually because of a classic split personality, he commits the most criminal acts, including the murder of his own brother. The novel's formal structure reproduces the double motif: the first part purports to be an objective account of "traditionary facts," using the third person point of view of an editor who is not James Hogg; the second part is the private memoirs of Robert Wringhim.

In the second part, the extent of Robert's madness is finally ascertained. In these confessions we see that all Robert's evil acts are sanctioned by his "friend" who he does not realize is the Devil until it is too late. Now demonology bows to pathology. Is his friend simply a projection of his mental aberration and a manifestation of his disorder? Not only is he completely driven by his belief in his own divine justification, but he reveals several psychotic symptoms. He hates women; he suffers from some nervous disease which he attributes to witchcraft.

> Immediately after this I was seized with a strange distemper, which neither my friends nor physicians could comprehend, and it confined me to my chamber for many days; but I knew, myself, that I was bewitched, and suspected my father's reputed concubine of the deed. I told my fears to my reverend protector, who hesitated concerning them, but I knew by his words and looks that he was conscious I was right. I generally conceived myself to be two people. When I lay in bed, I deemed there were two of us in it; when I sat up I always beheld another person, and always in the same position from the place

> where I sat or stood, which was about three paces off me towards my left side. It mattered not how many or how few were present: this my second self was sure to be present in his place, and this occasioned a confusion in all my words and ideas that utterly astounded my friends, who all declared that, instead of being deranged in my intellect, they had never heard my conversation manifest so much energy or sublimity of conception; but, for all that, over the singular delusion that I was two persons my reasoning faculties had no power. The most perverse part of it was that I rarely conceived *myself* to be any of the two persons. I thought for the most part that my companion was one of them, and my brother the other; and I found that, to be obliged to speak and answer in the character of another man, was a most awkward business in the long run.

In the end Robert accepts the idea of the demonic because, believing in an external moral order, he cannot accept any other explanation. "To be in a state of consciousness and unconsciousness, at the same time, in the same body and same spirit, was impossible." Only in very few instances, however, are the events unexplainable in psychological terms.

In the twentieth century the author's intentional use of the *Doppelgänger* is rarely in doubt. The rapid rise of Freudian psychology as a discipline and the gradual decline of the influence of religion as an absolute external sanction have determined the Devil's role in the Double novel. When inner duality is externalized as a Devil, that Devil is clearly a hallucination. After all, the *diabolus ex machina* is too naïve for modern taste; not so the *diabolus ex capite.* Or else realistic characters, by assuming traditional demonic attributes, symbolize the illicit freedom of unconscious processes. (pp. 334-36)

Claire Rosenfield, "The Shadow Within: The Conscious and Unconscious Use of the Double," in Daedalus: Journal of the American Academy of Arts and Sciences, *Vol. 92, No. 2, Spring, 1963, pp. 326-44.*

T. E. Apter

[*In the following excerpt, Apter examines the double theme from a psychoanalytic viewpoint.*]

The most common notion of the divided self, or of the double self, is the division between the good and the bad self. This division is remarked upon by Plato in the *Symposium,* and by St. Paul; it is at the root, too, of the plea not to lead us into temptation, for the assumption is that an evil self is ready, given appropriate circumstances, to emerge. R. L. Stevenson's *The Strange Case of Dr Jekyll and Mr Hyde* (1886) makes use of this assumption. A doctor who has had to suppress his more reckless and indulgent impulses on behalf of his career, devises a medicine which, he believes, will release his animalistic nature. The mixture works, and Dr Jekyll becomes Mr Hyde, free to enjoy the pleasures a respected member of society must deny himself: Mr Hyde becomes a front for Dr Jekyll's worse self. The change in character involves such a metamorphosis of appearance that the former cannot be recognised in the latter. Mr Hyde is shorter, and younger than Dr Jekyll, because (Jekyll presumes) Hyde has not lived as long as Jekyll; but these traits also link him to a satyr. Furthermore, in Hyde's appearance there is a deformity that all perceive but none identifies. He bears an aura of distaste and horror, which Jekyll diagnoses as others' unwelcome recognition of affinity.

Jekyll discovers that the creation (or release) of Hyde makes it impossible to keep his unacceptable impulses hidden. He had hoped to save his reputation while lust and anger had a heyday, but he failed to realise that society would not countenance Hyde in any form. Society will execute Hyde, and therefore, to save himself, Hyde must return to the form of Jekyll. But hidden impulses, once released, are out of control. Jekyll spontaneously reverts to Hyde, and the medicine eventually can no longer bring him back to his former self—because, he presumes, the original ingredients contained an unknown impurity which alone was effective.

It is Jekyll's pride, his belief that he can both enjoy and control his impulses, that leads to his destruction. Pentheus, too, in Euripides' *The Bacchae,* is destroyed by Dionysus and his followers because he proudly denies their status. In Hans Werner Henze's *The Bassarids* (libretto by Auden and Kallman) the notion of *hubris* is substituted by that of repression: Pentheus is destroyed by the Bacchae because he denies his affinity to them. Jekyll, however, does not deny his own wildness; he tries to find a way to avoid controlling it. Unlike Oscar Wilde's Dorian Gray, Jekyll cannot hide the marks of his crimes away in an attic, for Hyde functions independently, his own proud release mocking Jekyll's proud control.

Poe's 'William Wilson' (1839) divides the good and evil self into two different people who bear the same name, and who, at least in the narrator's mind, have not only disturbingly similar features but also an insidious affinity, so that the narrator's namesake acts as his controlling conscience—a relationship which is uncanny because it is a separate person, not Wilson's own conscience, who interferes with his dishonesty and lechery. Poe's tale is far less satisfactory than Stevenson's. The drama consists of a series of surprises and frustrations, increasing until the narrator finally murders his double. In doing so, he murders all hope of life or Heaven; but there is not, as there is in *The Strange Case of Dr Jekyll and Mr Hyde,* a drama which investigates the need for conscience and for control. As is usually the case with Poe's work, the tale is left to be filled in by the psychoanalytic interpreter. 'William Wilson' can be read as a parable about the id and the super-ego, but it offers no enlightenment on the tension between the two. The fact that it is amenable to such a reading stems from its shallowness, not its profundity.

The double theme is widely discussed in psychoanalytic theory and is explained in various ways. Melanie Klein sees the double as the product of projective identification: a person splits off from himself and ascribes to another those features which he denies as belonging to himself; but because he still unconsciously recognises the projected characteristics as his own, he identifies himself with the other. Thus Klein offers a psychodynamic model in which the mental acrobatics described are doomed to failure, since failure is built into the model: the projected features return home through identification and the attempted denial is ineffective.

Freud's most general analysis of the double theme is closer to the notion of the double as a product of the division between the good and bad self. The ego-ideal, which he eventually reformulated as part of the super-ego, is a psychic structure built up in accord with patterns of authority experienced in the people around the child. At this point Klein's projective identification may be employed to explain the various forms the double may assume: it emerges as the ego aligns itself with the super-ego and projects its worst impulses outwards, in which case the evil tempter is the double of a self that has been denied by this mental mechanism. On the other hand, the ego may align itself with the id, so that the projected figure (as in 'William Wilson') is the super-ego, the figure of conscience and authority. (pp. 48-50)

The obvious kinship the double theme has to that of two different personality types within an individual is a result of the fact that the double of one's self implies a tension between the self and the double; the presence of the double challenges the self 's existence; it is initially parasitic upon the self, and its aim is to destroy or displace the original self. Otto Rank traces, in psychoanalytic terms, the development of this theme ['Der Doppelgänger,' *Imago,* 1914]. Originally, in German folklore, the appearance of the double was an omen of death, since it represented one's ghost. Rank believed that this double figure was derived from an earlier, and more comforting, image—that of the soul which survives death. This image stems from narcissism: the libido returns to its initial object—the self and body—when disappointment and frustration are encountered in reality; thus, when faced with the prospect of death, the libido returns to the self, denying the possibility of annihilation. Hostility towards one's double arises from ambivalent feelings towards the self (which, Rank suggests, may be regarded as a defence reaction to narcissism), though the hatred of the double, and its persecutory character, indicate a connection with the sibling complex—the brother presents a rival for the mother's love.

Though the double initially emerged as a protection against extinction of the ego, it is associated with death and therefore represents impending death. It is a theme linked to the frustration of love, or to the destruction of a woman, because narcissism, when seriously threatened (for example, by rejection) becomes more active in compensation, and the double emerges. Freud endorses Rank's analysis: 'This invention of doubling as a preservation against extinction has its counterpart in the language of dreams, which is fond of representing castration by a doubling or multiplication of a genital symbol.' When primary narcissism is superseded, the double takes on its terrifying aspect and proceeds to develop apart from its narcissistic origins. The double represents a splitting-off of the mind's self-criticism so that it shadows its twin and often knows, even without apparent observation, what the original is doing or thinking. Also connected to the double concept, or in some cases represented by the double, are the many possible futures, or selves, to which one clings in fantasy (i.e., desire), 'all the strivings of the ego which adverse external circumstances have crushed, and all our suppressed acts of volition which nourish in us the illusion of Free Will.' The uncanniness of the double theme fits Freud's theory of the uncanny because the double dates back to an early mental stage when it bore an affectionate aspect; but the fact that it has been repressed, and that the double theme re-arouses the discarded fantasy, makes the activation of the theme terrifying.

Schubert's song (poem by Heine) 'Der Doppelgänger' (1828) can be read as a supremely concise realisation of Rank's thesis. The speaker is aghast to see his double standing by the window of his former beloved's house: the chilling and despairing music might be a product of the speaker's annihilation through loss of the love object: he identifies himself with the woman's present lover to mitigate his jealousy, yet the double, originally constructed as a defence, assumes the role of a harbinger of death. Indeed, the speaker's double does foretell his death, or the annihilation of the ego, in so far as it defends against (and thus admits the threat of) such annihilation. However, an interpretation like this, one directed and completed by psychoanalytic theories, is closer to a producer's interpretation of a play or opera which 'realises' the material than to a critic's interpretation which must draw a more definite line between the interesting and the valid. What we are given by the psychoanalyst is one possible framework for the emergence of the song, but this deteriorates to an idiosyncratic supposition when the woman (as she would in Rank's theory) is identified with the mother. (pp. 51-2)

Freud and Rank offer highly interesting formulations of the double, but literary themes range so far from the psychoanalytic explanations, which are themselves loosely thrown together (the narcissistic explanation gives way to an explanation in terms of a self-critical faculty) that the suggestion of analysis, as in the case of Freud's definition of the uncanny, is illusory. What we have from them is a provocative handful of double stories to be valued alongside other double tales, not to be seen as explanations of them.

E. T. A. Hoffmann's *The Devil's Elixirs* (1816) is a remarkable and utterly confusing novel in which the double theme is compounded by similar appearance, telepathy, including desire and guilt, and a splitting-up of motive and action between two characters who temporarily fuse and form a single but highly unstable personality. It might be viewed as a Gothic counterpart to *The Comedy of Errors* except that Hoffmann lacks Shakespeare's exuberantly deft manipulation of the material. The proffered explanations with which the novel concludes do not enlighten, but indeed, as Freud says, completely bewilder the reader. Terror and confusion are at the root of the drama, not coincidence and mistakes. *The Devil's Elixirs* might be placed in the picaresque tradition, for the protagonist endures many reversals of fortune, including narrow escapes from punishment and murder, and enjoys easily gained wealth and love; but Hoffmann's novel has none of the light-hearted energy of the picaresque novel, and the protagonist proceeds—or rather is compelled—upon his way not by his wits but by fate's design.

The starting point for the wayward plot is the father's sins which are visited upon his offspring. The protagonist, the Capuchin monk Medardus, is led from a holy path by lust and pride. He tries to suppress his lust by retreating to a monastery, but he is sent out to the world again, where he commits murder, among other crimes. Finally, he is saved when the woman who has inspired his lust takes holy vows, though she is murdered immediately by Medardus's double. Hoffmann's story belongs to the medieval tradition from which Thomas Mann derived the irony of *The Holy Sinner.* For in spite of Hoffmann's seriousness the repentance he depicts is grotesque, based upon a sickly, sensuous devotion, and the guilt depicted is hysterical, totally self-regarding, without any glimmer of moral perception.

The Devil's Elixirs does not actually deal with moral transgression, however concerned with it the characters may be. The novel shows the link between the double theme and the demonic, though the demon's horror rests not in his immorality but in his power to confound self-understanding and self-direction. Medardus's life is, from its beginning, spoiled. The theme of the visitation of the father's sins upon the children is Hoffmann's excuse for

Self-portrait of E.T.A. Hoffmann.

presenting a person whose thoughts, desires and actions are subject to laws which appear to be far removed from normal human functioning. Medardus's aggression is uncontrolled, not merely in the sense of being unsuppressed, but also in the sense of being undirected—at least by himself. In waking Victor (who, unknown to him, is his brother and his double in appearance) as he lies at the edge of the precipice, Medardus means to save him, yet instead precipitates his fall into the gorge. Here he causes harm without reason and, when he actually does intend to be aggressive to some degree, his aggression is effective in the highest degree. Thus in defending himself against Aurelia's brother, he strangles him. Nor can he protect himself from his own anger, which viciously works against the attainment of his desires. Medardus wants to marry Aurelia—that is the motivation of the main events of his life—and yet he is appalled at the idea of her being his wife. His desire for the woman he idealises becomes a desire to denigrate her, which he will do in marrying her, since in marrying he will break his holy vows, thereby involving her in a sacrilege. Haphazardly, but relentlessly, Hoffmann shows the self nervously jumping away from itself, defeating its own interests and wishes at any given point, but in defiance of any system or rationale.

One could, of course, construct from the story a psychoanalytic hypothesis: Medardus, deprived of his father and believing that his father committed some terrible deed, identifies himself with his father to deny the deprivation and, either to justify his sense of guilt or to exhibit his identification with his father, commits terrible deeds himself. This hypothesis, however, leaves out of account the dynamic self-abuse, terror, love and hatred (in Freud's theory of the melancholic's self-abuse, the abuse is pleasurable, since it is directed not towards the self but towards the person with whom the ego is now identified) that run throughout the novel, and which appear acutely in the following passage. Medardus, posing as a Polish nobleman, but also identified as Count Victor, has just been cleared of murder charges brought against him, for he is now believed not to be Medardus: the mad monk, who is really Count Victor, is now thought to be Medardus. Aurelia has confessed her love to Leonard, as she did earlier to Medardus, and they are about to marry. Medardus narrates the events:

> One of the Prince's servants announced that the company was ready to receive us. Aurelia quickly drew on her gloves, and I took her arm. Then the chambermaid suddenly noticed that Aurelia's hair had become disarranged, and hastened away to fetch some hair-pins. The delay seemed to disturb her. As we waited by the door, there was a dull rumbling in the street outside, raucous voices shouted and the noise was heard of a heavy cart, rattling slowly by. I hurried to the window. In front of the palace stood an open cart driven by the hangman's servant. Sitting backwards in it was the monk, in front of whom stood a Capuchin praying aloud with him. The monk was disfigured by a deathly pallor and an unkempt beard, but the features of the gruesome double were only too plain. Crowds were thronging round the cart, and as it moved off he

turned his terrible eyes upon me, laughing and howling:

'Bridegroom! Bridegroom! Come on to the roof! Up there we will fight with each other, and the one who pushes the other over will become king, and be able to drink blood!'

'Horrible wretch!' I screamed. 'What do you want with me?'

Aurelia flung her arms round me and tore me away from the window, crying:

'O Holy Virgin! They are leading Medardus, my brother's murderer, to his death! Leonard! Oh, Leonard!'

The demons of hell raged within me, and I seized her in fury.

'Ha, ha, ha! Mad foolish woman! I—I am Medardus! It is I who am your lover, your betrothed—I who am your brother's murderer! You, who are the bride of a monk, will you snivel and whine so that destruction will fall on your bridegroom's head? Ho, ho, ho! I am king and shall drink your blood!'

I let her fall to the floor, drew out my knife and stabbed at her. A fountain of blood gushed over my hand. I rushed down the staircase and fought my way through the crowd to the cart. Seizing the monk, I tore him from his seat. I felt myself gripped from behind, and stabbed about me with my knife. Wrenching myself free, I jumped away but the mob came after me. I felt a wound in my side, but with my knife in my right hand, and dealing powerful blows with my left, I fought my way to the nearby wall of the park and vaulted over it with a tremendous leap.

'Murderer! Murderer! Stop!' shouted voices behind me. I heard them preparing to burst open the gate to the park. I rushed on without stopping. I came to the broad moat which separated the park from the forest until I sank exhausted under a tree.

When I recovered my senses, it was already dark. My only thought was to flee like a hunted beast. I got up but hardly had I moved away when a man sprang out of the bushes and jumped on to my back, clinging to my neck. In vain I tried to shake him off. I threw myself on the ground, jammed my back against the tree, but all to no avail. He cackled and laughed mockingly. Then the moon broke brightly through the black pine-trees, and the pallid, hideous face of the monk, the supposed Medardus, my double, stared at me with glassy eyes as it had done in the cart.

'Hee, hee, hee! Hee, hee, hee! Little Brother! I . . . am . . . al-ways . . . with . . . you, will . . . not . . . leave . . . you. Can-not . . . run . . . like . . . you. Must . . . must . . . carry . . . me. Have . . . come . . . from . . . the . . . the . . . gal-lows. Wanted . . . to . . . to . . . break . . . me . . . on . . . on . . . the . . . wheel. Hee, hee!'

The horrible spectre laughed and howled. With the strength of wild terror I leapt up like a tiger in the stranglehold of a python, crashing against trees and rocks so as, if not to kill him, at least to wound him so severely that he would be forced to let me go. But he laughed all the more hysterically, and I was the one who received the wounds. I tried to free his hands which were locked under my chin, but he threatened to choke me.

At last, after a fit of frenzy, he suddenly jumped off. I had only to run a few yards when he jumped on me again, cackling and laughing, and stuttering those terrible words. Again that struggle in wild rage—again free—again in the grip of a hideous monster.

I cannot say how long I fled through the dark forest, pursued by my double. It seemed an eternity before I ate or drank anything. Of one vivid moment, however, I still have a clear impression: I had just succeeded in throwing him off, when a bright light shone through the forest I heard a monastery bell tolling the matins.

'I have murdered Aurelia!' At this thought the icy arms of death closed around me, and I sank unconscious to the ground.

The references to the Oedipal situation—the challenge of one brother to the other, whereupon one shall drink blood (i.e., spill one's own blood, the blood of the father in castration) and be king (father), the mockery of him as bridegroom before he accepts the challenge—are glaringly obvious because of Freud's persuasive genius, not because of anything we can find in the tale. The disarranged hair here, and elsewhere in the novel, where the arrangement of hair is crucial to Medardus's disguise and to the strange role the barber plays in the events, also stands out like a sore thumb in need of a psychoanalytic bandage; but the obvious madness in the writing, which with its ellipses of motive and meaning, invites psychoanalytic interpretation, provides other more satisfying, even if less complete, indications of meaning.

Medardus has not stabbed Aurelia: even though she was lying prostrate when he attacked her, he did not strike her, but himself. In trying to injure the awful pursuer, he only manages to injure himself. This is a phantom double, a mean, diabolical attacker—no subsequent explanation of Victor's mental state or motive can deny his splendid, fantastical status. Hoffmann shows the double as a thief, as obsession itself is a thief, stealing any possible integration of thought and purpose. The double is the arch-interferer, the arch-reducer, depriving Medardus of all other motives save the compulsion to escape him. The double here is not the bad self versus the good self, but rather an impediment to any self at all. Victor at times enacts Medardus's worst desires, which Medardus himself manages to restrain—Victor stabs Aurelia, who has just taken her vows, at the very moment Medardus has triumphed over the outrage at his loss of the woman—but Victor also at times takes on Medardus's guilt, suffering hysterically from it, and then at other times taunts Medardus as a diabolic conscience. The double here portrays total disintegration.

Despite the flaws of *The Devil's Elixirs,* despite the awkward handling of the religious themes, which really serve only as a background to the horror story, despite the highly unsatisfactory concluding 'explanations' of events, and despite the jolting discontinuity of purpose, *The Devil's Elixirs* has a vigorous and uncanny power, able to suggest issues beyond psychoanalysis. For whatever diagnosis—either of Medardus or Hoffmann—could place the diverse material into a pattern, the novel succeeds in portraying the terrifying instability of the self and the absurd drama of disintegration. This is not merely to say that Hoffmann depicts what it is like to be mad, while psychoanalytic theory describes the mechanisms of madness, for Hoffmann's presentation of the feelings of madness challenges the psychoanalytic model of the double theme in terms of a structured psyche divided within itself; or, rather, Hoffmann reminds us that the structured model itself is a fiction of the same kind as the double story drawn up from volatile and elusive material. *The Devil's Elixirs* defies the assumption, common both to double stories in literature and to double stories in psychoanalytic theory, that the divisions can be identified, that the warring factions have stable aims and comprehensible desires, that indeed the double theme is like a division between two different people. Whereas most double stories indicate the similarities between self-conflicts and interpersonal conflicts, Hoffmann insists upon the differences.

The panicky movement of the plot treads a very delicate balance between mirroring artistically the panic within the self and exhibiting, neurotically, symptoms of such panic. Yet it is fantasy's prerogative to tread this line unsteadily.

Forty years before the publication of *The Strange Case of Dr Jekyll and Mr Hyde* Dostoevsky's *The Double* was published (1846). This is the finest work on the double theme, though, as in *The Devil's Elixirs,* the proliferation of the protagonist's fears becomes a proliferation and fragmentation of themes. Whereas Hoffmann's tale deals with the double's annihilating effect as a breakdown of normal connections between desire and action, intention and effect, even between thought and the thinker, Dostoevsky shows annihilation to be the effect of rejection and redundancy. Golyadkin registers seriously and accurately his colleagues' and acquaintances' attitudes towards him, and his sensitivity to objective self-assessment is disastrous. Medardus on the other hand is merely a subject for confusion. He has little within the normal concept of a self and thus the acts he performs are not clearly assignable to an integrated person or character. Hoffmann's material is nearly impossibly elusive, and though he was able to offer a sketch of original horror, he could not give his fantasy its essential logical or psychological substance.

The Double is sub-titled *A Poem of St Petersburg,* indicating the conditions from which Golyadkin's madness arises. As in any fantasy, the schematic control essential to allegory is ruled out, yet the petty and secular take on a hieratic aspect from Golyadkin's respect which becomes the basis of his defeat.

The story itself is fairly simple. Golyadkin, a Titular Councillor in the Russian civil service (ranking ninth in a hierarchy of fourteen) attends a party to which he is not invited. After attempting to court the daughter of the house, he is thrown out. On his way home he meets someone who, presumably, is his double. At work the following day he meets the double again. Initially the second Golyadkin is friendly to the first Golyadkin and seems grateful for his help; but gradually the replicated self usurps Golyadkin's work and encourages people to mock him. Golyadkin receives a letter from the young woman he had tried to court, in which she proposes they elope. As he waits for her in the courtyard, he is attacked by a crowd of people and then abducted by his physician (presumably to some prison or madhouse) while the double skips gleefully behind the departing carriage.

Despite the relatively simple narrative it is nearly impossible to give a straightforward account of the story. It is presented from the real Golyadkin's viewpoint who, even at the opening of the tale, is highly disorganised and confused. It seems as though he believes he is invited to the dinner party and at the same time it seems as though he is persona non grata in that house since the servant claims he has orders not to admit him. Furthermore, prior to encountering his double he reports to his physician that enemies are plotting against him. The doctor is subsequently believed to be involved in the plot, for, as Golyadkin recalls the physician's advice to have his medicine dispensed always at the same pharmacy, he implicates the doctor in a plan to poison him. Golyadkin's former landlady, a German woman with whom his replica now lodges, is also perceived as the agent of attacks upon him as punishment for misbehaviour with women.

The fantastic confusion occurs within a pedestrian, realist setting. Golyadkin wakes and wonders whether he is still dreaming. His wakefulness is confirmed by the seediness and tawdriness of his surroundings. As he looks in the mirror the insignificance of his reflection satisfies him:

> 'It would be a fine thing,' said Mr Golyadkin half aloud, 'it would be a fine thing if something was wrong with me today, if a pimple had suddenly appeared out of the blue, for example, or something else disastrous had happened; however, for the moment, it's all right; for the moment everything is going well.'

His first concern is whether his world is the familiar one. His fear is that the common course of petty things will change and take him by surprise. His sense of disaster is as attenuated as his hopes. In comparison, Gregor Samsa's encounter with the morning's discovery is magnified: Gregor wakes to find himself transformed into a gigantic insect, a metamorphosis consistent with his normal order, whereas a facial pimple constitutes an attack upon Golyadkin whose pathological self-depreciation renders him sufficiently vulnerable to interpret anything as an affront.

Golyadkin's dissatisfaction with his identity—personality, name, position—is the source from which his double arises. Annihilation begins as a defence against self-revulsion. The quandary colloquially expressed as 'not knowing what to do with oneself' can be taken literally in Golyadkin's case. Carefully groomed and riding to the dinner party, he happens to pass in his carriage Andrey

Philippovich, his supervisor at work. He wonders, 'Ought I to bow? Should I speak to him or not? Ought I to acknowledge our acquaintance?' and, then,

> 'Or shall I pretend it's not me but somebody else strikingly like me, and look as if nothing's the matter?' said Mr Golyadkin, lifting his hat to Andrey Philippovich and not taking his eyes off him. 'I . . . It's all right,' he whispered, hardly able to speak, 'It's quite all right; this is not me at all, Andrey Philippovich, it's not me at all, not me, and that's all about it.'

Golyadkin does not value his own actions; he believes that his plans to become socially acceptable are ludicrous. He can admit these desires only by pretending that he is someone else. His belief that people are both right to exclude him and wrong for excluding him exist simultaneously in an imbalance which never leads to self-justification. He protests repeatedly that he is not an intriguer, that he does not wear a mask nor decieve with everyday graces. In reply to this protest his physician suggests that he undergo a radical transformation of character—not an obviously apt reply, but one which shows that even his statements of self-defence appear as self-complaints.

Golyadkin links his inability to wear a mask—that is, to act with composure or even sanity—with the power of his enemies. He views his disability as a symptom of honesty and forthrightness, but clearly loathes these virtues. He views social composure as self-assertion, and self-assertion as aggression. Thus as Golyadkin frantically endeavours to gain composure in his physician's presence, he sits, then stands, then re-seats himself, and protects

> himself against all contingencies with the same challenging stare that possessed such exceptional powers of mentally annihilating and reducing to ashes all enemies of Mr Golyadkin. The stare, moreover, fully conveyed Mr Golyadkin's independence, that is, it stated clearly that Mr Golyadkin didn't care, he was his own master, like anybody else, and his life was his own.

This is precisely what Golyadkin cannot believe. The emergence of his double confirms his worst fears: he is not his own master.

Golyadkin's voluntary actions, or those actions which would normally be considered voluntary, consistently run counter to his decisions. The morning after his initial meeting with his double on the bridge, he determines that he is ill and cannot go to work, but immediately puts on his overcoat and rushes to the office. When Golyadkin does act according to his impulses, those impulses, he believes, mislead him. Thus he reveals to the alternate Golyadkin all his secret hopes about Clara Olsufyevna, whom he had courted at the dinner party. He invites the new Golyadkin to live with him, and no sooner declares that they will be as brothers than he derides himself for his gullibility. On the other hand, if he suppresses his impulses, he also feels that he has made the wrong move. While hiding in the house of Clara Olsufyevna, watching for an opportunity to join the party and approach her, he hesitates and, believing he has missed his chance, he calls himself a coward and a fool, and derides himself not simply for his present behaviour, but for being himself. Yet again, when he behaves bravely, as he believes he does in writing to various people in quest of the new Golyadkin's address, he thinks:

> 'Why on earth did I write all those letters, like a suicidal idiot?—a suicidal idiot, that's what I am! I couldn't keep my mouth shut, I had to blab. And really, why? If you are ruined, be a doormat. But no, that wouldn't really do for you, you have to bring your pride into it . . .'

Thus Golyadkin continually turns against himself; indeed the abuse offers him almost voluptuous satisfaction even as he worries compulsively over others' abuse.

Golyadkin's see-sawing self-image issues in the fear that other people will not know how to distinguish between the two Golyadkins. They will say that one is a rogue and a scoundrel while the other is honest and virtuous, but how will they identify him as the latter and the other Golyadkin as the former? In short, he is uncertain of his status as the object designated by a proper name. His imbalanced view of the qualities of his character issues in confusion as to the identity of his person.

Golyadkin's insecurity arises not from concern with the good and bad self, but from concern with the approved and rejected self. He is obsessed by the notion of shame, and of being sullied. Golyadkin dreams that he is being praised by illustrious company, but suddenly a new figure emerges, the copy of Golyadkin, and shows up the old one as a counterfeit, thus destroying his brief feeling of triumph. Everyone now praises the new Golyadkin and spurns the old. The counterfeit Golyadkin is then multiplied; the city fills with perfect replicas of him. Finally a policeman grabs all the replicas by the collar and locks them up. Golyadkin wakes rigid with horror. He has seen his uselessness, his redundancy; he can be replicated perfectly and without cost. For his interest lies in others' views of him; and therefore whether he is praised or derided, he is inessential, even to himself. His neurosis is the death-throes of self-concern. The self must be considered, at least in its own view, as irreplaceable. Freud suggested that the notion of irreplaceability, when it is active in the unconscious, may appear as an endless series since every surrogate is inadequate, yet Dostoevsky's tale suggests the horror of discovering that something believed to be irreplaceable is in fact easily replaceable. The horror arises from the inability to sustain self-valuation which indeed often does seem to defy a realistic assessment of the self and which at the same time is so necessary to human functioning that it must also been seen as realistic. Dostoevsky brings objectivity into the self and in so doing challenges the feasibility of self-knowledge.

Golyadkin is anxious to have the whole affair settled and he believes, or seems to believe, he has a good idea of what the affair is about, though the reader does not. He believes that the case has actually been settled against him, and that all he has to do is to surrender to the enemy; then he could give up the struggle, then he could rest. As soon as he sees the double he believes that the verdict is signed and sealed; he tries to feel relieved, tries to feel that it does not matter to him (for, when he is acutely embarrassed or frightened, he pretends that it all has nothing to do with him, that he is someone else), yet he cannot suppress dread:

> [. . .] suddenly his whole body quivered, and involuntarily he leapt to one side. He began to look around him with inexplicable anxiety; but there was nobody, nothing particular had happened, and yet . . . and yet it seemed to him that just now, this very moment, somebody had been standing there, close to him, by his side, also leaning on the parapet and—an extraordinary thing!—had even said something to him, something hurried and abrupt, not altogether understandable, but about a matter touching him very nearly, something that concerned him [. . .] Mr Golyadkin was troubled and even afraid, and felt at a loss. It was not that he feared this might be some bad character, he was simply afraid [. . .] The fact was that the unknown now seemed to him to be somehow familiar [. . .] Mr Golyadkin knew this man thoroughly well; he even knew what he was called, knew his name [. . .] His situation at that moment was like that of a man standing above a terrible chasm when the ground has begun to break away [. . .] Mr Golyadkin knew and felt, was indeed quite sure, that some other evil thing would inevitably happen to him on the way, something else unpleasant would burst upon him; for instance, he might meet the stranger again; but, horrible to tell, he even wanted the meeting, felt it was unavoidable and only asked for the whole thing to be over and done with as quickly as possible . . .

Golyadkin chases his double back to his own flat where he finds the 'stranger' sitting on his bed, greeting him with a friendly nod; he does not want to flee his replacement.

Clearly Golyadkin's anxiety is not rational; that is, it does not arise from an external danger ('It was not that he feared this might be some bad character, he was simply afraid [. . .]') but from something that can be effected within himself. To speak of his anxiety in psychoanalytic terms as fear arising from an internal danger, however, is to neglect the logic of his thoughts and the way they register his external reality.

The following morning he acknowledges that for a long time something was being prepared, that 'there was *somebody else* in reserve.' In effect, given his objective value, there is always someone else in reserve; Golyadkin as Titular Councillor is easily replaceable, and he lacks either genuine attachments or necessary fantasies of self-importance as protection against this recognition. His acute sensitivity to impersonal forces leads him to suspect that they are directed against him in particular, and he thereby imparts to them personal features. He scans these features for confirmation of self-importance, or of the significance of his uniqueness, yet the impersonal cannot provide this confirmation. Dissatisfied, he avidly repeats his search for recognition, and repeated frustrations defeat him. Thus it is his dependence upon others' responses, alongside the recalcitrant impersonality of those responses, that annihilate him—or, rather, effect the annihilation of which such obssessive concern itself is a symptom.

The mockery Golyadkin endures as a result of his dependence is both cheap and violent. He continually broods upon the idea of having his reputation sullied; his concern with dirt can be taken literally. The stairs to his flat are filled with rubbish. When he first chases the double to the flat he is surprised that the 'stranger' knows his way about these dirty obstacles. When Golyadkin gets soiled walking along the street, he believes that it is all part of the plot against him. He associates himself with dirt, and when he sits at a restaurant table and notices a pile of dirty dishes at his table, he believes he is responsible for them, though everyone laughs at him when he asks how much he owes for the meal. (The rationale of this query is in past experience: his double takes meals at restaurants and then disappears, so that Golyadkin is deemed accountable for the bill. The double is, moreover, surprisingly greedy. While he has one patty, his double has ten so that Golyadkin has the responsibility for eleven.) The most humiliating moment occurs when his double greets their colleagues with the confident geniality of a popular man. Eagerly Golyadkin junior takes the hand of Golyadkin who responds with tearful emotion; but, suddenly, when the new Golyadkin realises whose hand he is clasping, he pulls, back, shaking his hand as though to rid himself of the attachment to filth.

In the wake of this humiliation the new Golyadkin teases the old about his association with women: 'Give me a kiss, darling!' he calls out, and everyone present enjoys the sly allusion. Clearly Golyadkin's defeat has some link to his relations with women. His initial self-inflicted humiliation occurs as he forces his attention upon Clara Olsufyevna, and his final defeat occurs as he waits for her in the courtyard in compliance with either a terrible prank or the message in a hallucinated letter which suggests that they elope. The 'letter' generates Golyadkin's most disagreeable thoughts. Angry at her suggestion, he considers that it proves how badly she, and indeed all women, are reared, expecting men to make love all the time, when, in fact, all a man really wants is someone to cook and clean and to be satisfied with an occasional little kiss. Previously he has suspected his former landlady, a one-eyed German woman, of leading the plot against him and of spreading the rumours which incite an acquaintance to accuse him of being dangerous to morally innocent and uncontaminated people; but now he sees the ex-landlady as the good woman and Clara Olsufyevna as the bad witch. Yet he waits for her in the courtyard, as the letter bids him. He waits for her, feeling only anger towards her: 'Here's a man on his way to destruction, a man losing his identity, and he can hardly control himself—and you talk about a wedding!'

Golyadkin does not have to repeat the assertion that he would cut off his finger to effect an instantaneous settlement, to involve the psychoanalytic theme of castration complex. Golyadkin looks upon his superiors as paternal figures—if he can win them over to his side, they will save him; but the new Golyadkin wins them for himself, and thereby renders the old Golyadkin helpless. He is even attacked for his desire for women, which he simultaneously repudiates and pursues, waiting in the courtyard to elope and deriding the notion of romantic attachment. While vainly expecting satisfaction, he is carried off by the physician, another paternal figure, as his double stands mocking him from behind. The double may be the just punisher of his desires, as well as the idealised other who succeeds where Golyadkin himself fails. The one-eyed landlady could bear her deformity as a sign that she is the avenging (i.e. castrating) woman, and therefore Golyadkin, in preparing to satisfy his desire with Clara Olsufyevna, thinks of her as the good woman (for she punishes forbidden desires) and Clara Olsufyevna as the bad woman (for she grants the satisfaction of forbidden desires).

Though one cannot legitimately argue against psychoanalytic interpretation in general by postulating one interpretation and showing it to be inadequate, since psychoanalytic theory does permit an enormous range of critical interpretation, it can be said that any such interpretation is in many respects closer to the creative realisation of the producer of a play or opera than the explication, emphases and registers of response attempted by the literary critic. The producer is free to distort so long as his distortions are enlightening, but critical re-writings tend to be far less interesting. Fiction does not lend itself as easily to creative realisation since it is not something to be performed. Moreover, in good fiction, the detail, the structure, the allusions offered within the work itself are usually too dense to be amenable to idiosyncratic translations. The castration theme may well be indicated in Dostoevsky's *The Double,* but in making use of this indication the story's strength must be seen as equal to that of the psychoanalytic theory, whereby the castration theme becomes enmeshed in more general problems of the self.

The double fantasy makes use of the fact that, when notions of the mind and self are involved, the metaphor becomes the only possible method of presentation. The double fantasy exploits the fact that the language of actuality is usually logically prior to metaphorical language: we must know what a red rose newly sprung in June is before we can understand how love is like it, and we must see a person against another identical person to understand what a conflict within the self is like. The double theme has therefore been exploited as a means of presenting as actual that which can only be presented in metaphor, and the exploitation has had such success because self-conflicts are felt as actual conflicts between separate but affinitive forces. For this reason, too, psychoanalysis has had such success: it presents fundamentally metaphorical material in the guise of historical explanation, and it can evade detection because its metaphors are peculiarly intricate and systematic, and because (given the material it deals with) it can be countered only by another metaphor. The supposition that psychoanalytic theory alone is not metaphorical but literal, is . . . highly misleading. (pp. 53-66)

T. E. Apter, "The Double: Stevenson's 'Dr. Jekyll and Mr. Hyde,' Hoffmann's 'The Devil's Elixirs,' Dostoevsky's 'The Double'," in his Fantasy Literature: An Approach to Reality, *Indiana University Press, 1982, pp. 48-66.*

PHILOSOPHICAL CONSIDERATIONS

Dmitri Chizhevsky

[Chizhevsky is a scholar noted for his work in various fields of Slavic scholarship. His books include Outline of Comparative Slavic Literatures *(1952),* On Romanticism in Slavic Literatures *(1957), and* History of Russian Literature from the Eleventh Century to the End of the Baroque *(1960). In the following excerpt, he interprets Dostoyevsky's profound psychological insights into thedouble as a warning against the depersonalization of the individual in a culture dominated by rationalism.]*

The double is one of Dostoevsky's most characteristic themes. It is almost a fixed idea—it recurs in his work many times and in several versions. Little, however, has been written about its deep meaning. The first version of the theme, *The Double* (1846) received rather unfavorable criticism, and until recently was considered an unoriginal work, influenced either by Gogol's "Overcoat" or his "Nose" or by Western European models.

Dostoevsky himself had a very different opinion of *The Double.* While working on the story, he wrote to his brother Michael (November 16, 1845): "This will be my *chef d'œuvre.*" On the day of publication (February 1, 1846) he wrote to him: "*Golyadkin* [the name of the hero of *The Double*] is ten times better than *The Poor People.* My friends say that there is nothing comparable since *The Dead Souls,* that it is a work of genius." Dostoevsky did not think such praise exaggerated. "Really *Golyadkin* turned out exceedingly well," he adds, "you will like it even more than *The Dead Souls.*" Still, the disappointment of his friends (Belinsky in particular) after the publication of the story affected Dostoevsky. "I am tired of *Golyadkin,*" he confessed to his brother (April 1, 1846). But Dostoevsky was persuaded only that the artistic *form* was not a success. He had not the slightest doubt that the *idea* of his "Petersburg poem" was important: "I have disappointed expectations and bungled the work which could have been a great achievement." A year later Dostoevsky wavered again and was ready to agree with those who spoke enthusiastically of *The Double.* "I hear about *Golyadkin* indirectly (and from many sources) wonderful things," he wrote to his brother (December 1, 1847). "Some people say openly that this work is a miracle and has not yet been properly appreciated. It will play an enormous role in the future, it is enough for me to have written only *Golyadkin* . . . it does one good to know that one is understood."

Even after the years of penal servitude Dostoevsky did not lose interest in the theme of *The Double.* In the very first letter (Omsk, February 22, 1854) to his brother Michael after his release from the camp Dostoevsky asked: "Who is Chernov who published a *Double* in 1850?" When he was planning a new edition of his writings, Dostoevsky did not want to include *The Double*—not because he did not think it worthy of inclusion, but because he wanted to publish it separately (May 9, 1859): "*The Double* could be published last—revised, or rather rewritten to perfection." He hoped that the new version would bring out what his contemporaries had misunderstood: "Believe me, brother, that this revision, with a preface, will be worth as much as a new novel. They will see at last what *The Double* is. I hope that it will arouse great interest. In a word I'll challenge them all." Also at that time Dostoevsky considered the *idea* of *The Double* most important (October 1, 1859): "Why should I abandon an excellent idea, a type of great social importance, which I was the first to discover and of which I was the first prophet?"

Even thirty years after the publication of *The Double,* when Dostoevsky surveyed his career, he held a high opinion of the idea of the story. He admits in *The Diary of a Writer* (November 1877) that *The Double* was "a complete failure," that "the story did not come off." But Dostoevsky wanted to draw attention to the idea of *The Double:* "The idea was very clever and I have never propounded anything more serious in literature." He considered the idea topical and urgent even for that time: "If I were today to take up this idea and propound it again, it would assume a very different form; but in 1846 I had not found the form and had not mastered the story."

But did Dostoevsky never return to the idea after *The Double*? Did he never attempt to give it "a very different form"? The idea which in Dostoevsky's own words was "more serious than anything he had propounded in literature," by which he would "challenge all," was not forgotten. It recurs throughout his writing in various metamorphoses. We can even say that this idea is an answer to the deepest spiritual problems of the nineteenth century and that it is still alive in the philosophy of our own time. It is really one of the main ideas for Dostoevsky: it leads us into the very center of his religious and ethical views. It will be our task to trace the role of the idea of the double in Dostoevsky's work and to uncover its philosophical meaning.

The starting point of our analysis is the fact that Dostoevsky's style is based on an interpenetration of "naturalistic" and "unrealistic" elements. The ordinariness of everyday life is strangely shot through with the fantastic, naturalistic portrayal alternates with the pathos of an abstract idea, the sober striving for reality with ecstatic visions of the world beyond the confines of reality. Dostoevsky's power as an artist lies precisely in his ability to avoid mixing or confusing these sharply contradictory elements, and to succeed in weaving them together, fusing them into an organic unity. No doubt this style is closely linked with literary tradition (E. T. A. Hoffmann, Gogol, Dickens, Balzac) and with the deepest personal experiences of Dostoevsky. The important thing for us is to recognize that Dostoevsky's "realistically psychological" analysis is at the same time also "transcendentally psychological," "existential," and that all events and the whole pattern of his theme are always an ideological construct as well. This duality, where the plot develops on two planes of meaning, is particularly important for our analysis.

From the very first pages of *The Double* Dostoevsky insists that the meaning of the younger Golyadkin's appearance lies exclusively in the peculiar psychic "situation" of the elder Golyadkin, even though the strange event might well be explained on the plane of reality. Just as in *The Landlady* the fantastic scenes appear always on the background of the almost delirious state of Ordynov, so also Golyadkin's double appears to him first while he is in an abnormal state of mind:

> Mr. Golyadkin halted in exhaustion . . . and began looking intently at the black and troubled waters of the canal. There is no knowing what length of time he spent like this. . . . At that instant Mr. Golyadkin reached such a pitch of despair, was so harrassed, so tortured, so exhausted, and so weakened in what feeble faculties were left him that he forgot everything . . . All at once . . . he started and involuntarily skipped a couple of paces aside. With unaccountable uneasiness he began gazing about him . . . he fancied that just now, that every minute, some one was standing near him, beside him, also leaning on the railing . . . a new sensation took possession of Mr. Golyadkin's whole being: agony upon agony, terror upon terror. . . . a feverish tremor ran through his veins.

At this moment Mr. Golyadkin's double—his "double in every respect"—appears out of the snow storm. Later, the double also appears side by side with him in the coffeehouse, and at his Excellency's "he made his appearance through a door which our hero had taken for a looking-glass." The double again appears next to Mr. Golyadkin "as if he had stepped out of his reflection in the shop windows of the Nevsky Prospekt" and, after his visit to Golyadkin Senior, he disappears so mysteriously—without leaving a trace—that one could doubt his reality altogether.

Mr. Golyadkin's double—whatever may be the status of his physical reality—is conditioned psychologically: it rises from the depths of Golyadkin's soul. Even if one could show from the point of view of psychopathology that there is a causal necessity for this appearance, it matters only that Golyadkin's psychic situation, depicted at the beginning, must inevitably lead to a tragic end. At the beginning of the story the delusion has not yet entered Golyadkin's soul. But even then his whole behavior testifies to the pathological character of his split personality. Dostoevsky has us meet his hero at the moment when he has to make a decision, when he is getting ready for an action that is to change his whole life. He behaves "as if" he had such a plan. But only—"as if." His very first steps show that he is by nature incapable of making a decision. Fear, anxiety, the feeling of being menaced from all sides, prepare the appearance of the double. Mr. Golyadkin goes so far as to deny his own existence not only in the momentary intention to "shoot himself, one way or another, that night," but also by his vain attempts to quiet himself by asking: "Should I pretend that I am not myself, but somebody else, strikingly like me?" Mr. Golyadkin tries to find a way out by asserting his "independence," if only in the sphere of his "private life." But the double—and it does not matter how far he is real—leaves neither Golyadkin's "official relations" nor his "private life" undisturbed as soon as he enters his life.

In the second part of *The Double,* after the appearance of

the double, Dostoevsky gives at last—through Golyadkin—a formula containing the idea of his work. Against the background of the same constant vacillation between decisiveness and passive withdrawal, between "humility" and pathological retreat from imaginary or real dangers, a new and much deeper tone is sounded. Mr. Golyadkin's double crowds him out of all spheres of his life; he replaces, "impersonates," him in the office and with his fellow clerks, and in his "private life" in the family of Olsufy Ivanovich; or, as Golyadkin phrases it: "he forcibly enters the circle of my existence and of all my relations in practical life." The double has "the strange pretension and dishonorable and fantastic desire to squeeze others out of the position which those others occupy, by their very existence in this world, and to take their place." The title of a chapter in the first edition of the novel was "The Depraved Man Takes the Place of Mr. Golyadkin in Practical Life." "Imposture and shamelessness do not pay nowadays . . . Grishka Otrepyev [supposedly the real name of the first false tsar Dmitri] was the only one who gained by imposture," says Golyadkin several times. "Otrepyevs are not possible in our time." "My views in regard to keeping one's own place are purely moral," he remarks.

In order to make it perfectly clear that what matters is not the behavior of a real younger Golyadkin, but rather the feelings and introspection of the older Golyadkin, Dostoevsky expounds the same situation in a (consciously unreal) dream of the older Golyadkin. In this dream the younger Golyadkin "takes his place in the service and in society" and succeeds in proving that "Golyadkin Senior was not the genuine one at all, but the sham, and that he—Golyadkin Junior—was the real one." Finally the Golyadkins multiply indefinitely.

> Beside himself with shame and despair, the utterly ruined though perfectly innocent Mr. Golyadkin dashed headlong away, wherever fate might lead him; but with every step he took, with every thud of his foot on the granite of the pavement, there leapt up as though out of the earth a Mr. Golyadkin precisely the same, perfectly alike and of a revolting depravity of heart. And all these precisely alike Golyadkins set to running after one another as soon as they appeared, and stretched in a long chain like a file of geese, hobbling after the real Mr. Golyadkin, so there was nowhere to escape from these duplicates; so that Mr. Golyadkin, who was in every way deserving of compassion, was breathless with terror; so that the whole town was obstructed at last by duplicate Golyadkins.

This weird dream is the center of the work. The answer to the question of "one's own place" is clear. Golyadkin (and here lies his typical—or, as Dostoevsky says, "social"—significance) has no place of his own, he has never achieved one in his life, he has no "sphere" of his own in life except possibly the corner behind the cupboard or the stove where he hides from the imaginary persecutions of his enemies. In this respect Golyadkin is very similar to other characters in Dostoevsky: the "dreamer" in *The White Nights*, and *The Petersburg Chronicle*, the heroes of *The Faint Heart*, and *Mr. Prokharchin* (in part, at least), and Marmeladov in *Crime and Punishment*. There is something inhuman, thing-like in this lack of a place of one's own. (Golyadkin feels that he is being treated like a "rag.") The appearance of the double and his success in squeezing out Golyadkin from his place only shows that Golyadkin's place was completely illusory to begin with. For even the double can keep all his "places"—from the office to his Excellency's cabinet—only through the purely external traits of his character: by the flattery and servility which the older Golyadkin would have liked to master himself but which are no less superficial, unessential, and inhuman and incapable of ensuring him a "place" in life. Here Dostoevsky raises the ethical and ontological problems of the fixity, reality, and security of individual existence—surely one of the most genuine problems of ethics. The reality of human personality cannot be secured simply on the empirical plane of existence but needs also other (non-empirical) conditions and presuppositions.

We do not know why, exactly, Dostoevsky was dissatisfied with the form of his "Petersburg poem." If we judge from the vicissitudes of the idea of the double in Dostoevsky's later writings, we have to conclude that one of the defects in the development of the theme of the double was the fact that a weak character in a dependent social position—in short, a petty official—was made the hero of the story. The ontological instability of a personality, however, is not necessarily connected with psychological instability ("weakness of character") or social instability ("dependence"). Dostoevsky links the further development of the theme of the double with characters of a very different type. The double occurs again in *The Possessed* (1872-73), *A Raw Youth* (1875), and *The Brothers Karamazov* (1879-80).

The theme of the double is handled in the simplest—even schematic—manner in *A Raw Youth*. There only one motif of the complex theme is used: the instability of the self, which is expressed by the ambiguity of Versilov's individual actions and general behavior. Versilov's instability is not explained by any psychological "weakness": his personality is in its way brilliant and sharply defined. Dostoevsky gives us no clue to understanding the division in Versilov. He merely describes it: "I feel as though I were split in two. . . . Yes, I am really split in two mentally, and I'm horribly afraid of it. It's just as though one's double were standing beside one." The description of this period in Versilov's life is concluded by a theoretical reflection: "What is the double, exactly? The double, according to a medical book written by an expert that I purposely read afterward, is nothing else than the first stage of serious mental derangement which may take a fatal turn." It is "a duality of will and feelings." An explanation of this loss of self, of its unity, is only hinted at, *e.g.*, when Makar Ivanovich alludes to "infidels" who "let themselves go and give up taking notice of themselves." But other traits, characteristic of Versilov's inner division, are clarified in *The Possessed* and *The Brothers Karamazov*.

A great deal of light is thrown on the figure of Stavrogin [in *The Possessed*] by the scenes which Dostoevsky dropped when the novel appeared in book form. In these scenes Stavrogin talks to Dasha about the appearance of a double, of a "demon":

> I saw him again . . . at first here in the corner, there near the stove and then he sat next to me, all night, and stayed there even after I left the house . . . Now begins a series of his visitations. Yesterday he was stupid and impudent . . . I got angry that my own demon could appear in such a miserable mask . . . I was silent all the time, on purpose: and not only silent, I did not move. He got furious at that and I was glad that he got furious. I don't believe in him. I don't believe in him as yet. I know that it is I myself divided in different ways and that I speak with myself. Still, anyhow, he got very angry: he terribly wanted to be an independent demon and that I would believe in him as a reality.

Stavrogin also tells Tikhon about him, how he suffered, especially at night, from certain strange hallucinations; how he sometimes saw or felt close beside him an evil being, derisive and rational: "It shows different faces and assumes different characters, and yet is always the same and always infuriates me. . . . It's myself in various forms and nothing else."

But the devil of Stavrogin does not remain a mere hallucination. Fedka the Convict—an incarnation of the same devil—tells Stavrogin in a deleted passage: "There were terribly many devils here yesterday—terribly many. They crept out of all the swamps. One of them suggested to me yesterday on the bridge that I should cut the throat of Lebyadkin and Marya Timofeevna." In reality, both Kirilov and Shatov are simply two emanations of the spirit of Stavrogin—each of whom accepts him from his own point of view—while Fedka the Convict only does what he thinks Stavrogin wants from him and Pyotr Verkhovensky is acknowledged by Stavrogin as his "ape." In Stavrogin there is great spiritual treasure, but it is somehow "spilt," "scattered," "wasted." Stavrogin (like Versilov but unlike Golyadkin) has a great enough spiritual force to become the ideologist of religious Slavophilism (Shatov), of the revolt against God (Kirilov), and of the revolution (Pyotr Verkhovensky). Shatov's whole ideology comes from Stavrogin. "It was a teacher uttering weighty words, and a pupil who was raised from the dead. I was that pupil and you were the teacher," confesses Shatov to Stavrogin. "You were sowing the seed of God and the Fatherland in my heart." Shatov feels "condemned to believe" in Stavrogin "through all eternity" for only he "could raise that flag"—*i.e.*, the flag of his particular brand of Slavophilism. Even though his ideology is too shallow to need the help of Stavrogin's spiritual midwifery, Pyotr Verkhovensky nevertheless feels that the fate of his plans is completely dependent on Stavrogin's "raising the flag": "I love an idol. You are my idol. . . . It's just such a man as you that I need. You are the leader, you are the sun and I am your worm." He expounds a half-crazy though grandiose plan for a revolution which Stavrogin the Pretender would head as Ivan the Tsarevich. Such a plan could have arisen in Pyotr Verkhovensky's shallow and petty mind only as a response to the great personality of Stavrogin. Finally, the mad genius of Kirilov too could rise only from the depths of Stavrogin's soul. "He is your creation," Shatov reproaches Stavrogin, "You were infecting the heart of that hapless creature with poison . . . you confirmed false malignant ideas in him, and brought him to the verge of insanity," Kirilov is the only one of the "emanations" of Stavrogin who never ceases to have a "warm and kindly" relation with his master though, also, he expected from Stavrogin that he "would undertake burdens nobody else can bear." Fedka the Convict too is—to a lesser degree—an "emanation" of the spirit of Stavrogin. But Stavrogin is right, after all, when he calls Fedka his "little devil." Fedka's last crime is a response to Stavrogin's perhaps unconscious wishes, though they are distorted and strained by the soul of Pyotr Verkhovensky.

Thus Stavrogin lives among the "emanation" of his spirit, in a world of phantoms, of "demons." Or more exactly: others live for him (especially the women of the novel) and "of him" but he himself does not really live; he is only a Pretender, in reality and in possibility, an "Ivan the Tsarevich," a "Grishka Otrepyev." Real people follow him, but they take him for something totally different from what he really is. For in reality he is "split," he is "split into two," he has no face, or many faces, or even all faces. Others see in him "faces" which he does not have. But in any case, two contradictory faces are clearly visible: one bright, the other dark. Some (Shatov, Kirilov, Dasha) expect a "great deed" from him, the "undertaking of burdens," and others (Pyotr Verkhovensky and his gang) see in him an "extraordinary aptitude for crime." He actually sees "no distinction between some brutal obscene action and any great exploit, even the sacrifice of life for humanity": "I am still capable of desiring to do something good, and I get a feeling of pleasure from it; at the same time I desire evil and feel pleasure from that too." It is not surprising that people consider him capable "of any mad action even when in full possession of his faculties." In other words Stavrogin is "neither cold nor hot" not because he does not know the difference between good and evil (like *e.g.* Pyotr Verkhovensky or Fyodor Karamazov). He knows what is good. He tries to "rise from the dead." He tries—more than once—to waken to the good: by revealing his marriage to Marya Timofeevna and by the publication of the "Confession" which he gave to Tikhon to read. But in order to "wake to the good" it is not enough to know what is good—it is not enough to know it theoretically or aesthetically. Stavrogin knows only this "theoretical" awakening. And even then Stavrogin with all his beauty, elegance, gentlemanliness, education, wit, courage, and self-reliance remains outwardly and inwardly passive in the face of life and concrete reality. He is torn off, isolated from all the world, absolutely alone; he has no point of support in the concrete world. He understands much, but he does not love anything. We are struck by Stavrogin's power—his enormous spiritual power—"illimitable, great power." But this power of Stavrogin's (in the original sketches of the novel called "Prince") is "immediate, it does not know on what to rely." This is the source of his indifference, boredom, absentmindedness, even his laziness. He does not have a human face; he wears some kind of mask. The cause of Stavrogin's loneliness is in himself: he is divided from living reality by his pride, his limitless presumption, his scornful relation to life, his contempt for his concrete neighbors.

Kirilov, we are told, was "consumed" by his idea. Possibly Stavrogin is partly right when he writes to Dasha that he can "never believe in an idea to such a degree as he [Kirilov] did. I cannot even be interested in an idea to such a degree." Still, Kirilov is right when he says that "the idea has also consumed" Stavrogin. Stavrogin is right—though these ideas may be contradictory—that "one may argue about everything endlessly, but for me nothing has come but negation, with no greatness of soul, no force." "Only negation"—that means that assertion needs not only knowledge, but also love, not only the "abstract reason" of Stavrogin but the *nous erōn* of Kirilov. Yes, even Kirilov, who perishes tragically, aims at something definite: the "Man-God," "self-will." But there is no "tension" in Stavrogin, no "magnetic meridian" of the soul, no "magnetic pole" to which, according to Dostoevsky, every living soul is drawn. He knows no God. A living, concrete human existence—a "place" in the world—is possible only through the living link of man with the Divine Being. The anecdote of Pyotr Stefanovich is certainly a central point of the novel:

> I was drinking with the officers . . . They were discussing atheism and I need hardly say they made short work of God. They were squealing with delight . . . One grizzled old captain sat mum, not saying a word. All at once he stands up in the middle of the room and says aloud, as though speaking to himself: "If there's no God, how can I be a captain then?"

Just as one cannot be an army captain without God, so Stravrogin cannot without God be a Slavophile, or a revolutionary, or even a militant atheist (like Kirilov). For his unlimited but godless power there remains then only one "place" in the world, similar to the "places" where Golyadkin was hiding. This "one place" is "in the mountains of Switzerland," "a gloomy place" to which he calls Marya Timofeevna. There he wants to hide again with Dasha: "a very dull place, a narrow valley, the mountains restrict both vision and thought. It's very gloomy. I don't want to go anywhere else ever." But even this "place" is not granted to him. We know the end: "The citizen of the canton Uri was hanging behind the door."

But one cannot deny that for Stavrogin there was a way open to concreteness. He does not take it, of course. It is the way of shame and disgrace. This sense of shame is possibly Stavrogin's last remaining link with other people and with human society. While he is completely indifferent to success, fame, and danger, he is deeply disturbed by the possibility of disgrace: "If one did something wicked, or worse still, something shameful, that is disgraceful, only very shameful and . . . ridiculous, such as people would remember for a thousand years and hold in scorn for a thousand years!" Liza has "a strong feeling" that Stavrogin "had something awful, loathsome, some bloodshed on his conscience . . . and yet something that would make him look very ridiculous. Beware of telling me, if it's true: I shall laugh you to scorn. I shall laugh at you for the rest of your life." Tikhon fears that he won't "endure the laughter of people . . . The ugliness of the crime will kill it. It is truly an unbeautiful crime . . . there are truly shameful, disgraceful crimes which are not redeemed by horror." Tikhon advises him "sincerely to accept the blows and the spittle . . . It is always thus that the most degrading cross becomes a great glory and a great power, if only the humility of the act is sincere." Stavrogin's way to life could have led through "shame and disgrace." But, unable to endure the "blows and the spittle," he chose the way to death. Possibly the motive for his suicide was not only his own crime but the crimes—the "unbeautiful"—crimes of his "doubles." For the crimes of Pyotr Verkhovensky and of Fedka the Convict "are too unbeautiful." And all the "doubles," all the "emanations" of Stavrogin (with the exception of Pyotr Verkhovensky) die symbolically before he himself commits suicide.

Stavrogin's "devil" was dropped by Dostoevsky in the book-form edition of the novel: possibly because the depiction of the devil seemed to him too bold at that time or because it might simply have changed the tragedy of Stavrogin into a psychic illness. Still, there is another devil in Dostoevsky's works: the devil of Ivan Karamazov.

Ivan Karamazov is not mentally ill, he has not committed any crime, and he is not at all indifferent to life as Stavrogin is. But, like Stavrogin, he is divided from the people, from his neighbors, by pride. Ivan is conceited: he exalts himself over other people and considers himself their judge. Dmitri and his father are, in his opinion, "serpents"; his father deserves death: he does not doubt that Dmitri was the murderer. The source of Ivan's pride is his rationalism; his pride is "the pride of reason." His way to ethical insight is not—like Alyosha's—the way of faith nor—like Dmitri's—the way of suffering, but the way of madness and breakdown, the way of a division of personality. This division of personality is shown in the scenes with Smerdyakov and with the devil. Smerdyakov is also in a certain sense a "double" of Ivan. Not only have they in common basic character traits—"enlightened" rationalism, conceit, contempt for other people, loneliness, and complacency—but they also share an interest in common "themes." Smerdyakov tries to prove the right of man to mortal sin, Ivan argues that "everything is permitted." Both have a low opinion of Russia and Europe, and both recognize that there are people who have a different relation to God: Smerdyakov tells of "two pilgrims," Ivan recognizes the limits of "Euclidean" reason. Ivan himself admits his agreement with Smerdyakov on this point. That is why Smerdyakov worships Ivan—a point which Dostoevsky emphasizes several times. This inner link between Ivan and Smerdyakov is revealed particularly in the conversation at the gate in which Ivan seems to make himself—unwittingly—an accomplice in the murder of his father. After the murder a consciousness awakes in Ivan's soul that he is—not empirically, but in some other sense—guilty with Smerdyakov, guilty because of their similarity and because "the lackey Smerdyakov sat in his soul." Ivan is ashamed of Smerdyakov and thus a recognition of his own guilt penetrates into Ivan's mind in accord with the main theme of the novel: "everybody is guilty for everything and everybody." Shame is the key to the moral awakening of the rationalist Ivan. Ivan's moral crisis is displayed in his "nightmare," in the appearance of his double—the devil—who is, as Ivan says:

> the incarnation of myself, but only of one side of me—of my thoughts and feelings, but only the nastiest and stupidest of them. . . . You are myself, myself only with a different face. . . . You choose only my worst thoughts, and what's more, the stupid ones. . . . All my stupid ideas—outgrown, thrashed out long ago, and flung aside like a dead carcass—you present me as something new. . . . I was never such a flunkey. How then could my soul beget a flunkey like you? . . . He is myself. All that's base in me, all that's mean and contemptible.

Thus Smerdyakov is not simply similar to Ivan but is in him. Ivan came to this recognition through shame. Dostoevsky has not shown us Ivan's moral rebirth. But in *The Brothers Karamazov* he has, in any case, revealed new and deep aspects of the problem of the double.

We have asserted that the philosophical problem of the double in Dostoevsky points to essential and central problems of nineteenth-century philosophy. To uncover this link (without stopping to enquire how far this answer to nineteenth-century philosophy lay in Dostoevsky's intentions) will be our further task.

The appearance of the double raises a question about the concreteness of man's real existence. It shows that simply "to exist"—"to be"—is not a sufficient condition for man's existence as an ethical individual. The problem of "stability," of the ontological "fixity" of an ethical being is the real problem of the nineteenth century; or, more accurately, the problem of the distinction of human existence from any other kind of existence, which could be defined generally and abstractly as anything specific in space and time. The problem was put very clearly by Kierkegaard, but not by him only. It is one of the central problems in the whole development of Hegelianism; it was stated expressly by Feuerbach, Bruno Bauer, Stirner; and in some respects it determined the development of Marx. The problem of individual existence also plays a central role in the philosophy of Nietzsche. Nietzsche's "new tables of values" are tables of ontological values that are to guarantee the concrete existence of the individual. I can only allude to the new formulations of the problem of concrete individual existence in recent philosophy, in Tillich and Heidegger, and in the tradition of the Hegelian Left and Nietzscheanism in Russian philosophy (*e.g.,* in Rozanov).

One could point out that though there is an indubitable similarity in the problem of the existence of the individual self as it confronts these thinkers and Dostoevsky, there is still a very great difference between their points of view. Kierkegaard and Nietzsche see the reasons for the loss of the ontological "fixity" of the self in abstract, theoretical, "pure," "immaculate" thought. But is the way Dostoevsky puts the problem really so different? We noted in Stavrogin his intellectual power combined with a complete absence of any living relation to concreteness, and Ivan is a typical intellectual. Stavrogin and Ivan are possible only on the soil of Russian "Enlightenment" and Dostoevsky expressly connects them with it. The Russian Enlightenment of the nineteenth century, with its universal rationalism, its conviction that reason is able to grasp all of reality and also to create a new and better reality, was the main thing in Russian life against which Dostoevsky fought all his life. The rationalization of the aesthetic sphere—the reduction of beauty to utility (see Dostoevsky's articles directed against Dobrolyubov); the rationalization of the ethical sphere—the substitution of rational arguments for immediate feeling (cf. *The Diary of a Writer, The Grand Inquisitor,* the whole moral personality of Ivan); the rationalization of social life—the ideal of the "anthill" (cf. the theories of Shigalev in *The Possessed* and *The Grand Inquisitor*)—these are the central ideas of Russian "Enlightenment" which Dostoevsky fought incessantly. Dostoevsky's rejection of the Enlighteners was expressed possibly with the greatest clarity in the "Fragment of a Novel Shchedrodarov" where he puts into the mouth of the editors of the *Contemporary* the whole program of the Enlightenment:

> Every writer's and poet's highest goal is to popularize natural science. . . . A real apple is better than a painted apple. . . . shoes are in any case better than Pushkin. . . . The enlightened Kurochkin who destroys prejudices in any case stands incomparably higher than the unenlightened Homer. . . . For the happiness of all mankind, and equally for the happiness of every separate individual, first and most important of all, is the belly, or in other words, the stomach. . . . The anthill is the highest ideal of social organization one can imagine. . . . People are stupid, because they cannot figure out where their real advantage lies, because they rush after some childish toy, called art, after the useless, because they are steeped in prejudice, live separately and haphazardly, according to their will, rather, than according to rational books.

Dostoevsky answers this through the mouth of Shchedrodarov:

> You are going against life. We are not supposed to prescribe laws for life and extract laws from life for ourselves. You are theoreticians . . . How can one stand on air, without feeling the soil under one . . . Before you can do anything you have to make yourselves into something, to assume your own shape, to become yourselves . . . But you are abstractions, you are shadows, you are nothing. And nothing can come from nothing. You are foreign ideas. You are a mirage. You do not stand on soil but on air. The light shines right under you. . . .

Here the same problem is put very clearly, as in Kierkegaard and Nietzsche—with the difference that Kierkegaard and Nietzsche fought the "professors," the "abstract thinkers," and the ideologists "of pure reason" while in the Russia of the 1860's and 1870's every mediocre liberal and every revolutionary member of the intelligentsia was a theorist.

Golyadkin belongs to this group of problems. Of course, he is not a "theorist" or a "thinker," but in Russia the "Enlightenment" infected not only society but also the government. The society of the period of Emperor Nicholas I was also an attempt to build a thoroughly organized "anthill." Pyotr Verkhovensky dreamt of it: "Nothing has more influence than a uniform. I invent ranks and duties on purpose; I have secretaries, secret spies, treasurers, presidents, registrars, their assistants—they like it awfully, it's taken capitally." Gogol had fought the government "anthill," and had confronted its rational organization with the ideal of "a religious organization" of society. Golyadkin is, so to say, the passive bearer of the rational principle—and its victim. He, like the other clerks depicted by Dostoevsky, is devastated, exploited by the rational principle, embodied in the government apparatus of the period of Emperor Nicholas I. Rationalism devours Stavrogin and Ivan from inside, not from outside.

Dostoevsky does not remain on the surface of the question. He moves from the social and psychological problem (*The Double*) to the ethical and religious (*The Possessed* and *The Brothers Karamazov*). He is not satisfied with an easy battle against Pyotr Verkhovensky, Shigalev and Smerdyakov. In the figures of Stavrogin and Ivan loom the two basic aspects of ethical rationalism. In Stavrogin we see primarily the "coldness," in Ivan "the abstractness," of ethical rationalism. These two sides are closely linked and arise from a common source.

The ethical action of man has three aspects. *Someone, somewhere,* and *somehow* are necessarily involved in any ethical action. The first two elements are thoroughly concrete and individual. The third, however, can be taken abstractly, in logical terms. The abstract is the most primitive, the simplest form of mind. (See Hegel, *"Wer denkt abstrakt?"*) This is why we note in the history of moral philosophy the tendency either to ignore the first two elements of ethical action or to schematize them in the manner of abstract thinking. This tendency expresses itself in the attempt to fix ethical laws or norms, devised on the model of natural laws or laws of logic, or on the model of norms of convention or of law. In other words the "how" of the ethical act is established by completely abstracting it from the "who" and the "where." The living subject of ethical action becomes an unnecessary adjunct to a system of ethical world-order—unnecessary because it can be replaced by any other ethical subject.

It is remarkable that even in thinkers who were not consciously ethical rationalists we find such lack of emphasis on the ethical subject. Even Kant's "categorical imperative" ignores the individual concreteness of the ethical subject. In Kant "moral prescriptions are to be conceived as general laws of nature" (*Grundlegung zu einer Metaphysik der Sitten*). The "ethical realm of ends," we are told, can be conceived "only on the analogy of the realm of nature." In other words the morality of man consists in his acting as if he would submit to mechanical causality, and thus the characteristic ethical act is one divorced from the concrete. The main trait of the ethical world is its uniformity and monotony. In such an ethical world live and act impersonal ethical subjects—the multitude of the "supremely similar oncs," "the many too many," as Nietzsche called them.

One would think that Nietzsche, the apostle of free individuality, who—like Dostoevsky—poses the question of the reality of the ethical subject, could not be accused of ignoring the role of the ethical subject in the ethical act. But Nietzsche also was unwittingly subdued by the spirit of ethical rationalism. As Georg Simmel has clearly shown, his teaching about the "eternal recurrence" gives only another form to Kant's conception of the uniformity and monotony of the moral world. The "eternal recurrence" is a criterion of value. For the ethical subject can recognize as ethically valuable only something in relation to which he can ask for repetition "not once but innumerable times." Thus Nietzsche sees the criterion of morality in the same acceptance of action as something infinitely repeatable, which Kant demanded with his law of nature, and, even more sharply, Fichte, when he formulated the imperative: "Act in such a manner that you could conceive the law of your will as the eternal law of your action." In all three thinkers, in Kant, Fichte and Nietzsche, the ethical subject loses the main trait of individual concreteness: it cannot be repeated, cannot be duplicated.

It is no chance that the devil of Ivan Karamazov appears as the defender of the theory of "eternal recurrence": "Our present earth may have been repeated a billion times . . . the same sequence may have been repeated endlessly and exactly the same to every detail, most unseemly and insufferably tedious." In the theory of "eternal recurrence"—at which (in one way or another) ethical rationalism must inevitably arrive—was concentrated the whole fierceness with which the meaning of the individual concrete being was rejected.

The feverish search for a "place" of one's own conducted by Dostoevsky's heroes appears as an expression of their insatiable desire for concreteness, for realization in a living "here" and "now." In the philosophy of the nineteenth century the problem of "one's own place" has been put by, among others, Fichte, who thinks it indispensable for an ethical subject to have its own special "sphere of freedom" and puts this conception into the center of his legal and social schemes. A paradoxical sharpening of this idea occurs in the teachings of Max Stirner. Stirner could not save the individuality of the ethical subject but asserted the concreteness, the "uniqueness" of the sphere of freedom of the "unique" subject, and thus arrived at an original kind of "ethical solipsism." But after all, the concreteness of a "sphere of freedom" cannot replace the concreteness of the ethical subject itself. Kierkegaard and Nietzsche struggled with that difficulty.

Dostoevsky construes "his place" ("the sphere of freedom") differently; he starts from the Christian concept of the "neighbor," *i.e.,* by accepting as the basic ethical datum the concretely individual existence of a multitude of ethical subjects. Ethical rationalism understands only love for man in general, while the "neighbor" is strange and distant. It is, however, precisely the concrete individuality of the "neighbor" that should be the object of our ethical action. The ethical rationalist is incapable of loving a concrete man, *i.e.,* the idea of man hides the living man for him. Thus the Enlightener Nekrasov, according to Dostoevsky, "loved, on the Volga, man in general in the bargeman and suffered, strictly speaking, not for the bargeman himself but for the bargeman in general. You see, to love man in general necessarily means to despise and, at times, to hate the real man standing at your side." Also Versilov reflects:

> To love one's neighbor and not to despise him . . . is impossible. I believe that man has been created physically incapable of loving his neighbor. . . . Love for humanity must be understood as love for that humanity which you have created in your soul. . . . To love people as they are is impossible. And yet we must. And therefore do them good, overcoming your feelings, holding your nose and shutting your eyes (the latter's essential).

Ivan Karamazov says the same: "I could never understand how one can love one's neighbors. It's just one's neighbors, to my mind, that one can't love, though one might love those at a distance." The elder Zosima tells of a doctor who said: "The more I love humanity in general, the less I love man in particular . . . the more I detest men individually the more ardent becomes my love for humanity."

In Dostoevsky's opinion, "not to judge" is the main condition of the specific relation to people through which they become our "neighbors." For Alyosha Karamazov "not judging" is the inescapable norm of ethics. "He did not care to be a judge of others—he would never take upon himself to judge and would never condemn anyone for anything." Alyosha asks Ivan: "Has any man a right to look at other men and decide which is worthy to live?" Such an attitude "restored the heart" to Grushenka—for Alyosha "did not speak as a judge but as the lowest of the judged." Aloysha "pierced the heart" of his father "living with him, seeing everything and blaming nothing." Fyodor says to him: "You are the only creature in the world who has not condemned me." Father Zosima says many times: "Remember particularly that you cannot be a judge of anyone." Precisely because of this unwillingness to judge, Alyosha gets to know his father, his brothers whom he had not known before, Grushenka, the boys, and the captain. In fact, he appears everywhere loving, near, and familiar; for him everybody is a neighbor in the genuine Christian sense of the world. His place—his "sphere of freedom"—is the whole moral world. Every special sphere, every "place," every "here and now" becomes "concrete" for him, and is filled with tasks which he does not flee but seeks out for himself. The whole world becomes to him ethically "transparent," becomes his own self through the active love which grows on the soil of "not judging."

Finally, the basis of Alyosha's active love and "not judging" lies in the sphere of religion; the ontological stability of his personality is due to his closeness to God. The religious and philosophical solution given by Dostoevsky is more essential than the "ethical and ontological" problem.

We can ask still another question: why does the specific ontological weakness and instability of the ethical subject that constructs itself according to rationalistic schemes express itself in a "splitting" of the personality which in pathological cases appears as an actual "doubling" and finally leads to madness?

First of all, rationalistic ethics carries a schism into the psychic life of man, setting abstract duty against concrete inclination. It sees the ethical aim of the individual as a sacrifice of the concrete to the abstract. The schism and the struggle in the soul of the ethical subject are declared to be his "dignity," the essence of his ethical being. It is not by chance that after the establishment of the radically abstract ethical system of Kant this principle of the inner split became the object of bitter attacks by Schiller, Fichte, Hegel, the Hegelians (Feuerbach, Stirner), and later, Nietzsche. Nietzsche sees the meaning of Kant's moral philosophy in the struggle of a "higher" with a "lower" self and sees that the concrete man "is completely divorced from his higher self and becomes often an actor of his self." Still, none of these philosophers succeeded in overcoming ethical dualism. But this schism makes the concrete nonexistent, and the abstract powerless.

The schism brought into the life of an ethical subject by rationalistic ethics, can be even more clearly demonstrated by the fact that the only living, *i.e.,* nonabstract, ethical motive remaining is shame. Ethical rationalism requires a quantitative comparison of the ethical subjects, a distribution over steps on a ladder, an evaluation of the "higher" and "lower"—in short, "judging." Actually, however, ethical subjects are essentially incomparable—or, rather, they must not be compared—for everyone has his own individual scale of ethical values, incommensurable with the other scales of other subjects. In the abstract principle of duty all men are identical. Hence comes the shame man feels for his concreteness insofar as it appears identical with the concreteness of the "least man," of the "many, all too many." Stavrogin is ashamed at the naïve enthusiasm of Shatov, at Fedka the Convict, at Pyotr Verkhovensky, at his "demon." Shame is also the only key to Ivan Karamazov's ethical self-knowledge—shame for Smerdyakov, for the "devil." Dostoevsky sees the weakness of Stavrogin and Ivan in sense of shame. But in Nietzsche contempt, revulsion, scorn, "the great satiety" are identical with shame for the "last man," "the many all too many," the petty man—man insofar as he is "an ape and a torturing shame" of the superman: this is the main ethical stimulus. Although Nietzsche reflects that shame is a great ethical power, in Dostoevsky shame—the inability to overcome shame—leads to the impasses of both Stavrogin and Ivan and their divorce from concreteness. For the shame at concreteness (one's own and that of others) weakens and reduces power and the life of concreteness and reaffirms the split in the soul of the ethical subject that was caused in him by ethical rationalism.

This splitting in two prepares the appearance of the double. For concreteness—living and ontologically stable concreteness—is rejected and repulsed by the abstract principle. Still, it cannot take on ontological power and firmness. The existential sphere of the ethical subject is weakened. Fear, *Angst,* the feeling of being threatened on all sides arises. This can become the living source of religious insight (Paul Tillich's argument), but it can also bring about a total psychological disbelief of the ethical subject in its ontological stability, and can create an unstable situation in the soul. The soul craves the blow which would throw it out of this torturing situation. And this blow falls, naturally, on the weakest, unprotected point of the ethical subject. The subject, having lost the source and base of its ethical concreteness—the concreteness of the "I," its "who"—also loses that sphere of concreteness which it had still preserved: its "place," its concrete "sphere of freedom," its "here." In extreme cases, such a blow must on the strength of the psychological cause we have described (the split in the soul of the ethical rationalist) result in the appearance of a double, whether imaginary or real. The ethical function of the appearance of the double is obviously the same as the ethical function of death, *i.e.,* the loss of existence of the subject. Or shall we say that the loss of concreteness brings about a depersonalization of the subject: it becomes a "thing," it loses existence as a subject. Thus the double puts with extreme power the question: will the individual discover a new stability and a new life in absolute being or will he perish in Nothingness?

Thus Dostoevsky's raising of the problem of the double appears as one of the most significant milestones in the nineteenth-century philosophical struggle against ethical rationalism, a struggle which has not by any means been concluded and which may even have barely begun. (pp. 112-29)

Dmitri Chizhevsky, "The Theme of the Double in Dostoevsky," translated by René Wellek, in Dostoevsky: A Collection of Critical Essays, *edited by René Wellek, Prentice-Hall, Inc., 1962, pp. 112-29.*

FURTHER READING

General Critical Studies

Coates, Paul. *The Double and the Other: Identity as Ideology in Post-Romantic Fiction.* London: Macmillan, 1988, 152 p.

Relates the appearance of the double in literature to social, historical, and ideological determinants.

Guerard, Albert J. "Concept of the Double." In *Stories of the Double,* edited by Albert J. Guerard, pp. 1-14. Philadelphia: Lippincott, 1967.

Attempts to define the various manifestations of the double in modern literature.

Herdman, John. *The Double in Nineteenth-Century Fiction.* London: Macmillan, 1990, 174 p.

An overview of the literary, psychological, philosophical, historical, and theological contexts of the double theme in European and American nineteenth-century literatures.

Miller, Karl. *Doubles: Studies in Literary History.* New York: Oxford University Press, 1985, 468 p.

A general discussion of the double in the Anglo-American literary tradition.

Porter, Laurence M. "The Devil as Double in Nineteenth-Century Literature: Goethe, Dostoevsky, and Flaubert." *Comparative Literature Studies* XV, No. 3 (September 1978): 316-35.

Attempts to account for the frequent use of the demonic double in nineteenth-century fiction.

Smith, James M. "The *Homo Duplex* in Nineteenth-Century French Literature." In *Studies in Honor of Alfred G. Engstrom,* edited by Robert T. Cargo and Emanuel J. Mickel, Jr., pp. 127-38. Chapel Hill: University of North Carolina Press, 1972.

Examines the principal types of the double in the works of Charles Baudelaire, Gérard de Nerval, Alfred de Musset, and other writers.

Waldeck, Peter B. *The Split Self from Goethe to Broch.* Cranbury, N. J.: Associated University Presses, 1979, 190 p.

A psychological interpretation of the double in modern European literature.

Comparative Studies

Gillman, Susan, and Patten, Robert L. "Dickens: Doubles:: Twain: Twins." *Nineteenth-Century Fiction* 39, No. 4 (March 1985): 441-58.

Analyzes Charles Dickens's and Mark Twain's fascination with alternate selves and compares their responses to doubling.

Ireland, Kenneth R. "Urban Perspectives: Fantasy and Reality in Hoffmann and Dickens." *Comparative Literature* XXX, No. 2 (Spring 1978): 133-56.

Discusses the parallels between the works of Dickens and Hoffmann, with particular emphasis on doubling.

Mahoney, Dennis F. "Double into Doppelganger: The Genesis of the Doppelganger-Motif in the Novels of Jean Paul and E. T. A. Hoffmann." *Journal of Evolutionary Psychology* 4, Nos. 1-2 (April 1983): 54-63.

A comparative study of two seminal German writers who developed the double theme.

The French Revolution and English Literature

INTRODUCTION

The French Revolution marked the transition from the *ancien régime* to the modern era in France, and represented for many the dawn of a new age founded on such principles as justice and equality. Historians have analyzed a number of factors that contributed to the Revolution, concurring that the chaotic state of government finances and growing bourgeois discontent with the feudal system provided the impetus for a coup d'état. Scholars also discuss the influence of such Enlightenment philosophers as Voltaire, Diderot, Montesquieu, and particularly Rousseau. These thinkers established an intellectual basis for revolution through their attacks on church and crown, advocating popular sovereignty while espousing concepts of natural law and human reason.

Most historians regard the storming of the Bastille as the decisive early incident that symbolizes the popular overthrow of the *ancien régime.* A medieval fortress used by the monarchy as a prison, the Bastille had become a hated symbol of the despotic Bourbon dynasty, and on 14 July 1789 a Parisian mob seized the prison and freed several inmates. An interim governing body, the National Assembly, drafted a constitution to replace the absolute monarchy of Louis XVI. The principles of this Revolutionary government were codified in the Declaration of the Rights of Man and of the Citizen. Reflecting the spirit of the American Declaration of Independence, the French document espoused the rights of the individual to liberty, property, and free speech, and advocated a republican government. In 1792, the National Convention was formed to create a new constitution; the legislature abolished the monarchy, ultimately executing the king for treason. Within the Convention, several factions emerged: the Girondists represented a moderate point of view, the Jacobins were slightly more radical, and a group of legislators led by Jacques Hébert represented the extreme left position. At the time, France was involved in military conflicts with other nations in addition to the tumult within its borders. In an attempt to present a unified republic both to the people of France and to potential foreign invaders, the Convention instituted the Committee of Public Safety, empowered to act as an emergency dictatorship. The inception of the committee marked the beginning of what came to be known as the Reign of Terror, during which thousands of people suspected of counterrevolutionary activity were arrested, tried by the Revolutionary Tribunal, and executed by guillotine or mass drownings. Maximilien Robespierre, a Jacobin, gradually rose to power within this controversial and powerful committee, eventually overthrowing the competing factions. By 1794, politically moderate Convention members asserted that military successes abroad reduced the need for drastic measures within France, and in an effort to avoid a backlash from the populace, Robespierre's enemies banded together to remove him from power. He was arrested, tried, and—on 28 July 1794—guillotined.

The French Revolution has exerted a profound influence on European art and thought. English writers of the nineteenth century expressed in their works both the hope associated with the early stages of the Revolution and the sense of horror and betrayal aroused by the Reign of Terror. Noted theorists of the period responded directly to revolutionary events with political treatises espousing particular ideologies. Edmund Burke's *Reflections on the Revolution in France,* for instance, voices his opposition to the Revolution, while Thomas Paine's *Rights of Man* and Mary Wollstonecraft's *Vindication of the Rights of Woman* defend revolutionary tenets. The Revolution is also manifested in the language, imagery, and structure of creative works of the nineteenth century, most notably in the genre of Romantic poetry. As Stopford Brooke has asserted, "[the Revolution's] ideas, or opposition to its ideas, underlie the whole of the great poetry of England from Cowper to Keats." Inspired by the political climate in France, English Romantic poets exalted the worth of the individual, incorporating into their works such themes as universal freedom and equality. When the Committee of Public Safety was established as a war dictatorship, many observers believed that the ideal of popular government had been abandoned, and such influential poets as Wordsworth, Blake, and Coleridge registered disappointment and anger that the goals of the Revolution had not been fulfilled. English novelists also interpreted the events of revolutionary France. For instance, though Gothic fiction did not necessarily treat the Revolution overtly, Ronald Paulson has suggested that, with its "tales of darkness, confusion, blood, and horror," Gothic novels "did in fact serve as a metaphor with which some contemporaries in England tried to come to terms with what was happening across the Channel in the 1790s." Events of the Revolution were also depicted in dramas of the nineteenth century, though these plays were strictly censored by the English government.

HISTORY AND THEORY

Ronald Paulson

[*Paulson is an American critic and educator who has written extensively on art and literature in eighteenth-century England. In the essay below, he examines Edmund Burke's representation of the French Revolution, and assesses responses to Burke in the works of Thomas Paine and Mary Wollstonecraft.*]

Burke's first response to the Revolution, written on 9 August 1789, adopts the metaphor of art. He expresses his "astonishment at the wonderful Spectacle": "what Spectators, and what actors! England gazing with astonishment at a French struggle for Liberty and not knowing whether to blame or to applaud!" At once, however, he detects "something in it paradoxical and Mysterious" because, in the act of destroying the Bastille with a "spirit it is impossible not to admire," he sees that "the old Parisian ferocity has broken out in a shocking manner." This passage was echoed near the beginning of his mature thoughts on the subject, *Reflections on the Revolution in France* (1790):

> In viewing this monstrous tragic-comic scene, the most opposite passions necessarily succeed, and sometimes mix with each other in the mind; alternate contempt and indignation; alternate laughter and tears; alternate scorn and horror.

By this time Burke's ambivalence had settled on the matter of whether the Revolution was a continuation of old revolutions—the English Civil War, not of course the Glorious Rebellion of 1688, which some of his colleagues liked to see as its analogue—or something absolutely and appallingly new. He starts off his *Reflections* with the metaphors of English radical dissent seen through the eyes of his literary mediator, Swift's *Tale of a Tub.* The "spirit of liberty" is a "wild gas," and once "the fixed air is plainly broke loose," Burke writes, "we ought to suspend our judgment until the first effervescence is a little suspended, till the liquor is cleared, and until we see something deeper than the agitation of a troubled and frothy surface."

Burke's argument is determined less by logic than by a Swiftean chain of association that links Richard Price's Revolutionary Society speech (which set him off) with the dissenters, their incendiary sermons, illumination and zeal, divine afflatus, the regicide Reverend Hugh Peters, memories of the Civil War, and the "leading in triumph" of King Charles I. The last becomes the type of (or analogue for) the conveyance of Louis XVI to Paris by the crowd, with (to complete the parallel with Charles I) the element of predictability or prophecy in the inevitable execution that lies ahead, and also the Augustan (Popean as well as Swiftean) evocation of the *Via Dolorosa* of Christ in the description of how the king and his queen "had been made to taste, drop by drop, more than the bitterness of death, in the slow torture of a journey of twelve miles, protracted to six hours. . . . "

But this is the climax of various interlocking series of images. The Swiftean metaphor of body-clothing is energized on the third page with French society now revealing itself "stripped of every relation, in all the nakedness and solitude of metaphysical abstraction." The Enlightenment metaphor of bright and undeflected light intertwines with Burke's own distinctive metaphor of organic growth. The imagery of light and dark of course plays a large part in Swift's *Tale,* and like Swift Burke begins with the words of the enemy, the source of his own transvaluation of the image. For he is reacting against the metaphor formulated by Richard Price shortly after the fall of the Bastille, addressed to the "friends of the Great and Glorious Revolution of 1688":

> I see the ardor for Liberty catching and spreading. . . . Behold, the light you have struck out, after setting America free, reflected to France, and there kindled into a blaze that lays despotism in ashes, and warms and illuminates all Europe! Tremble all ye oppressors of the world! . . . You cannot now hold the world in darkness. Struggle no longer against increasing light and liberality.

Price has raised the imagery of Enlightenment into one of conflagration, and Burke revises it into the false usurping sun of the human reason as "not the light of heaven, but the light of rotten wood and stinking fish—the gloomy sparkling of collected filth, corruption, and putrefaction." This is the false light cast by Swift's enthusiasts and Pope's dunces, the light of the "new philosophy" which only its *adherents* perceive as a "glorious blaze."

But Burke is also—and I think much more importantly—approaching the subject of light through the aesthetic context of his own *Philosophical Enquiry into the Origin of our Ideas of the Sublime and Beautiful* (which he published in 1757, thirty years before), where he argued that darkness is sublime, light is not: "But," he qualified his generalization, "such a light as that of the sun, immediately exerted on the eye, as it overpowers the sense, is a very great idea. . . . Extreme light, by overcoming the organs of sight, obliterates all objects, so as in its effects exactly to resemble darkness." This same fierce glare, this power or uncontrolled energy seen as sublime in his *Philosophical Enquiry,* becomes thirty years later in his *Reflections* the model for the Enlightenment rays that have been intensified by the revolutionaries into "this new conquering empire of light and reason" which dissolves all "the sentiments which beautify and soften private society." The true sun, as he sees it, enters

> into common life, like rays of light which pierce into a dense medium, [and] are, by the laws of nature, refracted from their straight line. Indeed in the gross and complicated mass of human passions and concerns, the primitive rights of men undergo such a variety of refractions and reflections, that it becomes absurd to talk of them as if they continued in the simplicity of their original direction.

His image of man's intricate and complex nature as the essential reality that must be preserved in society is the exact contrary of the revolutionary's view of man as an obstruction to the beneficent sunburst of human liberty. By implication, Burke posits two suns: the royal or natural sun, which is, in England at least, refracted through the prism of human nature or human possibility, and the false usurping sun of human reason, which he describes alternately in terms of the blinding sun of sublimity or the phosphorescence of rotten wood and stinking fish.

Burke's argument has been proceeding by a process of analogy like the one he recommends as the essential of government itself. He moves from the organic growth of the plant (the great British oak) to the countryside, the country house and the georgic ideal of retirement, the estate, the aristocratic family and its generations, the inviolability of inheritance. The house becomes a castle and the concept of patrilineal succession merges with the argument for "chivalry." "We wished," he says at the heart of his argument, ". . . to derive all we possess as an inheritance from our forefathers. Upon that body and stock of inheritance we have taken care not to inoculate any cyon alien to the nature of the original plant."

All of these image patterns, in themselves conventional, build and merge until they erupt in the double scene of the king being led in triumph by his rebellious subjects and the queen attacked in her bedroom as the mob cuts down her guard:

> A band of cruel ruffians and assassins, reeking with his blood, rushed into the chamber of the queen, and pierced with an hundred strokes of bayonets and poniards the bed, from whence this persecuted woman had but just time to fly almost naked, and through ways unknown to the murderers had escaped to seek refuge at the feet of a king and husband, not secure of his own life for a moment.

There is, it needs to be said first, no evidence of Marie Antoinette's fleeing "almost naked." The imagery of clothing, activated earlier, reemerges with the cruelly penetrating power of the sunlight, and when Burke tells how "All the decent drapery of life is to be rudely torn off," all those religious customs and illusions of the past stripped away, revealing "our naked shivering nature," he is thinking of the queen: "On this scheme of things, a king is but a man; a queen is but a woman; a woman is but an animal; and an animal not of the highest order." In this scene at the very heart of the *Reflections* the metaphoric stripping of society has become the literal stripping of the queen.

When you strip the queen, you expose the principle of equality, but you also prove your masculinity in relation to the king (the "father" of his people, the center of his universe, descendant of the "roi soleil"). You pierce the queen's bed "with an hundred strokes of bayonets and poniards" as a surrogate for the queen herself, and, as Burke intimates, were she captured she would best play "the Roman matron" and "save herself from the last disgrace by taking her own life." Burke is recalling the imagery of republican Rome adapted by the French themselves, focused on stories such as the Horatii, the rape of Lucrece, and all the deadly conflicts between love of family and loyalty to the state. But Burke sees much deeper, beneath the Roman costume to the most primal situations which only the sans-culottes revealed upon occasion, sometimes printed in the popular Paris papers.

The brutal sensuality of the ragged mob derives, of course, from memories of the sexual license traditionally detected under the idealistic claims as the real motivating force of the radical Protestant sects. The attack on the queen, her nakedness, and the capture of the king lead to "fervent prayer and enthusiastic ejaculation" as the marriage of religion, sex, and politics did in Swift's *Tale of a Tub.* But Burke's own particular concatenation of the natural, genetic, and inherited with the revolutionary's sexual license focuses on the traditional imagery of the king as father, his subjects as his family. He makes striking use of the topic in his allusion to Medea, who like the French, cuts up her father and boils him in order to "regenerate the paternal constitution."

As he refines the image of the queen's rape, however, in his later attacks on the revolutionaries what emerges is rather an insinuating seduction, for which his model (and, he believes, the revolutionaries') is Rousseau's *Confessions* with its young parvenus, "dancing-masters, fiddlers, pattern-drawers, friseurs, and valets de chambre," who enter the sacred family circle, seduce the wife or daughter, and undermine the authority, indeed take the place of the father-husband. Burke develops the model in the sequel to his *Reflections, A Letter to a Member of the National Assembly* (1791), where he argues that Rousseau has become for the revolutionaries a figure "next in sanctity to that of a father," and following his example, they encourage tutors "who betray the most awful family trusts and vitiate their female pupils" and they "teach the people that the debauchers of virgins, almost in the arms of their parents, may be safe inmates in their house. . . . " The National Assembly, he believes, hope that "the females of the first families of France may become an easy prey" to these dancing masters and valets, "and other active citizens of that description, who have the entry into your houses, and being half domesticated by their situation, may be blended with you by regular and irregular relations." For it is precisely the object of the revolutionaries "to destroy the gentlemen of France," and so, Burke concludes,

> by the false sympathies of this *Nouvelle Éloise* they endeavor to subvert those principles of domestic trust and fidelity which form the discipline of social life. They propagate principles by which every servant may think it, if not his duty, at least his privilege, to betray his master. By these principles, every considerable father of a family loses the sanctuary of his house.

If we place these passages back in the context of Burke's *Reflections* and the well-known passages idealizing Marie Antoinette, we see Burke opposing a vigorous ("active"), unprincipled, rootless masculine sexuality, unleashed and irrepressible, against a gentle aristocratic family, patriarchal and based on bonds of love. His point of departure, I should suppose, was Rousseau's well-known assertion in the *Confessions* that "seamstresses, chambermaids, and shop girls hardly tempted me; I needed young ladies. Everyone has his fancies, and that has always been mine. . . . " Rousseau is much concerned with the "servant's intimacy with his mistress," to which end in fact he used his own musical and pedagogical talents, and he refers to cases of servants who enter a household and seduce the wife or daughter under the father-husband's nose. Burke is probably recalling Rousseau's account of M. de Tavel, Mme. de Warens's philosopher-teacher, who slipped into her affections and first drew her away from "her husband and her duties" by inculcating her with philosophical sophistries ("He succeeded in persuading her that adultery was nothing").

But the most striking facts about Rousseau's own affairs with ladies at first seem at odds with Burke's model.

(These are facts, incidentally, which do not apply to his long affair with the working-class Thérèse.) One fact is his passivity and the other is that they are husbandless women. What Burke may have seen, or sensed, however, was the way Rousseau insinuated himself into this passive role to become an irresistible combination of both son and lover to the widow. For a third striking aspect of Rousseau's affairs beginning with Mme. de Warens is the oedipal dimension. She is "Maman": "By calling her Mamma and treating her with the familiarity of a son," says Rousseau, " . . . I felt as if I had committed incest. . . . " He tends to choose his ladies from among widows and otherwise husbandless women, after the rival has already been disposed of (and they are, of course, older women—after Mme. de Warens, Mme. de Larnage is forty-four and the mother of ten). But in Mme de Warens's case the servant Anet fills the role of husband, and (although Burke cannot have known this) his death may well have been suicide in response to Rousseau's superseding him in his mistress's affections. Anet "died in our arms," Rousseau, unruffled by the bizarre scene, tells us, "with no other spiritual exhortations than my own; and these I lavished on him amidst transports of such heartfelt grief that if he had been in the state to understand me, he should have received some consolation." And this is followed by Rousseau's "vile and unworthy thought . . . that I should inherit his clothes, and particularly a fine black coat which had caught my fancy," which he promptly puts into action. The pattern is completed by his taking over Anet's duties in Mme. de Warens's household, and finally by his being superseded himself by another young servant (a journeyman wigmaker who "succeeded in making himself all important in the house," he says): "In short I found my place filled." Rousseau does, in perhaps ways that Burke sensed, all too well fit his model.

There remains throughout Rousseau's relations with Mme. de Warens and other ladies a distinct ambivalence. He can say, in a personal context (a sentence that would have been significant to Burke), "that it is not only in the case of husbands and lovers that the owner and the possessor are so often two very different persons." Then in *La Nouvelle Héloise,* his novel about such a triangle, there is his praise of the young woman who has an affair before marriage but can regain her virtue as a wife, and in the second part of the *Confessions* there is his scathing opinion of the unfaithful wife: " . . . morality and marital fidelity . . . are at the root of all social order." And yet, as he tells us, the success of *La Nouvelle Héloise* made possible for him the conquest of any woman, "even of the highest rank." And finally, as was all too evident in the *Confessions,* an actual seduction and affair were not required for Rousseau to bring about the disruption of a family (recall the effect of his friendship with Mme. d'Houdetot on the d'Epinay household).

In psychological terms, then, Burke offers a rationale for repression: Avarice, ambition, and sexuality are passions in men which must be controlled and restrained by the state, but Rousseau and his followers, in both private life and public, would outlaw all repression. The two qualities he emphasizes are youth and energy. The revolutionaries are "bold, presuming young persons." "*One* thing, and *one* thing only" explains their success: "they have *energy,*" "this dreadful and portentous energy." Sheer energy, the energy of ability without property, Burke believes to be the most dangerous threat to ordered society; for "ability is a vigorous and active principle, and . . . property is sluggish, inert and timid. . . . " The *Letter to a Member of the National Assembly* ends with a peroration about the energy of the revolutionaries: "You are naturally more intense in your application," he says, than relaxed and detached Englishmen. "This continued, unremitted effort of the members of your Assembly I take to be one of the causes of the mischief they have done." What Burke finds appalling is that this energy or unchecked instinct can be directed with such fearful intensity toward finding ways to possess the master's wife or daughter and to overthrow the king (and lead him in triumph).

All this makes a fairly complicated model, with ramifications less corresponding to Rousseau's *Confessions* than suggesting that Burke fitted Rousseau into a prior model of his own. The peculiar obsession with sexuality in Burke's attacks on the revolutionaries can be explained, for example, as it has been by Isaac Kramnick, in terms of Burke's psyche, especially his childhood experiences. He himself was, after all, a parvenu, like Rousseau the music-master or philosopher who used his talents to insinuate himself into the lives of the great, toward whom his feelings were ambivalent. Long before reaching Burke's psyche, however, we have to acknowledge the extremely conventional literary elements of his attack which derive from the polemics of the English Civil War and its aftermath, in which religious enthusiasm leads to the unleashing of sexual drives and/or the overthrowing of government. In Swift's terms, we recall, the errant vapor (the "gas" Burke refers to) rises from semen adust to seek an outlet in orgasm or, when this is impracticable, it rises to the brain, overturns it, and causes the individual to overturn society as well. There is, in short, a high degree of the conventional in Burke's vocabulary and imagery.

Kramnick tends to go straight to the archetype or the biography, over the head, so to speak, of the literary text. He draws proper attention to Burke's excremental imagery: "the principle of evil himself, incorporeal, pure, unmixed, dephlegmated, defecated evil," Burke writes, referring to the Jacobins as Phineas's birds, who (in the *Aeneid*) "flutter over our heads, and souse down upon our tables, and leave nothing unrent, unrifled, unravaged, or unpolluted with the slime of their filthy offal." However, the scatology goes off into imagery of mere darkness ("black and savage atrocity of mind," "all black with the smoke and soot of the forge of confiscation and robbery"). Kramnick associates, quite correctly, the scatology, the anality, the darkness, and dirt of the the Jacobins with Satan, a black, sulfurous figure whose anus is saluted in the ceremony of the Sabbath. But the basis of such imagery is to be found in Swift's Grub Street hacks and Pope's dunces, and, insofar as it involves Satan, in the central paradigm of *Paradise Lost,* upon which Burke as well as Dryden, Swift, and Pope built their satiric fictions. For Burke Paris is Milton's hell (everywhere "rankness" and "refuse and rejected offal") and the story is of the troops of God opposing the Jacobin fallen angels, with all the old associations of pride, impiety, and overthrown order.

The best clue to what Burke makes of Satan appears in a speech he delivered in Commons on 11 April 1794 in which he describes the Jacobin hell:

> The condition of France at this moment was so frightful and horrible, that if a painter wished to portray a description of hell, he could not find so terrible a model, or a subject so pregnant with horror, and fit for his purpose. Milton, with all that genius which enabled him to excel in descriptions of this nature, would have been ashamed to have presented to his readers such a hell as France now has, or such a devil as a modern Jacobin; he would have thought his design revolting to the most unlimited imagination, and his colouring overcharged beyond all allowance for the license even of poetical painting.

This passage, with its reference to the "terrible" and to painting, recalls Burke's own *Philosophical Enquiry into the Sublime and Beautiful,* in terms of which he is now saying that the true sublime in government is a mixture of fear and awe or admiration, whereas the false sublime, a perversion of this (like the false *light* versus the true), generates only fear and a grotesque energy. It is not surprising that Burke's formulation in the *Philosophical Enquiry* is couched in terms of a family:

> The authority of a father, so useful to our well-being, and so justly venerable upon all accounts [i.e., the sublime], hinders us from having that entire love for him that we have for our mothers, where the parental authority is almost melted down into the mother's fondness and indulgence [i.e., the beautiful].

More interesting, however, is Burke's allusion to Milton's hell, seen in the light of the examples he offers in the *Philosophical Enquiry* of the terrible as the defining feature of sublimity. As in the *Reflections,* I believe the illustrations and metaphorical decoration take us closest to Burke's true intention, often saying more than he may have meant to say. One of the prime qualities that evoke the terrible (which certainly anticipates the imagery of the *Reflections*) is obscurity, and Burke illustrates this with Milton's description of Satan, who amid his fallen angels, "above the rest / In shape and gesture proudly eminent / Stood like a tower. . . . " About the passage Burke says:

> Here is a very noble picture; and in what does this poetical picture consist? In images of a tower, an archangel, the sun rising through mists, or in an eclipse, the ruin of monarchs, and the revolutions of kingdoms.

I think we can begin to see where Burke's imagery of revolution in fact came from and what it meant to him. It was the terrible of his sublime, with precisely the aesthetic distancing implied in his formulation that pain and danger "are simply painful when their causes immediately affect us [i.e., if we were in France]; they are delightful when we have an idea of pain and danger, without being actually in such circumstances." In his first *Letter on a Regicide Peace* (1796) Burke wrote of the Revolution:

> I can contemplate, without dread, a royal or a national tiger on the borders of PEGU. I can look at him, with an easy curiosity, as prisoner within bars in the menagerie of the tower. But if, by habeas corpus or otherwise, he was to come into the lobby of the House of Commons while your door was open, any of you would be more stout than wise, who would not gladly make your escape out of the back windows. I certainly should dread more from a wild cat in my bedchamber, than from all the lions that roar in the deserts behind Algiers. But in this parallel it is the cat that is at a distance, and the lions and tigers that are in our ante-chambers and our lobbies.

It is well to remember that Burke was originally galvanized into active opposition to the Revolution by the threat in Price's speech of a tiger closer to home than "distance" might suggest, and on 25 October 1790 he wrote to Calonne that in the *Reflections* "in reality, my object was not France, in the first instance, but this Country." Burke could come to terms with the Revolution by distancing it as a sublime experience, even while denying its sublimity and realizing that it might not keep its "distance."

But the description he quotes of Satan (from *Paradise Lost,* book 1) is preceded, two pages earlier in the *Philosophical Enquiry* (illustrating the same concept of "obscurity"), by the description of Death in book 2, confronting Satan at the Gate of Hell and shaking at him "a deadly dart," *as seen by* Satan. There is no portrayal of Satan in the passage describing his confrontation with Death, and so for the equivalent view of Satan Burke went back to the passage in book 1. Satan addresses Death as a rebel son (ll. 681–87), and Death replies in kind to Satan: "Traitor Angel, art thou hee, / Who first broke peace in Heav'n and Faith, till then / Unbrok'n, and in proud rebellious Arms / Drew after him . . . "; and he refers to himself as king (the one unobscure part of him is his "Kingly Crown") and to this realm "Where I reign King, and to enrage thee more, [am] / Thy King and Lord." Burke himself refers to Death as the "king of terrors," the ultimate sublime, the real father.

Our sensation in reading Burke's passage derives from viewing not a static figure, however powerful, but an aggressive action: not just Satan or Death but the two challenging each other, and not just a confrontation but consecutively Burke himself seen as facing Death and then facing Satan confronting Death, so that we see him assuming the role of each challenger in turn. Between Satan and Death in this scene (though not mentioned by Burke) is the figure of Sin, the daughter-lover of Satan, the mother-lover of Death, suggesting a single powerful image of the son who challenges his father for the person of his mother. The deep ambivalence of the emotion is patent in the fact that it is Satan, the arch rebel, who himself has become the father figure, and each insists on *his* being a king and father, the other a son and rebel.

Burke's solution to the confrontation with this unthinkable phenomenon, the French Revolution (one already adopted to some degree in his attacks on Hastings' Indian depredations), was to fit it into the framework of aesthetic categories he had worked out himself thirty years before. He is not unaware of that other category, the beautiful, associated by him with sentimental comfort and soft curving lines. But beauty, "that quality or those qualities in bodies in which they cause love, or some passion similar to it," he associates with the mother, the queen, the chivalry that surrounds her, while it is desire or lust to which "we must attribute those violent and tempestuous passions" of the sublime. "We admire what is large and submit to it; we love what is small enough to submit to us." For if Burke sees revolution as sublime, Rousseau presumably sees it as beautiful, emotions centering around the mother's breast (and a future pastoral state with gently rolling hills and blooming flowers).

The accepted definition of the sublime experience before Burke wrote and redefined it was transfiguration in the presence of some great and unknowable power such as tempest, hurricane, or vast mountain scenery. In *Spectator* 411 and 421 Addison defined it as a sense of immensity or abundance that cannot be contained; as a desire or need to go beyond confines and controls; and as the reaching for what is "too big for its capacity," implying the wish to extend oneself beyond what is rational, possible, or prescribed. Addison, however, sees the sublime as liberating and exhilarating, a kind of happy aggrandizement, whereas Burke sees it as alienating and diminishing. Beauty for both is repose, a comfortable, perhaps enervating status quo, but the sublime projects the mind forward to ultimates, positing a confrontation with power and change that for Burke at any rate is the essence of terror. To turn, as his examples imply, from the beautiful to the sublime is to turn from the comfort of the mother to the threat and incomprehensibility of the father, but more to be part of a confrontation with this father over the beautiful, mediating, desired mother.

The sexual dimension of the scene is plain in both the *Philosophical Enquiry* and the *Reflections.* He in fact tends to use the imagery of tumescence to describe the sublime experience, which begins with "an unnatural tension and certain violent emotions of the nerves." He writes of those confronting the sublime, that "their minds are erect with expectation"; and ambition, another aspect of the situation, is what "tends to raise a man in his own opinion, produces a sort of swelling or triumph, that is extremely grateful to the human mind." It is easy enough to relate this to Swift's analysis of enthusiasm in *A Tale of a Tub* and to Burke's own use of the imagery in his description of the rebels' "fervent prayer and enthusiastic ejaculation" in the *Reflections.*

On the next page of the *Philosophical Enquiry* after the account of Satan, Sin, and Death, Burke brings together Job and God, another son and father. The animals cited—the horse, wild ass, tiger, unicorn, leviathan—are examples of the power of God, the voice out of the whirlwind, over a presumptuous, weakly challenging man. And this congeries of allusions is followed a page later by the contemplation of God Himself, from which "we shrink into the minuteness of our own nature, and are, in a manner, annihilated before him." Job capitulates; he does not curse God and die but internalizes Him. If we look back at the famous passage about the public execution (to see which Burke believes we would abandon a tragedy being performed in a theater), we notice that he is referring to "a state criminal of high rank" (presumably Simon Lord Lovat), a traitor to the king; this is followed by the example of an earthquake—another Job-like confrontation of God and man.

It is the experience of the son's revolt, with its implications of sexual release, followed by his feelings of guilt, and the accommodation by which he comes to terms with the father, internalizes him as superego, and himself becomes a father. It is first the feeling of the son as he challenges Death, and then of the "son" Death facing his towering father Satan, as they confront each other, held apart by the mother-lover. The ambivalence of the rebel toward the act of revolt is both because it is an aggressive act and because the object remains beyond comprehension. It is also because Burke can imagine himself in one or both positions.

The oedipal formation is superimposed upon an original ambivalence (to authority—or to the idea of freedom) and so there is a rapid alternation of attraction and repulsion, evident in Burke's explanation of the initial effect the Revolution had on him, of "gazing with astonishment . . . and not knowing whether to blame or to applaud." But the pattern Burke at once detected in the Revolution—or assigned to it, prophesied, perhaps even in some sense brought about by his prophecy—was obtained by spreading out this ambivalence into the consecutive stages of a plot. As he says, these opposite passions "necessarily succeed, and sometimes mix with each other." In the scenario of the Revolution one first destroys the father and then of necessity internalizes him and becomes more repressive, more the tyrant than he was.

I must distinguish the sublime in which Burke himself is participating from the sublime as a rhetorician's tool. I have been speaking of the first, but a few words must be added about the second. While regarding the Revolution as a false sublime, Burke sees the terrors of something like the sublime experience as a warning to Englishmen who might see the Revolution as beautiful. He remembers his earlier words in the *Philosophical Enquiry* that "terror is a passion which always produces delight when it does not press too close," and now he wants it to press close. He does not want the Revolution to produce "delighted horror" because he intends for its "pain and terror to be so modified [by contact with reality] as to be actually noxious." He does not *want* his reader to feel safe: the tiger is not in Pegu but in London. In terms of Longinus's definition of the sublime, Burke has failed if he "carries his hearer . . . not to persuasion but to ecstasy," since he seeks to convince him that the Revolution is a clear and present danger.

Man's response to an ongoing process cannot be analyzed in the same way as his reaction to a discrete event like a scene in a play or in *Paradise Lost* (or a public execution) or to a static object like a tower. Accordingly Burke treats the Revolution in his *Reflections* as a series of isolated outrages, notably "the atrocious spectacle of the sixth of October 1789." But he projects not only a series of sublime scenes but a sublime plot of the sort I have outlined, only attempting to remove the "security" he insisted on as requisite to the sublime. This removal, which is an attempt by every rhetorical means to create immediacy, is the chief persuasive strategy of the *Reflections* and the works that followed.

Burke is also aware that this security was the safety-catch that functioned to protect the individual himself from becoming a revolutionary—from following a continuous process of psychic liberation and experimentation, like the Jacobins among whom "every counsel, in proportion as it is daring, and violent, and perfidious, is taken for the mark of superior genius." The momentary liberation and exultation, the purgation, which man experiences in his secure encounter with the terrible, the unconstrained, or the rebellious, cannot be allowed permanent sway without a disastrous breakdown of those habitual inhibitions which constitute civilization. In Burke's terms, a regression is taking place to earlier, less mediated stages of development.

Thus underneath the aesthetic and moral vocabulary (the grounding, for example, of social attitudes in a traditional Christian vocabulary), Burke allows us to sense the profound psychic forces of the Revolution that seemed to offer a permanent release from the necessary discontents of civilization. These were precisely the forces that had been given a sanctioned, carefully distanced airing in his aesthetic of the sublime but that in his final summation of the French Revolution in *Letters on a Regicide Peace* of 1796 showed the Jacobins regressing from oedipal to anal-oral manifestations, from demonic to bestial and from eucharistic to cannibalistic behavior. He opens the first "Letter" with another version of Milton's Death:

> . . . out of the tomb of the murdered monarchy in France has arisen a vast, tremendous, unformed spectre, in a far more terrific guise than any which ever yet have overpowered the imagination, and subdued the fortitude of man. Going straight forward to its end, unappalled by peril, unchecked by remorse, despising all common maxims and all common means, that hideous phantom overpowered those who could not believe it was possible she could at all exist. . . .

Death is now a Gothic fantasy confronting the writer directly, without mediation, like the tiger of Pegu who appears later in the "Letter," and it is a "she"—now not merely the son who rises from the tomb of his murdered father but, presumably, a fantasy based on those women Burke described in the *Reflections* who marched on Versailles and brought back the king and queen in triumph to Paris:

> . . . the royal captives who followed in the train were slowly moved along, amidst the horrid yells, the shrilling screams, and frantic dances, and infamous contumelies, and all the unutterable abominations of the furies of hell, in the abused shape of the vilest of women.

It was, he writes, "a spectacle more resembling a procession of American savages," leading their captives "into hovels hung round with scalps, . . . overpowered with the scoffs and buffets of women as ferocious as themselves."

If the first image sets the stage for Revolutionary monsters that will eventuate in Victor Frankenstein's creature, and the second in Blake's "Tyger," other images carry us back to the cannibalism that will be evoked in the graphic work of Gillray in England and Goya in Spain: "By cannibalism, I mean their devouring as a nutriment of their ferocity, some part of the bodies of those they have murdered; their drinking the blood of their victims, and forcing the victims themselves to drink the blood of their kindred slaughtered before their faces." It is not difficult to see how Burke's imagination takes him from the threatening specter that rises from the tomb of the murdered king to the primal horde that devours "as a nutriment of their ferocity" the body of the king. But the emergence of the specter as "she" draws attention to the whole movement of the *Letters on a Regicide Peace,* which is downward and backward into undifferentiation of the sexes as well as of the ruler and ruled, the hunter and hunted, and the eater and eaten.

. . . . .

The most famous metaphor in Thomas Paine's *Rights of Man* (1791-92) appears at the conclusion of the second part (1792):

> It is now towards the middle of February. Were I to take a turn in the country, the trees would present a leafless winterly appearance. As people are apt to pluck twigs as they walk along, I perhaps might do the same, and by chance might observe, that a *single bud* on that twig had begun to swell. I should reason very unnaturally, or rather not reason at all, to suppose *this* was the only bud in England which had this appearance. Instead of deciding thus, I should instantly conclude, that the same appearance was beginning, or about to begin, everywhere; and though the vegetable sleep will continue longer on some trees and plants than on *others,* and though some of them may not *blossom* for two or three years, all will be in leaf in the summer, except those which are *rotten.* What pace the political summer may keep with the natural, no human foresight can determine. It is, however, not difficult to perceive that the spring is begun.

Paine's metaphor of natural process is, among other things, a response to Burke's organic metaphor of the state and his plea for sexual repression. Paine refers to "the vegetable sleep" out of which man is just emerging, and even notes, thinking of Burke's British oak, that some trees may *not* blossom—"those which are *rotten.*" The natural, and so irresistible, process of nature is his point: the first of the old connotations of the word *revolution* to be developed as its meaning changed from the rotation of celestial bodies to the fundamental transformation of society. There is no sense of a winter returning, only of the progress from winter to spring and its irreversibility.

But also present are the connotations of spring, warmth, love, rebirth, youth, and happiness—in short, the beautiful, the green world we still encounter in the images of Russian revolutionary films in which the crowds of workers converging on the prison or factory or palace are related by montage to the bursting buds of spring, the melting ice, the opening of the water-flow, which becomes a raging torrent sweeping away all the locked, cold, and dead barriers.

To see how Paine arrives at his version of the Revolution we have to look back to Matthew 24.32-33, in a chapter devoted to a rehearsal of the Second Coming:

> Now learn a parable of the fig tree; When his branch is yet tender, and putteth forth leaves, yet know that summer is nigh: So likewise, ye, when ye shall see all these things, know that it is near, even at the doors.

The context includes Bunyan's phrase describing the millenarian fugure when it will be "always summer, always sunshine, always pleasant, green, fruitful, and beautiful," and, looking ahead, Burke's counterversion in which precisely such a pastoral scene is destroyed by the Revolution: "All the little quiet rivulets, that watered an humble, a contracted, but not an unfruitful field, are to be lost in the waste expanse, and boundless, barren ocean of the homicide philanthropy of France." The immediate precursor of Paine's passage, however, was Richard Price's sermon which ignited Burke's *Reflections.* The seeds of ideas, says Price, had been planted by philosophers since Milton and are now growing to be a "glorious harvest" in France, and this becomes his climactic metaphor of fire ("I see the ardor for liberty catching and spreading . . . "), which Paine develops some sixty pages earlier than the passage about the budding trees at the opening of his notorious chapter 5 (part II):

> From a small spark, kindled in America, a flame has arisen, not to be extinguished. Without consuming, like the *Ultima Ratio Regum,* it winds its progress from nation to nation, and conquers by a silent operation.

And that silent operation is the opening up of the buds that brings part II to an end, in a kind of sublimation of consuming fire in fructifying warmth and spring.

The image of the Revolution as beauty, peace, and a pastoral *locus amoenus* was made much of in France itself, especially in the graphic form of its great festivals marking the stages in the progress of the Revolution. The most symbolic gesture of these festivals was the transformation of the Champs de Mars into a pastoral setting for parades in which "animals of warfare were excluded, with only peaceful cows and doves permitted." The renaming of days to replace saint's days with trees, fruit, and domestic animals was a similar transvaluation. But in the depths of the Terror the dream was held by Girondin and Jacobin alike of a peaceful island in the midst of the stormy sea, and the festivals represented "in the navigation of life what islands are in the midst of the sea: places for refreshment and rest." In the background were memories of the island on which Rousseau was buried, but, as Paine's conjoint imagery of fire and spring sunlight suggests, the conflict lay between the initial impetus (the spark or fire) and the peaceful end of the conflagration, the good that must come out of necessary evil. Paine tried to elide the difference in his concluding passage, but the French more realistically joined the image (again graphically in their spectacles) of a tranquil island utopia with an erupting volcano, made of badly needed explosives held back from the front in the autumn of 1793 after the execution of Marie Antoinette. At the Feast of the Supreme Being a year later a volcano appeared again, this time transformed into "a peaceful mountain of floral beauty," but the fragility of the relationship between volcano and flowers became clear within the month when Robespierre, the author of the Feast, was himself beheaded.

For Paine also uses the burgeoning of plants in springtime as a final metaphorical statement of the individual French citizens rising as "the people," as a great crowd—a "vast mixed multitude of all ages, and all degrees" (as opposed to Burke's "swinish multitude")—leading to the central historical fact, whose symbolism did not escape Paine, the destruction of the Bastille. Paine brings the crowd as disorder, fire, and energy into conjunction with the Bastille, "the high altar and castle of despotism." He uses the destruction of the Bastille as the focus of *Rights of Man,* a materializing of those metaphors used by Adam Smith and the Physiocrats for the blockage of a laissez-faire economy and therefore of social, moral progress. But he is also responding immediately to Burke's "custom," which blocks the way, the "succession of barriers, or sort of turnpike gates . . . set up between man and his Maker," i.e., kings, parliaments, magistrates, priests, and nobility. If his primary images are of the release of the repressed, of natural rebirth and the irresistible force of a crowd breaking down a prison, behind the contrast of energy and constraint is a larger one between youth and age, between circumstances and what Paine calls contracts (and Blake calls "charters"). The words "control" and "bind" are repeated again and again, connected with those men of the past, "who existed a hundred years ago" and made "laws" that now resist the "continually changing" circumstances of the living. The past are the "dead," embodied in "musty records and mouldy parchments" and now in Burke's writings, and in his sources ("How dry, barren, and obscure"). Paine even notes, as he approaches the storming of the Bastille, that the Archbishop of Vienne, at the time president of the Assembly, was "a person too old to undergo the scene" that was about to unfold, while the actor called for by the circumstances was "a man of more activity, and greater fortitude," the young Lafayette. Indeed the "living" are embodied in Lafayette, "a young man scarcely then twenty years of age" when he assisted in the American Revolution, which itself was part of the larger opposition between the old moribund governments of Europe and the young one in America.

As Burke's plot (his "Jacobean tragedy") centered on the Via Dolorosa of the king and the attack on the queen, so Paine's centers on the taking of the prison, the march on Versailles, and his own version of the triumphal return with the royal family to Paris. What Burke treats in terms of the topos of the world turned upside down Paine treats in terms of a return to the natural and proper. His context is his own *Common Sense* (1776), which must in its way have influenced Burke's formulation as much as Burke's influenced Paine's in *Rights of Man.* What Burke would have seen in *Common Sense* was its insistent connection of family (bastardy versus heredity and primogeniture), the sundering of the family, the parting or "separation" of the colonies from the father country in American "independence."

In Paine's travesty of Burke's beloved law of primogeniture a bastard is the origin of the English monarchy: "A French bastard landing with an armed banditti, and establishing himself king of England against the consent of the natives, is in plain terms a very paltry rascally original.—It certainly hath no divinity in it." Paine's questioning of authority in *Common Sense* by no means stopped with the relationship of colonies to fatherland, as Burke must have seen. But starting with the case of the Americans, he calls for "a final separation" rather than leaving the next generation "to be cutting throats, under the violated unmeaning names of parent and child." And confronted with what was for him and the Americans the crucial day of 19 April 1775—the American version of 14 July, which was the massacre at Lexington—Paine brings together all his strands (including the bastardy), saying he will reject

> the hardened, sullen tempered Pharaoh of England for ever; and disdain the wretch, that with the pretended title of FATHER OF HIS PEOPLE can unfeelingly hear of their slaughter, and composedly sleep with their blood upon his soul. [*Common Sense*]

From the image of the false father, the Saturn-figure who can approve the slaughter of his own children, he moves (a few pages later) to the demand for something very like Freud's primal horde, which figuratively breaks up and ingests the royal symbols of the father, urging: "let the crown at the conclusion of the ceremony ['a day . . . solemnly set apart for proclaiming the charter'], be demolished, and scattered among the people whose right it is." Paine's wishes were carried out a few months later when the equestrian statue of George III in New York City was pulled down by the "Sons of Liberty," broken into pieces, and laid "prostrate in the dirt."

Indeed, Paine could draw upon the American Loyalists' (the Tories') references to England in their propaganda as the "parent trunk," independence as "forbidden fruit," and the revolution as the attempt to lop off "every excrescence from the body politic. Happy if they can stop at the true point, and in order to obtain the fruit . . . do not cut down the tree." He also had the transvaluation of this imagery in the Sons of Liberty's ceremony of setting up some "young oak" as a "Tree of Liberty." Winthrop Jordan has explored the mythic dimension of this American imagery, from which emerges a remarkable parallel to the Satan-Sin-Death situation at the heart of Burke's paradigm for both the sublime and the Revolution. Primitive man worships his father as a tree, or as Christ on a cross; Genesis tells of man's guilt at having eaten his father/god in the story of the "forbidden fruit"; and man sets up a maypole at Merrymount or a Liberty Tree in the town square. From Milton's regicide pamphlets onward, the equation of king and father was pretty clearly part of the republican tradition of polemics. Even the "youth" connected with the American Revolution was present for Paine to develop. He refers in *Common Sense* to the "infant state" of the Colonies: "Youth is the seed time of good habits, as well in nations as in individuals." Many of the leaders themselves were young, as were most of those who guided the fate of the French Revolution (from Danton and Robespierre to the very young Saint-Just and Napoleon).

Mary Wollstonecraft, whose Vindication of the Rights of Woman *(1792) extended the revolutionary notion of equality of women.*

The parental situation in England was the reverse of the one Paine had advocated at the end of *Common Sense.* Recalling perhaps Burke's metaphor of Medea, like the French, cutting up her father and boiling him to "regenerate the paternal constitution" (*Reflections*), Paine turns the metaphor around in *Rights of Man* and comes up with the father Saturn cannibalizing his sons (all except the firstborn):

> By the aristocratical law of primogenitureship, in a family of six children, five are exposed. Aristocracy has never more than *one* child. The rest are begotten to be devoured. They are thrown to the cannibal for prey, and the natural parent prepares the unnatural repast. [*Rights of Man*]

This is by no means the last we shall hear of Saturn in relation to the French Revolution. In the midst of the accusation of the Girondins (including Vergniaud) Paine told Danton that Vergniaud had been right about the Revolution devouring its young.

Paine brings together youth-age, father-son, primogeniture, and organic growth in a single powerful condensation some pages earlier, connecting the towering oak with "the despotic principles of the government" which are centuries old and "too deeply rooted to be removed . . . by anything short of a complete and universal revolution." "Lay then the axe to the root," he says, quoting Matthew 3.10 ("And now also the axe is laid unto the root of the trees: therefore every tree which bringeth not forth good fruit is hewn down, and cast into the fire"), completing the phallic dimension of the metaphor and projecting another version of what Burke saw the "cruel ruffians and assassins" doing to their king, the Rousseauist valets de chambre doing to their master.

From both the "Lay then the axe to the root" passage and the climactic passage about the burgeoning buds of spring, Paine moves to *The Age of Reason* (1793), where he turns to the greatest of "musty" texts, the Bible:

> I have . . . gone through the Bible, as a man would go through a wood with an axe on his shoulders, and fell trees. Here they lie; and the priests, if they can, may replant them. They may, perhaps, stick them in the ground, but they will never make them grow.

And this sums up *Rights of Man* also, in which Paine goes back to origins—to the time before the Normans ("we must trace it to its origin" he says of the English government), long before the artificial barrier of primogeniture was put between us and our heritage of freedom.

"Titles," he says, "are like circles drawn by the magician's wand, to contract the sphere of man's felicity. He lives immured within the Bastille of a word, and surveys at a distance the envied life of man." The "Bastille of a word" shows that Paine shares with many other predecessors (in literature Swift, Fielding, and even more, Sterne) the old topos of life versus (and being constricted by) the written or printed word of the past, with its "power of binding and controlling posterity to the 'end of time'." His own rhetoric includes the idea of clearing away these fetters and barriers, of freeing argument from Burkean art and artifice, leaving it plain, open, and unhindered. Although he parodies Burke's own images (most obviously the idea of chivalry becoming Don Quixote in search of windmills to tilt with), and so produces his own myth of bastardy, his true view expressed in the myth is that "The past was a tale told by an idiot." Plot, story, and history for him are only discontinuity and a total rejection of precedent of every kind. In *Rights of Man* he stopped with an upbeat ending, a myth of a pastoral future. Later, locked up awaiting possible execution at the hands of the Jacobins, he chose to write in *The Age of Reason* his ultimate demystification of the Christian "Book" or of any "Book," which included the French Revolution also.

. . . . .

Paine was quick to see that for Burke revolution is a theatrical performance, just as his hell derives from Milton's poem and painted representations of it, and the whole is a strange aesthetic experience, one important element of which is the inevitable distance of the Englishman from the immediate danger but with the undeniable potential for a reprise on his own soil. In a passage as brilliantly sustained as any in the *Reflections,* Paine ties together "the tragic paintings by which Mr. Burke has outraged his own imagination, and seeks to work upon that of his reader" (paintings "very well calculated for theatrical representation"—indeed "a composite of art," "a dramatic performance" which produces "a stage effect") with Burke's persistent clothing imagery, leading up to: "He pities the plumage, but forgets the dying bird." Burke himself, of course, may have been thinking of the passage in *Common Sense* where Paine had written: "Government, like dress, is the badge of lost innocence; the palaces of kings are built on the ruins of the bowers of paradise"—which neatly reversed in advance Burke's pastoral setting ravaged by revolution.

But Paine could also have been building on an even earlier response to Burke's *Reflections,* which emphasized the aesthetic dimension. A pamphlet called *A Vindication of the Rights of Men* was published by the end of the same month that saw the *Reflections.* Within a few weeks the second edition carried the name of its author, Mary Wollstonecraft. The addition of a woman's name was significant, for Wollstonecraft substitutes for the model of tyranny shared by Burke and Price—the religious plight of dissenters—one of her own: the plight of women in a male society. It was part of her answer to Burke's "letter" but also part of the female persona to choose the woman's literary form par excellence as the perfect vehicle for the "ef-

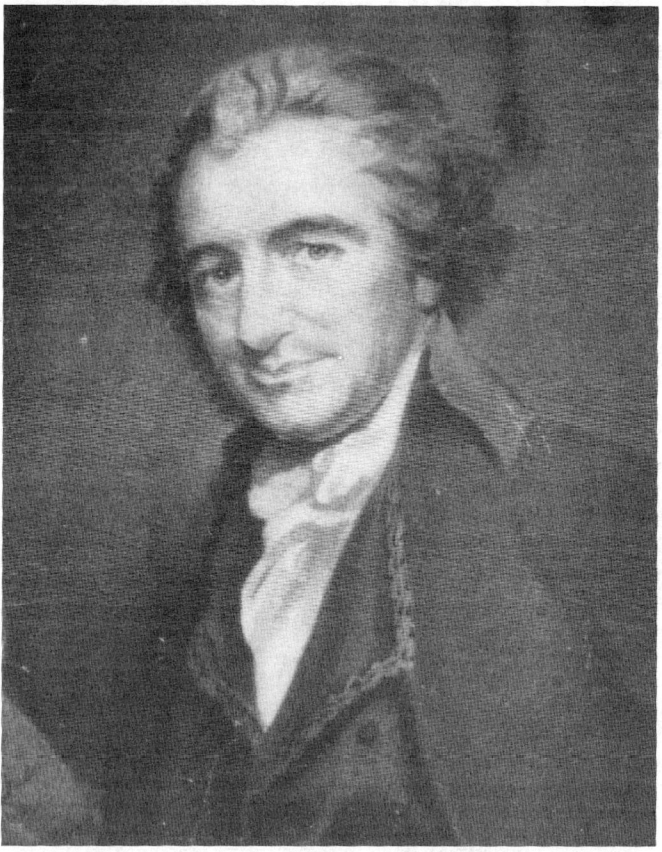

Thomas Paine, author of Rights of Man (1791), *which was both a response to Burke's* Reflections *and a defense of the Revolution.*

fusions of the moment" (as she describes them in her preface) and for "the spontaneity and vigor" of her attack.

In many ways Wollstonecraft's response is the closest in spirit to Burke's own book. It is an impassioned letter addressed directly, and much of the time intimately, to Burke. It shares Burke's rhapsodic structure and even more than the *Reflections* functions as a poem rather than an argument. But what makes the *Vindication* especially interesting is the fact that running counter to the general, somewhat vague and repetitious dithyramb (which turns our attention from the French Revolution to the plight of the English poor; which polarizes the images of the property-oriented Burke and the champion of liberty Price) is Wollstonecraft's powerfully original insight into the relationship between English liberty and the servitude of women.

It is very clear that Wollstonecraft, while consciously inspired by Burke's attack on her friend and mentor Richard Price, was far more deeply stirred by his two central images of the French queen as beautiful, sexually threatened, passive, and vulnerable in an age when chivalry is dead; and of the procession that carried her to Paris, to the accompaniment of "horrid yells, and shrilling screams, and frantic dances, and infamous contumelies, and all the unutterable abominations of the furies of hell, in the abused shape of the vilest of women." Wollstonecraft quotes these lines and replies: "Probably you mean women who gained a livelihood by selling vegetables or fish, who never had had any advantages of education." She is expressing exactly Burke's fear when she connects the Revolution and its "assembly of unlettered clowns" (and the crisis they have produced) with "the active exertions that were not relaxed by a fastidious respect for the beauty of rank, or a dread of the deformity produced by any *void* in the social structure." This "void" (versus "the beauty of rank") is also the "abused shape of the vilest of women," and elsewhere "the poor wretch, whose *inelegant* distress extorted from a mixed feeling of disgust and animal sympathy present relief." Wollstonecraft probes downward to Burke's fear that the beautiful will be overthrown by the sheer vagueness, size, and force of "sublime" energy.

These are the horrible, ugly, violent, aggressive *women* (versus Burke's more usual Rousseauistic men) of the Parisian mob who march to the royal palace and bring back the king and queen—women who in effect *are* the Revolution. Burke's contrast between the two kinds of women drew Wollstonecraft's attention to her own position as the female outsider in a male society and led to the tone of irate detachment which distinguishes her pamphlet (and to the identification of the author's sex in the second edition). But the contrast between the queen and the wretched women of the mob also allowed her to see to a level of Burke's argument only dimly sensed by other writers in their comments on his theatricality and the pleasure he seemed to take in the Revolution as a spectacle. Wollstonecraft's insight was far deeper: she saw that his categories were essentially his own aesthetic ones of the *Enquiry.* She bluntly asserts that "if we really wish to render men more virtuous, we must endeavour to banish all enervating modifications of beauty from civil society." Her contempt and indignation, she says, should not be taken as merely "a flight of fancy; for truth, in morals, has ever appeared to me the essence of the sublime; and, in taste, simplicity the only criterion of the beautiful."

She joins the images of the two kinds of women in passages she directly addresses to Burke:

> A *gentleman* of lively imagination must borrow some drapery from fancy before he can love or pity a *man.*—Misery, to reach your heart, I perceive, must have its cap and bells; your tears are reserved, very *naturally* considering your character, for the declamation of the theatre, or for the downfall of queens, whose rank alters the nature of folly, and throws a graceful veil over vices that degrade humanity; whilst the distress of many industrious mothers, whose *helpmates* have been torn from them [e.g., by press gangs], and the hungry cry of helpless babes, were vulgar sorrows that could not move your commiseration, though they might extort an alms.

The queen is recalled by the clothing imagery (drapery/fancy) and the "graceful veil" that makes vice charming; the women of the mob are represented by the "many industrious mothers," who eventually respond to the impressing of their husbands by marching to Versailles to get the queen. From passive observers, they have become an active force, filling the vacuum left by the pusillanimous males. The queen herself remains only a passive image of beauty, threatened by the irrational force of *other* women that is now unleashed.

Women readers of Burke's *Enquiry* "have laboured to be pretty, by counterfeiting weakness." They are the Marie Antoinettes of the greater world, convinced by Burke's aesthetic that "*littleness* and *weakness* are the very essence of beauty" and that "Nature, by making women *little, smooth, delicate, fair* creatures, never designed that they should exercise their reason to acquire the virtues that produce opposite, if not contradictory, feelings." In Burke she sees the civilization that uses the search for beauty to replace the correction of crimes against the people, that sees experience in aesthetic rather than moral categories—that, in short, "refines the manners at the expense of morals" or makes them "a painted substitute for morals."

Burke's beautiful, she makes clear, is only a prettifying, as when reason "is only employed to varnish over the faults which it ought to have corrected." It is the clothing—the veiling or covering over—that Burke argues for so fervently. The stripping of the woman (of Marie Antoinette), which Burke summons up as a horrible prospect, Wollstonecraft sees as the essential and necessary act. Echoing Burke on Marie Antoinette, she writes:

> Is hereditary weakness necessary to render religion lovely? and will her form have lost the smooth delicacy that inspires love, when stripped of its Gothic drapery?

Gothic is her favorite word for Burke's aesthetic: "These are gothic notions of beauty," she says, "—the ivy is beautiful, but, when it insidiously destroys the trunk from which it receives support, who would not grub it up?"

Edmund Burke, author of the conservative analysis Reflections on the French Revolution.

This grubbing up is the active, energetic, sublime part of the operation, and the part Burke fears. Again "Gothic gallantry" is opposed to a woman's "humanity," which "should have been better pleased to have heard that Lord George Gordon [inciter of the Gordon Riots] was confined on account of the calamities which he brought on his country, than for a *libel* on the queen of France." "Gothic" summons up ideas of chivalry and courtesy but also castles, cells, locked rooms, high walls, contracted marriages, and all the customs that make women fit into Burke's beautiful.

Marie Antoinette is the perfect focus because although queen she stands for the "weakness and indulgence" that "are the only incitements to love and confidence" in Burke's system. Woman is at the center of this problem because Burke and English society in general believe that God gave women beauty so that they would not be inclined

> to cultivate the moral virtues that might chance to excite respect, and interfere with the pleasing sensations they were created to inspire. Thus confining truth, fortitude, and humanity, within the rigid pale of manly morals, they might justly argue, that to be loved, woman's high end and great distinction! they should 'learn to lisp, to totter in their walk, and nick-name God's creatures.'

Love or admiration of women is the "homage [which] vitiates them, prevents their endeavouring to obtain solid personal merit; and, in short, makes those beings vain inconsiderate dolls, who ought to be prudent mothers and useful members of society."

This is Wollstonecraft's central insight: that beauty and seductiveness are men's fiction imposed on women to keep them weak and submissive, Marie Antoinette-like, so that such men as Burke can use them as his image of the ideal chivalric society; rather than the messy, gross, vigorous (to Burke grotesque) women who take the law into their own hands. These are masculine women who, utterly outside Burke's aesthetic categories, are implicitly contrasted with the men who are ordinarily "unmanly" or "effeminate." Wollstonecraft reveals the underlying experience of a woman: perhaps the most basic, personal revolutionary experience in England, since there were few black slaves, and since women could be upper class as well as eloquent without sharing the rights of their men—could experience in an aristocratic body the agonies of the poor and oppressed.

By *primogeniture,* which "enables the elder son to overpower talents and depress virtue," which is at the center of most revolutionary literature of the time, Wollstonecraft refers not to the brother but to the husband or father who overpowers his wife and daughter. The gross and obvious effect of her civilization on a female is the sacrifice "to family convenience," and the more subtle and insidious one is the inculcation of the "desire of shining," of being beautiful, witty, and vain.

So it becomes clear that Wollstonecraft was inspired by the passages about the queen who stood for everything beautiful and seductive, which to Burke meant the goodness, and to Wollstonecraft meant the tyranny, of society—and about the women of the "swinish multitude" that led the king and queen to Paris: the two aspects of women which she saw as the heart of the problem raised by the French Revolution. And from this insight she went straight into her sequel, *A Vindication of the Rights of Woman* (1792), where she attributes the social oppression of women to the assumptions that make them submissive and delicate objects of beauty. Here she carries her argument one step further:

> Women are, in fact, so much degraded by mistaken notions of female excellence, that I do not mean to add a paradox when I assert, that this artificial weakness produces a propensity to tyrannize. . . .

They "become either abject slaves or capricious tyrants." Although still talking of society in general, she is already thinking of women when she writes of "the freedom which has been bartered for splendid slavery"—a phrase which applies only to women. Her view can be contrasted with Burke's Swiftean thesis that idle and restless minds (imagining minds) are the causes of "revolutions" in philosophy, religion, and government. Taking women as her example, she sees their idle, restless, and imaginative minds as creating illusions that keep them happy—fools among knaves—or make them tyrants but prevent them from carrying out a revolution. She makes her revolutionary thesis explicit: "It is time to effect a revolution in female manners—time to restore to them their lost dignity—and make them, as a part of the human species, labour by reforming themselves to reform the world." In *Rights of Woman,* which is as directly aimed at Rousseau as *Rights of Men* was aimed at Burke, Wollstonecraft argues that women must not submit physically and mentally to the male-oriented world but must train both mind and body. "To preserve personal beauty, woman's glory! the limbs and faculties are cramped with worse than Chinese bands, and the sedentary life which they are condemned to live, whilst boys frolic in the open air, weakens the muscles and relaxes the nerves." Her favorite terms are *exercise* and *exert.* Because women have been brought up to feel "contempt of the understanding," they have failed to develop "that persevering ardor necessary to give vigor to the faculties, and clearness to the judgment."

The underlying image is of the female spirit struggling, through the energy of body and mind, to break out of social institutions, cultural assumptions, constricting dress,

Jean-Jacques Rousseau, the ideological patron of the French Revolution.

and her own body and sex, as well as from the prison of a specific marriage. She still contrasts Burke's categories, opposing "a pretty woman, as an object of desire" to "a fine woman, who inspires more sublime emotions by displaying intellectual beauty." In *Historical and Moral View* (1794) she refers to the "energetic character—A supple force, that, exciting love, commands esteem"—who *excites* rather than *exudes* love. Her figure is not the Burkean (or Blakean) revolutionary rapist but the female who attracts love but is energetic in other ways. She does not waste revolutionary energy on lovemaking.

"I do not wish [women] to have power over men," she writes in *Rights of Woman;* "but over themselves." Her image of the ideal situation for a woman (at least in society as presently constituted) is widowhood. Only the widow, she remarks in a passage on arranged marriages in the *Vindication of the Rights of Men,* shows that women can occasionally fall in love. In the ideal family Wollstonecraft virtually removes the male (as husband and father) altogether. Her longest and most central discussion of the family in *Rights of Woman* assumes the absence, indeed the death, of the husband-father. Widowhood offers the real test of womanhood: Now "she subdues every wayward passion to fulfill the double duty of being the father as well as the mother of her children." The absence of the husband-father also gives rise to beneficial suffering and struggle ("experience") for both wife and daughter. Earlier she has remarked that "An unhappy marriage is often very advantageous to a family, and . . . the neglected wife is, in general, the best mother." The woman should prefer struggle to the "present enjoyment" of sexual passion. Wollstonecraft's fear of transient love and sexual passion, and her consequent advocacy of enduring friendship, is less important than her thirst for some variety of struggle or adversity in the relationship between man and woman.

At one point Wollstonecraft remarks that "the contemplation of the noble struggles of suffering merit has raised admiration," and this naturally recalls Milton's Satan and his sense of "injured merit." She adds a footnote at the bottom of the page to "Milton's pleasing picture of paradisiacal happiness" of Adam and Eve:

> yet, instead of envying the lovely pair, I have, with conscious dignity, or Satanic pride, turned to hell for sublimer objects. In the same style, when viewing some noble monument of human art, I have traced the emanation of the Deity in the order I admired, till, descending from that giddy height, I have caught myself contemplating the grandest of all human sights;—for fancy quickly placed, in some solitary recess, an outcast of fortune, rising superior to passion and discontent.

This is a passage of some import for the whole drift of Wollstonecraft's writing. Like Blake, she has "turned to hell for sublimer objects," and within her purview is still Burke's "grandest of all human sights," not the deity but "an outcase of fortune, rising superior to passion and discontent"—a wronged woman, who in relation to men is a Satan to whom active evil is to be preferred to passive good. As widow—as mother in relation to her children—

woman is a self-sufficient Satan who has no need for man at all.

She has distinguished two categories: the sublime of the strong-willed, educated, struggling woman, and the beautiful of the faint-hearted passive "bird in a gilded cage." The underlying insight of Wollstonecraft's writings on the French Revolution is that the beautiful is no longer a viable aesthetic category. Poets and historians can no longer write about Burke's sad chivalric fantasy based on female beauty: "it becomes necessary to observe, that, whilst despotism and superstition exist, the convulsions, which the regeneration of man occasions, will always bring forward the vices they have engendered, to devour their parents" (*Historical and Moral View*). The eye of the poet and historian must inevitably move back toward the cannibalism and undifferentiation of the primal horde, indeed to the undifferentiation of aesthetic categories once the beautiful has been left behind. For a third category that remains unforgettable is the grotesque rout of women who march to Versailles, who could become sublime (she implies) were they to be educated. The force of her imagery (as opposed to her argument) lies in the grotesque shapes and energies of that mob. The second stage, she would insist, is the harnessing of this energy into a sublimity that rises above both weak negative beauty and the positive grotesque. But her contribution to the imagery of revolution lies in her vivid portrayal of the existential woman. (pp. 57-87)

Ronald Paulson, "Burke, Paine, and Wollstonecraft: The Sublime and the Beautiful," in his Representations of Revolution: 1789-1820, *Yale University Press, 1983, pp. 57-87.*

Steven Blakemore

[*In the following essay, Blakemore discusses Burke's seminal analysis,* Reflections on the Revolution in France. *Written in 1790,* Reflections *conveys Burke's opposition to the French Revolution.*]

Writing in 1827 about Burke's prose style, Thomas De Quincey observed that "in Burke, every thing figurative is part and parcel of the process of thinking, and [is] incarnated with the thought; it is not a separable descant *on* what . . . [he thinks], but a part of the organ *by* which . . . [he thinks]." The observation is especially germane to *Reflections on the Revolution in France,* where Burke's representations of the Revolution illustrate the various ways in which he understands it. In this context, he is concerned with the related issue of how the Revolution misrepresents reality. Perhaps the principal way that Burke makes representation a major theme is in the metaphors of madness and legitimacy through which he both envisions and condemns the revolutionary world he writes against. For instance, his vision of the Revolution is thematically encapsulated within a language of imprisonment, through which he attempts to contain the revolutionary madness he sees escaping into the vulnerable European world. Against this madness, he reproduces an alternative vision of Marie Antoinette as the cultural emblem of a legitimate order of reality, sexually besieged by rampant revolutionary forces assaulting the sublime and beautiful institutions she represents. The legitimacy of the traditional order is additionally expressed in terms of legitimate sexual mores and family lines, a legitimacy that clashes with the Revolution's illegitimacy—the bastard births and venereal disease infecting the body politic. Finally, as we shall see, Burke extends the theme of legitimate representation in his discussion of the Revolution's economic and electoral misrepresentations of reality.

One of Burke's first memorable comparisons in the *Reflections* occurs when he qualifies theoretic liberty by asking if it is "because liberty in the abstract may be classed amongst the blessings of mankind, that I am seriously to felicitate a madman, who has escaped from the protecting restraint and wholesome darkness of his cell, on his restoration to the enjoyment of light and liberty?" Burke then presses the point by another comparison: "Am I to congratulate an highwayman and murderer, who has broke prison, upon the recovery of his natural rights? This would be to act over again the scene of the criminals condemned to the gallies, and their heroic deliverer, the metaphysic Knight of the Sorrowful Countenance."

Various things happen in this passage. First, there is the conspicuous allusion to Don Quixote, the metaphysical knight maddened by chivalric romances and, by extension, English and French men maddened by revolutionary romances, such as Richard Price's anniversary sermon. The irony resides in the plight of metaphysical deliverers who, Burke suggests, will "act over again" Don Quixote's fate and be beaten and robbed by the revolutionary criminals they liberate (see *Don Quixote,* pt. 1, chap. 22). The cluster of associations suggests that defenders of the French Revolution, celebrating liberty "in all the nakedness and solitude of metaphysical abstraction" are themselves blindly subject to delusive fantasies resulting in their own psychological imprisonment. The image of the crazed ideological deliverer reappears subsequently when Burke refers to French politicians who are "delivered over blindly to every projector and adventurer, to every alchymist and empiric." In Burke's vision of the Revolution, madness and ideology are metaphorically equated, and metaphysical deliverance ends in imprisonment in a world where projectors spin out political fantasies allusively equivalent to the mad schemes of the projectors in Swift's Laputa. Burke uses these metaphors of madness to explain a revolution that continues to astonish him.

The initial images of the madman escaping from the "wholesome darkness of his cell" and the murderer who has "broke prison" are thus pertinent to Burke's comment, in the subsequent paragraph, that he should suspend his "congratulations on the new liberty of France" until he understands its true nature. Burke, of course, has already prejudged France's "new liberty," since he allusively evokes the madman who escapes his cell and the murderous highwayman who breaks prison and recovers his "natural rights." Just two sentences before, Burke had asked rhetorically if he should "congratulate" France upon its new freedom; this leads to the question whether he should seriously "felicitate" a liberated madman. The French Revolution is metaphorically equated with murder and madness, and revolutionary liberty is equated with the escape of madness and murder into the vulnerable eighteenth-century world. In contrast to his call for a total offensive war against revolutionary madness in his subsequent antirevolutionary works, Burke's imagery in the *Reflections* is essentially defensive, because he tries to contain revolutionary forces within the restrictive forms of his language. The logical corollary of Burke's discourse is that revolutionary forces should be confined within the "wholesome darkness" of civilization's protective cells. But Burke believes that the Revolution's seductive appeal makes this especially difficult, since revolutionary liberty seems better than it is—an abstract liberty that is actually "folly, vice, and madness, without tuition or restraint."

Burke continues to equate this specious liberty with threatening escapes from insane asylums and prisons. He contends that even revolutionary "speculatists" should be confined to "schools" lest their doctrines "break prison to burst like a *Levanter,* to sweep the earth with their hurricane, and to break up the fountains of the great deep to overwhelm us." He sees revolutionary dogma as an explosive form of subversive energy, figuratively destroying the world with a second flood; he sees it as a cosmic levanter—a frenzied eastern wind toppling traditional European values.

Revolutionary doctrines that "break prison" are reminiscent of other prison breaks closer to home, in England, where dangerous fanatics are reimprisoned, even after being liberated by frenzied mobs:

> We have Lord George Gordon fast in Newgate; and neither his being a public proselyte to Judaism, nor his having, in his zeal against Catholick priests and all sorts of ecclesiastics, raised a mob . . . which pulled down all our prisons, have preserved to him a liberty, of which he did not render himself worthy by a virtuous use of it. We have rebuilt Newgate, and tenanted the mansion. We have prisons almost as strong as the Bastile, for those who dare to libel the queens of France.

The reference to George Gordon, the anti-Catholic agitator prosecuted for the antipopery riots that inflamed London in June of 1780, is pertinent. First, Gordon was considered by many to be insane; second, his frenzied followers wore blue cocades, probably reminding Burke of the cocades worn by the Revolution's supporters in France, just as similar scenes of violence during the summer of 1789 undoubtedly reminded him of the marauding mobs ransacking houses and chapels in June 1780; third, the reference to Newgate is equally pertinent, since it had been, like the Bastille, a symbol of oppression for generations of Englishmen, and since its prisoners had also been liberated by violent mobs accompanying the prisoners into London's streets. In addition, Burke had been personally threatened by the rioters. In a letter to the duke of Portland (29 September 1793), he connected the "Partisans of Jacobinism" in Scotland with "the first Scene of Lord George Gordon's actions, and . . . his Spirit" (Gordon was a Scotsman and had begun his anti-Catholic activities in Scotland in 1779). Because Burke experienced the London riots both directly and indirectly—riots in which roving mobs attacked selected symbols of authority and London newspapers reported savage scenes of drunkenness and destruction—this lived imagery informs the *Reflections,* becoming, for Burke, the closest correlation to what he envisions happening in France; and the allusion to the Gordon riots suggestively evokes the correspondent anti-Catholic fanaticism Burke sees besieging France.

Burke's reference to English prisons as "almost as strong as the Bastile" is deliberately provocative, since the Bastille was a kind of bogey symbol for the Revolution's supporters, evoking all the monstrous oppression of the ancien régime. Burke implicitly reinforces the punitive structures of the traditional European order, and suggests that they are the legitimate and appropriate "cells" for frenzied revolutionary mobs. The imagery of the Bastille is curiously contrapuntal, however, for the Bastille had been sacked and opened by the very revolutionary forces he wishes to contain. Moreover, calling English prisons only "almost as strong as the Bastile" does not reassure an English audience fearing an outbreak of revolutionary madness in England. Madness seems poised to escape within and out of the very language with which Burke assures his countrymen that it is contained. But this is an essentially ingenuous deconstruction since Burke, throughout his antirevolutionary writings, consistently makes the Revolution a threatening possibility precisely because he wants the English people to fear its impending presence. Its potential "escape" into England is part of a strategy to awaken the people to a danger that alarms Burke.

Conversely, Burke sees the Revolution creating its own "cells" by converting France's traditional "edifices" into prisons that confine the legitimate representatives of the traditional order. Louis XVI is "lodged in one of the old palaces of Paris, now converted into a Bastile for kings." Burke thus suggests that the Revolution creates the very monster it supposedly destroys, for in imitating the oppressive structures they apparently efface, the revolutionaries reveal a secret attraction for the demonized power they supposedly reject; and the "Bastile for kings" also functions figuratively like those precarious English bastilles and, of course, the Bastille itself in reverse, for Burke threatens the Revolution with its own history by suggesting the possibility of the monarchy's liberation and the retributive return of the traditional order.

When we return to the fanatical anti-Catholic mob that "pulled down all our prisons," we find the image reappearing when Burke remarks that there is no skill in merely "destroying and pulling down": "Your mob can do this as well . . . as your assemblies. . . . Rage and phrenzy will pull down more in half an hour, than prudence, deliberation, and foresight can build up in a hundred years." As it echoes the Lord Gordon passage, the imagery seems to refer to both the razing of civilization's "protective" prisons as well as the very "foundations" of the traditional order Burke defends. Moreover, inasmuch as the revolutionary mobs destroying civilization's foundations react in "rage and phrenzy," Burke again evokes frenzied madmen escaping into the vulnerable European world.

There are additional references to the Revolution's madness. Burke refers to revolutionary imitators of the metaphysically insane Rousseau, who, if he were alive and "in one of his lucid intervals . . . would be shocked at the practical phrenzy of his scholars"; and throughout the *Reflections,* there are correspondences between revolutionary leaders and the revolutionary texts leading to the revolutionary "phrenzy" destroying civilization's fragile foundations as well as its "protective" prisons. After referring to the revolutionary mob, Burke quotes, in a footnote, "A leading member of the [National] assembly," who calls for the complete destruction of the old order, including its ideas, language, and manners. Burke adds the following commentary:

> This gentleman was chosen president in an assembly not sitting at the *Quinze vingt,* or the *Petites Maisons;* and composed of persons giving themselves out to be rational beings; but neither his ideas, language, or conduct, differ . . . from the discourses, opinions, and actions of those within and without the assembly, who direct the operations of the machine now at work in France.

Burke suggests that the revolutionary leaders within and without the assembly are equally insane, and even though they are not technically "sitting at the *Quinze vingt,* or the *Petites Maisons*"—respectively the foundations for the blind and lunatic asylums—their "ideas, language, or conduct" reveal they are ideologically mad, even though they give "themselves out to be rational beings." In addition, the reference to institutions for the blind and the insane initiates a metaphoric linkage between blindness and insanity, which Michel Foucault maintains approximates what was considered the "essence of classical madness." It also highlights Burke's thematic distinction between the sanity of England, where "madmen are not our lawgivers," and the madness of revolutionary France, where people are "besieged by no other enemies than their own madness and folly."

As we have seen, this contrast is precarious because revolutionary madness can potentially escape the defensive restraints of civilization as well as Burke's circumscribed language. It is, nevertheless, a distinction that Burke continually emphasizes, so that what emerges in the *Reflections* is an apocalyptic vision of the French nation's conversion into an opened lunatic asylum where madmen run loose, imprisoning or murdering those who are legitimate or sane. Burke's imagery indicts the Revolution in terms of escaped murder and madness, and he attempts to quarantine it rhetorically by controlling, containing, and encapsulating its linguistic presence within the confining categories of his language.

Conversely, Burke uses the language of "tradition" to depict the legitimate world he is defending; but whether he is extolling this world or castigating its antitype, the Revolution's presence and the pan-European crisis it represents are what inspire his antirevolutionary language. The revolutionary madness contaminating France constitutes for Burke a revolution in representation—a revolution in the way the European people had traditionally understood and experienced the world. In this context, the revolutionary crisis within France also caused a crisis in the paradigms of revolutionary representation (e.g., political, economic, and electoral paradigms), which Burke contends do not correspond to or represent reality. He presents the *Reflections* as an antidote to revolutionary madness, as a mirror that reflects the way the world really is and that simultaneously reveals the dangerous, distorted illusions insanely magnified and exalted in the French fantasy world. In this sense, the *Reflections* was intended as an injection of reality into the feverish European body politic—as a reintroduction of the reality principle into European discourse. While Burke's major preoccupation is protecting England from the French disease (a metaphor he uses continually in his correspondence), he also attempts to isolate and arrest the disease within France. Public and private modes of experience overlap because Burke's crisis is also the crisis the French people are experiencing: "In France you are now in the crisis of a revolution."

Burke felt this crisis so intensely that his antirevolutionary imagery was used against him. In the *Reflections* he had remarked that if he had asked whether the "privileged nobility who met under the king's precept . . . in 1789, or their constituents," deserved to be considered contemporary tyrants, he would "have passed for a madman" (suggesting that those who believe this now are indeed mad). He was soon depicted as a counterrevolutionary Don Quixote, the crazed defender of frivolous queens and obsolete chivalry. As he raged against the Revolution in the House of Commons, his Whig opponents suggested he was insane—an ironic suggestion in that Burke had earlier, in the same body, made George III's sanity an issue during the Regency Crisis when he had declared that God had "hurl'd" the king from his throne—an image reappearing in the *Reflections* in reference to the plight of Louis XVI. Burke was also depicted as a Don Quixote defending a sluttish Dulcinea; and since these caricatures resonate in discussions of his chivalrous defence of Marie Antoinette, a reconsideration of his defence is pertinent in connection with the crisis he contended was confronting European civilization.

In the *Reflections,* Burke reproduces his vision of the queen's connection with the civilization he is defending—a civilization, he notes, that for several generations has "appeared without much lustre" in the "eyes" of French iconoclasts, although it still shines in his vision of the queen:

> It is now sixteen or seventeen years since I saw the queen of France, then the dauphiness, at Versailles; and surely never lighted on this orb, which she hardly seemed to touch, a more delightful vision. I saw her just above the horizon, decorating and cheering the elevated sphere she just began to move in,—glittering like the morning-star, full of life, and splendor, and joy.

This "vision" of the queen seems to light not only the earth, "this orb," but also another orb, Burke's eye, shining, at second hand, on the reader's eye. Burke pictorially presents a vision that the reader sees reflected in Burke's eye, so when Burke sees the future queen "above the horizon," he establishes a sense of height, distance, and respect that he feels the English people share. The English people, in a different context, will not tolerate any "insolence" or "proud pretension, to look down with scorn upon what *they look up to* with reverence" (emphasis mine). Burke's imagery establishes a whole field of interrelated perspectives reinforcing a sustained vision of traditional European culture. For Burke, the French queen is important because she legitimately represents the traditional European order—the two-thousand-year-old inheritance of European civilization. He is defending an entire heritage, rather than a particular regime or person.

Another way to look at Burke's vision is through the aesthetic categories of his *Philosophical Enquiry into the Origin of Our Ideas of the Sublime and Beautiful* (1757). J. T. Boulton was the first to note how Burke's apostrophe to the queen reflects comments he had made in the *Enquiry* regarding Homer's description of the effects of Helen's beauty on observers. In fact, in the context of the *Enquiry,* Burke attempts a style of writing in which elements of the sublime and beautiful are artfully fused: the queen's rank is sublime, her sex, beautiful. Just before the apostrophe, for instance, he comments that it is natural to be moved by "the exalted rank of the persons suffering, and particularly the sex, the beauty, and the amiable qualities of the descendant of so many kings." He then eulogizes Marie Antoinette in terms of both her rank and the effect of her beauty on him: "distant, respectful love" evokes the code of chivalry and the chaste knights who protect their lovely ladies—in this case a very vulnerable queen, whereas respect or "veneration"—qualities restricted to the sublime in the *Enquiry*—evoke her sublimity. As we have seen, Burke describes the queen in a series of glittering images: she lights on an orb; then while suspended above the horizon, she floats in a sphere, "glittering like the morning-star, full of life, and splendor, and joy." In section XIII (Part II) of the *Enquiry,* Burke had considered magnificence to be a source of the sublime: "A great profusion of things which are splendid or valuable in themselves, is *magnificent.*" One of his examples is from *Ecclesiasticus,* in which, among images of light and fire, the high priest Simon is compared to *"the morning star"*—an image suggestively reappearing in the apostrophe to the queen. His principal point is that such a profusion of shifting images "dazzle[s]" the mind, making "it impossible to attend to that exact coherence and agreement of the allusions, which we should require on every other occasion." Although Burke's apostrophe does not consist of an extravagant profusion of images that dazzle or overwhelm the reader, a series of shifting images suggests the fusion of the sublime and beautiful he contends is the glory of Europe (*Reflections*).

Moreover, his celebration of chivalry as "that generous loyalty to rank and sex" is certainly at one with the values of both the sublime and beautiful and of the queen herself, whom he defends against the "revolution" (alluding simultaneously to the queen's "reversal" and the French Revolution) that precipitates her to fall metaphorically right before his eyes: "I saw her just above the horizon. . . . Oh! What a revolution! and what an heart must I have, to contemplate without emotion that elevation and that fall!" By depicting a revolutionary world devoid of chivalric defenders, Burke endeavors to gain the reader's sympathy for the beleaguered queen, since, as he noted in the *Enquiry,* "Beauty in distress is much the most affecting beauty."

This aspect of the queen is also highlighted in a preliminary passage dealing with the events of 6 October, when her chamber was invaded by a revolutionary mob:

> the queen was first startled by the voice of the centinel at her door, who cried out to her, to save herself by flight. . . . Instantly he was cut down. A band of cruel ruffians and assassins, reeking with his blood, rushed into the chamber of the queen, and pierced with an hundred strokes of bayonets and poniards the bed, from whence this persecuted woman had but just time to fly almost naked.

There are several things to note. First, the ruffians "reeking" with the sentinel's blood conjure up the men who had heard Richard Price's anniversary sermon and who had left "reeking from the effect of the sermon." The participle, which appears only in these two passages, may establish an allusive connection between revolutionary literature and the potential violence Burke feels it provokes. Second, Burke's version of the attempted attack on the queen is suggestively sexual: she escapes "almost naked," just as the potentially murderous "rapists" stab her bed with a series of frustrated phallic plunges. Finally, the "hundred strokes of bayonets and poniards" are textually situated to recall the "ten thousand swords" that fail to appear in her defence, which, for Burke, constitutes a stain on French honor now that "the age of chivalry is gone."

Burke's defence of the queen's honor and his depiction of her as a damsel in distress are especially revealing in context of her reputation as a woman of easy virtue. Having read an advance copy of the *Reflections,* Philip Francis, Burke's friend, informed him bluntly that "on this subject . . . you cannot but know that the opinion of the world . . . has been many years decided." He then proceeds to ask Burke if he is "such a determined Champion of Beauty as to draw . . . [his] Sword in defense of any jade upon Earth provided she be handsome?" Burke was aware of the queen's reputation. In his reply (20 February 1790) to Francis, he responds that he does not entertain "the Tales and all the anecdotes of the Coffeehouses of Paris and of the dissenting meeting houses of London"; he does not believe "the slander of those who calumniate persons, [so] that afterwards they may murder them with impunity." He then defends the queen by referring to the values of both the sublime and the beautiful:

> What, are not high Rank, great Splendour of descent, great personal Elegance and outward accomplishments ingredients of moment in forming the interest we take in the Misfortunes of Men? . . . Is it absurd in me, to think that the Chivalrous Spirit which dictated a veneration for Women of condition and of Beauty, without any consideration whatsoever of enjoying them, was the great Scource [sic] of those manners which have been the Pride and ornament of Europe for so many ages?

In his denial of the queen's stained reputation, Burke appears as her lone chivalric defender, his sword drawn, in Francis' metaphor, where ten thousand others failed to appear. He becomes the queen's textual defender against those who continue to violate and degrade her linguistically. Burke continually sees a connection between ideological violence and physical violence. He argues that the rampant gossip and rumor, the degrading pornographic insults issuing from coffeehouses, novels, and pamphlets, are a form of ideological violence, having causal repercussions for a queen who can be degraded and then murdered "with impunity." His account of the revolutionary mob invading the queen's bedchamber is an indictment of the correspondent revolutionary forces linguistically violating her honor and attempting physically to assault her and the institutions she represents.

Thus, in the *Reflections,* Burke endeavors to restore the queen's honor textually within a defensive, chivalric context. As he defends her with the last great statement of European chivalry, Burke writes within a tradition that, as Maurice Keen notes, "To sustain itself . . . required not only the swords of knights but the pens of clerks too."

The legitimacy of tradition is one of the *Reflections'* principal themes. For Burke, the Glorious Revolution's legitimacy was incarnated in Mary, the legitimate, eldest daughter of James II. In contrast, the illegitimacy of James' reign was represented by the questionable son of his second marriage, subsequently known as the Old Pretender, widely (and wrongly) believed to have been someone else's baby. In discussing tradition, Burke uses metaphors of genuine parentage and offspring—authentic blood lines—while the disruption of it is expressed in metaphors of bastard births and venereal disease.

For instance, the British monarchy was a line "of hereditary descent." Consequently, Burke sees the Glorious Revolution, as most Whigs did, as a "true" revolution, a return or restoration (*Oxford English Dictionary,* meanings #1 and 2). Applied to government, this implies the return to legitimate rights and a legitimate monarchy, the sense in which Burke understood the American and British Revolutions; but when discussing the French Revolution, he uses "revolution" in its modern sense of a complete overthrow of a government and the radical transformation of society (*O. E. D.,* #7). The Glorious Revolution was thus "a parent of settlement, and not a nursery of future revolutions." The imagery intensifies Burke's meaning, for in addition to being a place, "settlement" had a legal acceptation, as Samuel Johnson notes, of "the act of giving possession by legal sanction." The Glorious Revolution was the legitimate "parent" of a legal settlement; the French Revolution was a "nursery" for illegitimate revolutions. The shift from the singular "settlement" to the plural "revolutions" emphasizes the contrast between the former's legitimate stability and the latter's promiscuous proliferation of bastard revolutions. "Nursery" also suggests a place for illegitimate children, as in the Foundling Hospital that Burke accused Rousseau of casting his illegitimate offspring into (*Letter to a Member of the National Assembly*). There is an implicit contrast between private familial nurturing and public institutional "fosterage" (*O. E. D.,* #1 and 2). Because Burke's meaning is pejorative, other denotations of "nursery" are also possible, such as "A place which breeds or supports animals" (*O. E. D.,* #5).

Burke recognized, however, that some revolutions, depending on circumstances, could become legitimate. In this case, the people "would recognize, even in its cradle, the child as legitimate." He thus acknowledged that the violent revolutionary birth of a government could be transformed into a legal "parent" through prescription, "which, through long usage, mellows into legality governments that were violent in their commencement." He suggests, however, that the French people will not recognize the French Revolution, because it "has derived its birth from no law and no necessity; but . . . on the contrary has had its origin in those vices and sinister practices by which the social union is often disturbed and sometimes destroyed." The various metaphors suggestively stigmatize the Revolution as an illegitimately deformed child produced by "vices and sinister practices"—the illicit practices of political whoring and the consequential "venereal disease" that "disturbs" or "destroys" the "social union." As the Revolution begins to resemble a military colony, the "new commonwealth is born, and bred . . . in those corruptions, which mark degenerated and worn out republics. Your child comes into the world with the symptoms of death; the *facies Hippocratica* forms the character of its physiognomy."

In terms of the cradle metaphor (the people recognizing "even in its cradle, the child"), there is another contrast between the diseased Revolution unrecognized and unacknowledged in its "cradle" and the prerevolutionary France that Burke sees as *"gentis incunabula nostrae"* [the cradle of our people], the Virgilian phrase (*Aeneid,* III.105) Burke cites in connecting the traditional French order with the British political order. Burke also refuses to grace the revolutionary "cradle" in his old age, when revolutionary projectors would try to regenerate him or have him "squall in their new accents, or to stammer, in my second cradle, the elemental sounds of their barbarous metaphysics. *Si isti mihi largiantur ut repueriscam, et in eorum cunis vagiam, valde recusem!*" Burke's quotation from Cicero's *Cato Maior De Senectute,* slightly altered, insists—in the classical language of traditional Europe—that if revolutionary projectors "should allow me to return to infancy from my old age, to weep in their cradle, I should vehemently protest" (my translation). We will remember that revolutionary cradles are metaphorically contaminated; in addition, the reference to regeneration ("These gentlemen deal in regeneration," specifically that of Burke's "rigid fibres" by revolutionary experimentors) alludes to revolutionary children who, instead of approaching "the wounds of the father" with "solicitude," hack the "aged parent in pieces," putting "him into the kettle of magicians, in hopes . . . they may regenerate . . . their father's life." These two passages allusively complement each other, so that the revolutionary cradle is equated, à la the allusion to Pelias (the mythological king chopped up and boiled by his daughters who believed they were actually rejuvenating him), to the barbarous kettle and hence to both the death of the traditional paternal order and Burke himself.

Finally, just as revolutionary children fail to approach "the wounds of the father" with "solicitude," so the revolutionaries likewise lack "the tender parental solicitude which fears to cut up the infant [that which is cherished in a country] for the sake of an [ideological] experiment." By employing images of unnatural familial relations—"relations" that are "severed"—as well as images of tainted cradles and deformed bastards, Burke metaphorically quarantines a contagious Revolution he contends is pathologically illegitimate.

The theme of illegitimacy culminates in Burke's argument that the Revolution was the greatest assault on reality in the world's history. Thus, as we shall see, he links illegitimacy and madness with misrepresentations of economic and electoral reality. In this context, Burke argued that the Revolution radically misrepresented everything, including itself. For Burke, reality meant, *inter alia,* the traditional values embodied in the historical corporate institutions that the Revolution was attacking—values he assumed were normative, so his own representations became the criteria by which he judged revolutionary deviations from the reality he represented. Hence, Burke is vulnerable to inviting deconstructions, although he did have a commonsensical belief that reality is accessible to rational men and women; and therefore there was, to him, a genuine correspondence between reality and its legitimate representation, whether in the correspondent value of words and what they expressed or, more specifically, in the representative value of money and land. It followed that the Revolution was an unprecedented experiment in ideological insanity precisely because it violated these "natural" correspondences.

Burke had what Michel Foucault calls a "Classical" understanding of the world, in which words supposedly expressed the reality of things and specie represented true value. This traditional understanding had been steadily discredited since the seventeenth century, when attention was being focused on contradiction, divergence, and discrepancy. That words did not always mean what they said, or money did not always reflect an intrinsic value, was to Burke caused by the new revolutionary forces that had distorted the relationship between reality and representation. In the *Reflections* Burke's war against the Revolution is a war over the terms and values of representation; it is a war over whose representation will prevail.

Burke aggressively raises the issue of electoral representation, especially since English supporters of the Revolution argued that England was not free because there was no popular election of the House of Commons and therefore no "popular representation" of the people. Since neither the monarchy nor the House of Lords was elected to office, supporters of the Revolution stressed the inequality of representation, an inequality that rendered the English government illegitimate. As Burke points out, summarizing a revolutionary argument, "if popular representation, or choice, is necessary to the *legitimacy* of all government, the house of lords is, at one stroke, bastardized and corrupted in blood." Burke then proceeds to delegitimize the Revolution by applying the criterion of popular elections to revolutionary France. In effect, he uses the revolutionary standard to contradict the Revolution's representation.

His critique of revolutionary representation consists of showing how the representative is systematically separated from the citizen, how "there must be many degrees, and some stages, before the representative can come in contact with his constituent." First, he contends that the Revolution's democratic elections are based on a policy of exclusion, specifically the distinction between active and passive citizens, which restricts the vote to those active citizens paying a direct tax amounting to thrice the daily wage for unskilled labor. Thus, as Burke notes, the man who has nothing but his "natural equality" is excluded by a restrictive money qualification. Burke stresses the discrepancy between how the revolutionaries represent the Revolution and how they practice it. The revolutionary government resembles a "tyrannous aristocracy"—the demonized order it supposedly replaces.

Second, Burke notes that the active citizens in a particular canton gather in assemblies to elect deputies to the commune. The result, he contends, is a barrier "between the primary elector and the representative legislator"; but this is just the beginning, since those elected to the commune must pay an annual direct tax ten times the amount of the local daily wage—yet another economic qualification effectively excluding the primary elector.

Third, this process of exclusion continues as the representatives of the commune elect deputies to the *département,* and these, in turn, elect deputies to the National Assembly—deputies who must pay an annual direct tax equivalent of a mark (244.5 grams) of silver, or approximately 51 livres, in addition to owning land. (Burke only notes the first qualification.) In effect, Burke highlights revolutionary hypocrisy by arguing that the vaunted "rights of man" are only rhetorical; he suggests that revolutionary representation is more vicious since it is based on three economic qualifications and three successive elections of representatives removed from the original voter by three stages. The result is a series of exclusive barriers, a series of debased representations. Burke suggests that there is an ontological distance by which debased representations are more and more removed from a real source.

As Burke takes the reader through each cumbersome stage, there is a sense of both spatial and moral distance between the disenfranchised passive citizen and the revolutionary system contradicting those it supposedly represents. By illustrating these discrepancies, he exploits the contradictions of what to him is illusory representation: "there is little, or rather no, connection between the last representative and the first constituent. The member who goes to the national assembly is not chosen by the people, nor accountable to them"; he is "too far removed . . . [from the primary electors] in the chain of representation." Burke underscores the distinction between a revolutionary world of fantasy and illusion and a traditional European world based on correspondence and reality. He thereby depicts a Revolution interested only in representing itself and, therefore, a Revolution misrepresenting both itself and all that it supposedly stands for.

Burke's critique of electoral representation complements his critique of economic representation. He asks his English audience if they should imitate the economy of revolutionary France and substitute a "compulsory paper currency" for the "legal coin of this kingdom." Burke is suggesting that the revolutionaries are forcing their illegitimate values, their bastard currency, on the French people. Hence, the French *assignat* becomes the illustrative metaphor for fictitious representations of revolutionary reality. By tracing the circular cycle of the *assignat*—church and crown lands are confiscated and auctioned off as plunder purchased in the form of *assignats* used to pay off France's creditors, which the latter use to buy the confiscated lands—Burke documents a series of representations that contradict rather than complement each other. For example, the rationalization for the confiscation of the lands and the creation of the *assignats* is that they will pay off the national debt, yet the result is the enforced bankruptcy of France. The "madness of the project of confiscation" depreciates the value of the land, and revolutionary financiers exacerbate the financial crisis as inflationary *assignats* become the basis of "fictitious wealth." The new paper money creates inflation, not stability, because its true value does not correspond to what it supposedly represents.

Burke's economic indictment of revolutionary representation is a metaphor for the violation of what he believes are natural moral laws and a normative order of reality. What emerges is a kind of Burkean law suggesting that, in a revolutionary crisis, false representations replace true representations just as, in Gresham's law, bad money drives out good money (another of Burke's points). According to Burke, since the depreciated lands and the inflated *assignats* do not reflect an intrinsic value, the French people are forced to accept a paper fantasy similar to all the proclamations and pamphlets he sees inundating France. The depiction of revolutionary robbers establishing illusory values and attempting "to reverse the very nature of things" suggests an inverted world of uncontrolled madness. By making "their paper circulation compulsory in all payments," the revolutionaries force their false values on the French people—they force the people to accept their fictitious representation of economic reality. They attempt to sanction the illegitimate confiscations by binding "the nation in one guilty interest": the enforced acceptance of the *assignats* suggests a *de facto* acquiescence legitimizing revolutionary values.

The enforcement of these values is especially illustrative in the plight of the clergy, who have been reduced to state functionaries and compelled to receive their state allowance in *assignats,* "the depreciated paper . . . stamped with . . . the symbols of their own ruin." Burke is outraged that the Revolution's victims are forced to accept the very values that destroy them: "So violent an outrage upon credit, property, and liberty, as this compulsory paper currency, has seldom been exhibited by the alliance of bankruptcy and tyranny, at any time, or in any nation." Because real credit has been systematically discredited, the Revolution has no real money, no real credit; and there can be no correspondent faith, trust, or belief in it. He stresses this again when he refers to revolutionary managers: "for credit, properly speaking, they have none." The corollary is that despite the enforcement of these fictitious representations, the French people do not believe them because the discrepancy between illusion and reality cannot be papered over. The upshot is also obvious: when the revolutionaries "force a currency of their own fiction in the place of that which is real," they end by "establishing an unheard of despotism."

English currency, however, is soundly based on either deposited wealth or gold or silver specie; and even when Burke is referring to British paper currency, which is not valuable in itself, he assumes it corresponds to a real value because it is based on real wealth, rather like American Silver Certificates before the switch to Federal Reserve Notes. The representative order (money) consequently, for Burke, reflects the correspondent economic reality on which it is based.

This fundamental understanding of representation tinctures Burke's thinking about almost everything, whether it is a stable semantic vocabulary expressing linguistic continuity or traditional European values reflecting a genuine ontological order. While Burke recognized the discrepancies between reality and representation, he reaffirmed what to many seemed a beleaguered world view, because he believed that these discrepancies were deviations from a natural order of reality. It followed that the Revolution and all that it represented (and vice versa) was not based on anything real. Burke delights in documenting all the chaotic contradictions that he contends are destroying the revolutionary world. His emphasis on the need to contain this world within France was an effort to turn the Revolution against itself—to implode it on its own contentious contradictions.

It is fruitful to consider briefly how Burke's principal revolutionary respondents addressed Burke's critique, for certainly Burke's representation was ostensibly open to charges of misrepresentation by the very people who had challenged him on practically every other point. On the issue of revolutionary electoral and economic representation, they are, however, silent. Wollstonecraft and Paine are illustrative: they do not criticize or challenge Burke's representation, focusing instead on English electoral and economic representation. In *Vindication of the Rights of Men* (1790), Wollstonecraft concentrates on the notorious elements of the English electoral system—the rotten boroughs, the corruption, and the underrepresentation of the British people—a strategy Paine also employs in *The Rights of Man* (1791). By ignoring Burke's critique, they make English representation rather than revolutionary representation the issue. Their silence, however, tacitly concedes the force of Burke's criticism.

With regard to economic representation, Burke and his English enemies share the same value system: they assume a direct relation between real money (gold and silver) and the value it represents. In the *Vindication,* Wollstonecraft again does not respond to Burke's critique, while in *An Historical and Moral View of the French Revolution* (1794), she criticizes "the inflated system of paper" that contributes to France's debt, distinguishing between a real and inflated value: "Gold and silver have a specific value . . . Paper, on the contrary, is a dangerous expedient" (see Bk. 4, chap. 3). In *The Rights of Man,* Paine contends that there is actually more gold and silver specie in France than in England and contrasts France's "wealth" with England's "funding system"—a system that "in effect creates upon paper the sum which it appears to borrow, and lays on a tax to keep the imaginary capital alive by the payment of interest, and sends the annuity to market, to be sold for paper already in circulation." The funding system "is not money; neither is it . . . credit." Paine was obsessed with the dangers of paper currency (doubtless because of his experience with worthless continentals in the American Revolution), and he continually predicted the collapse of the English economy. In *The Rights of Man,* he throws Burke's representation back at him, making the same point about English paper that Burke had made about the *assignats;* but his silence on Burke's critique tacitly acknowledges again the relevance of Burke's criticism. That Burke and his English respondents share common assumptions about representation and the direct correspondence between signifier and signified in language, politics, and economics suggests that they are working within the same representational system, which opens a seminal area of investigation.

In France, the revolutionaries also share common assumptions about representation, although the emphasis radically changes whenever a competitive revolutionary clique insists that its privileged representation of the Revolution is the only true and correct one (the fate of the 1791 Constitution is illustrative). At one point, the representation of a transparent Revolution reified in the "General Will" creates the very contradictions that must then be erased. All opposition or difference suddenly becomes "counterrevolutionary," and a series of reductive explanations are employed to contain, control, and ultimately eliminate discrepancies the Revolution denyingly creates. Similarly, concrete flesh-and-blood repression corresponds to the repressive writing that reinforces and represents it.

In the end, Burke sees the Revolution imposing its dominant representations on the powerless French people. In deconstructing the Revolution's discrepancies, he isolates what he believes are its extraordinary misrepresentations and reinforces the interrelated themes of illegitimacy and insanity that reverberate through the *Reflections.* In a fundamental sense the *Reflections* is about a revolution in representation—a revolution that Burke felt was changing man's psychological perception of reality. As Burke and the revolutionaries proceeded to offer oppositional representations of both the Revolution and themselves and to accuse each other of misrepresentations at variance with reality, they waged a textual war that coincided with a larger war over the contested meaning of Europe. In this context, since language is our principal repository of what the Revolution means, Burke's *Reflections* remains, as Novalis noted two centuries ago, a revolutionary book against the Revolution. (pp. 1-16)

Steven Blakemore, "Revolution in Representation: Burke's 'Reflections on the Revolution in France'," in Eighteenth-Century Life, *Vol. 15, No. 3, November, 1991, pp. 1-18.*

Emmet Kennedy on the legacy of the French Revolution:

The French Revolution left people with a hope, a hope repeatedly acted out, in a revolution that would right the wrongs left untouched or actually created by the last revolution. This hope in an ever-future revolution became a secular messianism which, when it failed to materialize, left man with that *mal du siècle* that plagued him through the nineteenth century and beyond. Or, perhaps more commonly—especially after 1870, when the Revolution had been institutionalized safely in the Third Republic—the French could look back gratefully to 1789 for what they owed it without fearing that it would threaten their present. On the other side of the spectrum are those today who refuse to "celebrate" the bicentennial of the French Revolution but who wish to simply "commemorate" it as an important, historic event with too many positive and negative characteristics to allow unambiguous rejoicing or regrets. The historian's task is to sort it out, sift the evidence, understand it, interpret it. To almost all parties, 1789 retains mythic proportions—the Great Revolution, the Great Fear, the Great Terror, the Great Nation. Its grandeur is charged with meaning that ever waits to be deciphered.

Emmet Kennedy, in his Cultural History of the French Revolution, *1989.*

John Clubbe

[*Clubbe is an American educator and critic. In the essay below, he addresses Carlyle's treatment of heroism in his highly influential study,* The French Revolution *(1837). Clubbe also discusses the influence of Goethe on Carlyle's work.*]

Throughout the 1830s Carlyle pondered the meaning of heroism and continued to search for heroes who met his criteria for excellence. Hero-worship would form the basis of the new society that would arise after the great revolutionary conflagration that the French Revolution heralded had run its course. After this phoenix death-birth, heroes would lead and men would reverence them. "I should not have known what to make of this world at all," Carlyle told Froude, "if it had not been for the French Revolution." Not only did he view the Revolution as the most important phenomenon of his own times but he thought study of it necessary, for himself and for his generation, to understand the inevitable revolutions of the future. No part of this study had more value than a close scrutiny of the heroes who had attempted to control the rising tide of Sansculottism during the epic struggle that had taken place in France in the 1790s. In what had they succeeded, in what had they failed? In *The French Revolution* Carlyle's ostensible heroes are Mirabeau and Danton. Off in the wings, however, hovers a presence rarely seen but ominously felt—Napoleon. And behind these three heroes of action stands a hero of thought, the only hero not gravely flawed—Goethe.

Two circumstances influenced Carlyle's choice of the French Revolution as a subject. The first was his decision in the summer of 1833 to write *The Diamond Necklace,* a work that chronicles an episode involving corruption in high places in pre-revolutionary France. Writing it satisfied Carlyle that he could handle historical narrative. The second, ultimately the more important, was his reading early in 1834 of the *Iliad* in the original Greek. Once into the *Iliad,* Carlyle could not have enough of it. "Nothing I have read for long years so interests and nourishes me," he said. At the same time he struggled along with the *Iliad* in Greek, he also went through Johann Heinrich Voss's translation of it into German hexameters. Experiencing Homer's epic in Greek and German provided the catalyst for Carlyle both to write *The French Revolution* and to envision it as a modern epic.

Though the *Iliad* influenced Carlyle in numerous ways, its graphic depiction of character in action took especial hold of his imagination. Reading Homer's epic brought to life for him what he called a "Portici," or gallery, of characters. "All the *Antiquity* I have ever known becomes alive in my head," he wrote in February 1834. "There is a whole Gallery of Apelleses and Phidiases that I not only look upon but *make.*" During the winter months he spent his evenings studying Homer in Greek and German; his days he spent studying accounts of the French Revolution. The two readings coalesced in his heated imagination as he recreated the French revolutionaries in the molds of Homer's heroes.

Believing that the essence of history lay in biography, Carlyle encapsulates in his history numerous biographies of the revolutionaries. The example of Homer's world bulked large in his imagination. The *Iliad*'s myriad character portraits encompass great physical variety and psychological range. Unlike Carlyle, who overtly shapes his personages, Homer invariably lets his reveal themselves through their speeches. Even individuals who appear once in the *Iliad*—Thersites, Phoenix, Dolon—leave a striking impression. Similarly, Carlyle presents many of his cast of hundreds in unforgettable vignettes, with only a few figures—usually the heroes—receiving extended treatment. The interactions among all his portraits, major and minor, heroic and unheroic, give Carlyle's history tremendous kinetic energy as he depicts the dynamics of individuals in motion and colliding against each other. In virtually every portrait, even of lesser personages, Carlyle attempts chiaroscuro. His Marie Antoinette, for example, embodies the unthinking ways of the aristocracy—out-of-touch with reality, frivolous and vain, even if occasionally well-meaning—but under pressure she does reveal courage for which he grudgingly gives her credit. One whom Carlyle delights to paint in ambivalent, oxymoronic strokes is "that irreverend Reverence of Autun," Talleyrand. Even when Carlyle cannot sympathize with an individual he enters into his being: for example, he makes us experience Louis XV's oncoming death from Louis's own point of view.

Carlyle often succeeds better in cumulative portraits that develop over the course of the book than in drawn-out set pieces. In *The French Revolution* he rarely lingers long over a portrait, even one of a major figure like Mirabeau or Danton. Rather, he builds these portraits up to considerable complexity by returning to them often, recalling earlier acts, characteristic gestures, even physical appearance (e.g., Mirabeau's masses of black hair). Carlyle alerts the reader to what he has presented before by reminding him of it, or adding to it, or commenting upon it, or by all of these methods together.

Throughout *The French Revolution* Carlyle examines the attributes of kingship or, more broadly, of leadership. His primary structure for holding together a society constantly under enormous centrifugal pressures is the hero. Although for Carlyle the hero represents many things, primarily he exists to impose his will upon the chaos of life. "May we not say," Carlyle writes in the lectures on hero-worship, "while so many of our late Heroes have worked rather as revolutionary men, that nevertheless every Great Man, every genuine man, is by the nature of him a son of Order, not of Disorder." Disorder for Carlyle is "dissolution" and "death." Under Louis XVI a power vacuum gradually develops. After the Revolution breaks out, successive sons of order attempt to stem the rising tide of anarchy. Mirabeau establishes a precarious control; Danton maintains it with difficulty, only to have it denied by Robespierre and the Terror; finally, Napoleon as *deus ex machina* restores the principle of order.

Louis XVI has ruled ineffectually. A true king, Carlyle believes, emerged in primitive times, in a since rejected etymology, as our "Acknowledged Strongest (well named King, *Könning,* Can-ning, or Man that was Able)." No task facing the hero has more importance than that of providing direction for the society entrusted to him; "governing . . . is man's highest work, done *well.*" But Louis no longer governs well, or even at all. When the States General convene in 1789, Carlyle speculates which of its six hundred members will emerge to lead France. He does not speculate long. "*Gabriel Honoré Riquetti de Mirabeau,* the world-compeller, man-ruling Deputy of Aix" quickly assumes the mantle of kingship abandoned by Louis. As Mirabeau "steps proudly along," he "shakes his black chevelure, or lion's-mane; as if prophetic of great deeds."

Yet by the next paragraph Carlyle has qualified his enthusiasm for Mirabeau, "the Type-Frenchman of this epoch; as Voltaire was of the last." Voltaire fascinated Carlyle all his life, from his first reading while a university student of the Frenchman's works, to his 1829 essay, to his extended serial portrait, three decades later, in *Frederick.* Yet he had large reservations about Voltaire's character and achievement, as he had about the French in general. Briefly, although Carlyle admired French brilliance and wit, he condemned their frivolity, insufficient high seriousness, loose morality, and lack of reverence for the divine. Great peoples believed in God; the French did not. In 1824, as a young man making his first extended trip outside of Scotland, Carlyle had visited Paris and found French ways appalling. But in *The French Revolution* he presents on balance a favorable portrait of the French, at least as favorable as his stern northern prejudices allowed him. Once he even compares "the ready Gaelic fire" to "the Teutonic anthracite," concluding, "how happy is our Europe that has both kinds!" Although Carlyle admitted that "Gaelic fire" constituted a necessary component of European culture, nonetheless he felt that the French character lacked profundity. Whatever individual merits a Frenchman may possess, his tainted national origin adversely affects Carlyle's estimate of him. In sum, it is difficult to imagine any Frenchman rising to the highest rank in Carlyle's pantheon of heroes. To link Mirabeau with Voltaire by speaking of him as the "Type-Frenchman" of his day is thus mixed praise. Furthermore, Mirabeau lives and works during a time of revolution. Such epochs, in which the hero serves as a restraining rather than as a constructive force, do not allow the higher qualities of heroism to develop. Nor, in Carlyle's view, is Mirabeau by nature and temperament cast in the best mold. After the initial introduction, Carlyle returns almost immediately to Mirabeau's *chevelure,* now, however, become his "black Samson-locks." As Samson had often sacrificed duty to sensual pleasure, so will Mirabeau—a weakness, Carlyle implies, particularly French.

For twenty-three months Mirabeau becomes for Carlyle France's true king and "the Pharos and Wonder-sign of an amazed Europe." First, he is "royal" Mirabeau, then "King Mirabeau" lifting up his "lion-voice." When he confronts Louis XVI's representative, he "glares on him with fire-flashing face; shakes the black lion's mane." From the beginning, as Homer had Achilles, Carlyle identifies Mirabeau with fire; at culminating moments, "like a burning mountain he blazes heaven-high."

Yet even Mirabeau cannot control the accelerating lava-flood of events, nor even fully comprehend the revolutionary phenomenon. Contemporaries suspect him of loyalist sympathies. As he nears the end of his career, he becomes "a man travelling, comet-like, in splendour and nebulosity, his wild way," yet also "a questionable, most blameable man," questionable because his fixed "way of thought . . . *can* grow no further," blameable because moral lapses have sapped his character and concentration. To cease to grow in Carlyle's organic universe is to die; nor does he excuse Mirabeau his lapses. Death near, "giant Mirabeau walks in darkness." Hearing the cannon fire without, he asks, "Have we the Achilles' Funeral already?" His middle policy has aroused suspicion both on the royalist right and the Jacobin left, and, like Caesar in Shakespeare's play, he dies midway through the national upheaval. The struggle to become a Homeric "Cloud-Compeller," that is, a god who can sway the universe, destroys him before his time, a victim of his superabundant energies. The daimon in him does not know the meaning of "impossible." "*Ne me dites jamais ce bête de mot.*" He cannot stop, only cease.

As Mirabeau's star wanes, Danton's rises. Mirabeau dominates the first half of Carlyle's three-decker, Danton the second. Carlyle early associates him with Mirabeau as one who can discern the course of events, and, like Mirabeau, he represents a rallying point for order amidst the increasing chaos. When the new assembly meets in October 1791, Mirabeau is dead. "Our only Mirabeau now is Danton," Carlyle writes, "whom some call 'Mirabeau of the Sansculottes'." Danton has become the "cloudy Atlas of the whole." Yet with more than human greatness, he too stands doomed, as much by flaws within as by circumstances without. By September 1793 Danton has an official post: "Minister of Justice is his name; but Titan of the Forlorn Hope, and *Enfant Perdu* of the Revolution, is his quality." Although for a time Danton bestrides the onrushing Revolution, in the end it engulfs him. Like Don Quixote, the Knight of the Woeful countenance, he confronts a world unable to rise to his imaginative conception of it. He cannot will men to act in conformity with his ideal.

As with Mirabeau, Carlyle stands in uneasy relation to Danton. Danton, like Mirabeau, can get through "in brief space . . . immensities of business; not neglecting his own wages and trade-profits, it is thought." Carlyle quotes Madame Roland's opinion that Danton had too much of the "Sardanapalus character." Great as a leader but flawed as a man, his moral failings prevent him from attaining his heroic potential. Only as death approaches does he rise momentarily to full epic greatness. As Mirabeau had compared himself to Achilles, so Danton, in prison and facing execution, arrives at the "Bourne of Creation" like Ulysses in the Underworld. As Ulysses must journey to Hades to gain awareness of death and thus achieve maturity of vision, so too must Danton in prison make a spiritual pilgrimage. Even more than Mirabeau, Danton possesses extraordinary power of voice. It is his particular heroic gift, as it was one of Achilles'. As Achilles's voice struck terror into the Trojans when he first appeared before them in Book 18 of the *Iliad,* so Danton, defending himself at his trial, threatens to overwhelm his opponents with "passionate words, piercing with their wild sincerity, winged with wrath." "Speech will not utter what is in that man," writes Carlyle, impressed and moved. Danton's voice, like Achilles' on the wall, expresses the mysterious power of a great personality. His opponents dare not risk letting him speak again, and he is guillotined.

What Carlyle felt a true hero needed was a perspective that was inside the Revolution and yet detached from it. Mirabeau and Danton, both very much inside the Revolution, cannot envision it with sufficient detachment. Does anyone manage to attain a perspective that combines involvement with detachment? We must now consider Napoleon, who lurks in the wings throughout Carlyle's epic drama.

Virtually every mention of Napoleon by Carlyle in *The French Revolution* is gratuitous since Napoleon, though sympathetic and keenly observant, did not play a major role. In effect, Carlyle had little reason to bring him in at all, or to end his narrative in 1795 with Napoleon's dramatic quelling of the Parisian mob with a "whiff of grapeshot." No history of the French Revolution that I have looked at mentions Napoleon until 1795; none ends where Carlyle ends his. Nor, by and large, does Napoleon meet Carlyle's usual specifications for greatness, except that by finally controlling the mob he establishes order at a crucial moment.

In his first two volumes Carlyle mentions Napoleon, always unnecessarily, on several occasions. Early on, for example, we observe "a dusky-complexioned taciturn Boy" at a military school. Later, Napoleon's meteoric rise through the ranks attracts Carlyle's attention, as does his

The Declaration of the Rights of Man.

evident military genius. Every mention he makes of Napoleon gains in intensity. In July and August 1793 Napoleon helps put down royalists in skirmishes in the South of France. By November he has become "an Artillery *Chef de Brigade,* of extreme diligence, who often takes his nap of sleep among the guns." At Danton's trial Carlyle speaks of Napoleon in the same breath with him: ". . . Danton only . . . could still try to govern France. He only, the wild amorphous Titan;—and perhaps that other olive-complexioned individual, the Artillery-Officer at Toulon, whom we left pushing his fortune in the South?" By bringing Napoleon in at this point Carlyle wants us to realize that he has inherited Danton's mantle of leadership, even if he does not assume it immediately. Only Napoleon can now restore order, and the reader anticipates the moment when—a dozen chapters later—he will enter center-stage.

Carlyle's *French Revolution* ends on October 5th, 1795, with the famous whiff of grapeshot. When grapeshot is used against the people by one who has himself risen from their ranks, the Revolution will have come full circle. What began with the gradual collapse of the monarchy, moved through increasing disorder to a period of chaos, has finally arrived at a semblance of stability. The "Epic Ship" that was, or is, the French Revolution has reached its destined end.

Carlyle never gives Napoleon a full human dimension. Though a greater man on the world stage than either Mirabeau or Danton, he lacks their color, flair, and humanity. When in *Heroes and Hero-Worship* Carlyle explores his character in more depth, he found it unsatisfactory. Yet, despite his flaws and the aberrations of his subsequent career, Napoleon *"had* a sincerity" of a Cromwell to be sure, but withal impressive, for it comprised "a certain instinctive ineradicable feeling for reality." On St. Helena, Carlyle observes, Napoleon "still, to his last days, insists on the practical, the real . . . 'Say nothing, if one can do nothing'."

Simone Weil has described the *Iliad* as the "poem of force." More than any other work of literature, it embodies the enduring reality in human affairs that power determines relationships among individuals. The strongest in the *Iliad* are the physically strongest; the strongest in *The French Revolution* command the physical resources of their own being or of others'. In *Heroes* Carlyle depicts the universe "as a force, and a thousandfold Complexity of Forces . . . Everywhere Force," and "we ourselves a mysterious Force."

The pervasive fire imagery that hovers about the heroes of the *Iliad* and *The French Revolution* symbolizes not only their outward strength but this mysterious inner "force." Homer engulfs Achilles in images of fire. When he shouts to the Trojans from the wall, fire plays around his being. Fire is also of the essence of Carlyle's universe, the expression of its intensity, its life, its energy; those in harmony with its natural forces themselves emanate fire. Danton is "fiery-real, from the great fire-bosom of Nature herself." "Fire flashes from the eyes of him" as he defends himself before his accusers. Mirabeau burns with "a fret and fever that keeps heart and brain on fire." Fire for him is immersion in life, from dinners that "cost five hundred pounds," to "Syrens of the Opera," to "all the ginger that is hot in the mouth." His impassioned energy keeps him ablaze until the end: ". . . in the glare of the coming dissolution, the mind of the man is all glowing and burning."

Mirabeau meets several of Carlyle's criteria for greatness. He is sincere, in earnest. He reveals a vein of humor, a *fond gaillard.* Even more indispensable for leadership "in a most blinkard, bespectacled, logic-chopping generation" is the gift of vision, the ability to cut through at a glance a complex ever-changing situation. At one point in his narrative Carlyle asserts that, of men then living and endowed with vision, he finds "some Three." He does not name the three, but they are evidently Mirabeau, Danton, and Napoleon. "Nature," he writes, has gifted Mirabeau "with an eye." His strength, at least in the early stages of his career, is that he sees "a thing, how it is, how it may be worked with." Heroes, as Carlyle conceives them, possess to an extraordinary degree the power of sight. It is both sight and insight, and ultimately it is Carlyle's most original contribution to the nineteenth-century mythology of the hero.

Carlyle also admired in Mirabeau the gift of vivid, pictorial utterance, a quality he prized in his own father, in Burns, and in himself. The ability to speak well under pressure is, in the Carlylean pantheon of virtues, a test of genius and a usual component for leadership. Both Mirabeau and Danton have full, vibrant voices that pierce to the heart of the subject and of the hearer. Mirabeau's voice made him "a world-compeller, and ruler over men"; Danton's at his trial carries across the Seine. But excessive vocal power can detract from heroic stature. "Bellowing" characterizes the voice of the Marquis Saint-Huruge. "Cracked or half-cracked is this tall Marquis's head; uncracked are his lungs." We rarely see Napoleon talking, however, though (as Carlyle observes in *Heroes*) he "has words in him that are like Austerlitz battles." The glimpses we have of Napoleon are of a man in action or poised to act; Carlyle usually associates him with his guns. But when Napoleon speaks, he does so in terse, memorable utterances: his words are acts—swift, direct, annihilating. For Carlyle, the greatest heroes, like Cromwell, feel more than they can express. Cromwell speaks or writes, not in torrents of words, but in pithy, heartfelt pronouncements that immediately command attention. Even his undeniable obscurities Carlyle finds worthy of explication. The words are the tip of the iceberg, characteristic of the man but only a small external manifestation of latent strength.

Both Mirabeau and Danton ground themselves in reality, in things as they are. Overthrowers or "swallowers" of formulas, they reject the deadwood of antiquated societal forms for newer syntheses more in harmony with contemporary realities. Carlyle describes Danton as "no hollow Formalist, deceptive and self-deceptive." He is a "Swallower of Formulas; of still wider gulp than Mirabeau." Although Carlyle's heroic Frenchmen know themselves imperfectly and indulge in excess and corruption, they do not consciously deceive, themselves or others.

Nor can the Carlylean hero be passionate. Practitioners of epic from Homer to modern parodists of the form like

Joyce view erotic love for women as an obstacle preventing the hero from fulfilling his duty. In classical epic only the time-rich gods revel in love-making. Humans, bound by their mortality, have a nobler purpose. Achilles, though he sleeps each night with Briseis, regards her neither with passion nor sentiment; Odysseus, though he has liaisons with Circe and Calypso, retains his ideal of earlier domestic unity; Aeneas, though sorely tempted by Dido, rejects her to accomplish a higher design, the founding of New Troy. These heroes have commitments elsewhere, to the past and to a vision of the future.

Aware of this tradition of the epic hero commanding his passions, Carlyle uses it to undercut the heroic image of his protagonists. Except for Napoleon, his heroes give free rein to their amorous propensities—to the detriment of the task before them. With more than a hint of contempt Carlyle speaks of Mirabeau and Danton, when they succumb to sensual passion, as "love-heroes." Only Napoleon appears passionless. Carlyle makes no mention in *The French Revolution* of his relationship with women. Ascetic as Mirabeau and Danton are not, he sleeps with his guns.

Mirabeau, Danton, and Napoleon all in different ways fail to measure up to the potential residing in them as active heroes. We still seek a hero who more fully embodies Carlyle's ideal of heroism.

The only person who enjoyed a perspective both within, yet detached from, the Revolution was Goethe. As an observer attached to the Prussian forces he collided briefly with the Revolution in 1792. In *Campagne in Frankreich* he recorded his experiences and pondered their meaning. "Mark that man, O reader," exhorts Carlyle, "as the memorablest of all the memorable in this Argonne Campaign." In Carlyle's view, as the ephemeral disappears from historical view, Goethe's impact upon human affairs would become "visible more and more" in his character as one of the Immortals. Ultimately, although he has only the briefest of walk-on parts in Carlyle's epic drama, more than anyone else except Homer he and his ideas dominate it. Scholars still fail to recognize that Goethe's influence upon Carlyle persisted long after *Sartor Resartus,* that Carlyle's writings after 1834 cannot be adequately understood without taking into account Goethe's continuing impact upon them.

In *The French Revolution* Goethe's ideas, his aphoristic phrases, even the mottoes he supplies for the three volumes, are everywhere in and behind Carlyle's narrative, pervading its muscles and sinews, influencing its perspective, so much so that at times Goethe virtually takes on the character of a *persona.* At one pole, Goethe represents for Carlyle a model of rationality, of control over one's life, against which one measures the revolutionaries' behavior; at the other, he supplies Carlyle with the all-important concept of the daimonic. I limit myself here to what may seem a minor but is actually a highly significant indication of Goethe's influence: the mottoes from his works that Carlyle chooses to precede his three volumes.

As he had with *Sartor,* Carlyle drew upon Goethe for the motto, in this case mottoes, for *The French Revolution.* In *Sartor* the lines that serve as motto—"My inheritance, how wide and fair, /Time is my fair seed-field, of Time I'm heir"—signal Carlyle's underlying conception of the role of time in man's existence. Much in the same way, Carlyle in choosing the mottoes for *The French Revolution* indicates a perspective by which he wishes his readers to interpret the events described. Few critics of Carlyle have commented on these mottoes; in fact, the single available reprint of *The French Revolution*—the Everyman edition—omits them entirely. This cryptic quatrain from Goethe's *Venezianische Epigramme* (1791) precedes Carlyle's first volume:

> To this stithy I liken the land, the hammer its ruler,
> And the people that plate, beaten between them that writhes:
> Woe to the plate, when nothing but wilful bruises on bruises
> Hit it at random; and made, cometh no Kettle to view!

These lines as well as volume I's subtitle, "The Bastille", foreshadow a France prostrate, helpless under a monarchy that cannot lead. No more than a helpless "plate" can oppressed people resist arbitrary blows. In a larger sense, the quatrain questions the legitimacy of any leadership that allows such blows to fall at random. "The proper name of all Kings is Minister, Servant," Carlyle will write in *Past and Present;* the ruler has an overriding responsibility to rule effectively. The "hammer" (the state) exists to shape, not to abuse, the "kettle" (the people). If the ruler allows anarchy to prevail, the people have a right to seek leadership elsewhere.

To preface the second volume of history, "The Constitution", Carlyle takes quatrain No. 13 from Goethe's *Weissagung des Bakis* (1798):

> Walls I can see tumbled down, walls I see also a-building;
> Here sit prisoners, there likewise do prisoners sit:
> Is the world, then, itself a huge prison? Free only the madman,
> His chains knitting still up into some graceful festoon?

These brooding lines, in which Goethe reaches what Harold Jantz calls "the nadir of his historical pessimism," suggest that the revolutionaries become as much captives as those whom they incarcerate: "Hardly has one tyranny been crushed when another rises and man remains prisoner as before." The prisons, actual and metaphysical, into which the revolutionaries are thrown or throw themselves, foreshadow the madness of the Terror. Only the insane, who create their own worlds, are truly free. By implication, those who live in this world must learn to live within constraints. To legislate freedom is an impossibility. Walls are built as well as torn down; the Bastille may have disappeared but man remains hardly more free than before.

The *Venezianische Epigramme* again provide the quatrain (No. 50) that prefaces volume III, "The Guillotine":

> No Apostle-of-Liberty much to my heart ever found I;

License, each for himself, this was at bottom
their want.
Liberator of many! first dare to be Servant of
many:
What a business is that, wouldst thou know it,
go try!

"The French Revolution was also a revolution for me," Goethe confessed unhappily in 1790. Many of his writings on the Revolution remained in fragmentary form. Finding apostles of freedom abhorrent, he tried to make them abhorrent to others in these writings, which, in E. M. Butler's words, represent him "vainly struggling to stem the fearful flood-tide by deriding, or belittling, or impugning the manifestations of a spirit so incommensurable with his own." Carlyle uses this quatrain from Goethe to comment ironically on all those who, like Mirabeau and Danton, supported the Revolution from motives not entirely altruistic. We remember, too, that another apostle of freedom is Robespierre, who triumphs in the Reign of Terror only, in turn, to fall by his own instrument.

All three quatrains suggest an attitude detached from, yet ironically observant, of the human spectacle. Goethe's words obviously meant a great deal to Carlyle. In *Death of Goethe* (1832), written immediately after the event, Carlyle had spoken generally of Goethe's "Patriarchal Sayings, which, since the Hebrew Scriptures were closed, we know not were to match; in whose homely depths lie often the materials for volumes." That same year he followed this essay with a major statement, *Goethe's Works,* in which he tries to express Goethe's meaning for the present. At the end he ponders the three quatrains we have examined in a pregnant discussion of Goethe's political stance. Was Goethe "Ministerial or in Opposition?" Carlyle has him neither and both. The message he draws from the three quatrains is that the poet can most benefit society by remaining detached, practicing his art, and avoiding the political arena. The artist must strive, "in true manful endeavour, were it under despotism or under sansculottism, to create somewhat." In the end does not "the hope of the world lie," Carlyle asks, with the artist? When he admonishes his readers to go forth and create, he in effect admonishes himself. Better not be tempted to play an active role in the turbulent present; seek instead to "scan and interpret" it clearly to others. Such is the artist's role, and to fulfill it he must remain, as Goethe had remained, of all parties and of none—a practice "we could recommend to universal study, that the spirit of it might be understood by all men, and by all men imitated." When Carlyle ends the essay with the words, "of Goethe, with a feeling such as can be due to no other man, we now take farewell," he means his "farewell" in more than a rhetorical sense. In the almost fifty years remaining to him Carlyle does not write an extended piece on Goethe, though he did not lack opportunities to do so. Until the end of his life he will lament that the English know so little of the German sage, yet he makes little attempt to enlighten them. Why is this? Carlyle's major works after 1834 are saturated with Goethe's thoughts and phrases; his letters teem with incidental comments. In *Heroes,* while admitting that Goethe is the modern most worthy of consideration as "the hero as man of letters," he refuses to speak of him, alluding, in defense, to the imperfect state of English knowledge. This explanation does not hold up, for Carlyle had often written of Goethe before when English opinion had been even less well informed; in addition, he includes among his heroes both Odin and Mohammed, about whom English opinion was even less well informed.

In my view, Carlyle refused to write further about Goethe not because he thought English knowledge of him imperfect, nor because he had nothing more to say, least of all because he stopped learning from Goethe himself. Rather, Carlyle has now taken on for his age the mantle of *vates,* of poet and prophet together, that Goethe had relinquished through death. In a real sense, Goethe's influence begins anew in the mid-1830s as Carlyle attempts to become the "Vates and Seer" to his age that Goethe had been to his, the interpreter of the awesome forces of change that were taking place in the present. Consideration of the mottoes of *The French Revolution* can only be a miniscule part of any argument designed to show that after 1834 Goethe continued to exercise a pervasive influence upon Carlyle. But the mottoes do reveal Carlyle in his Goethean role as ironic and keenly-detached observer. Though seeing into the origins of the Revolution, Carlyle, Poet and Prophet like Goethe, retains his distance from it. Beyond insisting that, given the state of France's spiritual corruption, the Revolution was inevitable, he does not openly take sides. Indeed, contemporaries criticized him for his detached perspective and for not condemning the Revolution in his history.

In *Goethe's Works* Carlyle asserted that the German's "Spiritual History" was "the ideal emblem of all true men's in these days"; and further, that "the goal of Manhood, which he attained, we too in our degree have to aim at." It is impossible not to believe that when Carlyle writes "we too in our degree" he does not also intend the words to apply to himself. Similarly, at the end of *Death of Goethe* Carlyle had claimed that the spirit of the man whom he had loved "yet lives in us with an authentic life." He wished to follow in Goethe's steps, to be for his contemporaries the guide that Goethe had been for his, to chart his age's course as Goethe had his, to be, in short, as Goethe had been, the "Captain of spiritual Europe." Goethe's death, we must remember, had followed hard upon that of Carlyle's own father, whom in a different way he had admired as much as he had admired Goethe. Stunned and shaken by these deaths, Carlyle pondered what he should do, to what great purpose he, with all the gifts he knew he had, should direct his life. For several years he looked for a subject on which to write, one that would allow him to assume a Goethean role to his contemporaries as *magister vitae* and interpreter of the present. He did not decide on the French Revolution until mid-1834. In writing a history of this most important modern phenomenon, one which had tremendous significance for present-day England, what more inevitable and right for Carlyle than to preface his volumes with the quatrains, so charged with significance for him, with which he had closed *Goethe's Works*? These quatrains suggest that only an outsider, one who has looked hard and seen clearly—more clearly than Mirabeau and Danton or even Napoleon—could achieve the perspective necessary to grasp the revolutionary phenomenon. Goethe had done so in his time; now Carlyle's turn had arrived. In *The French Revolution* Goethe the *vates,* prophet as well as poet, emerges as the nearest approximation to Carlyle's ideal of heroism. The mottoes are Carlyle's bow to his spiritual mentor before striking off on his own. (pp. 165-81)

John Clubbe, "Epic Heroes in 'The French Revolution'," in Thomas Carlyle 1981: Papers Given at the International Thomas Carlyle Centenary Symposium, *edited by Horst W. Drescher, Peter Lang, 1983, pp. 165-85.*

ROMANTIC POETRY

Stopford A. Brooke

[*Brooke was an Anglo-Irish clergyman, poet, critic, and educator, whose* Primer of English Literature *(1876) was popular with generations of students. Among his other notable works on literature are* Theology in the English Poets *(1874) and* Naturalism in English Poetry *(1920). In the following lecture published in the latter volume, Brooke asserts that the main ideas expressed in Romantic poetry stem from the French Revolution.*]

It is quite necessary, at the date at which this study has arrived, to say something concerning that world-shaking movement which men call the Revolution, and which, in 1789, passed in France from floating thought into form and act. For its ideas, or opposition to its ideas, underlie the whole of the great poetry of England from Cowper to Keats—and in other forms, made, indeed, by its own working in the world, from Tennyson to Morris. We are now struggling to reshape them into a new poetry, but, as yet, with no clearness, no success.

Some say that the Revolution had but little influence on poetry; that its influence has been exaggerated. These persons do not seem to me to have grasped the ideas of the Revolution, nor studied its outbreak in France, and its temporary failure there; and without some steady study of the whole subject of the Revolution in France, the matter, the stuff and the passion which underlie and thrill like life through the poetry of the nineteenth century cannot be felt or understood. Even the minor poetry of the third-rate poets needs, for its useful and just reading, such a study. Nor, without it, is there any right appreciation possible of those poets, who, like Scott, were in revolt against the ideas of the Revolution. The ideas of the Revolution set a war on foot. They came not to bring peace but a sword. And the work, in poetry, of its opponents, as well as of its supporters, needs for its comprehension knowledge of the thoughts and passions which were then at issue. For such a study the best books that can be read on the matter are De Tocqueville's *Ancien Régime* and Taine's *Origins.*

The French Revolution, in its suddenness, violence and devastating power, and subsidence, may well be compared to the eruption of a volcano. But the comparison extends further than these analogies of suddenness, violence and the rest. A volcanic eruption is only sudden in its outburst. The forces which take violent shape in it have been gathering together in silence for many years. Age after age, the caverns below are slowly filling with tense elements seeking, for their escape, the path of least resistance. At last they reach the point where their upward thrust exactly equals the downward pressure of the earth and air. One touch then, the lightening by the hundredth part of an inch on the barometer of the weight of the atmosphere, and the imprisoned forces burst upwards to terrify and destroy the land. It seems then sudden, but it has been long preparing. Its point, its place of outbreak seems casual, but it has also been the result of a long-continued series of antecedents and sequences. It is fixed where previous events have produced the line of least resistance.

The ideas of the Revolution had been storing up their forces for at least two centuries under the surface of European society. They were ideas which were the contradiction and the destruction of the remains of the Feudal System. They were certain to break forth, and they found the path of least resistance in France. There, the Feudal System was weakest; there the people had had more liberty than elsewhere on the Continent, and there the ideas themselves had been most thrown into stimulating theories. A host of literary men sowed France, country and town, with thousands and thousands of books and pamphlets which put into every conceivable shape the ideas of the Revolution in opposition to the ideas of the Ancient Regime. The path of least resistance was there, and there the volcano broke forth. It burst, it blazed amain and the whole face of the world was changed. In England no such overwhelming outbreak took place. The ideas of the Revolution were, of course, moving in England as they were in Germany. In Germany they were crushed; in England they stole from thought to thought into the minds of men. There was no fixed point in the political history of the country where preparation ceased and fierce formation began—no two periods divisible from one another. But what did not exist in politics did exist in poetry and among the poets. The English poets felt the revolutionary ideas long before 1789 and expressed them with growing passion; but they did not take a clear form in their poetry. They floated through it like those airs of the coming spring which haunt the milder days of February and March, prophecies of the resurrection of the world. They rose into clear life and form after 1789. Wordsworth, Coleridge, Southey embodied them. Then they decayed after Walter Scott had represented the reaction against them; and they decayed in the hands of the very men who had expressed their youth. Out of their decay they sprang up again in Byron and Shelley; and then they died altogether for a time in Keats.

Of course, English poetry up to 1832, the period of Parliamentary Reform, was much more than a mere representative of these ideas. It took up a thousand other subjects of emotion, but the revolutionary conceptions concerning man, his origin, his rights, mutual duties and destiny, are the underlying spirit of all poetry, the main emotion in which all other emotions share. So far, then, as English poetry from 1780 to 1832 is related to the general history of mankind, a great part—a necessary part—of its history is best explained by its relation to the Revolution and to the form the Revolution took in France. It can best be grouped around this centre, and its sequence is thus best explained. I assert this, but I do not dwell upon it. It would be too historical; and our business here is not history, but poetry, not the frame, but the picture in the frame. Nor shall we dwell on the political or social forms in which the Revolution enshrined its movement, but the main idea of the Revolution, expressed in its most concise form, we must dwell upon. It dominates poetry. And there are also certain side issues of this main idea which, carrying with them worlds of emotion, are worth marking out, not only because they are represented in English poetry for at least thirty years before the outbreak of the French Revolution, but also because they have continued to be powers in poetry up to the present day.

The first, the main idea of the Revolution, an idea which had been growing up, for at least 200 years before 1789, was "That there was only one Man, if we may so style it, in all Humanity; that, therefore all divisions, classes, outside differences, such as are made by birth, by rank, by wealth, by power, or by separate nationalities, were to be wholly put aside as non-existent; that there was a universal Mankind, every member of which ought to be free, with equal opportunities, and bound each to each as brothers are bound. Hence, finally, all divisions made by caste, by colour, by climate, by aggressive patriotism, by all that we call nationality, were also dissolved. There was only one country, the country of Mankind, only one nation, the nation of Humanity."

This was the great conception which attacked the ideas of the Feudal System, and which will finally conquer the whole world. The war it initiated continues still. Even now, caste, rank, colour and wealth contend with it, and strive to hold their own against it, but day by day their armies of darkness or of oppression are being beaten back. The victory of this conception may be long in winning, but it is absolutely certain. The whole future of the race depends on that victory. The health, the honour, the greatness and great-doing of every nation depend on its obedience to the duties this conception imposes on it. Every disobedience to its duties entails—in proportion to the amount of the disobedience—national disgrace, dishonour, loss of influence for good, social disturbance and misery and sorrow and suffering on all mankind. That is as certain as any law of Nature. The sanctions of the idea are imperative and as inevitable as Death and Life. France proclaimed their conception in 1789 as a national confession. It violated it as the Terror went on; it violated it still more under the imperialism of Napoleon. It violated it again after Waterloo, returning like a dog to the vomit of Feudalism. It violated it still more, and in the meanest of all fashions, in the predominance of wealth, under Napoleon III. There is scarcely any form of its violation which France did not present as an object-lesson to the world; and to this day, even under republican institutions, it is suffering the results of these persistent violations of the conceptions it was the first publicly to proclaim. No States can say they have not been warned. No government aware of the history of France can say that it has been taken by surprise when the consequences of its disobedience to the first law of human progress fall upon itself and the people that it rules. We must dwell on this for a moment. France proclaimed the idea and smote it into form. Alas, it also exhibited, one after another, nearly all the false forms the idea could take. It also exhibited its resurrections. Again and again, in revolution after revolution, it strove to recall the original conception. Again and again, it let it go, or let it drift into baser shapes. But it never let it completely go. It rescued it even when it seemed quite lost, by the voice of its writers, by the uprising of the passion of its people. It has showed to the world, during a hundred years, how and why the idea fails, and where, how and why it succeeds, where it is pure and where it is debased. France has been sacrificed for the good and use of the human race. This is an exhibition in history which has educated humanity, and the deep gratitude which is due to her for this, both when it was conscious and unconscious, has been given to her in a measure pitiably small.

It was this great conception, with all the vast ocean of emotion which flows after it, which in 1730 began to influence the poets of England, and which moves through all great poetry and prophecy now in majestic power and kindling passion. For a century and a half it has mastered song.

It began . . . with James Thomson. When he was alive the only class the poets thought of was the cultivated class in London. Pope said that the proper study of mankind was man, but he meant by man the little aristocracy of culture by which he was surrounded; and I am inclined to believe that this aristocracy is the most exclusive and the most heartless, and therefore the least original and originating of all the aristocracies. At any rate, it is diametrically opposed to the great conception of the Revolution, and the result was that the poetry of Dryden, of Pope, of the whole of the critical and intellectual school, had no elements of continued life in it and died with the death of its finest exponent. While he was yet alive, Thomson threw himself on the other side; not, I think, with any consciousness of what he was doing, not with any fervour, but sufficiently to show that a new spirit had entered into English poetry; that the Elizabethan passion for man as man had recurred, with a plainer direction given to it. The humanity we meet in the *Seasons* ranges from Greenland to Italy and seems as interested in the Esquimaux as in the Englishman. It is not the learned folk whom Thomson cares for, but the shepherd in the snow, the ploughman in the fields, the poor girl crouching in the doorway on a bitter night and the country-maiden bathing in the summer stream. A new world opens before us. It is the spirit of the Revolution before the Revolution. Such a spirit could not die away. It had immortal youth and fire; and poet after poet was influenced by it. It even shows itself in Samuel Johnson, whose "London" cannot quite rest in London. It made the first great country novel in the hands of Goldsmith. In *The Traveller* Goldsmith passes from clime to clime beyond the English shores. In "Sweet Auburn, loveliest village of the plain," he sketches the poor with faithfulness and sympathy. We feel that they are of the same blood, of the same honourable passions, as the rich and powerful. Man is man in his poetry, independent of all differences. Nevertheless, it does not seem quite natural; the principle is rather worn as a fashion than felt from the heart. And this is still more the case with Gray, whose "rude forefathers of the hamlet," whose "mute inglorious Milton," whose "short and simple annals of the poor" are not much more than the play of a cultivated scholar with an idea beginning to be in vogue. But when we come to Crabbe, whose *Village* was published in 1784, on the eve of the French Revolution, we come to the conception on the eve, as it were, of its birth. The poor, their life, their one human nature with the rich: that is the very subject itself of the book. It is painted with stern feeling and with a grim intensity of sympathy. The poetry of the city is replaced by the poetry of a sordid village on the east coast of England with all its poverty and crime; and its rare and humble goodness and comfort. The poetry of fine society, court and palace is replaced by the poetry of the alehouse, the rude gatherings of the brutish fishermen and the miseries of the workhouse. The painting is direct from Nature; and the only part of the poem which is out of tune is at the end where he passes into a panegyric on the Lord of the Manor and his son; and that has at least this advantage that it throws, by its contrast with the previous wretchedness, a more lurid light upon it. In Cowper's *Task,* published in 1785, it is not only the poor, but man as man, which is his subject; man in his simplest elements, man not only in England, but over the whole world. The very next year, so swift and so exciting was this idea, Burns, himself a peasant, took up the whole conception and added to its passion, and especially that passion of love which, in its equalising and exalting power, lies more than all other passions at the root of the universal conception of humanity. In a multitude of poems we hear breathing in 1786, three years before it burst into fierce form in France, the impassionating, the primary idea of the Revolution.

This, then, is the main idea and this its progress. But it contained within it a number of related ideas; some of which were fitted for poetic treatment and received it. The first of these has been alluded to in what I have already said. It is the expansion of the love of country into the love of mankind, and especially the loss of the hating element in patriotism. Our highest country is mankind, and the interests of our own nation (our separate nation) are to be subordinated to the interests of the whole. There is a love greater than patriotism. It is the love of the great ideas on whose continued mastery depend the fortunes of the whole race. That this should arise in England, the most insular of all nations, is surely remarkable, but so strong was the leaven now, that before France proclaimed it in '89, England proclaimed it by the voice of Cowper. It was the first time that note was struck in England, and there was no response to it, save on the lips of a few politicians and philosophers, over the country. But this retired clerk boldly smote it out on the chords of his lyre. He transferred the inalienable brotherhood of man from England to Greenland, to Italy, to France, to Spain, to Africa, to South America, to the revolted States of America, and beyond them to the savage and the slave. His love of man was international.

This is a note which has gone on sounding in English poetry from that time. Wordsworth and Coleridge at the beginning of their career sympathised with France and denounced England for the crime of war against the young Republic. When they attacked Napoleon, they attacked him, not because he was at war with England, but because he strove to enslave the other nations to France; because he was at war with the principle that the love of man was a higher love than the love of country. Byron repudiated the insularity of England and died for another country than his own. Shelley was no isolated patriot; he loved Italy more than England; he loved mankind more than Italy. Keats was of no nation whatever, but the nation of loveliness. Tennyson reverted to the merely patriotic feeling, which contains a contempt of, or an attack on, other countries than our own; but Browning maintained, in a poetry which is Italian, French, Spanish more than English, the wider and nobler patriotism which loves man as man, independent of all national distinctions. That idea lasts. Wherever it lives in poetry, it keeps it young and fresh. Wherever it breathes, it also burns. Its fire is holier, its aspect is more bright, its song more thrilling than any insular or limited love of nationality; and its mightiest and noblest development is in the future. When it is fully grasped in action, as it is now by some of us in conception, poetry will receive its highest impulse and accomplish its most splendid and passionate song. May God be with it, and the crowning race of Man!

The second corollary from the original idea which took form in poetry was a protest for liberty and against oppression. We need not dwell on that, because it was not special to the Revolution. It has always been natural to mankind, and it has always formed one of the great motives of poetry. What region of the earth is not full of its song? Nevertheless, it took at this time in English poetry a more plain and practical turn than it had taken before; and it was new in its denunciations, in its appeal to God, in its foundation on the universal brotherhood of man, when Cowper took it up and gave it voice. He carried the poetry of human wrong into the prison with Howard and into the starving lives of the poor. He denounced, as Goldsmith had already done, the landowners who neglected their peasants and the merchants who built factories with blood, and the infamy of slavery. Patience itself, he said, is meanness in a slave. The English king, he thought and said, who covets more than freemen choose to grant, is a traitor, and rebellion is a duty. He had an example of that close at hand in the revolt of the American Colonies. I have often wondered whether Cowper in those famous lines was not thinking of those more famous days when Adams cried, as he heard the musketry at dawn from the fields near Woburn—"O, what a glorious morning is this!" *The Task* was published in 1785. He may have written these very verses shortly after the news of Lexington arrived in England in 1775. At any rate, he felt the wrath of the coming Revolution in France, four years before it came, when he suddenly places us in front of the Bastille:

> Ye horrid towers, the abode of broken hearts,
> Ye dungeons and ye caverns of despair,
> That monarchs have supplied from age to age
> With music such as suits their sovereign ears—
> The sighs and groans of miserable men!
> There's not an English heart that would not leap
> To hear that ye are fallen at last.

Wordsworth heard the news; Coleridge heard it; and both recorded their triumphant joy. From that day, poetry, which had always used this motive of love of liberty and hate of oppression, gave it a more practical turn. The right, so long considered divine, of the powerful, the well-born and the wealthy to use up the poor to support this right, was considered the vilest wrong; and wherever it was used, that special use was plainly named and directly attacked by the poets. This was the change that took place, and English-speaking poetry has done this close, defensive work, not negligently.

The third idea contained in the original conception, I have already dwelt on in its origins in England. It has been called "The Return to Nature." It is no harm in this introductory essay to isolate it again in different words before we treat of the poets who fully shaped it into song. It held that the true happiness of man consisted in a simple, almost a primæval life in accordance with Nature. This is an idea which was not peculiar to the Revolution. It has always arisen when luxury has corrupted society; when great wealth in a few hands has made it stupid; when life is made complex by selfish interests; when it is burdened with conventions and weary of knowledge. Let us get back, it says, to the breast of Mother Earth, where our own hands can win our own living from the woods and fields, when man is free from the slaveries of civilisation; away from the cities in which men lose their individuality and live like worms wriggling in a dish; away from the torment of intelligence and the uselessness of culture. And this included, of course, a belief that the natural man, man in his simplest form, and living the simplest life, was the best sort of man. In the peasant, the labourer, among shepherds and woodmen, the natural affections were most naturally felt, the primary emotions most free and noble, the virtues most manly, the heroism of life most noble. This was the idea; not new, but newly shaped. It may be said, at this time, to have first arisen in England, but it was Rousseau who gave it full vogue. He was himself inspired by it, and he inspired others with his passion. He put it into so attractive a form that men were convinced of it as it were against their will, and even the society of the Court and the noblesse took it up and played with it; fools, who did not understand that it held in it fire, earthquake and hurricane for their society. In England, it helped to destroy the school of Pope, which was eminently a school of citied culture. It dawned in the poetry of Thomson; it even influenced in his scholastic retirement the precise and careful verse of Gray. It moved through all the minor poets. Poetry left the city and took a country house. At first an air of unreality pervaded this poetry. The poetry called artificial left a kind of ghost behind it; and the ghost was sententious. The poets played with the new idea, but they were not passionate for it. However, as the French form of the Revolution drew near, the air grew warmer; this idea began to be a real power; and it was to be put into a form more luminous and more glowing. Goldsmith, Crabbe and Cowper developed it. It rose into passion in Burns. And when the French Revolution broke out, it became one of the vital spirits of English poetry. The poets themselves lived its life. Wordsworth fled the cities, dwelt in Somersetshire and finally settled in a remote village among the Cumberland mountains. He read few books; he let his own nature elicit its own poetry. He worked for his own living, and no one has ever clung closer than he to the heart of the common earth. Coleridge, when he was young, lived the same kind of life—Southey aspired to do so. They returned to Nature, and they made of natural things their dearest subjects. Moreover, they made the natural man, and his natural life, their main humanity. Wordsworth's new theory of poetry was based on the belief that in the natural phraseology of men educated by Nature and living a natural life, such as a shepherd lived in the dales, was to be found the true language of poetry. It was an absurd proposition and he sometimes carried it into a most absurd extreme, but it illustrates the passionate obstinacy with which this idea of the return to Nature was supported and the mastery it exercised over the minds of men. And the heroes of this new poetry were not warriors, princes, philosophers or great adventurers, but the shepherds of the hills and the ploughman at work, and the wives of the peasants and the children of the poor. It was a vast revolution, and its power has endured in poetry for more than a century. It ran, of course, into its extreme, but the extreme, in the end, did not hinder, but confirmed, its good. And its greatest good was the immense expansion which it gave to poetry. It opened out to the work of song not only the whole of country life, but also the emotional life of the largest and the most varied class in humanity, the class of the poor. Henceforth the range of poetry was as wide as human nature itself.

Connected with this was another subject of feeling and thought which also brought a new life into poetry. The transference which has just been described of the interests of the poets from man, considered as an intellectual and wealthy class in cities, to man independent of culture and wealth, as he was found in the country in his simplest elements—brought about, in time, or ran alongside of, a love of wild natural scenery. As the best of man was to be found where he was least spoiled by cultivation, so the greatest beauty was to be found, not in the trim gardens and landscape that Pope loved, but in the wild, untutored lands which man had not touched, where Nature went her own original way, and where, in consequence, we might get closer to her heart.

This is also a result of the Revolution ideas concerning man. Rousseau, who gave this love of wild Nature its most natural, one may say, its finest voice in France before the Revolution, connects it with the new interest in man, as seen in his simplest life. This love of wild Nature and the expression of it developed *pari passu* with the thought of man being at his best in the state of nature, and was kept hand in hand with the passion of humanity. We must always remember that the same poets who lived with the uncultivated people and found in them the most beautiful and unspoilt forms of human nature, found in the least cultivated natural scenery, in scenery wholly untouched by any hand but God's, the loveliest, the most spiritual natural beauty. Into that, as into an ocean of beauty, they plunged with passion, and some of them, especially modern poets, with so extreme and isolated a joy that they forgot in it their love of pure human nature—that is, forgot the origin of their love of wild Nature. But that was not the case at the beginning of the last century. Man was not then neglected. But the love of Nature, though it did not at that time extinguish the love of man, expanded—and especially after 1789, with the same rapidity and the same copiousness as the love of man as man expanded. This, at least, was the case in England.

The curious thing is that the idea thus struck into a finished form by Rousseau, had, for a long time, no growth in France as compared with its growth in England. The fact is that the tremendous rush of the new theories about man into violent political action in France overwhelmed at first this related idea. It took thirty years at least, after the Revolution was over, for the French poets fully to develop that solitary love of wild Nature which rose like a tree into full foliage in England ten years after the Revolution, which had begun to grow in England sixty years before its outburst, and which has continued to extend its branches—a mightier and a mightier tree—up to the present time. This then is a part of the revolutionary movement which especially belongs to England, and we owe its steady and vast expansion to our having kept the main idea of the Revolution in the midst of peace, apart from hasty, violent action, apart from despotism.

We . . . [can see] the development of this poetry of wild Nature from James Thomson, through Gray and Collins. We can trace it also in Goldsmith, Chatterton, Beattie, and in the faded verse of the Wartons. Then, as the outbreak of the Revolution drew near, this new poetry grew stronger and lovelier than before. Above all it grew more natural, closer to the actual sights and sounds of Nature, closer to the life of animals. The poets described what they saw, and lived with their eye on the subjects. This was the case with Cowper, Crabbe and Burns. But in these three poets, Nature is very rarely loved or haunted only for her own sake. Man is always with her. She is still, but with ever-advancing power, only a background for human nature. The poet is not lost in her alone. Neither Cowper, Crabbe nor Burns are capable of Wordsworth's isolation with the souls of lonely places, of temporary forgetfulness of man in Nature, it was not till the mighty, soul-shaking, past-destroying movement of the Revolution was thrown into passionate form in France that the English poets, set on fire by that flaming outburst, which burnt up every remnant of past conventions and artificial thought and made man naked of all that hampered his original emotions, became capable, when they chose, of forgetting man, of forgetting their very self, in the love of the Mighty Being, with whose spirit, in the wild and lonely places of the earth, they seemed to mingle, in whose doings they delighted, and whose very personality they loved, as a form of God Himself.

It seems strange to say that a movement for man should produce a passion for Nature in which man was at times forgotten. But it must be remembered that man was never really left aside by these poets. Nature came to be felt in this intense way through the intenser interest that they took in the humanity they found living among the wild mountains and the lonely streams. Wordsworth sketches in the *Prelude* the whole of the process. And, moreover, the fire of emotion they felt for man was so glowing that, when they came to look at Nature, they transferred the fire to their contemplation of Nature. Her beauty was now loved by the new poets, after the Revolution, as much as humanity was loved; and immediately all the poetry of Nature was transfigured into a new life. This was a wondrous change. It took fifty years to accomplish, but when it was accomplished, when in 1798 Wordsworth revealed to us, especially in that poem on the Wye, the passion of his soul for Nature, the life he felt in her, and the answer of his own being to the great Being of thought and beauty in the world—the poetry of Nature was utterly revolutionised. It was like the discovery of a new and lovely continent, opened for the first time to the eager voyaging of all the poets who should come after him. When we read those verses we feel that nothing resembling them in spirit, in emotion, in thought, had ever been written before.

Another idea which was adopted into poetry at this time, was also the direct outcome of the revolutionary thought. This was the vision and the prophecy of a universal regeneration of mankind, of a golden age, not mournfully looked back on as passed away, but joyfully anticipated in the future. It had existed long ago in the faith of the Church in a millennium, but there it was limited to the saved, who were then a small number; and it was to be realised after a great upturning of the earth for judgment. It was supernatural, not natural. It occurs even in the classical poets; it occurs now and again in the poets of England of the seventeenth and eighteenth centuries. But it occurs vaguely, and it is always limited to a class or a nation for want of a universal conception of man. But now, when man was conceived of as one people, as having one country of which all, without exception, were citizens, as being a universal brotherhood—and when, under the rule of that conception, all exclusive systems, whether poetical or religious, fell under the ban of humanity—then indeed, for the first time, the idea of an all-embracing restitution of mankind into a perfected state became possible. We find it first in Cowper, but somewhat limited by his theology. But when his poetic passion was upon him, he rose above his theology. He sees the time when love shall be master of all men, evil be annihilated, all climes have an eternal summer, and God be wholly at home with men. Coleridge and Wordsworth took up the same thought and sang of it in connexion with the outbreak of the Revolution. They ceased to sing of it when France smote freedom down by the hand of Napoleon. And then there was silence with regard to it for a time. But the silence did not last long. This universal thought took its highest form in the *Prometheus Unbound* of Shelley, the fourth act of which is the choral song of the whole universe for the regeneration of all mankind in Love and Peace and Joy. Nor has that conception ever died. It has formed, since Shelley's time, with a few sorrowful exceptions, one of the noblest motives of the English poets. The hopes of man had always put it forth, but it never could take a universal form as long as, under despotic kings, or feudal systems of any kind, all men were not considered equally worthy of love and justice. Christianity had always put it forth, but it never could take a universal form as long as priests, for the sake of retaining power, made its happiness belong only to a few rescued with difficulty from the sinful world. These limits to it lasted even through Wordsworth and Coleridge, so long does the exclusive take to die. But Shelley, flinging boldly overboard, and with fiery wrath, all the limitations made by political and religious systems, leaped straight to the heart of this great thought, derived from the original idea of Christianity and of the Revolution, and proclaimed the right of all mankind to completion and perfection. The whole world shall be redeemed. All men shall yet be equal, free and brothers in a Golden Age. It is the habit nowadays to smile at this, but if you deprive the world of that faith and its hope, you leave it to degradation. Let the poets keep it up. They can do no better work.

Then, in conclusion, when men were thus being set free, even before 1789, by the influence of worldwide ideas concerning man, from the oppressive and limiting powers of caste; when, in the air of this freedom, literature and art ceased to be the business of a few and became the possibility of all, a great development of individuality took place—and that to such a degree that, in poetry at least, men of the lower classes, and men who lived apart from the cultured caste in cities, were the chief speakers. The ideas of the Revolution kindled intellect and passion wherever they fell. Wealth, culture, rank, these did not count. A man is a man for all that. It is his right, his duty, to say what is in him; and if what he has to say is good or beautiful, he is above kings who are dull and rich men who may not love their fellows. Of course, such a belief, and the sentiment of it, awoke in all classes every latent germ of intelligence, imagination and emotion, and the whole field of literary and artistic work was as much enlarged as the field of social, political and warlike work. Men pushed everywhere to the surface like corn in spring, and the greater number were outside of the conventional society. We may recall that the chief leaders of the Revolution in France and of the Napoleon wars sprang from the common people. And the chief poets who sent forth the ideas, with all their emancipating and impassionating emotions which have been discussed in this chapter, were Cowper, a retired lawyer's clerk who lived away from towns in a lazy land, by a slow-moving stream, and Burns, a veritable peasant of the Lowlands, who

> in his glory and his joy
> Followed the plough along the mountain side.

And when the Revolution did break forth, it was not the critics and the comfortable folk of social intelligence who then opened the new fountain of song, but Coleridge, who was always on the verge of bankruptcy, and Wordsworth, who, educated among peasants, lived their life and, scraping through Cambridge, settled down with his sister to live in a silent country, in a tiny cottage, on £80 a year; and William Blake, the most curious example of the unrelated individualities which emerged at this time to astonish, irritate and impel the world. Blake's first poems preceded the French Revolution. The *Songs of Innocence* appeared in 1789, the year of its outburst. The *Songs of Experience* were engraved in 1794, when the Terror was dying. His poetic work, such as it was, continued while Wordsworth and Coleridge were writing. He, Cowper, Crabbe and Burns lived through that great uprising, and into the reaction against it. But he remained, while the rest fell away, its faithful follower. None of them were as poor as he was, none of them so unknown, none of them, save Wordsworth, so original, so plain an example of the remarkable individuality which arose out of the people in this creative and stormy time. None of them, though he dwelt in London, lived more close to Nature, more according to Nature, even to the violation of the maxims of society. He represented, better than the others, in his life and work the revolt from all conventional opinions, whether in art, literature, religion or social matters, which characterised the Revolution. He claimed his right to live as he pleased for the sake of man. He represented, briefly, often obscurely, but most determinedly, all the ideas we have dwelt on in this chapter—and one more on which we have not dwelt, for it did not, except in his case, arise at this time in England—an attack on priests, and on all religious doctrines which enslaved the conscience, weakened the reason, violated the love or limited the imagination of mankind.

I have thus sketched the poetic state of England before 1789. It was a state in which vague, prophetic ideas were flying about from mind to mind, ideas half-conceived, ideas that waited some outward touch to leap into as clear life as Athena from the head of Zeus. They had grown clearer and clearer among the poets as the poems they wrote grew closer to 1789. But they waited the event which should strike them into a shape which all the world could understand.

That event came when the noise of the fall of the Bastille rang through Europe. It was the tocsin of a new poetry which began in Wordsworth's *Lyrical Ballads* of 1798. (pp. 69-91)

Stopford A. Brooke, "The French Revolution and the Poets Who Preceded It," in his Naturalism in English Poetry, *E. P. Dutton & Company, 1920, pp. 69-91.*

Robert M. Maniquis

[In the following essay, Maniquis traces reactions to the Terror in the works of English Romantic poets.]

> Where is the patriot, even the enlightened one, who has never made a mistake? Ah, if we admit that there are moderates and cowards of good faith, why wouldn't there be patriots of good faith carried too far by laudable sentiments? . . . Who after all will sort out all these nuances?
>
> —Robespierre, *On the Principles of Revolutionary Government*

In the midst of the terror, Robespierre here conjures up and then abandons those nuances that usually disappear in divine wrath. Something of that wrath was appropriated in June of 1794 when the Convention officially recognized the existence of the Supreme Being, a typical republican sacralization. Political catechisms and hagiographies, Pantheonized glory, celebratory masses for Reason, patriotic fesivals—all infused the revolution with religious emotion for citizens who had known no other than Catholic sacraments. The Terror, however, was a strange, symbolic regression. Other forms of religion could be mocked or republicanized. But the Terror, invoked to protect the Revolution, seemed to turn society backward, conjuring up an ancient instrumental fear that had been, during the previous century, attributed only to savage gods. (p. 365)

After the Lisbon earthquake of 1755, philosophical polemics, of which *Candide* (1759) was only one brilliant example, disarmed the optimistic idea that natural catastrophes were all for the best. Philosophy was soon called upon again to confront the Terror, which seemed to be a moral catastrophe as incongruous with human reason as destroying cities was with divine mercy. Divine wrath, by rationalist principles, had always been only the sacralized projection of human violence. But until the French Revolution it was not for humanity to declare *itself* the source of its own terror.

Some writers, of course, were content with an ancient wild justice, invoked by satanic Jacobins who were finally crushed by truly divine wrath—as in Gillray's French giant, exploded by the heavenly lightning of God and British naval power. Popular in caricature and the newspapers, this providential theme was elaborately developed in anti-revolutionary French Catholicism. There were also, to be sure, republican Christians, like Louis-Claude de Saint-Martin, an *illuminé* who celebrated the Revolution as the incarnated word, with that chiliastic thrill common between 1789 and 1815. Out of Joanna Southcott's English womb Shiloh, the Second Messiah, was to have emerged in 1814, only a decade or so after the French had worshipped the Virgin Mary as a patron saint of Liberty and Jesus as the first sans-culotte. Between these extremes of revolutionary and anti-revolutionary Christians, others saw in the Revolution both Sin and Grace, a fortunate fall necessary to those desperate spiritual revivals of the kind theorized by Bonald and de Maistre in France and later trumpeted in England loud and long by Carlyle.

Rational optimists had even more thorny problems than revolutionary or reactionary Christians, for they had to answer Robespierre's rhetorical question about moral nuances with ideas the Terror had compromised. Like religious optimists before them, however, they usually found light amidst the darkness. Condorcet wrote his *Esquisse d'un tableau historique des progrès de l'esprit humain* (1793) in hiding, where he would die (perhaps by suicide), pursued to the end by the Jacobins. Neither the September massacres of 1792, nor the High Terror of 1793, nor his own persecution shook his faith in progress toward the virtuous human community. William Godwin in 1789, several years before his *Enquiry Concerning Political Justice* (1793), in which he warned against all violent revolution, immediately distinguished the passions of the "multitudes" from that which he desired: " . . . such political changes only as should flow purely from the clear light of the understanding, and the erect and generous feelings of the heart."

Whether Christian or rationalist, explanations of the Terror abounded, and even a brief account of their variety—from Catholic maledictions to philosophic meditations—would overflow these pages. Some explanations of violence had already emerged in the eighteenth-century shift from theodicy to psychology and anthropology. The attack on Leibnizian optimism, from the late 1750s on, centered attention on psychological projections in universal terror, while terror had been historically traced, since the seventeenth century, in well-known accounts of the Spanish conquistadors by Las Casas, Garcilaso de la Vega, and later by Marmontel. These factual and legendary reports often described human sacrifice in native American rituals, examples that, along with religious horrors of the Egyptians and Assyrians, would find their way into philosophical attacks on the vestigial cannibalism of Hebrews and Christians. But these accounts also described a constancy of racial extermination, war, and atrocities, confirmed as well throughout Gibbon's *The History of the Decline and Fall of the Roman Empire* (1776-88). European history often seemed a mnemonic grid of great exterminations from the massacre of the Albigensians to the ever-repeated horrors of St. Bartholomew's Night—memories commonly invoked in liberal reaction to the Terror. If St. Bartholomew of 1572 could be read in the guillotining and massacres of 1793, then the Terror became only regression and less a fatal interruption of enlightened progress.

And yet we know that the Terror produced a sense not of something old, but of something new. Carlyle would insist, in 1837, that the Terror was something for which history had no name: " . . . what if History were to admit, for once, that all the Names and Theorems yet known to her fall short? That this grand Product of Nature was even grand, and new, in that it came not to range itself under old recorded Laws of Nature at all, but to disclose new ones?" Forty years after the Terror, Carlyle fit this new historical thing to his ontological Yeas and Nays, christening Terror as "transcendental despair" to be answered in the spiritual progress of hope. But the long romantic reaction to the Terror, which ended in Carlyle and Dickens and began with the writers I shall emphasize here—Blake, Wordsworth, and Coleridge—had little effect in submerging the Terror in dystoles and systoles of organic rhythm or in progressive oppositions and antagonisms. On the contrary, in the last two hundred years, the Terror has been ideologically simplified into an *Ur*-form of modern political violence.

The reactions of Blake, Wordsworth, and Coleridge began in the political fray. But effects of the Terror upon them appear most dramatically in their poetry, which often speaks of violence untranscended, in images of the poet himself falling sadly silent. In poetry, sacramental exchanges of death for life, which replaced terror with hope, were threatened from all sides, dislocated by violent revolution and a European war waged almost continuously from 1792 to 1815. There was also a growing darkness in social thought that joined the Terror in its cultural effect. The publication, for instance, of Thomas Malthus' *An Essay on the Principle of Population* (1798) caused nearly as much intellectual shock as the Terror, and all romantic writers reacted vehemently to it. Malthus specifically brings the Terror into his demographic theories, while criticizing the optimism of Condorcet and Godwin, whose ideas, so he argued, were not so much false as irrelevant. Far from anthropomorphizing the Terror with either divine or evil human will, Malthus de-psychologizes and dehumanizes violence in an internecine social mass mechanically ruled by sex and hunger. As Marilyn Butler suggests, catastrophic changes in scientific narratives provided patterns of deep time against which perhaps even the Terror could fade into evolutionary processes. Transforming political violence, along with plagues and famines, into natural shifts certainly provided a congenial scientific parallel to social meliorism. English romantic forms of the idea, however, lie somewhere between eighteenth-century rational and nineteenth-century scientific optimism, as we see in Coleridge's version of violence leading to good: "Without advocating the exploded doctrine of *perfectibility,* we cannot but regard all that is Human in Human Nature, and all that in Nature is above herself, as together working forward that far deeper and more permanent revolution in the Moral World of which the recent changes in the Political World may be regarded as the pioneering whirlwind and storm." But the Malthusian appearance of such processes (as far as the romantics could see in the 1790s) brutally transformed history into only *material* history.

The Malthusian shock, in the oddest way, suggested a return to the subjection traditional Christians saw in divine extermination, except that the extermination had become mere periodic self-adjustments of the social mass. The dark implications of these ideas romantic poets always repelled. From *The Prelude* (1795-1850) to *Prometheus Unbound* (1820), wherever there are revolutionary floods, earthquakes, and volcanoes, there is also insistent human will. Sometimes adjusting human will to historical progress was awkward. Coleridge, writing in the margins of the *Essay on Population,* accused Malthus of confused moral views in thinking that European expansion could not proceed by exterminating other peoples: "If it be immoral to kill a few Savages in order to get possession of a country capable of sustaining a 1000 times as many enlightened and happy men, is it not immoral to kill millions of Infants and Men by crowded Cities, by Hunger, and by the Pox?" It would be silly to conclude much from a remark designed only to make a telling point against Malthus. Still, it is always morally awkward to suggest that one kind of collective murder is better than another. Malthus forced his readers into such moral awkwardness, one reason why readers like Coleridge abhorred his book. Poetry, of course, needs more moral nuance than is to be found in marginal scribblings. The presence of universal human good would have to be traced in that which Wordsworth constantly refers to—undercurrents of beneficent tendency, "something" running below, something "more deeply intertwined" in history. But tracing those lines also went on as the rationalist dismantling of anthropomorphic terror grew into its logical extension, the anthropological dismantling of humanism. Wordsworth's intertwinings of the human and the natural were already becoming, in the larger culture, dark entanglements.

Cultural and moral contradictions, of course, did not bring romantic writing to a halt. Sometimes the contradictions simply disappeared into journalistic tub-thumping for the British Empire. Southey, De Quincey, and Carlyle, for instance, had little trouble turning their attention from revolutionary violence in Europe to the productive use of violence elsewhere. But romantic writing during and just after the Revolution is painfully self-conscious of its moral dilemmas. Caught between humanist and materialist ideas, the romantic poet, after the Terror, attempts sacramental gestures in a new order of aesthetic imagination—unfortunately, just when the imagination was about to be decentered and the moral voice of poetry drowned out in vast, imperial noise.

• • • • •

> I would not willingly kill even a flower, but were I at the head of any army, or a revolutionary Kingdom, I would do *my Duty.*
>
> —Coleridge

The general reaction to the French Revolution in Great Britain is often reduced to one scenario. Sympathetic British witnesses hailed it in 1789, condemned it after the September Massacres in 1792, and abandoned it with the so-called Great Terror of 1793 to 1794, when disillusionment turned sunshine revolutionaries into gloomy reactionaries. All this is not so much false as too simple. Without a doubt, progressive reformers like Samuel Romilly were joyous in 1789 and shocked in 1793: "The French are plunging into a degree of barbarism which, for such a nation, and in so short a period, surpasses all imagination. All religion is already abolished; and the next proceeding will undoubtedly be a persecution as severe and as unremitting as any that has taken place in the darkest ages." And young radical poets like Wordsworth, Coleridge, and Southey did become middle-aged reactionaries. But what many wrote, at least as political explanation of the Terror, is neither shrill nor panicky. From 1792 to the 1840s sympathy for the plight of the French as a people forced into horrors was commonly expressed. Coleridge, Southey, Wordsworth, Blake, and later Shelley and Hazlitt were relatively restrained in their reactions after 1793. Robespierre, though often compared to Cromwell, had of course not yet acquired the satanic features assigned to him later as the supposed ancestor of Stalin and Hitler. Robespierre and the Terror were, for many English writers in the 1790s, repulsive but explainable, and explanation had a way of cushioning shock.

The common portrayal of the Terror as an explosive result of oppression is one Wordsworth repeats in *The Prelude* when he insists on understanding "the reservoir of guilt / And ignorance, filled up from age to age, / That could no longer hold its loathsome charge . . . ," when he suggests that the French, mired in "ignorance and immaturity," needed only the light of "one paramount mind" to put a stop to their barbarism (x.176-88). Their revenge he does not simply condemn. Saddened and depressed by this stain upon revolutionary ideals, he returns to England, where he undergoes his greatest depression. Like Coleridge, Thelwall, Godwin, Paine, Kant and others, Wordsworth suggests that the Terror was not really the fault of the French but of the British. As England set itself against France, he was himself filled with anger against the reactionary spirit that intensified the Terror:

> In France, the men who for their desperate ends
> Had plucked up mercy by the roots were glad
> Of this new enemy. Tyrants, strong before
> In devilish pleas, were ten times stronger now,
> And thus beset with foes on every side,
> The goaded land waxed mad; the crimes of few
> Spread into madness of the many; blasts

Cartoon depicting the English view of the sans-culottes *during the Reign of Terror.*

> From hell came sanctified like airs from heaven.
> (x.306-14)

Far from mysterious, at least in these lines, the Terror for Wordsworth had clear historical causes that go far towards, if not a defense, at least a distanced account of why the French became madly violent.

Nevertheless, these lines from *The Prelude* are tame compared to Coleridge's *Conciones ad Populum,* in which the common English radical theme is also taken up: it was the antipathy of England and Prussia towards France that caused the worst horrors:

> . . . in this inventory of guilt as the immediate and peculiar effect of the present War, and justly attributable to our Ministry, we must place the EXCESSES OF THE FRENCH, their massacres and blasphemies, all their crimes and all their distresses. This effect the War produced by a twofold operation of terror:—First, on the people of France, secondly, on their Rulers.
>
> First, on the people of France. Instant death was threatened to all taken in arms;—beheading and confiscation to the members of the departments, districts, and municipalities; military execution to the members of the national assembly, magistrates, and all the inhabitants of Paris; and total destruction to that City. All palaces and towns shall incur the same punishments as those inflicted on the inhabitants of Paris.—Such as Brunswick's manifesto. "The mode of civilized War will not be practised," says Burke. Our Government were projecting to *starve* the whole nation, and many of our senators did not scruple to proclaim the war a war of *extermination.*

Some historians find in the French Revolution the first modern appearance of a collective will to political and even racial extermination. They forget that this fear of extermination was exactly what French revolutionaries and sympathizers feared in reactionaries. The young radical Coleridge fervently believes this as he points in France to the "bloody fanatics," created by the policy of the initiating English Terror. It was common in the 1790s to turn the word *terror* around upon Britain; Godwin does as much in a preface to *Caleb Williams,* where he uses the word as if it could only refer to British repression. In countering this British terror, Coleridge the preacher sermonizes in the typical biblical language of dissenting radicals:

> . . . Hunted on all sides, insulted by unceasing

> and brutal menaces, they felt the blended influence of terror and indignation—by the first they were impelled to become voluntary slaves to the bloody fanatics, whose wild energies seemed alone proportionate to the danger; by the latter their gentler feelings were suspended, and the military spirit with all its virtues and all its vices seized at once a whole nation. In the truly prophetic words of Isaiah—"They have trod the wine-press alone, and of the nations there was none with them. They looked and there was none to help; they WONDERED that there was none to uphold. Therefore their own arm brought salvation unto them, and their FURY, *it* upheld them."

Biblical authority and political necessity converge in the French Terror, and indeed all revolutions, Coleridge asserts, may need to "dissolve the ordinary ties of morality." His moral condemnation is filled with sympathetic understanding: "I mean not to imply approbation of such systems of morals: but doubtless the Terrorists . . . knew that the general consequences of their actions would be evil, but they thought the occasion so vast and pressing, as to make the particular good consequences overbalance the general evil ones—especially as those actions could never be imitated in after times with any shew of reason, unless in the rage and tempest of some future Revolution." In support of this argument he quotes from his and Southey's play *The Fall of Robespierre* (1794). What he quotes suggests, in its dramatic context, revolutionary fanaticism, but in the foil of Coleridge's radical attack, the same words become a reasonable argument for justifiable violence:

> Are not the congregated clouds of War
> Black all around us? In our very vitals
> Works not the king-bred position of rebellion?
> Say, what shall counteract the selfish plottings
> Of wretches, cold of heart, nor aw'd by fears
> Of Him, whose power directs th'eternal justice?
> Terror? or secret-sapping gold? The first
> Heavy, but transient as the ills that cause it,
> And to the virtuous Patriot rendered light
> By the necessities that gave it birth:
> The other fouls the fount of the Republic
> Making it flow polluted thro' all ages;
> Inoculates the state with a slow venom,
> That once imbib'd must be continued ever!
> (i. 147-60)

The continuous political Terror that horrifies Coleridge less in France than in its source comes from the deep hostility to all that was progressive. As he builds to his sermonic climax, Coleridge exploits images of French violence in England of the 1790s, popular in caricatures of French sans-culottes drinking blood and chewing on human flesh—all this is turned back upon the British and on that satanic figure, Pitt:

> TERROR intoxicates more than strong wine; with the which, who forcibly drenches another man, is the real cause and sole responsible agent of all the excesses, which in the hour of drunkenness he shall have committed. . . . Alas! Freedom weeps! The Guillotine became the Financier-General.—That dreadful pilot, Robespierre, perceived that it would at once furnish wind to the sails and free the vessel from those who were inclined to mutiny.—Who, my Brethren! was the cause of this guilt, if not HE, who supplied the occasion and the motive?—Heaven hath bestowed on that man a portion of its ubiquity, and given him an actual presence in the Sacraments of Hell, wherever administered, in all the bread of bitterness, in all the cups of blood.

Coleridge's Unitarian distaste for the Eucharist made it easy for him to associate British savagery with sacraments sliding back into savage origins. Recalling eighteenth-century rehearsals of horror, he reaches back to the behavior of the British in America, where, he says, they hired Indians and tended to turn into savages and cannibals themselves. The language is familiar from *Reflections on the Revolution in France,* in which Burke describes black masses of revolutionary cannibals. Both Coleridge and Burke, like most radical and conservative, revolutionary and anti-revolutionary writers, participate together in the same cultural dissolution of sacramental order, portraying in each other a new yet ancient violence beyond any order of meaning. The world, in this revolutionary moment had left the domain of moral nuances—all writers seem to agree. And one of the common ways they mark it is to play upon one of the grand tropes of the day—humanity cannibalizing itself.

Years later in his *The Life of Napoleon* (1828-30) Hazlitt would rehearse the same and many more explanations of the Terror; though disdainful of the "effeminate" French, he refuses to grant the Terror any special historical status. His analyses of French revolutionary violence are, like the young Coleridge's, exercises in accepting political aggression and defense. Hazlitt continued to invoke a rough *Realpolitik* in defending the French long after Wordsworth, Coleridge, and Southey had fallen away into Toryism. Hazlitt also underlines the belief that the Revolution was particularly violent and savage because the French were Catholic:

> Perhaps a reformation in religion ought always to precede a revolution in the government. Catholics may make good subjects, but bad rebels. They are so used to the trammels of authority, that they do not immediately know how to do without them; or, like manumitted slaves, only feel assured of their liberty in committing some Saturnalian license. A revolution, to give it stability and soundness, should first be conducted down to a Protestant ground.

Nothing like the young Coleridge's radical invective erupts here, but Hazlitt makes a similar point about contagious blood-thirst, translated from English radical dissent into more restrained liberal disdain. He is emphasizing national traditions of authority, but his comparison also depends on Protestant psychological clichés about the Catholic sacrament. Eucharistic consumption, along with a "slave" mentality are closely allied with Saturnalian license and blood-letting; French Catholics run amok in revolution because something primitive has for centuries run amok in their superstitious minds. By the time of Hazlitt's *The Life of Napoleon,* however, in the late 1820s, the linguistic explosion of revolutionary and anti-revolutionary pamphleteering had ended. Understatement and irony were sufficient. Byron was never short of anticlerical vitriol, but in describing the shipwreck scene of *Don Juan* and Pedrillo about to be cannibalized, all he needs is a brief, ironic touch to suggest the savage core of sacrificial death:

> He died as born, a Catholic in faith,
> Like most in the belief in which they're bred,
> And first a little crucifix he kiss'd,
> And then held out his jugular and wrist.

The ironic reference recalls the Enlightenment theme of vestigial violence, themes that Byron can brilliantly play with just as he plays, again in *Don Juan,* with providential terror humanized: " 'Let there be light!' said God, 'and there was light!' / 'Let there be blood!' says man, and there's a sea" (VII.41). For poets like Blake, Wordsworth, and Coleridge, however, in the political heat and linguistic explosion of the Revolutionary decade, irony was no consolation in their earnest search for symbolic transformations of blood into a vision of purposive Nature.

Those transformations only became harder to make as writing in the 1780s and the 1790s continued the Enlightenment dismantling of the old sacrificial order. Goethe aligns sacrificial imagination under a holy savagery in *Iphigenia* (1787); Blake, in *The Mental Traveller* (1800-1804), demonstrates the dull mental round of sacrificial violence; in his political lectures Coleridge locates a social savagery of revenge in, what he calls, using Bacon's phrase, mere "wild justice" and a sacrificial instinct gone wild. Again and again, writers identify exhaustions of the symbolic exchange of death for life. After a century of both rationalist attack and the gentle spirituality of deism, some dismantling of mystery and terror was easy. Blake confidently turns an angry patriarchal God into his toothless Nobodaddy. Thomas Jefferson simply took his scissors to the New Testament, cut out all its offensive primitivism, and glued together what was left into a personal moral guide. But the writing *of The Prelude* or *The Four Zoas* or *Le Génie du Christianisme* or *Prometheus Unbound* could not be cut and pasted if art was to transform old into new sacramental forms. The aesthetic ambition stubbornly survived, though the poets themselves sometimes thought it was an ambition humiliated by history.

. . . . .

> . . . a humble, holy, sacred 'violence' must be used in prayer . . .
>
> —John Fletcher, *Meditations*

Explaining how the Terror came about politically, then, was obviously not the same thing as poetically explaining the Terror. Together with historical and psychological explanations of the Terror in *The Prelude,* there are also haunting lines on the September massacres unmediated by an explanation or by any symbol:

> Through months, through years, long after the last beat
> Of those atrocities, the hour of sleep
> To me came rarely charged with natural gifts,
> Such ghastly visions had I of despair
> And tyranny, and implements of death;
> And innocent victims sinking under fear,
> And momentary hope, and worn-out prayer,
> Each in his separate cell, or penned in crowds
> For sacrifice. . . . Then suddenly the scene
> Changed, and the unbroken dream entangled me
> In long orations, which I strove to plead
> Before unjust tribunals,—with a voice
> Labouring, a brain confounded, and a sense,
> Death-like, of treacherous desertion, felt
> In the last place of refuge—my own soul.
>
> (x.399-415)

This world of violence is neither juridical, nor sacrificial, nor apocalyptic. The tribunals are unjust, those to be sacrificed, which is to say *murdered,* are gathered like animals in pens, and there is nothing lying before the poet; he can only draw back in a naked confrontation with himself. Such moments are common enough in romantic dream accounts, where the self gazes upon the self, when as in Coleridge's dreams or De Quincey's nightmares the man-God of Christological imagination is split in two and becomes both the "idol" and the "priest," the sacrificer and the sacrificed. Such moments cannot be endlessly repeated; they are too psychologically radical. Wordsworth expanded the 1850 version of this passage, in order to deepen the sense of empty despair; this is the mind collapsed to a symbolic zero point. Justice has become a savage revenge grown ghastly. The sacrificial hope of finding in a symbolic exchange some sense of life in death is dissolved by indiscriminate massacre. From that point on, all that can be done is to imitate the sacramental process by which violence is transformed into something else.

These dark dreams are framed before and after by Wordsworth's descriptions of terror that he tries to locate metaphorically with allusions to *Hamlet, Paradise Lost,* or the Hercules myth. This is violence we remember from *Macbeth,* a spreading of evil and blood. It is also like the mere animal intensity of a child:

> . . . They found their joy,
> They made it, ever thirsty, as a child—
> If light desires of innocent little ones
> May with such heinous appetites be matched—
> Having a toy, a windmill, though the air
> Do of itself blow fresh and makes the vane
> Spin in his eyesight, he is not content,
> But with the plaything at arm's length he sets
> His front against the blast, and runs amain
> To make it whirl the faster.
>
> (x.336-45)

The poet remarks an inadequacy in his similes and while setting them forth, he also retreats from them. Can indeed the "light desires of innocent little ones" be compared to what he also describes as "heinous appetites?" Yet there is method in this poetic coyness, for having remembered the violence of the Terror in one frightening moment of self-confrontation, Wordsworth, as we shall see, turns that history back into imagined innocent moments of youth, when all such transformation of violence seems unnecessary.

When he describes "eternal revenge" in hearing of the death of Robespierre, it is not surprising to see Wordsworth typically enveloping the violent reaction, even his sense of vengeance, in descriptions of Nature seeming to absorb all calmly into itself. But it is important to see that in remembering how he heard of Robespierre's fall, Wordsworth describes nature enveloping *two* stages of the past. The first comes in the established eighteenth-century trope of the ruin. Wordsworth's evocation of the mass celebrated in a "ruined chapel" has nothing harsh in it. As with all his ruins of churches and abbeys, there is even something of nostalgia here for the kind of sacramental, and hence communal, order it represents. Yet it is, after all, a ruin, an empty space where once that communal symbolization, however primitive, worked its power "in ancient times." These two historical disappearing forms—a superseded sacramental order and a barbarous figure of violence—are presented already embedded in time as memory and even the chapel "like a sea rock" is run into continuous lines with Nature:

> Without me and within as I advanced
> All that I saw, or felt, or communed with
> Was gentleness and peace. Upon a small
> And rocky island near, a fragment stood—
> Itself like a sea rock—of what had been
> A Romish chapel, where in ancient times
> Masses were said at the hour which suited those
> Who crossed the sands with ebb of morning tide.
> Not far from this still ruin all the plain
> Was spotted with a variegated crowd
> Of coaches, wains, and travellers, horse and foot,
> Wading, beneath the conduct of their guide,
> In loose procession through the shallow stream
> Of inland water; the great sea meanwhile
> Was at safe distance, far retired.
>
> (x.515-29)

The religious vocabulary of his social memory is insistent. He "communed with" all that he sees and feels around him. The "variegated crowd" is caught in motion and only just linked, in their time, with the memory of those in the past who came for sacramental communion in their time. When he hears of Robespierre's death, it is as if the news will be received and dissolved into this communal and communing world:

> . . . I paused,
> Unwilling to proceed, the scene appeared
> So gay and cheerful—when a traveller
> Chancing to pass, I carelessly inquired
> If any news were stirring, he replied
> In the familiar language of the day
> That, *Robespierre was dead.* Nor was a doubt,
> On further question, left within my mind
> But that the tidings were substantial truth—
> That he and his supporters all were fallen.
>
> Great was my glee of spirit, great my joy
> In vengeance, and eternal justice, thus
> Made manifest. 'Come now, ye golden times',
> Said I, forth-breathing on those open sands
> A hymn of triumph. . . .
>
> (x.529-43)

This brilliant setting of the scene allows him to speak revenge and to call down "eternal justice" with, of course, little chance of confusing this mild invocation of divine terror with the kind he remembers in the Terror, when "blasts of hell" came "sanctified like airs from heaven." Wordsworth sometimes revised his poetry into tortuous nuance in order to make this kind of distinction.

In the 1805 version, for instance, where he speaks of spiritually surviving the "evil times" of those "enormities," he remembers the "wrath of Heaven," which gave him "Something to glory in, as just and fit, / And in the order of sublimest laws." These feelings "amid the awe / Of unintelligible chastisement" gave him "a kind of sympathy with power" (X.401-16). The 1850 revision of these lines, however, reveals how such feelings have also made him uncomfortable. This sense of the "sublimest laws" leads him to hope arising from "affliction." But it also suggests to him an awkward complicity from which, in the 1850 version, he disentangles himself. In 1805, the prophets are "enflamed" with vaguely defined "consolations" and "majesty of mind." In 1850, the prophets are "borne aloft / In vision, yet constrained by natural laws / With them to take a troubled heart." They are no longer "enflamed" in 1850, but moved by a "creed / of reconcilement." The most interesting revision of all qualifies the expression "sympathy with power." This becomes "sympathies with power," the plural form weakening the identification with sublime vengeance, diffused even more by defining this "power" as "motions not treacherous or profane, else why / Within the folds of no ungentle breast / Their dread vibration to this hour prolonged?" He distinguishes his feelings, these "motions" and their enduring "dread vibration" from both the "treacherous and the profane." He participates in the moral opposition to the Terror, while also carefully distancing himself from violence projected into God and history, the kind he sees in "glimpses of retribution, terrible" (X.437-60 [1850]). These are intricate lines, in which Wordsworth twists and turns to escape treacherous and simplifying violent oppositions.

His hearing of Robespierre's death in a landscape, where there is a happy crowd and a ruined chapel, is typical not only of Wordsworth's attempt to negate both historical violence and vast, opposing "terrible" retributions. That religious-social-natural—and personal—memorial scene both absorbs and distances the religious sacraments of the past. Only in such a prepared scene can he pronounce without any troubling complicity what is only a form of that which, in another circumstance, became madness in the Terror—the wild justice of revenge. This scenic circumstance, however, dissipates any sense of violence even in personal thoughts of vengeance; he is poetically exculpated from historical violence just as the textual revisions we have seen put a distance between him and any complete poetic identification with the "retribution, terrible."

He goes on talking about how the Revolution will actually proceed, how great hopes are still to be realized, but he brings all of history back to the memory of boyish joy, running swiftly past two historical moments of the past, one symbolized by the Romish chapel (associated with still another "mouldering fane"), and the other, by Robespierre:

> Thus, uninterrupted by uneasy bursts
> Of exultation, I pursued my way
> Along that very shore which I had skimmed
> In former times, when, spurring from the Vale

Of Nightshade, and St. Mary's mouldering fane,
And the stone abbot, after circuit made
In wantonness of heart, a joyous crew
Of schoolboys, hastening to their distant home,
Along the margin of the moonlight sea,
We beat with thundering hoofs the level sand.
(x.557-66)

As Time and Nature move forward, the recent, revolutionary violence and the previous monuments of sacrificial ceremony are absorbed into nature as they are absorbed into the poet's own memory, interrupting (but only just interrupting) the joy of the moment and the expectation of the future. Historical transformation is finally enveloped here in the personal remembrance of a time before violence, an innocence when all energy was only "wantonness of heart." It is tempting to describe this as sublimation, which suggests a completed psychological process and a poetic closure, and such passages do imitate poetic memory completely embracing pleasures, violence, and even past sacramental form. But Wordsworth also keeps a radical memory of unmediated violence constantly open in his poetry, imitating sacramentalism but never disguising those moments when symbolic exchanges of death for life are unperformed and closure impossible. We mystify organic form and narrative catharsis if we think that a carefully designed historical forgetting erases what the poet insists are often remembered fractures. It is hard to forget that moment when Wordsworth puts us close to the desolation of massacre.

. . . Then suddenly the scene
Changed, and the unbroken dream entangled me
In long orations, which I strove to plead
Before unjust tribunals,—with a voice
Labouring, a brain confounded, and a sense,
Death-like, of treacherous desertion, felt
In the last place of refuge—my own soul.
(x.409-15)

The poet confronts a kind of radical violence as if for the first time, as if the violence has no mediation. This is rather different from those "spots of time" in Book XII and others, when death, the signs of murder or brutality, or a brutalized soldier are suddenly come upon and then, as if inevitably, linked by memory to other restorative images. Memories of the Terror are spots of time never quite absorbed. They begin as symbolically empty places in time that then abound in conflicting images and colliding senses of evil and providential violence. The dreadful memories of isolation in the midst of the historical moment of the Terror need not be collapsed into one Freudian primal scene, nor need we imagine primordial violence transformed by the poet into some other, hidden story. Recurring memories and dreams of the Terror are of violence untransformed; part of their powerful effect is in their transparency leading to nothing beyond itself. In such moments an imaginative impasse is emblematized in the self set immediately before what is finally a desymbolized violence. Something of that feeling of coming upon violence, as if for the first time, apprehended without any symbolic mediation, is there in the description of the September massacres of 1792:

I thought of those September massacres,
Divided from me by a little month,
And felt and touched them . . .
(x.64-66)

Feeling and touching massacres, Wordsworth goes on to say, is mixed with "tragic fictions," "remembrances," "dim admonishments," but it is the feel and touch of unmediated violence that throws him into an eery state of perdition where symbolical transformation has disappeared. Obviously none of this produces permanent despair. As we have seen in the passages on Robespierre, Wordsworth finds ways both to engage and to extricate himself from a dialectics of violence, and to see hope always arising out of its opposite. But these moments are, even in their isolation, frightening in the halt they bring to *all* connection.

Even Blake, a poet of enthusiastic prophetic violence, records a moment of such fracture in *America: A Prophecy* when he hesitates before the terror in his own mythopoeic world—an unusual but a revealing moment for Blake—when the poet grows silent. *America* we can take certainly to be as much about the French Revolution and the Terror as it is about the American War of Independence; Blake treats the American uprising as if it produced apocalyptic violence, all couched in the language of religious prophecy—fire, blood, plagues, and pestilence. He thus radicalizes the American Revolution, displacing political violence of the years 1793 to 1795 into metaphorical violence, what Erdman calls "prophetic terror." Blake speaks in 1793 of terror that could have no other historical referent than the actual terrors of revolutionary France. Orc is, of course, biblically terrible. In his original awakening in the sexual embrace with Urthona, he is born in a wrenching of the world. And as a political force he is:

. . . a Human fire, fierce glowing, as the wedge
Of iron heated in the furnace; his terrible limbs
were fire
With myriads of cloudy terrors, banners dark &
towers
Surrounded: heat but not light when thro' the
murky atmosphere.
The King of England looking westward trembles
at the vision.

At the beginning of Plate 8, Orc is a terror that can simply declare itself: "The terror answered: I am Orc." All these references are common stuff in the rhetorical tradition of Hebrew and Protestant prophecy. Its language antedates all contemporary revolutionary violence and is derived not only from the Bible but from a long line of prophetic histories.

And yet it is impossible to ignore the fact that *America* was several times printed during the worst of French revolutionary violence and the worst of English reactionary oppression. It is a poem of those years when real violence directly mirrored prophetic violence, when history challenged the poet to absorb its violent moment in his mythopoeic system. We also cannot ignore those lines, in the Preludium, when the Bard momentarily stops his poem even before it begins. Just after Urthona completes her song in recognition of Orc: "This is eternal death: and this the torment long foretold," we read:

> The stern Bard ceas'd, asham'd of his own song; enrag'd he swung
> His harp aloft sounding, then dash'd its shining frame against
> A ruin'd pillar in glittring fragments; silent he turn'd away,
> And wander'd down the vales of Kent in sick & drear lamentings.

Why does the Bard dash his harp against a ruin'd pillar? Despite his transformative imaginative system of contraries of existence, is there a violence untransformable by the poet's song? "Silent he turn'd away," we are told, turning his back upon his song only to lament. The lines are not easy to interpret, especially since they are almost always masked and only twice printed by Blake himself, though it is not at all clear what determined Blake to print or not to print them. As G. E. Bentley, Jr. puts it [in *Studies in Romanticism* (Autumn 1966)], "Were these pessimistic lines part of Blake's first complete version of the poem, confidently omitted in most printings of the poem, or were they a gloomy addition, made after the hopes inspired by the French Revolution had been destroyed by Napoleon and by the English government?" And if the lines were present very early but masked between roughly 1793 and 1799 (as Bentley shows), why were they etched at all? Critics have a wealth of suggestions: Blake was pessimistic in the mid-1790s at the turn of violence in the French Revolution; or he was disappointed that the American Revolution, not radical enough, left British and continental tyranny in place; or he was pessimistic, like other radicals, at the growing weakness of their movement and the power of the English "terror." Interpretations like these, and their variations, suggest that the specific reasons for Blake's pessimistic lines will probably never be determined. But their fundamental significance lies in the plainest evidence. That he is "ashamed" of his own song, we may attribute to poetic hyperbole. That the song is at least sometimes imaginatively halted by Blake's own text suggests a scar usually removed, but always there to be hidden on the etched plate. In this confrontation with his own poem, the poet does not simply speak of a poetic difficulty; he walks out of its frame, "down the vales of Kent" as if away from the poetic moment into real historical time. After marking that break, he must then of course proceed, suppressing that early etched-in doubt through most of the mid-1790s. Later he again unmasks that doubt and twice prints the lines even before plunging forward once more with prophetic terror. *America* leads finally to a vision of peace and love, of sensuous and communal unity, arrived at through the prophetic but now also dangerous tropes of terror painfully reified by the very actors upon the historical scene in which the poet finds himself. Danton, Robespierre, and Marat also used a prophetic vocabulary of blood, pestilence, plague, and terrors, similar to Blake's, for this was, indeed, common language. They would have used that language even if there had never been an officially established Terror. But there was such a Terror and such traditional biblical phrases cannot help but be painful in a new sense when spoken in the echo of violence in the new State, almost immediately expanded by Napoleon into an even more massively violent empire.

How could Blake, to use a phrase of David Erdman, combine "prophetic terror with pursuit of the main chance?" One answer to this question is that he could not. Though some critics read this as an optimistic, others as a pessimistic poem, it only makes sense *poetically* as ambivalent prophecy, a poem partially self-fragmented. We underestimate Blake's humanity and his intelligence when we assume that he reacted little to Robespierre, to the Terror, or the general violence of the long European war, because he simply drew them into his system of contraries and played cruel violence out between Energy and Reason. Blake was nothing if not poetically self-confident, but he was never blithe or bumptious. As Erdman points out, Blake would never again "write such precisely dated prophecies as *America* and *Europe.* When Blake had 'called all his sons to the strife of blood' he had simply no idea how that strife would sear the inlets of the soul both in France and in England." There is at times an agony in Blake as there is in Wordsworth, glimpsed rarely, as in *America,* but which is nevertheless part of a contradiction between poetry and history that has nothing to do with contraries. Indeed, it was because of that real contradiction that an imaginative system of contraries was necessary.

And yet Blake's prophetic terror, the most powerful in all English romantic writing, elaborates itself into a linguistic implosion. The difficulty of the later books has many causes, but one of them is their multiple transformations of violence into imaginative process of which the natural world is always only a trope. The later books are not unlike the circling inward of mythical redemption in *Faust II*—the more historically and psychologically inclusive these poems become, the more difficult they are to read. Blake's shaping of terror and death with fragile displacement of religious and ordinary language is, at the same time, part of its brilliance, evident even in his simplest lines. If the "cut worm forgives the plow" (*The Marriage of Heaven and Hell*), we sacramentalize and psychologize the natural process; we agree to speak as poetry always has—with pathetic fallacies. We can also *think* the lines literally, rather than speak their imitation of sacrament, and insist on natural process in which the worm's forgiveness of the plow obviously makes no difference at all. Such a vulgar, Malthusian interruption of poetic prescription emphasizes the fragility in romantic sacramentalizing of natural—and historical—process. Like Wordsworth's use of the term *communing with,* designed both to invoke and dismiss old sacraments, the word *forgives* lies between the romantic imagination and the world as a memory of past sacrificial violence. If we drive the word *forgives* too far into natural process, it loses even this particular connotation, like the word *sacrifice,* in the midst of indiscriminate, terrorist violence turned into only another word for death or destruction or the anonymous enveloping of matter within matter. Romantic poetry commonly gestures with such sacramental words by which an imaginative order graces a natural or historical order of violence. But in this poetic gesture, the imaginative word is also constantly challenged not to dissolve into that which it tries to endow with significance.

In 1798, nearly four years after his spirited analysis of the

Terror, Coleridge published "France: An Ode," a poem about revolutionary France now drifting into its historical role as imperial aggressor. Like Blake, Coleridge could still summon prophetic biblical language to speak against tyranny and as his anger against France grew, in poems like "Fire, Famine and Slaughter" (1798), he calls down lightning and earthquake with old poetic thunder. But in the same year he also published *The Rime of The Ancient Mariner,* a poem set in opposition to prophetic terror, a poem about violence and its symbolic transformations.

When the Ancient Mariner recounts how he let the arrow of his crossbow fly and murdered the albatross, we are thrust into violence as yet untransformed and unsymbolized. The poem is the imagination of a pure act of violence before interpretation, not yet fitted into discourses of symbolic exchange. No other literary work in English literature so strikingly portrays violence stripped to such naked phenomenalism—portrayed as a mysterious act and a call to the mind to understand. The poem dramatizes how an original violence is turned into significance, filtered through discretely separable acts of interpretation, complicity, revenge, and a self-conscious repetition of sacrificial exchange that, as a form of imagination, is ultimately transcended. The crew members, witnesses to violence, communally decide at first that the violence was bad and then that it was good, becoming as the Gloss tells us, "accomplices in the crime"; like Europeans confronting the Terror, the crew is a community of interpreters. *The Ancient Mariner* is no simple allegory of revolutionary violence, but it does poetically concentrate the pervasive question of intellectual complicity in European reactions to the Terror. This cosmically tiny, yet ontologically giant act of killing the albatross seems to occur without purpose or meaning. As the sailors become not only witnesses but implicated actors in the scene of violence, they confer meaning upon it and suffer extermination in their complicity. An image of sacrificial death, symbolized in the albatross hung like a cross from the Ancient Mariner's neck occurs at the center of the poem. There everything turns around—from a world filled with interpretation, judgment, punishment, and sacrificial symbol to a world devoid of all determinate sacrificial meaning. Like the ruined chapel Wordsworth emphasizes in *The Prelude,* a sacramental place remembered with respect, even nostalgia, but dissolving into time, the sacrificial sacrament imitated in the hung albatross, must also be got beyond—in an act of love imagined without any primitive memory of *necessary* violence at its center. When that act of love is complete, the albatross falls from the Mariner's neck and the sacrificial memorial of violence falls away.

The framed narrative of *The Ancient Mariner* provides the perfect distancing from this most self-conscious of all romantic poems about the mythic imagination of violence. Like the Bard in Blake's *America* who, just for a moment, turns away from his own poem silenced and sad, the Wedding Guest is unforgettably silenced by the story. But the Wedding Guest is not both a sadder and a wiser man because the violence witnessed and all its subsequent—and disastrous—transformations have left him with any new symbology. He has only the injunction to love; in the poem, it is only by a thaumaturgic act of love that both violence and its sacrificial sublimations are got beyond. Yet Coleridge himself thought that injunction an inadequate issue out of the poem's symbolic complexity. The Wedding Guest stands outside just as the Mariner is inside his own story, doomed always to repeat his story from that zero point of initial, violent fracture, setting it again and again before another listener for reinterpretation. The different orders of violence—massive violence of the French Revolution and the killing of a seabird—do not make this poem any less a poem of the revolutionary 1790s, when the interpretation of violence was a dominant political and psychological topic. *The Ancient Mariner* simply pushes to the extreme moments like those we have seen in Wordsworth and Blake—moments of void from which all meaning must then be reconstructed.

In the notebooks and letters, Coleridge often returned to *The Ancient Mariner,* as if it were an exemplary text to reflect upon continually. Its themes can be followed forward into Coleridge's meditations on politics, society, and religion. Among those reappearing themes is the idea of a communal complicity in those interpretations and symbolizations which instrumentalize violence. That concern appears in an 1817 apology for his 1798 poem, "Fire, Famine, and Slaughter." Coleridge recounts a conversation he had in the presence of Sir Humphrey Davy and Sir Walter Scott and other unnamed friends. Scott had come upon "Fire, Famine, and Slaughter," a bloody poem indeed, published anonymously in the *Morning Post* in January of 1798. Scott read it aloud to the assembled company and afterwards Coleridge's host, William Sotheby, commented that whatever the merits of the poem, "they could not have compensated for that malignity of heart which could alone have prompted sentiments so atrocious." The charge was cruel, but obviously Sotheby thought the poem was too. Shaken by the remark, Coleridge noticed that Humphrey Davy (the only other person in the room aware of the author's identity) was also made uncomfortable. Coleridge summoned up, he says, "presence of mind enough to take up the subject without exciting even a suspicion how nearly and painfully it interested me." He then recounts what he said in 1798 to the charge of thinking cruelly and what he has since thought about the subject, quoting himself in passages from *The Friend* in 1810.

The real subject of the *Apologetic Preface to 'Fire, Famine, and Slaughter'* is the contamination of metaphoric by historical terror. Coleridge essentially says his violent language was just a way of speaking; it did not indicate his actual sentiments. We are reminded here of Wordsworth's revisions of those 1805 lines on "enflamed" prophetic wrath which turn into guiltless glimpses of the Terror and "terrific" retribution. Like Wordsworth, Coleridge extricates his poetic violence from its context of historical violence: "Could it be supposed, though for a moment, that the author seriously wished what he had thus wildly imagined, even the attempt to palliate an inhumanity so monstrous would be an insult to the hearers." Coleridge surely sensed the implication in this defense—that every intelligent reader knows that this is *only* poetry. That implication, however, would undermine Coleridge's idea that, in one sense, the poetic imagination is everything. Hence he takes the defense very seriously: " . . . it seemed to me worthy of consideration, whether the mood and the general state of sensations in which a poet produces such vivid and fantastic images, is likely to co-exist, or is even compatible with, that gloomy and deliberate ferocity which a serious wish to realize them would pre-suppose." After carefully building up psychological distinctions, he goes on to defend writers and poets of the past, as if the contamination he must defend against, in this historical moment, can be too easily projected back even upon them. Dante, Jeremy Taylor, Milton, those who spoke with terrible imprecation of the imaginary horrors of eternal justice, should not be imagined, Coleridge insists, as devoid of "humanity, or goodness or heart." He even feels obliged to distinguish Milton's violent seventeenth-century republican language from any "modern" associations with revolutionary violence: "Milton became more and more a stern republican, or rather an advocate for that religious and moral aristocracy which, in his day, was called republicanism, and which, even more than royalism itself, is the direct antipode of modern jacobinism." Coleridge is arguing against unnamed critics who, he suggests, see in poets of the past a horrifying complicity they could never have intended.

The poet protests too much. That he must distinguish between barbarous intentions and his metaphors indicates the deep effect upon a writer in a culture whose violence can no longer be contained in coherent symbolic form. His defense of himself is historically specific. His defense of his poetic predecessors is a defense of all poetry in the face of history. If this defense was truly necessary in 1817, then how could poetry ever achieve again that imitative prophetic power Coleridge, along with Blake and Wordsworth, admired in the example of Milton? How could the mantle of the prophetic poet be worn comfortably if the romantic poet had to point out that Milton's seventeenth-century republican wrath was not proleptic Jacobin excess? To be obliged to remind readers, at a time of vicious violence, that a poetry of violence is just a way of speaking implies that poetry had already lost one of its ways of speaking.

In these romantic hesitations, silences, and self-conscious gazes by the poet at his own language we read intimations of the complicity that Kant suggested rational beings were historically obliged to feel. Kant's word for this complicity was *enthusiasm,* which comes in witnessing a great event, the welling up of good feeling that became a self-affirming sign of the righteousness of the Revolution:

> The revolution of a gifted people which we have seen unfolding in our day may succeed or miscarry; it may be filled with misery and atrocities to the point that a sensible man, were he boldly to hope to execute it successfully the second time, would never resolve to make the experiment at such cost—this revolution, I say, nonetheless finds in the hearts of all spectators (who are not engaged in this game themselves) a wishful participation that borders closely on enthusiasm, the very expression of which is fraught with danger; this sympathy, therefore, can have no other cause than a moral predisposition in the human race.

Coleridge, as we have seen, argues generally the same idea when he says the Revolution was the "pioneering whirlwind" of "more permanent revolution in the Moral World." What Kant, however, emphasizes also is complicity with the total idea of the Revolution and, however imaginative, a morally dangerous complicity with its means. Despite the danger, Kant says, and all the bloodshed, humanity enthusiastically welcomed the Revolution, because, ultimately, humanity always means well. Coleridge suggests, in explaining "Fire, Famine, and Slaughter," that, despite their violent metaphors, the poets too always mean well. To be obliged to say that is sad and also revealing of where the poet most intensely feels moral complicity—in language itself. Certain forms of linguistic complicity are never gotten over. Though history and a thundering public voice continue to metaphorize violence (we speak today even of a balance of terror) the best of poetry after the Revolution never significantly recovers its ability to form prophetic terror or coherent images of sacrificial order. In this sense, the Terror is deeply imprinted in the rest of nineteenth-century English poetry.

Kant says that the French Revolution was "never to be forgotten" because it was an undeniable tendency to human improvement. Nineteenth-century writers indeed never forgot the French Revolution—both its hope and the challenge its violence posed to the imagination. Shelley remembered the Revolution in one way in 1809 as he translated, with revolutionary glee, the bloodiest lines of *La Marseillaise.* He remembered it differently as he planned *Hubert Cauvin,* a tale (never to be written) about the failure of the French Revolution. And he remembered it, in still another way, when in *Prometheus Unbound,* he would have to start all over again (like Blake, Wordsworth, and Coleridge before him) and portray social imagination as a denial especially of the replicating violence of vengeance and sacrifice.

It is not too much to say that the Terror affected the imagination of all violence in poetry. In 1818, Keats speaks of the "shapes, and shadows, and remembrances" of things "all disjointed" from a bust of Voltaire to Hazlitt to images of ancient sacrifice stopped in the aesthetic time of a painting. He tells also of looking "too far into the sea," and "into the core of an eternal fierce destruction," one that he can only chase from his mind, for this is a violence for which he has no philosophy, no system, no language, no transforming images. Though this particular "core of an eternal fierce destruction" is far removed from guillotining and massacre, Keats's intellectual nakedness here is typical of his post-revolutionary world, while it also reminds us of those radical moments of violence we have seen in Blake, Wordsworth, and Coleridge.

Nineteenth-century English poetry was often left in the lurch of what Keats calls these "horrid moods," memories of violence that he can make no sense of. In these moods, most subsequent poetry also stopped rehearsing romantic sacramental gestures, and by the 1840s it was no longer interesting to dismantle, as the romantics did, ancient sacramental order. On the contrary, a poet like Tennyson tried to call up, though only as failing reminiscence, the old sacramental order and images of Christian resurrection, as if somehow they might imaginatively work once more. Modern poetry is filled with desperate revivals of such symbolism as we come full circle in Lawrence's primitivist fascination with ancient Mexican gods or Eliot's anthropologically-laden sadness in *The Wasteland.* The body buried in the garden of that poem will always be just a body in the garden that will never rise again.

What I have described here is only a part of romantic poetry, which is also celebratory and filled with confident joy. Reactions of the English romantic poets to the Terror are, however, revealing of something disintegrating in the cultural order. Poetry could not put back together what the Revolution had begun to take apart. Romantic poets could provide few enduring images with which poets afterwards could confidently react to history's augmenting violence. What they did leave were brilliant expressions of a sacramental failure. (pp. 368-95)

Robert M. Maniquis, "Holy Savagery and Wild Justice: English Romanticism and the Terror," in Studies in Romanticism, *Vol. 28, No. 3, Fall, 1989, pp. 365-95.*

Norman Hampson on the myths of the French Revolution:

The French Revolution has been a fertile source of myth, and much of what it symbolizes for the general public is as untrue as the familiar story of Marie Antoinette saying, 'If they have no bread, let them eat cake.' It did not do away with the Bourbons: they were back in 1814 and, if they finally lost the throne sixteen years later, it was through the folly of Charles X, the former comte d'Artois. The Revolution did not drown France in blood: the total number executed in the whole country during the terrible year II was similar to the number that fell at Waterloo in a single day. Although the actual figures will never be known, it is likely that more people were put to death after the liberation of France in 1944. Judicial murder should not be quantified, but things must be kept in proportion. By twentieth-century standards the bloodshed was on a limited scale.

The Revolution did not exterminate the nobility; it did not even expropriate them. Noble birth excited suspicion and made a man more likely to be arrested, but it was never a crime in itself. Some distinguished families suffered very heavy casualties but, of the 14,000 victims of the Terror and civil war whose social origin is known, only 1,158 were nobles. About 16,000 more nobles fled the country and found their property liable to confiscation, but their ingenuity was often able to circumvent the law. After the Restoration the wealthiest men in France remained, as they had always been, noble landowners. Many bourgeois succeeded in making careers for themselves that would not have been possible before the Revolution, but neither under Napoleon nor the restored Bourbons did the middle class exercise any significant degree of political power.

Norman Hampson, in The French Revolution, *1975.*

Nicholas Roe

[In the following essay, Roe examines the political views of Wordsworth and Coleridge in the years surrounding the French Revolution.]

Twelve years after the fall of the Bastille, William Godwin recollected the response to that event in Britain. 'Where was the ingenuous heart which did not beat with exultation', he enquired, 'at seeing a great and cultivated people shake off the chains of one of the most oppressive political systems in the world, the most replenished with abuses, the least mollified and relieved by any infusion of liberty? Thus far we were all of us disinterested and generous.' Coleridge disagreed. In the margin of his own copy of Godwin's pamphlet *Thoughts Occasioned by the Perusal of Dr Parr's Spital Sermon,* Coleridge wrote beside this passage:

> Had this been the fact, which the whole History of the French Revolution in its first workings disproves a posteriori, it would have been *a priori* impossible that such a revolution could have taken place. No! it was the discord & contradictory ferment of old abuses & recent indulgences or connivances—the heat & light of Freedom let in on a half-cleared, rank soil, made twilight by the black fierce Reek, which this Dawn did itself draw up.—Still, however, taking the sentence dramatically, i.e. as the then notion of good men in general, it is well—and just.

While conceding that Godwin's immaculate revolution was true to 'the then notion of good men in general' in 1789, Coleridge emphasized that with hindsight it was not 'the fact'. When seen 'a posteriori' it appeared flawed from the outset, an abortive and 'contradictory ferment' that had deceived a generation of liberals and radicals throughout Europe and America. However, Coleridge's early poem 'The Destruction of the Bastille' reveals that he too had shared Godwin's 'disinterested' exultation,

> I see, I see! glad Liberty succeed
> With every patriot virtue in her train!

—and although they appear to differ in their later ideas of revolution, Godwin's pamphlet and Coleridge's note had a common purpose. Each was concerned to justify his former support for the French Revolution in the aftermath of its failure.

Godwin's immediate motive had been to rebuff recent criticism of *Political Justice* by invoking the generous spirit with which it had originally been written: 'My book, as was announced by me in the preface, was the child of the French revolution,' he claimed. William Hazlitt remembered that when *Political Justice* first appeared in February 1793 it was treated as 'the oracles of thought', its author 'talked of . . . looked up to . . . sought after'. Eight years later the popularity of Godwin's book had diminished, and he was at pains to explain why. 'If the temper and tone in which this publication has been treated have undergone a change,' Godwin wrote in his pamphlet, 'it has been only that I was destined to suffer a part, in the great revolution which has operated in nations, parties, political creeds, and the views and interests of ambitious men. I have fallen (if I have fallen) in one common grave with the cause and love of liberty . . . '. Godwin's 'great revolution' in public opinion was conditioned by the demise of revolutionary idealism and subsequent imperial expansion of France, and by repressive hostility to political and social reform in Britain during the 1790s and throughout the Napoleonic wars. In *The Prelude* Wordsworth dates his own experience of betrayal precisely to February 1793, and the outbreak of war between France and Britain:

> Not in my single self alone I found,
> But in the minds of all ingenuous youth,
> Change and subversion from this hour.

That drawn-out and disenchanting process of 'change and subversion' is Wordsworth's subject in *The Prelude,* Books Ten and Eleven, where it appears as the immediate context for his emergence as poet and friend of Coleridge. For Coleridge, on the other hand, the 'hour' of final disappointment did not come until February 1798 when France attacked Switzerland and threatened to invade Britain. That moment of disillusion is recorded in two poems, 'France, an Ode' and 'Fears in Solitude'; it stands at the threshold to Coleridge's declining creativity in the years following, and is bound up with opium dependence in the larger anguish of his family life and relation to Wordsworth and Sara Hutchinson. For Wordsworth as writer of *The Prelude* revolutionary disappointment was compensated in his power and calling as a poet; for Coleridge it issued as breakdown and creative paralysis. These differing experiences inevitably coloured the ways in which each looked back upon his earlier radical self.

'[J]uvenile errors are my theme', Wordsworth announces a little over half-way through *The Prelude,* Book Ten. In *Newspapers Thirty-Five Years Ago* Charles Lamb similarly recalled his first 'boyish heats' of political awareness 'kindled by the French Revolution, when if we were misled, we erred in the company of some, who are accounted very good men now'. But of course it only appeared that those good men had 'erred' in retrospect; there was no sense of being 'misled' at the time. Coleridge's note in Godwin's pamphlet registered this double perspective by allowing the generous welcome for revolution in 1789 but also pointing out that, 'a posteriori', another view might be possible. Elsewhere, Coleridge was less candid about his own politics during the revolutionary decade. In his letter to Sir George and Lady Beaumont of 1 October 1803, for instance, Coleridge announced that during the 1790s he had been

> utterly unconnected with any party or club or society—& this praise I must take to myself, that I disclaimed all these Societies, these Imperia in Imperio, these Ascarides in the Bowels of the State, subsisting on the weakness & diseasedness, & having for their final Object the Death of that State, whose Life had been their Birth & growth, & continued to be their sole nourishment—. All such Societies, under whatever name, I abhorred as wicked Conspiracies—and to this principle I adhered immoveably, simply because it was a principle. . . .

Not so: Coleridge never adhered 'immoveably' to a principle 'simply because it was a principle'. The grotesque and laboured disgust with which Coleridge emphasizes his distance from the popular reform movement betrays his own uneasiness at vindicating a position no one would have thought to challenge in 1803; rather than confirming his independence from such 'wicked Conspiracies', his letter to the Beaumonts is a memorial of personal complicity. Coleridge was ill, unhappy, and sleepless when writing it; granted, but he was also misrepresenting his former self to his 'dear Friends'. He repeated his claim to have been 'utterly unconnected' with other reformists in his essay 'Enthusiasm for an Ideal World' in *The Friend.* 'I was a sharer in the general vortex,' he concedes there, 'though my little world described the path of its revolution in an orbit of its own'. A little later in this essay Coleridge says that, while he rescued himself from 'the pitfalls of sedition, . . . there were thousands as young and as innocent as myself who, not like me, sheltered in the tranquil nook or inland cove of a particular fancy, were driven along with the general current!'

Robespierre.

By representing his then beliefs as 'a particular fancy' of his 'innocent' youth, Coleridge blurred and sentimentalized that period of his life. In 1817 he used an identical strategy to defend Southey's authorship of the recently pirated *Wat Tyler,* arguing in the *Courier* for Southey's 'lofty, imaginative, and *innocent* spirit' in writing the play while still 'a very young man'. By so doing Coleridge contrived to hide the past, but at a cost. He was deliberately betraying ideals and opinions once fundamental to his own identity and career, the disappointment of which had inevitably proved damaging and disabling. If Coleridge had indeed been 'sheltered' from the mainstream of British radicalism in the 1790s, there was no need for his later elaborate justifications of that position (why all the pother, if he had *not* been involved?). But this had never been the case. It was Coleridge's self-implication in that cause and its ultimate defeat which provided the motive for his subsequent evasiveness and falsification.

Coleridge's letter to George Dyer in February 1795 indicates that he was very much 'connected with a party' at Bristol, and by no means sheltered from the 'general current' of radical politics. 'The Democrats are . . . sturdy in the support of me,' he says, 'but their number is comparatively small,' and then goes on to tell Dyer about the 'scarcely restrained' threats of attack at his lectures. If one allows a little exaggeration for Dyer's benefit, it is nevertheless clear that Coleridge was a popular figure among the Bristol opposition; equally, his political concerns were not confined to a merely local 'orbit' as he later pretended in *The Friend.* In December 1795 one of his 'chief objects' announced in the Prospectus to the *Watchman* was explicitly 'to co-operate . . . with the PATRIOTIC SOCIETIES' in opposing Pitt's and Grenville's Two Acts, and in pressing for 'a Right of Suffrage general and frequent'. At this moment 'PATRIOTIC SOCIETIES' meant the London Corresponding Society and its provincial associates in the campaign for parliamentary reform—precisely those societies he later told the Beaumonts he had 'abhorred as wicked Conspiracies'—and, to underline the extent of his cooperation and commitment, he set out on 9 January 1796 on an extensive tour through the Midlands canvassing subscriptions for his journal.

Fourteen years after Coleridge's 1803 letter to the Beaumonts, reformists were once again active following the end of the Napoleonic wars. Coleridge's concern to distance himself from this revival was one encouragement to the misconstructions in Chapter ten of *Biographia Literaria* where, for example, he claimed that his opinions had been 'opposite . . . to those of jacobinism or even of democracy'. John Thelwall's memory did not coincide with this version of the past. In the margin of his own copy of *Biographia,* Thelwall replied:

> that Mr C. was indeed far from Democracy, because he was far beyond it, I well remember—for he was a downright zealous leveller & indeed in one of the worst senses of the word he was a Jacobin, a man of blood—Does he forget the letters he wrote to me (& which I believe I yet have) acknowledging the justice of my castigation of him for the violence, and sanguinary tendency of some of his doctrines. . . .

The point at issue here is not whether Coleridge's opinions had been democratic, levelling, 'Jacobin', or 'sanguinary', although I shall return to these matters later on. Thelwall's note is most salutary for identifying the reality of Coleridge's letters, lectures, and poems during the radical years that his later accounts in *Biographia* and elsewhere contrive to suppress or forget.

Wordsworth did not deliberately misrepresent his former revolutionary sympathies to the same extent. Although he had visited France at least twice between 1790 and 1793, his personal active commitment to a political life was never so extensive or as consistent as Coleridge's, nor was it integrated with religious belief as with Coleridge's unitarianism. Moreover, Wordsworth's successive experiences of hope and disappointment between 1792 and 1796 had a seminal relation to his imaginative life, in his poetry of achieved belief and lasting vulnerability in 'Tintern Abbey' and, later on, in *The Prelude.* Wordsworth did not share his friend's sense of personal failing as a motive for disguising his revolutionary self; rather the reverse, for in Books Six, Nine, and Ten of *The Prelude* he explores that self by way of assuming it within the history of his own mind. In that Wordsworth conceived *The Prelude* as preparatory to *The Recluse,* the philosophic poem ordained by Coleridge as a propitiation for revolutionary failure, his treatment of his own radical years would prove a worthless foundation for the greater work if not ideally honest. 'Thus, O friend', he says to Coleridge towards the end of Book Ten,

> Through times of honour, and through times of
> shame,
> Have I descended, tracing faithfully
> The workings of a youthful mind, beneath
> The breath of great events—its hopes no less
> Than universal, and its boundless love—
> A story destined for thy ear. . . .

When Wordsworth writes about his Godwinian self with a genial irony in Book Ten, therefore, one suspects that this oblique tone may have a specific point beyond acknowledging the drawbacks of *Political Justice* viewed with eleven years' hindsight in 1804. Looking back to the time when he had been much influenced by Godwin's ideas, he says that

> This was the time when, all things tending fast
> To depravation, the philosophy
> That promised to abstract the hopes of man
> Out of his feelings, to be fixed thenceforth
> For ever in a purer element,
> Found ready welcome. Tempting region that
> For zeal to enter and refresh herself,
> Where passions had the privilege to work,
> And never hear the sound of their own
> names—. . . .

The privileged working of 'passions' among devotees of Godwin's philosophy is a sly jibe at *Political Justice,* which had denied emotion for the 'purer element' of reason. The more subversive thrust of Wordsworth's irony is its covert eroticism, in the 'tempting region' of abstract thought with which Godwin had seduced his disciples much as Acrasia lured her lovers to the 'horrible enchantment' of her 'Bowre of Blis' in *The Faerie Queene.* The attractions of Godwin's rationalism had proved similarly deceptive and deadly; this had long been apparent to Wordsworth when he wrote these lines in 1804, and the passage confirms Godwin's own sense of the changed 'temper and tone' in public estimation of *Political Justice.*

Wordsworth's account of Godwin in Book Ten is of course infected by his memory of the intellectual confusion to which *Political Justice* had led him, and which coincided with his first meetings with Coleridge between 1795 and 1797. Coleridge himself had been alive to the shortcomings of Godwin's philosophy as 'turned aside / From Nature' since 1794, and he would have appreciated Wordsworth's portrait of his Godwinian self as a memorial to their earliest acquaintance at Bristol and Racedown. But in 1794 *Political Justice* had certainly not appeared to Wordsworth as it is recalled in Book Ten; the passage actually obscures the quality of Wordsworth's 'ready welcome' for Godwin's thought at that time, and the reality of Wordsworth's Godwinian self disappears. Nothing is said in *The Prelude* about Wordsworth's personal friendship with Godwin as it is, notably, with reference to William Taylor, Michel Beaupuy, Coleridge, and Dorothy. Godwin himself is not mentioned by name, unlike the revolutionaries Carra, Gorsas, Louvet, and Robespierre, and the political implications of Wordsworth's presence among Godwin's circle in London are left in silence. In retrospect perhaps these appeared ephemeral factors in his own development, an intellectual dead end. Contemporary evidence in Wordsworth's writing between 1794 and 1796 suggests otherwise; that Godwin was actually the immediate ancestor of Coleridge as Wordsworth's philosophic mentor and guide, and that this period of his life was a crucial precedent to his emergence as a poet. Its oblique treatment in *The Prelude,* Book Ten, can only be rectified by returning to those former times and reconstructing, so far as is possible, what actually happened. E. P. Thompson once said that there has been 'insufficiently close attention to [Wordsworth's and Coleridge's] actual lived historical experience' in the early 1790s. Given the various strategies with which both poets recollect this period in later writings, his comment deserves to be taken seriously, although recent critics, with one or two exceptions, have failed to take the hint. It is only by plotting Wordsworth's and Coleridge's immediate responses to events, and their contemporary relation to other good men and women, that their true radical selves emerge most clearly.

. . . . .

> To delineate with a free hand the different Classes of our present Oppositionists to 'Things as they are,'—may be a delicate, but it is a necessary Task . . .
>
> [Coleridge].

In his *Moral and Political Lecture* Coleridge differentiates four categories among the 'present Oppositionists'. The first he describes as 'indolent' and inconsistent, depending 'with weathercock uncertainty on the winds of Rumor, that blow from France'. His 'second class' are 'wild' and potentially violent, while the 'third class among the friends of Freedom' appear 'steadily' but selfishly interested, 'with narrow and self-centering views'. It was with the fourth category of oppositionists, 'that small but glorious band, whom we may truly distinguish by the name of thinking and disinterested Patriots', that Coleridge identified himself, along with four others: Joseph Gerrald, Maurice Margarot, Thomas Muir, and Thomas Fysshe Palmer.

All of these men welcomed the French Revolution in 1789, and agreed on the need for parliamentary reform and liberty of conscience in Britain. Nevertheless, Coleridge's 'small but glorious band' also represented three subsections of contemporary opposition. Gerrald and Margarot were leaders of the popular reform movement in the London Corresponding Society, and both were delegates to the first British Convention at Edinburgh where they were arrested on 5 December 1793. Thomas Muir was a lawyer and founder of the relatively moderate whig Friends of the People in Edinburgh. Thomas Fysshe Palmer was a Cambridge graduate and unitarian minister at Dundee where he also belonged to the Friends of the People, thereby representing the political radicalism of religious dissent. All four of Coleridge's patriots were tried for sedition between August 1793 and March 1794. They were found guilty and transported to Botany Bay; Margarot was the only one of the four who lived to return to Britain.

In Southey's poem 'To the Exiled Patriots', Gerrald, Margarot, Muir, and Palmer are hailed as

> Martyrs of Freedom—ye who firmly good
> Stept forth the champions in her glorious cause,
> Ye who against Corruption nobly stood
> For Justice, Liberty, and equal Laws.

—and for Coleridge too they were men of vision, perseverance, and patience, qualities that he later associated with his 'elect' in 'Religious Musings'. Coleridge's own position in 1795 was close to Thomas Fysshe Palmer in that both were Cambridge men, unitarians, reformists. But, while he shared Palmer's academic and religious background, Coleridge's political lecturing was more akin to John Thelwall's activities in London as a leader of the London Corresponding Society, and their opinions frequently and strikingly coincided between 1794 and 1797. Differentiating opposition in the 1790s remains a 'delicate task'. Superficially distinct groupings of radicals and reformists tended to overlap. The Friends of the People, the Society for Constitutional Information, and the London Corresponding Society all shared common interests and aims, and members concerted their efforts for reform in petitions, subscriptions, dinners, meetings, and so on. Godwin's circle of friends, to which Wordsworth belonged in 1795, also included the leaders of the London Corresponding Society and others actively involved in metropolitan opposition. Among them can be found John Thelwall, political lecturer; John Binns, plumber's labourer; William Frend, unitarian; Felix Vaughan and James Losh, radical barristers; Thomas Holcroft, atheist member of the Constitutional Society, acquitted of treason in December 1794. Not only does this suggest that Wordsworth was moving close to—and very probably within—the popular reform movement while in London during 1795, it should give pause to those who still cherish the image of Godwin holding himself discreetly aloof from active political affairs.

It is essential to unravel the complexities of Wordsworth's and Coleridge's radical years, not simply to identify where they agreed or disagreed, but because in a longer perspective those similarities and differences were to form the basis of their creative interaction in later years. The problem can be focused in their crucial early meetings at Bristol and Racedown in 1795 and 1797. The poets' first acquaintance at Bristol in August and September 1795 was apparently encouraged by sympathetic political opinions, subsequently reflected in Coleridge's admiration of 'Salisbury Plain' and Wordsworth's reciprocal esteem for 'Religious Musings'. Each had opposed the war since 1793, and they would have agreed on the urgent need for reform. Looking back to the period of their first meetings in *The Prelude,* though, Wordsworth reminds Coleridge of a significant difference between them: 'Ah, then it was', he says,

> That thou, most precious friend, about this time
> First known to me, didst lend a living help
> To regulate my soul.

Wordsworth's chronology is vague—'about this time'—because his concern here was to emphasize his need for the intellectual and philosophic guidance Coleridge was able to offer him over a period of years. *The Prelude* does not recall the coincidence of two like minds, but the dynamic potential released through disparity. While their political opinions were superficially identical and with their shared literary ambitions would have warmed each to each, it was the philosophic divergences within otherwise compatible politics that proved decisive in their emergent creative relationship. In *The Prelude,* Book Ten, Coleridge and Dorothy are presented as redeeming figures who sustained Wordsworth in the moral 'despair' to which Godwinian rationalism had brought him. When Wordsworth remembered that time, he did so in the knowledge that Coleridge's power to 'lend a living help' was related to his earlier rejection of *Political Justice* at a time when Wordsworth himself had been a worshipper at 'the oracles of thought'.

Coleridge's earliest recorded reference to Godwin occurs in his letter to Southey of 11 September 1794: 'Godwin *thinks* himself *inclined* to *Atheism*—acknowledges there are arguments *for* deity, he cannot answer—but not so many, as *against* his Existence—He is writing a book about it. I set him at Defiance—tho' if he convinces me, I will acknowledge it in a letter in the newspapers—'. In mid-1794 Wordsworth did not share Coleridge's desire to set Godwin 'at Defiance'. Three months before Coleridge's letter to Southey, Wordsworth had told William Mathews that 'every enlightened friend of mankind' had a duty to 'diffuse by every method a knowledge of those rules of political justice', and elaborated plans for their journal the *Philanthropist* in terms that demonstrate his familiarity with Godwin's book. Just over a year before they met, therefore, Wordsworth was drawing encouragement from *Political Justice* while Coleridge was in conflict with its author. The major issue on which Wordsworth and Coleridge would have differed was the question of Godwin's atheism. For Wordsworth it was not an obstacle; as Britain appeared to be following France towards a violent repression in 1793–4, *Political Justice* offered a philosophic justification for progress that eliminated recourse to revolutionary action. But for Coleridge Godwin's system threatened a moral and spiritual breakdown, in that it neglected the reconciling love of God which was vital to Coleridge's idea of human society. While Wordsworth and Coleridge would have agreed on any number of day-to-day issues in contemporary opposition, Coleridge's radicalism was inseparable from religious principles Wordsworth did not hold. This set their different bearings towards Godwin, and is perhaps well enough known. But the wider implications of their respective attitudes to Godwin have been misunderstood.

In the Introduction to their excellent edition of Coleridge's *Lectures 1795 on Politics and Religion,* Lewis Patton and Peter Mann allege that Coleridge's defiance of Godwin 'affected his attitude to the whole radical movement', and that it is 'the key to much of his social and religious thinking in 1795'. They elaborate this argument in some detail:

> Coleridge's complex and critical feelings about Godwin, Paine, Holcroft, Thelwall, and other radical figures, the majority of whom were 'infidels' of some sort, made it additionally difficult for him to sustain a strong and consistent attitude during the 1790's, when events in France, combined with repression and reaction at home, made political agitation difficult, dangerous, and dispiriting. In addition, his distrust of the political methods of the Corresponding Societies . . . necessarily isolated him to some extent from the most important active forces for reform. . . .

The precise extent of Coleridge's 'necessary isolation' is not defined, nor are his 'complex and critical feelings' about other leading political and intellectual radicals explained. Nevertheless, Patton and Mann acknowledge that their account is substantially what Coleridge wished the Beaumonts to believe in 1803, when he told them he had been 'insulated' from other reformists. It is unfortunate that the editors' final words on Coleridge's position in 1795 reiterate his later version of this year without question: 'By reason of his Christian, moral, and philosophical principles, which he attempted to clarify and justify in his lectures, Coleridge found himself in a state of 'insulation' (to use his own expressive word) from the democratic movement and its ideas'. This would have delighted the author of *The Friend,* but it seriously misrepresents Coleridge as an active political figure in Cambridge, London, Bristol, and the Midlands between 1792 and 1796. Yes, his religion did mean that his attitude to Godwin, Holcroft, and other radical leaders was complex and sometimes critical, but the corollary is not that he should have been 'necessarily isolated'. To differ with Godwin was not to reject the ideas and aspirations of other friends of liberty, as the Prospectus to the *Watchman* demonstrates. Nor is it the only 'key' to Coleridge's social and religious thinking, his relation to other radicals and to Wordsworth in particular. This must be sought in the 'Christian, moral, and philosophical principles' that influenced his response to Godwin in the first place and which, contrary to Patton's and Mann's argument, enabled Coleridge to maintain a remarkable stability in opposition through years when Wordsworth experienced

> sorrow, disappointment, vexing thoughts,
> Confusion of the judgement, zeal decayed—
> And lastly, utter loss of hope itself
> And things to hope for.

Wordsworth's radicalism was the product of his own experiences in France and was responsive to the changing course of the Revolution thereafter. As peaceful progress was succeeded by terrorism and war in 1793, he turned to *Political Justice* to sustain his 'solicitude for man', eventually to discover that Godwin's philosophy was inadequate to the practicalities of social change, and to his own experience of human nature. With that realization, Coleridge's critique of Godwin became relevant and accessible to Wordsworth as the 'regulating' and inspiring influence recollected in *The Prelude,* Book Ten. Coleridge was not forced to shift his political and philosophic allegiances to the same extent and there were, I think, two principal reasons for this. The first was Coleridge's consistent effort to reconcile 'all the affairs of man as a process' within God's providence; the second reason was that the religious principles on which he based his idea of political progress belonged in a tradition of radical dissent that was encouraged by the French Revolution, but not inextricably dependent upon its course from day to day. As late as January 1798, when other friends of liberty had been exiled, emigrated, gone underground, or withdrawn from politics, Coleridge was still preaching against war and the political and religious establishment to the unitarian congregation at Shrewsbury.

In this perspective Coleridge was not 'isolated' or 'insulated' at all. He relished the thought of himself as successor to such eminent dissenters as Richard Price, Joseph Priestley, Thomas Fysshe Palmer, and, most importantly, William Frend. Each of these men had welcomed the French Revolution in 1789 as the advent of political and religious liberty elsewhere in Europe; all of them had delivered political sermons and lectures, and published controversial pamphlets too. Not one of them was 'isolated' from the general current of radical affairs by his faith; on the contrary, their dissent urged them to the forefront of controversy in calling for the removal of Test Acts and an extension of the suffrage. Price's exultant welcome for revolution—'Tremble all ye oppressors of the world! Take warning all ye supporters of slavish governments, and slavish hierarchies!'—alarmed Burke into composing his *Reflections* as a counter to 'this spiritual doctor of politics'. Priestley's unitarianism offered no 'insulation' from the church-and-king mob at Birmingham in 1791; his radical dissent was precisely the reason for the attack on his home and laboratory. Two years later William Frend's 'Christian, moral, and philosophical principles' afforded no defence before the university court at Cambridge in May 1793, nor did Fysshe Palmer's dissent serve to mitigate his seven years' exile at Botany Bay in September of that year. When Joseph Gerrald protested to Braxfield that Christ himself had been a reformist, the judge chuckled in reply, 'Muckle he made o' that; *he* was hanget'. There is no reason to suppose that Coleridge's religious or philosophic thinking made him any less exposed than Priestley, Frend, and Fysshe Palmer, or that his opposition was in any way separate from the wider democratic reform movement as he later tried to claim. The anonymous *TLS* reviewer (E. P. Thompson?) of Patton's and Mann's volume puts the matter succinctly: 'the curve of Coleridge's commitment, in 1795–6, took him very close indeed to the popular societies—or towards their more intellectual component . . . and such a trajectory, if it had not been arrested by the retirement at Stowey, would almost certainly have led him to prison.'

On Sunday, 21 December 1794 Coleridge met Godwin for the first time at Thomas Holcroft's house. Godwin noted in his diary 'talk of self love & God', which suggests that Coleridge fulfilled his promise to challenge Godwin's atheism. A little over two months later, on 27 February 1795, Wordsworth also met Godwin over tea at William Frend's house—but as disciple rather than critic and in company with some of the most prominent radicals in London. By this time Coleridge had already written and delivered three political lectures at Bristol. His meeting with Godwin and his wish to counter Godwin's intellectual influence among other reformists served to accelerate his emergence as an active political figure, drawing him into contemporary controversy rather than pushing him off into an orbit of his own. The near coincidence of Wordsworth's and Coleridge's first meetings with Godwin reveal both of them in much the same company, at the epicentre of British radical life. Each had found his way to the author of *Political Justice* by a different path, but both had started in the same place: Cambridge University. (pp. 1-14)

Nicholas Roe, in an introduction to his Wordsworth and Coleridge: The Radical Years, *Oxford at the Clarendon Press, 1988, pp. 1-14.*

Eugene L. Stelzig

[*Stelzig is an Austrian-born American critic, poet, and educator. In the essay below, he examines the effect of the French Revolution on Wordsworth's intellectual and creative development.*]

The *Prelude* differs from other classic instances of Romantic autobiography, such as Rousseau's *Confessions* and Goethe's *Poetry and Truth,* in its treatment of major historical events witnessed first-hand—the French Revolution, in Wordsworth's case—as crucial in its author's intellectual development and the life of his imagination. Wordsworth's treatment in 1804 of his experiences in France in 1792 does not aspire to be objective or historically comprehensive, yet his powerfully subjective rendering of "the workings of a youthful mind, beneath / The breath of great events" achieves a representative status as the intellectual autobiography of the best and noblest minds of his generation—and does so perhaps precisely because of its ambiguous and ambivalent confessional presentation of a mind in which the millennial idealism of revolutionary aspirations is inextricably bound up with "juvenile errors" (*Prelude,* 10.637). My aim in this essay is to consider, principally in the context of *The Prelude,* how Wordsworth's problematic sense of "nature" relates to his responses to and reflections on the French Revolution, and particularly how his optimistic and quasi-Rousseauvian perception of man's natural goodness serves him effectively as a justification for the Revolution, but poses difficulties for him when confronted with the monstrous realities of the revolutionary terror. "Nature, be thou our goddess" might have been, to paraphrase Edmund in *King Lear* (I.ii.1), the republican slogan of Wordsworth and Beaupuy in their highminded philosophical-political conversations on the banks of the Loire in 1792, but the sinister side of human nature that emerged under the sign of the guillotine during the next two years is one not dreamt of in their philosophy, though well-known to Gloucester's natural son.

A student of the political ideas of the young Wordsworth, Leslie F. Chard [in *Dissenting Republican: Wordsworth's Early Life and Thought in their Political Context,* 1972] concludes that after his return from France in December 1792 Wordsworth's "philosophy" was "centered . . . on his belief in the natural goodness of man, and on his moral perfectibility." As Émile Legouis pointed out nearly a century ago, the key components of the "religion of humanity" shared by the young Wordsworth—"that nature is good, that man is born good, that liberty is a certain cure for every ill, that man is made to be happy"—had been current for half a century and were "accepted as axiomatic" at the outbreak of the Revolution. The general tenor of these ideas, promulgated in different forms and with different stresses by Enlightenment *philosophes*—and which found an extreme expression in the 1790s on both sides of the Channel in the writings of Condorcet and Godwin, with their intoxicating emphasis on human perfectibility—must have been familiar to Wordsworth before he went to France. Indeed, as Nicholas Roe points out in his recent examination [*Wordsworth and Coleridge: The Radical Years,* 1988] of the political thinking of the young Wordsworth, the poet's "radical identity" was well under way before his second visit to France at the end of 1791. Of course, once there, Wordsworth fell under the spell of Michel Beaupuy, that enlightened French officer who had a greater impact on Wordsworth's thinking, as Jonathan Wordsworth reminds us, than anyone other than Coleridge.

The republican idealist Beaupuy—"Man he loved / As man" (*Prelude,* 9.313–14)—was a type of the happy warrior on behalf of the Revolution, well versed in the intellectual currents of his age, whose discussions with Wordsworth turned on "Man and his noble nature" (*Prelude,* 9.363). General Beaupuy was also, like other philosophical supporters of the Revolution, indebted to Rousseau, whose influential early writings had put a sensational stamp on the notion that while man in modern society is corrupt and degenerate, he is "naturally good." Life in Rousseau's state of nature may be solitary, but it is not nasty or brutish, because, contrary to what Hobbes asserts, Rousseau theorizes that primitive man has "an innate repugnance toward seeing his fellow man suffer": "the pure movement of nature, prior to all reflection" is "the force of natural compassion" on which the social virtues of generosity, clemency, friendship, and benevolence are posited. If in Rousseau's second *Discourse* the pure movement of innocent nature is powerfully contrasted with the moral corruption of modern civilization, his monumental treatise on education, *Émile,* based on the premise that "there is no original perverseness in the human heart," pursues the revolutionary agenda of mapping out the terms of what he sees as an eminently *natural* education in a radically denatured society. Rousseau does not want to educate his ideal pupil to fit into the social structure of a moribund *ancien régime,* to "reduce him to never being capable of being anything but a lord, a marquis, a prince, and perhaps one day less than nothing." "We are approaching the state of crisis and the century of revolutions," he writes clairvoyantly: "All that men have made, men can destroy: there are no ineffaceable characters save those inscribed by nature, and nature makes neither princes, nor the wealthy, nor great lords." Because a natural education should be based on what is permanent in man, Rousseau's pedagogy aims at nothing less than raising Émile "to the condition of man." Émile, the artful product of Rousseau's cultivation, will be, not "l'homme de l'homme" but "l'homme de la nature." Conversely, the early books of Rousseau's posthumously published *Confessions* present a powerful case study of the disastrous consequences of an unnatural education, as the paradise of innocence that is Rousseau's early childhood disintegrates under the corrupting pressure of personal injustice and social inequality.

The Romantic primitivism of Rousseau's second *Discourse* is clearly reflected in the characterization of "primæval Man" of Wordsworth's *Descriptive Sketches,* written in France and published in 1793 after his return to England:

> Once Man entirely free, alone and wild,
> Was bless'd as free—for he was Nature's child.
> He, all superior but his God disdain'd,
> Walk'd none restraining, and by none restrain'd.
> (ll. 520–23)

The fact that this vision of "the native dignity" (l. 530) of natural man is called into question almost two decades later in Book 3 (composed ca. 1809-1812) of *The Excursion,* in the Solitary's description of the American Indian, may be, even if we make proper allowance for the speaker's jaundiced viewpoint, a reflection of Wordsworth's change of mind about the nature of man by the time he was writing his monumental dialogue. Having fled to the new world, after his hopes for the revolutionary regeneration of the old have failed, the Solitary discovers in the American wilderness not "Primeval Nature's child," "that pure archetype of human greatness" envisioned by Rousseauvians, but only a version of the old Adam, "A creature, squalid, vengeful, and impure; / Remorseless, and submissive to no law / But superstitious fear, and abject sloth." Similarly, the young Wordsworth's republican vision in *Descriptive Sketches* of the spread of "th' innocuous flames" of freedom that is the Revolution as a "lovely birth" resulting in the restoration of "Nature, as in her prime," (ll. 782–84), takes on a sinister coloring in the Solitary's bitter confession of the moral and intellectual downfall brought on by his "Gallic zeal" (*Excursion,* 3.743). Roused by the outbreak of the Revolution from the depression occasioned by the death of his two children and his wife, the Solitary is "reconverted to the world": "Society became my glittering bride, / And airy hopes my children" (*Excursion,* 3.733–35). His new-found revolutionary gospel, which he preaches from the pulpit with apocalyptic fervor, is the correlative of a self-alienation whose perverted energies become overtly destructive as his "airy hopes" are frustrated by the failure of the Revolution and he becomes a vicarious participant in the tyranny across the Channel: "For rights, / Widely—inveterately usurped upon, / I spake with vehemence" (*Excursion,* 3.793–95).

The Solitary is of course not the Wordsworth who wrote *The Excursion,* but an ironic and at times tragic dramatic portrait of how certain extreme elements latent within the new devotee of the Revolution might have formed into a perverse compound under the unremitting pressure of the great events of the day. In the Solitary's bitter hindsight the Revolution was indeed the oxymoron of the age, for "that righteous cause (such power hath freedom)" attracted at once "Ethereal natures and the worst of slaves" (*Excursion,* 2.227, 229). By the time of *The Excursion* there is a clear bifurcation in Wordsworth's vision of the larger possibilities of political freedom and the essential nature of man. Some two decades after the event, Wordsworth's questioning of human nature in the context of the political cataclysm in France in the early 1790s is split, as it were, between a Hobbesian sense of humanity's natural depravity and a Rousseauvian sense of humanity's natural goodness. Wordsworth's dualistic perception of humanity in its potentiality for good and evil is epitomized in the Solitary's terse acknowledgement that in his fanatical cleaving to the Revolution even during the reign of terror, "Here Nature was my guide, / The Nature of the dissolute; but thee / O fostering Nature! I rejected" (*Excursion,* 3.807-9).

This conflict, so memorably extrapolated in the long retrospect of the Solitary's confession, between a fostering and regenerative nature and one that is dissolute, destructive, and even entropic, seems also to be at the core of the agonized ambivalence of the at-times convoluted and disorientingly repetitive history of Wordsworth's feelings about the Revolution in *The Prelude.* As early as 1796 he had come to see that a corrupt intellectual seducer such as Rivers in *The Borderers* could use the rhetoric of nature—of "nature's law" and "the institutes / Of nature, by a cunning usurpation / Banished from human intercourse"—to justify his own crimes and to alienate the most basic impulses of compassion in the human heart. Is there any cause in nature that makes these hard hearts, Wordsworth might well have asked with Lear (III.vi.75–76), and the gloomy diagnosis provided by River's unwitting victim, the young Mortimer, after his disabusement—"the deeper malady is better hid— / The world is poisoned at the heart" (*Borderers,* ll. 1035–36) may stand as an indicator of a pessimistic undercurrent that calls into question the more optimistic rhetoric of "nature" and "liberty" of the account of the French Revolution in his autobiography completed nearly a decade later. Admittedly, like the later Solitary, Mortimer, the noble if rather naive leader of the band of borderers who succumb to the Iago-like sophistries of Rivers, is not Wordsworth, but a fictional character much less complex than the pessimistic young poet who wrote the play. Nevertheless, there is a confessional continuity between Mortimer's belated realization of a world poisoned at the core and Wordsworth's troubled vision (in the decade in which he wrote the first version of *The Borderers*) of a revolution that had taken a fundamentally wrong turn.

In the books of *The Prelude* devoted to the French Revolution nature is fairly consistently made the sanction of the Revolution, a revolution whose original ideals and principles are never repudiated, even in the more cautious and conservative text of 1850—which, strategically enough, places the later tribute to the "Genius of Burke" (*Prelude,* 7.512–43), which was added in 1832, not in the sequence dealing with Wordsworth's "Gallic" phase, but rather in the earlier book on London. Intellectually, Wordsworth's belief in the sanction of nature may have its sources in modern philosophers, including Rousseau, but emotionally, as *The Prelude* does not tire of stressing, its origin is closer to home, in Wordsworth's Lake District childhood and his exalted vision of the shepherd as "man free, man working for himself" (8.152), "a lord and master" (8.393), "all visible natures crown . . . instinct / With godhead" (8.634, 639–40). Love of nature may have led Wordsworth to the love of man, as he insists with the tendentious title of Book 8, but in France it also led him to the love of revolution, because, as he writes in Book 9, to one who like him had learned to look with "awe / Upon the faculties of man" the "first great outbreak" on behalf of "the government of equal rights / And individual worth" appeared "nothing out of nature's certain course— / A gift that rather was come late than soon" (9.245–46, 250, 248–49, 253–54). As he will remind us in the next book, his enthusiastic embrace of the Revolution was only an extension into the political sphere of "those affections . . . / That from the cradle had grown up with" him (10.753–54). For Wordsworth and Beaupuy a "living confirmation" of their republican creed is the image of "a people risen up / Fresh as the morning star" (9.390–92), and their "hatred of absolute rule" (9.504) is fueled by striking images of actual suffering epitomized by the "hunger-bitten" peasant girl at Blois—" 'Tis against that / Which we are fighting" (9.512, 519–20)—which in Wordsworth's more romantic imagination also assumes the chivalric guise, as Kenneth R. Johnston has noted, of knights rescuing damsels in distress.

In invoking the sanction of nature and of natural liberty, the young enthusiast was also willing to make allowances for certain excesses of liberty in the name of a better world to come. As he recaps it in Book 10, for the "active partisan" of the cause and "a child of Nature, as at first," the "throwing off [of] oppression must be work / As well of licence as of liberty," and as such he did not care "if the wind did now and then / Blow keen upon an eminence that gave / Prospect so large into futurity" (10.736, 752, 746–47, 749–51). For the child of nature and republican apostle of a liberty consistent with the high calling and intrinsic dignity of man, a certain amount of "licence" in the pursuit of these goals is thus justifiable. This license, or the revolutionary excess authorized by nature, asserts itself against the unjust social institutions of the *ancien régime,* and it is temporary—at least so Wordsworth believed or wanted to believe in the early 1790s. Writing of one of his juvenile errors, the assumption that after the fall of Robespierre the Revolution would return to its original course, Wordsworth gives a larger characterization of the period as one in which "Power had reverted" to "Nature": "habit, custom, law, / Had left an interregnum's open space / For her to stir about in, uncontrolled"

(10.609–13). This movement back from custom to nature is warranted because of a corrupt political order whose supporters in the eyes of a new generation have brought shame upon it and themselves, a "disgrace of which custom, and written law, / And sundry moral sentiments . . . Too justly bore a part" (10.852–55).

"A veil had been / Uplifted" (10.855–56), concludes Wordsworth, and "a shock had then been given / To old opinions" felt by "the minds of all men" (10.860–61). Yet there is something more sinister than comforting about his characterization of nature stirring about uncontrolled in the revolutionary interregnum in France. The young poet wanted to believe that these uncontrolled stirrings, even in their excesses, were ultimately for the greater good. In *A Letter to the Bishop of Landaff,* his spirited but never-published defense of the Revolution (including the execution of Louis XVI), written for an English audience shortly after his return from France, he attempts to address the moral dilemma posed by revolutionary violence and despotism: "a time of revolution is not the season of true Liberty. Alas! the obstinacy & perversion of men is such that she is too often obliged to borrow the very arms of despotism to overthrow him, and in order to reign in peace must establish herself by violence." That the eventual outcome of these regrettable excesses, however, will be a better political order is suggested by a revealing analogy. Arguing against those who assert that the democratic principle of giving power to the people is "but a change of tyranny," Wordsworth asserts that "the animal just released from its stall will exhaust the overflow of its spirits in a round of wanton vagaries, but it will soon return to itself and enjoy its freedom in moderate and regular delight" (1:38). The free animal—the people—is naturally good, its wanton vagaries are not inherent but only the temporary reaction to extreme and long-standing prior restraint. In letters written a year later to his friend William Mathews, Wordsworth still affirms his republicanism—"I am of that odious class of men called democrats, and of that class I shall for ever continue"—but recoils from the "bare idea of a revolution" in England and professes himself "a determined enemy to every species of violence." Clearly Wordsworth has already had second thoughts about the justification in the *Letter to the Bishop,* on the telling analogy of nature, of revolutionary violence and the licentious excesses of Gallic liberty.

Wordsworth's pervasive ambivalence in *The Prelude* about the revolutionary rationale of nature is correlated with his deeper uncertainty about the nature of human nature, and by extension, perhaps the nature of the revolution. Consider the famous trope in Book 10:

> I had approached, like other youth, the shield
> Of human nature from the golden side,
> And would have fought even to the death to attest
> The quality of the metal which I saw.
> (662–65)

The implication is that the proverbial shield has another and perhaps less precious side. The poet's recollection of his first encounter with the Revolution in 1790 on his foot journey to the Alps, though very much in the golden shield key with its invocation of "a time when Europe was rejoiced, / France standing on the top of golden hours, / And human nature seeming born again" (6.352–54), already has some suggestions of liberty verging on license in its description of the delegates returning from Paris: "Like bees they swarmed, gaudy and gay as bees; / Some vapoured in the unruliness of joy, / And flourished with their swords as if to fight / The saucy air" (6.398–401). The "glad rout" of this intoxicated and "boisterous crew" (6.422, 420) is in a sense a collective counterpart of the poet who has slighted his academic obligations, even if the professed motive of his waywardness is the prospect of the alps rather than the events going forward in France: "Nature then was sovereign in my heart, / And mighty forms seizing a youthful fancy / Had given a charter to irregular hopes" (6.346–48). If the joyful swarm of delegates becomes on Wordsworth's return to France two years later a "universal ferment" (9.165) that takes on the suggestion of a Biblical plague—"the land all swarmed with passion, like a plain / Devoured by locusts" (9.178–79)—the "irregular hopes" of the wandering student Wordsworth of 1790 are metamorphosed into the erotic waywardness of his confessional alter ego in the melodramatic tale of Vaudracour and Julia. Indeed, Vaudracour's sexual bond with Julia (consummated without the benefit of marriage, forbidden by his aristocratic father, who refused to see his son allied with a commoner) is a fitting metaphor of the revolutionary spirit of the age: Wordsworth speculates that Vaudracour, in getting Julia with child, "was inwardly prepared to turn aside / From law and custom and entrust himself / To Nature for a happy end of all" (9.602–4). The end of Vaudracour's romantic career—"his days he wasted, an imbecile mind" (9.935) in a blighted sequestration from which even the voice of freedom resounding through France cannot rouse him—can in fact be seen as a symbolic analogue to the dismal outcome of the Revolution.

To attempt a larger characterization: it is Wordsworth's reluctance to fully face up to the dark side of human nature, despite the fact that his deepest prophetic intuitions point him squarely toward it, that helps to account for the claustrophobic sense of moral ambiguity and disturbed conscience in Books 9–11 of *The Prelude,* the section dealing with the Revolution and its aftermath in the poet's troubled imagination. The most impressive instance of such prophetic urgency comes in the famous spot of time in which he contemplates, after his return from Orleans to Paris at the end of October 1792, all the bloodletting of this terrible season, climaxed by the September massacre of the prisoners by the Parisian mob. The revolutionary optimist in Wordsworth, who had returned to the capital "enflamed with hope" (10.38) and who is thus in a sense himself imaginatively implicated in the "lamentable crimes" (10.31) committed in the name of the Revolution, wants to think of these as "past": the "Earth [was] free from them for ever (as was thought), / Ephemeral monsters, to be seen but once, / Things that could only shew themselves and die" (10.34–37).

If such crimes are the sinister side of nature stirring about in the streets of Paris uncontrolled, these movements are, like the excesses of the unstalled animal of the *Letter to the Bishop of Landaff,* a temporary aberration. But the prophet in Wordsworth tasks him in his "high and lonely" (*Prelude,* 10.57) night vigil with a more dire and tragic foreboding, an apocalyptic sense of the eternal recurrence of such horrors:

With unextinguished taper I kept watch,
Reading at intervals; the fear gone by
Pressed on me almost like a fear to come.
I thought of those September massacres,
Divided from me by a little month,
And felt and touched them, a substantial dread

• • • • •

The horse is taught his manage, and the wind
Of heaven wheels round and treads in his own steps;
Year follows year, the tide returns again,
Day follows day, all things have second birth;
The earthquake is not satisfied at once'—
And in such way I wrought upon myself,
Until I seemed to hear a voice that cried
To the whole city, 'Sleep no more!'

(10.70–77)

The quotation from Shakespeare, which focuses Macbeth's sense of guilt and revulsion immediately after his murder of Duncan, appropriately points to Wordsworth's agonized waking up to the full extent of a political holocaust in which his own best aspiration—his *enflamement,* as it were—has played its vicarious part.

It is important to note how in the haunting hindsight of *The Prelude* the poet's younger self is imaginatively implicated, through his enthusiastic endorsement of the Revolution, with its horrific excesses. In this respect Wordsworth's autobiography is confessional in character, very much like Rousseau's, albeit in a different key—the young Rousseau's misdeeds (e.g., lying, theft, exhibitionism) were fundamentally breaches of conventional morality, whereas Wordsworth's errors here are primarily political, though the tale of Vaudracour and Julia carries the confessional imprint of sexual misconduct as well. Revolutions, as Wordsworth was to show nearly a decade later through the Solitary's confession, appeal to the best but also to the worst in us, individually and collectively, and here in the prophetic spot of time of Book 10 we have the poet's visionary confrontation with the latter. On his return to Paris, Wordsworth had visited some of the scenes recently "heaped up with dead" without realizing their deeper significance, as if looking at "a volume . . . written in a tongue he cannot read" (10.48–52); in the lurid light of his night illumination, he sees the metropolis as "a place of fear, / Unfit for the repose of night, / Defenceless as a wood where tigers roam" (10.80–83).

The summary metaphor of a primevally predatory nature is strikingly unusual for the poet of *The Prelude,* though it harmonizes effectively with the Shakespearean resonances of the passage, and its visionary sense of human monstrosity (cf. "Tigers not daughters, what have you performed?" in *Lear,* IV.ii.40). Paris, the seedbed of the Revolution, is not the place where man's best hopes for the millennial rebirth of humanity under the sanction of a benign and fostering nature have come to fruition, but one, to use the Solitary's distinction, where the nature of the dissolute has moved to the center of the stage of history. Because of the slaughter of innocents, this urban stage has become a place of sacrifice, like the Druid "altar, fed / With living men—how deep the groans!" (12.331–32) in the vision Wordsworth records as having had on Salisbury Plain in the summer of 1793, and which is the symbolic correlative and aftershock in Wordsworth's imagination of the sacrificial bloodletting across the Channel. As Wordsworth's characterizations of the revolutionary terror suggest, its licentious and orgiastic energies are marked by repetition, accumulation, and proliferation. Beset by external foes and internal division, "the goaded land waxed mad; the crimes of few / Spread into madness of the many" (10.312–13). "Domestic carnage," which "now filled all the year / With feast-days" (10.329–30), claims "head after head, and never heads enough / For those who bade them fall" (10.335–36)—the carnivalesque grotesqueries of London's Saint Bartholomew Fair (satirized in Book 7) have undergone a dreadful Channel-change in this terse account. Wordsworth confesses that "through months, through years, long after the last beat / Of those atrocities" (10.370–71) had finally ended, he was oppressed by nightmares that implicated him by correlating the excesses of the Revolution with a sense of personal guilt:

I scarcely had one night of quiet sleep,
Such ghastly visions had I of despair,
And tyranny, and implements of death,
And long orations which in dreams I pleaded
Before unjust tribunals, with a voice
Labouring, a brain confounded, and a sense
Of treachery and desertion in the place
The holiest that I knew of—my own soul.

(10.373–80)

For those who subscribe to theories of man's natural depravity—from dour Christian divines like Calvin, obsessed with original sin, to Hobbes and his concept of the brutish state of nature, to Freud with his bleak postulate of the death instinct—Wordsworth's night epiphany of Paris as a jungle where tigers roam is simply the revelation of a permanent aspect of human nature. As Freud puts it, with the help of a quotation from Plautus, "*Homo homini lupus.* Who, in the face of all his experience of life and of history, will have the courage to dispute this assertion?" Indeed, even the liberal Locke of the *Second Treatise,* whose concept of natural right was instrumental to the intellectual underpinnings of the American and French revolutions, grants that it is precisely "the corruption and vitiousness of degenerate Men" among us that necessitates the movement from the (unwritten) law of nature to the (written) statutes of civil society. The assumption that man is naturally *not* good leads readily to an essentially negative and repressive view of government, as it does for Burke, who in his conservative polemic against the French Revolution insists that "government is not made in virtue of natural rights," but is rather "a contrivance of human wisdom to provide for human *wants.* . . . Among these wants is to be reckoned the want, out of civil society, of a sufficient restraint upon their passions." The well-being of society requires that "the inclinations of men should frequently be thwarted, their will controlled, and their

Louis XVI at his execution.

passions brought into subjection" [*Reflections on the Revolution in France,* 1790].

But Wordsworth, even after his prophetic, Lear-like vision of the bestial side of human nature, refuses to take this negative turn, but insists instead on our essential human goodness. As Carl Woodring has written [in his *Politics in English Romantic Poetry,* 1970], "clearly the second half of *The Prelude* does not trace the conversion of a republican into a Tory." After he had recovered from the moral crisis precipitated by the "over-pressure of the times / And their disastrous issue" (*Prelude,* 11.46–47) with the help of the healing mercies of Dorothy and of nature, Wordsworth insists that his conviction "that the inner frame is good" (12.280) is stronger than it ever was. Indeed, even in the darkest days of the terror he seems to have clung to his deep faith in man's ultimate goodness, and hence also his hope for the eventual vindication of the founding principles of the Revolution. Robespierre is essentially a terrible but temporary deflection from the Revolution's true course; thus Wordsworth's prophetic glee at the demagogue's downfall. After the spot of time of visionary *Schadenfreude* that commemorates the very moment the poet received the news of Robespierre's death, his "trust" in the French "people" is unimpaired, "and in the virtues which [his] eyes had seen" (10.577–78).

If Wordsworth still insists on the golden side of the shield of human nature despite compelling intimations to the contrary, how is he to account for the atrocities of the Parisian mob and its despotic manipulators? He rejects out of hand the taunting and all-too-easy explanation of Burkean "scoffers in their pride, / Saying, 'Behold the harvest which we reap / From popular government and equality' " (10.430–32). "The blame," as he puts it with what may seem a sleight-of-hand distinction, "is ours, not Nature's" (429). Nature, then, is off the moral hook, as it usually is for Wordsworth, but then in what sense are *we* humans to blame? Wordsworth's well-known answer is cryptic yet suggestive: what "caused the woe . . . was a reservoir of guilt / And ignorance, filled up from age to age, / That could no longer hold its loathsome charge, / But burst and spread in deluge through the land" (10.435–39). The admittedly vague but metaphorically powerful notion of a bursting reservoir of guilt and ignorance seems to be an expression of Wordsworth's republican values: human nature is not intrinsically bad, but it is corrupted under royal absolutism—both the rulers and the people—through the extreme exercise of power and the ostentatious display of the wealthy few, and the ignorance and poverty of the abject many. Though Wordsworth disdained the more pedantic schemes of eighteenth-century educational theory, as is evident in the satirical "child prodigy" passage of the *Prelude* (5.290–349), he shared the Enlightenment's larger stress on human and social progress via the circulation of knowledge throughout society. As he put it in his *Letter to the Bishop of Landaff,* in a republican government, where "it would no longer be in [the] interest" of the rulers "to keep the mass of the nation in ignorance, a moderate portion of useful knowledge would be universally disseminated" (1:39). Seen in this light, the loathsome deluge of the reign of terror is not the function of an intrinsic flaw in human nature, but the result of the degradation of the people because of long-standing social injustice. That is, not the ideals of the French Revolution, but the corruption of the *ancien régime* casting its long shadow is what produced that foul discharge. A gloss from Paine's *The Rights of Man,* which is one of the important texts behind Wordsworth's *Letter,* is helpful in clarifying the enigmatic *Prelude* passage. Contra Burke, and like Wordsworth, the English radical insists that "what we now see in the world, from the revolutions of America and France, is a renovation of the natural order of things." In criticizing Burke for charging "a whole people" with the outrages of the Parisian mob, Paine maintains that the very existence of this mob is the product of the old despotic order: the former "inflict in their turn the examples of terror they have been instructed to practice" by the latter. Hence "these outrages are not the effect of the principles of the Revolution, but of the degraded mind that existed before the Revolution, and which the Revolution is calculated to reform." Is Wordsworth's explanation of the dynamics of the terror, read in the light of *The Rights of Man,* as the function of the mind-forged manacles left over from the old order, a glib liberal rationalization, or a substantial historical truth?

In any event, for the young Wordsworth in 1794, if not for the more chastened poet of a decade later who had seen the bright promise of the Revolution terminate in the nauseating prospect of Napoleon's imperial sway, the deluge ends with the tyrant Robespierre's death; the foul waters *have* receded. In the long section celebrating his demise (10.466–566), which follows almost immediately in the text after the deluge explanation, Wordsworth is crossing Leven Sands, a shallow estuary; in the archetypal landscape with which he communes "the great sea . . . [is] at a safe distance, far retired" (528–29). *The Prelude* is a deluge-haunted poem, but here Wordsworth's essential trust in himself and the outer world—"Without me and within me as I advanced / All that I saw, or felt, or communed with, / Was gentleness and peace" (10.515–17)—is such that the unexpected news of Robespierre's death leads to an Old Testament prophet's sense of vindication at the despot's downfall and joy at the "mighty renovation" (10.556) of France to come:

> Great was my glee of spirit, great my joy
> In vengeance, and eternal justice, thus
> Made manifest. 'Come now, ye golden times',
> Said I, forth-breathing on those open sands
> A hymn of triumph, 'as the morning comes
> Out of the bosom of the night, come ye.'
> (10.539–44)

In such an idyllic and symbolically charged English pastoral setting, it is easy for Wordsworth and his reader caught up in this visionary rhetoric of political renovation to forget the terrible burden of his Parisian night vigil, that all things have second birth, even deluges of ignorance and bloody despotism. (pp. 415-31)

Eugene L. Stelzig, " 'The Shield of Human Nature': Wordsworth's Reflections on the Revolution in France," in Nineteenth-Century Literature, *Vol. 45, No. 4, March, 1991, pp. 415-31.*

THE NOVEL

Margaret A. Doody

[*Doody is a Canadian novelist, dramatist, and critic. In the following essay, she surveys novels written by women in the years following the French Revolution, averring that these novels marked the beginning of the historical novel tradition.*]

In Fanny Burney's novel *The Wanderer,* a novel about the French Revolution, begun in the 1790's and finally published in 1814, we find a character called Mr. Scope, 'a gentleman self-dubbed a deep politician'. He addresses the heroine, who has just come from France, condescendingly, as follows:

> "And, if there were any gentlemen of your family, with you, Ma'am, in foreign parts . . . I should be glad to have their opinion of this Convention, now set up in France; for as to ladies, though they are certainly very pleasing, they are but indifferent judges in the political line, not having, ordinarily, heads of that sort. I speak without offence, inferiority of understanding being no defect in a female".

Things, we are tempted to say, have certainly changed since Mr. Scope's time. We no longer dismiss a woman and seek for her male relatives when we want opinions on matters of moment. But things were changing in Mr. Scope's time. He is behind the times, a comic figure. He represents both English insularity and assumed male superiority, and is a figure typical of characters in the novels with which I shall deal. His presence—in a novel by a writer who was no flaming radical—is a symptom of woman's concern with herself as a being with political and historical interests. 'Ladies' may have 'heads of that sort'. The comic presentation of Mr. Scope's views signifies a change in attitudes, noticeable in women's novels dealing with the French Revolution. (p. 176)

[When] we look at English books about the French Revolution, we are seeing France from an English point of view, and with that I can claim some familiarity. The novels with which I intend to deal were written in the 1790's, or in the very early years of the nineteenth century, and all are examining ideas and events of the '90's. The French Revolution was an experience for the English, although you must consider it experience at second-hand. Those who admired and those who detested it both felt they were living in a new era.

In this period in England, female writers were very much to the fore in the realm of fiction; until the advent of Scott, there is no major masculine novelist who dominates the literary scene. Women's works readily found an audience, and as writers they were treated by readers and reviewers on surprisingly equal terms. When we examine—however briefly—some of the material, certain questions come to mind. Why did women novelists play such a major part in the Revolutionary period in examining contemporary history in their works of fiction? I am not sure that this question is an easy one to answer—but I hope to deal with it to some extent [in this essay], especially at the end when some of the novels have been canvassed.

Roughly speaking, in eighteenth-century novels by women we find a movement from the novel of love to the 'novel of ideas' (this latter phrase is a bad one, but must serve). At the outset, novelists like Mrs. Haywood rest their claims on a special expertise in knowledge of affairs of the heart. As the century progresses, women deal with wider aspects of feminine experience, and exhibit a desire to write about their whole society in its larger aspects. Fanny Burney's *Cecilia* (1782) is a case in point.

When Fanny Burney, now Mme. D'Arblay, came to write her last novel, *The Wanderer; or, Female Difficulties,* set in France and England in [1794], she insisted that it was not a political work. Yet she knew that in another sense it is political, as her Preface explains:

> to avoid disserting upon these topics as matter of speculation, implies not an observance of silence to the events which they produce, as matter of fact: on the contrary, to attempt to delineate, in whatever form, any picture of actual human life, without reference to the French Revolution, would be as little possible, as to give an idea of the English government, without reference to our own: for not more unavoidably is the last blended with the history of our nation, than the first, with every intellectual survey of the present times.

She takes it for granted that a novelist is both portraying 'real life' and making 'an intellectual survey of the present times'—she seems even to equate the two. This is an interesting assumption about the nature of the novel—what it ought to be and do: the phrases would seem more descriptive of, for example, George Eliot's novels (such as *Middlemarch* and *Daniel Deronda*) than of Fanny Burney's own first novel, *Evelina* (1778). She expresses what writers of the '90's had felt: that the French Revolution has affected the whole of modern life and thought. Her historical analogy is interesting. The British constitution could be explained only by reference to our Civil War—but not constitutions or governments merely but the whole of modern contemporary life and thought can be understood only in the light of the French Revolution. It has permeated the whole of modern existence.

To all who thought about such things, the Revolution signified an experiment in living with great implications for the lives of states and of individuals. Women novelists were most eager to see the connection between the life of the state and the life of the individual. And writers felt called upon, as never before, to handle this contemporary experience.

The pioneer—the first novelist to use the French Revolution for theme and setting—was a woman, Mrs. Charlotte Smith. This very able writer had an unhappy life, suffering from an arranged marriage to an idle spendthrift with whom she had nothing in common, a union rather like Roxana's first marriage. They had an enormous brood of children, and Charlotte had to watch the family lose their estate, and was even forced (in 1789) to share a debtor's prison with her husband. She turned to writing in order to make money. In 1788 her first novel appeared. *Emmeline* (which Miss Seward thought an imitation of *Cecilia*) exhibits the novelist's characteristic combination of vivid social comedy with romantic beauty or terror, all bound together with some social thesis which controls the narrative. In *Emmeline* the author examines true and false relations between the sexes. In showing the heroine as right in breaking off an engagement because she falls in love with a better man, the author is rather daring, and anticipates Mary Wollstonecraft's views of rational and radical sexual rebellion. Other successful novels followed.

For a radical Whig fond of a *roman à thèse* the French Revolution provided an opportunity for a fictional proclamation of sympathies. Charlotte Smith nailed her colours to the mast in *Desmond* (1792), a novel solidly in favour of the late developments in France. Her Preface to the novel challenges the view that (as Mr. Scope would say) 'ladies' are 'indifferent judges in the political line'.

This Preface is an interesting political and literary manifesto:

> As to the political passages dispersed through the work, they are for the most part, drawn from conversations to which I have been a witness, in England, and France. . . . In carrying on my story in these countries, and at a period when their political situation (but particularly that of the latter) is the general topic of discourse in both, I have given to my imaginary characters the arguments I have heard on both sides; and if those in favour of one party have evidently the advantage, it is not owing to my partial representation, but to the predominant power of truth and reason, which can never be altered nor concealed.
>
> But women it is said have no business with politics—Why not?—Have they no interest in the scenes that are acting around them, in which they have fathers, brothers, husbands, sons, or friends engaged?—Even in the commonest course of female education, they are expected to acquire some knowledge of history; and yet, if they are to have no opinion of what *is* passing, it avails little that they should be informed of

what *has passed,* in a world where they are subject to such mental degradation; where they are censured as affecting masculine knowledge if they happen to have any understanding; or despised as insignificant triflers if they have none.

Knowledge, which qualifies women to speak or to write on any other than the most common and trivial subjects, is supposed to be of so difficult attainment, that it cannot be acquired but by the sacrifice of domestic virtues, or the neglect of domestic duties; *I* however may safely say, that it was in the *observance,* not in the *breach* of duty, *I* became an Author. . . .

• • • • •

For that asperity of remark, which will arise on the part of those whose political tenets I may offend, I am prepared; those who object to the matter, will probably arraign the manner, and exclaim against the impropriety of making a book of entertainment the vehicle of political discussion. I am however conscious that in making these slight sketches, of manners and opinions, as they fluctuated around me, I have not sacrificed truth to any party. . . . To those however who still cherish the idea of our having a *natural* enemy in the French nation; and that they are still more *naturally* our foes, because they have dared to be freemen, I can only say, that against the phalanx of prejudice kept in constant pay, and under strict discipline by interest, the slight skirmishing of a novel writer can have no effect: we see it remains hitherto unbroken against the powerful efforts of learning and genius—though united in that cause which *must* finally triumph—the cause of truth, reason, and humanity.

In her novel the author is consciously undertaking to exhibit real contemporary public political life in relation to individual characters, all of whom are more or less politically conscious or possess political attitudes. Some of these attitudes the author wishes to uphold; others she wishes to question or to ridicule. All of the characters are affected in some way by the Revolution and respond to it. Her Preface shows that she definitely sees that this is a new and different kind of novel—directly involved in contemporary political events, examining them and promulgating certain views. She sees clearly that both matter and manner will be adversely criticized. She feels called upon to defend—and does intelligently defend—women's right to create political novels dealing with contemporary events, pointing out that women too are concerned in them, even if only through their menfolk. And also 'Even in the commonest course of female education, they are expected to acquire some knowledge of history; and yet, if they are to have no opinion of what *is* passing, it avails little that they should be informed of what *has passed*'. What is the good of schoolgirls being taught history if women are to be cut off from the history of their own times, from what effects them? They have the right to investigate their own times. Nor need they be restricted to writing about female central characters. Both of Mrs. Smith's novels about the French Revolution have masculine central characters, and the love stories are subordinate to the political and social themes.

Desmond is set in France and England during 1790-91. (The story begins on June 9, 1790, and the main action ends in November, 1791, although the last letter of this epistolary novel, which forms a kind of epilogue, is dated February 6, 1792). The English hero is delighted with the France he first sees in the summer of 1790, and much of the novel consists of his descriptions of France under the new regime. The villains of the story are the heroine's brutal husband (a reactionary), and a set of rakish *émigrés;* men who abuse their power over women are political oppressors as well, and a direct connection is made between politics and sex.

The lecherous power-seekers are contrasted with the virtuous Desmond and the progressive ex-aristo, the *ci-devant* Marquis de Montfleuri, who is proud to co-operate with the new order, and voices pointed criticisms of the English who attack it. Various attitudes of French and English of different ranks and conditions are depicted. *Emigrés* and blind parasites of the old order are condemned—often, dramatically, through their own foolish utterances. For example, the ridiculous old servant of the stubborn aristocrat D'Hauteville shoots the partridges so the peasants shall not have them; when Montfleuri asks this loyalist if he realizes the danger he is courting, the servant replies

> "Soit, Monsieur le Marquis, j'aimerai mieux d'être pendu par ces gens détestables, moi, que de vivre où ils sont mes égaux, & où ils vont à la chasse."

The stupid insularity and entrenched prejudices of the English middle and upper classes are particular objects of attack. These stupidities are well brought out in some of the best comic and dramatic moments of a novel which sometimes errs in over-using exposition and harangue. There is, for instance, the conversation between Lord Newminster and General Wallingford about the decree abolishing all titles of nobility in France. Lord Newminster, irate at the upstart French plebeians, says "If I was king of France for three days, I would drive them all to the devil in a jiffy."

> The more sagacious General cast a rueful look at the wise and gallant projector of an impossible exploit: and then, without attempting to demonstrate its impracticability, he began very gravely to descant on the shocking consequences of this decree.
>
> . . . —"It will be impossible, I fear," said the General, "at least for some time, for any man of fashion to reside pleasantly at Paris, which I am extremely sorry for, for it is a place I always used to love very much; and I had a great inclination to pass the autumn there.—For my part, I've never observed but that the people had liberty enough—Quite as much, I am convinced, as those wrong headed, ignorant wretches, that form the canaille ought to have, in any country. . . . "

Part of the novelist's strength is that she can examine and

present various shades of attitude, particularly among the English; she also makes clear and consistent use of the different settings of France and England. One of her main concerns is to show the difference between what people think is happening, and what is really happening. Her tale is larded with careful (if doctrinaire) historical detail to amplify the sense of the misery of France under the *ancien régime.* Her hero refers to 'the furious manner in which the carriages of the *noblesse* were driven through the streets' in the old days; members of the nobility 'have been known to feel their rapid wheels crushing a fellow creature, with emotions so far from those of humanity, as to have said, *"tant mieux, il y a toujours assez de ces gueux."* ' The author herself in a footnote refers to the 'numerous anecdotes of this kind, that have been collected' and proceeds to relate more. Such a vivid image of callous oppression (whether derived from propaganda or with some basis in fact), as well as the fact that such stories were part of Revolutionary mythology, is of interest to the student of English in relation to a well-known sequence in Dickens's *A Tale of Two Cities.* (It seems quite probable to me that Dickens, working up background for that novel, read some of the English novels of the Revolutionary period, including those of Mrs. Smith.)

The historical progress of events during the time of the story is carefully marked by particular references. Burke's treatise appears and is indignantly criticized by Desmond. We hear of the King's flight to Varennes, and of his return, and then, later, of the signing of the Constitution. The characters' letters are dated, and the author is evidently careful to ensure that people mention events at the time when they would first have heard of them. She is clearly striving for a precise historical verisimilitude.

Throughout, we are made to feel that *émigré* conspirators and reactionary aristos are becoming weaker and weaker. The tale ends happily: the wicked husband dies and the right-minded progressives are united. So rational is her understanding that Geraldine, the heroine, is able to accept the fact that the hero, while in France, had an affair with a married woman; Geraldine accepts responsibility for the child, while the adulteress is seen as an honourable woman, not to be punished. Rational sexuality, like rational politics, triumphs in the light of understanding, and the monsters vanish.

To all who thought about such things, the Revolution signified an experiment in living with great implications for the lives of states and of individuals. Women novelists were most eager to see the connection between the life of the state and the life of the individual. And writers felt called upon, as never before, to handle this contemporary experience.

—Margaret A. Doody

Unfortunately, they didn't vanish. Events outran the novelist, for the situation was less stable than she had hoped. Her sympathies did not remain with the Revolution after the execution of the King and the events which shortly followed. The new waves of emigrants had her sympathy—but not intransigent aristos and the higher clergy. Her own daughter married an *émigré* in the summer of 1793. Her novel *The Banished Man* (1794) is about an *émigré;* it deals with the trials of a young dispossessed aristocrat and his wanderings in Europe and England. In this novel she is antipathetic to recent events in France—the destruction, the violence, the killings—and feels that earlier ideals have been betrayed. This novel has the first 'guillotine scene' in English fiction that I have been able to find—a predecessor of a number of later ones, culminating in those of Dickens's *Tale.*

Here, the author gives us the progress of D'Alonville's feelings; experience affects the hero so that he comes to curse and condemn the Revolution from its inception. At the same time, the novelist detaches herself from her hero, giving a different view: at its inception the Revolution was 'a glorious attempt'. The novel is not a betrayal of the views expressed in *Desmond,* but a modification of them in the light of contemporary events. The best of *The Banished Man* lies in its presentation of a life of exile. The author captures the difficulties and frustrations of living in another country with an alien culture, especially when important events in one's native land hold little deep interest for the inhabitants of one's refuge. D'Alonville's friend Ellesmere is an idealistic and progressive-minded young Englishmen, but most of the English are presented as insular and limited, without comprehension of what is going on in France. Of these, Lady Ellesmere is the most amusing example, and at least she is not unkind in her attitude to D'Alonville:

> she had at length been made to comprehend that he was a gentleman who had left his country in hopes of returning to re-instate his dethroned king; and seeing his situation in this light, she felt for him pity and respect; but to the strange scenes that had been passing for so long a time in France, her curiosity had till now been very little directed. She was one of those women, who content with an home prospect, never risk the sobriety of their understanding by attempting the giddy heights of science. Kings and politicians occupied her attention no otherwise than when she read of the places they had to give . . . but of despotic government, of limited monarchy, or republicanism, she had not a single idea; and never knew from whence originated the revolution in France, of which, without ever attending to it, she had been hearing for four years.

She thinks she knows how her son's young friend can be cheered up: 'Lady Ellesmere had heard that all the French were great dancers, and she concluded that D'Alonville would be very happy at a ball'. Others are less generous and more suspicious: "Jacobin emissaries are about and are so artful, that it is hardly possible to detect them". Many are ready to reject any Frenchman as a secret agent and a threat, or just as a foreigner. Charlotte Smith is very sharp when dealing with relativism, showing how various views and responses are conditioned by social factors, by historical situations. People's stupidities are the effects of social causes, combined with individual psychological tendencies.

This novel was treated seriously by the reviewers, and the more conservative magazines show a genuine appreciation of getting such an able author back—as they see it—in their camp. This may have been annoying, but Mrs. Smith must have been heartened by being treated as a serious and important political novelist.

At this time of political unease in England, unlike the previous periods of civil dudgeon, women were welcomed on all sides into the arena of political discussion. Hannah More's *Village Politics* (1792), aimed at the working class, was held in great esteem by conservatives; she was a major propagandist. I think members of Parliament and others of the governing classes might even persuade themselves that a woman, outside the corridors of power, would be writing sincerely and hence the more effectively, because she would not have the blatant personal interests at stake which men had. The respect accorded to female writers as propagandists is also to be seen in the several invitations made to Fanny Burney to write for the *Anti-Jacobin,* the most virulent organ of the Establishment; she always managed to refuse. And on the other side, Mary Wollstonecraft was an important writer for the *Analytical Review.*

We should not be surprised that women writers—and women novelists—are in evidence in all camps—radical, liberal, and conservative. We know that men have such different notions about the social good that their political life is split into parties. But women may also have different notions about the good of society, and even about what is good for women and for themselves as individuals. It is a mistake—and even an antifeminist one—to think that all women of any political consciousness ought to belong to one party of thought, as long as men are allowed, even if grudgingly, to have political differences. Modern radical feminists, and feminist historians of ideas, tend to get angry with women who do not think like themselves. This seems to me a mistake. If we allow woman to be a political creature, we must allow her as well as man to define herself as conservative, or radical, according to her lights. The word 'Woman' does not describe a political party.

Some women novelists of the '90's voluntarily turned to writing fiction supporting the conservative side. Charlotte Lennox, who had earlier been an innovator in portraying, in novels, the life of women at work, and in investigating the evils of a bad marriage, now turned out a witty reactionary tale. *The History of George Warrington; or, The Political Quixote* (1797) is set in England in 1792-3. [The critic adds in a footnote that "modern scholars such as Duncan Isles have concluded that Charlotte Lennox was *not* the author of *The Political Quixote.* Contemporary readers thought she was, as the title-page said 'By the Author of the *Female Quixote*'. It has been suggested that the book was written by the Misses Purbeck. It seems sad to have to rob Charlotte Lennox of what once could be thought of as one of her best-written books. . . . In any case the presentation of certain details and the description of various female characters in the novel make it quite certain that this book was written by a woman."] It describes the adventures of a political *naif* who, inspired by revolutionary writings, determines to go to France to assist the Revolution and support the cause of equality. He never leaves England. His experiences as he travels from North to South shake some of his convictions about equality, as he meets various ungentle and self-interested persons infected with the new philosophy. In London he innocently becomes involved with an insurrectionary society, and is misled by its leader, the evil intriguer, Mr. Davenport. Davenport has a personal grudge against Mr. Annesley, a neighbouring landowner and manufacturer. He works upon the feelings of Sir George so that the latter, stupid but well-meaning, advises the workers to demand an increase in wages, and promises to lead a party which will go to the employer and

> endeavour by remonstrances to prevail on Mr. Annesley to grant them the wished-for addition to their wages. Our hero meant only to remonstrate; but a lawless rabble is like a raging ocean. . . .

The violence that follows shows that movements once set going are not easy to control (an obvious parallel to the Revolution in France) and Sir George at last sees that he has been wrong. The author dismisses genuine radical ideology as a motive—all the 'revolutionary' characters are serving personal interest. The novel reflects British anxiety about secret societies, and social and economic unrest—there is a real fear of a possible re-enactment of the Revolution in Britain. The novelist unreservedly defends the British established order of things. The arguments used, dramatically, throughout, are witty and unfair, rather on the level of parlour debate: 'Would you let your daughter marry a footman?' There is real shrewdness in some points about the ignorance of those who think they understand current affairs but are culturally and historically half-educated, stupid and hence dangerous. The pushing shopkeeper who pretends to understand the Revolution speaks of 'Mounseer Eagle-ight', and the reader, like the hero, is left to puzzle out the meaning and find the reference to Philippe Egalité.

As the decade advances we find fewer lengthy descriptions of events in France and more attention to the potential effect of the Revolution in England. Increasingly, too, we find, in relation to questions about the Rights of Man in various social classes, questions about the Rights of Woman. Ideas about woman's moral and intellectual nature, her position in marriage and in the economic community, which had become traditional topics in novels during the century, receive new impetus from the interest in revolutionary doctrines. In *Desmond* connections between political and sexual matters are made evident. Although Charlotte Smith won't allow her high-minded heroine to commit adultery, we are made to feel that a bad marriage to a tyrannical husband is an unnatural injustice, like aristocratic power over the weak. Now, some women writers were even more outspoken in urging the right of women to revolt. The Revolution showed that all accepted notions of hierarchies and duties could be questioned, that past customs established no authority over the future. One novel in particular became notorious as signifying everything detestable and ridiculous in the new feminism (the word did not exist then, but the idea did). Mary Hays, a liberal radical, wrote out of her own experience a novel about a woman who asserts her right to make experiments in living, and carries her idea of equality so far as to make, repeatedly and argumentatively, her own proposals—or rather, propositions—to a man. As Mary Hays found out in her own life, this does not work, and the novelist insists that her story is a warning rather than an example. Nevertheless, *The Memoirs of Emma Courtney* (1796) is often quoted, attacked, and ridiculed. The situation was thought funny in itself. And the author's real insistence on a woman's right to go her own way and make her own mistakes was too disturbing not to be criticized. The heroine who carries out a sort of personal one-woman revolution in her private emotional and sexual life becomes a topic for the novelist, in works both for and against the new thought. Charles Lloyd's *Edmund Oliver* (1798), an obvious attack on *Emma Courtney,* shows the evils of 'a woman of warm affections, strong passions, and energetic intellect, yielding herself to these loose and declamatory principles'. The story traces the decline and fall of the freethinking Gertrude, who forsakes her doting fiancé to take as a lover a revolutionary member of a secret society. Sexual experiment and the violent subversion of society are seen as closely related, and as related to a rejection of family ties and the bonds of affection and duty.

Mary Wollstonecraft, after the success of her *Vindication,* returned to fiction as a way of expressing her ideas about the life of women. In her unfinished novel *The Wrongs of Woman, or Maria* (published posthumously in 1798) she asserts as she had in *Mary* (1788) the right of woman to think and act for herself. Unhappily-married Maria is imprisoned by the machinations of her husband in a lunatic asylum (an image analogous to the Bastille and the powers of *Lettres de cachet*). She escapes with her lover, a quondam American revolutionary. The lover is sued for alientating a wife's affection. Maria, refusing to be treated as a piece of property, makes an impassioned plea in the court of law, insisting on her adultery, denying any case of seduction for her lover to answer, and demanding the right to a divorce. Divorce, once thought of as the punishment of an erring wife, is now seen as a woman's road to freedom. One of the innovations in social customs in France, much commented on, had been the new freedom of divorce in the laws of 1792. Here, the Establishment is entirely opposed to Maria and to 'French principles'.

> The judge, in summing up the evidence, alluded to the fallacy of letting women plead their feelings, as an excuse for the violation of the marriage-vow. For his part, he had always determined to oppose all innovation, and the newfangled notions which encroached on the good old rules of conduct. We did not want French principles in public or private life. . . .

The revolution in private life is to be resisted as steadily as that in the public.

Another woman, a very sophisticated writer, took up the cudgels against Mary Wollstonecraft and Mary Hays. Elizabeth Hamilton, a Scotswoman, wrote *Memoirs of Modern Philosophers* (1800), a novel satirizing the new philosophies and the new definitions of woman's role. The masculine philosophers—two crooks called Myope and Vallaton—representing the views of Paine, Godwin, and some French philosophers, pervert the two young women, Julia Delmond and Bridgetina Botherim. These become female philosophers of the new school, with unhappy results. The romantic heroine Julia is seduced by Vallaton, reduced to emotional and intellectual confusion under the spell of his specious rhetoric about liberation from all traditional ties (such as duty to—or affection for—parents). Her sexual revolution is a disaster for this false lover is employing the new philosophy for the sake of old rakishness. The 'rights of women' are presented as being extremely hollow. The author evidently thinks women are yet again being led like sheep to accept notions which ultimately are injurious to women, allowing men more power and less responsibility. The new doctrines of sexual freedom are fool's gold for women, a libertine's charter. The comic anti-heroine, Bridgetina, an ugly and foolish girl, repeats Godwinian phrases parrot-fashion, and is in love with the notions as they give her an excuse for every form of egotism. She ridiculously enacts the part of an Emma Courtney in pursuit of the hero, Henry Sydney:

> "You tell me I have no share in your affection. You even hint that you love another; but you are mistaken if you think this makes any alteration in the decided part I have taken. No: I have reasoned, I have investigated, I have philosophised upon the subject; and am more than ever determined to persevere in my attacks upon your heart. . . . Why should I despair of arguing you into love? Do I want energy? Am I deficient in eloquence?—No. On you, therefore, beloved, and ah! too cruel Henry! on you shall all my energy and all my eloquence be exerted . . . It is your mind I wish to conquer, and mind must yield to mind. Can the mind of my rival be compared with mine? Can she energize as I do? Does she discuss? Does she argue? Does she investigate with my powers? You cannot say so; and therefore it plainly follows she is less worthy of your love."

The author has given her the name 'Botherim' because when she falls in love with a man she will bother him. The new doctrines support folly and egotism in those who are foolish and selfish enough to begin with.

Near the beginning of the novel we have an effective and horrific 'guillotine scene' in a context which connects the cruelty of private egotism and the cruelty of public violence. In Paris the unscrupulous Vallaton watches the procession go by:

> a crowd advanced towards him, in the midst of which he presently discovered the fatal cart, which had, alas! become too familiar to the eyes of the inhabitants of Paris, and which was now loaded with victims for the guillotine: He stood aside to observe them as they passed. Various were the expressions which might be read in the different countenances of these unhappy persons. On some was depicted the meekness of resignation; on others, the sullenness of despair.

> A youth of about seventeen or eighteen years of age, whose air of manly fortitude expressed maturity of virtue, appeared to exert his utmost efforts to comfort and support an aged mother, whose enfeebled mind was lost in the horrors that surrounded her. A young woman, who was placed in the most conspicuous part of the machine, still more forcibly attracted the notice of the spectators. A gleam of satisfaction illumined each fine feature of her beautiful countenance; and, as she turned her lovely eyes to Heaven, they appeared animated with the sweet enthusiasm of hope and joy.
>
> This young lady was the last remains of an honourable and happy family; she had, in the beginning of the reign of terror, seen her father, mother, and brother, perish on the scaffold; and last of all, a lover, to whom from childhood her heart had been united, was doomed to the same fate. After the death of this beloved youth, she seldom spoke, but to repeat the French translation of the lines of our English poet,
>
> "This is the desert, this the solitude;
> How populous, how vital is the grave!"
>
> Which words having been overheard by the reporter of the commune, she was accused of incivism, denounced, and sent to the guillotine.
>
> The person who imparted these circumstances to our hero, seemed willing to favour him with an equal degree of information concerning the rest of the unhappy groupe; but he was too much occupied by his own thoughts to listen to such uninteresting details, and hastily stepped on.
>
> "What a charming contrivance is this guillotine!" said he to himself, as he went along. "How effectually does it stop the mouths of troublesome people. Would that this good-for-nothing old man had made such a desirable exit! And why should he not? Of what utility is his life to society? Why should he deprive me of these seven hundred guineas?"

This description is typical of the way in which English novelists from the mid '90's throughout the nineteenth century have seen and presented that central image of the Revolution, and the Revolution itself. The novelist is no mere dogmatic conservative like the author of *The Political Quixote.* She is humane, and socially critical. She holds no brief for the establishment at large, and is often caustic about men in power and about polite society. As a novelist one of her best qualities is the dry wit which picks up and parodies English revolutionary rhetoric with such pointed effect. There is also a humour, a love of the absurd for its own sake, that goes beyond mere satire:

> Mr. Glib, who, like a true philosopher, despised all ceremony, took not the least notice either of Mrs. Botherim or her guest, but skipping at once up to Bridgetina, "Good news!" cried he, "citizen Miss. Glorious news! We shall have rare talking now! There are Mrs. Myope, and the Goddess of Reason, and Mr. Vallaton, all come down upon the top of the heavy coach."

It is delightful to think of the Goddess of Reason on the top of the heavy coach.

In Fanny Burney's *The Wanderer; or Female Difficulties* the wheel has come full circle. She had been an influence upon the writings of Mrs. Smith. Now she adapts techniques used by Mrs. Smith for her own novel of the Revolution. In this work many of the elements of the novel of the French Revolution with which we have become familiar reappear in new associations. The heroine (English by birth but French by education) is an *émigrée,* escaping from France in the winter of 1793; she has seen the guillotine at work in the square of a provincial town. The refugee, penniless, is cast upon the alien complacent world of England where she must make her own living. Like D'Alonville, but more subtly and intensely, she experiences the sadness of exile and the difficulties of being an alien. The difference between the real experience of the French characters and the shallow notions of the English who know and care so little about the Revolution is well brought out. Some passages between French characters are in French, emphasizing the reality of the other culture. Different attitudes to the position of women are discussed at the same time as political and cultural differences—or rather, at her best, Fanny Burney does not discuss, but present situations dramatically. There is a fine contrast between the rich middle-class English girl, Elinor, an admirer of the Revolution and its principles, who espouses feminism, and Juliet, the poor refugee, who has to assert feminine independence the hard way, by working for her living. Juliet experiences at first hand, in a variety of jobs, the difficulties of women and the degradation of the poor.

Elinor applies her doctrines egotistically only; with splendid unconscious egotism she describes how she values the Revolution because it has inspired her to change her own pattern of life:

> "The grand effect . . . of beholding so many millions of men, let loose from all ties, divine or human, gave such play to my fancy, such a range to my thoughts . . . that I frequently felt as if just created and ushered into the world—not, perhaps, as wise as another Minerva, but equally formed to view and judge all around me. . . . Every thing now is upon a new scale, and man appears to be worthy of his faculties; which, during all these past ages, he has set aside . . . holding it to be his bounden duty, to be trampled to the dust, by old rules and forms, because all his papas and uncles were trampled so before him. However, I should not have troubled myself, probably, with any of these abstruse notions, had they not offered me a new road for life, when the old one was worn out. To find that all was novelty and regeneration throughout the finest country in the universe, soon infected me with the system-forming spirit; and it was then that I conceived the plan I am now going to execute . . . ."
>
> "I am fixed to cast wholly aside the dainty common barriers which shut out from female practice all that is elevated, or even natural. Dennis, therefore, shall know that I hate him; Albert . . . Ah, Ellis! that I hate him not!"

There is a sense of the bathetic here—all that bloodshed and upheaval so that Elinor can break her engagement and ask another man to marry her. Her systems begin and end with herself; she professes to believe in equality, yet has no desire to understand, or sympathize with, the difficulties and limitations of the poor seamstress or milliner. Yet her impassioned speeches about women's rights are given straightforwardly by the author, without caricature, unlike the parodic statements in Mrs. Hamilton's novels. In Fanny Burney's book, when we look at the complacent and foolish men in polite middle-class society, and at the ill-educated and conventional women, we cannot but feel that some of Elinor's responses must be justified. The comfortable middle-class world of Brighton, jogging on its way in the momentous year of 1794 (as observed twenty years later), is seen as shallow and defective, itself historically conditioned and limited.

This often vivid novel asks some very pertinent questions about social life. The author is something of a pessimist. Fanny Burney, always fascinated by the violent and aggressive impulses of the human heart, sees the French Revolution during the Reign of Terror as licensing human lethal desires which are always present to some extent. The aggression which finds its bloody outlet in the Reign of Terror is the same as that which makes organized 'civilized' society the structure of restrictions and oppressions that it (to a great extent) really is. The author feels that political action is an inadequate answer to the human social condition. Human beings of the right, as well as of the left, have a knack of employing systems and codified pseudo-rational beliefs to justify, unconsciously, their own urges and lethal fantasies. The author's psychological interest, and her fascination with what is eccentric, even deranged, work in combination with her political themes to suggest, rather disturbingly, that almost all social arrangements are to a great extent manifestations of immature and self-centred fantasies. The 'guillotine scene' in her novel is an image of the brutality which is present (at least potentially) in most individuals and in all groups. Juliet is taken hostage (a disconcertingly modern situation, that) but in ordinary civilized life people use each other as hostages, and relationships, personal, economic and social, are conducted by blackmail. The novel is not just 'an intellectual survey of the times', it is a psychological survey of society. Not a single major issue raised by the novel has been settled comfortably by 1975. And it was a very short-sighted and complacent writer who wrote the review in *The British Critic* [1814]:

> The revolutionary spirit, which displays itself in the sentiments and actions of Miss Elinor Joddrel, is, fortunately for a bleeding world, now no longer in existence: few of our female readers can remember the *égalité* mania, which once infested the bosom of their sex. . . .

With a single fleeting exception, all the novels dealing with the Revolution that I have mentioned were written by women; yet, really, I have almost entirely covered the ground. Were I dealing with all the English novels connected with the Revolution written during this period, I would have said something about writers like Bage, Godwin, and Holcroft, and it is certainly true that the female novelists were affected by their fictions and were concerned with dealing with English political theories, especially Godwin's. Yet it is the women who take the lead in writing directly about the Revolution, using that as their theme and setting, examining the impact of public events on those living through a particular epoch—even in a particular year.

In the history of the novel—which is just as interesting a subject as the history of feminism—these women novelists all made a contribution, a discovery which was to have serious consequences for the later novel. In the eighteenth century novels had been increasingly valued because they reflected the manners of the age. Now these writers, led by Charlotte Smith, decided (as it were) that one of the things the novel can do is to reflect contemporary history and interpret it consciously and ideologically. There are earlier novels set in the past—often a vague past, as in Mrs. Radcliffe's works—and earlier novels refer incidentally to particular contemporary historical events (as in *Tom Jones* or *Roderick Random*). But these novels do not deal with the past or the present *as history*.

The novelists dealing with the French Revolution gave a new attention to the importance of public events and current ideas in relation to individual experience. The novelists' attention is directed by the sense that the historical moment can be explored and interpreted, and that the exploration demands fidelity to detail and comprehension of diversity. Their characters are creatures living in history. The novelist—each of these novelists—tries to show the impact of ideas and events on people whose names will not appear in any history books, who are yet the confused living material of which history is made. We are shown a variety of individuals making up the mass of those affected by the movements of their era, and in turn affecting them, however minutely: we see aristocrats, farmers, footmen, gentlemen, tavern-keepers, young ladies, milliners, shopkeepers, soldiers, intellectuals. These persons may or may not be conscious of their relationship to historical movements. The authors have already grasped the idea that an individual's understanding of the period of history through which he is living is often inadequate and inevitably partial. These novelists (the conservative satirists as well as the others) are interested in the variety of mundane living which goes on in a particular period, and is subtly shaped by the period and changes it.

If one examines a period of contemporary history, it is necessary to be scrupulously faithful to the details and events of the period described. These novelists of the '90's tried to be faithful to the minute detail of the period (often of one particular year, exactly chosen) which they described. From such an interest it is not a long step to turn to examination of a more distant past, to interpret a past era with its particular events and ideas, to imagine what it was like to be alive during that particular historical moment for a variety of people with particular assumptions and historically-formed beliefs.

The historical novel is born here. I should say that *Desmond* marks the beginning of the historical novel in England. It is no coincidence that Sir Walter Scott admired Mrs. Smith's works. He is usually thought of as the father of the modern historical novel. Like Charlotte Smith and all these others he exhibits a variety of views, is fascinated by the different ways in which historical events are seen and felt by those who are thrust (as we all are) into the *mêlée* of history. The novelists had their effect on history writing; a historian like Macaulay is not content with discussing battles or changes in the constitution but feels called upon to examine social history. From the school of writing which begins in the 1790's in England comes the impressive English tradition of the historical novel, which is so conspicuous a feature of the literature of our Victorian age: we have, for example, *Vanity Fair, Shirley, A Tale of Two Cities, Middlemarch*—to name but a few. In nineteenth-century France (where Scott was also an influence) we have the new French fascination with history in the works of Hugo, Dumas, and Balzac. The sense that human life is part of history, that it can be properly understood only if seen in its context in history, begins to grow in the English novels about the Revolution. These novelists are harbingers of the future. We have Hegelianism before Hegel. The novelists insist that a novelist should be an historian. As Mrs. Smith intimates, the novelist has a unique capacity to produce the present, 'what *is* passing', as history.

What made these women into historians? Or, less rhetorically, why are women novelists the first to write proper historical fictions?—and among the first to see in the novel a peculiarly proper vehicle for historical analysis? One reason, I think, is that attention to realistic mundane detail had been thought of as a feminine characteristic, and had been accepted in women's fiction. And this new fiction demands that the realistic and mundane be included if it is to succeed in convincing. Women did not accept, and did not have to accept, established categories of significance, hierarchies which predetermine what is trivial and what is important. Women novelists could the more readily include harp-lessons and stoves and clothes and wet-nurses and chit-chat and parties in their serious novels. They see and allow connections which the male writer, once he waxes philosophical, may the more readily ignore, and call to their aid objects and incidents which he would disdain. The women do not really write 'philosophically' in these novels like Holcroft or Godwin in their fictions. Female writers want to transmit the sense of felt life, to include objects and emotions. Even the most tendentious of women novelists were unlikely to adopt a system in too dry and meagre a fashion. The appeal of describing experience and emotional reactions, of probing instead of generalizing, was too strong, and the tradition of the female novel with its emphasis on the particular and the emotional gave them an inheritance which was a strength when they wanted to present experience in history as natural, real, and diverse. Women writers also had some unique advantages in presenting the whole of experience; they had a claim to particular authority in speaking about women, and thus in speaking about love, sex, marriage, childbearing, education, the family—about the basic relationships which are of the essence of human experience in historical conditions. Whatever a female novelist may say, no man, however much opposed to her views, can ever say 'no woman ever really felt like that'.

Albert Dieudonné in Abel Gance's Napoleon, *which chronicles the French Revolution and Napoleon's rise to power.*

None of this quite answers the question—why did women novelists become historians? Certainly, part of the answer lies in the education of women. From the middle of the century it had been increasingly accepted that learning history should form part of the education of the well-bred woman, and this is something of a new departure. Thus, Charlotte Smith can pertinently ask why a woman should be taught the history of the past if she is to take no notice of the history of the present. There was a new excitement in learning history—it was a mental weapon in the hands of the educated. More important still, I think women were and had been conscious of a change in their own historical condition during the course of the century. To be a woman novelist at all, to utter in public and be heard, to be reviewed and seriously discussed, meant a kind of break with the past. All of these writers knew they were doing something their grandmothers would not have thought of. For women, more than for men of the same class and interests, there had been a marked change in manners and in expectations. An educated woman, aware that she was not a citizen in the full legal sense, was yet made more conscious than ever before of her potential contribution to society. She knew that, if not a citizen, she was yet a participant in the history of her own times. It is no wonder that as women became novelists they took on the responsibility of observing their society more closely and more extensively. Women had a reason to be curious. They had questions to ask. What is this society of which I am now a more responsible and articulate member than most of my ancestresses have been? How has it become what it is? What is wrong with it? What is right? Should it be changed? How should people react to each other? How do people adapt their private selves to this complex public world?

The French Revolution brought these questions to the fore for all who thought at all about such things, and women novelists had the confidence and the interest to take up these questions in their works of fiction. (pp. 176-96)

Margaret A. Doody, "English Women Novelists and the French Revolution," in La Femme en Angleterre et dans les colonies américaines aux XVIIe et XVIIIe siècles: acte du Colloque tenu à Paris les 24 et 25 octobre 1975, *Publications de l'Université de Lille III, 1976, pp. 176-98.*

[The] writer is the hero of post-revolutionary society, for it is through the writer that Revolutionary Paris becomes literary France.

—Priscilla Parkhurst Ferguson, in **L'Esprit Créateur, *Summer 1989.***

Ronald Paulson

[*In the essay below, Paulson contends that Gothic fiction of the early nineteenth century is imbued with themes and symbols expressing the "negative, dark side" of the French Revolution.*]

In Chapter 5, Volume II, of Jane Austen's *Northanger Abbey* Henry Tilney regales Catherine Morland with his version of the Gothic fantasy she loves to read. When she arrives at Northanger Abbey, he says, she will be taken by the housekeeper "along many gloomy passages, into an apartment never used since some cousin or kin died in it about twenty years before." She will discover that the door has no lock, and shortly (a couple of nights later) there will be a violent storm. "Peals of thunder so loud as to seem to shake the edifice to its foundation will roll around the neighbouring mountains—and during the frightful gusts of wind which accompany it, you will probably think you discern (for your lamp is now extinguished) one part of the hanging more violently agitated than the rest." These details are punctuated by "Will not your heart sink within you?" The next step is to lift the tapestry, try the door found behind it, and proceed into "a small vaulted room." The walk through several such chambers reveals a dagger, some drops of blood, torture instruments, and an old cabinet in a secret drawer of which is found a roll of paper: "you seize it—it contains many sheets of manuscript—you hasten with the precious treasure into your own chamber, but scarcely have you been able to decipher 'Oh! thou—whomsoever thou mayst be, into whose hands these memoirs of the wretched Matilda may fall'—when your lamp suddenly expires in the socket, and leaves you in total darkness."

Certain elements of Ann Radcliffe's Gothic are here, including the passivity of the sensitive heroine, the labyrinthine passages and chambers through which she wanders, the violent storm, and the perusal of written documents that record experiences with which she never herself makes contact. Elsewhere in *Northanger Abbey,* the Gothic fiction is reflected in vocabulary—in, for example, Isabella's "amazing" or "inconceivable, incredible, impossible!" or Catherine's remark, "Udolpho [is] the nicest book in the world," to which Henry replies, "The nicest;—by which I suppose you mean the neatest. That must depend upon the binding." The adjective is just another sort of exaggeration, another expression of a point of view, a way of looking at the world as if it were a book.

Henry Tilney himself, we have learned in an earlier chapter, is a reader of history ("Yes, I am fond of history," he says). Catherine reads history only "as a duty, but it tells me nothing that does not either vex or weary me," whereas from Gothic novels she presumably gains comfort. Henry, however, has his own Quixotic version of sensibility: he is a student of the Picturesque, believing that a "beautiful" sky does not signify good weather but a drawable picture. He instructs Catherine in these mysteries until she views "the country with the eyes of persons accustomed to drawing"—and at length "voluntarily rejected the whole city of Bath, as unworthy to make part of a landscape."

At this point in the conversation, Tilney moves from the subject of the Picturesque to politics, "and from politics, it was an easy step to silence." It is in this context—of the Gothic, history, the Picturesque, and politics—that Catherine remarks, "I have heard that something very shocking indeed, will soon come out of London. . . . more horrible than any thing we have met with yet"—by which of course she means the publication of a new Gothic novel. Miss Tilney, however, thinks she means a riot. It is left to Henry to explain the discrepancy between a new publication "in three duodecimo volumes, two hundred and seventy-six pages in each, with a frontispiece to the first," and (in a fantasy parallel to the Gothic fantasy I have quoted above) "a mob of three thousand men assembling in St. George's Fields; the Bank attacked, the Tower threatened, the streets of London flowing with blood, a detachment of the 12th Light Dragoons . . . " and so on. This was written in 1797 or 1798 when Austen if not Tilney was thinking of history: the Gordon Riots of 1780 and the French Revolution of 1789.

In the context of *Northanger Abbey* the irony is that the exaggeration of the sign falls short of the grim reality. But precisely *what* reality? The lies of the Thorpes and the fantasy of General Tilney as wife-murderer generated by the Gothic-infatuated Catherine turn out to signify, but not something close to the sign, not a Gothic but rather a worse, because more banal, more historical evil—one perhaps like the French Revolution itself: General Tilney's abrupt dismissal of Catherine because he thinks she will interfere with his dynastic plans for Henry.

In *Northanger Abbey* there is posited something we might call the real, or the thing itself, and then something else we can call the word, and Austen shows that they can only come together in formalized, conventionalized ways. We notice the difference between the Gothic fiction and history, but also the similarity. General Tilney is indeed the reality beneath Manfred, Montoni, and the other Gothic villains: a man concerned with property, heirs, and wealth; a man who tries unscrupulously to preserve his family and fortune against the incursions of a penniless outsider, who in fact does disrupt it. In the real world, the Gothic casts up (or is bettered by) the reality of a General Tilney or a French Revolution in which, in Burke's terms, penniless parvenues infiltrate the aristocratic family—or the royal family itself, ultimately breaking through its doors into the bedroom of the queen—and ravish the wife-mother-daughter. The principal elements are the same: the Gothic only supplies the metaphors and the gushing response of the safely distant spectator, who hears the storm (remembering perhaps the metaphors of natural upheaval—hurricanes and erupting volcanoes—that were immediately applied to the Revolution), notices the bloody daggers and racks, and reads—or starts to, until her candle is extinguished—a letter from an actual participant.

The Gothic did in fact serve as a metaphor with which some contemporaries in England tried to come to terms with what was happening across the Channel in the 1790s. The first Revolutionary emblem was the castle-prison, the Bastille and its destruction by an angry mob, which was fitted by Englishmen into the model of the Gordon Riots of nine years before. But if one way of dealing with the Revolution (in its earliest stages) was to see the castle-prison through the eyes of a sensitive young girl who responds to terror in the form of forced marriage and stolen property, another was to see it through the case history of her threatening oppressor, Horace Walpole's Manfred or M. G. Lewis' Ambrosio—the less comforting reality Austen was heralding in the historical phenomena of London riots. In Lewis' *The Monk* (1795) the two striking phenomena dramatized are first the explosion—the bursting out of his bonds—of a repressed monk imprisoned from earliest childhood in a monastery, with the havoc wreaked by his self-liberation (assisted by demonic forces) on his own family who were responsible for his being immured; and second, the blood-thirsty mob that lynches—literally grinds into a bloody pulp—the wicked prioress who has murdered those of her nuns who succumbed to sexual temptation. Both are cases of justification followed by horrible excess: Ambrosio deserves to break out and the mob is justified in punishing the evil prioress, but Ambrosio's liberty leads him to the shattering of his vow of celibacy, to repression, murder, and rape not unlike the compulsion against which he was reacting; and the mob not only destroys the prioress but (recalling the massacres of September 1792) the whole community and the convent itself:

> The incensed Populace, confounding the innocent with the guilty, had resolved to sacrifice all the Nuns of that order to their rage, and not to leave one stone of the building upon another. . . . They battered the walls, threw lighted torches in at the windows, and swore that by break of day not a Nun of St. Clare's order should be left alive. . . . The Rioters poured into the interior part of the Building, where they exercised their vengeance upon every thing which found itself in their passage. They broke the furniture into pieces, tore down the pictures, destroyed the reliques, and in their hatred of her Servant forgot all respect to the Saint. Some employed themselves in searching out the Nuns, Others in pulling down parts of the Convent, and Others again in setting fire to the pictures and furniture, which it contained. These Latter produced the most decisive desolation: Indeed the consequences of their action were more sudden, than themselves had expected or wished. The Flames rising from the burning piles caught part of the Building, which being old and dry, the conflagration spread with rapidity from room to room. The Walls were soon shaken by the devouring element: The Columns gave way: The Roofs came tumbling down upon the Rioters, and crushed many of them beneath their weight. Nothing was to be heard but shrieks and groans; the Convent was wrapped in flames, and the whole presented a scene of devastation and horror.

The end, of course, as it appeared to Englishmen in 1794—remembering Thomas Paine's words ("From a small spark, kindled in America, a flame has arisen, not to be extinguished" [*Rights of Man,* 1792]) and the imagery of light and fire associated with the Revolution—was the destruction of the revolutionaries themselves in the general collapse.

I do not mean to suggest that Ann Radcliffe or Monk Lewis was producing propaganda either for or against the French Revolution. Lewis' treatment of the lynching scene, for example, is far removed from the morally clear-cut renderings of anti-clericalism exemplified by the *drames monacals* popular in the theaters of Revolutionary Paris. In one of these plays—de Menuel's *Les Victimes cloîtrées* of 1791, which Lewis saw, admired, and translated—the wretched prisoners held in the dungeons below a convent are finally rescued by a Republican mayor brandishing the *tricouleur.* Lewis exploits the dramatic resonances of the Revolution and its anti-clericalism, but simultaneously portrays the rioting mob as blood-thirsty, completely out of control, animal-like in its ferocity. The convent of St. Clare represents corruption, superstition, and repression, but its overthrowers, no more admirable than the tyrants, are capable of the same atrocities or worse. In the same way, many observers (conservative and otherwise) by 1793 saw the brutally oppressed masses of France usurping the tyrannical roles of their erstwhile oppressors.

In his critical essay "Idée sur les romans" (1800) the Marquis de Sade, who considered *The Monk* superior to all other works of its kind, asserted that the bloody upheavals of the French Revolution had rendered everyday reality so horrific that contemporary writers necessarily had to invoke the supernatural and demonic realms for material which could still shock or startle their readers. I do not think there is any doubt that the popularity of Gothic fiction in the 1790s and well into the nineteenth century was due in part to the widespread anxieties and fears in Europe aroused by the turmoil in France finding a kind of sublimation or catharsis in tales of darkness, confusion, blood, and horror.

The Gothic, however, had existed from the 1760s onward, and we are talking about a particular development in the 1790s, a particular plot which was either at hand for writers to use in the light of the French Revolution, or was in some sense projected by the Revolution and borrowed by writers who may or may not have wished to express anything specifically about the troubles in France. As a descendent of Walpole's Manfred, for example, Ambrosio has to be seen as a conflation of rebelling son and tyrant father. Manfred was the servant who murdered his master in order to usurp the family castle—or the castle of his father or older brother, in later versions of the story—and then sacrificed his own children to retain his property. But Ambrosio is notably unconcerned with property—only with liberty of a sexual sort. This is why he is sympathetic in a way that Manfred is not, even given Walpole's assurances that Manfred is otherwise a great soul. Ambrosio's story is of his insane, uncontrolled rush into freedom and, incidentally, of its consequences, which include repression of other people's liberty for the end of self-gratification. In short, *The Monk* is about the act of liberation, whereas *The Castle of Otranto* was about a man's attempt to hold together his crumbling estate and cheat others of their rightful inheritance. One is a fable of revolution, the other of the *ancien régime.*

The earlier phase produced fictions that continued to be copied throughout the period of the Revolution. Not long after the notorious September Massacres, the *Monthly Review* attacked a Gothic novel called *The Castle of St. Vallery* in the following terms:

> Of all the resources of invention, this, perhaps, is the most puerile, as it is certainly among the most unphilosophical. It contributes to keep alive that superstition which debilitates the mind, that ignorance which propagates terror, and that dread of invisible agency which makes inquiry criminal.

The critic sees the Gothic practiced in this novel as the representation of tyranny which was a central contribution of the pre-1789 genre, and so an example of everything the French Enlightenment and Revolution was seeking to correct. He detects nothing of either the analysis of unrestrained energy that appears in some of Radcliffe's work of the 1790s or the representation of the energy of revolution itself in *The Monk.* Many such writers simply ignored the fact of the French Revolution. As John Garrett writes of one of these, Mary Meeke, her "conservatism was based on a belief that the 1789 revolution was some sort of aberration of history," and so she continued to portray France of the *ancien régime* as if nothing had happened.

Other writers *were* concerned about the significance of the events in France. But the castle as prison was already implicit in *The Castle of Otranto* and Radcliffe's *Castles of Athlin and Dynbayne* (1789), and it may have been only this image and this frame of mind that made the Fall of the Bastille an automatic image of revolution for French as well as English writers. By the time *The Mysteries of Udolpho* appeared (1794), the castle, prison, tyrant, and sensitive young girl could no longer be presented naively; they had all been sophisticated by the events in France.

At this point another strand of novel, the novel of reform (the so-called "Jacobin" novel), joins the Gothic in the representation of tyranny and revolution. The Gothic tended to be the form adopted by those who were either against or merely intrigued by the Revolution, or by problems of freedom and compulsion. The reformers Godwin, Holcroft, Bage, and Inchbald are *for* the Revolution; they call their works "Things as they Are," "Man as he Is" or "Man as he is Not"; they avoid the Gothic and theatrical trappings Burke associated with the Revolution; they have a sometimes dismaying singleness of purpose and go straight to the contemporary Englishman, the General Tilney, illustrating Arthur Young's insistence that "The true judgment to be formed of the French revolution, must surely be gained, from an attentive consideration of the evils of the old government" [*Travels during the Years 1787, 1788, and 1789,* 1793]. This was, of course, what the English Jacobins usually represented in their novels, tracts, and poems, for their real subject was not France but forms of compulsion in England.

Gothic and Jacobin novels had a similar ancestry in Richardson's *Pamela* and *Clarissa;* both show the family as a compulsive force on the children, in particular on the marriageable daughter or the young wife. The distinction is rather between a novel about the tyranny seen from the point of view of the helpless (most helpless because female) individual, and a novel about the rebel. William Godwin's *Things as They Are: or the Adventures of Caleb Williams* appeared just a year before *The Monk,* combining the two fictions in a more schematic, more coherent form. The relationship between Falkland and Caleb is the same explored by Inchbald and Holcroft between society the cruel hunter and the suffering individual, its victim. But by the time Godwin was writing, the French Terror had cast its shadow on libertarian dreams, and his work reflects that constant potential for simple inversion of the persecutor-persecuted relationship which events in Paris had so terribly exemplified.

In his initial, discursive response to the Revolution, *Political Justice* (1793), Godwin argued that "the great cause of humanity" is hindered by both the ancient tradition of Burkean thought (in his *Reflections on the Revolution in France* of 1790) *and* by the "friends of innovation." He focuses on the second, bringing to bear Burke's own argument that "to dragoon men into the adoption of what we think right is an intolerable tyranny": the French have shown that to overthrow tyranny is to have to become greater tyrants themselves. Godwin's own point is that the orderly process of growing philosophical awareness—a passive process—was dangerously interrupted by the Revolution, and perhaps directed into the wrong channels. His second point is that "Coercion first annihilates the understanding of the subject upon whom it is exercised, and then of him who employs it." For Caleb Williams, in his way, becomes as much a persecutor (and ultimately a murderer) as his master—and is eventually brought to commit similar crimes through an equally obsessive concern to protect the "honour" he no longer possesses.

The potentially invertible relationship in *Caleb Williams* is between two wholly isolated beings who play out their equally agonizing parts in a series of physical and psychological hunts and flights, wherein they repeatedly exchange the roles of persecutor and victim, hunter and hunted. Their final miserable realization of the simultaneity of both roles in their natures (each having previously viewed only the other as the real persecutor) results in the climactic moment in the novel when Falkland collapses into Caleb's arms and confesses to the murder of Tyrrel—and when Caleb realizes that his own awakened sense of guilt and responsibility must deny him the possibility of ever receiving any happiness from his long-desired liberty.

Both *The Monk* and *Caleb Williams* offer embryonic versions of the titanic Romantic hero who comes into being with the blurring of the old black-white morality of earlier Gothic fiction. This figure is in part characterized, as was the French Revolution, by the appalling ease with which his nature could be inverted, either by assuming the vices of the tyrant he has overthrown, or by a simple shift of moral perspective. Ambrosio seen from one point of view is the cruel hypocrite, matricide, and incestuous rapist, who lets no barrier stand between him and the fulfillment of his lust; but from another he is the helpless, passive victim of his repressive environment and of Satanic persecution, rendered vulnerable by his miseducation, seduced by a demon, tricked into ravishing his own sister, driven to sell his soul when an earthly reprieve is at hand, and finally betrayed and destroyed by the Arch-Fiend.

Some of the ambivalent feelings we have registered to Ambrosio, Caleb, and the crowd that destroys the prioress and her convent can be sensed in the meditations of a first-hand witness to the early stages of the Revolution. Arthur Young argues that release—the violent, destructive explosion of release Lewis depicts in Ambrosio—was a consequence of oppression, signifying only in relation to that original oppression. He asks whether it is "really the people to whom we are to impute" the excesses they are committing:

> —Or to their oppressors who had kept them so long in a state of bondage? He who chooses to be served by slaves, and by illtreated slaves, must know that he holds both his property and life by a tenure far different from those who prefer the service of well treated freemen; and he who dines to the music of groaning sufferers, must not, in the moment of insurrection, complain that his daughters are ravished, and then destroyed; and that his sons' throats are cut.

The fact that neither Lewis nor Godwin stresses the cruelty of the masters of Ambrosio and Caleb does not alter the general point that the revolt is understood only in terms of the oppression against which it acts. As to the crowd, which does react against specific and monstrous cruelty on the part of the prioress (who, after all, is a minor character in the novel), Young admonishes: "Let it be remembered that the populace in no country ever use power with moderation; excess is inherent in their aggregate constitution . . . ."

From the Fall of the Bastille to the September Massacres, and to the *levée en masse* and Napoleon's armies, this crowd is in many ways the central phenomenon of the Revolution. The crowd, with the related terms "natural sovereignty" and "General Will" (or Burke's "swinish multitude"), was among the most ambiguous concepts to arise from the Revolution. Ambrosio, it should be recalled, was at the very outset presented as a spell-binding orator, the master of the crowd that later proves beyond mastering. The crowd, the *mobile vulgus,* was an image that was ready to hand in the literature of conservative Anglo-Catholic royalists like Dryden and Swift, but materialized by the Gordon Riots and the actual events in France. With this past history, and with its own development in France, the crowd merged with the conflicting or overlapping fictions of, on the one hand, the cabal or small secret society that governs the crowd and determines events, or, on the other, the single great man who expresses in himself the General Will.

The disturbances in Ireland, for example, the *Times* of 22 February 1793 reported, "arise from the pure wantonness of a set of desperadoes called Defenders . . . encouraged and abetted by a secret junto, that like the French Jacobins, wish to throw all government into confusion. . . ." The largest such fiction was the one woven by the Abbé Augustin de Barruel, who argued that the *illuminati* masterminded the whole Revolution. As J. M. Roberts has written in his *Mythology of the Secret Societies:*

> Educated and conservative men raised in the tradition of Christianity, with its stress on individual responsibility and the independence of the will, found conspiracy theories plausible as an explanation of such changes: it must have come about, they thought, because somebody planned it so.

Such myths as plots of the Freemasons, *philosophes,* and *illuminati* were "an attempt to impose some sort of order on the bewildering variety of changes which suddenly showered upon Europe with the Revolution and its aftermath." The assumption of individual agency (as opposed to the more popular modern explanation of social and economic determinism) is evident not only in the allegorizations of revolution as the actions of a single man—an Ambrosio—but also in the comforting retreat to Satanic responsibility in the Miltonic fictions of rebellion in heaven and in the Garden of Eden—in Rosario-Matilda, the Devil who in fact determines all the events that Ambrosio seemed responsible for.

The crowd could thus mean either complete uncontrol of unruly passions or the carrying out of the designs of a single man or a very small group of schemers—or even diabolic possession or inspiration. The historical villain (as in many of the theories Barruel collects) is the Duc d'Orléans type (Philippe Egalité), the cadet who wants power himself and therefore topples the rightful older brother or cousin by masterminding a plot that moves the crowd (Satan in heaven, jealous of the raising of his "brother" Christ, or Schedoni in Radcliffe's *The Italian*), and is himself swept away by the tempest he has unleashed. The force then becomes the Jacobin Club or a Robespierre, who eventually loses his own head, and ultimately a Napoleon.

General Tilney (or Montoni or Schedoni) and the rioters are, of course, polarities: one concerned with the preservation and the other with the destruction of property, but both with its appropriation. Tilney is the malign individual, the Radcliffe villain; the rioters, something she only hints at in the vague figures of the sexually threatening soldiers of Montoni whom Emily fears (in this sense related to Burke's mob that threatens Marie Antoinette), are mere misdirected action, chance, the natural force of a crowd—in some ways even more terrifying to contemplate. Both, however, were historical phenomena, not exactly unthinkable before 1789, but largely Gothic fantasies or satiric exaggerations. Taken together, however, they represent the two chief explanations offered for the phenomenon of the Revolution by conservative theorists, the spokesmen of counter-revolution.

The sense of unresolved mystery that was one aspect of the Gothic fiction of Walpole, Clara Reeve, and Radcliffe also fitted the way many contemporaries "read" the Revolution. The feeling the reader has in Gothic fiction is of never knowing exactly where he is, where he is going, or what is happening. This is a feeling which corresponds to the puzzlement of the protagonist too, whether a passive Emily or an active plotter like Ambrosio. The Gothic describes a situation in which no one can understand or fathom anyone else's motives or actions. The narrative structure the Gothic inherited, and carried to its greatest degree of subtlety in Radcliffe's novels (and of formal innovation in Maturin's *Melmoth the Wanderer* and Hogg's *Confessions of a Justified Sinner*), was one involving a theme of communication, the unresolved difficulty of understanding actions; this was expressed in the aposiopesis of Sterne's and Mackenzie's novels, in the authentic manuscript lost in gun-wadding or hair curlers, the resort to typographical excesses, and the alternative accounts that leave the reader as uncertain of the responsibility for the protagonist's actions as the protagonist himself. This is, of course, also a feature of the sublime style, "where half is left out to be supplied by the hearer"—and so a logical and syntactical obscurity joins revolution and sublimity.

Behind all of this obscurity, however, is the elaborate plot, masterminded but slipping out of control, which involves the overthrow of a property owner. When the Revolution itself came, and as it progressed, it was precisely this inability to make out the events on a day-to-day basis, but with the suspicion of personal skulduggery beneath each new changing-hands of property, that made the Gothic novel a roughly equivalent narrative form. But this is not to say that the Revolution produced no plot structures of its own. There was a discernible scenario that began with the Fall of the Bastille and progressed to the march on and back from Versailles, the flight to Varennes, the September Massacres, the Terror, Thermidore, Brumaire, and so on. Even Waterloo was followed, for Englishmen, by Peterloo, an ironic, domestic extension. Depending on what stage one looked back from, he had a different structure, though it was increasingly colored on the dark side by the Terror, by the further disillusionment of the Directory, and by the threat to national security of the Empire.

Behind all of this was a new sense of history, of what could or should happen in history, and what history was in fact about. From being about the kings, it became, in certain ways, about larger groups of subjects and their attempts to come to terms with, or create a new order from, the disorder consequent upon the overthrow of the old established order. The process was one of evolution or revolution, probably of both, involving circular motion but in a spiral that was either ascending or descending, as Caleb overthrows while at the same time becoming Falkland, as Orc overthrows and then becomes Urizen, and so on. The standard features that emerged were the rebellion itself with the enormous possibilities and hopes it opened up; this was followed by a stage of delusion, dangerous and unforeseen consequences, and disillusionment.

It is difficult not to agree with Nelson Smith that in many ways Emily St. Aubert is used by Radcliffe in precisely the critical way Jane Austen uses Catherine Morland. The (remote) potential of Ambrosio in Emily is broached at the beginning in M. St. Aubert's death-bed warning to her, "do not indulge in the pride of fine feeling" or "ill-governed sensibility," which is dangerous to its possessor and to others as well; and it is materialized at the end in the nun Agnes' expostulation to Emily based on her own slip from sentiment into sexual passion. In general, however, Radcliffe contrasts Emily's gentle sentiments in Udolpho with the "fierce and terrible passions . . . which so often agitated the inhabitants of this edifice," "those mysterious workings, that rouse the elements of man's nature into tempest." Emily's, she assures us,

> was a silent anguish, weeping, yet enduring; not the *wild energy of passion, inflaming imagination, bearing down the barriers of reason and living in a world of its own* [*The Mysteries of Udolpho*].

The terms I have emphasized are precisely those applied by contemporaries like Burke to the Revolution. The deeply intuitive feelings of Emily are the quiet English virtues of the spectator of sublime overthrow across the Channel; the "wild energy" of Montoni is what Burke associates with the French rabble. Both derive from the sentimental novel, but one is the delicate sensibility of a Toby Shandy or a Harley, the friendship and compassion that can join parental duty, justice, and prudence; the other is the dangerous love of a Clarissa, even the benevolence of a Charles Surface, and the "Jacobin" view that "It is the quality of feeling that sanctifies the marriage; not, as the anti-Jacobins were to have it, the other way around."

Emily is therefore, as Mary Poovey has argued, the susceptible young spectator who *might* be seduced by the real center of energy into becoming another Agnes; and this center of energy, Montoni, is based on a need to dominate that draws on the conventions of both Gothic and revolutionary mythology. There is, in short, a distinction between misperception—believing a General Tilney to be a Montoni, or (to take Blake's contemporary case, in "The

Tyger") a lamb to be a tiger, a gallant French Revolution to be a bloodthirsty uprising or vice versa—and exploitation either of the sensitive soul by others or of others by the sensitive soul expanded until out of control. Emily is obviously the former, but this is because she never allows herself to slip completely out of control, and because Radcliffe has already given us this rebel figure in the male villain, whose motives are unrelievedly bad.

If Radcliffe produces a fiction about a spectator of revolutionary activity who can be confused by her experience, whose response though virtuous is both ambivalent and liable to the temptation to misperceive, then Lewis' *Monk* reproduces the exhilarating but ultimately depressing experience of the revolutionary himself.

I have already rehearsed the trajectory of Ambrosio's explosion of energy. Although this pact with the Devil introduces the Faustus story, it is significant that Ambrosio does not want the intellectual, spiritual, or specifically political power we associate with the Enlightenment. He wants only sexual power. The world of the Enlightenment no longer represented intellectual knowledge; the Revolution had, in Burke's and Lewis' terms, exposed the reality under Enlightenment to be unrestrained sexual "knowledge." Faustus' Mephistopheles becomes Ambrosio's Matilda. It is Ambrosio's desire for her that drags him into the world of Lucifer, and his lust for Antonia that draws him further into the Satanic power. At the same time, Raymond's violent love for Agnes permits the supernatural to penetrate the human world, for it is as he waits to elope with her and consummate his desire that the Bleeding Nun appears to him in her place. In *The Monk* it is the unleashing of repressed sexual desires that shatters the barrier between the natural and supernatural worlds.

Caleb Williams is also a Faustus figure, who describes his "crime" or "offence" as "a mistaken thirst of knowledge." Although he is, unlike Ambrosio, in pursuit of an intellectual goal—knowledge of his master's crime—he describes his obsessive quest in sexual terms. Such words as "pleasures," "pains," "perpetual stimulus," "insatiable desire," "satisfaction," and "gratification"—all directed to the subject of his quest—have sexual resonances. When he realizes that Falkland is the murderer, he says "My blood boiled within me"—as we are told that Ambrosio's "blood boiled in his veins" when he looked upon Rosario-Matilda's bosom. "I was conscious to a kind of rapture for which I could not account," Caleb goes on. "I was solemn, yet full of rapid emotion, burning with indignation and energy." Based on Godwin's brilliant insight into the nature of the servant-master relationship for both parties, Caleb's almost sexual curiosity releases all the darker potentialities of Falkland's inner self, and lays Caleb open to inhuman pursuit and persecution, as well as to the corruption of his own nature.

Man searches for body equivalents for any important, unexplained phenomenon, from unordered nature to economics to revolutions. But there is probably some connection between love and revolution in the political experience itself—or at least in the mind (or vocabulary) of the person who writes about revolution, who is imaginatively recreating the experience. "Revolution is the sex of politics," as H. L. Mencken said. But if at the outset the most common metaphor was of sexual release—whether spring's bursting buds (in Paine's *Rights of Man*) or Blake's Orc breaking his chains and raping his tyrant-captor's daughter—by the end it had become images of parturition, of giving birth to creatures like Victor Frankenstein's, regarded as (depending on the point of view) a victim or a monster.

The plot of *The Monk* can be seen as a version of the revolutionary scenario as far as the Terror; Mary Shelley's *Frankenstein* (1818, the year in which *Northanger Abbey* was finally published) was to some extent a retrospect on the whole process through Waterloo, with the Enlightenment-created monster leaving behind its wake of terror and destruction across France and Europe, partly because it had been disowned and misunderstood and partly because it was created unnaturally by reason rather than love in the instinctive relationships of the Burkean family.

One aspect of Shelley's fable we can see by recalling her remarks, on her elopement journey across France in July 1814, on the swath of devastation cut across France by the Russian troops following Napoleon's retreat from Moscow. The Cossack terror was in some sense the final consequence of Napoleon's—ultimately the French Revolution's, or the French *ancien régime*'s—Frankenstein monster. In this crescendo of destruction can be read an allegory of the French Revolution, the attempt to *re*create man and the disillusionment and terror that followed, not ending until Waterloo in 1815, the year between the Shelleys' two trips to Switzerland.

We also know that Mary Shelley read in 1815 the Abbé Barruel's *Mémoires pour servir à l'histoire du jacobinisme* (1797-98) as well as her mother Mary Wollstonecraft's *Historical and Moral View of the Origin and Progress of the French Revolution* (1794). In the first of these, Barruel uncovered sources of the Revolution in the occult practices of the Freemasons, the *illuminati,* and the Albigensians, Manicheans, and Assassins. Victor Frankenstein initially apprentices himself spiritually to Cornelius Agrippa, Albertus Magnus, and Paracelsus, and he goes off to college at Ingoldstadt. Munich or Heidelberg would have been closer to his home in Geneva, but Ingoldstadt (as Shelley knew from the *Histoire du jacobinisme*) was where Adam Weishaupt, the symbolic archdemon of revolutionary thought, founded the Bavarian *illuminati* in 1776, and from this secret society supposedly grew the French Revolution. The *illuminati* were sworn to further knowledge for the betterment of mankind, no matter what the cost or the means. The words of M. Waldman to Victor could have been Weishaupt's own: "These [Agrippa and Paracelsus] were men to whose indefatigable zeal modern philosophers were indebted for most of the foundations of their knowledge. . . . The labours of men of genius, however erroneously directed, scarcely ever fail in ultimately turning to the solid advantage of mankind."

We can feel the pervasive influence of Barruel, who saw the essence of the *illuminati* and of the Revolution he believed they propagated to be atheism, universal anarchy, and the destruction of property. The three elements of the Frankenstein syndrome are the aim to replace God the creator with man, to destroy the family and its ties, and to destroy property and human life. Barruel offered an extremely symbolic explanation (down to the detection of the Masonic triangle in the guillotine blade, invented by Dr. Guillotine, a Freemason), one that could be called Gothic in its bias toward historical explanations and extreme causality, on devious and secret plotting, and on pseudo-science and occult philosophy.

The reading of her mother's book on "the Origin and Progress" of the Revolution was for Mary Shelley a way of connecting the personal and the public reality of history with Barruel's Gothic fictions of origins. Mary Wollstonecraft, writing about this "revolution, the most important that has ever been recorded in the annals of man," made it very clear that its cruelties were the consequence of the *ancien régime.* From the court's imprisonment of representatives to the assembly, the troops' crushing public demonstrations, and the king's substituting retaliation for justice, she says,

> we may date the commencement of those butcheries, which have brought on that devoted country so many dreadful calamities, by teaching the people to avenge themselves with blood!

The origin of the Revolutionary bloodbath was in the cruelty of the tyrant himself, much as Arthur Young and Godwin had asserted. Percy Shelley offered the same explanation in his preface to *The Revolt of Islam* (1817-18): "Can he who the day before was a trampled slave suddenly become liberal-minded, forbearing, and independent?" And he wrote in his review of *Frankenstein:*

> Treat a person ill, and he will become wicked. Requite affection with scorn:—let one being be selected, for whatever cause, as the refuse of his kind—divide him, a social being, from society, and you impose upon him the irresistible obligations—malevolence and selfishness.

If these texts were the ambience, the immediate experience behind Mary Shelley's writing was the trauma of her giving birth to a dead child in February or March 1815 and the memory of her own birth, which had killed her mother nearly twenty years before in 1797. Birth trauma is one of the central concerns of *Frankenstein,* as it was metaphorically of Wollstonecraft's history of the "Origin and Progress" of the Revolution, and in Mary Shelley the points of view of the parent and child merged.

Private and public life first joined in Mary Wollstonecraft's love affair with Gilbert Imlay (as it had also in Wordsworth's with Annette Vallon), their idyll in Paris during the Revolution, and his betrayal of her at the same time the Revolution itself betrayed her. The result was the commonplace similitude between revolution and sexual love. Wollstonecraft's recovery was through her relationship with Godwin, and this time the offspring was Mary Shelley—in whose birth (the symbolic joining of these two revolutionary spirits) the mother died, leaving Mary with the trauma of seeming rejection by the mother-creator, as well as by the father who held her responsible for the death of his beloved wife. At the age of four she was further rejected by her father when he took Mary Jane Clairmont as his second wife. Now to the guilt of having killed her mother was added the birth and death of her own first child, and the birth in January 1816 of her second (who survived until 1819), not long before the trip to Switzerland, and at a time when she was seeing the French Revolution in its final stage: political reaction following the rejected and rejecting Revolution.

The construction of the monster, as of the makeshift, nonorganic family, is the final aspect of the *Frankenstein* plot. Burke's conception of the state as organic and of the Revolution as a family convulsed was joined by Mary Shelley with the fact of her own "family," the haphazard one in which she grew up with other children of different mothers and with a stepmother. This creation of a family of children by some method other than natural, organic procreation within a single love relationship is projected onto the Frankenstein family, a family assembled by the additive process of adoptions and the like, and so to Victor's own creation of a child without parents or sexual love. The autochthonous family, made up of bits and pieces, a substitute for organic growth, begins with Victor's father and leads to his own putting together of his creature from a variety of different bodies. The construction of the "child" is then followed by its rejection by its "father"; and then by the creature's desire for a proper mate in order to carry on its own line, the "father's" refusal, and the creature-son's systematic destruction of the father's whole family—including his bride (who would have been the mother had there been one).

The conventional tyrannical family (Turkish in this case) is contrasted with the new rational family Frankenstein projects:

> A new species would bless me as its creator and source; many happy and excellent natures would owe their being to me. No father could claim the gratitude of his child so completely as I should deserve theirs.

Frankenstein predictably sees himself as the father who "deserves" the gratitude of his children more "completely" than any other, and in saying so becomes the tyrant himself. As an allegory of the French Revolution, his experiment corresponds to the possibility of ignoring the paternal (and maternal) power by constructing one's own offspring out of sheer reason, but it shows that the creator is still only a "father" and his creation another "son" locked in the same love-tyranny relationship Mary's own father had described so strikingly in *Caleb Williams* (another book Mary had reread as she undertook her novel).

We have by now distinguished two phases of the Revolution, one seen from the point of view of a lover, and the other from the point of view of the child of the union. These are not as distinct as they might at first appear. The first is an Oedipus, or, in Blake's terms, the Orc who becomes a rival to his father; and the second is Electra or Polyneices, the child of the incestuous union, the offspring of the Revolution. It is precisely this juxtaposition (or conflation) of points of view, including the parallel one of the author (expressed again, looking back from the Preface of 1831, when she says, "And now, once again, I bid my hideous progeny go forth and prosper"), that distinguishes Frankenstein as a fictional work.

The description of the creator and his creature looking at each other in turn, and thereafter reporting the same scenes from their respective viewpoints, inevitably evokes the passage in Burke's *Philosophical Enquiry* (1757) in which, as an example of how the sublime operates, Milton's Satan and Death are described as if facing each other, each seeing the other from his own point of view, as mutual challengers. There is, of course, no mother in the case of Frankenstein's creature, and so no Sin of the Satan-Sin-Death paradigm, because Victor thinks he can create out of himself alone (as Satan originally did Sin). But the mutually destructive conflict proves to be over the creature's mate, and the victim is Victor's own mate. As in Burke's example, Sin is the invisible third party standing between the father and son.

The world seen by creator and creature is constructed of the most familiar image patterns of the Revolution, beginning with Barruel's *illuminati.* The word *illuminé* was, of course, radically ambiguous, "used by people in diametrically opposed ways" as reason and as revelation, as right and as wrong, as royal authority and as human liberty. When Victor reads Cornelius Agrippa, he finds that a "new light seemed to dawn upon my mind," and this is the familiar illumination which (in terms similar to Paine's) becomes fire in the thunderstorm that first suggests the idea of how to galvanize inert matter into life:

> on a sudden I beheld a stream of fire issue from an old and beautiful oak, which stood about twenty yards from our house; and so soon as the dazzling light vanished, the oak had disappeared, and nothing remained but a blasted stump. When we visited it the next morning, we found the tree shattered in a singular manner. It was not splintered by the shock, but entirely reduced to thin ribbands of wood. I never beheld any thing so utterly destroyed.

This description of lightning-electricity as both life-giving and utterly destructive, aimed at "an old and beautiful oak," is a final echo of the vocabulary in which Shelley's mother and her opponents (in particular Burke with his British oak) had described the Revolution. The effect is that of the crowd's vengeance in *The Monk,* but the image leads into the Promethean associations of light and fire, benevolence and destruction. (Napoleon was associated with Prometheus by Byron and by his own propaganda machine.)

The creature is born into light, so strong that "I was obliged to shut my eyes," and darkness and light alternate as he closes and opens his eyes. While light allows him to move about and "wander on at liberty," it leads him to seek relief in its opposite: "The light became more and more oppressive to me; and, the heat wearying me as I walked, I sought a place where I could receive shade." His enlightenment-oriented master, we recall, was given to remarking that "Darkness had no effect upon my fancy."

As the creature's eyes become "accustomed to the light" so that he can now "perceive objects in their right forms," he comes upon light in its next higher incarnation, fire:

> I . . . was overcome with delight at the warmth I experienced from it. In my joy I thrust my hand into the live embers, but quickly drew it out again with a cry of pain. How strange, I thought, that the same cause should produce such opposite effects.

Frankenstein's monster runs the gamut of the associations of birth, springtime, and the heat that becomes destructive fire, found in so many of the writings of the Revolution. His birth is described as a kind of emergence into spring, and his progress is to the beautiful spot of the cottagers, from winter to spring, followed by the disastrous confrontation and dispersal of himself and the foster-family he had tried to join. Victor describes his own breakdown following the "birth" of the monster, and then his recovery, in terms of the seasons:

> I perceived that the fallen leaves had disappeared, and that the young buds were shooting forth from the trees that shaded my window. It was a divine spring; and the season contributed greatly to my convalescence. I felt also sentiments of joy and affection revive in my bosom. . . .

The irony is that Victor fails to recognize the connection between his production of the monster and this rebirth and the conventional imagery going back to Paine and Mary Wollstonecraft of the Revolution seen from a positive point of view as the beautiful. Victor sees it instead as the terrible, the sublime, the threatening, and the tragedy of his reaction is that, like Burke, he turns the creature into the sublime destructive force he reads into his aesthetic response to it—when his response presumably should rather have been that of a sensitive parent. What is needed is the beautiful love of a mother, not the sublime fear of a father.

The warmth of spring ends, however, as destructive and then self-destructive fire. The creature tells us that he is going to end his life on a funeral pyre at the North Pole:

> Soon these burning miseries will be extinct. I shall ascend my funeral pile triumphantly, and exult in the agony of the torturing flames. The light of that conflagration will fade away; my ashes will be swept into the sea by the winds. My spirit will sleep in peace. . . .

And having said this, he makes off on his ice raft, and the novel ends: "He was soon borne away by the waves, and lost in darkness and distance"—a final sublime object.

It seems not possible to write about the Revolution and avoid the aesthetic categories first introduced by Burke in his *Reflections.* Victor has made the creature out of beautiful features, but the scale is too large and the juxtapositions ugly—and the whole inspires terror. Thus, as Victor says when he sees the creature for the first time instilled with life: "the beauty of the dream vanished, and breathless horror and disgust filled my heart." And the beautiful cottage, its surrounding scenery, "the perfect forms of my cottagers" (as the creature says), and Safie with her "countenance of angelic beauty and expression," are set against the looming presence of the monster which destroys the *locus amoenus* and disperses this, another family.

Mary Shelley is summing up all we have seen about the

Gothic as a fiction in which to describe the French Revolution. The positive representations of the Revolution tended to stop—insofar as they remained positive and did not move on to the next phase of response—at the burst of sexual energy, which was creation. Beyond that, Paine, Price, Blake, and others suggested a vaguely pastoral life, an ideal of a Golden Age of leisure defended by Godwin and predictably attacked by Malthus, Crabbe, and Burke. The negative, dark side of the Revolution thus not unnaturally tended to fall into the fiction of the Gothic; and this suited Burke's way of thinking in his *Reflections,* for precisely what was being destroyed was the beautiful, passive, feminine, chivalric, pastoral world that is embodied in the maiden fleeing down dimly lit, tortuous corridors, followed by the active, masculine, sublimely aggressive force of the French revolutionaries who threatened the queen and abducted, humiliated, and overthrew her husband, the father of his people, the king. (pp. 532-52)

Ronald Paulson, "Gothic Fiction and the French Revolution," in ELH, *Vol. 48, No. 3, Fall, 1981, pp. 532-54.*

David D. Marcus

[*In the following essay, Marcus addresses Dickens's novel,* A Tale of Two Cities *(1859), and Carlyle's historical account,* The French Revolution *(1837). He asserts that Dickens owed Carlyle a conceptual as well as factual debt, noting that in these works "both writers seek ways in which people can socialize their energies in an age whose institutions seem at odds with any humanly valuable purpose."*]

A Tale of Two Cities is the most disparaged and least understood of Dickens's late novels. Overwhelmingly, the critics have judged the work a failure and dismissed it as intellectually superficial. According to this view, Dickens held only the most simpleminded view of history, and although the novel fictionalizes events whose memory haunted the Victorian era, it never places those events in the context of a coherent understanding of the processes of social change; the book is an amalgam of romantic melodrama based on Dickens's experience as an actor in Wilkie Collins's *Frozen Deep* and fragments taken from Carlyle's *French Revolution,* a work from which Dickens unsystematically borrowed details but not any conceptual framework. Thus understood, the novel splits in two; its connection between romance and the French Revolution seems tenuous and contrived. As George Lukács complains [in his *Historical Novel,* 1969], "neither the fate of Manette and his daughter, nor of Darnay-Evrémonde, and least of all of Sidney Carton, grows organically out of the age and its social events." Taylor Stoehr's very different approach to the novel [in his *Dickens: The Dreamer's Stance,* 1765] also admits this split by disregarding Dickens's political ideas and interpreting the historical events as a ritual expiation through violence for the sexual violation that is the original cause of the action.

But in fact, the two plots are closely related, and that relationship points toward a much more complex vision of history than criticism has so far allowed. My discussion of this relationship will also suggest that Dickens's conceptual debt to Carlyle is much greater than recent criticism has recognized. Dickens and Carlyle share a common quest that informs the historical vision of *A Tale of Two Cities:* both writers seek ways in which people can socialize their energies in an age whose institutions seem at odds with any humanly valuable purpose. Dickens's exploration of revolutionary France resembles Teufelsdröckh's spiritual pilgrimage in *Sartor Resartus* and the exhortatory social criticism of *Past and Present* in the connection that it draws between the social and the psychic dimensions of historical crisis; the humane man finds himself caught in the mechanism of historical processes that move according to their own laws and that destroy any possibility of useful action. It is precisely this tie between the social and the psychic that unites the romantic and revolutionary plots of *A Tale of Two Cities.*

As Robert Alter has noted [in his "The Demons of History in Dickens' Tale," in *Novel: A Forum on Fiction* 2 (1969)] of the novel's French episodes, they are "intended to dramatize the ways in which human beings become the slaves of impersonal forces, at last are made inhuman by them." But the English as well as the French episodes deal with the problem of historical dehumanization. At the end of the novel, Darnay and Dr. Manette retreat into the tranquillity of a secluded domestic circle, and that retreat has to be seen in the light of their failure as public men to influence the course of events. Thus their retreat and the quasi-religious redemption through love and self-sacrifice are actually strategies for coping with the characters' need to find a sense of fruitful relatedness in the face of the impossibility of solving social problems. For Dickens, the family and religion serve much the same function as religion and the corporate spirit did for Carlyle: they are means of humanizing the void left in the individual life by mechanistic social institutions.

In describing the relationship between Carlyle and Dickens, I am emphasizing the social and secular sides of Carlyle's works and his role as the interpreter of the Romantic tradition to Victorian England. In commenting on Carlyle's phrase "natural supernaturalism," M. H. Abrams has said of the Romantic era that "the general tendency was, in diverse degrees and ways to naturalize the supernatural and to humanize the divine." Certainly this description applies to Carlyle himself; for all of his explicitly religious interpretation of experience, the end result even in *Sartor Resartus* is a reorientation of the individual that allows him to experience a sense of purpose in his work. As George Levine has pointed out [in his *Boundaries of Fiction: Carlyle, Macaulay, Newman,* 1968], Carlyle's contemporaries as well as many later readers saw Teufelsdröckh's spiritual pilgrimage as a call for "a moral and social as well as a religious revolution." Whether Carlyle is historically the only source of Dickens's efforts at dealing with the problem of the individual's relationship to his culture is not strictly demonstrable, although Dickens's own sense of himself as a disciple of Carlyle's certainly lends an air of plausibility to such speculation. But Carlyle did crystallize these problems for his age, and both men saw the crisis of their culture in similar terms. Thus Carlyle provides at the very least a useful model for understanding Dickens, and for seeing Dickens as the heir to the

Romantic era's tendency to internalize historical phenomena. Like Carlyle and the Romantic poets, Dickens is concerned with defining the possibilities for self-fulfillment in a society whose institutions seem inimical to all that is distinctively human.

From the beginning of *A Tale of Two Cities,* Dickens concentrates on the difficulty of understanding public events for those immersed in them. The famous opening paragraph presents the reader with a series of neat antitheses that in sum offer confusion rather than clarity:

> It was the best of times, it was the worst of times, it was the age of wisdom, it was the age of foolishness, it was the age of belief, it was the epoch of incredulity, it was the season of Light, it was the season of Darkness, it was the spring of hope, it was the winter of despair, we had everything before us, we had nothing before us, we were all going direct to Heaven, we were all going direct the other way—in short, the period was so far like the present period, that some of its noisiest authorities insisted on its being received, for good or for evil, in the superlative degree of comparison only.

At first, this passage seems to be a direct authorial commentary, but the attribution of these extreme opinions to some of the age's "noisiest authorities" invites us to question whether the noisiest and most extreme authorities of any age are to be trusted. The patterned rhetoric of the passage reveals confusion rather than understanding. The difficulties of reaching any clear knowledge of one's own era emerge through the novelist's explicit comparison of the past to the present and through the irony that both history and the novelist lend to the eighteenth-century's view of itself: "In both countries [England and France] it was clearer than crystal to the lords of the State preserves of loaves and fishes, that things in general were settled for ever." As Dickens points out immediately afterwards, the year is 1775, and with both the American and French Revolutions impending, things in general are anything but settled forever. As the novel's first paragraph makes clear, both the age's noisiest authorities and its powers that be are unaware of the significance of the historical forces that are shaping the future.

Only in retrospect do events assume a clear order. The novel's French episodes invite the reader to view every incident in the light of his historical knowledge and to recognize events as pieces in a larger pattern that is known a priori. All of the French action appears first as a foreshadowing and later as a realization of the Revolution, and Dickens eschews subtlety in favor of a directness that always keeps before the reader the relationship of each action to larger historical forces. Thus the opening French scene with its broken wine cask flooding the street suggests in its sacramental overtones the blood that will one day flow in the streets; but Dickens is not content to leave matters at the level of suggestion: "The time was to come, when that wine too would be spilled on the street-stones, and when the stain of it would be red upon many there." Taylor Stoehr's rhetorical analysis of this and succeeding French episodes very thoroughly points out the linguistic methods through which Dickens creates a strong sense of the links among all of these events. Even the novel's web of closely interrelated characters is only a transformation of French historical forces into personal terms.

Similarly, the French characters have no individuality but exist only to play their roles in the revolutionary drama. They are defined exclusively in terms of their class. Our first glimpse of the Marquis is at a reception at which he is singled out only after a very Carlylean critique of a degenerate aristocracy whose only function has become self-aggrandizement: "Military officers destitute of military knowledge; naval officers with no idea of a ship; civil officers without a notion of affairs; brazen ecclesiastics, of the worst world worldly . . . all totally unfit for their several callings, all lying horribly in pretending to belong to them, but all nearly or remotely of the order of Monseigneur, and therefore foisted on all public employments. . . . " Although the Marquis is out of Monseigneur's favor, he is nevertheless the perfect aristocrat: he can respond to others only in terms of their class and recognizes no common bonds of humanity. His carriage kills a child, and he can see the event only in terms of his contempt for the poor: "I would ride over any of you very willingly, and exterminate you from the earth." To his nephew Charles Darnay, he laments the deterioration of the power of the aristocracy: "Our not remote ancestors held the right of life and death over the surrounding vulgar." The Marquis despises Darnay for his humane feelings. And of course, there are the events related in Dr. Manette's prison diary in which the Marquis and his brother destroy a peasant family in order to exercise their *droit du seigneur.*

If the French Revolution is a form of retribution for such distortions of humanity, it is also paradoxically a continuation of them; the new order merely perpetuates the dehumanizing class-consciousness of the old. Just as the Marquis and the society he represents were trapped within a system that allowed them to perceive others only in terms of their position within the social system, so too are the revolutionaries trapped within their own inversion of that system. Charles Darnay's journey into France most clearly dramatizes how little the overthrow of the old institutions has changed the premises behind French society's judgments of human beings. As he prepares to leave England, Darnay comforts himself with the belief that his renunciation of his social position and his efforts to assist his impoverished tenants will protect him; but the reader, who has seen the condemnation of the Evrémonde race by Defarge and his fellow conspirators, recognizes that Darnay's very reasonable point of view is a misunderstanding, a projection of his own humanity into a very inhumane situation. To the new order, Darnay can be nothing more than the representative of a doomed aristocratic family.

One's position as a citizen subsumes all other ties, and revolutionary France has as little respect as the late Marquis for the feelings that bind families together. Dr. Manette's belief that his suffering now has value as a means of saving his son-in-law from the guillotine proves an illusion; the Revolution is unconcerned with the purely personal. The populace has revived the "questionable public virtues of antiquity," so that the President of the court that is about to condemn Darnay draws cheers from the crowd by telling Dr. Manette "that the good physician of the Republic would deserve better still of the Republic by rooting out an obnoxious family of Aristocrats, and would doubtless feel a sacred glow and joy in making his daughter a widow and her child an orphan. . . ." Madame Defarge plots to destroy the remaining members of the Evrémonde family—Lucie, her child, and Dr. Manette—by using their human feelings against them; she is going to accuse them of grieving for Darnay, and in revolutionary France even grief is subject to legal regulation: mourning for a victim of the guillotine is itself a capital offense.

Dickens emphasizes the inhumanity of the French Revolution not merely for sentimental reasons but as a means of distinguishing social upheaval from substantive change. On the one hand, social upheaval comes about as the inevitable result of oppression and exploitation. As the tumbrils roll through the streets of Paris toward the guillotine, Dickens gives a direct warning: "Crush humanity out of shape once more, under similar hammers, and it will twist itself into the same tortured forms." On the other hand, substantive change can occur only when people discard the "mind-forg'd manacles" within which they are trapped, the state of mind that remains long after the external exploiters and oppressors have been destroyed. Of course, such change can occur only within the individual, but that is not to say that Dickens is naive: for if the true instrument of oppression is a state of mind, what possible institutional solution is there? Dickens's lack of faith in political action and the inward direction of his social criticism is more than the Victorian fear of revolution. He is the heir to the inward turning that took place in Wordsworth and Coleridge in the wake of the failure of their faith in the French Revolution. As Carlyle counseled his readers in *Past and Present.*

> It were infinitely handier if we had a Morrison's Pill, Act of Parliament, or remedial measure, which men could swallow, one good time, and then go on in their old courses, cleared from all miseries and mischiefs! Unluckily we have none such; unluckily the Heavens themselves, in their rich pharmacopoeia, contain none such. There will no "thing" be done that will cure you. There will a radical universal alteration of your regimen and way of life take place; there will a most agonising divorce between you and your chimeras, luxuries and falsities, take place . . . that so the inner fountains of life may again begin, like eternal Light-fountains, to irradiate and purify your bloated, swollen, foul existence, drawing nigh, as at present, to nameless death.

Without such an inner transformation, the new order in France can only perpetuate the old oppression by continuing the inherited class-based assumptions about what human beings are. For Dickens, revolution is institutional, but change is psychic.

The religious transformation that takes place within Sidney Carton illustrates both this concern for the inner life of the individual as the only possible means of change and Dickens's use of religious motifs as a way of talking about that inner life. As Carton stands at the guillotine ready to die, he has, according to the observers that Dickens places at the scene, "the peacefullest man's face ever beheld there." He is in the grip of a prophetic vision, one that even offers him a form of redemption through Lucie's as yet unborn child: "I see that child who lay upon her bosom and who bore my name, a man winning his way up in that path of life which once was mine. I see him winning it so well, that my name is made illustrious there by the light of his. I see the blots I threw upon it, faded away." But Carton's vision secularizes the religious theme of immortality by substituting the continuity of generations for religious mystery. There is no suggestion that he will survive in any other sense; he refers to his coming death as a "far, far better rest . . . than I have ever known." Carton's vision simply asserts the newfound sense of relatedness that has led him to sacrifice his life; he now feels himself linked by human ties to a future that he will not personally see. He is no longer the "disappointed drudge" who cares for no one and is cared for by no one. The spirit of optimism in his prophecy arises not out of a faith in God but from a faith in the best that men can become.

The novel's religious symbols follow this pattern: they reflect human attitudes and actions within social boundaries rather than a teleology. Dickens strips religion of any necessary connection with God so that it becomes simply the human potential for good or ill, for the loving self-sacrifice of a Sidney Carton or the indiscriminate destruction of the French revolutionaries. Religious feeling at its best now functions as a basis for human community, a way in which men can reach beyond themselves, experience a sense of fruitful relatedness, and grow beyond the loneliness that many other Victorian writers—Marx, Mill, Arnold, and especially Carlyle—describe as a universal malady of their age. But Dickens recognizes that this positive relatedness is only one possible recasting of Christianity in human terms. The fury of the Carmagnole—"a something once innocent, delivered over to all devilry"—is another form of community; the Cross can also be transformed into the guillotine: "It was the sign of the regeneration of the human race. It superseded the Cross. Models of it were worn on breasts from which the Cross was discarded, and it was bowed down to and believed in where the Cross was denied." In popular mythology, the French now worship St. Guillotine "for the great sharp female was by that time popularly canonised." Thus in France, the redefinition of religious faith precludes those human values that have been traditionally associated with Christianity. As an enraged mob finally hangs the hated Foulon on a lamppost after repeated failure, the author remarks "then, the rope was merciful," a pointed reminder of the virtue that is lacking in the mob.

Similarly, as Robert Alter points out, the four incendiaries who burn the Marquis' chateau suggest the four horsemen of the apocalypse. We do not, however, have the biblical apocalypse, but a fear that the death of the old order may also be a foreshadowing of the death of all order. The one incendiary Dickens describes at length appears in the midst of a barren, unproductive landscape and is ominously portrayed as "a shaggy-haired man, of almost barbarian aspect." As he sleeps, the reader comes to see him through the eyes of the road-mender who is the sole observer within the scene:

> Stooping down beside him, the road-mender tried to get a peep at secret weapons in his breast or where not; but, in vain, for he slept with his arms crossed upon him, and set as resolutely as his lips. Fortified towns with their stockades, guard-houses, gates, trenches, and drawbridges, seemed to the mender of roads, to be so much air as against this figure. And when he lifted his eyes from it to the horizon and looked around, he saw in his small fancy similar figures, stopped by no obstacle, tending to centres all over France.

In each sentence, Dickens reminds us that this vision of destruction is taking place within the mind of the road-mender. Apocalypse thus acquires a social meaning in two ways: it figures the widespread devastation that actually takes place within France, but it also conveys the consciousness of that devastation, the disappearance of any faith in the stability of things. Historically and psychically, the symbolism of apocalypse is, like the symbolism of the guillotine, an inversion of tradition that leaves only the horror with none of the hope.

English society, by contrast, does offer some hope, although of a very limited sort. Dickens creates a number of similarities between Britain and France, similarities that undermine any self-satisfied confidence in the inherent superiority of British institutions and attitudes. England has no special historical foresight as the references to the American Revolution in the opening chapter and at Darnay's trial make clear. Dickens also suggests that the English have a potential for violence very like that of the French. He labels the crowd at Darnay's English trial "ogreish" in its interest. And the spectator who describes "with a relish" the gruesome penalty for high treason is as much the connoisseur of death as Jacques Three who contemplates "like an epicure" his vision of Lucie and her daughter in the hands of the executioner. The mob that turns the supposed funeral of John Barsad, the spy, into a near riot palely but surely echoes the grotesque French mobs that dance wildly through the streets of Paris. And like both the French monarchy and the revolutionaries who succeed it, the English law indiscriminately employs the services of the executioner who can be seen "to-day taking the life of an atrocious murderer, and to-morrow of a wretched pilferer who had robbed a farmer's boy of six-pence."

But in England, unlike France, it is impossible to see all events as parts of a pattern. Much to everyone's surprise, Charles Darnay is acquitted in England. Moreover, there is a disjunction between public and private life. Despite his assurances that he is "a mere machine" in the service of Tellson's, Mr. Lorry does develop an emotionally rich personal existence through his acquaintance with the Manette family. In contrast to the French scenes that show the relationships of people to one another and to the events around them as controlled by the pattern of French history, the early English scenes emphasize the uncertainty of both the reader's and the character's perceptions and how little the characters know of one another. As Mr.

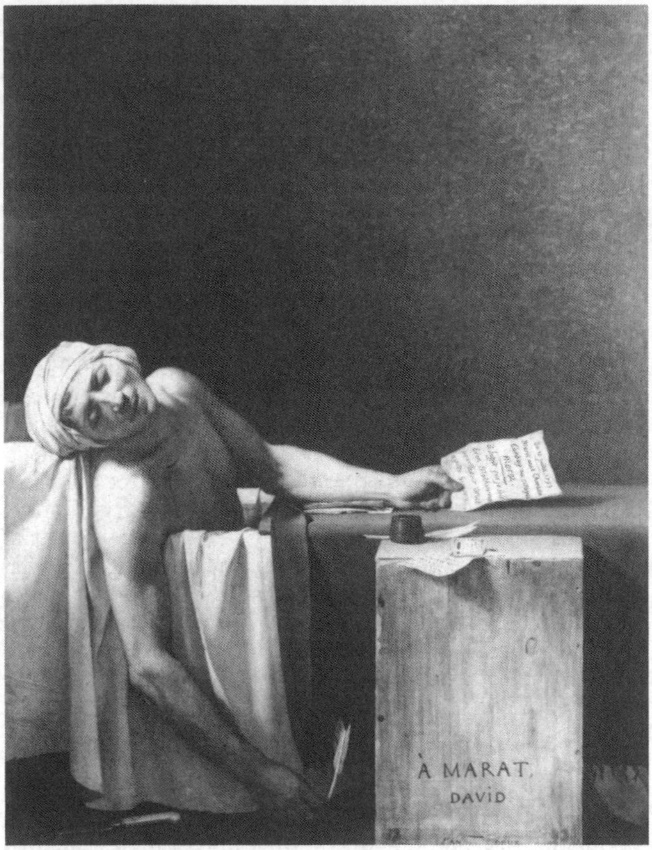

Jacques-Louis David's 1793 painting of Jean-Paul Marat's murder in the bathtub at the hands of Charlotte Corday.

Lorry rides toward Dover, Dickens tells us that the coach "was in its usual genial position that the guard suspected the passengers, the passengers suspected one another and the guard, they all suspected everybody else, and the coachman was sure of nothing but the horses. . . ." The passengers keep themselves so separated from one another that at Darnay's English trial, Mr. Lorry is unable to say—and indeed we never learn—whether Darnay was in the coach. As Jerry Cruncher returns to London bearing Mr. Lorry's cryptic message, the narrator meditates on human isolation and concludes with a rhetorical question: "In any of the burial-places of this city through which I pass, is there a sleeper more inscrutable than its busy inhabitants are, in their innermost personality, to me, or than I am to them?" In England, there are limitations on one's ability to perceive, and in sharp contrast to France, the reader is no longer able to place data in context, to see the coherence of events.

Dickens treats this secrecy that shrouds every individual with characteristic ambivalence. The early coach scenes portray a social atmosphere of constant distrust and fragmentation; as Dickens tells us, "the highwayman in the dark was a City tradesman in the light. . . ." The example of Jerry Cruncher makes abundantly clear that one's private existence is not necessarily a haven in which domestic virtue flourishes. Moreover, the narrator's commentary on the inability of people to know one another implies a loneliness that is developed more fully in the portrait of Sidney Carton. But for all these limitations, the possibility of a private identity has the great advantage of making England a culture in which personality can be multidimensional, in which the publicly visible self is but one part.

In such a society, the individual can think of himself and others in a variety of contradictory terms, and this process of conflict allows the individual to change. This most clearly takes place in the tensions that beset Dr. Manette. At his first appearance in the novel, he is a man completely stripped of his identity by the ordeal of his imprisonment; he works quietly at his shoemaking and passively submits to others. But after a period in England, another side of his personality dominates, a side that completely reverses the passivity of the prisoner: "He was now a very energetic man indeed, with great firmness of purpose, strength of resolution, and vigour of action." This reversal of his personality does not mean that he has escaped the past, for he continues to bear the prisoner within him. At crucial moments, he reverts or attempts to revert to his shoemaking: when he suspects Darnay's true identity, when he finally learns it, and when he ultimately feels himself responsible for Darnay's condemnation by the revolutionary tribunal. Doctor Manette is able to accept Darnay and to recover from his ordeal because he thinks of himself not only as the wronged prisoner but as Lucie's father. As Darnay hints of his actual descent, the doctor responds that if there are "any fancies, any reasons, any apprehensions, anything whatsoever, new or old, against the man she really loved—the direct responsibility thereof not lying on his head—they should all be obliterated for her sake." As the doctor's final relapse makes clear, that obliteration is an incomplete process, but he is able to achieve a new inner balance in which the old wrongs are outweighed by his love for his daughter.

Such change has effects that are felt only within the sphere of immediate relationships. It is not the result of dedication to great causes but of following the injunction that Carlyle borrowed from Goethe: *"Do the Duty which lies nearest thee."* Thus Sidney Carton finds a sense of purposefulness through his devotion to Lucie to whom he has said "For you, and for any dear to you, I would do anything." Like Dr. Manette, Carton exemplifies the contradictory possibilities inherent in human nature. He has told Darnay after the courtroom scene of his sense of emotional isolation, and he tells Lucie, "I am like one who died young. All my life might have been." But as he walks through Paris with his mind set on sacrificing himself to help Lucie and her family, a sense of relatedness returns;

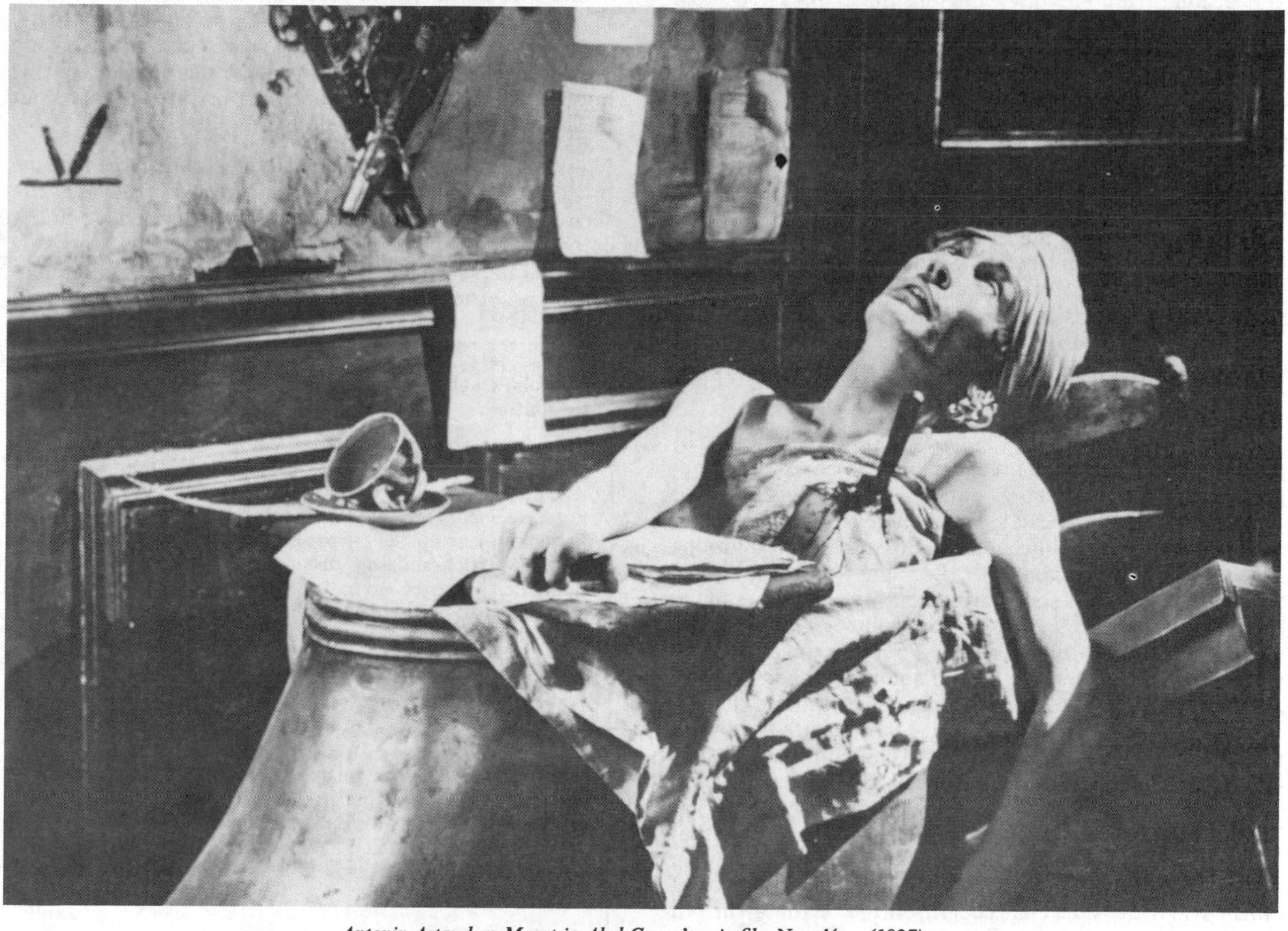

Antonin Artaud as Marat in Abel Gance's epic film Napoléon *(1927).*

he remembers his father's funeral, and the words of the burial service pass through his mind. And his changed state appears to the very last not only in the dramatic act of dying in the place of another but also in the kindness that he displays toward the seamstress who precedes him to the guillotine. Carton's love for Lucie has aroused the sympathetic capacity within his nature, and by caring for another, he finally emerges from the self-imposed prison of indifference. He is finally able to respond to those around him.

Clearly Dickens is not giving us any formula for the regeneration of the human race; the most radical effect that individual change brings about is reconciliation within families. This emphasis on intimate relationships does imply a view of society, but that view is largely negative: the individual must not be excessively burdened by his social identity, he must have room to develop with the contradictory fullness that is distinctively human. But even within a culture that offers that possibility, society does not offer any encouragement to the best human impulses. If Doctor Manette is recalled to life from the grave of his imprisonment, John Barsad parodies that same theme in his mock funeral and reappearance in France as precisely what he has always been, a spy. If Charles Darnay uses the freedom from the past that England offers him to make a new and productive life, Sidney Carton, the character who so uncannily resembles Darnay, is too paralyzed to realize either his emotional or professional capabilities except in his final self-sacrifice. The love of Lucie Manette acts as a regenerative force, but not all women have that power. Miss Pross maintains an unquestioning loyalty to her brother, a loyalty that has no effect other than relieving her of all her property, and Jerry Cruncher remains through most of the book insensible to his wife's prayers. Lucie is clearly a force for the good, but the French episodes, with their portrait of the bloodthirsty Madame Defarge and her companions, effectively undercut any notion that Dickens uncritically idealizes women as moral forces. In *A Tale of Two Cities,* no external circumstance can do more than create an atmosphere in which change is possible; the individual's readiness is all.

A Tale of Two Cities does not pose domesticity and religion as remedies for the great social problems of the nineteenth century; at most, Dickens's versions of faith and family offer the individual some refuge from the void left by the futility of public action. For whatever solutions Dickens offers are given with the same awareness that is the basis of Carlyle's social criticism: the old clothes of society—its beliefs, its institutions, its politics—are worn out and no longer fill human needs. Thus the novel's tale of private romance becomes a confession of public despair. At the end of the book, the characters retreat into domesticity only after both Darnay and Dr. Manette have tried to influence the course of public events and have clearly failed. Institutions seem impervious to human effort: good men waste their lives if they engage in activism. What Dickens can do on a miniature scale—redefine traditional institutions so that a small group can be based on human values—he cannot do for his culture. Like the author of *Sartor Resartus,* Dickens recognized the death of the old world but could not visualize the birth of a new.

Certainly as so many critics have claimed, this novel leaves the reader dissatisfied, and part of that dissatisfaction is rooted in Dickens's tendency toward facile moralizing. But the novel also deliberately engenders dissatisfaction through its presentation of the extreme disparity between public and private life. Institutions exist not only as social mechanisms but also through the states of mind they create within their culture, and to destroy the mechanisms cannot in itself bring about substantive change. The old order in France had created a society of unidimensional men who in the overthrow of the past could not break away from the enslaving spirit of their history. The French Revolution abolishes the monarchy, abolishes the aristocracy, abolishes the financial exploiters, but in its perverse way, it embodies the values of these traditional oppressors.

The malaise that Dickens sees in the French Revolution is characteristic of his anatomy of society in his late novels. *A Tale of Two Cities* presents in its most extreme form the same inability to translate private virtue into public action that in other novels plagues English society; the Circumlocution Office in *Little Dorrit* and the Court of Chancery in *Bleak House* poison the will of Englishmen. These institutions work according to their own internal logic and not to fulfill any human need, and as Daniel Doyce and Richard Carstone learn, they dehumanize anyone who comes into contact with them. Such institutions respond to nothing outside of themselves. It is better, Dickens says, to retreat into a sphere of a few close relationships where action becomes meaningful, to make one's garden grow; but whatever hope Dickens offers for private life grows out of an acceptance of social despair.

Unlike Dickens, Carlyle seems to offer some hope that the process by which men change themselves and dedicate their energies to the fulfillment of their immediate duties can perhaps in the long run transform society. It is likely that this hope struck a responsive note in his contemporaries and brought Carlyle to the height of his popularity

Malcolm Cook on propagandistic fiction of the French Revolution:

Critics of the literature of the revolutionary period have, to say the least, been disparaging. The French Revolution may not have encouraged works of literary quality, but it did use fictional forms for the purposes of propaganda, and this in itself is worth examining. Just as the moral literature which flourished in the second half of the eighteenth century needed to persuade its readers of the truth of the edifying message, so the aim of political works was to convince. Many writers appeared to choose fictional forms as the most effective method of persuasion. At the same time, it was vital that the reader should not simply reject works of a fictional nature as pure fiction. When a character in a novel was known to have existed in reality, the reader had to be prepared to accept the account as possibly true. It is then that two worlds, the real and the fictional, are balanced and modified to promote a particular view.

Malcolm C. Cook, in Studies on Voltaire and the Eighteenth Century, *1982.*

in the late 1830s and the 1840s. It is also probably the extinction of that hope that brought to the fore Carlyle's more authoritarian tendencies and that to some degree alienated him from a part of his audience. But the differences between Carlyle and Dickens should not obscure the basic similarity of their outlooks: both writers believe that man's self-realization can occur only in a social context and yet that contact with society is inherently destructive. Like Wordsworth and Coleridge in the aftermath of the French Revolution, both Carlyle and Dickens are seeking a means by which people can experience a sense of purposeful action in a society whose institutions are devoid of all human purpose and whose populace has come to reflect that inhumanity. (pp. 56-67)

David D. Marcus, "The Carlylean Vision of 'A Tale of Two Cities'," in Studies on the Novel, *Vol. 8, No. 1, Spring, 1976, pp. 56-68.*

Lee Sterrenburg

[*In the following essay, Sterrenburg examines Mary Shelley's* Last Man, *characterizing the novel as one of several post-Revolutionary works sharing apocalyptic themes.*]

> There never was a vaster project conceived in the interests of civilisation with more generous intent or one that came closer to realisation. And here is the remarkable thing: the obstacles that made me fail did not come from men; they all came from the elements. In the south, the sea has been my undoing; in the north, the burning of Moscow and the cold of winter. Thus water, air, and fire, all of Nature, nothing but Nature—these have been the enemies of a universal regeneration which Nature herself demanded! The problems of Providence are insoluble.—Napoleon Bonaparte in *Conversation with Las Cases* (1816)

Between the fall of the Bastille in 1789 and the July Days Revolution of 1830, nature and revolution were allied to one another in at least three distinctly different ways. The second two are clearly Romantic. The first is the almost Rousseauian faith of the French revolutionaries that nature was on their side. If the old regime represented corrupt society in decline, then the revolution represented the restorative forces of nature. The latter, if properly pursued, could revitalize the former. The revolutionaries of the early 1790's regarded nature as a helpful, benevolent ally who, in Napoleon's later phrase, had demanded a "universal regeneration" in the political realm. Perhaps the greatest monument to this faith in nature is the republican calendar of 1793. The social millennium of the Year 1 is marked by the beginning of a new season. The new calendar commences on what had formerly been 22 September, the day of the autumnal equinox and also the day upon which the monarchy was officially abolished. The republican calendar begins in fall—thus commemorating the fall of the monarchy—and goes on through to the fruition of late summer. The renamed months of the calendar imply a corollary between nature and revolution, moving as they do from *Vendémiaire* through *Fructidor,* or, in English, through the months of Vintage, Fog, Sleet, Snow, Rain, Wind, Budding, Flower, Pasture, Heat, Harvest, and Fruit. The regeneration of nature and society are one. As the Chartist writer James Bronterre O'Brien later remarked of the early 1790's, "nature appeared just then to conspire with politics, in giving *eclat* to the new Revolutionary æra."

This utopian optimism did not last long. It was soon superseded by a second attitude toward nature which M. H. Abrams, in *Natural Supernaturalism,* describes as the preeminently Romantic one. In this Romantic phase, nature often replaces politics and offers a haven from the struggles of the Jacobin Revolution. After the Reign of Terror and the official reactionism of Thermidor, the Romantic poets in England had lost faith in the Revolution. As Abrams points out, they renounced their former utopian and revolutionary aspirations and turned instead to nature. Abrams documents at length how the generation of Wordsworth and Friedrich Hölderlin, beginning in the mid-1790's, sought out the beauties of nature as an antidote for post-revolutionary despair. A typical passage from revolution to nature appears in Hölderlin's *Hyperion,* which was published in two parts in 1797 and 1799. Hölderlin's protagonist steeps himself in utopian hopes and plunges into a revolution against the despotic Turks. But his millennial hopes are shattered when his own revolutionary troops run wild and instigate a reign of murder, plunder, and general terror. Hyperion abandons all hope for a political utopia. He succumbs to apathy and despair. But then he recovers through the regenerative forces of nature. As Abrams observes, Hyperion metaphorically enters "into a union with nature as a bride" and thereby compensates for his dashed revolutionary hopes.

Nature was also associated with revolution in a third, more pessimistic way. In some writings, visions of utopian social reform simply gave way to premonitions of apocalyptic annihilation. Throughout Augustan and Romantic literature there had long been a concern with catastrophes, the ruins of empire, and the collapse of civilizations. These decline-and-fall themes took on a new resonance and intensity after the defeat of the Napoleonic Empire in 1815. Napoleon's complaint that he was defeated in Russia by nature—water, air, and fire—anticipates the growing pessimism over the prospects of politics and empire. Far from demanding a universal regeneration in the realm of politics, nature now seemed to be conspiring to destroy all of civilization through such catastrophic agencies as fire, storm, flood, earthquake, or epidemic. Nature was no longer a refuge; if she was a bride, she was a destructive one. George Steiner [in his *In Bluebeard's Castle: Some Notes towards the Redefinition of Culture,* 1971] aptly describes this revival of apocalyptic themes in art: "An odd school of painting develops: picture of London, Paris, or Berlin seen as colossal ruins, famous landmarks burnt, eviscerated, or located in a weird emptiness among charred stumps and dead water."

Mary Shelley contributed to this apocalyptic milieu when she published *The Last Man* in 1826, a novel about the advent of a great plague which exterminates the human race at the end of the twenty-first century. Her disaster novel can be placed among a number of other post-Napoleonic works of literature and painting which shared analogous themes of the end of the race or the end of empire. The theme of the end of the human race appeared in such works as Lord Byron's poem "Darkness" (1816), Thomas Campbell's poem "The Last Man" (1823), Thomas Lovell Beddoes's fragmentary play *The Last Man,* (1823–25), and Thomas Hood's poem "The Last Man" (1826). The end-of-empire theme surfaced in such works as Alfred Tennyson's early poems "Lamentations of the Peruvians" (1827), "Babylon" (1827), and "Timbuctoo" (1829); in many of John Martin's paintings, including *The Fall of Babylon* (1819) and *The Fall of Nineveh* (1828); and in Thomas Cole's series of paintings *The Course of Empire* (1834–36), which concluded with *The Destruction of Empire* and *The Desolation of Empire.* Of all these disaster visions, Mary Shelley's *The Last Man* is probably the most expansive in its allusions to political writings and events from the era of the French Revolution, the Napoleonic Empire, and the Greek revolution against the Turks during the 1820's. Indeed, the political emphasis of Mary Shelley's novel would seem to support Steiner's contention that the characteristic "counterdream" of apocalyptic violence in nineteenth- and twentieth-century art dates back to the collapse of revolutionary hopes in the years after 1815.

Since it first appeared in 1826, reviewers and critics have often sought out the autobiographical meanings of Mary Shelley's disaster novel. The work has been described as a dispirited postmortem on Percy Shelley and Lord Byron, both of whom died in the early 1820's. The two deceased poets appear in the novel, thinly disguised, as Adrian, Earl of Windsor, and Lord Raymond. Both characters perish in the course of the story. They do so in a manner recalling the deaths of their real-life counterparts. Like Percy Shelley, Adrian drowns at sea; like Lord Byron, Lord Raymond dies while attempting to aid a Greek revolution against the Turks. The novel, in fact, is so obviously a *roman à clef* that critics sometimes tend to see it as little else. One early reviewer, citing Mary Shelley's personal involvement in her story, snidely asked why she did not write a novel about being *"the last Woman"* because then "she would have known better how to paint her distress at having nobody left to talk to." This line of reasoning does have its merits. But I shall follow another course and stress the political ramifications of Mary Shelley's apocalyptic vision.

Mary Shelley does more in *The Last Man* than memorialize the personalities of Percy Shelley and Lord Byron. Her novel is intellectually ambitious. Formally, it combines confession and anatomy. In part, the novel is an anatomy or encyclopedic survey of a number of political positions, including utopianism, Bonapartism, and revolutionary enthusiasms of various kinds. *The Last Man* deals with politics, but ultimately it is an antipolitical novel. The characters in the novel discuss and try to enact various reforming and revolutionary solutions, but all such endeavors prove to be a failure in Mary Shelley's pessimistic and apocalyptic world of the future.

The antipolitical import of *The Last Man* might not fully reveal itself, however, until we look seriously at Mary Shelley's disease metaphors. Mary Shelley often engages political issues on the level of metaphor. She works dialectically, adapting old metaphors to new ends. In *Frankenstein* (1818), she grapples with the conflicting heritages of William Godwin, Mary Wollstonecraft, and Edmund Burke by recasting a familiar political metaphor, the parricidal monster who destroys his own creator. She does something analogous to this in *The Last Man.* She takes up a set of nature metaphors—diseases and plagues—which previous writers had used as hopeful symbols of the revolutionary process. She reinterprets those symbols in a pessimistic and apocalyptic way and, in so doing, rejects the meliorative political views of her parents' generation.

Writers who conceive of revolution as a disease are sometimes the heirs of eighteenth-century universalism. They regard the enthusiasm of rebels as a passing fever. They know, from their lofty historical vantage point, that it has all happened before and will probably all happen again, like the periodical eruptions of a disease. It is expected that society will recover from its revolutions, just as natural organisms recover from sickness and fevers. Politically, the disease metaphor has been a favorite among those who do not wish to embrace a total or permanent theory of revolution. Some writers are quite self-conscious about this when they symbolize revolution as a disease. For a useful modern example of the disease metaphor, we can turn to Crane Brinton's *The Anatomy of Revolution* (1938), an encyclopedic survey or "anatomy" of the revolutionary process. Brinton presents a wide historical overview, and he fills out his taxonomy with examples from the English, American, French, and Russian revolutions. But the metaphor is central. As Brinton notes, "the distinction between a conceptual scheme and a metaphor is still an uncertain one."

What I wish to emphasize is how Brinton's disease metaphor resembles earlier Enlightenment models dating from the 1790's. Brinton's anatomy of revolution is a useful articulation of the kinds of assumptions to which Mary Shelley was also heir. He writes in his introduction:

> We shall regard revolutions as a kind of fever. The outlines of our fever chart work out readily enough. In the society during the generation or so before the outbreak of revolution, in the old regime, there will be found signs of the coming disturbance. . . . Then comes a time when the full symptoms disclose themselves, and when we can say the fever of revolution has begun. This works up, not regularly but with advances and retreats, to a crisis, frequently accompanied by delirium, the rule of the most violent revolutionists, the Reign of Terror. After the crisis comes a period of convalescence, usually marked by a relapse or two. Finally the fever is over, and the patient is himself again.

As in the writings of the 1790's, nature and politics are closely identified. Brinton's model of revolution places a traditional emphasis upon recovery and regeneration. His references to the natural course of diseases suggest, by way of analogy, the natural course of revolutions. They pass like fevers. The patient recovers and is the better for the experience. As Brinton argues, the revolutionary disease strikes organisms that have "structural weaknesses," and it actually leaves them in some respects "strengthened" by the encounter and "immunized at least for a while" from the threat of further revolutionary upsets.

During the 1790's, many writers conceived of revolution in terms of disease metaphors. Most assumed, in one way or another, that society would recover from the revolutionary disease if the right measures were taken. For Mary Shelley's mother, Mary Wollstonecraft, the correct cure was simply to let nature run her course. The disease will out. Like Brinton, she assumed that the revolutionary disease began because of structural weaknesses in the old regime, and like Brinton, that the violent fever is really the unpleasant cure, made necessary because the old regime failed to reform itself voluntarily. In the final paragraph of her *An Historical and Moral View of the French Revolution,* Wollstonecraft announces in a balanced, periodic, Enlightenment style:

> Thus had France grown up, and sickened on the corruption of a state diseased. Burt, as in medicine there is a species of complaint in the bowels which works it's own cure, and, leaving the body healthy, gives an invigorated tone to the system, so there is in politics: and whilst the agitation of its regeneration continues, the excrementitious humours exuding from the contaminated body will excite a general dislike and contempt for the nation; and it is only the philosophical eye, which looks into the nature and weighs the consequences of human actions, that will be able to discern the cause, which has produced so many dreadful effects.

Speaking in the abstract, Latinate phraseology of the eighteenth century ("the excrementitious humours exuding from the contaminated body"), Wollstonecraft assumes the posture of an Enlightenment rationalist. She examines her subject philosophically in terms of cause, effect, and consequence. Her disease metaphor is progressive. Politically, the keywords are "cure," "healthy," "invigorated," and "regeneration." Here again, we see nature and disease metaphors sanctioning a regeneration in the realm of politics.

Significantly, diseases also play an important role in the writings of Wollstonecraft's conservative archenemy, Edmund Burke. Wollstonecraft and Burke share the same metaphor: they merely apply it to different political ends when it comes to interpreting the recent events in France. Both claim to be creatures of compromise and heirs of the Glorious Revolution of 1688. Both contrast the healthy British ways of doing things—that is, the peaceful ways of 1688—with the diseased and convulsive phenomenon of violent revolution in France. Burke writes in his *Reflections on the Revolution in France* (1790): "An irregular, convulsive movement may be necessary to throw off an irregular, convulsive disease. But the course of succession is the healthy habit of the British constitution." In Burke, violent revolution emerges as a very un-British disease that should be quarantined and kept out of Britain. Rhetorically, he asks whether the revolutionary "panacea" in France is not in fact a plague. Answering his own rhetorical question, he opines: "If it be a plague; it is such a plague, that the precautions of the most severe quarantine ought to be established against it." This is also Burke's posture toward the role of revolutionary ideas in Britain: they ought to be quarantined and kept out, and the corresponding societies put down.

Mary Shelley obviously had Burke's *Reflections* in mind when she wrote *The Last Man* in the mid-1820's. Her narrator Lionel Verney quotes directly from Burke several times. He also footnotes his source, lest the reader miss the connection. Metaphorically, however, Mary Shelley shifts the equation in favor of the plague. Her plague is no longer revolutionary opinions, nor even simply revolutionary violence, but rather a real plague that cannot be censured or quarantined or fought or stopped. No political remedies whatsoever will avail against it, nor will society survive in the face of its ravages. Mary Shelley copes with the problem of revolution by cancelling out history itself.

It might be objected that this solution is anti-intellectual. In a way this is true. Mary Shelley sacrifices some of the political ambivalence and metaphorical subtlety in Wollstonecraft and Burke when she renders the plague into a literal fact of nature. But Mary Shelley has not wholly sacrificed her intellectual interests, nor is she simply succumbing to political reactionism. The very literalmindedness of her plague imagery is in some ways a source of strength in her debate with her forerunners. It enables her to swerve dramatically from their eighteenth-century visions of history.

Mary Shelley, after all, is quite aware of what she is doing: she is rebelling against the political faiths of her parents' generation and writing an obituary on the idea that the social organism has a natural imperative toward survival and improvement. For these reasons, she has Lionel Verney quote verbatim one of the most famous passages in Burke's *Reflections.* The novel's references to Burke are ironic, especially when we know the catastrophic outcome of the entire story. Verney quotes from Burke in order to buoy up his own spirits after the plague has already begun its deadly rampage across the globe. The plague is marching relentlessly toward Britain, and Verney, who has returned from the revolution in Greece, is living near Eton where his young son Alfred attends school. One day Verney muses on the dismal fate of the youngsters who were to have been the future governing classes of England. He ruefully rehearses Burke's claim that society is a permanent body, which survives while individuals pass away. As Verney recalls, Burke attributes to human society "the mode of existence decreed to a permanent body composed of transitory parts; wherein, by the disposition of a stupendous wisdom, moulding together the great mysterious incorporation of the human race, the whole, at one time, is never old, or middle-aged, or young, but, in a condition of unchangeable constancy, moves on through the varied tenour of perpetual decay, fall, renovation, and progression." For Burke, writing at the end of the eighteenth century, the "permanent body" of society still has the resilience and strength to resist the plagues of revolution. Mary Shelley echoes this faith in order to subvert it. In her novel the social organism sickens and dies. She gives us the decay and fall without the renovation and progression. And she does so by greatly expanding the chaotic forces that assail the social organism from without.

When Verney quotes the long, periodic sentence from Burke on the "unchangeable constancy" of human society, he deletes the opening clause which reads: "Our political system is placed in a just correspondence and symmetry with the order of the world." In *The Last Man,* this orderly, eighteenth-century vision of society has broken down. There is no longer a stupendous wisdom governing all, and the orderliness of nature no longer serves to buttress and sanction the idea of an orderly society. Nature has turned demonic and to be in "correspondence" with it is to be destroyed. To put the matter in other terms, one of the central philosophical issues in *The Last Man* is the decline of mind and wisdom as forces for governing and ordering the world. Mary Shelley dispenses with Burke's deistic "stupendous wisdom" behind all things, and she also cancels out the corporate wisdom of human institutions. She rejects not only Burke's organic metaphor but also the philosophical system that goes along with it.

Mary Shelley's plague novel also stands as a response to the writings of her father, William Godwin. Her intellectual relationship with Godwin is tangled and suffused with personal ambivalence. It is further complicated by the changes Godwin underwent during and just after the 1790's, when his writings evolved from what Isaac Kramnick calls the "characteristic intellectualism of the Enlightenment" to an incipient form of Romanticism. This shift is especially apparent in Godwin's novels; but it is also evident in the second and third editions of his *Enquiry Concerning Political Justice,* where he places increasing emphasis upon emotions and feelings and also offers a sharper critique of certain forms of Enlightenment optimism. Mary Shelley takes her father's early rationalism and utopianism to task in *The Last Man.* But her novel also echoes—often in exaggerated form—some of the images and literary devices of his emerging gothic sensibilities. Godwin's writings of the 1790's contain a running debate on the elimination of diseases. Mary Shelley picks up where her father leaves off and pursues the subject to new and demonic ends.

In the first edition of his *Enquiry Concerning Political Justice* (1793) Godwin assails earlier rationalists and their theories of natural law. But at the end of the book he becomes a visionary and offers his own highly rational scheme for the improvement of the human race. Godwin still believes in the powers of the human mind, if freed from institutional restraints and rightly applied. One of his most utopian arguments in *Political Justice* is his contention that disease and perhaps even death can be conquered and canceled out by the powers of mind. "We are sick and we die," Godwin asserts, ". . . because we consent to suffer these accidents." He looks forward to a future "improvement of mind" when we will be empowered to resist disease and even death. When that utopian future arrives, Godwin confidently asserts, "there will be no disease, no anguish, no melancholy and no resentment." Humans will not merely be freed from disease, but in addition, he speculates, they "will perhaps be immortal." As Judith N. Shklar wryly observes, there is sometimes in Godwin's writings "a degree of reasonableness that borders on the irrational."

Godwin's prophecy of the rational anarchist future is so extreme that it virtually invites rebuttal. His critics, including Mary Shelley, tend to go to opposite extremes. Godwin forecasts a utopia that could come about once human population is brought under control. Thomas Malthus rebutted Godwin by envisioning a nightmare world of overcrowding, depleted resources, and human suffering. Mary Shelley rebutted her father's rationalism by envisioning the annihilation of the entire human race. But Godwin, in fact, had anticipated the response of his critics. He too had engaged in speculations about the end of the human race.

In the second edition of *Political Justice,* published in 1796, Godwin added a lengthy critique of the "optimists," such as Leibnitz, who insisted that we live in the best of all possible worlds. Along with his emphasis on social injustices and things as they are, Godwin also countered the optimists by suggesting the catastrophes that might befall the human race. He asks, "has improvement been the constant characteristic of the universe? The human species seems to be but, as it were, of yesterday. Will it continue for ever? The globe we inhabit bears strong marks of convulsion, such as the teachers of religion, and the professors of natural philosophy agree to predict, will one day destroy the inhabitants of the earth." Were Godwin completely thorough and systematic about the "convulsion" theory, it would doubtless call into question his own utopian speculations about social perfection, the elimination of disease, and the evolution of humanity into a possibly "immortal" species. But convulsions and catastrophes remain a relatively minor theme in *Political Justice.* With only slight rhetorical qualifications, Godwin retains his utopian speculations in the revised editions of his treatise.

Mary Shelley, however, takes up an analogue of the convulsion theory and works out its ultimate consequences in narrative form. She echoes her father's utopian speculations about the elimination of disease in order to reverse and negate them. Disasters displace utopian speculations. Adrian, who is Earl of Windsor and sometimes Lord Protector of England, experiences several spasms of utopian longing in the course of the novel. He wishes that England could be governed by Godwinian principles. But his articulation of Godwin's ideas suggests the terms of their own negation. Adrian wants to eliminate disease in a world where disease reigns supreme. He says to Verney at one juncture: "Oh, that death and sickness were banished from our earthly home! that hatred, tyranny, and fear could no longer make their lair in the human heart! . . . The choice is with us; let us will it, and our habitation becomes a paradise. For the will of man is omnipotent, blunting the arrows of death, soothing the bed of disease, and wiping away the tears of agony." Echoing Godwin's *Political Justice,* Adrian suggests that we suffer because we consent to do so; he asserts that sickness and even death can be banished if we exert our will to overcome these adversities. These utopian hopes prove futile in *The Last Man* because nature is impervious to human will and human rationality. In fact, Mary Shelley diminishes human mind virtually to the vanishing point when everybody but the narrator dies in the great cataclysm. Whereas Godwin's philosophy touches upon disasters as a minor theme, Mary Shelley enlarges them into a root-and-branch attack upon his utopian system.

The demonic plague in *The Last Man* cancels out the utopian rationality of Godwin as surely as it cancels out the conservative organicism of Edmund Burke. The end-of-the-world melodrama represents a departure from the assumptions and the organizing metaphors shared alike by the republican and the conservative polemicists during the decade of the French Revolution. Although writers like Burke, Wollstonecraft, and Godwin have their occasional apocalyptic moments, they usually adhere to a faith in the survival or even the gradual improvement of the human lot. In the disease metaphors of her precursors, there is an assumption that the social organism can survive the fevers of revolution. Mary Shelley retains the metaphor of illness, but transforms it into an absolute that effaces all human endeavor.

Susan Sontag [in *Illness as Metaphor,* 1978] suggests that "with the French Revolution [political] disease metaphors in the modern sense came into their own." Political ills came to be represented in more "virulent" and "demagogic" terms, and accordingly, when solutions were imagined at all, they tended to be violent and extreme ones. For writers like William Godwin and Mary Shelley, the experience of the revolutionary era not only rendered disease metaphors more virulent, but it also prompted a shift in literary form. In place of the abstract universals of eighteenth-century philosophy, Godwin and Mary Shelley turned to the novel and experimented with confessional and gothic conventions.

Peter Brooks [in *ELH* 40 (1973)] observes that the gothic novel arose in reaction to the pretensions of rationalism. This is certainly the case in William Godwin's gothic novel *St. Leon* (1799), which was an important influence upon both *Frankenstein* and *The Last Man.* Godwin's novel shifts the struggle against disease from philosophy to gothicism. In the process, he qualifies and retracts some of the rationalist positions set forth in *Political Justice.* The novel is narrated as the confessions of Reginald de St. Leon, a Faustian adventurer and nobleman from the sixteenth century who acquires the secrets of the "philosopher's stone" and the "elixir of immortality." Like Godwin's prophetic race of the future in *Political Justice,* St. Leon's powers render him "invulnerable to disease." But now immunity to disease is no longer an attainment of universal rationality: it is rather the demonic secret of someone who traffics with the nether forces.

St. Leon wants to use his powers to improve mankind in general, but finds that his forbidden powers lead him from one disaster to another. At one point in the novel he goes to Hungary to "revive" a populace that has been oppressed by Turkish invasion and despotism, much as Mary Shelley's protagonists Raymond and Adrian go to help Greece in *The Last Man.* As in Mary Shelley's novel, diseases symbolize the impediments to social reform. The nobility of Hungary has already "fallen a victim to the merciless plague of war," and the savage neglect of a country despoiled by despotism has produced in repeated instances "contagious air and pestilential diseases," as well as widespread famine and death. St. Leon tries to provide leadership, but he finds that he cannot control the economy, the unruly populace, or the despots who hold sway over the country. The powers of philosophy cannot alter social reality. St. Leon is finally forced to withdraw from Hungary, and he concludes darkly about future prospects for improvement and reform: "I had made a sufficient experiment of the philosopher's stone, and all my experiments had miscarried. My latest trials in attempting to be the benefactor of nations and mankind, not only had been themselves abortive, but contained in them shrewd indications that no similar plan could ever succeed."

Mary Shelley also deals with lofty, utopian ambitions by reversing them in melodramatic fashion. Projects for the improvement of mankind produce demonic results, and characters are often forced by circumstances to abandon and renounce their schemes for the betterment of the race. The protagonist of her first novel, Victor Frankenstein, sounds like an updated version of St. Leon when he plunges "with the greatest diligence into the search of the philosopher's stone and the elixir of life." Victor wants to benefit humanity and exclaims hopefully: "what glory would attend the discovery, if I could banish disease from the human frame, and render man invulnerable to any but a violent death!" Turning his attention to even grander experiments, Victor tries to revive the dead and bring forth a whole "new species" of mankind, thus parodying the theme of immortality in a more literal fashion. But this Godwinian experiment fails when Victor's creature turns out to be a parricidal monster.

An analogous melodrama of failed expectations recurs in *The Last Man.* Lord Raymond, under whose reign as Protector of England "disease was to be banished," becomes a Napoleonic-style liberator of oppressed peoples abroad. He goes to Greece, a land which he believes should be "rescued from slavery and barbarism, and restored to a people illustrious for genius, civilization, and a spirit of liberty." But again, as in *Frankenstein,* there is a melodrama of failed expectations. And, once again, that failure is personified by the rise of a demonic monster.

As I have argued elsewhere, the monster metaphor derives from political polemics during the age of the French Revolution. Victor's lone, parricidal monster echoes the collective revolutionary monsters in writings of the 1790's. In *Frankenstein,* Mary Shelley turns from the politics of the 1790's to the more subjective realms of necromancy and gothicism. In *The Last Man,* she hesitatingly returns to the realm of collective politics. But her concerns are largely the same: the failure of lofty ambitions. Those ambitions now play themselves out on a world-historical scale. Victor is merely trying to revive a dead creature; Raymond is trying to revive the glory and liberty that was Greece. Victor works alone; Raymond goes to Greece and becomes the commanding general of a revolutionary army. Victor pursues hidden ambitions; Raymond announces his ambitions publicly and claims his place in the exalted tradition of Alexander, Caesar, Cromwell, and Napoleon.

The Last Man contains far more references to actual history and politics than *Frankenstein,* yet in both novels a previous age of revolution gives way to isolation, demonism, and death. Collective movements dissolve and the narrators are left trapped in the envelopes of their own subjectivity. When Raymond and his imperial crusade disappear from the stage of history, Verney signals a shift to subjectivity by infusing his narrative with portentous gothic symbols, which efface and blot out political realities. As in *Frankenstein,* the world becomes haunted with phantoms and monsters that are a fatal nemesis.

This shift from politics to gothicism takes place most explicitly in Lionel Verney's nightmare, which occurs when Raymond dies in the ruins of Constantinople. Just as Raymond had promised in his earlier conversations with Verney, he goes to Greece, defeats the Turks, and captures Constantinople. But he captures an empty city. The plague has reached there first and annihilated the Turkish population. Raymond plunges into the city anyway and there he meets his doom. Verney follows into the smoldering ruins in search of his friend, but he eventually succumbs to exhaustion and collapses into a deep sleep. He has a surrealistic, highly literary dream about Raymond, the pestilence, and the coming apocalypse. According to his dream symbolism, a phantom has been set loose upon the world:

> Methought I had been invited to Timon's last feast; I came with keen appetite, the covers were removed, the hot water sent up its unsatisfying steams, while I fled before the anger of the host, who assumed the form of Raymond; while to my diseased fancy, the vessels hurled by him after me, were surcharged with fetid vapour, and my friend's shape, altered by a thousand distortions, expanded into a gigantic phantom, bearing on its brow the sign of pestilence. The growing shadow rose and rose, filling, and then seeming to endeavour to burst beyond, the adamantine vault that bent over, sustaining and enclosing the world.

This nightmare recapitulates a familiar pattern in the writings of Mary Shelley. Desire and appetite quickly give way in melodramatic fashion to death and demonic persecution. The emergence of the "gigantic phantom" also echoes another of her pervasive concerns, the symbolic resurrection after death. Like Edmund Burke's "hideous phantom" that arises from the tomb of the murdered monarchy in France, and the Frankenstein monster that arises from the tomb in Mary Shelley's first novel, her phantom—at least in the dream—appears to arise from the dead as well. Raymond turns into a gigantic phantom, who spreads an empire of death across the skies.

Verney's demonic style extends beyond his dreams. The phantom is abroad in the world at large. Verney uses gothic imagery to narrate the plague's advance. When Raymond brings his army before the dead city of Constantinople, he orders his troops to breach the walls so that he can enter. His men do so, but then, according to Verney, they "shrank back; they seemed afraid of what they had already done, and stood as if they expected some Mighty Phantom to stalk in offended majesty from the opening." Their fears are justified. The pestilence follows them to Greece and soon reigns supreme in the Peloponnesian peninsula. Verney apostrophizes upon this disastrous turn of events in gothic metaphors. He exclaims how "that same invincible monster, which hovered over and devoured Constantinople—that fiend more cruel than tempest, less tame than fire, is, alas, unchained in that beautiful country" of Greece.

This relentless force of nature differs significantly from the monster who speaks so eloquently of social injustice in *Frankenstein.* Mary Shelley creates a deadly, rebellious monster in *Frankenstein,* but she endows that monster with human sympathies and a human conscience. Like his creator, the monster can think and speak. Although a vengeful rebel, he is also an articulate, civilized creature who can be interviewed at length by Frankenstein and Robert Walton. After completing his rebellion, and destroying the family of Victor Frankenstein, the monster gives way to remorse and eventually kills himself in a ritual purgation by fire. Even among parricidal monsters, a moral order obtains.

In contrast, the "monster" in *The Last Man* is a totally inhuman, disembodied force of nature. It rises mysteriously from Asia and the Nile basin and spreads relentlessly, destroying all in its path. There is no possible way to debate with this monster. One can only exclaim, apostrophize, or lament upon its ravages. As a narrator, Verney is forced into the role of an apocalyptic prophet, who warns of a dire fate he can neither forestall nor alter. His narrative takes on almost biblical overtones, and he repeatedly gravitates toward final, melodramatic encounters with the forces of doom. Thus his analogy for the demise of the Greek army before the walls of Constantinople:

> I have heard a picture described, wherein all the inhabitants of earth were drawn out in fear to stand the encounter of Death. The feeble and decrepid fled; the warriors retreated, though they threatened even in flight. Wolves and lions, and various monsters of the desert roared against him; while the grim Unreality hovered shaking his spectral dart, a solitary but invincible assailant. Even so was it with the army of Greece.

The figures and metaphors of Verney's apocalypse are highly traditional: demonic hosts appear in the skies; monsters and phantoms stalk abroad; wolves and lions roar in the deserts; mass panics and frenzies erupt; riots and invasions follow. These outbreaks are accompanied by storms, fires, floods, famines, shipwrecks, and, of course, by the contagious spread of the monstrous pestilence from country to country, until everybody but Verney is conquered by death.

In *The Last Man* Mary Shelley leaves behind the domestic gothicism of *Frankenstein* and invents a new confessional format. On the one side, she greatly expands the demonic threat, changing it into a disembodied, all-pervasive, mindless onslaught. On the other, she narrows and diminishes the role of the narrator, who emerges as a largely passive observer of political and natural disasters. The narrator writes in total isolation and frequently despairs of ever finding a readership. Verney writes his confessional narrative during the last year of the twenty-first century, after Adrian and Clara, his only surviving companions, have died at sea. He compares himself "to that monarch of the waste—Robinson Crusoe," but he quickly points out the fatal difference. Crusoe knew that humanity still existed beyond the horizon and that someday the events of his solitude might become a "fire-side tale" known to many. Verney laments in contrast: "To none could I ever relate the story of my adversity; no hope had I." He knows it is likely that only his eyes will "read these pages" as he ponders: "And who will read them? Beware, tender offspring of the re-born world. . . . Let not day look on these lines."

Structurally, the communal aspects of literature are significantly diminished in *The Last Man.* Writers on revolution and reform during the 1790's address one another in open, public "Letters." This convention is superseded by the private letters in *Frankenstein* and by the confessional memoir that is told to nobody in *The Last Man.* The complex network of domestic communication which informs the narrative in *Frankenstein* no longer survives intact in *The Last Man.* The monster confesses to his creator Victor Frankenstein, who in turn confesses to Robert Walton, who in turn writes home to his sister Margaret from the arctic wastes. In *The Last Man* Adrian and Raymond confess their lofty reforming ambitions to Verney before they die, but Verney, who is even more isolated than Robinson Crusoe, has no friend or sister to whom he can impart his dismal tale. He decides that he will leave his completed manuscript behind in Italy, acting on the remote hope that somewhere, in a "to me unknown and unattainable" nook, there might exist the "children of a saved pair of lovers," who, wandering to Rome to visit the relics of the "ante-pestilential race," might someday find and read his book. But this remote prospect does not really convince Verney, who despairs: "No one has entered Rome. None will ever come." The audience has vanished. Verney therefore dedicates his narrative: "TO THE ILLUSTRIOUS DEAD. / SHADOWS, ARISE, AND READ YOUR FALL! / BEHOLD THE HISTORY OF THE / LAST MAN."

Walter J. Ong has reminded us that the writer's audience is always a fiction. Part of the fiction in *The Last Man* is that the narrator has no audience. Moving away from the chains of confessional interaction that shape *Frankenstein,* Mary Shelley turns her attention in her "Author's Introduction" to the work of composition itself. She anticipates Thomas Carlyle's *Sartor Resartus* (1833–34) by setting up an elaborate hoax about a found and scattered manuscript of supposedly prophetic import, which her author/editor works upon in "long hours of solitude." Endeavoring to explain how a confessional tale supposedly written in the year 2099 came to be published in 1826, the "Author" recounts how she and a companion, exploring near Naples in December of 1818, accidentally stumbled upon the confessions of Lionel Verney in the depths of the Sibylline Caves. Mary Shelley's "obscure and chaotic" prophetic "fragments" supposedly come to us via the timeless cave of the Cumæan Sibyl, and Carlyle also echoes this classical myth when his Editor describes the "fragments" of Diogenes Teufelsdröckh's manuscript as "Sibylline." Mary Shelley's "Author" also anticipates the intellectual labors of Carlyle's Editor when she says of Verney's pages: "Scattered and unconnected as they were, I have been obliged to add links, and model the work into a consistent form."

The edited fragments of Shelley and Carlyle are both encyclopedic fictions that contain "prophecies" of the future, and both *Sartor Resartus* and *The Last Man* rely upon central, integrating metaphors as a way of anatomizing philosophical ideas, political theories, and revolutionary events. Mary Shelley's novel is over-long, partly because she is trying to write a triple-decker so as to conform to the format of the circulating libraries, but it is also over-long because she is trying to survey such a wide variety of utopian and revolutionary theories that she believes have failed. Northrop Frye [in his *Anatomy of Criticism,* 1957] suggests that fictional anatomies typically deal with "diseases of the intellect" and that they often present the reader with masses of erudition, dialogues, and colloquies in which the "dramatic interest is in a conflict of ideas rather than of character." Mary Shelley borrows from the anatomy tradition in *The Last Man* when she has Verney and other characters discourse at length on various reforming ideas, which are eventually canceled out by the advent of the plague.

Mary Shelley maintains an ironic, editorial-like distance from the reforming ideas presented in her novel. She anticipates Thomas Carlyle in that she strives to close her Byron, her Shelley, and her Napoleon. But in contrast to Carlyle she has nothing to open in their place. She remains squarely in the Everlasting No. Writing in *Sartor Resartus* Carlyle could urge his readers to "Close thy *Byron;* open thy *Goethe.*" And he could also suggest—albeit somewhat cryptically—that the July Days rebellion in Paris was the augury of the coming phoenix rebirth of European society. By 1837, he could open his French Revolution and warn of more such phoenix conflagrations if society did not set about reforming itself. But Mary Shelley could find no such formula for rebirth, either on a personal or a collective level. She reflects upon this impasse in her introduction when she admits she has been "depressed, nay, agonized" while transcribing Verney's vision of the end of the world. And she muses aloud: "Will my readers ask how I could find solace from the narration of misery and woeful change?" What Mary Shelley lacks in the way of optimism and solutions she strives to compensate for with a sweeping historical overview of the revolutionary age. Her novel surveys intellectual expressions from the French Revolution of 1789 to Napoleon and the Greek revolution of the 1820's, which was still in progress when she wrote her novel.

Although I can only briefly touch upon the subject here, a full investigation of Mary Shelley's disease imagery would suggest how it reflects upon the Philhellene movement and the disillusioning events of the Greek revolution, including Byron's death at Missolonghi in April of 1824. Her novel also reflects symbolically upon the writings of Percy Shelley, who was the leading European poet who wrote in support of the Philhellene cause. He composed two major poems about rebellions against the Turkish hegemony, *The Revolt of Islam* (1818) and *Hellas* (1822). Both works make significant use of plague imagery. Percy writes in his preface to *The Revolt of Islam* that the results of despotism are "civil war, famine [and] plague," and in the poem itself he narrates how a deadly "Plague" arises from the battlefields to threaten despotism with ruin. In *Hellas* he shifts the site of the revolution to Greece, where the Turkish despots are again threatened by the "Spirit of the Plague." Echoing the meliorative traditions of the 1790's, Percy's poem suggests that the plagues of revolutionary war will eventually give way to a "brighter Hellas" of the future.

In his prose prefaces Percy Shelley announces his support for the insurrection in Greece and voices his hope that the revolutionaries of the early 1820's would prove to be a "new race" who could overthrow the "holy alliance" of "despots" reigning throughout Europe. Calling upon metaphors of racial rebirth, he sees the Greeks, through their acts of revolution, "rising as it were from the ashes of their ruin." Mary Shelley, however, does not believe in Percy's heroic "new race" any more than she believes in Victor Frankenstein's "new species" in her first novel. For Mary, all revolutionary experiments breed monsters. The monsterlike holocaust that descends upon the Greek revolution in *The Last Man* is a graphic fictional rebuttal of Percy's political views.

In *The Last Man,* Mary Shelley goes out of her way to demonstrate that Percy had been too idealistic about the Greek revolution before he died in July of 1822. Byron once reportedly said that Percy planned to accompany him to Greece. Adrian, Earl of Windsor, who is Mary's fictional surrogate for Percy, does go along as a "volunteer" to her imaginary Greek revolution of the future. He comes face to face with the grim realities of revolutionary war and quits Greece disillusioned with the prospects of national regeneration. Mary has Adrian witness and narrate the Greek capture of a Turkish-held town in which "every breathing creature within the walls was massacred." Adrian tries to intervene and save innocent civilians, but the Greek soldiers turn upon him and bayonet him in the side. Like Hölderlin's Hyperion, the idealistic Adrian initially supports the revolution, but later becomes disillusioned when it issues forth in a general reign of terror.

Mary Shelley's anatomy of failed revolutions does not place all the blame upon the "blood-thirsty war-dogs" (116) of Greece, however. She also indicts the Romantic cult of the heroic leader. She combines attributes of Napoleon and Byron in the figure of Lord Raymond, who leads the Greeks to their rendezvous with doom at Constantinople. Thomas Carlyle, writing in *Sartor Resartus* in 1831, remarked that "the very Napoleon, the very Byron, in some seven years, has become obsolete." Mary Shelley anticipates this critique in her portrait of Lord Raymond. Raymond boasts to Verney that he will free the Greeks, capture Constantinople, and "subdue all Asia"—an achievement which eluded even Napoleon. Raymond brashly predicts: "Napoleon's name shall vail to mine; and enthusiasts, instead of visiting his rocky grave . . . shall adore my majesty, and magnify my illustrious achievements." The plague, however, eliminates not only the Romantic hero, but also the multitudes who would have preserved and glorified his memory.

When Carlyle rejects the Romantic heroes of the past in *Sartor Resartus,* he does so for different artistic and philosophical reasons. Like Mary Shelley, Carlyle writes an encyclopedic fiction, closes his Byron and his Napoleon, and anathematizes the past heoric age as sick and diseased. But Carlyle also fashions a dual narrative structure which keeps us aware of the disease metaphor as metaphor. Carlyle juxtaposes the voices of the Editor and Diogenes Teufelsdröckh so that we remain aware of the subjective and personal nature of the latter's prophetic utterances. When the Editor tells us, in mock surprise, how Teufelsdröckh is "content that old sick Society should be deliberately burnt . . . in the faith that she is a Phœnix," we are no longer in the holocaust world of *The Last Man.* Carlyle not only retains an emphasis upon recovery and regeneration, but he also foregrounds and reflects upon the act of prophecy itself. It is Diogenes Teufelsdröckh who sees the age as sick—history may or may not bear out his apocalyptic prophecies about the July Days and the coming phoenix regeneration.

Mary Shelley, however, turns the metaphor into fact. This is both her weakness and her strength in *The Last Man.* Artistically, it is a weakness because she also retains a traditional novelistic emphasis upon character, even while the plague completely obliterates humanity. Mary Shelley's characters, except for the narrator Verney, have little to do except struggle briefly and die. The domestic and political plottings of the novel work at cross purposes with the monolithic advance of the plague. But Mary Shelley's plague novel is also of considerable historical and intellectual interest. The plague enables her to survey the past heroic age from a consistent point of view; it enables her to comment on the ideas and metaphors of her forerunners; and it also enables her to suggest, by implication, some of the genocidal atrocities of the Greek revolution. It also places her as an artistic forerunner of modern science fiction. The structure of her novel, with its isolated narrator-witness who is surrounded by disasters and holocausts, looks forward to such works as H. G. Wells's *Time Machine* and *War of the Worlds.* Mary Shelley may well have been responding to a sense of personal grief when she wrote *The Last Man,* but she translated her personal suffering into an ambitious, historically significant anatomy of the revolutionary age. (pp. 324-47)

Lee Sterrenburg, " 'The Last Man': Anatomy of Failed Revolutions," in Nineteenth-Century Fiction, *Vol. 33, No. 3, December, 1978, pp. 324-47.*

DRAMA

Jeffrey N. Cox

[In the essay below, Cox asserts that censorship, among other factors, prompted early nineteenth-century English playwrights to mythologize their depictions of the French Revolution.]

During the grand and terrible days of the French Revolution, history itself seemed to become theatrical. The Revolution had its stages in assembly halls, courtrooms, and scaffolds. It had its great actors in Mirabeau, Danton, St. Just. And events seemed to follow the rhythms of the drama, particularly dramatic tragedy. When Jean-François Ducis, playwright and adaptor of Shakespeare, was asked why he abandoned the drama in 1792, he responded, "Why talk to me . . . of composing tragedies? Tragedy walks the streets."

Dramatists and theatrical managers were quick to seize upon the potential of these enormously theatrical events. Many of the more interesting plays of the late eighteenth and early nineteenth centuries can be read as attempts to dramatize the Revolution; as Victor Hugo proclaimed, "The physiognomy of this epoch will be determined only when the French Revolution, which personified itself in society in the form of Napoleon, personifies itself in art." English writers would have agreed—with Shelley, for example, seeing the Revolution as the "master theme" of the epoch. The attempt of romantic dramatists to "personify" the Revolution follows an interesting path. We often think of literature arising within myth, then passing through such idealizing forms as the romance and high tragedy, before descending to such "realistic" forms as the novel and the prose drama. The dramatizers of the Revolution, however, moved in the opposite direction, from the direct representation of actual events to the displacement of revolutionary acts into neoclassical and Gothic parallels and finally to the re-creation of the Revolution in mythic terms. As we will see, both governmental censors and revolutionary sympathizers had reasons for translating the representation of revolt from history to myth.

It comes as no surprise that Parisian theaters often moved events directly from the streets to the stage. Numerous plays celebrated the taking of the Bastille and the various national fêtes. Central events such as the flight of the king and his family to Varennes would throw theaters into a frenzy of competition to see which one would first and most successfully put the latest news on stage. Military victories often gave rise to such plays as *The Entrance of Dumouriez into Brussels (L'Entrée de Dumouriez à Bruxelles;* Théâtre-Français, Rue de Richelieu, 1793), which depicted a key French triumph but was a theatrical failure. We also find pieces devoted to revolutionary martyrs; Marat, who was celebrated as the "friend of the people" in a very successful play by that name (Gassier Saint-Armand's *L'Ami du peuple ou La Mort de Marat;* Variétés Amusantes, 1793), had his life and death dramatized at least six times.

There was initially a parallel interest in bringing the deeds of the Revolution to the London stage, with key events sometimes being staged at several theaters at the same time. For example, in August of 1789, the Royal Circus, the Royal Grove (later Astley's), and Sadler's Wells all produced versions of the taking of the Bastille; and Covent Garden had a drama based on the events of 14 July in rehearsal only to have the play blocked by the Lord Chamberlain and his censor. The next summer found the same three "minor" theaters offering dramatizations of the national fête of 14 July 1790 in honor of the Federation. We can find less direct echoes of events in France in many plays, including popular spectacles such as J. C. Cross's *Julia of Louvain: or, Monkish Cruelty* (Royal Circus, 1797), which is taken, the published version tells us, "from a paragraph in a Newspaper during the French Revolution." Revolutionary events could even find their way into the popular harlequinade, with Charles Bonnor's *The Picture of Paris Taken in the Year 1790* (Covent Garden, 1790) mixing scenes of life under the Revolution with the antics of Harlequin and Columbine. Of course, not all these plays were sympathetic to the Revolution. For example, William Preston's *Democratic Rage: or, Louis the Unfortunate* castigated the rebels on stage in Dublin in 1793, in Charleston, S. C., in 1795, and in Boston in 1797. Coleridge and Southey joined this attempt to bring history into the theater when they wrote their *Fall of Robespierre* (1794).

John Dent's *The Bastille,* which ran for 79 successive nights at the Royal Circus beginning in August 1789, provides a useful example of these early and usually popular attempts to stage the Revolution. The play's plot is simple. Henry Dubois meets with his beloved Matilda at the beginning of the play. They have a personal as well as political motive for wishing the Bastille to fall, for Matilda's father has been imprisoned after refusing to grant Matilda's hand to Henry's powerful rival. The play alternates between essentially public scenes—in which we see the people preparing to storm the Bastille—and scenes treating the private concerns of Henry, Matilda, and her father, who faces torture at the hands of the demonic governor of the prison. The people finally storm the Bastille with Henry at their head; they free Matilda's father, and the

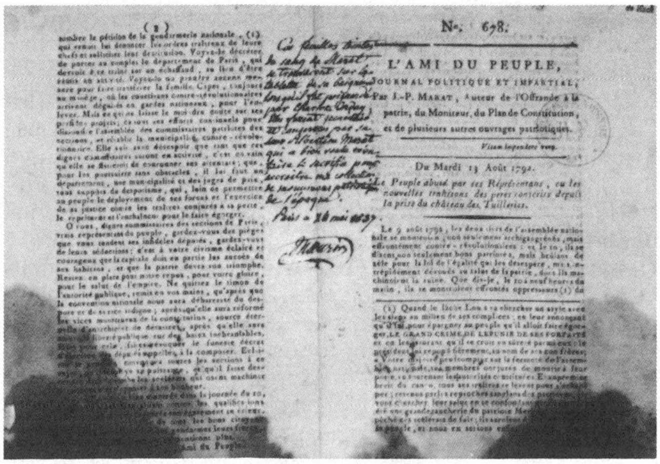
N°. 678.

L'AMI DU PEUPLE,

JOURNAL POLITIQUE ET IMPARTIAL;

Par J.-P. MARAT, Auteur de l'Offrande à la patrie, du Moniteur, du Plan de Constitution, et de plusieurs autres ouvrages patriotiques.

Du Mardi 13 Août 1792.

An edition of Marat's radical revolutionary newspaper Ami du peuple, *stained with his own blood from the stabbing that caused his death.*

governor is led off to execution as his Cross of St. Louis is stripped from him and given to Henry. The play concludes with a grand celebration of liberty that culminates in praises of England, as an allegorical figure of Britannia descends holding portraits of the English king and queen while the statue of liberty is seen trampling the figure of despotism.

The play is in many ways a romance of revolution, with Henry snatching the imprisoned father from the instruments of torture and thus proving himself worthy of Matilda's love. The plot follows the three-part pattern Northrop Frye identifies with romance, as it moves from the preliminary minor adventures with Henry and the people readying their assault to the central struggle of the attack upon the Bastille itself and finally to the exaltation of the hero in the closing processional scene.

However, Dent clearly intends this romance as in some sense documentary. Not only does he take pains to re-create actual places and events, but he also has Henry deliver in the final scene a long speech we are told is a translation of an oration delivered on 29 July to the French troops by Moreau de Saint-Méry. Part of the play's appeal clearly lay in its claim to accuracy, as we can see from a favorable notice in the *Times* [8 August 1789] praising the drama as an entertainment in which "the bloody business of the Bastille . . . is dramatized into a regular story and brought to a denouement founded in truth." We see similar claims in other plays where stage directions testify to the attempt to evoke revolutionary events and Parisian scenes in great detail. Covent Garden's *Picture of Paris Taken in the Year 1790,* for example, includes such sets as a "faithful representation of the celebrated Convent of the Jacobins, situated in Rue St. Honoré, part of which, according to an inscription on the Gate, is converted by the National Guard into a Guard House, or Rendezvous for the first Batallion of the Division of St. Roch."

Of course, direct portrayals of actual revolutionary events were not tolerated for long by the government, as represented by the lord chamberlain and John Larpent, the examiner of plays. After the success of plays such as Dent's *Bastille* at minor theaters, the patented theaters royal of Covent Garden and Drury Lane sought to offer plays that capitalized on these exciting events. In the autumn of 1789, Covent Garden prepared a play on the fall of the Bastille; but, as the author Frederick Reynolds tells us, "when the parts were studied, the scenery completed, and the music composed, the Lord Chamberlain refused his license." Drury Lane was allowed to stage a play centering upon the Man in the Iron Mask—*The Island of St. Marguerite,* by John St. John (1789)—but only after allusions and parallels to the Bastille were dropped. Apparently, it was felt that such performances at London's central theaters would lend a sanction to the reenactment of revolutionary events different in kind from performances at the minor theaters. Increasingly, any references to the Revolution were prohibited. For example, in November 1789 Covent Garden decided to revive a pantomime entitled *Harlequin Touchstone* and to include within the play a new scene depicting the procession of France's three Estates; the examiner of plays first banned the play and then apparently insisted that the procession be transferred to Rome while deleting several passages that might seem to embrace republican sentiments. Again, *The Death of the Queen of France,* although a violently antirepublican play, was denied a license twice, in 1794 and in 1804, which suggests that the government was so squeamish about revolutionary events that any portrayal of them was suspect. Censorship was sufficiently prevalent by 1793 that almost all political comment was excluded from the drama. In fact, the lord chamberlain rarely had to exercise his power because theater managers became so sensitive about contemporary allusions that they became censors in their own right. As the author of the rejected *Helvetic Liberty* (1792) put it, the playwright who sought to bring political matters into the theater found "in that paradise . . . politics to be the forbidden fruit, lest the people's eyes should be opened and they become as gods knowing good and evil: in brief my Piece was politely returned, with an assurance, that it was too much in favor of the liberties of the people, to obtain the Lord Chamberlain's licence for representation."

Apparently, the official fear was that the theatrical re-creation of revolutionary events would lead to their reenactment on the streets. Herbert Lindenberger has noted that defenders of the drama—and of the historical drama in particular—have praised the theater's ability to inspire by offering great historical figures that the audience will then desire to emulate; Lindenberger quotes Thomas Heywood, who says of convincing historical re-creation that "so bewitching a thing is lively and well spirited action, that it hath power to new mold the h[e]arts of the spectators and fashion them to the shape of any noble and notable attempts." Similar views were expressed during the Romantic period. Hazlitt, for example, in reviewing *Coriolanus* as a play that he says includes all the ideas in "Burke's 'Reflections,' or Paine's 'Rights of Man,' or the debates in both Houses of Parliament since the French Revolution," argues that "we may depend upon it, that what men delight to read in books, they will put in practice in reality." Again, John Haggit in his reactionary *Count de Villeroi* (1794) notes that the drama is "most powerfully calculated to influence the public mind" and laments that the English have not followed the French National Assembly who "by the pieces which they have ordered to be acted, as well as those composed for the purpose . . . have gained an astonishing increase of popularity to their cause, astonishing to those who have never considered the influence of theatrical performances." And, of course, the revolutionary government's extensive use of the drama as a means of molding opinion testifies to their belief in the power of the theater.

The problem was that, if the historical drama inspired to "noble and notable attempts," it could also—at least in the eyes of the powers that be—"bewitch" audiences into imitating dangerous, rebellious acts. The British government, concerned about any avowal of republican sentiments on the stage, was particularly bothered by the representation of mass or mob action. Although we can find crowd scenes in Dent's *Bastille* and in *The Picture of Paris,* they were prohibited in other cases, as we can see from the examiner's copies of the *Island of St. Marguerite,* which reveal the censor's anxiety to control the drama's inflammatory potential. Larpent had the theater recast the climactic scene in which a mob descends upon the evil Commandant's castle where the Man in the Iron Mask is imprisoned. In the original version, the crowd frees the prisoner and hauls the Commandant off to be executed—that is, the ending was essentially an exact parallel to the scene in which the Bastille is taken in Dent's play. In the version finally licensed, however, the Commandant comes out to the mob to tell them that the Man in the Iron Mask is within the castle and warns them not to turn "from liberty to license." He remains unharmed. Larpent also had potentially dangerous words removed from the mouths of the mob; republican sentiments were apparently less dangerous if voiced by a figure of authority, in this case an officer. As L. W. Conolly argues, giving the officer the potentially radical lines "lessens the *rapport* between gallery and stage and gives an air of respectability to the sentiments expressed." If the populace was presented with the portrait of a unified and radical populace on stage, then it too might rise up. Shelley understood this potential, and tried to evoke and provoke the power of mass action in *The Mask of Anarchy,* a poem that owes much to dramatic precedent. The authorities feared the potential of communal dramatic experiences to create a revolutionary community; a vision such as that in *The Mask of Anarchy* could not be printed let alone performed.

Despite such censorship, playwrights could not ignore this revolutionary master theme; instead they sought to present it obliquely. One strategy—rarely successful, given the watchful censor—was to find historical parallels to the French Revolution in earlier uprisings. Plays were written—but not staged—about Wat Tyler and the Peasant's Revolt (e.g., Richard Cumberland's *Richard the Second,* revised as the uncontroversial *The Armorer* before the censor would allow it to be performed at Covent Garden in 1793; or Southey's *Wat Tyler,* written in 1794 but not published until 1817) or William Tell (e.g., *Helvetic Liberty*); anti-republican authors also found historical parallels, as in Arthur Murphy's unacted *Arminius* (1798). However, the writers of the romantic period did find ways to dramatize the issues surrounding the French Revolution in two more distant and more useful displacements of current events: in neoclassical tragedy they found the means to portray tyranny—not just the tyranny of individual rulers but the subtler tyranny that the past and tradition hold over the future; and in the Gothic drama, they discovered the means to explore their ambivalence toward the individual liberated by revolt.

The choice of neoclassical tragedy to represent the Revolution or revolutionary themes—a strategy we find in Goethe's *Natural Daughter* (*Die natürliche Tochter;* 1803), Byron's history plays, and innumerable, long forgotten dramas that filled the theaters of the French Republic—might surprise us. In the age of Romanticism and revolution, neoclassicism might strike us as a preeminently conservative form. In France, however, in the works of artists such as David and dramatists such as Marie-Joseph Chenier, neoclassicism became the style of the Revolution, and this ideological tie was not without impact in England. Plays on classical themes often received a political reading. We have already noted Hazlitt's comments on Shakespeare's *Coriolanus.* Sheridan Knowles's classical *Caius Gracchus* (1823; Drury Lane, 1823) and *Virginius* (Covent Garden, 1820) were both censored for their liberal ideas. This provoked Hazlitt to complain, "Is the name of Liberty to be struck out of the English language, and are we not to hate tyrants even in an old Roman play?" The answer was given by George Coleman, examiner of plays after the death of Larpent, who told Bulwer-Lytton's parliamentary panel investigating the status of the theater that he would ban from the stage "anything that may be so allusive to the times as to be applied to the existing moment, and which is likely to be inflammatory." He then went on to note that the word *reform* might provoke a disturbance in a theater and that he would not permit a play about Charles the First, "because it amounted to everything but cutting off the King's head upon the stage." For him any historical incident that paralleled the Revolution was a dangerous provocation: neoclassicism could be another disguise for radical sentiments.

The most intriguing attempt to use neoclassical form to treat revolutionary matters occurs in Byron's three history plays, *Marino Faliero, The Two Foscari,* and *Sardanapalus* (all three 1821; *Marino Faliero* was performed that year at Covent Garden). That these plays, which all center upon a struggle between tyranny and liberty, have a political, even revolutionary, theme has been noted by reviewers, both in Byron's day and our own; *Marino Faliero* was performed only in a heavily censored version; and Byron himself wrote to Kinnaird that the play "is full of republicanism." Given this subject matter, readers often have been puzzled by Byron's choice of a neoclassical style. Still, we can see the appropriateness of his neoclassical form to his vision of revolt: the neoclassical form images the power of the past over the future that revolt would create. Significantly, when at the close of *Sardanapalus,* his most severely classical play, Byron wants his hero to offer a vision of the future—"a light / To lesson ages" (V, i, 440-41)—he shatters the play's neoclassical fetters in a grand romantic finale that inspired Delacroix's painting.

The power of the past over the future is asserted throughout the two Venetian plays. In *The Two Foscari,* all of the central male characters are fixated upon the past and tradition: Loredano is obsessed with revenge against the elder Foscari, for he believes the Doge to have murdered his father and uncle; the Doge himself is so tied to the traditional forms of Venetian law that he will do nothing to prevent the torturing of his son; and that son has brought this torture upon himself by an obsessive need to return to his ancestral home in Venice after he has been banished from it. The central image in the play sums up this entrapment in the past: the play opens with Loredano speaking of his account book in which he has entered Foscari's debt to him for the two lives of his kinsmen; it closes after the deaths of the two Foscari with Loredano closing out his account book over the collapsed body of the Doge. *The Two Foscari* is a play in which the present owes a debt to the past that binds the future to the patterns of violence that have marked previous history.

This vision of history—in which the future can never

break free of the rhythms of the past—dominates Byron's vision even in *Marino Faliero, Doge of Venice,* which presents a revolutionary effort to free Venice from tyranny. The play analyzes a political situation in which a party of aristocrats have robbed Venice's nominal ruler, the Doge, of any power and denied the people their rights. The Doge thus joins a plebeian revolt, hoping that a popular revolution will re-create Venice as a republic within which he can act freely and win the public acclaim he identifies with his heroic honor; his goal is to "free Venice and avenge my wrongs." Yet this revolt for an ideal Venice is beset by contradictions that arise from Faliero's ultimate commitment to an idealized past rather than to a vision of the future. The heroic self-image that Faliero struggles to reassert is bound up with the city's traditional hierarchy and with the very nobles he must kill, for he is an aristocrat himself; as he realizes, "Each stab to them will seem my suicide." If he does not act, he loses his powerful sense of himself to the political realities of a debased present. If he does act, he must move to destroy the social and political forms that in the past have been the supporters of his identity. Although he fights for the revolutionary regeneration of his society, his problems can be resolved only by a revival of a neoclassical world of honor and hierarchy.

Faliero's inability to escape the past is reinforced by the fact that the rebels come to commit the same crimes for which they condemn the aristocrats. They talk of ideals but repeat the kind of violence that has marked Venetian history. As in *The Two Foscari,* the neoclassical form becomes an image of society's inability to break free from the past and into the future. For example, in order to preserve the unities that Byron embraced as the hallmark of the "regular" drama (see "Preface" to *Marino Faliero*), he has the key elements of the political crisis—Steno's insult to Faliero's wife and the assault by a noble upon the rebel leader, Israel Bertuccio—occur prior to the opening of the play; by the end of the first act, we have already witnessed Faliero's movement toward the rebellion as he reacts angrily to the light reprimand Steno receives. The rest of the play can offer (within its twenty-four-hour limit) the rise and fall of the revolt. This structure gives the play unity and inevitability; but inevitability also arises from the sense that what occurs within the play's present has already been determined by what has occurred in the past. Largely given over to exposition, the play is firmly tied to events that occurred prior to the first act, and the conclusion appears as the fateful closing off of the future as only destruction looms for Venice. *Marino Faliero* goes further than does *The Two Foscari,* presenting not just society's entanglement in the past but that of the revolutionary himself: the tragedy is not just that man has failed to change society, but that the rebel finds himself—as in Blake's "Orc cycle"—becoming a new tyrant.

If neoclassical tragedy was a form tied to the past, and thus an appropriate choice to portray humanity's entrapment in the past, the popular Gothic melodrama seemed as immediate as the Revolution itself. The melodrama arose alongside of the Revolution; Pixérécourt, the "father" of the French melodrama, fought both for and against the revolutionary government and escaped the Terror to create the kind of dramatic fare that pleased audiences who had experienced with him the splendors and miseries of their day. The shape and mood of the melodrama were often close to such revolutionary plays as Monvel's *Cloistered Victims* (*Les Victimes Cloîtrées;* 1791) and Maréchal's *Judgment Day for Kings* (*Le Jugement dernier des rois;* 1793). The ties between the melodrama and the Revolution that saw its birth were asserted by Charles Nodier, who argued that melodrama was "the only popular tragedy appropriate to our age"; he saw the violence and moralism that marked the melodrama as an image of the chaos and restoration of order that had marked French history.

English melodrama in its early Gothic form could also appear to embrace republicanism, as in Monk Lewis's *The Castle Spectre,* a smash hit at Drury Lane in 1797. As in most Gothic plays, the action centers upon the struggle of the beautiful heroine, Angela, against the evil aristocrat, Osmond, who has killed her mother and attempted to assassinate her father. Though she too will prove of noble birth, she has been raised by humble folk and comes to represent the domestic values of family, home, and purity against the amoral power of Osmond. Much of the plot concerns attempts by Angela and the heroic Percy to escape from Osmond's decaying castle, which seems to symbolize a ruined aristocratic past. In that their escape and their liberation of Angela's imprisoned father are aided by comic rustics and servants opposed to the villainous Earl, the play could be seen to embrace a republican view of natural equality; and, in fact, the drama included attacks upon slavery by the villain's black henchman that were marked for omission by the examiner.

The truly radical feature of the Gothic melodrama, however, lay not in its plot—which was finally a moralizing one—or in individual speeches—which were subject to censorship—but in its characterization of the villain, who increasingly becomes a villain-hero, a complex, inwardly divided, charismatic figure, far more attractive than the bumbling, official hero. Lewis's Osmond, for example, is much more appealing than the dull Percy; whereas Percy seems largely ineffectual (it is Angela who finally saves her father), Osmond not only controls the action but is also granted considerable sympathy as he struggles with his present love for Angela and his remorse over past crimes against her parents. That such figures were considered as "revolutionary"—and as potentially dangerous—can be seen in Coleridge's attack upon Maturin's Gothic tragedy *Bertram* (Drury Lane, 1816), in which he rejects the Gothic as the "modern Jacobinical drama," because it finds grandeur in immoral figures. Within the plot the villain-hero acts as a feudal aristocrat bent upon maintaining the system of rank and power that sustains him, even if he must commit crimes to do so; but as a sympathetic character, he embraces the liberation of the self from any social code, any system of power. He may oppose social change, but he embodies a more individual revolt, a stand against all authority that would reduce the self. The Gothic villain-hero reminds us that the age of the French Revolution also had room for more personal rebellions.

Of course, the Gothic drama was not truly revolutionary. It remained escapist rather than inflammatory. Indeed, the melodrama always insisted upon a return to moral order. The domestic virtues of the hero and heroine overcome the liberated selfhood of the villain-hero. As Peter Brooks has argued, the violence that marks the melodrama thus becomes a means of reinstating order—a way of revealing the moral valence of the characters—not a path to a radically new society. The revolutionary motto of Saint-Just was that the Revolution rules through Virtue, not Terror, but the melodrama embraces terror to recover virtue. Within the melodrama the Revolution becomes a necessary and temporary testing of an eternal moral order.

Still, romantic dramatists found in the Gothic villain-hero a vehicle for exploring both the glory and the danger they discovered in the self liberated by revolt. In plays closely allied to the Gothic drama, such as Schiller's *Robbers* (*Die Räuber;* 1781) and its two descendants, Wordsworth's *Borderers* (1795-96; published 1842) and Coleridge's *Remorse* (Drury Lane, 1813), the rebel figure's revolt leads him into crime, but we still find him superior to the world he rejects. The fear raised by such plays is that his revolt severs the conventional ties that would otherwise check the revolutionary's deeds; it enables him—much like the villain-hero—to see himself as an amoral superman: Karl Moor, for example, comes to realize that two men like himself would wreck the moral universe.

The younger romantics continued to draw upon the Gothic heritage. *The Cenci* is in many ways a Gothic tragedy, and Wasserman and Behrendt among others have found in it a treatment of revolution. The debt of the Byronic hero to the villain-hero is well known; in *Werner* Byron works to transform the Gothic into historical tragedy, and in *Manfred* and *Cain* he offers vastly refined examples of the Gothic self's revolt against authority. Such Gothic characters offended the government censors, whose opposition suggests the ideological import of the Gothic villain-hero. Larpent blocked the performance of a translation of *The Robbers* because, the translator tells us, "the grandeur of his [Moor's] character renders him more likely to excite imitation than aborhence" and this "conjunction of sublime virtue with consummate depravity, though it may be found in nature, should never be dragged into view:—the heroism dazzles the mind, and renders it blind to atrocity." Larpent's successor, Coleman, offered a broader objection to Gothic characters, stating that he would not license plays that "pourtray [*sic*] the disaffected as gallant heroes and hapless lovers." Rebellious characters could be granted no sympathy lest such sympathy be extended also to actual ideas and causes.

The censors were not very successful in eliminating Gothic villain-heroes or the tragic rebels of neoclassical drama from the stage. But, then, such figures were less dangerous than direct political comment or the representation of the Revolution itself. After all, these plays did not present successful revolutionary movements; in fact, they hardly represent movements at all, despite conspiracies such as the one in *Marino Faliero.* Both the Gothic melodrama and neoclassical tragedy refocus attention upon the individual—and an aristocratic individual at that. There are no dangerous scenes of mob action in these plays. They pit an individual against a society, and it is usually a solitary such as Faliero with as little sympathy for the people as he has for tyranny. It is, thus, interesting that in what I see as the third or mythic phase of the romantic attempt to "personify" the Revolution we find playwrights creating—if not mass movements—at least archetypal human figures rather than unique individuals.

This phase is best represented by Shelley, who gave his dramas on political events a mythological frame in *Prometheus Unbound, Hellas,* and *Swellfoot the Tyrant.* Shelley is not, however, the only poet to turn revolution into myth. The ideological concerns of Byron's metaphysical plays have been noted by a number of critics; and Goethe sought in the second part of *Faust* to work out his attitudes toward the French Revolution in the struggle between "Neptunism" and "Vulcanism" in the "Classical Walpurgisnacht."

Still, Shelley provides the fullest example. His reasons for turning history into myth are complex, but in a curious way he ultimately shares with the government censors a basic objection to the direct representation of recent French history: they fear the impact that the spectacle of the Revolution might have on an audience. Like these censors Shelley believes in the ability of poetry to shape behavior. In *The Defence of Poetry,* he argues that those who read Homer, for example, "were awakened to an ambition of becoming like to Achilles, Hector, and Ulysses"; and Athenian drama presented "that ideal perfection and energy which every one feels to be the internal type of all that he loves, admires, and would become." Given this belief in the power of art, Shelley is concerned about the direct portrayal of revolutionary events: dramas of revolt might lead audiences to embrace the brand of violent political action that Shelley clearly rejects; or, more ominously, in depicting the collapse of the Revolution, the drama might inculcate despair in the remaining defenders of liberty. Shelley saw such political despair—and the quietism and conservatism it can bring—as a key problem for Restoration Europe. Wordsworth's embrace of private over public solutions and Southey's political apostasy were vivid examples for him of what could happen to men who had internalized the Terror, Napoleon, and war as despairing rejoinders to their youthful revolutionary hopes. Harold Bloom has suggested that the literal is, for the poet as poet, death. I would suggest that, for the romantics as dramatists of the Revolution, the literal recreation of history was death for revolutionary hopes. It is significant that the period's two most despairing treatments of revolt turn to the literal: Musset's *Lorenzaccio* (1834) closes with the actual speech given by Cosimo de Medici as he took control of Florence, this literal recreation signaling the end of the dreams of revolution set forth earlier in the play; and Büchner's *Danton's Death* (*Dantons Tod;* 1835) relies heavily upon transcripts of speeches by key revolutionary figures, the literal reiteration of historical documents adding to that play's sense of entrapment and inevitability. Shelley, however, set out to write dramas that would replace the literal with the mythic, that would translate events from what he saw as the "sad reality" ("Dedication" to *The Cenci*) of historical events to a visionary plane where hope for a future revolution could be nourished. From Shelley's perspective all the dramatic attempts to stage the Revolution I have been discussing fail. As Shelley knew well, the project of portraying the Revolution was beset by difficulties. Ronald Paulson has argued that the French Revolution challenged the artist to assimilate within traditional forms what were felt to be unprecedented events. Simply put, playwrights faced a tension between the astonishing new content presented by the events of the French Revolution and the conventional dramatic models they might select to give shape to those events. Shelley understood this tension; in writing *Hellas*—a play about revolt and liberation in Greece—he adopted the strictures of Greek tragedy; yet in speaking of the content of the play, he apologized for relying upon "newspaper erudition" ("Preface"). Shelley outlines here two directions playwrights turned in their attempts to stage the Revolution: they adopted traditional forms into which the writers molded current events, even though they might thus discount the very novelty of those events; alternatively, they allowed contemporary content to determine form, even though this might result in the sacrifice of vision to fact—or, worse yet, to the narrow political opinions of the moment. As Paulson argues, the dramatist seemed to be caught between the poles of the present and the past.

Shelley hoped to escape this bind by creating dramas directed toward neither the past nor the present but the future. It is interesting to note that the worst thing that Shelley's Christ in the fragmentary prologue to *Hellas* has to say about Satan is that "Thou seest but the Past in the To-Come." For Shelley the drama of the day was trapped in patterns of repetition, tied to the past, not creative of the future. Documentary plays literally repeat the past—even if it is the recent past—and threaten to drown us in despair. The Gothic melodrama reiterates the morality of the past, no matter what its theatrical innovations or plunges into daring characterization. Neoclassical tragedies of revolt, even those of Byron, were incapable of staging any moment of liberation without shattering their form. Shelley explicitly criticizes neoclassical tragedy and the melodrama in the *Defence:*

> In periods of the decay of social life, the drama sympathizes with that decay. Tragedy becomes a cold imitation of the form of the great masterpieces of antiquity, divested of all harmonious accompaniment of the kindred arts; and often the very form misunderstood: or a weak attempt to teach certain doctrines, which the writer considers as moral truths; and which are usually no more than specious flatteries of some gross vice or weakness with which the author in common with his auditors are infected. Hence what has been called the classical and the domestic drama.

Imitations of past forms and presentations of fleeting contemporary ideologies are signs of social decay, not signposts to a revitalized future.

Prometheus Unbound contains within itself a critique of these opposing attempts to "personify" the Revolution. The attempt to portray directly the true but sad tale of the Revolution receives the clearest criticism; for the staging of revolutionary failure is one of the tortures brought to bear on Prometheus by the Furies, as they call to him:

> See! a disenchanted nation
> Springs like day from desolation;
> To truth its state, is dedicate,
> And Freedom leads it forth, her mate;
> A legioned band of linked brothers
> Whom Love calls children—
> 'Tis another's—
>
> See how kindred murder kin!
> 'Tis the vintage-time for Death and Sin:
> Blood, like new wine, bubbles within
> Till Despair smothers
>
> The Struggling World, which slaves and tyrants win.

As Prometheus himself states when the Furies first approach, the danger in watching such spectacles is that "Whilst I behold such execrable shapes, / Methinks I grow like what I contemplate / And laugh and stare in loathsome sympathy." A preoccupation with the failures of the past leads us to repeat these failures. Shelley explores more fully this possibility of becoming what one beholds in the companion piece to *Prometheus Unbound, The Cenci,* a sad reality counterposed to the high idealisms of his mythic drama. In his history play, Shelley's Count Cenci describes what he hopes to do to Beatrice in forcing her into an incestuous relationship:

> She shall become (for what she most abhors
> Shall have a fascination to entrap
> Her loathing will), to her own conscious self
> All she appears to others. . . .

Of course, most readings of *The Cenci* find Beatrice in fact becoming what she most abhors, that is, becoming a duplicate of her father; and Wasserman has suggested that Beatrice's decision to use her father's violence to overcome her father's tyranny parallels the course of the Revolution: *The Cenci,* then, becomes an example of what happens when man cannot free himself from the patterns of the past. Prometheus's great victory is that he overcomes the past—even the revolutionary past with its high hopes and deadly despair. He refuses to repeat the past in refusing to repeat his curse, in "unsaying" that curse. He liberates himself from historical time, just as Shelley liberates his play from the historical time of documentary reconstruction.

Shelley's objections to neoclassical re-creations of the French Revolution are partially grounded in his rejection of hackneyed forms, outlined in the passage from the *Defence* quoted above; but his reservations went further, as can be seen in his comments on Byron's use of a neoclassical model for his history plays. He remarked of *Marino Faliero* that Byron "affects to patronize a system of criticism fit only for the production of mediocrity, & although all his fine poems & passages have been produced in defiance of this system: yet I recognize the pernicious effects of it in the 'Doge of Venice.' " As Charles Robinson has argued, Shelley felt that Byron's traditional form forced him to adopt a predestined action that finds reform inevitably leading to violence; and insofar as that action appeared fated, there also seemed to be an excuse for that violence. Byron's neoclassical plays can be read as embracing the two results of the Revolution that most concerned

Shelley: the turn to violence as the only way to combat tyranny, and despair over what appears to be the inevitable corruption of the forces of liberty when they adopt such violence. Byron shared Shelley's liberal views, but Shelley believed that Byron's neoclassical aesthetic ultimately betrayed those views. Shelley saw, as Starobinski and Paulson have seen, that neoclassicism—even when it was adopted by the Revolution itself—could not portray the liberation of revolt, its leap toward the future. The traditional form came to embody man's entanglement in historical patterns, and thus, in Starobinski's words, "such tragedy was doomed to mere repetition."

Shelley, of course, offers his own brand of classicism in *Prometheus Unbound,* but he clearly overturns classical traditions in his revisionist handling of Aeschylus. In inverting Aeschylus's ending, Shelley liberated his play from any pattern of inevitability; the play depicts not the force of fate but the power of the will and the imagination. The grand romantic finale of the fourth act stands as an emblem of Shelley's rejection of traditional versions of classicism, as he leaves behind all models to celebrate a world remade.

Even the melodrama is subsumed and transformed in Shelley's play. Stuart Curran has noted the generic label for *Prometheus Unbound*—lyric drama—which marks its ties to the opera. But "lyric drama" might also remind us of the *melo-* or *music*-drama. The melodrama typically followed a four-act structure in which a virtuous hero and heroine struggle against an oppressive villain, as the action moves toward the overthrow of the tyrant and the union of the lovers; the plot was often resolved through the uncovering of some mysterious relationship—usually some question of paternity or kinship—here, the paternity of that ultimate mysterious stranger Demogorgon. I do not want to render *Prometheus Unbound* into a melodrama. What I want to suggest is that Shelley includes the outlines of that form to respond to its vision of narrow moralism, of terror issuing in virtue, a vision worthy of Jupiter. In Shelley's play terror is laid to rest, and traditional morality is overturned as man frees himself to rule the world through imagination and love.

In a sense all of these alternative dramatic forms create plays written within the language of Prometheus's curse, a language bound to past tyranny and violent resistance. In seeking to replace this language with a visionary language that will be a "perpetual Orphic song," Shelley seeks to displace these rival "personifications" of the Revolution: in the place of the "sad reality" of historical chronicles, he offers the "dreams of what ought to be" provided by myth ("Dedication," *The Cenci*); to counter the restrictions of neoclassical tragedy, he offers his own romantic classicism with its open form; and rather than a moralizing melodrama, he offers his lyric drama with its celebration of "the great secret of morals," love (*Defence*).

Of course, one can argue that this mythic "personification" of the Revolution is not a personification at all but an impersonation, a sublimation of the Revolution's actual violence in order to create a metaphoric or mythic "beau ideal" of revolt, to quote Shelley's own description of his *Revolt of Islam.* These plays clearly participate in what Jerome McGann has called the "romantic ideology": "The poetry of Romanticism is everywhere marked by extreme forms of displacement and poetic conceptualization whereby the actual human issues with which the poetry is concerned are resituated in a variety of idealized localities." The question to be asked is what is gained by such displacement. The movement away from actual historical events and issues can appear as an evasion, a turn to ideal solutions over complex human problems. Such may be the case with Coleridge's dramatic corpus. It begins with the historical *Fall of Robespierre* (1794), which treats the Revolution as an example of usurpation, then turns to *Osorio/Remorse* (1797/1813), which again depicts an example of political usurpation but now within a Gothic framework, and concludes with *Zapolya* (1817), a romance in which the usurpers are defeated and a conservative ideal of stability and succession is discovered. In moving from documentary play to Gothic parallel to romance, Coleridge seems to be fleeing the troubling historical realities of his day in pursuit of a form within which his vision of the Revolution as a simple act of usurpation can be brought to a satisfactory conclusion.

However, Coleridge's development is not that of Shelley, for example. There *is* in the romantic dramatists' move to myth an increasingly ambiguous attitude toward history and politics. Romantic plays dealing with revolt—from Goethe's *Götz* (1773) and Schiller's *Robbers* to Hugo's *Hernani* (1830) and Büchner's *Danton's Death*—typically depict the rebel's involvement with the historical realm as part of the tragedy. It is, for example, because Byron's Foscari and Faliero must adopt the means available to them in their time and place—Foscari is forced to accept the rituals of the law and Faliero finds himself allied with a plebeian rebellion that contradicts his own sense of himself—that they are unable to find a path of action that breaks free from Venice's doomed history. Again, it is because Beatrice Cenci lives in a particular historical reality dominated by patriarchal systems of authority and the ideology of the church that she makes what Shelley calls her "pernicious mistake" and kills her father ("Preface" to *The Cenci*). The heroes of romantic drama remain time-trapped as long as they remain within the confines of the early nineteenth-century stage, the stage of John Dent's documentary romance, Sheridan Knowles's neoclassical plays, Monk Lewis's Gothic dramas. They can, however, be liberated on the mythic or visionary stage. Faliero and Foscari cannot find a mode of action that does not compromise their sense of honor, but Manfred walks through his play shunning any compromise to remain master of his fate. Beatrice must succumb to violence or react with violence, but Prometheus can move beyond violence to vision. Although in these visionary plays the historical past—and particularly the revolutionary past—is in part lost, that past is translated into a myth whose goal is to shape future history. (pp. 33-50)

Jeffrey N. Cox, "The French Revolution in the English Theater," in History & Myth: Essays on English Romantic Literature, *edited by Stephen C. Behrendt, Wayne State University Press, 1990, pp. 33-52.*

Marvin Carlson on Revolutionary drama:

The Revolution left its mark everywhere on the theatre, and from time to time it is not surprising to find that the theatre left its mark on the Revolution. So we find, for example, a troupe of actors setting off to war in stage chariots and presenting battle re-creations on fields where the blood was scarcely dry. Or . . . , we see the leaders of the Revolution concerning themselves with great theatrical festivals, offering to the masses entertainments such as only monarchs had previously enjoyed.

Marvin Carlson, in his Theatre of the French Revolution, *1966.*

Peter Brooks

[*Brooks is an American educator and critic. In the essay below, he presents a Freudian interpretation of the prison liberation theme, which was prevalent in European literature after the French Revolution.*]

In a dusty corner of the Musée Carnavalet in Paris, one can find the ladders, constructed from bedsheets and firewood, that purportedly were used by Henri Masers de Latude in his escape from the Bastille in 1756. Latude spent little time at liberty; he was apprehended, returned to the Bastille, then transferred to other prisons—Vincennes, Charenton, Bicêtre—and finally released in 1784 after a total of thirty-five years in confinement for having insulted Madame de Pompadour. He became celebrated through his Memoirs, the first version of them, in 1787, apparently apocryphal, a later authorized version prepared by the lawyer Thiery. When the Bastille was stormed on July 14, 1789, Latude's ladders, and various other tools manufactured for his ingenious escape, were found in the *greffe* of the prison. They were put on public display in 1834, in the foyer of the Théâtre de la Gaîté, for the opening of Guilbert de Pixerécourt's "mélodrame historique," *Latude, ou trente-cinq ans de captivité.* This was the last great success of the playwright known as the "Corneille of the Boulevards," and the play he chose to close the fourth and final volume of his *Théâtre choisi.* It sums up not only dominant themes and situations in Pixerécourt's vast melodramatic production, but as well an obsessive imaginative focus of melodrama from the moment of its creation, during the Revolution. Pixerécourt's play is about the nightmare of captivity, life constrained in the dungeon, unable to assert its rights, unable to make heard its claim to innocence. Latude's rightful name is even changed in the prison registers, to ensure that he will never be able to nominate himself as what he is, the victim of arbitrary tyranny. His companion in imprisonment and confederate in his ill-starred escape, Dalègre, finally goes mad from the deprivations of captivity, and by the end hallucinates himself in the role of jailer and torturer rather than victim. The opening of the prison, performed in the last act of the play by the enlightened minister Malesherbes, reveals a sorry spectacle, the underside of the Age of Reason.

From July 14, 1789, onwards, the Bastille will be taken and opened up and torn down hundreds of times in the theatres of Paris, in vaudevilles and melodramas using various story lines to reach this glorious moment. The prison and the aspiration for liberation become dominant themes in the French and European imagination, as Victor Brombert has so well shown. From those popular plays entitled *La Prise de la Bastille* or some slight variant thereof to the melodramas of the Empire and the Restoration—*Le Château des Appenins, Les Mines de Pologne, La Forteresse du Danube*—to the memoirs of Silvio Pellico and Alexandre Andryane, to the novels of Stendhal and Hugo, to Beethoven's *Fidelio* and the operas of Verdi, the prison is everywhere, the act of liberation a salutation to a new era in which the rights of man will be a fundamental guarantee, the freedom to dispose of one's own mind and body an irreducible test of civilization.

But what interests me here is less the aspiration to liberty than what one finds when the liberators open the prisons, what lies concealed in the depths and comes to light with the gesture of liberation. Here, I think, one encounters something less clearly progressive and beneficent than the simple setting free of prisoners. The act of opening up releases a certain repressed which reason has ignored. It is here that the structure of fortress and prison, with moats, drawbridges, towers and, especially, layer upon layer of subterranean *cachots* and *oubliettes,* comes to resemble a Freudian conceptualization of the mind as a spatialized construct of the conscious, the preconscious, and the unconscious, and the uncovering of repressed material as an archeological excavation into ever more deeply buried strata of psychic life. Some of the best representations of this structure come in those Revolutionary dramas sometimes labeled as *théâtre monacal:* dramas of forced religious vocations and diabolical abbots and abbesses which always include subterranean crypts and *in pace* where the virtuous are confined and tortured until release arrives. While this Gothic situation can be found in novels and plays that predate the Revolution—for the Revolution was culturally as well as politically prepared, anticipated in the realm of *l'imaginaire* as well as in those of *le politique* and *le social*—the storming of the Bastille and then the attacks on the clergy and on monasticism give it a new vigor and popularity during the Revolution, in plays such as *Les Rigueurs du cloître,* by Fiévée (1790), *Le Couvant, ou les voeux forcés* (1790), by Olympe de Gouges, *Les Victîmes cloîtrées* (1791), by Boutet de Monvel, *Fénelon, ou les religieuses de Cambrai* (1793), by Marie-Joseph Chénier, *Julie, ou la Religieuse de Nismes* (1796), by Charles Pougens, among many others. Particularly following the liberation of the theatres on January 13, 1791, there was full flowering of melodramatic treatments of the theme.

I want to dwell for just a moment on Boutet de Monvel's *Les Victîmes cloîtrées,* which has often been called the first melodrama (though the label had not yet come into use), presented to the acclamations of the audience by the Comédiens-Français on March 29, 1791. In this play, monastic, political, and erotic intrigue converge to the point where they are indistinguishable. The evil Pére Laurent cloisters the innocent Eugénie against her will—ostensibly to please the aristocrat Madame de Saint-Alban, who wants to prevent her mésalliance with the merchant Dorval—but really in order to pursue his own libidinous designs on her; while Madame de Saint-Alban's brother, the virtuous Francheville, has been elected mayor by *his concitoyens,* and combats Dorval's desperate resolution to cloister himself (abetted by Père Laurent, who wants Dorval's fortune) through arguments that a young man should put his talents at the service of *la patrie.* To no avail. By the fourth act, both Eugénie and Dorval have been consigned to the deepest *in pace* cells of the convent and the monastery, respectively, which, it so happens, are built side by side, and share a common wall. So that the decor of the fourth and final act shows two prison cells, one stage left, the other stage right, the one containing Eugénie, the other Dorval, each of whom pursues a soliloquy of despair. But before Père Laurent comes to pursue his designs on Eugénie, Dorval discovers a tunnel from the one cell to the other, nearly completed by a predecessor prisoner who spent twenty years at labor on it before expiring. To the cry of "Liberté! liberté! soutiens-moi!" Dorval completes the tunnel, and comes through to Eugénie's cell. Noises are heard on the stairs leading down to the cells. Eugénie and Dorval prepare to die fighting, when the door opens to reveal the party of the virtuous, escorted by the municipal police and led by Francheville draped in his mayoral *tricolore* sash, who have overcome Père Laurent and his henchmen and come to free the victims. Francheville sums up: "O mes concitoyens! vous voyez les bienfaits de la loi. . . ." And a virtuous monk, Père Louis, has the curtain line, announcing that he will leave the monastery: "je vais briser les chaînes que la violence m'imposa si longtemps."

The chains of violent constraint are broken, the victims of tyrannical oppression are liberated from the depths, republicanism triumphs. Yet there remains the image of that fourth-act setting, the deepest dungeon, where prisoners are deprived of justice and of their very identity, and where the female victim is subject to the erotic will of her persecutor. One may be reminded of Robert-Fleury's famous painting of Pinel ordering the chains taken off the madwomen of the Salpêtrière when he assumed its direction in 1795: along with the gesture of liberation, we remain forcibly impressed by the anguished faces and twisted bodies of the madwomen. If the Revolution constituted a solar myth, as Jean Starobinski puts it, the light of reason that it shed kept illuminating situations of unreason, shadows of the human heart and mind that could not be so simply dispersed.

Among the members of the audience at *Les Victîmes cloîtrées* was a young Englishman, Matthew Gregory Lewis, who was so impressed by Monvel's work that he translated and adapted it as *Venoni, or the Novice of St. Mark's,* which was staged at Drury Lane in 1808. As the title implies, Lewis has changed the place of the drama—to Sicily—and the identity of some of the characters, especially Francheville, "who in the original," he notes, "was a Republican Mayor, whose sentiments and conduct were by no means adapted to the present times or to the British taste." Lewis goes on, in his preface, to concede that while his first two acts were well-received at the first performance, "the last was by no means equally successful, and the concluding scene operated so strongly on the risible muscles of the audience, as to make it evident to me on the third night, that unless I could invent an entirely new last act, the piece must be given up altogether." So he substituted a new third act, and the play continued a successful run—interrupted only by the burning down of Drury Lane Theatre. Lewis maintains that the original last act was nonetheless preferable. Yet it could not work, I think, because once stripped of its political symbolism, the scene of liberation lost much of its power. Surely there were no "risible muscles" at work at the Théâtre de la Nation in 1791: the stakes of the opening of the depths were clear.

I mention Lewis's drama because between seeing *Les Victîmes cloîtrées* and producing *Venoni,* Lewis wrote his masterwork, *The Monk* (published in 1795 or 1796), a novel that was clearly inspired by Monvel's play and which, despite the nationality of its author and its transposition of events to other times and places, may legitimately, if somewhat perversely, be considered the greatest novel to come out of the French Revolution. And it was in fact a work that at once returned to France, in the form of numerous translations, imitations and, especially, theatrical adaptations, including one by Pixerécourt himself. *The Monk* takes as its setting Spain, at an unidentified date but one at which the Inquisition appears to reign supreme. Through his masterful evocation of the penetrating omnipresence of the Inquisition, Lewis creates a powerful image of any regime of unreason and arbitrary tyranny. And in the churches, monasteries and, especially, the Convent of St. Clare that stand at the center of his novel, he creates the essential spaces of claustration, and within them the horrible monsters engendered by the sleep of reason and freedom.

I won't attempt to rehearse the complex plot of *The Monk,* which turns on the gradual conversion of Ambrosio, the holy abbot of the Capuchins, into a lustful monster who enters into pacts with the infernal powers in order to pursue his erotic needs. Ambrosio is first seduced by the novice Rosario, who turns out to be not a young man but a woman in disguise, Matilda, who has in fact served as the model for the icon of the Madonna that Ambrosio worships. So that the very vehicle of his sublimation of profane love in love divine becomes the instrument of the return of the repressed: the ambiguous figure of Rosario/Matilda unleashes the nether side of a passion Ambrosio thought to be wholly spiritual. Once she has seduced Ambrosio, Matilda initiates him into the practice of diabolical conjurations in order to perpetrate the seduction of the beautiful and virginal Antonia, whose mother he is forced to kill along the way, while he has Antonia drugged and removed to the deepest cell of the sepulchre of St. Clare, the better to practice upon her virtue. Meanwhile—in the novel's even wilder subplot—the pregnant Agnes has been separated from her lover, Don Raymond, and also entombed living in the underground sepulchre of St. Clare, in a punishment meted out by the hypocritical Domina of the convent, where she will have her baby amidst skeletons and decaying corpses. Thus the climax of all the tales of passion in *The Monk* will have to be played out in the deepest dungeons of the convent, accessible only through a hidden door concealed under the base of the statue of St. Clare, and by way of Piranesi-like staircases into the subterranean gloom. At the same time, the

The taking of the Bastille.

disappearance of Agnes and other young women has become public knowledge, and the populace rises in revolt against the Domina and the convent, murdering the one, setting fire to the other.

This, in brief, is the context in which both Don Lorenzo, brother of Agnes and renamored of Antonia, and Ambrosio go into the depths in the final chapters of the novel. First Lorenzo: he discovers a door into the sepulchre from the cemetery, and hears the sound of footsteps leading deep into "the labyrinth of passages." Leaving behind daylight and rationality, Lorenzo finds himself "impelled by a movement secret and unaccountable" into the sepulchre, until he undercovers the grate hidden under the statue of St. Clare, which, raised, shows the entrance to the true underworld: "A deep abyss now presented itself before them, whose thick obscurity the eye strove in vain to pierce." The fearful nuns gathered at the statue refuse to accompany him in his descent. "Alone therefore, and in darkness, he prepared to pursue his design. . . . " Down, down into the "gulph" he descends, as by compulsion, until finally in a "loathesome abode" he finds his beloved Agnes, clutching a bundle that turns out to be the corpse of her baby.

Agnes will fill in the full narrative of her prison sojourn momentarily, a story of lizards, toads, worms, and the excruciating agony of the slow death of the child. Meanwhile, we return to another part of the sepulchre, where the drugged Antonia has been confined, and Ambrosio prepares to further his designs on her: "By the side of three putrid half-corrupted bodies lay the sleeping beauty." Ambrosio's words of seduction suggest the identity of the dungeon with the deepest recess of forbidden desire: "This sepulchre seems to me Love's bower. This gloom is the friendly night of Mystery, which he spreads over our delights! Such do I think it, and such must my Antonia. Yes, my sweet girl! yes! Your veins shall flow with the fire which circles in mine, and my transports shall be doubled by your sharing them!" But she resists such seductions, and he is reduced to raping her. Immediately thereafter, he is seized by "disgust" (which may be the most frequently-repeated word in the novel) at his despoiling of innocence. But he cannot release her to tell her tale. The only solution he can propose is a life in the sepulchre: "Wretched girl, you must stay here with me! Here amidst these lonely tombs, these images of death, these rotting, loathesome, corrupted bodies! Here shall you stay, and witness my sufferings; witness what it is to be in the horrors of despondency, and breathe the last groan in blasphemy and curses!" When Antonia attempts to flee, he finally murders her.

To heighten further this frenetic drama it turns out that, all unbeknownst to the actors, Ambrosio and Antonia are brother and sister, thus the rape also an incest, the murder a fratricide, and the killing of Antonia's mother a matricide. It is in the logic of Ambrosio's towering sexual passion, once it has broken through the layers of denial and repression, that it should violate all the ultimate taboos. If the depths represent the effects of repression, pushing eros down into the deepest recess, once one penetrates into those depths one finds sexuality gone berserk, playing out scenarios of an unconscious that does not recognize contradiction. Incest in particular, as the taboo demarcating culture from nature and thus founding society, will have a long history in Romantic texts, as a temptation barely escaped, and often will be associated with the claustral space: think, for instance, of Chateaubriand's *René,* where Amélie's confession of her incestuous desire for her brother comes at the moment she is stretched out on a gravestone, during the *office des morts* that prepares her taking of the veil. The convent, the dungeon, the sepulchre are where the most intense and interdicted passions—interdicted because intense, intense because interdicted—come to be confined, and when one penetrates into the place of confinement, one finds the enactment of desires that reason and the daylight self do not avow.

This is the image that *The Monk* most forcefully impresses upon us: that in opening the depths, we not only perform an act of beneficent liberation, we also discover something much more troubling, something that political versions of liberation are not adequate to account for or deal with—an image already implicit in *Les Victîmes cloîtrées.* Claustration is itself the space of a psychic liberation, but of forces that political liberation needs to repress. Consider, in a final reflection on *The Monk,* Ambrosio's trial before the Inquisition, in the last chapter. The narrator tells us: "In these trials neither the accusation is mentioned, nor the name of the accuser. The prisoners are only asked, whether they will confess. If they reply, that, having no crime, they can make no confession, they are put to the torture without delay." Such a procedure appears in some ways as the very opposite of the Revolutionary tribunal, where denunciations are specific and often made in person. It is, one might say, the procedure appropriate for a world in which everyone is guilty, of unspecified crimes which are in the nature of man himself. It gives an image of guilt appropriate to post-Freudian man, living in the knowledge that psychic recesses harbor a freight of repressed desires normally excluded from consciousness.

The person who best understood the complicity of the claustral space with the release of repressed desire—indeed their mutual interdependence—was, of course, the Marquis de Sade, whose whole *oeuvre* narrates and dramatizes this connection. And in the work in which he brings his most sustained analytic attention to the Revolution—the tract "Français encore un effort si vous voulez être républicains," inserted into *La Philosophie dans le boudoir*—Sade argues that the Revolution will fail if it does not push forward to a total unrepression of manners and morals. The revolution must attain a state of permanent insurrection which is by definition a state of immorality. As Sade claims: "l'état *moral* d'un homme est un état de paix et de tranquillité, au lieu que son état *immoral* est un état de mouvement perpétuel qui le rapproche de l'insurrection nécessaire, dans laquelle il faut que le républicain tienne toujours le gouvernement dont il est membre." All of Sade's legislative project derives from this premise that the morality of the Republic is immorality, and that one must pursue the premise to its logical consequences, allowing all desires a full field for their exercise. Why marriage, since all children should be, not members of a family, but "uniquement les enfants de la patrie?" Incest? Does anything in nature outlaw it? On the contrary. "J'ose assurer, en un mot, que l'inceste devrait être la loi de tout gouvernement dont la fraternité fait la base." Sodomy? "L'habitude que les hommes ont de vivre ensemble dans les républiques y rendra toujours ce vice plus fréquent. . . . " At the climax of his argument, Sade reaches the "singular reflection" that an old and corrupt nation that throws off the yoke of tyranny can only maintain itself by crime: "car elle est déjà dans le crime, et si elle voulait passer du crime à la vertu, c'est-à-dire d'un état violent dans un état doux, elle tomberait dans une inertie dont sa ruine serait bientôt le résultat." One recognizes here a kind of hyper-logical extension of Robespierre's and Saint-Just's discourse of the necessity of Terror, carried into an inner realm.

Sade's fierce logic constitutes a charge, which perhaps can never be answered, against any political revolution: that it will remain superficial, and hence ultimately unsatisfying to the humanity it claims to benefit, if it does not address the liberation of what lies in the psychic prisons—what Sade does not hesitate to call the *crimes* of love. This critique of revolution was well captured for our own time by Peter Weiss' play, *The Persecution and Assassination of Jean-Paul Marat as Performed by the Inmates of the Asylum of Charenton under the Direction of the Marquis de Sade.* In this imagined debate between Marat and Sade, Sade finally argues the irreducible importance of the individual body and its desires: "Marat/ as I sat there in the Bastille/ for thirteen long years/ I learned/ that this is a world of bodies/ each body pulsing with a terrible power/ each body alone and racked with its own unrest/ In that loneliness/ marooned in a stone sea/ I heard lips whispering continually/ and felt all the time/ in the palms of my hands and in my skin/ touching and stroking/ Shut behind thirteen bolted doors/ my feet fettered/ I dreamed only/ of the orifices of the body/ put there/ so one may hook and twine oneself in them." Sade goes on to say: "Marat/ these cells of the inner self/ are worse than the deepest stone dungeon/ and as long as they are locked/ all your Revolution remains/ only a prison mutiny/ to be put down/ by corrupted fellow-prisoners."

In Peter Weiss's remarkable recreation of Sade, we have the paradox made explicit: that it is in the deepest dungeon that one discovers the existence and the meaning of the psychic crypt, the inner spaces of claustration—*diese Gefängnisse des Innern*—which harbor drives that political Revolution ignores—and ignores at its peril, since political liberation may in fact stumble upon the possibility of, and perhaps the need for, another kind of liberation, one that politics cannot address, and which indeed threatens to deconstruct the whole meaning of political revolution. Only in prison is the truly revolutionary potential of the psyche and the body set at large. It is notable how close to Weiss' troubling vision some of the plays of the Revolution and its aftermath come, particularly Monvel's *Les Victîmes cloîtrées* and Pixerécourt's *Latude.* For if these are ostensibly plays about the liberation from political and social tyranny, they are, in their darker aspect, equally about what one finds when one goes to perform liberation from the space of claustration. What one finds is deeply disturbing, the content of those inner psychic cells that both demands liberation, and—from the point of view of the political—must not be liberated. The body cloistered, imprisoned, constrained is not a political body alone. It is a sexualized body, dreaming of its orifices, a body in a state of insurrection against the psychic mechanisms of repression and sublimation. The political sense of imprisonment in the Bastille is matched by the psychic and bodily meanings of confinement in the madhouse of Charenton.

I will give the last word to one of the Revolutionary party, to Saint-Just, who, in a famous line of his "Institutions républicaines," exclaims: "Le gouvernement républicain a la vertu pour principe; sinon, la terreur. Que veulent ceux qui ne veulent ni vertu ni terreur?" What do they want, indeed? Saint-Just uses the logic of melodrama, the exclusion of the middle ground. But somewhere between republican virtue and republican terror lies a denied space that clamors for attention, and satisfaction. (pp. 113-22)

Peter Brooks, "The Opening of the Depths," in The French Revolution, 1789-1989: Two Hundred Years of Rethinking, *edited by Sandy Petrey, Texas Tech University Press, 1989, pp. 113-22.*

CHILDREN'S LITERATURE

Margaret R. Higonnet

[*Higonnet is an American educator and critic. In the following essay, she addresses the representation of the French Revolution in Victorian children's literature.*]

For Victorians, the French Revolution was "the greatest, the most animating event in history" (Matthew Arnold). They read their own history, whether complacently or with prophetic fear, through French history. Through fictions about the Revolution, they also sought to give their children a vision of an ideal social order and an understanding of historical processes. For historical fictions rarely have documentation as their sole intent. To be sure, the particulars about events or historical personages serve to color in a historical moment and thus to preserve one image of the past, among many possible images. In the same mirror, however, we read ourselves and the present. After the Chartist riots of 1831, writers like Thomas Carlyle saw "a second edition of the French Revolution" as "distinctly within the realm of chances" for England.

What type of historical vision might a nineteenth-century English or American child encounter? We must bear in mind that the boundary between adult and children's texts was not clearly drawn, nor was that between scholarly and popular texts. Patterns of reading in family circles meant that authors even of "high" literature, encrusted with political philosophy and moral reflections, also deployed melodramatic incidents, romances, and slapstick that might appeal to children. As a result, young people then read writers like Wordsworth and Hugo whom we now think of as addressing adults, while other, more popular writers such as Dickens or Dumas found their works adopted as children's classics.

A second point to be made is that the line between history and fiction was less clearly drawn then than it is today; history was not just a science but an art. Influenced by Sir Walter Scott's novels, the historian Carlyle strove to avoid the "mere abstractions and dead formulas" of Mignet and Thiers. He struggled to record the "life-tumult," "the bodily concrete colored presence of things," in bold strokes, so "that it may look like a smoke-and-flame conflagration in the distance."

One of the tools of seduction that Carlyle and his contemporaries drew on in interpreting the French Revolution was metaphor. They used organic and other natural imagery to imply that an inevitable process had led to this sequence of events. They evaluated that process morally: a violent deluge had inundated and wiped out a corrupt and effete system, whose royal and noble leaders had, as a class, provoked a historical retribution not unlike that which swept Noah's fellow men from the face of the earth. Victorians could not know the kind of evidence historians have subsequently compiled—that the September massacres struck poor and petty criminals as well as nobles or clerics, that the "white terror" of counter-revolutionaries was as costly in human lives as the official Terror, or that the property system survived virtually intact through this period. Instead, what fascinated them was the tensions between their sympathy for a Revolution that seemed divinely justified at the outset and their horror at the bloodshed that marked 1792 and subsequent years.

These were the two sides of the picture drawn by the poet laureate Wordsworth in his autobiographical epic, *The Prelude,* written between 1798 and 1805 but not published until after his death in 1850. A Girondin sympathizer and follower of Godwin, Wordsworth reacted with fervent idealism to "France standing on the top of golden hours,/ And human nature seeming born again." At first he defended the September massacres as a "return" of the "tide": "all things have second birth;/ the earthquake is not satisfied at once" (10:83-84). Gradually, however, in respose to the "tyranny and implements of death" of the Terror, he charted a turn away from hopes of political reform, toward introspection and a belief that "brotherhood" could be found only in the bosom of nature (12:87). He closed—or foreclosed—his experience of the Revolution by a return to "Home at Grasmere," where the sisterly love of Dorothy restored him to his love of nature and sense of self. His manifest political message, then, was conservative.

If in many ways the poet laureate embodied what Hazlitt called the Spirit of the Age and shaped late Victorian views of the Revolution, he wisely left to another writer the task of composing "some dramatic tale" about the general lessons of the Revolution. In the event, that tale was penned by Charles Dickens, whose *Tale of Two Cities* (1859) he first conceived when acting with his children and friends in a play about the triumph of self-sacrifice over the desire for vengeance. Since he aimed to "add something to the popular and picturesque means of understanding that terrible time," it is not surprising that the novel became standard fare in family reading circles and remains a children's classic, included in school curricula.

Intertwining scenes of Paris and London between 1775 and 1793, Dickens's story sums up the fundamental contradictions of the English view. In the first half of the novel, we follow the eminent Dr. Manette, who after long and unjust imprisonment in the Bastille, recovers his sanity and makes his life in London. Ironically, his daughter there marries the son of the very nobleman who had had the doctor imprisoned to avoid a scandal about his criminal abuse of seigneurial privileges. Though this young man has left France and renounced his inheritance, the latter part of the novel takes him back to Paris, to face the Revolutionary tribunal for the sins of the past.

Dickens closely studied the mid-nineteenth-century historiography of the Revolution. He read Rousseau, Mercier's *Tableau de Pris,* even the tax tables, besides English works like Trollope's *La Vendée.* A decade before he had met Jules Michelet in Paris. Above all he studied the massive *French Revolution* (1837), by his friend Thomas Carlyle, who sent Dickens two cart-loads of books. Like Carlyle, Dickens represented the Revolution as a natural and inevitable flood. "As a whirlpool of boiling waters has a centre point, so all this ranging circled round Defarge's wine-shop," where arms are collected and the assault initiated. The people are a "living sea." Time likewise is an organic "mill" grinding the present out of the material provided by the past, just as the oppressive feudal order is a "mill" that grinds young people old. "Hunger" walks the streets of Paris like a gigantic figure out of Goya.

But the Revolution also punctuates this love-story with moments of terror, when the mob rises up in brute revenge to sharpen their knives and dance the Carmagnole. Disorder, wine, and blood flow in the streets; they take form in Mme Defarge, a female figure of revenge and of the world turned upside down, an echo of Théroigne de Méricourt who foreshadows Michelet's later identification of female menstrual flow with revolutionary bloodshed.

In a typical Dickensian grotesquerie, social types shrink into caricatures of themselves. "Monseigneur" is represented as an irresponsible "class," guilty of Lucifer's pride, Sardanapalus's luxury, and a mole's blindness. As in the fable, this sorcerer's apprentice, having raised the Devil with infinite pains, at the sight "took to his noble heels." Lukács complained that Dickens severed the human drama from its social basis; it would be more accurate to say that Dickens flattened his characters in order to stress their social representativity and to give a satiric edge to his fiction.

Dickens brings to life the movement of social forces through the central characters of the novel: the two wicked Marquis d'Evremonde, the relentless sansculottes Monsieur et Madame Defarge, the victimized bourgeois Doctor Manette. Even the innocent noble-born Charles (Evremonde) Darnay plays his schematic role, as he reveals the great historical contradiction between the class-struggle and the principle of civic equality (or the legal principle, "crimes are individual").

By their personal values and experiences, these characters motivate social change. Through Doctor Manette we learn of *lettres de cachet* and are reminded of the importance of careers open to talents. Through the Evremonde family we see the evils of seigneurial dues and rights, insistently driven home not only by their persecution of Doctor Manette, but by their wanton murder of a child in the street and their willful destruction of the family of Mme Defarge, father, brother, sister, and brother-in-law alike. Indeed the famine of 1788-89 becomes their personal responsibility. Through the Defarges, we glimpse Dickens's conception of the sansculotte: a wine-merchant and his wife, literate, politically active as leaders of a (misnamed) "Jacquerie" long before 1789. Their hostility to the Ancien Regime is not ideological, but a response to their own experiences and those of their fellows (Ernest Defarge presents a petition to the king on behalf of a friend condemned to hang for avenging the murder of his child); they maintain a network of information that reaches into the provinces. In an imaginative condensation of history, they participate in the taking of the Bastille, the beheading of Delaunay, the September massacres, the Terror.

Greatest of the Victorian novels on the Revolution, *Tale of Two Cities* also articulates many of the clichés that permeate renditions of this moment for children. Most important, the stress is on moral principles rather than political events. The haven of social order is located in the bosom of the family: at the close, an act of love and individual self-sacrifice saves Darnay; social justice and reform find no definitive, concrete expression. The same features that make the novel radically innovative in its form—dramatically juxtaposed scenes in Paris and London, proleptic and ironic intrusions ("the time was to come")—also make it exemplary of romance. The argument by antithesis, the melodramatic juxtaposition of innocent love with grim reality, Charles Darnay's daring last-minute escape from the guillotine thanks to the self-sacrifice of his double—these all typify the novel of adventure and foreshadow the popular fictions of Baroness Orczy.

One of the central features of children's literature, however, is missing from Dickens's novel: the child protagonist. Already in 1839, Anna Eliza (Stothard) Bray had published a tale for children that exploited this perspective: "The Orphans of La Vendée." Indeed, "The Orphans" is notable for depicting a girl in disguise, who fights and dies at Doué, suicidally avenging her beloved brother's death. When her brother joins the royalists led by Henri de Rochejacquelein, Jeanne, who had shared as a child in such "masculine exercises" as hunting, abandons "feminine employments" to don men's garb and practice the quarter staff so that "she might share his fate if he fell." For all its apparent embrace of a healthy gender equality, this basically conservative tale of "the demoniacal spirit of the French Revolution," exploits the violent civil-war setting to set off youthful courage and fidelity to the values of family, church, and king.

Such exploitation of a violent setting for fundamentally conservative ends also marks two novels published fifty years later by the most popular nineteenth-century English writer of historical fiction for boys, George Alfred Henty. *In the Reign of Terror: The Adventures of a Westminster Boy* (1887), collapses together for the sake of plot the Terror, the massacres at Nantes, and the notorious drownings of priests and nuns. In a typically Wordsworthian alignment, Henty's middle-class English hero sympathizes with the oppressed peasantry but tries to protect his adoptive noble French family from the terror. Frank and pragmatic, the hero Harry (!) embodies liberal virtues of individual courage and accomplishment, as opposed to those of revolutionary levelling.

Henty's *No Surrender! A Tale of the Rising in La Vendée* (1899), was probably influenced both by Balzac's *Chouans* and Trollope's *La Vendée* (1850) in its sympathetic rendition of the Vendéan insurrection and capture of Saumur. When children's literature draws on war, it seems, the opportunities for youthful heroism are rarely depicted as apolitical; traditional social values serve as a counterbalance to the setting of social upheaval.

The Anglo-Saxon fascination with the counter-revolutionary context of the Vendée also reflects a tendency in children's literature to represent the French Revolution through geographic displacement. This curious phenomenon shifts the focus from Paris to the more conservative provinces, from France itself to the high seas. It is not that violence is thereby avoided—children's books on the subject are full of it—but perhaps that these events and the principles they bring into question can best be examined on the margins.

Such a move is made by Samuel Goodrich, better known as Peter Parley, whose story about *The Adventures of Philip Brusque* (1845) may start at the iron gates of the Bastille, but shifts scenes immediately to "a home in the sea" on a Robinsonian island. Ardent and inspired by faith in "a political millennium, when every man should walk forth in freedom and happiness," young Philip helps to destroy the Bastille, but in 1793, he goes into exile, sickened by "the shocking and brutal insults offered to the queen." The bulk of the novel depicts Philip's constitutional experiments after he is shipwrecked: first, the pure anarchy possible in isolation, then a compact to allocate goods between two castaways by lot, followed by tyrannical license imposed by a pirate, and finally a tripartite government modelled on the American constitution that guarantees—a most important point—private property. The French Revolution, in short, caricatured as the deployment of the guillotine, provides a mere springboard for the study of American principles of government. In some very abstract sense, to be sure, Goodrich's tale is about the stakes of the Revolution, but cut completely free from their historical context.

One novel stands out for the immediacy of its vision of life in the revolutionary moment: S. Weir Mitchell's *Adventures of François* (1897), a popular novel written for adults but read by children, which traces a foundling's adventures from choir-boy, sheltered but also oppressed by the Church, to Revolutionary adolescence. Whereas most texts for children veer toward romance, this one has a strong infusion of irony, for François's distinctive trait is his laughter, his clown-like enjoyment of life, a gift he uses to entertain the crowds to maintain his hold on life through the worst scrapes.

It is the strength of this novel that Weir Mitchell shows society from the bottom up, through the daily life of a thief. He paints daily life in broad strokes, stressing the lack of luxuries to be stolen, the barriers to free travel, and the memory of injustices that motivates revolt against chateau-owners. At best, his hero is an anarchist, who distrusts demagogic appeals to the masses. Gradually, however, the poison spread by his rapacious landlady, an informer called Quatre Pattes, the experience of imprisonment, and the fear for his life push François to reject the Revolution and drive the novel to its intrinsically conservative close.

Here too, then, we find a fascination with a quasi-Fayettiste, a liberal noble who does not leave France or reject the Revolution but does oppose the Jacobins. Avoiding such historical refinement as a mention of Girondins or Hébertistes, Mitchell draws a simple contrast to the ruthless idealism of such figures as Robespierre, Amar, and l'abbé Grégoire. The historical compression that marks this typically antinomian view of the Revolution can be summed up in Mitchell's two main female characters: "la marquise," beautiful and innocent victim of a peasant uprising, whom François tries to save, and the grasping, self-interested, crab-like figure of Quatre Pattes, who is nearly responsible for the death of François.

How has the heritage of the French Revolution been traced for English-speaking children? At the threshold of this world-historical event, it was described as the "sister" of the American Revolution. The differences between the two, however, quickly became apparent. For many writers and thinkers, this political upheaval was summed up by the Terror, a focus that led to novels of adventure and romance surrounding the escape of gentle men and women from the guillotine. Even those more sympathetic to the ideals of the Revolution tended to approach the representation of its historical course as at once inevitable and treacherous, a slippage into madness and the maelstrom.

In English-language fiction, the situation is positively discouraging: the French Revolution serves as a backdrop for dashing romance and rescue: swordplay to save duchesses, the mystery of the dauphin's rumored escape from prison, heroic battles. The baroness Orczy rather than Michelet is the model. A startling number of texts are set in the

Vendée or among the Chouans in Brittany. This geographic displacement sharply distinguishes historical fiction from the mainstream of history (in French as well, viz. the fictions of Balzac, Dumas, and Hugo). Several questions of genre seem to influence this selection of subject matter and location.

One is the simple temptation of recasting history in the form of romance, exploiting social upheaval for its dramatic narrative curves of imprisonment and escape, threat of defeat followed by victory. James Fenimore Cooper's *Wing and Wing: or Le Feu Follet* (1842) (like C. S. Forester's series a century later about Midshipman Hornblower) accordingly locates its adventures aboard a privateer, in the period of the Directory. So does Cyrus Townsend Brady's *Two Captains* (1904), which moves from a provincial showdown between a marquis and a bloodthirsty sansculotte to the greater showdown on the sea between Nelson and Bonaparte at Aboukir. Not the political moment but the dramatic occasion for a display of character is what matters.

More important probably is the circumscription or displacement of violent death, paired with the trend toward social conservatism in books for children. Children may not in fact differ radically from adults in their understanding (or misunderstanding) of the aphorism that a little bloodshed can water the tree of liberty. But it is not surprising that Anglo-Saxon literature, especially that for reading in a family circle or by children, should deplore the September massacres, the Terror, and the Jacobin repression of provincial uprisings.

Third, just as children are marginal to the play of politics, so children's literature tends to stay on the margins of history. Indeed this is one of the features that makes historical fiction for children so interesting to historians influenced by the French *Annales* school. For children's literature offers an appropriate space for the study of *mentalités,* of popular culture, and the ways we represent the history of daily life. (pp. 196-99)

Margaret R. Higonnet, "Victorian Children and the French Revolution: Views from Below," in Children's Literature Association Quarterly, *Vol. 14, No. 4, Winter, 1989, pp. 196-200.*

FURTHER READING

Carlson, Marvin. *The Theatre of the French Revolution.* Ithaca, N. Y.: Cornell University Press, 1966, 328 p.

Centers on French theater during the Revolutionary era, asserting that "every major upheaval, indeed every significant shift in political opinion, was reflected with remarkable alacrity in the theatres of Paris—in their audiences, actors, producers, authors, and the theatre organizations themselves."

Cook, Malcolm C. "Politics in the Fiction of the French Revolution, 1789-1794." *Studies on Voltaire and the Eighteenth Century* 201 (1982): 237-335.

Examines the political content of French prose fiction written during the years of the Revolution.

Dickens Studies Annual 12 (1983): 117-24, 177-266.

Contains several articles comparing Dickens's *Tale of Two Cities* to Carlyle's *French Revolution.*

Dowden, Edward. *The French Revolution and English Literature.* 1897. Reprint. Port Washington, N. Y.: Kennikat Press, 1967, 285 p.

Studies the relationship between the events of the French Revolution and English literature of the eighteenth and nineteenth centuries, addressing in particular the major political theorists of the era.

Kennedy, Emmet. *A Cultural History of the French Revolution.* New Haven, Conn.: Yale University Press, 1989, 463 p.

Social history, treating the Revolution as "a profound cultural event."

Klancher, Jon. "Romantic Criticism and the Meanings of the French Revolution." *Studies in Romanticism* 28, No. 3 (Fall 1989): 463-91.

Traces evolving views of the French Revolution in Romantic criticism. Klancher asserts: "Pressing the aesthetic, psychological, and ideological claims of romantic discourse has always entailed making a claim for what the French Revolution meant, and above all what it means now in the critic's own historical moment."

Saine, Thomas P. "A Peculiar View of the French Revolution: The Revolution as German Reformation." In *Aufnahme—Weitergabe: Literarische Impulse um Lessing und Goethe,* edited by John A. McCarthy and Albert A. Kipa, pp. 233-61. Hamburg: Helmut Buske Verlag, 1982.

Examines the responses of German intellectuals to the French Revolution, highlighting the impact of revolutionary events on German literature.

Sturm und Drang

INTRODUCTION

The scholar Roy Pascal has called the Sturm und Drang movement "the first flowering of the greatest period of German literature." Typified by fervent nationalistic sentiments, the evocation of passionate emotions, and the depiction of intensely individualistic characters, the works of such figures as Johann Gottfried von Herder, Jakob Michael Reinhold Lenz, Friedrich Maximillian von Klinger, and above all Johann Wolfgang von Goethe develop an original conception of society, history, art, and nature.

The objective of the Stürmer und Dränger, as propounded in the critical writings of Herder and Goethe, was to assert the unique qualities of individuals, nations, and languages and proclaim the supremacy of the imagination as realized in the figure of the genius. Most scholars regard these contentions as both a critique and a further refinement of the Enlightenment, the eighteenth-century philosophical movement that celebrated human reason and rationality. The Stürmer und Dränger distrusted the Enlightenment application of reason, which they viewed as the prop of social convention. In particular, they reacted against the empiricism of such British philosophers as George Berkeley and David Hume and the rigorous materialism of the French *philosophes* as expressed in the *Encyclopedia* edited by Denis Diderot and d'Alembert. In the field of social criticism the Stürmer und Dränger denied the Enlightenment's view of human progress as essentially the collective effect of the illumination of individual minds, concentrating instead on the issues which arise when the individual's will is obstructed by society. Typical Sturm und Drang themes concern family conflicts among fathers, sons, and brothers, the damaging effects of aristocratic privileges on lower social classes, and the man of genius who is thwarted by traditional attitudes in his attempts to improve conditions. In treating such themes, the Stürmer und Dränger were influenced by the theories of the French philosopher Jean-Jacques Rousseau regarding natural man and the superiority of the primitive condition to the perceived decadence of civilization. The Sturm und Drang generation extended Rousseau's ideas and developed an organic and dynamic view of human societies as well as an interest in the hitherto disregarded lives of the common people.

Although the members of the Sturm und Drang did not formulate a coherent literary or philosophical theory, they were united in their skepticism regarding the eighteenth-century conception of reason. Instead, they emphasized the value of subjectivity, spontaneity, and eccentricity. As a result, Sturm und Drang writings are typified by the use of nontraditional literary forms, extravagant language, and grotesque imagery. Such techniques are in keeping with the Sturm und Drang view of artistic creation as a matter of passionate self-expression rather than communi-

cation. This emphasis led the noted Romantic critic A. W. Schlegel to maintain that the Stürmer und Dränger were gifted but misguided writers who were overly concerned with strident castigations of the prevailing social order at the expense of developing a well-supported body of thought. Despite Schlegel's contention, most critics have concurred that the contributions of the Sturm and Drang movement to lyric poetry, drama, and the novel are landmarks which have exerted a lasting influence on the development of German language and literature.

REPRESENTATIVE WORKS

Goethe, Johann Wolfgang von
Rede zum Shakespears Tag (criticism) 1771
Gotz von Berlichingen midt der eisernen Hand: Ein Schauspiel (drama) 1773
[*Goetz of Berlichingen with the Iron Hand,* 1799]
Clavigo: Ein Trauerspiel (drama) 1774
[*Clavigo: A Tragedy in 5 Acts,* 1798; also published as *Clavigo,* 1897]
Die Leiden des jungen Werthers (novel) 1774
[*The Sorrows of Werter,* 1779; also published as

Werter and Charlotte, 1786; and *The Sorrows of Young Werther,* 1929; and *The Sufferings of Young Werther,* 1957]
Faust: Ein Fragment (poetry) 1790
Herder, Johann Gottfried von
Uber die neuere Deutsche Litteratur. 3 vols. (essays) 1767
Kritische Walder. 3 vols. (essays) 1769
**Abhandlung über den Ursprund der Sprache, welche den von der Konigl* (essay) 1773
[*Treatise upon the Origin of Language,* 1827]
**Briefwechsel über Ossian un der Lieder alter Völker* (essay) 1773
*"Shakespear" (essay) 1773
Volkslieder [editor] (folk songs) 1778; also published as *Stimmen der Völker in Liedern,* 1807
Vom Geist der ebräischen Poesie. 2 vols. (essay) 1782-1783
[*The Spirit of Hebrew Poetry,* 1833]
Klinger, Friedrich Maximillian von
Sturm und Drang: Ein Schauspiel (drama) 1776
[*Storm and Stress,* 1978]
Die Zwillinge: Ein Trauerspiel in fünf Aufzügen (drama) 1776
Faust's Leben, Thaten und Höllenfahrt in fünf Büchern (novel) 1791
[*Faustus: His Life, Death, and Descent into Hell,* 1825]
Leisewitz, Johan Anton
Julius von Tarent: Ein Trauerspiel (drama) 1776
Lenz, Jakob Michael Reinhold
Ammerkungen übers Theater nebst angehängten übersetzten Stück Shakespeares (criticism) 1774
Der Hofmeister oder Vortheile der Privaterziehung: Eine Komödie (drama) 1774
[*The Tutor,* 1972]
Die Soldaten: Eine Komödie (drama) 1776
Schiller, Friedrich
Die Räuber: Ein Schauspiel (drama) 1781
[*The Robbers,* 1792]

*These works are included in the essay collection *Von deutscher Art und Kunst* edited by Herder in 1773.

DEFINITIONS

E. L. Stahl and W. E. Yuill

[*In the following excerpt, taken from their study* German Literature of the Eighteenth and Nineteenth Centuries, *Stahl and Yuill provide an overview of the Sturm und Drang. They highlight the movement's relationship to the Enlightenment and other eighteenth-century thinkers and detail the contributions of individual Sturmer und Dranger in the genres of drama, poetry, and the novel.*]

After Klopstock and the intervening group of poets called the 'Göttinger Hain', the writers of the 'Sturm und Drang' represent the culmination of the pre-Romantic trends which began with Bodmer and Breitinger's opposition to Gottsched well within the era of Enlightenment. But although these writers decisively reacted against the Enlightenment, the complexity of the historical processes leading to the 'Sturm und Drang' is so great and the impetus behind the Enlightenment so considerable, that in several important respects the 'Sturm und Drang' appears as a further development of the 'Aufklärung' as much as its revocation.

In both movements writers demanded social equality and individual autonomy, but equality and freedom meant different things in the two cases. Adherents of the 'Sturm und Drang' no longer believed that progress was assured by the 'enlightenment' of the human mind and they rejected the rationalists' view of the relationship between individual and society. Social criticism became much sharper and was principally directed against abuses of privilege by the upper classes. The lower orders are therefore shown in a new light and a host of figures appear in literature who had not been previously written about in the same way—simple folk from the countryside as well as from the cities. Rousseau was a powerful influence: his ideas on nature and society determined much of the thought of 'Sturm und Drang' writers. New distinctions were made or were newly emphasized, such as those between society and community, state and people, civilization and 'culture', the positive valuation in each case resting on the second entity.

Rousseau's primitivism came to be allied to another view of nature. A characteristic feature of 'Sturm und Drang' thinking here is the interest in organic and dynamic processes as against the static image of nature prevalent in the previous era. Genesis, origin, development are the categories which now claim primary attention. They influenced the production and the evaluation of literature to a considerable extent. Stress was laid on energy of character and strength of feeling. Passionate involvement was ranked above intellectual detachment in life as in artistic presentation. This led to a form of expressionism in language and style. At the same time the interest in hitherto neglected representatives of society—the life led by simple people and the downtrodden classes—brought a greater measure of realism, even a kind of naturalism, into the dramatic literature of the movement. Here the pre-Romantic character of the 'Sturm und Drang' gives way to different trends which will reach full expansion only in the nineteenth century.

The cult of energy enabled the writers of the movement to evolve a new heroic ideal: the strong individual as leader, the creative mind rivalling the deity in fashioning human beings in its own image, genius proclaiming and demonstrating its autonomy in life and art. These predilections reveal a dichotomy of values which the members of the 'Sturm und Drang' could not resolve until they reached classical maturity. The common man and the heroic 'titan' ('Kraftkerl') are brought together in many works, novels as well as dramas, and frequently clash in the motivation of the actions presented in them. A similar discrepancy appears in the evaluation of literature and art. The supreme artist, a 'genius' like Shakespeare, was regarded as autonomous and in his works appeared to be a law unto himself. On the other hand such a genius was seen to be the spokesman of his times, and no less a product of the age in which he lived, the country in which he had his being, than its ordinary citizens. As Herder put it in his review on Thomas Abbt: 'Der führende Geist . . . steht in seinem Jahrhundert wie ein Baum in dem Erdreich wurzelt, aus welchem er Säfte zieht.' In his essay on Shakespeare it is difficult to reconcile the image of Promethean creativity with the idea of conditioned art whereby he accounts for the difference between the types of tragedy written in ancient Greece and the Elizabethan age.

Many conditioning factors were now recognized as contributing to the processes of history. Compared with the views put forward in the 'Aufklärung', 'Sturm und Drang' concepts of history placed far greater emphasis on the process itself than on its ultimate goal. More than one writer disavowed teleological thought, even in its Aristotelian form, and eschewed rationalist beliefs in progress, affirming instead the differences between individual historical manifestations. 'Sturm und Drang' individualism contrasts with the abstract idealism of the Enlightenment. Moreover, its primitivism led writers to pay increased attention to the origins as well as the processes of historical development. The essence of a phenomenon was seen to lie in its original form, as Herder stated in *Fragments:* 'In dem Ursprung eines Phänomens liegt aller Schatz der Erklärung, durch welche die Erklärung desselben genetisch wird.' This point of view explains why the beginnings of individual and collective man, childhood and primitive society, came to occupy an increasingly important place in the literary interests of the 'Sturm und Drang' period.

Primitivism also accounts for the revival of folk poetry which had been given an inferior position by Gottsched and most of his followers. 'Sturm und Drang' individualism likewise enhanced the expression of personal experiences in poetry. By contrast, the assessment of poetry as a craft tended to be neglected and remained in abeyance until the advent of Classicism.

In spite of the prominence given to originality in 'Sturm und Drang' thought, foreign influences decisively affected the trends of the movement. In dramatic theory and practice Sebastien Mercier's essay on dramatic art was translated by Heinrich Leopold Wagner and this helped to sharpen the break with the drama of the preceding period. His eulogy of Shakespeare's genius was linked with opposition to the canons of Aristotelian criticism and so went far beyond Lessing who still attempted to justify Shakespeare in Aristotelian terms. Shakespeare was the major foreign influence: different aspects of his dramatic art engaged most German dramatists in the later eighteenth century as well as throughout the nineteenth. In the 'Sturm und Drang' Shakespeare criticism was largely moulded by English writers like Edward Young in whose *Conjectures on Original Composition* of 1759 (translated by Teubner in 1760) many of Herder's thoughts on genius, the rules, imagination and creativity are prefigured.

In poetry major English influences were James Macpherson's *Fragments of Ancient Poetry* (1760-3), and Percy's *Reliques of Ancient English Poetry* (1765). They helped 'Sturm und Drang' writers to formulate their views on the nature of poetic language and composition and on the difference between 'natural' and 'artificial' modes of expression. These trends were enforced by the revaluations of Vergil and Homer contained in Wood's *Essay on the Original Genius and Writings of Homer* of 1769.

Within Germany Johann Georg Hamann (1730-88) made the strongest impact on writers of the 'Sturm und Drang'. A radical critic of the Enlightenment, he arrived at his 'irrationalist' view of human nature after his religious conversion during a visit to London. His opposition to rationalism allowed him to exalt feeling, intuition and the imagination above man's intellectual faculties and to propound the principle of 'docta ignorantia' (*Sokratische Denkwürdigkeiten,* 1759). His own unsystematic fragmentary writings are full of improvisations and contradictions and his style, like that of his pupil, the young Herder, is a compact of oracular, allusive and associative utterances. One of the most influential ideas he stated in his *Aesthetica in nuce,* a chapter of *Kreuzzüge des Philologen, eine kabbalistische Rhapsodie* (1762), is contained in the parallel he drew between divine and human creativity: God is 'der Poet am Anfang der Tage'. His creation is 'Weltdichtung', a work of art. Aesthetically this view is of doubtful value since it tends to obscure the essential quality of any work of art. The young Schiller similarly equated the divine creation with a human work of art: he did not advance towards a truer estimate of aesthetic phenomena until he adopted Kantian principles under the guidance of J. G. Körner. Hamann's aesthetic ideas had greater validity when he applied them to literary topics. He described poetry as an imitation of the 'Tatendichtung Gottes', human language as the medium of revelation, poetry as the 'mother tongue' of mankind. The Old Testament, 'älteste Urkunde des Menschengeschlechts', is essentially a poetic work. Hamann viewed the poetry of primitive people in the same way and prepared the ground for Herder to enunciate his ideas on language and poetry in *Fragmente über die neuere deutsche Literatur* (1767-8) and *Kritische Wälder* (1769) which represents the authentic 'Sturm und Drang' doctrine on these topics.

Johann Gottfried Herder (1744-1803) was the intellectual leader of those 'Sturm und Drang' writers who gathered in Strasbourg during the formative years of the movement. His conversation made an even greater impact on his disciples than his writings, many of which remained fragmentary. He inaugurated a new era in criticism by rejecting judgements based on the application of set standards and instead relating individual works and authors to embracing historical trends. His importance lies in the fact that he contributed in equal measure to the formulation of 'Sturm und Drang', Classical and Romantic ideas.

During his first phase his most influential work was on drama and poetry. It is contained in his essay on Shakespeare and in *Briefwechsel über Ossian und die Lieder alter Völker,* from *Von deutscher Art und Kunst,* a collection of essays by different hands which he edited in 1773. No contemporary writer stated the new ideas on lyric style more suggestively and forcibly than Herder did in his appreciation of Ossian's songs. Such 'popular' poetry represents the direct communication of feeling through irregular rhythmic patterns, concrete and sensuous imagery, impromptu and 'dance-like' articulation (Würfe und Sprünge), obscure and even ineffable sentiments, dynamic word combinations and the use of inversions and repetitions without regard for logical consistency. He followed up the essay with the collection of *Volkslieder* (1778, later called *Stimmen der Völker in Liedern*), which contains poems by Pindar, Sappho and Shakespeare as well as folk-songs from a large number of countries including Iceland and Peru. He helped to mould the 'Sturm und Drang' style of German poetry until, with the advant of Classicism, the practice of craftsmanship again prevailed over spontaneity. Herder himself promoted the change as early as 1775 when, in *Ursachen des gesunkenen Geschmacks bei den verschiedenen Völkern da er geblühet,* he commented adversely on the excesses which his own enthusiastic pronouncements had in good part fostered, and demanded the renewed exercise of Good Taste in the interests of order and harmony.

Herder had an intuitive grasp of lyric values. By contrast, his contribution to dramatic theory has less significance. The essay on Shakespeare in *Von deutscher Art und Kunst* (1773) makes an interesting comparison with Goethe's *Rede zum Shakespeare Tag.* Goethe praised Shakespeare's Promethean creativity; Herder's interest was largely historical. In his 'Sturm und Drang' phase one of his main concerns was to establish the relativism of history against the view held by Enlightenment thinkers, to demonstrate the individuality of each era and to show how it differed from other eras: he put greater emphasis on the variety of historical phenomena than upon their fundamental uniformity. This is the principal theme of the treatise *Auch eine Philosophie der Geschichte zur Bildung der Menschheit* (1774) where he states: 'Jede Nation (und freilich auch jede Zeit) hat ihren Mittelpunkt der Glückseligkeit in sich, wie jede Kugel ihren Schwerpunkt.' Thus all ages must be judged by their own standards, none is essentially more perfect than any other, each represents a characteristic totality of constituent forces. Later, in his Classical phase, Herder sought to find the force that links the ages of history together and eventually discovered it in the idea of 'Humanität'.

His 'Sturm und Drang' attitude is also evident in *Kritische Wälder,* especially in the influential dissertations on the origins of language and on the 'Laokoon' problem. In the latter essay he went further than Lessing had done by distinguishing more clearly between poetry and music on the one hand, and between painting and sculpture on the other. In characteristic 'Sturm und Drang' fashion he described poetry as a manifestation of energy ('Kraft') and explained sculpture in terms of tactile sensation ('Gefühl') which exhibits its three-dimensionality. This point of view enabled him to add the category 'In- und Hintereinander' to Lessing's 'Nacheinander' and 'Nebeneinander'; it again demonstrates a focal quality of 'Sturm und Drang' thought.

Drama

The conflicts presented in the dramatic works of 'Sturm und Drang' writers reflect the current ideas on the rights of man, particularly the claims of vigorous personalities against an effete society. A strongly propagandist strain enters the depiction of those conflicts where in the previous era even Lessing had sought to moderate the political bias. Similarly, whereas Lessing had avoided metaphysical issues, the dramatists now showed their heroes as representatives of mankind battling against tyrannous supernatural forces. For this reason they used ancient myths and legends more often than had been the case hitherto: Prometheus was the prototype of the hero in revolt. The favourite historical background, however, was the Renaissance, from which dramatists of the 'Sturm und Drang' took some of their leading figures. Their attitude of revolt went beyond the choice of theme in their disregard for the traditional rules of dramatic composition.

In a revised version of his essay Herder asserted that Shakespeare portrayed events ('Begebenheiten'), while the Greek dramatists presented actions ('Handlungen'). This distinction is symptomatic of the practice followed in the 'Sturm und Drang'. Rejecting the unities dramatists now tended to present a series of episodes in preference to constructing actions in the strict sense: their works have an epic quality. Moreover, disregarding one of the main contentions Lessing had made in *Laokoon* on the difference between the pictorial arts and poetry, they used the words 'Gemälde' and 'Schilderung' for their dramatic presentations. The blurring of distinctions between tragedies and comedies led in the same direction. With their lyric interpolations, dramatic structures resembling the Romantic 'Gesamtkunstwerk' in rudimentary form resulted from these efforts to combine effects from different areas of art and literature.

The first plays to show 'Sturm und Drang' features are *Julie* (1767) by Helfrich Peter Sturz (1736-79) and *Ugolino* by Heinrich Wilhelm Gerstenberg (1737-1823). In the former play the heroine's refusal to submit to parental authority and the attention paid to environmental conditions show the new trends. But Sturz observes the unities, as does Gerstenberg in *Ugolino* (1768), although here the theme enforced observance of the unity of place. The play is a dramatization of an episode from Dante's *Divine Comedy,* the action representing the last phase when father and sons are faced with death by starvation. The principal interest aroused in this remarkable work are the different reactions of the characters to their situation, the contrasts of mood and expression ranging from the heroic to the macabre. In theme and tone German drama took a new turn with *Ugolino* which was written five years before Lessing completed *Emilia Galotti.*

The first 'Sturm und Drang' drama in the technical sense is Goethe's *Götz von Berlichingen* (1773), a model for many contemporary playwrights. But while these dramatists conformed to one and the same trend, they also showed individual predilections in their choice of themes and their treatment of common topics. Criticism of contemporary society is not the salient feature of Goethe's dramatic work as it is that of much of the dramatic work of Lenz, Wagner and the young Schiller. Klinger shared with Goethe a preference for dramatizing the fortunes of 'titanic' individuals in conflict with their times rather than with their society. In his 'Sturm und Drang' period Goethe treated this theme by choosing historical figures who had become legendary, such as Götz von Berlichingen and Faust, while Klinger also used contemporary material.

In his earliest plays, *Die Laune des Verliebten* (1768) and *Die Mitschuldigen* (1769), Goethe to a large extent followed the Rococo fashion, although in the former work he modified the idyllic theme by introducing touches of psychological realism while the latter play bears the stamp of Goethe's style in the handling of the rhyming alexandrine couplets: he frequently splits up individual lines by distributing parts among two or more speakers, thus loosening the traditional form. This indicates a certain break with convention and foreshadows the greater changes represented in the composition of *Götz von Berlichingen* which began in 1771.

Goethe's idea of tragedy in his 'Sturm und Drang' is best seen in his *Rede* on Shakespeare. He follows the trend of the time in pointing to Shakespeare's plays as examples of Promethean creativity: 'Er wetteiferte mit dem Prometheus, bildete ihm Zug vor Zug seine Menschen nach, nur in Kolossalischer Grösse.' In a later passage he reads into these works a problem that is in fact more his own than Shakespeare's, the clash between the claims of individual freedom and external necessity: 'Seine Stücke drehen sich alle um den geheimen Punkt . . . in dem das Eigentümliche unseres Ichs, die prätendierte Freiheit unseres Wollens mit dem notwendigen Gang des Ganzen zusammenstösst.' This is the problem of 'Sturm und Drang' titanism which Goethe, unlike other dramatists of the movement, from the beginning saw as a tragic issue. He did not exaggerate the claims of the individual against society to the same extent as Klinger, and he took more trouble to portray the conditions which fashioned the attitude of his titanic heroes, especially of Götz and Faust. In dramatizing the autobiography of the German knight he does present a 'grosser Kerl' who fights for his own right and that of others. But Götz is also the last of the barons who opposes social change, the 'notwendigen Gang des Ganzen' that led to the rise of the middle class. Götz is politically a reactionary far more than a revolutionary, the defender of an outworn system, not a protagonist of social progress. Here Goethe's play differs from those 'Sturm und Drang' works which advocate social change outspokenly or implicitly.

In other respects, however, Goethe gave a lead which his contemporaries followed. He presented a series of events in Herder's sense and included two sub-plots. The first concerns the relations between Adelheid (a 'Machtweib' modelled on Lady Macbeth) and Weislingen, and brings in the theme of infidelity, a motif which Goethe also treated in his other 'Sturm und Drang' plays, *Faust, Clavigo* and *Stella.* The second sub-plot of *Götz von Berlichingen* sketches the historical background of the Peasants War and the Reformation (represented in Bruder Martin). This diversity of scene and action endangers the unity of the work: only Goethe's skilful control avoided the pitfall of formlessness to which other dramatists of the time succumbed. But he chose a technique of multiple scene changes which atomized the action and made Herder deplore the excess to which his own commendation of Shakespeare had led. Goethe accepted the censure and acted upon it when revising the play for publication. This second version lost in liveliness what it gained in cohesiveness. In making these changes Goethe studied *Emilia Galotti* and so laid the foundation for his later 'classical' technique.

At this time he planned to write dramas on several legendary or historically attested 'titanic' figures: Faust, Prometheus, Socrates, Caesar and Mohammed. None materialized except the first. *Faust* became Goethe's life work because the material allowed him the greatest scope for diversification. In its first stage (the 'Urfaust') the unity of conception was endangered by the disparity of the Faust-Mephistopheles and the Faust-Gretchen actions. The latter is a 'bürgerliches Trauerspiel' in strong contrast with the supernatural aspects of the Faust-Mephisto action. Lessing had met the same difficulty when he began to dramatize the Faust legend. His two plans show that the supernatural elements presented him with a problem which he proposed to solve either by making Mephistopheles into a human being ('Erzbösewicht') or by presenting the hero's temptation in a dream sequence to enable him to escape damnation. It is not known whether Goethe from the beginning likewise planned to save Faust: his 'Sturm und Drang' idea of tragedy makes this unlikely. The first extant version lacks the scenes when Mephisto makes his appearance and when he concludes the pact with Faust. This 'grosse Lücke' may be due to the fact that Goethe hesitated at that stage of writing the work about the question of Faust's damnation: upon this issue the terms of the pact clearly depend. The solution he finally arrived at takes us into his classical era.

The principal tragic theme in the 'Urfaust' is centred on Faust's seduction of Gretchen and her act of infanticide. These are favourite topics with those 'Sturm und Drang' writers who wished to voice their social criticism. Goethe is not among them, nor is his dramatization of Faust's urge to achieve universal knowledge characteristic of the period. He gave titanism a tragic bias by allowing it to reveal the limitations of the hero's nature and to provide the motivation for Faust's practice of magic as well as his search for experience to which Gretchen falls victim.

Although the work remained a fragment for many years, even the 'Urfaust' is Goethe's most representative 'Sturm und Drang' creation in real no less than potential achievement. This is shown in his formal and structural virtuosity. He fashioned a flexible medium comprising 'Knittelvers', prose and song with which he expressed a great variety of moods and feelings in monologue, dialogue and repartee, in reflective and emotional utterance.

Faust's dualism has its origin in religious doubt. By comparison, *Clavigo* (1774), based on the memoirs of Beaumarchais, presents the problem less searchingly. Carlos is a representative of 'Sturm und Drang' morality, but Clavigo himself falls short of it. He is a 'genius', yet a vacillating character. By divorcing strength from genius, Goethe cast doubt on a salient aspect of 'Sturm und Drang' ideology. He also moderated his own earlier practices of dramatic construction and expression. The inconclusive end of *Stella* (1776) where, with infidelity forgiven, general accord prevails, indicates a similar transition from 'Sturm und Drang' radicalism towards acceptance of the 'classical' principles of harmony and reconciliation.

Egmont, begun in 1775 but not completed until 1788, testifies to the transition in a different way. As Goethe reports in Book XX of *Dichtung und Wahrheit,* a new awareness gained ground with him at the time he began to write the drama. The 'daimonic' impulse he describes here is different from the titanic urge of his 'Sturm und Drang' heroes. Goethe saw it operating within the individual as well as externally in nature, and manifesting itself in contradictory attributes, rational and irrational, beneficent and malevolent. Accepting the reality of this 'incalculable' power, he transmuted his experience of it into poetic images: 'Ich suchte mich vor diesem furchtbaren Wesen zu retten, indem ich mich nach meiner Gewohnheit hinter ein Bild flüchtete.' He also says: 'Am furchtbarsten aber erscheint dieses Dämonische, wenn es in irgend einem Menschen überwiegend hervortritt.' When 'der grosse Kerl' of 'Sturm und Drang' provenance is ruled by this daimonic power it inspires fear. In other circumstances it evokes admiration and love. Such is the case with Egmont: in him it appears merely as carefree bravery, but nonetheless leads him to doom.

The play is an historical drama different from *Götz von Berlichingen* although both deal with the theme of liberty. Exercising the right of poetic licence in dealing with his material, Goethe invented the figure of Klärchen and made Egmont her lover for obvious dramatic reasons which Schiller failed to recognize in his review of the play. Some of the broadly epic features of Goethe's earlier drama recur in *Egmont,* particularly in the crowd scenes. But Goethe succeeded in exploiting the dramatic potentialities of the historical material in a new way. He amplified the technique of contrast which he had practised in *Götz* and *Faust* and produced even greater diversity of interest within a more balanced total action. The final scenes show his new approach. They have, without justice, been called 'operatic', if this is a term of censure. They are intentionally untragic. Egmont's resignation and his vision of Klärchen as an emblem of freedom achieved, prefigure the kind of conclusion Goethe was to find for *Faust* nearly sixty years later. More immediately, *Egmont* points to Goethe's mature style of dramatic language. He did not finish the work until he had written *Iphigenie auf Tauris.* Embedded in the prose of the final act are numerous blank verse lines, the metre he chose for his classical plays.

None of the other 'Sturm und Drang' dramatists except Schiller had the talent or good fortune to progress far beyond the confines of that movement. Jakob Michael Reinhold Lenz (1751-92) had the gift to do so but succumbed to madness. There is much tragic violence in the plays he called 'comedies'. He used the term in a more than ordinarily embracing sense: he combined tragic and comic effects for purposes of realistic presentation: 'Daher müssen unsere deutschen Komödienschreiber komisch und tragisch zugleich schreiben, weil das Volk . . . ein solcher Mischmasch von Kultur und Rohigkeit, Sittigkeit und Wildheit ist.' He shared with his 'Sturm und Drang' contemporaries a strong antipathy against the abuse of privilege but avoided one-sided motivation of its consequences. In *Der Hofmeister* (1774) the tutor Läuffer and Gustchen's parents are equally to blame. In true 'Sturm und Drang' manner, however, Lenz treats his main theme against a composite background. He includes a satirical portrayal of student life and introduces much realistic detail in characterizing such figures as the schoolmaster Wenzeslaus and the musician Rehaar. The epic interest is sustained to an excessive degree: for the thirty-five scenes there is an inordinate number of changes of locality.

Lenz practised a similarly impressionistic and epic technique in *Die Soldaten* (1776) with the aim of impartially presenting the privileged position of the officer class and the moral instability of the lower middle class section of society. As a play devoid of heroic intent it entitles Lenz to be called a 'Maler der menschlichen Gesellschaft'. His objectivity eschews the idealistic quality this attitude begins to assume in German Classicism, but it won the approval of Bertolt Brecht and gives his dramas their modern appeal.

The dramas of Friedrich Maximilian Klinger (1752-1831) have a more subjective bias. The deprivations he suffered in youth made him an outspoken critic of society. Following Rousseau, his chosen theme is the thwarting effect of institutions and conventions upon the self-esteem and freedom of action of exceptional human beings. He modelled his first tragedy, *Otto* (1775), on *Götz von Berlichingen* but added the favourite 'Sturm und Drang' theme of family feuds and treated it in characteristically explosive language. Fratricide resulting from the hero's revolt against the law of primogeniture is the content of *Die Zwillinge* (1776), emancipation and the battle against oppression the subjects Klinger treated with equal vigour in *Das leidende Weib* (1775) and *Die neue Arria* (1776). His next two plays, *Simsone Grisaldo* and *Sturm und Drang* (originally called *Wirrwarr*) are again written in this uninhibited manner, but they indicate the beginning of a change in his outlook: the feuds and conflicts end in reconciliation. In the oddly chosen setting of *Sturm und Drang,* in America, there are typical characters like the 'Kraftkerl'. Wild, violent passions and intentionally chaotic scenes: so much so that the work appears to be an ironic presentation of those features of the movement to which it gave its name.

Klinger was in Weimar on a visit to Goethe when he wrote the play. It shows him in process of outgrowing his youthful exuberance. Among his later dramatic works are the comedies *Der Derwisch* (1780), *Stilpo und seine Kinder* (1780) and *Die falschen Spieler* (1782). They treat some of his 'Sturm und Drang' themes with greater restraint. Despite his association with the Seyler group of actors, he did not succeed in the theatre but turned instead to writing 'philosophical' novels after entering the Russian military and civil services where he achieved considerable eminence. His farewell to the 'Sturm und Drang' is the satirical novel *Plimplamplasko oder Der hohe Geist (heut Genie).*

Heinrich Leopold Wagner (1747-79) was an even more

outspoken critic of society than Klinger. After imitating Wieland's *Komische Erzählungen* in his *Confiskable Erzählungen* (1774) and the satire *Prometheus, Deukalion und seine Rezensenten* (1775), he wrote two dramas which are characterized by stark realism bordering on naturalism. In theme and style *Die-Reue nach der Tat* (1775) anticipates the late-nineteenth-century treatments of love frustrated by class prejudice. Wagner's frankly propagandist intentions are evident from his characterization of the coachman Walz who, like Wenzeslaus in *Der Hofmeister* and Wesener in *Die Soldaten,* represents human nature unspoilt by civilized society. The butcher Humbrecht in *Die Kindermörderin* (1776) is another sympathetically drawn man of the people but here Wagner's presentation is less partial than in his earlier play. His condemnation of the privileged class is not so sweeping as in *Die Reue nach der Tat.* His main concern in writing *Die Kindermörderin* appears to have been a plea for legal reform in the punishment of infanticide. Evchen Humbrecht's seduction and its aftermath have striking similarities with Gretchen's tragedy in *Faust,* justifying Goethe's accusation of plagiarism. But Wagner's realism and his propagandist line resulted in a play that is quite different from Goethe's, even in the treatment of the 'Kindermörderin' motif.

Johann Anton Leisewitz (1752-1806) treated the other favourite 'Sturm und Drang' theme, fratricide, in *Julius von Tarent* (1776). However, he was not a member of the Strasbourg group (he did not meet Herder and Goethe until he went to Weimar in 1780) but rather of the 'Göttinger Hain'. Unlike Klinger he focussed attention on the weaker brother and divorced the tragic issue from social criticism. On the other hand he followed the trend in condemning tyranny when he wrote the 'Dramoletten' *Der Besuch um Mitternacht* and *Die Pfändung.*

Aspects of the 'Sturm und Drang' are also apparent in the work of Friedrich ('Maler') Müller (1749-1825). Like Goethe he dramatized legends in *Niobe* (1778) and the fragmentary *Fausts Leben dramatisiert* (1778). In a Preface to the latter work he stated his reasons for treating his material in the 'Sturm und Drang' manner: 'Faust war in meiner Kindheit immer einer meiner Lieblingshelden, weil ich ihn gleich vor einen grossen Kerl nahm; ein Kerl, der alle seine Kraft gefühlt den Zügel, den Glück und Schicksal ihm anhielt, den er zerbrechen wollt' und Mittel und Wege sucht—Mut genug hat, alles niederzuwerfen, was im Weg trat und ihn verhindern will—Wärme genug in seinem Busen trägt, sich in Liebe an einen Teufel zu hängen, der ihm offen und vertraulich entgegentritt.' This is a good statement of 'Sturm und Drang' ideology, but in the parts of the play which Müller executed, the titanic side of Faust's character is not much in evidence. Instead, Müller dwells largely on the domestic side of his hero's life and the reasons (among them lack of money) which led him to make the pact with the devil. Maler Müller did not have Goethe's gift of portraying a forceful personality: his strength lay in depicting the student and merchant milieu at Ingolstadt where the action takes place.

His 'painterly' approach to his subjects comes out in the idylls he wrote in 1775 and 1776: *Der Satyr Mopsus, Bachidon und Milon, Die Schaf-Schur, Das Nusskernen.* Here he succeeds remarkably in evoking the actuality of life in the Palatinate countryside. He was not equipped to write a drama in the 'Sturm und Drang' style. This is confirmed by *Golo und Genoveva* written between the years 1775 and 1781, in which he again aimed at portraying titanic figures in the unscrupulous Golo and in Mathilde, a virago with obvious likeness to Adelheid in *Götz von Berlichingen.* Instead, he succeeded well in creating 'Stimmung', the forest atmosphere of medieval Germany. The play contains scenes of great poetic beauty and for this reason, not because of its realization of 'Sturm und Drang' qualities, it may be ranked as one of the best dramatic productions of the time.

The last representative 'Sturm und Drang' writer was Friedrich Schiller. When he began writing, the movement had lost its impetus, nor was he associated with any member of the Strasbourg group until he went to Weimar at a time when the movement was a thing of the past and he had himself changed. His literary antecedents were different from those of the other 'Sturm und Drang' dramatists. Swabian pietism and relics of Enlightenment philosophy determined his outlook even when he revolted against the political and social inequalities of the time. His protests have a strongly religious flavour and when he wrote his defence of the stage, justifying it as a 'moralische Anstalt', he paid more than lip-service to the philosophy of the 'Aufklärung', retaining, in particular, the belief in universal harmony until his friend Körner disproved it in Kantian terms. His youthful poem 'Die Kindesmörderin' has far more moral fervour directed against the seducer than is found in Goethe's and Wagner's plays.

The starting point of Schiller's 'Sturm und Drang' was different from Goethe's: he did not go through a Rococo phase. From the beginning he showed keener awareness of social problems. In a sense Goethe amalgamated his two earlier phases (Rococo and 'Sturm und Drang') when he evolved his Classicism. Schiller moved away from his 'Sturm und Drang' in a straighter line. The more Goethe developed as a dramatist, the less he concerned himself with historical themes: for Schiller history yielded increasingly rewarding topics the more he outgrew his 'Sturm und Drang'. He became the first consistent writer of historical dramas in modern German literature.

The 'Sturm und Drang' ethos of his first three plays is very pronounced. It is unmistakable in their themes and their language. Yet there are characteristic differences which place them apart and account for the direction of Schiller's later development. In *Die Räuber* (1777-80) he does deal with fraternal enmity, the theme stated in the sub-title. It may have been the subject of Schiller's original conception and only later gave way to the robber motif. At any rate, both aspects of the plot show his 'Sturm und Drang' interest in crime as a social phenomenon. Franz Moor is the younger 'disinherited' son of 'Sturm und Drang' tragedies on fratricide without being a 'grosser Kerl': in *Die Räuber* Karl Moor fulfils this function and he is the avenger of social injustice. By distributing the roles in this way and making such a combination of themes, Schiller produced a new kind of 'Sturm und Drang' drama.

Furthermore, he added another facet: Franz represents frustrated materialism, Karl embodies idealism gone astray. The antithetic structure of the whole work is characteristic of Schiller's art. It accounts for the superiority of his dramas as theatre over the 'epic' forms chosen by his predecessors. By turning his 'grosser Kerl' into a misguided idealist he was able to include in his dramatic scheme a credible presentation of change of heart, thus safeguarding his moral priorities. Karl Moor comes to recognize his own guilt and atones for it with an act of generous magnanimity. This is a motif which Schiller found capable of further development in his classical phase. In this sense Karl prefigures the later 'sublime' heroes.

Schiller's second tragedy, *Die Verschwörung des Fiesco zu Genua* (1782), is noteworthy for being his first attempt at dramatizing historical material. It remained an immature endeavour because he had not made a careful study of historical sources as he was to do for his later plays, but relied on a secondary account of dubiously 'romantic' character. The interest accordingly lies less in the dramatization of a phase of Genoese history than in Schiller's handling of a psychological motif: the corruption of Fiesco the republican idealist through the lure of power, the making of a potential tyrant out of a genuine lover of freedom. This project involved Schiller in dealing largely with deceit and intrigue. He made skilful use of imagery denoting acts of cloaking, veiling and masquerading, a motif which runs through the work and culminates in Fiesco's killing his wife when she is in male disguise. He had not yet mastered the technique of weaving love intrigues and political cabals together, a problem he faced more successfully in his next play. But he was able to put the love episodes to good account in constructing his tragedy on antithetical lines. *Fiesco* has many shifts of mood and attitude in language of appropriate diversity; its main feature is the contrasts Schiller establishes between the representatives of the two political camps as well as within the Republican fold.

Antithesis and variety of mood and language characterize Schiller's next play, the 'bürgerliches Trauerspiel' *Kabale und Liebe* (1783). An improvement of his technique is evinced by his ability to exploit contrasts of personality and to express them by differentiating the speech of the lovers Ferdinand and Luise from that of the courtiers and of the heroine's middle-class parents. In Hofmarschall von Kalb he also satirized the Gallic mannerisms affected in aristocratic speech of the day. In this way he developed the realism of 'Sturm und Drang' drama without going to the lengths practised by Wagner.

A further indication of Schiller's originality within the current tradition is his treatment of the middle-class theme. Social distinctions and their destructive effect for the individual are still the principal content of *Kabale und Liebe,* but Schiller went beyond the traditional scope by adding an internal process of disintegration to the externally motivated destruction. The relationship between Ferdinand and Luise is undermined and their love destroyed no less by Ferdinand's jealousy than by Wurm's machinations. If Shakespeare is an influence here it has changed its quality since the days of Strasbourg. By amalgamating themes from *Othello* and *Romeo and Juliet*

Title page of Schiller's play Die Räuber *depicting Karl Moor swearing revenge on his brother Franz for cheating him out of his inheritance.*

Schiller gave a more mature presentation of dramatic conflict than he had hitherto achieved. This meant that the way lay open to him to evolve a new style at about the same time as Goethe did when he published his first classical play. An important figure in *Kabale und Liebe* is Lady Milford. She had the makings of an Orsina or of a 'Sturm und Drang' virago. Instead, she acts on principles which Schiller increasingly used in his later dramas to demonstrate sublimity in his heroes and heroines.

Don Carlos (begun in 1782, completed in 1787) is the great work of Schiller's transition from 'Sturm und Drang' to Classicism. His original theme, enmity between father and son, became less important for him in the course of writing the play. This is partly accounted for by the fact that while his original intention was to write a 'domestic tragedy', it could not have been a 'bürgerliches Trauerspiel'. The plot was fairly easily shorn of its 'Sturm und Drang' bias when Schiller's growing historical interests influenced his writing. At the beginning he had based himself largely on Real's romantic fabrication, but as he realized the potentialities of his material he went more carefully into the historical background with the result that the rivalry between

King Philip and Don Carlos in their love for the queen faded into relative insignificance. Marquis Posa, a character of subordinate interest in Schiller's first draft, now gained in importance as he came to represent the ideal of freedom in the struggle of the Netherlands against Spain.

Again, however, what might have remained a 'Sturm und Drang' conflict between a tyrant king and one of his liberal-minded subjects changed when Schiller made Posa into an egotistical schemer, an idealist who resorts to intrigue and deceit in carrying out his plans. Now a revision of the king's character became possible: in the completed work he is no longer the traditional tyrant but an intensely vulnerable man who is capable of generous acts yet demeans himself by outrageous behaviour towards his queen. Elisabeth, by contrast, gains in majesty in persuading Don Carlos to give up his love for her. Posa shares in the process of rehabilitation when he sacrifices himself for Carlos. But the defeat of idealism is made finally manifest when the Grand Inquisitor rebukes King Philip at the final juncture of the play and when he is seen to exercise real power over him.

This drama of inordinate length is best remembered for isolated scenes such as the confrontation between the king and Posa in Act III. It compares in dramatic interest with that between Nathan and Saladin in Lessing's play. *Don Carlos* is likewise written in blank verse, a medium which Schiller made his own in a remarkably short time after writing his previous tragedy. Its cadence of eloquence compares with Lessing's conversational and Goethe's poetic use of the form. These three writers fashioned the medium of classical German drama in less than a decade and in different ways impressed upon it the stamp of their personalities.

Poetry

Elements of the 'Sturm und Drang' are first to be found in the work of some members of the 'Göttinger Hain', a group of poets at the Hanoverian university in the sixties and early seventies. Klopstock's influence was paramount (the name of the association derives from his poem 'Der Hügel und der Hain'), while Wieland was rejected as representing alien trends. A 'Bund' was formed by contributors to the *Göttinger Musenalmanach* which Heinrich Christian Boie (1744-1806) and Friedrich Wilhelm Gotter (1746-97) began to edit in 1770. When Gotter, who later became an opponent of the 'Sturm und Drang', left Göttingen, Boie enlisted the aid of Bürger for a short while; the *Almanach* was edited by Johann Heinrich Voss during the years 1776-80. In the later issues Voss, Hölty and Miller became contributors, as did Klopstock, Wieland, Herder, Leisewitz, Goethe, the brothers Stolberg and Claudius at different times. None of the last named except Klopstock and the Stolbergs joined the 'Bund'. It ceased to exist in 1776 while the *Almanach* continued to be published from Hamburg until the end of the century.

The poets of the 'Göttinger Hain' formed an organized group. They held regular meetings at which they discussed each others' poetry and they kept a record of these transactions which has been lost. They were agreed on some general matters such as the need to promote national feeling in poetry and shared a love of nature and of country life, but there are considerable differences in the content and the quality of the poetry they produced. In terms of literary history, the work of some members points towards Classicism, that of others towards Romanticism. The most important representatives are Voss, Friedrich Leopold Stolberg and Hölty: it is in their work that these divergent trends are most clearly seen.

Johann Heinrich Voss (1751-1826) had the greatest influence with his hexameter translations (1781-93) of Greek and Latin poets, especially Homer and Virgil; they became standard works and continued the dissemination of classical literature begun by Lessing and Winckelmann. In his original verse he showed a preference for pastoral and idyllic poetry, his most successful work being the idyll *Luise.* It first appeared in the form of three cantos in the *Göttinger Musenalmanach* of 1783 but was re-issued in 1795 and in 1800 with many prosaic additions in the form of an epic under the title *Luise, ein ländliches Gedicht.* In other examples of idyllic poetry Voss introduced a polemical note on contemporary social topics. He attacked aristocratic privileges in the 'Sturm und Drang' manner. On the other hand he also wrote idylls with the aim of spreading 'Volksaufklärung' by attacking superstition and ignorance. Here the continuance of Enlightenment tradition is evident. As time went on he increasingly showed this side of his interests: he became an outspoken critic of some aspects of romanticism, notably opposing the Catholic trends of the Heidelberg School, especially in *Anti-Symbolik.*

Friedrich Leopold Graf zu Stolberg (1750-1819) had little sympathy with the Enlightenment. When he belonged to the 'Göttinger Hain' he wrote defiant and forceful odes and hymns on freedom and kindred subjects, e.g. 'Die Freiheit', 'Freiheitsgesant'. The 'Sturm und Drang' quality of his verse is also evident in the language, metre and themes of his mature poetry. At the same time he showed a liking for idyllic scenes and tranquil moods of nature. The coexistence of both attitudes in Stolberg's work shows itself in his treatment of similar themes with contrasting effect as in 'Die Meere' and 'An das Meer', 'Der Felsenstrom' and 'An die Wende bei Göttingen'. This conjunction of the revolutionary and the pacific is a feature of the poetry of the whole period. Stolberg's idyllic trend is best seen in poems like 'Die Ruhe' and 'Der Abend'. It increased in significance after the death of his first wife in 1789. When he was converted to Catholicism in 1800 he belonged to the circle of Gräfin Gallitzin which played an important part in the development of Romanticism in Germany. In Stolberg's later poetry Romantic features are frequently found, for example in 'Lied auf dem Wasser zu singen' (1782), 'Die Bitte' (1789) and 'Sehnsucht' (1790). These melodious and suggestive poems are among his best work.

Stolberg's treatment of the quest for tranquillity when he was a member of the 'Göttinger Hain' is paralleled in the poetry of another adherent, Ludwig Christoph Heinrich Hölty (1748-76). His early death prevented him from fulfilling the promise he amply showed. He began as a follower of Anacreonticism and in this phase wrote some of his best known poems, such as 'Lebenspflichten'. When Bürger introduced him to Boie and he became a founding member of the 'Bund' he developed a different style and treated new themes. This is shown in his nature poetry, particularly in the groups of poems he called 'Mai- und Mondlieder' and 'Erntelieder'. The 'Mondlieder' are clearly pre-Romantic in theme if not in treatment. In none of his mature work are 'Sturm und Drang' features noticeable, although he wrote many poems in the 'Volkslied' style and in his ballads was influenced by Percy's *Reliques.* Another English writer whose work he followed was Thomas Gray. Hölty wrote a number of elegies between 1770 ('Elegie auf eine Rose') and 1775 ('Elegie bei dem Grabe meines Vaters'). His imitation of Gray's elegy as well as his relative independence can best be seen in the two poems he wrote in 1771, 'Elegie auf einen Dorfkirchhof' and 'Elegie auf einen Stadtkirchhof'. By making the contrast between village and city, Hölty introduced a rudimentary form of social criticism into the subject matter of Gray's poem and so showed some affinity with 'Sturm und Drang' tendencies.

Matthias Claudius (1740-1815) shared little of the growing interest in these tendencies. He cultivated the simple style of folk poetry without accepting Herder's theories, and distrusted the fervent expressiveness of *Der Messias.* It is one of the works he admitted finding incomprehensible. He spent most of his adult life in rural parts of Westphalia writing poetry which differs from that of his contemporaries in that it is genuinely 'naiv' in Schiller's sense of the term. His cradle songs ('Ein Wiegenlied beim Mondschein zu singen' and 'Noch ein Wiegenlied') and the poems on death, including the justly famed 'Der Tod und das Mädchen', are among his best work. His fundamentally affirmative attitude enabled him to indulge a quizzical sense of humour devoid of satirical thrust. An example is 'Wandsbeck—eine Art von Romanze'.

Some of the diverse influences brought to bear on German poetry between Anacreonticism and the Classical era show themselves in the work of Gottfried August Bürger (1747-94). His outstanding achievement was the creation of a new kind of ballad at a time when Gottsched's condemnation of the genre was still influential. 'Lenore' justly gained for its author a European reputation. It is his best known work but not the only one of its kind: he wrote other ballads in a comparable style.

Before writing 'Lenore', Bürger had an Anacreontic phase, traces of which remained in his later work. However, he deepened the Rococo mood in his treatment of love as a cosmic force, e.g. in 'Die Nachtfeier der Venus' (1769), 'Die Elemente' (1776) and similar poems. He published 'Lenore' in the *Göttinger Musenalmanach* for 1774. It is one of the first works partly written under the impact of Herder's Ossian essay. But it is essentially not 'folk poetry' in Herder's sense: far from being a spontaneous effusion of feeling proceeding in a series of 'Würfe und Sprünge', it is carefully composed and it achieves its telling effect with an intricately assembled stanza form and a judicious mixture of repetition and variation, narration and dialogue, description and onomatopoeic jingle. These devices enabled Bürger to convey speedy movement and the mounting tension of the ghostly atmosphere. He wrote other poems, e.g. 'Die Entführung', in the same style but with less success. In some ballads ('Das Lied vom braven Mann', 'Der Ritter und sein Liebchen', 'Der wilde Jäger') a moral tone which he kept under control in 'Lenore' became obtrusive. In a further group ('Der Kaiser und der Abbt', 'Die Weiber von Weinsberg', 'Frau Schnipps', 'Jupiter und Europa') Bürger employed satire, in yet another he used 'Sturm und Drang' motifs that deal with oppression ('Der Raubgraf', 'Der Bauer') and infanticide ('Des Pfarrers Tochter von Taubenheim').

He is in line with 'Sturm und Drang' writers in another respect. His 'Mollylieder' are examples of 'confessional' poetry. In these he did not achieve Goethe's distinction of creatively transmuting personal experience. In 1791 Schiller severely criticized this side of Bürger's work, unjustly, since he was not given to write his poetry to Schiller's precept: 'Nur die heitere, die ruhige Seele gebiert das Vollkommene.' But without reaching such classical perfection, Bürger did attempt formal control by composing sonnets. He did this at a time when few German poets wrote in the genre. His enterprise in this field has no little merit, but his place in the history of German literature is mainly assured by his writing 'Lenore' and by translating and expanding Raspe's *Münchhausen* (1786).

Goethe's poetic pre-eminence during the 'Sturm und Drang' remained unchallenged. The range and depth of his experiences and, more tellingly, his creative apprehension of them in the process of composing his poetry, qualified him as 'Erlebnisdichter' in a unique and unrivalled way. He achieved this distinction not only because of his ability to express his experiences in memorable form but because these very experiences were of a poetic order: experience and creation were complementary manifestations of Goethe's personality.

As in his dramatic work, so in his poetry he began by adopting established conventions. His first collections *Annette* (1767) and *Neue Lieder* (1770) owe much to Anacreontic models. Even here, however, some of his abiding themes make their appearance, as in his use of images like water and moonlight which he employed more significantly than other poets at that time. But a fuller realization of his true potentialities came with the composition of the three odes to his friend Behrisch which are notably original in theme and style.

During the years 1770-5 Goethe brought 'Sturm und Drang' poetry to full efflorescence. He has no equal in any of the different forms practised by the members of the group. The ballads, songs, odes and hymns he wrote in Strasbourg and Frankfurt are supreme examples of pre-Romantic poetry excelling even Klopstock's contribution in depth and range. The quality of his achievement may be gauged from the richly varied poetic dispositions he had at his command: directly communicative expression of emotion ('Mailied', 'Willkommen und Abschied'), suggestive narration and the evocation of mysterious presences in nature ('Der Fischer', 'Erlkönig'), idyllic description ('Anacreons Grab'), defiant challenge ('Prometheus', 'An Schwager Chronos'), rapture in acceptance of personal destiny ('Mahomets Gesant', 'Ganymed', 'Wanderers Sturmlied'), humorous self-assertion ('Lilis Park').

Goethe's lyric dynamism was greater than at any other time. This is shown by his preference for expressions denoting movement and by the actions he incorporated in poems like 'Wanderers Sturmlied', 'Auf dem See', 'Mahomets Gesang' and 'Ganymed'. These poems illustrate two other features in which he differed from some of his fellow 'Stürmer und Dränger'. The will to shape was strong in Goethe long before it found supreme fruition in his Classical era. Even when his 'Sturm und Drang' dynamism was in full spate he made this pronouncement: 'Ich finde, dass jeder Künstler, so lange seine Hände nicht plastisch arbeiten, nichts ist.'

The second characteristic feature is his choice of images which were capable of embodying his personal experience in correlative form. Such an image is the 'Wanderer' in 'Wanderers Sturmlied', 'Der Wanderer' and the two 'Wanderers Nachtlied' poems. Another instance is the imagery derived from natural phenomena like water and moonlight ('Mahomets Gesant', 'An den Mond'). From his use of these images we can trace the continuity and the changes of his poetry in transition from 'Sturm und Drang' to Classicism.

The last representative writer of the 'Sturm und Drang' in poetry as in drama is Friedrich Schiller. He is one of the major poets of the age (Hölderlin is another) whose lyric style was not moulded by the revival of the 'Volkslied'. It also lacks the quality of song which Goethe so eminently possesses. Some of his poems were occasioned by actual events, such as the death of a friend, but Schiller invariably left the occasion behind in order to dwell in cosmic realms of the imagination. His early poetry is characterized by the kind of abstraction he later censured in Klopstock, a typical example being 'Die Grösse der Welt'. His love poetry in particular is strangely unreal. If it is appropriate to call such poems as 'Die Entzückung an Laura', 'Melancholie an Laura', 'Phantasie an Laura' and 'Laura am Klavier' products of the 'Sturm und Drang', the difference between them and Goethe's 'Friederikelieder' is unmistakable. Similarly, Schiller's evocation of spring in 'An den Frühling' is less direct than Goethe's in 'Mailied': his feelings towards the world around him were far from sanguine. There is a strain of pessimism, a sense of bitterness and rancour in all his early work which derives from personal deprivations but can also be analysed as frustrated idealism. These notes are heard in poems like 'An Minna' and 'Eine Leichenphantasie'. Compared with Hölty's gentle laments, Schiller's 'Elegie auf den Tod eines Jünglings' is intentionally macabre and acrimonious.

Yet even at its most exaggerated Schiller's lyric utterance had potentialities of development towards more balanced forms. The intellectual bent of his imagination remained inviolate, and when he subjected it to new influences he found the strength to produce an individual kind of Classical poetry.

Novel

Although Goethe's *Die Leiden des jungen Werthers* (1774) may belong superficially to the category of the 'sentimental' novel inspired by Richardson and Rousseau's *Nouvelle Heloise,* it goes far beyond the other members of this category, both in its radically subjective morality and its aesthetic quality. What Goethe had said of *Sternheim* applies with even greater force to his own novel: it is indeed a human soul that is laid bare. Gone are all the sensational elements that had marked the novel up till now: *Werther* appealed to its contemporaries, and appeals to us still, by its artistic economy, and by its authentic emotional intensity. The 'plot' may be summed up in a few words: Werther, still smarting from an unhappy love affair, makes the acquaintance of Lotte, idealizes her and falls in love with her, only to find that she is engaged to Albert, whom he cannot but respect; he tears himself away and seeks distraction in a career which brings him only frustration and rebuffs. He is drawn back to Lotte, now married to Albert, ultimately confesses his love, and then shoots himself with one of Albert's pistols. The story rings true, not simply because it is known that these events reflect, on the one hand, Goethe's situation in Wetzlar vis-à-vis his friend Kestner and Charlotte Buff, and, on the other, the suicide of a colleague at the 'Reichskammergericht', but because the character of the hero is so utterly consistent. Werther, typical of his generation, is incapable of mastering a situation resolved with relative ease by Gellert's Swedish countess. His suicide is, however, not merely the consequence of a forbidden passion, much less the heroic solution which he conceives it to be. It is the inevitable end of an unstable character, whose idealistic visions and ineffable experiences could not be accommodated to the prosaic circumstances of his time. Unhappiness in love is compounded by disgust with pedantry and social prejudice; Lotte merely focusses a wider experience of rejection. Werther plunges helplessly from rapture to despair, for he has nothing of the rationalist's 'Gelassenheit'. His perception of the world is constantly coloured by his emotions. Nature captivates him with mystic intimations of divine unity, or horrifies him as a destructive monster, he turns from the sunny world of Homer to Ossian's Celtic twilight. The integration of every detail and circumstance to form a picture of a mind in torment gives *Werther* its inner form and carries it from the sphere of fiction into the realm of poetry. It is unique in its age and one of the first characteristically modern works of literature. It articulates the sense of alienation that goes with the purely subjective mode of feeling and demonstrates that suffering may spring not from guilt and malice but from sheer discord of mind and milieu. Goethe draws the tragic conclusion from which Rousseau, with his basically optimistic morality and didactic purpose, still shrank.

Werther was the first German novel to achieve almost world-wide fame. It fired the imagination of youth and incensed the older generation; it stimulated imitation and provoked parody in almost every country of Europe. Its German successors include J. M. Miller's *Beiträge zur Geschichte der Zärtlichkeit* (1776) and his more famous *Siegwart, eine Klostergeschichte* (1776), J. M. R. Lenz's thinly disguised account of life in the Weimar circle, *Der Waldbruder* (written 1776), and F. H. Jacobi's *Aus Eduard Allwills Papieren* and *Woldemar.* Such works represent the more elegiac and sentimental aspect of the 'Sturm und Drang' as it was satirized by Nicolai in his *Freuden des jungen Werthers* (1775). The aggressive titanism of the movement which so revolutionized the drama is less evident in the novel and manifested only in relatively late works by Wilhelm Heinse and F. M. Klinger. Heinse's *Ardinghello oder die glücklichen Inseln* (1787) is a Utopia glorifying vitalism and the aesthetic life. Heinse's enthusiasm for a return to nature is more vigorous than Rousseau's, his advocacy of Greek sensuality more robust than Wieland's, his vision of a Greece restored to pristine glory cruder than Hölderlin's, but he has affinities with all three. The dionysiac amorism of Heinse's work disturbed Goethe and Schiller, but he exercised a strong influence on the Romantics and has even been seen as a forerunner of Nietzsche.

In a cycle of ten novels, of which nine were more or less completed, Klinger sought to 'embrace the entire moral existence of man'. The archetypal figure of Faust recurs again and again as the author grapples with a welter of philosophical and political problems: the nature of evil, free will and necessity; the conflict of nature and culture; the dialogue of poet and pragmatist; the abrogation of aristocratic privilege and the improvement of the peasant's lot. The ultimate view of man's destiny is embodied in the Faustian philosophy of constant striving—even although God remains inscrutable and mute: 'nichts beantwortet dieses schreckliche Schweigen als unsere innere moralische Kraft, und auch sie selbst nur durch ihr Wirken.' In his concern with the corrupting effects of civilization Klinger is linked to Rousseau and Wieland; his vision of man's triadic development from innocence through depravity to higher harmony anticipates a typical Romantic pattern of thought. Klinger employs a variety of forms and idioms—myth, Märchen and satire, and it is hardly surprising that the vast enterprise barely achieves the unity he sought and that its extravagance reminds us of the baroque novels of an earlier age. (pp. 51-81)

E. L. Stahl and W. E. Yuill, " *'Sturm und Drang',* " *in their* German Literature of the Eighteenth and Nineteenth Centuries, *Barnes & Noble, Inc., 1970, pp. 51-81.*

An excerpt from Johann Wolfgang von Goethe's poem "*Prometheus*" (1778)

Cover thy spacious heavens, Zeus,
With clouds of mist,
And, like the boy who lops
The thistles' heads,
Disport with oaks and mountain-peaks;
Yet thou must leave
My earth still standing;
My cottage too, which was not raised by thee;
Leave me my hearth,
Whose kindly glow
By thee is envied.

I know nought poorer
Under the sun, than ye gods!
Ye nourish painfully,
With sacrifices
And votive prayers,
Your majesty;
Ye would e'en starve,
If children and beggars
Were not trusting fools.

Johann Wolfgang von Goethe in his Poems of Goethe: Translated in the Original Metres *translated by Edgar Alfred Bowring, George Bell and Sons, 1885.*

Werner Kohlschmidt

[In the following essay, Kohlschmidt traces the origins of the Sturm und Drang to both the philosophical rationalism of the Enlightenment and the religious subjectivity of pietism. He also examines typical Sturm und Drang concerns as expressed in poetry, drama, and prose.]

Whatever the differences, and indeed conflicts, between *Sturm und Drang,* classicism and Romanticism, they share certain important determining features. They are heirs to the Enlightenment and to pietism, both of which had a decisive influence on the German language around 1770. Rationalism made the language more precise and gave it a power of intellectual differentiation and abstraction that it had not had in the baroque age. The religious intensity of pietism, on the other hand, found a power of expressiveness which left far behind the mystic-subjective terminology of baroque and found a new range of subtleties through the act of self-observation. Both these linguistic developments underlie the position that German literature attains between 1770 and 1830. One may also apply to the situation Goethe's remark that his generation had rediscovered the language of Luther; but at the same time the urge to break new ground must surely have derived to a greater extent from Lessing's achievement in intellectual precision and flexibility and Klopstock's language of passionate insistence.

The condition for this linguistic development, which was inherited by *Stürmer und Dränger* and classicists alike, was the release of that subjectivity which produced in the secular sphere the philosophy of the Enlightenment, and in the religious sphere the sentimental introspection of pietism. The Bible-based world view of the baroque age, unshakeable and binding on both confessions, had completely disintegrated in the first half of the century—or at least had taken up its stance on completely different foundations. The new rationalist view was based on natural law and human justice, and the religious aspect was at best incidental. The changed role of the problem of a theodicy is significant, for God is now called before the judgement-seat of Reason, in contrast to Anselm's *fides quaerens intellectum.* And where, as in pietism, God is still at the centre, the theocentric concept no longer has absolute validity—and orthodoxy has even less. Orthodoxy could give rise to a Lessing but could no longer move men's minds. For its part pietism concentrated on the figure of Christ, retained its cult-image only in restricted circles and introduced a liberalizing tendency through the idea of tolerance—an idea it shared with the Enlightenment. The power with which philosophy from Locke and Hume down to Kant made human subjectivity aware of its rights and the responsibilities of its maturity could no longer be held back. As the new science had replaced a geocentric universe with a heliocentric one, so the philosophical emphasis now became anthropological rather than theological.

Corresponding to this is the movement of the age, first found in England, towards empiricism, which in turn uncovered new human faculties and new areas of reality. Kant's *Critiques* had the effect of heightening man's sense of responsibility in his newly attained 'state of majority' (cf. its later destructive effect on Kleist) but served at the same time as a logical corrective to English empiricism, which also led to a new view of reality. Kant's thought thus offered legitimate support to Schiller's aesthetics, which aimed at a far subtler conception of aesthetic reality than the static conception held by the age of Gottsched.

This shift of values is already apparent in the way in which the Enlightenment treated the philosophy of Shaftesbury. The aesthetic assumes equal importance with the ethical, and from here it is only a step to Young's concept of Original Composition. The line of development leads from the release of aesthetic subjectivity in Shaftesbury to the release of aesthetic originality in Young; it was in fact already manifested by the great English novelists, Sterne, Richardson and Fielding. This development also contains within itself, however, the concept of education and self-development, for the notion of universal history and world-literature—the Middle Ages, folksong, Shakespeare, Milton, Greek and French classicism—was not a creation of Herder, Goethe and the Romantics but was already pursued by Gottsched, Bodmer and Breitinger, and the Bremer Beiträger. Classical antiquity is studied, not only with ever-growing critical acumen but from different starting-points: Winckelmann, Lessing, Voss, Heyne, F. A. Wolf give a new view of Homer and a revolutionary assessment of the values of classical art.

The exploitation of these two worlds—medieval/baroque and neoclassical—comes with *Sturm und Drang,* classicism and, in a more modern way, with the Romantics. Initially it was the universalism of Lessing, Winckelmann and Herder that showed the breadth of this world-literature, a universalism stimulated by the urge to educate and instruct which is so marked a characteristic of the age. Enlightenment attitudes and activities provide the basis of the age of Goethe in both its emotional and irrational, classical and didactic aspects. The changes that occur in the 1770s, therefore, are only partly revolutionary in nature; they also have their characteristics as entirely organic developments.

An organic development from the situation in the early 1770s comes with the 'Göttinger Hain', a group of poets, one of whom, Johann Heinrich Voss, turned the name into 'Hainbund' to convey the corporate nature of their activities. The group was founded on 12 September 1772 under the spiritual aegis of Klopstock, from whose ode *Der Hügel und der Hain* they took their name. This group of Göttingen students went out one night by full moon to an oak-lined glade where they pledged eternal friendship and moral uprightness, danced and crowned each other with wreaths. On the one side this is the sentimental aspect of the Enlightenment, on the other it is a youthful revolutionary outburst.

The important thing is not that such a group met formally, elected a leader, kept records of its meetings, celebrated anniversaries, etc.—the linguistic societies of the seventeenth century had already done such things—but that it should have produced the literary results it did. As well as Voss (1751–1826), the first leader, the members included Hölty (1748–76), the two Counts von Stolberg (Christian (1748–1821) and Friedrich Leopold (1750–1819), Leisewitz (1752–1806) and Johann Christian Boie (1744–1806), publisher of the famous *Göttinger Musen-Almanach.* These are all North Germans—indeed, the Göttinger Hain can be seen as the North German counterpart to *Sturm und Drang.*

However, the revolutionary self-confidence of the *Stürmer und Dränger* was foreign to the Hain, whose links with *Sturm und Drang* in the narrow sense come with Leisewitz's drama *Julius von Tarent* (1776) and with the Stolbergs' meeting with Goethe in the course of the latter's first journey to Switzerland, as a result of which the Stolbergs acquired something of Goethe's mood of *épater le bourgeois.*

The most significant literary achievements of the Hain lie in the field of lyric poetry. The title of Friedrich Stolberg's little essay *Fülle des Herzens* (1777)—a title only possible in these changed times—fully conveys the attitudes and aims that link the Hain to *Sturm und Drang.* These young disciples of Klopstock turned the experience of time and place into a matter of pure rapture without entering the theoretical field of aesthetics. Much of their poetry is simply 'Fülle des Herzens', and it is not surprising that a great deal of it should have acquired such wide currency. 'Fülle des Herzens' also designates the odes of Hölty and the Stolbergs, even down to their metrical characteristics, such as the use of very short lines. There are idyllic overtones reminiscent of the Anacreontics but they are often infused with a new sincerity and subjectivity, so that imagination, love, nature, friendship and the fatherland become truer, more authentic than before, although as themes they are not new. There is a new intensity: lines like Hölty's, addressing the imagination—

> Reiß mich flügelgeschwind über die Wolken-
> bahn
> In den goldenen Sternensaal
>
> (Gather me up like a bird through the banks of
> clouds into the company of the golden stars)

—have a dynamic power derived from Klopstock. In the strophic idyll, too, we find verses which make Gleim, Ewald von Kleist and Gessner seem like formalists and which approach Goethe:

> Noch tönt der Busch von Nachtigallen
> Dem Jüngling süße Fühlung zu,
> Noch strömt, wenn ihre Lieder schallen,
> Selbst in zerrissenen Seelen Ruh.
>
> (From out of the bush the call of nightingales
> rouses sweet feelings in the youth, and the sound

of their songs brings peace even to tormented minds.)

(Hölty)

The subjectivization of the material world is only possible when there is an awareness of spiritual conflict. In the lyric poetry of the Enlightenment, based on optimism and a logical outlook, such an awareness was hardly possible, even in idyllic, Anacreontic verse. Most of the poets of the Hain share both the Anacreontic fervour and the inner conflict. Friedrich Stolberg's 'Süße heilige Natur', for instance, perhaps the most intense of their nature-poems, exists alongside the Alcaic strophes of the ode 'Genius', with its original vocabulary of words and phrases like *Urkraft, Sonnendurst, Durst nach Unsterblichkeit, Toben in der Brust, geistiger Flug*—words with a Promethean tendency (and almost contemporary with Goethe's *Prometheus*). Also of Klopstockian origin is the somewhat 'Germanic' mixture of poetic self-confidence and patriotism which, in the imagination, was to outstrip the national feelings of the 'Britons and the French'. In this respect too, and even including the theme of opposition to tyranny, the Hainbund made common cause with the more radical *Sturm und Drang.*

The second spiritual father to the Hainbund was Gottfried August Bürger (1747–94), who lived in Göttingen and whose career offered the young, enthusiastic poets, in a form far more intense than that presented by their own existence, a picture of the tormented life of the poetic genius. For Bürger was not simply the poet of the 'panting soul'—he *was* this soul, as much as Goethe at the time of *Werther* and as much as Lenz and Klinger. This makes Göttingen, home of the movement to establish the ballad as the prime form of folk art, the equal of Herder's Strasbourg in the folk movement: Bürger's *Lenore,* published in Boie's *Musenalmanach,* the literary journal of the Göttingen circle, is the paradigm of this success.

Whereas with the new subjectivism of the Göttingen poets the emphasis lay on poetic practice—apart, that is, from Bürger's essays on poetics, which, like Klopstock's, are in the nature of a self-justification—the pamphlet published by Herder (1744–1803) under the title *Blätter von deutscher Art und Kunst* (1773) is the manifesto of a revolutionary attitude towards poetry. The essays by Goethe and Herder in this publication represent the credo of a new generation, although the elderly Justus Möser's *Vorrede zur Osnabrückischen Geschichte* is also included with them. The most important items, Herder's rhapsodic essays on Ossian and on Shakespeare, were originally intended for the continuation of the *Schleswiger Literaturbriefe* of Gerstenberg (1737–1823), whose critical attitudes—with their disclosure of the *Edda,* Ossian, old English ballads, the Danish *Kaempeviser,* and their defence of *Don Quixote,* Klopstock, even Hamann, the 'Magus im Norden'—played a considerable part in the destruction of the Enlightenment. When Gerstenberg's journal did not materialize, Herder, who was at that time court chaplain at Bückeburg, decided to make his own plans and produced this manifesto by adding Goethe's and Möser's contributions to his own.

His *Auszug aus einem Briefwechsel über Ossian und die Lieder alter Völker* opens the work. It is only of secondary importance that Macpherson's 'Ossian' was a fraud which skilfully appealed to the prevailing mood of sentimentality. Far more important is that it became a symbol for the new generation of the absoluteness of the emotions and the senses. A Nordic counterpart to Homer, the quintessence of spontaneity, Herder's Ossian—the antithesis of all that Berlin Rationalism stood for—turns into Goethe's Werther. His concern is not with beauty but with authenticity—the authenticity of originality and genius.

In the realm of language too this shift of values goes far beyond Gerstenberg. Genius is originality, spontaneity, immediacy, and synonyms or near-synonyms like 'wild, sensuous, powerful, vital, immense, tangible, independent' acquire a new meaning, that of the force of nature in the human spirit.

The most spontaneous and most natural spirit, however, is also the most lyrical, represented above all by the 'bard' (Klopstock and the Hain poets were also primarily lyricists). This establishes a link with the old English, Scottish and Scandinavian ballads in which passion, sensuousness and fantasy triumph over logic. The folksong, too, remained uncouth and unpredictable, dark and mysterious, not subject to the pressures of conformity. Herder's German version of the *Edward* ballad from Percy's *Reliques of ancient English poetry* (1765) symbolize the ideal, and the folksong illustrates the new conception of genius. Originality thus becomes vested in the common people, and *Volk* assumes vital thematic importance from *Götz von Berlichingen* to Romanticism.

As Herder's Ossian essay was concerned with deep lyrical forces, with the primeval depths of folk-culture, so his essay on Shakespeare seeks to illumine the vision of the supreme artist who draws on both the outer and the inner world. Right from the opening picture of the gigantic figure of the genius on the rocky pinnacle, towering above the world of common mortals, everything is aimed at conveying the impression of grandeur.

The concept of grandeur, indeed, dominates *Sturm und Drang.* Ossian, Homer, Shakespeare, Sophocles, the power of nature and the power of human creativity, the figure of Prometheus (the second creator, as Shaftesbury, following late classical and Renaissance interpretations of the myth, called him)—such are the dominant forces, culminating in Goethe's ode and dramatic fragment of *Prometheus.* Also symbolical of the age is the story that Lessing's Spinoza-inspired interpretation of Goethe's myth brought about the death of Moses Mendelssohn, Enlightment philosopher of moderation and reason.

In Herder's picture Shakespeare is just such a Promethean figure. But it was not a question of 'rescuing' Shakespeare, as Lessing, Johann Elias Schlegel and Gerstenberg had defended him against Gottsched. It was a totally new view, based on empathy—*Einfühlung* (Herder's coinage)—on spiritual kinship, on a new view of history. Indeed, a whole new view of history is involved, for Shakespeare could not be expected to share the single-mindedness of the Greeks. In Herder's eyes he was the genius of modern times, the voice, in Dilthey's phrase, of 'the poetry of fantasy' in the modern age: 'As genius is more than philosophy, and a creator is greater than a critic, so Shakespeare was a mortal with divine powers.' These creative powers enabled him 'to combine the most varied elements into a wonderful new whole', and the simplicity of Sophocles is offset by a greater breadth and wealth of material, a combination of new and more varied experiences, making Shakespeare a historically more highly developed figure.

Compared with this profusion of ideas and this exuberant, rhapsodical language, which expresses a new anti-rational aesthetic, Goethe's 'Rede zum Shakespearestag' (1771) is but a shadow. Goethe writes as Herder's disciple, Herder as Hamann's, whose concept of poetry as the mother tongue of the human race Herder conveyed to a whole generation that was looking for the language of the emotions wherever it could be found, from the Greeks to Rousseau. This generation saw in Shakespeare the perfect exemplification of the divine freedom of the creative genius, and saw themselves, in the same spirit, as free of the rules of Aristotle, Opitz, Boileau and Gottsched. The *Sturm und Drang* answer to the *Querelle des anciens et des modernes* lies in the image of Shakespeare presented by the young Herder and the young Goethe. Dream, passion, magic, the wisdom of the fool, madness, thoughts of darkness and death, with an awareness of the comic and the grotesque hovering overhead—these become the proper constituents of an independent modern art, and the *Stürmer und Dränger* lost no opportunity to employ them in their works, above all in drama and lyric poetry.

Goethe's contribution to *Von deutscher Art und Kunst* does not go further than Herder's but it does cover a different field—and that, if anything, in an even more subjective spirit. His panegyric on Strasbourg Cathedral and its legendary architect Erwin von Steinbach is simply called *Von deutscher Baukunst*— and 'German' here reflects an emphasis which corresponds to Gerstenberg's and Herder's 'Nordic'.

In a sense Goethe's essay is a synthesis of Herder's *Volk* ideas from Ossian and the subjective philosophy of genius in the Shakespeare essay. The latter, seen in a Faustian, Promethean spirit, dominates in that Steinbach's passionate vision is portrayed as a force that set him among the gods, an irresistible force that demanded expression. For Goethe's essay is not just a rehabilitation of Gothic architecture—something which Herder had already concerned himself with—but an assertion, more powerful than Herder's, of the *Sturm und Drang* philosophy of genius. Goethe's greater assertiveness derives from the *Deus sive natura* of Spinoza and from his own Prometheus concept. His study of mystico-natural forces at this time can be followed from the experiments in alchemy in which he indulged with the pietistically minded Susanne von Klettenberg and of which his diary contains a record. Spinoza is a logical conclusion to these interests, which, starting from man's affinity to God, led first to complete pantheism and then to the fashioning of human genius by God. Prometheus can mock Zeus and force the gods to restore his own direct link with fate; the 'enlightened', rational citizen can be reduced to the status of an insect because he has betrayed the potentiality of genius within himself. Human creativity, obligated to no principles and no schools, recreates beauty in truth, and nature in both—an act of creation that draws forth the epithet 'godlike'; trust in the artistic genius is boundless, for he is *natura sive Deus ipse.*

The reinstatement of Gothic art—the art denigrated by the rationalists and Renaissance theorists but to the understanding observer a symbol of the majesty of the creative urge in art—is merely the application of the concept of genius to the plastic arts. A rhapsody in the passionate Herderian style, it testifies to the spirit of enthusiasm for everything of stature. Yet in all such works it is the main concern of *Sturm und Drang* writers to create an appropriate atmosphere for the launching of their own work, to become themselves part of the free nature which they set out to portray.

Despite the enthusiasm of the young Herder and Goethe, however, *Von deutscher Art und Kunst* was not utterly original, a pioneer work, but the expression of an anti-Enlightenment tendency which had been growing for more than a decade and which is to be seen in the first instance as springing from Johann Georg Hamann. At the same time it must be seen in the context of the whole of Herder's writings from 1760 to the mid-1770s.

It is virtually impossible to dissociate these writings from the most important aesthetic and theological works of Hamann (1730–88). The 'Magus im Norden', possessed of the learning of the rationalist and the religious conviction of the pietist (he was converted in London in 1757), was a man of strong passions and intense reactions. The works that had the most lasting effect on his age were his *Sokratische Denkwürdigkeiten* (1759), together with the sequel *Wolken* (1761) and, of interest to aestheticians, the *Kreuzzüge des Philologen* (1762); in addition there is the *Abälardi Virbii Chimärische Einfalle . . .* (1761), which is a polemic against the *Literaturbriefe* of Lessing and Mendelssohn and in favour of Rousseau's *Nouvelle Héloïse.* The *Sokratische Denkwürdigkeiten,* ultimately religious in intent, present in the figure of Socrates, opponent of the rationalistic Sophists, a picture of the genius as represented over ten years later by the *Stürmer und Dränger*—the genius whose 'ignorance', in the rationalistic sense, was interpreted as 'feeling', the opposite of dogma. In Homer genius makes unnecessary a knowledge of the rules which Aristotle subsequently thought out. The same is true of Shakespeare.

The connection with *Von deutscher Art und Kunst* is obvious. It is even more so in the *Aesthetica in nuce,* the core of Hamann's *Kreuzzüge des Philologen,* where the link is apparent in style as well as in substance; even its subtitle 'A Rhapsody in Cabbalistic Prose' shows where Herder derived his picture of himself as a 'rhapsodist'. The terse, anacoluthic style, with its emphasis on images and sense-impressions, is reproduced in Herder's essays on Ossian and Shakespeare, and from Hamann comes the principle of all *Sturm und Drang* aesthetics: 'Poetry is the mother tongue of the human race.' Similarly: 'The senses and feelings deal exclusively in images.' Such theories anticipate in its entirety Herder's concept of folk-poetry and at the same time justify the use of the rhapsodical style with its mysterious allusiveness yet directly sensuous appeal. And behind this aesthetic stands a view of history which sees the challenge of the present as the reattainment of the true, natural naïvety of the unspoiled past—a view that takes its place in the contemporary trend towards irrationality and anti-rationalism. We are urged to become children again—cf. this motif in *Sturm und Drang* drama and in the realm of *Volkslied.*

The anti-rationalist barb appears in Hamann's vicious attack on Mendelssohn in his *Aesthetica in nuce:* 'Your deceitful philosophy has destroyed nature. And why do you urge us to imitate nature? So that you can have the pleasure of destroying the disciples of nature as well.' Small wonder that Hamann takes Rousseau's side. In his *Leser und Kunstrichter nach perspektivischem Unebenmaße,* an attack on Ludwig von Hagedorn, he states the logical, anti-rationalist, aesthetic viewpoint: 'If a man tries to remove arbitrariness and imagination from the realm of art, he is a charlatan who knows his own rules even worse than he knows the nature of ailments. . . . If a man tries to remove arbitrariness and imagination from the realm of art, he is attempting an assault on the honour and the life of art itself.' This attitude justified the attitudes not only of *Sturm und Drang* but also, subsequently, of Jean Paul and the Romantics.

Herder's early work *Über die neuere Literatur, Fragmente* (1765), written in Riga, already reflects Hamann's principle of a detached, non-optimistic, anti-Enlightenment view of the present age, which Herder regards as poor in original works but far richer in diaries and the like. Any great work of literature, he maintains, presupposes a great language; hence Luther's writings proceed from his 'revivification of the language', which contrasts with the artificiality and affectation of eighteenth-century style. He also praises the sublimity of the Gothic spirit at the expense of the fashionable 'cultured' values of the time.

In his *Journal meiner Reise im Jabre 1769,* written on a journey from Riga to Nantes, he keeps even closer to Hamann, both in substance and in style. Building on Hamann's invective against the desiccated world of rationalism, he draws a picture of a fully developed human being towards which he seeks to educate himself in the spirit of modern ideas of what constitutes genius. Much in this *Journal* anticipates *Von deutscher Art und Kunst,* Goethe's *Prometheus, Urfaust* and *Götz.*

Herder's yardstick is that of sensuous reality, i.e. a concept of man as a blend of mind and body which the intellectual bias of rationalism had destroyed. The whole man, the whole of reality, the conception of genius, of the arts, of language, God's plan for the world as the philosophy of history based on the Bible—all these are just different aspects of the view, derived from Hamann, which Herder held up to the time when he went to Weimar (his stay in Bückeburg, if one looks on his career as a whole, is not really to be seen as a moment of pietistic self-alienation, though it has sometimes been so interpreted).

Vom Erkennen und Empfinden der menschlichen Seele (sketched in Bückeburg, finished in Weimar, 1778); *Die älteste Urkunde des Menschengeschlechtes* (1774/6); *Über den Ursprung der Sprache* (printed 1772); *Plastik; Auch eine Philosophie zur Geschichte der Bildung der Menschheit* (1774): these are the works which, together with *Von deutscher Art und Kunst,* had a decisive effect as a virtually complete cycle of works testifying to the *Sturm und Drang* conception of man, God, history, the arts and especially language. They are all informed, theologically, psychologically, aesthetically and historically, by the view that the manifestations of human life form an organic whole and are emanations of an original sentient being. The theological framework for this outlook is given in *Die älteste Urkunde des Menschengeschlechtes,* and on its deistic foundation is built the notion of a sensuous life which God has ordained for man to experience. Its beginnings in the Old Testament are the beginnings of the history of mankind itself, and this Eastern origin conditions the nature of the human imagination.

The conflict between *Die älteste Urkunde* and *Über den Ursprung der Sprache* is only apparent. In the latter Herder opposes the rationalistic theory by which language arose as a kind of arbitrary convention, but he also opposes the conception of language as a gift of God, a kind of ready-made bequest. God remains the Creator, but man's pre-ordained path of self-expression is made to start as close to the act of Creation as possible, and language is thus present at the very beginning of man's development—'the sounds of the soul', as Herder put it. The sounds of language emerge to correspond to man's growing stock of emotions and sensations; like Hamann, he sees original language as the sounds of nature, as opposed to the 'later, refined language of metaphysical usage' which insists on logic and 'correctness'. Both Hamann and Herder see a process of refinement in the development of language as an expression of the rationalist view of progress, both on theological and aesthetic grounds, but this refinement means a loss of strength, and the *Stürmer und Dränger* saw it as the mark of decadence.

The praise of childlike qualities as reflections of a one-time unspoilt and undivided consciousness runs right through *Sturm und Drang.* It plays its part in the background to Herder's *Auch eine Philosophie,* for example, in which is expressed, as well as the belief in man's progress to reason, a penchant for the oneness with the world which characterizes the childhood of man, a state governed by 'wisdom rather than knowledge, fear of God rather than wisdom, love rather than convention'. The conflict between 'impulse' and 'reflectivity' is a product of later centuries of decay, which means the loss of simplicity, the destruction of unity, the exaggeration of reason—in short, the mechanization of the whole of life.

These are the elements behind the bold new judgements on art and history first pronounced in *Von deutscher Art und Kunst* and in the *Frankfurter Gelebrte Anzeigen* for 1772, where Goethe and Herder were joined by the friend of their Strasbourg days, Johann Heinrich Merck, in the production of a literary journal which for a short while was to enable them to propagate their ideas in a vigorous, almost presumptuous manner.

On such foundations, and in this changed atmosphere, there arose in the first instance a new lyric poetry. The trend is already observable in some of Goethe's Leipzig poems ('Die Nacht'; 'Hochzeitslied'; 'An den Mond'), which break through the Anacreontic tradition, and from these to his Sesenheim poems is only a short step, for the main characteristic, the directness of expression, was present before Goethe became a disciple of Herder and entered his Shakespearean, Promethean phase: the sincerity of 'Erwache Friederike' and 'Mayfest', with their short lines, and the insistent rhythm of 'Es schlug mein Herz, geschwind zu Pferd' are extensions of this directness. The same is true of the emotive vocabulary of these poems, including some of rococo type, such as 'Kleine Blumen, Kleine Blätter', or in traditional rondeau form, like 'Ob ich dich liebe, weiß ich nicht'. The new feelings and attitudes are, however, still simply expressed, partly because of Goethe's temperament and partly under the influence of the *Volkslied,* to which, at Herder's instigation, he had directed his attention, collection them in the surrounding Alsatian countryside. 'Heidenröslein', which Herder quotes in his Ossian essay as a folksong—though it had in fact only just been composed—shows how close the Friederike lyrics are to *Volkslied,* while 'Ach wie sehn ich mich nach dir', addressed to Friederike, derives its personal tone from its folksong-like use of repetition.

The spirit of *Sturm und Drang* shows itself in a different form in the hymns and odes which Goethe wrote at this time. Their starting-points are Klopstock, Ossian, Pindar and a number of free-verse poems of Herder, in which Goethe found a concreteness and directness of expression in such subjects as the power of nature, the irresistibility of the artistic impulse, the impelling forces behind human life and the relationship of man to the gods and to fate. Subjects of such magnitude cannot be absorbed in a simple subjectivity but demand a certain detached tone of awe, of mystery, with an intense, dynamic vocabulary that reflects an unmistakable singlemindedness of purpose and style.

Such, for example, is 'Wandrers Sturmlied', a poem of loosely connected, unequal strophes in free rhythm which Goethe tells us he recited aloud as he walked through the countryside during a storm. The shadow of Pindar hangs over it, but the vocabulary, full of neologisms, reflects what Gundolf called '*Sturm und Drang* Titanism'—the mighty spirit lifts the poet above everyday life to the eminence of the gods. The personal passion of 'Wilkommen und Abschied' becomes in 'Wandrers Sturmlied' the consuming passion of the artistic vocation. The image of a headlong journey through life recurs in 'An Schwager Kronos' and is also close to the 'Prometheus' poem of 1773, in which the theme of the artist's equality with the gods returns. This was the poem that F. H. Jacobi showed to the ageing Lessing and which both interpreted as a poetic transmutation of Spinoza. It is dominated by the ego's expression of confidence in itself as a creature in which the divine power resides and which is therefore in no need of a mediator. This creative self-sufficiency also underlies 'Ganymed' and 'Mahomets Gesang'. Ganymed, like Prometheus, symbolizes the transformation of the myth of suffering into a myth of creation; the image of the river in 'Mahomets Gesang' also embodies the dynamic concept of relentless forward movement, ending in universal unity; likewise 'Elysium', 'Pilgers Morgenlied' and 'Felsweihegesang', written in Darmstadt, are sustained by the dynamic concept of immediacy that transcends all restrictions. Particularly striking in all these hymns and odes, and to a far greater extent than in the love-poems, is the originality of language: logical, grammatical constructions are done away with, new, vivid compound verbs are coined, and hyperbole dominates the whole scene.

These qualities continue to characterize Goethe's lyrics in the succeeding period, such as the noble transcriptions from Pindar and Ossian (these latter merge into *Werther*) and the Lili poems, above all 'Neue Liebe, neues Leben' and 'An Belinde' (with its superb rhythm). In 'Seelied', written in 1775 on his first journey to Switzerland, with its blend of love and nature, there is an urgency, a passion and an identification with the forces of fate that cannot be compared with anything the eighteenth century had yet produced.

There is no lyric poet among the *Stürmer und Dränger* to match Goethe. Herder's strength lay not in his original lyrics but in his understanding of the poetry of others; his poetic gifts are perhaps best displayed in his epigrams—'Amor und Psyche auf einem Grabmahl', for instance, is one of the most attractive poems of the time. Hölty occasionally strikes notes that anticipate Goethe; more striking, however, is Matthias Claudius (1740–1815), whose *Wandsbeker Bote* (1771–5) shares with *Von deutscher Art und Kunst* a conception of the *Volk* as the repository of the naïve and the spontaneous. The poems that Claudius published in *Der Wandsbeker Bote* are personal variants of the *Volkslied* manner; 'Der Mond ist aufgegangen' is the most beautiful evening-song since Paul Gerhardt, while 'Der Tod und das Mädchen'—the theme of death strikes the deepest chords in him—is a moving blend of the objective and the subjective. At the same time his reflections on life contain a genuine popular humour which, unlike the idyllic tone of Gleim or the sometimes childish efforts of the Hainbund poets, is both realistic and direct.

Another lyric poet of importance is the unhappy Lenz (1751–92), Goethe's shadow in Strasbourg and Weimar. Parts of his poems to Friederike Brion can hardly be distinguished from Goethe's, but in its total effect his poetry appears as a somewhat exaggerated copy of Goethe's. His life consisted of sharing the love-affairs of others, or even of falling in love with portraits, as in the case of Henriette von Waldner; and in the same way his poems, including those to Friederike, are interventions in Goethe's poetic world, however moving some of these interventions may be, such as 'Wo bist du jetzt, mein unvergeßlich Mädchen?' and 'Ach bist du fort? Aus welchen güldnen Träumen / Erwach ich jetzt zu meiner Qual?' In his 'Freundin aus der Wolke' he imitates Goethe's short lines, while 'Nachtschwärmerei' is an outright imitation of Goethe's hymns and their Rousseau/Spinoza-inspired language. The song 'Rösel aus Hennegau' from the play *Die Soldaten* serves the same function as 'Der König in Thule' in *Faust* and is similarly dominated by emotional values.

There was, however, another direction for *Sturm und Drang* lyric poetry to follow, with one root in the emotionalism of Klopstock but a more important one in a side of Goethe's poetry that emerges most clearly in 'An

Schwager Kronos' and 'Künstlers Morgenlied'—the tendency to naturalism. This is the realm of Bürger, of Schubart and of Schiller. In his *Anthologie* poems Schiller echoes this dissonance of the *Sturm und Drang* lyric, which is concerned, not with the eternal verities but with naturalistic directness and sensuous immediacy, while with Bürger and Schubart it is an expression of their own tortured lives.

The Titanism of Goethe's hymns and the fervour of Herder's odes are in the first instance the forceful expression of emotion, not the expression of an inner conflict or of an irrepressible urge which leads to naturalistic results, such as are found in Gottfried August Bürger. This is true not only of the unrestrained, macabre features of his ballads, above all 'Lenore', with its extremes of emotional outburst and gruesome description, and 'Der Raubgraf ', in which the count devours himself limb by limb—such motifs being, despite their unpleasantness, the perverted expression of the characteristic *Sturm und Drang* passion for the fully committed and the totally demanding—but also of his early love-poems, which sometimes show a naturalistic directness that would be unthinkable in Goethe's early lyrics. This directness that would be unthinkable in Goethe's early lyrics. This directness is a kind of pre-Expressionist scorn of all restriction or discipline in life—as, indeed, was Bürger's own existence.

Bürger's other side is that of the 'calculating reasoner', which is logically connected with a personal sense of genius which, unruly by nature, despises convention, demands its own freedom and will not be led. This attitude is seen in his 'Elegie' ('Als Molly sich losreißen wollte').

There is no better description of the conflict in Bürger than that given by Schiller in his review of Bürger's poems, which was to usher in his friendship with Goethe. The language of these poems reflects the almost paradoxical tensions of his personality—his love of life and his ardent emotions, yet his wish to escape 'into the empty void'; and on the one side anti-middle-class attitudes, with a publicly declared hatred of oppression, and on the other side a thinly disguised hankering after the idyllic—reminiscent of his association with the Hainbund poets. Indeed, alongside his rapturous passion, his motifs of killing and punishing, and the corresponding naturalistic style of his ballads, in which, for example, a duel could be described through the image of butchery, he is a master of that most cultured of traditional forms—the sonnet. This is endemic both to his psychology and to the nature of his imagination: for a poet of his type it was an almost more reckless task to attempt a strict formal exercise than to follow where his abandoned 'genius' led, and this situation reappears when we remember Bürger's disciple August Wilhelm Schlegel and the delight which certain Romantics found in the sonnet form.

A similar figure to Bürger is Christian Friedrich Daniel Schubart (1739–91), whose life and work show the same dichotomy and inner contradiction. His poetic career starts with his *Todesgesänge* (1769) in the Klopstockian style and then divides into, on the one hand, political poetry, which led to his imprisonment by Karl Eugen of Württemberg on the Hoher Asperg and, on the other hand, pietistic lyric verse in the contrafacture style.

His significance in his own age lies in the radical nature of his polemical response to authoritarianism. Poems such as 'Die Fürstengruft' and 'Deutsche Freiheit' reflect the same strained relationship to Karl Eugen as that of the young Schiller. Today one tends to draw attention to the Duke's humane wisdom under the mollifying influence of Franziska von Hohenheim, but at the same time his actions provided the starting-point for the *Stürmer und Dränger* of Swabia in their concern for political liberty. Schubart's 'Fürstengruft', with its realistic descriptions of physical decay and the dance of death, is an expression of this desire for liberty in what was probably the only form that could escape the censor, the theme that the aristocracy, like the common man, had to go the way of all flesh. The twenty-six strophes of this poem become increasingly bitter in their anti-aristocratic tone, and the macabre side of death is employed as a means of destroying the pride, the glory, the lust, the intrigue and the un-Christian attitudes of the nobility. With overtones of this kind, in a manner that resembles the naturalistic side of Bürger's poetry, it is not surprising that even one of the more tolerant rulers like Karl Eugen should have taken exception to Schubart's verse and seen it as a threat to his rule. And when one recalls that Schubart's well-known 'Kap-Lied', which was aimed at stirring up feeling against foreign alliances, was sung throughout the state like a folksong, one can understand that conflicts between men like Schiller and Schubart and the ruling powers were inevitable. Again the posture struck by the *Sturm und Drang* anticipates that of the Expressionists.

In contrast to Schubart Schiller did not write any political poetry in the strict sense until 1785, and it is only in a few social poems from the *Anthologie* (1781), like 'Rousseau' and 'Die Kindesmörderin', that we find any trace of what might be called a revolutionary mood. This is partly due to Schiller's greater powers of generalization, which found expression in poems such as 'Hymne an den Unendlichen', 'Größe der Welt' and 'Resignation', in which one can already sense the philosophical poet that was to come. They are not all in free rhythms like Goethe's odes but in free strophic forms in which the combination of short and long lines is intended to convey a turbulence of spirit. It is perhaps in vocabulary that they are closer to Goethe, with words like 'Zackenfels', 'Adlergedanke', 'Gewittersturm', 'Sonnenwanderer', 'Riesenschatten', 'Götterschwur' conveying concentrated emotion; the verbs too have a dynamic quality, possibly with a stronger tendency towards the naturalistic, but it is above all in the nouns that the linguistic power lies.

In Schiller's love-poetry and poems on death, however, or in occasional poems like 'Die Schlacht' and 'Gruppe aus dem Tartarus', where the emphasis is not on concepts, it is the colourful verb, and to a lesser degree the adjective, that predominates, again, as in Bürger and Schubart, with a boldness that presages the lyric of Expressionism. Poems of death, such as 'Brutus und Cäsar', 'Eine Leichenphantasie' and 'Elegie auf den Tod eines Jünglings' have the same power of language. A key climactic word in

Schiller's vocabulary at this time is 'dumpf' or 'dumpfig'; the elemental and the passionate is everywhere in control, even in his love-poems, e.g. 'Amalia', the 'Phantasie an Laura' and 'Der Kampf' (addressed to Charlotte von Kalb). Schiller's early love-poetry burns, glows, rages, rises and falls—in short, attempts to convey, directly and without regard to convention, the dynamic intensity of the elemental force of love. This intensity characterizes the whole of Schiller's *Anthologie* period, its Elysian as well as its Tartarean aspects, its Dionysian as well as its macabre moments. There is everywhere an urge towards the depiction of opposites, extremes and exaggerations—in a word, the mannerist aspect of *Sturm und Drang.* Yet all this does add up to a style, even if an extravagant one, and whatever similarities of detail there may be, it is a style that cannot be confused with that of any other *Sturm und Drang* poet.

It is no accident that Herder should have illustrated his views on literary genius by reference to Shakespeare as well as old folksongs, for in addition to lyric poetry it was logically drama that was the form which best expressed the impulses of *Sturm und Drang.* Here too certain key motifs were in the air: the Faust theme was treated not only by Goethe but also by Maler Müller and Klinger, while the motif of the child-murderess underlies not only the *Urfaust* but also Wagner's drama and Schiller's ballad. Italy, the land of passion, provided the setting for Gerstenberg's *Ugolino* (1768), Leisewitz's *Julius von Tarent* (1776), Klinger's *Zwillinge* (1776) and *Simsone Grisaldo* (1776) and Schiller's *Fiesko* (1783).

Farce, literary satire and political satire become vehicles for views on contemporary events: attacks on tyranny are contained in Schiller's *Räuber* (1781), *Fiesko* (1783) and *Kabale und Liebe* (1784) as well as in Leisewitz's short drama *Der Besuch um Mitternacht* (1775) and, with a bigger element of social criticism, Lenz's so-called comedies *Der Hofmeister* (1774) and *Die Soldaten* (1776). Outspoken literary satire is found in Lenz's farce *Pandaemonium Germanicum* (not printed until 1819) and in Goethe's *Götter, Helden und Wieland* (1774) and *Satyros* (1773). Voltaire also comes in for criticism, e.g. Wagner's *Voltaire am Abend seiner Apotheose* (1778). Goethe's *Götz,* on the other hand, takes the great conflicts of the moment—justice *versus* injustice, loyalty *versus* intrigue, the courtier *versus* the common man, freedom *versus* oppression—and treats them not satirically but with a Herder-like passion and sense of history. Finally there is that subjective dramatic outburst which gave its name to the whole movement, Klinger's unperformable *Wirrwarr* (1776), which the Swiss *Stürmer und Dränger* Kaufmann rechristened *Sturm und Drang.*

The *Urfaust,* only discovered in 1885, and that by chance, combines virtually all the important elements in *Sturm und Drang* drama: scenes loosely assembled without regard to the unities; *Knittelvers* metre derived from old German sources via Herder; and interpolated scenes in prose, imitative of Shakespeare and also naturalistic in the manner of Bürger.

The motivation derives from two sources. The theme of infanticide is used to criticize social convention and justify the killing; the Faust theme, as yet without its universal application, is pregnant with potential power. Faust is the product of Goethe's alchemical studies after his return from Leipzig. He is not yet the restless, questing traveller through life but he already shows a dissatisfaction with the dead world of book-learning and a determination to penetrate the secret of the world of which his imagination has already given him an inkling. The only way to do this is by magic. Behind these parts of the opening monologue—from the spirits in Old Norse ballads to the celebration of the infinite and the universal—stands the figure of Herder. The confident, self-assertive Faust is mockingly called a 'superman' by the Erdgeist, but the superman is not created in the image of God, for in the next moment he discusses professional scholarly matters with Wagner like a man of earth and is ironically parodied by Mephisto when he makes his unmotivated appearance in the scene with the student.

The link between these elements and the motif of infanticide in the Gretchen scenes is forced, for whereas in the study scenes Faust is the powerful, unique personality in the *Sturm und Drang* sense, in the Gretchen scenes he appears only as the conventional seducer, his originality, stimulated by Mephisto, declining into an exaggerated sophistication. The two aspects are not really compatible. Thus he is finally defeated by Gretchen's innocence. This too makes the *Urfaust* a mere torso—but as such it is the epitome of *Sturm und Drang.* Nature; mystery; the world of spirits and fantasy; the vitality of youth (Auerbachs Keller); the quality of childlike innocence in its union with the world and in the moment of its betrayal (Gretchen), expressed in folksong ('Der König in Thule'); middle-class degeneration (Frau Marthe); the motif of the dead letter (Wagner, scene with the student); the undogmatic, mystical, emotion-dominated interpretation of religious faith: all this is the purest *Sturm und Drang* in its conscious originality—so too is the philosophy of love, which is that also found in Goethe's lyrics of the period.

As mentioned above, the defence of moral protest against conventional ideas of right and wrong is one of the main concerns of *Sturm und Drang.* This is what links Schiller's *Räuber,* for instance, with the motif of infanticide in Goethe and Leopold Wagner. At the same time this is only one of the forms taken by social criticism at the time. There would have been no need for the *Stürmer und Dränger* to be followers of Rousseau or to have their own cult of genius and nature if they had not questioned the whole social structure. Everything in this field—the power of the aristocracy, whether despotic or 'enlightened' (in the latter case they saw it as a mechanistic, intellectual curbing of the ego); the prescribed rigidity of the class structure; religious and bourgeois prejudices—appeared to them as an attack on liberty.

Thus to the ethical critique in the motif of infanticide Lenz, in *Der Hofmeister* and *Die Soldaten,* adds a specific critique of social conditions. These are comedies with a strong satirical flavour, attacking contemporary conventions and making seduction the point of crisis. In *Die Soldaten* it is the usual seduction of an innocent middle-class girl by an immoral officer—the situation in *Emilia Galotti* but with the seducer one degree lower on the social scale, and also resembling Lessing's play in its dramatic exposure of the utter defencelessness of the middle class and the infamy of the officers' cadres. In *Der Hofmeister* it is the hero, with the sinister name of Läuffer ('fleer'), who seduces his employer's daughter; thus the guilt of the classes is virtually the reverse of that in *Die Soldaten,* or at least is more fairly apportioned. This appears illogical, but one must remember that the uprightness and geniality that characterize the aristocracy in *Der Hofmeister* are not intended to be conservative but rather that an unsatisfactory kind of middle condition should be uncovered through the motif of fashionable education at the hands of *Hofmeister* (private tutors). The guilt of the upper class lies in its frivolity and in matters of education. The comedy has become the medium for an attack on conventionality in the spirit of Rousseau's ideal of education.

The element of social criticism is also integrated, though in a very different way, into Schiller's first three plays, written during the unsettled period between leaving Swabia for Mannheim and then for Jena. It is most prominent in *Fiesko,* whose historical theme is least connected with it; in *Die Räuber* and *Kabale und Liebe* it is subsidiary to the problems of the main characters. The basic concept in *Die Räuber* (like that of infanticide in the *Urfaust*) is that of the Prodigal Son in the context of a family intrigue: this intrigue destroys Karl Moor's relationship with his father and his fiancée and also, as a consequence of his passionate self-assertiveness, with society as such. Robbery becomes the extreme expression of freedom, a symbol of the refusal to compromise in matters of honesty. The agonizing price he has to pay for this consists not only of his own banishment but also of a break with those dearest to him, and he becomes both a victim and a seeker after vengeance, a tragic figure in both aspects.

His is the tragedy of the 'man of genius' who, driven by the demonic power within him, opposes the limitations and the treacheries of the world by fighting convention from an emotional rather than an intellectual standpoint. Schiller invests him with greatness not only in his final moment of renunciation and self-sacrifice but at an earlier stage, even when he acts unlawfully; yet the deepest suffering and the most agonizing decisions spring from the nobility of his character and his self-dependence—this is what remains of the theme of the Prodigal Son. The end is never happiness—but it is destiny and thus greatness, and it is here, far more than in the somewhat obtrusive moralizing of the end of the play, that the remarkable effect of the work lies.

Kabale und Liebe, in contrast to Lenz's comedies, is a 'domestic tragedy' like *Emilia Galotti,* and as such its social criticism is sharper than that of *Die Räuber*—which, incidentally, received its motto 'In Tyrannos' from the publisher, not from Schiller. Yet the conflict of depraved court and noble citizen is not political like that of oligarchy and republic in *Fiesko.* Lady Milford, for instance, outwardly the most dubious representative of court society, has human sympathy, humanity and social conscience, while Ferdinand, Luise's real lover, who kills both her and himself in his delusion that she does not love him, is the son of the President, who is the great rogue at court: class distinctions are not the simple reflection of ethical distinctions, as critics used to think. Wurm, too, the President's intriguer, is portrayed as a middle-class citizen. The tragic irony lies in that, from the social point of view, Wurm is Luise's legitimate suitor, whereas Ferdinand, the nobleman, is excluded from her company both by her father and by his own. The object of attack here is class barriers themselves: nobility of character brings the nobleman and the middle-class girl together, while Wurm, the degenerate middle-class citizen, is as unworthy a partner for Luise as Franz Moor is for Amalie.

Even more important than such facts is the argument behind them: the aristocracy is largely degenerate, but so too is the middle-class world, witness Wurm and Miller's eagerness for Ferdinand's money. This is not a question of black *versus* white, and Schiller is not taking up a class-position; rather he is portraying the tragedy of human qualities which are made to bow before the callousness of inhumanity, and this is independent of matters of class.

In contrast to *Die Räuber* and *Kabale und Liebe,* human tragedies with only peripheral political elements, Schiller's one historical play of his *Sturm und Drang* period, *Fiesko,* is basically political. The venerable Doge Andrea Doria rules the Genoese oligarchy, but his regime is threatened by the Pretender Gianettino, his nephew, a violent autocrat, who is described in the *dramatis personae* as 'of stunted education'. It is against him that the conspiracy is directed, led by Fiesko, a nobleman whose conscience is represented by Verrina, who seeks to lead the opposition to the establishment of a real republic. After seemingly overcoming the Dorias, however, Verrina comes into conflict with Fiesko's selfish ambition to acquire the fruits of the rebellion for himself; Verrina kills Fiesko, and the old Doge regains his former position which, in the final scene, the Republican Verrina also pledges himself to support. This is not a contradiction, for the drama is concerned with the temptations of power: Fiesko fails as a conspirator and as a man because he covets the title of Duke, and the most dramatic scenes are his conflicts with Verrina on this issue. Verrina sees that a change of roles will achieve nothing and that therefore Doria is the more rightful ruler, though he detests his regime; and Fiesko's trial at Verrina's hands is the expression of a deep disillusionment with the man who had betrayed the republic.

The fundamental human motif in the drama is the conflict between egoism and service in Fiesko's soul, and the notion of power as something inherently evil besets his inconsistencies and inconstancies, taunting him and ultimately destroying his far from despicable personality. If one is to set the interests of the community above one's own—as does Verrina alone—one needs an unconditional moral altruism, and until such an altruism conquers the world, the world will naturally remain an object which the forces of tradition will seek to dominate. *Sturm und Drang* thus represents here not only the republican view in politics but the absoluteness of the moral imperative.

Perhaps the summit of *Sturm und Drang* drama is the language of these early plays of Schiller. It has not the forced casualness or affected *naïveté* of Klinger and Lenz, and its richness of imagery and vocabulary is the expression of a youthful dynamic passion not found in the *Anthologie* poems of the same period. It is the language both of primitive emotion and of spirituality, accessible to all ranks of society, sensuous, the vehicle of men of passion who yet reflect upon life; the passionate outbursts of Schiller's heroes have thus far more conviction than those of the other *Stürmer und Dränger:* examples are Franz Moor's cynical confession at the end of the first scene of *Die Räuber;* Lady Milford and Miller in *Kabale und Liebe;* Verrina the Republican and Gianettino the villain in *Fiesko.* Karl Moor's self-characterization in Act I, Scene 2 is like a list of all the *Sturm und Drang* motifs, while at the same time glowing with all manner of imagery and rhetorical devices.

A comparison with the historical dramas of the earlier *Stürmer und Dränger* reveals the same. Gerstenberg's *Ugolino,* for instance, has the macabre motif, taken from Dante, of the father together with his three sons thrown into the tower by his mortal enemy, the father being forced to watch his sons starve to death one by one, his agony made all the more poignant by the arousing of false hopes of their survival and by hopeless attempts to console himself over their fate. No depiction of suffering in Schiller's works is so cruel as this. It is the tragedy of greatness which is rendered powerless and made to witness its own defeat and the suffering of others—a hyperbolic presentation typical of *Sturm und Drang.* There are linguistic anticipations of Schiller, but a sense of effective, gripping theatre, with a growing climax and a final catastrophe, is missing.

From this latter angle J. A. Leisewitz's *Julius von Tarent* and F. M. Klinger's (1752–1831) *Die Zwillinge,* both treatments of the same subject—the jealousy of two brothers and its tragic outcome—are closer to Schiller than is Gerstenberg. In both plays it is the selfish, hot-blooded, yet more interesting brother who loses his self-control and kills his gentler, more congenial, yet duller twin, and in both plays the father takes the law of retribution into his own hands. This is clearly the same attitude towards fate as is found in classical drama, where a whole family can be cursed, and as a type it recurs in Schiller's *Braut von Messina.* Yet at the same time the *Sturm und Drang* concept of genius contradicts this. In both these plays the murderers are portrayed in a naturalistic and quite unclassical manner and their self-centredness is utterly modern, while the climax of the works takes the form of fury at the world and against the laws that restrict the expression of the individual ego. The gentleness and goodness of the other brothers, on the other hand, achieves no dramatic effect.

In the last analysis, and quite logically, this kind of *Sturm und Drang* drama is a monodrama, for even though the five-act form, the climax and the final catastrophe are preserved, they have lost their traditional power to convince, and give way to the concept of genius as the unifying force. The hero cannot tolerate a rival but at the most a partner of his own breed who can add to the singleminded power of the action. Klinger's *Der Wirrwarr,* virtually the last product of the South German 'genius'-worshippers before they broke up after Goethe's departure for Weimar, also shows this. Such colourful language as that used by Guelfo in *Die Zwillinge* shows the typical tendency to excess and exaggeration, and these features appear all the more prominent because there is no Schillerian thought to sustain them. Such language, found also in *Der Wirrwarr,* abounds in words of violence and extremes, in hyperbole and in onomatopoeia; it is consciously ungrammatical and elliptic in syntax, and goes to lengths never attempted by Schiller or Goethe, or even Lenz. In fact this is *Sturm und Drang* at its superficial level, not in its profoundest meaning, such as one finds in the young Goethe and the young Schiller, and even occasionally in Bürger.

The action of the play too, which is set in America, is a veritable 'Wirrwarr' (confusion), based on the vagaries of chance, the glorification of instinct and primitive urge, and a delight in the repellent, with the merest coincidence as *deus ex machina.* Three typical abandoned *Sturm und Drang* rapscallions give vent to their confused emotions; a tribal feud, in whose name the most horrible deeds of hatred are committed and in which lords talk and behave like privateers, ends improbably with a partly sincere, partly reluctant reconciliation brought about through the stilted device of a marriage between the youngest children of the warring families. There is no psychological motivation, and there could have been other endings equally logical. It is not surprising that even in Weimar under Karl August, Klinger could not get himself accepted with such a play. It is eloquent in destruction but leaves nothing in its place, and even its crude naturalism is a form of arbitrary realism barely more authentic than the middle-class world it was attacking. This is *Sturm und Drang* existing merely for itself, without a goal.

More substantial was the literary farce, which the *Stürmer und Dränger* developed into an original genre. In this they portrayed the contrast between their own conception of literature and that of the Enlightenment, attacking above all Wieland, also Nicolai, Voltaire and even Herder (in Goethe's *Satyros*). The form used is either *Knittelvers* (doggerel) or prose satire. Goethe later added, in Weimar, a stylistically authentic parody of a baroque drama in alexandrines to his *Jahrmarktsfest zu Plundersweilern,* mocking the emotionalism of the courts and the orderly baroque world. There is also much parody of contemporary conditions in this work, but today it is only possible to identify a small part of it—most obviously, perhaps, in the mockery of the prim and proper middle-class onlookers.

The position is different with the 'perverted' antiquity of *Götter, Helden und Wieland,* in which Wieland, in a nightcap, cuts the worst possible figure in his satirical confrontation with true antiquity, like a little man confronted by giants. The narrow-minded, tiny man of the Enlightenment, respectable and conceited, a petty moralizer who does not even worry himself about the dream in which he is destroyed, cannot grasp the standards of an Alcestis or a Hercules. It is interesting to note that when Wieland visited Weimar shortly afterwards, he made no effort to take his revenge on the author of this piece.

Related to this exuberant and direct satire of the young Goethe are works such as Wagner's farce directed against Voltaire and Klinger's *Prometheus, Deukalion und seine*

Recensenten, aimed at Nicolai. In his *Pater Brey,* an attack on Leuchsenring, and his *Prolog zu den neusten Offenbarungen Gottes,* directed against Bahrdt, Goethe himself satirized pietists and religious hypocrites in his *Knittelvers* style. All these works reflect the *Sturm und Drang* demand for openness and honesty, qualities which lead to the choice of *Knittelvers* as a form and of the market place as the scene of the *Jahrmarktsfest zu Plundersweilern,* both of which are true reflections of the *Volk.* There is also a clear connection with *Götz.* In his *Satyros oder der vergötterte Waldteufel* Goethe even satirizes Herder, the idol of *Sturm und Drang,* but in a more refined, more subtle, allusive style than his attacks against Wieland and Bahrdt. Satyros's proclamation is a perfect parody of *Sturm und Drang* effusiveness and the fascination that is exerted. All these works, written between 1773 and 1775, have the bold, irreverent spirit of *Sturm und Drang,* with a playful quality about them. The last works in this style, however, starting with *Der Triumph der Empfindsamkeit* (1777), belong to Goethe's early classical period.

Lenz's literary farces remained unpublished: one of them, now lost (*Wolken*), followed the line of Goethe's Wieland polemic, while the other, *Pandaemonium Germanicum,* is an outspoken literary review in which Lenz attempts to parody whole classes, such as 'the Imitators', 'the Philistines', 'the Journalists'. They all tumble around at the foot of a mountain—the symbol of genius—at whose summit sit Goethe and Lenz himself. (This is the image at the opening of Herder's essay on Shakespeare and also influences Goethe's Aristophanic *Die Vögel.*) The symbol of the mountain is characteristic of *Sturm und Drang,* though in the second act of *Pandaemonium Germanicum* it gives way to the allegorical Temple of Fame, where French and German men of letters (among them Wieland again) converse—whereby the Germans emerge in an unfavourable light; otherwise the work is concerned with the passing of literary judgements. The image of the mountain is also very Goethean and serves to symbolize the *Sturm und Drang* conception of genius, pre-eminent among whose representatives were Lessing, Herder, Shakespeare, Klopstock, Goethe and (in Lenz's eyes) Lenz himself. Certainly much of the work preaches to the converted, and it is quite unperformable and often ridiculous, but it does state a firm position, and as such is a highly revealing utterance of the movement.

In Goethe's *Götz*—both the first version, *Die Geschichte Gottfriedens von Berlichingen mit der eisernen Hand dramatisiert* (1771), and the final play, *Götz von Berlichingen mit der eisernen Hand* (1773)—the individual, human, historical, revolutionary, Herderian-Rousseauesque elements of *Sturm und Drang* all come together. Both versions are Shakespearian in their freedom from the unities, and their prose has the same spontaneity as the prose scenes in the *Urfaust*—a greater freedom from stylization, moreover, than the prose version of *Iphigenie* or *Egmont,* both of which have concealed four- and five-stress iambic lines in them. *Götz* is the pure expression of *Sturm und Drang* naturalism, without, however, the unbridled exaggerations found in the language of Klinger and, to some extent, Lenz. Underlying this naturalism is Herder's concept of the unity of the *Volk* within itself and with the world, and the unity of the hero or man of genius within himself. This concept shows itself in the language of knights and peasants alike, as in that of the hero, his wife, his sister and his son, in contrast to the affected court speech of the opposing party—Weislingen, Adelheid and the Bishop. Linking this contrast is Goethe's striving after a Lutheran style of simplicity and directness, with elision, apocope, inversions and archaisms, giving a primitive richness of vocabulary which is nevertheless far from being an exercise in historical imitation. Unlike the *naïveté* deliberately affected by Klinger and Lenz, Goethe's language serves a basic unity of time and character.

The same is true of the subject-matter. Götz and Elisabeth, together with their followers, represent an ideal picture of *Sturm und Drang* man, as their treacherous opponents represent the side of Wieland and Voltaire in the literary farces. Part of Götz's tragedy is that he, the man of action, sees in his hesitant, simple-minded son a kind of punishment, an embodiment of feelingless degeneration, and in true *Sturm und Drang* style he is allowed to perish as a heroic, ideal figure. Particularly significant in this respect is the scene from Act II of the original version (later omitted) in which the boy's parents decide, because of his weakness and effeminacy, to send him to a monastery: his mother sees him as a knight of doubtful quality, and when her sentimental sister suggests that he might have a noble role to play in life, she claims that that could not happen in an age of 'real men' but only in a hundred years' time, when human beings will have sunk to some inconceivable low level—a thought that obviously springs from Herder's view of the decadence of men and cultures as expressed in *Auch eine Philosophie.* Götz knows that he marks the end of an epoch in which simplicity of mind, sensuous awareness and the morality of chivalric loyalty could still be combined, and all the subsidiary plots—Georg, Bruder Martin, Weislingen and Adelheid—serve only to underline this. No other drama of the *Sturm und Drang* era is so thoroughly and richly typical of the driving forces of that era, or so original and satisfying in its Shakespeare-inspired form.

The formal influence of pietism is seen at its most fruitful in the realm of the novel. Apart from Church hymns, such as those of Susanne von Klettenberg, the elderly friend of Goethe's youth, and her spiritual consort Lavater, together with some of those of Klopstock, it is above all in lyric poetry that the feeling of confidence in one's aesthetic message, or in the passion of one's love, or in the sincerity of one's self-absorption into nature is at its most powerful. The drama tends to reveal rather than to conceal, even in the religious sphere, and is furthest removed from didactic tendencies, above all where the career of the active 'hero' is concerned.

The novel, on the other hand, had already become in the whole of Europe a repository both of sentimentality and self-analysis by about 1770. From Gellert's *Schwedische Gräfin* to Sophie von la Roche's *Fräulein von Sternheim* (1771)—praised in Lenz's *Pandaemonium Germanicum*—the moral sentimentality of the Enlightenment and the moral self-investigation stimulated by pietism united in order to uncover, to confuse and then to reconcile the

Portrait of Goethe at the age of thirty by G. Oswald May

destinies of human beings. Alongside the traditional narrative form pietism contributed the letter and the diary as familiar media for the expression of guilt, ecstasy and violent emotion.

All this is present in Goethe's *Werther* (1774), as it is, in a different form, in *Götz.* At the same time the ego reveals itself here, not in a less direct manner than in the lyric, but in a less typical form than in the drama. For all his individuality, Götz is the representative of true manhood, and is supported as such by Sickingen, Georg and Lerse; Werther, on the other hand, is a unique, untypical man of passion, notwithstanding the fact that his famous attire became fashionable among young people. For he was not a product of this fashion but created it himself. And when Goethe warned his readers against following Werther, it was not only an expression of shock at the effects of his autobiographical novel but a legitimate interpretation of it.

Who, then, is this individual called Werther? Certainly not the pitiful young Jerusalem, whose suicide gave Goethe the outer framework; certainly not the Goethe of Wetzlar days, who vied with Kestner for the favour of Charlotte Buff. This is clear, and was so long before Thomas Mann's *Lotte in Weimar.* But Goethe has breathed into these two historical characters a highly personal *Sturm und Drang* yearning and produced a character who has to perish through his emotional imbalance and his excess of passion. The second sentence of the first letter could stand as a motto for the whole work: 'Bester Freund, was ist das Herz des Menschen!'

It is significant that Werther does not just live out his life but consciously and consistently poses this question. The epistolary form is in itself reflective rather than active, and the inner form of the book rests on the tension between what Werther knows himself to be and what he would wish to become, i.e. a man who lived by his emotions and lived life to the full. Again the epistolary form encourages this intimacy of expression, as a comparison with the epic narrative style of *Wilhelm Meister* reveals.

This symbolizing of Werther's conflict both in the inner and the outer form underlies the well-known letter of 10 May and similar passages. It is the letter which recalls *Ganymed,* with its self-immersion in the universality of nature—though while *Ganymed* is pure lyricism, *Werther* is the confession of a man who knows, and is reflecting on, his own nature, so that his descriptions of his violent emotional experiences are fundamentally epic, however lyrical the means he employs. From the psychological standpoint the latter form meant to the *Stürmer und Dränger* complete frankness and, at the same time, self-exposure to the limits of human endurance, even to the possibility of self-annihilation. Thus the epistolary form of the novel itself foreshadows Werther's ultimate tragedy; or, put the other way round, the force of Goethe's emotions compelled him to use this particular form. From all angles, therefore, and not only that which makes his suicide the natural outcome of his passion, Werther is a logical character.

Of *Sturm und Drang* inspiration is Werther's Herder-like longing for the peace of childhood, such as in the scene after the introduction of Wahlheim and the scene through which he finds his way to Lotte. This is the happy presence of nature in man, the nature that symbolizes man's yearning. Werther's views on art, too, stimulated by his own drawings, are *Sturm und Drang* realism, for his first sketch of children was made, as he said, without adding anything of his own, which strengthened him in his determination to allow nature to dictate to him as she had to all great artists. The meditation that follows, on the 'rules' which can produce Philistines and mediocrities but not even remarkable villains, let alone geniuses, recalls Goethe's *Von deutscher Baukunst* and *Rede zum Shakespearestag*—indeed, the whole of Herder's influence. Genius must burn itself out, independent of common canons of judgement: this is Werther's concept of his own life, and it is the concept by which he perishes.

As in other genres, Lenz copied Goethe in the novel also. His fragmentary *Der Waldbruder,* largely written during his unhappy visit to Weimar in 1776, is a personal *roman à clef* and also an epistolary novel in the wake of *Werther.* Where Goethe is to the point, Lenz is exaggerated. The hero is a thinly disguised self-portrait depicting his passion for Henriette von Waldner, whom he knew only from a picture and who was already betrothed to another man (cf. *Werther*); the picture is stolen from the hero, which causes his utter collapse—again, a typical *Sturm und Drang* exaggeration, turning an almost ridiculous illusion into an all-consuming passion. The hero bears the symbolic name Herz ('Heart'), modelled on the symbolism of Wild ('Savage') and Feu ('Fire') in Klinger's *Wirrwarr.* The hero's renunciation of the world to become a hermit—significantly called a 'romantic' decision in the book—is a crude derivative of *Werther,* though Werther's loneliness remains spiritual. In form too it shows its obvious descent from *Werther,* except that it has no epic, descriptive sections but relies entirely upon letters, and there are no fewer than eight different writers from whose correspondence the inner and outer biography of the hero's unhappy love emerges.

1776 also saw the publication of the sentimental novel *Siegwart,* set in a monastery and not unrelated in theme to *Der Waldbruder,* by Martin Miller (1750–1814), a pietist pastor from Ulm. Here the hero already dreams in his youth of renouncing the world. His love-story, like the pietistic religious content, is sentimental, not in the passionate style of *Sturm und Drang* but rather in the general mode of sensibility, with many motifs of little more than contemporary sociological interest. Nevertheless it shows far more direcctly than *Werther* the employment of pietistic emotions and values in a prose narrative genre.

This process can, however, be traced in terms of more significant works, genuine autobiographical novels of pietistic inspiration which, unlike *Werther,* whose centre of gravity lies in the aesthetic sphere, are the true representative works of *Sturm und Drang* in the realm of prose narrative. They are both autobiographies and confessions, for religious principles require strict honesty; they are also both descriptions of spiritual development and accounts of the divine educative forces which press upon the personality. There is also a link with Herder at this point.

This range of aspects is particularly apparent in J. H. Jung-Stilling (1740–1817), whose *Heinrich Stillings Jugend,* published by Goethe in 1777 and later expanded into a full-length autobiography, combines the educative, the philosophical and the physical. From the dawning of consciousness in the child, his conflicts with the world of parents and grandparents, of the village and all its practical concerns, we pass to the question of his education, of nature and of God, whom the author is concerned to present as a living force. There is a certain inner similarity to the affectionate realism of the world of Matthias Claudius, who did not, however, employ the novel as a form.

Theodor Hippel's *Lebensläufe nach aufsteigender Linie* (1776 onwards) started as a family chronicle but turned into a four-volume autobiography. In a realistic manner, like Jung-Stilling, Hippel (1741–96) treats his own youth as a series of events of virtually equal importance.

The psychology of human development, however, is far more deeply treated, also in terms of a sensitive childhood, in *Anton Reiser* by Karl Philipp Moritz (1757–93), a friend of Goethe's with whom he discussed aesthetic questions in Rome in 1786. Hippel and Jung-Stilling saw experience, meditation, instruction and sermon as means of education, as did Moritz, but there is in Moritz's work a psychological depth, shown, for example, in Reiser's meeting with the quietist sect of Madame de Guyon, which even anticipates Dostoevsky and the French, German and Scandinavian naturalists, while the amphibolic effect of this confessional Christianity, free, as it is, of all trace of religious dogma, on a young, impressionable mind gives Moritz's work a greater realism than that of either Stilling or Hippel.

Thus the *Sturm und Drang* novel not only shows the sublimation of passion, the conquest of aesthetic isolationism, worldliness and the realities of a childlike world, as in Werther and its successors, but demonstrates how, as in drama, self-observation develops from a starting-point in pietism, an objective self-analysis beyond the reach of Gellert's or Nicolai's sentimentality or even the emotional-cum-rationalistic moralizing of Sophie von la Roche's *Fräulein von Sternheim.* (pp. 166-92)

Werner Kohlschmidt, "*'Sturm und Drang',*" *in* German Literature: A Critical Survey, *edited by Bruno Boesch, translated by Ronald Taylor, Methuen & Co Ltd, 1971, pp. 166-92.*

An excerpt from Herder's essay on Ossian (1773):

The wilder, i.e. the more living, more freely active a people is, the wilder, i.e. the more living, more sensuous, freer, fuller of lyrical action must be its poetry. The further away from artificial, scholastic modes of thought, speech, and writing a people is, the less its songs will be made for paper and be dead literature. The essence and purpose of these songs depends alone on the lyrical, living, as it were dance-like character of song, on the living presence of the images, on the connection and as it were dire urgency ['Nothdrang'] of the content and feelings, on the symmetry of word, syllables, yes often even of letters, on the movement of the melody, and on a hundred other things which belong to the living world and these national songs. . . . Hence the whole magic power that makes of these songs the entrancement, the spur, the everlasting inheritance of joy of a people.

Johann Gottfried von Herder, On Ossian and the Songs of Ancient Peoples, *quoted in* The German Sturm und Drang, *by Roy Pascal, 1953.*

Roy Pascal

[Pascal was an English educator specializing in German literature. In the following excerpt, he demonstrates that the guiding principle uniting the Sturmer und Dranger was a desire to forge a new conception of society, history, consciousness, nature, and art.]

The term *Sturm und Drang* has less ambiguity than most categories of literary history; it raises few of the questions which are necessarily provoked by such terms as 'Baroque' or 'Romanticism'. It is applied to a group of writers who were allied in a very personal and real way, and whose cohesion scarcely needs proving. It is however advisable to define the composition of the group, since lack of precision in this respect has caused confusion in the interpretation of its work. It was publicly identified for the first time, I believe, by Wieland [in *Teutscher Merkur,* 1774], who spoke disparagingly, in 1774, of the 'Hamann sect', including Herder, Goethe, and Lenz. Merck, Klinger, H. L. Wagner, and Maler Müller may be added as personal associates and literary allies. Hamann was an older man who in many ways remained apart from the others and who is best considered as a precursor; Klopstock and Justus Möser may be given a similar title. Leisewitz is usually accounted one of their number, but he did not know the others, and touches the *Sturm und Drang* only in his one play, *Julius von Tarent.* There were a number of men who went along with them for a short time—Lavater, Jung-Stilling, F. L. Stolberg, Bürger, F. H. Jacobi and Heinse in particular—but careful study reveals important differences between their views and those of the *Stürmer und Dränger,* even when they seem most akin. The movement might be said to start in 1770, when Herder and Goethe met; it remained a movement of young men, and in all the important members a marked change or development is to be observed by about 1777 or 1778. Herder and Goethe, the most profound and comprehensive of them, form the heart of the movement, though Lenz's contribution is by no means negligible.

One of the most troublesome problems is the position of Schiller. Ten years younger than Goethe, he had no personal contact with any other *Stürmer und Dränger,* and began to write only after the others had emerged from their *Sturm und Drang.* In spite of an obvious resemblance with their views and outlook, one finds in fact many important points of difference, in his general temperamental make-up, his mode of life, and his literary style and themes. It is always necessary to bear these differences in mind, if the *Sturm und Drang* is to be accurately and fully understood.

The importance of the *Sturm und Drang* as the first flowering of the greatest period of German literature cannot be contested. Yet there have been remarkably few comprehensive studies devoted to it, since the first beginnings by Erich Schmidt and Jakob Minor in the nineteenth century. With some justification, but much over-emphasis, it is usually treated as a stage in a development, but is then subsumed under some such heading as 'irrationalism', 'the German spirit', and is frequently treated as a mere preparation for German romanticism (e.g. by Kindermann, Benz and Ruprecht). It was a movement of young men; but, unjustly, juvenile rebelliousness has been taken to be a predominant characteristic. Specialized studies fail to relate its various aspects, so that both the range and the unity of its achievement are underestimated; in particular the new conception of poetry, and the new poetry itself, are often treated as something apart from the new interpretations of society, history, consciousness, and nature. There is a lack of precision as to the composition of the *Sturm und Drang* group and, for instance, its distinctiveness from the Klopstockians; the peculiarity of Schiller's position is overlooked. The best and most comprehensive study is the first volume of Korff's *Geist der Goethe-Zeit,* though this work suffers from some of the failings mentioned above, and especially from Korff's abstract conception of his work as 'die Geschichte des ideellen Wachstums einer über die Individuen und individuellen Leistungen hin verteilten Idee'. One still returns with profit to the great biographies like Haym's *Herder* (1880-5) and Unger's *Hamann und die Aufklärung* (1911) where the richness of the principal figure, at least, is expounded in its fullness.

We know enough of great poetic achievement to recognize that it is not the outcome solely of a felicitous gift, and that the gift of poetic utterance is not something apart from life, thought and feeling. The poet is the whole man, and issues out of innumerable factors that his times present to him: thus history is a necessary pre-condition to literary criticism in the fullest sense. While doing justice to individual character and variation, an adequate study of the *Sturm und Drang* must start from that common stock of experience, practical and spiritual, out of which its unity of response grew—and indeed we have a model in the two great autobiographical statements of the group, Goethe's *Dichtung und Wahrheit* and Herder's *Journal meiner Reise.* It was of course a sharply discriminating response and in view of the pugnacity of the movement's expressions one hardly runs the danger of breaking up the uniqueness and unity of their achievement into a number of 'influences'.

Here there is no space to discuss the *Stürmer und Dränger* in all their variety, but it is necessary to reach some guiding principle which will account, in the fullest possible sense, for their indebtedness and their hostility to predecessors and contemporaries, for what links them to the past and what constitutes their specific achievement. All definitions which are couched in purely ideal terms, especially those which would claim a clear repudiation of humanism or rationalism, break down on closer examination—'subjectivism', 'irrationalism', 'a new religion', 'Germanism', 'individualism', 'freedom' are either false or only partially true; or like 'humanism' are not sufficiently precise. We find an immense debt to British and French humanists, rationalists, and empiricists, as well as conflict with them. If the German *Aufklärung,* so feeble a reflexion of European humanism, provoked their contemptuous hostility, we must remember what they owed to Lessing—when he died Herder wrote: 'Ich kann nicht sagen, wie mich sein Tod verödet hat; es ist, als ob dem Wanderer alle Sterne untergehen, und der dunkele wolkigte Himmel bliebe.' Herder wrote this in full consciousness of his differences with Lessing, but he recognized what he owed the older man for his personal independence, his courage in face of secular and ecclesiastical authorities, his vigorous realism in thought and art, his bold struggle for tolerance, even his pantheism.

The relationship of the *Sturm und Drang* to the 'eighteenth century' can perhaps most conveniently be summed up in terms of their relationship with Lessing. He, in close sympathy with writers like Richardson and Diderot, sought to break through dogmas of every sort and to reshape thought and art on the basis of experience and reason. Neither of these two terms interprets an absolute; they mean the experience and reason or knowledge available, and they define essentially the experience of the contemporary middle class, often in polemical distinction from that of other classes, particularly of courts and nobility. In this respect the *Stürmer und Dränger* continue their work. But they take it much further, for they delve much deeper into the inner life of the burgher world and assert its values with a far greater confidence and passion, even recklessness. They overthrow the 'reasonable' compromises, the caution of the realists, and the half-heartedness of the 'pre-romantics', among their European contemporaries. True to their experience as Germans, their work has not the practical, political or economic range of the British and French; but, less restrained by social responsibilities in a country without public life or a cultural centre, they undermine more radically than any contemporaries (more even than Rousseau) the rule of 'polite society' in the sphere of culture. Thus we may see the *Sturm und Drang* as a stage in a most significant and vast development—not in a purely ideological movement or towards a limited 'objective' such as Romanticism or Idealism, but a stage in a whole complex of human relationships, principles, and problems, that become characteristic of the nineteenth century and still have significance to-day.

Social and Political Attitude

In the sphere of social and political thought the *Stürmer und Dränger* were more successful in grasping problems than asserting principles. They were all of burgher families, and academically educated; the Germany in which they grew up was split into innumerable principalities and free towns all governed by absolute rulers or hereditary patriciates. In revolt against the narrowness of public office and of normal burgher occupations, they failed to discover any political or social movement to which they could give their allegiance. Resolutely bourgeois in outlook, there is no lack of criticism of despotism and courtiers in their works, and equally of the spirit of subservience in the middle class. Criticism of courts is, indeed, as a rule excessive and frequently betrays a juvenile ignorance of court circles; but Merck knew what he was talking about when he warned Lenz against court-life in which 'alle Eigenthümlichkeit des Menschen verloren geht'. Goethe writes from Weimar of 'das durchaus Scheißige dieser zeitlichen Herrlichkeit'; though we can see the beneficial influence of experience when we compare the court in *Egmont* with that in *Götz*. One must note that Schiller's criticism of social oppression and of a corrupt court in *Die Räuber* and *Kabale und Liebe* is far more precise, and more to the point, than that in other *Sturm und Drang* works; while at the same time he subscribes in *Don Carlos* (and to some extent in *Die Räuber*) to positive national and social principles far less ambiguously than the others, here closer to Lessing than to them. But the characteristic *Sturm und Drang* situation is the abrupt repudiation of the political world, devoid of value, in favour of the private life where the individual can live according to his own feelings.

This is the first wish of Karl Moor, and the limit of Ferdinand von Walter's personal ambition. Klinger finds this solution in *Das leidende Weib* and *Sturm und Drang*. In *Julius von Tarent* Leisewitz more challengingly opposes the idea of private domestic bliss to government, even when the ruler is a model. Werther also seeks a refuge in simple circumstances, though Goethe's deeper insight shows the insecurity of the ideal itself. In *Götz* Goethe finds the most firmly established form in which this ideal may be realized, a historic mode of life sustained by warm personal relations and practical activity. In all cases, however, the worthy life appears as something insecure or unattainable, and the struggle for it is tragic, either through the might of political power or (and in addition) through the tragic conflict within the hero's own self. It is noteworthy that, much as the *Stürmer und Dränger* owed to Rousseau, they do not follow him in his attempts, in *La nouvelle Héloïse, Emile,* and *Du contrat social,* to find some way of reconciling inner values with outer social obligations; more drastically than he, they assert the conflict as an insoluble one.

Together with many outbursts against despotic rule and against the pettiness of public life, there is a remarkable lack of direct political interest in the *Sturm und Drang.* Herder could ascribe the decline of culture to the lack of a homogeneous public, to the lack of 'Freyheit und Menschengefühl', but such terms are not linked with their meaning in the modern political sense. Occasionally he utters an outburst against Charlemagne for having enslaved the Germans. But their concern with the nation arises almost entirely from their concern with culture and their desire for a poetry which will truly interpret German life. They were as obdurate to Klopstock's idealization of freedom as they were to his nationalism; both ideals they felt to be 'phantoms', meaningless, mere tirades; and in retrospect both Goethe and Herder condemned such excesses as the product of a time in which there was no great cause to enlist energies. Their distrust of this high-sounding vehemence was reasonable and shrewd, for in practice Klopstock, like the capable and free-speaking administrator C. F. von Moser (for whom the *Stürmer und Dränger* had a healthy respect), admired the enlightened despot and hankered after a restoration of the medieval empire under the Habsburgs.

The American War of Independence broke out at the height of the *Sturm und Drang,* and their response to it shows how little they understood or sympathized with the political idea of independence. Klopstock supported the insurgents, as did Stolberg and Schubart; Schiller sympathized with their aims. But Lenz (the great politician!) called the colonists idiots. He and Klinger were ready to enlist on the English side, like Werther and many other characters of *Sturm und Drang* works. Indifferent to the issue of freedom, they sought in this war, in war in general, merely an attractive outlet for their energies. 'Where war is, there am I.' Their attitude to the American War throws considerable light on the ambiguity of their use of the word 'freedom', yet it is usual to consider them champions of political freedom. They might have a bad conscience about it, like Goethe's Fernando (in *Stella*), who escapes the turmoil of his emotions by taking part in the suppression of the rising of the 'noble' Corsicans. Bodmer, the good republican, was astonished at Goethe's admiration for the tyrant Caesar.

Political power and aggrandisement were devoid of all meaning in their view. Here again they must be distinguished from men like Heinse or Schubart, who, for all their worship of 'freedom', were fascinated by the success of Frederick the Great. The two Prussians among them, Hamann and Herder, had nothing but loathing for Prussia, for its despotism and its ruthless efficiency—like Winckelmann and Lessing before them. They might feel sympathy, with Goethe, for Frederick's personal heroism, but not for his system, nor for the extension of Prussian power, which in Herder's view was the negation of all true social and personal welfare. In *Auch eine Philosophie der Geschichte* Herder delivers a broadside on all power-politics, all imperialism, whether political or economic, including with Prussian expansionism that of England and France. Their main attack was, however, delivered at the German system, at the bureaucratic despotisms characteristic of the German states; even if these were efficient, in their view they brought a fatal impoverishment of personal life and initiative. With an eye to Prussia Merck wrote that departments of state are now organized like army battalions:

> Der tabellarische Geist hat den individuellen verdrängt. Und da es jeder gleich gut machen soll, so macht es nicht leicht einer besser als der andere. Jedes Mannes Gewalt und Redlichkeit ist so enge controlliert, und jeder so subaltern von dem andern, daß es kaum der Mühe lohnt, das Zutrauen zu verdienen, das man ihm zum voraus versagt hat.

In such a situation, the temptation to repudiate all social obligation, as do so many figures in their works, was strong; Hamann in fact gave them a lead in this direction, in his actual life and his writings. But the *Stürmer und Dränger* were haunted by the idea of worthy practical activity—we see this in Herder's *Journal* or his letters to Caroline Flachsland, his welcome to the calls to Bückeburg and Weimar; in Lenz's 'Handeln sey die Seele der Welt'; in poetic symbols like Götz or Prometheus. And in what framework could they find activity? All the political theorists of their time were at one in recommending enlightened (benevolent) despotism as the best framework for social advance, however differently A. L. von Schlözer, C. F. von Moser, Klopstock, Kant, or Justus Möser himself, might interpret the term 'advance'. It is therefore not surprising that the *Stürmer und Dränger* themselves thought and worked within the assumptions of enlightened despotism. Weimar was not an accident, but a principle.

Goethe tells us that, on his first meeting with Karl August, they discussed Möser's writings; Möser is nearer to the *Stürmer und Dränger* than any other political thinker. He wrote from the experience of an absolutism, but in a very small state without a hereditary ruler, where the administrators could be in close contact with all social strata and could interest themselves in all aspects of life. He was a consistent opponent of the large state and the bureaucratic apparatus necessary in a large autocracy. While he was deeply concerned for welfare and efficiency, he was equally anxious to strengthen the social ties which promote the cohesion of social groups, and link them to the whole society. He valued all those traditions and customs which weld the individual to the group, and thought of the individual not as a 'subject' but as a participant in a community. The state itself was for him not a power-unit, but a historical entity made up of most diversified groups, whose purpose was realized only if it strengthened the vigour of these groups. Thus he defended traditional corporations and sought to maintain privileges and rights which ensured corporate existence. He pointed out that the abolition of serfdom was no unmixed blessing. In strong contrast to the general trend of *Aufklärung* thought he sought to strengthen the separate identity of the social estates, seeing in them a means to check the power of the ruler.

Goethe says in Book 15 of *Dichtung und Wahrheit* that Möser's standpoint gave meaning to the anarchy of Germany, since he showed how the mass of small states gave the opportunity to tend the peculiar culture of each district. Through him the *Stürmer und Dränger* were fortified in their interest for the local, provincial, concrete forms of life. Loathing despotism and the impersonality of the bureaucratic state, they saw the traditional estates as a defence of 'freedom'—we find Herder, in *Auch eine Philosophie der Geschichte,* condemning the 'mixing of social estates' and putting in a word for feudalism and serfdom. But this backward-looking ideal involved them in characteristic and almost unavoidable contradictions.

They learnt from Möser that the nobility was a defence against despotism. Even the boldest German spirits echoed this theme, C. F. von Moser and Schubart among them. In *Sturm und Drang* works one often meets with the honest nobleman, the country squire, who seeks to improve conditions or to check corruption. Most of their heroes are noblemen, and it might well be thought that in their view only noblemen, like Götz, Julius von Tarent, Karl Moor or Ferdinand von Walter, had the spirit to assert themselves against the earthly powers. At the same time there is the sharpest criticism of noblemen, of their arrogance and class-conceit—see *Der Hofmeister, Werther,* and their private correspondence (Brander's remark in *Urfaust* is not untypical: 'Das ist was vornehmes inkognito, sie haben so was unzufriednes böses im Gesicht'). This contradiction runs through all Goethe's and Herder's work, till their death; and there is a personal note in Herder's remark about Swift: 'Was den Dechant am meisten niederdrückte, waren die obern Stände. Sie hielt er für unverbesserlich; und an sie hatte er sich so sehr gehangen, und sie so sehr getrauet' (in his *Sturm und Drang* days, Herder liked to call himself 'der Dechant', after Swift). There is a similar contradiction, or ambiguity, in the attitude of the *Sturm und Drang* to marriage between burgher and noble. Misalliance is the theme of many of their works, and there is no mistaking the sympathy with which they treat two lovers separated by class. But even Schiller conceives such an alliance as possible only outside society. Indeed, they criticize the sentimental novel because it untruthfully shows that love may conquer social prejudice (e.g. in Lenz's *Soldaten* or Klinger's *Das leidende Weib*), and in *Die Soldaten* Lenz roundly asserts that a young burgher girl must not raise her eyes to the nobility.

Their attitude to the feudal constitution is equally contradictory. In *Auch eine Philosophie der Geschichte* Herder writes contemptuously of the 'freedom' which has shackled the lawless barons, dissolved the guilds, and emancipated the serfs—as one reads one thinks of *Götz.* But in Riga he had commended a nobleman who had emancipated his serfs, and he welcomed the breaking of feudal privilege in France at the time of the Revolution. Merck on a visit to Russia recommended the emancipation of the serfs. It is a significant comment on the German situation that Herder, Merck, and Lenz, when they were associated with Russian affairs, keenly participated in the schemes of enlightened reform that were circulating at that time in Catharine's court; in Germany they were bitterly frustrated and uncertain of themselves.

The attitude of the *Stürmer und Dränger* to the common people was less ambiguous, though very complex. It was determined by cultural considerations—at no time do they envisage the bourgeoisie or the *Volk* as a political force. In the common people they found the real substance of the nation. In his review of an English book which summed up the characteristics of Germany in terms of 'polite society', Goethe exploded against the whole notion of 'good society', 'polite nations'; the German character is to be found, he wrote, in the domestic family, the farm, the workshop, the inn and coffee-house. Their works show how they claimed cultural intercourse between burgher and noble. But there is no admiration for merchants and bankers in their writings; the noble merchant of the English and French tradition is absent, and on the contrary there is much vexation expressed with the dull routine of bourgeois employment. The dissatisfaction of a Werther or a Wilhelm Meister turns into sharp criticism when the professional classes come on the scene, and all through the *Sturm und Drang* we find vehement and contemptuous attacks on 'Stubengelehrten' as men who neglect living for the sake of ideas or learning. Most drastically in the Ossian essay Herder opposed to the learned 'pedants' of his time the untutored, 'natural' classes—'unverdorbne Kinder, Frauenzimmer, Leute von gutem Naturverstande, mehr durch Thätigkeit, als Spekulation gebildet'. It is one of the great achievements of *Sturm und Drang* writing to have captured the reality and charm of these practical social groups, young women in the home, children, tradesmen, peasants. But again, they do not make them an ideal, or attribute to them more than the virtues of their limited sphere, as the Romantics were to do; or, if they tended to do so, they checked themselves. Herder and Bürger, in the first flush of their enthusiasm for folksong, thought they found in artisans and peasants the true bearers of poetic culture. But they were too faithful to their intellectual heritage (and too intimidated by hostile critics) to maintain this standpoint, and they hastily assured everyone that by *Volk* they did not mean the *Pöbel.* With fine tact Goethe makes Faust say, of Gretchen's room:

> In dieser *Armuth* welche Fülle!
> In diesem *Kercker* welche Seeligkeit!

The *Stürmer und Dränger* appreciated the richness and 'warmth' of burgher existence and grasped the critical points at which burgher values were threatened, but they became involved in contradictions when they sought to suggest ways in which these values might be secured. But in their very contradictions they were most true to the life around them. Not only are their imaginative works full of vivid realistic observation, but their social and political ideas are distinguished too by a greater concreteness than those of Nicolai, Schlözer, or even Kant, and truthfully reflect a stagnant, bewildering social reality. One may suggest that it was this obduracy of the political and social structure of Germany that made, not Herder's political ideas, but his theory of history, the finest flower of their social thought. It was his repudiation of the bureaucratic state, of unhampered absolutism, or power-politics and expansionism, his longing for a social community where thought and practical life were in harmony, that led him to understand the cultural qualities of early society and of the Biblical patriarchate, that gave him insight into the dependence of governmental forms on the mode of life of a people, that enabled him to appreciate how complex is the law of social development. There are many palpable faults in his theory of history, in its early and late form; but the value of his insight cannot be contested, and, in its strength and weakness, it is an integral part of the *Sturm und Drang.*

Man and Nature

The *Sturm und Drang* conflict with *Aufklärung* philosophy springs from the same root as their political thought. It is essentially a conflict about the powers of man. The *Stürmer und Dränger* refused to accept the cramping interpretation of man as an etiolated intelligence; they were savagely contemptuous of men who turned the universe into a web of ideas, and who defined man and his destiny in terms of abstractions. 'Metaphysics', 'speculation', 'abstractions' are always terms of vituperation with the *Stürmer und Dränger,* directed against the pedestrian arrogance of Nicolai, the idealistic constructions of Mendelssohn, and the speculative theology of the time. For the Berlin rationalists, the toleration to speculation allowed by Frederick the Great was a great stride towards 'perfection'. Lessing had already bitterly contrasted this 'freedom to utter follies' with the actual slavishness of life in Berlin. Herder was more extreme in his fury: 'Das liebe, matte, ärgerliche, unnütze Freidenken, Ersatz für alles, was sie [die Menschen] vielleicht mehr brauchten—Herz! Wärme! Blut! Menschheit! Leben!' In *Dichtung und Wahrheit* Goethe put this principle positively in his (rather overgenerous) summing-up of Hamann's thought: 'Alles was der Mensch zu leisten unternimmt, es werde nun durch That oder Wort oder sonst hervorgebracht, muß aus sämmtlichen vereinigten Kräften entspringen; alles Vereinzelte ist verwerflich.'

Herder's philosophical works, on language, knowledge, and poetry, are part of a consistent effort to work out the fundamental principles of this revolt against the degradation of human capacities, to justify on the broadest basis this desire for the full employment of all human faculties. It brought him into conflict not only with minor figures, but also with Kant, and his criticism of Kant, over the theory of history, epistemology, and aesthetics, has not received the attention which is its due. Too often his philosophy is summed up as 'irrationalism', and we shall see how misleading this definition is. Like Hamann he owed an immense debt to English empiricists like Bacon and Locke, French sensualists like Diderot and Condillac, and to

Hume's scepticism. But while Hamann utilized the arguments of empiricists and sceptics to justify his 'Köhlerglauben', Herder built out of them a philosophy which is essentially humane and secular.

This philosophy asserts the primacy of being over thinking. In contrast to the Cartesian idealists of his time, he insists that sense and activity are as fundamental to man as thought. The theme of his *Vom Erkennen und Empfinden der menschlichen Seele,* at which he was writing between 1774 and 1778, is that there is no knowing without feeling, and neither without will and activity. Philosophy must be, in his view, an induction from experience—metaphysics should be, he writes, an 'after-physics'; and his own experience taught him that thoughts and feelings impregnate one another, and both are shaped by particular and local situations (it was this interwovenness that he so admired in Shakespeare). He eagerly embraced Leibniz's dynamic conception of matter, and asserted that all human capacities are functions, operations; thus he opposed the mechanical materialism of a Helvétius as sharply as he did the idealism of Descartes or dualism in any form, particularly the dualism of Leibniz and Kant. He answered the question, is mind or matter primary, by asserting that both are energies and, in the last resort, identical. The distinction between them is, in his view, of historical origin, due to the division of labour in civilized society which separates thinkers from doers; and his remedy is typical of the *Sturm und Drang,* a practical one—thinkers must break out of their studies and begin to feel and to act. 'So sind die Theorien gestiegen, bis endlich die höchste Philosophie wieder gebietet, zur Praxis zurückzukehren'; 'die vollständige Wahrheit ist immer nur That'—Goethe's *Faust* seems to be the quintessence of Herder's epistemological treatise.

It is clear that Herder's theory powerfully reflects his own experience and feeling, his frustrations and aspirations. But we do him a serious wrong if we consider it as of merely subjective validity. His studies in language and poetry, in history and anthropology, and not least his attentiveness to contemporary science, all fortified him in his view. Too much attention has been paid to the influence of alchemy on *Sturm und Drang* thought, and too little to that of the best science of their time. Herder's works show a constant and growing preoccupation with scientific works. To some extent, the change-over from the mechanistic, deistic picture of the universe to the dynamic pantheistic conception is due, as Diderot several times asserted, to the rise of the biological sciences—and, we may add, to the beginnings of the science of electricity. In *Vom Erkennen und Empfinden,* and all later works, Herder finds substantiation for his views in the biologists' and physicists' and chemists' discovery of the energy within living organisms, within apparently 'dead' matter; and these discoveries fortified him, as they did Goethe, in his instinctive feeling of the unity of all natural phenomena, of man and nature, in his pantheism.

Herder's thought, though consistent in general, is not disciplined; sometimes he seems to dissolve the universe into a 'realm of unsubstantial forces', sometimes he expresses a thoroughgoing materialism; sometimes he personalizes God as a loving father, usually he dismisses any transcendental or anthropomorphic conception of the divinity; his vocabulary is emotive, and his use of many terms, for instance of 'Seele', is confusing. His philosophy is rather a starting-point than an end, and it might lead to an idealistic or a materialistic dynamic monism. There is a curious offshoot from it in Lenz's essays. Lenz, too, struggled with two opposing factors of experience: the conviction of the determination of thought by environment, as expounded for instance by Helvétius, and the conviction of the dynamic energy within himself, or at least of the irrepressible urge within him to assert himself over environment. Lenz comes to the suggestion that in this struggle the 'soul' comes into being and makes itself an independent realm—a little-known anticipation of Schelling's 'Naturphilosophie', even of the theory of 'emergent evolution'.

Goethe, known to his friends as a powerful thinker, wrote very little directly upon this theme in his *Sturm und Drang* years. All his work testifies, however, to his feeling of unity with nature, to his awareness of the identity between the 'living forces' of nature and of man. The essay, *Die Natur,* of which he was the spiritual father, is his Magnificat to the author and originator of his being. Averse from philosophical generalities, he always keeps truer to observed and experienced nature than Herder. While Herder writes [in his *Ideen zur Philosophie der Geschichte,* Book 9] 'Wer seinen Sinnen nicht traut, ist ein Tor und muß ein leerer Spekulant werden', Goethe avoids the pitfall of dogmatic sensualism by writing [in his *Sprüche in Prosa*]: 'Der Mensch ist genugsam ausgestattet zu allen irdischen Bedürfnissen, wenn er seinen Sinnen traut *und sie dergestalt ausbildet, daß sie des Vertrauens wert bleiben.'* Faust is uneasy with 'Im Anfang war die *Kraft'* (Herder's phraseology) and prefers the more concrete and practically helpful 'Im Anfang war die Tat'. These examples are taken from Goethe's maturity; but one finds as clear and pregnant a statement in his *Sturm und Drang.* What attracted him about Lavater's physiognomical studies was the identity they presupposed between spiritual qualities and physical appearance; so, in a short jotting meant to serve as a preface to the work, he sketched the guiding principle governing inner and outer change, the self and the environment:

> Was den Menschen umgiebt wirkt nieht allein auf ihn, er wirkt auch wieder zurück auf selbiges, und indem er sich modificieren läßt, modificiert er wieder rings um sich her. Die Natur bildet den Menschen, er bildet sich um, und diese Umbilding ist doch wieder natürlich.

With the inner clarity and self-confidence that Herder so sadly lacked, Goethe finds a lucid and productive formulation that puts the new attitude in a form which directs to further intellectual and practical labour.

Although Herder alone of the *Stürmer und Dränger* can claim to rank as a philosopher, we can, I believe, justifiably call his work the philosophy of the *Sturm und Drang,* since it is built out of insights and values that find other forms of expression (dramatic, lyrical, etc.) in their works and lives. It will be recognized that Schiller's way of thinking, though his dissertation deals with the 'connexion between the animal nature of man and his spiritual', stands quite apart from earlier *Sturm und Drang* thought; with his adoption of the basic concepts of Kant it becomes in many ways its opposite. There is no space here to investigate the extension of this basic *Sturm und Drang* thought into the later 'classical' period of Herder and Goethe; it must suffice to assert that in Herder's later historical and philosophical work, in the *Ideen* and *Gott. Einige Gespräche,* and in Goethe's scientific work and *Weisheit,* we find its fulfillment.

Religion

It is well-known that the *Stürmer und Dränger* found in religion support, even inspiration, for their onslaught on the *Aufklärung,* but it is extremely easy to misinterpret the part religion played in their thought. Almost all Hamann's works were avowedly religious in character. Herder was a clergyman; Lenz was (very fitfully) studying theology. All three were brought up in pietistic homes. Goethe kept in sympathetic touch with pietists throughout his *Sturm und Drang* period, and, like the others, enjoyed close personal relations with religious men like Lavater or Jung-Stilling. Yet none had sympathy with dogma or cult. Hamann was a thorn in the flesh not only of the orthodox, but also of pietists. Herder was charged with being an atheist, a free thinker, a Socinian, an enthusiast (*Schwärmer*), as he told Hamann. Goethe avowed himself a 'non-Christian'. In the controversy over Lessing's pantheism Herder and Goethe both acknowledged themselves to be pantheists, Spinozists.

Herder's first religious publications fall in 1774, when he was hoping for a Chair of Theology: one can hardly believe that either *Die Älteste Urkunde des Menschengeschlechts* or *Provinzialblätter* could have strengthened his claims, and he himself heard that he failed 'because his orthodoxy was in question'. The former is an ostentatious justification of the Biblical account of the Creation, directed both against rationalists who ridiculed it on rational and scientific grounds, and against theologians who tried to justify it as a symbolical expression of the truths available to modern science. Yet Herder's arguments are ambiguous in the extreme. He admits the truth of the modern cosmology of Newton and Euler and does not slur over the conflict between the conclusions of science and the statements of Genesis. But he asserts that while one is true for modern experience and consciousness, the other is equally true for the experience of the Biblical shepherds who created it. He then interprets Genesis as a mythical statement of the sunrise, and dwells upon the superiority of the ancient conception of God, which interprets the daily experience of a pastoral people, and is alive in their daily need and joy. The God of the deists is 'a metaphysical Something' that means nothing to the feeling and daily life of the individual; but this God of the patriarchs is a vital summation of their being. All truth worthy of the name must arise from experience, from the whole man—from 'Anschauen, Evidenz, Zeichen, Erfahrung'; it must lie 'im ganzen, unzerstückten, tiefen Gefühl der Sachen'. It is easy to understand the theme as a defence of the poetic value of Genesis, as a defence of the religion of a simple pastoral people; it is also clear that Herder was demanding from a religion or philosophy that it should not be a matter of mere intellectual deduction, but should arise from the totality of experience and appeal to the whole man. But few of his religious readers would have been content with his statement that the truth we arrive at is 'nichts als eine Sammlung und Fachwerk Menschlicher Begriffe, von außen, in unserm Kreise, nach unsern Organen gesammlet'; and, if the form of religion is thus determined subjectively, according to the varying experience of peoples and generations, why should a modern man hold to the forms of a pastoral people?

The theme of the *Provinzialblätter* is less ambitious and speculative; the book is made up of short homilies to parish priests. Here again we see Herder arguing against dogmatic and theological abstractions, and calling on clergymen to preach a religion that 'opens eyes and senses, ears and thoughts'. He recommends the use of the Bible because it 'nourishes most deeply the soul', because it is 'a primer for the development of human powers through the revelation of God'. There is no special organ of religion in man, the faculties are not divided into higher and lower, he says, in words that might be Hamann's:

> Die ganze Religion in Grund und Wesen ist Thatsache! Auf Zeugnis der Sinne und nicht der Oberkräfte allein; bei dem Empfangenden auf Glauben, der alle Kräfte faßt, gebaut: nach Zweck und Inhalt ans Volk, den grössten sinnlichern Theil der Menschheit, und nicht an Grübler gerichtet; in Art und Sprache sie mit allen Trieben umzuschaffen und zu lenken.

It is of importance that this work was primarily concerned with the sort of religious teaching that was suited to the common mass of people, the 'greatest, more sensuous part of mankind', not to philosophers. Many times we note this preoccupation in Herder, his recognition that the common man can find no greater spiritual sustenance than in the tangible factual Biblical teaching. This is a typical *Aufklärung* point of view, shared by Lessing and Voltaire, who neither of them wished to disturb the faith of the masses. Merck, a non-believer, likewise regretted that religion had been deprived of all its sensuous elements, its relish, and adds the characteristic remark that fortunately the 'productive class' had not been affected by this enlightened religion, and therefore 'no plough or wheel has been brought to a standstill'. We remember that Faust understands and fully respects Gretchen's literal faith. How far is Herder expounding his own faith, and how far is he demanding religious instruction suited to the common man, as part of his campaign against a self-centred intellectual class?

It is difficult to answer this question. The duties of his office, his memories of childhood, his own impressionable and emotive nature, all combined to fill Herder's works with religious terms and tones. There is a never-ending battle in his mind. But the prevailing theme of his religious works—especially those not concerned directly with religious edification and Biblical exegesis—is 'decidedly non-Christian'. He polemises openly against the idea of a transcendental or anthropomorphic God, he ignores problems such as sin, grace, and salvation, he is unconcerned for dogma. Religion is above all trust in the goodness of the universe, trust in the goodness of man's powers. He denies the possibility of expressing truth or the nature of God in the limited terms of human understanding. In *Auch eine Philosophie der Geschichte* God becomes identical with an inscrutable fate, undiscernible to human intelligence, working through entirely natural means but with a good purpose. In *Vom Erkennen und Empfinden* and his later works, particularly his fullest statement, *Gott. Einige Gespräche,* the earlier emotive exaltation at the thought of fate becomes a serene acceptance of divine Necessity, of the law governing the whole universe, in which man finds his fulfilment and his 'freedom'. In the *Ideen* he more fully works out his earlier idea that religion takes different forms according to the total circumstances of the life of a people. His mature philosophy, his pantheism, reconciles the idea of God with his trust in man's intellectual powers and dynamic energy—a God who lives and moves in every particle of Creation, who is justified by sense and feeling as well as thought, who is present in man's energy but who cannot be contained in any dogmatic formulation or restricted to any cult. 'This philosophy makes me very happy.'

Several of Lenz's essays are theological in character, and the inconsistency of his views corresponds to the instability of his character—one finds in them theological argumentation in the style of *Aufklärung* theologians, pietistic reminiscences, and moral puritanism. In his most emphatic passages, however, where we can detect a distinctive and personal note, he approximates to Herder. He writes that 'the central intention of Christ's doctrine' lies in the word Μετανοειτε—

> μετα! μετα! überweg über alle eure vorigen Meinungen von Vollkommenheit und Glückseligkeit, überweg über euer *non plus ultra,* über euer Ideal selbst, und unaufhörlich überweg, solang ihr noch weiter kommt. . . . Glaube beschwingt, befacht, entzündet unsere Kräfte alle. . . . Es ist also der Glaube eine gewisse Zuversicht des, das man hofft.

Religion is for Lenz, therefore, a principle of energy engaging all man's powers; and in the most profound religious poem of the *Sturm und Drang* ["Edward Allwills einziges Geistliches Lied"], he implores God, with the violence of despair, to satisfy his heart's longings, or destroy him:

> Nein, ich schreie—Vater! Retter!
> Dieses Herz will ausgefüllt,
> Will gesättigt sein; zerschmetter
> Lieber sonst dein Ebenbild!

The religious views of Goethe, the 'non-Christian', reflect in all essentials the same principles as Herder's. He spoke of the 'Mährgen' of Christ, detested 'proofs' of Christianity ('Brauch ich Zeugniß daß ich binn? Zeugniß daß ich fühle?'), hated dogma and dogmatists; laughed at Puritans; detested the feeling of sinfulness and repentance, 'Zittern und Beben'; and turned in vexation from the intellectual narrowness and unproductive brooding of pietists. But he respected that faith which sustains men in the fullness of their personality, for instance the belief of Fräulein von Klettenberg or Lavater, which he recognized as the intense expression of their capacity for love and friendship. He sympathetically tolerated Jung-Stilling's naïve fundamentalism, 'sein unverwüstlicher Glaube an Gott', because it was 'das Element seiner Energie'. In his *Brief des Pastors* he says that the essence of religion is 'unaussprechliche Empfindungen', while dogma is 'tyrannischer Unsinn'. 'In unsers Vaters Apotheke sind viele Rezepte'. He told Betty Jacobi that she should bring up her children to believe, though it was immaterial what form the belief should take: 'Ob sie an Crist glauben, oder Götz, oder Hamlet, das ist eins, nur an *was* lasst sie *glauben.* Wer an nichts glaubt verzweifelt an sich selber'. He recalls this attitude in *Dichtung und Wahrheit:*

> Beim Glauben, sagte ich, komme Alles darauf an, *daß* man glaube; *was* man glaube, sei völlig gleichgültig. Der Glaube sei ein großes Gefühl von Sicherheit für die Gegenwart und Zukunft, und diese Sicherheit entspringe aus dem Zutrauen auf ein übergroßes, übermächtiges und unerforschliches Wesen.

As we see from Faust's 'Gefühl ist Alles', religion both interprets this subjective feeling of trust and confidence, and confirms and strengthens it, by attaching it to the whole universe, to a 'supermighty and inscrutable being' about whom it is wisest to say nothing.

One may then speak of a *Sturm und Drang* religious philosophy. They gained from religion confidence in their own instinctive feeling, and they treasured in it those elements which sustain men in their emotive and practical life. For themselves, they let fall all the dogmatic and specific form of Christianity. 'Faith' meant for them confidence in the delight and meaning their senses, feelings, and inner energy provided. From the beginning it expressed their consciousness of forming part of nature, like all Spinozism it sanctified matter, and it sustained them in their later, more objective study of the universe, of history and nature, in which they found the same principles, the same 'mighty being', as stirred in their own hearts. Their 'religion' runs counter to the transcendentalism of the Romantics or the 'existentialism' of Hamann; it belongs to the great tradition of humanism and was justified, in their view, by its productive function in the totality of a man's existence.

Morals

The burden of Herder's criticism of the thinkers of his century was, that everything was turned into a 'gaunt ghost', into an abstraction: philosophers, he wrote of Hume, were content 'mit Sachen zu spielen, die man brauchen und nicht besehen sollte'. In his view, and in this he fully represents the *Sturm und Drang,* ideas are meaningful only if they interpret and contribute to 'das tiefe, unersetzliche Gefühl des Daseins', and as they could be realized in actual life. Actions likewise were worth doing only if they arose from, and contributed to, this vital feeling. 'Jeder handle nur ganz aus sich, nach seinem innersten Charakter, sei sich selbst treu, das ist die ganze Moral'. Such principles entailed a conflict, not only over the theoretical fields of philosophy and religion, but also in the religion of morals. In fact, a great deal of the hostility to the *Stürmer und Dränger* arose from the alleged immorality of their works. *Werther* was called 'eine Schule des Selbstmordes', *Stella* 'eine Schule der Entführungen und Vielweiberei'. *Faust,* once it was published, was to give rise to a stream of charges against its immorality. Other *Sturm und Drang* works laid themselves open to the same charge, against which Schiller had to defend himself in the prefaces of his early works. Heyne, Herder's Göttingen friend and abettor, sadly regretted that Herder was so obstinately determined to banish morality from art.

It was not mere moral theory that was at issue. The *Stürmer und Dränger,* including Hamann, were all at odds with practical obligations, however much they sought scope for activity. They had and expressed no respect for normal burgher professions. In their manners they shocked decorous burghers and flouted public opinion. Among themselves they cultivated a frank, easy intercourse, freer and more spontaneous than propriety allowed. Goethe, above all, made himself the centre of a lively, uninhibited circle. His letters are as original in content, form and vocabulary as his poetry. Nicolai's 'rectification' of the morals of *Werther* is paralleled by F. H. Jacobi's criticism of *Sturm und Drang* lack of restraint in *Eduard Allwills Papiere.* Often enough, in the minor members of the *Sturm und Drang,* this spontaneity degenerated into the rampageous excess of the 'Kraftgenie', juvenile not youthful, the literary expression of which is found in such figures as Klinger's Simsone Grisaldo, in the Dedication of Maler Müller's *Fausts Leben.* The self-conscious and ostentatious amoralism of Heinse's *Ardinghello* is the aberration of a weak and frustrated character. But it would be wrong to identify the moral challenge of the *Sturm und Drang* with these excesses.

In some of their works, moral questions are discussed which belong to the whole trend of the *Aufklärung.* The prevailing criticism of unnatural sexual continence belongs to the tradition of the Enlightenment, as does the sympathy with the victims of the harsh law against infanticide. Lenz's attack on private tuition (in *Der Hofmeister*) fits in with normal *Aufklärung* thought. But even in such matters, the manner of the *Stürmer und Dränger* is very different from that of the more cautious, socially responsible *Aufklärer;* it is sharp, assertive, absolute; the evil causes not only suffering, but a dismaying perversion of character in the victims. In fact, it is from a practical point of view less effective than more restrained criticism: the attention is drawn away from thoughts of social or moral reform to absorption in the experience and response of the individual characters. The fate of Gretchen hardly moves us to reflect at all on the law governing infanticide: Faust does not protest against it, and Gretchen herself accepts death as punishment and retribution.

Normal reforming thought of the time sought to adjust prevailing morality to the needs of personal happiness; but, equally, it sought to adjust personal need to the unavoidable claims of social and religious authority, to the moral principles which corresponded to the social structure. The ideal of contentment implied a voluntary self-restriction and self-control; the ideal of perfection was bound up with the effort to subject instinct and feeling to reason. The sentimentalists postulated a sort of feeling which was, by its nature, virtuous and consonant with religion, and because of this, in their plays and novels, they could reward such feeling, as Sophie de la Roche rewarded her Fräulein von Sternheim with marriage and happiness. In Julie Rousseau himself described a character whose instinct is good. F. H. Jacobi and F. L. zu Stolberg continually asserted that deep feeling chimed in with Christian morals and religion.

There are evidences of this view here and there in the works of the *Stürmer und Dränger*—for instance in the first version of Herder's *Vom Erkennen und Empfinden.* But for them, in general, happiness and contentment were aims to be despised, or at least aims that could never be achieved; pretty pictures with which men beautified the walls of their prison, in Werther's words. They sought an outlet for their feeling, room for action, experience; a perpetual movement and striving, as Lenz said, towards an infinite goal. They did not wish to avoid pain and effort, but accepted them as a necessity of existence, as the stuff of existence:

> Ich fühle Muth, mich in die Welt zu wagen,
> All Erden Weh und all ihr Glück zu tragen.

Thus they were not primarily concerned to patch up the social and moral world, but to show what capacity for experience man possesses, how the world cramps and distorts the best in man. They do not provide, and scarcely suggest, solutions, for a solution would suggest that a man might come to that 'Ruhepunkt' that Lenz cursed. Or, one might say that when they suggest solutions, like Fernando's *ménage à trois,* or Lenz's state-nursery for officers' women, they tend to the fantastic, even idiotic. But what is characteristic is that they represent the collision between the individual and morality as irremediable, fatal, something akin to the tragedy they felt in Othello, Macbeth, or Lear: one thinks of *Werther* and *Faust,* Müller's *Fausts Leben,* Klinger's *Die Zwillinge,* Lenz's *Der Engländer* or *Die Soldaten* (Marie).

Thus we find in the *Sturm und Drang* a double development from earlier eighteenth-century criticism of morals. On the one hand, social or moral authority and 'Sitte' is much more profoundly implicated in human tragedy; and on the other hand, the individual hero himself is in his own character much more tragic, lost. In *Emilia Galotti* Lessing criticizes precisely the irresponsibility of the absolute sovereign, who is the contriver of the tragedy. The victims have no share in guilt and no fault; and we feel that if the prince were 'benevolent', or if the ruler were subject to civil law, tragedy would be obviated. By contrast, in Schiller's *Kabale und Liebe,* the *Sturm und Drang* play nearest to Lessing's, one finds, instead of a mere wicked prince, a whole system of prejudice and corruption, in which the 'good' characters are lost and lose themselves. But Schiller still maintains the fiction of feelings absolutely good in themselves, which become disastrous only through the impact of evil circumstances. Goethe shows in *Werther* the insufferable narrowness of burgher routine and idea and the arrogance of the nobility, but also the disastrous tensions in Werther himself, which in these circumstances drive him to self-destruction. Gretchen is destroyed not merely by public opinion and law, but also by the insoluble conflict within herself between the morality she accepts and the 'goodness' of her love—a conflict within her instinct itself. Klinger's Guelfo is destroyed by his own perverted passions, as is Lenz's Marie, with her innocent desire for pleasure and elegance which the burgher world cannot satisfy.

Thus Goethe felt the untruth of Sophie de la Roche's neat and precise differentiation between good and evil: 'Ist das böse nicht gut und das gute nicht bös?' Werther can explain to Albert that the rational and sensible condemnation of suicide is meaningless for the loving soul cheated of its happiness. Gretchen puts it simply:

> Doch—alles was mich dazu trieb,
> Gott! war so gut! ach war so lieb!

The same contradiction exists in nature as a whole, parallel to the moral contradictions in man. Werther discovers the destructive power in all-creative nature, and must worship what he knows to be 'all-engulfing'. 'Schaffen und zerstören', writes Klinger in noisy jubilation. Goethe's essay, *Die Natur,* is a hymn to this amoral force of nature, destroying as it creates. Death appears to them not as a bleak ending, nor as a gateway to a transcendental existence, but as the concomitant to life, as essential to life as birth. 'Leben ist ihre schönste Erfindung [der Natur], und der Tod ist ihr Kunstgriff, viel Leben zu haben.' Nearly all the great works of Goethe's maturity centre in this interpretation of good and evil, and the completed *Faust* is true to the earliest conception in this respect. The energy within Faust is his 'good'; but this good is compounded to the very end of evil and destruction, not just unfortunate attendants of the good, but inescapable conditions of the good.

It is perhaps characteristic of the 'youthfulness' of the *Sturm und Drang* that this problematical character of good so deeply engrossed their thought, to the (relative) exclusion of positive moral views. It is clear that Herder, Goethe, and Lenz were also aware that their views and imaginative figures represented not ideals, but the difficult truth; 'Sey ein Mann und folge mir nicht nach', Goethe affixed to the second edition of *Werther.* And it was quite consistent that, in working out the principles of practical existence, Goethe should both continue in the *Sturm und Drang* and emerge from it. But in the *Sturm und Drang* we see something of the profoundest significance: the fragility of established social morality and its religious sanctions is investigated; and the reluctance of the *Stürmer und Dränger* to reconcile their dearest values with the demands of morality constitutes the deepest criticism of the social world in which such conflicts could arise, a deeper and more productive criticism than emerges from more limited, sensible, practical proposals for reform. Their attitude was not satisfactory; they themselves knew it, sometimes excusing themselves on the grounds of youth; but it is deeper and even to-day more moving and more disturbing than that of their contemporaries.

The Function of Poetry

It remains to investigate the relationship between their attitude to art, or rather to poetry, and the general body of their thought. I cannot hope to do more than sketch the main features of their poetic theory and work; but it is necessary to ask, not only what was their attitude towards poetry and conception of its function, but also why poetry takes so important a place in their thought and achievement. By 'poetry' should be understood imaginative literature in its widest sense, *Dichtung.*

Even the treatises of the *Stürmer und Dränger* are written in a 'poetic' style; by ellipses, elisions, inversions, questions, unfinished sentences, colloquial phrases, they seek to present not only thoughts in the abstract, but an emotive attitude, a response, gesture, a tone of voice. Herder insisted that truth is compounded of sense, thought, and will, that abstract language interprets the dessicated *Stubengelehrter* and that man in his fullness needs for self-expression a much richer language. Good German, Herder wrote, is to-day spoken only by the uneducated sections of society, children, young women, artisans and practical folk, and thus the poetic language of the *Stürmer und Dränger* was deeply refreshed through the rehabilitation of the vocabulary, phraseology, and rhythms of vigorous colloquial speech. At the same time, they did not confine themselves to the limited range of the *Volk,* but borrowed widely from poetic language which has in it the power they sought—Pindar, Homer, Shakespeare, folksong. Goethe was able to marry the earthiness of the *Knittelvers* with the sublimity of deepest thought and emotion.

In accordance with their attacks on metaphysical and dogmatic idealism, they overthrew the authority of the Rules; and at the same time the notion that poetry is mere embellishment. Poetry, they felt, must be meaningful within the experience of the individual poet, not constructed on some abstract principle. Herder's delight in early poetry, in folk-

Pastel drawing of Klinger by Goethe, 1775.

song, was due to his perception that this poetry was a creative element in social and personal life, the accompaniment of social tasks, battle and work, 'die Entzückung, die Triebfeder, der ewige Erb- und Lustgesang des Volks'. He continually criticized poets like Gessner who substituted a pretty or sentimental world for the true one; the only true poetry he told Caroline, was that which stirs the passions, 'the springs of mankind'. The essay on Ossian [*Briefwechsel über Ossian*] is devoted to this theme of the active function of poetry in simple society, in the *Volk.* But, in a time where there was no real national community, Herder recognized that Klopstock had marked the way for the renewal of poetry—a poetry of individual experience, expressing the individual's deepest emotions—'Gefühl ganzer Situation des Lebens! Gespräch Menschlichen Herzens—mit Gott! mit sich! mit der ganzen Natur!' And if Klopstock failed him through his excessive etherealism, Goethe came fully to realize Herder's principles. Hamann had put the same view in his sybilline way in *Aesthetica in nuce.* Here he asserted that art is the expression of the divine force through the creative reproduction of nature, and that it must speak to sense and passions, the organs of the Divine. Poetry is no place for trivialities and abstractions; it must be characteristic, concrete, individual, not idealizing nature but reproducing its vigour and working vigorously upon the reader.

This rupture with the old idea of absolute rules led in some respects to a disregard of form altogether. Hamann showed a complete failure to appreciate form. The first response to Shakespeare led Herder and Goethe to see his works as 'history', 'the world', 'a raree show'. Lenz compares the ideas of the poet to an unruly garrison, which may 'ohne Anführer, Kommando und Ordnung herumschwärmen'. Many *Sturm und Drang* works show a deliberate flouting of accepted formal principles, even of necessary technical conditions such as the stage imposes. The genius, they could believe, was above rules. Abandoning the rules associated with the principle of verisimilitude, Herder, following Gerstenberg, asserted that the poet's task is to create illusion, to impose his own world on us. Often the essence of the *Sturm und Drang* is held to be a cult of wilful 'genius'.

But their critical and poetic work shows in fact a new and profound insight into the problem of form—so difficult and elusive a problem that it is not surprising that their formulations are not always consistent. In the *Fragmente,* Herder was always struggling with this problem, investigating the characteristics and determinants of poetic language and poetic traditions, in order to discover the secret of the variations and function of form. His great review of Klopstock's odes shows his understanding of the formal properties of these poems, each with its own tone and colour, with a form which arises from the nature of the theme. The Ossian essay is an extended investigation of the formal properties of folksong, so different from those conventionally required. Above all in the Shakespeare essay, Herder shows how the form of Greek and Shakespearean drama is of equal validity, since each arose from a mass of historical conditions, social, religious, and artistic, through which they acquired their deep human significance. He comes to the idea of organic form: a form he calls comparable to that of nature, which gives 'jedem Kraut, Gewächse und Thier seine Gestalt, Sinn und Art, die Individuel ist und eigentlich nicht verglichen werden kann'. This is the theme of Goethe's rhapsody over the Strassburg Minster. He seeks to understand Gothic architecture as the development of the primitive hut, as a natural process, and concludes: 'wie in Werken der ewigen Natur, his aufs geringste Zäserchen, alles Gestalt, und alles zweekend zum Ganzen.'

Herder's aesthetic historicism is of capital importance in the history of aesthetics as well as of literary criticism; beauty, he asserted in conformity with his general philosophy, is not an abstract ideal, but a product of a dialectical relationship between subject and object, between a society and nature, a man's experience and his environment. Goethe supplemented Herder's general critical insight by equally significant remarks on the formal element in poetic creation. Even Lenz realized, at times, that the poet was not an arbitrary creator, but created according to principles which followed from his standpoint, his experience. In *Von deutscher Baukunst* Goethe speaks of the 'bildende Natur' in man; in the *Dritte Wallfahrt* he writes that 'Schöpfungskraft im Künstler sey aufschwellendes Gefühl der Verhältnisse, Maase'. If Herder wrote of the 'Nothdrang des Inhalts' of early poetry, Goethe puts the same idea in the image of the charioteer, guiding his spirited horses according to his will, guiding them though at the same time carried along with them. 'Alles schreibens anfang und Ende ist die Reproduktion der Welt um mich, durch die innre Welt die alles packt, verbindet, neuschafft, knetet und in eigner Form, Manier, wieder hinstellt.' Bürger seems to echo Goethe when he writes that the poet must have the courage 'ein Ding zu packen, zu halten, zu schleudern und in die Luft emporzureissen'. But by contrast Goethe's remarks emphasize that the poet is not so arbitrary with his material, that the form it takes is partly determined by its own nature.

So, when Goethe wrote his comments on L. S. Mercier's *Du théâtre,* he emphasized above all the problem of form. One must remember, he says, that the stage is an artificial structure, and must study and observe the conditions it imposes; the drama is not a 'raree show', but must have form. All form is artificial; but it is the way in which reality, truth, may be presented to the soul of man. 'Jede Form, auch die gefühlteste, hat etwas Unwahres, allein sie ist ein für allemal das Glas, wodurch wir die heiligen Strahlen der verbreiteten Natur an das Herz der Menschen zum Feuerblick sammeln.' Reproduction of nature, but condensed and intensified through the poet's vision: the image of the burning-glass sums up his view admirably. Thus, in the later part of the jottings, Goethe refuses to take sides in the great contemporary controversy over the relative merits of Rembrandt, Raphael and Rubens; each in his view is great in that he presents the world as he experiences it. 'Der Künstler mag die Werkstätte eines Schusters betreten oder einen Stall, er mag das Gesicht seiner Geliebten, seine Stiefel oder die Antike ansehen, überall sieht er die heiligen Schwingungen und leisen Töne, womit die Natur alle Gegenstände verbindet.' Goethe defines the attitude of the artist to his material as 'love', a love which discovers in the object the same harmonies, proportions, 'holy vibrations', as the poet feels within himself. These jottings, which belong to the end of his *Sturm und Drang* period, and perhaps prepare us for the preoccupation with art in the early Weimar years, interpret both the widening of aesthetic appreciation by the *Stürmer und Dränger,* and their own search for an individual form, consonant with their mode of experience and their inner values, such as Goethe found for his lyrics, for *Werther* and for *Faust.*

Hamann had combated the conception that art must beautify nature by justifying nature and the senses as creations and instruments of the Divine; but he had also rebelled against contemporary realistic theories of art, e.g. that of Diderot, since they denied the imagination and feeling their proper function. 'Willkühr und Phantasie' are essential, he cries, to art. His own imagination ran to caprice, there is no doubt; but he raises here a problem that lies at the heart of the *Sturm und Drang:* the relation of imagination and reality. These two elements in their work were noted by Justus Möser. He praised the healthy grasp of the real world shown in their best writings, and at the same time ascribed such realism to the poet's ability to 'schöpfen aus sich selbst und seine Empfindungen allein ausdrücken'. It is a peculiar and often ignored achievement of the *Sturm und Drang* to have 'reproduced' actual reality with an intensity no German generation of the nineteenth century surpassed.

It is true that German literature, for Wordsworth, was distinguished by a delight in the fantastic and macabre that he properly detested, and some works of the *Sturm und Drang* show an unhappy indulgence in unreal fantasies. Herder complained of his own 'aufgeschwellte Einbildungskraft' which tended to 'distort' reality grotesquely, and Merck addressed to him the sympathetic words: 'Ewig wirst du Träume jagen.' Goethe wrote the lines:

> Doch du warst mein Zeitvertreib
> Goldne Phantasie.

Lenz suffered immeasurably, in his life and works, from 'imaginaire Leiden', from an inability to see the world clear and true. Yet this was a tendency they all sought to combat, training themselves to observe objectively, to pierce through the mist of subjective fancy and feeling. Merck wrote of *Faust:* 'es ist ein Werk, das mit der grössten Treue der Natur abgestohlen ist.' He criticized minor works of the *Sturm und Drang* because they were taken from 'dunkle Träume poetischer Begierde', instead of the 'Markt des Lebens', and Goethe attributes to him the salutary advice: 'Dein Bestreben, deine unablenkbare Richtung, ist, dem Wirklichen eine poetische Gestalt zu geben; die andern suchen das sogenannte Poetische, das Imaginative zu verwirklichen, und das gibt nichts als dummes Zeug.' Merck's attitude on these points was in full conformity with the main tendency of the *Sturm und Drang.* Lenz felt it necessary to excuse the 'willkührliche Ausschweifungen der Phantasie' of *Der Engländer,* and proudly claimed *Die Soldaten* was taken from life.

Herder wrote of early poetry that it 'webt um daseiende Gegenstände, Handlungen, Begebenheiten, um eine lebendige Welt'. In like manner, all the *Stürmer und Dränger* sought to interpret in their works their actual experience. But they rejected any dogmatic realism, realism for its own sake; they sought to reproduce that reality which had significance for them, for which they had 'love', to use Goethe's word. The realism of Nicolai's *Sebaldus Nothanker* was tedious and dispensable for them. Goethe demanded that the poet should describe his own circumstances, his own feelings; then his poetry would have poetical worth. 'Nur da, wo Vertraulichkeit, Bedürfniß, Innigkeit wohnen, wohnt alle Dichtungskraft. . . . Geh vom Häuslichen aus und verbreite dich, so du kannst, über alle Welt.' The 'burning-glass' of the poet alters this reality, the imagination uses all sorts of 'unreal' instruments, metaphors, rhyme, images, 'den dunklen Gang der Melodie', supernatural figures and symbolic events; but these unrealistic means serve to interpret a human reality, in which nature and things are impregnated with human vitality, and vice versa. It is a remarkable feature of *Urfaust* that Goethe has stripped the folkplay of almost all its macabre and fantastic elements, and that what he retains or invents is of direct human relevance. This poetic realism is characteristic of all his work; it infinitely surpasses the flat realism of Lessing in that it calls into play a great mass of feelings and responses, and sets the reader vibrating with the work; it is of course equally different from the empty subjectivism of much German romanticism. With him, the imaginative is not the opposite of the real; it is a means of evoking and interpreting the real. Imagination is something akin to what it was in Wordsworth, a means of deepest insight and sympathy. It is, as Goethe later called it, a surmise, an anticipation of reality; not as with the German romantics or Coleridge an alternative to experienced reality, the organ of a transcendental world. Even before Goethe met Herder, he detested the unreality of Klopstockian enthusiasm, and yet could see 'auch ein Mährgen hat seine Wahrheit'. Illusion and reality were interwoven for him, as companions in the developing process of life:

> Ich hatte nichts und doch genug,
> Den Drang nach Wahrheit und die Lust am Trug.

In this respect, once again, we see an application of the general philosophy of the *Sturm und Drang.*

Poetry therefore acquires a new meaning for the *Stürmer und Dränger,* or rather they understand the meaning great poetry always has had. It is not embellishment, not a routine craft, not the handmaiden of established morality or a pleasant way of uttering moral or philosophical arguments. It is a mode of grasping reality and strengthening men's full participation in life, both in the process of poetic appreciation and in that of poetic creation. Herder expresses over and over again the feeling of vigorous joy, the enhancement of his vital consciousness, that he gained from folk-poetry, which 'uns ganz einnimmt, uns aber doch nie zu etwas mehr als Menschen macht'. Shakespeare gave him the same sense of human power and dignity. Goethe wrote how, on reading Shakespeare for the first time, he felt his existence 'um eine Unendlichkeit erweitert'—Wilhelm Meister uses almost the same expression. K. P. Moritz, whose autobiography gives us something of the basic 'Problematik' of the *Stürmer und Dränger,* wrote in a similar strain:

> Nachdem er den Shakespear, und so wie er ihn

> gelesen hatte, war er schon kein gemeiner und alltäglicher Mensch mehr—es dauerte auch nun nicht lange, so arbeitete sich sein Geist unter allenseinen äußern drückenden Verhältnissen, unter allem Spott und Verachtung, worunter er vorher erlag, empor. . . . Durch den Shakespear war er die Welt der menschlichen Leidenschaften hindurch geführt—der enge Kreis seines idealischen Daseyns hatte sich erweitert—er lebte nicht mehr so einzeln und unbedeutend, daß er sich unter der Menge verlor.

He described the effect of *Werther* in similar terms, for after reading it he no longer thought of himself as 'ein unbedeutendes weggeworfenes Wesen'. Lenz demanded from poetry 'Zuwachs unserer Existenz', 'den lebendigen Eindruck, der sich in Gesinnungen, Taten und Handlungen hernach einmischt'.

So also, poetic creation was for the *Stürmer und Dränger* a function of living, necessary in their effort to develop the totality of their capacities. Often enough their works express too directly their own too personal needs and frustrations, and fail to impart that enhanced consciousness of human worth which came to them from Shakespeare. Moritz' powerful response to Klinger's *Die Zwillinge* shows exactly where this play fails, for it only increased his 'Abscheu vor sich selbst'. Goethe, incomparably the greatest poet of the *Sturm und Drang,* repeatedly seeks words to indicate the function of poetic creation in himself. He compares art with the instinct of animals 'sich gegen die zerstörende Kraft des Ganzen zu erhalten'; 'O wenn ich ietzt nicht Dramas schriebe ich ging zu Grund.' And, more subtly, he describes himself

> immer in sich lebend, strebend und arbeitend, bald dic unschuldigen Gefühle der Jugend in kleinen Gedichten, das kräfftige Gewürze des Lebens in mancherley Dramas, die Gestalten seiner Freunde und seiner Gegenden und seines geliebten Hausraths mit Kreide auf grauem Papier, nach seiner Maase auszudrücken sucht, weder rechts noch lincks fragt: was von dem gehalten werde was er machte? weil er arbeitend immer gleich eine Stufe höher steigt, weil er nach keinem Ideale springen, sondern seine Gefühle sich zu Fähigkeiten, kämpfend und spielend, entwickeln lassen will.

The sentence is a whole aesthetic. Experience and environment provide the material of his work; different grades of experience find appropriate forms; the expression is shaped according to his peculiar 'measure'; and the artistic labour is a means of self-development; through it his feelings develop into capacities. Reflecting later in life on the imperious inner necessity that drove him to write *Werther,* Goethe wrote that the composition of this work had 'saved' him from the 'stormy element'—'Ich fühlte mich, wie nach einer Generalbeichte, wieder froh und frei und zu einem neuen Leben berechtigt'.

This exalted vital function that poetry had for the *Stürmer und Dränger,* in theory and practice, explains in part why so much of their work was concerned with imaginative writing. Poetry was not at end in itself, but a means to life, to activity. With such a purpose, the limitations and pettiness of their social world gave to poetry a peculiar significance. Their ideals crashed against actuality, and we see the reflexion of this fateful collision in work after work, above all in *Werther* and *Faust;* in the imagination, in the imaginative self-projection of their works, the intensity of being which was their ideal could be realized. Professor Bruford [in his *Theatre, Drama and Audience in Goethe's Germany,* 1950] has brought out the significance of the fact that the theatre was the only public forum in eighteenth-century Germany, and this circumstance, combined with the tensions and 'pungent spice' of their experience, accounts for the predominant significance of the drama in the *Sturm und Drang.* Lenz expresses the point with rueful whimsicality, when he writes [in *Über Götz von Berlichingen*] that the best his friends can do, since they are 'stumme Personen auf dem grossen Theater der Welt', 'da uns itzt noch Hände und Füße gebunden sind', is to put *Götz* on the stage and learn from *Götz* how to think and behave. In poetry they could express that fullness of being they sought, could see it in relation to the outer world, could follow some of its implications; through poetic appreciation and poetic activity they could release some of their actual stresses, could come to clearer self-understanding, could move towards that 'Läuterung' of which Goethe often writes in the late Frankfurt and early Weimar period. Only Goethe was so favoured, both in personality and in outward circumstance, as to be able to move forward in a steady development; and one sees in his assumption of practical duties at Weimar, in his scientific interests, in the steady broadening of his life, the true fulfilment of the *Sturm und Drang,* according to the possibilities that German society offered. (pp. 129-51)

Roy Pascal, "The 'Sturm und Drang' Movement," in The Modern Language Review, *Vol. XLVII, No. 2, April, 1952, pp. 129-51.*

Thomas Mann on the impact of Goethe's *Werther:*

The extreme, nerve-shattering sensitivity of this little book, which made it the horror and detestation of the moralists, evoked a storm of applause which went beyond all bounds and fairly intoxicated the world with an ecstasy for death. It ran like a fever and a frenzy over the populated earth, acting like a spark in a powder magazine, setting free a dangerous amount of pent-up force. We must be aware that an audience already existed for the book before its appearance. It seemed to fill the world with a very rapture of death; it was as though the public in every country had been secretly and unconsciously waiting for this very work, produced by an unknown citizen of a German city, to release for them, as though by a revolution, the suppressed yearning of their entire world. It was as though a bullet had hit the bull's-eye; it was the word of salvation. There is a story told of a young Englishman who in later years came to Weimar, saw Goethe walk past, and fainted in the street, overpowered by the sight of the author of *Werther* in the flesh.

Thomas Mann, in his Freud, Goethe, Wagner, *1933.*

Alan Menhennet

[In the following excerpt, Menhennet defines the Sturm und Drang as a literary revolution, comparing its ideological attitudes with those of the Enlightenment and focusing in particular on the importance of the Self and Nature to the Sturmer und Dranger.]

The 'Stürmer und Dränger' hated restriction much more than they feared disorder. They sometimes seem to cultivate disorder deliberately, nowhere more strikingly than in the approach and method of their literary theory, which seems to be symbolized in Hamann's provocative subtitle for his *Aesthetica in Nuce:* 'a rhapsody in cabbalistic prose.' They were much less willing than the Sentimentalists had been to submit their feelings to the authority of reason or conventional 'virtue'. Herder, awaking to a realization of the emotional self-mutilation often practised in the name of virtue, addresses a woman he once knew in Riga: 'You have been virtuous; show me your virtue. It is a tissue of renunciations, a grand total of zeros.' Nature, for the 'Aufklärer' [thinkers of the Enlightenment], prescribes rules and restrictions; for Heinse, 'all compulsion inhibits and constricts nature.' While an inherent balance normally prevents total and overt endorsement of criminality, there is in the period a significant proportion of not unsympathetic treatment of characters who infringe the commandments of morality and the law, including even the sixth commandment. One thinks of Guelfo in Klinger's *Die Zwillinge,* Golo in Müller's *Golo und Genoveva,* and above all of Karl Moor in Schiller's *Die Räuber.*

Whatever the exact reasons—and it seems too facile to refer simply to political and social conditions, for there is no startling change in these at this time and the French Revolution is still a decade away—leading German writers quite suddenly began to feel an intolerable constriction in what previously had been acceptable. 'Freedom! Freedom!', the final cry of Goethe's Götz von Berlichingen, became the war-cry of the whole generation.

It is a vague, but extremely strong feeling and its expression is often violent. Images of a violent, often destructive nature are common, whether in the 'quieter' realm of inner feelings or in the more active and heroic context. One of the finest is that of the chariot-race in Goethe's poem 'Wandrers Sturmlied', which is associated with Pindar and with a thunderstorm. This, and not the idyllic world of Theocritus or the light-hearted one of Anacreon which had been the haunt of Gessner and Gleim, is the medium which Goethe's mood demands. The thunderstorm reference reminds us of the enthusiasm shown for Klopstock's 'Frühlingsfeier' in *Werther.* But whereas the earlier poet, for all his emotional involvement, still uses the image as a link in a definite train of thought, one suspects that Goethe's response is less specific and intellectual and that it is the inherent expressive force of the image, its fitness as an outlet for a mood rather than its metaphorical potential, which interests him. There is, in other words, a strong constructive and orderly element in Klopstock's use of it which is not necessarily present in Goethe's understanding of it.

The restoration of a certain degree of order to a landscape fundamentally disrupted by the great outburst of the 'Sturm und Drang' is a central factor in the process of Goethe's development into a 'Classicist'. That he, and Schiller and Herder, were able to ride through this storm and effect such a restoration without reverting to the more negative, restrictionist attitude of the 'Aufklärung' is a measure of the stability and flexibility of their characters. It was certainly no easy victory. Goethe, in later years, always felt a deep unease when returning, spiritually, to the landscape of the 'Sturm und Drang', particularly to *Werther,* the work in which he experienced the inherent destructiveness of that mood to its full extent.

The dangers which go together with the exhilaration of the 'Sturm und Drang' attitudes are best illustrated by the case of J. M. R. Lenz, a gifted, but unstable, and not entirely welcome disciple of Goethe's. Writing apropos of *Götz von Berlichingen,* he lays exclusive stress on the theme of freedom:

> We learn [from all this] that the active power within us does not rest, does not cease to work, to move, to rage in us until it has procured freedom all around, room in which to act . . . and even if it were a Chaos that thou [i.e. God] hadst created, desert and empty, if only freedom resided there and we could brood over it in imitation of thee until something came out of it—what a blissful, blissful, divine feeling that would be!

This kind of language, which is not more passionate, but more extravagant and vague than Goethe's, gives a clear warning light.

After we have read Lenz in this vein, we can see why not all those 'Stürmer und Dränger' who cultivated sentiment so assiduously, escaped unscathed. Lenz himself was destroyed mentally and G. A. Bürger at least materially. It is not at all surprising that the mature Goethe and Schiller looked somewhat askance at the confusions of the younger generation, even of a Hölderlin or Heinrich von Kleist. They would have called too vividly to mind the often unhealthy extravagances of days not too far gone by. Goethe, for example, had had experience at first hand of the instability of Lenz and of the embarrassing *démarches* of Lavater, who, 'seized by the freedom- and nature-spirit of the time', in the words of *Dichtung und Wahrheit,* could control neither his emotions nor his prosyletizing zeal. And there had been even more dubious figures who had enjoyed a vogue and had taken in even the great, including Goethe himself. The most famous of these was Lavater's compatriot Christoph Kaufmann. This man, who is described as having had an imposing presence, was half charlatan, half Rousseauistic prophet and gave himself out to be a kind of divine emissary, seeking out the elect. Jakob Minor describes him, in the *Allgemeine Deutsche Biographie* as travelling about 'mounted on a white horse, his jerkin open and his hair flowing freely down'—no doubt an impressive sight! Schiller, when he attacked the extravagances of others, may well have had at the back of his mind a memory of the excessive emotings of his own youthful poetry, or of his youthful friendships, which are reflected in letters such as those to Scharffenstein and Boigeol of 1776.

'The only thing the Kraftgenies [i.e. 'Stürmer und Dränger'] could not learn was restraint,' says [W. H. Bruford in his *Theatre, Drama and Audience in Goethe's Germany,* 1950]. There is irritation in this comment, and on occasion, when confronted by an example of self-indulgent adolescent iconoclasm, one is inclined to sympathize with it. 'Sturm und Drang' could be a mere manner, like any other style, and there is little that is more tiresome than conventional unconventionality. But the 'Stürmer und Dränger' usually act from positive principle, even if it is only hazily realized in terms of conscious thought. Their throwing-off of restraint was not merely a negative gesture; it was itself an expression of something positive, and the positive ideals were nearly enough and often enough realized to make the aberrations and wildnesses not too high a price to pay.

If there is a central point in the superficially rather confused mass of positive ideals and ideas of the period, it lies in the liberation of the Self. Society, theological and philosophical orthodoxy, poetic theory, conventional morality and many other orders within which men lived and which originated outside the individual, imposed on him restraints of various kinds. Previously, the impulse to individual self-expression and self-assertion had certainly existed, but had always been contained. At some stage, the discipline of an outside authority had been accepted. Now, these restraints were rejected along the whole front. This included the rejection of 'reason', as conceived by the 'Aufklärung', since in this form it is a kind of general, unvarying essence, extraneous to the individual and attempting to exert authority over him from without: a person's feelings, however inchoate, lacking in intellectual value, even 'immoral', could be seen as having more validity.

If we focus on the central position of the individual Self, we are also better able to understand the primacy of feeling as such in the scheme of things of the 'Sturm und Drang'. Lenz writes:

> Lieben, hassen, fürchten, zittern,
> Hoffen, zagen bis ins Mark,
> Kann das Leben zwar verbittern;
> Aber ohne sie wär's Quark.

He says this in a poem addressed 'to the heart', the organ for which the generation of the 'Stürmer und Dränger' had most respect. Knowledge, a thing acquired from outside, was infinitely inferior in value to the riches of the heart. 'What I know,' says Werther, 'anyone can know. My heart belongs to me alone' (letter dated 9 May in Book II). The heart is not, like the 'reason' of the 'Aufklärer', a universal norm: it embodies the principle of individuality. Thus Lenz, in his 'Versuch über das erste Prinzipium der Moral', resists the tendency of the rationalistic thinker to reduce everything to one principle. He rejects the reason as chief guide and substitutes the heart, which will produce harmony, but not uniformity, in human activity.

No one who has any acquaintance with the literature of this period will have failed to be struck by its dynamism. It is dominated by the language and imagery of power. There is something approaching a cult of 'Kraft' (power, energy), hence the common title of 'Kraftgenie' for this generation. The great hero of the 'Sturm und Drang' is the man, like Götz von Berlichingen, who has innate strength and power and leads a life of freedom in which these qualities can be expressed. This freedom for individual action explains the enthusiasm of sophisticated eighteenth-century Germans for the 'Faustrecht' (right of private justice) of the sixteenth-century knights, as for more 'primitive' ages in general (Homer, Ossian, the Patriarchs). The concept of genius is their most effective practical embodiment of the ideal. Here, some kind of fulfilment was possible, some satisfaction for the 'sweet impulse to create', as Müller calls it in the dedication of *Fausts Leben.*

The Storm and Stress generation felt almost suffocated in the atmosphere which surrounded them. They felt within themselves the 'great and warm heart' which the young Schiller says is 'all a man needs for bliss', and yet that heart could not find sufficient scope or sustenance:

> Nein, ich schreie—Vater! Retter!
> Dieses Herz will ausgefüllt
> Will gesättigt sein. Zerschmetter
> Lieber sonst dein Ebenbild.

Ironically, the 'Sturm und Drang', in which the religious urge was considerably stronger than in the 'Aufklärung', was more likely to come into collision with orthodoxy. However much he disliked the specific structure, the 'Aufklärer' would dislike even more the destruction of the order which it represented. In the form in which it appeared in the eighteenth century, however, orthodoxy offered little nourishment for the heart and little scope for the Self to feel and fulfil itself. Both the positive and the negative poles of the religious consciousness of the young Goethe, as represented by the poems 'Ganymed' and 'Prometheus' respectively, lead us back to a common origin—what in the latter is called the 'heilig glühend Herz' ('heart glowing with holy warmth'). God, for the 'Stürmer und Dränger', lived in the individual heart or conversely, the heart became God. There was an oscillation—reminiscent of the Renaissance—between the mystically oriented position of the founding father of the 'Sturm und Drang', Hamann, and that represented, for example, by Faust, especially as conceived by Müller, or by Heinse in *Ardinghello.* The latter work is set, significantly, in sixteenth-century Italy, and the hero proclaims the self-sufficiency of the individual in correspondingly bold terms: 'I believe that every man has a daimon in him which tells him what he should do . . . in every man there dwells a god and he who has sufficiently purified his inner feelings can perceive the oracles of that god without words or signs.'

'Nature' is another watchword of the movement, and here again one comes back ultimately to the inner Self as the fountain-head. The nature now admired and sought was not, as in the 'Aufklärung', the truth deducible by the reason from the general run of things, but rather those things themselves, in their own individuality, before the intellect could detach them from their roots and reduce them to a characterless common denominator. Civilization was conceived, following Rousseau, as the enemy of nature: civilization, that is, in its generalizing, intellectualizing function. Goethe, reviewing a 'Characterization of the most prominent European nations' in the *Frankfurter Gelehrte*

Anzeigen denies all true character to a 'polished' (i.e. sophisticated) nation:

> As soon as a nation becomes polished it has acquired conventional ways of thinking, acting and feeling, it has ceased to have a character . . . What, then, is the 'character' of a polished nation? What can it be, other than . . . drapery, the most one can say of which is how well it suits a nation.

Goethe seems sceptical as to the possibility of any kind of harmonious relationship between 'Politur' and the 'Naturstoff' underneath it. Later, Classicism was to attempt a reconciliation of the two. For the time being, it is the latter which needs to assert itself. The aggressive tone in which the 'Stürmer und Dränger' asserted their 'German-ness' is one reflection of this, and it was for this purpose that the ordinary people were particularly dear to them and were so affectionately portrayed by them, as, for example, in the figure of the coachman Walz in Wagner's *Die Reue nach der Tat.* All these things reflect the importance attached to natural, individual 'character', just as Goethe uses the word 'characteristic' to epitomize his new ideal of an art which, whether it originates from a primitive or a civilized source, should arise organically, and be shaped by a single, unified emotion into a 'characteristic whole'.

The shift of taste in gardens from the formal lay-out which appeals to the intellect to one which, like that at Wörlitz which so impressed Goethe, or Werther's favourite haunt (Book I, letter of 4 May), has more to offer to 'the feeling heart', is another feature of this same phenomenon. It leads to a consideration of the special relationship in which Goethe, particularly, felt himself to stand to the world of what we call inanimate nature which seems to have been more truly alive for him than sophisticated human society. Even if he asserts that Lili Schönemann carries 'Natur' with her wherever she goes, the antipathy he feels to the 'Lichter' and 'unerträgliche Gesichter' of the brilliant society into which she leads him is unmistakable. That world is clearly *not* nature for him, and it is a world in which he cannot feel free and be himself.

Among the trees and meadows, on the other hand, Goethe seems to be enjoying a personal relationship, and he is free:

> Und frische Nahrung, neues Blut
> Saug ich aus freier Welt,
> Wie ist Natur so hold und gut
> Die mich am Busen hält!

There is an intimate, indefinable relationship between the personal feelings of the individual and the surrounding natural world. The great poem 'Mailied' is the supreme expression of this, together with several key passages in *Werther,* but even within the consciously artificial context of the pastoral 'Singspiel', it emerges quite distinctly. In *Erwin und Elmire,* Valerio speaks of the way in which 'all around, a spring-like weather rises out of our full souls'.

Nature is rarely there for its own sake in 'Sturm und Drang' writing. If the nature-poetry of the time carries conviction, it is because the perspective is so completely given by the 'Ich', the Self which over and over again turns out to be the central point from which the sometimes quite complicatedly ramified growth takes its origin.

The assertion of the Self, its realization (this is the purpose for which freedom is sought), does not mean simply the reinstatement of feeling to the exclusion of the other faculties. The ideal is the complete man, which includes the mind; but the system of the 'Aufklärung', which chose the intellectual faculties as the centre and therefore subjected the individual to the general, naturally evoked a strong reaction which tended to overestimate the importance of feeling. Subconsciously at least, the 'Stürmer und Dränger' did not mean the primacy of the heart to imply mindlessness, and it could be argued that the word 'heart', as it was then understood, was a more fitting one to represent the unity and interaction of all man's spiritual faculties than was 'head'.

The writings of the new generation are not, in fact, anti-intellectual. Theoretical discussion still bulks large in their production, and art, philosophy and other such subjects continue to be discussed at a sophisticated level, if not always in a sophisticated spirit. The spirit, rather than the substance of the popular is what interests them in such things as the 'Volkslied', and this is because it represents a state in which the unity of the individual's spiritual life has not been lost. They do not want to go 'back to nature' in any literal sense. Herder disclaims any idea of reverting to 'walking on all fours' and Goethe expresses impatience with the intellectual limitation of the Pietists of Strassburg.

It would have been an inconsistency for the 'Sturm und Drang' to have substituted one-sided emphasis on a single aspect of human nature for the different one-sidedness of the 'Aufklärung', for they were imbued with a longing for wholeness and universality. 'All', and 'ganz' (whole) are keywords of the movement. The appeal of figures like Faust is at least in part a result of this impulse. Both Goethe's hero and Müller's react against restraints on their self-fulfilment in this way. 'O, sie müssen noch alle hervor, all die Götter, die in mir verstummen . . . ' says Müller's Faust, and the idea of completeness is implicit here. Goethe has a more definite vision. His Faust desires knowledge of the ultimate in cognition ('Was die Welt Im innersten zusammenhält'), and the ultimate in experience. The great ideal of the movement, the demi-god hero, is not only free, but complete and creative.

The artistic variant of this ideal, the genius, shows this in a particularly clear form. He obeys no rules that one can codify, he confines himself within no plan that one can see clearly. 'His plans,' says Goethe of the great embodiment of the 'Genie'-concept, Shakespeare, 'are in the ordinary sense, no plans at all.' Herder, in his characterization, constantly stresses Shakespeare's infinite variety and tangled disorder: he does so, indeed, to the point of distortion. An 'ocean of events,' without shore or shape, is what he sees. 'Drunkenness and disorder' seem to characterize the creator of this dramatic world. But this is not meant to be understood merely negatively. All these jumbled pieces are 'symbols towards . . . a Theodicy of God': the particular chaos is the direct result of a universal vision. Herder's description of *King Lear* as a 'father-and-children-and king-

and-fool- and beggar-and-wretchedness-*whole*', sums up the tendency of the critique.

The literary theory of the 'Sturm und Drang' cultivates a deliberate disorder. Hamann, the first theorist to write in a consistently 'Sturm und Drang' spirit, gives his *Aesthetica in Nuce* the provocative sub-title: 'A rhapsody in cabbalistic prose' and always glories in his 'non-philosophical' (i.e. non-rationalistic) approach. Philosophy, as practised by the 'Aufklärung', is for him the enemy of nature: 'your lying philosophy has swept nature aside'. The hostility to rationalism which—in spite of denials by some critics—pervades the literary theory and practice of this generation is not, therefore, a totally negative thing. The *merely* rationalistic philosophy must be destroyed, if nature is to be restored. Poetry, the direct and sensuous 'mother-tongue of the human race', in Hamann's famous phrase, has been overlaid by the language of the intellect, and needs to be set free.

There is primitivism of a kind in the 'Sturm und Drang', but it is neither negative nor truly unsophisticated. The wide range of learning deployed by Hamann, Herder and others, is sufficient evidence of this. G. A. Bürger, who even wanted to elevate 'popularity' to the status of canon for all poetry, by no means departs entirely from the concept of poetry for the educated. He advocates a poetry which is 'by educated people [literally, scholars] but not for educated people *as such*'. The ruling concept should be that of 'Volk', which is understood as meaning 'those characteristics in which approximately all, or at least the most reputable classes, agree'. The most important of the 'Stürmer und Dränger' were, indeed, harder to understand than their predecessors. Only relatively peripheral and minor figures like Schubart or Bürger himself were really 'popular', even in Bürger's sense.

The enthusiasm of this generation for folk-poetry, and the role which it plays in literary theory, especially that of Herder, is a symptom of a more wide-ranging attitude. The qualities of this literature appeal because they help the writer to throw off the restrictions on the feelings which are most important to him. Folk-poetry is precious because it is alive; because it is sensuous and immediate in expression and sets no restrictions on feeling, imagination or 'Kraft' (the inner energy which was always seeking an outlet); because it has 'character' and individuality and because it is a natural, organic growth.

Art should be the direct and complete expression of individual experience.

The idea of the norm is inconsistent with the outlook of the 'Stürmer und Dränger': his mirror reflects the complete panorama of nature, in all its diversity. As Hamann puts it in his reply to critics of the *Sokratische Denkwürdigkeiten*:

> . . . our muse is suckled at the many breasts of the fruitful, shapelessly sprawling mother [i.e., presumably, nature], a pupil of that swarm of bees in the lion's carcass, where food came forth out of the Devourer and sweetness out of the Strong One.

In the vision of the untrammelled creativity of genius, as in that of art as an organic and individual growth, the 'Sturm und Drang' expresses its fundamental requirement that the Self should be free, and able to fulfil itself. The subjectivity of some of the 'Stürmer und Dränger' is extreme. Schiller shows an insight into this when he writes to Reinwald (14 April, 1783): 'In the last analysis, it would seem that all the creations of our imagination are no more than—ourselves.'

The most important passage in Goethe's essay on the Strassburg minster is the one in which he talks about the crude artistic endeavours of the savage. He is able to find in this a particularly clear example of art that is, as he puts it, 'characteristic'; art, that is, in which a personal experience grows, or seems to grow naturally into a product which is an acceptable artistic whole ('Ganzes'), but is so without loss of individuality: 'a single feeling formed it into a characteristic whole.' Then, in a sentence which comes as close as any written in this period to putting the artistic credo of the movement in a nutshell, Goethe continues:

> When it [i.e. art] produces out of a heartfelt, unique feeling, a feeling which is independent and belongs to the one artist alone, unconcerned about, indeed ignorant of everything alien to it, then it matters not whether it is born of crude savagery or of cultured sensibility, it is whole and alive.

This 'characteristic' art (which, as we see, is not necessarily unsophisticated) is the art of the free Self, and according to Goethe it is 'the only true art'.

The negative aspects of the 'Sturm und Drang', though their effects are often spectacular, are not there for their own sake. The willingness to accept disorder and the undeniable hostility of the movement to the rationalism of the 'Aufklärung' are caused, at least in the truly important 'Stürmer und Dränger', by the fact that the order and the rationalism with which they found themselves confronted were a barrier to the complete and organic growth which they demanded. It was when social conventions had this effect that they became a stumbling-block to the young generation. Differences as such were not particularly objectionable. As far as the social structure was concerned, it would seem to have been not inequality, but the domination of the centralized system, the swallowing-up of the individual by his rank or office so that men no longer related to one another as individual men, that they hated most. 'Aufklärer' and 'Stürmer und Dränger' alike detested the *tyranny* of despots, but the former could appreciate the rational orderliness of the centralized despotic system as it had culminated in the eighteenth century, whereas the 'Stürmer und Dränger' hankered after a kind of 'family' structure, where there was authority, but also more organic, personal relationships.

Just as the individualism of outlook discussed above tends to seek integration in a greater whole, there is in the 'Sturm und Drang' concept of art a premonition of a greater form and order towards which their apparent formlessness is the first important step. Freedom does not mean the denial of form. It is 'better to produce a confused piece than a cold one', says Goethe. But there is an 'inner form', one which cannot be intellectually arrived at, but must be 'felt'. The work must take the form which the artist intuitively feels in the material and which, as it were, emerges from within it. This form is much less unnatural than the rationalistic norm of the 'Aufklärung', but it is still form; it still, as Goethe admits, has something 'untrue' about it. Complete lawlessness, the kind of freedom which is in fact licence, is no part of the 'Stürmer und Dränger's' basic desire. There is such a thing as beauty; a greater order within which the individual belongs and to whose heights he can aspire. Unless his genius and his heart are functioning without let or hindrance, he has no chance of making contact with the higher order at all. The freedom of the individual is an essential precondition, but there are gradations in the artistic feeling for beauty and hence there must be an objective measure for it, even if its inner secrets are accessible only to intuitive feeling. Goethe continues the section of 'Von deutscher Baukunst' from which we have just quoted:

> In nations and in individual men, you will see innumerable gradations. The more the soul raises itself towards a feeling of those proportions which alone are beautiful and eternal, whose chief chords can be shown but whose secrets can only be felt, and in which alone the life of the godlike genius rolls round in blissful melodies, the more this beauty penetrates into the being of a spirit so that it seems to have originated with him . . . the more deeply we bow and adore the anointed of God.

Goethe in fact employs the word 'beautiful' in two senses: that in which it is used by 'Aufklärer' like Sulzer, and that of the higher beauty of the passage just quoted. The former is restrictive and is rejected when Goethe assigns the formative ('bildend') element priority over the 'beautiful' ('schön') in art. The second sense is in harmony with the full expression of the individual and is the true end of the forming process.

That Herder did not appreciate disorder for its own sake is evident from his prize essay of 1773, 'Ursachen des gesunkenen Geschmacks bei den verschiedenen Völkern, da er geblühet'. The unpolished, natural force of genius must come first, if true taste is to develop at all. An historical development brings the crude forces into a state of 'order'; reason (though it is a more dynamic, creative reason than that of the 'Aufklärer') is a vital motive force in bringing about the desired result:

> Given that taste is nothing but order, the capacity of [man's] forces to achieve beauty, however quickly it operates and is felt, it can only operate through reason, judgement and due consideration, through which alone order comes about. Even the bee's cell (if I may compare genius with animal instinct, and perhaps they are at bottom the same), even that needs the most excellent bee-understanding ['Bienenverstand'] if it is to be brought to perfection, and the more noble a genius is, the more worthy the sphere towards which it strives and the more worthily it fulfils its striving, all the more does it need to show an apt and comprehensive reason, even in the most swift-flowing fiery river of activity and feeling.

What is envisaged here is something more complex than the straightforward, methodically calculating ratiocinative process of the 'Aufklärung': rather, a synchronization of the rational and non-rational.

The emotional energy of this generation was so comprehensive that artistic creation was possibly the only practical activity in which it could have found fulfilment. A restructuring of society, for example, would hardly have sufficed: it desired a rebirth. Its preoccupation with the inner life explains the stress it laid on receptivity as well as creativity. 'Ganymed' is a poem of great dynamism, but its central figure is blessed at least as much in receiving as in giving. He is 'umfangend umfangen' ('embracing, embraced'). The receptive and active sides of the 'Sturm und Drang' sometimes come out in dramatic dualisms (e.g. Weislingen-Adelheid in *Götz von Berlichingen* or Luise-Ferdinand in *Kabale und Liebe*), sometimes in uneasy oscillation between two poles of a single character, like Goethe's Clavigo. Ideally, they are complementary and intimately interrelated which is why, when all is said and done, the one complete work which can count as a successful epitome of the movement is *Die Leiden des jungen Werthers* which, for all its apparent limitation, manages, without loss of unity, to encompass the themes of love, religion, art, society and the human heart in general, in their full range.

We have reached the stage at which we must take up . . . the theme of idealism in German literature. For all its surface 'realism', its concern for nature as it is in the individual instance rather than in rationally conceived general terms, the 'Sturm und Drang' in fact represents the first stage in the development of that idealism of outlook which is a continuous thread throughout the literature of the 'Goethezeit'. In so far as the writing of this time has the *quality of reality* (and it does not often have it to a marked degree), it is an incidental element. The 'Sturm und Drang' is *less* close to it, indeed, than Classicism. It enjoys the feel and smell of the details of real life for their individual nature, their immediacy, their non-intellectual and sensuous quality. When, in the *Ammerkungen übers Theater,* he advocates imitation of the nature that lies around us, Lenz stresses its sensuousness and its quality of being 'gegenwärtig' (literally, 'present'). It is the distillation of a certain spirit out of reality rather than a careful, objective re-creation of it which seems to be the aim.

For a time, of course, these two lines can run parallel. In *Die Soldaten,* in particular, Lenz gives a convincing picture of the milieu in which the action takes place. But the actual world is not able to satisfy the demands of mind and spirit completely. Even in *Die Soldaten,* we find the Countess saying: 'What has life left to offer by way of appeal if our imagination does not introduce it?' And Lenz expresses elsewhere the Faustian desire to know and experience everything immediately and totally, 'all bliss in one feeling'. Reality has immediacy, but it lacks totality; at least, it did for the 'Goethezeit'.

The 'Stürmer und Dränger' had a sense of history which is much closer to the modern one than that of the 'Aufklärung'. As [R. G. Collingwood in his *The Idea of History,* 1946] points out, historians like Hume and Voltaire wrote in a polemical and anti-historical spirit, measuring the past by the standards of the eighteenth century. Writers like Herder and Möser write in conscious opposition to this trend, so that Herder's *Auch eine Philosophie der Geschichte,* the precursor of the more famous *Ideen,* is itself in large measure a polemical work. Criticism of the 'Aufklärung' is the strongest single thread. But it is more than just a criticism of Herder's own time. It is imbued with the idea, which is foreign to Montesquieu even, that each nation and age has its own character and should be understood in its own context. Against Montesquieu's 'esprit' and his attempt to reduce the tremendous mass of material to a small number of general principles, so that every age and nation should 'hang up all its belongings on three weak nails', Herder puts a sympathetic understanding of the individual character and validity of each unit in the 'Taumel aller Zeiten, Nationen und Sprachen'.

But we are still a long way from the history of truly 'objective' realism, the kind which sets out, as did Ranke, to see 'how things in fact were'. The 'Stürmer and Dränger' have more interest than the 'Aufklärer' in the factual details in themselves, because they contain life, character and individuality. But the detail is a stepping-stone to something bigger. It is not so much the actuality which interests Herder and Möser, but the spirit ('Geist') which informs it, without being comprehended by it. Möser, for example, writing of 'Faustrecht' [in] the twelfth and thirteenth centuries, says that this is the age in which 'our nation showed most feeling for honour, most physical virtue and a national greatness of its own.' The nation 'would do well to study that great period and become acquainted with the genius and the spirit which worked, not on stone and marble, but on human beings and ennobled their feelings and their strength in a way of which we can hardly have any conception today.'

To a significant extent, then, if not quite so exclusively as with the Romantics of the nineteenth century, Möser's main interest is in the 'Geist' of the past. This is even truer of Herder, who is concerned with the spirit in which men lived rather than the day-to-day details of their lives and sees human history as a unified whole, as 'the progress of God through the nations', the ultimate goal being a kind of millennium of humanity, an idea more composedly worked out in the *Ideen zu einer Philosophie der Geschichte* of his Classical phase.

But already, in the different atmosphere of the 'Sturm und Drang', Herder is thinking in strongly idealist terms. He urges his fellow men to work together towards 'a great future' and sees all noble and worthy acts, in whatever age, as seeds for 'the noblest plant of humanity'. Contemplated in this light, all these acts lose their incidental, merely actual qualities:

> All the merely corporeal and political [i.e. presumably, practical] aims involved fall away like the broken casing and dead body ['Scherb und Leichnam']; the soul, the spirit, the content relevant to humanity as a whole remains, and happy the man who has been able to drink deeply of this pure, unsulliable spring of life!

In the more specifically literary field, the great source from which authors were able, according to Herder, to imbibe the spirit of real, living, unstultified nature, was the poetry of the 'Volk'. This concept, which Herder was largely responsible for introducing into German cultural and political thought, and which later caused such unparalleled havoc when men of a very different character set out to apply it in practical life, represents a kind of ideal essence for Herder. It is not synonymous with 'nation', in a political sense, nor with 'people', in a social, class-sense. It represents a quality which the cultured man can and should strive to possess, but it is not the result of culture or education: in fact, civilization, with its increasing intellectualization of life and culture, has militated against it. It is rather like the immediacy, sensuous life and simplicity of the 'natural' character projected on to the national plane.

Herder certainly believes in the reality of a German national character, one which needs to be rediscovered and revitalized, having been overlaid with an intellectualistic pseudo-character of foreign origin. This idea of national character goes together with the wider and more important concept of 'Volk' as such, whose qualities are life, power, sensuous immediacy, individual being, rather than generalized and anonymous ratiocination—in a word, 'that rich Nature which everyone is capable of feeling', as he puts it in the Preface to Part Two of the *Volkslieder.* The prime example given in that work is Homer; elsewhere, it is Ossian: both together fulfil this function in Goethe's *Werther.* In both cases, it is the spirit which Herder is most concerned to stress.

'Volk', then, stands for a spirit which is, in the biblical sense of the word, 'lively', a way of being which is natural and organic rather than controlled by an intellectually calculated pattern, and in which individual character finds expression and fulfilment. A similar formulation would apply to life at the personal level. This is the spirit which informs the 'Sturm und Drang' call for freedom. It is a revolutionary spirit up to a point: order, when it acts in a constricting way, is anything but sacred to the 'Stürmer und Dränger'. But to use a political analogy, the revolution is more right- than left-wing in its approach to problems. The Self desires to be free to be, and to fulfil itself, and has a destructive urge to smash what prevents this. At the same time, it is more interested in the spirit, the way of being, than in the power to plan and organize life. It does have a longing for integration into a greater whole, a complementary, perhaps quasi-religious urge to surrender itself. Conscious of itself when it is constricted, it is not afraid of losing that consciousness by merging itself with something bigger, as does Goethe's Ganymede, for example. Conflict is an integral part of its experience, but resolution of conflict is a central part of its deepest desire. The impression which emerges from Herder's ideal of the Patriarch is of simple *being,* diverse, individual, but with a real streak of passivity:

> Siehe diesen Mann voll Kraft und Gefühl Gottes, aber so innig und ruhig fühlend, als hier der Saft im Baum treibt, als der Instinkt, der, tausendartig dort unter Geschöpfe verteilt, der in jedem Geschöpfe einzeln so gewaltig treibet, als dieser in ihn gesammlete, stille, gesunde Naturtrieb nur wirken kann! . . . Langes Leben,

Genuss sein selbst auf die unzergliederlichste Weise, Einteilung der Tage durch Ruhe und Ermattung, Lernen und Behalten—siehe, das war der Patriarch für sich allein. Aber was für sich allein? Der Segen Gottes durch die ganze Natur, wo war er inniger als im Bilde der Menschheit, wie es sich fortfühlt und fortbildet: im Weibe für ihn geschaffen, im Sohn seinem Bilde ähnlich, im Gottesgeschlecht, das ringsum und nach ihm die Erde fülle!

[See this man, full of power and the feeling of God, and yet whose feeling is as deeply inward and as peaceful as the sap moving through this tree, as instinct, that quiet, healthy, self-possessed natural urge which is distributed among creatures in a thousand forms and impels each single creature so powerfully, is capable of being! . . . Long life, enjoyment of himself in the most completely integrated way, division of his days through rest and exhaustion, learning and retaining—see! such was the Patriarch in himself alone. But how can I say "in himself alone"? The blessing of God through all nature, where was it deeper and warmer than in the image of mankind, as it went on feeling and developing: in the woman created for him, in the son who resembled his own image, in the divine race of beings which was to fill the earth around him and would go on doing so?]

It is not surprising that this generation was not politically revolutionary. That it produced a literary revolution, on the other hand, there can be no doubt. (pp. 119-35)

Alan Menhennet, " 'Sturm und Drang': The Struggle for Freedom," in his Order and Freedom: Literature and Society in Germany from 1720 to 1805, *Weidenfeld and Nicolson, 1973, pp. 119-35*

POETRY AND POETICS

Roy Pascal

[*In the following excerpt, taken from his book,* The German Sturm und Drang *(1953), Pascal examines the poetic theory of the Stürmer und Dränger and illuminates the differences which separate their poetry from that of earlier eighteenth-century German verse.*]

The essential principle of the new poetry of the Sturm und Drang was . . . that enunciated by Herder in his essays in *On German Character and Art:* that is, the demand for a literature that should fully express the experience, the 'living world', of the writer. Goethe put it very plainly in his review of a volume of poems by a Polish Jew. He writes that he opened the book with keen anticipation, in the hope of finding the specific feelings of a Polish Jew. But alas, here is the usual devotee of the 'fine arts', with his fashionable clothes, powdered hair, and hairless chin! Everything about his girl and his feelings is generalised and abstract. Let a poet arise, Goethe cries, who will live fully and joyously in his circle, however restricted it be, who will tell us of his experiences as they are: 'Then there will be truth in his songs, and living beauty, not iridescent soap-bubble ideals such as float about in a hundred German songs.'

The Stürmer und Dränger were the founders of modern German poetry because they insisted that poetry is not an abstract self-contained activity, but a function of living individuals in a concrete situation. In a little work published when the Sturm und Drang was over, Justus Möser grasped many of the essentials of their attitude. His *On German Language and Literature* of 1781 was an answer to Frederick the Great's condemnation of German literature as provincial and formless. Möser considers that the inadequacy of German was due to its bookish, academic character, and he holds up English as an example of good language.

> The English language, like the nation itself, is the only one that is afraid of nothing, but lays its hands on everything. . . . It is the only folk-language which is written in Europe, a provincial dialect raised to the throne, which stands upon its own lush soil, and does not, like our book-languages, wither in the barn.

He praises Lessing for having introduced provincial turns of speech into literature, and goes on to commend the Sturm und Drang for having shown Germans as they really could be (he is referring to *Götz* in particular). And with this realism he associates the subjectivism of the Sturm und Drang. This healthy grasp of reality, he says, can be acquired only by following the principles of Rousseau and Klopstock, 'one must create out of oneself and only express one's feelings'. Even if this subjectivism leads to extravagance, it is the only way to grasp the external world as it really is, the only way to true poetry.

Of course, the unity in the natural and social circumstances of a nation gives a unity to its culture; but at the same time there is continual change in a national cultural tradition, corresponding to the changes in outer life and social constitution. Cultural affinities can be sought according to the feeling of any particular generation, and forms will necessarily develop and change. The affinity in spirit that Herder found between Greek and Shakespearian tragedy was possible, he asserted, only through the total dissimilarity of their form, since each form won its validity from its relationship to the total experience of the poet. And this principle must be valid within all national cultures and languages. Thus the Sturm und Drang did not even discuss any supposedly indigenous characteristics of Germanic art, except in the sense that, in order to be true art, it must reflect the inner nature of the poet and the external nature and society in which he is placed. But though this insight was of profound truth, and of profound significance in freeing them from outworn formulas of art, it left them, as creative artists, with a great dilemma. How was subjectivism, inner feeling, to be associated with realism, as Möser claimed? How were imagination and true experience to be combined? The Klopstockian surrender to feeling often led to 'tirades', to an etherealism and unrealism that irritated them; the realism of a Diderot, Mercier, or Lessing, or Nicolai, was without wings, without poetry. Not all the Stürmer und Dränger saw this problem; but some did, and their efforts to solve it again sound a peculiarly modern note.

Eighteenth-century poetry shows many signs of discontent with the prevailing temper of sobriety and rationalism. Gray and Mason in their 'Pindaric' odes, Smart in the *Hymn to David,* find pleasure in sublime feelings and obscure, grandiose expressions. The growing taste for the world of chivalry, for Tasso and Spenser, was largely based on a delight in the sublime, exotic, fantastic, and finds an extreme form in Warton's discovery of the charm of ruins and decay, in the 'romanticism' of Strawberry Hill. But this taste was recognised to be only 'poetical', and did not constitute a challenge to the normal values of intercourse and life. Hurd could define the poet's world as 'marvellous and extraordinary', a frank admission that poetry is a separate activity of the mind, dissociated from the truths that we gain from experience. The first book of *La nouvelle Héloise* constituted a serious challenge to this equanimity, for the lonely reveries of St.-Preux are weighed against the wise conclusions of common sense and sober social experience; but even Rousseau's ultimate purpose was to show that the exalted imagination was the product of a diseased temperament in a harsh society. Klopstock transplanted the taste for sublime feelings into Germany, but he and his disciples were conscious that they were often giving way to expressions and feelings that were not true, neither as they were related to the external world nor to themselves.

Despite the debt that Herder owed Klopstock, he always felt uneasy about the idealising trend of the latter's poetry. He corrected his betrothed's adoration of the 'sweetness and grace' of Klopstock, the attraction of which he admitted, because it transported the reader beyond the human sphere into unearthly regions. Goethe expressed the same unease, but more drastically, referring particularly to the bardic odes of the Klopstockians: 'Noise and shouts instead of pathos . . . Tinsel and that's all. . . . The most unbearable thing about a picture is untruth.' Bürger wrote to Boie, criticising a bombastic Klopstockian ode of Schönborn: 'In poetry, in spite of all divine sublimity, everything must be tangible and visual; if not, it is no poetry for this world, but perhaps for a different world which, however, does not exist.' And the same strain is heard in the mature Schiller, for while he deplores the moral effects of Klopstock's 'everlasting straining of the emotions', he also points out its aesthetic failings—'he always leads us out of life . . . without refreshing the mind with the tranquil presence of an object'.

But poetry for the Stürmer und Dränger was a realm neither of pastime nor of sublime unearthliness. It expressed their deepest subjective need, their deepest truth. They therefore protest continually against an attitude to poetry which would segregate feeling and imagination in a separate compartment of the mind. They felt that Homer and Shakespeare and folksong expressed fundamental values, the nature of life in its deepest sense and highest dignity; the truth of poetry was something infinitely more necessary to man than the indifferent conclusions and wisdom of common sense and reason. Were they merely to revel in feeling and imagination at odd times, in their leisure hours, but at other times behave 'seriously' like the rest? This was what Nicolai suggested in his *Joys of Werther the Man;* and this they repudiated.

Shakespeare was one of their guides, for in his plays they found true man and true history. But Shakespeare could also be a danger, for his power of illusion, of which Herder wrote, might be understood as the power to transport into a world of imagination attractive just because it was different from the sober world of real experience. Herder clearly recognised this attraction. He wrote to Merck: 'In my frenzy for Shakespeare I had long ago settled down specially to [translate] the scenes where he opens up his new world of ghosts and witches and fairies.' It was this side of Shakespeare that particularly appealed to Bürger, who thought it a special merit that the witches of Macbeth belong 'to fancy and feeling, not reason and wit'. The poets of the Sturm und Drang all succumb at times to the fascination of the unreal, the fantastic, for its own sake; in this respect they anticipate the extravagance and morbidity of the later German romanticism that Wordsworth found so distasteful. Bürger's ballad, *Lenore,* which had so great a success, is an exercise in the macabre. He told his friends that it would scarify like the ghost in *Hamlet,* and recommended them to read it at twilight in a ghostly room, with a skull on the table. In *Fausts Leben,* Maler Müller takes over much of the terrifying trappings of the puppet-play, the ludicrously awesome antics of the devils. The stage directions of the first scene are: 'Midnight. Tempest. Ruins of a decaying Gothic church, overgrown with debris' (*sic*!). The last setting is a cross-roads before a dark forest, with a bell tolling midnight in the distance. Ghosts and premonitions play their part in many plays, which borrow from Shakespeare the thrill of the supernatural, of storms and the blackness of night. Goethe has a gruesome scene in *Götz,* the sitting of the secret court, the 'Vehme', at which Adelheid is condemned with solemn and mysterious rites. The last act of *Clavigo* uses to the full the tension of a midnight setting, with torches and cloaked men. In Klinger's *Otto* there is a wild mixture of all such macabre elements, and it may be considered to be the first of the lugubrious extravaganzas which were later such popular German exports.

It must be emphasised, however, that settings of this kind, and the use of the supernatural, are rare in the works of the Stürmer und Dränger. It is one of the extraordinary achievements of Herder in his essay on Shakespeare that he treats the supernatural elements of the plots, the witches in *Macbeth* and the ghost in *Hamlet,* in the same way as he does the blasted heath and the midnight battlements, not as 'pleasures of the imagination', but as constituents of the real human scene. His, and Goethe's, love for folk-ballads did not lead them to revel in hallucinations, like Bürger, to whose *Lenore* Herder took up a somewhat critical attitude. The folk-ballads Goethe collected, and his own compositions, are essentially, in this period, songs of human feeling and human relationships, like the *König in Thule;* ballads like *Erlkönig* and *Der Zauberlehrling* belong to later periods—though, of course, for all their evocation of supernatural beings and weird or macabre situa-

Maler Müller depicted as a faun in a drawing by Genelli.

tions these too are securely anchored in real experience. Goethe's works are the living evidence of his Strassburg habit of utilising nocturnal expeditions to lonely spots, churches and graveyards, for the purpose of hardening himself against 'the attacks of imagination'.

But even when fantastic means are employed in the works of the Stürmer und Dränger, they are rarely used arbitrarily for the mere purpose of thrilling the reader or audience with a feeling of mystery and horror. In Maler Müller's *Fausts Leben* it is necessary that scenes of devilry and exorcism should have a mysterious, abnormal setting. The ghost that the hero of Klinger's *Die Zwillinge* sees is justified as an emanation of a diseased and guilty mind. The masked figures of *Clavigo,* the midnight burial, are not arbitrarily introduced and belong legitimately to the theme. It is perhaps most surprising that, in Goethe's *Urfaust,* the product of his Sturm und Drang, there are scarcely any of the supernatural elements that belong to the traditional story. The Earth-Spirit is an emanation of nature, and speaks as 'nature'. The Mephistopheles we see is the most human devil imaginable, an evil and subtle, malicious and sarcastic fellow, whose magic does not go further than helping Faust to conjure up wine, and providing him with treasures as gifts for Gretchen. If he can help Faust to break into prison, he has no power over Gretchen. When we consider Goethe's task in face of the legend and puppet-play, it is clear that he denudes the story almost entirely of its supernatural, fearsome aspects, and concentrates all his attention on the human tragedy. It was a later Goethe who showed Faust's exorcism of the poodle, the Witch's Kitchen, the Walpurgis Night—and, of course, not in order to bemuse or scarify, but in order to show the barrenness of Mephistopheles' world and its inherent incapacity to satisfy Faust's yearnings.

Of all the Stürmer und Dränger, Lenz comes closest in this respect to the mystifications of German romanticism. In his plays there is a plentiful admixture of fanciful elements, castles and arbours, moonshine and twilight, particularly in *Der Engländer* and *Henriette von Waldeck.* In those works which directly express his own spiritual torment he often yields to the temptation to find solace in unreality; nothing in these two plays is in perspective, nothing clear, but all vague, blurred. But he had a bad conscience about the 'capricious aberrations of fancy' of such plays. The works of which Lenz was most proud, *Der Hofmeister* and *Die Soldaten,* are full of realistic observation of persons from his own environment—he told Herder emphatically that the latter play was 'true history, in the strictest sense of the word'. When Lenz succumbed to the charm of imaginations which seemed to compensate the harshness of the real world, he was aware that he was failing in his poetic mission, and betraying the very spirit of poetry. The imagination, he writes in his *Observations on the Theatre,* must serve to reveal the characteristic individuality of scenes and characters, not the ideals of the poet which are real only to him.

From Shakespeare the Stürmer und Dränger received the confirmation of their own experience that feelings and imagination acquire their substance from actual situations, and can be expressed in poetry only through the evocation of this sensuous environment and source. There is an individuality and particularity in the settings of their works, their lyric poems, their novels, and their plays, which is new in German literature. Goethe's poems nearly all reflect the very scene in which his feelings were formed, the nocturnal ride and sunlit departure in *Willkommen und Abschied,* the lake, sky, mountains, and ripening grapes in *Auf dem See;* or, in a transposed sense, the noble ruins and fruitful earth of *Wandrer,* the actual movement and sound of the spinning wheel in Gretchen's *Meine Ruh ist hin.* As he was to say, much later, his poems reflect 'the particular character of some state and circumstance'. The Lotte of *Werther* comes to life in the midst of the tasks of the home, and Werther himself is understandable only in relation to the thronging world around him, the countryside, the peasants, Lotte's home. In the normal sentimental novel, like Gellert's *Schwedische Gräfin,* the characters flit across the vaguest backcloth, and even in the more precise *Fräulein von Sternheim* of Frau von la Roche, the court and country mansion and 'Scottish lead-mines' are at best background, just sufficient to indicate the moral struggles and stresses of the heroine. With *Werther,* however, the setting is not mere background, it enters into the substance of the hero's soul, it constitutes his experience. Lenz achieved the same substantial quality in his *Liebe auf dem Lande,* and, not quite so successfully, in his tales, *Zerbin* and *Der Waldbruder.* Müller's idylls *Das Nusskernen* and *Die Schafschur* owe their charm to the reality of the peasants and activities described, as do the earlier parts of Jung-Stilling's autobiography, when he does not seek to do more than describe the circumstances of his early life and development.

In comedy the realistic tradition was established, since even Gottsched had asserted that comedy is the representation of the 'vices' of the middle class. But while neoclassical comedy had sought to confine the setting to one scene, a drawing-room, or as in Lessing's *Minna von Barnhelm* an inn, Lenz allows himself in his comedies much greater freedom of action. The plot of *Der Hofmeister* moves through many milieux, the tutor's home, the mansion of his employers, a student's lodgings, a village school-house, a hovel, etc., so that we see the characters in the actual environment which interprets, and partly determines, their ideas and feelings. But this is one of the very few Sturm und Drang works which can rank as comedies. Their satire is usually interwoven with a sentimental theme, and 'comedies' like *Die Soldaten* are better described as plays of common life. In this play, the characters again move through different milieux, and as tragedy begins to envelop Marie, we are thrown with bewildering rapidity through the scenes of her downfall, which as they change interpret her abandonment. One of the chief weaknesses of plays like *Der neue Menoza* or *Die Freunde machen den Philosophen* arises from Lenz's failure to give any precision or real relevance to the situations in which he places his characters.

The Sturm und Drang polemic against French tragedy had its roots in a protest against the flatness of characters assembled against an indifferent or unchanging background. They resented this background in so far as it always reflected the environment of polite company; but even more because it deprived the characters of the substantiality that individual settings give. This is the burden of their frequent criticism of the sentimental novel. 'What is Grandison, the abstract figure of a dream, compared with a partridge that stands there before us?' [Lenz, *Anmerkungen über Theater*]. Thus an essential characteristic of the literature of the Sturm und Drang is its realism, the concrete substantiality of its figures, scenes, and language; a realism which, as Auerbach [in his *Mimesis,* 1946] has pointed out, surpasses anything before it or since in German literature. Yet this realism is not the opposite of imagination, of poetry, as is the realism of Diderot's or Lessing's plays. It is imaginative; it is poetic. The fusion of imaginative experience and reality is one of the great achievements of the Sturm und Drang, through which it is the spiritual parent of both the romanticism and the realism of the nineteenth century.

Often enough the Stürmer und Dränger fail. The characters of Klinger are rootless and abstract, their language rhetorical. Leisewitz's and Schiller's characters too often slip into impersonal discourses. Some of Goethe's smaller works, like *Stella* or *Erwin und Elmire,* lack the substantiality of a real background and existence. At times the world of fancy attracts them as more seductive, more beautiful, than the real world. Merck wrote in sympathetic criticism of Herder:

> Ewig wirst du Träume jagen, fangen,
> Dürstend an dem Kelch der Liebe hangen,
> Dich äfft Wiederhall der Sympathie,
> Doch als Zephyr küsset sie Dich nie.

> You will for ever hunt and catch dreams, hang thirsting on the cup of love; the echo of sympathy will mock you, yet never kiss you like a zephyr.

Goethe also felt the comfort of dreams.

> Als ich noch ein Knabe war,
> Sperrte man mich ein.
> Und so sass ich manches Jahr
> Ueber mir allein,
> Wie im Mutterlieb.
>
> Doch du warst mein Zeitvertreib,
> Goldne Phantasie;
> Und ich ward ein warmer Held,
> Wie der Prinz Pipi,
> Und durchzog die Welt.
>
> When I was a lad
> They'd lock me in my room,
> And I sat for many a year
> Close within my lair,
> As within the womb.
>
> Yet thou wert my pastime,
> Golden fantasy;
> I became an ardent knight
> Like the Prince Pipi,
> Journeying far and wide.

So Goethe could contrast, in the poem *An Belinden,* the richness of his dream-world with the vexations of polite amusements. But far more characteristic of him and Herder is the effort to overcome the seductions of dreams, to grapple with reality, and find self-fulfilment in experience and activity. 'Away, thou dream, golden as thou art; here also is love and life.' In *Werther* Goethe describes the tragedy of a young man who 'loses himself in dreams', as he wrote. But before the tragic turning-point in Werther's life, when he succumbs to his dreams, his imagination leads him to appreciate in a new intensity the reality of simple and vital forms of existence, nature, the children and the peasants, Lotte in her home.

With the Stürmer und Dränger, despite their aberrations, we find the imagination restored to the function which they recognised it had in Homer or Shakespeare: not a means of escaping from reality, of beautifying reality, but a means of penetrating to its innermost truth and meaning. Merck was always prompt to criticise them when they surrendered to unreal fancies. Of Maler Müller's *Situation aus Fausts Leben* he wrote vexedly that few writers 'feel the detail, the character in every work of nature with sufficient respect', and that Müller, like other young dramatists [of the Sturm und Drang], had taken his material 'from obscure dreams of poetic desire, and not from the market of life'. He often corrected Goethe's tendencies in this direction, and Goethe reports him as telling him:

> Your endeavour, your unswerving tendency, is to give reality a poetic form; the others seek to turn the so-called poetic, the imaginative, into something real, and that produces nothing but stupid stuff.

So the highest praise he gives to *Faust* is that it is 'stolen with the greatest faithfulness from nature'.

This phrase has a totally different meaning from the traditional 'imitation of nature'. It is not a question of a mechanical observation of reality, but an imaginative grasp of reality, which synthesises in an intense experience the complex and successive factors of reality, and presents it in a specific poetic form. Lenz discusses this poetical process in his *Observations on the Theatre.* He begins with the subjective purpose of poetry, the feeling of 'an accretion to our existence', which results from poetry. Our experiences of normal life are successive: the poet has to turn these successive experiences into something instantaneous, into a single, all-embracing experience. 'We would like to penetrate with one glance into the innermost nature of all beings, to absorb with one feeling all the joy that is in nature and combine it with ourselves.' Analysis and synthesis go hand in hand: 'It is our constant endeavour to unwrap all our collected ideas and see right through them, and make them visual and present.' The supreme achievement of the artist is 'to grasp firmly all our knowledge until it has become visual ["anschaulich"]'. This operation is neither mechanical nor arbitrary—'the true poet does not combine in his imagination according to his own whim . . . He takes a standpoint and then he has to combine accordingly.'

It is not surprising, in view of the difficulty of the problem, that we find little theoretical discussion of the relation between imagination and reality. The Sturm und Drang restoration of the imagination to its vital function is largely an intuitive assertion, expressed in occasional criticism and in their poetical works. Poetry for them must be impregnated with reality, the poet must be, in Herder's phrase, 'the interpreter of nature', but his tools and methods have their own characteristics and speak to the imagination. Words are not objective descriptions of a material or intellectual reality, as the Aufklärung thought, but statements of a relationship between man and nature; they are 'energetic', active, interpreting vital impulses in man and a process in nature. Thus, in place of the flat prosaism or conventional rhetoric of contemporary poetry, they love the earthy idiom and plastic phrase of the peasantry—not because it is more 'realistic' in the simple sense, but because of its evocative, sensuous power. They grasp the function of rhythmic speech, anticipating Coleridge's criticism of Wordsworth's view that the language of poetry is that of 'ordinary men'. Through rhythmic speech, 'the dark stream of melody', through image, the poet recaptures the total significance of an experience, and transmits it to the 'inner sense' of the hearer. Herder's emphasis on song, on actual music, in his essay on folksong indicates how fully he recognised that poetry, while arising from a concrete situation and interpreting in sensuous imagery the peculiarity of this experience, speaks in specific imaginative terms. The imagination is the instrument which collects all the elements of experience, sensuous, emotive, and intellectual, and condenses them into a unity which sets the whole man tingling.

Willey [in *Nineteenth Century Studies,* 1949] has pointed out how dependent Coleridge's conception of the imagination was on his metaphysics. With Hamann and Lavater we find indeed the imaginative impulse justified as a link with a supersensual reality. For the chief Stürmer und Dränger, as for Wordsworth, the imagination places us 'in the presence of truth', of deepest reality. But their conception of reality is far less mystical, less metaphysical than that of the later Wordsworth or Coleridge. Imagination gives insight into reality because it issues from the ultimate identity of the poet, of man in general, with the observed world. It does not point, for Herder and Goethe, to a transcendental realm of reality opposed to that of experiential 'appearance', it is not evidence of a dualism of Reason and Understanding such as Coleridge and the German Romantics postulated. It establishes the correspondence of inner and outer life. It is the expression of that mysterious and fundamental sympathy of man with nature, to which Goethe and Wordsworth often give the name love, and which is the kernel of Herder's and Goethe's pantheism. In the framework of this general pantheistic interpretation of the universe they can justify the most mysterious function of imagination, what Goethe calls 'anticipation', and which may variously be described as intuition, surmise, foreboding. It is the specific poetic quality to anticipate reality, to grasp it imaginatively. Goethe commented in later life on the truth of his *Götz von Berlichingen,* in which he 'anticipated' the knowledge of human relations which he did not as yet 'possess'. When his friend Zelter wrote to him, in 1831, to say that near Naples he had identified the place and person of the poem *Wandrer,* Goethe answered that he had written the poem long before he had visited Italy—'but that is the advantage of the poet that he can anticipate and value in imagination what those who seek reality must doubly love and delight in, when they find it in real existence'. The young Goethe was not distinguished from his contemporaries by a wider experience or knowledge, but by the intense vividness with which his imagination turned experience into general symbols.

Mysterious as are the workings of imagination, it is given no mystical character by the Stürmer und Dränger. It is for them the key to real experience, as anticipation or as synthesis. Quite logically it guided Herder to his new understanding of history, of man in the varied circumstances of the past, as it did Goethe in his study of nature, in his scientific work. When Goethe wrote that 'a fairy-tale too has its truth' he was asserting the fundamental identity of intuitive and experiential knowledge which he associates in the 'Prologue on the Stage' in *Faust:*

> I had nothing, yet profusion,
> The urge for truth and joy in delusion.

Imagination is thus, for the Stürmer und Dränger, the counterpart in the individual of the creative force in the universe, operative in all essential human energies as in the process of nature. It is, in Herder's word, an 'inward sense', which synthesises all the outward senses, which grasps what is meaningful in the world of daily experience and behaviour, and presents it 'through a burning-glass'. Poetic imagination thus has more truth than the most punctilious description in the naturalistic manner. The language of poetry is therefore not that of everyday life, its truth is not tested by its rationality; it is necessarily imaged, rhythmic, for it has to evoke a truth which is both on the surface, sense-given, and a truth under the surface, which links the poet and the world outside him; it links inner knowledge with that given by experience. Imagination is not a substitute for reality, but penetration of reality in its fullest form. Wordsworth's words are not far from the belief of the Sturm und Drang:

> This spiritual Love acts not nor can exist
> Without Imagination, which, in truth,
> Is but another name for absolute power
> And clearest insight, amplitude of mind,
> And Reason in her most exalted mood.
> [*The Prelude*]

In relating poetry to inward and outward experience, the Stürmer und Dränger necessarily placed the whole problem of poetic form in a new context. When Herder wrote in the Ossian essay of the 'dire urgency' of the content of poetry, and when he asserted that he was not concerned to 'excuse or slander' Shakespeare, he was implicitly condemning as frivolous every purely formalistic approach to poetry. Thus, in all the Stürmer und Dränger, we find continual indignation with critics who carp at their works in the name of general rules and abstract critical principles. Hamann led the way in deriding such pedants, who ignore all the effect of art in order to chatter about indifferent formalities. Goethe, in his customary manner, wrote farcical little poems on such 'connoisseurs'. In one of these he describes how he offers a guest the best fare he can provide, and how, after eating his fill, the ungrateful fellow goes next door and complains to his neighbour that the soup might have been tastier, the roast browner, the wine more mature. And Goethe concludes: 'Devil and damnation! Strike him dead, the dog, it's a reviewer!' [*Ein Gleichnis*]. 'You don't look a gift-horse in the mouth!' [*Der Welt Lohn*]. Equally derisive is his poem *The Connoisseur.* He takes the connoisseur to meet the girl he loves, but the expert does not notice her 'fresh, young, warm life', he merely comments that she is too thin and has too many freckles. When they go to a picture gallery, the connoisseur can only make pedantic objections while Goethe is transported by the 'ardour of the human spirit'.

Herder had defined literary criticism as something quite different. The task of the critics is not to judge all art by a dogmatic system of rules, to make the poet their servant; it is their function to serve the poet and the public. His insight into poetry had brought him to an historical and relativistic conception of form, and his criticism of dogmatic pedantry arose from his conviction that the critic must seek for 'the concrete qualities and modes of the beautiful in history'. The critic must be able to empty himself of preconceived dogmatic notions, must be able, as he defined his own purpose in the Shakespeare essay, 'to expound, to feel how the poet is'. 'Feel yourself into everything', he charged the historian, and this is also the principle of his literary criticism. The traditional relationship of critic and poet is reversed; the critic, instead of claiming to be the instructor of the poet, becomes his interpreter. His task is, not to show where the poet's work corresponds to his own taste, but to reveal the spirit and purpose of the poet, to show the inner structure of the poem and the experience in it, to make it easier of access to others, perhaps too to make the poet more conscious of his own purpose and intention. Klopstock indeed sent Herder a striking tribute, telling him that Herder was the only critic of whose comments he took note, 'because you are a critic through your own very strong feeling', that is, not a critic by theory and rules.

Goethe wrote some verses which assert that nature and art can be appreciated only if the observer, the critic, himself feels within himself the creative power that drives to form:

> Was frommt die glühende Natur
> An deinem Busen dir?
> Was hilft dich das Gebildete
> Die Kunst rings um dich her?
> Wenn liebevolle Schöpfungskraft
> Nicht deine Seele füllt,
> Und in den Fingerspitzen dir
> Nicht wieder bilden wird?

> What avails your heart the glow of nature, what use to you is art, the shapely forms all round you, if loving creative power does not fill your soul, and if it does not drive your finger-tips to mould and form?

These expressions, 'creative power', 'mould and form', are extremely characteristic of the Sturm und Drang, and were so often repeated that they called down the ridicule of rationalists like Lichtenberg. The conception of form that is involved is totally different from the traditional one of writers of poetics. Just as the lyrics of Goethe or Lenz burst the framework of the traditional lyric, so the Stürmer und Dränger felt uneasy even about such relatively clear terms as tragedy or comedy, and prefer other names. Herder would prefer to call Shakespeare's tragedies 'plays', 'dramas', 'histories'. Goethe called *Götz* 'a dramatised history', *Stella* a 'play'. Lenz uses the looser term 'Trauerspiel' for tragedy, and says that his *Soldaten,* which was published as a 'comedy', should properly have been called a 'play' ['Schauspiel']. Bürger attacked the whole division of plays into comedy and tragedy and suggested that all should be called 'Schauspiele'. Indeterminacy and mixtures of form are characteristic of the works of the Sturm und Drang, and indicate their unwillingness to admit any absolute validity to established forms. Form they felt to be merely a function of a peculiar experience and personality; or, in the widest sense, of a particular historical and social situation. Therefore it must vary accordingly.

To some extent, this new insight into the character of form encouraged the Stürmer und Dränger to disregard the need for communicability, and some of their works are deliberately rank in form and obscure in diction—Nicolai and Lichtenberg charged them repeatedly with wilful esotericism. But such extravagances, which may be found even in Goethe, are only incidental to their main purpose, the discovery of a principle of form which would be applicable to all the great literature of the past, and serve as well as a guiding principle for their own times. Gerstenberg had already drawn their attention to statements in Shakespeare which associate nature and art:

> This is an art
> Which does mend nature—change it rather; but

The art itself is nature.

It was along these lines that their thought ran—not without disturbance from the Rousseauistic derogation of art in favour of nature.

Herder's Shakespeare essay is essentially an exposition of the dependence of dramatic form on the changing nature of society and man. He had attributed the peculiarity of Homeric song to the circumstances in which it was sung and the nature of the Greek language. He had compared the unity of folksongs and the form of Klopstock's odes with that of a plant, an animal, a natural landscape. Goethe defined the unity of the Gothic structure of the Strassburg Minster in similar terms. In contrast to Herder's criticism of 'the artificial, gloomy, and monstrous vaults of Gothic', to which he prefers 'the free Greek temple, with its lovely, regular colonnade', Goethe discovered the harmony of Gothic. 'All these masses', he wrote in face of the minster, 'were necessary. . . . As in works of everlasting nature, down to the least fibre, all is form, all a purpose in a whole.' This form is as justifiable as that of the Greek temple; and Goethe continues:

> In man there is a formative nature, which actively asserts itself as soon as his existence is secured. As soon as he is free of anxiety and fear, the demigod, active in his repose, stretches out his hand for matter into which he may breathe his spirit.

Goethe is not comparing the formative power of the artist with that of the gardener who beautifies nature, but with that of nature herself, as evident in all her parts. In the same way, in the poem *Connoisseur and Artist,* he compares artistic creation with physical procreation:

> O rathet! Helft mir!
> Dass ich mich vollende!
> Wo ist die Urquell der Natur,
> Daraus ich schöpfend
> Himmel fühl' und Leben
> In die Fingerspitzen hervor!
> Dass ich, mit Göttersinn
> Und Menschenhand,
> Vermög' zu bilden,
> Was bey meinem Weibe
> Ich animalisch kann und muss!
>
> O counsel! help me!
> That I fulfil myself!
> Where is nature's primal source,
> Drawing at which I may
> Feel heaven and life
> Right into my fingertips!
> That I, with sense divine,
> And a human hand,
> May have power to form,
> What, with my wife,
> In the flesh I can and must!

On his third visit to the Strassburg Minster, when returning from his first visit to Switzerland, Goethe was again overpowered by the feeling of the kinship between the formative process of nature and art, and humorously admitted that it seemed to be his fate 'to stammer poetically about the proportions of masses'. Again he apostrophises the minster:

> Thou art one and living, begotten and evolved, not pieced together and patched. Before thee, as before the foam of the rushing fall of the mighty Rhine, as before the radiant crown of the eternal snow mountains, as in the sight of the serene expanse of the lake, and, gray Gotthard, of thy cloud-rocks and desolate valleys: here, as before every great thought of Creation, there stirs in the soul whatever of creative power it possesses. It stammers over in poetry, in scrawling lines it hurls on to paper adoration to the Creator, eternal life, all-embracing, inextinguishable feeling of what is and was and is to come.

But this creative feeling is not chaotic; it has within it the principle of organic form. As he climbs the steps of the tower with Lenz he reflects:

> The creative power in the artist is this swelling, soaring feeling of proportions, of masses, and what belongs to them, and only through these can an independent work, like other creatures, spring into being through its individual germinal force.

Each work of art is then, for Goethe, individual; individual in its source and setting, individual in its form. The task of the artist is to feel the specific individuality of each experience, and to establish its inner structure and proportion, as it is grasped in the 'inward world', the imagination. He wrote to F. H. Jacobi:

> The beginning and end of all writing is the reproduction of the world around me, through the inward world which lays hold of everything, combines it, re-creates it, and kneads it, and reproduces it in its own form and manner—that remains for ever a mystery, God be praised, and one I shall not reveal to the onlookers and gossips.

Compelling experience, the impact of the outer world, goes hand in hand with the inward effort to grasp and shape it.

> The good spirit has revealed to me the source of my being. It came to me as I thought over Pindar's επικατειν δυναδθαι. When you stand boldly in the chariot, and four fresh horses rear up wild and distracted at the reins, and you guide their strength, whip in the one who's kicked over the traces, force the other to stop rearing, and you gallop and guide them and turn, whip them, and stop, and then dash off again until all sixteen feet keep time as they bear you to your goal. That is mastery, επικατειν, virtuosity. But I have only just sauntered around, only taken a peep here and there. Nowhere really set to. To lay hold, get a firm grasp, that's the essence of mastery.

Bürger wrote something apparently similar, yet characteristically different . To write poetically one must have, he says, 'courage and strength enough to feel, to lay hold of a thing, to hold it, to hurl it and toss it into the air'. Here the arbitrary character of his own poetry is evident, he can play with the 'thing'. For Goethe 'the world around him', the 'wild horses', have to be mastered, but they have to be mastered in a form which they themselves impose. Mastery is not merely an assertion of will, but a product of understanding, of self-identification and self-fusing with the outer stimulus or experience.

Like Herder, then, Goethe repudiates the notion of absolute form, but at the same time is aware that what distinguishes the artist is not only emotive and imaginative power, but also feeling for form, for proportion, for measure. In unconscious refutation of his own earlier interpretation of Shakespeare's plays as a 'raree-show', in 1775 he distinguishes the artist's feeling for form from the formless impressions of normal men, for whom 'the world is a raree-show, whose illusions flit past and disappear, leaving shallow and isolated impressions on the soul'. His comments on Mercier's *Du théâtre,* which were published in 1776 as an appendix to Wagner's translation, are extremely interesting in this connection. Mercier's work was a scathing attack on the formalistic neo-classical theatre, and a defence of the modern realistic social drama. Goethe sympathised with the theme of the book, but found that though Mercier asserted that style is the expression of the individuality of an author, the real problem of form was not really dealt with. After recommending the book he goes on:

> It is time that people stopped talking about the form of dramatic plays, their length or shortness, their unities, beginning, middle and end, and all the rest of it. And our author goes pretty direct to the question of content, which as a matter of fact seemed to follow of itself.
>
> Yet there is a form, distinct from that other sort of form as much as the inner sense from the outer, which cannot be caught in one's hands, and must be felt. Our head must survey what another head can hold, our heart must feel what can fill another's. . . . If this feeling of inner form, which embraces all forms in itself, were more widespread, we should have fewer distorted products of the mind. One would not get the idea of turning every tragic event into a drama, or breaking up every novel into a play! I wish some wit would parody this doubly vexatious error and turn, say, Aesop's fable of the wolf and the lamb into a five act tragedy.
>
> All form, even the most deeply felt, has some untruth about it, but it is once for all the glass through which we focus the holy beams of dispersed nature into a fiery ray on to the heart of man. But the glass! Those who have not got it won't get it by hunting, it is like the mysterious philosopher's stone. . . .
>
> And if you do really want to write for the stage, be sure to study the stage, the effect of paint in the distance, of the lights, make-up, glazed canvas, and tinsel, leave nature in her own place, and take careful thought to contrive nothing but what can be carried out on the boards, between laths, cardboard and canvas, through puppets, before children.

These remarks indicate a much deeper understanding of the problem of art than his earlier statements, in which Goethe had emphasised above all the need to subject oneself to experience and master it. He recognises that art must have a significant content, but is here mainly concerned with the 'mystery' of form, the process by which art is produced. Form he still calls something 'untrue', unnatural, but it is the means by which nature, experience, can be focused in the poet's mind as in a burning-glass, and communicated to the hearts of men. The artificiality of this medium is stressed as he enumerates the properties of the theatre; it is the problem of the artist to work through these trivial, unnatural means, to accept these conditions, as a means to present nature in its essential quality:

> So in this narrow wooden mansion,
> Pace out the circle of creation.

The rest of these jottings are concerned mainly with pictorial art, and circle round the same theme. Art, Goethe writes, cannot come into being in the frivolous salons of the great, nor in frigid academic institutions. 'Poetry dwells only where dwell intimacy, need, inward feeling.' The artist must love, and describe the world as he loves it. Goethe cuts across the great controversy of his times over the relative merits of Rembrandt, Raphael, and Rubens, by asserting that in this all are alike, all are true artists. That Rembrandt confined himself to a particular group of articles, 'old household gear and strange rags', does not limit his power, but 'leads him into the mysteries through which the thing presents itself to him as it is'. 'Start from domestic concerns, and then spread yourself, if you can, over the whole world.' These great artists are not to be criticised for their one-sidedness; it is the peculiar character of their minds that 'magically' transforms their themes into 'true human sympathy and participation'. The harmonies of nature are everywhere, and they are the inspiration of the artist; but he must reproduce them in his art according to the character of his material and his individuality.

> The artist does not only feel the influences [of nature], he penetrates to their very source. The world lies before him as before its Creator, who in the moment when he rejoices over his creation enjoys also the harmonies by which he has produced it and in which it consists. Therefore do not think you can so quickly understand what it means to say: feeling is harmony and vice versa. And it is this that weaves through the soul of the artist, that in him presses on to the most understood expression, without having gone through the intellect. . . . The eye of the artist sees these harmonies everywhere. He may enter the workshop of a cobbler, or a stable, he may gaze upon the face of his beloved, his boots or antique statues, he sees everywhere the holy vibrations and subtle tones, by which nature links all objects. At every step a magic world is revealed to him.

These comments of Goethe are the profoundest commentary on poetry to be found in the Sturm und Drang, and at the same time they indicate Goethe's emergence from his Sturm und Drang. Here once again the unity of nature and art is asserted, and yet in a way which distinguishes them sharply. Art is the reproduction of nature, whose energy can be recognised more easily in the work of art 'because of the simple and strong effect'; but the emphasis is not so much on the chaotic creative force of nature as on the unity, the 'wondrous harmonies' of nature. The poet is 'the interpreter of nature', as Herder called Shakespeare, but in a medium totally different from nature, with its own specific conditions. The environment and inner feeling, impact from outside and energy from within, are necessary conditions of the structure of aesthetic experience and poetical production, but the main problem of art appears as the problem of form, the process by which experience is turned into art—the very problem which Herder avowedly shirks at the end of his Shakespeare essay.

Goethe's little essay was written when he was composing *Faust,* and it seems to be the very definition of this play. Its form is a development of the popular folk-play, built therefore, as Herder demanded, on the myths and 'theatrical illusion' of a popular tradition. It is an historical play, yet interpreted in a way specific to Goethe, so that we forget its historicism and think of it essentially in terms of its present, immediate relevance. It starts 'from domestic concerns', from the inward and outer knowledge which was the stuff of the author's experience, and is universal, as Goethe said of Rembrandt's paintings. It struck all its contemporary readers, Merck, Boie, and the rest, as being overwhelmingly true and real, yet it is poetic, unrealistic in form. Its language is full of the idiom and variety of natural speech, yet it is unnatural, poetic, rhythmical. Its construction is like that of a ballad, springing from scene to scene, without the detail and complex transitions of real events. It is, indeed, nature focused in a burning-glass; nature intensified, nature transformed: art.

It can be seen that, for the Stürmer und Dränger, poetry had a dynamic function of which the eighteenth century before them had little or no inkling. Their predecessors pursued poetry as a reputable conventional activity, and justified it in the main either as an intellectual recreation, or as a pleasant means of moral instruction. For the fashionable poets of the 1760s, like Gleim, Ramler, Uz, Georg Jacobi, poetry was a graceful game. They chose their themes without reference to any significant personal experience, and they even assured their readers that, if they wrote about wine and women, their sentiments were not to be taken seriously. Their poetry was appreciated as an agreeable relaxation, and they themselves judged poetry on purely formal grounds, according to its smoothness of metre, neatness, its conventional imagery, its 'propriety' of diction. In folksong men like Ramler saw only vulgarity of theme and clumsiness of form; and in Batteux' formalism they found the highest statement of poetics. At times the Stürmer und Dränger confessed to a liking for these graceful nothings. Herder sometimes praised Ramler's poems, and was always a friend of Gleim; Goethe and Lenz composed little poems, even operetta-like texts, in the anacreontic vein. But they were aware that this sort of poetry was at best a minor matter, an agreeable pastime. When they were writing seriously about poetry they tended to explode in gutsy ridicule of all this frivolity, as Lenz did in *Pandämonium Germanicum,* and Wagner in *Prometheus, Deukalion und seine Rezensenten.*

The formalist poets were in no sense aesthetes; that is, they did not consider art to be an end in itself, and in fact, when in serious mood, they fell back on a moralism little different from that of Goeze or Nicolai. But they tried to find an aesthetic justification for the pleasures of art. Sulzer, their magistral spokesman, asserts that nature has fashioned men so that they find aesthetic delight in pleasant scenes, and that men are thus intended to be educated to gentle and humane sentiments. Art has the duty of presenting this pleasant side of nature and of human relationships; its principle is not imitation of nature but beautification of it. Thus, in his extremely pedantic review of the fine arts, Sulzer indicates the formal rules for presenting the agreeable sides of nature and love, etc. Both Merck and Goethe exploded at this conception of art, which completely ignores all the subjective necessity of art, as it distorts the character of life. Merck wrote:

> If only Herr Sulzer were himself a practising artist, his system of art would be not gloomy zealotry, but serene faith, that never reviles.

And Goethe:

> If a man has no sensuous experience of art, better leave it alone. Why should he occupy himself with it? Because it is the fashion? Let him bear in mind that all this theory bars the way to real enjoyment, and that a more harmful inanity has not been invented.

The great mass of criticism in Germany was religious or moralistic in character. Klopstock asserted that the highest poetry was religious in character, and that all poetry must have a moral purpose; the most serious criticism of his *Messias* came from writers, like Lavater, who considered his work primarily as a religious document. Mendelssohn condemned Rousseau's *La nouvelle Héloise* for its immorality. Nicolai, the leader of a great group of Aufklärung critics, wrote very frankly to Herder: 'A certain part of poetry, the imagination, in so far as it does not directly improve or impair the intellectual forces and society, is off my path.' Lessing was far more sensitive towards poetical expression than most of his contemporaries, and sought to define in *Laokoon* and the *Hamburgische Dramaturgie* the specific technique of artistic forms. But his own works, and his evaluation of others, were largely shaped by moral considerations, even though his outlook was much broader, more humanitarian, than that of his rigid, dogmatic, utilitarian contemporaries. It is not an accident that his plays all bear a definite moral lesson. In the best of them there is evident a delight in human personality and tensions which goes beyond his theory, but there is no doubt that he, like all his associates, would have subscribed to the view of the Hamburg zealot, Goeze, who wrote in indignant horror at Goethe's *Stella:* 'I thought that the stage had the aim of showing virtue to be charming, and vice abominable and disastrous.'

The publication of Goethe's *Werther* marshalled the forces of the moralists of all camps. Goeze led with a review that condemned the book as being a defence of suicide, and called for its confiscation. His criticism was supported by quotations from the Bible to prove how immoral and irreligious Goethe's work was. He carried the attack further in his review of *Stella,* where he repudiates the distinction drawn by another critic between poetic and moral ethics. The *Reichs-Postreuter,* which attacked sentimental novels because 'they make young folk incapable of becoming useful members of society', called Goethe's *Erwin und Elmire* a 'damnable' play because it ridiculed religion, and dismissed *Werther* as 'a school for suicides', *Stella* as 'a school of abduction and polygamy'. Nicolai put the crown on this type of criticism by giving *Werther* a new and moral ending. Others 'rescued' *Stella* by adding a sixth act in which the hero is punished for his bigamous frivolity.

Some of the fellow-travellers of the Sturm und Drang shared this attitude, though not in quite so simple a form. Klopstock had asserted that poetry, in order to achieve 'moral beauty', must 'set the soul in motion' and represent the passions in their truth, but he and his followers believed that only noble, moral themes were susceptible of poetic treatment. Lavater and F. L. Stolberg succumbed to the charm of Goethe's poetry and personality, and championed poetry as the expression of feeling. But they convinced themselves of the ultimate coincidence of feeling with moral goodness and the Christian religion. Bit by bit, as they discovered the implications of the new poetry, they turned from it. Stolberg's ecstatic essay, *On Fullness of the Heart,* which has been defined by Ermatinger as a paraphrase of Goethe's 'Feeling is All', is on the contrary a moralising distortion of Goethe's view, for Stolberg insists here that feeling is and must be noble and good, and must lead to 'admiration of the good, horror of the bad'; feeling for nature and the Christian religion are identified. Such men did not share the narrow-minded moralism of clergymen like Goeze and deny to Goethe outright any poetical worth. But they were puzzled and worried, like Fritz Jacobi, by the contradiction between his immoralism and his poetical achievement, and tried to suggest some way in which poetry could be brought back to the fold.

Die Leiden
des
jungen Werthers.
Erster Theil.
Leipzig,
in der Weygandschen Buchhandlung.
1774.

Title page of Die Leiden des jungen Werthers.

To this doubt the Stürmer und Dränger answered with the assertion of the necessity of truth in the representation of nature and passion, irrespective of its goodness. Heyne, Herder's good friend at the university of Göttingen, was alarmed at Herder's 'obstinate determination to ban morals outright from the fine arts'. Heinse anticipated the criticism of the moralists when he wrote, in the preface to his translation of Petronius:

> Poets, painters, and novelists have their own morality. It would be very inappropriate to demand of them that they should bring to birth nothing but Grandisons, Madonnas and crucifixes and Messiads. The morality of the fine arts shows men as they are and always were, in outstanding actions, for the pleasure, instruction, and admonition of all men. A genius is therefore allowed to describe and paint everything that has happened or may happen. He is permitted to relate and paint in the most expressive words the fairest and ugliest actions and thoughts of men. He is in the wrong only when he praises the most abominable vices as good.

Thus Heinse answered all the criticism of *Werther* by saying 'it is just the description of the sorrows of young Werther'. In an essay on the 'Goethe-school', *Über das Göthisiren,* a writer asserts:

> The ideal of poetry is the impassioned man. Its matter is action, and the sum of the energies that produce the action is the measure of its perfection. Othello, the throttler of the chastest woman that ever lay in the arms of a man, is poetically more perfect than the whole of that divine Grandison.

The Stürmer und Dränger do not, however, deny a moral function to poetry. Some of their works are indeed centred on social or moral problems, as we have seen. Schiller's essay *On the Stage as a Moral Institution* of 1784 considers the drama entirely as a supplement to the pulpit and the legal code. But in general their conception of nature and man is infinitely more complex than that of their contemporaries, just as they make many more demands on social life. Poetry is for them not a means by which human feelings and relations are arranged into a pattern corresponding to the demands of the dominant religion and morality, but it is the expression of things ignored and combated by the moralists, it asserts new values, and by its actual being it moulds personality anew. It is not a means of arguing about the known, but the discovery of the unknown, and with this the re-creation of personality.

At the bottom of their poetical activity and theory lies the fundamental discovery of the supreme joy of aesthetic experience. This is the theme of Herder's essays on folksong and Shakespeare, in which he finds rhapsodic expression for the tumultuous rapture that poetry brings, for 'those obscure, ineffable impressions that flood our soul'. This aesthetic experience is not separate from the moral part of man; through it one becomes enlarged, fuller, richer in total personality. So Goethe could write that, on reading Shakespeare, 'I felt my existence enlarged by an infinity.' In almost the same words Lenz wrote that poetry brings 'an accretion of our being'. This joyous response to poetry is not due to any moral theme or intention of the poet's, but simply to his poetic activity, to the character of poetry. This is the meaning and justification of poetry, its essential function.

How closely related this new response to poetry—or this new awareness of its permanent character—was to the narrowness and deprivations of German social life is made clear by K. P. Moritz's account of his reading of Shakespeare and *Werther.* A sensitive and intelligent child, he was oppressed by the poverty of his parents, the humiliations he had to suffer at school and at the hands of his betters, the narrowness of the pietistic beliefs and practices of his relatives and patrons. At school he discovered Shakespeare.

> After and as he had read Shakespeare, he was no longer an ordinary and everyday man—before very long his spirit worked its way up out of its external oppressive circumstances, out of the derision and contempt to which he was succumbing. . . . Through Shakespeare he was led through the world of human passions—the narrow circle of his ideal being was enlarged—he was no longer so isolated and insignificant as to be lost in the crowd—for in reading Shakespeare he had experienced the feelings of thousands.

And further:

> After reading Werther, as with Shakespeare, he felt himself elevated above all his circumstances; the intensified feeling of his isolated existence, which brought him to consider himself a being in whom heaven and earth are mirrored, gave him pride in his humanity, and he felt himself no longer to be the insignificant outcast he thought he was in the eyes of other men.

It is an interesting comment on the comparative poetic quality of Klinger's *Die Zwillinge* that, after seeing this play, which fascinated and harrowed him, Moritz describes how conscious it made him of his own humiliations and spiritual suffering, and how it intensified his melancholia, his 'horror of himself'.

If we compare this psychological analysis of the effect of poetry with Herder's rhapsodic utterances on folksong, we can see how closely linked, for the Stürmer und Dränger, are the two aspects of the function of poetry—the inner expansion of being that it brings, and the communion it establishes between men, between men and nature. Herder attributed the power of primitive poetry to the community of life of primitive peoples, whose poetry expresses the common basis of their experience and, binding them imaginatively together, is a 'spur' to activity. He demanded for his own time a poetry which would inspire modern men to joyous existence in the same way as the 'songs of war, heroes, and ancestors' inspired ancient peoples. This is the theme of Goethe's criticism of the *Love Songs of a Polish Jew* in 1772, where he links the true poet's capacity for deep and 'hallowed' feeling with that for friendly, gay, social intercourse in his own circle. Lenz even proposes a new test for poetry. In his little essay on *Götz von Berlichingen* he writes that a literary work must be judged not by its formal qualities, but by its power to stir the reader to a new way of life:

> So, qui bono? what effect do the products of all the thousands of French geniuses have on our mind, our heart, our whole being? Heaven forfend that I should be unjust. We take a nice, blissful, sweet feeling home with us, as if we had emptied a bottle of champagne.—But that is all, too. Sleep on it, and it is all blotted out. Where is the living impression, which expresses itself afterwards in convictions, deeds, and actions, the Promethean spark which has stolen so imperceptibly into our inmost soul and inspires our whole life—unless we let it die away through complete lethargy. . . . And now give your opinion on *Götz.* I would like to shout to the whole German public: All of you, first behave like Götz, first learn how to think, feel, act, and then, if you like the change, give your opinion on *Götz.*

This function of poetry, to change men inwardly and establish new relationships between men, was defined most clearly by Herder in his essay on folksong. But how could it be fulfilled in a time when there was no German nation and no national purpose, when the social classes were separated by occupation, custom, even language, and when the literary class was divorced from practical life? This was a problem the Stürmer und Dränger could not solve. Thus Herder's Ossian essay closes with a panegyric of Klopstock's odes, poems which lack any tangible social function and are, in his words, 'meditations of the human heart with God, with itself, with the whole of nature'. Though the Stürmer und Dränger could see that the reinvigoration of man through poetry was at the same time the re-establishment of man's communal nature, for their own times they could only assert the subjective side of this function, the psychological restoration that poetry brings. The community that poetry strengthens is a spiritual, not an actual community: it is made up of a few like-minded individuals, not a whole society.

But even with this restriction—a restriction imposed on them by the character of their times—the Stürmer und Dränger give poetic production a significant function in personal life. Poetry must well up from inner experience, imaginative or actual; it is not the result of intellectual intention, shaped by a moral or formal purpose. But it also reacts back upon the poet, it is a deep and necessary function in his moral existence. Goethe, the greatest poet of the Sturm und Drang, insisted on this inward necessity of his imaginative writing. When he met Kestner's reproaches with his 'Werther must must be', or when he got furious with critics who said he should not have written in the way he did, he was not only asserting that something within him drove him to write, but also that his poetry was the means to an inner 'purification' ['Läuterung'], a word he often uses in 1775 and afterwards. He describes himself to a correspondent he had not met:

> ever living in himself, striving and working, seeking to express according to his measure the innocent feelings of youth in small poems, the pungent spice of life in many sorts of dramas, the figures of his friends, his circumstances, and his beloved house-gear in chalk on gray paper—and asking neither to right nor to left, what people think of what he is doing; for as he works he always rises a step higher, because he does not want to jump after an ideal, but let his feelings develop into capacities, through struggle and play.

His attentiveness to his feelings, to his inner tensions and joys, was not morbid, but a means to self-development.

An early review of Goethe's expresses in a more general form the same appreciation of the function of art. It was written before *Götz* had appeared or *Werther* was thought of, and has some obvious immaturities of expression, but it is highly characteristic. Goethe was expostulating against the conception of nature as a kindly mother, who leads man only to agreeable experiences, and against the conception of art as the reproduction of the pleasant aspects of nature:

> What we see of nature is force that swallows up force, nothing present, all transitory, a thousand seeds crushed, every moment a thousand born, great and significant, manifold to infinity; beautiful and ugly, good and evil, everything existing side by side with equal right. And art is its very counterpart, it arises from the endeavour of the individual to preserve himself against the destructive force of the whole. Animals themselves define themselves, preserve themselves by their artistic instinct; man in all his circumstances affirms himself against nature, to avoid its thousand-fold evils, and to enjoy his measure of good; until he manages in the end to enclose the circulation of all his true and invented wants as far as is possible in a palace, to lock up all dispersed beauty and happiness in his glass walls, where he can become more and more mild, can substitute the joys of the soul for the joys of the body; and thus his energies, no longer braced as in the natural world to resist vexations, may be resolved into virtue, benevolence, and sentiment.

The ideal of resistance to the 'pains and evils' of life interprets Götz rather than Werther or Faust, and Goethe was in other jottings to emphasise the need for unreserved experience of the process of nature; the ideal of 'virtue, benevolence, and sentiment' was to be replaced by a much more complex conception of man's purpose. But this early definition of the intimate relation between nature and art, and of the profound psychological function of art as a mental restorative, anticipates his later development and thoughts.

In his autobiography Goethe found the classic formulation for this function of poetry as he himself experienced it. Reflecting on the imperious inner necessity which drove him to write *Werther,* and the effect the composition of this work had on him, he writes:

> By this work I rescued myself more than by any other from a stormy element, upon which I had been tossed to and fro in the most violent manner, through my own and others' fault, through accident and deliberate choice, through intention and over-haste, through obstinacy and acquiescence. I felt, as after a general confession, cheerful and free again, and entitled to a new life. My old specific had this time done its work excellently.

This 'specific' was his innate instinct to turn reality into poetry, to objectivise his own stresses in poetical, imaginative form. And in this passage he not only claims as a function of poetry the declenching of almost unbearable tensions, but, because of this, its function as releasing the poet for 'new life'—leading him out of 'murk and mist' into clarity, out of tortured feeling into serenity, out of isolation into society, out of introspection into activity. The theme of self-education, which is ever-present in Goethe's later works, in *Iphigenie, Tasso, Wilhelm Meister,* in *Faust* itself, continues on an ever-widening scale the earliest experience of self-education through art, and Goethe distinguishes himself from all earlier thinkers through his appreciation of the educative function of beauty.

Whether considering poetry from the point of view of the reader or the poet, then, the Stürmer und Dränger introduce totally new conceptions of its function. They see it as a subjective necessity, but one that in enriching the personality links it up with the community; they see it as arising from internal stresses, as subjectively determined, and yet as liberating the personality from encumbering experience, and freeing it for living. It mirrors the experience of the writer, and reproduces the world 'according to his measure', and yet at the same time gives the truth of existence. It is seen, not as pastime or morals or philosophy,

An excerpt from Goethe's *Rede Zum Shakespears Tag* (1771):

When I had finished the first play of Shakespeare's . . . I felt most intensely my existence enlarged by an infinity. . . . I hesitated not for a second to renounce the regular theatre. The unity of place seemed as oppressive as a prison, the unities of action and time burdensome fetters on our imagination. I leapt into the open air, and felt at last that I had hands and feet. . . . Shakespeare's theatre is a lovely raree-show, in which the history of the world moves past our eyes on the invisible thread of time. His plots are, to speak in conventional style, no plots, but his plays all turn round the mysterious point, which as yet no philosopher has seen and defined, at which the essential characteristic of our ego, the alleged freedom of our will, comes into collision with the necessary motion of the Whole. . . . Most of these gentlemen [Shakespeare's critics] niggle at his characters. And I cry Nature! Nature! nothing so completely Nature as Shakespeare's characters.

Johann Wolfgang von Goethe, Rede Zum Shakespears Tag, *quoted in* The German Sturm und Drang *by Roy Pascal, 1953.*

but as a dynamic and necessary function of the totality of man, arising out of vital experience, and modulating his being, preparing him for life and work. (pp. 267-99)

Roy Pascal, "The Revolution in Poetics," in his The German "Sturm und Drang," *1953. Reprint by Manchester University Press, 1967, pp. 233-99.*

Werner Kohlschmidt

[*In the following excerpt, taken from his* A History of German Literature: 1760-1805, *Kohlschmidt explores the Sturm und Drang fascination with Shakespeare and old Nordic and Celtic poetry and analyses the poetry produced by the Gottingen Grove, an offshoot of the Sturm und Drang centered around the University of Gottingen.*]

The area of literary evaluation [of the Sturm und Drang] was affected by the philosophical insights into language and history, as advanced by Hamann and Herder. There was indeed need of examples and proof for the early ages so full of strength and sensuousness of perception and expression, for the decisive function of imagination and originality characterised by its wealth and energy. Quite certainly they could not be found in classical antiquity as the Enlightenment understood it, much less in French Classicism, not to mention Voltaire. And least of all in the German tradition from Opitz to Gottsched. The mature Lessing had already advanced beyond these models and he was joined by Johann Elias Schlegel and the Baron von Gerstenberg, who were hardly aware of their being precursors of the 'Storm and Stress'. For these a new world opened up at the very height of the Enlightenment: the world of Shakespeare and old Nordic and Celtic poetry of early times, which had first been introduced, in fact, by Klopstock. It was in these areas that one looked, first tentatively and then with increasing determination, for values that equalled the achievements of the Ancients. The discovery of an indigenous old Germanic tradition began in the midst of the Rationalistic Age. Firstly with Gottsched, who drew no conclusions from it, then Bodmer, whose rediscovery, above all, of the *Minnesang* coincided with his interest in English imaginative poetry. Klopstock's bardic period, too, fitted in programmatically, so to speak. The immediacy and the inventiveness of that past age still did not allow a distinction to be drawn between old Germanic and old Celtic, not even when Macpherson appeared on the scene in England and his allegedly Gaelic bard Ossian became fashionable. By the time the forgery—which was characterised by an enormously subtle understanding for current tastes—was recognised as such in England, it had crossed to the Continent and continued its triumphal march *via* Herder and subsequently Goethe's *Werther,* even reaching Napoleon. Its very impetus was increased through the effect exerted by another English book, namely Thomas Percy's *Reliques of Ancient English Poetry* (1765). The result in Germany was not only interest in that vague mythology extending from Klopstock to Macpherson's translation, but also the concrete discovery of those values of expression and feeling which had lain untapped in old folk poetry in general, above all in the *Volkslied* and *Volksballade.* It now unleashed a lyrical effusion that at last seemed to do justice to the cult of creative genius after a long and sterile period of imitating the Ancients. It led *via* Herder and Bürger to Goethe's Odes and early ballad poetry, and at the beginning of the following century was still to fascinate the Romantics and invite them to continue in the same strain.

Hand in hand with all this went the development of the new Shakespeare image, the historical significance of which has been demonstrated in Gundolf's very fine book. Folk poetry was for the most part anonymous. Even the names that were known could scarcely be grasped in their historical context, or, as in the case of Ossian, it was the myth of the figure that remained in man's consciousness. The need for a comprehensible incarnation of poetic genius remained unappeased. In Shakespeare, however, (Shakespearean criticism was still somewhat dormant), there was felt to be at one's disposal a positive countersymbol to classical antiquity, and this symbol was then subsequently taken in the 'Storm and Stress' to represent the epitome of Nordic genius, a model of originality.

Both these very themes—Ossian and Shakespeare—Herder had brought to Goethe's attention in Strassburg, and, what is more, he had given them memorable treatment in two essays in 'dithyrambic prose' for Gerstenberg's *Schleswiger Literaturbriefe.* But just then these *Literaturbriefe* ceased publication and so Herder resolutely combined his 'rhapsodies' with Goethe's *Von deutscher Baukunst* and Möser's *Vorrede zur Osnabrückischen Geschichte* to form that manifesto of the 'Storm and Stress' concept of art and history, which bore the title *Von deutscher Art und Kunst.* An inorganically added piece on Gothic architecture was merely a rehash from the Italian. Herder's contributions were loaded with ingenious antirationalistic dynamite. Nowhere else did he keep closer to Hamann's style than in his *Shakespeare* essay. The mode of expression employed in these 'Rhapsodies' in which he hammered away at point after point, arbitrarily selected, suppressing what was non-essential in the sentence, conjuring forth the main points in larger than life-size terms with untiring interjections and exclamations, his choice of vocabulary and word-formations containing unprecedented nuances—this mode of expression achieved here an extraordinary suggestiveness. This was true of all parts of speech, but perhaps especially so in the case of the dynamic verbal language. Here it was possible to 'pour forth sensations to the full', 'stammer', 'hear and perceive with an inner ear', 'feel with an immediacy and precision', but also to 'over-refine'. 'Fortreißen', 'fortfühlen', 'einfühlen', 'eindichten', 'zusammendichten' ['carry away by emotion', 'absorbed by empathy', 'enclose in poetic form', 'condense by means of poetry'] are certainly introduced here as verbs, not to mention the innumerable participles with the same level of meaning and importance which appear as dynamic epithets. In the case of the latter, namely the adjectival formations, the combination and accumulation of words created the same effect:

> Ossian so kurz, stark, männlich, abgebrochen . . .
>
> [Ossian so short, strong, manly, abrupt . . .]

Or again, in relation to the Skaldic poems:

> Der Geist, der sie erfüllet, die rohe, einfältige, aber große, zaubermäßige, feierliche Art . . .
>
> [The spirit which fills them, the rough, simple but mighty, magical, solemn nature . . .]

It is felt possible to trace *ab ovo,* so to speak, a dionysiac joy in language everywhere. Everything expresses movement, a groping and listening for new possibilities of expression—everything confidently original. The noun compositions and compounds are no less fascinating, where the vocabulary of energy and immediacy, of ('inner') feeling, of rapture and bliss, but also that of nuance and intermediate shades of response can attain full expression, in the sense in which it was said of Klopstock that he produced 'fine nuances, often intermediate shades of feeling' together with the full flood of emotional outpourings in his writings. And highly characteristic was the devaluation of the word 'beautiful', which Herder denigrated almost to the level of a synonym for 'artificial', 'regular', 'useful' by connecting it with the classical *bon goût.*

The *Auszug aus einem Briefwechsel über Ossian und die Lieder alter Völker* was based right from the outset on a passionate bias in favour of originality. The German translation of Macpherson by the Jesuit Michael Denis (whose *nom de guerre* was the 'bard Sined') had been completed in hexameters. For the 'Storm and Stress', however, that was a *crimen laesae majestatis* against the original, the allegedly genuine bard Ossian:

> Ihnen wollte ich nur in Erinnerung bringen, daß Ossians Gedichte Lieder, Lieder des Volks, Lieder eines ungebildeten sinnlichen Volks sind . . .
>
> [I merely wanted to remind you that Ossian's poems are songs, folksongs, songs of an uncultured, sensuous people . . .]

Songs, however, are something other than a fine flowing epic. One has to feel one's way into their style, otherwise one destroys them. Characteristically Herder leapt directly to Shakespeare to furnish proof for this assertion and showed by example from the latter's songs the senselessness of translating them into epic verse. The empathic translator has to be 'flexible', Herder argued, he must have 'an inner feeling for the sensuous qualities in form, sound, tone, melody, all those dark and ineffable impressions which flood our soul when we hear the poem sung'. The translator is then seen as a trustee of original genius, in this instance the genius of the folksong, which has 'the miraculous power of being the rapture, the mainspring, the eternal hereditary and joyful song of the people'. But what is folksong? (Including Ossian's Skaldic poetry?) Herder heaps up a pile of epithets to define it: wild, lively, unhindered, sensuous, strong, dynamic, hence full of 'leaps and sallies', and hence alogical too in the scholastic sense. The decisive thing is the ear as an organ for rhythm, tone, melody:

> Nichts ist stärker und ewiger und schneller und feiner als die Gewohnheit des Ohrs!
>
> [Nothing is more powerful and lasting, quicker and finer than the habit of listening!]

All this found verification in the old English and old Scandinavian ballads which Herder knew of from Percy's and other collections, quite apart from Ossian and Shakespeare too. And it was also put to the test in Herder's own translations, excellently so, for example, in that of the old Scottish ballad *Edward, Edward.* But Herder did not romantically narrow the limits of his subject to the past. He took just as seriously as original compositions in this genre pieces that were composed in his own day, such as Ewald von Kleist's *Lied eines Lappländers* or Goethe's *Sah ein Knab ein Röslein stehn.* In the selection for his own collection of folksongs (which later bore the title *Stimmen der Völker in Liedern* (*Voices of the Nations in Song*)) he was to claim the same liberty by placing on one and the same plane something that had originated as an 'art-song' with a folksong from the past. All this, from the *Edda* and Skaldic poetry in the broadest sense, to medieval ballads, the old Lutheran Hymn, Shakespeare and contemporary poetry (in the style of the folksong), i.e. even Gleim's ballads, and Ewald von Kleist's and Goethe's verse, was 'folksong' in Herder's eyes. The standard was provided by the original sensuality, in word and tone (and dance), which distinguished such poems from all artificiality and abstraction. Here too Herder took up again a position of absolute opposition to 'bourgeois' Classicism and Rationality. The folksong was in no way a phenomenon of importance for him as another example of antiquarian greatness to be held against classical antiquity, but as an instance of human genius, which Herder saw as stemming, like the poems of wild, savage peoples, from 'the immediate present, from the direct inspiration of the senses and the imagination'.

His picture of Shakespeare, which was to help testify to the concept of originality as already presented in the *Ossian* essay, was in the same vein. Except that, as already indicated, the semi- or total anonymity of the creative genius, as was the case with the songs of the people, could now give way to the glorification of the individual historical artist as the 'second creator' (in Shaftesbury's sense) and the secularised *creator spiritus* of Christianity. In fact, Herder was at least as concerned with the poet's greatness as a 'dramatic God' and with his promethean originality as with the work itself, however penetratingly, indeed powerfully, this was interpreted and characterised. Since Shakespeare was more easily understood than the nebulous figure of Ossian, he became the representative of artistic originality in general—moreover, right from the start, in apocalyptic, larger-than-life dimensions:

> Wenn bei einem Manne mir jenes ungeheuere Bild einfällt: hoch auf einem Felsengipfel sitzend! zu seinen Füßen Sturm, Ungewitter und Brausen des Meers, aber sein Haupt in den Strahlen des Himmels! so ist's bei Shakespeare!—Nur freilich auch mit dem Zusatz, wie unten am tiefsten Fuße seines Felsenthrones Haufen murmeln, die ihn—erklären, retten, verdammen, entschuldigen, anbeten, verleumden, übersetzen und lästern!—und die Er alle nicht höret!
>
> [If ever one man appears to me in a mental image sitting high up on a rocky pinacle, at his feet the storm and tempest and raging of the sea, his

> head however high in the radiant firmament, then that is Shakespeare. Except, of course, with this addition, that down below at the very bottom step of his rocky throne there are crowds murmuring, who set out to explain him, save him, curse him, excuse him, idolise him, deny him, translate and slander him—and all of whom HE does not hear!]

This was the standard of greatness the 'Storm and Stress' applied to the artist, a supernatural, mythical dimension. Corresponding to this was the annihilation of the 'gaggle' of defamers, commentators, but also the apologists and uncritical admirers. The 'Storm and Stress' furnished a similar example in Lenz's grotesque comedy. *Pandaemonium Germanicum,* but with Goethe in place of Shakespeare on the throne of genius. Shakespeare's 'defenders' also included Johann Elias Schlegel, Lessing and Gerstenberg. They had already transformed the timorous *apologia* for a Shakespeare who at least did not vanish completely in the face of classical antiquity, into an assertion that he was of a different species altogether; now fields of characterisation and realism were allotted the 'modern' poet over against the idealising Greeks. If we recall all this, we become aware of the total, vehement passion manifested in this antithesis between greatness and insignificance. That antithesis remained the dominant theme.

It was, in fact, given support through a masterly application of the empathic and comparing historical sense. Naturally Shakespeare had to be compared with the Greeks and measured against them. And everything that Herder in his philosophy of language and history, in biblical exegesis and revaluation of the concept of education, had so far achieved in versatility of comparisons and wealth of suggestive ideas, he resolutely staked on this favourite theme of his. Here, in accordance with the basic principle, the individuality of the Greeks must be preserved just as much as that of Shakespeare:

> In Griechenland entstand das Drama, wie es in Norden nicht entstehen konnte . . . In Norden ist's also nicht und darf nicht sein, was es in Griechenland gewesen.
>
> [In Greece drama rose as it could not arise in the North . . . In the North, therefore, it is not and cannot be, what it has been in Greece.]

The whole Aristotelian doctrine of the three Unities was hereby historically relativised and robbed of its timelessness. By the same token, however, the possibility of making its non-observance by Shakespeare an argument for his non-conformity to rules, as classicistic poetics made out, lost its validity. But on the other hand, what French Classicism itself represented and achieved, Herder argued, became anachronistic and also unhistorical and led to the destruction of originality. Herder accordingly called French Classicism 'the puppet of the Greek Theatre'. That held good in his eyes right from Corneille to Voltaire. Their art was but second- or third-hand:

> Spanish-senecasche Helden! galante Helden, abenteuerlichtapfere, großmütige, verliebte, grausame Helden, also dramatische Fiktionen, die außer dem Theater Narren Heißen würden . . .
>
> [Spanish-Seneca-type heroes; gallant heroes, adventurous, brave, magnanimous, amorous, cruel heroes and for that very reason dramatic inventions whom one would call fools outside of the theatre.]

But what was its counterpart? The answer lay in self-invented drama, which for the author of the *Reisejournal* could be based only on its own historical reality. The direct consequence was the call for the one genius who 'would produce from his material a dramatic creation as natural, great and original as the Greeks did from theirs'. That person was Shakespeare, who had to be understood, of course, in the light of his own historicity. But this historicity was no longer that of the Greeks in their simplicity, but of the Modern writers in their complexity; in drama, for example, it was no longer the epoch of the Greek chorus, but of historical plays and puppet plays. And from these, his own times he moulded 'social classes and individuals, peoples and modes of speech, king and fools, fools and king into one glorious Whole'. The form it took was that of joint experience of what was encountered. The creative genius became the 'interpreter of nature in all its tongues':

> Mir ist, wenn ich ihn lese, Theater, Akteur, Kulisse verschwunden! Lauter einzelne im Sturm der Zeiten wehende Blätter aus dem Buch der Begebenheiten, der Vorsehung der Welt!—einzelne Gepräge der Völker, Stände, Seelen!
>
> [Whenever I read him, the theatre, actors and scenery vanish from my mind's eye. Just individual leaves blowing about in the storm of the times, leaves from the Book of Events, of World Prvidence—individual impressions of peoples, conditions, souls!]

It is unmistakable how Herder the subjectivist placed everything on the Individual and his Rights. Individuality demanded, if one wished to experience it, total identification. For Herder *Ossian* had already found its inimitable scene of comparability: 'on the foundering ship' and the stormy sea at night. And likewise now with Shakespeare there was the matter of identification of poet, landscape and work. And whether it was the fate of Lear or Othello and Macbeth, there was always the sense of involvement in the play, which was made up into 'a living Whole comprised of father-and-children-king-and-fools-and-beggar-and-misery', involvement in the drama which 'transports one's heart, all one's emotions, one's whole soul from beginning to end'. It was not Goethe nor Schelling, but Herder who repeatedly used the word *Weltseele* ('universal spirit') long before them as a symbol of this 'totality' in Shakespeare. And it was also no accident that the philosophical godfather of the 'Storm and Stress', 'that giant God of Spinoza: Pan! Universum!' was likewise invoked as the God of Shakespeare's world. This hallmarked the creative writing of the modern dramatic genius. The limitations of Time and Place disappeared. The dream that could transcend everything, ruled supreme. The concluding note was the sad reflection that 'even this great creator of history and the universal spirit was more and more receding into the past'. It was the inevitable consequence of Herder's way of proceeding by which the timelessness was transformed into something belonging to a point in history. But he tore himself away from the temptation to be melancholy by appealing to Goethe's drama which had just been completed, namely *Götz von Berlichingen,* in which he felt he saw the guarantee of a renewal of Shakespearian original genius and creative style. This consolation, however, was not tenable, strictly logically speaking. It was empirical. Shakespeare is—even today—topical. The 'rhapsodist'—even today—has proved his Right. But it was a Right taken directly from Life itself, wholly in accord with the 'Storm and Stress' meaning. (pp. 24-32)

. . . . .

About the same time that a group was forming around Herder and Goethe in Central and Southern Germany, an even closer cultural circle was coming into being in Lower Germany at Göttingen. The focal point was the university. Here too there were students with whom an older man, namely Gottfried August Bürger, benevolently associated himself, just as Herder had done in the South. For the most part they originated from North or Central Germany, a fact which was easily recognisable in the peculiar make-up of the circle. It too was a product of Enlightenment sensibility and of the influence of Pietism, but the opposition to Enlightenment as such did not emerge so absolutely as in the 'Storm and Stress' movement that stretched from Strassburg to Frankfurt and Darmstadt. And so the subjectivism here scarcely grew to 'titanic' proportions, nor did it lead to creative works of art like Goethe's Odes or *Werther,* not even in the case of Bürger. But there was a high degree of youthful sentimentality and a heightened sensitivity involved. This found expression primarily in lyric verse. The drama, which predominated in the 'Storm and Stress' south of the river Main, was represented here only by Leisewitz. The Göttingen Grove did not remain without contact with Herder and Goethe, but it derived more in actual fact from Klopstock, and, to be precise, from the Klopstock of the bardic period. Last but not least, the rather mild northern character of the Göttingen landscape, wooded mountains of medium height and water meadows close by (despite the Klopstockian and Goethean myth about the Harz) struck a chord in the enthusiasm for nature that was displayed here. True, there was also revolutionary pathos in the tyrant-theme, in verse particularly with Bürger. In the case of the Stolbergs and Voss, however, this was subdued by the tone and rhythm appropriate to the ode.

Where the real 'Grove' was situated in the rural surrounds of Göttingen has not even been determined. It was really more a question of the genus, which from the outset bore a literary accent borrowed from Klopstock's bardic language. In his ode *Der Hügel und der Hain* Klopstock dealt with the contrast between classical antiquity and the early Nordic times, between Parnassus and the Grove of the Bards, between grace and 'soulful nature'. And that was the theme-song of this student group chosen at their founding ceremony; they produced first of all in 1770 the *Göttinger Musenalmanach* and in 1772 established the formal association under the name 'The Grove'. (The term *Hainbund* was in fact later coined by Voss.)

Heinrich Christian Boie (1774–1806) from Schleswig-Holstein started it all. The later *Landvogt* and Finance Councillor came to Göttingen in 1769 to continue his law studies, and that same year he was joined by Johann Heinrich Voss (1751–1826) from Mecklenburg, who though of a very humble peasant background had worked his way up despite great hardships, rising to the position of private tutor. Boie became the founder and first editor of the *Göttinger Musenalmanach,* Voss the first Elder of the Grove. Both too were excellent organisers. Boie immediately succeeded in getting not only Klopstock and Bürger, but also Goethe to contribute to this influential and thoroughly German imitation of the Parisian *Almanac des Muses.* The Göttingen group quickly developed an identity of their own, as a result of which Bürger could write to the old man Gleim: 'In Göttingen a quite new Parnassus is sprouting forth and growing as quickly as the willows fringing the brook.' The 'new Parnassus', however, grew into a collection of youthful enthusiasts conscious of the *Geniebewegung,* which admittedly only in the case of Bürger assumed those somewhat obstreperous and foolish forms in which Lenz and Klinger, for example, took delight in south Germany. From being close friends Voss and Boie became brothers-in-law. Voss acquired in Ernestine Boie the wife who corresponded to his own nature. In his later stations in life as rector in Otterndorf and Eutin it was she who ran the hospitable household from which the classical idyll *Luise* would result, as also the Homer translation (1781) which became the standard version for generations.

Ludwig Heinrich Christoph Hölty joined these Göttingen friends as the third member. Hölty (1748–76) was the son of a Hannoverian parson, and a theologian himself. He had a delicate constitution and succumbed early to consumption. He was the really ethereal member of the Circle. Talent and illness perhaps interacted upon him to conjure forth a lyricism which forms a direct part of the background to Novalis and Hölderlin in literary history. Other north Germans who were accepted into the Circle included Karl Friedrich Cramer (1752–1807), the son of the *Bremer Beiträge* contributor and friend of Klopstock (in Göttingen 1772–74), later classical scholar in Kiel, and Johann Anton Leisewitz (1752–1806), a lawyer, and finally as a significant addition, the Stolberg brothers, Friedrich Leopold (1750–1819) and Christian (1748–1821), both likewise lawyers, whose subsequent diplomatic and Court posts one would hardly have prophesied at that time, despite their background. The two Counts established together the personal connections with the 'Storm and Stress' Circle around Goethe; together with Goethe on their Swiss journey of 1775 they had shocked Bodmer in his old age in Zürich through their boisterousness. On the other hand Johann Martin Miller (1750–1814) came from Swabia; he was in Göttingen from 1770 on, later becoming Dean in his home town of Ulm. His sentimental novel of the post-Göttingen period *Siegwart, eine Klostergeschichte* made him more famous than had his Göttingen lyrics. And then along with others who joined the group were Friedrich Wilhelm Gotter (1746–97), a Thuringian, and

Johann Friedrich Hahn (1753-79) from Hesse. Several times, in fact, Gotter crossed Goethe's path in Wetzlar and later in Gotha, which was close to Weimar. Yet beside Boie and Voss, Hölty and the Stolbergs, Leisewitz and even Miller too, all the others were only peripheral figures, so that essentially the Grove remained dominated by north German elements.

There is an exact description of the founding ceremony of the Grove on 12 September 1772 in one of Voss's letters:

> Ach, den 12. September, mein liebster Freund, da hätten Sie hier sein sollen. Die beiden Millers, Hahn, Hölty, Wehrs und ich gingen noch des Abends nach einem entlegenen Dorfe. Der Abend war außerordentlich heiter und der Mond voll. Wir überließen uns ganz den Empfindungen der Natur. Wir aßen in einer Bauernhütte eine Milch und begaben uns darauf ins freie Feld. Hier fanden wir einen kleinen Eichengrund, und zugleich fiel uns allen ein, den Bund der Freundschaft unter diesen heiligen Bäumen zu schwören. Wir umkränzten die Hüte mit Eichenlaub, legten sie unter den Baum, faßten uns alle bei den Händen, tanzten so um den eingeschlossenen Stamm herum—riefen den Mond und die Sterne zum Zeugen unseres Bundes an und versprachen uns eine ewige Freundschaft. Dann verbündeten wir uns, die größte Aufrichtigkeit in unsern Urteilen gegeneinander zu beobachten und zu diesem Endzwecke die schon gewöhnliche Versammlung noch genauer und feierlicher zu halten. Ich ward durch Los zum Ältesten erwählt. Jeder soll Gedichte auf diesen Abend machen und ihn jährlich begehen.
>
> [Oh, my dear friend, you should have been here on the 12th September. The two Millers, Hahn, Hölty, Wehrs and I went whilst it was still evening to an outlying village. The evening was extraordinarily serene and the moon full. We abandoned ourselves completely to the sensations of nature. We drank some milk in a small farmhouse and then went into the open. Here we found a dell of oak-trees and it occurred to us all simultaneously that we should swear a bond of friendship under those sacred trees. We garlanded our hats with oak leaves, laid them under the tree, all clasped hands together and danced around the sequestered tree-trunk—we summoned the moon and the stars as witnesses of our bond, and pledged eternal friendship. Then we promised to observe the utmost sincerity in our judgment of one another, and to this end to hold a regular gathering with even greater detail and solemnity. I was chosen by lot to be the Elder. Each person was to compose poems to this evening and celebrate it annually.]

This then was the style: a feeling for the beauty of nature with a rustic and Rousseauistic touch, oak-wreaths, dancing, enthusiastic oaths of friendship. Whether the immediately established rites of constitution entirely coincided with the basic feeling that prevailed, need not be discussed. From his standpoint as the sarcastic intellectual, Lichtenberg had some grounds for pouring forth his scorn upon the subjectivity and sentimentality of the *Hainbündler,* who did not even understand 'what it was they hummed to the listening circle with lips pale and trembling, and arms moving as if reaping corn in time to the droning bagpipe sounds of ecstasy'. The form of their sentimentality corresponded to the Bardic and Ossianic motif. Each had his bardic name: Voss was called Sangrich, Boie Werdomar, Hölty Haining. Then there were names like Minnehold, Teuthard, and Raimund. This practise was not basically part of the new idea of subjectivism, but rather of the old heritage, namely of the Baroque *Sprachgesellschaften.* And the constitution had much in common with this too. There was the Society Elder, the Journal, the weekly gatherings at which one's own and others' poetry was recited and discussed. It was a custom that continued in Germany well into the nineteenth century (e.g. the Berlin *Tunnel*). Anniversaries and farewell parties were highspots in the history of the 'Grove'. The celebration of Klopstock's birthday on 2nd July 1773 was, next to the actual founding of the 'Grove', its most important and historic day. Klopstock himself was in fact not even present. His garlanded works had to take his place. As with the southern 'Storm and Stress' movement, Wieland represented for them the counter-trend, and a work of his was symbolically torn up and stamped upon. However in the September of 1774 Klopstock did participate on just one occasion as an official member. It was natural that the tears flowed liberally when departure celebrations were held.

The guiding principle of the Circle stemmed from Voss's *Bundesgesang* (1772), namely a strong patriotism in the spirit of Klopstock's *Hermannsschlacht.* In marked contrast to the frivolous passion for fame and glory of the French was his own

> . . . rauhe[s] Lied,
> (Ach! kein Mädchen und kein witziger Höfling
> liebt's)
> Das, in holpernden Tönen, Gott
> Dieses Märchen! und ha! Freiheit und Vaterland
> Und altväterische Tugend singt!—
>
> [. . . rough song (Oh, no maiden nor witty courtier loves it), which in unpolished tones, sings of God—that fairytale character—and with gusto of freedom and fatherland and ancestral virtue!]

Clearly this patriotism could also be seen as a kind of anti-Rationalism. Hölty's ode *Der Bund* was far more sentimental and impassioned than Voss's *Bundesgesang.* The poet himself 'glows with joyous rapture'. The 'soul of German song pours forth with burning fire'. In the Klopstockian style Haining's sworn bond includes his friends in one embrace. Both poems are rhymeless and in classical form, that of Hölty is expressly an ode. This points to the kind of poetry whose history, of all the genres, owes most to the Göttingen Grove. Moreover it has its historical significance as far as song is concerned, an importance still further strengthened by Abraham Peter Schultz's compositions. It was with Bürger's *Lenore,* first published in the *Göttinger Musenalmanach,* that the ballad, in line with Herder's suggestion, took a further step forward along its victorious path from Göttingen. So the Grove's compass reached from the classical form treated in a specifically

German manner, but with a technique that revealed uncanny understanding, to the old Nordic and old English ballad verse. The central position was held by the *Lied*—still with clearly traceable anacreontic elements, yet at its best, like the other forms, pulsating with a new feeling for life.

Like Voss's *Bundesgesang,* his ode *An Goethe* (1773) was a programmatic poem in the literary sense:

> Der du edel entbranntst, wo hochgelahrte
> Diener Justinians Banditen zogen,
> Die in Roms Labyrinthen
> Würgen das Recht der Vernunft;
> Freier Goethe, du darfst die goldne Fessel,
> Aus des Griechen Gesang geschmiedet, höhnen!
> Shakespeare durft' es und Klopstock,
> Söhne, gleich ihm, der Natur! . . .
> Deutsch und eisern wie Götz, sprich Hohn den Schurken—
> Mit der Fessel im Arm! Des Sumpfes Schreier,
> Schmäht der Leu zu zerstampfen,
> Wandelt durch Wälder und herrscht!

> [You who were so nobly enflamed, when Justinian's learned servants bred but bandits who choke the Right of Reason in Rome's labyrinths, you, Goethe, free as air, you may sneer at the golden chains forged from Grecian song! Shakespeare was able to, and Klopstock, both sons of nature! . . . German and iron-hard like Götz, pour scorn on the rogues—in chains! The lion is above stamping underfoot these bawlers from the morass, he roams the woods and rules supreme!]

This is nothing less than an identification with the 'Storm and Stress' Goethe, yet at the same time too with Herder's position as literary critic: namely, *contra* the rules of classical antiquity, *pro* the freedom of a Shakespeare or Klopstock, the Germanic ideal of Götz (no longer the *Teutschheit* of Hermann). At the same time it is a panegyric to dominating and unfettered promethean genius. Friedrich Leopold von Stolberg's ode *Genius* had no less promethean an effect. As the lion symbolised sovereign genius with Voss, so the eagle did here, the eagle 'full of primal energy'. Corresponding to the thirst for the sun was the 'wing of lofty inspiration', which bears genius that here appears in the first-person form:

> Mir gabst du Feuer! Durst nach Unsterblichkeit!
> Dies Toben in der Brust! Dies Staunen,
> Welches durch jegliche Nerve zittert.

> [You gave me fire! A thirst for immortality! This raging in my breast! This awe that vibrates through every nerve.]

This verse is constructed in accordance with the regular alcaic form. The theme, however, follows the new feeling of self-confidence of freely creative genius.

Compared with such highly gifted utterances from the young Voss and the younger Stolberg, Hölty's verse has a much more gentle and lyrical quality, even in the ode. Here he provided in the favoured second asclepiadaic, the alcaic and sapphic strophe some of the finest examples in the German tradition, such as *Mainacht, An die Grille* or *Sehnsucht.* He favoured the ode to friends, Love and Nature, the last with a strongly idyllic ring. Of his real idylls, *Das Feuer im Walde* (1774) has become a classic of its kind. Just as *Die künftige Geliebte* with its theme common to Klopstock (and Rilke) sounded somewhat muted as against Klopstock's elegy, so too did his ballads suffer in comparison with those of Bürger. A political song such as *Der befreite Sklave* with its theme of freedom from tyranny sticks out like a sore thumb in his total output that was predominantly purely lyric. The sounds of enchantment and bliss had their truest ring in his love poems. The vitality of the drinking-songs, on the other hand, appeared still rather conventional in the anacreontic sense. The same could be said of the nature poems, although (as in Stolberg's famous *An die Natur*) a new note of intimacy could occasionally break across the anacreontic scheme of things in Hölty, as seen in *Mailied.* In the whole of this circle of friends, however, he probably remained the member with the least sense of revolutionary awareness.

This self-assertion was perhaps most succinctly expressed in Leopold Stolberg's inspired prose rhapsody *Über die Fülle des Herzens* (1777). Here the 'gutless century' and its 'silken little men' and 'short-sighted petty rationalists' are attacked, those who analyse everything and hence lose all touch with Nature. The prayer which the poet would say for his first child stands in contrast:

> Gib ihm die menschlichste aller Gaben, die eine göttliche Gabe, gib ihm die Fülle des Herzens!

> [Grant him the most human of all gifts, the one divine gift, grant him fulness of heart!]

This finds expression firstly in the ability to love, celebrated in words which could have been inspired by Goethe: 'How it fires him, how it courses through him . . . ' After love, it bestows an immediate awareness of nature:

> Aus deiner Fülle möcht' ich nun schöpfen, o du, die ich als Mutter ehre, die ich liebe als Braut, Natur! an deren Brüsten ich allein ungestörte reine Wollust atmen kann!

> [From your fulness should I now like to draw, O nature, you whom I honour as my mother, love as my bride, at whose breast I alone can breathe pure and peaceful bliss!]

Experience must go hand in hand with this passionate feeling for Nature: 'The heart grows sick in the town.' From all this springs the self-assertion of the 'fiery, highly sensitive' genius, who is master over time: 'His is the past, his the future.' Certainly, when he wrote this, Stolberg was no longer in Göttingen, but was already influenced by his friendship with Goethe. Nevertheless he did express what could at least develop in terms of new self-awareness through contact with the essential spirit of the *Hainbund.*

Besides their larger-than-life vitality together with this 'fullness of heart', Johann Anton Leisewitz's *Julius von Tarent* and one-act plays reveal connections with the 'Storm and Stress' dramas in other respects. Leisewitz embodied the radical element within the Göttingen circle, though he later found his way back into the bourgeois world as a Privy Justice.

By contrast Gottfried August Bürger reflected 'Storm and Stress' confusion and chaos in his whole way of life. He was born in 1747, the son of a parson from the Harz region. His parents were well-to-do, though difficult. After an unregulated early upbringing he first awoke to an awareness of his talent during a visit to the Foundations established by the Pietist Francke. But his education in the grammar-school section of the Foundation was abruptly terminated by his grandfather, so that the seventeen-year-old began his theological studies in Halle without having matriculated. Bürger was never able to compensate for this deficiency which marked his education, particularly since the grandfather made him interrupt his studies again and again later on. So lack of restraint and immoderation characterised Bürger's path from the outset. As early as 1767 he was sent down whilst still a student of theology. But in fact he had already shown a preference for philological studies in Halle (and, to make it worse, under Klotz, a figure of vain and questionable character). The now enforced change of university led him to Göttingen. For a short time (roughly 1770-1771), as a result of his contact with Boie and his circle, through which he became friendly with Gleim in Halberstadt, he seemed to pull himself together. Percy's *Reliques* made a decisive impression upon him at that time and opened up for him a new world besides the classical one of Homer, Lucian, Catullus, with which he nevertheless continued to persevere. And it was now that the arch-poet of ballad and 'folk' poetry emerged (the description under which Schiller was to review him so harshly later on in the *Jenaische Allgemeine Literatur-Zeitung*). Yet the fame that soon came his way did not in the long run contribute to an ordering of his life, any more than did his (rather patronising) relationship with the *Hainbund.* A bungled Civil Service career as district administrator which ended in 1780 with his dismissal, a botched private life through his universally-known bigamous relationship with the sisters Dorette and Auguste (Molly) Leonhart, his passion for drinking and gambling, which completely dissipated his not inconsiderable inheritance, and finally after Dorette's death his marriage to Molly, and following her demise an eccentric third marriage which resulted in an early divorce—all this made him quite impossible in bourgeois eyes, although he was made a don at Göttingen University in 1784. Bürger had to blame himself rather than society, which let him fall by the wayside, for his death in 1794, in misery and debt and following a long illness, when he was only forty-six years of age. Next to Lenz, Bürger was probably the person who, in his whole mode of existence, most strikingly represented the extreme freedom of genius which must accept from society the consequences of an asocial attitude and way of life. As an example of unruliness, he had much in common with the wretched Johann Christian Günther, even in the way that he wrested with a certain desperate defiance a considerable poetic achievement from a life totally wrecked by unbridled passions.

Bürger's contribution owed much to the classical world, interspersed as it was with elements of Catullus and Anacreon (obviously still in the fashion of Hagedorn and Uz). *Die Nachtfeier der Venus* (referring to the pseudo-catullan *Pervigilium Veneris*) was not only influenced by the songs to Joy, and hence by German anacreontic poetry, but also displayed an individualistic form of enraptured mythology (a prelude to Schiller) in fervid rhymes and excited enjambement. The verse on the birth of Venus sounds almost like a paraphrase of Botticelli's famous picture:

> Ahnend, welch ein Wunder werde,
> Welch ein Götterwerk aus Schaum,
> Träumten Himmel, Meer und Erde
> Tief der Wonne süßen Traum.
> Als sie, hold in sich gebogen,
> In der Perlenmuschel stand,
> Wiegten sie entzückte Wogen
> An des Ufers Blumenrand.
>
> [Wondering what miracle would take place, what divine creation would emerge from the foam, Heaven, Sea and Earth dreamed a deep sweet dream of rapture. When she, gently arched, stood in the pearl conch, enchanted waves rocked her gently to the flower-fringed shore.]

This goes beyond Uz and Gleim, and is representative of Bürger's early developed sensuality, harnessed through form. Between *Nachtfeier* and *Lenore,* which established Bürger's fame (1773), there emerged some relatively insignificant poetry of an idyllic / anacreontic type. The ballad then seemed, however, to fulfil what Herder, in his *Ossian* essay, had hoped for, and demanded from German poetry if it accepted the pattern of primitive ballad verse. It is known that a German *Kunstballade* or literary ballad did not exist before Bürger. Gleim's *Romanzen* ('Romances'), with their affinity to the popular song and *Moritat,* composed though they were in somewhat childish fashion, rank here at most as a prelude. Bürger's ballad tone too has occasionally something of the style of the *Moritat:*

> Als nun das Heer vorüber war,
> Zerraufte sie ihr Rabenhaar,
> Und warf sich hin zur Erde
> Mit wütiger Gebärde.
>
> [When the army was now past, she tore her raven hair and cast herself to the ground with frenzied gesture.]

Something like this could be found too in the low popular ballad, yet there it is in *Lenore,* the 'classic' German model of the literary ballad. The connection exists even in the theme, e.g. the demonstrated atonement of guilt. Here, however, it was not disadvantageous, for the *Lenore* ballad set up no 'artificial literary' form as a counter to the historically accepted tradition in Germany, but on the contrary was embedded in it in a certain sense: it demonstrated Bürger's keen sense of the possible. At the same time the *Lenore* theme was 'Storm and Stress' subject matter *par excellence.* Not only because it treated a thoroughly contemporary theme, namely a theme from the Seven Years War, which had raged but a decade earlier. Not only because, as in *Julius von Tarent,* uncontrollable passion led to blasphemy, that the sensual was here raised to the status of an absolute; the contemporaneity of the topical and the historical reflected too the spirit of Herder. For Lenore's desperate mourning for her loved one missing in the Battle of Prague then led, on the wild ride with the spirit of the fallen man to the common grave as the bridal bed (the old image from the folk ballad), to a totally realistic and contemporised *danse macabre.* The theme of expiated blasphemy can in the end be associated with this. Furthermore, the repeated *Chevy Chase* verse relates directly to Percy, the source common to Herder, and the style with its numerous interjections, its 'leaps and sallies', becomes almost a realisation of Herder's ideal. If all this is borne in mind, Bürger's ballad can then be understood as an event that belongs to the history of the 'Storm and Stress'. Bürger conceived it as just that, as the correspondence with Boie on *Lenore* (1773) confirms. From this it is clear that through Boie he had first become acquainted with Herder's *Blätter* whilst working on the ballad, so that he himself assessed its completion as a realisation of Herder's ideal:

> O Boie, Boie, welche Wonne! als ich fand, daß ein Mann wie Herder eben das von der Lyrik des Volks und mithin der Natur deutlicher und bestimmter lehrte, was ich dunkel davon schon längst gedacht und empfunden hatte. Ich denke, Leonore soll Herders Lehre einigermaßen entsprechen.
>
> [O Boie, Boie, what joy when I found that a man like Herder taught more clearly and decisively about the lyric poetry of the people, and consequently nature itself, that which I had thought about and perceived but darkly for a long time. I think *Lenore* shall correspond in some way to Herder's doctrine.

Yet another standard work of the 'Storm and Stress' inspired him to new Lenore verses—Goethe's *Götz:*

> Hu, wie wird mich der Unverstand drüber anblöcken! Aber der kann mir—! Frei! frei! Keinem untertan als der Natur!—
>
> [Oh, how those who lack understanding will taunt me! But the hell with it—for I am free, free, subject to none but Nature!]

The style itself reveals the atmosphere of intense excitement in which the poem came into being. And a stylistic preference for the same intensity lies behind Bürger's type of ballad in general. This aimed at starkly contrasting effects and was based largely on macabre (mythical as well as realistic) themes. It could be grotesque with a measure of black humour as in *Der Raubgraf,* or a moralistic extreme as in *Der wilde Jäger,* the piece most closely related to *Lenore* in its presentation of horror. As in the ballad *Des Pfarrers Tochter von Taubenhain,* with its theme of seduction, it can be linked in a social critical vein to the 'Storm and Stress' theme of infanticide, with tones that anticipate Annette von Droste-Hülshoff. It can also, in a serious or joking manner, be linked to the medieval tradition of song and jest, as in *Der Kaiser und der Abt, Graf Walter, Das Blümchen Wunderhold* or *Volkers Schwanenlied.* Finally, it can be topical material, as in *Lied vom braven Mann.* Almost everywhere Bürger's characteristic style is the decisive factor, a style which he saw, even in theoretical terms, as forming a totally consistent whole, bearing the imprint of ideas akin to Herder's (e.g. *Herzensausgußüber Volks-Poesie*). Proceeding from the inescapable fact that the vernacular and the scholarly tongues are two separate entities in Germany, just like imagination and wit, poetry and 'versifying', Bürger establishes in this last-named piece his passion for *Naturpoesie,* a passion with which he 'listens in the evening twilight to the magic sound of the ballads and street songs, under the linden trees in the village, in the open air and in the spinning-rooms'. From these ballads he hopes too for the rebirth of a folk-epic. Admittedly this would first entail 'the emergence at long last of a German Percy'. Bürger's whole hatred, however, was reserved for the 'philosophunculis' of the Nicolai type, whose *Feiner kleiner Almanach* (1777), the parody of Herder's enthusiasm for the folk-song, he himself in turn parodied. In the accompanying piece 'On the Popularity of Poetry' he attempted similarly a kind of *Aesthetica in nuce* with the definition of poetry as an imitation of the 'original subject' induced for 'the interior sense'. This imitation, however, is a representation, determined by the power of imagination. But as such it must not be poetry for individual classes and ranks, but simply poetry for the people: 'All poetry shall be popular.' The term 'people', though, has to be comprehended correctly not as the *hoi polloi,* but as that totality for which Homer, Shakespeare and Ossian wrote.

Herein lay the key to Bürger's concept of the *Volksdichter.* He was not conceived in a narrow, limited sense, but in a vast universal literary context. It was all the same whether he composed his ballads under the influence of Percy and the 'vulgar ditties' heard at first hand, or whether he vied with Goethe and Stolberg in translating Ossian, with Voss and Stolberg in translating Homer, as in fact was the case. The same applied when as a narrator he compiled the tall stories of Baron Münchhausen and when he thus produced not only a book of funny tales, but also a book for children that has few equals. This too was an epic of 'man's sensitivity', here appealing to man's sense for the comic.

Bürger's poetic work covered a wide range of subject matter, even outside of his ballads. First of all it was a reservoir of 'Storm and Stress' subjects with aesthetic as well as political themes. Then it served at the same time to expose the bourgeois figure as in *Prometheus,* rationalistic conformity as in *Mamsell La Regle* with its deliberately insolent punch-line *à la* Klinger:

> Laßt, Brüderchen, die alte Strunsel gehn!
> Nur Kinder mag also ihr Laufzaum schürzen!
> Was tut's, ob wir mal stolpern oder stürzen?
>
> [Brothers, let the old hag go! Her apron string can then be a hindrance only to children! What does it matter if we stumble or fall?]

Finally, denigration of the 'august tyrant' as in *Der Bauer.* None of this was well-tempered, but rather eccentric, without a mean temperature between boiling- and freezing-point. Thus the well known *Zechlied* too manifests a state of intoxication between extremes, a bacchanalian self-awareness, where the drunken genius can say:

> Sind Homer und Ossian
> Gegen mich nur Stümper.
>
> [Homer and Ossian are but bungling amateurs beside me.]

Bürger was half-seriously, half-jokingly aware that there would be a flood of dissertations on him one day. For he also had at his command a kind of tortured humour. So it is no wonder that it was Bürger of all people who made the formula for the age so expressly his own in verse:

> Wie wird mir so herzlich bange,
> Wie so heiß und wie so kalt,
> Wann in diesem Sturm und Drange
> Keuchend meine Seele wallt.
>
> [How my heart is so afraid, will beat so hot and cold, when my soul heaves pantingly in this Storm and Stress.]

These words appear in *Elegie,* one of the poems to Molly, in which the most intimate passion struggles for expression. Here too is an echo of the related sounds of Johann Christian Günther, but in a new, unchained vocabulary of passion. 'Shriek out', 'pour out', 'burn', 'grow together as one', 'ferment'—this is the temperature of just the verbal imagery in this poem. In addition to this, and hardly by chance, one could find for probably the first time in Bürger's lyric poetry the term 'feeling for life'.

It is scarcely a contradiction to Bürger's 'panting' style of originality, that he was also one of the first masters of the sonnet since the Baroque age. Indeed from the literary historical point of view it is of the utmost significance. For he practised his skill in this genre together with a pupil who was also very famed in it later: namely with August Wilhelm Schlegel, whose Romantic period had then not yet dawned. If we recall that it was Romanticism, that largely formless movement seeking the infinite, which resurrected the sonnet, a form that was to attract even Goethe, the seeming contradiction in terms of Bürger is then resolved. The stimulus that forced Goethe's *Mächtiges Überraschen* into sonnet form, may be ascribed to Bürger's passion for the sonnet.

From the literary sociological point of view, with the specifically German social patterns in mind, one can understand the—at first sight, rather curious—fact that from the year of the French Revolution onwards the majority of the companions from the one-time *Göttinger Hain* circle, which also included other 'Storm and Stress' figures and Pietists, assembled at a rural centre, namely at the castle of the Reventlov-Schimmelmann family in Emkendorf (Holstein). Over the years Voss, the Stolbergs, Claudius, even Klopstock too, met there, but in addition Friedrich Jacobi, the Princess Gallitzin and other exponents of the religious movement that laid emphasis on (religious) feeling. This 'Emkendorf Circle' is a familiar concept in modern literary history. It is historically interesting in that it represented in almost model fashion the rapid change in the mirroring of the French Revolution in German intellectual life. As, for example, in the case of Klopstock and Schiller: at first they displayed enthusiasm stemming from that century's feeling for human rights, soon however an imperious assertion of a conservative abhorrence of the tyrannical attitude shown by the revolutionaries themselves. Thus, whilst maintaining total intellectual alertness, they slipped, culturally-politically speaking, into a reactionary attitude, corresponding to the predominantly aristocratic composition of the circle. This circle therefore belongs, more than fifteen years after the youthful exuberance of the Göttingen Grove, to an intervening phase between the 'Storm and Stress' and classical forces bent on maintaining the *status quo,* not dissimilar to the intellectually interested society that dominates Goethe's *Unterhaltungen deutscher Ausgewanderten.* (pp. 33-47)

Werner Kohlschmidt, "The Ossianic World and Shakespeare" and "The Göttingen Grove," in his A History of German Literature, 1760-1805, *translated by Ian Hilton, The Macmillan Press Ltd., 1975, pp. 24-33, 33-47.*

DRAMA

F. J. Lamport

[In the following excerpt, Lamport examines the major practitioners of Sturm und Drang drama, particularly Goethe, focusing on their rejection of the classical unities and rules of dramatic form in favor of a drama concerned primarily with the presentation of character.]

Alongside the work of Lessing, many other attempts were being made, in the 1750s and 1760s, to create a serious German drama. The experimenters included men distinguished in other branches of literature—Klopstock, the great pioneer in lyric poetry; Wieland, the father of the modern German novel—as well as many who are now forgotten. They essayed a variety of forms and of subject-matter: they wrote in prose and in verse, in neo-classical and in freer styles, on historical, mythical, biblical and modern subjects. Klopstock dramatised both Hermann's defeat of Varus and the Roman legions and Cain's murder of his brother Abel. But none of these experiments met with more than passing success. The next stage in the awakening of German drama comes in the 1770s, sometimes called by German literary historians the Age of Genius or, more commonly, the age of 'Sturm und Drang' (Storm and Stress), after the title of one of its most characteristic dramatic products, a play by F. M. Klinger, dating from 1776.

The German 'Sturm und Drang' is the first major outburst of the European Romantic movement. Suddenly the most culturally backward of the European peoples sprang into the limelight and created a new style in which to embody the attitudes and feelings characteristic of a new generation. Above all, the movement was the work of one man of extraordinary genius, Johann Wolfgang Goethe, who, born in 1749, had the good fortune to be coming to manhood at a time when in all the literary genres the pioneering work had been done, and lyric, drama and novel only awaited the 'golden touch' to bring them fully to life. But the pioneers had had to do their work first. And it is not surprising that the new movement should thus break out in backward, disunited, frustrated Germany, for it was a movement born of frustration: born of a generation of young men's passionate desire for self-expression, and of their often angry impatience with the existing norms—literary, cultural, social, and even, at least implicitly, political—which seemed to exist only to deny them what they desired. Sometimes, it is true, they seem to have little to express save the burning desire to express themselves. Typical is the description of the hero, Wild (his very name is of course characteristic), in Klinger's *Sturm und Drang* itself: 'He uttered a curse and looked up to Heaven, as if possessed by some deep, genuine feeling' (I, iv). But at their best they were genuine idealists, longing for a better world in which men could enjoy what the founding fathers of the American republic proclaimed in that same year of 1776 to be their self-evident and inalienable rights to 'life, liberty and the pursuit of happiness'. Klinger's play is actually set in America: his characters have crossed the seas in pursuit of their ideals.

Literary historians often date the epoch of Storm and Stress from 1767, when the great theorist of the movement, Johann Gottfried Herder, published his *Fragmente über die neuere deutsche Literatur* (*Fragments on Modern German Literature*); and Heinrich Wilhelm von Gerstenberg's *Ugolino* of 1767-8 is sometimes claimed as the first Storm and Stress play. It is a dramatisation of an episode from Canto 33 of Dante's *Inferno,* depicting the starving to death of Ugolino and his sons, who have been imprisoned by their enemies' intrigues. It is a strange but characteristic piece, strictly classical in external form but very unclassical in substance and effect. A conventional dramatist might have chosen to portray something of the intrigues which have led to Ugolino's imprisonment, but Gerstenberg ignores this possibility and concentrates exclusively on the slow agony of his death. The process is inevitable, lacking in all tension and therefore, as Lessing argued in a letter to Gerstenberg, quite undramatic; Gerstenberg, however, was not concerned with dramatic tension in the conventional sense, but only with the evocation and progressive intensification of a mood of claustrophobic horror. To this end the observation of the unities—the action takes place in the course of a single stormy night in a dimly lit prison cell—makes its own contribution, and mood and setting were to be profoundly characteristic of the new movement. Passionately committed as they were to the ideal of freedom, the 'Stürmer und Dränger' came again and again to dwell upon its antithesis, the image of the prison.

Gerstenberg (1737-1823) also wrote critical essays in which, in the mid-1760s, he was already advancing some of the theories which were to typify the movement. But the real beginnings, especially as regards the drama, are to be sought in Strasbourg in 1770-1. Here Goethe, who had come to Strasbourg University in the course of his legal studies, met Herder, who had come from a series of eye operations, and subsequently J. M. R. Lenz, who was employed there as a private tutor. Herder was five years older than Goethe, Lenz two years younger. Essays by these three writers, all dating from 1771-2, sum up the dramatic creed of the 'Stürmer und Dränger': Herder's 'Shakespeare', published in 1773 in the collection *Von deutscher Art und Kunst* (*Of German Character and Art*), which may be called the manifesto of the movement; Goethe's *Rede zum Shakespeares-Tag* (*Address for Shakespeare's Name-day*), composed in October 1771; and Lenz's *Anmerkungen übers Theater* (*Notes on the Theatre*), published in 1774 as the preface to a translation of *Love's Labour's Lost.* Around their adulation of Shakespeare the three young men build up a reasonably coherent theory of drama for their own age. There are some variations, in Lenz in particular, but a great deal of common ground. Goethe's Shakespeare address echoes indeed not only Herder's ideas but also Herder's characteristic rhapsodic, ejaculatory and enthusiastic prose style.

The theory of these young writers differs fundamentally from that of earlier ages. First and foremost, they see writing, like all forms of art, as a matter not primarily of communication but of expression: whereas Gottsched and Lessing alike had been much concerned with the effect a piece of writing had or was intended to have upon its audience—the inculcation of a moral lesson, the arousal of compassion—the 'Stürmer und Dränger' lay a new emphasis upon individual genius and its powerful creative force or energy ('Kraft'). And as a natural corollary of this, they are no longer interested in the classification of works of literature into genres by the application of what seem to them merely external rules. Gerstenberg had already demanded 'Away with the classification of drama!' To Herder and Goethe, such divisions as that between tragedy and comedy, whether determined by social considerations or by the difference in their presumed or intended effect, are irrelevant to the dramatist's true aim, which is simply to portray his experience of the world; and Shakespeare's mixture of the genres seems to them therefore exemplary rather than reprehensible. The further restrictions of the neo-classic style are similarly rejected as a falsification of life and as unnecessary limitations on the free expression of genius. When Goethe read Shakespeare, he declares: 'I hesitated not a moment in renouncing the regular theatre. The unity of place seemed to me timid and narrow like a prison, the unities of action and time irksome fetters upon our imagination.' The rejection of the French style also takes on a new note of nationalistic intensity. Here Lessing had shown the way, but in Herder's eulogies of Shakespeare there are intimations of deeper affinities of blood between the Germans and the English. Finally there comes a point of a rather different, but also related kind. The drama, above all the tragedy, of earlier ages was concerned with actions and events: tragedy, Aristotle tells us, is an imitation not of persons but of action, and a tragedy without character portrayal, though it might not be very good, was nevertheless perfectly possible, while a tragedy without a plot was inconceivable. But modern drama, for the 'Stürmer und Dränger', is a drama of character. This development in dramatic theory is already prefigured in Lessing, who despite his almost unquestioning reverence for Aristotle lays great emphasis on psychological motivation and on the self-identification of the spectator with the stage figures. But in the 'Stürmer und Dränger' the shift of emphasis is complete, and Lenz makes the point in flat contradiction of Aristotelian precept. Here too Shakespeare is seen as exemplary, as a creator above all of characters, of human beings ('Menschen'). As Goethe puts it: 'He vied with Prometheus, copied his human creatures feature by feature, but made them of colossal greatness; . . . then he breathed life into them all with the breath of *his* spirit, he speaks through all of them, and we recognise their kinship.' Twenty-five years later Schiller was to argue very differently, that Shakespeare, the 'naive' poet, presents his characters to us in pure objectivity, and that his own personality is completely inaccessible to us. But Goethe, at all events in his Storm and Stress period, is concerned to emphasise the expressive nature of Shakespeare's character portrayal.

Goethe also declares that all Shakespeare's plays (though he is presumably thinking primarily of the tragedies) have the same theme: 'All his plays turn upon the secret point, which no philosopher has yet seen or defined, where the vaunted freedom of our will collides with the inexorable course of the whole.' The critic Gundolf observed [in his *Shakespeare und der deutsche Geist,* 1914] that this is a truer description of Goethe's own Storm and Stress plays than of the plays of Shakespeare. In fact Goethe has defined a theme which is common in some form to all tragic drama, but is perhaps particularly characteristic of the drama of emergent German classicism: the struggle of individual human beings—their individuality recognised and valued at this period more strongly than ever before—to assert their autonomy in the face of seemingly all-powerful, hostile, indifferent or uncomprehended alien forces. These forces may be identified as gods or as fate; as the impersonal forces of mechanical causality or of historical necessity; as the inherent limitations of the human mind in its understanding, and hence in its control, of external reality; or finally as some kind of world-spirit or immanent Idea. And the philosophers of German idealism did indeed seek to define that 'secret point', in a variety of ways, so that the history of the German classical drama runs parallel to that of the great age of German philosophy which was also just beginning. Many connections and parallels can be observed, sometimes conscious, sometimes subconscious, sometimes apparently merely coincidental: Schiller and Kleist with Kant and Fichte, Hebbel with Hegel, Grillparzer with Schopenhauer.

Pencil sketch of Lenz, circa 1777, by an unknown artist.

The dramatic theory of Storm and Stress may thus be said to have set the German drama of the period on a philosophical kind of course. It is from the start a self-conscious drama, even, as has been argued, a drama of self-consciousness. This makes it from the start essentially a drama of sophisticated, rather than popular, appeal. And for all the enthusiasm of the 'Stürmer und Dränger' for popular culture, for ballad and folk-song, for all their imaginative sympathy with the lives of the common people, this tendency finds support in other elements of their thought. Their emphasis on individual genius and creativity, and their view of writing, even dramatic writing, as primarily an expression of individuality, lead to a neglect of the public, social aspect of drama, of which Gottsched and Lessing had both in their different ways been so keenly aware. In Herder the genius seems no longer to speak *to* his fellow-men, even if by some mysterious, almost mystical embodiment of the collective identity of the 'Volk' he may be seen as speaking *for* them.

This neglect of the public dimension is compounded by a considerable indifference to the practical exigencies of the theatre. In their enthusiasm for Shakespearian freedom of form—and in their general ignorance of the conditions under which Shakespeare's plays were designed to be performed, for the apron stage was unknown in Germany and even the travelling players used a picture stage with a front curtain—they assumed that Shakespeare had disregarded these matters and that in imitating him they might do likewise: hence the fifty-six scene-changes of Goethe's *Götz von Berlichingen* and the fifty-three of Klinger's *Otto,* or Lenz's scenes consisting of only five or six words. A certain amount of rapid scene-changing would, however, have been well within the technical capacities of a reasonably well equipped eighteenth-century German theatre, which would have a variety of painted backdrops and movable wings. Moreover, the young writers' literary discovery of Shakespeare is indeed paralleled by a theatrical discovery: in the 1770s Shakespeare was brought, albeit in imperfect prose translations and often in drastically modified form, to the German stage as well as to the German reading public. Here the pioneer was Schröder, who took over the running of the theatre in Hamburg in 1771. Another important event of that memorable year 1776 was Schröder's production of *Hamlet,* the first significant performance of a Shakespeare play in Germany, and the model for the description of Wilhelm Meister's performance of *Hamlet* in Goethe's novel.

The Germans' discovery of Shakespeare was thus not purely a literary phenomenon, nor was the drama of the young Goethe and his associates. The 'Stürmer und Dränger' wrote plays which, albeit with a certain amount of difficulty, could be, and indeed were, performed upon the contemporary stage. The increased realism and immediacy of their dramatic style also reflects the ever-increasing realism of contemporary acting styles, as exemplified in that of Schröder when compared with Ekhof. But the young dramatists were undoubtedly as impatient of the limitations of the stage as of other 'irksome fetters upon the imagination', and they lacked the practical commitment to the theatre as a social institution which had impelled Gottsched and Lessing. The result of this is that in the 1770s the gap between literary drama and the stage begins to widen again. The theatre-going public had enthusiastically accepted the realistic middle-class domestic drama which Lessing had introduced, and for the next generation and beyond, plays of this type enjoyed far more box-office success than any other. The most successful stage dramatists around the turn of the century were not Goethe, nor any of the other 'Stürmer und Dränger', nor Schiller, nor even Lessing himself, but August Wilhelm Iffland (1759-1814) and August von Kotzebue (1761-1819). Both were prolific writers, largely in the mode of contemporary realism, though Kotzebue also wrote some historical plays. Iffland was also a distinguished actor-manager, noted for the moderated realism of his performances, in which he continued the tradition of Ekhof. But their dramatic works make plain the weaknesses of the eighteenth-century 'bürgerlich' manner. All too easily—as we see from the beginning in *Miss Sara Sampson*—it degenerates into melodrama and sentimentality. It also dates: as the society which produced it disappears, its contemporary concerns lose their relevance and appear trivial. It is in fact, if not in the same kind of way as the French neo-classic style which it had supplanted, an essentially limiting style, and the 'Stürmer und Dränger' were right to try to escape from its limitations.

The first great work in which the dramatic imagination of Storm and Stress burst from its fetters was Goethe's historical drama *Götz von Berlichingen.* Sprawling, disorganised, but with a basic unity of character and theme and a great deal of rough immediacy and vigour, it presents all the characteristics of a work of spontaneous creative genius such as the theory of the young Shakespeare-worshippers had called for. In fact the familiar version of 1773 is a fairly radical revision of the original of 1771, but the original does appear to have been written in a fairly rapid burst of inspiration. The title of this original version, *Geschichte Gottfriedens von Berlichingen mit der eisernen Hand, dramatisiert* (*The History of Gottfried von Berlichingen with the Iron Hand, dramatised*) indicates its loose, 'epic' character, its closeness to its historical source, and its lack of concern for the exigencies of the stage. Despite some tidying-up, all these qualities are still evident in the revised version, whose subtitle 'Schauspiel' (play) indicates not so much an increased regard for theatrical practicality as a continued disregard for the accepted generic subdivisions of the drama. However, though it is not designated a tragedy, *Götz* is the most unambiguously, and probably the most convincingly, tragic of all Goethe's major plays.

It is indeed a Shakespearian play, at any rate as Goethe and Herder had understood their idol's work: Herder's reported comment to Goethe that 'Shakespeare has been your ruin' was unfair, for it was very much Shakespeare seen through Herder's eyes. It is the first great example of drama as expressive utterance, revealing the creative personality of its author through the portrayal of a figure himself understood to be a 'creative' personality: strong, noble, magnanimous, straightforward, loyal and honest, devoted to the cause of freedom. One might even describe Götz as a genius, even if he is not himself a creative artist (though we do see him, in the course of Goethe's play, embarking upon the writing of the autobiography which was to be Goethe's source). The whole play is concerned, directly and indirectly, with the evocation of this character, loved and revered by his family, his friends and servants, and the common people—'this man whom the princes hate and to whom the oppressed will always turn' (Brother Martin in Act I), 'the model of a true knight, brave and noble in his freedom, and calm and faithful in misfortune' (Götz's wife Elisabeth in Act IV). Götz finds himself increasingly at odds with an age of selfishness, dishonesty, disloyalty and political intrigue: history makes him a rebel against the Empire to which he unceasingly professes his loyalty. The watchword of 'freedom' echoes through the play from Götz's first speech to his last, when he dies in prison with the word on his lips. The expression of this theme reaches its grandest climax in Act III, where Götz and his few faithful, beleaguered friends drink a toast to freedom with their last bottle of wine, evoking a vision not simply of individual freedom and anarchy—for which Götz's aggressive forthrightness and self-reliance can easily be mistaken—but of a world in which under a benevolent patriarchy all men of good will can live together in harmony.

The theme of freedom is also of course reflected in the form of Goethe's play—seemingly anarchic, ostentatiously defiant of all the neo-classical unities and proprieties. As has been mentioned, there are fifty-six changes of scene (in the original version there are sixty), ranging freely and evocatively over much of southern Germany. There is no precise time-scale, but the action evidently spans a good number of years: the historical events upon which the play is based took place between 1495 and 1562, the year in which the real Götz von Berlichingen died (not in prison, incidentally, but at home in his own bed). The stage is filled with violent action—battles, storms, burnings and plunderings—and with violent language: Götz's invitation in Act III to the Imperial officer, sent to demand his surrender, to 'lick my arse' has earned undying notoriety, even though Goethe himself deleted it from later editions of the play. The unity of action is abandoned in favour of a series of loosely connected episodes and subplots and a continuous switching of focus between contrasting groups of characters—Götz and his associates, courtiers, soldiers, peasants, gypsies. Whereas neo-classic drama aims at the heightened uniformity of the 'grand style', Goethe makes each of these groups of characters speak its own distinctive language, in the Shakespearian manner—though apart from some interpolated songs (another Shakespearian feature) the play is written entirely in prose. Some of the subplots attain an almost disproportionate importance, notably the story of Götz's weak and vacillating friend Weislingen, his defection to the court party, and his betrayal by the *femme fatale* Adelheid—herself a figure who plainly fascinated Goethe (particularly in the original version of the play) more than her role in the dramatic economy would strictly warrant.

In all these respects *Götz von Berlichingen* was a landmark. But Goethe's most momentous innovation was his completely new treatment of historical subject-matter. Dramatists had hitherto used history to illustrate general truths about life, in accordance with Aristotle's distinction between poetry and history: the names of historical characters had given the drama dignity, as Gottsched had stated, or had served as a convenient shorthand for certain types of character, as Lessing had suggested (*Dramaturgie,* No. 24). But Lessing had also argued that the dramatist would do just as well to invent his own characters and names—as he had indeed done in his own plays. Lessing was in fact not much interested in historical drama, seeing it largely as an encomium upon the doings of the great, which was not in his view a proper use of the dramatist's art. But in *Götz* Goethe was doing something different. He was not simply using the figure of Götz to express timeless, universal human truths—though they are undoubtedly there in the play. Nor was he simply celebrating a great individual, though this was very much part of his intention: as he wrote to one of his friends in November 1771, 'I am dramatising the story of one of the noblest of Germans, restoring the reputation of a fine man.' Nor was he simply writing a patriotic play, though this again is an important element. He was also evoking the characteristic spirit of a past age, and dramatising the process of historical change; and with this discovery of history as a theme in itself he gave the German drama one of its most constant preoccupations. The view of history conveyed in *Götz* is of course a highly romantic one—though if we use that adjective it is because *Götz* is one of the works in and through which the romantic vision of history was created. Götz's ideals of liberty and fraternity are those of the young Goethe and his contemporaries. Goethe, however, presents them as qualities of life which did in the past exist, but have since been lost, and shows us in his play when and how he believes them to have been lost. Götz fights for the values of the 'good old days' against the encroachments of 'progress': if he is a rebel, he is a conservative or even a reactionary one. Goethe portrays what was indeed a crucial period of German history, the age of the Emperor Maximilian, of the religious Reformation (the name of the character Brother Martin hints strongly at Luther himself), of the Peasants' Revolt and of the attempts of political reformers to reshape the structures of German society and to create a greater sense of unity and nationhood. . . . [The] tragedy of German history in the sixteenth century was the failure of Germany to emerge from medieval feudalism into the modern world. But Goethe's hero is an unrepentant champion of feudal values, and his play is designed to show a natural way of life and a natural, organic society being supplanted by a corrupt and artificial one. Whether we agree with this view or not, Goethe's portrayal of the way in which in the course of history one way of life, one society, one set of values gives way to another was profoundly influential. Nor was its influence confined to Germany. It was partly through reading *Götz von Berlichingen* (which he translated into English) that Scott was moved to explore the changing face of Scottish society, and to portray the disappearance of the old, tribal Scotland in *Waverley* and the novels which succeeded it; and Scott's work in turn inspired further generations of European writers, and Americans such as Fenimore Cooper—so that Götz von Berlichingen can be described as the direct literary ancestor of the Last of the Mohicans. This, of course, is not what Frederick the Great, still unwavering in his exclusive admiration of the French classical style, had in mind when he described *Götz* as 'digne des sauvages du Canada'. Nor was Lessing favourably impressed, for *Götz* seemed to him little more than a reversion to the old-style 'Haupt- und Staatsaktion'. And indeed the immediate theatrical progeny of Goethe's play was a host of 'Ritterstücke', or, as we might say, 'robber-baron plays', anticipating the style of Hollywood medievalism: swashbuckling historical costume melodramas, full of spectacle and violence but of very little literary merit. The proliferation of works of this kind has perhaps made it harder to appreciate the originality and power of *Götz* itself. But if Ronald Peacock, in the major English monograph on Goethe the dramatist [*Goethe's Major Plays,* 1959], could describe *Götz* as a 'rather a tedious play for non-Germans' and 'of all Goethe's plays, the one that has to be appreciated essentially by historical evaluation', the playwright John Arden evidently felt very differently, making his own adaptation of *Götz* (*Ironhand,* London 1965) as well as treating a similar historical subject himself in *Armstrong's Last Goodnight.*

A historical vision similar to that of *Götz* again inspires Goethe's next major play, *Egmont,* which was also begun about this time although it was not completed until 1787. Again it shows the destruction of a traditional, natural, harmonious society and its values by the imposition of an alien system—in this case, the suppression of the traditional liberties of the Netherlands by Philip II of Spain and his agent the Duke of Alba; and again, the traditional values are embodied and supremely exemplified in the play's hero, Egmont, who was trapped and executed by Alba's orders in 1568 (the period, we note, is the same as that of *Götz:* evidently in Goethe's view the lights were going out all over Europe in the mid-sixteenth century). Again the hero is presented as a noble, forthright character, innocent of guile, a natural leader beloved and respected by the common people, especially by his mistress Klärchen, a simple but equally forthright 'Bürgermädchen' in whose company Egmont feels blissfully free of the cares and responsibilities which go with his noble rank. In conversation with his secretary in Act II Egmont describes himself as a sleepwalker, a man instinctively treading a dangerous path who will fall if he wakes up; and as a charioteer, drawn on inexorably by the 'sun-horses of time', steering his course between boulder and precipice as best he may, but unable to check his pace. He is a cheerful fatalist, allowing himself willingly to be driven on by an irresistible personal destiny, a *daimon* as Goethe later described it.

He insists on living dangerously, on taking no thought for the morrow, refusing to play the devious game of politics which is the chosen element both of Alba, his jealous enemy, and of William of Orange, his anxious, prudent friend. Natural ruler though he is, born (like Götz) to govern his people with light but firm, benevolent, patriarchal hand, he is no match for Alba, the ruthless totalitarian politician: he refuses to believe that King Philip will send Alba to the Netherlands, or that Alba will act against the native nobility, Orange and himself. Like *Götz von Berlichingen, Egmont* depicts, on the political plane, the extinction of traditional liberties by a 'modernising' despotism, and on the individual plane the defeat of an essentially unpolitical man by the alien force of modern politics itself. Egmont falls as a result of his own innocence, an innocence which others often see as mere irresponsibility. These others have included not only his friends and foes within the play, but also generations of critics, beginning with Schiller in 1788, who have found fault with Egmont as a tragic protagonist: the controversies on this point show no sign of abating. They also, inevitably, extend to the dramatic efficacy of Goethe's play, held together as it is almost solely by the personality of its hero. Many have found it wanting, while others have drawn attention to the originality and to the poetic, rather than conventionally dramatic, unity of its form.

Unlike *Götz von Berlichingen, Egmont* has very little external action, and the kaleidoscopic procession of short scenes, which in the earlier play so effectively, if at times a little confusingly, conveys the complexity and turbulence of the historical period, here gives way to a more leisurely series of static tableaux. In a sense *Egmont* can be said to observe a unity of action: the first three acts are all exposition, and nothing actually happens until Egmont's arrest in Act IV, followed inevitably by his execution in Act V. But whereas a Racinian exposition is a complex web of stresses and strains, a tense system of interrelationships, the scenes of *Egmont* are self-contained and discontinuous—a series of portraits of the hero from different points of view, first through the eyes of others (he does not himself appear in the first act), then face to face. And as Egmont himself lives for the moment, refusing until it is too late to consider the consequences of his actions, so the scenes of the play do not really lead on consequentially, one into the other: major figures like the Princess Regent, Orange, even Alba, each make only one appearance, in a single scene in which their part in the action is, so to say, placed before us complete rather than developed in the usual way from scene to scene, from act to act. The unity of *Egmont* is thus not a unity of action in a classical sense, but reflects the 'Sturm und Drang' theory of drama as being above all expressive of character.

The ending of the play is particularly remarkable. Like Götz, Egmont is last seen in the fatal setting of the prison—'the dungeon, image and foretaste of the grave, hateful alike to hero and to coward' (Act V). And like Götz too he goes to his death with the word 'freedom' on his lips. But Götz's last despairing cry is consistent both with the situation to which the action of the play has finally brought him, and with the pessimism of the historical vision which the play embodies. Egmont's last speech, delivered as the stage fills with Spanish soldiers who are to lead him to execution, takes the form of an ecstatic evocation of future liberation, inspired by a dream-vision, shared by the audience, in which we see Klärchen transfigured into an allegorical embodiment of Liberty, anticipating the spirit of Delacroix's famous painting celebrating the Paris revolution of 1830. Schiller objected to what he called the '*salto mortale* into the world of opera' by which Goethe transforms tragedy into triumph: the effect is brilliantly captured in the overture which Beethoven wrote for the play in 1810, but in terms of ordinary dramatic psychology it remains questionable. It seems that here, even in his Storm and Stress period when the play was conceived, Goethe was already aiming at a new and specifically poetic form of drama, to which such prosaic considerations would not apply. Certainly by 1787, when it was completed, poetic rather than realistic drama had become his ideal, and he sought to impose a measure of classical discipline on a work parts of which, as he then wrote, had come to seem to him too 'unbuttoned' in character. The texture and rhythm of the prose, less richly varied and less earthy than that of *Götz,* often take on a distinctly poetic quality: pervasive images, such as that of horse and rider, underpin the play's thematic unity, and the cadence of its speech often falls into that of blank verse. Memorable above all, even if frustrating in terms of conventional drama, are the great confrontation scenes between Egmont and Orange, Egmont and Alba; and Alba's powerful soliloquy in Act IV as he waits for Egmont to ride into his trap, culminating as from the window he watches Egmont dismount from his horse: 'Step down!—So, now you stand with one foot in the grave! and now with both!'

In his early years Goethe made a number of other plans for dramas on the Shakespearian model, as he conceived it, portraying 'human beings of colossal greatness': titanic, heaven-storming individuals like Prometheus and Faust, or prophets and leaders of men like Socrates, Julius Caesar, Mahomet. Shakespeare's Caesar did indeed 'bestride the narrow world / Like a Colossus'; in Goethe's version, he is described with earthy colloquialism as 'ein Sackermentskerl', which might be rendered 'a hell of a guy'. (The 'Stürmer und Dränger' were particularly fond of the colloquial word 'Kerl' for 'man', so much so that they themselves, as well as their heroes, are often referred to as 'Kraftkerls'.) In these fragments, Goethe experiments further in form and style, notably in the use of verse of different kinds. But fragments they remained. He salvaged excerpts from *Prometheus* and *Mahomet* and published them as separate lyric poems, in which form they remain some of the most familiar and important works of his early years. The 'Prometheus' ode is the supreme expression of defiance, in which the Titan issues his powerful challenge to the divine authority of Zeus:

> Hier sitz ich, forme Menschen
> Nach meinem Bilde,
> Ein Geschlecht, das mir gleich sei,
> Zu leiden, zu weinen,
> Zu genießen und zu freuen sich,
> Und dein nicht zu achten,
> Wie ich!
>
> Here I sit, forming men

In my own image,
A generation to resemble me,
To suffer and to weep,
To delight and to rejoice,
And to ignore you,
As I do!

Artists of a later generation, such as Beethoven and Shelley, were again to use the figure of Prometheus to symbolise the struggle of the human spirit to break free from the fetters of the old order. And Goethe himself was to complete the tragedy of that other, more modern rebel against divine authority, Faust, but not until many years later.

Götz von Berlichingen was not, however, the only dramatic work which Goethe had managed to complete before his move to Weimar in 1775, which marks the beginning of the end of his 'Sturm und Drang' years. The two domestic dramas *Clavigo* and *Stella* continue the vein of contemporary middle-class realism which Lessing had initiated. *Clavigo* is basically a fairly conventional 'bürgerliches Trauerspiel', which, however (or perhaps for that very reason), has long maintained a place in the German repertory. It is based, albeit loosely, on a contemporary real-life source, the memoirs of Beaumarchais, already a well-known figure of the time, although he had yet to earn his greatest fame as the author of *Le Mariage de Figaro;* Beaumarchais was, it seems, not amused by Goethe's portrayal of him as a fire-eating 'Kraftkerl'. In *Stella,* subtitled 'a play for lovers' ('ein Schauspiel für Liebende'), Goethe modifies the convention in a daring and original way, producing something much more like a modern 'problem play', steeped though it is in the sentimentality of its period. The bigamous hero Fernando (another vacillating figure in the mould of Mellefont and Weislingen) and his two wives Cäcilie and Stella end the play resolved to attempt to live together in a *ménage à trois.* Schröder produced *Stella* in Hamburg in 1776 and it was well received by the public, but soon banned by the authorities as immoral. In 1806, for a production in Weimar, Goethe was to revise the ending, turning it into a tragedy: Fernando shoots himself and Stella takes poison, and traditional propriety, both moral and dramatic, is thus restored. The original, less conventional version was, however, translated into both French and English, and in more recent times has enjoyed a number of successful revivals.

Goethe also completed in the early 1770s a number of minor works which explore other theatrical possibilities. *Erwin und Elmire* and *Claudine von Villa Bella* are plays with musical numbers ('Singspiele'), a form which attracted a good deal of attention at this time and reached its apogee with the German operas of Mozart; the text of *Claudine* was subsequently set by a number of composers, including Schubert. Goethe also wrote a number of farces, burlesques and revue-like pieces, including *Götter, Helden und Wieland* (*Gods, Heroes and Wieland*), an affectionate satire (Wieland took it in good part) on the latter's Rococo travesty of the Greek world in his 'Singspiel' *Alceste* (1773), and *Das Jahrmarktsfest zu Plundersweilen* (*The Lumberton Fair*), a revival of the Sachsian 'Fastnachtsspiel'. These are vigorous and lively works, distinctly popular and, in the latter instance, specifically national in flavour, and showing a considerable interest on Goethe's part in forms of theatrical entertainment far removed from the 'serious' literary drama as it had come to be understood in his day, and as he himself conceived it in *Götz* and *Egmont.* But it was only in *Faust* that he was eventually to achieve a synthesis of these very disparate styles.

The other 'Stürmer und Dränger' of the 1770s stand very much in Goethe's shadow: they were indeed often referred to as 'Goetheaner'. Lenz is undoubtedly the most original of them, even if his originality at times verges on perversity, betraying the pathological streak which mars his work and was to destroy his life. Lenz in both his theory and his plays manifests a much keener social awareness than most of his contemporaries, perhaps indeed than any European playwright or dramatic theorist before him. He argues that the 'rules' of Greek drama are intimately related to the Greek view of life and the world, and in particular that the Greeks regarded the individual human being as much less autonomous, much more a creature of the gods or of fate than is the modern view. Like Goethe, Lenz advocates that modern tragedy should portray great, towering, heroic characters, rather than 'actions' in the classical sense: we want, he says in the *Anmerkungen,* to see 'a whole series of actions, following one upon the other like thunderclaps', all issuing from the character of the protagonist, so that at the end we can cry out in wonder and admiration 'Das ist ein Kerl!' (which again we might render 'What a guy!'). But at the same time Lenz argues that the modern theatre-going public is not capable of appreciating tragedy, and that therefore comedy is for the moment, until 'the comic playwright creates the tragedian's public for him', the more appropriate form. By comedy, however, Lenz understands something much more like modern critical social drama than the traditional form. Articulating more precisely the feeling already voiced by Diderot that the traditional genres were no longer appropriate to the needs of a modern audience, he writes: 'Comedy is a depiction of human society, and when the state of society is serious, its depiction cannot be a laughing matter.' Although, in accordance with his theories, his play *Die Soldaten* (*The Soldiers,* 1776) was originally to have been designated a comedy, Lenz changed this before publication to the neutral 'Schauspiel'. This and the earlier *Der Hofmeister* (*The Private Tutor,* 1774) are his best and his most familiar plays (*Der Hofmeister* was adapted by Brecht for the Berliner Ensemble in the 1950s). In both of them potentially tragic elements, notably the theme of seduction and abandonment, are treated with a degree of intellectual detachment; but both plays also convey a keen sense of the suffering caused by social injustice and class divisions, which Lenz himself knew only too well at first hand. His work is a more radical development of Lessing's domestic realism: it does not really belong in the history of German classicism, but points forward, as we have already suggested, to later developments of a quite different character.

The other most important dramatist of the 1770s was Friedrich Maximilian Klinger, author of the play by which the whole movement came subsequently to be known. His best play, however, is undoubtedly not *Sturm und Drang* but *Die Zwillinge* (*The Twins*), yet another product of the *annus mirabilis* 1776, when it won a prize offered by Schröder in Hamburg. It is a practicable piece of theatrical writing, having a very small cast and keeping close to the classical unities in form, despite its explosive content and style. It depicts the fatal rivalry of twin brothers, the passionate and dynamic Guelfo and the gentle, melancholy and reflective Ferdinando. The motif of hostile brothers is one which Klinger made very much his own: a familiar tragic subject, but one to which he gave a new intensity and expressive force. The Promethean revolt of the 'Stürmer und Dränger' against the literary, cultural, moral and social values of earlier generations is here expressed through the revolt of a son against family ties and paternal authority. But even in *Die Zwillinge,* though Guelfo does kill Ferdinando and is himself killed by their father in punishment, the energy of the theme is drained through rhetoric rather than channelled into genuine dramatic conflict. Klinger is more interested in histrionic gesture—Guelfo smashing his reflection in the mirror (IV, iv)—than in action or even than in serious character portrayal. His heroes—Guelfo, Wild in *Sturm und Drang,* Otto in the play of that name—in their passionate desire for self-fulfilment and self-expression seem to epitomise the ideal of the 'Kraftkerl', but in reality they do very little but rant and strike attitudes. For the true realisation of the dramatic potential of the theme of rebellion, we have to wait for Schiller. (pp. 32-51)

F. J. Lamport, "The Revolt of Prometheus (i): Goethe and the 'Sturm und Drang'," in his German Classical Drama: Theatre, Humanity and Nation, 1750-1870, *Cambridge University Press, 1990, pp. 32-51.*

An excerpt from J. M. R. Lenz's "Eduard Allwills Only Hymn" (1775?):

Once I tasted, it is true,
Moments full of sheerest bliss.
But in moments, God, so few,
Thy reward should lie in this?

Sparks they were of high delight,
Birds that told the fall of land,
When its sorrows' depth and height
Passed what mind could understand.

Will they never burst to flame?
Can it be thy Word should lie,
Seeking like a nurse to tame
With a cunning lullaby?

No, I cry—O Saviour! Father!
My heart's yearning must be stayed,
Must be sated; if not, rather
Smash the image thou hast made!

Must I strain then to the last,
Hope and trust in wind and wild?
No, my Life, I'll hold thee fast
Till thou bless with joy thy child.

J. M. R. Lenz, "Eduard Allwills Only Hymn," quoted in The German Sturm und Drang *by Roy Pascal, 1953.*

Friedhelm Radandt

[In the following excerpt, Radant provides an overview of the lives and careers of some of the Sturm und Drang movement's most prominent playwrights.]

The enormous success of Goethe's *Götz* inspired other *Sturm und Drang* authors to use their talents for the writing of drama. As the active group moved from Strasbourg to Frankfort, drama became more and more the central subject of their discussions. The admiration of the *Sturm und Drang* writers for Shakespeare kindled their fascination with the stage even more. Since in *Götz* Goethe had, in their opinion, achieved the characterization of a powerful individual by following the principles of Shakespeare's dramas, it seemed possible to write more such plays for the German stage. Goethe himself was working on his *Faust* drama, but was also soon making plans for his *Egmont.* In addition, there was the influence that Heinrich Wilhelm von Gerstenberg (1737-1823) exerted on the *Sturm und Drang.* In his *Briefe über Merkwürdigkeiten der Literatur* (1766-1770) he had discussed Shakespeare's dramas. His approach to the English playwright was not different from Herder's, for Gerstenberg too wanted Shakespeare's work to be judged by criteria that were particular to Shakespeare, and to the times in which Shakespeare wrote. Unlike Herder, however, Gerstenberg also sought to put into practice what he considered to be Shakespeare's greatness. Gerstenberg's *Ugolino* (1768)—the drama builds on the story of Count Ugolino Gherardesca in Dante's *Divine Comedy*—was intended to dramatize a great and morally strong character who maintains his own dignity in the face of death.

Ugolino was overthrown as ruler of Pisa and, together with his three sons, condemned to death by starvation in the tower of that Italian city. Their emotions and struggles in the face of death, but mainly Ugolino's successful fight against the temptation to take his own life, once he has watched his sons die, make up the plot of the drama. Gerstenberg's language gives full expression to Ugolino's range of feelings, from rage to despair to quiet composure. *Ugolino* was well received by Lessing who immediately following its publication summarized his impressions in a letter to Gerstenberg: 'Ihr *Ugolino* bleibt immer ein Werk von sehr grossen, ausserordentlichen Schönheiten. . . . ' But Lessing also had some questions which arose from his understanding of the nature of the medium of drama. How is it possible, he wonders, for Ugolino to refrain from taking his and his sons' lives if in fact their death is inevitable? Only uncertainty about their fate, Lessing argues, could keep Ugolino from hastening that end by his own intervention. That uncertainty does not exist, given the nature of the genre and the objective of the playwright. Gerstenberg replies a few months later with the observation that starvation was the topic of the drama, and that therefore it was necessary to show 'ob die Vorsehung den unglücklichen Menschen retten, ob er seinem Charakter gemäss ausdulden wird. . . . '

In the meantime, the great and strong character that Gerstenberg had demanded of drama had been achieved by Goethe in his *Götz.* The *Sturm und Drang* authors took up the challenge and developed the new drama in various directions. Lenz, Klinger, Wagner, Maler Müller and Leisewitz all concentrated their efforts on creating for Germany plays that were no longer intended to teach but to portray real life. In this they were successful, and most of them produced their work within a short time, between 1774 and 1778.

Jakob Michael Reinhold Lenz (1751-1792), who was driven to insanity by the disparate forces of his personality, wrote within the span of some three years (1774-1776) several dramas which give expression to the period's belief in the complexity of human life, and which in form and language attest to the movement's protest against the cult of wit and rationalism as well as against the existing social system. Lenz's plays also show his unusual talent for achieving a life-like portrayal of his times. His work therefore proved to be of singular influence on other playwrights. The Romantic Tieck published Lenz's work in three volumes in 1829. That edition was available to Büchner, whose indebtedness to the *Sturm und Drang* dramatist has been convincingly shown. In our century Brecht prepared his own version of the Lenz play *Der Hofmeister,* thus helping Lenz's play to a belated stage success. Even more recent is a new adaptation of Lenz's *Die Soldaten* by Heinar Kipphardt (1968), who considers the play to be of extraordinary importance in the history of German drama. There can be no question that Lenz's contribution to the development of drama is pivotal to its success during the *Sturm und Drang.* The leading literary figures of his day recognized that fact when they corresponded with him actively, especially following his debut as dramatist in 1774. Hamann, Herder, Lavater, and especially Goethe acknowledged Lenz's talent as shown in his successful techniques he uses for the portrayal of social reality. Lenz's artistic accomplishments, however, must not be overrated. There is not the parsimonious economy of language and dramatic structure that is the hallmark of Büchner's *Woyzeck,* a play that imitates and uses so effectively linguistic elements and poetic inventions of *Die Soldaten.* Besides, Lenz's pervasive social and cultural criticism lacks logical cohesiveness and thus the power to be convincing. Nor are his plays dominated by the one overpowering character as is the case in Goethe's *Götz.* The greatness of Lenz's dramas lies in the telling use of highly idiomatic and vivid language, as well as in the feeling of constant movement, achieved through the frequent change in scenery, and the suggestion that a multiplicity of forces shapes the life of an individual.

The son of a Pietistic minister and theologian, Lenz attended the University of Königsberg as a student of theology. He became quite familiar with the general cultural scene of rationalistic Germany, came to admire Rousseau—who was read by all *Sturm und Drang* writers—but probably also knew Hamann, who by this time had published his major works. Lenz's first creative writings made use of the conventional forms of Enlightenment literature, the philosophical poem and the sentimental comedy. He was still in Königsberg when he began translating Shakespeare's *Love's Labour's Lost.* At the time of his arrival in Strasbourg he was ready for the ideas and ideals of the emerging *Sturm und Drang.* Lenz went there in 1771, accompanying two young noblemen who were to receive army training near Strasbourg. Since Lenz lived with them he experienced army life and became thoroughly familiar with the mentality of eighteenth-century military officers. The experience was to provide him with ample material for his drama *Die Soldaten.* The Strasbourg *Sturm und Drang* group was high-spirited at the time, and the impressionable and somewhat romantic Lenz was susceptible to the spirit of the genius cult and to its poetry. His review of Goethe's *Götz von Berlichingen* is a vivid testimony of his new literary ideals. Arguing that action is at the center of all life and must be the central issue of literature, he holds up Goethe's *Götz* in its first version, widely considered impossible to perform, and proposes to prove its viability by mounting it himself: 'Lassen Sie mich für die Ausführung dieses Projekts sorgen, es soll gar so viel Schwürigkeiten nicht haben als Sie anfangs einbilden werden. Weder Theater noch Kulisse noch Dekoration—es kommt alles auf Handlung an.' The assertion that the abundance of scenes and frequent changes in the scenery make a staging of *Götz* almost impossible is countered by the opinion that intricate theatricals are not essential, whereas the portrayal of action is. He is willing to dispense with props and scenery altogether, is willing to indicate a change in locale by playing music that would function as a kind of identifying leitmotif, to create the impression of immediacy of action and of multifariousness of human life.

Lenz stayed in Strasbourg longer than the other *Sturm und Drang* writers and lingered on until 1776. It was the most fruitful period in his life. After Goethe left Strasbourg in 1771, Lenz initiated a correspondence with him. He idolized Goethe and relied on his relationship with him as a source of personal strength and encouragement, particularly since Goethe was willing to comment on Lenz's manuscripts. The first of these was *Der Hofmeister oder Vortheile der Privaterziehung* (1774) which treats the bitter lot of private tutors in houses of nobility, and demonstrates that the alleged advantages of private tutoring are in reality only disadvantages. It is dehumanizing to the tutor because it perverts his sensibilities, and is apt to turn the students into rash and reckless young people. Public education receives praise, and the public school teacher Wenzeslaus, who is not without his idiosyncrasies, plays the role of the honest and morally courageous man. A representative of the nobility, the privy councilor Berg is the outspoken advocate of public schools, who admonishes his son and his niece to live in the world of reality and not of fancy: ' . . . keine Romane spielen wollen, die nur in der ausschweifenden Einbildungskraft eines hungrigen Poeten ausgeheckt sind und von denen ihr in der heutigen Welt keinen Schatten der Wirklichkeit antrefft' [I, 6]. Indeed, his son shows himself as having accepted this advice when he in turn seeks to instill a sense of decency in a fellow student, the licentious Pätus: 'Wir sind in den Jahren; wir sind auf der See, der Wind treibt uns, aber die Vernunft muss immer am Steuerruder bleiben, sonst jagen wir auf die erste beste Klippe und scheitern' [IV, 6]. Lenz uses here a characteristic *Sturm und Drang* metaphor: the young sailor out on the stormy sea, in danger of shipwreck on a cliff. Goethe liked this image as well because it captured the feeling of uncertainty and the experience of adventure that the genius cult welcomed. Interestingly enough, Lenz appeals in this context to reason and assigns to it the role of the pilot in a person's life. The piteous tutor, the hero of the play, does not use reason, running away from problems instead, as his name 'Läuffer' suggests, he ruins his life when he castrates himself in a moment of over-zealous striving for virtuousness, but subsequently has no compunctions about marrying a young girl.

The awkwardness or even uncanniness of the situation is not uncommon with Lenz, who likes such stark and rude sketches of life. They do have a certain comical effect, and the reader and viewer can hardly accept them as serious. Nor are they intended to be taken seriously, just as the play's subtitle was merely a ploy to get the question about the advantages of private education into the open, jokingly raising expectations that the author was not about to meet. Lenz classified all his plays as comedies. It is probably more accurate to call them tragi-comedies, as is commonly done. At any rate, uncanny humor is part of all of Lenz's plays. Lenz distinguished between tragedies and comedies by reserving portrayal of the development of the individual character for the former, and treatment of a problem for the latter. The distinction marks Lenz as a Shakespeare follower, as might be expected of a *Sturm und Drang* playwright. For the comedy, in particular, he claimed poetic subjectivity as a way of underscoring the poet's freedom to deal with a given subject matter as he pleases. Since all his plays are billed as comedies Lenz felt free to include many episodes which do not bear on the hero's character or personality, but which do elucidate the complexity of human life, and to invent scenes of the stark comical nature found in *Der Hofmeister.* Lenz's most important ideas on the theater are contained in the lively critical treatise *Anmerkungen übers Theater* (1774), a basic work for *Sturm und Drang* drama. His dominating interest in drama is documented through his versions of five Plautus comedies, all published in 1774.

The good reception of *Der Hofmeister* encouraged Lenz to continue with his approach to play-writing. In a short time followed *Der neue Menoza,* still in 1774, *Die Freunde machen den Philosophen* and *Die Soldaten,* both in 1776, and *Der Engländer, eine dramatische Phantasey* in 1777. A number of fragments of plays have also been preserved. Besides *Der Hofmeister,* the plays *Die Soldaten* and *Der neue Menoza* have contributed most to the development of drama. The latter play with the subtitle *Geschichte des kumbanischen Prinzen Tandi* treats the problem of decadence in European culture. The name 'Menoza' was taken from a contemporary Danish novel by Erik Pontoppidan. The 'Menoza' of the novel is an Asian prince who had traveled to enlightened Europe in search of true Christians. Lenz did not retain the name 'Menoza', except in the title. He calls his hero Tandi and declares him an African prince, actually a European by birth, who expects to find in Europe a society of enlightened people adhering to a rigid code of moral and ethical behavior. In that expectation he is disappointed. There is a good deal of Rousseauism in *Der neue Menoza,* as when the morally impeccable prince from Africa uses harsh language to castigate the Europeans:

> In Eurem Morast ersticke ich. . . . Das der aufgeklärte Weltteil! Allenthalben wo man hinriecht, Lässigkeit, faule ohnmächtige Begier, lalender Tod für Feuer und Leben, Geschwätz für Handlung. . . . Was ihr Empfindung nennt, ist Schmincke, womit ihr Brutalität bestreicht.

This sort of cultural criticism reminds one of Herder's attacks on contemporary European culture in his *Auch eine Philosophie. Der neue Menoza* is an all-encompassing denunciation of society in Germany. The narrow thought pattern of the middle class is depicted in the representative Biederling, for he is 'bieder' in his views and activities. The prophet of doom, Beza, embodies the self-righteous Pietist-theologian who counterbalances the optimistic world view of the Enlightenment. Zierau serves as an example of the arrogant young pedantic man who has returned home from the university and now attempts to put into practice the ideas of the rationalistic age which he has not even understood. In contrast, his father, the unschooled but level-headed mayor, employs common sense in all areas of life, even in aesthetic matters. As a result he is able to enjoy the escapades of a harlequin on stage and naively looks for entertainment in a theatrical performance, and not for the strict observance of the dramatic unities, as does his son. The world of nobility is captured in Count Camäleon, who, true to his name, possesses many personalities, but tries to hide his true identity. His wife, the alleged Spanish countess Donna Diana, a fury of jealousy, eventually turns out to be Biederling's daughter, for she had been exchanged as a baby. Concurrently the romantic middle-class Wilhelmine, who in the play is Biederling's daughter, turns out to be a countess. The fact frees her from the guilt of incest because the African prince to whom she has become married has in the meantime been identified as Biederling's missing son. Confusion throughout the drama is great. Lenz causes it because he employs two such extreme plot elements as the exchange of babies and the unexpected return of a long lost son. Lenz's liking for the uncommon and unbelievable again comes to the surface here. The more the African prince becomes entangled with European society the less he can fulfill his active and outspoken role as cultural critic. Yet his reaction to what he believes to be his participation in incest is vastly different from that of all others. While he seeks to do penance, the others merely try to explain it away. The theologian Beza looks for ways to justify it after all, and Biederling for excuses to avoid embarrassment. Thus it is precisely the prince's relationship to Wilhemine and the ensuing confusion that broadens the portrait of eighteenth-century society in Germany, a society that lives by artificial standards. The prince, a learned but humble man, is at odds with this society because he uses common sense. That is the point Lenz wants to drive home, and is apparently the reason why the play ends with a scene that exemplifies once more the dichotomy between the artificial rule-consciousness of an alleged age of reason and the positive existence that is possible where common sense rules.

Die Soldaten emerges not only as Lenz's strongest stricture against existing social conditions, but also as his best play because it goes beyond mere social accusations. It is a moving document of human frailty in the unrelenting clutches of temptation. Both the middle-class dealer in jewelry and other fancy goods, Wesener, and his daughter, Marie, are blinded by glitter. Glitter is the stuff of Wesener's business, and the glitter of the military as evidenced in the uniform and free life of the high officers, all of them representatives of the nobility, captures Marie's fancy. Neither can withstand the strong pull of this temptation, and in the penultimate scene of the play father Wesener finds his daughter begging in the streets. Upon mutual recognition they fall into each other's arms and to the ground. 'Beide wälzen sich halb tot auf der Erde,' reads the stage direction at this point. Their final fate remains uncertain, allowing the playwright once more to return to the topic of social improvement in the final scene.

The plan for improvement is advanced by a high military officer who is shocked over the plight that has befallen the Wesener family. His proposal recognizes the custom that military men were not permitted to marry, a fact which he views as the root of many social and moral problems. Realizing the ineffectuality of suggesting that the king should permit marriage, he envisions a group of women in the employ of the king sacrificing, as it were, their honor and their concept of love and marriage, and by their sacrifice guaranteeing the moral safety of young girls from middle-class families. The totally unrealistic and even grotesque plan is typical for Lenz, who wants to arouse the reader's reaction by describing such stark, inhuman courses of action. The officer's plan is not advanced as a possible solution. Rather it calls attention to the fundamental unacceptability of the existing situation better than any real improvement plan could do. The fact that Lenz did make a similar proposal in a separate essay does not alter the function of the plan within the context of the play. Indeed, the presentation of the self-centered life and the contemptible world of thought of army officers was a daring denunciation of the military, certainly at a time when soldiery in Prussia was admired.

At no time did Lenz consider literature a means of changing the world, but he certainly thought it a means of branding its wrongs. Lenz did not choose the form of the idyl to describe a world free from present social evils because he was afraid that readers might confuse a literary fictive reality with actual reality. Thus he has the Countess La Roche, who presents Lenz's own views in *Die Soldaten,* warn Marie not to read the idyl in Richardson's *Pamela* in terms of social reality in which a marriage between members of different social classes is possible. Marie's happiness, which would have been assured in a marriage with Stolzius, the middle-class dealer in cloth, is destroyed because she responds to Baron Desportes' flirtings. Her weakness for glitter makes it easy for her to brush aside the occasional pangs of conscience she feels about the way she has been treating Stolzius, whose mental torment and psychological anguish are caused by Marie's unfaithfulness, and even more by the contemptuous manner in which the officers who take delight in his suffering inform him of Desportes's escapades with Marie. These officers find pleasure in sadistic pranks. Their military existence has subverted their humanity completely. The creation of Stolzius is one of the great literary accomplishments of Lenz's work. Büchner would draw on this figure when he created the character Woyzeck for his well-known play by that name. Lenz's careful observance of speech patterns and dialect peculiarities constitutes the basic device used to lend this figure an aura of general hauntedness and insecurity. His worry about Marie leads to stages of mental depression which cause his seemingly absentminded remarks. The ominous seriousness of his responses to the jocular comments of the officers testifies how badly he feels hurt by them. Yet they do not perceive that their pranks and jokes threaten his very existence, and drive him toward madness and revenge.

More and more Lenz's plays began to reflect the author's growing alienation from society. This is strongly the case with his prose works, especially with the novel fragment, *Der Waldbruder,* written in 1776, and published in Schiller's influential journal *Die Horen* in 1797. The novel's hero is given the name Herz, thereby reaffirming the period's faith in the right of an individual to trust his own feelings. Herz speaks of this dimension of personal freedom when he writes: 'Nur Freiheit will ich haben, zu lieben was ich will und so stark und dauerhaft, als es mir gefällt.' It is unrequited love, love for a countess whom he has never even seen, that drove Herz to become a hermit. The novel consists of letters from Herz to his friend Rothe, as well as those written by Rothe and others who discuss the hermit's motives and views. The work is a semi-autobiographical account, including the aspects of love for a woman he had never met and the plan to go to America and fight in the Revolutionary War. Lenz wrote this work at the beginning of his estrangement from Goethe. In 1775 Goethe had visited Lenz in Strasbourg, and Lenz put his enthusiastic admiration and veneration for Goethe into words in his *Pandemonium germanicum.* The critical work ridicules outright all contemporary German literary works which will not bear comparison with those of Goethe. Written in 1775, it was not published until 1819. But when the Goethe admirer showed up in Weimar in the spring of 1776, disagreements developed quickly, leading by the year's end to an almost formal expulsion from Weimar. Lenz returned to the Strasbourg region. There he experienced prolonged periods of depression and madness. He sought help from Pastor Oberlin, who lived in an Alsatian village. Oberlin's carefully kept diary of his encounters with Lenz would serve later as the basis for Büchner's novella *Lenz.* The illness eventually forced the young author to return to his home in Riga. His mental health improved for a time, and he went to St Petersburg and to Moscow where he did some teaching. In 1792 he was found dead in a street in Moscow.

The dramatic work of Friedrich Maximilian Klinger (1752-1831), which in many ways offers the most characteristic *Sturm und Drang* writing, does not simply glorify the titanic person or heap praise on the unbridled challenger of all human order. Goethe had moved from portraying the powerful individual Götz, who felt so sure about his principles that he was willing to battle even the emperor, to describing the life of the emotion-filled Werther, who could not cope with the strength of his feeling. Lenz, meanwhile, showed preference for the individual who is destroyed by unjust social realities, and Klinger constructed his dramas around the egocentric person of unusual strength, who is given to rage and acts of violence and madness, and who is totally unrestrained and unrestrainable in his passionate outbreaks of anger. For that very reason his work has been cited whenever someone wanted to point to the boisterousness of *Sturm und Drang* personalities and utterances. Yet the question has been asked correctly whether the obstreperous, frenzied and boastful heroes of Klinger's plays are to be taken as positive representatives of the age, or whether the author criticized his own age for producing such self-styled 'geniuses'.

Klinger, like Goethe a native of Frankfort, found in the circle of *Sturm und Drang* authors what his searching mind needed. He was only nineteen in 1771 when Goethe returned home from his university studies in Strasbourg. Meeting Goethe and other like-minded adherents of the movement influenced Klinger decisively. Goethe took a liking to the aspiring writer who came from a humble background. He even supported his studies at the university, and Klinger followed in Goethe's footsteps by choosing law, although play-writing was Klinger's major activity at the university. Given that Goethe had written his *Götz* late in 1771, and that this work was to be discussed and admired most by the young authors and intellectuals involved in the new literary movement, it will not come as a surprise to discover that Klinger's first drama, *Otto* (1775), was another example of the increasingly popular type that sought to glorify the age of knighthood. Klinger completed four plays during the two years at the university between 1774 and 1776, *Das leidende Weib* (1775), *Die Zwillinge* (1776), *Die neue Arria* (1776), and *Simsone Grisaldo* (1776). Being separated from his friends in Frankfort, for he studied in Giessen, Klinger felt a strong need to express himself in writing. The plays he wrote there deal with the battle an individual may experience within himself, as well as the problems such an individual may encounter in his relationships to others. The play that gave the period its name, *Sturm und Drang* (1776), he wrote after he had demonstrated his opposition to the existing cultural and educational institutions by leaving the university. Yet only a very short time later Klinger would reach the conscious decision to change his writing style and disassociate himself from the *Sturm und Drang* movement. While he did not return to a university to complete his studies formally, embarking rather on the successful career of a military officer, he did later on play an important role in university life as the curator of the University of Dorpat in Russia.

When he left Giessen, he was at the height of his involvement with the ideas and ideals of the movement, and he was in inner turmoil. That probably was the reason for his going to Weimar to be close to Goethe once again. Yet Goethe's interests had shifted away from the subjective *Sturm und Drang* life. He was a high public official in Weimar by now, no longer experiencing individual emotional turmoil and tensions, if indeed he ever had identified in reality, and not merely in imagination, with the extreme *Sturm und Drang* position. As a result, Goethe had little appreciation of Lenz's and Klinger's plight when they showed up in Weimar in 1776. Lenz took revenge for Goethe's coldness by creating the figure of Rothe in the novel fragment *Der Waldbruder,* who is accused by the novel's hero Herz of having compromised his convictions when he joined the court society. Klinger also felt alienated by Goethe, and he too rejected the comfortable life at the Weimar court. His inner turmoil became even more intense. Klinger left Weimar in the early fall of 1776, for almost two years associating with a traveling theater troupe, and then choosing for himself the military life which proved to be satisfying to him, and which was to bring him many honors, take him to Russia, and eventually make him an influential person at the Russian court. That fact is important because it tells us that in Klinger's case being a high officer in the Russian military afforded the kind of intellectual challenge that he needed. He remained extremely active as a writer, turning his attention primarily to the novel, treating topics of concern to the general climate of the period, and doing so in a fashion that holds the fascination even of today's reader, especially his treatment of Faust. Klinger's biography exemplifies why the life story of a *Sturm und Drang* author is of interest. Klinger admittedly used writing as a way of contending with his own passionate feelings, just as being a soldier was to him a way of maintaining strength of character.

Recent analyses of Klinger's dramatic *Sturm und Drang* work have called attention to a recurring motif that throws an interesting light on the author's view of the literary movement of which he was a part. The characters he creates, these titanic, boisterous, screaming, God-and-world-accusing, self-centered, raging heroes let themselves be guided exclusively by uncontrolled urges and exaggerated outbursts of feeling. They are, to be sure, representatives of the *Sturm und Drang* generation. Yet their Promethean defiance stems from childish stubbornness, and is not the result of a reasoned protest against the world. Klinger's portrayal of his characters as childlike heroes is the recurring motif which reflects his critical view of the *Sturm und Drang* rebel. His sympathies lie not simply with these powerful characters for whom life has become a game in which outbreaks of passion determine the nature of each move. Klinger's plays show the sufferings of these passionate characters who are unable to control themselves. The author views this kind of inner turmoil as a result of the *Sturm und Drang* cult of genius in which feeling and passion reign supreme, and he warns against it.

In *Das leidende Weib* Brand—his name is suggestive of the consuming desire he feels for the ambassador's wife—strikes us as a person totally without any self-control. This impression of him is vividly portrayed in the fifth scene of the first act: 'Soll ich hingehen? soll ich? du trinkst mehr Gift. Soll ich? will ich? Da liegt's. Ich will, will immer, weil meine Sinne trunken sind.' His inability to even want to resist the desire of being with the ambassador's wife corresponds to her feeling as well, when she confesses to be weeping over her sin: 'Über meine Sünde, Brand! Und in meiner Brust brennt's—o fühl's, ich bin bereit, neue zu begehen' [I, 7]. While the ambassador's wife is torn between her love for her husband and the desire to be with Brand, the latter's uncontrolled passion for her is matched by Count Louis's desire to possess her. He feels betrayed by Brand and is eager to prove that Brand enjoys an illicit relationship with the ambassador's wife. Klinger's masterful presentation of feelings and jealousies, of sufferings and passion, which lead to the destruction of these characters, provided the most important literary source for Büchner's *Woyzeck*.

Die Zwillinge exposes the reader to a kind of literature which has often been regarded as a portrayal of the extreme rule of emotions and passions. Guelfo is outraged against his twin brother Ferdinando, who is the first-born, and who has won the Countess Camilla, whom he, Guelfo, loves. This plot permits Klinger to develop the themes of the prodigal son and of fratricide—themes which are prominent in *Sturm und Drang* literature. Klinger bases the hero's denunciation of his father, and his murder of his brother, solely on Guelfo's inability to deal with his own emotions and feelings in a rational way. His is not a case of rebellion against apparent injustice. Neither father nor brother have tried to deceive him, although he makes the unfounded and unsubstantiated charge that he was the first-born and not Ferdinando. His pathological condition is betrayed in his own words with which the first scene closes. He sees his own senseless raging as building castles in the air:

> Was hilft das nun all, wenn ich mir mit geballter Faust vor die Stirne schlag und mit den Winden heule—droh und lärme, und bei alledem nur Luftschlösser, Kartenhäuser baue! . . . Nichts lautet närrischer, als wenn ich mir selbst rufe. Guelfo! [I, 1]

Guelfo withdraws again and again from his family to be by himself. He can never be completely by himself, for Grimaldo is always with him. However, since Grimaldo is merely the symbolic personification of Guelfo's raging self, this technique works to remind the reader and viewer of Guelfo's schizophrenic existence. Those around Guelfo treat him as a sick person and demonstrate love and even patience for the tormented member of the family. Still, their kindness does not bring healing to him, but rather increases Guelfo's anger. He is the irrational hero *par excellence,* and the play a characteristic example of *Sturm und Drang* drama. That does not mean, however, that it should be read as an endorsement of the autonomy of feeling.

Nor is Klinger concerned with outward social reality, although he has often been featured as a social critic. His dramas are peculiarly devoid of impressive settings or particular events. The reader may be told that a certain play takes place in Italy or in America, but nothing further in the drama will reinforce this piece of information. What is described could happen anywhere and is not tied to any special locale. The major place of action is in the minds of the heroes. Klinger writes about the worlds his heroes create in themselves. What Drullo in *Die neue Arria* says of the play's hero, Julio, can be said of Klinger: 'Das ist ein überspannter Mensch von einem Poeten, wie ich immer sagte, der neue Welten in sich schafft, und die würklichen vergisst' [II, 5]. The entire play revolves around the question whether Julio can escape the normality of life and achieve the greatness which would correspond to the greatness of his feelings and win him the respect and love of the power-hungry Solina.

The great person is also the theme of *Simsone Grisaldo.* General Grisaldo's accomplishments on the battlefield are enhanced by his humane actions and wise decisions. Grisaldo has found harmony within himself and has adjusted to political reality. Although it may appear that Klinger created more mature heroes after *Die Zwillinge,* such an impression is certainly not appropriate in view of his play *Sturm und Drang*—initially given the title *Wirrwarr*—which he wrote after *Simsone Grisaldo.* Klinger assigns the telling name 'Wild' to the play's hero, and indicates its setting as America, which may simply underscore the idea of wildness, for there is nothing else in particular that would remind the reader of being in the midst of the Revolutionary War in America. A feud between two English families is settled in America after much confusion about the identity of persons. Before the outbreak of hatred between the families the children had been promised each other in marriage. Now Lord Bushy's son Wild finds Lord Berkley's daughter Jenny Caroline in America, and the appearance of Lord Bushy, who had been presumed dead, ends plans for revenge and brings about reconciliation. To be sure, Klinger borrowed from Shakespeare names and plot details. But the emphasis here is on finding harmony and inner peace. Several sub-plots serve as a foil to Wild's and Jenny Caroline's love experience. In contrast to their strong love the courtship of the minor characters ridicules forms of love which are not based on mutual attraction and consuming feeling. Wild's impetuousness is soothed by Jenny Caroline's unswerving love for him. He confesses that only his love for her has sustained him, that he has been searching for her all over the world, and has come to America to seek death in battle: 'Ja, Miss! nur die Liebe hat diese Maschine zusammengehalten, die durch ewigen, innern Krieg ihrer Zerstörung jede Stunde so nah war' [II, 4]. Even though Wild's words in the first scene speak of restlessness, of the happiness of taking part in a war and of blaming himself for his misfortunes, the language of the entire play conveys a much calmer mental attitude than was the case in *Die Zwillinge.* The playwright Klinger had reached a point in his life when he was more interested in dealing with philosophical issues of human existence. He was no longer the *Sturm und Drang* author who was seeking to portray the turbulence and confusion of uncontrolled feeling. This is documented outwardly when he employs the novel as a carrier of his ideas, although he does not abandon the dramatic form.

His novels in particular—he planned a cycle of ten and executed nine—testify to his sharp analytical mind. In them he deals with diverse topics as he intended to portray human society in all its forms of existence. *Fausts Leben, Taten und Höllenfahrt* (1791) is an example of the philosophical novel that seemed to correspond to his own interests. The work captured the imagination of the public, partly because the Faust theme had become so timely by 1791, but mainly because Klinger's treatment, with its satirical overtones, is a fascinating and highly intellectual commentary on human nature. That intellectualism imbues the novel with a sense of timelessness which holds the interest of today's reader as well. In the novel *Der Weltmann und der Dichter* (1798) Klinger addressed the problem of the relationship between the artist and society. He provided an early example of a historical novel in *Geschichte Raphael des Aquillas* (1793), and touches on basic questions of the period in *Geschichte eines Teutschen der neuesten Zeit* (1796/98). It is the story of the liberal, political reformer, Ernst von Falkenburg, whose idealism is in irreconcilable conflict with the system as it represents itself in his uncle. Ernst's tutor, spurred on by Rousseau's *Emil,* has awakened in him a desire to be human rather than a nobleman, and to distinguish between true virtue and mere rule observance. Accordingly, the uncle dismisses the tutor who achieves one of Klinger's own dreams when he goes to America. The new tutor is willing to teach a moral system that knows only the criterion of usefulness and allows for sensuality without the restrictions of virtue. Ernst knows, and that is the point of the novel, that the two philosophies exclude each other. He must choose one or the other. The choice is, of course, not difficult since he represents a generation that is influenced by Rousseau. The theme of the generation conflict reminds us of the *Sturm und Drang* period in general, and of Klinger's early plays in particular. It is just as noteworthy that in some aspects Ernst removes himself from Rousseau's ideas for he does not necessarily advocate a return to nature.

The *Sturm und Drang* writers were not oblivious to technical requirements of the stage even though they often were writing for a reading public. Heinrich Leopold Wagner (1747-1779) became more involved in stage production than the other *Sturm und Drang* playwrights, and his plays were especially successful as theater pieces. In that respect he is similar to Lenz, with whom he shares also the desire to display on the stage a realistic social milieu. Wagner was the oldest of the *Sturm und Drang* writers who were attached in some way to the circle around Goethe. Yet he was one of the last to join, and his name is connected mainly with only one play, *Die Kindermörderin.* The title indicates that the play treats a topic similar to that of the Gretchen episode in Goethe's *Urfaust.* Goethe even accused Wagner of plagiarism. That charge was unfounded, for Wagner had made radically different use of the motif of an unwed mother murdering her child out of fear and desperation than had Goethe. It was not until 1775 that Wagner came to know Goethe in Frankfort, even though Wagner, who was born in Strasbourg, had been there when Goethe pursued his studies in the Alsatian town. Wagner's early interest in literature was along traditional lines, and he continued to write Anacreontics even after he had made the acquaintance of Lenz in Strasbourg and had become a member of the circle around Josef Daniel Salzmann, Goethe's mentor during his Strasbourg stay. He did not seem to become convinced of the value of the new literary ideals until he spent two years as a tutor in Saarbrücken. There he came into contact with the life of the lower classes, an experience which appeared to make him more sensitive to the aims of the *Sturm und Drang,* and which influenced his views of society. When he met Goethe and other *Sturm und Drang* authors in Frankfort in 1775, he began writing dramas almost immediately. *Der wohltätige Unbekannte,* a one act play, appeared in 1775, as did *Die Reue nach der Tat.* His successful *Die Kindermörderin* was published in 1776. After that he broke with Goethe and returned to Strasbourg to complete his studies. His old friends there gave strong approval to *Die Kindermörderin.* As soon as he received his doctorate and was licensed as a lawyer in the fall of 1776, Wagner devoted his energies entirely to the theater. He worked with the then famous Seyler troupe, translating for them, directing at times, and adapting plays for them to perform. In this capacity he prepared Shakespeare's *Macbeth,* which he published in 1779. His active interest in the theater led him also to translate Mercier's *Du théâtre ou nouvel essai sur l'art dramatique* (1773). The *Sturm und Drang* authors were attracted to Mercier's views whose insistence on genius rather than rules appealed to them, especially because he, too, had praise for Shakespeare. Wagner applied Mercier's dramatic precepts when he attempted life-like portrayal in his dramas. He also made considerable use of dialect language in his writings and created characters who were representatives of the lowest classes.

Both *Die Reue nach der Tat* and *Die Kindermörderin* have six acts, a demonstration of Wagner's freedom from the usual dramatic rules. Madam Langen in *Die Reue nach der Tat* thwarts a marriage between her son and the daughter of the coachman Walz. When the unrebellious girl becomes seriously ill over her fate Madam Langen is willing to give in. Her consent comes too late to save the life of either the girl or her son. Wagner did not create convincing characters in this play, but he was successful in evoking a sense of reality by paying attention to details. If the play reminds the reader of nineteenth-century realism and naturalism this is even more true of *Die Kindermörderin.* It evokes impressions one gains from reading Friedrich Hebbel's *Maria Magdalene,* which treats a similar subject. Hebbel's famous Meister Anton has his precursor in the butcher Martin Humbrecht. Their moral and ethical views, their dealings with their children, their treatment of legal officials and their inability to compromise are features which they share. Wagner had to defend the realism of the play because the seduction scene in the first act had been attacked and eliminated by Lessing's brother, who had prepared an edition of the play. When the poet himself published an edition for the stage he, too, cut the first act and added a happy ending. He did so maintaining that the original play had been written to be read, not played. Wagner refused to take out, however, what was to him an extremely important dramatic device, the theft of a silver snuff-box which brought the legal officers to the house of the self-righteous butcher where they revealed that the butcher's wife and daughter had been to a brothel, albeit unknowingly. The snuff-box links Madam Humbrecht's vanity, which permits her daughter's seduction to happen, with the butcher's assertive self-righteousness, which forces his daughter to flee from home and kill her child. Wagner does not employ the frequent scene changes so popular with other *Sturm und Drang* playwrights. While the first act takes place in a brothel-inn and the sixth act in a poor washerwoman's hut, the remaining four acts are all set in Humbrecht's house, the place which is ruled solely by Humbrecht's moralizing views and questionable actions. Our knowledge of this house can explain why it was possible for a virtuous girl to become the victim of a seducer, and why a tragic ending was inescapable.

Maler Müller and Leisewitz are two writers whose contributions to *Sturm und Drang* drama deserve mention because of the choice of subject matter and the form of treatment. Müller's seizing upon the Faust theme, and his independence and originality in treating it, and Leisewitz's subdued yet thoughtful and almost traditional presentation of the *Sturm und Drang* fratricide motif have preserved for both of them a place in literary history. Friedrich Müller (1749-1825) chose for himself the name Maler Müller because he was a painter and etcher before he also became a poet. Apart from his interest in dramatic idyls, which goes back to his admiration for the writer and painter Salomon Gessner, Maler Müller was only loosely connected with the Strasbourg circle, even though he came from the nearby Palatinate. It was not until 1775 that he met Goethe, and not until 1776 that he became acquainted with Lenz, Klinger and Wagner. Before that time he felt a literary kinship with Klopstock and the 'Göttinger Hainbund', which may account for his interest in writing idyls. As the *Sturm und Drang* group broke up, Maler Müller began laying plans for an extended stay in Rome. He left in 1778 and was never to return to Germany. Neither was he ever to complete his literary presentation of Faust, although he continued working on the theme for many years.

Maler Müller was fascinated by the popular moralizing presentations of the Siegfried and the Faust legends. The first he formed into the drama *Golo und Genoveva,* and the second into *Fausts Leben.* Only the first part of the five part *Faust* drama was published in 1778, written mainly between 1776 and 1778. He continued reworking the other four parts in Rome. Goethe's publication of *Faust I* in 1806 gave him the impetus to rewrite the *Faust* drama in verse but he never finished it. We have already noted that Lessing, Goethe and Klinger were drawn to the Faust topic. Contrary to the popular portrayal of a smallish, deceiving Faust, the *Sturm und Drang* writers saw in him the strong person. Maler Müller claims in the preface to the drama that he desired to defend Faust because of his striving 'ganz zu sein, was man fühlt, dass man sein könnte.' In Müller's *Faust* the metaphysical realm does not take on importance. Scenes depicting the spirits in hell are much like those in the familiar puppet play. Faust's goals are simply to live independently, to scorn conventions, to enjoy gambling and to gain honor. He is the kind of person Mephistopheles can admire because he dares to live without restraints. Faust's yearning to rise above the lowness of life remains unfulfilled. Yet the forcefulness and richness of the language, as well as the poet's ability to create the impression of real life scenes, mark Müller's *Faust* fragment as an important event. The play *Golo und Genoveva,* which was written during the second half of the seventies, treats the change of the desperate lover Golo into a violent person when Genoveva, Siegfried's faithful wife, rejects his advances. The passion and singlemindedness of Golo's love force the change upon him. In this drama, too, the author is unduly preoccupied with the colorful and realistic detail, which provides poetic quality, but which often detracts from the dramatic tension.

Johann Anton Leisewitz (1752-1806) is the only dramatist of the period who had no connection with any members of the Strasbourg circle. He studied in Göttingen and joined the 'Göttinger Hainbund' in 1774. In the fall of that year he returned to his native Hanover, practicing law and, for a few years, devoting much time to writing. Besides a few short poetic dialogues the play *Julius von Tarent* (1776) is his only extant literary work. The short but poignant dialogue *Die Pfändung* betrays the convictions which he shared with the other members of the 'Hainbund'. A peasant and his wife philosophize about the personal and spiritual freedom they will retain even though they know that their unjust immoral prince will take from them the very bed in which they are lying. Schiller was attracted to the deep religious feeling and the belief in final justice that are manifested in Leisewitz's work. As in Klinger's *Die Zwillinge* and later in Schiller's *Die Räuber,* so we find in *Julius von Tarent* two brothers, sons of a nobleman, who are in love with the same girl. But only in Leisewitz's play is love itself described as the one force in human experience that is not subject to reason. Guido's greed for honor and Julius's love for Blanca constitute the conflict. It would please Guido's honor to possess Blanca, and satisfy Julius's innermost longing for Blanca, if she could be his. Julius would gladly not become prince, although he knows that running away with Blanca would put his brother Guido, a tyrant, on the throne. The father's solution is to make Blanca a nun. Yet cloister walls cannot shut out the force of love. The conflict ends when Guido stabs his brother. Blanca is seized by madness when she sees the dead Julius. But it is the father who establishes justice when he kills Guido, not in a moment of rage, but rather deliberately and after having rejected the easier solution of suicide. The play is characterized by such deliberate actions and by reasoned discussions about the tension between personal freedom and social responsibility. This deliberateness is paralleled by a tight and well-balanced plot, a fact which may well betray Leisewitz's admiration for Lessing. (pp. 155-73)

Friedhelm Radandt, " 'Sturm und Drang'," in his From Baroque to Storm and Stress, 1720-1775, *Croom Helm, 1977, pp. 126-85.*

Victor Lange

[*In the following excerpt, Lange discusses several Sturm und Drang plays and asserts that their violent and excessive nature expresses a rational view of existence in conflict with existing social conventions.*]

The dramatic writing which appeared in Germany in the 10 years after 1770 is more remarkable for its documentary fury than for any lasting effect upon the subsequent history of German intellectual, social or literary life. In so far as it offers the sort of consonance which is commonly thought of as the Sturm und Drang sensibility, this is the result of a challenge as passionate as its programmatic focus was indistinct, thrown defiantly at the political realities of the age. On the other hand, the radicalism of its gestures and the flamboyance of its protests all too frequently conceal a profound melancholy as to the prospects of a more humane life. It shares, of course, Rousseau's conviction, set forth in his eloquent (and immensely popular) psychological novel *Émile* (1762), of the alienation of man from his authentic self, and the conclusion that all is fundamentally good as it comes from the hand of the Creator and that all degenerates under the hand of man.

But it would be difficult to point to a single philosophical model to which the Sturm und Drang poets subscribed. They thought to an important degree in the terms of contemporary materialist and sensualist theories and were inclined to see merit in d'Holbach's conclusion that the all-compelling laws of nature could only lead to a fatalistic acquiescence in the inevitable; they were, at the same time, parodoxically, persuaded by Helvetius' doctrine that the objective unreason of the existing social order could be modified by the demonstrative assertion of spontaneous subjectivity. The essentially empirical character of this central Sturm und Drang proposition distinguishes it from the speculative subjectivism of the later romantic faith.

Many of those who were most deeply affected by Herder's questioning of accepted modes of judgement were, during the next few years, to produce plays, prose, even poetry of a defiant, rough-cast and disturbing style. Their common impulse, later designated as the 'Sturm und Drang' mentality, was defined in confessional essays and letters—none attempted anything like a critical statement of systematic coherence. They were far from thinking of their work, published or merely circulated in manuscript, as representing a clearly focused literary doctrine. What links the diffuse and multi-faceted efforts by men of varying intellectual disposition and talent is the resolution to declare, in blunt and deliberately offensive terms, their deep distrust in the contemporary practice of reason, and a determination to question prevailing forms of thought and conduct. The Sturm und Drang rebellion is, in fact, the first in that succession of European (and American) anti-cultural protests that have challenged the social and intellectual assumptions of an establishment whose inherent contradictions and whose obsolescent conventions can be attacked most forcibly by asserting the superior power of incoherence, formlessness and eccentricity.

The violent tone of many of the Sturm und Drang plays and their extravagant topics may seem nihilistic; they are, however, even at their most aggressive, with few exceptions, built upon a fundamentally rational view of life. They presume the stability of 'nature' and 'man' which needs now to be reasserted in their deep estrangement from the prevailing cultural conventions. The belief in the rationality of existence remains, but the proclamation of 'reason' as the justification of the existing political and aesthetic systems henceforth becomes suspect.

What gives an unmistakable tone and texture to the most interesting work of these artists, poetry, critical reflection, painting and even music, is not merely the discovery of 'feeling'—this had earlier been an ingredient in the religious pathos of the pietists and in the demonstrative sentimentality of rococo manners and art. It was a new sense of place and time through which the claims of inspiration and spontaneity were now asserted within distinctly secularized notions of greatness and genius against the traditional (aristocratic) assumptions of civilizing decorum. The benevolent function and the conciliatory effect of feeling upon social conduct is now bluntly denied. Radicalized and freshly explored, it is now sanctioned not by its social efficacy but by the integrity of its sheer and sublimely 'natural' force. In its fullest awareness, it is the as yet unfathomed and undefined resource of a life whose primary feature is not balance and equanimity but indeterminacy and openness. 'Sentiment' now takes on a spurious and trivial connotation: as 'sentimentality' it becomes the despised instrument of convention.

The recurrent topics of the Sturm und Drang writers are, in Herder's sense, 'nature' as a creative resource, history as a projection of local and collective experiences, man and his total perception, the poet as the supreme example of 'genius'—all these dramatized in figures (like Goetz) of powerful energy and defiant authenticity. In so far as these ideas are cohesively stated and not merely as brief critical asides or scattered in the creative works themselves, they are, above all, polemical and tend, like Goethe's address commemorating Shakespeare's birthday (1771), to take the form of ironic advice to the bemused elders who, with their polite and impotent philosophy, are about to be driven from the Elysian shelter, critics whose aridity has made them blind to the over-whelming life-force that is Shakespeare.

Shakespeare was, henceforth, to be the touchstone of greatness. Lessing had briefly referred to his original genius; Herder was to sum up the shared admiration in a measured essay (1774); Lenz, Goethe's friend, concludes his *Anmerkungen übers Theater* (1774) with an emphatic paean to the great innovator; H. W. von Gerstenberg's *Briefe* had praised his superiority over French classicist dramaturgy. For the Sturm und Drang dramatists, Shakespeare and his contemporaries supplied the justification for a radical dissolution of the dramatic form. In 1765 Gerstenberg translated Beaumont and Fletcher's *The Maide's Tragedy (Die Braut)* and, in his own play, *Ugolino* (1769) makes use of Dante's episode of the incarceration of the rebel Ugolino and his three sons, and their death by starvation. Before Gerstenberg later modified the hero's end, the play offered an almost expressionist scenario without any dramatic motivation of the issue of guilt: existential anguish is constantly asserted by the four characters during the stormy night in the oppressive confinement of a tower; it is a gauche but powerful piece of ecstatic lyricism, affecting by its sustained projection of suffering in the face of death.

The most impressive talent among the Sturm und Drang dramatists was undoubtedly J. M. R. Lenz. Like Hamann and Herder, he was born in the northeast; while a student of theology and a tutor in an aristocratic family, he met Goethe and his circle in Strasbourg. An extraordinarily restless mind, he later became insane and died miserably in Moscow. The intricacy and complexity of Lenz's character and the curiosly 'literary' nature of his life were later sharply recorded by Goethe: in *Dichtung und Wahrheit* he recognizes his profound and inexhaustibly productive talent; but tenderness, restlessness and sophistry seemed in him to be in constant conflict, and his sublime gifts were touched with sickness:

> his imagination was that of a rogue, his love as well as his hatred were unreal, he was wilful in his ideas and feelings so as to be constantly occu-

> pied. He tried to give reality to his affections as well as his dislikes by the most absurd means; again and again he destroyed his own work. And thus he never benefited any of those he loved, and never hurt any of those he hated; he seemed to sin only in order to punish himself, and to plot against others only in order to be able to graft a new fable upon an old.

Georg Büchner was to make him the subject of a haunting short story (1836).

Lenz's first play, *Der Hofmeister* (1772-73), is in form and subject-matter original and striking. Although subtitled a 'comedy', this sharp and desperate account of a tutor's precarious and humiliating position in a noble family is far from amusing; its social criticism is carefully distributed among a group of plausible and well drawn representatives of contemporary life.

The design of the play corresponds to Lenz's own definition of comedy as a 'performance which is intended for everyone'.

> Our German writers of comedy must write in a tragic and comic mode at the same time, because the audience for whom they write—or should write—is itself a mixture of culture and brutality, decency and savagery. Thus the comic poet may well create a public for the writer of tragedy.

Yet, however severe its attack on the inhumanity of class-bound individuals, *Der Hofmeister* ends in resignation. Written, like *Goetz,* in brief and pointed scenes with a remarkable feeling for the milieu and the speech of the characters, it has remained exemplary for the subsequent masters of German social theatre, for Büchner, Wedekind and Brecht. Attached to Lenz's *Anmerkungen übers Theater* (1774) is his translation of Shakespeare's *Love's Labour's Lost* under the title *Amor Vincit Omnia*—the first German version of the play to do justice to Shakespeare's wit.

As defiant in spirit and dramatic structure is Lenz's *Die Soldaten* (1776), once more a 'comedy' that tends towards the grotesque and verges on the tragic; a loosely strung sequence of 35 fast-moving scenes, indifferent to the traditional requirements of unity of time and of place. Lenz conducts a double-barrelled attack upon a dissolute corps of aristocratic officers and upon bourgeois eagerness to satisfy ambition and vanity. Marie, the seducible daughter of a merchant, is the victim and in turn the instrument of corruption and dishonour. It is clear that Lenz's social criticism concerns less the inherent weakness of a political system than certain remediable malpractices within it. His astonishing linguistic virtuosity in differentiating characters and in creating moments of high tension assures theatrical effectiveness; the 'open' structure of the play gives it a peculiarly modern texture. Yet, interlarded and barely integrated discursive passages as well as an unnecessary distribution of the action over three localities indicate the shortcomings of Lenz's experiment. It is one of a number of such comedies (consciously fashioned after Plautus) with which he hoped to contribute contemporary material for an emerging national theatre.

No less indicative of the fluid form of the 'new' drama is the extensive body of early work of Maximilian Klinger. The title of one of his plays, *Wirr-Warr* was changed to *Sturm und Drang* (1776) at the urging of Christoph Kaufmann, a Swiss religious fanatic, a friend of Lavater and an ardent follower of Rousseau. It was this title which later suggested to the Romantic critic A. W. Schlegel the designation of the movement as a whole.

Sturm und Drang is the least interesting of the six plays which Klinger wrote within barely two years as a supplier of material for a well-known troupe. We are given very little theatrical action: three young Europeans, stock characters—one impetuous, one delicate and sentimental, one melancholy—tired of their pointless adventures, have just arrived in America, 'where everything is new and interesting'. They deplore their empty life in an age of disarray—'our misfortune comes from the mood of our own heart; the world has contributed, but less than we ourselves'—and are ready to become involved in amorous affairs. These lead, in a series of absurd coincidences to the discovery of earlier and hostile family relationships that are at the end amicably resolved. *Sturm und Drang* has a trite plot and much sententious exclamatory language without the energy that galvanizes Klinger's other efforts, especially *Das leidende Weib* (1775) and *Die Zwillinge* (1776), both outstanding examples of Sturm und Drang dramaturgy.

In *Die Zwillinge* the motif of two hostile brothers is developed in a set of discrete moments of animosity, during which Guelfo is, in a sheer rage of self-assertion, driven to killing his twin. He is at the end left confused and exhausted, suggesting in flashes of terrified insight and in bursts of intense and fragmented speech the tragic impasse of total subjectivity. Klinger's drama demonstrates the failure of the rebellious self within a social context that is merely invoked in its oppressive mood and violently denounced, without even the suggestion of an intelligent analysis of its inherent conflicts.

The same tension between impulsive action and superficial reflection, between libertarian wilfulness and a questionable social order make Klinger's *Das leidende Weib* a characteristic if absurdly melodramatic play. Once again, as in Lenz's *Hofmeister,* the basic conflict is between aristocratic and middle-class ways of life, here generalized by a critique of fashionable sentimentality and of pretentious notions of social privilege. The violent confrontations and deaths that make up the plot are awkwardly resolved by the withdrawal of the survivors from life at court to the bucolic peace of a Rousseauean retreat. The powerful, ejaculatory prose and attempts at distinguishing individual and social attitudes give a measure of interest to a Sturm und Drang document which is more impressive in its theatrical energy than in any coherent social philosophy.

Whatever Klinger's merits or shortcomings as a singularly prolific playwright, his career after 1780 as an official in Russia is more notable—especially from 1803 to 1817 as Curator of the University of Dorpat. The artistic and intellectual scope of his life is not as yet fully appreciated: detached from the German scene and closer to French ways, he was to recover his faith in a rational culture which the Sturm und Drang experience had attacked or by-passed. He returned to the masters of the Enlightenment: Kant, Voltaire, Diderot and Rousseau whom he now recognized as the progressive precursors of the French Revolution. In his later plays, his philosophical novels, and his exceptionally rewarding *Betrachtungen und Gedanken über verschiedene Gegenstände der Welt und der Literatur* (1803-05) he represents a critical modern humanism, not always relished by the society he judged, but enlivened by the memory of his participation in the impetuous protest movement of the Sturm und Drang.

The titanic rebel and his instinctual revulsion against convention is one of the central themes of the decade: it supplies the plot of J. A. Leisewitz's *Julius von Tarent* (1776), a tragedy of fratricide, much admired by Lessing and Schiller. Sophisticated in its structure and disciplined in its prose language, it is the work of a man of wide intellectual and social interests, a member of the *Hainbund* in Göttingen, a close acquaintance of Lessing and Nicolai and later a distinguished lawyer and public servant.

The Duke of Tarent rejects, because of her inferior rank, the girl loved by both his sons. The two brothers, each in his own way pursuing an enlightened political career, are by temperament incompatible. Guido is the proud soldier, Julius the dilatory philosophical mind who longs for a life in distant parts of the world, dedicated to the serene 'reasons of love'. In an attempt to free the girl from the convent to which she has been banished, Julius is killed by his brother, who is in turn murdered by the Duke. Rousseau's social criticism is here sharply confirmed: 'Must the human race, in order to be happy, be imprisoned in a state in which everyone is the slave of the other and none is free? Is everyone welded to the chain by which he holds his slave?' Leisewitz tells the story in the hope that justice and equity, illuminated by that love for which Julius dies, may modify the despotism that is mirrored in the harsh conflicts of the play.

The year 1776, in Germany so rich in dramatic statements of protest and defiance, produced one work of distinct historical interest: Heinrich Leopold Wagner's 'tragedy in six acts', *Die Kindermörderin* (1776), is concerned with the topical case of a mother's killing her illegitimate infant. The play proved successful precisely because of its strands of Richardsonian class morality, bourgeois sentimentality such as Diderot and Lessing had made appealing, and sudden flashes of that private despair which crystalized in so many incidents in Sturm und Drang writing. Goethe's later suggestion that Wagner plagiarized the 'Gretchen' episode in his *Faust* which he had read to him at the time has little weight; instead of the touching seduction and despair of a loving girl, the entanglement of Wagner's 'little Eve' is part of a facile mechanism by which the morality of the lower middle class and the transparent game of an irresponsible officer are brought into a conflict made pathetic more by the rhetoric of anger and denunciation than by an inescapable demonstration of true passion.

The stylistic and thematic mixture, here and elsewhere, of the trivial and the esctatic, of a momentary assertion of defiance and a relapse into the accepted social clichés is thoroughly characteristic of Sturm und Drang writing. Their aesthetic horizon was, at best, delineated in Louis-Sebastian Mercier's *Du Théâtre ou Nouvel Essai sur l'Art Dramatique* (1773), which attacked Boileau's neo-classicist poetics and called for a theatre close to contemporary life and providing moral and, by implication, political education. On Goethe's urging, Wagner translated it (in 1776). The Sturm und Drang playwrights turned away, particularly, from Diderot, the master of Lessing and of popular critics such as J. J. Engel and J. J. Eschenburg, and rejected Diderot's concept of a 'domestic' drama as tepid sentimentality.

In his *Geschichte der romantischen Literatur* (1803-04), A. W. Schlegel roundly scores the misguided manner of the Sturm und Drang fraternity. Theirs was, indeed, a disputation between strident voices, often more intent on shouting than on being considered. These gifted writers, impatient with the prevailing social and aesthetic order, who proclaimed in life as well as literature the cleansing power of irregularity, tended to discredit sustained thought and discourse, and preferred the man of violent action to the scholar, the aphoristic declamation on the stage to the book or the study. (pp. 64-70)

Victor Lange, "Strident Voices: 'Sturm und Drang' Drama," in his The Classical Age of German Literature, 1740-1815, *Holmes & Meier Publishers, Inc., 1982, pp. 64-70.*

FURTHER READING

Brook, Barry S. "Sturm und Drang and the Romantic Period in Music." *Studies in Romanticism* IX, No. 4 (Fall 1970): 269-84.

Traces "the pervasive kinship between music and literature" during the Sturm und Drang period, focusing in particular on the works of Haydn and Mozart.

Brown, M. A. L. "Lenz's *Hofmeister* and the drama of Storm and Stress." In *Periods in German Literature, Volume II: Texts and Contexts,* edited by J. M. Ritchie, pp. 67-84. Chester Springs, Penn.: Dufour Editions, 1970.

Argues that the social criticism implicit in *Der Hofmeister* is consistent with other Sturm und Drang dramas.

Bruford, W. H. *Theatre, Drama and Audience in Goethe's Germany.* London: Routledge & Kegan Paul, 1950, 388 p.

Pioneering study of eighteenth-century German drama and its historical context.

Duncan, Bruce. "Some Common Themes in the Reception of *Sturm und Drang* Drama." In *Momentum dramaticum: Festschrift for Eckehard Catholy,* edited by Linda Dietrick and David G. John, pp. 149-60. Waterloo, Ontario: University of Waterloo Press, 1990.

Questions traditional assumptions regarding the social concerns addressed in Sturm und Drang drama.

Kayser, Wolfgang. "The 'Spirit of the Grotesque' in the Drama of the Sturm und Drang." In his *The Grotesque in Art and Literature,* translated by Ulrich Weisstein, pp. 40-7. Bloomington: Indiana University Press, 1963.

Discusses the relevance of the theme of the grotesque to Sturm und Drang drama.

Liedner, Alan C. "A Titan in Extenuating Circumstances: Sturm und Drang and the *Kraftmensch.*" *PMLA* 104, No. 2 (March 1989): 178-89.

Analysis of the Promethean rebelliousness and cult of the genius which typify the Sturm und Drang movement.

McIlvenna, Estelle. "The 'Philistine' in 'Sturm und Drang'." *The Modern Language Review* XXXIII, No. 1 (January 1938): 31-9.

Argues that the application of the term "Philistine" to signify "the narrow bourgeois, lacking insight and wanting in appreciation of all the finer things in life" is a coinage of the Stürmer und Dränger.

McInnes, Edward. "The Drive Toward Realism: Some Underlying Affinities in the Drama of *Sturm und Drang* and Naturalism." In *Patterns of Change: German Drama and the European Tradition: Essays in Honour of Ronald Peacock,* edited by Dorothy James and Silvia Ranawake, pp. 89-101. New York: Peter Lang, 1990.

Asserts that the revolutionary realism employed by the Sturm Drang dramatists derived from their efforts to present "a more immediate, vivid image of everyday existence and . . . a more discriminated psychological portrayal of the dramatic figures" than their predecessors had.

Natan, Alex. "Introduction." In *German Men of Letters, Volume VI: Literary Essays,* edited by Alex Natan and Brian Keith-Smith, pp. 13-18. London: Oswald Wolff, 1972.

General essay which places the Sturm und Drang movement against the backdrop of the Enlightenment.

Nicolson, Harold. " 'Sturm und Drang' (1770-1778)." In his *The Age of Reason,* pp. 330-48. London: Constable and Company, 1960.

General discussion of the Sturm und Drang movement and its background.

Stamm, Israel. "*Sturm und Drang* and Conservatism." *The Germanic Review* XXX, No. 4 (December 1955): 265-81.

Argues that the Sturm und Drang partook "of the conservative reaction to rationalistic progressivism."

Stewart, Walter K. *Time Structure in Drama: Goethe's Sturm und Drang Plays.* Amsterdam: Editions Rodopi, 1978, 308 p.

Discusses the dramatic innovations of Goethe's early plays.

Vail, Curtis C. D. "Lessing's Attitude Toward Storm and Stress." *PMLA* LXV, No. 5 (September 1950): 805-23.

Discussion of Enlightenment thinker Gotthold Ephraim Lessing's perceptions of various members of the Stürmer und Dränger.

Vaughan, William. *German Romantic Painting.* New Haven: Yale University Press, 1980, 260 p.

Explores the influence of the Sturm und Drang on late eighteenth- and early nineteenth-century painters.

Victorian Autobiography

INTRODUCTION

Many critics have called the Victorian era the golden age of English autobiography. Victorian writers, inspired by the zeal for self-discovery and recognition of the value of the individual that marked the period of their Romantic predecessors, became increasingly fascinated by the mystery of the individual's development in relation to the external factors of his or her environment. Novels of the period, many of which were quasi-autobiographical, frequently traced the lives of their protagonists from infancy, prompting—according to Barbara Charlesworth Gelpi—"even greater numbers of mid-Victorians to meditate on the facts of their own particular lives." At the same time, Victorians living in an age of change and uncertainty developed a penchant for retrospection and nostalgia that fostered both the writing and the eager reception of autobiographical works. Mrs. Humphry Ward's desire to "seize and record" the moment, for example, has been cited as indicative of a "distinct consciousness of *change*" that, according to E. D. Mackerness, "lies behind all the great Victorian autobiographies."

Reflecting Thomas Carlyle's philosophical emphasis on activity and self-sacrifice rather than introspection and self-consciousness, Victorian autobiographers largely rejected the confessional mode (patterned after Augustine's fifth-century *Confessions*), fearing that an excessive indulgence in self might result in what Ira Bruce Nadel has termed a "morbid, paralyzing self-consciousness." Instead, these writers opted for a seemingly impersonal tone and the more modest and objective form of the apology, wherein the author defended his life course without anguished admissions of guilt or expressions of regret. Best exemplified by John Henry Newman's acclaimed *Apologia pro vita sua* and Charles Darwin's *Autobiography,* the apology is characteristic of what Margaret Oliphant referred to as a "fashion of self-explanation which belong[ed] to the time." For female authors, self-explanation often entailed a justification for or a defense of their choice of a literary career, with a focus on facts and accomplishments rather than on their personal experiences and feelings. The extent to which writers of the period eschewed these latter elements in constructing a history of their lives is indicated by Anthony Trollope in the preface to his *Autobiography,* where he facetiously asserts: "It will not, I trust, be supposed by any reader that I have intended in this so-called autobiography to give a record of my inner life." In later decades of the nineteenth century, as authors grappled with disillusionment and despair over their loss of religious faith, confessional elements were reintroduced into autobiographical writings. However, these writers used the device of a mask or alternate self (for example, Henry Ryecroft in George Gissing's *Private Papers*) to circumvent their discomfort with self-revelation. Characterizing the period as a whole, Howard Helsinger maintains that the Victorians, feeling a sense of urgency to impart the lessons they had learned in their own lives, "write not only for themselves and their contemporaries, but for posterity. They grow concerned about propriety, avoid introspection, and produce work which is predominantly memoir." Critics continue to analyze the form, function, and content of Victorian autobiography both for its social and literary interest, acknowledging its role in providing historians with valuable insights into the thought and temper of the time.

REPRESENTATIVE WORKS

Butler, Samuel
The Way of All Flesh (novel) 1903
Carlyle, Thomas
Sartor Resartus (prose) 1833-34
Darwin, Charles
Autobiography (autobiography) 1876
Dickens, Charles
The Personal History of David Copperfield (novel) 1850
Gissing, George
The Private Papers of Henry Ryecroft (novel) 1903
Gosse, Edmund
Father and Son (novel) 1907
Hunt, Leigh
The Autobiography of Leigh Hunt (autobiography) 1850
Kemble, Fanny
Record of a Girlhood (autobiography) 1878
Martineau, Harriet
Autobiographical Memoir (autobiography) 1877
Mill, John Stuart
Autobiography (autobiography) 1873
Moore, George
Confessions of a Young Man (fictional autobiography) 1888
Newman, John Henry
Apologia pro vita sua (prose) 1864
Oliphant, Margaret Oliphant Wilson
The Autobiography and Letters of Mrs. M. O. W. Oliphant (autobiography and memoirs) 1899
Pater, Walter
"Child in the House" (short story) 1878
Ruskin, John
Praeterita (unfinished autobiography) 1885-89
Sewell, Elizabeth Missing
Autobiography of Elizabeth M. Sewell (autobiography) 1893 [enlarged edition by Eleanor L. Sewell, 1907]

Spencer, Herbert
Autobiography (autobiography) 1904
Stephen, Leslie
Mausoleum Book (autobiography) 1895
Trollope, Anthony
An Autobiography (autobiography) 1883
Wilde, Oscar
De Profundis (prose) 1905

DEVELOPMENT AND MAJOR CHARACTERISTICS

Keith Rinehart

[In the following excerpt, Rinehart traces evolving conceptions of the nature and function of autobiographical writing in Victorian England.]

[The] Victorian attitude toward autobiography may be divided into two aspects which have a rough correspondence to the traditional definition of the functions of literature—to instruct and to delight. The early Victorian emphasis was upon autobiography as a moral influence; the later, upon autobiography as art; but both united in their emphatic appreciation of autobiography: "Autobiography is allowed, by common consent, to be one of the most universally agreeable kinds of reading," said a reviewer in *Blackwood's Magazine* for November, 1829. In 1849 [also in *Blackwood's Magazine*] Sir Archibald Alison wrote: "Autobiography, when skilfully and judiciously done, is one of the most delightful species of composition of which literature can boast." And in 1881 Sir Leslie Stephen said: "Nobody ever wrote a dull autobiography."

Prior to the Victorian era the most widely known nineteenth-century essay in English on autobiography was John Foster's "On a Man's Writing Memoirs of Himself," first published in 1805. Since the book in which it was published (*Essays in a Series of Letters*) had so large an audience, going through numerous editions in England in pre-Victorian and Victorian years, and since the essay is in itself a remarkable document in the literary criticism of the genre, it deserves extensive comment here.

Foster's essay consists mainly of advice to the autobiographer. The kind of autobiography which concerned Foster was a man's account of his own life for his own use, "endeavoring not so much to enumerate the mere facts and events of life, as to discriminate the successive states of the mind, and the progress of character." Foster's concern is very largely moral. "It is in this progress that we acknowledge the chief importance of life to consist." In these words Foster comes nearest to defining autobiography—the serious record of the progress of character.

The justification of such autobiography is, of course, to know one's character more adequately and to improve it: "One of the greatest difficulties in the way of executing the proposed task [i.e., writing an autobiography] will have been caused by the extreme deficiency of that self-observation, which, to any extent, is no common employment, either of youth or any later age." Only by the deliberate attempt to observe ourselves can we know "what our character was, and what it was likely to become." Foster makes this further, rather chilly, observation: "We may regard our past life as a continued, though irregular course of education; and the discipline has consisted of instruction, companionship, reading, and the diversified influences of the world." He draws a melancholy picture of what the honest records of the lives of a hundred men taken at random would reveal, for they would disclose "how many things may be the causes of irretrievable mischief" and "into how many forms of intellectual and moral perversion the human mind readily yields itself to be modified." To recognize some of these perils and perversions and to help himself to escape them, the autobiographer should "maintain the feeling in earnest that it is really at a confessional, and a severe one, that he is giving his account."

Foster's prescriptions could scarcely be considered of much interest to the history of literary criticism, were it not that he does see some of the literary problems involved in the writing of autobiography. He believes, for instance, that autobiographies should not be day-by-day accounts—such as diaries—but should be written after longer intervals of time have elapsed: " . . . they should not be composed by small daily or weekly accumulations . . . but at certain considerable intervals, as at the end of each year, or any other measure of time that is ample enough for some definable alteration to have taken place in the character or attainments." This advice suits his "definition" of autobiography as a kind of literature not so much enumerating facts as discriminating successive states of mind. He suggests that the occasions of writing autobiography coincide with "those short intervals of illumination which sometimes occur without our knowing the cause, and in which the genuine aspect of some remote event, or long-forgotten images, is recovered with extreme distinctness by vivid, spontaneous glimpses of thought, such as no effort could have commanded; as the somber features and minute objects of a distant ridge of hills become strikingly visible in the strong gleams of light which transiently fall on them." The recommendation reveals not only that Foster may have read Wordsworth to advantage but that he recognized something of the aesthetic nature of the recollections embodied in autobiography. For autobiography is to reveal the true shape of the progress of character—not in a chronological narrative of daily events but in a description of character traits as seen from a distance at a peculiarly opportune time.

Nevertheless, his final emphasis is moral, not aesthetic. The style of the autobiography "should be as simple as possible—unless indeed the writer accounts the theme worthy of being bedecked with brilliants and flowers." And autobiography may become "only a temptation to an indulgence in vanity" unless the author honestly records his vicious, as well as his virtuous, tendencies. Such an autobiographer must "keep his record most sacred to himself, unless he feels such an unsupportable longing to relieve his heart by confiding its painful consciousness, that he can be content to hold the regard of his friend on the strength of his penitence and recovered virtue."

Apparently, some of the autobiographers of a later, though still pre-Victorian, decade were not so fortunate in their confidences, for an unsigned review, "Autobiography," in the *Quarterly* in 1827 laments the fact that "low" people are writing memoirs and autobiographies—" . . . beings who, at any period, would have been mean and base in all their objects and desires" had demanded "with hardihood the attention and the sympathy of mankind, for thoughts and deeds that, in any period but the present, must have been as obscure as dirty." This "garbage of Confessions, and Recollections, and Reminiscences, and Aniliana" had polluted "the ear of that grand impersonation, 'the Reading Public,' " so that it "had become as filthily prurient as that of an eaves-dropping lackey." This article shows less moral disapproval of vice than aristocratic disapproval of "lowness," yet both are present.

Looking to the past, the *Quarterly* reviewer thinks that autobiography should be written by one who has "some considerable portion of talent, or at least by a person of some considerable celebrity in one way or another." And it is these touchstones which prompt another reviewer to say in *Blackwood's* in 1829 that reading autobiography "affords relaxation from laborious investigation, or from intense abstract thought, combined with valuable information" and "unites much of the entertainment of the novel, with the proud satisfaction of seeming to be engaged with an instructive book."

Critics of the genre in the early nineteenth century recognized most of the problems which were to concern their successors—the problem of moral and aesthetic values, of narrative form imposed upon stubborn fact and calling for a selection and arrangement consistent with truth, and of the differing points of view of author and reader.

With Carlyle, we enter the Victorian period proper, and the difference in the criticism is not so much one of content as of attitude and emphasis. Carlyle recognizes a "poetic" as well as a "scientific" value in autobiography, but both, as is so often the case for Carlyle, are really moral:

> A scientific interest and a poetic one alike inspire us in this matter [i.e., the study of biography and autobiography]. A scientific: because every mortal has a Problem of Existence set before him, which, were it only, what for the most it is, the Problem of keeping soul and body together, must be to a certain extent *original,* unlike every other; and yet, at the same time, so *like* every other; like our own, therefore; instructive, moreover, since we also are indentured to *live.* A poetic interest still more: for precisely this same struggle of human Free-will against material Necessity, which every man's Life, by the mere circumstance that the man continues alive, will more or less victoriously exhibit,—is that which above all else, or rather inclusive of all else, calls the Sympathy of mortal hearts into action; and whether as acted, or as represented and written of, not only is Poetry, but is the sole Poetry possible [Carlyle, "Biography," in his *Critical and Miscellaneous Essays,* 1859].

Carlyle thinks that, as "science" or "poetry," the importance of the genre lies equally in its moral usefulness. What pleases him above all else is the belief that in autobiography and biography he is dealing with fact, not fiction: " . . . let any one bethink him how impressive the smallest historical *fact* may become as contrasted with the grandest fictitious event"; and many more words to the same effect.

Carlyle has the happy faculty, in this as in other respects, of sensing and underlining some of the main intellectual currents of his age. A chief problem confronting the Victorians was how to combine aesthetic interest and moral value with fact—in their case the facts of growing industrial activity and scientific knowledge and the consequent growing dissatisfaction with traditional religious creeds. Autobiography promised to be a suitable literary medium in the Victorian attempt to cope with this problem. It was, thought the early and mid-Victorians (led by Carlyle), moral and practical, and it could be aesthetically satisfying.

A chief problem confronting the Victorians was how to combine aesthetic interest and moral value with fact—in their case the facts of growing industrial activity and scientific knowledge and the consequent growing dissatisfaction with traditional religious creeds. Autobiography promised to be a suitable literary medium in the Victorian attempt to cope with this problem.

—Keith Rinehart

Thus, in 1849, Sir Archibald Alison, after an emphatic encomium on the genre, finds that the main appeal of autobiography lies in its providing a "window by which we may look into a great man's mind." He praises Gibbon's autobiography as a perfect example, because it steers a middle course between over- and under-exposure and because it is written simply, without the affectations of either vanity or modesty. He condemns Rousseau's *Confessions* for its affectation.

Less aristocratic in his outlook, Thomas McNicoll, in 1853 and again in 1861, is at pains to show that there is a "charm derived from the study of even the lowest type of character," a kind of scientific interest, he suggests, analogous to the study of vermin. The value of autobiography for him does not depend upon the genius of its subject, as it does for Alison; it does not even depend on its truthfulness, but "it seems to demand only, what may be termed *genuineness* in the narrative, and *directness* in the narrator."

Though Foster's comments imply a serious concern with the problem, McNicoll is the first of the Victorians to deal directly with the thorny problem of truth in autobiography, thorny because it involves distinguishing between fact and fiction, history and literature, creative and "scientific" writing. He is not entirely successful in answering the question he has raised; but a careful examination of how he does handle it is important preparation for the understanding of such subsequent critics of the genre as Sir Leslie Stephen. McNicoll says:

> . . . The plainest class of these writings [autobiographies] are commonly the most interesting; or rather, the interest of them is more strictly of the kind proper to auto-biography. This class consists of memoirs of persons remarkable for neither their gifts, nor attainments, nor even extraordinary fortunes. Not always does the life described present any novel features to the imagination of the reader, nor is it even necessary that either in style or sentiment should the narrative rise above the level of mediocrity . . . but in the meanest subject of these memoirs, and in the most ordinary scenes depictured from the daily life of man, if there be only that sincerity in the memorialist which engages confidence in the narrative, we shall find attraction and instruction in a high degree. The picture, indeed, may be wanting in the elaboration and suggestiveness of a true work of art; but it will have the excellence peculiar to a daguerreotype portrait,—a literal and detailed truth to nature.

In his essay McNicoll seems to be saying that autobiography requires a faithful portrait of the subject, though not necessarily a truthful one. A liar, such as Falstaff (McNicoll's own example), can be known better by means of his lies.

In 1861 McNicoll published [in his *Essays on English Literature*] a revision of his essay, "Autobiographies," in which the following statement occurs:

> In all these confessions . . . we look for a certain openness and freedom, . . . insisting only that the writer reveal himself, with real candour, or through some transparent artifice, and that all his cunning and duplicity, though so great as to include self-deception, *shall not deceive us.*

McNicoll, in fact, does not solve the problem of truth in autobiography. He is in fundamental agreement with Carlyle: the true story of each man's life reveals him to be "the central figure of some imaginable moral circle, and the hero of a true dramatic unity" which "illustrate a thousand natural truths." Yet he goes more deeply into the study of autobiography than Carlyle did, perhaps because, unlike Carlyle, he did not consider autobiography a kind of biography. In biography the problem of truth is not so subtle or so significant. McNicoll's last word on this aspect of the genre is to advise against "extra-literal matter" in autobiography because it might destroy "vraisemblance." Truth, however humble, could not of itself "produce the morally absurd"; however desultory, truth would "manifest a beauty of its own." Though keenly aware of special problems, McNicoll favors an essentially moral interpretation of autobiography.

A remarkable unsigned essay, "Autobiographies," in the *North British Review* in 1870, is the only representative of what might be called the "scientific" approach to the genre in Victorian times. This essay attempts to classify autobiography in terms of Comtean philosophy and to deal with individual autobiographies, generally, as interesting psychological and historical phenomena.

The *North British* essayist begins his analysis by saying that the autobiographical intent is customarily an intent to attain immortality—certainly an easily understood human motive. The success of the autobiographer's achievement, "apart from questions of style, depends for its value and interest upon the measure of common human passion and experience concentrated in its pages, or on the degree of vividness with which they depict common human situations and sentiments." The key word in this passage is "common," for this is what makes the subsequent classification possible. " . . . Every autobiographer is a representative man, and one not of a representative class, but of a class of representative men." Thus autobiographies are clues to the ideas of the age itself—primary sources in the history of ideas:

> In point of fact, existing autobiographies may be arranged in three principal groups, corresponding roughly to Comte's three historic periods, though the chronological order is different, and subject to individual aberrations. These groups may be distinguished critically as the Monumental or Elementary, the Positive, and the Analytic, or, to keep up the analogy, the Metaphysical. The first of these schools is epic in style and heroic in substance; each of its works is that of an imaginative autocrat—a story of action told with primitive energy, unmixed self-approval, and spontaneous art. The second school contains artists of a sort, but no heroes. It is literal, realistic, and in form dramatic. The writers depict themselves only as a means or accessory to the age in and for which they live. They write with an unsurpassed depth of conviction what everyone knows and believes; they give expression to a sublimated common sense; and, as their observations are authentic and their judgments unimpeachable, the universal reason of mankind admires and applauds. The last variety of autobiographical writing is more complicated. To the autobiographer, at any rate, humanity consists of the ego and the non ego. It is possible to him to view the world in subordination to himself, or to treat himself in subordination to the world; but a third alternative is not easy to find. Decaying originality may take refuge in a sort of criticism: but criticism of the outer world does not naturally take the form of autobiography, criticism of the writer's self paralyses the course of a narrative, and criticism of the relations of the two are not naturally suggested by the events of an ordinary life. The only remaining possibility is to chronicle thought instead of action, changes of opinion instead of succeeding experience, or else to represent the influence of imaginary circumstances upon a real mind.

The real models for these comments seem to have been (though the author nowhere clearly says so) Cellini, Pepys, and Cardinal Newman. Newman's *Apologia* had appeared just five years before (1865) and had, perhaps, opened the eyes of the essayist to the art of autobiography, even though his view seems to have been channeled through the philosophical medium of Comte. Such autobiographies "have a clearness resembling that of direct poetic intuition." At the moment of writing, such an autobiographer sees his past life as "a complete artistic whole . . . an unbroken block of nature chiselled by the force of a single human will into the form we see." In an autobiographer like Pepys, however, "it is perception rather than memory that rises to the dignity of inspiration." The essayist suggests that the "Epic" and the "Analytic" autobiographers (or, to cite examples, Cellini and Newman) have egoism in common and that the "Epic" and the "Positive" autobiographers (Cellini and Pepys) have "outwardness" in common. In speaking of the genre as a whole, he says:

> . . . The intensification of any common taste or tendency is enough to make the subject of a good autobiography. The essential point is to present the maximum of life and motion compatible with the calm of self-analysis and the composure of unalterable self-respect; the rest is only an affair of skill in style or composition. The subtle genius which delineates character is midway between the art of the portrait-painter and the historian.

This essayist, "scientific" though he is, is no philistine. His introductory remarks and the entire slant of his essay may imply an approval of Comte's philosophy and forecast a sociological approach to his discussion; but, in fact, his essay contains much comment appropriate to the literary critic. He emphasizes the importance of style, of creative imagination, of organization, and of other matters having to do with literary form and literary appreciation.

Although this essay may be regarded in some ways as the climax of Victorian criticism of autobiography and as the most serious attempt during the era to discover in autobiography an art form which satisfied the Victorian desire for a moral and aesthetic presentation of facts, it is also transitional in our short history. We see in it a weakening of moral concern, an attempted objectivity, and a strengthening of critical aesthetic appreciation. The pattern which Carlyle had outlined thirty-eight years before is still dimly visible, but the newer aesthetic element is strong.

In 1877 William Bell Scott published his *Autobiographical Notes,* the prologue of which contains some new and heretical notions about autobiography. Scott was an earnest and thoughtful man; apparently, he had tried writing autobiography as a means of self-improvement in his various early attempts to write about his own life, but he had found the effort unsatisfactory:

> These [autobiographical] attempts on my part have had a self-educational excuse. I have thought to understand myself better by their means. But it has not been so; the difficulty of looking upon oneself from an outer standpoint is too great. It is not impossible to do so; but if we could "see ourselves as others see us," the poetical interest at least is gone, the record is worthless. It is no more a true picture of what we saw, felt, enjoyed, or suffered, but of mistakes and reasons—the dead elements of the scene. The result is a *caput mortuum.* I come to the conviction that autobiographic writings may be instructive to others; not to the writers. The best excuse for them is to be found in the pleasure they may afford, the luxury of again experiencing early emotions and scenes, however faintly, and communicating them to the friendly and sympathetic.

Scott thinks that the autobiographer is more an artist than a historian or moralist and that the autobiographic impulse is perverted and worthless unless aesthetic considerations are primary. Scott says nothing to contradict what Carlyle had written about autobiography—but Scott is writing from the author's point of view; Carlyle, from the reader's.

Scott discerns, however, that this aesthetic concern may lead the reader to doubt the truth of his autobiography, and this is the second problem that he deals with. He does not propose to "create" or to indulge in a narration of his dreams, hopes or fears: " . . . there will be little of the subjective, little introspection, not much allusion to the pains and penalties of over-sensibility and other constitutional weaknesses." On the other hand, he does not plan to write a literal exposé of his life:

> The motives, passions, and speculations of the transitional periods of boy and man, however important in physical, moral, or mental progression, were only transitional, and are better forgotten. We live surrounded by so many social conventions, we go about with so many deceptive coverings, that a sincere attempt at self-portraiture in writing is like walking into the street naked, and is only likely to frighten our neighbors.

Scott adds:

> All that I propose, then, in these pages, is to describe with some degree of accuracy some of the scenery of my life, and of the lives of my dear and intimate friends. And to do so as an artist should who has his model before him, I must premise that I shall endeavour to present realities, not merely appearances. What degree of truth there may be found on the canvas must be the measure of its value.

McNicoll in 1853 had used the portrait metaphor, too, but McNicoll's illustration was daguerreotype, not canvas and paint. By just so much did the two men differ in their conception of truth.

Scott seems to have felt that if the autobiographer sets out with serious aesthetic purpose, the result will be a self-portrait in his own style and with his own selection of detail. What more, we may ask, did Dürer or Holbein or Rubens? Yet neither the artistic merit nor the verisimilitude of their self-portraits has been called in question—nor has anyone rejected the portraits because they are lacking in moral emphasis.

In the last important Victorian essay on autobiography [*Cornhill Magazine* (April 1881)], Leslie Stephen approaches the genre with keen analytic insight and a curious mixture of gentle satire and relish. After roundly stating that "nobody ever wrote a dull autobiography," he notes:

> The autobiographer has *ex officio* two qualifications of supreme importance in all literary work. He is writing about a topic in which he is keenly interested, and about a topic upon which he is the highest living authority. It may be reckoned, too, as a special felicity that an autobiography, alone of all books, may be more valuable in proportion to the amount of misrepresentation it contains.

Stephen approaches the aesthetic problem of Scott from the analytic rather than the artistic point of view. He seems interested in the psychological motivation of the artist who produces an autobiography. An autobiography, in his opinion, "is the man's own shadow cast upon the coloured and distorting mists of memory." Foster, too, had used a visual image in describing the process of writing one's life-story, but he saw the twilight sun illuminating clearly the distant important events of the autobiographer's life. In Stephen, who probably had a more modern conception of memory, the picture is more vague, a shadow floating on mist. The artistic possibilities of Stephen's definition, when one is trying to set down a definite impression, are obvious; there is plenty of opportunity for "creativity."

It is on this basis, this distortion of memory, that Stephen distinguishes between biography and autobiography—for the first time in the Victorian era. As a student of autobiography, he says, one must recognize that "human nature is in some sense a contradictory compound," and one must be able to "delight in the queer results" which, in autobiography, grow out of that fact. "Your proper biographer glides over these difficulties, or tries to find some reconciliation. The man who tells his own story reveals them because he is unconscious of their mixture." The inconsistencies of autobiography are not necessarily dishonest, because autobiography is not simply the life-story of a man, as biography is, but the life-story of a man *as he himself sees it.*

Stephen thinks that the autobiographical motive is an "irresistible longing for confidential expansion"—akin, perhaps, to the need for self-expression that writers in a later era have asserted. He is not sure but that vanity may be the source of all autobiography. In a statement that may well make all future "moral" autobiographers hesitant, he says: "The autobiography takes so much the form of a philosophical sermon on the true principles of conduct, that we quite forget that the preacher is his own text." And he uses Mill's *Autobiography* as an illustration. In Stephen, the Carlylean and pre-Victorian synthesis of the morality and historicity of autobiography breaks down. All that is left is the aesthetic appreciation of the genre.

Subsequent Victorian essays on autobiography add nothing new to the discussion. Later writers re-present and re-digest the principles of earlier Victorian critics. No one follows Leslie Stephen, to approve or contradict what he had to say. From the beginning of the nineteenth century it was recognized that autobiography fulfils an aesthetic as well as an ethical function. Indeed, the history of the Victorian approach to autobiography turns on the problem not so much of what autobiography does as what it is. There was little attempt to define it; Foster and Stephen come closest to defining it, and their definitions measure the distance that critics had traveled between 1805 and 1881. Foster's "progress of character" seemed quite reliable as a moral guide until Scott and Stephen pointed out how uncertain are the processes of memory and how destructive of true art is the "self-educational" impulse in autobiography.

A new kind of autobiography came to be written in the late Victorian era. In 1888 George Moore pioneered with *Confessions of a Young Man,* an autobiography with deliberate fictional passages—a defeat for truth in autobiography, and for morality as well. Walter Pater's "Child in the House" (1894) and "Gaston de Latour" (1896) are still more remote from factual autobiography. Oscar Wilde's *De profundis* (1905, 1950) is written in a deliberately contrived "musical" form. And some modern works are difficult to classify as either autobiography or novel, because they share so many of the characteristics of both genres. Yet, at the same time, the traditional autobiography has increased in popularity, if we are to judge by its rate of production. It seems likely that each decade of the present century has seen as many new English autobiographies as the entire Victorian era saw.

The Victorians never found an adequate definition or a satisfactory classification of the genre, but they did study it as one of the important branches of literature—a study which has been much neglected by the literary critics who followed them. Perhaps within the studies of autobiography which they made lies the nucleus of a critical theory which can restore autobiography to the literary status it once enjoyed. (pp. 178-86)

Keith Rinehart, "The Victorian Approach to Autobiography," in Modern Philology, *Vol. LI, No. 3, February, 1954, pp. 177-86.*

Ira Bruce Nadel

[*Nadel is an American-born Canadian educator and critic who has written extensively on Victorian and biographical literature. In the following essay, he examines the forms and techniques that characterize Victorian autobiography, commenting especially on the authors' use of narrative masks.*]

Epitomizing the melodrama of my title is Lady Isabel's exclamation in Act III of *East Lynne:* "Alas!" she cries, "What is to be the end of my sufferings? How much longer can I bear this torture of the mind, this never dying anguish of soul?" But unlike Lady Isabel, I shall not isolate moments of passionate unburdening in Victorian autobiography, although I shall use confession and apology as historical paradigms for an analysis of the patterns and practices of Victorian autobiographical writing. Additionally, I shall analyze the complex relationship that emerged between autobiography and fiction in the Nineteenth Century.

In brief, Victorian unease with confession as an autobiographical form led to its expropriation as a device for the novel. This, in turn, elevated the apology as the fundamental convention of autobiographical expression but the preponderance of objective, descriptive and limiting autobiographies that appeared created a conflict over form resolved only through the emergence of the mask as an autobiographical strategy late in the century. The first dilemma of the Victorian autobiographer was the selection of his form; the second was how to integrate that form with his natural desire but social resistance to personalizing experience.

The religious connotations of the confession made its appeal inherent to the Victorians. Traditionally, it meant the examination of one's conscience and the admittance of one's guilt, an act simultaneously professing knowledge of God and of one's self. Duty and self-discovery became united in the literary form of confession as seen in Augustine and Rousseau. The Romantics, however, exploited the confession and initiated what Carlyle labeled "the Era when all manner of Inquiries into what was once the unfelt, involuntary sphere of man's existence, find their place, and as it were occupy the whole domain of thought." This danger threatened the Victorian autobiographer who might have chosen to write a confession but could not because he might engage himself with a debilitating, over-involvement with the self in his pursuit of self-knowledge. The danger was double: unburdening the self might lead, on one hand, to a morbid, paralyzing self-consciousness. This is what Harriet Martineau complained of when she wrote in her *Autobiography* that "I had now plunged fairly into the spirit of my time,—that of self-analysis, pathetic self-pity." The apology, the defense of the self, became a necessary antidote to the self-indulgence brought about by the confession.

Augustine and Plato provide the classical models of the confession and the apology. In the *Confessions* (397 A.D.), Augustine creates a focused, internal private self who offers an inner-most truth for edification, not for art. His confessions particularize faults and admit errors while establishing a dialogue between himself and God, and between the reader and the work. Plato's account of Socrates' defense of his actions remains the *locus classicus* of the apology which originated in the forensic or judicial oratory of classical rhetoricians. Aristotle describes its method in Book I of his *Rhetoric.* Throughout Plato's *Apology* (ca. 399 B.C.), Socrates asserts his sincerity and projects his absolute moral belief in himself. "I am confident in the justness of my cause," he declares. This public expression of trust united with rationality and presented in a rhetorical pattern are the hallmarks of the apology. The confession is, or appears to be, spontaneous; the apology, planned.

As the confession and apology evolved, autobiographers altered their features. The confession became more immediate, personal and discontinuous in its structure while it became more inspirational, self-imagining and subjective in its content. The private nature of the confession created sincerity and authenticity through the intimate dialogue between the narrator and reader which in turn intensified believability in the text. Revelation not justification became the major impulse, while its major action was a crisis or conversion. The confession became ontological, projecting the uniqueness of the self, although encouraging what the Victorians would oppose: a fatal pride in one's individual glory. This quality led to an attempt to codify the self through external record, an element that modified the nature and form of the apology.

In contrast to the confession, the apology was a conscious composition reflecting organizational detail, control and rationality. Its primary purpose was to justify, defend or explain. Ideas, not the self, were its central focus as seen in the title of Sir Philip Sidney's *Apology for Poetry* (1595). The concern of the apology with love and friendship was minimal, preferring instead to be a record of convictions. The effort of the apology, especially in the Nineteenth Century, was to summarize and survey and it proceeded in an objective, detached manner. Authority appeared to be its most powerful effect as it narrated a life in context, not isolation. Integrity was its goal, ethics its character, a journey or ascent its principal metaphor.

For the Nineteenth Century, Rousseau and Coleridge restate the basic paradigms of the confession and apology. In his *Confessions* (1781-88), Rousseau relentlessly pursues the naked self, exposing, revealing, and at times even embarrassing himself with his candor. Voyeurism, pecadillos and cheating become common in his account of his youth and maturity. Often, he intimidates his readers into viewing acts they may not want to see, insisting they witness what they have personally avoided or could not face. The very choice of his title, *Confessions,* instead of the more accepted term "Memoirs" for French eighteenth-century autobiographies, was shocking at best and revolutionary at worst. His work also conveys no guilt or hesitation about his actions. Secularizing the form Augustine introduced, Rousseau gives it new momentum and direction, altering its concentration on repentance through a detailed examination of conscience.

By contrast, Coleridge in the *Biographia Literaria* (1817) establishes the harmony of this life through intellectual rather than personal details. Erratic in its presentation of personal details, private education and public career, the text substitutes philosophy, aesthetics and literary criticism for autobiographical details as found in conventional autobiographies. The work is an apology, a justification of himself as a poet, prompted by what he understands to be vicious attacks on his poetry by anonymous reviewers. The second sentence of the book makes this clear: "Most often it [my name] has been connected with some charge which I could not acknowledge, or some principle which I had never entertained." In this personal tone Coleridge begins the work he consciously subtitled "Biographical Sketches of my Literary Life and Opinions." As the work progresses, the personal voice of the narrator lessens and private details virtually disappear to be replaced by criticism and literary theory.

The subject of the *Biographia,* its autobiographical content, is "intellectual power" while the self, in Coleridge's words, "pauses and half recedes." The digressive, associational structure of the work reflects the intellectual progress of the subject, a progress that is convoluted, unsure and, at times, without direction. But the primary autobiographical feature of the text is the narrator's self-defense, marked by a shift in narrative voice from a personal to didactic tone as the journey of the intellect courses upward. This ascent and transformation is an important characteristic of the apology. Ironically, the text becomes the very work the author declares he is now prepared to write—his autobiography—and explains why Coleridge never started that work. He had in fact completed it. The unity of the *Biographia* is illustrated by its ending which is another personal defense from yet another attack, this time a misreading of "Christabel." Fixated on its own defense, the self reasserts its claim to be heard as the final paragraph of the work echoes its opening: "This has been my Object, and this alone can be my Defence—and O! that with this my personal as well as my LITERARY LIFE might conclude!" Coleridge clearly perceives the integration of the two as one and the *Biographia* as a declaration of his principles and defense of his actions.

Coleridge was being practical in his decision to write an apology rather than a confession because the English, as De Quincey knew, would never countenance personal revelations. The first part of the 1821 version of *Confessions of an English Opium Eater* makes this clear:

> Nothing, indeed, is more revolting to English feelings, than the spectacle of a human being obtruding on our notice his moral ulcers or scars, and tearing away that 'decent drapery' which time, or indulgence to human frailty, may have drawn over them.

In his own work, however, De Quincey sidesteps the embarrassments of the confession by anticipating and answering reader reactions, emphasizing the earnestness and understanding with which he tries to confront his problem and stressing "the blended and intertwisted" quality of his life, a quality reflected in his prose style and mixture of fact and fiction. But the confessional element dominates the narrator as discontinuities of plot and structure, unallowable in the apology, shape the text.

The means of De Quincey's evasion and maintenance of harmony in the *Confessions* is the dream. The dream structure of the book enhances the spontaneity necessary for a confession through its irregular presentation of time, recognition of the importance but incompleteness of memory, synchronic interweaving of events and shifting narrative form. No single unifying autobiographical element such as a consistent sensibility or sustained tone dominates the work except that of the unconscious and its datebook, the dream. The flow of life and the mind dictates the shape and content of the text as imagination reconstructs experience. And true to the unfinished quality of a confession—when is the need to confess ever eliminated?—De Quincey briefly and incompletely presents his recovery from opium as a testing ground of the real and the imagined. But liberation from the drug is of less literary interest than enslavement.

Victorian autobiographers, however, soon recognized the dangers of the confessional form; it led to excess, to an exposure of unknown aspects of the self and to morbid introspection. They preferred to rely on accomplishments, on the record and the facts of a life, an approach which paralleled Carlyle's emphasis on work rather than self-consciousness. Fiction was a safer form of self-revelation because few would mistake (so they thought) the fictive with the real; furthermore, the imagination permitted a greater freedom of expression. The more private the experience, the greater the need to fictionalize it because the confession became an unacceptable method of autobiographical discourse. *Sartor Resartus, David Copperfield, The Autobiography of Mark Rutherford, Confessions of a Young Man* and *The Private Papers of Henry Ryecroft* are several of the better known examples. The adoption of the confession by fiction, however, meant that Victorian autobiography required an alternate paradigm which it found in the apology.

Thomas Carlyle.

In the discursive, factual and explanatory form of the apology, autobiography for the Victorians could thrive because it met the moral requirement of reticence and maintained the social need for privacy. Furthermore, the apology permitted self-evasion through its facade of impersonality and the narrative strategy of modesty. The writer could conceal himself behind the barrier of his deeds and avoid the troubling engagement with his feelings. The apology was self-protective; it promoted a public accounting without personal cost. Through his self-deprecation—

in contrast to the confessor's self-celebration—the apologist could sustain his self-protection by down-grading certain aspects of his life or character and in that way never have to explain them. The persona Darwin creates in his *Autobiography* (1887) is a clear example. In addition, the large number of life and times biographies written in the Victorian period descended from the *res gestae* autobiographies, works that emphasized the activities and duties of the subject rather than the personality and meaning of his life. An infatuation with the past, reverence toward documents, absorption with history and bias toward induction further added to the fascination with the recorded as distinct from the recreated life.

The apology permitted and even encouraged the autobiographer to detail and defend his life. Mill could explain the nature of his education, Newman could clarify his changing religious opinions, Darwin could survey his passion for collecting, Spencer could present his "natural history" of himself, Trollope could report on how methodic was his success as a novelist. But only in momentary glimpses or not at all do we perceive the inner selves of these figures. In the security of its objectivity and defensiveness, the apology as an autobiographical form became the vehicle for endorsing the public career of the author, functioning as a summation of his life and as a key to understanding its success. The apology required minimal introspection, and a moderately clear memory; often a reliance on chronology supplanted any invention caused by forgetfulness. The posthumous publication of the autobiographies of Mill, Darwin, Spencer and Trollope further illustrates the need of the autobiographer as apologist to protect his private self. The author permits an account of his life to appear only after that life is over—when he can be sure to preserve an identity free from criticism, conflict or correction.

The principal examples of the apology in Victorian autobiography are, of course, Mill and Newman and at the risk of rehearsing the obvious, I want to indicate how conscious was their awareness and use of the form. In a diary passage from January, 1854, Mill distinctly calls attention to the apologetic nature of his autobiography as he reproaches himself for the delay in failing to justify his actions. "I feel bitterly," he begins,

> how I have procrastinated in the sacred duty of fixing in writing, so that it may not die with me, everything that I have in mind which is capable of assisting the destruction of error and prejudice and the growth of just feelings and true opinions.

The intention of Mill is as noble as it is clear: to correct any misconceptions about his relationship with his father and about his education. His desire is "to make acknowledgment of the debts which my intellectual and moral development owes to other persons."

With the exception of his mental crisis, Mill's narrative tone in the autobiography remains distant. He avoids criticism of his father, commentary on Harriet Taylor or personal reactions to society. His style remains aloof and objective as in this passage of advice: "A person of high intellect should never go into unintellectual society unless he can enter it as an apostle; yet he is the only person with high objects, who can safely enter it at all." In his critique of selfishness, for example, Mill limits his self-presentation; a general comment on English society can apply equally well to his personal presence and development in the text: "though they have thrown off certain errors, the general discipline of their minds, intellectually and morally, is not altered." In the autobiography, Mill's determination to provide a complete record blocks his feelings and lends an ironic element to the entire effort because his mental crisis was precipitated by a reaction against the emotionless existence of a life of fact.

Newman, equally if not more consciously, also writes a defense as he answers the charges of Kingsley. The *Apologia* (1864) is both a legal and spiritual defense, while his "Preface" is a pointed rebuke to the accusations elaborated in the text as a whole. Significantly, Newman's apology involves the entire Catholic priesthood, not just himself: "I was making my protest in behalf of a large body of men of high character . . . who were [also] insulted by my Accuser" he declares. Throughout the early sections of the work, battle images supplement the legal metaphors and extend the defensive nature of the text. And as Socrates believed in the justness of his cause, a characteristic attitude of the apologist, so, too, does Newman with increasing rhetorical force.

Not surprisingly, it is Newman who articulates the purpose of the apology as an autobiographical form when he writes "I am doing no more than explaining myself, and my opinions and actions. I wish . . . to state facts. . . . It is not at all pleasant for me to be egotistical" he adds. The chronological account of Newman's religious crisis supplants his resistance to revealing the private self in the work which is pointedly not a confession but, in his words, "my own testimony on the matter in question and there to leave it." Correspondingly, he titles four of the five chapter headings "History of My Religious Opinion" with the appropriate date; the fifth he calls "Position of My Mind Since 1845." "My main purpose," he announces, "is a defence of myself." Only in the proem to Chapter 3 does Newman digress to consider the problem of autobiographical method and the possible difficulties in reconstructing a life:

> who can recollect, at the distance of twenty five years, all that he once knew about his thoughts and his deeds. . . . It is both to head and heart an extreme trial, thus to analyze what has so long gone by, and to bring out the results of that examination.

In the text of the *Apologia,* however, such moments of introspective analysis are brief.

Echoes of Newman's concentration on the facts and action of his life appear in a number of later Victorian apologias, Trollope's perhaps being the most direct. "It will not, I trust, be supposed by any reader that I have intended in this so-called autobiography to give a record of my inner life" Trollope boldly and confidently asserts. Additional apologists such as Darwin, Spencer, Besant and Huxley focus on similarly external accounts of their lives.

Although the majority of Victorian autobiographers perceived autobiography to be a defense of the self, several began to recognize the limitations of the apology as a vehicle for self-expression. John Ruskin, Leslie Stephen and Edmund Gosse are three principal examples. Increasingly, they express in their own autobiographies the inability to *remain* totally objective and impersonal. Indeed, personal character has not been concealed consciously nor has it been displayed intentionally, Ruskin remarks at the opening of *Praeterita* (1885-89). But objectivity and observation, witnessing and recording, nonetheless remain his major activities in the autobiography: "My entire delight was in observing without being myself noticed—if I could have been invisible, all the better." The lyrical, confessional passages in *Praeterita* are guilty pleasures that increase in appearance as a sense of meditative retrospection expands in the work. A late passage about a hayfield illustrates the increasingly dominant theme of self-identity:

> There used to be always a corncrake or two in it. Twilight after twilight I have hunted that bird, and never once got glimpse of it: the voice was always at the other side of the field, or in the inscrutable air or earth.

The retrospective confession competes with the immediacy of the apology here, suggesting a tension that will become more substantial in later autobiographical works.

Written only a few years after *Praeterita,* Leslie Stephen's *Mausoleum Book* (1895) contains an equally ambivalent attitude towards recording and revealing and in its directness clarifies the tension autobiographers experienced in the late Victorian period. Stephen attempts to be personal and confidential, asserting that his account is initially only for the eyes of his seven children. But he is unsure of whether or not he can sustain the necessary personal tone: "I am so much of a professional author that I fear that what I am about to say may have the appearance of being meant rather for a book than for a letter." His distinction is revealing because the two forms embody the two voices that Stephen recognizes to be in conflict. One is external and public; the other internal and private. Stephen is careful to enunciate, however, that he does not intend to write an autobiography as later authors such as Beatrice Webb and Virginia Woolf were also to declare. He gives as reasons his poor memory for facts and inability to recall any momentous incidents. Furthermore, he explains he could not provide any of "those inward events, conversions or spiritual crises which give interest to some autobiographers." Curiously, he is forgetting such moments as his 1875 renunciation of Holy Orders in a document witnessed by none other than Thomas Hardy. Stephen values his privacy, admitting that while he remembers some struggles in his past, there is "a certain sense of satisfaction reflecting that I shall take that knowledge with me to the grave."

These introductory remarks to what is in fact a doleful autobiography expose the insecurities prompted by the autobiography as apology. Stephen resists the writing of an autobiography for the very reasons that made the confession essential and the apology popular: confidentiality in the former and public record in the latter. He chooses to refer the reader to his other publications for details of his life. But as he proceeds with his account, ostensibly about his recently deceased wife, Stephen cannot prevent himself from disclosing a variety of personal struggles and private thoughts such as his taking orders. He reveals that he did so only to secure a fellowship at Cambridge and thereby "relieve [his] . . . father of the burthen of supporting me." Increasingly, Stephen exposes more and more about himself but always with hesitancy, self-consciousness and reticence. Criticizing the sincerity of a compliment, for example, he adds, with self-reproach, "in saying this, I know that I am confessing a weakness." But as the autobiography continues, what Stephen calls "memory pictures" intervene and supplement the narrative while altering the chronology. This feature parallels Ruskin who included episodes from his life where they made thematic but not always chronological sense in *Praeterita.*

Victorian autobiographers . . . recognized the dangers of the confessional form; it led to excess, to an exposure of unknown aspects of the self and to morbid introspection. They preferred to rely on accomplishments, on the record and the facts of a life, an approach which paralleled Carlyle's emphasis on work rather than self-consciousness.

—Ira Bruce Nadel

Writing on death, the initial motive for composing *The Mausoleum Book,* Stephen is particularly tense and unsure. After describing his wife's convulsion and his rush for a doctor, Stephen says "I remember only too clearly the details of what followed; but I will not set them down." But at the death of Herbert Duckworth and its effect on his future wife, Julia, Stephen emotionally writes that "Life . . . becomes under such trials a dream, a futile procession of images." Such commentary, however, is infrequent. *The Mausoleum Book* is fundamentally an autobiography that exposes through self-doubt the tension between wanting to confess and the need to justify one's actions, exactly illustrated in his account of his role in the Anny Stephen-Richmond Ritchie marriage or in the nature of his courtship with Julia Duckworth. Nevertheless, the sense of personal disclosure in the autobiography is limited and only occasionally present. The work is basically an apology, although the following statement suggests the confusion of purpose that underlies the book: "I will not knowingly either soften or darken a shadow." While this is true for what Stephen chooses to include, he prevents a great number of shadows from appearing.

A similarly divided self appears in the narrative, style and them of Edmund Gosse's *Father and Son* (1907). Late in the work, Gosse uses images of human growth to represent a division repeated throughout the text:

> My spirits were divided pathetically between the

> wish to stay on, a guarded child, and to proceed into the world a budding man. . . .

This dichotomy expresses the structural and narrative dilemma of the late Victorian autobiographer trapped by the convention of the apology while seeking to employ the confession. The aesthetic problem of how to narrate the work, the psychological problem of how to present the self, and the moral problem of what to reveal or hide are all manifestations of the autobiographer's quandary caused by conflicting impulses and limiting forms. The most significant aspect of *Father and Son* then becomes the consciousness of the speaker trying to find a means by which he can honestly and convincingly represent his record of the two temperaments.

Gosse states the problem early in the work: "I fancied that one of my two selves could flit up, and sit clinging to the cornice, and look down on my other self and the rest of us, if I could only find the key." He expresses this duality in moral terms later in the book writing "I was at one moment devoutly pious, at the next haunted by visions of material beauty and longing for sensuous impressions. In my hot and silly brain, Jesus and Pan held sway together. . . ."

By his own account, Gosse discovers an alternate self and from this realization emerges his freedom from his father and sense of individuality. Imaginative language in the form of metaphor, imagery and dream project his new sense of wholeness. But seeking certitude, he finds flux:

> Everything seemed to be unfixed, uncertain; it was like being on the platform of a railway-station waiting for a train. . . . I became miserable, stupid, as if I had lost my way in a cold fog.

Contradictions and disruptions mar the announced thematic goal of constancy and reflect the shifting character of the autobiographer resolved only through the use of a mask expressed by Gosse's objectification of himself as "the Son." The mask permits a welcomed comedy in the autobiography, a quality generally absent in the form which seems to breed only seriousness. But *Father and Son* is conscious of how it orders, and re-orders experience, and is aware of its own theatricality. No passage in the autobiography more consciously renders the need for a mask than the following. With its understated attention to its own importance, the passage expresses the paradox of the autobiographer at the end of the century:

> Once more I have to record the fact, which I think is not without interest, that precisely as my life ceases to be solitary, it ceases to be distinct. I have no difficulty in recalling, with the minuteness of a photograph, scenes in which my Father and I were the sole actors within the four walls of a room, but of the glorious life among wild boys on the margin of the sea I have nothing but vague and broken impressions, delicious and illusive.

The language here alternates between the romanticism of the confession and the objectivity of the apology. The language, however, betrays the writer's allegiance. In writing of what he says he records with photographic exactness, he is vague—we see a room with four walls, no more; yet he describes the actions with the boys in vivid detail calling it a "glorious life . . . on the margin of the sea . . . delicious and illusive." That Gosse is able to recount both in a modulated, urbane manner attests to the presence and need (and undeclared presence) in the work of a mask. The autobiographical act is one of both self-discovery and self-disguise which may seem a commonplace today but was less evident to the Victorians.

Father and Son shares with *Praeterita* and *The Mausoleum Book* an awareness of the limitations of the apology as an autobiographical form. Collectively they prepare us for autobiographies that rely totally on the mask such as those of Yeats and Gertrude Stein. But before discussing this final stage of autobiographical evolution, it is necessary to recognize two parallel developments in the status of autobiography.

The first is a growing distrust of autobiography and fear of its power to expose hidden elements of the self. This is a backlash against the tension in late Victorian autobiographies between reticence and admission. Reaction to the desire to reveal more in fact created a counter-reaction which emphasized the protection of the self. This resistance was called by one critic in 1907 an objection to "the nude in autobiography" which consisted of "those facts . . . [of] life which people generally hide through interest or shame." "Even when it is not intrinsically shocking," continued the author, "the revelation of it [the nude] is shocking."

Beatrice Webb, whose Edwardian autobiography, *My Apprenticeship* (1926) signals a change in early modern autobiographies, expressed this fear of autobiography more privately and exactly when she wrote in her diary that "there is an unpleasantness of selling your personality as well as your professional skill, you are displaying yourself like an actress or an opera singer—you lose your privacy." "The difficulty," she remarked, was "to tell the truth without being self-conscious in the telling of it." On re-reading her diaries and dictating extracts, Beatrice Webb recorded that she wrote "so as to base my autobiographical element in it [*My Apprenticeship*] not on memories but on contemporary evidence exactly as if it were about somebody else." The passage both summarizes the struggle between remembering and recording while posing a solution: a mask, the vehicle for the creativity and truthfulness autobiography seeks to convey. Ironically, for Beatrice Webb, however, the very substance of her autobiography consists of its two voices which alternate between personal feeling and objective knowledge. Her work seeks definition as an apology but achieves its meaning and importance as a restrained confession.

Virginia Woolf was equally perplexed by autobiography, disliking it because it was too intimate, although she continued a family tradition of autobiographical writing with her "Reminiscences" written in 1908 and "Sketch of the Past" written in 1939, in addition to other, shorter pieces. But to Ethyl Smyth she wrote that personal details diminished every autobiography: "I hate any writer to talk about himself; anonymity I adore. And this may be an obsession. I blush, I fidget, I turn hot and cold. I want to pull the curtain over this indecency." Shaw summarized this response to autobiography when he unabashedly announced that

> All autobiographies are lies. . . . No man is bad enough to tell the truth about himself during his lifetime. . . . And no man is good enough to tell the truth to posterity in a document which he suppresses until there is nobody left alive to contradict him.

Such a reaction to autobiography was in part a reaction to what caused the use of the mask in autobiographical writing: the need to find a way to maintain the self-protective quality of the apology while formalizing the freedom of the confession. The dominance of the apology was challenged by the practice of those autobiographers who found it too limiting but saw the confessional form as still too threatening and used almost exclusively by fiction. Only a mask or "anti-thetical self," to borrow Yeats' term, seemed an appropriate alternative. This means of autobiographical expression permitted the integration of the psyche, free to express itself in the confession, with history, limited by time and event as found in the apology. Turning oneself into a work of art, a concept originating with the aesthetes and decadents, then allowed the inner self-realization of the individual denied by late Victorian attitudes and use of the confession. A mask, furthermore, permitted the unity of a retrospective point of view—what happened—with a prospective view—what happens. Time could be apprehended in two directions at once by the author as he interpreted events (the past) and treated interpretation as events (the present) without exposing any secrets or revealing too much of the self. This is not, however, a cover-up as Yeats explained: "the anti-self or the antithetical self. . . comes but to those who are no longer deceived, whose passion is reality." The mask enables one to pass beyond conflict. Logos and mythos find unity in autobiography through the employment of a mask.

The mask emerged because it was undesirable as well as impossible to lay bare the self. With a mask one could simultaneously be confessor and apologist, allowing for intensity and detachment without jeopardizing identity. This development coincided with a change in the novel, a second parallel to the shift in the status of autobiography. As the narrator disappeared from prominence in the Victorian novel and was virtually eliminated in the work of the early moderns (James, Woolf and Joyce), he reappeared more distinctly in autobiography. Wilde, Gosse and Yeats illustrate this change. The confession consciously suppressed the mask, having no need for it because it interfered with the spontaneous "I" that shaped the work and maintained its character of honesty. The apology, finding itself unable to integrate a private self with a public character, discovered the usefulness of a mask. In short, the increased presence of a public voice in the apology reversed what the confession achieved, the repudiation of a literary narrative convention. Resorting to a conscious narrator who functioned as a mask was the ironic means of reconciling the divergent demands of the confession and apology. While uniting opposite psychological and aesthetic requirements, the mask also combatted the fear of autobiography being too personal by creating an alternate self. This shift in autobiographical technique validated Wilde's remark that "man is least himself when he talks in his own person. Give him a mask, and he will tell you the truth."

Wilde, to no one's surprise, initiates the conscious use of the mask in autobiography and provides a fascinating example of its application in his long letter to Lord Alfred Douglas published posthumously as *De Profundis* (1905). Wilde himself was aware of the over-circumstantial quality of autobiography, noting in "The Critic as Artist" that while "the highest criticism" is the "record of one's own soul" it is also the "only civilized form of autobiography, as it deals *not* with the events, but with the thoughts of one's life." The confession also deals with these elements as *De Profundis* demonstrates.

Wilde, who had a compulsion to confess, admits his errors frankly in his lengthy lament, although the work ironically exposes another man's faults more thoroughly than his own. Wilde never particularizes his sins, although he assumes the pose of self-admonishment and gentle remorse required of every gentlemanly confessor: "I blame myself for allowing an unintellectual friendship. . . . From the very first there was too wide a gap between us" he writes. The tension in autobiographical form finds projection in the tension between Wilde and Lord Alfred which he expresses in a witty fashion:

> Whether at Torquay, Goring, London, Florence or elsewhere, my life, as long as you were by my side, was entirely sterile and uncreative. And with but few intervals you were, I regret to say, by my side always.

Throughout the autobiographical work, Wilde empurples his sense of guilt, overstating, enlarging, distorting his repentance to such a degree that it loses its sincerity and conviction for the reader. His confession is closer to pantomime than tragedy, a condition confirmed by his concern over where and how he and Lord Alfred will meet immediately after his release. Wilde's earnest plea to reunite undermines the extended critique of Lord Alfred's negative effect upon himself and undercuts his loss of reputation and financial ruin. The situation highlights the ironic use of a mask in that the persona of the confessor is weaker than the ostensible desires of the author. *De Profundis* confirms the truth of Wilde's 1894 comment that "in so vulgar an age as this we all need masks."

In autobiography the mask becomes a conscious persona of the author that frees or, at times, betrays him from an identity he may find too inhibiting in a form he found too limiting. In response to the fictional use of the confession in the Victorian novel and the weakness of the apology as an autobiographical form, the mask became a means of handling the desire to confess and the demands of the apology. In short, as the tension between the obligation to record and the need to interpret grew, a fear and distrust of autobiography emerged which was overcome only by the employment of a mask to act as a vehicle to contain the private and public self. This autobiographical strategy corresponded with narrative changes in the novel which suggests that the dilemma of Victorian autobiography is both an aspect of literary history as well as a stage in the evolution of a literary form. (pp. 189-203)

Ira Bruce Nadel, "Apologize or Confess!: The Dilemma of Victorian Autobiography," in Biography, *Vol. 5, No. 3, Summer, 1982, pp. 189-204.*

THEMES AND TECHNIQUES

Howard Helsinger

[*In the following essay, Helsinger discusses the various methods by which Victorian autobiographers sought to ensure the credibility of their narratives.*]

In Book X of the *Confessions* St. Augustine confronts a problem intrinsic to autobiography when he asks, "What have I to do with men, that they should hear my confessions . . . ? When they hear me speak about myself, how do they know if I speak the truth, since none among men knows 'what goes on within a man but the spirit of man which is in him.' " Testifying to his own character, the autobiographer is a suspect witness whom even the least skeptical auditors might doubt. We know our own tendencies to present ourselves, even to ourselves, as better or worse than we are, and so inevitably suspect the autobiographer of similarly painting himself in colors too light or too dark. The more personal his testimony, the less liable to corroboration by public knowledge, and hence the paradox: the greater the autobiographer's effort at introspective honesty, the more subject he grows to doubt. Even if he does not consciously suppress or distort information, he may do so unconsciously. But if memory consciously and unconsciously shapes the past to fit the needs of the present, how then can the autobiographer escape the imputation of falsehood and lying?

The autobiographer's defense against these charges reveals his conceptions of the nature of autobiography. Augustine, for example, takes autobiography to be a form of speech which is both intimate and influential—intimate in that it is both introspective and among friends; influential in that it shapes both his own life and theirs. He says:

> Because 'charity believes all things' among those whom it unites by binding them to itself, I too, O Lord, will confess to you in such a manner that men may hear, although I cannot prove to them that I confess truly. But those men whose ears charity opens to me believe me. . . . Charity . . . tells them that I do not lie when I make my confessions: it is charity in them that believes in me.

By charity—that is, caritas—Augustine means the love by which men are properly bound to God. According to him, the things of this created world, including our fellow mortals, are to be loved not in themselves, which would be cupidity, but in God, for only God may properly be loved in himself. The *civitas dei* is a society bound together by its common love of God; bound, that is, by charity. As God is Truth, so truth and belief are characteristics of this society. By binding men together in a common love, charity binds them together as brothers enabled to see through potentially deceitful surfaces to the truth within. Charity, in other words, defines a relationship, and it is on the basis of that relationship that Augustine presumes to validate his speech. Augustine's honesty is thus confirmed by his intimacy with his readers, which is in turn a correlate of his intimacy with himself and, ultimately with God.

Few Victorian autobiographers shared Augustine's recognition of the innate difficulties in telling the truth about one's own life. Their response to that suspicion of deceit from which no autobiography can be wholly free suggests they conceived this literary mode not as intimate speech but public discourse. They write not only for themselves and their contemporaries, but for posterity. They grow concerned about propriety, avoid introspection, and produce work which is predominantly memoir. In general they lack self-consciousness. Thus, the embarrassing depths of self-pity and regret which Ruskin reveals to us in *Praeterita* are insights for us, but not for him, because he does not watch himself looking at himself. Carlyle's elaborate framework in *Sartor Resartus* serves as a conscious means of avoiding the appearance of self-consciousness. Due to this lack or avoidance of self-consciousness, the Victorians make a limited and distinctive response to the question of autobiographical honesty. Unlike Augustine, whose claim to belief rests on the relationship he affirms with himself and his audience, most Victorian autobiographers rest their claim to belief on their denial of any such relationship.

THE TWO DEFENSES: EX VITA AND EX MORTE.

We can illustrate the two opposite modes of defense in the writings of David Hume and Edward Gibbon. In April of 1776, four months before he died, the terminally ill David Hume wrote a brief account of his life, intended as a preface to the next edition of his works. This abbreviated autobiography begins:

> It is difficult for a man to speak long of himself without vanity; therefore I shall be short. It may be thought an instance of vanity that I pretend at all to write my life; but this Narrative shall contain little more than the History of my Writing; as indeed, almost all my life his been spent in literary pursuits and occupations.

The fear of seeming vain and thus guilty of self-interest and distortion is almost enough to silence Hume, but by his consciousness of that suspicion he seeks to weaken it. He will, moreover, speak briefly and write factually, a mere "History of my Writings." His strongest defense, however, is that in his debilitated condition "it is difficult to be more detached from life than I am at present." That very detachment from himself, from others, and from life in general is to be the guarantee of his honesty. Thus he says "I am, or rather was (for that is the style I must now use in speaking of myself, which emboldens me the more to speak my sentiments); I was, I say, a man of mild dispositions." By speaking of himself in the past tense, like a voice from the grave, Hume claims to be beyond self-interest, and therefore without motive to distort. We may call this, therefore, the defense *ex morte*. By its aid Hume

Craigenputtoch, the hill-farm in Scotland where Carlyle worked on Sartor Resartus.

can treat himself objectively, and by speaking quasi-posthumously, speak frankly. But this is of course pretense, a not very effective rhetorical pose, for since the beginnings of history men seem to have been concerned for their reputations after death. Rather than solving the problem of autobiographical credibility, the defense *ex morte* avoids it. The autobiographer hopes such an approach will transform him into an historian, and hence enable him to escape his difficulties. But, as Hume himself seems to have realized, the escape is impossible, for he concludes, "I cannot say there is no vanity in making this funeral oration of myself, but I hope it is not a misplaced one: and this is a matter of fact which is easily cleared."

Edward Gibbon is less tempted by the pose of historical detachment. He began his autobiography in 1786, and worked on various versions of it until 1791. The earliest version, wherein Gibbon first faced the difficulty of autobiography, opens as follows:

> In the fifty-second year of my age, after the completion of a toilsome and successful work, I now propose to employ some moments of my leisure in reviewing the simple transactions of a private and literary life. Truth—naked unblushing truth, the first virtue of more serious history—must be the sole recommendation of this personal narrative. The style shall be simple and familiar. But style is the image of character, and the habits of correct writing may produce, without labor or design, the appearance of art and study. My own amusement is my motive, and will be my reward; and if these sheets are communicated to some discreet and indulgent friends, they will be secreted from the public eye till the author shall be removed from the reach of criticism or ridicule.

The expectation of posthumous publication allies this to the defense *ex morte,* as does the identification with "more serious history," but Gibbon's sensitivity to style indicates how conscious he is of an audience. He proposes to adopt a "simple and familiar" style fit for both his subject matter and the relationship he seeks with his audience. He aims at "truth—naked unblushing truth," and a simple and familiar style will encourage belief because "style is the image of character." We will believe him because he seems familiar, i.e., intimate and known. But character is constant, and his own may be so habituated to the forms of "correct writing," Gibbon goes on, that strive as he may to be simple, he may yet unwittingly and unintentionally "without labor or design," give the "appearance of art and study," and thereby seem false and deceitful. In short, if his style is true to his character he will be taken for a liar, and only by borrowing a style and thereby masking his character can he be sure of making a truthful impression. Unable to embrace Wilde's paradox that "Truth is entirely and absolutely a matter of style," Gibbon softens the effect of his art by apologizing for it, and thereby takes us further into his confidence. To these means of enhancing his credibility Gibbon can add his reputation as an historian, which lends weight to, and is in turn reinforced by, his tendency to generalize, for as his generalizations ring true, and are confirmed in our experience, we give credence to his account. This reliance on reputation, together with an explicit consciousness of style and its effects, indicate in Gibbon an awareness and acceptance of his relationship to his audience. His words may be published posthumously, but they are spoken by a man in touch with society, and with himself. As a means of affirming autobiographical truth such assertion of relationship, which resembles the brotherhood of charity on which Augustine relies, may be termed the defense *ex vita.*

We will find a clearer example of this defense *ex vita* in Wordsworth's *Prelude,* which was, as McConnell has recently stressed, known in manuscript as "the Poem to Coleridge." The poem's primary claim to our belief is its intimate voice. It is, like Augustine's confession to God, private, privileged discourse on which we are merely eavesdropping. By adopting a private voice the poet can deny all public role-playing. Whereas the defense *ex morte* claims truth by denying relation to living men, the fully realized defender *ex vita,* like Wordsworth, affirms so intimate and immediate a relationship with his audience as to allow no self-conscious separation, no division, no duplicity. He assumes, or if necessary creates, such a community as Wordsworth lauds in *The Recluse:*

> Society is here
> A true community—a genuine frame
> Of many into one incorporate. (ll.614-16)

That sense of community seems to have diminished as the century wore on, and by 1850, when the *Prelude* appeared posthumously, the defense *ex vita* had fallen into disuse.

In that year, in the Preface to his *Autobiography,* Leigh Hunt seems to refer to a familiar intimacy with his readers: "I have been so accustomed during the greater part of my life to talk to the reader in my own person . . . that I fall more naturally into this kind of fireside strain than most writers, and therefore do not present the public so abrupt an image of individuality." Hunt's purpose here, however, is not to evoke relationship, but to apologize for personality. Propriety, far more than veracity, concerns Hunt as he admits, to the despair of anyone hoping for frankness, that: "I have lived long enough to discover that autobiography may not only be a very distressing but a very puzzling task, and throw the writer into such doubts as to what he should or should not say, as totally to confuse him." Such statements may stir in the reader doubts about what he should or should not believe. Although Hunt recognizes the value to his undertaking of a charitable sympathy, which he calls intuition, between author and reader, he does little to encourage that relationship, and the prayer with which he closes his Preface suggests only the difficulty of achieving it: "And so Heaven bless the reader, and all of us: and enable us to compare notes some day in some Elysian corner of intuition, where we shall be in no need of prefaces and explanations." The true community where explanation is unnecessary has withdrawn to an Elysian corner, and the autobiographer withdraws into himself. Whatever influence his work can have is purely reflexive—it makes him feel better: "I will liken myself to an actor, who though commencing his part on the stage with a gout or a headache, or perhaps, even with a bit of a heartache, finds his audience so willing to be pleased, that he forgets his infirmity as he goes, and ends with being glad that he has appeared." Were the issue of honesty and credibility as sharp for Hunt as it is for Augustine, his resemblance to an actor would trouble him. That it does not is an indication of how mute the issue has become.

The Autobiographer As Gentleman: Trollope.

I have suggested that the autobiographer is compelled to defend himself against the suspicion of falsifying or holding back the details of his life, but this is true only if he desires to seem entirely frank, if his goal is the "naked unblushing truth" Gibbon aimed at. One may aim elsewhere, and when Hunt considers what he "should not say," truth has begun to clothe herself with modesty. To at least one sensitive Victorian autobiographer, the naked truth seemed not merely improper, but unattainable. Writing in 1875, Anthony Trollope opens [his *Autobiography*] by asserting, "That I, or any man, should tell everything of himself, I hold to be impossible" and he closes on the same note: "It will not, I trust, be supposed by any reader that I have intended in this so-called autobiography to give a record of my inner life. No man ever did so truly—and no man ever will." Trollope asserts here not the rhetorical difficulty of convincing his audience of his honesty, but the prior epistemological impossibility of entirely accurate or honest self-knowledge, and the secondary difficulty of the complete expression of such self-knowledge as can be attained. When he says "who could endure to own the doing of a mean thing? Who is there that has done none?" he seems to embrace modesty as inevitable, but he has more than just conscious modesty in mind. "Rousseau probably attempted," he admits, "a record of [his] inner life," which includes to be sure the doing of mean things, "but who doubts," Trollope goes on, "but that Rousseau has confessed in much the thoughts and convictions rather than the facts of his life?" However honest a man's intentions, "A man does, in truth, remember that which it interests him to remember." The exclamatory "in truth" has full adverbial weight. One cannot report "the facts of his life," because "in our lives we are always weaving novels." In the end there remain no facts at all.

Such thorough skepticism does not, however, relieve the autobiographer of the need to convince his audience that he has at least aimed at such honesty as can be attained. Memory may be determined by interest, but it can be at least undertaken "in truth." Trollope may hold that to tell everything of himself is impossible, but he goes on to say "that nothing that I say shall be untrue." His defenses, however, are strangely limited.

As Trollope had intended, his *Autobiography* was published posthumously, but he uses the defense *ex morte* only to explain and apologize for what would be otherwise socially unacceptable frankness. After speaking fondly of John Everett Millais, he concludes: "These words, should he ever see them, will come to him from the grave, and will tell him of my regard,—as one living man never tells another." As a voice from the grave he "may dare to say what no one now does dare to say in print,—though some of us whisper it occasionally into our friends' ears. There are places in life which can hardly be well filled except by a Gentleman." He excuses his speaking well of the moral influence of his own novels by evoking "that absence of self-personality which the dead may claim." Despite Trollope's awareness of the problem of honesty, he cannot, as a gentleman ("one of us"), manifest "self-personality."

In so far then as Trollope seeks to convince us of his honesty, it should be the defense *ex vita* on which he relies. Even the posthumous voice serves the ends of this defense, by allowing him to speak as if whispering into friends' ears. An expectation that we will believe and trust him because he is known and familiar would be consonant with the *Autobiography* as a whole, which is conceived as an anti-romantic polemic against the idea of writer as genius. Writing, we are to understand, is a profession like others, allied more to hard work than to inspiration. "It is my purpose as I go on," says Trollope,

> to state what to me has been the result of my profession in the ordinary way in which professions are regarded, so that by my example may be seen what prospect there is that a man devoting himself to literature with industry, perseverance, certain necessary aptitudes, and fair average talents, may succeed in gaining a livelihood, as another man does in another profession.

Writers, indeed, will do well to learn from cobblers:

> I had . . . convinced myself that in such work as mine the great secret consisted in acknowledging myself to be bound to rules of labour similar to those which an artisan or a mechanic is forced to obey. A shoemaker when he has finished one pair of shoes does not sit down and contemplate this work in idle satisfaction. 'There is my pair of shoes finished at last! What a pair of shoes it is!' The shoemaker who so indulged himself would be without wages half his time. It is the same with a professional writer of books. . . . Having thought much of all this, and having made up my mind that I could be really happy only when I was at work, I had now quite accustomed myself to begin a second pair as soon as the first was out of my hands.

The writer, in short, is a day-laborer, not a wool-gathering poet who sits "nibbling his pen, and gazing at the wall before him, till he shall have found the words with which he wants to express his ideas": "All those I think who have lived as literary men,—working daily as literary labourers,—will agree with me that three hours a day will produce as much as a man ought to write."

If statements such as these convinced us that writers are just ordinary folk, they might encourage us to trust Trollope as "one of us," but pride in his own singular achievements regularly undercuts his claim to be common. Even the community of "literary men" invited to agree with him is meant to marvel when Trollope illustrates these precepts by his own practice: "It had at this time become my custom . . . to write with my watch before me, and to require from myself 250 words every quarter of an hour. I have found that the 250 words have been forthcoming as regularly as my watch went." We are struck more by the singularity of his diligence than by the familiarity of his effort. The labor may be common, but the laborer is extraordinary: "I feel confident that in amount no other writer contributed so much during that time to English literature." What is to encourage us to share that confidence?

There are "two kinds of confidence which a reader may have in his author," explains Trollope, "a confidence in facts, and a confidence in vision." (These correspond to the defenses *ex morte* and *ex vita.*) For the first a writer employs research, strives for accuracy, and demands of the reader faith; for the second he employs observation, aims for sensitivity and imagination, and demands judgment. Although Trollope explains that he himself employs the subjective way of vision, his *Autobiography* seems rather more a reporting of facts demanding faith. His account of his schooling is characteristic:

> When I left Harrow I was all but nineteen, and I had at first gone there at seven. During the whole of those twelve years no attempt had been made to teach me anything but Latin and Greek. . . . The assertion will scarcely be credited, but I do assert that I have no recollection of other tuition except that in the dead languages. . . . I feel convinced in my mind that I have been flogged oftener than any human being alive. It was just possible to obtain five scourgings in one day at Winchester, and I have often boasted that I obtained them all. Looking back over half a century, I am not quite certain whether the boast is true; but if I did not, nobody ever did.

These are ostensibly facts, although they are guaranteed only by Trollope's assertion. They are, as it were, subjective facts, for which Trollope's own character, or his reputation as a truthful gentleman, can be the only ground of belief. To support our faith in his facts, we need to judge him, to know him. But his character is unique, as he has been at pains to have us realize, and hence hard to know and difficult to judge.

Trollope's difficulty in establishing a basis for belief stems from his ambivalent desire to be both common and unique, of the masses and above them. Success mattered to him intensely, but he never quite trusted the success he achieved. "To be known as somebody,—to be Anthony Trollope if it be no more,—is to be much," he acknowledges, but he made the extraordinary experiment of publishing several novels anonymously to see if they would sell without his name. Perhaps Trollope's visit with Brigham Young is emblematic. "I called upon him," Trollope says:

> sending to him my card, apologising for doing so without an introduction and excusing myself by saying that I did not like to pass through the territory without seeing a man of whom I had heard so much. He received me in his doorway, not asking me to enter, and inquired whether I were not a miner. When I told him that I was not a miner, he asked me whether I earned my bread. I told him I did. 'I guess you're a miner,' said he. I again assured him that I was not.

> 'Then how do you earn your bread?' I told him that I did so by writing books. 'I'm sure you're a miner,' said he. Then he turned upon his heel, went back into the house, and closed the door. I was properly punished, as I was vain enough to conceive that he would have heard my name.

Although he can, as here, laugh at his presumption, Trollope nonetheless presumes that we too will have heard his name, that we will know who he is. He pretends to be a laborer, but expects to be trusted as a gentleman.

When he seems to really take us into his confidence, he successfully evokes confidence in turn, but that happens only once, in the next to last paragraph. Speaking of his surviving sources of pleasure, he says: "Could I remember, as some men do, what I read, I should have been able to call myself an educated man. But that power I have never possessed. Something is always left—something dim and inaccurate,—but still something sufficient to preserve the taste for more. I am inclined to think that it is so with most readers." Most readers at that point may want to say "ah, one of us at the very last," but the need in Trollope to seem singular reasserts itself, and he closes his book on the otherwise inconsequential note that he has been reading the English dramatists, and that "if I live a few years longer, I shall, I think, leave in my copies of these dramatists, down to the close of James I, written criticisms of every play. No one who has not looked closely into it knows how many there are."

The sharpness of Trollope's sense of the impossibility of accurate self-knowledge or honest self-expression may have contributed to his limited response to the rhetorical problem of creating an appearance of honesty. He tells us once at the beginning that he shall say nothing untrue, and relies thereafter on his reputation as a gentleman among equals, and on our corresponding trust. But by assuming such an audience, he assumed certain limitations on frankness. There were things he might not say, even if he wished to. Manifest self-consciousness, for instance, would have been improper. The community of gentlemen does, in fact, guarantee Trollope's honesty, but it is an honesty restricted to a range much narrower than we may hope to find in autobiography, where politeness is not always a virtue.

The Autobiographer As Natural Historian: Darwin, Spencer, Mill.

Few Victorian autobiographers share Trollope's skepticism about the possibility of honesty. Darwin, for example, claims in 1876: "I have attempted to write the following account of myself as if I were a dead man in another world looking back at my own life." In Darwin this defense and its claim to objectivity suggests scientific method. The principal uncertainty of autobiography rises from the encounter of living self with deceitful memory, but Darwin's stance, "as if I were a dead man," fixes for observation his own life as surely as formaldehyde had fixed his collection of limpets. Beyond this defense *ex morte* Darwin's *Autobiography* hints at a community with the audience of his family: "A German Editor having written to me to ask for an account of the development of my mind and character, with some sketch of my autobiography, I have thought that the attempt would amuse me, and might possibly interest my children or their children." Later, when he momentarily adopts the second person, all other audience than his family seems forgotten: "You all know well your Mother, and what a good Mother she has ever been to all of you." Despite his immediate relation with his audience in this passage, the invocation of community is entirely naive, and made with no sense of its effects or consequences. As we read further we cannot, I think, fail to grow skeptical: "She has ever been my greatest blessing, and I can declare that in my whole life I have never heard her utter one word which I had rather have been unsaid. . . . I have indeed been most happy in my family, and I must say to you my children that not one of you has ever given me one minute's anxiety, except on the score of health." That account may, just possibly, be true in substance, but its style reeks of fiction, of those novels "which are works of the imagination, though not of a very high order," of which Darwin says "a surprising number have been read aloud to me, and I like all if moderately good, and if they do not end unhappily—against which a law ought to be passed." Darwin is basically unselfconscious. He doesn't hear himself speak in this passage, and is unaware of how suspicious we may be of his Pollyanna tone. It is precisely Gibbon's sensitivity to style, and the concomitant sense of audience, which Darwin lacks.

Herbert Spencer, writing between 1886 and 1894, continues the scientific tradition and calls his *Autobiography* a "natural history of myself." He chooses explicitly between modes of defense: "In years to come, when I shall no longer be conscious, the frankness with which the book is written may add to whatever value it has, but while I am alive it would, I think, be out of taste to address the public as though it consisted of personal friends." Good taste does not make good autobiography, but the English sense of reserve and decorum is at work. Self-exposure is indecent, and vanity is shameful, but some appearance of vanity is almost inevitable:

> It is a provoking necessity that an autobiography should be egotistic. A biography is inevitably defective as lacking facts of importance and still more as giving imperfect or untrue interpretations of those facts which it contains; and an autobiography, by exhibiting its writer as continually talking about himself, is defective as making very salient a trait which may not perhaps be stronger than usual. The reader has to discount the impression produced as well as he can.

Having expressed his generation's distaste for manifest egotism, Spencer here goes on to imply that the defects of biography are rectified in autobiography, which will have all the facts and interpret them correctly; and that the autobiographer's (i.e., his own) apparent egotism is a false impression generated by the medium itself. Although in this second point he is astutely aware of style, in both points Spencer reveals his basic unself-consciousness. Regarding the first, autobiographers such as Augustine have made clear the elusiveness, even in autobiography, of truth in fact or interpretation. Regarding the second, which is intended as self-defense, Darwin gives contrary testimony, having written of Spencer: "I think that he was extremely egotistical." Spencer's comments may be a response to Darwin, but if so the defense is even less convincing.

In so far as Darwin and Spencer are writing "natural history," it seems appropriate that they should adopt posthumous publication and the associated defense *ex morte* to establish themselves as disinterested observers objectively reporting the facts. But posthumous publication is adopted also by John Stuart Mill, for whom subjective experience has major importance. Actually, Mill makes no defense at all, says nothing about when the book is to be published, says nothing about the difficulty or inaccuracy of reminiscence, nothing about vanity, nothing about truth. Lucid prose and clear intentions go far toward encouraging our belief, but we may still wonder at Mill's apparent unconsciousness of the imputations to which autobiography may be subject.

The gloomy crisis in Mill's mental history was first resolved by his reading in Marmontel's *Memoires* a sentimental passage that sounds today highly self-conscious and artificial. In the aftermath of his emotional response Mill adopted a theory "having much in common with . . . the anti-self-consciousness theory of Carlyle": "Ask yourself whether you are happy, and you cease to be so." He might also have said, "ask yourself whether you are truthful, and you cease to be so." In each case self-consciousness is the canker in the bud. Darwin, Spencer, and Mill avoid introspection and thus avoid doubts and anxiety about the veracity of their self-image. It is not surprising that they should do so, for they are, professionally, men dedicated to objective truth, to fact. Mill's discovery of the importance of feeling and emotion, his discovery, that is, of the inner life, doesn't bring him to doubt the possibility of describing that life accurately, because he immediately objectifies what he discovers. Mill urges on his friend Roebuck that

> the imaginative emotion which an idea, when vividly conceived, excites in us, is not an illusion but a fact, as real as any of the other qualities of objects; and far from implying anything erroneous and delusive in our mental apprehension of the object, is quite consistent with the most accurate knowledge and most perfect practical recognition of all its physical and intellectual laws and relations.

He thus redeems the inner life, imagination, and emotion by identifying them with the real world of objects. If the emotions associated with perception are not erroneous and delusive, the autobiographer's fear that his highly charged memories may falsify experience becomes groundless. Mill is converted to an appreciation of individuality and imagination, but the imagination remains subject to "intellectual laws" and rational analysis and the individual escapes self-consciousness. The extent of Mill's self-consciousness may be his observation, in a letter to Harriet of 1855, that "I know how deficient I am in self-consciousness & self observation."

The Autobiographer Accused: Newman.

The only Victorian who equals Augustine in his awareness of the difficulty of securing unqualified belief for autobiography, or approaches his sensitivity to the elusiveness of truthful self-expression, is John Henry Newman. But, then, Newman was impelled to write the *Apologia Pro Vita Sua* by Kingsley's accusations, from among which he chose one against which to make his stand: "there is only one about which I much care,—the charge of Untruthfulness." Confronting Kingsley's quotation of his own words that "it is not more than a hyperbole to say, that, in certain cases, a lie is the nearest approach to truth," Newman necessarily makes his defense against the charge of lying detailed, elaborate, and explicit.

Newman was not merely accused of telling a lie, but of being a liar, and the effect, as he observes, is to "poison the wells." Until that comprehensive charge is dispelled nothing that Newman says can escape its taint:

> If Mr. Kingsley is able thus to practise upon my readers, the more I succeed, the less will be my success. If I am natural, he will tell them. 'Ars est celare artem'; if I am convincing, he will suggest that I am an able logician; if I show warmth, I am acting the indignant innocent; if I am calm, I am thereby detected as a smooth hypocrite; if I clear up difficulties, I am too plausible and perfect to be true. The more triumphant are my statements, the more certain will be my defeat.

Kingsley here serves Newman as the traditional voice of autobiographical self-doubt, accusing him of artful deceit,

John Henry Newman.

hypocrisy, and acting. "He called me a liar," says Newman, and "what I needed was a corresponding antagonist unity in my defence," for his very identity had been challenged. Newman responds to Kingsley's question "What does Dr. Newman mean?" by pointing out the implications of his antagonist's question: "He asks what I mean; not about my words, not about my arguments, not about my actions, as his ultimate point, but about that living intelligence by which I write, and argue, and act. He asks about my Mind and its Beliefs and its Sentiments." Words, arguments, and actions are the stuff of superficial autobiographies, the "natural histories" of self; but the charge of lying, whether leveled by an external adversary like Kingsley or by the adversary in one's own soul, stimulates autobiography of a different sort: "I must, I said, give the true key to my whole life; I must show what I am that it may be seen what I am not, and that the phantom may be extinguished which gibbers instead of me. I wish to be known as a living man, and not as a scarecrow which is dressed up in my clothes." Newman's task is to distinguish surface from substance, to discover the real to extinguish, as did Augustine, the Manichean phantom of the false and divided self.

Newman thus faces the familiar autobiographical task of affirming his own true unity. Like other converts, he must "distinguish between his past self and his present" to show that he was not *then* what he is now; not only to affirm the change, but also to prove that he was not then already converted—was not then lying. At the same time, to make us understand the connection between past and present and their basic unity, he must indicate how minute were the increments of change.

Newman's own self-consciousness fed the suspicions leveled against him. When Tract 90 was published he saw, from the reaction, that "Confidence in me was lost," but he had, he says, "already lost full confidence in myself." "How was I any more to have absolute confidence in myself? how was I to have confidence in my present confidence? how was I to be sure that I should always think as I thought now?" He had, he says, a "secret longing love of Rome, . . . And it was the consciousness of this bias in myself . . . which made me preach so earnestly against the danger of being swayed by our sympathy rather than our reason in religious inquiry." This self-consciousness becomes an element of Newman's defense as it enables him so exactly to express the position of his opponents.

Among the other elements of Newman's self-defense, his articulate style, careful logic, clear ideas, and precise facts, we must also recognize the impression he gives of self-exposure. "I mean," he says, "to be personal . . . to speak out my own heart." It is commonplace to say that "It is not at all pleasant for me to be egotistical; nor to be criticised for being so," but Newman's expressions of distaste are made so elaborate, and placed so significantly once at the end of the Preface, and again at the beginning of the central "History of my Religious Opinions from 1839 to 1841," that we come to credit them. The sense of self-exposure he generates works to suggest an intimacy with his readers, and hence a sense of community with them. Very early he evokes that community by reminding his readers of how well they know him:

> Whatever judgment my readers may eventually form of me from these pages, I am confident that they will believe me in what I shall say in the course of them. I have no misgiving at all, that they will be ungenerous or harsh with a man who has been so long before the eyes of the world; who has so many to speak of him from personal knowledge; whose natural impulse it has ever been to speak out. . . .

He goes on to characterize himself in such a way as to impart a sense of precisely such personal knowledge. Our larger sense of intimacy comes from Newman's meticulous introspection, which encourages us to believe (as we never do Gibbon) that he is indeed naked before us. But there is also at work to encourage our belief a real community, a brotherhood of auditors, to which Newman directs this work; and which he invokes on his last page: "my dearest brothers of this House, the Priests of the Birmingham Oratory," with whom he prays to be "brought at length, by the Power of the Divine Will, into One Fold under One Shepherd."

The affirmation of his veracity can occupy so large a place in Newman's thought because conversion yields him, as it did Augustine, a conviction of truth to which both life and autobiography must testify. Unified in soul, he must be on guard against the disunity of life. Unlike his contemporaries, he is therefore intimate, introspective, and wholly conscious of his own style.

THE AUTOBIOGRAPHER AS ARTIST: GOSSE.

Self-consciousness and sensitivity to the issue of autobiographical honesty are natural correlates. The self-conscious autobiographer recognizes the autobiography itself as part of his self-characterization; he sees with Gibbon that "style is the image of character," and is therefore aware of the artificial element in any image of character he may create. His task becomes that of convincing us of the congruence of style and character, and it is to that end that he aims at a sense of intimacy. The would-be natural historian of himself, on the other hand, not wanting to admit to watching himself, puts on an objective style, and pretends to be talking about someone else. He thus presents himself as not only unbiased, but as free of any possible duplicity. Lying speech is always duplicitous, aware of itself and of the truth it is not. Deceit, in other words, is always self-conscious, and so the natural historian avoids the appearance of self-consciousness to avoid the suspicion of deceit. But that can only be pretense, and it is really more honest to admit to self-consciousness. The difficulty this creates for an autobiographer like Augustine or Newman who has a personal truth to convince us of is not, as we have seen, insurmountable. Indeed, they find their way to truth through self-knowledge, according to the ancient injunction *nosce te ipsum.*

When self-consciousness becomes an end in itself, as it does for Edmund Gosse, the issue of honesty is transformed. The account which Gosse gives of his education in *Father and Son* is, as he says, "the record of the struggle between two temperaments, two consciences and almost two epochs." In broadest terms it records the struggle between Truth and Imagination, between the rigid Evangelical Puritanism of his father and his own dawning imaginative sensitivity. In the world of his parents all fiction, indeed, all art, was rejected. His mother noted in her diary that from early youth she "considered that to invent a story of any kind was a sin," his father burned Gosse's copy of Jonson and Marlowe, and Gosse reports that " . . . not a single fiction was read or told to me during my infancy." By all their denial of the imagination his parents had, he says, "desired to make me truthful; the tendency was to make me positive and skeptical."

We might imagine that as a skeptic Gosse would deal rigorously with the autobiographical claim to truthfulness, but he raises the issue only once, in his opening sentence:

> At the present hour, when fiction takes forms so ingenious and specious, it is perhaps necessary to say that the following narrative, in all its parts, and so far as the punctilious attention of the writer has been able to keep it so, is scrupulously true. If it were not true, in this strict sense, to publish it would be to trifle with all those who may be induced to read it.

Like the more conventional opposite disclaimer that "any resemblance to persons living or dead is purely coincidental," Gosse's statement acknowledges the similarity of his account to fiction, but denies the identity. The similarity seems scarcely to trouble him, and, he shows little sensitivity to the role of style in creating the appearance of honesty. If this book is, as he claims, "nothing else if it is not a genuine slice of life," we may wonder how a plum such as the following got into the loaf from which the slice was cut:

> This, then, was the scene in which the soul of a little child was planted, not as in an ordinary open flower-border or carefully tended social parterre, but as on a ledge, split in the granite of some mountain. The ledge was hung between night and the snows on one hand, and the dizzy depths of the world upon the other; was furnished with just soil enough for a gentian to struggle skywards and open its still azure stars; and offered no lodgment, no hope of salvation, to any rootlet which should stray behind its inexorable limits.

Like Darwin's idealized account of his family, this is the stuff of fiction. But the "positive and skeptical" Gosse, trained to truthfulness, was not stylistically naive, and we must wonder why he felt no greater need to distinguish his account from fiction, and affirm his veracity.

The discovery of untruth was the central event in Gosse's mental history. He confused his father, he says, "in some sense with God," so that when one morning in his sixth year, he heard his father say something which "*was not true,*" "the shock to me was as that of a thunderbolt." "The most curious" and for us most important consequence of this crisis is that "I had found a companion and confidant in myself. There was a secret in this world and it belonged to me and to somebody who lived in the same body with me. There were two of us, and we could talk with one another." The rest of his childhood is dedicated to the preservation of that secret self: "Through thick and thin I clung to a hard nut of individuality deep down in my childish nature. To the pressure from without, I resigned everything else, my thoughts, my words, my anticipations, my assurances, but there was something which I never resigned, my innate and persistent self." In the "consciousness of self " Gosse gained through this newly discovered inner duality we may recognize the potential for lying. Duality enables duplicity; if you can keep a secret you can choose to not tell the truth. In protecting that duality Gosse aims at a goal directly opposite to St. Augustine's.

Gosse's deconversion is, in significant detail, just the reverse of Augustine's conversion. Augustine's education began with literature. As a schoolboy he loved theatre, and won a prize for his reading of a speech of Juno's from the *Aeneid.* His training in rhetoric was training in the surface rather than the substance of words, and he moved only gradually toward a penetration of the surface and an insistence on Truth. Augustine was tormented by the duality he discovered in himself, which he refers to as "this debate within my heart . . . of myself against myself," and he devoted all his effort and prayer to resolving that duality and restoring his soul's unity in God. At the climactic moment of conversion he refers to theater as a temptation away from Truth ("If one of us debates with himself . . . whether he should go to the theatre or to our church" and when, finally, he takes to heart the words of Scripture, "Not in rioting and drunkenness, not in chambering and impurities . . . but put you on the Lord Jesus Christ," he rejects the world of theater and "all the dark shadows of doubt fled away."

The setting of Gosse's climactic deconversion is an "open window at the top of the school-house," a sort of tower from which he "gazed down on a labyrinth of gardens sloping to the sea," a setting, we may note, remarkably like one in Ostia, "a certain window, where we could look into the garden" wherein Augustine and his mother shared their mystic vision. But for Gosse the tower is not a way of ascent to God, but a prison, keeping him from the world. As a child he was, he says, "most carefully withdrawn, like Princess Blanchefleur in her marble fortress," and even later "my soul was shut up, like Fatima, in a tower to which no external influences could come." Like Augustine at a comparable climax, Gosse's sense of his double nature is particularly strong: "I was at one moment devoutly pious, at the next haunted by visions of material beauty and longing for sensuous impressions. In my hot and silly brain, Jesus and Pan held sway together." It is the moment of sunset, and he prays for Jesus to come "and take me before I have known the temptations of life, before I have to go to London and all the dreadful things that happen there." He concludes:

> This was the highest moment of my religious life, the apex of my striving after holiness. I waited awhile, watching; and then I had a little shame at the theatrical attitude I had adopted, although I was alone. Still I gazed and still I hoped. Then a little breeze sprang up, and the branches danced. Sounds began to rise from the road beneath me. Presently the colour deepened,

> the evening came on. From far below there rose to me the chatter of the boys returning home. The tea-bell rang,—the last word of prose to shatter my mystical poetry. 'The Lord has not come, the Lord will never come,' I muttered, and in my heart the artificial edifice of extravagant faith began to totter and crumble. From that moment forth my Father and I, though the fact was long concealed from him and even from myself, walked in opposite hemispheres of the soul, with 'the thick o' the world' between us.

What interrupts this would-be ecstasy, this yearning for surrender and unification, is self-consciousness, "shame at the theatrical attitude I had adopted," the recognition that he is acting. The world that had been stilled, stirs, and stirs desire; the shadows which had fled from Augustine fall; and the completed separation from his father, as if in "opposite hemispheres of the soul," seems a figure for the confirmed duality of his own nature.

As Gosse moves away from the unity of faith and the belief in Truth, he moves towards a theatricality which implies not only an acceptance of lying but almost a defense of it. Not that he advocates dishonesty, but rather such polite prudence as we have seen in Hunt and Trollope. "Even at the age of eleven," says Gosse, "one sees that on certain occasions to press home the truth is not convenient." In the epilogue, as he judges his father who was a natural historian, Gosse defends "prudence" as part of the civilized life:

> My Father was entirely devoid of the prudence which turns away its eyes and passes as rapidly as possible in the opposite direction. The peculiar kind of drama in which every sort of discomfort is welcomed rather than that the characters should be happy when guilty of 'acting a lie' was not invented in those days, and there can hardly be imagined a figure more remote from my Father than Ibsen. Yet when I came, at a far later date, to read 'The Wild Duck' memories of the embarrassing household of my infancy helped me to realise Gregers Warle, with his determination to pull the veil of illusion away from every compromise that makes life bearable.

Gosse comes down in favor of the veil of illusion, in defense of the lie that makes life bearable. Even if complete honesty were possible it would be undesirable, for he wants to preserve the privacy of his hard-won inner world. Like Trollope, therefore, he rests his credibility on his identity as a gentleman, one who would not "trifle with all those who may be induced to read," and thereby establishes his right to privacy.

The most celebrated defense of lying is of course Oscar Wilde's essay "The Decay of Lying," where he laments the increasing factuality of novels. Like Gosse, Wilde wants his veil of illusion whole: "What is interesting about people in good society," he says, ". . . is the mask that each one of them wears, not the reality that lies behind the mask." "Truth is . . . a matter of style," and reality and identity matters of appearance, for beneath the surface "we are all of us made out of the same stuff." Wilde nonetheless finds autobiography irresistible: "when people talk to us about others they are usually dull. When they talk to us about themselves they are nearly always interesting." Because autobiography interests Wilde he presumes it to be the work of liars, whose aim he has defined as "simply to charm, to delight, to give pleasure."

Augustine's self-searching pursuit of Truth marks the discovery of the individual. Wilde's defense of lying, which is part of his response to the Victorian avoidance of introspection and transformation of autobiography into public, objective history, is really a reaffirmation of the individual, but it mocks the autobiographical claim to veracity because all the available truths have become truths of imagination. Gosse, speaking of himself in the third person, says that "the young man's conscience threw off once for all the yoke of his 'dedication' and, as respectfully as he could, without parade or remonstrance, he took a human being's privilege to fashion his inner life for himself." He might be describing Stephen Dedalus, flying by the "nets of religion, nationality, and language," to "forge in the smithy of my soul the uncreated conscience of my race." Gosse, like Dedalus, has become an artificer, because the inner self is no longer considered a scientific fact but is recognized as an imaginative creation.

It may be, as Trollope suspected, that no autobiographer can tell the whole truth, but no autobiographer can wish to be taken for a liar either. What he writes can have no standing as autobiography if it is not thought to be true, at least as far as it goes. Narratives we know to be untrue we call fictions. Almost all autobiographers make some gesture, therefore, toward affirming their honesty, although some, like Mill, may assume that the identification of their narrative as autobiography is gesture enough. To the Victorian autobiographers who approached themselves objectively the problem of honesty apparently seemed slight, and the defense *ex morte* sufficient. More introspective and self-conscious autobiographers see the claim to objectivity as a rhetorical pose, and aim instead at intimacy and sincerity. But this defense *ex vita* is rhetoric too. Because self-consciousness seems to preclude sincerity, or at least its appearance, even if you could tell the whole truth of your self, you still might be unable to convince people you were doing so. As the objective standards of truth with which Augustine and Newman could identify themselves grew inaccessible, therefore, defenses against the imputation of lying gave way to a defense of lying itself. This is not only the result of an increase in self-consciousness, or the willingness to appear self-conscious, although that plays its part too. There is also a concomitant shift in the conception of the self that autobiography intends to reveal. For the natural historians, the self was an object of description. Gosse, on the other hand, can speak of "fashioning" his inner life because the self has become something discovered, revealed, or created by the autobiographer. The self has come to be seen as the creation of its language. What I have spoken of as Gosse's defense of lying is really therefore a defense of style; a defense of language as the instrument of self-creation, self-discovery, and self-preservation. As some autobiographers embraced once again Buffon's dictum that "le style est l'homme même," they may have felt that protestations of honesty were unnecessary, since far more effectively than by historical fact, their naked truth would inevitably stand revealed by their very words themselves. (pp. 39-63)

Howard Helsinger, "Credence and Credibility: The Concern for Honesty in Victorian Autobiography," in Approaches to Victorian Autobiography, *edited by George P. Landow, Ohio University Press, 1979, pp. 39-63.*

Jonathan Loesberg

[*In the following essay, Loesberg theorizes that the Victorians turned to the form of autobiography because it enabled them to assume a mediating position in the intellectual debate regarding experiential and intuitional knowledge.*]

To talk about Victorian autobiography is to discuss that most Victorian of myths, the story of the self-made man. Autobiography is self-making because in writing of himself an author necessarily makes a story of himself. He transforms the structureless experience of his life into a patterned whole, a form that is of his own making. But to the extent that creating a pattern of one's own life falsifies it, the autobiographer would seem to invite the standard criticism of many great Victorian novelists and social critics: hypocrisy. The archetypal figure of hypocritical self-making in Victorian literature is perhaps Josiah Bounderby in Dickens's *Hard Times.* Bounderby constantly buttonholes anyone who will listen to the tale of his hapless childhood. He claims he was born in a ditch full of water and deserted by his mother, yet emerged, not only dry, but a rich and successful businessman. His moral is the moral of the Victorian middle-class capitalist: the good man creates his own advantages, and success is therefore a sign of goodness. But Bounderby is unmasked. From his mother—who had not deserted him—we learn that he was given an education and apprenticed to a good master by poor parents who sacrificed their comfort for his advancement. His self-making is fraudulent not only because he did not have to carve out his own opportunities in the world of business but also because the story of the carving, the retrospective self-making, has been a lie.

The reader does not have to wait for Bounderby's unmasking, however, to respond to him as a hypocrite. His insistent and repeated telling of his history brands him. Bounderby seems to feel that his past and present selves are one, that the necessity of acting as an opportunist during a deprived childhood sanctifies his adult ruthlessness, that this success has always been his goodness. It is not the specific lies he tells but his insistence on generalizing and structuring his past experiences into a morality tale, and then reliving that past to justify and explain his present, that constitutes his hypocrisy. The revelation that his autobiography is a lie only reinforces a conclusion we have already reached. Yet to relive one's life and to make a pattern of it are the most basic activities of the autobiographical process. Of course, one can, theoretically, justify oneself without being duplicitous or hypocritical. Newman's *Apologia,* his self-justification, successfully cleared him of those charges. But the figure of Bounderby reminds us of the risk Newman took. For the Victorians autobiography as justification, if it did not necessarily lead to hypocrisy, pointed ominously in that direction.

By making one's self-involvement its own end one could avoid the perils of hypocrisy implicit in self-justification. An autobiographer might then investigate himself not to justify his life but to understand it. He would escape the spectre of Bounderby, however, only to be confronted with a state of mind that many Victorian poets and social critics feared just as much: a morbid, debilitating overinvolvement with self. Carlyle's work-ethic and his concomitant insistence on self-forgetfulness were only the most extreme of Victorian reactions to an immobilizing self-consciousness. Even Mill noted in his *Autobiography,* a work necessarily concerned with the status of self-consciousness, that Carlyle's principle of anti-self-consciousness was one of the discoveries which led him out of his mental crisis. And Newman, who viewed self-consciousness more positively than most Victorians, was criticized for having a 'Hamlet's temperament.' Again, morbidity does not necessarily result from a desire to understand oneself fully any more than justification necessarily involves hypocrisy. But the Victorians were acutely aware of the connections.

Despite this awareness autobiography was by no means an unusual form of expression in the nineteenth century. Why were so many writers willing to face these alternative threats and write their autobiographies? The Romantic theories of art and philosophy had created not only an increased interest in subjectivity but also a sensitivity to the problems of inauthenticity and morbid inaction. The Victorians wrote autobiography, I shall argue, because that form offered them the ability to elucidate a mediating position between those philosophies which claim that all knowledge is experiential and those which insist on the central importance of an intuitional knowledge of *a priori* truths about the world. Moreover, since that compromise was formulated in terms of an autobiographer's definition of self-consciousness, the very quality that made self-justification and self-investigation threatening, autobiography seemed to [offer] the opportunity, not merely of skirting the threats of morbidity and inauthenticity in the quest of a philosophic mediation, but of transforming those threatening qualities and making them part of that mediation.

We can see the importance a mediation between intuition and experience had for the Victorians by recalling the meeting of the British Association at Oxford in June 1860. Bishop Samuel Wilberforce and Professor T. H. Huxley, among others, discussed Darwin's theory of evolution, then only one year old. Their interchange is famous. Wilberforce turned to Huxley and 'begged to know, was it through his grandfather or his grandmother that he claimed descent from a monkey?' The audience laughed, and Huxley patiently waited his turn. When it came, he responded that he was not ashamed to be descended from a monkey but he would be 'ashamed to be connected with a man who used his great gifts to obscure the truth.' The effect is supposed to have been electric. A hostile audience was converted. As one critic [William Irvine, *Apes, Angels, and Victorians,* 1959] has put it, 'Huxley had committed forensic murder with a wonderful artistic simplicity, grinding orthodoxy between the facts and the supreme Victorian value of truth-telling.'

The war between orthodoxy and fact was really an externalized version of the older war between intuitional and experiential knowledge. Orthodoxy, depending upon tradition, rests on our faith in the testimony of others or on our intuition of that testimony's truth. The existence of a fact, however, is apprehended through our experience, or our reasoning from our experience of another fact to it. Huxley had won a skirmish by connecting truth with fact and obfuscation with orthodoxy, but the war, of course, was far from over. Autobiography offers the possibility of mediating this conflict because it occupies an ideal middle ground in the dispute. One could honestly describe the facts of one's life, experiences, and intuitions. If the intuitions were irrational, it might still be a fact that one had had them.

The way in which formulating a compromise in the debate between intuition and experience leads a writer towards autobiography and, conversely, the way writing autobiography depends upon having formulated such a compromise can be seen most easily by looking at writers whose gestures towards autobiography necessitated at least minimal compromise even as their extremist positions finally pushed them away from that form. Carlyle's *Sartor Resartus,* for instance, is so scornful of empirical reality's significance, and therefore of the value of experience of that reality as a way of learning truth, that it is doubtful whether the book can be called autobiography at all. Here, for instance, is Teufelsdröckh on facts:

> What are your historical Facts; still more your biographical? Wilt thou know a Man above all Mankind, by stringing together beadrolls of what thou namest Facts? . . . Facts are engraved Hierograms for which the fewest have the key.

Facts here have no inherent value. Nor may their meaning be ascertained by reasoning from their appearance of phenomenal aspects. As 'Hierograms' they can be deciphered only by the initiate who has the key.

But when Carlyle discusses the intuition that perceives the significance of nature, the key to the Hierogram, he smuggles experience back into the picture in a way that allows for the possibility of autobiography. To elucidate the relationship between intuition and experience which Carlyle outlines I would like to discuss his use of Kantian terminology in the following passage:

> Our Professor's [Teufelsdröckh's] method is not, in any case, that of common school Logic, where the truths all stand in a row, each holding by the skirts of the other; but at best that of practical Reason, proceeding by large Intuition over whole systematic groups and kingdoms.

Even though practical reason is here contrasted to logic, it is not to be taken as an aspect of Kantian pure reason but as a form of Kantian understanding, of phenomenal knowledge, as the chapter's headnote to this section, 'Intuition quickened by Experience,' makes clear. Intuition is the Carlylean cognate to Kant's pure reason; but by using the term Carlyle makes distinct changes in Kant's philosophy. Intuition was a part of Kant's understanding in the sense that there are certain aspects of phenomenal reality which we do not experience but the intuition of which are a condition of experience itself. The pure reason which apprehends the Kantian ideas, the supersensible truths closest in Kant to the kind of significance Carlyle has intuition obtaining from experience, was split from this process entirely. Kant insisted that we had no experiential or tangible knowledge of noumenal essence. By taking intuition to be the same as pure reason but maintaining its place in experiential perception, Carlyle effectively connects experience of material reality with an intuition of spiritual essence. In such a situation a description of an author's experiences would clearly be relevant to a statement of his intuitions.

But Carlyle's connection between intuition and experience is a light, nearly an aleatory, one. Teufelsdröckh's knowledge develops not by logic, not by reasoning upon experience, not even by any real compromise, but by 'Intuition quickened by Experience.' It is not the particular shape of experience that gives us intuitional knowledge but the simple act of experience which ignites our intuition of spiritual reality. With no very close connection between the type of experience and the intuition it sets off, no reason exists for a close concern with the particular experience behind an intuition. Thus, though the Editor begins by claiming that a knowledge of Teufelsdröckh's life will aid our understanding of the ideas, he ends his account of the life with the suggestion that the biography he has offered may indeed be fictional, one of Teufelsdröckh's fancies. The suggestion here that the account of the experiences behind a perception of spiritual truth need not be accurate draws Carlyle away from the need to offer reliable spiritual autobiography and towards the playfulness of *Sartor Resartus.*

Carlyle is enough of a mediator in the dispute between intuition and experience to see experience as a necessary aspect of apprehending truth. *Sartor*'s Editor frequently counteracts Teufelsdröckh's metaphysical declamations when they seem to depart from all dependence upon empirical experience. Still, since experience can be fictionalized, different experiences interchanged, and we can still arrive at the same intuitional truths, *Sartor* seems less concerned with presenting particularized autobiography than with archetypalized versions of experience.

If Carlyle's sense of the interchangeability of experience and the unity of intuitional truth eliminates that need for sticking to the details of one's life upon which autobiography depends, Darwin so insists on a scientific approach that his *Autobiography* lacks cohesion. [William Irvine] characterized Darwin's work as 'the evolution of Charles Darwin treated in a thoroughly scientific spirit.' Indeed, Darwin's own subtitle, 'Recollections of the Development of my mind and character,' puts it clearly within the body of the rest of his scientific work. As he has discussed evolution of the species, he will also discuss his own development.

The problem is that the particular experiences of one's life are not precisely the same as the external facts of biology which, as a scientific observer, Darwin can generalize into a theory. He may be empirical about the external world, may deny any integral status to the species, but he is not an associationist:

> I am inclined to agree with Francis Galton in believing that education and environment produce only a small effect on the mind of any one and that most of our qualities are innate.

This assertion would seem to place Darwin in league with Carlyle: we do not learn from experience, but have an innate, integral self. Yet Darwin, unlike Carlyle, never expresses his intuitions, never tries to make his *Autobiography* a manifestation of his innate self. He simply and logically records the fact that certain qualities that he perceives in himself have no experiential basis and must therefore be inherent.

Darwin's withdrawal from intuition into science is never explicitly discussed in the *Autobiography.* Its reasons, though, may be implicit in the fate of his father. Robert Darwin is described as having an overwhelmingly comprehensive memory and an intuitive grasp of psychology so incisive that to Charles he seemed able to read minds. The result of this sensitivity and memory is not positive, however:

> I once asked him, when he was old and could not walk, why he did not drive out for exercise; and he answered, 'Every road out of Shrewsbury is associated in my mind with some painful event.'

Robert Darwin ends his life paralysed by his ability to remember everything and by his sharp sensitivity to everything he remembers. Moreover, his 'mind was not scientific, and he did not try to generalise his knowledge under general laws.' The suggestion is clear: intuition, memory, and excessive sensitivity paralyse one's ability to think and act in the world.

In contrast to his father, Darwin insists on his own ability to generalize: 'From my early youth, I have had the strongest desire to understand or explain whatever I observed,—that is to group all facts under some general laws.' But scientific observation can be a very mechanical process. Indeed, Darwin laments, 'my mind seems to have become a kind of machine for grinding out general laws out of large collections of facts.' The details of one's life, however, are not amenable to scientific generalization since, as innate, they are not in the realm of science. They can be understood only with the kind of intuition which paralyses his father and from which Darwin withdraws.

Darwin's *Autobiography* may be seen as a machine constantly grinding to a halt. It is filled with detail after vivid detail, but the evolution of the mind as a whole never takes form. The poignant last lines are almost an avowal of the failure of the autobiographical project: 'With such moderate abilities as I possess, it is truly surprising that I should have influenced to a considerable extent, the belief of scientific men on some important points.' Darwin cannot even manage to explain the first thing about himself, how he became a scientist. Both Carlyle and Darwin made autobiographical gestures to the extent that their theories pushed them away from their preferred position in the debate between intuition and experience. Carlyle's sense that intuition was grounded in experience influenced him to consider the connection between one's philosophy and one's autobiography. Darwin, to record the facts of his life correctly, had to mention his intuitions, his innate self. But Carlyle so stressed intuition over experience that even when he described experience it was fictionalized. Darwin so insisted on scientific method that when his method came upon an intuition it broke down; his *Autobiography* remains simply recollections.

If Carlyle and Darwin edged around autobiography because its form demanded compromise that ran counter to their theories, many Victorians sought it because it offered them the ideal medium for elucidating a compromise. They were willing to risk passing between the Scylla and Charybdis of self-consciousness—hypocritical self-justification and morbid self-concern—because autobiography offered a special mode of discourse, a valuable form in which to construct a philosophy mediating between the claims of intuition and experience. In using autobiography in this way a writer was also presented with the possibility of transforming these types of self-consciousness from alternative threats into complementary opposites. If one used self-consciousness as the epistemological quality that resolved the conflict between intuition and experience, it would then become not simply the medium but the proper subject of autobiography. Self-justification, now under the guise of formulating a philosophic compromise, would protect self-consciousness from becoming morbid and self-destructive. One must give one's self-consciousness a purpose to create an autobiography. Similarly, morbid self-involvement, now under the guise of a conscientious concern for reaching an accurate understanding of one's life, would protect self-consciousness from becoming hypocritical. If one understood one's life fully and properly, the result of the understanding might be philosophy, and would not be the hypocrisy of a Bounderby.

This theoretical structure of complementary opposition, however, breaks down. In the first place, autobiography can never be a completely honest and straightforward reflection on experience. John Freccero [in his introduction to his edition, *Dante: A Collection of Critical Essays,* 1965] outlines the problems of that assumption in his discussion of the special place that Augustine's *Confessions* has in the history of autobiography. He argues that the form of the *Confessions* followed the Pauline model of conversion in which there was 'a burial of the "old man" and a putting on of the new.' Such a model creates a straightforward explanation for self-detachment, which is the first requirement for being able to see the self in unity, the basic activity of autobiography. Modern psychology, however, allows no radical breaks in the personality: 'only death can close the series, lock the door of the self so that inventory may be taken. Death being what it is, however, it is impossible for the self to "take stock" of itself.' This is to say that any position one finds or creates, from which one may draw firm conclusions about one's life, must be essentially fictional because no such position exists within a chaotic series of experiences that is terminated only by death. I am not denying the possibility of conversion or change, sudden or gradual. But, if one assumes that there is no ultimate change prior to death that sums up one's life and makes it whole, then any position one creates from which to see one's life whole is fictional, at least in the sense that it imposes an order upon the life which cannot be inherent in the life. Yet such a position of self-conscious reflection is obviously vital to an autobiography. To call it fictional is, then, to say that autobiographies are fictional.

Autobiographies are not intended as fictions, however. If they did not exist *as evidence* for mediating positions in the dispute between intuitional and experiential theories of knowledge, they would be valueless in that dispute. They therefore insist upon their truthfulness and honesty. Even at the end of the Victorian period, when experiments in fictional form were raising questions about the nature of the distinction between autobiography and fiction, Edmund Gosse, in his autobiography *Father and Son,* felt constrained to begin his work with the following reminder:

> At the present hour, when fiction takes forms so ingenious and so specious, it is perhaps necessary to say that the following narrative, in all its parts, and so far as the punctilious attention of the writer has been able to keep it so, is scrupulously true. If it were not true, in this strict sense, to publish it would be to trifle with all those who may be induced to read it. It is offered to them as a *document,* as a record of educational and religious conditions which, having passed away, will never return . . . It offers, too, in a subsidiary sense, a study of the development of moral and intellectual ideas during the progress of infancy.

Other autobiographies have, of course, begun with the claim of being strictly true. Noteworthy here, however, are the terms Gosse insists upon in describing the work. It is a 'document,' a 'record,' a 'study.' When we remember that almost immediately after this description, the author falls into the allegorical labelling of himself as the Son and his father as my Father (surely there were less suggestive ways of hiding the real names), the insistence upon the documentarity of the text is even more remarkable. Gosse sees his life as exemplifying, most importantly, historical and religious development. If it is only 'in a subsidiary sense' an exemplum of epistemological development, one wonders how subsidiary are the actual details of the life which create such a universal emblem. Nevertheless, Gosse insists that his account is strictly evidential. *Father and Son*'s existence in a historical or theoretical context in fact is justified only by its literal truthfulness. Otherwise, Gosse felt he would be trifling with his readers.

To say, then, that the self-concern which protects the validity of an autobiographer's philosophic position ends not in discovery but in fiction is to undermine the philosophic position. If discovery ends in fiction, the philosophy of the autobiographer in question becomes, if not Bounderby's self-justification, at least inaccurate and faulty theory. I have been reversing cause and effect here. A thinker does not arrive at a flawed philosophy because he has fictionalized an account of his life any more than Bounderby was a ruthless hypocrite because he falsified his account of his childhood. The fictions of autobiography are the results of

Victorian autobiography begins with a process that was gravely problematical, self-consciousness, and uses its problematical nature to bridge philosophical gaps, construct fictional compromises in the contemporary debate between intuition and experience.

—Jonathan Loesberg

the flaws in the philosophy. One turns to autobiography to substantiate through narrative description what cannot be substantiated through philosophical discourse; one turns to a self-conscious narrative structure when a philosophy cannot adequately support a theoretical formulation of self-consciousness as a faculty mediating the claims of intuition and experience.

The links in the chain moving from philosophy through autobiography were particularly strong in the nineteenth century, as we can see by returning to Freccero's theory. It is not quite a discovery of modern psychology, nor at all a scientific fact, that the self is only the sum of one's experiences, that therefore only death provides a vantage-point from which to view a life whole. The theory is datable to Hume's *Treatise of Human Nature,* which argued that there is no identity or self independent of one's sense perceptions, that there is no *a priori* relationship between those perceptions, that therefore one is merely the sum or 'bundle' of one's chaotic sensations and there is no unified self. This theory need hardly be taken as definitive. In one sense, it was not much more widely believed in the nineteenth century than it was in St Paul's time, and certainly a writer who opposed to it his own definition of a unified self and a vantage-point from which to view that self had as much reason to be confident of the validity of his position as St Paul had to be confident of his model of the self as divided by conversion into 'old man' and 'new man.' Even Hume was aware of the controversial quality of his theory, as he indicates by classifying it in his anonymously published abstract of the treatise as one of 'two opinions peculiar to himself.'

In another sense, however, Freccero is right about nineteenth-century autobiographers. If Hume's labelling of any unification of the series of perceptions into a self as 'fiction' was not accepted as accurate, it was generally believed that his theory was logically sound and that the problem with it was that any theory that ran so obviously counter to the beliefs of common sense showed more the limitation of reason than the fallibility of common sense. Consequently, to define self-consciousness in the nineteenth century was an act that was both liberating and suspect: liberating because no definition was going to be subjected to logical inquisition if the very existence of the thing defined was unprovable; suspect because any likely definition could be offered since one could not easily dispute about a quality that no one could prove existed in any case. The only possible defence of a definition would be either simple assertion or the marshalling of empirical evidence.

And here something interesting happens. Up to now I have been using the term 'fiction' to mean something like an order imposed upon the world or some aspect thereof by man's mind as opposed to any order inherent in the world. But there would seem to be no necessary problem about being factually and empirically accurate within the boundaries of the controlling fiction. In other words, we might allow that autobiographers necessarily select and shape without claiming that they necessarily falsify. But if the formulation of self-consciousness with which one shapes one's life has an extra-autobiographical importance in its status as the delineation of a philosophic mediation, the events one relates become valuable not simply as descriptions of what has happened, but as ostensibly empirical defence of one's theoretical position. For a writer concerned to support a particular formulation about self-consciousness, then, the next step was, through the fictional shaping of an autobiography, to create the empirical evidence that defended the theory. At this point autobiography becomes fictional in the full sense of the word and the movement from philosophy to fiction via autobiography is complete.

So far I have been discussing the role of self-consciousness in autobiography rather generally. The only way to indicate fully an autobiography's existence in an epistemological context, to show the process by which a writer moves from philosophy through autobiography to fiction, is to discuss in some detail an author's philosophical theories and their relation to his autobiography. This I propose to do in a consideration of Newman's *Apologia pro Vita Sua* (1864) and his one finished work devoted centrally to epistemology, *A Grammar of Assent* (1870).

A Grammar of Assent is concerned not with assent *per se,* despite its title, but with that form of assent Newman called certitude. We do not have far to search for the reason behind this concern. Newman was in constant conflict with what he saw as one of the most prominent fallacies of his time:

> In this day, it is too often taken for granted that religion is one of those subjects on which truth cannot be discovered, and on which one conclusion is pretty much on a level with another. But on the contrary, the initial truths of divine knowledge ought to be viewed as parallel to the initial truths of secular: as the latter are certain, so too are the former.

Now the fact that a man holds an unconditional assent can never, for Newman, imply that he is therefore undeniably correct or that the assent necessarily is to certain knowledge. Assents are arrived at in too many questionable ways, too often based on prejudice, and too often proved to be mistaken, for Newman to argue that, because we assent to a thing, therefore the thing is true. Nor is he willing to argue that only assents based on irreproachable reasoning are true since clearly religious assents do not fit that description. Consequently he posits a particular kind of assent, a certitude, which mixes reasoning from experience with intuitive assent and always provides true knowledge: 'it is the characteristic of a certitude that its object is a truth, a truth as such, a proposition as true . . . if it is not right with a consciousness of being right, it is not a certitude."

Certitude differs from assent, according to Newman, in that it is the result of reflection. It

> is the perception of a truth with the perception that it is a truth, or the consciousness of knowing, as expressed in the phrase, 'I know that I know,' or 'I know that I know that I know,'—or simply 'I know;' for one reflex assertion of the mind about self sums up the series of self-consciousness without the need of any actual evolution of them.

Now at first blush, and taken out of context, this is a rather curious argument. Why should our consciousness of the fact that we hold an assent prove that assent's validity? The answer is that, for Newman, reflection or self-consciousness is not simply being aware of our sensations or thoughts. Certitudes result from a rigorous, reasoned investigation of the bases of our assents. Only after such an investigation can we be said to assent self-consciously, to have arrived at a certitude. An assent based on a conscious investigation of its own grounds, if not necessarily certain knowledge, is at least a more reliable kind of belief.

For the moment I am less interested in whether this reflexive activity is enough of a protection against error to allow us to be rightfully certain than in the suggestion that self-consciousness necessarily entails reasoning. The implication that we can only know that we know if we know why we know, that self-consciousness is also conscious reasoning, is unmistakable in the *Grammar.* If a certitude is simply knowing that one knows, yet if this knowing cannot occur without a reasoned investigation, then knowing that one knows must mean knowing why one knows.

The implication of the *Grammar* is made explicit in a passage from the *Philosophical Notebooks* where Newman confronts the associational theory of knowledge:

> My point is not to deny that our knowledge comes from experience, not to advocate inner forms, but to say that our experience is not so much of external things, but of our own minds.

This passage is perhaps not quite as conciliatory as Newman thinks. If we can have an experience of our own minds that is separate from our experience of the external world, the suggestion is that the mind is an entity separable from the external sensation it receives, a contention which a consistently held belief that all knowledge is experience cannot really uphold. Newman's separation from associationism is confirmed in a statement immediately following which contends that, while the soul does not think when in the complete absence of external stimuli, nevertheless, 'as soon as it is roused, it reflects on itself, and thereby gains a number of ideas, quite independently of the external world.' Whether Newman realizes it or not, this statement depends upon 'innate forms,' a mind with a pre-existing formation. If the statement is not quite as uncontentious as he would like to suggest, it is nevertheless a clear attempt at compromising between the claims of intuition and experience. And the compromising agent is self-consciousness. The mind may contain ideas independent of the external world, but those ideas can only be obtained through the mind's reflection upon itself, and that reflection is set off by external experience. Self-consciousness here, in opposition to the mind or soul, is clearly a reasoning entity. It experiences, reflects, learns. We may assent intuitively; but to arrive at certitude the reasoning process of self-consciousness is also necessary.

Even if self-conscious certitude involves knowing why one knows as well as that one knows, a crucial question remains: theoretically, at least, the fact of our being aware of our reasoning does not endow that reasoning with any greater reliability. If no reasoning, except that of a self-enclosed logical system, can attain the status of demonstrative proof, why should we be certain of an assent given on grounds of greater or lesser probability simply because we are aware of those grounds and their strength? In fact, Newman allows the possibility of incorrect reflective assents and does not argue that all reflective assents are certitudes. He defines reflective assent in the first case as conviction and then divides convictions into convictions of things that are true and of things that are false: 'There are right and wrong convictions, and certitude is a right conviction.' But how can we know whether we hold a false conviction or a true certitude? If there are no distinguishing marks other than the objective status of the proposition held, then we would seem to be left in the state of perpetual uncertainty from which Newman has been trying to extract us. When pushed to the limit—and he is honest enough to push this problem to the limit—Newman has no solution to this dilemma. He can only argue that convictions of false propositions, false certitudes, are extremely rare and that their falseness calls into question only the particular process by which they were attained and not the state of certitude *per se:* 'false certitudes are faults because they are false, not because they are (supposed) certitudes.'

Now the whole burden of the *Grammar of Assent* is to extract humanity from the perpetual uncertainty of scepticism by claiming that, while no proposition can be proved objectively true, there are subjective processes by which we may reach the truth, and if we can recognize these, we will know when we know a truth even if we cannot prove it to be true conclusively. But if we finally cannot know whether our conviction is a certitude or not, it would seem we are thrust back into the sceptic's dilemma. Newman's response here is that certitude is a natural human faculty, and we have so little alternative to trusting our faculties that it is absurd even to speak of trusting them:

> It seems to me unphilosophical to speak of trusting ourselves. We are what we are, and we use, not trust our faculties . . . Our consciousness of self is prior to all questions of trust or assent. We act according to our nature, by means of ourselves when we remember or reason. We are as little able to accept or reject our mental constitution, as our being. We have not the option; we can but misuse or mar its functions.

If Newman were speaking only of the faculties of sensation, there would be little problem. Although theoretically it is possible to deny that we are right to trust our senses, practically we have no alternative, just as we have no alternative to believing that our consciousness of our own existence is accurate. It is true that hallucination is possible, that our consciousness can play tricks upon us, but, after taking all due precautions, we have no choice except to rely on its informations. The alternative is the end of thought and discourse. But Newman has extended this situation to our reason and our judgment, and this does not seem as irrefutable. We may not be able to test the validity of sense-data, but the generalizations and judgments that reason leads us to are far more frequently found to be mistaken than are our sensations, and far more easily tested.

The sentence which allows Newman his extension is: 'Our consciousness of self is prior to all questions of trust or assent.' Self-consciousness, it will be remembered, was the reasoning, experiencing faculty in the passages I discussed earlier. Not consciousness but the unconscious mind had ontological priority. If we accept both Newman's tenets, that consciousness reasons, judges, experiences and that it is an unquestionable given of our existence, then the problem of distinguishing between a false conviction and a certitude becomes academic. Certitude, as a faculty natural to ourselves, a product of consciousness, must be accepted as we accept our sensations. Hallucinations are possible; faulty certitudes are possible. But as, after due precaution, we must trust our sensations, so after due precaution must we trust our certitudes. To accept both these tenets of consciousness, however, would seem to involve accepting an equivocal definition of the content of consciousness, to regard consciousness as on the one hand divorced enough from the mind, the self, to reason upon it in reflection, and on the other hand integral enough to the self to be an unquestionable primary faculty.

We can see the equivocal nature of Newman's definition of self-consciousness in a passage in the *Grammar* which offers an analogical explanation for the reliability of certitude despite the fact that one can never be strictly certain whether one's reflex assents are merely convictions or certitudes. It is here that we can see philosophical discourse breaking down, being replaced by metaphor. Here too we can see the place for Newman's *Apologia* in his philosophy:

> We do not dispense with clocks, because from time to time they go wrong and tell untruly. A clock, organically considered, may be perfect, yet it may require regulating. Till that needful work is done, the moment-hand is at the quarter-past, and the hour hand is just at noon, and the quarter-bell strikes the three-quarters, and the hour-bell strikes four, while the sun-dial precisely tells two o'clock. The sense of certitude may be called the bell of the intellect; and that it strikes when it should not is a proof that the clock is out of order, no proof that the bell will be untrustworthy and useless, when it comes to us regulated from the hands of the clockmaker.

The evasions of this passage lie in the phrases 'organically considered' and 'hands of the clockmaker.' If one considers the normal—normal at least since Burke and Coleridge—opposition between an organic and a mechanistic system, it is odd to hear a clock being spoken of as 'organi-

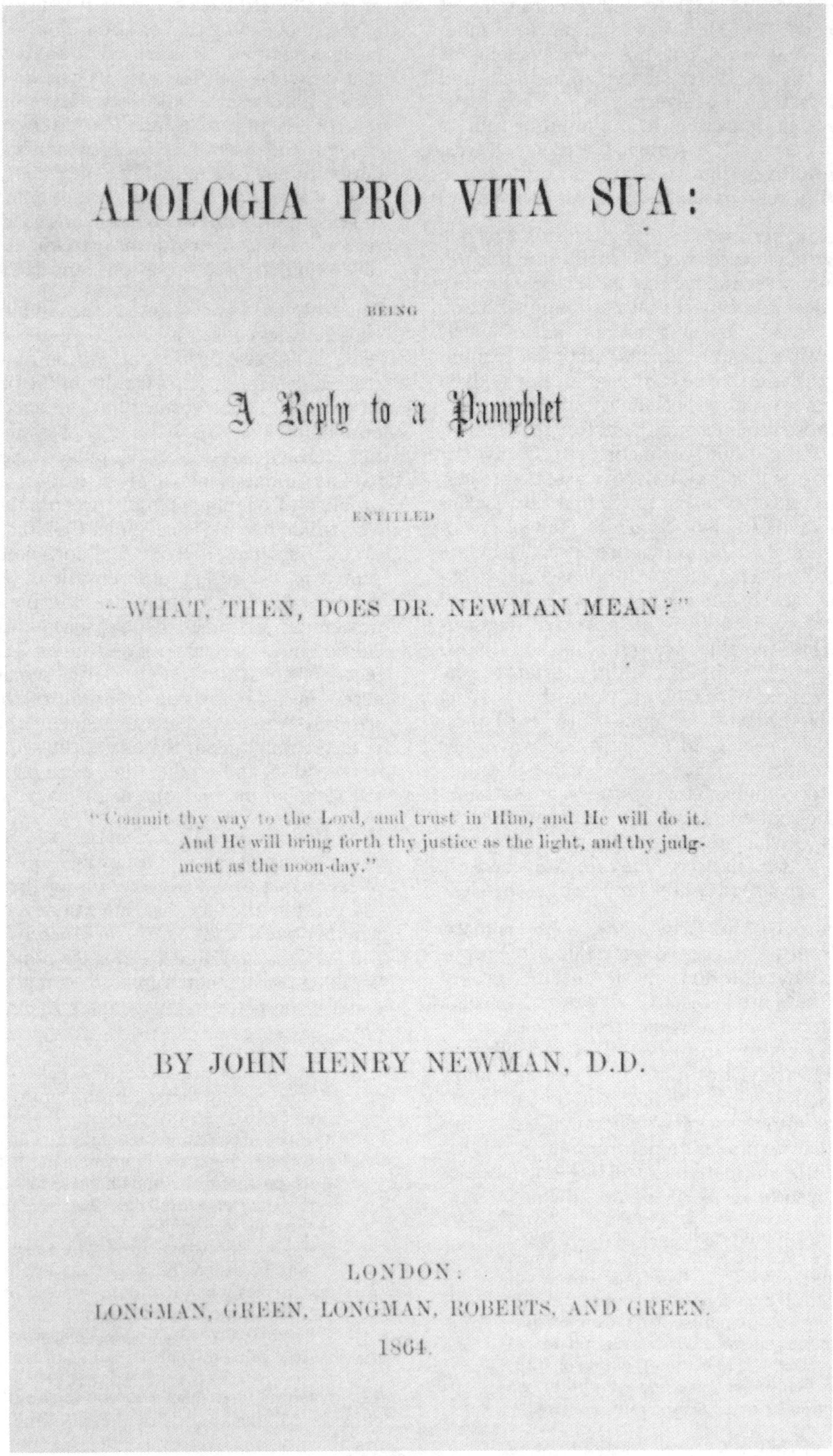

APOLOGIA PRO VITA SUA:

BEING

A Reply to a Pamphlet

ENTITLED

"WHAT, THEN, DOES DR. NEWMAN MEAN?"

"Commit thy way to the Lord, and trust in Him, and He will do it. And He will bring forth thy justice as the light, and thy judgment as the noon-day."

BY JOHN HENRY NEWMAN, D.D.

LONDON:
LONGMAN, GREEN, LONGMAN, ROBERTS, AND GREEN.
1864.

Title page for Newman's "spiritual autobiography."

cally considered.' The whole point about mechanisms, for those who reject them as fit analogies in certain cases, is that they are not organic, and therefore to compare them with things organic, to compare a clock with the universe or the mind, is a profound mistake, the mistake in fact of eighteenth-century rationalists. If one takes the phrase in an older sense as meaning simply 'considered as a system,' or 'considered as something organized,' it makes more sense, but the comparison of the mind to a clock runs directly contrary to everything Newman says in the *Grammar* about the mysterious, unmechanical, organic methods of the mind's reasoning process, about the intuitive qualities of the illative sense. Consciously or not, Newman wants the phrase to work both ways, I suspect. The intended meaning of the phrase would seem to be 'a clock considered as an organized system.' But the force of the phrase is the suggestion that a clock can be considered as like an organism, and therefore can be compared to the mind. Thus the mind has the organized, reliable, comprehensible quality of a machine and yet that mysterious integrity, superseding reason, with which we endow organic wholes.

The next and most obvious problem is the identity of the clockmaker. If the bell of the clock is certitude, Newman cannot mean the regulator to be ourselves since the process of arriving at a certitude is precisely the process by which we regulate our assents. Surely the clock cannot be its own clockmaker, regulating itself. But if the clockmaker, as in the frequent use of the simile, is God, then the passage becomes a monumental case of question-begging. Certitude is a state in which we can know certainly of God's existence despite the absence of logical proof or conclusive evidence. But how can we assume as the regulator of our certitudes the object of one of them? If we are wrong in our certitude of God's existence, who is to do the regulating?

As the word 'organic' has to be taken in contradictory senses for the passage to make complete sense, so the term 'clockmaker' must be taken to mean both God and ourselves. The regulator is God to the extent that clocks need clockmakers if they are to be regulated, that despite the attempt of the *Grammar* to make the process of acquiring sure knowledge an entirely internal one, an external object is needed to assure the validity of our certitude. Yet the regulator must be ourselves because the starting-point of the *Grammar* is that demonstrative proof exists only in closed systems, that we can never have a definitive external measurement of the accuracy of our thought. The images of clockmaker and organic clock in effect contain in their metaphoricity the equivocal role that consciousness plays in the philosophy as a whole. The clock, as organic, is both a reliable machine and a living entity. The clockmaker is the thing outside ourselves that is still of ourselves. Newman seems to be defending equivocal definitions with equivocal similes.

To turn this equivocation back into the compromise between the demands of reason and those of intuition is the role of the *Apologia,* which gives to Newman's definition the only kind of defence to which it is amenable, an empirical one. In his autobiography Newman can show that his consciousness is both a primary faculty, and therefore dependable, and a separated reflector, and therefore employable as a judge of reasoning and propositions.

Newman describes his own consciousness in the opening of the third chapter of the *Apologia* along precisely the lines laid out by his theory. This chapter is vital to his description of his conversion because it describes the one aspect of that conversion which had never been generally known and which has since been the cause of critical dispute: the theological bases, apart from his problems over Tract 90, for his decision that Catholicism was the one true faith. Those reasons for conversion are important to Newman's account not simply because they make that conversion seem the act of an incisive intelligence and not merely of a fanatic but because they constitute the inquiry and investigation into the bases of one's assents that the *Grammar* makes a condition of certitude. Since the *Apologia* first appeared, however, there have been many who felt that the reasons outlined in this chapter, particularly Newman's discovery of the historical significance of certain heresies and the theological significance of Augustine's statement about the value of Catholicity, were afterthoughts, that the real reason for conversion was resentment over his treatment by Anglican authorities.

This interpretation faces one serious problem, however. Newman documents his responses between 1839 and 1841, the time period of Chapter 3, fairly profusely. And there is seeming substantiation in sources outside the *Apologia* for the central incident of his troubled reaction to Wiseman's article on early church heresies and its citation of Augustine. Newman tells us in the *Apologia* that he read the article in the middle of September, 1839, after his troublesome reading into the Monophysite heresy. And there is a letter of 22 September 1839 to substantiate his claim for its unsettling influence:

> Since I wrote to you, I have had the first real hit from Romanism which has happened to me. R. W., who has been passing through, directed my attention to Dr. Wiseman's article in the new 'Dublin.' I must confess it has given me a stomach-ache. You see the whole history of the Monophysites has been sort of an alternative. And now comes this dose at the end of it . . . I seriously think this a most uncomfortable article on every account . . . I think I shall get Keble to answer it . . . but you don't suppose I am a madcap to take up notions suddenly—only there is an uncomfortable vista opened which was closed before. I am writing upon my first feelings.

The letter seems to indicate a reaction very much along the lines described in the *Apologia.* Newman is troubled but willing to wait upon further thought. Still, though there is a seriousness about the magnitude of the problem, there is also a clear playfulness about the letter, especially in its extended medicinal analogy. Moreover, there is a real confidence that the problem will be answerable, even an attempt to relegate it to Keble—who was not, it should be remembered, the foremost theorist of the movement.

There was good reason for Newman not to be very concerned. The arguments from his reading of the Monophysite heresy and from Wiseman's article were not new to him. In the 1836 article 'How to Accomplish It,' he had already confronted the issue of Catholicity, both with regard to Augustine's commentary on the Donatists and with regard to the Monophysite heresy. Moreover, even if we assume that the problem was suddenly brought home to him by the article, we find that he has returned by 1841 to his standard response:

> People shrink from Catholicity and think it implies want of affection for our National Church. Well, then, merely remind them that you *take* the National Church, but only you do not date it from the Reformation. In order to kindle love of the National Church, and *yet* to inculcate a Catholic tone, nothing else is necessary but to take our Church in the Middle Ages.

Catholicity is indeed a *desideratum.* But there is no reason to assume that at the points of divergence it is the Roman Catholic Church that has remained stable. The Anglican Church may also be given roots in the Middle Ages.

The *Apologia* is on even flimsier ground in asserting that it was Augustine's phrase *'securus judicat orbis terrarum'* that really struck Newman as vital. Ultimately, of course, we cannot be sure that he did not react to the phrase. The fact remains, however, that while he mentions Wiseman's article frequently, and his concern with the various heresies even more constantly, in letters both before and after the conversion, he never mentions the importance of the phrase itself, or even quotes it. And there is a suspicious aspect to the description of its import in the *Apologia.* Augustine was supposed to be telling him in 1839

> that the deliberate judgment, in which the whole Church at length rests and acquiesces, is an infallible prescription and a final sentence against such portions of it as protest and secede.

But deliberation, rest, and acquiescence are the marks of certitude in the *Grammar of Assent* and the theories he started to develop only after his conversion.

There is one final indication that the importance Newman placed on the theoretical justification of authority was very much in the nature of an afterthought. He realized when he was writing Tract 90 that he was responding to a crucial question: 'the question of the Articles came before me. It was thrown in our teeth; "How can you manage to sign the Articles? they are directly against Rome." ' Yet he states of the public reaction: 'I was quite unprepared for the outbreak, and was startled at its violence.' Ostensibly, between 1839 and 1841 Newman had been undergoing serious doubts about the Catholicity of Anglican authority. In Tract 90 he was consciously testing whether he would be allowed to take Anglican tenets in a Catholic fashion. Why then was he surprised at the outspoken denial of such an interpretation? Would not his studies have led him to expect such a reaction? The attitude he ascribes to himself at the end of the third chapter seems much more in accordance with his supposed doubts:

> I was indeed in prudence taking steps towards eventually withdrawing from St. Mary's, and I was not confident about my permanent adhesion to the Anglican creed; but I was in no actual perplexity or trouble of mind. Nor did the immense commotion consequent upon the publication of the Tract unsettle me again.

This seems a more likely reaction, an expectation of trouble coupled with resignation to it. There is an explanation of the contradiction inherent in these passages. The second chapter, though the dates of its title are 1833 to 1839, actually carries Newman through to 1841; the third, covering the years from 1839 through 1841, is thus a chronological interpolation and not a simple linear extension of the narrative. It seems at least possible that the narrative technique of doubling back and re-interpreting is a reflection not of the complexity of the period but of an actual reinterpretation, that the theoretical knots of that period are only seen to be important after 1845.

The highly wrought proem to Chapter 3 contains both an implicit recognition of and implicit response to this possible charge:

> For who can know himself, and the multitude of subtle influences which act upon him? And who can recollect, at the distance of twenty-five years, all that he once knew about his thoughts and his deeds, and that, during a portion of his life when, even at the time, his observation, whether of himself or of the external world, was less than before or after, by very reason of the perplexity and dismay which weighed upon him,—when, in spite of the light given to him according to his need amid his darkness, yet a darkness it emphatically was? . . . yet again, granting that calm contemplation of the past, in itself so desirable, who could afford to be leisurely and deliberate, while he practices on himself a cruel operation, the ripping up of old griefs, and the venturing again upon the 'infandum dolorem' of years, in which the stars of this lower heaven were one by one going out? I could not in cool blood, nor except upon the imperious call of duty, attempt what I have set myself to do. It is both to head and heart an extreme trial, thus to analyze what has so long gone by, and to bring out the results of that examination.

This passage tacitly admits that the reasons Newman is about to give are later discoveries, that at the time of the conversion he was 'amid darkness.' Yet the reasons are guaranteed as accurate because they are discovered by a self-consciousness that relives, as well as reflects, the original events.

The experiment in self-consciousness starts calmly enough as the kind of investigation which leads to or reconfirms certitude. Newman will 'analyze what has so long gone by,' and from that distance 'bring out the results of the examination.' A cool and unimpassioned act, seemingly, but it involves a conscious reliving of an old event, 'the ripping up of old griefs, and the venturing upon the "infandum dolorem".' Newman's consciousness reasons upon the old event, but the separation of time creates the effect of a doubling of rather than a severance from the self. Thus, as described in the *Apologia,* consciousness has both the attributes given to it by the theory outlined above: it reasons but, in its reduplication of the self, it also has the quality of unquestioned priority with which Newman endows the self. Even the citation of the *Aeneid* adds to this binding of equivocal qualities. Within the passage the *infandum dolorem* is part of the years of the conversion, but in the *Aeneid* that grief refers to the pain of *reliving* the fall of Troy in having to tell of it. Newman is here precisely in Aeneas's position of having to relive through telling. By having the pain of the original event compared to the pain of retelling Newman almost suggests that it is the pain of reliving, of consciousness, that is the primary sensation.

By describing his experience of self-consciousness Newman seems to give a basis to the reasons he is about to describe and an empirical defence of his theory of self-consciousness. The content of the passage, however, coils relentlessly back upon itself. It is frustratingly self-referential, describing no moment in Newman's life so much as the moment of writing. When it describes a pain, it describes it in terms of a poem, thus supporting an equivocal theory with an equivocal citation. It is even more an interpolation than the interpolation it is about to introduce. Newman's defence of a theory of consciousness turns out to be quite literally a fiction of consciousness, almost purely a linguistic construct.

If I am right about Victorian autobiography's place as philosophical defence, then the existence of interpolation in it should not surprise us. As we have seen, the Victorians had what they took to be excellent reasons for being cautious about being too concerned with their own lives, about being too self-conscious. They turned to autobiography—when they did turn to it—not so much because they overcame their caution as because they transformed self-consciousness by placing it in a different context. As an agent that created a philosophic compromise between the claims of intuition and of experience, that formulated a combination of those two modes of perceiving and knowing, autobiographical self-consciousness could no longer be hypocritical because its concern was not self-justification but theoretical justification; nor could it be morbid because its primary concern was not finally the self but the process by which the self was known. With the attention of autobiography always directed away from the ostensible concern of the work, the life, and towards the process by which the life was known, self-consciousness, interpolations, and re-interpretations become not an accidental incident in autobiography but a central part of its procedure.

We must remember, however, that autobiography's place in philosophy was as an empirical defence of the formulation of self-consciousness which mediated. But what was being asserted as empirically existing in the life, a particular form of self-consciousness, was also the narrative process by which the life was seen and told, and therefore the place where the fictions of an ordering mind could become prose fictions. In calling the *Apologia* a fiction of consciousness, then, I am not reviving the hoary old question of whether Newman was sincere or not. I am saying that the *Apologia*'s central mode of discourse, its self-conscious narrative, far from being an empirical fact, is purely a creation of language and that, in the light of that, it is hard to see the point of wondering whether events described by that process really happened or not.

A reader's suspicion of Bounderby's constant need to recite his past may turn out, then, to be more deeply justified than even *Hard Times* intended. Victorian autobiography begins with a process that was gravely problematical, self-consciousness, and uses its problematical nature to bridge philosophical gaps, construct fictional compromises in the contemporary debate between intuition and experience. My point here is not to dismiss autobiography as a failed form but to suggest that the implications of the recent critical impulse to call it fictional are not straightforward. Autobiography's fictional nature is not simply a matter either of the use of rhetoric or of the felicitous ordering of the events of one's life. Rather, we face, at least in the *Apologia* and many other nineteenth-century autobiographies, a transitional mode of discourse, one that offers philosophical defence and empirical evidence even as it delivers the convolutions and self-referentiality we have often come to expect from fiction. (pp. 199-217)

Jonathan Loesberg, "Self-Consciousness and Mediation in Victorian Autobiography," in University of Toronto Quarterly, *Vol. L, No. 2, Winter, 1980-81, pp. 199-220.*

LuAnn Walther

[In the following essay, Walther examines Victorian cultural attitudes toward childhood, analyzing literary conventions associated with the depiction of this stage of life in autobiographical writings of the period.]

Yeats, in his autobiography, said that he could remember little of childhood but its pain; Gide, in his, that he could recall nothing in his childhood soul that was not "ugly, dark, and deceitful." Neither man was subjected to any extraordinary unpleasantness or to the rigors of that infamous Victorian method of upbringing, "the breaking of the will." Ruskin, on the other hand, to whom denial and deprivation were central in his early life, who was whipped summarily for crying or tumbling on the stairs, thought that childhood was a blessed time, the happiest time of life. Augustus J. C. Hare's adoptive mother approved of and often aided her pious sister-in-law in treating Augustus in a way which can only be described as abominable (in order to teach him to "give up my way and pleasure to others", for example, his mother made him sacrifice his adored cat Selma to the formidable Aunt Esther, who promptly had it hanged), yet in later life Hare wrote of his relationship with this strange mother with a sincere overflow of love and affection, with, it is not unfair to say, a sadly maudlin nostalgia.

Clearly not only the conditions of but the attitudes toward childhood change considerably from age to age. Childhood, the invention of adults, reflects adult needs and adult fears quite as much as it signifies the absence of adulthood. In the course of history children have been glorified, patronized, ignored, or held in contempt, depending upon the cultural assumptions of adults. The autobiographical evaluation of one's early life has in turn reflected these assumptions. In an age like the seventeenth century, when babies were wrapped tightly in swaddling bands in order that they might grow not only physically but morally straight, and might not, moreover, crawl on all fours like distasteful little animals, we should hardly expect an autobiographer to dwell at length upon the particular details of his early life; infancy, except in the abstract, was a kind of larval stage to be passed through as quickly as possible. Modern autobiographers, in contrast, often examine the events of their first years for insights into their adult selves: Gide's account of having bitten the beautiful white neck of a cousin whom he was supposed to kiss, or his description of having acquired "bad habits" with the concierge's son as early as he could remember, are meant to serve as signals of the pleasures and perversities he was to find in his later life. Victorians, for whom the realities of early life were sometimes brutal or at least unpleasant, nevertheless participated in a culture which regarded childhood so ambivalently that many autobiographers praised parents whom they might have blamed, and recalled comfort and happiness when they had reason to remember otherwise.

If childhood is in one sense a historical "invention," the Victorian autobiographical childhood is in another sense a literary one, since never before this period had so many English writers been interested in recalling their early lives at length within the form of sustained prose autobiography. I would like to look at Victorian autobiography as having developed within a culture in which to be a child was both a privilege and a hardship. In so doing I hope to illustrate certain inter-relations between the history of childhood and the development of the autobiographical child figure, and to demonstrate the literary uses to which this relatively new creature was put. Autobiography is neither fiction nor history, yet it is often read as if it were fiction and cited as if it were history. Among other things the discussion will show that, as historical evidence, autobiography is unreliable; no autobiographer can be free of the fictionalizing impulse, and, even if he were, his memory itself is creative. At the same time I wish to note the very real effects which Victorian cultural attitudes had upon the development of a literary genre and its conventions. Finally I would like to ask what one can generalize about the role of the "self as child" in the Victorian adult imagination, if one can generalize at all.

. . . . .

> Family is the first, the permanent, the elemental sphere of social life, of morality; and consequently, it is the source of religion. . . . Here and there a few single men and women with intellectual aspirations, and here and there a few childless and unencumbered adults, may nurse the idea that they are living for themselves alone: but their condition is so abnormal, so unnatural, and their mental and moral constitution so morbid, that their opinion is not worth considering, and their demands should excite nothing but pity.

These remarks were delivered by Frederic Harrison in 1893 in a lecture entitled "Family Life." Though he speaks with the passion of a man who almost seems to know that he is supporting a losing cause, Harrison represents attitudes toward the home and the family which were by no means uncommon throughout much of the Victorian period. Without the family unit, it was feared, society would be endangered, religion would crumble, individuals would fall into unrestrained and base activity: in short, anarchy would result. The childless adult was unnatural, "morbid," a threat to the order of society. At the same time, however, he was admittedly "unencumbered," and, at least potentially, intellectual. That Harrison did not see a conflict here is typical of the way in which many Victorians were able to maintain, simultaneously, two contradictory notions of "home," and, more specifically, of the place of the child in it. On the one hand the child was a source of hope, of virtue, of emotion: along with the angelic wife, he was the repository of family values which seemed otherwise to be disappearing from an increasingly secular and brutal world. "Household happiness, gracious children, debtless competence, golden mean" [Alfred Lord Tennyson, in his "Vastness"]: these were ideals. But at the same time, and of course much less obviously, the child was a hardship, an obstacle to adult pleasure, and a reminder of one's baser self. He might be innocent, untainted by sexual knowledge, uncorrupted by the world of business, free from the agony of religious doubt; yet he was also potentially wicked and needed constant guidance and discipline. These contradictions are apparent throughout the children's literature of the period: while there is much sentimentality about the natural goodness of children and their clear, unspoiled view of things (*Sweetheart Travelers, Little Lord Fauntleroy*), there is also a strong element of admonition against following natural desires because they are likely to be selfish or sinful ("Rosamund and the Purple Jar," *The Fairchild Family*).

In this context it is not surprising that children were much favored while they were much denied. It was during Victoria's reign that the Christmas tree was introduced to England, that penny and halfpenny and farthing toys became popularly available, that the children's book trade reached previously unparalleled heights in volume and quality. It was also the age in which the early isolation of children from their parents—through the growth of the nursery and Nanny traditions—became established and acceptable in middle class homes; and the child for whom new games and amusements were being created was also painfully familiar with the cane, the strap, and the riding whip as disciplinary methods. As children became the focus of more attention due to the increased emphasis on "family life," the large injustices they had suffered for centuries were attacked by many legal and philanthropical reforms (such as Lord Shaftesbury's Factory Acts or his "Ragged Schools" for the poor), yet the more disguised kinds of abuse seem to have increased. There was common use of Godfrey's Cordial and other opiates to keep babies quiet; there was administering of horrifying punishments "for the child's own good" (in *The Fairchild Family,* for example, the children are taken to the gibbet to see the hanged criminals in order to teach them respect for the law; real-life Nannies sometimes did this too, and seem very often to have used bedtime horror stories as preventive discipline); there was a general burdening of small children with overbearing moral expectations and religious demands. Illustrating the disparities of freedom for the Victorian child, A. O. J. Cockshut noted [in his *Truth to Life: The Art of Autobiography in the Nineteenth Century,* 1974] that "the child was free to find God for himself, but not to leave the prunes upon his plate, to criticise his father, or to choose his own books."

Thus, while one social historian can say that for the nineteenth century the "privileged age" is childhood (as is "adolescence" for the twentieth and "youth" for the seventeenth), another can dwell grimly upon the difficulties through which children had to pass (floggings, malnutrition, and the like), and both can be right. There was indeed a strong tendency to idealize childhood—to see in the child such qualities as an enviable imagination, a naive spontaneity, an unspoiled sense of beauty. There was great popular sentiment for the child's innocent vulnerability—poor little Nell!—and great praise for his innocent goodness—perfect little Fauntleroy! "I love thee . . . with my childhood's faith," says the speaker in Elizabeth Barrett Browning's famous sonnet, thus granting superiority to the child's pure ability to believe over that of the polluted adult. The simplification and dilution of Romantic child-images to their sentimental extremes became a staple of the popular novel. And melodrama was not the only literary product of this concentration on childhood perception: Lewis Carroll's Alice, in addition to being a nice and mannerly middle-class girl, was allowed to become a complex (if unrecognized) spokesman for her time.

But despite the wave of interest and solicitude toward children which can be found in the literature and the social movements of the period, one can understand why Peter Pan's "I'll never grow up" was not heard until after 1901: the fun was too often complemented by discomfort and fear. Icy cold baths, distasteful medicines, long sermons, and teachers who flogged their students are typical memories in accounts of the period, and all took place in the name of healthy upbringing. Popular Victorian attitudes toward the amusement of children were similar to the attitudes toward sex described by Steven Marcus in *The Other Victorians:* the vital supply was limited, therefore one must be economical, one mustn't have too much. Alice Meynell [in her *Childhood*] advises her readers that

> . . . the evil to be feared is not that of making the child too happy; it is that of using up the capital estate of pleasure. If a child is to continue happy, to continue amused and gay, he must be entertained upon the usufruct and not upon the capital of pleasures. . . . The child over-amused is in peril of losing amusement itself within his own heart. . . .

If the child was in some ways superior to the man and in other ways his pet or his slave, if he was sometimes God's spokesman (as in certain Evangelical story books) and sometimes the object of cruel yet "necessary" punishments (as in fairy-tales by Knatchbull-Hugesson and Christina Rossetti), if, in short, he was both an ideal innocent and a selfish fallen creature, how did this cultural double standard affect the writing of the autobiographical childhood? Without wishing to draw any simple lines between large cultural motifs and the writing of specific books of literature, I would yet like to suggest two impulses which these attitudes may have encouraged in autobiographers. First is the need to emphasize childhood adversity, to portray oneself as not having been spoiled by overindulgence, even, in some cases, to have deserved hardship. Second, and in conflict with this, is the desire to present childhood as an Edenic, blissful state, a time of past blessedness, a world completely different from the grating present.

The first tendency has in some ways created a false view of the period, and since the interpretation of history through the "history of childhood" has in recent years become more and more popular, this is an important area for examination. The second tendency had a special function. It provided the autobiographer with a workable approach to the past and it allowed him to create, in the richness of memory, a place of repose from the harsh, indifferent "fast-hurrying stream of Time" which threatened him. In his vacillation between the need to have suffered and the need to have been blissfully innocent, the Victorian autobiographer reflected the cultural ambivalence of his age regarding children, yet at the same time discovered facets of himself which were emotionally restorative and which ultimately had their own literary power.

. . . . .

Though English autobiographers are generally more reticent about personal matters than, for example, their French counterparts, they do exhibit a willingness to discuss their early sufferings in print. When the military man William Butler wrote his autobiography he spent little time on his childhood; after all, it had nothing to do with

John Stuart Mill with his stepdaughter, Helen Taylor.

the battles past and battles to come, the politics, and the impersonal events of history which were his primary concern, his "life." This is predictable in autobiographies of men of state. Butler did, however, manage to pause long enough to express admiration for his hardworking parents, and to describe certain of the early hardships of their family. Anthony Trollope, writing for entirely different reasons yet with a similar desire for objectivity, also felt that the miseries endured by his family could and must be told: the poverty of his father, the hopeless depression of his schooldays, the unceasing efforts of his mother to save the family from the creditors. "Ah! how well I remember all the agonies of my young heart," he confesses. Thomas Carlyle chose to portray his strict father as a hero in *Reminiscences* (he was "perhaps among Scottish peasants what Samuel Johnson was among English authors," his "noble head" was like Goethe's, his "natural faculty" like Burns'); yet a different view of this stern man emerges out of the loose fictional disguises of *Sartor Resartus,* as Carlyle allows himself to reveal his own childhood unhappiness. Teufelsdröckh "wept often; indeed to such a degree that he was nicknamed *Der Weinende* (the Tearful)"; the same was true of Carlyle. And in the first person: "I was forbid much: wishes in any measure bold I had to renounce; everywhere a straight bond of Obedience inflexibly held me down . . . my tears flowed. . . ." Sara Coleridge, the daughter of Samuel Taylor Coleridge, began her autobiographical recollections with the intention of pointing out whatever "chief moral or reflexion" the various stages of her life might illustrate, but she only got so far as describing such things as the displeasure Coleridge showed when she preferred her mother to him, the "nervous sensitiveness and morbid imaginativeness" she developed early in life, the nightmares she had, at Grasmere, of terrible lions, of the ghost of Hamlet, of Death at Hell's Gate. The ability to remember and describe the painfulness of family struggle and childhood isolation was perhaps best accomplished at the end of the period in Edmund Gosse's *Father and Son,* in which the melancholy details of his mother's death, and the seemingly interminable dullness of his father's narrow religious life afterward, are painstakingly told.

What is striking in many of these accounts is the autobiographer's willingness to accept the blame for his own unhappiness or to see his suffering as having been, in retrospect, "good for him." Trollope said that his misfortunes were caused not only by his gentleman father's poverty but also by "an utter want on my own part of that juvenile manhood which enables some boys to hold up their heads even among the distresses which such a position is sure to produce." Though his father "knew not what he did" in passion, and in that state "knocked me down with the great folio Bible which he always used," Trollope insists that this form of punishment was simply the result of ignorance: "no father was ever more anxious for the education of his children, though I think none ever knew less how to go about the work." Samuel Smiles, the writer of self-help books, revealed his old schoolteacher Hardie to have been a tyrant and an indefatigable flogger, but then praised him for his "fairness." Similarly, Leigh Hunt described the humiliating methods of "Old Boyer," the famous teacher at Christ Hospital school. Though Boyer knocked Hunt's tooth out with the back of a Homer, and ridiculed his essays by "contemptuously crumpling them up in his hand, and calling out, 'Here, children, there is something to amuse you,' " Hunt saw him in retrospect as a "conscientious" and "laborious" man, and Christ Hospital school remained a dear memory.

Evidently a child was expected to be stoical when misfortune befell him. In Victorian popular novels there are many pathetic orphans, dying children, and neglected waifs; these young martyrs were attractive for various reasons, not the least of which was a horror of that worst and most dreaded alternative, the "spoilt" child. It would seem that any child who was poor and abused was superior to one overly coddled. When the illustrator Dorothy Tennant Stanley [in her *London Street Arabs,* 1890] decided to reject, for her "ragged life" drawings, the very widespread and popular images of "pale, whining children with sunken eyes, holding up bunches of violets to heedless passers-by; dying match girls, sorrowful watercress girls, emaciated mothers clasping weeping babes," in favor of more robust and happy urchins and "street Arabs," she too was operating under the assumption that the most interesting children in London were those whose "ingenuity" and "charm" were born of extreme adversity, in this case poverty. The feeling against spoilt children was so common that even so unlikely (and confessedly spoilt) a person as Lord Alfred Douglas echoed the general disapproval: "I would rather see a child badly treated than spoilt," he said; "suffering is good for the soul."

This may account in part for the lack of autobiographical reticence regarding childhood troubles. Victorians did not wish to think of themselves as having been "over-amused" as children. They were moreover quite ready to feel guilty for not having been strong or "manly" enough in times of distress. Childhood suffering was bracing; it was good for you. Learning obedience at the point of the rod was cause for tears, perhaps, but, as Teufelsdröckh says, "it was beyond measure safer to err by excess than by defect. Obedience is our universal duty and destiny; wherein whoso will not bend must break: too early and too thoroughly we cannot be trained to know that Would, in this world of ours, is as mere zero to Should, and for the most part as the smallest of fractions even to Shall."

Hence the harshness of parents and other authorities was forgiven and justified. Though Ruskin [in his *Praeterita*] portrayed himself as a lonely, suppressed child, often whipped, who was denied all toys, sweets, and even companions, he rationalized each of these denials by praising its beneficial result. The "utter prohibition" of wine and sweets, he said, had left him with "an extreme perfection in palate and in all other bodily senses." The whipping had given him "serene and secure methods of life and motion." The lack of toys and other distractions had given him a "formed habit of serenity," an ability to concentrate contentedly upon the patterns in the carpet or the wallpaper and thereby to learn "the main practical faculty" of his life, "the habit of fixed attention with both eyes and mind" through which his future in art was established. Gosse too [in his *Father and Son*] felt that parental severity had had its value. Even though the zoological illustrations which his father helped him paint had been "wrung" from him, "touch by touch, pigment by pigment, under the orders of a taskmaster," the mental discipline gained by working according to the strict requirements of his father had finally been worth the agony: "It taught me to concentrate my attention, to define the nature of distinctions, to see accurately, and to name what I saw."

Neither man protested, as a modern autobiographer might, that his talent had been damaged or his creativity stifled by such restrictions. Ruskin in fact wondered whether his childhood had not been *too* luxurious; perhaps, he thought, his mother had been right in suggesting that he had been "too much indulged." Mill also thought that he might have had too much too soon in his boyhood, and that easy success had spoiled his appetite for living: "I had had (as I reflected) some gratification of vanity at too early an age . . . little as it was which I had attained, yet having been attained too early, like all pleasures enjoyed too soon, it had made me *blasé* and indifferent to the pursuit." Like Meynell's "child over-amused," he felt that he had lost the very capacity for enjoyment: ". . . neither selfish nor unselfish pleasures were pleasures to me."

In a reaction against overindulgence some autobiographers not only did not judge their parents as harshly as they might have done, but tended to select details which suggested more hardship than may necessarily have been the case. Ruskin, for example, gives his readers some slightly exaggerated impressions of how much he was denied. He was, no doubt, called upon to crack nuts slavishly for the guests at dinner without being allowed to eat any himself; he did, probably, remember after sixty or more years the first three raisins he was given to eat, so rare a treat were they; he must certainly have had to grow up without elaborate toys and, as he relates, to give up the beautiful Punch and Judy dolls which his aunt had given him because it was "not right" that he should own such things. Yet occasionally a glimmer of luxury peeps through all this grey suppression, and causes one to wonder. The dolls were forbidden, but we soon enough learn of the rather splendid gift of a silver-mounted postilion's whip from the young traveller's increasingly well-off father. Food being so important to children, we marvel at the poor boy's misfortune to have had no sweets, nuts, "nor anything else of dainty kind" to eat, but we then read of the "ethereal flavor" of cherry pies which were cooked from the cherries he himself had chosen—in the very garden of which he had said earlier that "*all* the fruit was forbidden." It is not that Ruskin deliberately wishes to mislead but that like many others he selectively remembers the difficulties of his "poor little life" with a kind of unconscious pride; he creates of himself a character worthy to stand beside the rest of the unspoilt, brave, heroic children of collective Victorian fantasy.

If there was, as I am suggesting, a certain cultural encouragement to feel that one had suffered, then there is some question as to how to read a book like Augustus J. C. Hare's *The Story of My Life.* This six-volume autobiography is a mine for anyone looking for incriminating testimony against Victorian authority figures and the "breaking-of-the-will" school of upbringing. It begins with the story of how Augustus, an unwelcome birth, was shipped off by his parents to his widowed aunt Maria when she offered to raise him as her own. ("My dear Maria, how very kind of you! Yes, certainly, the baby shall be sent as soon as it is weaned; and, if any one else would like one, would you kindly recollect that we have others," Mrs. Hare wrote.) Then starts the long and pitiful account of Maria's sincere but clumsy campaign to teach him obedience and unselfishness. There was the lesson of the puddings:

> The most delicious puddings were talked of—*dilated* on—until I became, not greedy, but exceedingly curious about them. At length 'le grand moment' arrived. They were put on the table before me, and then, just as I was going to eat some of them, they were snatched away, and I was told to get up and carry them off to some poor person in the village.

There was the hanging of Selma. There was, alas, the all-too-frequent presence of Selma's murderess, Aunt Esther. This woman made Augustus sleep in an austere, freezing cold back room *because* he had chilblains and gave him sauerkraut to eat *because* it made him sick. (Esther said of another aunt's children when they were ill with measles: "I am *very glad* they are so ill: it is a well-deserved punishment because their mother would not let them go to church for fear they should catch it there." "She had the inflexible cruelty of a Dominican," Hare wrote.)

The horrors go on and on. Augustus was made to wear a miserable and unnecessary back brace—"a terrible iron frame"—when he went to Harrow. Christmas at home meant "having to sit for hours and hours pretending to be deeply interested in the six huge volumes of Foxe's 'Book of Martyrs,' " and "being compelled—usually with agonizing chilblains—to walk twice to church, eight miles through the snow or piercing marsh winds, and sit for hours in mute anguish of congelation, with one of Uncle Julius's interminable sermons in the afternoon. . . ." In the midst of all this anguish burns an undying flame of affection for Maria, "my darling mother." Hare justifies all her complicity with his more-than-Murdstonian aunts by referring to Maria's high religious principles: when persecuted, one must turn the other cheek; it grieved her that Augustus had to suffer, but as a good Christian he too

---

Victorians, for whom the realities of early life were sometimes brutal or at least unpleasant, nevertheless participated in a culture which regarded childhood so ambivalently that many autobiographers praised parents whom they might have blamed, and recalled comfort and happiness when they had reason to remember otherwise.

—LuAnn Walther

---

must follow Christ's meek example. And so Aunt Esther's tyranny prevailed, year after miserable year.

Multitudes of questions arise from a reading of Hare's book, but the one which concerns us here is how to read it in light of the autobiographer's impulse to entertain, at some level, the vision of himself as a child of adversity. With Hare, one senses a definite authorial relish in the description of family eccentricities and calamities. There are some very humorous passages, and there are moments when a character may be perfectly captured in a laughably grotesque image: at one point Esther is seen, spade in hand, marching off to the church-yard to bury two grinning skulls which have interested Augustus during his imprisonment in the church vestry. Dickens might have written it better, but the image itself cannot be improved upon for its delightfully apt placing of Esther in her proper setting. When social historians use Hare's book as factual evidence of the kind of discipline which Victorian parents were capable of inflicting, are they not misunderstanding the workings of a literary imagination? The young Hare, one is bound to note, often bears an uncanny resemblance to David Copperfield in *The Story of My Life;* one can also find echoes of *Praeterita* in the book. Hare was an experienced travel book writer who loved to repeat quaint stories and eerie legends to enhance his factual material. I do not mean here to claim that autobiography and fiction are one, or that Hare was a marvelous liar, but simply to suggest that in the case of an autobiography like this one, it ought to be read as existing within literary and cultural traditions which encouraged the selection of certain memories over others. In addition to noting Hare's habit of storytelling and his eye for the macabre and the unusual, we have to remember the increasing ease with which his culture allowed him to discuss the severity of former generations. Just as the claim that "I was the chief of sinners" became a kind of convention in Puritan autobiography, so the retelling of childhood woe became, if not conventional, at least common enough to be seen as part of a pattern. A man whose will had truly been broken, of course, would not have written the book at all.

The willingness to have suffered may perhaps be more clearly seen when viewed in contrast with its equally strong opposite: the desire to have inhabited an Edenic "other world" as a child. The ideological struggle in nineteenth-century children's literature between the didactic tale and the fairy-tale parallels this division. A fairytale need not have any relation to the world of Would, Should and Shall; its eventual triumph over the moralistic stories of writers like Mrs. Sherwood and Charlotte Mary Yonge is an indication of the adult writers' recognition that the realm of childhood fantasy could be as real and necessary as the world of adult rules and restrictions. Alongside the child as martyr, the Victorian mind was able to see the child as a free spirit, sporting idyllically on Echoing Greens, drinking in perceptions with a power which would later be lost. Ruskin praised the "large eyes of children," equating the child with the man of genius in having "infinite ignorance, and yet infinite power; a fountain of eternal admiration, delight, and creative force within him, meeting the ocean of visible and governable things around him." Froude [in his *Nemesis of Faith*] thought that the child's simple ability to believe was worth all the world's knowledge. He would gladly give away all he was, he said, "but for one week of my old child's faith, to go back to calm and peace again, and then to die in hope."

In this spirit, then, though somewhat less dramatically, autobiographers called forth memories of early happiness. Frances Power Cobbe describes a pleasant nursery, a mother who often cuddled up close to her on the sofa, a house full of relatives at Christmas with all the children playing "romping games" through the halls and corridors. In her childhood drawing room "the happiest hours of my life were passed." Lord Alfred Douglas also passed his "happiest days" in a family country house and remarked that "when you go to heaven you can be what you like, and I intend to be a child." Douglas, like Hare, idealized his mother as she had appeared to him in the early days, remembering that she had had an "angel's beauty"; she was so beautiful, he said, that when she and her sister went driving in the Park, "people stood on chairs to see them."

Angelic mothers, paradise in the form of a childhood garden—these are images which appear to have been very important to the formation of one's concept of early childhood. Frances Hodgson Burnett remembered an "enchanted garden which, out of a whole world, has remained, throughout a lifetime, the Garden of Eden" [in Ann Thwaite, *Waiting for the Party: The Life of Frances Hodgson Burnett,* 1974]. Her biographer could not place this garden, since the most likely spot housed only a small garden, not the "imposing mansion ensconced in trees" described by her son and first biographer, but the image was nevertheless real enough to Mrs. Hodgson Burnett, who transformed it into *The Secret Garden,* her best children's book. Ruskin of course began and ended *Praeterita* with images of "Eden-land" and "the rivers of Paradise." William Michael Rossetti grew up in the dinginess of Charlotte Street, Portland Place, but found that his earliest recollections were of his grandfather's country cottage in Buckinghamshire: though he was there only about three times after his infancy, he still clearly remembered as an adult the pigs, dogs, spiders, earwigs, and slugs of those early rural visits.

Sometimes it is not so much the content of the memory which is important in the establishment of an idyllic feeling. The very act of remembering can also be a source of unusual pleasure. As "the past grows holier the farther we leave it" [Carlyle], so the recapturing of lost time through memory may seem to carry an almost mystical significance. Leigh Hunt found that the accidental appearance in a music stall of songs he had sung as a boy caused him to remember the intensity, the reality of the past; this moment of childhood clarity made all his adult life seem stale and unreal:

> What a difference between the little smooth-faced boy at his mother's knee, encouraged to lift up his voice to the pianoforte, and the battered grey-headed senior, looking again, for the first time, at what he had sung at the distance of more than half a century! Life often seems a dream; but there are occasions when the sudden reappearance of early objects, by the intensity of their presence, not only renders the interval less

> present to the consciousness than a very dream, but makes the portion of life which preceded it seem to have been the most real of all things, and our only undreaming time.

This perhaps describes the kind of pleasure which Dickens felt while writing *David Copperfield,* and which made him so regretful finally to put his pen down when the book was finished. The memorialization of the past, through objects (Hunt's songbooks) or through narration (Dickens' story), creates not only a pleasant sense of nostalgia, but can also confer the energy and the purity of the former time to the present. The following passage on David's reaction to his mother's death is interesting because it seems also to describe the process by which the autobiographer is able to revive those images which seem most pure and eternal:

> From the time of knowing of the death of my mother, the idea of her as she had been of late vanished from me. I remembered her, from that instant, only as the young mother of my earliest impressions, who had been used to wind her bright curls round and round her finger, and to dance with me at twilight in the parlour. . . . In her death she winged her way back to her calm untroubled youth, and cancelled all the rest.

The ability to write *David Copperfield* must have begun with a similar cancellation, imaginatively, of Dickens' grown-up life; this then opened the door to the past, that fascinating other world, in all its seeming innocence and clarity.

Though the psychologist Emma Plank [in her "Memories of Early Childhood in Autobiographies," in *The Psychoanalytic Study of the Child,* 1945-1954] found that, of all the autobiographies she studied, only those written by "men of letters" revealed "genuine recollections" of very early memories (as opposed to "screen memories," or to repetitions of what an author had heard from other people about himself as a child), one should also note that men of letters can recollect things that may never have happened at all. Memory is not only creative in that it may "screen" or "conceal," in the Freudian sense, the significant event; a writer's memory, especially, may easily blend the real and the written event. Thus when Matilda Betham-Edwards describes [in *Reminiscences,* 1898] her "first recollection" as a baby in her nurse's arms, she may simply be inadvertently revealing her admiration for the work of Thomas Hardy:

> The scarlet coat so strikingly contrasted with the blue sky and green hedges, the ingratiating smiles of the wearer, who, whilst making love to the maid, warily ministered to the good humor of her charge, the animation of the pair, all these things make up a clear, ineffaceable whole.

For Betham-Edwards, this pleasant scene is clear and ineffaceable; but the fact that it is so like the famous appearance of Sergeant Troy in *Far From the Madding Crowd,* which she has read, suggests the effect other writers may have on autobiographers. The "other world" of childhood may also be a literary world.

Whether the autobiographer chooses to describe his former happiness in metaphors of enchanted gardens or visions of mother, whether his memories are "genuine" or screened or second-hand, the important point is that the tendency toward the idyllic is as common in descriptions of childhood as the previously discussed portrayal of adversity. Both are in part the result of cultural attitudes, though of course it would be much too limiting to see them only in this light. Both tendencies may exist side by side in the same writer, as when Hare portrays himself as a persecuted child raised by an angelic mother. The inclination is to swing from one to another, but never to reverse them; so far as I know, there are no spoilt children nor ugly mothers in Victorian autobiography. Each form of selection has its function for the writer. He is able, through the recounting of troubled times, to relieve his own sense of guilt, to reassure himself of his worth, and to implicate, without actually accusing, those who may have persecuted him or failed to help him. More importantly, the journey back to the imagination's "fair Life-garden" of childhood, where "everywhere is dewy fragrance, and the budding of Hope" allows the writer to escape his grown-up world of anxiety and limitation and to participate in an ideal which nevertheless seems "the most real of all things, and our only undreaming time" [Carlyle, in his *Sartor Resartus*]. In the furthest reaches of memory he finds a measure of repose.

> . . . as yet Time is no fast-hurrying stream, but a sportful sunlit ocean, years to the child are as ages: ah! the secret of Vicissitude, of that slower or quicker decay and ceaseless down-rushing of the universal World-fabric, from the granite mountain to the man or day-moth, is yet unknown; and in a motionless Universe, we taste, what afterwards in this quick-whirling Universe, is forever denied us, the balm of Rest.

(pp. 64-81)

LuAnn Walther, "The Invention of Childhood in Victorian Autobiography," in Approaches to Victorian Autobiography, *edited by George P. Landow, Ohio University Press, 1979, pp. 64-83.*

THE AUTOBIOGRAPHICAL TENDENCY IN VICTORIAN PROSE AND POETRY

Avrom Fleishman

[Fleishman is an American educator and critic who has written extensively on Victorian and modern English literature. In the following excerpt, he analyzes the use of symbolism as a structural device in Victorian autobiography, focusing especially on Carlyle's Sartor Resartus *as "the seminal Victorian autobiography."]*

It would not be enough to say that in the Victorian age self-writing becomes widespread; it becomes specialized as well. This is the period in which we discover gypsy autobiographies—or at least would-be gypsies like George Borrow; erotic autobiographies, of which at least one authentic example, *My Secret Life,* has come down to us; and even, if only as a fictional construct, an equine item: *Black Beauty: The Autobiography of a Horse.* With the tendency to play up one or another aspect of the self, there develops a wider range of metaphorical resources and an extension of the name and notion of autobiography to works of poetry and fiction. (*Aurora Leigh* and *Jane Eyre,* while not their authors' autobiography, are cast in that mold, and the latter is subtitled with that term.) At the start of any investigation of the undisputed masterpieces of Victorian self-writing, one notes their placement before a broad hinterland of pseudo-, quasi-, and neoautobiographies.

The Victorian period is still widely regarded as an age of egoistic authoritativeness, even though the studies initiated by Walter Houghton have opened up its underside of doubt, anxiety, and shunning of the self. The leading intellectual currents all stress selfhood in one or another way: Elie Halévy's famous thesis establishes a parallel between such unlikely bedfellows as laissez faire individualism and Evangelical religious activism; the philosophical hedonism at the base of Utilitarian ethics encouraged self-scrutinizing even as the doctrine widened to calculate the common good beyond personal satisfactions; and the applications of Darwinism in social thought compensated for the individual's insignificance, by comparison with the species's fortunes, with manly encouragement to struggle and endure. In this cultural climate, the leading proponents of one ideology or another become heroes—and are required to be models—of individualism. One result of this veneration of the heroic image is the sorry history of burnt letters, official biographies, and—a Victorian invention?—a self-created biography (or autobiography posing as biography), *The Life of Thomas Hardy.*

Thus, it comes about that we think of the great Victorians as creatures of biography—either as subjects for hagiography, as in the vest-pocket religions of the Browning societies and their like or as objects of ridicule, in the wake of Lytton Strachey. We might do better to think of them as creators of commanding self-images, in many cases surviving into our own age of skepticism and research. It is a short step from this awareness to the perception, now on the verge of general acknowledgment, that the Victorian age was one of great autobiographical activity, in which a number of masterpieces were created and in which the variety and importance of this aesthetic enterprise were thoroughly explored. Prefiguring the trend in contemporary English letters, in which every important writer and many a literary hanger-on must write his autobiography well before resigning himself to creative silence, the Victorians exhibit self-writings in prose and poetry, fiction and nonfiction, by almost all the leading figures of the age. In *In Memoriam,* "Switzerland," *Modern Love,* and Hopkin's "terrible sonnets," the poets devised new versions of or alternatives to the sonnet sequence—the series of distinct lyrics linked by a narrative line—to make a way for their impulse toward self-writing. And each of the major novelists is represented by at least one autobiographical novel—although in Trollope's case, he is better represented by an autobiography.

How did such an outpouring come about, given the firm restraints on public posturing and the apparent inappropriateness of seventeenth- and eighteenth-century and even Romantic models of self-writing? A man does not sit down to write his autobiography in cold blood, without a language somewhere at hand for the enterprise. (pp. 111-13)

Perhaps the most examined passage of Romantic poetry, at least in quarters where literary terminology comes under discussion, is Wordsworth's paean to natural objects at the Simplon Pass in Book VI of *The Prelude:*

> Characters of the great Apocalypse,
> The types and symbols of Eternity,
> Of first, and last, and midst, and without end.
> (lines 638-40)

The very magniloquence of the rhetoric may tend to dampen the vibrations of religious language in which this and much of *The Prelude* is couched. This use of the word "types" has, however, drawn attention in the recent revival of interest in typology, and Wordsworth's apocalyptic note has been connected to its primary source in biblical prophecy. We do not know precisely what Wordsworth understood by *type,* but it is likely to have come to his pen as readily as the phrase "types and emblems" did to his contemporary Francis Jeffrey, editor of the *Edinburgh Review* and least likely of typologists. As the observer of a parallel phenomenon in American letters has observed: "Throughout the nineteenth century, the terms 'symbol,' 'emblem,' 'type,' 'allegory,' and 'figure' were, through carelessness, often interchangeable and therefore largely negligible. The variety of concepts about metaphor does not correspond to the variety of terms" [Karl Keller, in *Literary Uses of Typology,* edited by Earl Miner, 1977]. Perhaps a low but liberating note was sounded when Blake punned on the term in referring simultaneously to his substitute for printing type and to his use of biblical figures in *Jerusalem*—"Therefore I print; nor vain my types shall be" ("To the Public").

The operative word in the Simplon Pass epiphany is, in any case, "symbols." For all Jeffrey's use of "types and emblems" to refer to the signifying action of natural objects—and despite contemporary attempts to construct a poetics of natural typology, in which such objects are seen substituting in the traditional role of biblical elements—the poetics of symbolism were already in place for Wordsworth and were being codified by Coleridge for the nineteenth century. In this poetics, typology had, indeed, a role to play, and it was Coleridge [in his *The Statesman's Manual: or, The Bible the Best Guide to Political Skill and Foresight,* 1816] who made the most vigorous call for the revival of the Bible and its language as a primer for poets as well as statesmen. For all their "modernity," the Romantics were instrumental in reviving biblical reference so as to foster its interplay with other symbolic resources. What was lost, and no small loss, was the historical sense of reenactment that orthodox typologists could enjoy, the viability of a social enactment by the after-type of the ideals manifested by types and the possibility of seeing the entire shape of a man's life under the sign of biblical heroism.

It is this provision and dearth bequeathed by their Romantic ancestors that made the grandeur and misery of Victorian autobiography. In the absence of a stable symbolic mode for self-writing, the Victorians were led to invent new techniques of composition, developing a palette of the myths, symbols, and other debris of classical and Christian culture. Recent commentators on nineteenth-century art have made us aware of the vivid and self-conscious way in which a number of Victorians employed typology, but their greatest contribution to our grasp of the poetics of the age lies in highlighting the expedients to which those authors were put. Thus, George Landow has not only shown the systematic use of typology in the art of William Holman Hunt [*William Holman Hunt and Typological Symbolism,* 1978] but has also indicated [in *Studies in Romanticism* 17 (1978)] the severe displacement which types must undergo in the hands of a lapsed Christian poet like Dante Gabriel Rossetti. Similarly, Linda Peterson [in *Approaches to Victorian Autobiography,* edited by G. P. Landow, 1979] has traced a series of types in Browning's self-conception at various stages of his career; the broad implication of these varied figures is that the poet could rest content with none of them but availed himself of one after another to express the special pangs of his vocation at crucial junctures. It is the absence of an overarching form for his life that one misses in the local applications of typology by Browning and other poets (Browning's own term for such references is *symbol,* in a passage quoted but misread by Peterson). If we are to find types functioning as structural principles that order the shape of a career, it is to the autobiographies of the period that we must look. But structural figures need not be exclusive and totalizing in a given life; it is the extended juxtaposition and dramatic interplay of competing self-images that is the life of autobiographical language. Such a dynamic of self-imaging may also be found in a number of autobiographical novels of the period, which splendidly exhibit this symbolic action.

The power generated by symbolic interactions in structuring a life precludes the possibility of establishing a single set of figures as the dominant one in Victorian self-writing. Some scholars have elected the Exodus pattern of wandering and return to a promised land as the Victorians' most potent inheritance from the spiritual autobiography tradition, but the proliferation of these motifs throughout post-Renaissance literature diminishes the particularity of their appeal in the nineteenth century. But the Victorians were endowed with widespread sources of imagery, in which the Christian *peregrinatio* (filtered through the Romantic poets) was only one strand. In the exfoliation of these patterns in Western art and literature, traditional typology is not left behind, but a new symbolic action is generated: the enriching of a biblical heritage with the whole history of its aesthetic versions, where what counts is not the specific content of the original figure but its malleability for life fashioning. The type becomes a palimpsest, and the developing schemas of using such overdetermined or polysemous figures make up a grammar of self-writing.

If one were to elect a single figure as the central one for the nineteenth century, however, it might well be the large possibilities offered by the myth of the Fall. A useful article by Martha Lifson [in *Genre* 12 (1979)] has collected the evidence of a widespread appearance of the Fall pattern throughout Western autobiography, and in this larger fund the Victorians have an important share. But here the universality of the figure leads one to doubt its distinctive presence in Victorian or modern culture; Lifson tends to employ archetypal terminology and to invoke universal human experience in order to explain the ubiquity and abundance of the figure. Nevertheless, one may observe a host of Victorian writers appealing to their Adamic qualities, setting their childhood in an Edenic garden or leafy landscape, and bewailing the loss of their original endowment and their difficulties in resuming a state of innocence to take relief from the busy, vicious world. In this complex of attitudes and the biblical imagery attached to it, however, a number of associated trains of imagery may be traced to other sources. The garden scenes are often couched in the language of the classical *locus amoenus,* reminding us that the educational texts of these writers were as often pagan as Christian. Similarly, the figure of the child who stands in these gardens is laden with secular attributes, which the Romantic poets had added to the store of virtues that the Gospels had allegorized with it.

The Victorians, to adapt Dylan Thomas's phrase, "dreamed [their] genesis" but showed no inclination to leave their exodus and return out of account. Neither one phase nor another of the biblical process was to be preferred in imaging a life, if only because the experience of alienation and recovery was as widespread as the memory of initial bountifulness. Just as the myth of the Fall is spelled out in a complex of figures—Adamic innocence, paradisal fruitfulness, diabolic temptation, etc.—so the sequence of figurative stages following upon that original state could be variously worked out in narratives of individual life.

Yet the potentialities of the biblical sequence for providing figures in which to register the successive stages of a life do not ensure that every—or that any—autobiographer will systematically take them up. Not only the special features of each man's experience but the selective leaning of every imagination toward one or another evocative symbol ensures that the autobiographical monomyth will remain an ideal reconstruction rather than an operative design. Several Victorian and modern autobiographers specialize, as it were, in one or more figural stages: Carlyle and Muir, the phases of exile and return; Dickens and Sassoon, those of childhood and Fall; Newman and Joyce, crisis and epiphany; etc. Curiously, we shall find that certain turn-of-the-century authors like Gissing and Gosse are among the most comprehensive employers of such figures, leading to speculation that their more or less self-conscious role was to recirculate the working symbolism of their predecessors and to give it a critical new turn before it passed into the hands of modern writers. When we come to Lawrence, Yeats, Richardson, and Woolf, some of these figures achieve a powerful reassertion on the same grand scale on which the Victorians employed them.

The experience of exile from an initial state of security is often expressed in figures that have as their burden the problem of self-consciousness as the Victorians inherited it from the Romantics. In place of the traditional gentlemanly apology for excessive self-regard in writing one's autobiography, the Romantics substituted *anxiety*— that their inwardness was either unmanly (Keats), or poetically unproductive (Byron), or unfathomable (Coleridge). These anxieties did not have to await the Victorians for full expression, but they emerge dramatically among them. In response to similar misgivings, Carlyle adapted from the Germans his "anti-self-consciousness theory," in Mill's phrase; describing his own adoption of it, Mill affirms the value of "the internal culture of the individual" but adopts the Carlylian strategy for maintaining it: "Those only are happy (I thought) who have their minds fixed on some object other than their own happiness. . . . Aiming thus at something else, they find happiness by the way." This strategy of indirect progress through oblique self-promulgation is merely a special application of the broad awareness fostered by the Romantics that though self-consciousness—indeed, consciousness itself—is at the root of our problems, having brought alienation into the world, it is nevertheless only through self-consciousness that this separation is to be transcended:

> The modern age, unhappily, has moved to the very extremity of dividedness, for "never since the beginning of Time was there . . . so intensely self-conscious a Society." . . . Carlyle echoes Schiller's assertion that the culture which had inflicted this wound must heal it, and like his predecessor, he suggests that the fall of man was a happy division that will lead to a greater good. Is not "the symptom of universal disease, yet also the symptom and sole means of restoration and cure?" [M. H. Abrams, *Natural Supernaturalism: Tradition and Revolution in Romantic Literature,* 1971]

It is this willingness to undertake the fallen condition of self-consciousness and to express it in the fallen language of symbolism that enables Carlyle to write the seminal Victorian autobiography. (pp. 113-20)

Carlyle was the transmitter, from the Romantics to the Victorians, not only of philosophical organicism but of its associated theory of symbolism. The new note he added to the accepted wisdom about the organic symbol was a volitional and creative one, to complement, if not fully to replace, its attributes of quasi-biological passivity and quasi-mystical unconsciousness. To invigorate a poetic symbolism that was said to come as naturally as leaves to the tree or not at all, Carlyle envisaged a universal human activity of symbol making in which not only pragmatic worldly skills but spiritual aspiration and imaginative conception were made concrete life in the form of symbols.

The strength of the transcendental imagination in Carlylian symbolism has long been acknowledged but at the expense of the Puritan element in his culture, to which it has often been juxtaposed. Although the immediate influence of Scottish Calvinism may well have been as stultifying in its literalism and antipathy to fiction as some have proposed, the larger Protestant tradition that Carlyle inherited was laden with representational systems of which he could readily avail himself. Allegory, typology, and the broader mythic resonance attached to the first books of the Old Testament were part of the grain and tissue of his mind, and we have only to consult a recent summative article [Joseph Sigman, "Adam-Kadmon, Nifl, Muspel, and the Biblical Symbolism of *Sartor Resartus,*" *English Literary History* 41 (1974)] on the biblical references in *Sartor Resartus* to sense how close the language of Scripture was to the nub of his pen.

The figures of this language were not so much normative for Carlyle as generative. They are the materials out of which he fashions a rhetoric for his thought and a poetics for his self-promulgation. After collecting the several biblical figures in which one of the Carlylian personae in *Sartor* is portrayed—Diogenes Teufelsdröckh as Old Testament prophet, Christ figure, exiled Israel, fire-baptised martyr, all-but-returned Moses, and microcosm of the macrocosmic Adam Kadmon—one is assured only of the synthetic tendency of the book's figurative mode. Neither typology, allegory, nor even a worldwide mythic lexicon will do justice to Carlyle's symbolic imagination, for it is larger and more interesting than the sum of its parts. It may well be true, as one student of nineteenth-century symbolism has claimed, that Carlyle creates a personal version of typological thinking and that his category of "intrinsic symbols," as opposed to the received and arbitrary extrinsic ones, is really a formula for traditional typology [Herbert L. Sussman, *Fact into Figure: Typology in Carlyle, Ruskin, and the Pre-Raphaelite Brotherhood,* 1979]. But the symbolism of *Sartor* and other high-Carlylian writings operates by superimposing varied biblical references over figures derived from classical and other cultures, by deliberately blurring the liaisons between symbols and the systems from which they are derived, and by building up larger structures for its figural personae—of which Teufelsdröckh is only one. This synthetic mode of symbolism is engineered not only to prophetically exhibit a heroic, transcendentalist view of modern life but also to promulgate the figure of the prophet himself—which is the autobiographical burden of this nongeneric work.

The origins of *Sartor Resartus* have been so often rehearsed that they can be seen to anticipate almost any of the faces this multifaceted book ultimately reveals. It is well known, for example, that Carlyle in 1827 was writing an autobiographical novel, *Wotton Reinfred,* that deals with an unhappy love affair and conflates his experience with at least three women. To express the personal, Carlyle seized so firmly on the popular fiction conventions of the day—the plot which turns on a revelatory locket, the appearance of a mysterious stranger, a setting in wild, vaguely Gothic scenery—that writing this sublimated version became unsatisfactory, and a new set of conventions became desirable. Similarly, the germ of *Sartor*'s symbol and subject has been located in Carlyle's 1830 journal entry: "I am going to write—Nonsense. It is on 'Clothes.' " But an equally decisive turning may have been made when the first version of the theme, the two articles he wrote for *Fraser's Magazine,* were rejected in 1831, and he recognized another desideratum: "I can devise some more biography for *Teufelsdreck.* . . ." Looking at the origins of the book prospectively rather than from our critical distance, the problem for the still struggling and no longer young author who had confined himself mainly to translation and literary hack work was to find a language, a set of figures that could sustain the speculative thought, the personal experience, and the peculiar personality of one of the most distinctive men of any age, who nevertheless insists on establishing himself as the spokesman and prophet for his age.

Writing and publishing, then, become acts of promulgating oneself before the world, but the ironies that attend every such interaction of the public and the private self become particularly attenuated in Carlyle. Not only in his personality but in his social vision and eventually in his metaphysics as well, the distance between the individually held core of truth and the dissipation of that thought in its various forms of manifestation—in language, in journalistic or other media, in the marketplace of ideas—becomes a fall from original purity. More concretely, the would-be social reformer must communicate his radical, if not revolutionary, critique to the very society he finds blind and corrupt; the pharmacist-physician of social disease must adjust his prescriptions to the claptrap of political shibboleths—the reformer must claim to be more profoundly conservative than the Tories. It is the traditional problem of the prophetic voice crying in the wilderness, not mitigated even when the outlander (a Scotsman in this case) arrives at the babel of voices in the metropolis.

In the absence of a stable symbolic mode for self-writing, the Victorians were led to invent new techniques of composition, developing a palette of the myths, symbols, and other debris of classical and Christian culture.

—Avrom Fleishman

To mediate that discordance, to place himself both within and without the community of discourse, Carlyle falls back on a narrative option that later became a hallmark of modern fiction, the device of multiple narrators or personae. For his radical and alien side, he erects the outlandish image of Diogenes Teufelsdröckh to convey the mystical, intellectual, Germanic, Promethean, heroic, and faintly absurd side of himself and his message—burdens emblematized in the six bags of autobiographical fragments and the Germanic text, which he opens to the British public. To receive this burden and to convey it to his compatriots, there is raised the equivalent of Scott's dry-as-dust editor, in this case a comically befuddled, skeptical, and resistant but earnest inquirer into the vagaries of the documents set before him. It should be evident that this artful multiplication of entities for conveying the message is no arbitrary convenience or mere means, for it corresponds to the twin elements in Carlyle's personality, vision and doctrine.

Although the initial splitting of the narrative focus between Teufelsdröckh and the editor represents a structural division within Carlyle's internal dynamic and stance in the world, the proliferation of figures that goes into the making of the former persona alone reflects the infinite nuances of that face of the self. From Diogenes's initial associations with the devil and his modern avatar, the Sansculottist, the Wandering Jew, a comic version of the Faustian polymath (Professor of Things in General at the New University of Don't-know-where), the Menippean satirist at his lofty elevation above the earth (although his "watch-tower" has also been taken as a biblical prophetic one), we become aware of a tropology of vast and devious knowledge, as much a condition of alienation, perhaps of original sin, as of authority and wisdom.

To this synthetic wisdom figure, severely marked by the taint of forbidden and self-destructive knowledge, another equivocal figure is added in Part II, as the biographical fragments are sifted to compose a narrative of the hero's origins. Adamic motifs have been employed earlier, but we now find a full passage of preference for the Edenic imagination of innocent youth: "a certain prospective Paradise" from which even the Tree of Knowledge is not excluded. The tale of Teufelsdröckh's delivery to his foster parents by a mysterious stranger is, of course, straight out of the storehouse of *Märchen* conventions, and he is further specified as a Fortunatus when making his *Wanderjahre* wanderings. Even his "unchristian" Christian name is given point when its reference to divine origins rather than to fallen wisdom (re: the Cynic philosopher) is foregrounded. To the equivocal figure of the prophet of Part I there succeeds an equally equivocal figure of everyman, born in unknowable circumstances and pursuing an iron but imponderable fate.

The common function of these explanatory metaphors and mythological associations is to obscure as well as to reveal the hero. As Carlyle, or his editor-persona, puts it: "From this point, the Professor is more of an enigma than ever. In figurative language, we might say he becomes, not indeed a spirit, yet spiritualised, vaporised. Fact unparalleled in Biography. . . ." It is not only the present sentence that resorts to figurative language but, as we have seen, the entire characterization of the protagonist and the associated self-imaging by his creator. So extended and self-conscious an enterprise cannot have been made *in spite of* its evident shortcomings as a clarification. There is here at work a systematic program to obscure as well as to reveal the hero and the author behind him. Nor is this a mere sportive coyness or early-Victorian diffidence on Carlyle's part; it is well known how much trouble his *Reminiscences,* written late in life, caused him, but the present mode of concealment shows less a bashful anxiety than a disciplined and controlled ambiguity. It is not to Carlyle's guilty egotism that we must account his powerfully presented and as powerfully withdrawn self-image but to his larger vision of things—to the philosophy of clothes, language, and symbolism that is the subject of *Sartor.* The thought and the thinker, form and content of the work, are inextricably entwined, and the "open secret" is written into the portraiture—the autobiography given/denied in the work—just as it is in the universe it envisages.

Carlyle's symbolic theory has been so heavily commented upon that a further review must aim to touch only on its characteristic turns of mind. The consequence of the view that "all visible things are emblems," beyond its transcendentalist reformulation of a Platonic-Christian idea, is the dual attitude that such a view entails toward the realm of matter in particular and toward symbolization in general. " 'Whatsoever sensibly exists,' " writes Teufelsdröckh in his oracular style, " 'whatsoever represents Spirit to Spirit, is properly a Clothing, a suit of Raiment, put on for a season, and to be laid off'." This ascetic ambivalence toward the body is extended then toward the realm of culture, to which the clothes philosophy metaphorically extends. Human nature is seen under the same rubrics: " 'Nay, if you consider it, what is Man himself, and his whole terrestrial Life, but an Emblem; a Clothing or visible Garment for that divine ME of his, cast hither, like a light-particle, down from Heaven?' " The condition of human life thus presupposes a fall of spirit into the realm of matter, but it carries the irradiating force of light, which can transfer significance from spirit to spirit. In this double role, all cultural forms are implicated in communication and imposture: " 'Clothes gave us individuality, distinctions, social polity; Clothes have made Men of us; they are threatening to make Clothes-screens of us'." And it is especially language that bears the double marks of its more general origins: " 'Examine Language; what, if you except some few primitive elements (of natural sound), what is it all but Metaphors, recognised as such, or no longer recognised; still fluid and florid, or now solid-grown and colourless?' " Metaphoric language has two states, both native to it: fluid and solid, energetic and material, communicative and stultifying, alive and dead (as the passage goes on to say).

Carlyle anticipates, it would appear, not only the post-Kantian philosophy of cultural forms in Ernst Cassirer's symbolic theory but also the more ironic view of culture—indeed, of reality—in the poststructuralist theory of *differance.* Where Carlyle's idealism would part company from Jacques Derrida's antimetaphysics is in holding fast to an ultimate reality that is not deferred, that does not come into play in the course of a differential system of symbolic relations; what they share is the same lively sense of imposture in the process, the same readiness to pinprick the naïve assumptions of truth and value traditionally ascribed to mere signs. Given this corrosive insight into the mere formality of what passes as stable and natural, there should be no surprise in discovering that autobiography is a prime target for Carlylian deconstruction.

The text of *Die Kleider* in hand, the sanguine editor wants to take the style-is-the-man theory a step toward its revelatory potential: "His Life, Fortunes, and Bodily Presence, are as yet hidden from us, or matter only of faint conjecture. But, on the other hand, does not his Soul lie enclosed in this remarkable Volume . . . ?" The autobiographical text is, then, a place for hiding a "Bodily Presence" as well as revealing a soul, and even the latter is "enclosed." Thus, the committing of life to language entails the same dual movement and effect as symbolism in general: Speak, and thou shalt hide.

To the editor, historical specialist in biographical documentation and representative of Carlyle's professional self, there is, of course, a norm of truth for autobiography and biography. Their usual guarantees as historical disciplines are, however, broadly undercut by the satire of the editor and his opening procedures. The appeal to historical data is lampooned in the image of the six bags' full of fragments, arranged and perhaps arrangeable only by zodiacal signs. The historian's commitment to truth telling is burlesqued as a form of gossipiness when the bags' supplier, Hofrath Heuschrecke, is allowed to dilate on the popular rage for exact information about celebrities: " 'Biography is by nature the most universally profitable, universally pleasant of all things: especially Biography of distinguished individuals'." And the final grace of the historian's craft, his urge toward chronological ordering and causal intelligibility, is annulled by the character of the materials that go to make up a man's totality, his theoretical work and indeed the *mental* character of his life: "Then again, amidst what seems to be a Metaphysico-theological Disquisition, 'Detached Thoughts on the Steam-engine,' or 'The continued Possibility of Prophecy,' we shall meet with some quite private, not unimportant Biographical fact." The editor is wise enough to conclude his own project: "Biography or Autobiography of Teufelsdröckh there is, clearly enough, none to be gleaned here: at most some sketchy, shadowy fugitive likeness of him may, by unheard-of efforts, partly of intellect, partly of imagination, on the side of Editor and of Reader, rise up between them." These words apply, *pari passu,* to *Sartor Resartus* as an autobiography of Carlyle.

The dual energy of *Sartor* in concealing as well as in revealing its author is at work in the two primary materials of Carlyle's being, which correspond to the divisions of *Die Kleider,* the "Historical-Descriptive" and the "Philosophical-Speculative." That is, Carlyle needs to imbed his thought in the living tissue of his personality and in at least selected aspects of his career, in order that it be understood as the sincere expression of a committed thinker. But the synecdochic relation of thought and life may readily be reversed, as in the above quotation in which the biographical facts are found imbedded among the larger texts of Teufelsdröckh's thought. The quandary of the hermeneutic circle applies to the creator of autobiography as much as it does to its interpreter. He cannot tell his life without images, yet these images obscure as much as they convey his pure self-conception. The constriction of this circle is felt with particular acuteness when these images are the traditional figures of autobiography.

The notion that to tell the story of a life, there may be recourse to a myth or other pattern of life as found in history or legend is open to the same duality of perception and attitude as that appropriate to all symbolism. The voice of the editor merges with Teufelsdröckh's story of his life in Book II, producing a series of allusions by which the early life of the hero is both magnified and mocked. This merger of mythologizing and skepticism is performed by the editor in quoting Teufelsdröckh's Romantic version of biblical figures, yet he is willing to believe in its efficacy: "This Genesis of his can properly be nothing but an Exodus (or transit out of Invisibility into Visibility)"; " 'The Andreas and Gretchen, or the Adam and Eve, who led thee into

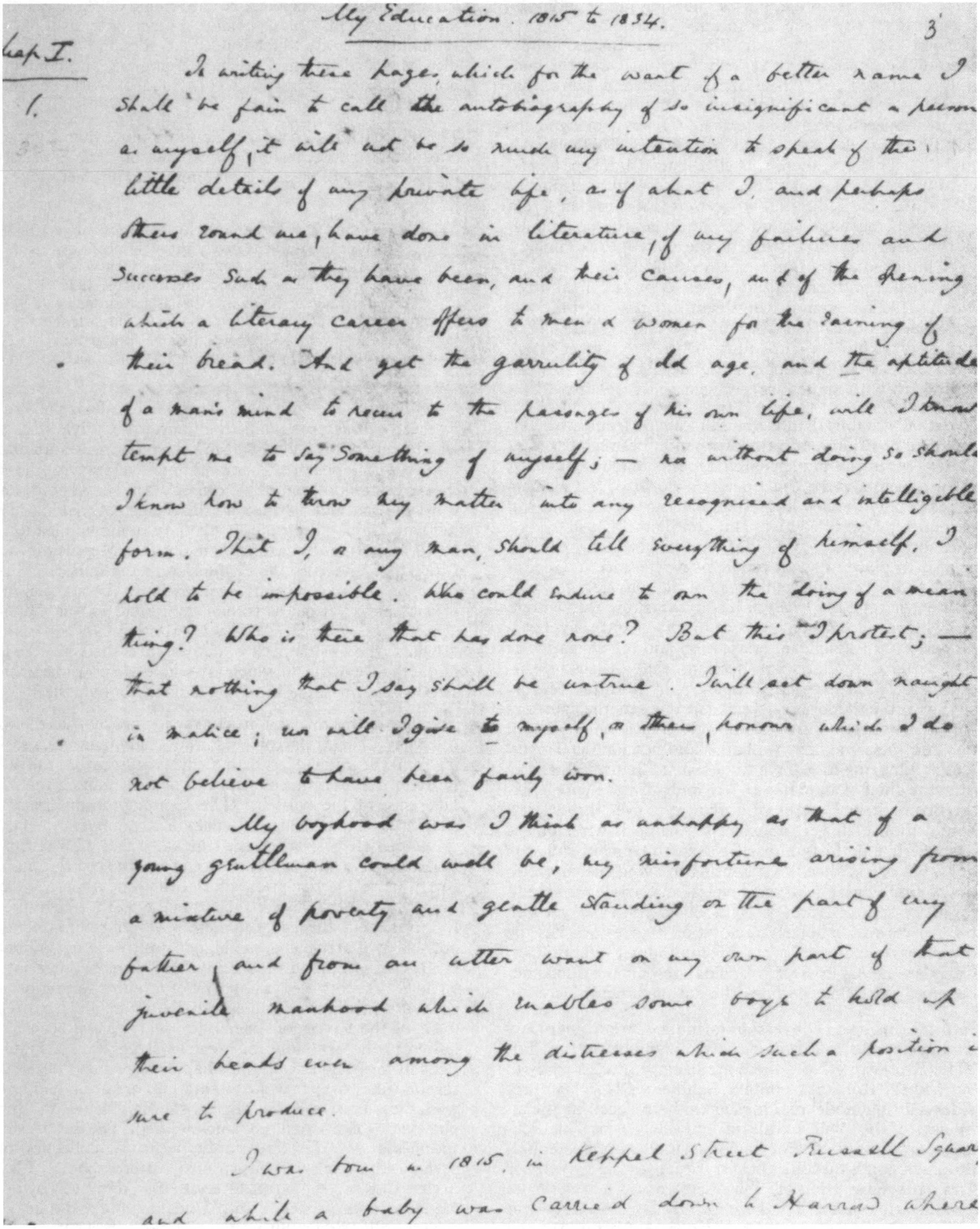
My Education. 1815 to 1834.

3

Chap. I.

1. In writing these pages, which for the want of a better name I shall be fain to call the autobiography of so insignificant a person as myself, it will not be so much my intention to speak of the little details of my private life, as of what I, and perhaps others round me, have done in literature; of my failures and successes such as they have been, and their causes, and of the opening which a literary career offers to men and women for the earning of their bread. And yet the garrulity of old age, and the aptitude of a man's mind to recur to the passages of his own life, will I know tempt me to say something of myself; — nor without doing so should I know how to throw my matter into any recognised and intelligible form. That I, or any man, should tell everything of himself, I hold to be impossible. Who could endure to own the doing of a mean thing? Who is there that has done none? But this I protest; — that nothing that I say shall be untrue. I will set down naught in malice; nor will I give to myself, or others, honours which I do not believe to have been fairly won.

My boyhood was I think as unhappy as that of a young gentleman could well be, my misfortunes arising from a mixture of poverty and gentle standing on the part of my father, and from an utter want on my own part of that juvenile manhood which enables some boys to hold up their heads even among the distresses which such a position is sure to produce.

I was born in 1815, in Keppel Street Russell Square, and while a baby was carried down to Harrow where

Page from the manuscript for Anthony Trollope's Autobiography.

life . . . were, like mine, but thy nursing-father and nursing-mother: thy true Beginning and Father is in Heaven . . .' "; " 'the fair Life-garden rustles infinite around, and everywhere is dewy fragrance, and the budding of Hope' "; " 'Those hues of gold and azure, that hush of the World's expectation as Day died, were still a Hebrew Speech for me; nevertheless I was looking at the fair illuminated Letters, and had an eye for their gilding' "; " 'The past, then, was all a haggard dream; he had been in the Garden of Eden, then, and could not discern it!' "; "He quietly lifts his *Pilgerstab* (Pilgrim-staff), 'old business being soon wound-up'; and begins a perambulation and circumambulation of the terraqueous Globe!"; " 'A hundred and a hundred savage peaks, . . . there in their silence, in their solitude, even as on the night when Noah's Deluge first dried! Beautiful, nay solemn, was the sudden aspect to our Wanderer' "; "Poor Teufelsdröckh! . . . Thus must he, in the temper of ancient Cain, or of the modern Wandering Jew, . . . wend to and fro with aimless speed"; etc.

Eventually, biblical allusion falls away from even this qualified centrality, and the distinction between Old Testament types and modern after-types is made explicit: "It is all a grim Desert, this once-fair world of his; wherein is heard only the howling of wild-beasts, or the shrieks of despairing, hate-filled men; and no Pillar of Cloud by day, and no Pillar of Fire by night, any longer guides the Pilgrim." In place of strict typological reference to Genesis and Exodus as a coherent image of the self, Carlyle yields to the syncretic tendency of his mythmaking throughout. In the three famous chapters of his crisis and conversion, he performs a significant adaptation and reformulation of the pattern of Christian heroism that Augustine bequeathed to the spiritual autobiography tradition. Side by side with the models of *askesis,* Carlyle sets the figures of Romantic selfhood that descend from classical myth. On one and the same page we find: "Did not Paul of Tarsus, whom admiring men have since named Saint, feel that *he* was 'the chief of sinners' . . . ?" and: "To the unregenerate Prometheus Vinctus of a man, it is ever the bitterest aggravation of his wretchedness that he is conscious of Virtue, that he feels himself the victim not of suffering only, but of injustice." Attempting to avoid the opprobrium of autobiographical self-revelation, Carlyle has his editor dismiss these figures as "symbolical myth all," yet with the network of scholarly annotation that establishes the literalness of many of his statements about Teufelsdröckh-Carlyle's mental crisis and suicidal despair the disclaimer becomes truer than perhaps the author intended.

Into the crisis and conversion formula, Carlyle pours layers of reference to a wide variety of symbol systems. For "The Everlasting No," there are literary models ready to hand in the Romantic context: Schiller's *Die Räuber* provides a fitting model of a tormented hero declaring the ultimacy of his will to affirm himself despite his self-lacerating impulses. For religious models of (potential) prophets going through their spiritual testing by worldly fires, there is a string of biblical references that needs no amplification here. To these primarily Old Testament sources, Carlyle adds the Christian lore of baptism, fused with the imagery of fire that attends the Pentecost and its issuance in inspired speech. And to round off the syncretic movement of his prose, he adds a grace note allusion to Baphomet, a figure which is itself a compound of mishandled Moslem, deviant Christian (Templar), and contemporary literary texture—a sort of symbol of synthetic symbolism itself.

The most striking image—an auditory more than a visual one—that emerges from the crescendo of "The Everlasting No" is that of the Protestant mind and its chief spokesman, Luther:

> Thus had the EVERLASTING NO (*das ewige Nein*) pealed authoritatively through all the recesses of my Being, of my ME; and then was it that my whole ME stood up, in native God-created majesty, and with emphasis recorded its Protest. Such a Protest, the most important transaction in Life, may that same Indignation and Defiance, in a psychological point of view, be fitly called.

Unwilling to take on himself the Romantic figure of Promethean self-assertion and rebelliousness, Carlyle finds a way to endow his individualism with a religious aura and his ego with a positive, liberating function. Having traced the Augustinian "trial of the center" (self versus soul) toward the self and alarmed by the danger of making it a self-worshipping deity, he avoids the Satanic implications of world defiance by casting them onto the Mephistofelian figure that underlies the chapter from the outset. In its place, he rears a figure that can say no to the no—empty of content as yet but as sure of its ground as was Christ against his adversary: " 'The Everlasting No had said: "Behold, thou art fatherless, outcast, and the Universe is mine (the Devil's)"; to which my whole Me now made answer: "*I* am not thine, but Free, and forever hate thee!" ' "

The succeeding stages of the conversion process have been traced by Charles Harrold and other commentators, moving from the initial, blatant, but empty affirming of the self through the intermediate stage of acknowledging the indifference of the not-self. "The Center of Indifference" chapter is an assemblage of scenes of meaningless worldly existence, whether in history (the battlefield of Wagram) or nature (the "infinite Brine" seen from the North Cape). But Carlyle's articulation of the dialectical process at work suggests that his advance from the positive but merely formal self, through the merely negative rejection of not-self, will arrive at some higher positive plane ("from the Negative Pole to the Positive"). The emergence into "The Everlasting Yea" is by way of a return to origins, a renewal of exilic and Promethean figuration, and a divestment of the figures of redemption which have been acquired in the exultation of previous struggles. "Temptations in the Wilderness!" the chapter begins and declares several times over that the temptations are at an end, the wilderness traversed, the pilgrim staff laid aside, and the possession of a promised land assured. The hero even specifies a New Testament antitype for his collection of prefigurative trials and purgations: " 'Here, then, as I lay in that CENTER OF INDIFFERENCE; cast, doubtless by benignant upper Influence, into a healing sleep, the heavy dreams rolled gradually away, and I awoke to a new Heaven and a new Earth. The first preliminary moral Act, Annihilation of Self (*Selbst-tödtung*), had been happily accomplished; and my mind's eyes were now unsealed, and its hands ungyved'."

But the figure of an entry into an apocalyptically redeemed world is surely hyperbolic—not an assertion of the antitype but a metaphorical exultation—for the hero and his author have not won through to a transcendental realm or beatific state. Indeed, the third phase of the conversion process is not transcendence but a return to the desert of this world; its vigorous cry of affirmation is not directed to a redeemer but to the conditions of life in this world. " 'Not so easily can the old Adam, lodged in us by birth, be dispossessed. Our Life is compassed round with Necessity; yet is the meaning of Life itself no other than Freedom, than Voluntary Force: thus have we a warfare; in the beginning, especially, a hard-fought battle'." And afterwards? Work, the fate of the old Adam. Self-annihilation, the return to the desert, the acknowledgment of fallen nature, the ethic of renunciation (*Entsagen*), which Carlyle imports from Goethe, the "Worship of Sorrow," which he resurrects from medieval and latter-day pietists—these elements of asceticism are carefully picked over among the debris of Christian culture to make a "new Mythus." It is no accident that precisely at the juncture between his conversion and his going forth to prophecy, Carlyle places the figure of George Fox, the man who made himself a suit of leather—and an autobiography to boot.

It is true that Carlyle translates Fox's gospel message in his own terms: "A man God-possessed, witnessing for spiritual freedom and manhood." But this set of values is the moral equivalent of the burden of the spiritual autobiography of the seventeenth century, one of the foremost carriers of the strain of Augustinian piety into the modern world. *Sartor Resartus* may be seen, then, as traditional not only in its figures but in its purport; what is new is its symbolic method and its grasp of that two-edged sword. Although its pattern of conversion departs in many respects from the formulas of Puritanism, its outcome is a modern renewal of the Protestant work ethic: " 'Produce! Produce! . . . Work while it is called Today; for the Night cometh, wherein no man can work'."

It was this image of the self—of himself—that Carlyle established for Victorian autobiographers in whatever forms they chose. Coming as it does (in book form) within a year of the start of Victoria's reign, *Sartor* becomes the paradigmatic text for a line of autobiographical novels of crisis and conversion while the most significant autobiographies of the time (Mill's, Ruskin's, and even Newman's) are written, as it were, in its margins. Carlyle's position as the "major prophet" of the age has, of course, been widely attested, and the role of his protective self-images in enforcing his claims to authority has been ably described. Equally, the peculiarities of *Sartor Resartus* as a prose work have been observed since Wilhelm Dilthey's groundbreaking review [in *Clio* I, no. 3 (1972)] of J. A. Froude's biography of Carlyle, which located the homology of form, content, and personal presence in the peculiarities of the style: "All these eccentricities do not hide the ingenious and appropriate structure of the work from a careful reader, for it makes transcendental idealism incarnate in a man, a life, and a symbolic expression of its doctrine." Yet it needs to be specified that this homology is not accidentally related to the autobiographical character of the work but is of its essence.

The conversion that takes up the center of *Sartor*'s narrative is, after all, only the middle phase of its autobiographicality. The dual personae of outcast hero and mediating editor may stand as a composite self-image for the author on beginning his autobiography. But how can we redeem the third and final book for autobiographical activity? A hint comes from a probing extension of the idea of conversion in an article by Walter Reed [in *English Literary History* 38 (1971)]. It is not simply the hero who is converted in the crisis narrative, but the materials of the philosophy and of the life are converted from dead to living matter by the power of metaphorical transformation. The personae act upon one another in the internal dynamics of the prose so that the editor is gradually converted from a skeptical and apologetic presenter to a lively advocate of Teufelsdröckh and his ideas; and the reader is handsomely invited to join in a social conversion that is already at hand in society: "Have many British Readers actually arrived with us at the new promised country?" That "actually" means *now,* as the seed working toward its flowering is now in place: "Our own private conjecture, now amounting almost to certainty, is that, safe-moored in some stillest obscurity, not to lie always still, Teufelsdröckh is actually in London!"

The several conversions which take place in Book III of *Sartor*—from a personal to a social range of reference, from a complex view of the power of symbolism to a simpler stripping away of the detritus of outworn symbols, from a metaphorical to a sententious style heavily committed to formulation in maxims—all these are aspects of the major conversion of the self that is dramatically enacted in the prose. For the ultimate aesthetic triumph of *Sartor* as autobiography lies in its enactment of the dual function of all symbolism, according to Carlyle's precocious insight—that it simultaneously hides as it reveals, absents as it presents, defers as it manifests. So with the autobiographical symbol by which this autobiography operates. Its final movement is to take away all that has been given and leave only the space of Carlyle without his substance. Like the seed of regeneration waiting to sprout, like Teufelsdröckh lying latent in London, Carlyle makes himself available for the Victorian age, but only as a potency. It is for the age to make his prophecy come true, to heed if not fully to grasp his message, to make the words take on flesh. Yet like all prophets, Carlyle can never be fully known by the populace. There must always stand between them the symbols in which they meet but which persist in their oddity and distraction. Thus, *Sartor Resartus* is the book in which Carlyle reveals and hides himself, like the absconding god whom he witnesses. (pp. 121-37)

Avrom Fleishman, "The Figures of the Prophets" and "Carlyle's 'Sartor': The Open Secret," in his Figures of Autobiography: The Language of Self-Writing in Victorian and Modern England, *University of California Press, 1983, pp. 109-20, 121-37.*

David J. DeLaura

[*DeLaura is an American educator and critic who has written extensively on Victorian literature. In the following excerpt, he discusses the importance of nostalgia and self-examination as unifying forces in Victorian prose.*]

George Saintsbury, himself an advocate of something very close to style-for-its-own-sake, once complained—amusingly, and instructively—that the mid-nineteenth-century polemicists had *meant* so intensely that they neglected their styles. And it is true: various kinds of prose experiment, as well as some of the famous passages of "heightened" prose, often seem to exist quite apart from both the more plainly argumentative passages and from more pervasive elements of purpose and meaning. It remains, in short, very difficult to describe the *unity* of Victorian prose works. Certainly, the familiar vehicle of the review-essay gave scarcely a semblance of pre-existing form and pattern of the sort available to novelists and poets, and a great deal of the most notable prose of the century—even whole books-full—consists of "passages" and highly digressive "essays." The unities I want to suggest here are "modal," manifestations of a unique meditative or reflective strain, in which certain identifiable themes, attitudes, and concerns intersect with special stylistic qualities that are considered their adequate embodiment, the whole bound together by a continuous, or at least intermittent, readiness for self-exploration and self-manifestation and the manipulation of one's own personal presence for highly diverse ends.

I want to examine some of these modes of procedure, these favored "situations" and ways of exploring "history," both one's own experience and (intimately connected with it) the larger shifts and movements of the culture. . . . I want, in short, to specify so far as I can how a simultaneous concern for style, for an implicit theory of mind, consciousness, and language, and for the exploration of personality creates an inter-region of its own, lying between the two more familiar kingdoms of explicit "content" on the one side, and "style," "form," and device on the other. I am trying to suggest the unity of Victorian prose in ways not so readily evident in the usual "philosophical" groupings and counter-groupings; the process allows us to discern some unexpected alignments and continuities.

I am particularly concerned to account for the role in the nineteenth century of nostalgia and personal memory, those controlling emotions in so many of the heightened passages in De Quincey, Carlyle, Newman, and Arnold. We need an approach to this pervasive reminiscential mood that does not confine itself to autobiography in any formal sense. Wordsworth is a key figure for understanding this backward-looking mood of the century. The "humble" fact to which he (like George Eliot after him) submitted himself turned out, again and again, to be the remembered fact, autobiographical or quasi-autobiographical. And personal memory, again and again, was the re-experiencing of the "something that is gone," those "Fallings from us, vanishings," that in their turn led to more universal perceptions of the "still, sad music of humanity," the thoughts that "lie too deep for tears." The elegiac, in the nineteenth century as earlier, involves not only a look backward and inward, but "up," to a more general or even transcendent perspective on the human situation. It is precisely the *present application* of these "shadowy recollections," their forward-looking and propulsive function, as well as the inference of "something far more deeply interfused," that are increasingly called into question in the colder climate of the latter half of the century.

For the most part, I think the Victorians inherited the Wordsworthian mode, even while putting it to new uses. Pater captures another, weaker, side of the cult of nostalgia, in describing "the ennuyé": "More than Childe Harold, more than Werther, more than Réné himself, Coleridge . . . represents the inexhaustible discontent, languor, and home-sickness, that endless regret, the chords of which ring all through our modern literature." After about 1825, Byronic pageants of the bleeding heart and Shelleyan musical wails—despite some shreds attaching to the early Tennyson and Browning, and of course to the reviled Spasmodics—seemed embarrassing, and "subjectivity" itself was the constant object of critical attack, starting with critics as diverse as Peacock, Macaulay, and Carlyle, and culminating in the onslaught on the feeble Spasmodics in the fifties.

Still, a good deal of the somewhat diffuse emotionality we associate with early- and mid-Victorian literature unquestionably centers on, precisely, memory and its melancholy inventory of past experience and loss. Though the theme of loss and the elegiac emotions is pervasive in the Old Testament, and in both Greek and Roman literature, it is especially the new Victorian experience, a newly intensified and reorganized set of emotions derived from a sense of cultural crisis, which a great many people, following the lead of their literary betters, learned to regard as their own "essential" and personal emotions. A kind of Victorian specialty, melancholy is as intense and as intimate as it was in Coleridge, Byron, and Shelley, but at the same time more consciously restrained; it is the Wordsworthian mood, though no doubt colored in stronger tones. (The mood found its perfect musical embodiment in the adagio movements of Elgar at the turn of the century and later.) The elegiac lies very close to the heart of what was considered essentially "poetic," in all the forms employed by the Victorians; it became, finally, for reasons I think worth exploring, a central defining element of the specifically "human."

But the nineteenth century explored the passion of the past, and expressed its own broken-heartedness and its barely controlled sobbing, at several levels of seriousness and with varying degrees of adequacy. We know its more popular and unpersuasive manifestations in the continual re-appearance of medieval ruins in the poetry and fiction of the century, even for un-"Gothic" purposes. The merely picturesque use of ruined castles and abbeys is a fairly harmless if persistent aspect of that often-overrated and all too "literary" phenomenon, nineteenth-century medievalism. But *below* the level of, say, Scott's undemanding picturesqueness, there were low-lying swamps of lachrymosity and self-pity; *above* it, there was a more serious and permanently available range of attitudes expressive of the personal and cultural losses suffered in a time of widespread and rapid change. These are among the *kinds* of feeling, however adequately embodied, that surprise us so frequently in Victorian writing, when the author (in Walter Houghton's words ["The Rhetoric of T. H. Huxley," *University of Toronto Quarterly* (January 1949)] "is suddenly swept by a gust of personal emotion which he cannot check or master sufficiently to integrate it with his theme." My own view is that such passages, especially in nonfictional prose, though abrupt and sometimes ill-managed, are often not nearly so out of keeping with an author's overt argumentative point as may at first appear. Such passages have a supplementary "purposive" value of their own; they become part of the more or less implicit campaign to change England's self-awareness, and instruments for fighting the battle with the Philistines by other methods.

The special Victorian version of backward-looking emotions, with a constant implicit reference to one's own experience, is in part to be explained by the very rapid growth in historical awareness during the second quarter of the century—that time of "transition" when again and again writers analyzed their historical moment under such titles as "The Spirit of the Age," "Characteristics," and "Signs of the Times." Kathleen Tillotson [in her *Novels of the Eighteen-Forties,* 1956] has spoken of "the drag of the past" in the novels of the period, the great divide coming in the thirties and symbolized in the transformation of the English countryside by the coming of the railway. This sense that the chasm in one's own personal history coincides with the great and decisive watershed of modern history is particularly strong in those born around 1820, a group who came to adulthood in the troubled forties—the generation of John Ruskin, George Eliot, A. H. Clough, Matthew Arnold, and J. A. Froude.

The union of the universal and the personal, *without* reference to the historical moment, is no doubt most common, though even this variant operates at different levels of generalization. One thinks of the scene of the younger George Osborne, in Chapter Sixty-One of *Vanity Fair,* as he comes across the letters G. O. scratched on the glass in his grandfather's house, and his mother's unspoken thoughts of the past; here the universality of human loss is totally implicit—though not without its strong effect. In contrast, the great elaborateness of Philip Pirrip's revisitings of the scenes of his youth in *Great Expectations,* as part of his growing sense of the loss of youthful innocence, suggests Dickens' conscious attempt to link Philip's experience to a more universal pattern of loss and gain, in the tradition of the *Bildungsroman.* But here the latent, but important, element is that third factor, the strong and continuous autobiographical pressure of Dickens' self-awareness and painful self-exposure in his anti-hero's progress. There is even an identifiable Victorian "situation," in which a young person, often a girl, coming upon "the happy Autumn-fields" and the beauty of a "Goldengrove unleaving," experiences not the Keatsian fulness of being and momentary stasis, but shocked tears, the result of a sudden inrush of the fact of mortality, including one's own, followed sometimes by a religious reflection. For us the chief examples are, perhaps, the revisiting of Helstone in Chapter Forty-Six of Mrs. Gaskell's *North and South* (1854), and Hopkins' "Spring and Fall" ("Margaret, are you grieving?"). The tears that rise while "thinking of the days that are no more" are Tennyson's "Tears, idle tears," but for the Victorians, as I want to argue, they were not idle at all.

My examples of personal memory and the universal meaning derived from it have so far been drawn from fiction and poetry. Granted, the background of industrial strife adds an extra dimension to Mrs. Gaskell's and Disraeli's treatment of loss and memory. But nonfictional prose is particularly well-suited to the new "uses" of memory, because of its free interplay between the author's personal remembrance and intimate self-revelation, on the one hand, and its virtually unlimited scope in exploring universal significance, on the other. It could then treat the changes in nineteenth-century society and sensibility as a "third" or inter-area, a fresh analogue, and in the process help grasp the significance of the new, disturbing, and characteristically "modern" experiences which all sensitive readers were confusedly undergoing. This presentation of one's own past, as part of a search for new meanings in a deteriorating cultural situation, is perhaps the most central binding activity of serious nineteenth-century literature. It is the great "task," a kind of implicitly shared program for the century. This everywhere evident autobiographical pressure of the period, deriving most obviously from the example of Wordsworth, reaches a kind of climax around mid-century—most obviously, in such works as *In Memoriam,* the poetry of Arnold and Clough, the fiction of Charlotte Brontë, Thackeray's *Pendennis,* Dickens' *David Copperfield* and *Great Expectations,* and George Eliot's *The Mill on the Floss.* The prose writers also played an essential, and unique, role in carrying out the program—and it has an untold history of its own.

Of course the free "interpretative" power of essayistic prose is not always exercised, and some of the most famous passages work best when memory bears its own meaning without explication and explicit "higher" reference. Hazlitt, who is mostly remembered today for his mode of "abrupt" opinionatedness, can I think be credited with virtually inventing that mood of "lofty thought or mournful memory" that is so central to the "high" passages of Victorian prose at all periods. In treating the Lake Poets, especially, Hazlitt's mixture of brokenhearted affection and blame for the betrayal of youthful social and political ideals offered a useful pattern for the interpenetration of personal feeling and larger intellectual and social considerations. In fact, it seems likely that Matthew Arnold, from a very early date, borrowed his double-edged mode of treating Newman—as a man of the highest spiritual and imaginative power, who had exercised a great attraction over him in his youth, but who had almost perversely misused his gifts—from Hazlitt's treatment of Coleridge.

We forget that Carlyle, too, for all the "rugged" tone and the exhortations to endeavor and endurance, is a great master of pathos. *The French Revolution* modulates between scenes of rather helpless and inexplicable mob violence, and portrait after portrait of human folly and failure. Against a Luther, or a Cromwell, or a Frederick, there is a counterbalancing John Sterling. Even in *Heroes,* with its praise of vehement self-exertion, when the theme most closely touches Carlyle himself the tone darkens and the texture softens. Of the two greatest poets, the "sorrowstricken" Dante is "most touching" to Carlyle, for his loneliness, his "silent pain," his "grief." Even the "complete and self-sufficing" Shakespeare "had his sorrows," "suffered," and had his share of "the troubles of other men." The "notablest of all [modern] Literary Men," Goethe, is the merest wraith, partly no doubt because Carlyle had come to suspect that the "victory" allegedly achieved in Goethe's career was only dubiously of the sort that Carlyle could in fact endorse. Of the three Heroes as Men of Letters presented, Rousseau in his "misery" is least adequate or sympathetic; but Carlyle virtually identified himself with Johnson, who lived "in an element of diseased sorrow," "stalking mournful as a stranger in this earth," and even more with his fellow-Scot Burns, "dying broken-hearted as a Gauger," "swallowing down his many sore sufferings daily into silence," his life "a great tragic sincerity." His *Reminiscences,* mostly written late in life, with their tremulous evocations of his father and Jane and Edward Irving, rehearse in sorrow the semi-autobiographical experiences rather burlesqued in *Sartor.* Carlyle only *asserted* (as he did in *Sartor*) that Time is one of the "deepest of all illusory Appearances." Closer to his continuous and almost passionate *experience* of Time is the remark made the following year, on his father's death: "Strange Time! Endless Time, or of which I see neither end nor beginning! All rushes on; man follows man; his life is as a Tale that has been told." He only *hoped,* "under Time does there not lie Eternity?"

Charles Darwin at age sixty. Photograph by Julia Margaret Cameron.

De Quincey can perhaps be called Wordsworth's chief imitator in the continuous use of personal experience, recollected in tranquillity. A very large proportion of what remains readable in De Quincey is in fact not, as he called it, "impassioned prose," but the mode of "deep, melancholic reverie" with which he treats the things of his own remembered past—in the dream-visions of the *Confessions* and *Suspiria,* and even more in the *Literary Reminiscences* (especially those of the Lake Poets) and the *Autobiographic Sketches.* The mode and treatment in the latter (written between 1834 and 1854), with their detailed evocation of childhood consciousness, would repay comparison with not only the best "childhood" novels of mid-century, but with Wordsworth before him (though not the *Prelude,* published in 1850), and later, with Ruskin's "The Two Boyhoods" (in *Modern Painters* V) and *Praeterita,* the opening chapters of Mill's *Autobiography* and Newman's *Apologia,* Pater's "A Child in the House" and the early chapters of *Marius*—and for that matter the opening of Joyce's *Portrait of the Artist,* since Joyce certainly knew most of these authors well and even parodied some of them in the Oxen of the Sun episode of *Ulysses,* where among his numerous imitations of nineteenth-century prose he includes a Lamb-like passage on "young Leopold," "precociously manly." We have heard much lately of children, parents, and orphans in Victorian fiction; the memory of childhood in nonfictional prose, though it has complex relations with poetry and fiction, forms a distinctive tradition of its own. Its central figure is a small lonely boy in the receding distance, separated from his creator—his later self—by impassable historical and cultural barriers. The attention given the orphaned or "lost" child figure in the nineteenth-century—usually a version of one's own lost childhood—becomes in prose another continually available mode of treating personal experience not only as a universal pattern of loss and gain, and apart from "doctrine," but as an analogue of the "losses" of modern culture. This search for one's own childhood carries its authenticity in its continually "exploratory" character; it is a specific and centrally adaptable variant of the nineteenth-century's search for an almost pre-lapsarian "wholeness" of personality and consciousness, also sought in classical culture (as in Schiller's discussion of "naive" poetry) or distant civilizations—in any event, before the "fall" and the ensuing dissociation of sensibility, whether that took place in fifth-century B.C. Athens, or Ruskin's fifteenth-century Venice, or the Scholar-Gipsy's seventeenth-century Oxfordshire.

But it is finally Newman and Arnold who most effectively combine "heightened" prose, personal reminiscence, and a larger historical and cultural pattern. I refer to both their inherent literary and emotional power and to their virtually unprecedented influence on later consciousness. Those passages in Newman's prose that were continually cited throughout the century—such as the ending of "The Parting of Friends," the "invitation" concluding *The Development of Christian Doctrine,* and the farewell to Oxford in the *Apologia*—exhibit a precisely calculated pathos and self-pity, all the more effective for being carefully restrained in rhythm and figure and refraining from the more obvious kinds of rhetorical elaboration. This restraint is especially evident in the farewell, at the end of Chapter IV of the *Apologia,* where Newman speaks of leaving Oxford "for good" in February 1846, and saying farewell to various friends, the last of whom was Dr. Ogle, who had been his tutor when Newman was an undergraduate:

> In him I took leave of my first College, Trinity, which was so dear to me, and which held on its foundation so many who had been kind to me both when I was a boy, and all through my Oxford life. Trinity had never been unkind to me. There used to be much snapdragon growing on the walls opposite my freshman's rooms there, and I had for years taken it as the emblem of my own perpetual residence even unto death in my University.
>
> On the morning of the 23rd I left the Observatory. I have never seen Oxford since, excepting its spires, as they are seen from the railway.

But something much more intellectually ambitious is attempted in the great, almost symphonic climax of Chapter V. Newman ends his account of his life, much of it written as he says in tears, by offering his book as "a memorial of affection and gratitude" to his brother priests of the Oratory. Of these he finally singles out Ambrose St. John, an Oxford convert, as "the link between my old life and my new." Newman goes on:

> And in you I gather up and bear in memory those familiar affectionate companions and counsellors, who in Oxford were given to me, one after another, to be my daily solace and relief; and all those others, of great name and high example, who were my thorough friends, and showed me true attachment in times long past; and also those many younger men, whether I knew them or not, who have never been disloyal to me by word or deed; and of all these, thus various in their relations to me, those especially who have since joined the Catholic Church.
>
> And I earnestly pray for this whole company, with a hope against hope, that all of us, who once were so united, and so happy in our union, may even now be brought at length, by the power of the Divine Will, into One Fold and under One Shepherd.

Here, Newman's personal pain in surrendering his place of power and influence at Oxford is more clearly caught up in the more widespread personal, and even national, calamity, of the breaking up of the Movement in which Newman's defection was both cause and effect. Newman is at once the pathetic victim driven out by his one-time friends and the strong man beckoning from the farther shore, daring them on to a new and even more dangerous "venture of faith." The tangled emotions *toward Newman* which this excruciatingly painful situation brought to his former hearers, and to those who looked on at a greater distance—whether those who followed him across the divide, or those who remained in the High-Church party, or even those who as a result drifted away from serious preoccupation with religion altogether—could include pain, sorrow, pity, love and, something close to despair; all these Newman plainly intended. They also included, for some of the participants—and Newman could foretell these, without quite intending them—blame, reproach, repudiation, bitter incomprehension. It is, I think, the most complex, clearly identifiable "situation" of the nineteenth century, extending over many years and renewed periodically, for the largest number of participants.

This carefully staged pathetic self-presentation, in which Newman's personal experience is made to symbolize perfectly the decisive breakup of the "old" culture and the instatement of a triumphant Philistinism and Liberalism, is of a piece with Newman's deepest view of man's perennial situation as a scene of loss and failure. Newman's "anthropology," his view of man's terrestrial condition—as well as one of the reasons for his insisting on the "classical" sources of consciousness—can best be grasped in his notable attempt to explain why medieval men viewed Vergil "as if a prophet or a magician": "his single words and phrases, his pathetic half lines, giving utterance, as the voice of Nature herself, to that pain and weariness, yet hope of better things, which is the experience of her children in every time." This was in *The Grammar of Assent,* published in 1870; six years earlier, in the *Apologia,* an even grimmer vision of the "heart-piercing, reason-bewildering fact" of human history, without even that "hope of better things," had joined the handful of most impressive passages in all of Newman's writing.

> To consider the world in its length and breadth, its various history, the many races of man, their starts, their fortunes, their mutual alienation, their conflicts, and then their ways, habits, governments, forms of worship; their enterprises, their aimless courses, their random achievements and acquirements, the impotent conclusion of long-standing facts, the tokens so faint and broken of a superintending design, the blind evolution of what turn out to be great powers or truths, the progress of things, as if from unreasoning elements, not towards final causes, the greatness and littleness of man, his far-reaching aims, his short duration, the curtain hung over his futurity, the disappointments of life, the defeat of good, the success of evil, physical pain, mental anguish, the prevalence and intensity of sin, the pervading idolatries, the corruptions, the dreary hopeless irreligion, that condition of the whole race, so fearfully yet exactly described in the Apostle's words, 'having no hope and without God in the world,'—all this is a vision to dizzy and appal, and inflicts upon the mind the sense of a profound mystery, which is absolutely beyond human solution.

Whether the inference drawn by Newman from this Pascalian vision of the "incompleteness" of man and human history is valid—that is, that an infallible Church is the providential means to preserve religion in such a world, given up to such purposes—is of course another question. But the fact is that these various passages are all cut from the same cloth: the personal, the cultural, and the universal planes intersect—and all are caught up in a religious vision of the "meaning" of these various levels of experience. Even for those who broke with Newman, and in some cases with all religion, the images continued to reverberate. Part of Newman's continuing power lies in his uncompromising willingness to fling a "dark" and melancholy view of human nature into the teeth of liberal optimism and progressivism, evident even in the easier forms of contemporary religion. Again, Newman's view of man's nature and history is both pre- and sub-theological in its universality, as well as exactly (and quite explicitly) calculated to arrest the new and growing popular consciousness of the day by making it aware of its own shallowness and complacency, as well as its unhistorical character.

Somewhere very central in Matthew Arnold's lifelong campaign to change the consciousness of his English contemporaries lay this multi-level structure of feelings and images presented by Newman; and Arnold, unsurprisingly, was not behindhand in seizing them and shaping them to his own purposes. What is most notable about the famous elevated passages in Arnold is, first, that they form a more or less coherent "myth" regarding Arnold's life, and second, and perhaps more startlingly, that they are the elaboration of, as well as the response to, the pattern established by Newman. Arnold's favored emotions in his most "personal" passages are not merely reminiscential in the general way some critics have noted; instead, they rehearse the experiences of a specially situated group of young men at Oxford in the 1840's, who had felt in various degrees the attraction of Newman, and who in his defection and the collapse of Tractarianism had been—as one of them [Goldwin Smith, in his *Lectures on Modern History,* 1861] put it—cast up as intellectual "wrecks . . . on every shore." Many of them remained permanently unsettled, wandering between two worlds, the "impossible" old and the unspeakable new. Arnold in effect established a new mode in his early poetry for describing the intellectual, emotional, and spiritual situation of a generation of disciples and near-disciples of Newman. Especially in the troubled poetry of the 1852 volume, including the lightly veiled autobiography of "Empedocles on Etna" itself, as well as in "Dover Beach," "The Scholar-Gipsy," "Stanzas from the Grande Chartreuse," and the major poems of the sixties, Arnold again counted the personal costs of honestly facing the new dislocation. More than in Wordsworth, and at least as much as in Byron, he takes as his ostensible subject an elaborate body of historical and literary criticism, but constantly implies that its meaning is inseparable from the special experiences of a small "band" of uniquely placed and specially alert participants—himself and a very few "children of the second birth." Arnold explains (in his first Obermann poem) that *his* generation was born too late to share in "Wordsworth's sweet calm, or Goethe's wide / And luminous view," but that of course they were deeply affected by the still powerful "voices" of that generation during the 1840's; implicitly, and just as importantly, those born too late even to witness the upheaval of the foundations in that decade are perforce cut off from full contact with those sources of deepest poetic and spiritual power, now defunct. (It was *literally* true, as he says of Wordsworth in "Memorial Verses" in 1850, that "The last poetic voice is dumb.")

In effect, Arnold created a powerful myth of a "lost" generation, a myth explored at least as coherently as the individual traumas of that even more cataclysmic decade, the 1790's, and perhaps not so distant from the perennial "lost" mood of the 1920's, caught by Hemingway and Fitzgerald. So successful was Arnold, throughout his career, in embodying this myth of generational loss that the description of his wandering and in-between state became a continually renewable experience (with whatever force of logic) for a host of readers thereafter: sorrow over the "end" of the old world and a bitter distrust of the new, combined with a restrained self-pity and a certain unwillingness to put one's hand firmly to the work of the world—all of these became a permanent "structure" of consciousness for literarily-oriented people. Uncounted readers who have never seen Oxford, and have only the most general impression of the scope of Newman's career and of the issues of the 1840's, regularly feel the "Matthew Arnold" emotions, and have continued to use them to explain their own experience.

Arnold's exploration of his own situation in the poetry, in close proximity to the deeper stratum of contemporary problems, was continued in the prose, but in a somewhat more hopeful vein, and with a shift in the balance of forces. For where in the poetry the center had been the *personal experience* of cultural crisis, now both the framework and the explicit content tended to be the intellectual or spiritual problem itself, "objectively" viewed, and the more personal voice is heard only in momentary, though not ineffective, glances dramatically "lighting up" the intellectual battleground. When this cooler intellectual balance of the prose is shaken and more private passions are glimpsed, the sudden surge of emotion, and sometimes pain, brings the realization that the speaker is indeed the same specially privileged and uniquely placed participant more steadily observable in the poetry. Perhaps the most extraordinary glimpse of this sort occurs at the end of "Pagan and Medieval Religious Sentiment" (1863), where medieval Christianity, up to this point the winner in an apparent struggle with late-pagan religion, is suddenly put aside in favor of the "balance" of Sophocles and his century. But the elevated religious tone of the illustration from Sophocles is followed by a jolting descent into a final fling, of questionable taste but startlingly personal: "Let St. Francis,—nay, or Luther either,—beat that!"

The continual revisiting, and revaluation, of Arnold's own youthful experience is clear enough in the famous passages—such as those on Oxford and Newman, George Sand, the four "voices" heard in the forties, and the virtually autobiographical salute to Falkland. It is important to note that the emotions of these personal passages—loss, regret, separation, alienation—are in effect supplemented by the melancholy and the strong pathos of the controversial touchstones that stud Arnold's prose from the time of the Homer lectures in the 1860's, culminating in "The Study of Poetry" in 1880. The secular touchstones stress, as one critic [John Shepard Eells, *The Touchstones of Matthew Arnold,* 1955] puts it, "the grimness and darkness of the human adventure," centering in loss, pain, grief, death, and the transience of both glory and happiness. The touchstones thus "fill in" the landscape of Arnold's writings and become more universal variants of his most private emotions. Arnold's "Homeric" insistence that "in our life here above ground we have, properly speaking, to enact Hell" is not, I think, very far from Newman's reading of man's life, in the passage on the Vergilian "pain and weariness," and more especially in the "appalling" panorama of human life, in the *Apologia,* as a "profound mystery," the scene of an "aboriginal calamity"—and Newman dwells, precisely, on states of alienation, disappointment, defeat, pain, and anguish.

Still, Arnold's standpoint is *not,* after all, that of Newman, and in the difference lies a crucial divergence of tone and a contrast in artistry. For although Arnold can freely "share" in Newman's own pathos and associate himself with the Tractarians and other Oxford causes ("we in Oxford," "our attachment to . . . beaten causes"), there is a persistent irony, a deep-running doubleness of effect, in some of the most intensely felt passages. The apparent paean to Oxford as the "home of lost causes," in the Preface of 1865, written obviously in the after-glow of the *Apologia,* is a jangle of doubtfully juxtaposed tones. Beautiful and venerable herself, Oxford calls us to perfection and beauty—but as is not uncommon in Arnold, beauty (like "poetry") is distressingly connected with *illusion:* the moonlit adorable queen is a figure of "romance" and "dream" and "enchantment," a worthwhile ideal no doubt, but "unravaged" precisely because not in the *real* world where Philistines have to be engaged frontally, and because in a disabling sense the "home of lost causes, and forsaken beliefs, and unpopular names, and impossible loyalties." The ambiguity of the word "impossible" in the mouth of this "son" of Oxford becomes even clearer in Arnold's companion portrait of Newman in 1883. Even the perceptive Lewis Gates found in the opening a "half-restrained pulsation in the rhythm, an emotional throb that at times almost produces an effect of metre." He finds in the rest of the essay "Arnold's usual colloquial, self-consciously wary tone" [Gates, *Three Studies in Literature,* 1899]. But Saintsbury is far closer to the point when he notes: "In the words about Newman, one seems to recognize very much more than meets the ear—an explanation of much in the Arnoldian gospel, on something like the principle of soured love . . . " [Saintsbury, *Matthew Arnold,* 1899].

There are of course marked differences between the two parts of the Emerson essay, and Gates is correct about the high-pitched tone of the opening. But he entirely misses the complexity and calculation of effect, and finally the pained rejection, in the portrait of Newman. The language is very close to that of the 1865 Preface, and as double-edged. Newman appeals to the "imagination" by "his genius and style"; his is the "charm" of a "spiritual apparition, gliding in the dim afternoon light"; his words were "a religious music,—subtle, sweet, mournful." We are not surprised when Arnold explicitly refers back to the words of 1865 and finds in Newman those "last enchantments of the Middle Age." There is, I think, a half-hint that Newman *staged* his "haunting" mysterious presence; there is an even clearer hint that this "apparition" and figure of "enchantment" is unreal and somehow unsound; above all, *before* he presents this skillfully managed portrait, Arnold could not be more explicit in stating the ground of his reservation: "he has adopted, for the doubts and difficulties which beset men's minds to-day, a solution which, to speak frankly, is impossible." There is, then, an evident element of blame and reproach, and something like heart-broken personal sorrow, in Arnold's dealings with Newman and Oxford, as well as a certain need to put both in their place. Both are among the vital sources of his own most central values, and what he meant by a full and complex humanity: but they had forfeited their right to leadership by neglecting "criticism," "knowledge," "light."

The central cleavage in Arnold's own career lies exposed here: imagination, beauty, emotion, poetry, charm, history, and a full humanity, on the one side, and Arnold's deep and painful commitment not to blink the implications of modern naturalism, on the other. Again, it is a question of one's placement in time, and of having lived through the moment of crisis in the forties: the blankness and "unpoetrylessness" of Arnold's position and that of all who share his views is poignantly evident in the easily overlooked words, "No such voices as those which we heard in our youth at Oxford are sounding there now"—or, he implies, anywhere else! The generation of "Our fathers," "the former men"—Newman, Carlyle, Goethe, Emerson, Wordsworth—is not a repeatable phenomenon for each succeeding generation; at best, they are a receding "source," to be revisited and drawn upon by those who can in fading imagination relive the "in-between" experience of Arnold's own generation. And they, the "fathers," are partly to blame for "our" plight. The result, I think, is that Arnold never quite got over the fear, expressed by the age of thirty, that he was "three parts iced over"; the need for a "second birth" that he preached to Clough meant for himself something like a revival to a half-life, a tentative and somewhat fragile Lazarus-like existence.

If there is a single key passage in which Arnold expresses his mature, and more positive, sense of his relationship to his Oxford past and the possibilities of the future, it occurs in *Culture and Anarchy,* where he describes rather vaguely a "new power" in politics, which rejects the values of middle-class liberalism:

> And who will estimate how much the currents of feeling created by Dr. Newman's movement, the keen desire for beauty and sweetness which it nourished, the deep aversion it manifested to the hardness and vulgarity of middle-class liberalism, the strong light it turned on the hideous and grotesque illusions of middle-class Protestantism,—who will estimate how much all these contributed to swell the tide of secret dissatisfaction which has mined the ground under the self-confident liberalism of the last thirty years, and has prepared the way for its sudden collapse and supersession? It is in this manner that the sentiment of Oxford for beauty and sweetness conquers, and in this manner long may it continue to conquer!

This is, in effect, a kind of allegory of Arnold's own career. He is the newly anointed figure, who relying on Newman's "Oxford" virtues of beauty and sweetness, will continue the work of undermining liberal complacency. It is Arnold's "secret"—and unverifiable—program; as his critics promptly and stingingly complained, since these are intellectual and spiritual attitudes, they somehow exempt him from the task of social amelioration of the usual humdrum and tedious sort. He is the ultimate tightrope-walker, and the stealer of divine fire: the man who barely escaped with his life from the "thrilling summons" of Newman (in "The Voice") also took with him the divine sources of inwardness and high spiritual percipience, guarded by the older "priest" figure. Again, he—Arnold—is specially placed, by history and temperament, to save the world, if it will listen; he has unique control over the necessary secret he has managed to carry over into the new era. Taken as a whole, Arnold's writings form a kind of complex *Bildungsroman,* or even a quest-romance, in which the son (of Thomas Arnold and Newman) who is the apparent failure, succeeds to a position of leadership, by carrying on more adequately the program which the "fathers" were unable to carry to completion.

The strongly autobiographical flavor of much of the Victorian prose I have been discussing provides an implicit but effective unity, linking apparently diverse modes and tones of expression. Whole careers in Victorian prose can be legitimately read as being as intensely and continuously "autobiographical" as the career of any novelist or poet. A number of writers—De Quincey, Carlyle, Newman, Ruskin, Arnold, and even Pater—spend their lives defining and redefining their own vocations, shaping and reshaping their past experience for present purposes, while ostensibly talking about something else: society, literature, or religion. Most importantly, Victorian "argumentative" prose uses memory as a medium of indirect persuasion, authenticating its more explicit views in a body of palpable and not easily refuted experience. I have dwelt at length here on Newman and Arnold because of the extraordinary complexity of their positions, and because Arnold's conception of his own career is so continuously, if ironically, intertwined with Newman's strategies of self-presentation, and because both men have remained vital forces even into our own time—their vitality being proved by the periodic need felt by many to "expose" or resist their claims on us. Moreover, their most famous personal and emotive passages, when examined closely, reveal—sometimes more exactly than their explicit argumentation—an "inner structure" of feeling and attitude that is the organizing pattern of their entire careers. (pp. 3-17)

David J. DeLaura, "The Allegory of Life: The Autobiographical Impulse in Victorian Prose," in Wascana Review, *Vol. 12, No. 1, Spring, 1977, pp. 3-20.*

Barbara Charlesworth Gelpi

[Gelpi is a Colombian-born American educator and critic specializing in Victorian and women's studies. In the following essay, she examines parallels between several Victorian autobiographies and popular fiction of the day, focusing especially on the novels of Charles Dickens.]

Through the winter months of 1853-54, just at the time when Dickens was visiting Preston to get material for *Hard Times,* John Stuart Mill was writing his *Autobiography.* The fact that Dickens' fictional version of utilitarian education is remarkably close to Mill's factual description of his own upbringing has already been noted, and the resemblances are probably not mere coincidence. It is surely possible and even likely that when Dickens described Thomas Gradgrind's catechizing of Bitzer he had in mind stories which he had heard about James Mill's education of his son, even though he could not, of course, have read the *Autobiography.* For by the time that John Stuart Mill met John Sterling in 1828, the story of Mill's childhood training had already become legend. Mill writes that Sterling "told me how he and others had looked upon me (from hearsay information) as a 'made' or manufactured man, having had a certain impress of opinion stamped on me which I could only reproduce." Then, too, by 1854 it seems more than likely that Carlyle, to whom *Hard Times* was dedicated and whom Dickens knew well, was keeping that legend alive—and, since Carlyle and John Stuart Mill were no longer friends, making the Mills, *père et fils,* both into mechanical men, satanic Mills to whom the very name of Gradgrind may punningly allude. So the facts of Mill's life may have been grist for Dickens' mill; that is a straightforward enough possibility. Yet is it not also feasible that the fantasies of Dickens' novels had an effect on Mill's account of his facts?

In his study of the autobiographical form [*Design and Truth in Autobiography,* 1960] Roy Pascal has discussed the importance to the Victorian novel of the great autobiographies of Goethe, Rousseau, and Wordsworth. Peter Coveney in *The Image of Childhood* and Jerome Buckley in his essay on the *Bildungsroman* have noted the impress particularly of Wordsworthian autobiographical feeling and beliefs about childhood upon Dickens and the incalculable but certainly enormous influence that Dickens' vision of childhood had in turn upon all Victorians. Say then that Dickens, moved by Wordsworthian theory and practice and motivated as well by obsessive images drawn from memories of his own childhood, writes *David Copperfield.* The character he portrays draws into himself all his author's ideas and feelings and then becomes a focus, an "archetypal image" if you will, for thoughts and feelings of Dickens' readers. Therefore I think it a mistake to say, as Wayne Shumaker does in *English Autobiography,* that the rise of the novel and of the autobiography are parallel but that one does not stand in "causal relation" to the other. The relationship may not be simply "causal," but neither are the two forms parallel and unrelated. They are interlaced: the rise in the number and quality of autobiographies becomes marked with the beginning of the Romantic period; that rise leads to a new emphasis in early Victorian novels on the mystery of the individual's growth and change through the interaction of all those things that make up his or her character and circumstances; that emphasis in turn brings even greater numbers of mid-Victorians to meditate on the facts of their own particular lives against the backdrop of the novelists' and—since he was the most widely read—especially Dickens' fantasies.

Therefore the nature of those fantasies which a society finds most compelling is very important: like the beautiful statues which pregnant Greek women were to gaze upon in order to produce beautiful children, a compelling story in art works its influence upon life. It forms, and, if it is unbalanced or untrue or misunderstood, it may deform. Both Peter Coveney [*The Image of Childhood,* 1967] and Angus Wilson ["Dickens on Children and Childhood," *Dickens 1970,* ed. Michael Slater, 1970] in their studies of the children in Dickens' novels believe that in mediating the Romantic image of the child to the Victorians Dickens marred it and sentimentalized it by his self-pity. Wilson, however, does not entirely agree with Coveney; he, like Jerome Buckley, sees Dickens as growing out of that self-pity by the time he wrote *Great Expectations,* and he has a good argument. But before Pip came Little Nell, Oliver Twist, Paul Dombey, David Copperfield, and Jo the street sweeper. Their stories were read by John Ruskin, John Stuart Mill, and Walter Pater, and it is my belief that these men in their autobiographical writings were influenced to "see" themselves as Dickensian waifs, those small people who cast such long shadows over the Victorian sensibility. Using Mill's *Autobiography* as a focus, I would like to consider the similarities between the autobiographers' relation of facts and Dickens' heart-wringing fantasies.

First: loneliness. When Mill was growing up, his family lived in a small, cramped house. The large table at which he and his father worked filled one end of a room occupied also by his harassed mother and the many younger children. In the *Autobiography* only the table remains and the figure of his father. Brothers and sisters who must be tutored appear, but only as potential or actual sources of difficulty, never as companions. Mill had no friends, or, to put it in his own words, "He [James Mill] completely succeeded in preserving me from the sort of influence he so much dreaded." Pater too lived in a small house with his mother, grandmother, aunt, two sisters, and a brother, but save for a mother and a little sister, his semiautobiographical figure, Florian Deleal, in "The Child in the House" is always alone. Ruskin was, in fact, an only child, born to middle-aged parents; nevertheless he had some visits with cousins, and from the time he was ten he had his cousin Mary as a companion. Yet he considers it the "dominant calamity" of his upbringing that, as he flatly states, "I had nothing to love." Like so many of Dickens' children all three writers have little or no sense of emotional bond with loving parental figures, and their interaction with other children, when it occurs at all, if happy, is brief—if unhappy, is only another cause for feelings of alienation.

Like Dickens' waifs too all three autobiographers are extraordinarily observant. The child Ruskin, deprived of almost all toys and turning his quick eyes to "examining the knots in the wood of the floor, or counting the bricks in the opposite houses," is a figure to haunt the imagination, and Pater's Florian lives with extraordinary awareness of "the material objects" about him. Can the same be said of Mill, however? There are no descriptions of place in the *Autobiography,* no attempts to describe faces or to give exact conversations. For the effectiveness of his story, however, such particulars are better absent. On what, after all, *should* the eyes of young Mill be fixed? On books. And so they are. The titles of the books lying on that large table, the Greek words written on cards: these come before us with extraordinary clarity. "The green fields and wild flowers" through which he walked with his father, repeating his lessons all the while, are described with only the words I have quoted, but "the account I gave him daily of what I had read the day before," the slips of paper containing notes, the books discussed and what was said about them: all that detail is seen and heard again through the eyes and ears of a quick, docile child.

Their intelligent sensitivity to impressions and ideas gave all three autobiographers a great need for parental love and understanding to help them deal with the ideas flooding in upon them, but, like Dickens' lonely children, they did not get such love or do not remember getting it. Pater's father died when he was very young, as did the fathers in "The Child in the House" and *Marius the Epicurean.* The mothers in these stories are vaguely beneficent but withdrawn, shadowy figures. Very telling, however, is the note of resentment in "Emerald Uthwart," a story based in part on Pater's experiences at King's School, Canterbury. Since his older brother seems not to have gone to the school, nor, of course, did his sisters, there is significance in the narrator's comment on Emerald's schooling: "Little by little he [Emerald, youngest of the brothers but "not the youngest of the family"] comes to understand that, while the brothers are indulged with lessons at home, are some of them free even of these and placed already in the world, where, however, there remains no place for him, he is to go to school, chiefly for the convenience of others . . . "

Mill has no sense of having been loved by his father, for none of the considerable attention that James Mill gave him had for the boy any tinge of loving-kindness or concern. Mill writes: "The element which was chiefly deficient in his [James Mill's] moral relation to his children, was that of tenderness." He goes on to describe his father as a "typical" Englishman in that, although originally a man of strong feelings, he had habitually repressed them until, to all intents and purposes, they disappeared. Add to this his father's constitutional irritability and the child's continual state of fear, and one gets the result baldly stated in Mill's early draft but then canceled: " . . . my father's children neither loved him, nor, with any warmth of affection, any one else."

Surprisingly, it seems to have been Mill's conscious intention in writing the *Autobiography* to pay tribute to his father. At least, after writing it he believed that he had done so. In 1865 he wrote to George Grote, thanking him for a review in which he alluded to James Mill's distinction in history and philosophy. "I am glad," Mill writes, "that you take the opportunity of doing justice to my father. My own contribution to his memory is already written in a MS designed for posthumous publication . . . " So he seems to have remembered what he had written eleven years before, but in fact the scenes described between James Mill and his son can well match those between Mr. Dombey and his daughter Florence, Mr. Bumble and Oliver Twist, or Mr. Murdstone and David Copperfield. Not that Mill's scenes are presented with any of the overt pathos that Dickens uses; they are, indeed, underplayed, but Mill's litotes has its own powerful effect.

In one scene, for instance, we are presented with a three- or four-year-old John and his father sitting at the single table, John working at his Greek, his father writing *The History of India.* No Greek-English lexicon was yet in print, and John, who knew no Latin, could not use the Greek-Latin lexicon. Therefore, "I was forced to have recourse to him for the meaning of every word which I did not know. This incessant interruption he, one of the most impatient of men, submitted to. . . . " We have all the information we need, and Mill, with filial delicacy, withdraws, leaving it to the imagination of his readers to reconstruct *how* his impatient father submitted to interruption and how he, the child, felt, torn between fear of interrupting and fear of making a mistake in his lesson.

Occasionally Mill allows himself a negative comment. For instance, describing his lessons in Greek elocution he writes: "Of all the things which he required me to do, there was none which I did so constantly ill, or in which he so perpetually lost his temper with me," and adds meekly, "but I even then remarked (though I did not venture to make the remark to him) that though he reproached me when I read a sentence ill, and *told* me how I ought to have read it, he never, by reading it himself, *shewed* me how it ought to be read." *Praeterita* is filled with examples of a similar meekness masking still-felt bitterness and at last getting its revenge, not the resounding last word which Betsy Trotwood inflicts on the Murdstones, but powerful nonetheless.

The effect of constant "negative reinforcement" upon Ruskin and Mill as upon Dickens' waifs is a haunting sense of their inadequacy and clumsiness. (In Pater's case there is only the negative evidence that he was too self-conscious about what he took to be his physical ungainliness and ugliness to write about them; his semiautobiographical figures bear no physical resemblance to him.) Just as her father's presence is a constraint upon "the natural grace and freedom" of Florence Dombey's thoughts and actions and as David Copperfield becomes "sullen, dull, and dogged" under the tutelage of Mr. Murdstone, so Mill describes himself as clumsy, inept, and awkward. For these qualities he says that he "merited reproof," but in fact he turns the reproof on his father for harassing him with "severe admonitions" about his "slackness" while providing him with only the stimulus of mental activity. Ruskin too blames his parents for everything from his shyness in company to his inability to swim or to ride a horse.

Ruskin's situation was the opposite of Mill's in that his mother was the domestic tyrant, his father the passive observer of her rules, and without much reading between the lines one can sense the reproach Ruskin feels toward his father, who might have given him so much more had he not worried about "infringing any of mother's rules." The end result was the same for both Mill and Ruskin, however, in that (again like so many children in Dickens' novels) intellectually and emotionally browbeaten yet painfully intelligent and aware, feeling their "backwardness" while at the same time resenting the overbearing figure who made them so conscious of inadequacy, they had no consoling mother to whom they might turn for comfort.

Dickens' children are usually bereft of their mothers through death, that absence being then no fault of the mothers. So Oliver Twist, Little Nell, the Dombey children, David Copperfield, Esther Summerson—all are motherless. As a novelist Dickens was thus able to take much though not all of the sting out of his portrayal of these mothers' inadequacy, but his own autobiographical sketch helps to explain why he took the mothers offstage. After Dickens' father was released from debtors' prison, he quarreled with the relative for whom Dickens worked at the blacking factory, and Dickens lost his job there. His mother went down the next day to try to get it back. "My father said, I should go back no more, and should go to school. I do not write resentfully or angrily: for I know how all these things have worked together to make me what I am: but I never afterwards forgot, I never shall forget, I never can forget, that my mother was warm from my being sent back."

. . . [A] new emphasis in early Victorian novels on the mystery of the individual's growth and change through the interaction of all those things that make up his or her character and circumstances . . . brings even greater numbers of mid-Victorians to meditate on the facts of their own particular lives against the backdrop of the novelists' and—since he was the most widely read—especially Dickens' fantasies.

—Barbara Charlesworth Gelpi

Mill, without the novelist's privilege of killing the mother in symbolic portrayal of the child's utter loneliness, achieves a similar effect, perhaps finally a more telling effect, by never mentioning her at all. The reader is left to suppose that, like the well-brought-up child, he is saying nothing when he cannot say something nice, and therefore the silence about his mother is a speaking void. It conveys its message even better than the statement made in the early draft of the *Autobiography* and then canceled. There he puts the final "blame" for the coldness and fear of the house in which he was brought up not on his father but on his mother: "That rarity in England, a really warm hearted mother, would in the first place have made my father a different being, and in the second would have made the children grow up loving and being loved. But my mother, with the very best intentions, only knew how to pass her life in drudging for them." Mill's bitterness is irrational and his contemptuous dismissal of the drudging unkind. Anything we can infer about James Mill's character suggests that not a single goddess alone but a combination of Aphrodite and Minerva, just for a start, would have been needed to make him a totally different being. Mill's fantasy of an all-powerful, all-healing mother figure is an interesting one, however, and not unrelated to similar fantasies in Dickens' work, but consideration of it lies outside the scope of this essay.

In sum, Mill's descriptions of his childhood self give him the qualities of "typical" Dickensian waif-children, although the method by which he achieves his characterization is the precise opposite of Dickens'. He works more through what he does not say than what he says; an aristocratic and quiet aloofness or a carefully precise concern to give praise or credit where due and assign blame as charitably and quietly as possible: this is his manner. There are in his work no death scenes, no whippings, no descriptions of poverty or loneliness or terror, no denunciations of man's inhumanity—none of the things, in short, that we tend to consider Dickensian. But to take Mill's seeming rationality and his calm interest in pedagogical method at face value is to misread the *Autobiography.* The interior life it describes (albeit unconsciously) is as tempestuous as that of any Dickens novel and indeed closely resembles the Dickensian "plot."

If it be granted that there are parallels between Dickens' fantasies and the autobiographers' remembrance of their facts, what then? How is it significant that the Dickensian waif strays off the written page and into life? A sociologist might find in the similarities between literature and life a proof that Dickens' novels are more factual and less fantastical than they seem, and the parallels open interesting lines of speculation about the "politics" of the Victorian home. That approach, however, deals with these events as facts, and my interest here is not so much with the facts themselves as with what the autobiographers made of the facts—with the incidents and personalities they chose to remember and with the emotions surrounding remembered events in a luminous haze. Since self-pity is dominant among those emotions, the case I have made might be used as further evidence in justification of Coveney's position and Buckley's on the destructive effects of self-pity; it works against "perfection of the life" just as, in Dickens' novels, it was damaging to "perfection of the work."

Thus the self-pity evident in Pater's semiautobiographical pieces might be another explanation besides that of T. S. Eliot ["Arnold and Pater," in his *Selected Essays, 1917-1932*] for the note of "inexhaustible, discontent, languor, and homesickness" in Pater's work. Eliot ascribes it to the loss of genuine religious faith, and his dislike of Pater's ideas makes him overstate his case. The note is not as all-pervasive as he suggests, but it is there, and a curious passage in *Marius the Epicurean* may help to explain it. Marius's mother dies while away from home, and the narrator comments: "For it happened that, through some sudden, incomprehensible petulance of his, there had been an angry childish gesture, and a slighting word, at the very moment of her departure, actually for the last time . . . the thought of that marred parting having peculiar bitterness for one, who set so much store, both by principle and habit, on the sentiment of home." Pater makes Marius's domestic feeling sound like a virtue, but "the sentiment of home," if based on unresolved bitterness, guilt, and self-pity, makes only for awareness of homelessness—makes then for alienation.

Ruskin's self-pity makes him see his life as failed and indeed does frustrate the full effectiveness of what is nonetheless a towering achievement. Moving restlessly from project to project, he can take little or no pleasure in what he has done but broods instead about unfulfilled and now unrealizable ambitions: "And if only . . . my father and mother had seen the real strengths and weaknesses of their little John . . . they would have made a man of me there and then, and afterwards the comfort of their own hearts, and probably the first geologist of my time in England."

The stultifying effect of self-pity may also help to explain the halt in Mill's mental growth after a certain point in his life: "From this time [around 1840] I have no further changes to tell of," he writes in 1854. And it is true that once he has described the importance of his relationship with Harriet Taylor, whom he met in 1830, he chronicles external events almost exclusively and describes no further inner changes of attitude. James Olney in his study of autobiography called *Metaphors of Self* attributes this halt to Mill's lack of feeling, but in my opinion his reading of Mill's personality is entirely wrong. Not lack of feeling but violent feelings of pity for his childhood self, of bitterness at the loss of potential selves he could imagine but could not become, may have kept Mill from coming to a final totality of vision.

Just as in *Art and Illusion* E. H. Gombrich has shown Ruskin's aesthetic theory of "the innocence of the eye," the perception of colors as he imagined a child would see them, to be based on a false physiology and a false psychology, so, as Coveney has pointed out, Sigmund Freud earlier proved the theory of an originally "innocent I" to be false psychology creating in turn false pedagogy and false sociology. It is Coveney's hunch that the whole feeling for childhood and innocence in the Victorian period may be an aspect of the Victorians' sexual repression; the child is a symbol of "purity," and when he does not live up to the symbol he embodies, he is treated savagely. Freud, by destroying the idea of childhood's sexual innocence, was actually preserving the "original romantic assertion of childhood's importance, and its vulnerability to social victimization."

That Mill, Ruskin, and Pater all show the effects of Victorian sexual repression goes without saying. But again, Coveney's use of Freudian theory turns more on the treatment of actual children and the children's remembrance of their upbringing than it does on the idea of the child and the symbolic significance for adults of their childhood years. There remains the question: what in the first place (putting aside, perhaps unfairly, for argument's sake the beauty and power of its language) gave a poem like "Ode: Intimations of Immortality from Recollections of Early Childhood" the impact it had on Dickens and through him on the Victorians? What in turn gave Dickens' fictitious children such a hold on Victorian imaginations?

The vision of the child for which Wordsworth found expression in the "Ode" and which, of course, our autobiographers experienced through the work directly as well as through its effects upon Dickens—is one of potential, perhaps infinite potential, frustrated by finite circumstance. To appreciate the power of the image Wordsworth called up one must consider not only Freudian theory on the importance of actual childhood but also Carl Jung's theories about the archetype of the child, an archetype which, he writes [in his *Archetypes and the Collective Unconscious*], "symbolizes the pre-conscious and post-conscious essence of man. His pre-conscious essence is the unconscious state of earliest childhood; his post-conscious essence is an anticipation by analogy of life after death. In this idea the all-embracing nature of psychic wholeness is expressed." When he uses the phrase "by analogy" Jung means, as Wordsworth seems to mean in the "Ode," that the sense of earlier "glory" leads to a sense of future glory, not necessarily in an afterlife but in certain states of mind that the notion of "afterlife" symbolizes. The child is a "mighty Prophet" of the soul's infinity; the sense of that infinity may time and again be lost, but through the image of the child it can at moments be recaptured.

Jung's explanation of the symbol, then, would be that it arises in answer to the human desire for all that is contained by the phrase "fullness of life." His thoughts about the image of the child also help to explain the great importance it takes on in early nineteenth-century literature. It is Jung's belief that the image of the child appears when the unconscious aspects of the psyche have been "repressed to the point of total exclusion." Thus it arises—and Blake, Wordsworth, and Coleridge were all consciously so using it—as an answer to the excessive rationality of the eighteenth century's dominant cast of mind. The children in *Songs of Innocence,* the little girl in "We Are Seven," "the limber elf" at the conclusion to part 2 of *Christabel* all effortlessly enjoy a vision, a sense of themselves, that the rational adults around them cannot fathom but can resent and try to frustrate. Dickens in the same way sets up Sissy Jupe's childish wisdom as an answer to Gradgrind's methodology, and in Mill's *Autobiography,* suffering little John becomes a similar reproach against and answer to the systematizing James. Excessive rationality divides mind from feeling and at least destroys feeling, as, according to his son's theory, it destroyed James Mill's feeling. Excessive morality (related to rationality) divides action from instinct as it divided Margaret Ruskin's methods of child rearing from her maternal instinct. The child is an image of wholeness set up against these divisions. "It represents," writes Jung, "the strongest, the most ineluctable urge in every being, namely the urge to realize itself"—and to realize itself as a whole: mind and feeling, will and emotion, act and instinct, psyche and soma.

This archetypal significance casts what Jung would call a "noumen" around the image of the child; the portentousness of the child as symbol, then, may offer another explanation besides Angus Wilson's for the mysterious wisdom often found in Dickens' "little people." Wilson calls children like Paul Dombey, Little Nell, and Tiny Tim "gnomic" and sees their characterization as deriving from Dickens' "reminiscence of himself in those castaway months [at the blacking factory]." While interested in these children, Wilson finds fault with the qualities of morbidity and sentimentality in their characterization and blames these artistic lapses on Dickens' constant memory of his childhood suffering. Without denying his interpretation, I would add the possibility that in portraying children Dickens is moved not only by self-pity but at a deeper level by the archetypal image of the child. The symbolic "weight" of the archetype is not applicable to any particular child, whether actually or imaginatively "real." In trying to bring the symbol and the fact together Dickens has the same difficulties that Wordsworth suffered when he devoted a stanza of the "Ode" to "a six years' Darling of a pigmy size."

Jung's description of the archetype of the child offers an insight, then, into the meaning of the symbol itself and helps explain as well the significance of its appearance early in the nineteenth century. But perhaps most interesting of all is the rationale his essay gives for those qualities of personality that I found both Dickens' fictional children and the autobiographers' remembered ones to have in common—and here, lest I seem to have set up those qualities with Jung in mind from the beginning, let me say that I had noted the parallels and written my description of them before I came across Jung's essay on the child symbol. An explanation for the relevance of his insights to my theme must lie in what Jung himself might term "synchronicity" and not in scholarly artful dodging.

The child's loneliness and separation from parents are concomitants of the way in which the archetype finds expression in myth, dream, or story because, according to Jung, "the motifs of 'insignificance,' exposure, abandonment, danger, etc., try to show how precarious is the psychic possibility of wholeness, that is, the enormous difficulties to be met with in attaining this 'highest good'." He gives another explanation as well: the child symbolizes a move toward greater consciousness, greater understanding than that previously available, and such consciousness is necessarily *"all alone in the world."*

To a world that simply cannot understand it the potentially new consciousness expressed through the child may seem clumsy and stupid, but the awkward-looking child possesses an intelligence and awareness far greater than those around it: "It is a striking paradox in all child myths that the 'child' is on the one hand delivered helpless into the power of terrible enemies and in continual danger of extinction, while on the other he possesses powers far exceeding those of ordinary humanity. This is closely related to the psychological fact that though the child may be 'insignificant,' 'unknown,' 'a mere child,' he is also divine."

The archetype appears, Jung believes, as prognostic of a change in consciousness, and ideally that change should involve a departure from earlier, more restricted ways into a new vision of life and life's meaning. For the process to come to completion, however, the fantasist, poet, visionary, autobiographer, or taleteller must separate what Jung calls his "personal infantilism"—that is, his memories of himself as an abandoned or misunderstood or unjustly treated child—from his sense of what the memories signify. He must come to see that the oppressed child of his imagination is at least partly the expression of the heart's hunger for totality of being and that the blame laid upon his parents and his upbringing is in fact a cry against all that divides the self. Paradoxically, if he does not make that dissociation, the image of the child instead of serving to integrate consciousness has the effect of creating a deeper alienation because it stirs up the divisive emotions of anger, bitterness, and self-pity, and the vision of an innocent "I" entangles the visionary in an ever deeper loss of innocence.

A way of thinking about Dickens' and the autobiographers' self-pity, then, is to see it as arising from their failure to dissociate the archetypal symbol of the child from memory's image of their childhood selves. Of such a failure the *I Ching* would say "no blame," and besides, of course, all had some cause to pity themselves. Still the genuine pity of it is that the image of the child if properly understood says that no one need feel sorry for himself. It invites us to rejoice. (pp. 57-71)

Barbara Charlesworth Gelpi, "The Innocent I: Dickens' Influence on Victorian Autobiography," in The Worlds of Victorian Fiction, *edited by Jerome H. Buckley, Cambridge, Mass.: Harvard University Press, 1975, pp. 57-71.*

Elizabeth K. Helsinger

[In the following essay, Helsinger examines Ruskin's Praeterita *as the most noteworthy of a number of "poetic alternatives to spiritual or crisis autobiography" in Victorian English literature. According to Helsinger,* Praeterita *typifies the Victorian poet's rejection of Romantic introspection and his deviation from the traditional objectives and conventions of prose autobiography.]*

Ruskin's *Praeterita* is a strangely self-destructive autobiography. It was evidently written by a man who did not like himself. He measures his achievements, professional and personal, and concludes he is a failure. The book seems deliberately to refuse the minimum we expect from autobiography: a retrospective account of the writer's life which discovers some order, consistency, and purpose in past actions, a progress toward his present self. *Praeterita* lacks focus. There are no definable principles of inclusion. It is digressive in form. Unimportant people provide subjects for much anecdotal reminiscence, while many people of particular importance to Ruskin are barely mentioned or entirely omitted. The absence of introspection in all his memories is striking. Regret for lost opportunities is so frequent that it becomes obtrusive. The tone of discontent is pervasive. *Praeterita* is hardly adequate as personal history or apology. It is an apparently perverse undertaking, almost a sabotage of the self.

In place of a completed self Ruskin offers something much more tentative: a peculiar sensibility. A sensibility is not an achieved identity, but a given receptiveness. Friendships and accomplishments, even education, seem to have affected this core of identity very little. This, I think, is one reason why the expected autobiographical content of *Praeterita,* presented in chronological fashion, is often so unsatisfactory. Ruskin's minimal sense of self was powerfully touched by places, not people, and his accounts of certain scenes are the most emotionally charged passages in the book. These experiences do not, however, form a pattern of growth, a progressive development toward the achieved self of the moment of writing. They give us instead a series of repetitions and returns through which Ruskin's sense of his original identity, the peculiar sensibility of his "tadpole" self, is steadily intensified. These descriptive passages, closely linked by imagery and by conscious recall, give *Praeterita* a definite structure it first seems to lack.

That structure, depending on the metaphoric and affective connections between place and state of mind, is potentially a powerful one for autobiography—we think of Proust, of course. It was also closely fitted to Ruskin's habits of mind and attitudes toward himself. He had successfully used a similar structure in his critical writing for thirty years. But in the process of writing *Praeterita* Ruskin seems to have tried to follow two conflicting models for autobiography. On the one hand, he was drawing a portrait of a sensibility reflected in the scenes to which it characteristically responded. At the same time he was also attempting to discern a more traditional historical pattern: the growth of a mind in a single direction, marked by spiritual crisis revealing that direction, and culminating in a present identity confirmed by achievement. *Praeterita* is of special interest because Ruskin's dissatisfaction with the aims and structures of autobiography was shared by other Victorians, who, like him, experimented with new ways of writing about themselves.

Praeterita is part of a shift in ways of viewing one's life which took place between Wordsworth's *The Prelude* and Pater's "Conclusion" to *The Renaissance.* Wordsworth, at the beginning of his autobiographical poem, is lifted by the "gentle breeze" of inspiration to one of the imagination's lookout points, from which he sees spread out before him both life and poem as a single path from past to present. "With a heart / Joyous, nor scared at its own liberty," he cries out, "I cannot miss my way." Pater concludes his *Renaissance* on a note of subdued sadness, apologizing for the impressions which he has substituted for biography: "To such a tremulous wisp constantly reforming itself on the stream, to a single sharp impression, with a sense in it, a relic more or less fleeting, of such moments gone by, what is real in our life fines itself down. It is with this movement, with the passage and dissolution of impressions, images, sensations, that analysis leaves off—that continual vanishing away, that strange, perpetual weaving and unweaving of ourselves." For Pater, the road connecting past and present is no longer an appropriate image for the self. One's life is not a stream but "a tremulous wisp constantly reforming itself on the stream." The self has no continuous existence in time which memory can retrieve, and so cannot define itself through chronological narrative. Representative experience may evoke memories of similar situations or responses ("a single sharp impression, with a sense in it . . . of such moments gone by"), but to extend this atemporal sense of recognition into a consistent progressive sequence is to construct a fiction which is psychologically false and philosophically impossible.

Autobiographers earlier in the century, like Tennyson's Ulysses, "cannot rest from travel." They share his "gray spirit yearning in desire / To follow knowledge"—self-knowledge, the end of the quest which is a shaping metaphor of life itself and of the autobiography which narrates it. Tennyson's Ulysses is already strangely slow to depart. Pater gives up the voyage entirely, turning from Ulysses' mode of self-exploration to Penelope's, "that strange, perpetual weaving and unweaving of ourselves." In 1868 and 1873, when Pater's "Conclusion" was published, his Penelope was condemned for seducing young men from the Ulyssean quest. Twenty years later in 1888, when Pater reprinted the suppressed "Conclusion," an increasing number of Victorian Ulysses were dead or permanently shipwrecked. The time of the Penelopean autobiographer was at hand. Ruskin began the last volume of *Praeterita* in the same year.

The prose autobiographies of the high Victorian period show few radical departures from a tradition which reaches from Wordsworth back to Saint Augustine. In this context, *Praeterita* is a disappointing and puzzling anomaly in style, structure, and the attitudes toward the self which underlie it. The major Victorian poets, however, expressed in the 1850s their discontent with Wordsworth's sublime egotism and experimented with poetic structures which would allow them to explore a different concept of selfhood. These poetic alternatives to spiritual or crisis autobiography prepare the way for Pater's Penelope. In both form and content they provide the closest contemporary parallels for *Praeterita.*

Neither Ruskin nor Tennyson, Browning, and Arnold were comfortable with sustained self-reflection as a subject for their writing. Their common judgment of introspection, especially in public, was that it was "morbid," unhealthy both for the poet and for his readers. Arnold puts it succinctly: "the dialogue of the mind with itself" is a characteristic subject of modern poetry, and too often it creates a situation "in which the suffering finds no vent in action; in which a continuous state of mental distress is prolonged, unrelieved by incident, hope, or resistance. . . . In such situations there is inevitably something morbid, in the description of them something monotonous. When they occur in actual life, they are painful, not tragic; the representation of them in poetry is painful also." Ruskin called modern poetry the poetry of pathetic fallacy: a poetry of feeling in which the poet's concern with himself colors all his perceptions. "The temperament which admits the pathetic fallacy" he judged "weak," and its perceptions not only "inaccurate" but "morbid." Tennyson spoke out against "all those morbid and introspective" modern tales, and once advised a young man to "develop his true self . . . by casting aside all maudlin and introspective morbidities. . . . " John Stuart Mill, after reading the young Browning's "Pauline," wrote that "the writer seems to me possessed with a more intense and morbid self-consciousness than I ever knew in any sane human being." Browning never forgot Mill's acerbic comment on his first long poem.

There are several possible reasons for the Victorians' dislike of direct exploration or exhibition of the self in literature. In the first place, they find introspection fruitless; it does *not* lead to a visionary knowledge of self and world, the prelude to action which autobiographers from Augustine to Wordsworth promised. The isolated quest for private identity is, in the Victorian experience, almost always a failure. Empedocles' "dialogue of the mind with itself" leads him to despair and death; Childe Roland's quest gives him at most a final revelation of the futility of his questing life. The Victorians know what Wordsworth never quite admitted: that self-discovery has become not the prelude to an active life but a substitute for it.

Arnold is spokesman for those who see these failures as a phenomenon peculiar to their times, to "an age wanting in moral grandeur," "an age of spiritual discomfort." Ruskin also associates the poetry of pathetic fallacy with what he calls the "cloudy" modern temper, a quality of mind distinguished by its preference for vagueness, darkness, and change. Poets like Dante whose perceptions were not affected by strong personal feeling saw more clearly than modern poets—they "saw life steadily and saw it whole," in Arnold's phrase. Ruskin concludes that they saw by the light of faith, which the moderns do not have. But there is something strange in these explanations. Both Arnold and Ruskin include the romantics together with themselves in their condemnation of the age. When they talk about the handicap of belonging to the modern age or temper, they do not simply mean the difficulty of being last romantics in a time of material prosperity. That is our analysis of their failure to follow romantic example. Both men did aspire to imaginative quests for identity through poetry, but they found the experience painful and fruitless. Their explanation is that solitary questing is itself a symptom of the moral atmosphere of the times. The best poets, Arnold declares, "do not talk of their mission, nor of interpreting their age, nor of the coming Poet; all this, they know, is the mere delirium of vanity." Arnold's last phrase is telling. The strongest reason for the Victorian objection to self-revealing literature seems to be not that it fails to lead to identity and action, but that it is "the mere delirium of vanity," an act of selfish pride. Their objection is profoundly moral. It is an attitude which can be found throughout the literature of the period. Tennyson's Princess, for example, is a blatant egoist. "On me, me, me, the storm first breaks," she cries: "*I* dare / All these male thunderbolts." Her precipitate fall is not just Tennyson's condemnation of her masculinity; it is a punishment for the moral sin of pride. In fact, Victorian critics and poets were right when they said that the quest for identity was usually painful and fruitless; their conviction that it was ethically wrong insured that they would find such selfhood a burden and turn aside from internal quests.

The injunction to forget oneself to find oneself is, of course, a commonplace of Christian and romantic tradition, but the Victorians took it further. Christians must remember God, and God, according to Augustine, will "recollect" the Christian, giving him a sense of himself he will only discover in the experience of conversion. The romantic poet seeks self-forgetfulness in imaginative experience, which will, in turn, offer the poet an identity. For many Victorians, such pursuits remained too self-involved, especially when they became subjects for literature. The way out was a deliberate shift in focus from the self to mutuality: friendship and marriage; or to community: the writer's concern for his audience and the reformer's vision of society. At the very least, the escape from self-involvement led the writer to complain of isolation, to criticize his romantic predecessors, and to subvert the forms of introspective literature, even when he continued to practice them.

Tennyson's *In Memoriam* is the clearest and earliest example of an autobiographical poem which opposes the internal quest for identity. For Tennyson, an identity independent of other people and even of achievements other than the act of self-discovery is an isolating identity. It is the child's painful sense of self to which his loss of Hallam threatened to return him.

> The baby new to earth and sky,
> What time his tender palm is prest
> Against the circle of the breast,
> Has never thought that "this is I";
> But as he grows he gathers much,
> And learns the use of "I" and "me,"
> And finds "I am not what I see,
> And other than the things I touch."
>
> So rounds he to a separate mind
> From whence clear memory may begin,
> As thro' the frame that binds him in
> His isolation grows defined.
>
> [Sec. 45]

At the deepest point of his despair at Hallam's death, Tennyson is further reduced to the baby's helpless inability to say that "this is I":

> . . . but what am I?
> An infant crying in the night;
> An infant crying for the light,
> And with no language but a cry.
>
> [Sec. 54]

The loss of Hallam is the loss of the sense of himself which their friendship had given Tennyson—a mature sense of self which had replaced the baby's fears of nonexistence and the child's isolating identity. The most frightening consequence of the death is not Tennyson's loss of faith in a fatherly God and a benign Nature, but his sense of a dissolving self, the return of what he sees as the infant's terror that he and the rest of his world will cease to exist when the lights go out. The infant's cry in the night is Tennyson's cry to Hallam in the great section 50: "Be near me when my light is low. . . . Be near me when I fade way." Without Hallam, Tennyson must, like the infant, begin again the isolating process of self-discovery. To learn that "I am not what I see, / And other than the things I touch" will protect him from the infant's night fears, but at the price of erecting a "frame that binds him in" and secures his isolation.

In Memoriam makes clear, however, that Tennyson has no desire to seize the occasion of Hallam's death to forge an independent identity for himself. The resolution of his poem is his recovery of Hallam's companionship: "A friendship as had master'd Time; / Which masters Time indeed, and is / Eternal, separate from fears" (sec. 85). The closing lyrics assert again and again that Tennyson has not recovered *from* Hallam's death; he has recovered Hallam himself: "Mine, mine, for ever, ever mine" (sec. 129); "I shall not lose thee tho' I die" (sec. 130). Hallam's friendship provided Tennyson with an alternative to the burdensome identity of isolation: identity through mutuality. The epithalamion which concludes the poem is Tennyson's praise of mutuality in its most firmly recognized social form: the institution of marriage. His conviction that a lasting and more satisfying identity can be achieved through a turning outward of the self in love is expressed throughout his poetry: it lies behind his early dramatizations of futile introspection ("The Two Voices," the "Supposed Confessions of a Second-Rate Sensitive Mind") and his brilliant portrait of an isolated mind in "Maud." The *Idylls* envision an entire social order created through a communal sense of identity—and dependent on the commitment to mutuality of a representative marriage.

Browning maintained that he had always intended to write dramatic rather than introspective poetry. After "Pauline" he made certain that his monologues did not suggest their author's public exploration of his own identity. But Browning had once been attracted by lyrical, openly autobiographical poetry. He wrote Elizabeth Barrett that "you *do* what I always wanted, hoped to do. . . . You speak out, *you,* I only make men and women speak—give you truth broken into prismatic hues, and fear the pure white light, even if it is in me. . . . . " The poet of "the pure white light" was, of course, Shelley, the "sun-treader" whom he had evoked as inspiration in his "Fragment of a Confession" and "Pauline," and whose spirit he deliberately banished from "Sordello" and the poetry that followed. Shelley was the type of the "subjective" poet, as Browning was later to describe him, for whom song and self were the same: "what he produces will be less a work than an effluence . . . indeed the very radiance and aroma of his personality, projected from it but not separated." In his own poetry self was to have no such role. "*My* poetry is far from 'the completest expression of my being.' "

This deliberate suppression of self had potentially frightening consequences, as Browning hinted in an extraordinary description of himself to Elizabeth Barrett: "To be grand in simile, for every poor speck of a Vesuvius or a Stromboli in my microcosm there are huge layers of ice and pits of cold water—and I make the most of my two or three fire-eyes, because I know by experience, alas, how these tend to extinction—and the ice grows and grows. . . . I am utterly unused, of these late years particularly, to dream of communicating anything about *that* to another person (all my writings are purely dramatic as I am always anxious to say). . . ." Purging his poetry of morbid introspection, the young poet felt he risked extinguishing vital emotion in himself altogether, risked condemning himself to a kind of Dantean hell where "the ice grows and grows." Elizabeth Barrett did not require him to extinguish the "fire-eyes" he showed to her, and in the next twenty years Browning articulated his new method for exploring the "layers of ice and pits of cold water," without introspection, in his poetry.

"Fra Lippo Lippi" (1855) first described the redirection of the autobiographical impulse which Browning defended at length in his own voice at the beginning of *The Ring*

John Ruskin.

and the Book (1868). Fra Lippo will paint only what he sees outside himself. He refuses to maintain artistic isolation, moving back and forth over the walls of monastery or Medici mansion. And the artistic process itself, he argues, permits him an imaginative participation in the society he paints, like that he claims when he follows pretty girls down Florentine alleys. "Lending our minds out" (line 306) we embody ourselves in what we see and paint. This desire is graphically realized at the end of the poem when Fra Lippo imagines how he will paint himself into his picture. His art becomes a means, not for direct self-exploration, but for the affirmation of an identity based on community. Returning to this conception of the artist in *The Ring and the Book,* Browning describes how "by a special gift, an art of arts . . . / I can detach from me, commission forth / Half of my soul" and send it out to reanimate the shades of the dead. The artist or poet who

> bounded, yearning to be free,
> May so project his surplusage of soul
> In search of body, so add self to self
> By owning what lay ownerless before
> [1:722-25]

can not only, as Browning claims, give dramatic life to the past, he can also free himself from the restrictions of morbid introspection or of a deliberate suppression of identity in his work. Under the guise of a dramatic fiction, the poet can "add self to self," reaching out to affirm his own, now multiplied identity through his sympathy for the people for whom he speaks. He finds a route through poetry to the identity of mutuality. At the same time, of course, he permits himself and his readers to regain the distance necessary for moral judgment—a distance which the youthful author of "Pauline" could not achieve. In the dramatic monologue, Browning finds a way for the objective poet to make his work, too, "the very radiance and aroma of his personality, projected from it but not separated."

Arnold does not share Browning's and Tennyson's radical struggles to alter the metaphors, form, and structure of the greater romantic lyric in order to praise mutuality. He does articulate more exactly and powerfully than any of his contemporaries their conviction that neither Christian remembrance of God nor romantic imaginative experience could change a painful isolation of the self. "Yes! in the sea of life enisled, . . . / We mortal millions live *alone,*" his "To Marguerite—Continued" begins. The perplexing word is "Yes!"; the tone of the poem is hardly affirmative. Between the first and last stanzas something happens which makes that "Yes!" impossible. Isolation, at the beginning of the poem, may even be fruitful. Through it, the islands know "their endless bounds." The phrase is marvellously ambiguous. If "endless" is temporal, the mortal millions discover that individual identity is permanent, and as such, a kind of bondage. The "Yes!" is contradicted even before the "But" of the second stanza. But "endless" is also spatial, and suggests that the individual, circular bounds of each island may potentially be extended infinitely—to include every island. The character of the sea in the preceding line strengthens this possibility. The mortal islands perceive it as "enclasping," folding each of them in a common embrace. They also feel it as "flow": the "sea of life" has suddenly become something very like a river of life. The islands perceive in it not only a shared embrace but also a shared directional movement. Individual identity then becomes the means to mutual identity, and a shared sense of purpose. We are probably not mistaken if we are reminded of "the sea of faith" in "Dover Beach," and follow the metaphor back to Donne's "No man is an island."

The desire which is kindled in the next two stanzas, however, ignores the uniting potential of the sea and regrets the absence of more solid connections ("For surely once, they feel, we were / Parts of a single continent!"). The setting (moonlit hollows, balmy spring, singing nightingales) allows us to recognize this impulse as a specific romantic one. But Arnold's poem ends very differently from Keats's. The last stanza allows neither uncertainty nor ambiguity: the romantic desire is "cool'd" and "render[ed] vain"; the "enclasping flow" is altered to "The unplumb'd, salt, estranging sea." Both romantic and Christian attempts to nullify individual isolation are declared void. Song is abandoned, verbal paradox is given up, metaphor is progressively reduced to single, separate terms. The sea of life is lifeless, the sea of faith, faithless. The link established in metaphor is destroyed, and we are left with seas and lives and a memory of faith, which the imagination cannot unite. Figurative connection becomes literal isolation, a characteristic movement in Arnold's poetry. This disintegration of metaphor can be as moving as its incredible extensions by Ruskin, but both lead, as Arnold recognized, to the end of poetry.

Ruskin shared the poets' distaste for solitary self-discovery in print, and for very similar reasons. *Praeterita,* like "The Two Voices," "Empedocles on Etna," and "Childe Roland to the Dark Tower Came," portrays introspective journeying as isolated, self-involved, and finally fruitless: incapable of yielding a confident sense of self, or an exhilarating view of a purposeful life. Ruskin began his autobiography with the sense that the solitary quest for identity had failed, and, indeed, had been mistaken from the start.

A passage from an early version of *Praeterita* is a quite candid confession of shapelessness: "I was a mere piece of potter's clay, of fine texture, and could not only be shaped into anything, but could take the stamp of anything, and that with precision." So far of his twenty-three-year-old self, but Ruskin continues in the present tense: "Which is the real virtue of me as respects other people. What shape of vase or cylinder I may arrive at myself is really of small consequence to them, but the impressions I take of things of them are trustworthy to the last line, and by the end of the forty years became sufficiently numerous." Ruskin's familiar arrogance is there in the assertion that his impressions are "trustworthy to the last line." There is also a note of apology or defense, perhaps for the absence (and indeed, the condemnation) of introspection: Ruskin's self is "of small consequence" to his readers. But the final admission, which Ruskin may have wished to suppress when he canceled the passage, is telling: at the age of sixty-five he felt he still had no shape, no identity beyond that of passive and precise observer. He was too amorphous to impress himself upon others. Shape or shapelessness may have been "of small consequence" to his readers, but it was of great concern to Ruskin himself. Again and again in *Praeterita* he regrets lost opportunities to *be* something or someone more definite than a sensitive eye: a geologist, a skilled draftsman; or a lover, friend, or husband.

Ruskin's distaste for his Protean identity is reflected in his playful epithets for his younger self. At twenty-one, for example, he is "simply a little floppy and soppy tadpole,—little more than a stomach with a tail to it, flattening and wriggling itself up the crystal ripples and in the pure sands of the spring-head of youth." He is as unformed and self-contained as "a squash before 'tis a peascod," a "codling or cocoon" (p. 261), as ludicrously but pathetically inept in social situations "as a skate in an aquarium trying to get up the glass." Ruskin's humor, for all its deliberate grotesqueness, allows him to convey an important perception about himself while keeping "morbid" introspection out of the autobiography. The unformed or amorphous creatures to which he compares himself are almost totally self-contained or self-involved. Their innocent, stubborn self-sufficiency is both ridiculous and sad, seen from any other perspective than their own. Though the bitterness in the observation is muted, Ruskin portrays the process through which his identity was formed as excessively isolated and self-absorbed, a chrysalid period which, however, failed in the end to yield the expected psyche.

Ruskin is sure, as the poets were not, that his lonely and unproductive cocoon stage is unique. Arnold blamed the age; Ruskin implicated his parents. He makes little attempt to appeal to the reader's experience—quite the opposite. He is constantly remarking on the enormous differences between himself and practically everyone else, even removing himself from the human race altogether, like the rejected prince of a perverse fairy tale who is changed back into skate or frog. As an autobiographer, he perpetuates the very isolation he deplores.

The Ruskin family, firmly enclosed in the house at Herne Hill, was indeed unusually small by Victorian standards. Yet much of what Ruskin describes sounds less strange now than it appeared to him because we recognize in it the characteristic experience of the only child. He is entirely confident that he is the center of his parents' world. Nothing intrudes into that magic domain but that which he can view as an extension of himself. All his needs are met, and little is demanded—or given—in excess of them. "My parents were—in a sort—visible powers of nature to me, no more loved than the sun and the moon: only I should have been annoyed and puzzled if either of them had gone out; . . . I had no companions to quarrel with, neither; nobody to assist, and nobody to thank. Not a servant was ever allowed to do anything for me, but what it was their duty to do; and why should I have been grateful to the cook for cooking, or the gardener for gardening . . . ?" Home and the family *are* the self, if an idea of "self" can be said to exist at all where there is as little distinction between "me" and parents or servants as, Ruskin's simile suggests, the primitive man makes between himself and the sun and moon which minister to him.

Ruskin recaptures the child's view of the world with exceptional vividness. He remembers sitting in a recess in the drawing room while his parents talked or read, a small figure throned like "an Idol in a niche"; or playing alone in the walled garden which, except "that, in this one, *all* the fruit was forbidden; and there were no companionable beasts . . . answered every purpose of Paradise to me." That he should have once been as unconsciously self-centered as an Adam or a god is not unusual, but that he should remember the sensation so distinctly is rather surprising. It suggests that the child's view persisted long enough for him to recognize it and articulate it—and make it part of the conscious memory which constitutes the self.

The child's view seems to have colored Ruskin's memories even in old age. John James and Margaret Ruskin's letters to each other while their boy was growing up contradict the picture of social isolation which *Praeterita* conveys. Apparently Ruskin's parents' love for their only son did not exclude other attachments for him, which might have drawn him out of his niche and turned his secluded garden into an ordinary pleasant back yard. Yet Ruskin remembers differently. He records few opportunities in his later childhood when he might have altered what he judged to be the "mischief, [which] by the chances of life up to seven years old, had been irrevocably determined for me" because, for first of "chief calamities," "I had nothing to love." In *Praeterita* the senior Ruskins bear the responsibility for depriving their son of the power to choose identity through mutuality and leaving him to the unsatisfying shapelessness of identity through isolation.

Praeterita, like *In Memoriam,* is autobiography which opposes a self-involvement which it must nonetheless record. In Ruskin's case the persistence of the child's view of the world, shaping the memories of the older man, is itself the best evidence that he is right: he has not escaped the self-involvement of his childhood, in spite of opportunities to do so. He has, however, consciously rejected it, and he presents in *Praeterita* an alternative to introspective isolation. Each of the three major Victorian poets had preceded him in the attempt to replace a program of internal questing, identified with romanticism, with a deliberate turning outward of the self. For Tennyson this outward turn was a movement of the heart and feelings, first experienced in his friendship with Hallam, then lost and recovered in a subversive romantic lyric, *In Memoriam.* Arnold's movement outward is accomplished by giving up poetry for criticism, where the concern for self-expression is consciously replaced by a concern for the needs of his audience. Browning's turn is a change of voice, from lyric to dramatic monologue, displacing and multiplying the "self" of his poetry. For Ruskin the change is learning to see in a different way, turning the self outward through the eyes. The most important episodes in *Praeterita* are those in which Ruskin's eyes are opened—to mountains at Schaffhausen and the Col de la Faucille, to ivy or aspen structure at Norwood and Fontainebleau, to art in Italy, to Veronese in the sunlight at Turin.

But Ruskin's escape from isolating forms of self-discovery and self-involved writing is only partly successful. He calls the new way of seeing the study of "the science of aspects"; his masters in it are Turner and Byron. But he also follows his first master, Wordsworth, and a romantic and religious way of seeing, introspective vision. The descriptions of his childhood perceptions show us that visual study of everything outside the self tended to become a form of self-regarding vision after all. The "secluded years" in the "self-engrossed quiet of the Herne Hill life" appear in *Praeterita* as one long process of morbid introspection because everything the young Ruskin sees *becomes* himself. Throned in his niche at home or sealed in the family carriage abroad, he is always the spectator, never the participant. He devours with his eyes what greater contact might have prevented him from appropriating. As spectator, he never really leaves himself. This is the pattern of Ruskin's response to the world, and it remains essentially unchanged for the rest of his life. The sights to which Ruskin travels in *Praeterita* bring him back, at its close, to the home garden, the first bit of the world which he had seen and recognized as an extended self. The book suggests that his later choice of a different way of seeing did not entirely relieve him of the burden of an unsatisfying identity, conceived in an isolation which the hungry eye could not alter.

Discontent with solitary self-discovery appears also as direct criticism of the romantic program, especially of the private quest, in the poetry of the 1850s. It was almost always a critique from within: poems whose nominal form and kind were introspective, like *In Memoriam* (1850), or in which quests were major metaphors ("The Scholar-Gypsy" in 1853, "Childe Roland" in 1855), yet which questioned the validity of this pursuit of self-knowledge and fulfillment. Ruskin's *Modern Painters III* is one of the finest critiques of what the Victorians felt were the fallacies of the romantic program they inherited. The poets, however, first turned the forms and metaphors of the introspective romantic lyric inside out. The ambivalent attitudes and competing structures of *Praeterita,* thirty years later, continue in a different genre the poets' quarrel with romantic models for discovering the self.

Perhaps the most influential of these models was Wordsworth. *The Prelude,* published posthumously in 1850, invites comparison with the Victorian alterations of introspective poetry in the decade that followed. There are two points of particular importance to be noted from *The Prelude:* first, Wordsworth is as confident at the beginning of his poem as he is at its end that he can perceive his life as a movement in a single direction. Second, his confidence is confirmed in the famous spots of time, moments of private vision which give him what is really self-revelation. This is the pattern which both Ruskin and the poets attempt to follow and finally reject.

Book 1 of *The Prelude* closes with Wordsworth's anticipation of shape in the life he is about to recount:

> forthwith shall be brought down
> Through later years the story of my life.
> The road lies plain before me;—'tis a theme
> Single and of determined bounds. . . .
> [1:638-41]

At the end of book 14 he again describes a view of his life attained before the beginning of his song:

> I said unto the life which I had lived.
> Where art thou?
> Anon I rose
> As if on wings, and saw beneath me stretched
> Vast prospect of the world which I had been
> And was, and hence this Song
> [14:377-82]

To the road and the prospect he adds a third metaphor for his sense of an inner life forming a continuous, clearly visible whole, the stream:

> we have traced the stream
> From the blind cavern whence is faintly heard
> Its natal murmur; followed it to light
> And open day; accompanied its course
> Among the ways of Nature, for a time
> Lost sight of it bewildered and engulphed;
> Then given it greeting as it rose once more
> In strength, reflecting from its placid breast
> The works of man and face of human life;
> And lastly, from its progress have we drawn
> Faith in life endless, the sustaining thought
> Of human Being, Eternity, and God.
> [14:194-205]

The tracing of the stream makes explicit what the image of the road already promised: that Wordsworth's life is not only continuous movement, but purposive movement in one direction: it is progress toward a goal, "The Growth of a Poet's Mind" to maturity, a journey to a now-achieved identity which is profoundly satisfying to the poet.

The prospect of his life as road or stream is attained in the ascent to vision. Wordsworth revisits "spots of time" which "retain / A renovating virtue . . . [which] enables us to mount / When high, more high, and lifts us up when fallen." (12:210, 217-18). The remembered spots of time reveal to reflection what the vision on Mount Snowden—the classic moment of revelation—immediately illuminated: the imagination or "Power of mind" which both shapes the poet's life and gives it its purpose, to celebrate the "mind of Man" in poetry. The mind reveals itself to itself, both in Wordsworth's visions and, for the reader, in the experience of the poem.

Tennyson's subtitle for *In Memoriam,* "The Way of a Soul," suggests that he will, like Wordsworth, trace a single movement or progress in time. Some structural features of the poem confirm this, notably the periodic measurement of passing time in the Christmas sections. Tennyson also makes an ascent to visionary experience (sec. 95) following a major depression, and after that vision accepts his present life. The poem ends with the celebration of a marriage. All these elements link his poem not only with Wordsworth's but with the long tradition of spiritual autobiography descending from Augustine. But external structure and subtitle—imposed, in fact, after much of the poem was written—do not entirely correspond either to what the poem says or to how it is said. More accurately, the poem subverts the form which it nominally resembles. The effect of Hallam's death on Tennyson is to make him reject the idea of life as a way, road, path, or track, and to try to replace it with a different sense of life's shape.

The speaker's attitude toward the traditional autobiographer's view of his life changes only gradually in the course of the poem. In section 22 he recalls "the path by which we twain did go" in their four years of friendship. This view of their entwined lives is quite adequate; in fact, he remembers, "we with singing cheer'd the way." In section 23, abandoned by Hallam, Tennyson is left to "wander, often falling lame." In this and the next three sections, he looks "back to whence I came, / Or on to where the pathway leads" (sec. 23), but the prospect is in both cases painful. Looking back, he cries "How changed" (sec. 23); looking forward, he finds "still onward winds the dreary way; I with it" (sec. 26). "I know that this was Life,—the track / Whereon with equal feet we fared" (sec. 25), he reflects, but his perception of life as a track is strongest when it has become least appealing, when he is left to walk it alone. By section 38, Tennyson's progress along the track has slowed almost to a halt, and his views, both forward and backward, have disappeared.

> With weary steps I loiter on,
> Tho' always under alter'd skies
> The purple from the distance dies,
> My prospect and horizon gone.

Once Tennyson's and Hallam's paths diverge (sec. 40), the single motion and prospect of which Wordsworth was so confident become, for Tennyson, first a burden and finally an impossibility. Section 46 confirms the viewlessness as a general human phenomenon. Memory, especially, fails to provide us with a sense of continuous life, "The path we came by, thorn and flower, / Is shadow'd by the growing hour / Lest life should fail in looking back." Autobiography, in the usual sense of the word, is under such conditions impossible. There is, for Tennyson, only one perspective from which a view is possible:

> . . . there no shade can last
> In that deep dawn behind the tomb,
> But clear from marge to marge shall bloom
> The eternal landscape of the past.
>
> [Sec. 46]

From that perspective, however, life does not appear as a track or path or way at all. It is fully occupied space, not time stretched like a road from point to point. It is a flowering "eternal landscape," "a lifelong tract of time" with rich fields and "fruitful hours of still increase"—where "still" is a wonderful paradox of silent, stopped motion which nonetheless suggests continued fruitfulness. This view of life as a fruitful landscape, in which loitering will be a pleasure, is already Hallam's, and it resembles the view which Tennyson and Hallam took of their lives when they were together and still unconscious of passing time. Tennyson does not want to ascend to Wordsworth's clear view of his life as road or stream progressing to a goal. He wants to see it as a landscape, preferably fruitful, of course: a whole in which progress or purposive action do not exist. Hallam holds the memory of Tennyson's past, and thus his identity; he also holds the secret of a way of viewing that identity which Tennyson finds far more satisfactory.

There are only two ways for Tennyson to attain this vision: to die, or somehow to regain Hallam's companionship. This is what he achieves in section 95, after he has at last relaxed his conscious will (sec. 70) which clings, like the yew tree, to the memory of the dead Hallam. Gradually and involuntarily, in dream, daydream, memory, and trance, Tennyson moves outward from himself to his friend, until he has recaptured the experience of mutuality which had once given him a different sense of his identity. Section 95 is not, like Wordsworth's Snowden experience or Augustine's vision in the garden, the revelation to Tennyson of who he is, or where he is going. It is a reunion ("The living soul was flash'd on mine, / And mine in this was wound") accompanied by a new, musical harmony in what Tennyson, treading the weary path, had heard as "the steps of Time—the shocks of Chance— / The blows of Death." The reunion makes possible the marriage at the poem's end, a "happy hour" which recalls the "fruitful hours" of Hallam's view of life, or of Tennyson's and Hallam's mutual experience. The marriage itself may exemplify the harmonization of temporal steps which Tennyson, united with Hallam, could hear, for he says, "In that it is thy marriage day / Is music more than any song." His own poem is not that music; "the songs I made" sound to him, after his reunion with Hallam, "As echoes out of weaker times, / As half but idle brawling rhymes." This is harsh, but we should recognize that Tennyson's poem is a mixed vision and a mixed music. Its external structure is that of the spiritual autobiography. But as we follow the poem, we, like Tennyson, lose our way, and find ourselves loitering and viewless, turned back on ourselves in beautiful lyrics of enclosing rhymes—by a poet who is curiously indirect about what is happening to him. The poem means to question, I think, the essential elements of the pilgrimage autobiography, both Christian and romantic: the view that one's self can be discovered by tracing the temporal path of one's life, that the self must be a solitary figure, and that that figure can or should pursue an introspective journey toward a self-revealing vision.

Yet, paradoxically, Tennyson recovers the identity of mutuality when he is most alone. Hallam touches him, in section 95, after his friends leave him. His final vision of Hallam as the type of a perfected humanity comes when he retires from the marriage feast to watch the moon rise. And in that vision Tennyson finds a perspective from which life *can* be seen as temporal path. The way of the soul which cannot be traced by the isolated traveler reappears as a collective destiny. Tennyson finally has it both ways: for the individual, identity is conferred through mutuality, and life assumes the aspect of the fruitful field. But through friendship and marriage the individual also affirms his membership in a larger community. The evolution of the human race possesses that linear shape which the isolated individual cannot see in his own life. *In Memoriam* does not dispense with solitary vision or linear progress, but it does deliberately frustrate our expectations of an introspective journey toward that vision, and alter the content of that vision as well. If Tennyson succeeds, he will finally convince us that his strangely atemporal wanderings among regretful and happy memories, daydreams, and dreams, constitute a different approach to exploring and presenting the self.

The "river of our life" ("The Buried Life," line 39) proves as unsatisfactory a metaphor for Arnold as "life's track" for Tennyson. Arnold's stream cannot be traced as Wordsworth's could and was. It is buried permanently, not just "for a time / Lost sight of." "Unregarded" (line 39) and indeed "indiscernible" (line 40), the stream cannot fulfill its major function, to assure a perception of purposive movement in a single direction. Even if one's life really does have such a shape (and Arnold, unlike Tennyson, does not deny that it does), the knowledge is useless to the individual in search of himself, who can only perceive that we "seem to be / Eddying at large in blind uncertainty" (lines 42-43). The ascent to vision is as impossible as the preliminary view. The most one can hope for is a momentary awareness "of his life's flow" (line 88), which comes, significantly, not through introspection but through the hand, the eyes, the voice of someone else. Mutual recognition *may* lead to self-cognition, but the moment is hardly visionary. At best, "he thinks he knows / The hills where his life rose, / And the sea where it goes" (lines 96-98).

The speaker in "The Scholar-Gypsy," like the modern man of "The Buried Life," is a latter-day romantic quester, but the man he seeks and finds is not himself. The speaker follows the scholar-gypsy, who is looking for a lost art. It is the art of questing which the speaker has lost, however. His quest provides him with a kind of identity, but only by contrast with the quester of old:

O life unlike to ours!
Who fluctuate idly without term or scope,
Of whom each strives, nor knows for what he strives,
And each half lives a hundred different lives;
Who wait like thee, but not, like thee, in hope.
[Lines 166-70]

Arnold's scholar-gypsy, Tennyson's Ulysses and Galahad, and Browning's Childe Roland, are sadly out of date. Their solitary journeys are possibly glorious but almost certainly suicidal. They bring back no visions and no gospel. The would-be modern quester, like Arnold's speaker, does not even attain the prospects afforded to his ill-fated models. In place of the single life, he is likely to perceive "a half a hundred"—loose threads attached to no ends, which only later autobiographers will discover are perpetually woven and unwoven, Penelope-fashion, into the fabric of a differently conceived self.

Childe Roland, last of the late questers of the 1850s, outlives his companions but not his quest. He has no emulators. His quest has none of the appeal to which someone like Arnold's speaker can respond. The scholar-gypsy is immortally young; the "childe" is a perpetual adolescent, still seeking his adult identity. The scholar-gypsy wanders through an anachronistically pastoral landscape; the childe tries vainly to see symbolic significance in what might well be an industrial wasteland. The childe's path behaves very much like Tennyson's track: it disappears behind him and darkens in front of him. The reasons for the shadowing may be the same: "Better this present than a past like that" (line 103), the childe says. The fading path is not replaced by any vision of fruitful space like that Tennyson can imagine, however. The childe remains committed to his path and his goal; he sees everything else as "gray plain all round: / Nothing but plain to the horizon's bound" (lines 52-53). The childe's goal is quite dark, too, and what is more, it remains so when he finally reaches it—not only dark, but viewless: "blind as the fool's heart" (line 182). The signs of the long-expected revelation are all there: recognition ("This was the place!" line 176), light ("why, day / Came back again for that!" lines 187-88), and annunciatory sound ("it tolled / Increasing like a bell" lines 193-94). But the tolling bells are doubly ominous; they announce his death, he assumes, but to us they may also echo a forlorn return "to my sole self." The childe's arrival at a tower "blind as the fool's heart" supports that possibility, but it doesn't promise much in the way of self-revelation. Sight and sound do tell the childe something, but he does not directly apply it to himself. "Names in my ears / Of all the lost adventurers my peers,— . . . / Lost, lost! one moment knelled the woe of years" (lines 194-95, 198). "In a sheet of flame / I saw them and I knew them all," he continues, "And yet . . . " (lines 201-2). The childe blows his horn to proclaim an arrival already stated in the past tense.

The poem ends, but the "sheet of flame" has not illuminated either the Dark Tower or the disappearing path along which he has come. His consciousness of his past, of his present identity, and of his apparently achieved goal is no different than it has ever been. The ascent to vision, if that is what it was, was a hoax: it gave him no new prospect. His life is what he experienced while he lived it, not to be transformed by a single moment of action or vision, no matter how faithfully pursued. We don't know whether the childe sees even this much before he blows his horn. It is a wonderful gesture, but just how blindly heroic we can't tell. Is he still looking for his moment of truth, in a final confrontation with the unknown? Or does he realize he has had it, that the end of his quest is only to be able to announce, "Childe Roland to the Dark Tower came"?

Browning's poem is a radical critique of the romantic program, yet it acknowledges the attraction as well as the dangers of the solitary quest to a Victorian. It is in some ways the most personal of Browning's poems, to be read together with the essay in praise of Shelley which he finished only two years later. Yet the personal material—the same that he used in the "intense and morbid" "Pauline" seventeen years earlier—is brilliantly controlled in "Childe Roland." The means by which this poetic control is achieved, lending the mind out to realize itself in dramatic fictions, is Browning's alternative to Childe Roland's suicidal heroism.

"The way of a soul," when Browning, Arnold, and Tennyson explore it in the 1850s, turns out to be far more devious than the open road which beckoned Wordsworth. To follow a single, temporal path seems difficult, perhaps impossible. Worse than that, to pursue it is to be misled, and for the poet, to be misleading as well. A growing concern with consciousness rather than simple action points to a new view of individual life not as a pilgrimage but as an intricate, unfinished web of memory and human connection, "that strange, perpetual weaving and unweaving of ourselves." Explicit concern with consciousness isolated from moral action is not acceptable to the Victorians any more than the old view of self-discovery as a form of moral action, a quest for individual truth. The deliberate pursuit of patterns of consciousness, Pater discovers, seems as morbid, self-involved, and probably fruitless as romantic questing. But those patterns can be suggested indirectly, by using literary forms and structures new to autobiographical writing. Tennyson and Browning are the great Victorian pioneers, using fictional more often than actual autobiography for their experiments. Ruskin, thirty years later, follows the way of the poets.

As one might expect from *Praeterita*'s condemnation of a self-absorbed "tadpole" childhood, Ruskin is as reluctant to assume the role of the self-conscious autobiographer as were his predecessors in the 1850s. His narrative, discontinuous and incomplete, cries out for the shaping presence of a self-reflective author. He is not there. On the rare occasions when he does allow his readers to glimpse his present self reflecting on the past, he is almost always calling attention to the shapelessness of his life. At the end of the first book of *Praeterita,* for example, he comments on the peculiar blend of feeling and ability in his eighteen-year-old self: "But so stubborn and chemically inalterable the laws of the prescription were, that now, looking back from 1886 to that brook shore of 1837, whence I could see the whole of my youth, I find myself in nothing whatsoever *changed.* Some of me is dead, more of me stronger. I have learned a few things, forgotten many; in the total of me, I am but the same youth, disappointed and rheumatic." Nearly fifty years are wiped out; there is no growth, no progress, no change. Ruskin at sixty-seven and Ruskin at eighteen are like Childe Roland; the aging youth, disappointed when he arrives at a viewpoint, discovers only a heart which, if not blind, is at least diseased. "Looking back" is not illuminating; the distance traveled between past and present disappears. Identity is not life shaped by time, but something else whose "laws" are "chemically inalterable" by temporal or spatial journeying.

As with the poets, Ruskin's complaints of shapelessness, isolation, lost ways, stopped progress, and unreached goals go on to imply a criticism of the linear view of life as progress and achievement, and to suggest an alternative. Ruskin characteristically approached both literal and metaphorical paths as more than the shortest distance between two points. Digressing from a description of Herne Hill, in the second chapter of *Praeterita,* he laments the loss of a favorite walk down the ridge from his old home. The field through which it passed has been walled off, though the path itself remains. He remarks that "questions of right-of-way are now of constant occurrence; and in most cases, the mere *path* is the smallest part of the old Right, truly understood. The Right is of the cheerful view and sweet air which the path commanded." Ruskin cares far more for his view of the field than for his progress through it. He takes the same attitude in all his longer travels—which is why he prefers the more leisurely pace of the carriage to the efficient speed of the railroad. "We did not travel for adventures, nor for company," he says of his first trips to the Alps, "but to see with our eyes, and to measure with our hearts. . . . Even in my own land, the things in which I have been least deceived are those which I have learned as their Spectator." When Ruskin envisions the course of his own life, he speaks not of roads, tracks, paths, or streams, but of fruitful fields: "my granted fields of fruitful exertion," "the Holy Land of my future work." Like Tennyson, he finds it oppressive or impossible to pursue a single dreary way, and gives up the quest. He chooses instead the flowers and fruits of his own "eternal landscape," secured not to the friend but to the Spectator.

The life described in *Praeterita* is a domain which Ruskin possesses visually, that he may labor to cultivate it by articulating his experience to others. That domain is first glimpsed in 1833 and not complete for several years, but it has already been imagined as the proper field of his vision by the child who watches the glittering springs of Wandel and asks to be painted in a landscape of blue hills. Ruskin's constant traveling is never progress; it is the means by which he revisits the territory of a visually extended self. *Praeterita* follows the course both of real journeys and of the voyages of memory that each new visit provokes. It is a history of continual return, of constant circling, a circumscription of a self identified with what it saw. Except for its dedication to his parents, Ruskin wrote in the preface, *Praeterita* would "have been little more than an old man's recreation in gathering visionary flowers in fields of youth." The description is just, but it needs no apology. The fields of Ruskin's youth are the fields of his maturity and his old age, and he recreated their flowers and "sweet air" by a lifelong series of mental and physical returns. The last of these revisits were accomplished in *Praeterita.*

Ruskin had no real model for an unprogressive autobiography. Even *In Memoriam,* as we have seen, is a subversion of an old mode rather than the straightforward creation of a new. *Praeterita* reflects several stages in Ruskin's struggle to make his book conform to the shape of his life and yet meet the demands of another form of autobiography. The first two chapters were not written as part of an autobiography at all, but as illustrations for *Fors Clavigera.* Ruskin incorporated them into *Praeterita* with the addition only of titles and closing paragraphs. He commented on what he had done, pointing out the differences between these chapters and the body of his book:

> . . . I fear the sequel may be more trivial, because much is concentrated in the foregoing broad statement, which I have now to continue by slower steps;—and yet less amusing, because I tried always in *Fors* to say things, if I could, a little piquantly; and the rest of the things related in this book will be told as plainly as I can. But whether I succeeded in writing piquantly in *Fors* or not, I certainly wrote often obscurely; and the description above given of Herne Hill seems to me to need at once some reduction to plainer terms.

Ruskin was aware that the two chapters bear an almost emblematic relationship to the life he must go on to recount "by slower steps" and in "plainer terms." They are remarkably unspecific about actual dates or chronology of events, recounting scenes from various periods of early childhood. And they clearly attempt to represent the essential experiences, not only of childhood, but of Ruskin's adult life as well: his fascination with water, his delight in the garden, his patient visual exploration of the patterns on his carpet, his role as removed spectator looking out at the world. Joining these chapters to a full account of his life, Ruskin is careful to note that not only will the rest of the account, progressive rather than emblematic, be slower and less "piquant," it will also, to some extent, be unnecessary. He said of his early travels that "although, in the course of these many worshipful pilgrimages, I gathered curiously extensive knowledge, both of art and natural scenery, afterwards infinitely useful, it is evident to me in retrospect that my own character and affections were little altered by them." At this point in *Praeterita* Ruskin is clear that a progressive model will not reflect what is of most importance about him the peculiar sensibility which time and events will not change.

He uses the new titles and conclusions to the first two chapters to further underline their emblematic status. The method of composition was one which he had used often in his critical writing. "The Springs of Wandel" (as the first chapter is called) refers in the first place to the stream behind his aunt's house in Croydon. The chapter's concluding sentence, in characteristic fashion, moves from an incident in the past (the Ruskins' early carriage travels in England) through an indefinitely extending future of repeated travels ("in the course of these many worshipful pilgrimages . . . ") up to the present ("it is evident to me in retrospect"). The sentence goes on with a return to the early time, where "the personal feeling and native instinct of me had been fastened, irrevocably, long before," and comes to rest, finally, on a single detail, "the cress-set rivulets in which the sand danced and minnows darted above the Springs of Wandel." The focus on this detail is not entirely unprepared; the Croydon spring has been mentioned only once, in passing, but there are several other watery memories through which Ruskin has presented his childish fascination with watching water, in particular that of "the filling of the water-cart, through its leathern pipe, from the dripping iron post at the pavement edge; or the still more admirable proceedings of the turncock, when he turned and turned till a fountain sprang up in the middle of the street." Ruskin's responses to the Croydon spring and the water-cart are picked up and woven together in the final image of the springs of Wandel, which becomes emblematic of one aspect of the visual domain which his sensibility established. "The Springs of Wandel"—and puns are always intentional with this most word-conscious of writers—describes both source and springtime of Ruskin's unique sensibility.

George Moore, about the time of his Confessions of a Young Man.

Chapter 2, "Herne Hill Almond Blossoms," ties an apparently loose collection of reminiscences to a single significant image of multiple repercussions by a similar procedure. The Herne Hill garden has been described earlier in the chapter as an Eden where all fruits were forbidden, and Ruskin returns in the last paragraph to state, in "plainer terms," what those fruits were and when they could be eaten. But he does not stop with the literal description. The forbidden fruits remind him "that the seeds and fruits . . . were for the sake of the flowers, not the flowers for the fruit." The childhood experience is the seed of the adult love of visual beauty for its own sake. The fully flowered thought dominates the concluding sentence, which makes the same imaginative excursion as the last sentence of the first chapter. The almond blossoms are part of "an unbroken order" of constant seasonal change repeated "for many and many a year to come." Memory moves forward on that wave of natural change to the present, and returns again to the past, praying for the protection of the fragile almond blossom: "The first joy of the year being in its snowdrops, the second, and cardinal one, was in the almond blossom, every other garden and woodland gladness following from that in an unbroken order of kindling flower and shadowy leaf; and for many and many a year to come, until indeed, the whole of life became autumn to me, my chief prayer for the kindness of heaven, in its flowerful seasons, was that the frost might not touch the almond blossom." The sentence combines temporal change with the stasis of perpetual motion, rhythmic progression with circular return. It summarizes neither life nor chapter, but it connects them to an image which it fills with new significance gathered in the course of a journey of circumspection. The structure reminds us of Proust, who recognized in Ruskin's prose many of his own strategies. Proust constructs even longer sentences, where a word or an image echoes repeatedly while it accumulates meaning, and repeats in miniature the process of affective memory which the book recreates.

Although Ruskin declares his intention to continue *Praeterita* in a different manner, the titles of most of his subsequent chapters also focus attention on a single scene. Usually the experience is one which is repeated many times—typically, a place which Ruskin visits often, like "The Simplon," or "L'Hotel du Mont Blanc." The responses Ruskin describes on any one visit are also habitual. Of the Hotel du Mont Blanc, he confesses "How to begin speaking of it, I do not know; still less how to end." *Where* to begin or end is also a problem, for the chronological narrative itself is constantly interrupted by references to other visits at other times. The chapter's subject is less what happened in 1849, the point which Ruskin has reached in his narrative, than what the hotel means to him after many revisits. The place of the title becomes, in the course of the chapter, first the stimulus and then the emblem for a recurring state of mind. The cumulative effect of these chapters, where places become images for the responses they evoke, is to establish a discontinuous mental geography which takes the place of direct introspective analysis, the guided tour from past to present.

The mental landscape of individual views, flowery fields seen from the right-of-way, does not provide Ruskin with a sufficient structure for his book, however. He acknowledges that an autobiography must above all be a chronological narrative. It is, he maintains, "my needful and fixed resolve to set the facts down continuously." After his indulgence in "piquant" style in the first two chapters, he was determined to set his life out as path and follow it. *Praeterita* was to consist of three books of twelve chapters, each book covering roughly twenty years. For the remaining ten chapters of book 1 and most of book 2, Ruskin keeps his narrative plan very much in mind. Yet in spite of the pressure of the genre to select a single line of development, he cannot make his own life conform to that pattern. *Praeterita's* central chapters are peppered with apologies for narrative deviations. "Whether in the biography of a nation, or of a single person," Ruskin confesses, "it is alike impossible to trace it steadily through successive years. Some forces are failing while others strengthen, and most act irregularly, or else at uncorresponding periods of renewed enthusiasm after intervals of lassitude. For all clearness of exposition, it is necessary to follow first one, then another, without confusing notices of what is happening in other directions." In place of a single life, Ruskin, like Arnold, discovers "a hundred different lives," each with its own time scheme. Autobiography threatens to splinter into multiple temporal narratives. Chronological structure is clearly breaking down, with no very satisfactory substitute for the vital and literary unity it provided. And even multiple narratives may not be enough to cover everything essential. "I shall have to return over the ground of these early years," Ruskin warns, "to fill gaps, after getting on a little first." A proliferation of paths is only a temporary expedient. Ruskin's real desire is to cover *all* the ground of these early years. He is most successful when he digresses from narrative traveling to take emblematic views like those his chapter titles suggest.

The record of facts continues, in spite of the signs directing us to broader views, but it is accompanied by notices of Ruskin's increasing discontent. He complains at the beginning of book 2 that "for any account of my real life, the gossip hitherto given to its codling or cocoon condition has brought us but a little way." But progress still seems to promise the best solution, and Ruskin goads himself to run faster: "I must get on. . . . " A few chapters later he expresses more serious dissatisfaction: "In my needful and fixed resolve to set the facts down continuously, leaving the reader to his reflections on them, I am slipping a little too fast over the surfaces of things; and it becomes at this point desirable that I should know, or at least try to guess, something of what the reader's reflections *are*! and whether in the main he is getting at the sense of the facts I tell him." Chronological narrative gives us the facts, but not what the facts mean. Ordinarily we would expect the self-reflective author to help us, and Ruskin seems to announce just that: "I think it, however, quite time to say a little more fully, not only what happened to me, now of age, but what was *in* me." But what follows is a series of passages from his diary contemporary with the events he is recording, not a statement of progress and direction from the perspective of the present. Eager to avoid the dangers of morbid introspection, the author refuses to speak up.

Even without the author's guiding presence, however, the narrative of his life can convey direction and purpose by recounting a moment of insight, the traditional resolution to a crisis of indirection in spiritual autobiography. Ruskin's letters and diaries indicate how ardently he had looked forward to such a moment, and how often he had been disappointed. On at least seven different occasions between 1845 and 1882 he thought he had achieved religious conversion, only to discover, in retrospect, that the turning had not been definitive. The middle chapters of *Praeterita* present a different series of illuminative moments. They are aesthetic rather than religious revelations in any traditional sense: Ruskin's first sight of the Alps at Schaffhausen in 1833; insights into leaf and branch design achieved at Norwood and Fontainebleau; his first real understanding of early Italian religious art at Lucca and Pisa, in 1845; further significant mountain walks in 1841, 1849, and 1860; and the blended impressions of music and color received in the Veronese gallery at Turin in 1858. Each experience stands out from the narrative by the intensity with which it is rendered. Ruskin himself also tells us we have reached a critical point, and his language on each occasion is very nearly the same: "blessed entrance into life," "I had found my life again," "I began the best work of my life," "a new epoch of life and death begins." Yet these passages span a period of seventeen years and refer to eight different occasions on which Ruskin says his "true," "best," or "new" life began. The conversion or turning point we expected has multiplied. Ruskin climbs the mount of contemplation again and again—"my most intense happinesses have of course been among mountains"—but once there, he gains no simple prospect of the past or future course of his life. He knows only that it must lie among mountains. His vision is not of the road he will follow, but of the view he will continue to enjoy. That view is, it is true, progressively enriched with new details of fore- and middle ground. In the aftermath of each new revelation, Ruskin was disappointed to discover how limited the view, how small the change in the direction of his life. In writing *Praeterita,* however, he arranges this series of views to suggest, if not a linear pattern of development, at least a spiral movement rather than a totally unprogressive series of returns. With each repeated vision, the familiar view is amplified—and Ruskin sees himself closer to a sense of his identity. The revelation is painfully gradual, not wonderfully sudden. The sequence of visionary moments in *Praeterita* does not show a dramatic development of identity or self-consciousness. It reveals instead a sensibility which remains fundamentally unchanged.

Ruskin also includes in *Praeterita* a number of false visions, similar experiences among mountains or before paintings which proved misleading. He describes, for example, an abortive conversion at Nyon in 1845. He puts special emphasis on his early passion for Venice.

> Thank God I am here; it is the Paradise of cities.
>
> . . . . .
>
> This, and Chamouni, are my two homes of Earth

he quotes from an 1841 diary. But the Byronic vision of Venice is given only to be retracted as false. "Venice I regard more and more as a vain temptation." The false visions cast further doubt on the usefulness of the "true" visions at Schaffhausen and elsewhere. Ruskin is too honest to leave out his wrong turnings, the roads which peter out, but by including them he blurs our sense of his progress or purpose.

In the last third of *Praeterita* the narrative structure breaks down. "This gossip has beguiled me till I have no time left to tell what in proper sequence should have been chiefly dwelt on in this number," he confesses. Scattered memories of people and places distract him from his chosen course as he nears the end of book 2. The decision to give up his sequential plan was nevertheless deliberate. He recognized the signs of imminent mental collapse and felt himself running out of time. "Lest I should not be spared to write another [number of] *Praeterita,*" he determined to indulge "an old man's visionary recreation" without regard for further progress toward the present.

Except for the masterful account of his unconversion ("The Grande Chartreuse"), the last chapters of *Praeterita* are diffuse, even chaotic, but in them we find repeated an exchange of vividly seen space for chronologically reconstructed time as a principle of order. When Ruskin surrenders the artistic control he had exercised in the middle of the book he returns to something like the emblematic method of his opening chapters. Places continue to provide the connections, the guides for memory. Ruskin seems to have lost track of time, but he recurs again and again to the hills of Scotland. "And there is no other country in which the roots of memory are so entwined with the beauty of nature," he explains. Such rooted memories, entwined with place, give "design and fixed boundaries" to Ruskin's wandering. But the scenes he revisits do not become emblems—not, that is, until the brilliant last paragraphs of *Praeterita.* Before we reach these, however, we should take another look at the intended and actual structures of the book as a whole.

Ruskin originally planned to take his narrative down to the 1880s, but at an early stage in his writing he decided to end the account with the 1860s. The actual *Praeterita* follows this second plan through the first four chapters of book 3, when Ruskin was permanently silenced by a final attack of madness. The book remains, in one sense, unfinished. Yet according to his second plan, the story would not have continued much beyond the point where he was forced to end it. The last chapters of book 3 were to have been a series of farewells to the places to which he felt himself most closely tied. They would effectively have turned the linear movement of the narrative back on itself, returning to the scenes of Ruskin's youth. They would also have shifted the book's emphasis from temporal progression to spatial views and reviews.

But place, not time, had determined the parts of *Praeterita* all along: all but seven of the twenty-eight chapter titles—or thirty-six intended titles—are place names. And Ruskin found his titles before he wrote his chapters, as we see from the plans for the unfinished book 3. On the rare occasions when he directs his readers how to see his life, he gives them what was evidently his own procedure, suggesting emblematic views, not setting out road maps. "I must here, in advance, tell the general reader," he warns in book 1, "that there have been, in sum, three centres of my life's thought: Rouen, Geneva, and Pisa." The projected final chapters return to these scenes, Rouen in France, Geneva in Switzerland, and Pisa in Italy. They also include a return to a fourth "home," though at Dover he barely sets foot on English soil. The conclusion would not have altered the structure of *Praeterita.* It would have clarified a pattern which, though submerged in the chronological narrative, is already present.

Granted that Ruskin designs chapters around significant places, generally prefers views to paths, and tells us we should look for geographical centers of his thought, a string of twenty-one locales organizes but does not structure the autobiography. There are, however, five chapters which receive special emphasis. "Schaffhausen and Milan," "The Col de la Faucille," "The Simplon," "The Campo Santo," and "The Grande Chartreuse" each present an experience of heightened visual and emotional intensity which gives the chapter its title and is the subject of its opening or concluding paragraphs. No other chapters combine formal emphases with the same visual and affective intensity of description.

If we examine those views to which Ruskin gives special weight, we discover that although they are geographically distinct, they are visually almost identical. "Schaffhausen and Milan" is memorable for its description of Ruskin's first sight of the Alps:

> We must still have spent some time in town-seeing, for it was drawing towards sunset, when we got up to some sort of garden promenade—west of the town, I believe; and high above the Rhine, so as to command the open country across it to the south and west. At which open country of low undulation, far into blue,—gazing as at one of our own distances from Malvern of Worcestershire, or Dorking of Kent,—suddenly—behold—beyond!
>
> There was no thought in any of us for a moment of their being clouds. They were clear as crystal, sharp on the pure horizon sky, and already tinged with rose by the sinking sun. Infinitely beyond all that we had ever thought or dreamed,—the seen walls of lost Eden could not have been more beautiful to us; not more awful, round heaven, the walls of sacred Death.

Though the mountains dominate this view, the city's "garden promenade" in the foreground, and the river and plain across which the unsuspecting eye travels, are essential elements in Ruskin's visual experience of Alpine glory. At Milan, later in the chapter, the experience is twice repeated: the distant Alps are seen once through the ornate pinnacles of the cathedral, and a second time, at sunset, from a park which looks across the town. "The Col de la Faucille" concludes with a magnificent prospect of Alps across the lake and valley of Geneva—a vision, Ruskin says, of his Holy Land. The foreground of garden and city and gothic tracery, missing from this prospect, is supplied by a lengthy, almost cinematic exploration of the town of Abbeville at the beginning of the chapter. The reader, traversing the intervening time and space imaginatively as "the modern fashionable traveller," forms a composite prospect. When Ruskin reaches "The Campo Santo"—literally the holy land—he discovers a familiar and satisfying view at both Lucca and Pisa: sunset walks, marble towers, a city at his feet, and clouds and mountains in the distance. "The Grande Chartreuse," recounting Ruskin's unconversion, opens with his disappointed expectations of the same scene at the Carthusian monastery and closes with his discovery of it in an unexpected place, the city of Turin. There, when Ruskin leaves the viewless grey Waldensian chapel, he climbs to an upper gallery with an open window. The afternoon light brings out a glow of "perfect colour" in the Veronese painting which is his richly sensuous foreground. Accompanied by music, bathed in rosy light, opening on a view of remembered, if not literally seen mountains, the secular Veronese painting in the gallery at Turin is justified and sanctified as it takes the place of natural and religious art in the foreground of Ruskin's visual domain.

The most extensive description of that domain occurs in the chapter which would have fallen almost at the center of *Praeterita.* "The Simplon," third in order of the five chapters which present this landscape most intensely, describes the prospect of and from Geneva. Our first view of it is from the Simplon, "that mighty central pass" through the Alps, and it reveals "this bird's nest of a place, to be the centre of religious and social thought, and of physical beauty, to all living Europe! . . . it rules them, is the focus of thought to them, and of passion, of science, and of *contrat social.* . . . Saussure's school and Calvin's, Rousseau's and Byron's,—Turner's,—And of course, I was going to say, mine. . . . " There is no mistaking Ruskin's intention. We are to see Geneva as more than geographically central; to regard it as the focus of a mental landscape which is both public ("to all living Europe") and personal. The seven pages that follow present the city exclusively in visual terms, but Ruskin's description is charged with such energy that we read it as a mythical landscape of desire.

On every side of this island city, surrounded by gardens and approached by "the delicatest of filiform suspension bridges," he discovers variations of an ideal view. From bridge, terrace, or "sycamore-shaded walk," he shows us now an expanse of lake, now of orchard and vineyard, which carry the eye up to more "ghostly ranges of incredible mountains." Finishing his circuit of the town, he turns inward to examine the foreground of this visual feast more closely. In the high, dark, secluded center of the town, we are admitted to Mr. Bautte's, the jeweler whose workmanship in "purest gold" achieves a unique "subtlety of linked and wreathed design." We come away from this *sanctum sanctorum* "of treasure possessed"—the visual treasure of intricate pattern which was the first and nearest of Ruskin's private domains. From there we move outward to the great river which encircles the town. The "not flowing, but flying water" has in it "the continuance of Time." But this is time which is never wasted, never exhausted, motion which is constant and therefore never progresses, and never ends.

> But here was one mighty wave that was always itself, and every fluted swirl of it, constant as the wreathing of a shell. No wasting away of the fallen foam, no pause for gathering of power, no helpless ebb of discouraged recoil; but alike

> through bright day and lulling night, the never-pausing plunge, and never-fading flash, and never-hushing whisper, and, while the sun was up, the ever-answering glow of unearthly aquamarine, ultramarine, violet-blue, gentian-blue, peacock-blue, river-of-paradise blue, glass of a painted window melted in the sun, and the witch of the Alps flinging the spun tresses of it for ever from her snow.

It is the perfect visual stasis of living natural design, as Mr. Bautte's gold and enamel brooches are a Byzantine perfection of artistic invention. In this ideal city, art and nature are interchangeable: the river has "currents that twisted the light into golden braids, and inlaid the threads with turquoise enamel." It is itself "one lambent jewel." And here the jewel and gold change places, and "the dear old decrepit town" with its golden center is embraced by the river "as if it were set in a brooch of sapphire."

At the center of his book, Ruskin's landscape of desire is realized in its most perfect form. "Foreground" and "background" are no longer adequate to describe it, for the spectator is now at the center of a view which extends outward in every direction: from the city, the nearest perfection of timeless natural and artistic design, across the plains of human dwelling and cultivated garden, and up and out into the infinite rosy distance of mountain, cloud, and open sky. The eye finds no limits to its motion, but the spectator remains fixed and motionless. From Geneva one travels everywhere, but need never leave home. It is the perfect image for Ruskin's life, and the antithesis of Christian or romantic pilgrimages: perpetual traveling, for the sake of the view; a series of circular journeys, with no direction and no goal; total visual possession of a universe whose center is completely human, yet completely impersonal. The unseen spectator loves what he sees passionately, and he becomes what he loves. In *Praeterita,* he is what he sees, and the landscape of "The Simplon" is the geography of a self, a geography perhaps not wholly conscious, but quite consciously placed at the center of the autobiography.

Had Ruskin ended *Praeterita* as he wished, he would evidently have given us four more views of his visual universe, returning to the landscapes he had come to possess since his first European trip in 1833. The larger structure of the book, with its center at Geneva, would have been a circle connecting the end of part 3 with the middle of part 1, abolishing the temporal distance between the 1830s and the 1860s or 1880s. The intended design could not be completed; perhaps, I am tempted to propose, it would have been left without conclusion even had madness not intervened. Ruskin had encountered the same difficulty bringing an equally digressive work to an end twenty-nine years earlier. "Looking back over what I have written," he began the last chapter of *Modern Painters,* "I find that I have only now the power of ending this work,—it being time that it should end, but not of 'concluding' it; for it has led me into fields of infinite inquiry, where it is only possible to break off with such imperfect result as may, at any given moment, have been attained." Ruskin's life had led him into fields of infinite inquiry too, and though it was time that it should end, its unprogressive course so far suggested no point at which it could arrive which would feel properly final. But Ruskin did end his autobiography. *Praeterita's* two closing paragraphs give it a formal completeness which the planned four chapters of review would not, for in the actual *Praeterita* Ruskin finds his way back, not only to the familiar European landscapes of his middle years, but to the founts and springs of perception emblematically presented in the first two chapters.

"I draw back to my own home . . . permitted to thank Heaven once more for the peace, and hope, and loveliness of it," the first of these last paragraphs begins. The home to which he now returns is Denmark Hill in 1869, but the scene which he recalls combines the crystal waters of "The Springs of Wandel" with the pink-blossomed garden at Herne Hill. Combines but improves; the child was lonely in his Eden of forbidden fruit; but in this return Ruskin takes his

> Elysian walks with Joanie, and Paradisiacal with Rosie, under the peach-blossom branches by the little glittering stream which I had paved with crystal for them. I had built behind the highest cluster of laurels a reservoir, from which, on sunny afternoons, I could let a quite rippling film of water run for a couple of hours down behind the hayfield, where the grass in spring still grew fresh and deep. There used to be always a corncrake or two in it. Twilight after twilight I have hunted that bird, and never once got a glimpse of it: the voice was always at the other side of the field, or in the inscrutable air or earth. And the little stream had its falls, and pools, and imaginary lakes. Here and there it laid for itself lines of graceful sand; there and here it lost itself under beads of chalcedony. . . . Happiest times, for all of us, that ever were to be.

The glittering stream absorbs Ruskin's gaze like "the gay glittering" Rhone of his Geneva landscape. But the lovely peace of this paradise is nearly all foreground. Only the voice of the unseen bird for an instant leads the eye to "the other side of the field, or in the inscrutable air or earth"; it returns to lose itself in the "falls, and pools, and imaginary lakes" of the little stream under the peach-blossoms. Vision is contracted, as if to the child's perspective; the stream forms a landscape in miniature. The distant heights to which the man's eye travels exist as yet only in the child's imagination. We remember what Ruskin told us at the end of his first chapter: "that the personal feeling and native instinct of me had been fastened, irrevocably, long before, to things modest, humble, and pure in peace, . . . by the cress-set rivulets in which the sand danced and minnows darted above the Springs of Wandel." From 1889, by way of 1869, Ruskin has returned to his earliest memories, the peaceful foreground of his visual domain.

But the book does not end here. There is no single completed circle, no simple joining of end and beginning, in memory. "How things bind and blend themselves together!" the second of these last paragraphs opens. The "glittering stream" at Denmark Hill led him back to the "spring of crystal water" at Croydon, but memory does not stop when it has found its source. The last paragraph of *Praeterita* recapitulates the process it has just articulated. Memories of fountains and crystal waters multiply: Trevi of Rome, 1872; Brande of Siene, 1870; the Brande of Dante's poetry; "the crystal and ruby glittering" of water changing into wine in Joseph Severn's unfinished "Marriage at Cana." Visual similarities—light playing on water in the foreground of a larger scene—bind and blend together disparate experiences which neither simple chronology nor purposeful progression can adequately connect. The visible fountains accumulate emotional significance. When their source is discovered and all are revisited, they come to designate an aspect of the self: "the personal feeling" which is "fastened . . . to things modest, humble, and pure in peace." But behind that single foreground feature, Ruskin recreates a familiar view, a landscape which places "the personal feeling" attached to sunlit water in a perspective we now recognize. From the Fonte Brande Ruskin walks to the hills above Siena. Glitter and movement continue to occupy his foreground, though now they come not from light on water but from fireflies at sunset in nearby dark thickets. Beyond this living design the town of Siena is seen through its gates. Behind gates and city rise "mountainous clouds still lighted from the west, and the openly golden sky," the furthest reaches of the Holy Land which Ruskin visually occupies.

As Ruskin again creates the same view, Pater's description of the only possible self-consciousness is graphically realized. The fabric which is perpetually woven and unwoven has a visual counterpart in *Praeterita:* the landscape which Ruskin dissolves into its elements, so that he may trace them to their sources in memory and recompose them into landscape again. The web of consciousness which emerges is always the same. Pattern and self correspond, but they can be known only through the process by which they recreate themselves.

There is a change in the Siena view, however, and it brings autobiographical recreation of the Penelopean kind to its only possible end. Ruskin's eye moves from fireflies to clouds and sky, but it also returns, by Siena's gate, to his foreground, if not to his heart, there to lose itself forever among those tiny, glittering lights. For the first time, foreground overwhelms background; perspective disappears. Ruskin's visual space collapses to a single plane of moving lights. How like, and yet how different from, the sun that Turner saw at his death, or the stars that close Dante's great visions: "*How* they shone! moving like fine-broken starlight through the purple leaves. How they shone! through the sunset that faded into thunderous night as I entered Siena three days before, the white edges of the mountainous clouds still lighted from the west, and the openly golden sky calm behind the Gate of Siena's heart, with its still golden words, 'Cor magis tibi Sena pandit,' and the fireflies everywhere in sky and cloud rising and falling, mixed with the lightening, and more intense than the stars." For all their wonderful brilliance, the fireflies are very small, and very near.

Ruskin was what he saw; *Praeterita* continually recreates that self as he sees again all that he loves most deeply. As long as memory leads and the eye responds, there can be no end to that perpetual recreation. But in *Praeterita*'s last paragraph, Ruskin reverses the visual movements of a lifetime. From background, he returns to foreground; from the brilliance of sunset cloud, to the tiny lights of fireflies; from the intense happinesses of mountains, to the pure peace—perhaps—of home. The Spectator has lost his view, and with it his hold on self-consciousness.

The record of Ruskin's development and achievements is unfinished, but the formal symmetry of *Praeterita* is completed in its brilliant ending. In the paradisiacal walks we have already returned to the emblematic scenes of the book's beginning. The fireflies of Siena take us there too, but only after we have seen the child's foreground placed in the larger visual domain of the book's middle chapters. The last two scenes perfectly balance the first two chapters, but they revolve no less about the book's real center, Geneva, and the landscapes which resemble it.

Like Arnold, Browning, and Tennyson, Ruskin had for years pursued in imagination the questing Ulysses. *Praeterita* bears the marks of his long vigil for the Ulysses in himself. But like the poets, again, Ruskin was not faithful to a marriage which proved uncongenial. *Praeterita* abandons purpose and chronology, and when it does a new kind of self-consciousness takes over. The patterns it creates may not have fulfilled Ruskin's expectations, but they are none the less there. The man reviewing his life still looked for the wandering Ulysses, but the artist, bringing his book to an abrupt close, was sufficiently aware of the form he had created to tie up the threads of his Penelopean web and leave it whole. (pp. 142-70)

Elizabeth K. Helsinger, "Ruskin and the Poets: Alterations in Autobiography," in Modern Philology, *Vol. 74, No. 2, November, 1976, pp. 142-70.*

VICTORIAN WOMEN'S AUTOBIOGRAPHIES

Mary Jean Corbett

[In the following essay, Corbett discusses several autobiographies written by Victorian women, contending that these works often reinforce rather than challenge cultural dictates regarding gender and class.]

In a recent book on women's autobiography [*A Poetics of Woman's Autobiography: Marginality and the Fictions of Self-Representation,* 1987], Sidonie Smith has argued that "the woman who writes autobiography is doubly estranged when she enters the autobiographical contract," with her estrangement founded on woman's historical subordination to male discourse and on her problematic relation to a reading audience always already configured as male. By usurping the male power of speech and writing, the female self-representing subject "unmasks her transgressive desire for cultural and literary authority" when she takes up the pen to author herself. Feminist Victorianists will find this scenario familiar, for in its basic elements, it replicates the argument elaborated by Sandra

M. Gilbert and Susan Gubar in *The Madwoman in the Attic* (1979) and extends it to the genre of self-representation, positing a "repressed desire" for literary—and thus masculine—authority as the subtext of every woman's life. In making this case, however, Smith's work also invites us to reconsider this interpretive model in relation to autobiography and to feminine authorship, and, as I will demonstrate below, to modify its totalizing claims about women's writing.

Smith locates "the repressed desire of a life like a man's" as the motivating principle in the Victorian text she examines, Harriet Martineau's *Autobiography* (1877). Reading Martineau's text as a paradigmatic example of how the feminine subject who "transgresses" the gendered boundary between the public and private spheres inscribes and is inscribed by the splits that structure gender itself, Smith exposes the contradictions that inhere in being a "public woman" in the Victorian period and thus in a woman's representing herself publicly as well. But her analysis is skewed because her basic and, until recently, quite orthodox feminist assumption—that only men possess authority and that women can only rebel against it—does not adequately account for the ways in which Victorian women *were* invested with authority, literary and otherwise.

I would adduce a very different reading of woman's role in relation to literary authority and cultural production from Martineau's history, the contours of which I can only suggest here, a reading I base on my understanding of Martineau as occupying a privileged position within Victorian culture. As the popularizer of a major hegemonic discourse, Martineau reproduced the lessons of high male theory for myriad private readers, male and female alike; her *Illustrations of Political Economy* (1832-34) were the fictional works primarily responsible for disseminating Utilitarian doctrine among the newly literate classes. Only when what she advocated—Malthusian principles of population control, for example—was perceived as inappropriate to "feminine" discourse did contemporary conservatives launch their scurrilous attacks against her; more sympathetic readers hailed her as a valuable spokesperson and propagandist for the new political economy, which legitimated the oppression of women and the working class. Martineau thus textually participates in perpetuating patriarchal discourse even though her life as a public woman challenges some of its assumptions about women's "proper sphere"; she is, then, not marginal but central to her culture, for her literary work supports the capitalist values on which that culture depends. And her *Autobiography* reenacts her ideological positioning as a woman empowered to speak and to represent herself publicly so long as her speech and writing do not threaten the basic socioeconomic principles that structure the culture, including the separation of the domestic world from the public one. To constitute Martineau as "transgressive," then, in the way that Smith does, is to downplay the ways in which her work upholds the categories her life is presumed to undercut.

In short, Smith's paradigm contains three assumptions contested by recent socialist-feminist analyses of Victorian women's writing: first, that all writing women have a marginal relation to structures of "cultural and literary authority"; second, that women have played little or no part in reproducing the ideological and material conditions that underwrite their own oppression; and third, that for women to represent the self under patriarchy is always an act of transgression. Without denying the heuristic power of her model, I would like to offer an alternative to it, for I believe that scripting a scenario in which women are always at the margins, and indeed are shown to derive their power from that outsider's perspective, occludes the ways in which certain women, primarily middle-class ones, have been empowered under patriarchy—and in its interests—by being positioned at the center, as cultural producers and reproducers of bourgeois values.

I would agree that in authoring their lives under patriarchal ideology, Victorian women writers confront the difficulty of representing female literary identity within a culture that, by and large, denies them the authority to do so in the public, secular realm; to say that, however, is not to say that women's different relation to that realm necessarily bars them from representing the self according to cultural criteria for femininity. Autobiography is, of course, one of the literary forms that most clearly displays its indebtedness to social conventions for representing personal identity, however that elusive concept is defined at any given historical moment; canonical nineteenth-century British autobiographies by male writers, for example, generally legitimate the individualist liberal values of capitalist culture by narrating the development of the self as a vocational history. Martineau's adaptation of this "masculine" form is, as Smith points out, clearly atypical in its time, for not until the end of the century do most middle-class women have access to the liberal rights and opportunities that allow them to map their self-representations onto a developmental model. Yet even though gender difference always continues to be constitutive of other differences, women's autobiographies throughout the century often wind up reinscribing—not challenging—cultural fictions such as fixed norms of gender and class.

In order to demonstrate how some women's autobiographical texts are produced not by transgressing but by conforming to bourgeois norms, I will look here at how one nineteenth-century discourse of the self, a religious discourse that extends interpretive authority to all believing Christians, enables and encourages writing women to represent themselves; within certain patriarchal constraints on what she can represent, the Evangelical emphasis on individual authority enables the woman writer to invoke a system of values that sanctifies her work as useful and important and designates her self-representation as exemplary. Acting in conjunction with the economic logic that assigns women to the private realm, Christian discourse gives the autobiographer authority over that domestic space, which is redefined as the new locus for cultural and even literary authority. Far from being marginal, then, the woman who writes herself in relation to God and the home is at the center of the private sphere, newly invested with the power of producing and reproducing the ideologies that structure Victorian culture. Today, neither the names of these women autobiographers—Mary Martha Sherwood (1775-1851), Charlotte Tonna (1790-1846), and Mary Anne Schimmelpenninck (1778-1856)—nor their works are familiar, while in their own day, the first two at least were amazingly prolific and popular writers. Sherwood's *The Fairchild Family* (1817) and Henry Milner tales were among the most popular children's stories of the period, while Tonna's tracts and novels of the thirties and forties, of the strictest Evangelical tenor, were also widely read. By the time the two came to write their autobiographies, they were well known as "authors," even if they lacked the public profile of their more illustrious male and female contemporaries. And in their autobiographies, the literary space in which we might expect them to represent themselves as authors, they do not establish claims to authorial status, but rather delineate the boundaries within which feminine authorship can be constituted.

Their different rationales for working in this genre, as they explain them, do not overtly involve a wish to capitalize on their popularity: publicity, as we ordinarily think of it, is the last thing the spiritual woman writer would seek. Moreover, their explicit intention in representing themselves is to control the way in which their readers, contemporary and future, will read them. In her *Personal Recollections* (1842), Tonna attempts to seal off what she has constituted as her private self from public view; asserting the sanctity of "private domestic history" and "the sacredness of home," and defending the absence of any remarks on that aspect of her life, she yet acknowledges "that when it has pleased God to bring any one before the public in the capacity of an author, that person becomes in some sense public property; having abandoned the privacy from which no one ought to be forced." Writing about ten years later, and commenting on "the propensity of the age for writing and recording the lives of every individual who has had the smallest claim to celebrity," Sherwood presents *The Life of Mrs. Sherwood* (1857) as a necessary defense against what others might write if she were to leave it unwritten: "Could I be quite sure, that when I am gone, nobody would say anything about me, I should, I think, spare myself the trouble which I am now about to take." She, too, assumes that the text of her life is vulnerable to all sorts of appropriation, and makes her move to autobiography a defense against that possibility of being appropriated.

Both choose to represent the self out of a desire not to be misinterpreted and misused by others; since as "public" figures they cannot count on the silence Sherwood seems to find preferable to speech, they assert a control over how they will be represented by putting their own versions of themselves into discourse. And in explaining their motives, they also signal a particular conception of the relation between the private and the public spheres not as separate realms, but as concentric circles, a conception that allows them to represent themselves without disturbing the line that demarcates their sphere from the public world. While Tonna suggests, for example, that her rhetorical representation of her "person" will become "public property," she posits some familial, interpersonal experience as prior to and privileged over public discourse; the "sacredness" of the private realm, its integrity as a space theoretically sealed off from the public world, must be preserved inviolate for, as we will see, it is precisely the sanctity of the interior that enables the spiritual woman who writes to represent herself publicly. What remains innermost and goes unrepresented—the intricacy of family life—is condensed in the figure of the woman herself.

Tonna's anxiety about making the familial public is linked to women's cultural positioning on the inside, at the center of the domestic circle, which is itself circumscribed by the larger circle of the public world. Because nineteenth-century middle-class women derived their primary social and cultural self-definition from their identification with the private realm, for the writer to maintain her placement in that realm even as she symbolically moves outside it through writing is a difficult, though not impossible, task. A woman's "public" work in representation threatens to undercut her gendered, class-based identity by figuratively connecting her act of self-exposure with acts performed by other public women, who sell not just an ordinary commodity, but their very bodies, in a male-dominated market-place: as Catherine Gallagher asserts [in her "George Eliot and *Daniel Deronda:* The Prostitute and the Jewish Question," in *Sex, Politics, and Science in the Nineteenth-Century Novel,* edited by Ruth Bernard Yeazell, 1986], Victorian writing and Victorian prostitution are metaphorically "linked . . . through their joint habitation of the realm of exchange." But by enabling her to represent her work and her life as part of her ordinary course of duties, the discourse of Christian piety invests the middle-class Christian woman with authority even as it minimizes the risks of her engagement in autobiographical discourse; she negotiates the crossing from the inner circle to the outer one by always representing herself through the signifiers of domesticity and by refusing to locate herself permanently in the public realm of exchange.

If she is thus retroactively to establish her claim to the authority that enabled her to begin writing, and also to legitimate the act of self-representation she engages in at the time of writing, the spiritual autobiographer must not upset the distinction between the norms that constitute appropriate feminine behavior and the eccentricities displayed by those who exceed the prescribed bounds of middle-class femininity. Asserting her own claim to be considered representative of the norm, Sherwood expresses her desire not to be thought exceptional—and thus unwomanly—mainly in terms of her distaste for the stereotypical literary woman, the bluestocking who, forfeiting femininity in her quest for publicity, comes to represent the extraordinary and unnatural woman rather than the conventional and unexceptionable one. Recalling her father's repeated claim that she "was to grow up a genius," Sherwood recollects that back then, as at the time of writing, to be "a celebrated authoress" was not her wish: "even then I felt, if it were necessary to be very singular, I would rather not be a genius"; while "it was a matter of course to me that I was to write, and also a matter of instinct . . . I had a horror of being thought a literary lady; for it was, I fancied, ungraceful." When "forced into public" (her father suggested that she should help an impoverished family friend by publishing her first work and donating the proceeds to him), "my heart sunk at the proposition": "to be set down so soon in that character which I had always dreaded," to feel "the mortification which I felt at being thus dragged into public" made her wish "that I had never known the use of a pen." Her choice of the term "mortification," a word Burney and Austen also use to describe what Evelina and Elizabeth Bennet experience when publicly exposed, either physically or psychologically, suggests that for the woman writer to enter the public world, even through the impersonal medium of print, is to incur the risk of social or moral death; Sherwood constructs the passage from the home to the world as symbolically representing the loss of the feminine self.

At this border, where the public and the private meet in self-representation, we see how competing tensions—the woman writer's need to remain situated within the domestic realm and her simultaneous engagement in the public process of writing, in which her name (if not her body) circulates at large within public discourse merely by the fact of publication—produce an anxiety about literature and literary production itself, about how texts function in the world and how their circulation affects their producers. As Mary Poovey notes [in her *Proper Lady and the Woman Writer,* 1984], while an "objective text" like a novel "serves as a more general mediator between self and public," the avowedly "subjective" text the autobiographer composes, which formally and thematically negotiates the line between private feminine experience and the public masculine world, presents itself as neither mediated nor mediating, as a window that opens directly onto the soul. For some women writers, opening that window onto the private is so fraught with danger that only fiction, or a masculine pseudonym, can provide them with the curtain necessary to shield them from public view. But by invoking a higher power than the self as the legitimating Author of their lives and their texts, by writing from the position of the Christian subject, whose life and work are always oriented toward an eternal goal, the outer circle which circumscribes all human life, women writers find a viable way of representing female experience. The combination of religious and domestic authority sanctions female authorship.

Although most feminists have, with good reason, tended to see religion as enforcing the patriarchal values that consign women to silence, recent revisionist work has begun to establish the counterpoint to the monolithic view that casts all religious discourse as inherently oppressive: as Gail Malmgreen puts it [in the Introduction to her edition, *Religion in the Lives of English Women, 1760-1930,* 1986], "it is surely neither possible nor necessary to weigh up, once and for all, the gains and losses for women of religious commitment . . . the dealings of organised religion with women have been richly laced with ironies and contradictions." If religion helped produce the ideology that assigned women to the domestic sphere, it also enabled them, within that realm, to write and act in ways that women who sought access to literary authority on purely secular grounds could not.

As Elizabeth Jay writes in her study of Evangelicalism and the Victorian novel [*The Religion of the Heart: Anglican Evangelicalism and the Nineteenth-Century Novel,* 1979], "the religion of the heart" invested its believers with "the onus of interpreting God's Word": "no appeal to any authoritative body of dogmatic pronouncements" could relieve the individual of her responsibility to establish her relation to the Bible and to God, for the eternal welfare of her soul ultimately depended on that relationship. And gender, here as everywhere else in the nineteenth century, plays its role as a determining factor in prescribing the possible limits and acceptable range of feminine discourse. For example, the cultural prohibition against women engaging in public activity, in conjunction with the spiritual imperative to meekness and humility, while dictating style and content does not absolutely prevent writing. Adhering to those unwritten laws, in fact, keeps the writing woman from the spiritual and moral death Sherwood fears, as in Tonna's invocation of the religious bent of her works as a safeguard against the ever-present temptation of taking too much satisfaction in her own literary abilities:

> . . . the literary labour that I pursued for my own sustenance was perfect luxury, so long as my humble productions were made available for the spiritual good of the people so dear to me. My little books and tracts became popular; because, after some struggle against a plan so humbling to literary pride, I was able to adopt the suggestion of a wise Christian brother, and form a style of such homely simplicity that if, on reading a manuscript to a child of five years old, I found there was a single word above his comprehension, it was instantly corrected to suit that lowly standard.

In a move that oddly recalls Wordsworth's transvaluation of work in the opening lines of *The Prelude,* Tonna's "labour" becomes "luxury"; "literary pride" is transformed into the "homely simplicity" of her style and her very self once she orients her writing toward a spiritual end. The "wise Christian brother," figure of patriarchal authority, is to Tonna not an oppressor but a benefactor, for it is his warning that keeps her on the appropriate path for the righteous Christian woman.

In these terms, the religious woman's writing entails not public "mortification," but the private mortification of the self before God, which leads to eternal life, for the writer herself and for her readers as well, to whom Tonna can relate through a shared system of values and beliefs. By erasing all traces of art and artfulness, she shows herself willing and able to mortify her "literary pride" before those readers in order to establish a reading community of comprehending converts. While writing demands that she present herself to an unfamiliar audience, the religious woman writer reduces the risk of entering discourse by appealing to values, specifically religious ones, that require her self-effacement even as they invest her with a voice to which other Evangelical Christians will listen.

For a reader of other nineteenth-century autobiographies, the lack of information provided in these women's texts about the actual activity of writing can be quite maddening, or, at the very least, startling: when juxtaposed with Mill's *Autobiography* (1877), that classic case of the life that, without Harriet Taylor, would have almost solely consisted of readings and writings, or with Trollope's *Autobiography* (1883), with its detailed description of all aspects of his literary work, including the ledger that sums up the total of his emoluments, these texts hardly seem to be by writers at all, so thoroughly do they repress the signs of literary production. But this silence, too, supports the exemplary status of the author-autobiographer: the publicity that writing entails, even the most minimal engagement with publishers, editors, and printers, is banished, thus enabling the writer to root her identity in the private sphere, where the middle-class woman neither calls attention to whatever undomestic talents and ambitions she may possess nor trespasses on male territory by commenting directly on political events. Keeping both her discourse and her body within the limits of the feminine sphere insures that the religious woman writer will not be subjected to the kind of criticism the autobiographer Mary Sewell leveled at a mid-Victorian woman evangelist who delivered her message directly to a public audience: a public proselytizer, unlike a private didact, is cut off from the legitimating power and protection of the family, for " 'a lone woman who speaks in public,' " Sewell intones, " 'is *a very lone creature* indeed.' "

Remaining private empowers the religious woman writer; keeping silent on certain subjects is a definite necessity for maintaining that power, and politics is thus a topic these texts do not speak of. Tonna, for instance, does not refer at all to her political beliefs, even though they deeply informed the rhetoric of her industrial novels; while she claims that she has been "often charged with the offence

Harriet Martineau.

of being too political in my writings," her autobiography reveals nothing to substantiate that charge. While Schimmelpenninck was an adolescent at the time of the French Revolution, contemporary politics never enter her self-representation: she writes not of "public events, with which I have nothing to do," but promises to trace "the effects which they produced on the domestic sphere with which I had experience," a promise she does not fulfill [*Life of Mary Anne Schimmelpenninck,* 1858]. The possibility of writing an account that would draw on the happenings of the public world is held out and then withheld; the actuality of public history is invoked only to be dismissed according to the implicit dictum that confines the woman autobiographer to writing solely about what is proper to her sphere. She cannot construct herself as "author," nor will she textually engage with public events.

What the female Christian autobiographer, like her counterpart, the female novelist at mid-century, is presumed to know best and encouraged to confine her attention to is, of course, character, and, specifically, female character. And everyone's character appears to best advantage in the private sphere, for it is "in the private lives of the children of God," as Sherwood puts it, "that we are enabled best to discern the wonderful beauty of the Divine influence . . . in the most private intercourse with the humblest and feeblest persons . . . we find the best and most lovely exhibitions of the Christian graces." Like Sarah Ellis [*The Wives of England,* 1843], who conceived the influence of a woman's "individual character" as "operating upon those more immediately around her, but by no means ceasing there; for each of her domestics, each of her relatives, and each of her familiar friends, will in their turn become the centre of another circle," Sherwood sees developing and shaping individual character as woman's special province.

Her school for doing so is the home, the realm of affective ties which is counterposed to the heartless world; the Christian household, in Nancy Armstrong's words [in her *Desire and Domestic Fiction,* 1987], "[detaches] itself from the political world and [provides] the complement and antidote to it," as the place where private virtue arms the family against public vice. Ideologically endowed with the responsibility for molding moral character, and particularly in relation to girls, the private-sphere writer must protect herself from "the danger of celebrity" (Sherwood) and avoid all traffic with the public world; her sphere is located on the inside, in the home and the heart, and her place is at the center. By eliminating everything external to the domestic, everything in the public world, from her texts, she both accedes to and reinforces the limits on the range of possible discourse, and so maintains her right to instruct her audience within her own realm, in the formation of everyday private-sphere virtues.

That writing itself, rightly conceived, does not conflict with women's prescribed role but, on the contrary, amplifies and extends it, proves to be a point to which all three autobiographies attest in their affirmation of the writing religious woman. Womanhood is itself valorized in these texts, in part for its disinterestedness: " 'Remember, it is a privilege to be a woman instead of a man,' " writes

Schimmelpenninck, recording her mother's words; " 'men, heroes, and others, do things partly to do good and partly to gain a great name; but a woman's self-denial and generosity may be as great, and often greater, while it is unknown to others, and fully manifest only to her own conscience and to God: to work for this, and for this alone, is the highest of all callings'." But invoking the language and concept of calling to define and deify womanhood, as conservative writers on femininity from Hannah More to Sarah Ellis repeatedly do in their writings, does not strictly predicate the ways in which that vocation may be practiced; it rules out only the love of fame as an end while presenting as the paramount object the necessity of making one's conscience fit for God's sight.

The way to keep that conscience clear is, paradoxically, to make its workings readable, not only to God, but to other readers: the Christian woman's self-examination, conducted through and throughout her life, externally expresses what would otherwise remain hidden from all eyes but God's, the subject's heart and mind. While the interpersonal and the political fall outside the circumscribed area of what the religious woman writer can represent, the most personal experience—the writer's relation to God—must be made legible in her text: reversing the logic of inside and outside, private and public, spiritual autobiography makes what is ostensibly most private, the inner self, the substance of the public representation.

As Carol Edkins' work on eighteenth-century American women's spiritual autobiographies ["Quest for Community: Spiritual Autobiographies of Eighteenth-Century Quaker and Puritan Women in America," in *Women's Autobiographies: Essays in Criticism,* edited by Estelle C. Jelinek, 1980] establishes, the religious woman can publicly represent this individual (but not unique) experience because her readers understand the conventions of religious discourse: the shared values held by autobiographer and reader "[create] a symbolic bonding with the group" such that her exemplary spiritual progress can be read and imitated by others. Spiritual autobiography, then, not only permits but demands of its writers an excruciatingly thorough self-inquisition, and particularly on the issue of writing itself, for those who produce literature and self-representations are responsible not only to God, but to other Christian readers as well, as a crisis of authorship reported in Tonna's text illustrates. Caught between the need to make a living and the demands of her husband, who apparently tried to annex her earnings as his own even after they separated, Tonna must decide between continuing to write her religious works under her own name, thereby forfeiting the income garnered by her pen, and beginning to write secular fiction under a pseudonym, which would disguise her identity and protect her income. She submits her case not to a court of law, as Caroline Norton did when entrapped in a similar situation, but to God's will:

> The idea of hiring myself out to another master—to engage in the service of that world the friendship of which is enmity with God—to cause the Holy One of Israel to cease from before those whom by the pen I addressed—to refrain from setting forth Jesus Christ and Him crucified to a perishing world, and give the reins to an imagination ever prone to wander after folly and romance, but now subdued to a better rule—all this was so contrary to my views of Christian principle that, after much earnest prayer to God, I decided rather to work gratuitously in the good cause, trusting to him who knew all my necessity, than to entangle myself with things on which I could not ask a blessing.

To serve "another master"—the world or Mammon—is an option she will not choose, since it is only her dissemination of God's word that authorizes her writing in the first place; by prayerful, conscientious self-examination, she arrives at the correct spiritual and moral decision. Moreover, to write for the secular world would entail a personal fall as well: by losing the audience of converts and believers already constituted for her, by "[giving] the reins to an imagination ever prone to wander after folly and romance," and thus undoing the labor to submit all human desires "to a better rule" which the autobiography records in painstaking detail, she would feed her body while starving her soul and the souls of others who live and labor in "a perishing world."

Again we see that writing must come under God's rule, but we see as well the way in which Tonna conceptualizes her self, God-given but marred by "indwelling sin," as a battleground between opposing forces of good and evil. Her duty, then, is to overrule the depravity of the self, including the innate tendency of the imagination to focus on vain and worldly things, by opening it to the intense scrutiny of God's light, and her readers' eyes, and by keeping careful watch over herself; in Schimmelpenninck's metaphor, which nicely illustrates the spatial relation between inside and outside and the permeable barrier that separates them, the self is a tabernacle and "an efficient company of porters and doorkeepers should guard every gate of access into the temple." Only a constant self-surveillance can insure that one's soul and one's writing will not be invaded by God's enemies, but that policing of the temple only restricts access; it does not prevent the autobiographer from representing the inner sanctuary.

For middle-class women, invested as they are with the responsibility for the moral life of children and, to a great extent, of adult men, interrogating the self is particularly crucial; for the woman writer, however, it is even more so. By writing and publishing, and thereby extending her influence to include not only like-minded middle-class Christians, but often the working class as well, she could as easily become a force for evil as for good, particularly since her position makes her so much more susceptible to the "temptations" and "mortification" of the public sphere. In order to mold the character of others, her own character must be scrutinized, continually searched for signs of moral and doctrinal failure. Thus the imperative to examine the self in writing throughout one's life, through letters and journals, and as one's earthly life draws to its close, in autobiography, is necessary for maintaining the fiction of authority that enables her to begin writing in the first place. God's sanction allows her to write, and to write the self is to test and re-test the validity of that sanction.

Writing for the marketplace is not, of course, the most decorous way for the middle-class woman to carry out her civilizing function, nor can the writer ever fulfill the true womanly ideal as it is configured by patriarchy: as George Henry Lewes comments sardonically in 1850 ["A Gentle Hint to Writing-Women", *The Leader,* 18 May 1850], "*My* idea of a perfect woman is of one who can write but won't; who knows all the authors know and a great deal more; who can appreciate my genius and not spoil my market." Sarah Ellis's far less ironic view, as quoted above, which imagines the exemplary domestic woman's influence as inspiring others to create perfect circles of their own, is shared, surprisingly, by Mary Russell Mitford, who portrays her ideal woman in much the same terms:

> the very happiest position that a woman of great talent can occupy in our high civilisation, is that of living a beloved and distinguished member of the best literary society . . . repaying all that she receives by a keen and willing sympathy; cultivating to perfection the social faculty; but abstaining from the wider field of authorship, even while she throws out here and there such choice and chosen bits as prove that nothing but disinclination to enter the arena debars her from winning the prize. [*Recollections of a Literary Life,* 1852]

The ideal woman Lewes and Mitford construct is the amateur *par excellence;* like Ellis's woman, she rests at the still center of the domestic sphere, defined not so much by what she produces as by what she reproduces, the cultured, leisured middle-class existence that approximates an earlier, but still operative, aristocratic ideal of unproductive gentility. As a later formulation of this model suggests, the true work of women, "a mission quite as grand as literary authorship," is not to write, but to "[keep] alive for men certain ideas, and ideals too, which would soon pass out of the world in the rush and hurry of material existence if they were not fed and replenished by those who are able to stand aloof from the worry and vexations of active life" ["Literary Women," *The London Review,* 26 March 1864]. Women's role in literary production, then, should be to protect and transmit culture, virtue, and private values; "feeding" and "replenishing," reproducing the material conditions of existence as well as the spiritual "ideas, and ideals" that have no home in the "arena" of the public world, domestic women also insure that art will continue to be produced.

The secular model for professional authorship suggests that male artistry requires female subordination; the ideal woman is confined to the home, where she carries out the unpaid labor of biological and cultural reproduction. Yet the religious woman who writes, whether or not she does so, as Mitford did, from financial necessity, makes up for what she might appear to lack in perfect womanhood by using literature itself as her medium for reproducing and exchanging domestic values. She sends her book out into the world only so that it will enter homes other than her own, where its influence will operate on other readers.

The autobiographers considered here definitely see literature's role in forming and disseminating the private-sphere virtues as central: that "the spiritual good of the people" of which Tonna speaks is actively advanced by their writing is not an assumption she and Sherwood ever question, and each also assumes that secular literature, which Schimmelpenninck calls "pestilential" and of "evil influence," does the devil's work in the world. These women can thus construct their writing as one of their womanly duties, a Christian duty to push back the powers of darkness by spreading the light of truth and salvation, a duty which the middle-class woman may carry out in print along the same lines as she does in her home and in her personal relations with others. Putting the values of the domestic into a public form for public circulation, the spiritual woman writer projects what she represents (which is equivalent to who she is) into a book, a tract, or a self-representing text, which passes through the public world en route to other middle-class homes; there it will be consumed in the service of the continuing reproduction of the values her life and her text embody.

In Ellis's terms, the exemplary woman's text spawns other domestic circles, other moral centers; that task, however, is not accomplished by women's "[entering] the arena," or "the wider field of authorship," but rather through reconstituting literature, and the scene of reading, as a private-sphere activity—women do not go outside, but literature comes in. Redefined as a private agent of private values, the religious woman's work exemplifies the powerful moralizing force of private femininity, a force which in its textual form actively combats the influence of secular novels, those "gin-palaces of the mind," in Schimmelpenninck's words, and "all that stimulates unproductive sensibilities."

Schimmelpenninck argues, in appropriately circular fashion, that women have both acted upon and been acted upon by literature, and that the mutual interchange has altered both in the process. Casting the history of literature from her youth at the time of writing as the history of its feminization, she asserts an identity between women's role and literature's purpose:

> The great increase of literary taste amongst women has wrought a wonderful change, not only in collections of books, but in their composition. Books were then written only for men; now they are written so that women can participate in them: and no man would think of forming a library in his house, without a thought that its volumes must be the companions of his wife and daughters in many a lonely hour, when their influence must sink into the heart, and tend to modify the taste and character. Thus, in literature, as in other things, and especially in domestic life, has the mercy of God bestowed on women the especial and distinguishing blessing of upholding the moral and religious influence, that spirit of truth and love by which man can alone be redeemed from the fall she brought upon him.

Women's education in the principles of "literary taste" makes for a change in how the domestic library, the physical locus for reading, is structured as well as in how each individual constituent part, each book, is composed: the fact that more women read requires the production of books that invite and allow "feminine participation" in them as readers. While the patriarch still determines the shape of the collection, he must choose more judiciously now than he did at some earlier point in time when books were "written only for men," for books are, anthropomorphically, "companions" for women, capable, as women in particular are, of molding human lives: "their influence must sink into the heart," the innermost center of the reading subject, "and tend to modify the taste and character."

Books become, in short, like women: they are moral agents whose influence shapes the interior life of their readers, and in doing so, they also prepare women to become writers who will send back into the world the lessons they have learned from reading the primers of the heart. Schimmelpenninck projects feminine moral force into a material object that can save all readers—and the woman writer herself—from the consequences of the first woman's sin, the desire for knowledge, for if the world fell through Eve's weakness, then it can only be "redeemed" through her stronger daughters' labor as readers and writers: Adam's curse is women's "especial and distinguishing blessing." And literature shapes the character of its readers within the confines of the gentleman's private library (rather than the eighteenth-century public coffeehouse, accessible only to men) as women themselves do in their private roles as wives and mothers; it acts as an agent of that private "moral and religious influence" which, implicitly because of their role as public beings, few men can supply. Thus the religious woman writer need never even leave the home to do her work, which is spatially, spiritually, and socially centered in her father's house.

In the moral economy of the Christian Victorian household, domestic women produce and reproduce the spiritual food necessary for the whole family's consumption: in its self-sufficiency and autonomy from what lies outside it, woman's sphere appears to constitute itself as the realm that saves the fallen public world from its own sins. What we see in looking at these autobiographies is that within a conservative ideological framework, writing need not be constructed as a threat to the feminine self, for writing itself is privatized and feminized by women's influence, transposed from the public world to the private one. Nor does their writing threaten to undermine the naturalness of the public-private split, for the confluence of the norms of femininity and those of Christianity produces a powerful ideology of the private sphere that simultaneously legitimates women's writing and puts it in the service of the continuing reproduction of bourgeois hegemony, since the goal of the exemplary self-representing text is to elide the differences between lives and texts, realities and representations. In the religious woman writer's self-representation, then, writing one's life as an exemplary text testifies to the ideological importance of the woman writer's leading an exemplary life. (pp. 13-27)

Mary Jean Corbett, "Feminine Authorship and Spiritual Authority in Victorian Women Writers' Autobiographies," in Women's Studies: An Interdisciplinary Journal, *Vol. 18, No. 1, 1990, pp. 13-29.*

Valerie Sanders

[*In the following essay, Sanders examines the autobiographies of four female Victorian authors, noting how these help define and promote nineteenth-century beliefs concerning the roles of women in society.*]

"My work and I have been fitted to each other, as is proved by the success of my work and my own happiness in it." Few Victorian female autobiographers celebrate the outcome of their professional lives with comparable satisfaction; yet even Harriet Martineau, populariser of political economy, novelist, journalist, traveller, and historian, surrounds this statement in her *Autobiography* with a wall of protective disclaimers and qualifications explaining why she did not marry and have children, as a "normal" woman would have done. Attributing her unsuitability for marriage and the care of a family to defects in her own personality, especially a lack of self-respect, she presents her choice of single life and a career in terms that strike an acceptable compromise between ambition and conformity: "The simplicity and independence of this vocation first suited my infirm and ill-developed nature, and then sufficed for my needs, together with family ties and domestic duties, such as I have been blessed with, and as every woman's heart requires."

The question of what "every woman's heart requires," at least in the view of potential readers, was to dog most Victorian women who attempted any form of autobiographical writing. If, as Patricia Meyer Spacks has argued [in her *The Female Imagination: A Literary and Psychological Investigation of Women's Writing,* 1975], "all autobiography must rest on a foundation of self-absorption," if the genre must, by definition, entail self-display, and the discovery, through writing, of an enduring and separate identity, Victorian women faced special problems in justifying to their first audiences their decision to pursue a professional career. As Elizabeth Winston has suggested [in *Women's Autobiography: Essays in Criticism,* ed. by Estelle C. Jelinek, 1980], women writing before 1920 "show ambivalence about being professional writers at a time when the usual pattern for a female was immersion in domesticity." This ambivalence is often felt throughout an autobiography, but it becomes especially acute when the author starts writing about how she started writing; when she comes to detail the course of events which rescued her from what was usually a monotonous domestic life, and made her, suddenly, a professional success. A survey of autobiographies by Victorian women who were subsequently successful in their professional lives, shows that though many were ambitious as girls, and believed in their own special destiny, generally as writers, most dismiss such ambitions as comically immature or egocentric. Most try to minimize the selfish impulses that thrust them into a full and stimulating career; most try to convince their audiences that their professional acclaim was, initially, at least, fortuitous and unimportant.

In each of the four autobiographies I have selected for discussion, the moment of breakthrough is preceded by a period of dullness and depression, roughly corresponding to the mood of hopelessness associated, in spiritual autobiographies, with a first conviction of sin. In each of the secular autobiographies, the writer is acutely conscious of her boredom or emotional turmoil; she feels isolated, or somehow different from the rest of her family, but is unable to do anything positive to help herself. She waits, like Bunyan, in *Grace Abounding to the Chief of Sinners,* in a state of active passivity, to be "called" by a force outside herself. When Rachel Curtis, heroine of Charlotte M. Yonge's novel, *The Clever Woman of the Family* (1865), declares "My mission has come to seek me," she expresses succinctly that fusion of longing and inertia which characterizes the mood of many Victorian women immediately before the discovery of a fulfilling occupation. It seems especially fitting, in this context, that terms such as "vocation," "calling," and "mission," have both a spiritual and a secular significance, relieving the author of some degree of responsibility for her choice of career. Additional detachment is achieved through self-mockery or belittlement, reference to fairy tales, or mention of pressing family problems, which their success, to some extent, relieved. Through much of the narrative, there survives a strong sense of exhilaration and release, constantly deflated by the apologetic nature of the author's voice and the shaping of her story, as she identifies closely with her early self at the point of crisis, yet reasserts the rational, mildly ironic tone of her present self as narrator.

The four autobiographers I have chosen to discuss are Harriet Martineau (1802-76), Fanny Kemble (1809-93), Margaret Oliphant (1828-97) and Elizabeth Missing Sewell (1815-1906): women largely forgotten today, but all, in their time, professionally successful. All, except Fanny Kemble, were prolific writers; all four pursued a career largely for economic reasons. Harriet Martineau and Elizabeth Sewell were single and childless; Fanny Kemble and Margaret Oliphant married relatively young and had children, but lost their husbands through divorce or death. They tend to dwell on the difficulties they experienced, and the misery of their early lives. Mrs Oliphant's excepted, their autobiographies recall an unhappy, or, at best, patchily happy childhood, disturbed by bouts of illness, neurotic fears, and insensitive treatment by severe or unsympathetic adults. This pattern is, of course, common enough in Victorian autobiography of all kinds, both fictional and formal, male and female. Nor is adolescence often seen as a happy time. Either the miseries of hypersensitivity increase, or the author resorts to mockery of an awkward appearance, flighty temper, fanaticism, or early attempts at courtship or literary composition. With the advent of a professional life, however, the divergence between male and female modes of autobiographical writing becomes more apparent. Whereas young Victorian men were encouraged to choose a lucrative, or, at least, "steady" career, or were summarily directed to a career chosen for them by their fathers, their sisters were kept at home, to improve themselves for marriage, and assist in the running of their father's household before removal to their husband's. Their close participation in family affairs was usually inevitable; few educated, middle-class women felt entitled to seek paid work on their own account, unless death or economic pressures drove them into it, and endowed their gesture of independence with all the sanctity of an unselfish, altruistic rescue. Frances Power Cobbe, for instance, describes her "home duties" as ending at her father's death, when, at the age of thirty-six, she felt entitled to start working how and where she pleased. In each of the four autobiographies I have selected, as in many others, there is a direct link between the daughter's vocational fulfilment, and the death, illness, or failure of her parents.

The moment of choice and success is trammelled, in each narrative, by a web of conflicting impulses. At the beginning, the author tries to explain her triumph in a calm, rational manner; then she starts to fantasize, to fictionalize, to relive the episode with vivid dialogue, and the revival of feelings sometimes half a century old. She may express, on the one hand, indifference, or hostility to her new-found role; on the other, her reconstructed memories of a personal victory recreate a mood of intense exhilaration and excitement, which, in turn, heightens the tension between the call for modesty, and the temptation to boast of triumphs honestly won, and against family expectation. Underlying the whole episode, and dictating its form, is the constant need to win sympathy and understanding from an unknown audience; to say nothing that will antagonize, while retaining the right to recall a success which was, in its time, the opening to emotional and economic release.

In Harriet Martineau's case, the miseries of childhood and adolescence were complicated by growing deafness, the coolness of apparently undemonstrative parents, and relentless teasing by her older brothers and sisters. When she was sixteen, and away at boarding-school in Bristol, her religion reflected the joyless, fanatical character of her mind: "and it was harsh, severe and mournful accordingly" (*Autobiography,* I). Returning home with "an abominable spiritual rigidity and a truly respectable force of conscience curiously mingled together," she earned for herself "the no less curiously mingled ridicule and respect" of her family. From 1819 until November 1832, she lived at home in Norwich, for what seemed to her a distinctively "marked period": the years extending from the beginning of adulthood, to the winning of an independent position in society. In tribute to the importance of these years, she devotes a separate section to them, opening with an account of her "early aspirations after authorship."

She recalls that these aspirations were encouraged by her mother, but her eldest sister made fun of her "conceit": whereupon she "instantly resolved 'never to tell anybody any thing again.' " By driving Harriet's ambition underground, her sister inaugurated the process of secrecy and concealment which was to surround the publication of her first article: "and when I did attempt to write, it was at the suggestion of another, and against my own judgment and inclination." It is worth pausing for a moment over the circumstances of this first publication, since the terms in which she describes it emphatically cleanse the episode of all self-interested initiative, and place the responsibility for her success squarely at the feet of her two favourite brothers, Thomas and James. Devotion to a brother is a recurrent motif in Victorian women's autobiography, from *The Mill on the Floss* to Elizabeth Missing Sewell's *Autobiography,* which is partly, at least, a memorial to her brother William's work at Radley College. Whether we see this as sublimated sexual feeling, especially in women who remained single, or as a sign of submerged intellectual rivalry, close relationships with brothers often served to legitimize a first practical attempt at professional authorship.

It was James Martineau, the future Unitarian minister and philosopher, who first encouraged Harriet to write, as consolation for her unhappiness when he returned to college after the vacations. "I said, as usual, that I would if he would," she remembers, again emphasizing her evident passivity in the process that was to lead directly to the publication of her first article. "What James desired, I always did, of course," she adds, linking her passivity with a habit of obedience, even to a younger brother. During her next period of "widowhood," as she calls it, she began a letter to the Editor of the Unitarian *Monthly Repository,* on "Female Writers on Practical Divinity," humbly signing herself "Discipulus." The choice of subject-matter was respectable, but with interesting feminist implications. Adopting the authoritarian voice that was to become a hallmark of her mature writing, she proposed to discuss, not only the special strengths of Mrs Barbauld and Hannah More as moral writers, but also, in a future article, "to examine some of the prejudices which still exist on the subject of female education." When her eldest brother, Thomas, read aloud and praised the first article [published in October, 1822], and she surprised him by her lack of enthusiasm, she was obliged to confess:

> I replied, in utter confusion,—'I never could baffle any body. The truth is, that paper is mine.' He made no reply; read on in silence, and spoke no more till I was on my feet to come away. He then laid his hand on my shoulder, and said gravely (calling me 'dear' for the first time) 'Now, dear, leave it to other women to make shirts and darn stockings; and do you devote yourself to this.' I went home in a sort of dream, so that the squares of the pavement seemed to float before my eyes. That evening made me an authoress.

This piece of dialogue raises many central issues. Primarily, it heightens the moment of achieved success, by isolating her brother's praise and her own exhilaration in a magical story. It also posits writing as a clear alternative to needlework, and all that needlework represents, with a man's authority to support her; though, as she insists elsewhere in the *Autobiography,* she was always a competent needlewoman, and could even earn her living by her needle, "as it once was necessary for a few months." She also remembers the episode as the occasion of her brother's first notable demonstration of love, in an undemonstrative family. Finally, it ends with the memory of triumph and excitement, removing her from a humdrum domestic routine into a private dream-world where she could enjoy an inward celebration of her fulfilled ambition.

Her career, as she describes it, was launched by the younger brother, and sanctioned by the elder; while she, as "widowed" and secretive sister, submitted quietly to their combined wills, but wrote, as she would throughout her life as a journalist, on a subject directly concerned with silent minorities. Her father's death in 1826, and the subsequent failure of his firm, in 1829, set the final seal on her choice of career. With only a shilling in her purse when the crash came, she was free to earn her living as she thought best. Though once again a passive victim of circumstances, she makes no attempt to conceal her sense of triumph:

> In a very short time, my two sisters at home and I began to feel the blessing of a wholly new freedom. I, who had been obliged to write before breakfast, or in some private way, had henceforth liberty to do my own work in my own way; for we had lost our gentility. Many and many a time since have we said that, but for that loss of money, we might have lived on in the ordinary provincial method of ladies with small means, sewing, and economizing, and growing narrower every year; whereas, by being thrown, while it was yet time, on our own resources, we have worked hard and usefully, won friends, reputation and independence, seen the world abundantly, abroad and at home, and, in short, have truly lived instead of vegetated.

From its muted beginnings, the passage builds to a triumphant climax, reversing the experience of "growing narrower" to seeing "the world." Yet it would be difficult to predict that the girl who needed her brothers' permission to write, and her father's business failure to legitimize her writing as a career, would become one of the most controversial public figures of the mid-nineteenth century, shocking her readers with her advocacy of birth-control, agnosticism, mesmerism, easier divorces, abolition of the Contagious Diseases Acts, and recognition of women's wage-earning capacity. Consequently, relations with the implied audience of her *Autobiography* often seem uncertain and restless. There can be no doubt that she genuinely enjoyed her professional life, despite its toll on her health, and of all the autobiographers under discussion, she felt most at ease in the career she had chosen. Yet, as she insists in a later passage of her *Autobiography,* authorship was not, for her "a matter of choice. I have not done it for amusement, or for money, or for fame, or for any reason but because I could not help it." Her comment represents, in its purest form, the denial of personal choice, which becomes the central theme of a woman autobiographer's professional life.

Fanny Kemble's three-volume autobiography, *Record of a Girlhood* (1878), itself only the first part of a three-part succession of memoirs, is relaxed and gossipy, with many extracts from letters to her friend, Harriet St. Leger, and lengthy digressions full of theatrical anecdotes. She devotes over sixty rambling pages to an account of her stage début as Juliet just before her twentieth birthday; yet despite the gossip and humour, this passage of her autobiography is troubled and contradictory in tone, as she insists on her dislike of the stage, while showing that she triumphed as Juliet and had a natural aptitude for the part. Entrance on a theatrical career was clearly even more compromising to a woman's modesty and family duties than was the life of a popular author. A novelist could, at least, choose what she wrote, and direct it towards some acceptable end, as Elizabeth Sewell did in her church novels, *Amy Herbert* and *Laneton Parsonage;* but an actress must act a part laid down for her by someone (generally a man) with possibly unreliable moral standards. She was, in any case, required to display, in performance, an exhausting range of artificial emotions: to weep and scream and laugh on demand. Fanny Kemble felt that acting was "a business which is public exhibition, unworthy of a woman." Yet in 1828, she had secretly decided that a stage career would be more lucrative than writing, and could be made "respectable" by "honourable conduct."

Fanny's moment came in 1829, when her father's involvement in the financial affairs of Covent Garden brought him to severe straits. "My life at home at this time became difficult and troublesome, and unsatisfactory to myself and others," she recalls, evoking the conditions of mental and emotional uncertainty, which, in so many autobiographies by Victorian women, occurred in the gap between the completion of their education, and the opening of a career. Like Harriet Martineau, she associates her unhappy state of mind with the absence of a brother, though in rather different circumstances: John Kemble, the family's great hope, had failed his examinations at Trinity College, Cambridge, much to his parents' disappointment, and had gone abroad. Her friend Harriet's brother was dangerously ill: "and I was thrown almost entirely upon myself, and was finding my life monotonously dreary, when events occurred that changed its whole tenor almost suddenly, and determined my future career with less of deliberation than would probably have satisfied either my parents or myself under less stringent circumstances."

When news came of the theatre's collapse, Fanny was "seized with a sort of terror, like the Lady of Shallott [sic]": she comforted her mother, and wrote to her father, who was away in Ireland, offering to find a job as a governess, so as to relieve him of her maintenance. Her mother, however, had other ideas: she asked her to learn a part for the stage, and Fanny chose Portia—"then, as now, my ideal of a perfect woman." Although her first part was actually Juliet, Fanny lingers significantly with Portia:

> the wise, witty woman, loving with all her soul, and submitting with all her heart to a man whom everybody but herself (who was the best judge) would have judged her inferior; the laughter-loving, light-hearted, deep-hearted woman, full of keen perception, of active efficiency, of wisdom prompted by love, of tenderest unselfishness, of generous magnanimity; noble, simple, humble, pure; true, dutiful, religious, and full of fun; delightful above all others the woman of women.

Fanny's analysis emphasizes Portia's generosity of spirit and obedience (even to a man unworthy of her): a role that no woman need be ashamed of acting in the theatre. As it was, Mrs Kemble considered the part too passionless, and requested Juliet instead. When Fanny acted well before her parents, her achievement, like Harriet Martineau's, brought her new demonstrations of love, in the form of "many kisses and caresses." Her next ordeal was a voice-trial in the deserted theatre, where the unreal darkness and silence of the place inspired an uninhibited performance:

> Set down in the midst of twilight space, as it were, with only my father's voice coming to me from where he stood hardly distinguishable in the gloom, in those poetical utterances of pathetic passion I was seized with the spirit of the thing; my voice resounded through the great vault above and below me, and completely carried away by the inspiration of the wonderful play, I acted Juliet as I do not believe I ever acted it again, for I had no visible Romeo, and no audience to thwart my imagination.

The structure of every sentence accentuates her lack of responsibility for what she was doing: she was "set down," she was "seized with the spirit of the thing," she was "completely carried away" by the power of Shakespeare's writing, and perhaps by the God-like quality of her father's voice speaking invisibly from the gloom. She was mesmerized into obedience, with no audience, and, more importantly no Romeo, to inhibit her display of passion; and from this passive obedience sprang, paradoxically, a new kind of self-activity, expressed by "my voice resounded" and "I acted Juliet as I do not believe I ever acted it again." The hint of contradiction traceable here returns, greatly augmented, whenever she abandons her cheerful anecdotes, and resumes the story of her own début.

The rest of this section is concerned with family relations, and her sense of loyalty to her parents, so that the decision to begin a theatrical career is seen as an act of family duty:

> My frame of mind under the preparations that were going forward for my *début* appears to me now curious enough. Though I had found out that I could act, and had acted with a sort of frenzy of passion and entire self-forgetfulness the first time I ever uttered the wonderful conception I had undertaken to represent, my going on the stage was absolutely an act of duty and conformity to the will of my parents, strengthened by my own conviction that I was bound to help them by every means in my power.

As frenzied lover, Fanny Kemble was risking herself in an anarchic role; as dutiful daughter, helping to save her family from economic ruin, she was behaving with exemplary unselfishness and fortitude. But as the passage goes on, it reveals a fundamental conflict between her moral objections to her chosen profession, and the exhilaration she experienced in performance:

> The theatrical profession was, however, utterly distasteful to me, though *acting* itself, that is to say, dramatic personation, was not; and every detail of my future vocation, from the preparations behind the scenes to the representations before the curtain, was more or less repugnant to me. Nor did custom ever render this aversion less; and liking my work so little, and being so devoid of enthusiasm, respect, or love for it, it is wonderful to me that I ever achieved *any* success in it at all.

Perhaps she protests too much. She certainly uses every opportunity to stress her reluctance to act, cancelling every positive assertion with a stream of earnest denials, and assuring her readers that she continued to live, as far as she could, a normal ladylike existence. On the day of her first appearance, she spent her morning much as usual: "practising the piano, walking in the inclosure of St. James's Park . . . and reading in 'Blunt's Scripture Characters'," a book in which she was then "deeply interested." Having already mentioned the "incessant excitement and factitious emotion," which were unavoidable by-products of a theatrical career, she took all possible measures to restrain "the irregular and passionate vehemence" of her temperament. Whenever she was not on stage, she resumed a monotonous round of occupations designed to calm her down:

> Amid infinite anguish and errors, existence may preserve a species of outward symmetry and harmony from this strong band of minute observance, keeping down and assisting the mind to master elements of moral and mental discord and disorder, for the due control of which the daily and hourly subjection to recurring rules is an invaluable auxiliary to higher influences. The external practice does not supply, but powerfully supplements, the internal principles of self-control.

This interjection of wholesome advice comes immediately before Fanny's account of her first night, for which this section of the book has been steadily preparing the reader. Its prim, didactic tone would fit it admirably for a conduct-book of the type written by Sarah Stickney Ellis in her *Women of England* series. Her choice of words gives special prominence to the inward powers of self-repression: "strong band," "keeping down," "master," "control," "daily and hourly subjection," "recurring rules," "internal principles": all ideas that were alien to Juliet, but essential to the preservation of any young girl going on the stage for the first time.

With her aunt in the dressing-room, her mother playing Lady Capulet, and her father Mercutio, she was impeccably chaperoned; yet every detail of the opening night reconstructs the picture of a defenceless victim being prepared for sacrifice. She herself calls it "execution," as she remembers how she waited backstage, her eyes brimming with tears, which then trickled down her rouged cheeks; the other members of the cast trying to help her through her ordeal: " 'Courage, courage, dear child! poor thing, poor thing!' reiterated Mrs. Davenport. 'Never mind 'em, Miss Kemble!' urged Keeley . . . 'never mind 'em! don't think of 'em, any more than if they were so many rows of cabbages!' " The balcony-scene, on this first night, proved a sore trial to her virginal feelings, "the passion I was uttering sending hot waves of blushes all over my neck and shoulders." Yet her performance was received with "a tumultuous storm of applause, congratulation, tears, embraces, and a general joyous explosion of unutterable relief." A set of enthusiastic young gentlemen in the audience became known as her "bodyguard": already, the factitious excitement was beginning.

Fanny Kemble insists that she never became used to an acting career, and that whenever she did act, it was for reasons of economic necessity. At four different periods of her life, she was, as she puts it, "constrained by circumstances" to maintain herself by acting. The excited, breathless quality of the narrative shows how closely she identified with her former self as trembling novice, and how much greater, in proportion to her fears, was her sense of triumph and relief when the performance was over. She cannot resist adding the information that she became "a little lion in society," and that "approbation, admiration, adulation" were showered upon her. Aware of the need to retain her readers' sympathetic interest in her fate, she tries to prove herself unspoilt, still modest, conscious of the many dangers surrounding her rise to theatrical stardom.

One way in which she minimizes her own responsibility for her success is by recourse to fairy story. The chapter closes with a picture of Fanny as a latter-day Cinderella, the "faded, threadbare, turned, and dyed frocks" that she normally wore, exchanged for "fashionably made dresses of fresh colours and fine texture," in which she seemed to herself "transfigured." As she concludes, every condition of her life had been altered, "as by the wand of a fairy." The fairy-tale analogy both reduces the extent of her own active participation in the metamorphosis, and provides an emotional outlet for her retrospective exhilaration. But to placate any contemporary reader who might still harbour doubts, she mingles delight with dark warnings. "God knows," she ends balefully, "how pitiful a preparation all this tinsel sudden success and popularity formed for the duties and trials of my after-life." With the reference to "duty," Fanny Kemble returns her readers to safe and familiar territory.

She succeeded, at least, in reassuring Mrs Oliphant. This prolific novelist, and reviewer for *Blackwood's Edinburgh Magazine* was, by the late 1870s, developing a critical interest in the genre of autobiography. She had already attacked Harriet Martineau's *Autobiography* for its disrespect for relatives and contemporaries, and its self-absorbed celebration of a literary success that seemed to Mrs Oliphant in 1877 both incredible and undeserved. "How such a commonplace mind could have attained the literary position she did fills me with amazement," she told John Blackwood. For Fanny Kemble's *Record,* however, she had nothing but admiration, praising especially its cheerfulness, sincerity, and avoidance of all bitter recriminations. She found the picture of family life particularly attractive and "highly toned," the most interesting part being "that which describes the way in which Fanny stepped into the breach, and did her best to prop up the big theatre and the family fortune on her own delicate girlish shoulders." Transforming Cinderella-Fanny into a kind of teenage-girl-Atlas, Mrs Oliphant is more than willing to play along with the myth-making. "Her life became a fairy life after this for a time," she comments on the aftermath of Fanny's début, noting in this episode and Fanny's account of it a "total absence of all self-assertion and independence." To Mrs Oliphant, still indignant at Harriet Martineau's apparent arrogance, this was clearly something to admire.

Seeing Fanny Kemble as Atlas, Mrs Oliphant was perhaps reminded of her own hard life, which had made her the sole dependable breadwinner for her own and her brother's children. As Linda H. Peterson has shown in her discussion of the *Autobiography* [in *Approaches to Victorian Autobiography,* edited by George P. Landow, 1979], Mrs Oliphant felt "miscast" in the role of artist, and her account of herself is composed of many shifting tones. Hers

Margaret Oliphant.

was certainly a tragic experience, exceptionally disaster-ridden. All her children predeceased her, her daughters before reaching maturity, and her sons while she was writing the *Autobiography* for them; her husband died, leaving her a thousand pounds in debt; and her writing never brought her the glamorous "lionizing" that seems to have been predominantly a feature of artistic life in the 1830s, when Harriet Martineau complained of it. Her professional life was a tale of unceasing labour in largely unfavourable conditions, to pay off debts, and educate her two surviving sons; yet it is one of the curious ironies of her story that a career that was to prove so essential to the maintenance of two families was regarded at its outset as a delightful joke.

Mrs Oliphant describes her entrance into the literary world in the familiar mixed style of exhilaration and apology. Again, her first attempts at writing followed a period of stagnation and depression, caused, in the young Margaret Wilson's case, by a broken engagement, followed by her mother's serious illness. To pass the time, she started composing a story:

> I had to sit for hours by her bedside and keep quiet. I had no liking then for needlework, a taste which developed afterwards, so I took to writing. There was no particular purpose in my beginning except this, to secure some amusement and occupation for myself while I sat by my mother's bedside.

Her writing is introduced as a natural, quiet bedside occupation, and, as in Harriet Martineau's story, as an acceptable alternative to needlework: though both authors assure their audiences that they later became very competent at needlework. Here, the very purposelessness of Mrs Oliphant's bedside writing demonstrates the lack of any egocentric ambition, its subject-matter as virtuous as Fanny Kemble's conception of Portia:

> I wrote a little book in which the chief character was an angelic elder sister, unmarried, who had the charge of a family of motherless brothers and sisters, and who had a shrine of sorrow in her life in the shape of the portrait and memory of her lover who had died young. It was all very innocent and guileless, and my audience—to wit, my mother and brother Frank—were highly pleased with it.

The prophetic irony of a plot in which the heroine assumes responsibility for "a family of motherless brothers and sisters" is apparently lost on its author, who adds only that it was "very silly . . . poor little thing." She was also embarking on her lifelong practice of writing especially for a family audience, which again reduced the element of public display in her professional career. It follows that her first attempt at writing for publication is mainly treated as an accident, and the exact circumstances of her inspiration and the nature of her ambitions left indistinct. "From the time above spoken of," she continues, "I went on writing, and somehow, I don't remember how, got into the history of Mrs. Margaret Maitland." A brother, like Harriet Martineau's two brothers, becomes the necessary intermediary between the inner, creative world of his sister's imagination, and the largely masculine outer world of publishing and public recognition. He took the manuscript of *Margaret Maitland* to Colburn's, who eventually agreed to publish it. "The delight, the astonishment, the amusement of this was not to be described," Mrs Oliphant recalls. "First and foremost, it was the most extraordinary joke that ever was. Maggie's story! My mother laughed and cried with pride and happiness and amazement unbounded!"

By treating her authorship as an immense, secret joke (even her first review left her "half-amused" at the idea of being seriously discussed in the newspapers), Mrs Oliphant, too, finds a way of combining both inbuilt audience-conciliation with her own remembered elation, without, in any way, compromising her position as a self-effacing widowed mother. She professes even to have forgotten whether *Margaret Maitland* was published in 1849 or 1850:

> I thought the former; but Geraldine Macpherson, whom I met in London for the first time a day or two before it was published, declared it to be 1850, from the fact that *that* was the year of her marriage. If a woman remembers any date, it must be the date of her marriage! so I don't doubt Geddie was right.

In fact, "Geddie" was wrong—at least about *Margaret Maitland;* but it is typical of Mrs Oliphant's attitude to her own writing that she should introduce her first published novel by way of another woman's (inaccurate) memory for marriage dates. *Margaret Maitland* itself appeared in 1849 as the supposed recollections of "a quiet woman of discreet years and small riches," a woman who accepts the care of a motherless child, and shows her audience how well-woven are the "threads of Providence." The desire for anonymity, the inward sense of doing something that may seem "unfeminine" or arrogant, is not necessarily incompatible with an assumed air of knowledge and wisdom in the writing itself, as Harriet Martineau proved in her first articles for the *Monthly Repository* in 1822.

"Maggie's" success is seen very much as a family event, which cheers the Wilsons in their anxiety about her brother Willie (who had "fallen once more into his old vice and debt and misery"), but it remains something of a comic-fantastic interlude in their troubled lives. She continues to regard writing as a variation on the normal female occupation of sewing, an activity to be carried on among the family, without special provisions. "I had no table even to myself, much less a room to work in," she remembers, comparing her family with Jane Austen's, "but sat at the corner of the family table with my writing-book, with everything going on as if I had been making a shirt instead of writing a book." Unlike Jane Austen's family, Margaret Wilson's were not ashamed of her apparent oddity: indeed, they were quite pleased to magnify her, and be proud of her work—"but always with a hidden sense that it was an admirable joke, and no idea that any special facilities or retirement was necessary." Nor was her head ever turned by excessive praise, for she had no one to praise her except her mother and her brother Frank: "and their applause—well, it was delightful, it was everything in the world—it was life,—but it did not count." As so often in the *Autobiography,* the tone is wistful and ambivalent—one suspects she would have liked some praise that did count—but she assures her audience that she was "wonderfully little moved by the business altogether," even when *Margaret Maitland* ran into three editions. Only the inadvertent reference to three editions admits a hint of pride in her achievement.

The "extraordinary epoch of the publication of my first book" has, for Mrs Oliphant, the same mythic qualities as those framing the recalled successes of Harriet Martineau and Fanny Kemble, whose autobiographies she had read and reviewed, before attempting one of her own; yet in all three, the rational, self-aware voice of the narrator speaks directly to her readers, supplying a steadying undercurrent of common sense and proportion. Each tries to convince her audience that success left her essentially unchanged; each insists on her modest abilities, and refers to the pressure of family problems, which were ultimately far more important than the unreal, artificial elevation to a position of public acclaim.

The familiar pattern recurs, with variations, in Elizabeth Missing Sewell's *Autobiography,* which appeared posthumously in 1907, edited by her niece, Eleanor Sewell. Author of a series of church tales, Tennyson's neighbour on the Isle of Wight, and acquainted with several members of the Oxford Movement, Elizabeth Sewell was "nearly the youngest of twelve children," and aunt to an increasing brood of motherless nieces and nephews, whom she and her sisters housed and educated. Like Mrs Oliphant, she became the mainstay of a family constantly in difficulties. She also taught her own younger sisters, began a school for poor cottagers' children, and took some pupils at home, to eke out her resources. Although, as a girl, she had vowed never to be a "useful aunt," arguing that if her brothers married, "they must take care of their own children," Elizabeth Sewell divided much of her adult life between the care and education of children who were not hers, and the writing of books, which she dreaded having praised to her face. Another of her "girlish declarations" was that "women ought not to write books."

Like Mrs Oliphant, Elizabeth Sewell had written stories for her family, and read them aloud to a domestic audience. She suggests that the ambition to write (and, as Sarah C. Frerichs has suggested [in Landow's *Approaches to Victorian Autobiography*], there is a good deal of repressed ambition in the *Autobiography* and appended Journal entries) must have been a latent wish which required positive stimulation to make it active. "I think that I must always have had a vague consciousness of being able to do something in that way," she concludes, "but it had never been brought out." The passive structure of her sentence, and avoidance of precise terms, transfers the responsibility for this discovery of her talents to something beyond her self-will and personal volition. When she was about fifteen, she thought of writing "a historical story" for two other sisters:

> but it never came to anything though I spoke of it to my mother, and I can recollect saying to her, "You know, mamma, Miss Edgeworth has written stories, and so perhaps I might be able to do the same"; a speech followed by a painful consciousness of having been terribly conceited, for I had all the time a great dislike to authoresses, and once startled a young lady who was dining with us by stating it as my opinion that women had no business to write. No one certainly could have had less perception in childhood or youth of possessing any power of imagination, or indeed of having any talent of any kind than I had.

This resembles Fanny Kemble's firm condemnation of the stage as a career for women, despite (perhaps because of) youthful plans to earn her own independence by acting and writing. The lengthy, breathless sentences seem to tumble out in headlong apology, the boast about Miss Edgeworth obliterated by a stream of starchy denials, and the final disclaimer that she has "any talent of any kind," at least that could be recognized in childhood. And yet, as she remembers, she could trace back to childhood "a pleasure in the exercise of the imagination," when she used to picture her ideal town, and describe its houses and shops. When she went to school, her "favourite topic" for the Sunday afternoon walk was

> a plan for a college for girls; the idea being suggested by my brothers having distinguished themselves at Winchester and Oxford. Happily there was no one near to make remarks upon anything I said or did, and I was such a very naughty child, and so continually in disgrace, that the question of ability was always kept in

> the background, whilst my education was so deficient as regarded information, that whenever I did compare myself with others it was to wonder at the extent of my own ignorance.

Significantly, her imaginative fantasies were all concerned with practical schemes: the provision of clean streets, and a girls' college (with some slight suggestion that girls, too, should be offered the chance to "distinguish themselves"); but even from these philanthropic ambitions she shrinks away, covering her shame with reminders that she was a thoroughly undistinguished child, whose abilities never demanded serious attention.

Her first attempts at written expression sound similar to Mrs Oliphant's: short, pious pieces with a moral purpose. An early play was "decidedly heavy," and she was "very much ashamed" of having it known that she had attempted anything of the kind; an unfinished story was meant to "bring out the working of religion in the mind of a young girl, who had been allowed to grow up with very little teaching upon the subject." Most of Elizabeth Sewell's mature works were to derive from a similar religious-didactic impulse; but at this stage, she protests, she had no intention of publishing her writing: "and only wrote it for my own amusement, and could never make up my mind whether it was good for anything." The formula is familiar enough; but it is marked in Elizabeth Sewell's writing by a particularly guilt-ridden need to counteract every forward impulse with a ritual repetition of self-doubts and apologies twice as long as the original escape of mild assertiveness. A paragraph that begins optimistically, with an account of some new literary enterprise, breaks into a rush of disavowals, ending repeatedly with the flat assumption that her work had little value in itself, or would prove too difficult for her to complete. This obstructive mechanism was largely inbuilt, supplying a system of conventional answers to questions about her own potential, and effectively destroying her initial pleasure in the exercise of her imagination. She recalls, for instance, coining a new simile, which compared a calm sea with a child sleeping in its mother's arms. "It sounded well, but I had a distinct suspicion that it might be great nonsense." As she grew up, however, she became increasingly critical of published works, especially those with a religious or moral purpose. In the chapter entitled "My First Literary Essay" (the separate chapter at least concedes that the event had some importance), Elizabeth Sewell locates the source of her inspiration firmly in the context of religious and social duty, the "parish work" undertaken with her sister Ellen; but her explanation betrays an undercurrent of irritation with the lifeless tracts which she was supposed to distribute:

> The blessing bestowed upon a Christian by baptism was the point which most impressed me, and this I tried to bring out in the first thing I ever wrote which was published—*Stories on the Lord's Prayer.* I meant it at the time for a tract. I used to give away the Christian Knowledge Society tracts in our district, and thought them intensely dull; and as I had a good deal of time to myself from not being very strong, and going out very little into society, I thought I would try and write something more interesting. I wrote one or two chapters, and then put them by—always having the feeling that I was attempting what was beyond me.

No entrance on a professional life could be announced more diffidently, or with less suggestion of egocentric impulse. The book was inspired by a wish to tell people about the blessings of Christian baptism, it was intended as a tract, and she was entitled to write it because she led a quiet, invalidish life, with few other demands on her time. Even when she began to write, doubts about her own abilities often halted her work. The only sign of ambition surfaces in her criticism of the "dull" tracts, and her evident belief that she could write a better one herself. Her first novel, *Amy Herbert,* was begun in similar circumstances, through a sense of rivalry with published writers, though its inception sounds nearly as aimless as *Margaret Maitland's:* "Then I began *Amy Herbert*—I scarcely know why—only I had been reading some story of Mrs. Sherwood's, which struck me as having pretty descriptions, and I fancied I could write something of the same kind." She decided to try her hand, as "a matter of curiosity"; but both works were repeatedly "put aside," victims of the crippling self-distrust, which becomes the *leitmotiv* of her *Autobiography.*

It was her elder brother William, like the brothers in Harriet Martineau's and Margaret Oliphant's autobiographies, who sanctioned his sister's first publication, in 1840:

> I had finished the little book, *Stories on the Lord's Prayer,* and it struck me that if I sent it to the *Cottager's Monthly Visitor,* which was the only magazine I knew likely to accept such a contribution, it might be inserted. I asked William whether there could be any objection, and when he said "No," it was sent.

It was published anonymously, while *Amy Herbert,* which came out four years later, carried the ascription "By a Lady. Edited by the Rev. W. Sewell, B. D., Fellow of Exeter College, Oxford."

From this point in the *Autobiography,* attention shifts to the background of family problems: economic pressures, the deaths of her father and two sisters-in-law, and her mother's grief. "The feeling that kept me to my work," she wrote of *Amy Herbert,* which she continued at "odd moments," was "the hope that, if great sorrow should be coming upon us, my writing might be an interest to my mother when she would not care for anything else; and so it proved. After my father's death, the only reading except the Bible, which, for weeks, she would listen to, was *Amy Herbert.*" Here, for once, the positive assertion is left unchallenged: but then, if *Amy Herbert* did her mother good, there was no need for her to feel ashamed of having written it. Still unsure of its worth, however, she left it incomplete; until William looked at the first few chapters, liked them—"and begged me to finish the story." In the circumstances, she could hardly refuse.

Of all the autobiographers in this group, Elizabeth Sewell displays the least joy in her success. From the first, she seems to have been too anxious about her family responsibilities, and her religious duties, to have had much interest in celebrating what was essentially a personal achievement; and though she was excited "in a way" when *Amy Herbert* was published, she felt already "the weight of that great pressure of pecuniary anxiety and personal responsibility, which has ever since crushed any feeling except that of momentary pleasure connected with the success of my books." After *Amy Herbert,* she felt, too, that she had exhausted her powers: "and I quite smiled to myself when William one day said to me, that having begun writing tales I could go on and write some more."

With this gracious permission, Elizabeth Sewell did "go on and write some more"; but she, like the other autobiographers I have discussed, never fully resolved the lifelong conflict between the will to write, and false shame at having done so. Writing their autobiographies seems less to help them dominate their experience, as Patricia Meyer Spacks has argued [in *Yale Review* (October 1973)], than to entangle them still further in the dilemmas that troubled them when they were young. Signs of excitement, delighted disbelief that a publisher has accepted and printed the "story" they wrote for "amusement," ambition to go on and publish more, are kept down by a recital of self-deprecating formulae that make the autobiographer's response to her success essentially a matter for public consumption, rather than private, or personal analysis. The sense of an audience is unceasing, if largely unspoken; and the moment of professional breakthrough, when a life irrevocably takes a public dimension, is the point where relations between author and audience face their severest test. For many Victorian women autobiographers, of whom these four are representative, a direct account of their feelings was impossible. Harriet Martineau's *Autobiography,* because of its author's fundamental enjoyment of her career, which she felt no need to deny, comes closest to the open confession of her thoughts, which a modern audience's familiarity with the mode has made both desirable and more readily attainable. For Fanny Kemble, Margaret Oliphant and Elizabeth Sewell, however, all positive recognition of self is buried in a mass of doubts and formal disavowals. If the implied relationship between author and reader gains in psychological complexity, the author, in attempting to arrest her former self at the moment of choice, retreats still further into an inaccessible personal past. (pp. 54-69)

Valerie Sanders, " 'Absolutely an Act of Duty': Choice of Profession in Autobiographies by Victorian Women," in Prose Studies, *Vol. 9, No. 3, December, 1986, pp. 54-70.*

FURTHER READING

Buckley, Jerome Hamilton. *The Turning Key: Autobiography and the Subjective Impulse since 1800.* Cambridge, Mass.: Harvard University Press, 1984, 191 p.

Study of nineteenth- and twentieth-century autobiography exploring " 'the subjective impulse,' the writer's assumption that he or she may or even must confess, explain, divulge, or simply display an innermost self to a putative audience."

Cockshut, A. O. J. *The Art of Autobiography in 19th and 20th Century England.* New Haven: Yale University Press, 1984, 222 p.

Analyzes English autobiographers' perceptions of "their own nature and development," discussing the literary forms employed by these writers in presenting their personal histories to readers.

Davis, Philip. *Memory and Writing: From Wordsworth to Lawrence.* Totowa, N.J.: Barnes & Noble Books, 1983, 511 p.

Explores the manner in which an autobiographical work "discloses within itself the memory of its creator's own processes of thought-composition."

Eakin, Paul John. *Fictions in Autobiography: Studies in the Art of Self-Invention.* Princeton, N.J.: Princeton University Press, 1985, 288 p.

Examines the autobiographical writings of Mary McCarthy, Henry James, and Jean-Paul Sartre, attempting to "identify the fictions involved in autobiography and the sources—psychological and cultural—from which they are derived."

Egan, Susanna. *Patterns of Experience in Autobiography.* Chapel Hill: The University of North Carolina Press, 1984, 226 p.

Elucidates narrative patterns and conventions common to nineteenth-century autobiographical writings.

Fleishman, Avrom. "The Fictions of Autobiographical Fiction." *Genre* IX, No. 1 (Spring 1976): 73-86.

Illustrates three recurrent types of "symbolic self-creation" with examples from novels by Dickens, George Eliot, and D. H. Lawrence.

Mackerness, E. D. "Victorian Autobiography: A Survey." *The Wind and the Rain* VII, No. 1 (Autumn 1950): 142-53.

Assesses the content and focus of several nineteenth-century English autobiographies.

Morris, John N. *Versions of the Self: Studies in English Autobiography from John Bunyan to John Stuart Mill.* New York: Basic Books, 1966, 242 p.

Traces the development of autobiographical writings from the seventeenth to the nineteenth centuries.

Peterson, Linda H. *Victorian Autobiography: The Tradition of Self-Interpretation.* New Haven: Yale University Press, 1986, 228 p.

Seminal analysis of form and content in autobiographical writings by Thomas Carlyle, John Ruskin, John Henry Newman, Harriet Martineau, and Edmund Gosse.

Shumaker, Wayne. *English Autobiography: Its Emergence, Materials, and Form.* Berkeley and Los Angeles: University of California Press, 1954, 262 p.

Includes chapters on the autobiographies of John Stuart Mill and Anthony Trollope.

Spengemann, William C. *The Forms of Autobiography: Episodes in the History of a Literary Genre.* New Haven: Yale University Press, 1980, 254 p.

Argues that autobiographical writings are linked by "a single evolving tradition that arose in the early Middle

Ages and arrived at the conclusions of its own internal logic in the nineteenth century."

Nineteenth-Century Literature Criticism

Topics Volume
Cumulative Indexes

Volumes 1-40

How to Use This Index

The main references

Calvino, Italo
1923-1985.....CLC 5, 8, 11, 22, 33, 39, 73; SSC 3

list all author entries in the following Gale Literary Criticism series:

CLC = *Contemporary Literary Criticism*
CLR = *Children's Literature Review*
CMLC = *Classical and Medieval Literature Criticism*
DC = *Drama Criticism*
LC = *Literature Criticism from 1400 to 1800*
NCLC = *Nineteenth-Century Literature Criticism*
PC = *Poetry Criticism*
SSC = *Short Story Criticism*
TCLC = *Twentieth-Century Literary Criticism*

The cross-references

See also CANR 23; CA 85-88;
obituary CA 116

list all author entries in the following Gale biographical and literary sources:

AAYA = *Authors & Artists for Young Adults*
AITN = *Authors in the News*
BLC = *Black Literature Criticism*
BW = *Black Writers*
CA = *Contemporary Authors*
CAAS = *Contemporary Authors Autobiography Series*
CABS = *Contemporary Authors Bibliographical Series*
CANR = *Contemporary Authors New Revision Series*
CAP = *Contemporary Authors Permanent Series*
CDALB = *Concise Dictionary of American Literary Biography*
CDBLB = *Concise Dictionary of British Literary Biography*
DLB = *Dictionary of Literary Biography*
DLBD = *Dictionary of Literary Biography Documentary Series*
DLBY = *Dictionary of Literary Biography Yearbook*
HW = *Hispanic Writers*
MAICYA = *Major Authors and Illustrators for Children and Young Adults*
MTCW = *Major 20th-Century Writers*
SAAS = *Something about the Author Autobiography Series*
SATA = *Something about the Author*
WLC = *World Literature Criticism, 1500 to the Present*
YABC = *Yesterday's Authors of Books for Children*

Literary Criticism Series Cumulative Author Index

A.
See Arnold, Matthew

A. E. . . . . **TCLC 3, 10**
See also Russell, George William
See also DLB 19

A. M.
See Megged, Aharon

Abasiyanik, Sait Faik 1906-1954
See Sait Faik
See also CA 123

Abbey, Edward 1927-1989 . . . . . . **CLC 36, 59**
See also CA 45-48; 128; CANR 2, 41

Abbott, Lee K(ittredge) 1947- . . . . . . **CLC 48**
See also CA 124; DLB 130

Abe, Kobo 1924-1993 . . . . **CLC 8, 22, 53**
See also CA 65-68; 140; CANR 24; MTCW

Abelard, Peter c. 1079-c. 1142 . . . **CMLC 11**
See also DLB 115

Abell, Kjeld 1901-1961 . . . . **CLC 15**
See also CA 111

Abish, Walter 1931- . . . . **CLC 22**
See also CA 101; CANR 37; DLB 130

Abrahams, Peter (Henry) 1919- . . . . . **CLC 4**
See also BW; CA 57-60; CANR 26; DLB 117; MTCW

Abrams, M(eyer) H(oward) 1912- . . . **CLC 24**
See also CA 57-60; CANR 13, 33; DLB 67

Abse, Dannie 1923- . . . . **CLC 7, 29**
See also CA 53-56; CAAS 1; CANR 4; DLB 27

Achebe, (Albert) Chinua(lumogu)
1930- . . . . . **CLC 1, 3, 5, 7, 11, 26, 51, 75**
See also BLC 1; BW; CA 1-4R; CANR 6, 26; CLR 20; DA; DLB 117; MAICYA; MTCW; SATA 38, 40; WLC

Acker, Kathy 1948- . . . . **CLC 45**
See also CA 117; 122

Ackroyd, Peter 1949- . . . . **CLC 34, 52**
See also CA 123; 127

Acorn, Milton 1923- . . . . **CLC 15**
See also CA 103; DLB 53

Adamov, Arthur 1908-1970 . . . . . . **CLC 4, 25**
See also CA 17-18; 25-28R; CAP 2; MTCW

Adams, Alice (Boyd) 1926- . . . **CLC 6, 13, 46**
See also CA 81-84; CANR 26; DLBY 86; MTCW

Adams, Douglas (Noel) 1952- . . . **CLC 27, 60**
See also AAYA 4; BEST 89:3; CA 106; CANR 34; DLBY 83

Adams, Francis 1862-1893 . . . . **NCLC 33**

Adams, Henry (Brooks)
1838-1918 . . . . **TCLC 4**
See also CA 104; 133; DA; DLB 12, 47

Adams, Richard (George)
1920- . . . . **CLC 4, 5, 18**
See also AITN 1, 2; CA 49-52; CANR 3, 35; CLR 20; MAICYA; MTCW; SATA 7, 69

Adamson, Joy(-Friederike Victoria)
1910-1980 . . . . **CLC 17**
See also CA 69-72; 93-96; CANR 22; MTCW; SATA 11, 22

Adcock, Fleur 1934- . . . . **CLC 41**
See also CA 25-28R; CANR 11, 34; DLB 40

Addams, Charles (Samuel)
1912-1988 . . . . **CLC 30**
See also CA 61-64; 126; CANR 12

Addison, Joseph 1672-1719 . . . . **LC 18**
See also CDBLB 1660-1789; DLB 101

Adler, C(arole) S(chwerdtfeger)
1932- . . . . **CLC 35**
See also AAYA 4; CA 89-92; CANR 19, 40; MAICYA; SAAS 15; SATA 26, 63

Adler, Renata 1938- . . . . **CLC 8, 31**
See also CA 49-52; CANR 5, 22; MTCW

Ady, Endre 1877-1919 . . . . **TCLC 11**
See also CA 107

Aeschylus 525B.C.-456B.C. . . . . . . **CMLC 11**
See also DA

Afton, Effie
See Harper, Frances Ellen Watkins

Agapida, Fray Antonio
See Irving, Washington

Agee, James (Rufus)
1909-1955 . . . . **TCLC 1, 19**
See also AITN 1; CA 108; CDALB 1941-1968; DLB 2, 26

A Gentlewoman in New England
See Bradstreet, Anne

A Gentlewoman in Those Parts
See Bradstreet, Anne

Aghill, Gordon
See Silverberg, Robert

Agnon, S(hmuel) Y(osef Halevi)
1888-1970 . . . . **CLC 4, 8, 14**
See also CA 17-18; 25-28R; CAP 2; MTCW

Aherne, Owen
See Cassill, R(onald) V(erlin)

Ai 1947- . . . . **CLC 4, 14, 69**
See also CA 85-88; CAAS 13; DLB 120

Aickman, Robert (Fordyce)
1914-1981 . . . . **CLC 57**
See also CA 5-8R; CANR 3

Aiken, Conrad (Potter)
1889-1973 . . . **CLC 1, 3, 5, 10, 52; SSC 9**
See also CA 5-8R; 45-48; CANR 4; CDALB 1929-1941; DLB 9, 45, 102; MTCW; SATA 3, 30

Aiken, Joan (Delano) 1924- . . . . **CLC 35**
See also AAYA 1; CA 9-12R; CANR 4, 23, 34; CLR 1, 19; MAICYA; MTCW; SAAS 1; SATA 2, 30, 73

Ainsworth, William Harrison
1805-1882 . . . . **NCLC 13**
See also DLB 21; SATA 24

Aitmatov, Chingiz (Torekulovich)
1928- . . . . **CLC 71**
See also CA 103; CANR 38; MTCW; SATA 56

Akers, Floyd
See Baum, L(yman) Frank

Akhmadulina, Bella Akhatovna
1937- . . . . **CLC 53**
See also CA 65-68

Akhmatova, Anna
1888-1966 . . . . **CLC 11, 25, 64; PC 2**
See also CA 19-20; 25-28R; CANR 35; CAP 1; MTCW

Aksakov, Sergei Timofeyvich
1791-1859 . . . . **NCLC 2**

Aksenov, Vassily . . . . **CLC 22**
See also Aksyonov, Vassily (Pavlovich)

Aksyonov, Vassily (Pavlovich)
1932- . . . . **CLC 37**
See also Aksenov, Vassily
See also CA 53-56; CANR 12

Akutagawa Ryunosuke
1892-1927 . . . . **TCLC 16**
See also CA 117

Alain 1868-1951 . . . . **TCLC 41**

Alain-Fournier . . . . **TCLC 6**
See also Fournier, Henri Alban
See also DLB 65

Alarcon, Pedro Antonio de
1833-1891 . . . . **NCLC 1**

Alas (y Urena), Leopoldo (Enrique Garcia)
1852-1901 . . . . **TCLC 29**
See also CA 113; 131; HW

Albee, Edward (Franklin III)
1928- . . . **CLC 1, 2, 3, 5, 9, 11, 13, 25, 53**
See also AITN 1; CA 5-8R; CABS 3; CANR 8; CDALB 1941-1968; DA; DLB 7; MTCW; WLC

Alberti, Rafael 1902- . . . . **CLC 7**
See also CA 85-88; DLB 108

Alcala-Galiano, Juan Valera y
See Valera y Alcala-Galiano, Juan

Alcott, Amos Bronson 1799-1888 . . **NCLC 1**
See also DLB 1

Alcott, Louisa May 1832-1888 . . . . **NCLC 6**
See also CDALB 1865-1917; CLR 1; DA; DLB 1, 42, 79; MAICYA; WLC; YABC 1

Aldanov, M. A.
See Aldanov, Mark (Alexandrovich)

Aldanov, Mark (Alexandrovich) 1886(?)-1957 .... **TCLC 23**
See also CA 118

Aldington, Richard 1892-1962...... **CLC 49**
See also CA 85-88; DLB 20, 36, 100

Aldiss, Brian W(ilson) 1925- .... **CLC 5, 14, 40**
See also CA 5-8R; CAAS 2; CANR 5, 28; DLB 14; MTCW; SATA 34

Alegria, Claribel 1924-............ **CLC 75**
See also CA 131; CAAS 15; HW

Alegria, Fernando 1918-........... **CLC 57**
See also CA 9-12R; CANR 5, 32; HW

Aleichem, Sholom .... **TCLC 1, 35**
See also Rabinovitch, Sholem

Aleixandre, Vicente 1898-1984 ... **CLC 9, 36**
See also CA 85-88; 114; CANR 26; DLB 108; HW; MTCW

Alepoudelis, Odysseus
See Elytis, Odysseus

Aleshkovsky, Joseph 1929-
See Aleshkovsky, Yuz
See also CA 121; 128

Aleshkovsky, Yuz .... **CLC 44**
See also Aleshkovsky, Joseph

Alexander, Lloyd (Chudley) 1924- .. **CLC 35**
See also AAYA 1; CA 1-4R; CANR 1, 24, 38; CLR 1, 5; DLB 52; MAICYA; MTCW; SATA 3, 49

Alfau, Felipe 1902-............... **CLC 66**
See also CA 137

Alger, Horatio, Jr. 1832-1899..... **NCLC 8**
See also DLB 42; SATA 16

Algren, Nelson 1909-1981 .... **CLC 4, 10, 33**
See also CA 13-16R; 103; CANR 20; CDALB 1941-1968; DLB 9; DLBY 81, 82; MTCW

Ali, Ahmed 1910- .... **CLC 69**
See also CA 25-28R; CANR 15, 34

Alighieri, Dante 1265-1321 .... **CMLC 3**

Allan, John B.
See Westlake, Donald E(dwin)

Allen, Edward 1948-.............. **CLC 59**

Allen, Roland
See Ayckbourn, Alan

Allen, Woody 1935- .... **CLC 16, 52**
See also AAYA 10; CA 33-36R; CANR 27, 38; DLB 44; MTCW

Allende, Isabel 1942- .... **CLC 39, 57**
See also CA 125; 130; HW; MTCW

Alleyn, Ellen
See Rossetti, Christina (Georgina)

Allingham, Margery (Louise) 1904-1966 .... **CLC 19**
See also CA 5-8R; 25-28R; CANR 4; DLB 77; MTCW

Allingham, William 1824-1889 ... **NCLC 25**
See also DLB 35

Allston, Washington 1779-1843.... **NCLC 2**
See also DLB 1

Almedingen, E. M. .... **CLC 12**
See also Almedingen, Martha Edith von
See also SATA 3

Almedingen, Martha Edith von 1898-1971
See Almedingen, E. M.
See also CA 1-4R; CANR 1

Alonso, Damaso 1898-1990 .... **CLC 14**
See also CA 110; 131; 130; DLB 108; HW

Alov
See Gogol, Nikolai (Vasilyevich)

Alta 1942- .... **CLC 19**
See also CA 57-60

Alter, Robert B(ernard) 1935-...... **CLC 34**
See also CA 49-52; CANR 1

Alther, Lisa 1944-.............. **CLC 7, 41**
See also CA 65-68; CANR 12, 30; MTCW

Altman, Robert 1925-............. **CLC 16**
See also CA 73-76

Alvarez, A(lfred) 1929-.......... **CLC 5, 13**
See also CA 1-4R; CANR 3, 33; DLB 14, 40

Alvarez, Alejandro Rodriguez 1903-1965
See Casona, Alejandro
See also CA 131; 93-96; HW

Amado, Jorge 1912- .... **CLC 13, 40**
See also CA 77-80; CANR 35; DLB 113; MTCW

Ambler, Eric 1909-............ **CLC 4, 6, 9**
See also CA 9-12R; CANR 7, 38; DLB 77; MTCW

Amichai, Yehuda 1924- ...... **CLC 9, 22, 57**
See also CA 85-88; MTCW

Amiel, Henri Frederic 1821-1881 .. **NCLC 4**

Amis, Kingsley (William) 1922- ...... **CLC 1, 2, 3, 5, 8, 13, 40, 44**
See also AITN 2; CA 9-12R; CANR 8, 28; CDBLB 1945-1960; DA; DLB 15, 27, 100; MTCW

Amis, Martin (Louis) 1949- .... **CLC 4, 9, 38, 62**
See also BEST 90:3; CA 65-68; CANR 8, 27; DLB 14

Ammons, A(rchie) R(andolph) 1926- .... **CLC 2, 3, 5, 8, 9, 25, 57**
See also AITN 1; CA 9-12R; CANR 6, 36; DLB 5; MTCW

Amo, Tauraatua i
See Adams, Henry (Brooks)

Anand, Mulk Raj 1905-........... **CLC 23**
See also CA 65-68; CANR 32; MTCW

Anatol
See Schnitzler, Arthur

Anaya, Rudolfo A(lfonso) 1937- .... **CLC 23**
See also CA 45-48; CAAS 4; CANR 1, 32; DLB 82; HW; MTCW

Andersen, Hans Christian 1805-1875 .... **NCLC 7; SSC 6**
See also CLR 6; DA; MAICYA; WLC; YABC 1

Anderson, C. Farley
See Mencken, H(enry) L(ouis); Nathan, George Jean

Anderson, Jessica (Margaret) Queale .... **CLC 37**
See also CA 9-12R; CANR 4

Anderson, Jon (Victor) 1940- .... **CLC 9**
See also CA 25-28R; CANR 20

Anderson, Lindsay (Gordon) 1923- .... **CLC 20**
See also CA 125; 128

Anderson, Maxwell 1888-1959 ..... **TCLC 2**
See also CA 105; DLB 7

Anderson, Poul (William) 1926- .... **CLC 15**
See also AAYA 5; CA 1-4R; CAAS 2; CANR 2, 15, 34; DLB 8; MTCW; SATA 39

Anderson, Robert (Woodruff) 1917- .... **CLC 23**
See also AITN 1; CA 21-24R; CANR 32; DLB 7

Anderson, Sherwood 1876-1941 ...... **TCLC 1, 10, 24; SSC 1**
See also CA 104; 121; CDALB 1917-1929; DA; DLB 4, 9, 86; DLBD 1; MTCW; WLC

Andouard
See Giraudoux, (Hippolyte) Jean

Andrade, Carlos Drummond de ...... **CLC 18**
See also Drummond de Andrade, Carlos

Andrade, Mario de 1893-1945..... **TCLC 43**

Andrewes, Lancelot 1555-1626 .... **LC 5**

Andrews, Cicily Fairfield
See West, Rebecca

Andrews, Elton V.
See Pohl, Frederik

Andreyev, Leonid (Nikolaevich) 1871-1919 .... **TCLC 3**
See also CA 104

Andric, Ivo 1892-1975 .... **CLC 8**
See also CA 81-84; 57-60; MTCW

Angelique, Pierre
See Bataille, Georges

Angell, Roger 1920- .... **CLC 26**
See also CA 57-60; CANR 13

Angelou, Maya 1928-.... **CLC 12, 35, 64, 77**
See also AAYA 7; BLC 1; BW; CA 65-68; CANR 19; DA; DLB 38; MTCW; SATA 49

Annensky, Innokenty Fyodorovich 1856-1909 .... **TCLC 14**
See also CA 110

Anon, Charles Robert
See Pessoa, Fernando (Antonio Nogueira)

Anouilh, Jean (Marie Lucien Pierre) 1910-1987 ...... **CLC 1, 3, 8, 13, 40, 50**
See also CA 17-20R; 123; CANR 32; MTCW

Anthony, Florence
See Ai

Anthony, John
See Ciardi, John (Anthony)

Anthony, Peter
See Shaffer, Anthony (Joshua); Shaffer, Peter (Levin)

Anthony, Piers 1934- .... **CLC 35**
See also CA 21-24R; CANR 28; DLB 8; MTCW

Antoine, Marc
See Proust, (Valentin-Louis-George-Eugene-)Marcel

Antoninus, Brother
See Everson, William (Oliver)

Antonioni, Michelangelo 1912- ..... **CLC 20**
See also CA 73-76

Antschel, Paul 1920-1970....... **CLC 10, 19**
See also Celan, Paul
See also CA 85-88; CANR 33; MTCW

Anwar, Chairil 1922-1949 .... **TCLC 22**
See also CA 121

Apollinaire, Guillaume .... **TCLC 3, 8**
See also Kostrowitzki, Wilhelm Apollinaris de

Appelfeld, Aharon 1932- .... **CLC 23, 47**
See also CA 112; 133

Apple, Max (Isaac) 1941-........ **CLC 9, 33**
See also CA 81-84; CANR 19; DLB 130

Appleman, Philip (Dean) 1926-..... **CLC 51**
See also CA 13-16R; CANR 6, 29

Appleton, Lawrence
See Lovecraft, H(oward) P(hillips)

Apteryx
See Eliot, T(homas) S(tearns)

Apuleius, (Lucius Madaurensis)
125(?)-175(?) .... **CMLC 1**

Aquin, Hubert 1929-1977.......... **CLC 15**
See also CA 105; DLB 53

Aragon, Louis 1897-1982........ **CLC 3, 22**
See also CA 69-72; 108; CANR 28; DLB 72; MTCW

Arany, Janos 1817-1882......... **NCLC 34**

Arbuthnot, John 1667-1735.......... **LC 1**
See also DLB 101

Archer, Herbert Winslow
See Mencken, H(enry) L(ouis)

Archer, Jeffrey (Howard) 1940- .... **CLC 28**
See also BEST 89:3; CA 77-80; CANR 22

Archer, Jules 1915- .... **CLC 12**
See also CA 9-12R; CANR 6; SAAS 5; SATA 4

Archer, Lee
See Ellison, Harlan

Arden, John 1930- .... **CLC 6, 13, 15**
See also CA 13-16R; CAAS 4; CANR 31; DLB 13; MTCW

Arenas, Reinaldo 1943-1990 .... **CLC 41**
See also CA 124; 128; 133; HW

Arendt, Hannah 1906-1975 .... **CLC 66**
See also CA 17-20R; 61-64; CANR 26; MTCW

Aretino, Pietro 1492-1556 .... **LC 12**

Arguedas, Jose Maria
1911-1969 .... **CLC 10, 18**
See also CA 89-92; DLB 113; HW

Argueta, Manlio 1936-............ **CLC 31**
See also CA 131; HW

Ariosto, Ludovico 1474-1533......... **LC 6**

Aristides
See Epstein, Joseph

Aristophanes
450B.C.-385B.C. .... **CMLC 4; DC 2**
See also DA

Arlt, Roberto (Godofredo Christophersen)
1900-1942 .... **TCLC 29**
See also CA 123; 131; HW

Armah, Ayi Kwei 1939- .... **CLC 5, 33**
See also BLC 1; BW; CA 61-64; CANR 21; DLB 117; MTCW

Armatrading, Joan 1950- .... **CLC 17**
See also CA 114

Arnette, Robert
See Silverberg, Robert

Arnim, Achim von (Ludwig Joachim von Arnim) 1781-1831 .... **NCLC 5**
See also DLB 90

Arnim, Bettina von 1785-1859.... **NCLC 38**
See also DLB 90

Arnold, Matthew
1822-1888 .... **NCLC 6, 29; PC 5**
See also CDBLB 1832-1890; DA; DLB 32, 57; WLC

Arnold, Thomas 1795-1842 ...... **NCLC 18**
See also DLB 55

Arnow, Harriette (Louisa) Simpson
1908-1986 .... **CLC 2, 7, 18**
See also CA 9-12R; 118; CANR 14; DLB 6; MTCW; SATA 42, 47

Arp, Hans
See Arp, Jean

Arp, Jean 1887-1966............... **CLC 5**
See also CA 81-84; 25-28R

Arrabal
See Arrabal, Fernando

Arrabal, Fernando 1932- ... **CLC 2, 9, 18, 58**
See also CA 9-12R; CANR 15

Arrick, Fran...................... **CLC 30**

Artaud, Antonin 1896-1948 ..... **TCLC 3, 36**
See also CA 104

Arthur, Ruth M(abel) 1905-1979.... **CLC 12**
See also CA 9-12R; 85-88; CANR 4; SATA 7, 26

Artsybashev, Mikhail (Petrovich)
1878-1927 .... **TCLC 31**

Arundel, Honor (Morfydd)
1919-1973 .... **CLC 17**
See also CA 21-22; 41-44R; CAP 2; SATA 4, 24

Asch, Sholem 1880-1957 .... **TCLC 3**
See also CA 105

Ash, Shalom
See Asch, Sholem

Ashbery, John (Lawrence)
1927- ..... **CLC 2, 3, 4, 6, 9, 13, 15, 25, 41, 77**
See also CA 5-8R; CANR 9, 37; DLB 5; DLBY 81; MTCW

Ashdown, Clifford
See Freeman, R(ichard) Austin

Ashe, Gordon
See Creasey, John

Ashton-Warner, Sylvia (Constance)
1908-1984 .... **CLC 19**
See also CA 69-72; 112; CANR 29; MTCW

Asimov, Isaac
1920-1992 ...... **CLC 1, 3, 9, 19, 26, 76**
See also BEST 90:2; CA 1-4R; 137; CANR 2, 19, 36; CLR 12; DLB 8; DLBY 92; MAICYA; MTCW; SATA 1, 26, 74

Astley, Thea (Beatrice May)
1925- .... **CLC 41**
See also CA 65-68; CANR 11

Aston, James
See White, T(erence) H(anbury)

Asturias, Miguel Angel
1899-1974 .... **CLC 3, 8, 13**
See also CA 25-28; 49-52; CANR 32; CAP 2; DLB 113; HW; MTCW

Atares, Carlos Saura
See Saura (Atares), Carlos

Atheling, William
See Pound, Ezra (Weston Loomis)

Atheling, William, Jr.
See Blish, James (Benjamin)

Atherton, Gertrude (Franklin Horn)
1857-1948 .... **TCLC 2**
See also CA 104; DLB 9, 78

Atherton, Lucius
See Masters, Edgar Lee

Atkins, Jack
See Harris, Mark

Atticus
See Fleming, Ian (Lancaster)

Atwood, Margaret (Eleanor)
1939- .... **CLC 2, 3, 4, 8, 13, 15, 25, 44; SSC 2**
See also BEST 89:2; CA 49-52; CANR 3, 24, 33; DA; DLB 53; MTCW; SATA 50; WLC

Aubigny, Pierre d'
See Mencken, H(enry) L(ouis)

Aubin, Penelope 1685-1731(?)........ **LC 9**
See also DLB 39

Auchincloss, Louis (Stanton)
1917- .... **CLC 4, 6, 9, 18, 45**
See also CA 1-4R; CANR 6, 29; DLB 2; DLBY 80; MTCW

Auden, W(ystan) H(ugh)
1907-1973 ..... **CLC 1, 2, 3, 4, 6, 9, 11, 14, 43; PC 1**
See also CA 9-12R; 45-48; CANR 5; CDBLB 1914-1945; DA; DLB 10, 20; MTCW; WLC

Audiberti, Jacques 1900-1965 ...... **CLC 38**
See also CA 25-28R

Auel, Jean M(arie) 1936-.......... **CLC 31**
See also AAYA 7; BEST 90:4; CA 103; CANR 21

Auerbach, Erich 1892-1957 .... **TCLC 43**
See also CA 118

Augier, Emile 1820-1889 .... **NCLC 31**

August, John
See De Voto, Bernard (Augustine)

Augustine, St. 354-430........... **CMLC 6**

Aurelius
See Bourne, Randolph S(illiman)

Austen, Jane 1775-1817 .... **NCLC 1, 13, 19, 33**
See also CDBLB 1789-1832; DA; DLB 116; WLC

Auster, Paul 1947- .... **CLC 47**
See also CA 69-72; CANR 23

Austin, Frank
See Faust, Frederick (Schiller)

Austin, Mary (Hunter) 1868-1934 .... **TCLC 25**
See also CA 109; DLB 9, 78

Autran Dourado, Waldomiro
See Dourado, (Waldomiro Freitas) Autran

Averroes 1126-1198 .... **CMLC 7**
See also DLB 115

Avison, Margaret 1918- .... **CLC 2, 4**
See also CA 17-20R; DLB 53; MTCW

Ayckbourn, Alan 1939- .... **CLC 5, 8, 18, 33, 74**
See also CA 21-24R; CANR 31; DLB 13; MTCW

Aydy, Catherine
See Tennant, Emma (Christina)

Ayme, Marcel (Andre) 1902-1967 ... **CLC 11**
See also CA 89-92; CLR 25; DLB 72

Ayrton, Michael 1921-1975 .... **CLC 7**
See also CA 5-8R; 61-64; CANR 9, 21

Azorin .... **CLC 11**
See also Martinez Ruiz, Jose

Azuela, Mariano 1873-1952 .... **TCLC 3**
See also CA 104; 131; HW; MTCW

Baastad, Babbis Friis
See Friis-Baastad, Babbis Ellinor

Bab
See Gilbert, W(illiam) S(chwenck)

Babbis, Eleanor
See Friis-Baastad, Babbis Ellinor

Babel, Isaak (Emmanuilovich) 1894-1941(?) .... **CLC 73**
See also CA 104; TCLC 2, 13

Babits, Mihaly 1883-1941 .... **TCLC 14**
See also CA 114

Babur 1483-1530 .... **LC 18**

Bacchelli, Riccardo 1891-1985 ..... **CLC 19**
See also CA 29-32R; 117

Bach, Richard (David) 1936- .... **CLC 14**
See also AITN 1; BEST 89:2; CA 9-12R; CANR 18; MTCW; SATA 13

Bachman, Richard
See King, Stephen (Edwin)

Bachmann, Ingeborg 1926-1973 ..... **CLC 69**
See also CA 93-96; 45-48; DLB 85

Bacon, Francis 1561-1626 .... **LC 18**
See also CDBLB Before 1660

Bacovia, George .... **TCLC 24**
See also Vasiliu, Gheorghe

Badanes, Jerome 1937- .... **CLC 59**

Bagehot, Walter 1826-1877 ...... **NCLC 10**
See also DLB 55

Bagnold, Enid 1889-1981 .... **CLC 25**
See also CA 5-8R; 103; CANR 5, 40; DLB 13; MAICYA; SATA 1, 25

Bagrjana, Elisaveta
See Belcheva, Elisaveta

Bagryana, Elisaveta
See Belcheva, Elisaveta

Bailey, Paul 1937- .... **CLC 45**
See also CA 21-24R; CANR 16; DLB 14

Baillie, Joanna 1762-1851 .... **NCLC 2**
See also DLB 93

Bainbridge, Beryl (Margaret) 1933- .... **CLC 4, 5, 8, 10, 14, 18, 22, 62**
See also CA 21-24R; CANR 24; DLB 14; MTCW

Baker, Elliott 1922- .... **CLC 8**
See also CA 45-48; CANR 2

Baker, Nicholson 1957- .... **CLC 61**
See also CA 135

Baker, Ray Stannard 1870-1946 ... **TCLC 47**
See also CA 118

Baker, Russell (Wayne) 1925- ...... **CLC 31**
See also BEST 89:4; CA 57-60; CANR 11, 41; MTCW

Bakshi, Ralph 1938(?)- .... **CLC 26**
See also CA 112; 138

Bakunin, Mikhail (Alexandrovich) 1814-1876 .... **NCLC 25**

Baldwin, James (Arthur) 1924-1987 ..... **CLC 1, 2, 3, 4, 5, 8, 13, 15, 17, 42, 50, 67; DC 1; SSC 10**
See also AAYA 4; BLC 1; BW; CA 1-4R; 124; CABS 1; CANR 3, 24; CDALB 1941-1968; DA; DLB 2, 7, 33; DLBY 87; MTCW; SATA 9, 54; WLC

Ballard, J(ames) G(raham) 1930- .... **CLC 3, 6, 14, 36; SSC 1**
See also AAYA 3; CA 5-8R; CANR 15, 39; DLB 14; MTCW

Balmont, Konstantin (Dmitriyevich) 1867-1943 .... **TCLC 11**
See also CA 109

Balzac, Honore de 1799-1850 .... **NCLC 5, 35; SSC 5**
See also DA; DLB 119; WLC

Bambara, Toni Cade 1939- .... **CLC 19**
See also AAYA 5; BLC 1; BW; CA 29-32R; CANR 24; DA; DLB 38; MTCW

Bamdad, A.
See Shamlu, Ahmad

Banat, D. R.
See Bradbury, Ray (Douglas)

Bancroft, Laura
See Baum, L(yman) Frank

Banim, John 1798-1842 .... **NCLC 13**
See also DLB 116

Banim, Michael 1796-1874 ...... **NCLC 13**

Banks, Iain
See Banks, Iain M(enzies)

Banks, Iain M(enzies) 1954- .... **CLC 34**
See also CA 123; 128

Banks, Lynne Reid .... **CLC 23**
See also Reid Banks, Lynne
See also AAYA 6

Banks, Russell 1940- .... **CLC 37, 72**
See also CA 65-68; CAAS 15; CANR 19; DLB 130

Banville, John 1945- .... **CLC 46**
See also CA 117; 128; DLB 14

Banville, Theodore (Faullain) de 1832-1891 .... **NCLC 9**

Baraka, Amiri 1934- ... **CLC 1, 2, 3, 5, 10, 14, 33; PC 4**
See also Jones, LeRoi
See also BLC 1; BW; CA 21-24R; CABS 3; CANR 27, 38; CDALB 1941-1968; DA; DLB 5, 7, 16, 38; DLBD 8; MTCW

Barbellion, W. N. P. .... **TCLC 24**
See also Cummings, Bruce F(rederick)

Barbera, Jack 1945- .... **CLC 44**
See also CA 110

Barbey d'Aurevilly, Jules Amedee 1808-1889 .... **NCLC 1**
See also DLB 119

Barbusse, Henri 1873-1935 .... **TCLC 5**
See also CA 105; DLB 65

Barclay, Bill
See Moorcock, Michael (John)

Barclay, William Ewert
See Moorcock, Michael (John)

Barea, Arturo 1897-1957 .... **TCLC 14**
See also CA 111

Barfoot, Joan 1946- .... **CLC 18**
See also CA 105

Baring, Maurice 1874-1945 .... **TCLC 8**
See also CA 105; DLB 34

Barker, Clive 1952- .... **CLC 52**
See also AAYA 10; BEST 90:3; CA 121; 129; MTCW

Barker, George Granville 1913-1991 .... **CLC 8, 48**
See also CA 9-12R; 135; CANR 7, 38; DLB 20; MTCW

Barker, Harley Granville
See Granville-Barker, Harley
See also DLB 10

Barker, Howard 1946- .... **CLC 37**
See also CA 102; DLB 13

Barker, Pat 1943- .... **CLC 32**
See also CA 117; 122

Barlow, Joel 1754-1812 .... **NCLC 23**
See also DLB 37

Barnard, Mary (Ethel) 1909- .... **CLC 48**
See also CA 21-22; CAP 2

Barnes, Djuna 1892-1982 ... **CLC 3, 4, 8, 11, 29; SSC 3**
See also CA 9-12R; 107; CANR 16; DLB 4, 9, 45; MTCW

Barnes, Julian 1946- .... **CLC 42**
See also CA 102; CANR 19

Barnes, Peter 1931- .... **CLC 5, 56**
See also CA 65-68; CAAS 12; CANR 33, 34; DLB 13; MTCW

Baroja (y Nessi), Pio 1872-1956 .... **TCLC 8**
See also CA 104

Baron, David
See Pinter, Harold

Baron Corvo
See Rolfe, Frederick (William Serafino Austin Lewis Mary)

Bierce, Ambrose (Gwinett) 1842-1914(?) ..... **TCLC 1, 7, 44; SSC 9**
See also CA 104; 139; CDALB 1865-1917; DA; DLB 11, 12, 23, 71, 74; WLC

Billings, Josh
See Shaw, Henry Wheeler

Billington, Rachel 1942- .... **CLC 43**
See also AITN 2; CA 33-36R

Binyon, T(imothy) J(ohn) 1936- .... **CLC 34**
See also CA 111; CANR 28

Bioy Casares, Adolfo 1914- .... **CLC 4, 8, 13**
See also CA 29-32R; CANR 19; DLB 113; HW; MTCW

Bird, C.
See Ellison, Harlan

Bird, Cordwainer
See Ellison, Harlan

Bird, Robert Montgomery 1806-1854 .... **NCLC 1**

Birney, (Alfred) Earle 1904- .... **CLC 1, 4, 6, 11**
See also CA 1-4R; CANR 5, 20; DLB 88; MTCW

Bishop, Elizabeth 1911-1979 ..... **CLC 1, 4, 9, 13, 15, 32; PC 3**
See also CA 5-8R; 89-92; CABS 2; CANR 26; CDALB 1968-1988; DA; DLB 5; MTCW; SATA 24

Bishop, John 1935- .... **CLC 10**
See also CA 105

Bissett, Bill 1939- .... **CLC 18**
See also CA 69-72; CANR 15; DLB 53; MTCW

Bitov, Andrei (Georgievich) 1937- ... **CLC 57**

Biyidi, Alexandre 1932-
See Beti, Mongo
See also BW; CA 114; 124; MTCW

Bjarme, Brynjolf
See Ibsen, Henrik (Johan)

Bjornson, Bjornstjerne (Martinius) 1832-1910 .... **TCLC 7, 37**
See also CA 104

Black, Robert
See Holdstock, Robert P.

Blackburn, Paul 1926-1971 ...... **CLC 9, 43**
See also CA 81-84; 33-36R; CANR 34; DLB 16; DLBY 81

Black Elk 1863-1950 .... **TCLC 33**

Black Hobart
See Sanders, (James) Ed(ward)

Blacklin, Malcolm
See Chambers, Aidan

Blackmore, R(ichard) D(oddridge) 1825-1900 .... **TCLC 27**
See also CA 120; DLB 18

Blackmur, R(ichard) P(almer) 1904-1965 .... **CLC 2, 24**
See also CA 11-12; 25-28R; CAP 1; DLB 63

Black Tarantula, The
See Acker, Kathy

Blackwood, Algernon (Henry) 1869-1951 .... **TCLC 5**
See also CA 105

Blackwood, Caroline 1931- .... **CLC 6, 9**
See also CA 85-88; CANR 32; DLB 14; MTCW

Blade, Alexander
See Hamilton, Edmond; Silverberg, Robert

Blaga, Lucian 1895-1961 .... **CLC 75**

Blair, Eric (Arthur) 1903-1950
See Orwell, George
See also CA 104; 132; DA; MTCW; SATA 29

Blais, Marie-Claire 1939- .... **CLC 2, 4, 6, 13, 22**
See also CA 21-24R; CAAS 4; CANR 38; DLB 53; MTCW

Blaise, Clark 1940- .... **CLC 29**
See also AITN 2; CA 53-56; CAAS 3; CANR 5; DLB 53

Blake, Nicholas
See Day Lewis, C(ecil)
See also DLB 77

Blake, William 1757-1827 .... **NCLC 13**
See also CDBLB 1789-1832; DA; DLB 93; MAICYA; SATA 30; WLC

Blasco Ibanez, Vicente 1867-1928 .... **TCLC 12**
See also CA 110; 131; HW; MTCW

Blatty, William Peter 1928- .... **CLC 2**
See also CA 5-8R; CANR 9

Bleeck, Oliver
See Thomas, Ross (Elmore)

Blessing, Lee 1949- .... **CLC 54**

Blish, James (Benjamin) 1921-1975 .... **CLC 14**
See also CA 1-4R; 57-60; CANR 3; DLB 8; MTCW; SATA 66

Bliss, Reginald
See Wells, H(erbert) G(eorge)

Blixen, Karen (Christentze Dinesen) 1885-1962
See Dinesen, Isak
See also CA 25-28; CANR 22; CAP 2; MTCW; SATA 44

Bloch, Robert (Albert) 1917- .... **CLC 33**
See also CA 5-8R; CANR 5; DLB 44; SATA 12

Blok, Alexander (Alexandrovich) 1880-1921 .... **TCLC 5**
See also CA 104

Blom, Jan
See Breytenbach, Breyten

Bloom, Harold 1930- .... **CLC 24**
See also CA 13-16R; CANR 39; DLB 67

Bloomfield, Aurelius
See Bourne, Randolph S(illiman)

Blount, Roy (Alton), Jr. 1941- ..... **CLC 38**
See also CA 53-56; CANR 10, 28; MTCW

Bloy, Leon 1846-1917 .... **TCLC 22**
See also CA 121; DLB 123

Blume, Judy (Sussman) 1938- ... **CLC 12, 30**
See also AAYA 3; CA 29-32R; CANR 13, 37; CLR 2, 15; DLB 52; MAICYA; MTCW; SATA 2, 31

Blunden, Edmund (Charles) 1896-1974 .... **CLC 2, 56**
See also CA 17-18; 45-48; CAP 2; DLB 20, 100; MTCW

Bly, Robert (Elwood) 1926- .... **CLC 1, 2, 5, 10, 15, 38**
See also CA 5-8R; CANR 41; DLB 5; MTCW

Bobette
See Simenon, Georges (Jacques Christian)

Boccaccio, Giovanni 1313-1375
See also SSC 10

Bochco, Steven 1943- .... **CLC 35**
See also CA 124; 138

Bodenheim, Maxwell 1892-1954 ... **TCLC 44**
See also CA 110; DLB 9, 45

Bodker, Cecil 1927- .... **CLC 21**
See also CA 73-76; CANR 13; CLR 23; MAICYA; SATA 14

Boell, Heinrich (Theodor) 1917-1985
See Boll, Heinrich (Theodor)
See also CA 21-24R; 116; CANR 24; DA; DLB 69; DLBY 85; MTCW

Bogan, Louise 1897-1970 ..... **CLC 4, 39, 46**
See also CA 73-76; 25-28R; CANR 33; DLB 45; MTCW

Bogarde, Dirk .... **CLC 19**
See also Van Den Bogarde, Derek Jules Gaspard Ulric Niven
See also DLB 14

Bogosian, Eric 1953- .... **CLC 45**
See also CA 138

Bograd, Larry 1953- .... **CLC 35**
See also CA 93-96; SATA 33

Boiardo, Matteo Maria 1441-1494 .... **LC 6**

Boileau-Despreaux, Nicolas 1636-1711 .... **LC 3**

Boland, Eavan 1944- .... **CLC 40, 67**
See also DLB 40

Boll, Heinrich (Theodor) 1917-1985 ... **CLC 2, 3, 6, 9, 11, 15, 27, 39, 72**
See also Boell, Heinrich (Theodor)
See also DLB 69; DLBY 85; WLC

Bolt, Lee
See Faust, Frederick (Schiller)

Bolt, Robert (Oxton) 1924- .... **CLC 14**
See also CA 17-20R; CANR 35; DLB 13; MTCW

Bomkauf
See Kaufman, Bob (Garnell)

Bonaventura .... **NCLC 35**
See also DLB 90

Bond, Edward 1934- .... **CLC 4, 6, 13, 23**
See also CA 25-28R; CANR 38; DLB 13; MTCW

Bonham, Frank 1914-1989 .... **CLC 12**
See also AAYA 1; CA 9-12R; CANR 4, 36; MAICYA; SAAS 3; SATA 1, 49, 62

Bonnefoy, Yves 1923- .... **CLC 9, 15, 58**
See also CA 85-88; CANR 33; MTCW

Bridie, James .... **TCLC 3**
See also Mavor, Osborne Henry
See also DLB 10

Brin, David 1950- .... **CLC 34**
See also CA 102; CANR 24; SATA 65

Brink, Andre (Philippus)
1935- .... **CLC 18, 36**
See also CA 104; CANR 39; MTCW

Brinsmead, H(esba) F(ay) 1922- .... **CLC 21**
See also CA 21-24R; CANR 10; MAICYA; SAAS 5; SATA 18

Brittain, Vera (Mary)
1893(?)-1970 .... **CLC 23**
See also CA 13-16; 25-28R; CAP 1; MTCW

Broch, Hermann 1886-1951 .... **TCLC 20**
See also CA 117; DLB 85, 124

Brock, Rose
See Hansen, Joseph

Brodkey, Harold 1930- .... **CLC 56**
See also CA 111; DLB 130

Brodsky, Iosif Alexandrovich 1940-
See Brodsky, Joseph
See also AITN 1; CA 41-44R; CANR 37; MTCW

Brodsky, Joseph .... **CLC 4, 6, 13, 36, 50**
See also Brodsky, Iosif Alexandrovich

Brodsky, Michael Mark 1948- ...... **CLC 19**
See also CA 102; CANR 18, 41

Bromell, Henry 1947- .... **CLC 5**
See also CA 53-56; CANR 9

Bromfield, Louis (Brucker)
1896-1956 .... **TCLC 11**
See also CA 107; DLB 4, 9, 86

Broner, E(sther) M(asserman)
1930- .... **CLC 19**
See also CA 17-20R; CANR 8, 25; DLB 28

Bronk, William 1918- .... **CLC 10**
See also CA 89-92; CANR 23

Bronstein, Lev Davidovich
See Trotsky, Leon

Bronte, Anne 1820-1849 .... **NCLC 4**
See also DLB 21

Bronte, Charlotte
1816-1855 .... **NCLC 3, 8, 33**
See also CDBLB 1832-1890; DA; DLB 21; WLC

Bronte, (Jane) Emily
1818-1848 .... **NCLC 16, 35**
See also CDBLB 1832-1890; DA; DLB 21, 32; WLC

Brooke, Frances 1724-1789 .... **LC 6**
See also DLB 39, 99

Brooke, Henry 1703(?)-1783 .... **LC 1**
See also DLB 39

Brooke, Rupert (Chawner)
1887-1915 .... **TCLC 2, 7**
See also CA 104; 132; CDBLB 1914-1945; DA; DLB 19; MTCW; WLC

Brooke-Haven, P.
See Wodehouse, P(elham) G(renville)

Brooke-Rose, Christine 1926- ...... **CLC 40**
See also CA 13-16R; DLB 14

Brookner, Anita 1928- ...... **CLC 32, 34, 51**
See also CA 114; 120; CANR 37; DLBY 87; MTCW

Brooks, Cleanth 1906- .... **CLC 24**
See also CA 17-20R; CANR 33, 35; DLB 63; MTCW

Brooks, George
See Baum, L(yman) Frank

Brooks, Gwendolyn
1917- .... **CLC 1, 2, 4, 5, 15, 49**
See also AITN 1; BLC 1; BW; CA 1-4R; CANR 1, 27; CDALB 1941-1968; CLR 27; DA; DLB 5, 76; MTCW; SATA 6; WLC

Brooks, Mel .... **CLC 12**
See also Kaminsky, Melvin
See also DLB 26

Brooks, Peter 1938- .... **CLC 34**
See also CA 45-48; CANR 1

Brooks, Van Wyck 1886-1963 ...... **CLC 29**
See also CA 1-4R; CANR 6; DLB 45, 63, 103

Brophy, Brigid (Antonia)
1929- .... **CLC 6, 11, 29**
See also CA 5-8R; CAAS 4; CANR 25; DLB 14; MTCW

Brosman, Catharine Savage 1934- .... **CLC 9**
See also CA 61-64; CANR 21

Brother Antoninus
See Everson, William (Oliver)

Broughton, T(homas) Alan 1936- ... **CLC 19**
See also CA 45-48; CANR 2, 23

Broumas, Olga 1949- .... **CLC 10, 73**
See also CA 85-88; CANR 20

Brown, Charles Brockden
1771-1810 .... **NCLC 22**
See also CDALB 1640-1865; DLB 37, 59, 73

Brown, Christy 1932-1981 .... **CLC 63**
See also CA 105; 104; DLB 14

Brown, Claude 1937- .... **CLC 30**
See also AAYA 7; BLC 1; BW; CA 73-76

Brown, Dee (Alexander) 1908- .. **CLC 18, 47**
See also CA 13-16R; CAAS 6; CANR 11; DLBY 80; MTCW; SATA 5

Brown, George
See Wertmueller, Lina

Brown, George Douglas
1869-1902 .... **TCLC 28**

Brown, George Mackay 1921- .... **CLC 5, 48**
See also CA 21-24R; CAAS 6; CANR 12, 37; DLB 14, 27; MTCW; SATA 35

Brown, (William) Larry 1951- ...... **CLC 73**
See also CA 130; 134

Brown, Moses
See Barrett, William (Christopher)

Brown, Rita Mae 1944- .... **CLC 18, 43**
See also CA 45-48; CANR 2, 11, 35; MTCW

Brown, Roderick (Langmere) Haig-
See Haig-Brown, Roderick (Langmere)

Brown, Rosellen 1939- .... **CLC 32**
See also CA 77-80; CAAS 10; CANR 14

Brown, Sterling Allen
1901-1989 .... **CLC 1, 23, 59**
See also BLC 1; BW; CA 85-88; 127; CANR 26; DLB 48, 51, 63; MTCW

Brown, Will
See Ainsworth, William Harrison

Brown, William Wells
1813-1884 .... **NCLC 2; DC 1**
See also BLC 1; DLB 3, 50

Browne, (Clyde) Jackson 1948(?)- ... **CLC 21**
See also CA 120

Browning, Elizabeth Barrett
1806-1861 .... **NCLC 1, 16; PC 6**
See also CDBLB 1832-1890; DA; DLB 32; WLC

Browning, Robert
1812-1889 .... **NCLC 19; PC 2**
See also CDBLB 1832-1890; DA; DLB 32; YABC 1

Browning, Tod 1882-1962 .... **CLC 16**
See also CA 117

Bruccoli, Matthew J(oseph) 1931- .. **CLC 34**
See also CA 9-12R; CANR 7; DLB 103

Bruce, Lenny .... **CLC 21**
See also Schneider, Leonard Alfred

Bruin, John
See Brutus, Dennis

Brulls, Christian
See Simenon, Georges (Jacques Christian)

Brunner, John (Kilian Houston)
1934- .... **CLC 8, 10**
See also CA 1-4R; CAAS 8; CANR 2, 37; MTCW

Brutus, Dennis 1924- .... **CLC 43**
See also BLC 1; BW; CA 49-52; CAAS 14; CANR 2, 27; DLB 117

Bryan, C(ourtlandt) D(ixon) B(arnes)
1936- .... **CLC 29**
See also CA 73-76; CANR 13

Bryan, Michael
See Moore, Brian

Bryant, William Cullen
1794-1878 .... **NCLC 6**
See also CDALB 1640-1865; DA; DLB 3, 43, 59

Bryusov, Valery Yakovlevich
1873-1924 .... **TCLC 10**
See also CA 107

Buchan, John 1875-1940 .... **TCLC 41**
See also CA 108; DLB 34, 70; YABC 2

Buchanan, George 1506-1582 .... **LC 4**

Buchheim, Lothar-Guenther 1918- ... **CLC 6**
See also CA 85-88

Buchner, (Karl) Georg
1813-1837 .... **NCLC 26**

Buchwald, Art(hur) 1925- .... **CLC 33**
See also AITN 1; CA 5-8R; CANR 21; MTCW; SATA 10

Buck, Pearl S(ydenstricker)
1892-1973 .... **CLC 7, 11, 18**
See also AITN 1; CA 1-4R; 41-44R; CANR 1, 34; DA; DLB 9, 102; MTCW; SATA 1, 25

Buckler, Ernest 1908-1984 .... **CLC 13**
See also CA 11-12; 114; CAP 1; DLB 68; SATA 47

Buckley, Vincent (Thomas) 1925-1988 .... **CLC 57**
See also CA 101

Buckley, William F(rank), Jr. 1925- .... **CLC 7, 18, 37**
See also AITN 1; CA 1-4R; CANR 1, 24; DLBY 80; MTCW

Buechner, (Carl) Frederick 1926- .... **CLC 2, 4, 6, 9**
See also CA 13-16R; CANR 11, 39; DLBY 80; MTCW

Buell, John (Edward) 1927- .... **CLC 10**
See also CA 1-4R; DLB 53

Buero Vallejo, Antonio 1916- ... **CLC 15, 46**
See also CA 106; CANR 24; HW; MTCW

Bufalino, Gesualdo 1920(?)- .... **CLC 74**

Bugayev, Boris Nikolayevich 1880-1934
See Bely, Andrey
See also CA 104

Bukowski, Charles 1920- .... **CLC 2, 5, 9, 41**
See also CA 17-20R; CANR 40; DLB 5, 130; MTCW

Bulgakov, Mikhail (Afanas'evich) 1891-1940 .... **TCLC 2, 16**
See also CA 105

Bullins, Ed 1935- .... **CLC 1, 5, 7**
See also BLC 1; BW; CA 49-52; CAAS 16; CANR 24; DLB 7, 38; MTCW

Bulwer-Lytton, Edward (George Earle Lytton) 1803-1873 .... **NCLC 1**
See also DLB 21

Bunin, Ivan Alexeyevich 1870-1953 .... **TCLC 6; SSC 5**
See also CA 104

Bunting, Basil 1900-1985 .... **CLC 10, 39, 47**
See also CA 53-56; 115; CANR 7; DLB 20

Bunuel, Luis 1900-1983 .... **CLC 16**
See also CA 101; 110; CANR 32; HW

Bunyan, John 1628-1688 .... **LC 4**
See also CDBLB 1660-1789; DA; DLB 39; WLC

Burford, Eleanor
See Hibbert, Eleanor Alice Burford

Burgess, Anthony 1917- ..... **CLC 1, 2, 4, 5, 8, 10, 13, 15, 22, 40, 62**
See also Wilson, John (Anthony) Burgess
See also AITN 1; CDBLB 1960 to Present; DLB 14

Burke, Edmund 1729(?)-1797 .... **LC 7**
See also DA; DLB 104; WLC

Burke, Kenneth (Duva) 1897- .... **CLC 2, 24**
See also CA 5-8R; CANR 39; DLB 45, 63; MTCW

Burke, Leda
See Garnett, David

Burke, Ralph
See Silverberg, Robert

Burney, Fanny 1752-1840 .... **NCLC 12**
See also DLB 39

Burns, Robert 1759-1796 .... **LC 3; PC 6**
See also CDBLB 1789-1832; DA; DLB 109; WLC

Burns, Tex
See L'Amour, Louis (Dearborn)

Burnshaw, Stanley 1906- ..... **CLC 3, 13, 44**
See also CA 9-12R; DLB 48

Burr, Anne 1937- .... **CLC 6**
See also CA 25-28R

Burroughs, Edgar Rice 1875-1950 .... **TCLC 2, 32**
See also CA 104; 132; DLB 8; MTCW; SATA 41

Burroughs, William S(eward) 1914- .... **CLC 1, 2, 5, 15, 22, 42, 75**
See also AITN 2; CA 9-12R; CANR 20; DA; DLB 2, 8, 16; DLBY 81; MTCW; WLC

Busch, Frederick 1941- ... **CLC 7, 10, 18, 47**
See also CA 33-36R; CAAS 1; DLB 6

Bush, Ronald 1946- .... **CLC 34**
See also CA 136

Bustos, F(rancisco)
See Borges, Jorge Luis

Bustos Domecq, H(onorio)
See Bioy Casares, Adolfo; Borges, Jorge Luis

Butler, Octavia E(stelle) 1947- ..... **CLC 38**
See also BW; CA 73-76; CANR 12, 24, 38; DLB 33; MTCW

Butler, Samuel 1612-1680 .... **LC 16**
See also DLB 101, 126

Butler, Samuel 1835-1902 ...... **TCLC 1, 33**
See also CA 104; CDBLB 1890-1914; DA; DLB 18, 57; WLC

Butler, Walter C.
See Faust, Frederick (Schiller)

Butor, Michel (Marie Francois) 1926- .... **CLC 1, 3, 8, 11, 15**
See also CA 9-12R; CANR 33; DLB 83; MTCW

Buzo, Alexander (John) 1944- ...... **CLC 61**
See also CA 97-100; CANR 17, 39

Buzzati, Dino 1906-1972 .... **CLC 36**
See also CA 33-36R

Byars, Betsy (Cromer) 1928- .... **CLC 35**
See also CA 33-36R; CANR 18, 36; CLR 1, 16; DLB 52; MAICYA; MTCW; SAAS 1; SATA 4, 46

Byatt, A(ntonia) S(usan Drabble) 1936- .... **CLC 19, 65**
See also CA 13-16R; CANR 13, 33; DLB 14; MTCW

Byrne, David 1952- .... **CLC 26**
See also CA 127

Byrne, John Keyes 1926- .... **CLC 19**
See also Leonard, Hugh
See also CA 102

Byron, George Gordon (Noel) 1788-1824 .... **NCLC 2, 12**
See also CDBLB 1789-1832; DA; DLB 96, 110; WLC

C.3.3.
See Wilde, Oscar (Fingal O'Flahertie Wills)

Caballero, Fernan 1796-1877 ..... **NCLC 10**

Cabell, James Branch 1879-1958 ... **TCLC 6**
See also CA 105; DLB 9, 78

Cable, George Washington 1844-1925 .... **TCLC 4; SSC 4**
See also CA 104; DLB 12, 74

Cabral de Melo Neto, Joao 1920- ... **CLC 76**

Cabrera Infante, G(uillermo) 1929- .... **CLC 5, 25, 45**
See also CA 85-88; CANR 29; DLB 113; HW; MTCW

Cade, Toni
See Bambara, Toni Cade

Cadmus
See Buchan, John

Caedmon fl. 658-680 .... **CMLC 7**

Caeiro, Alberto
See Pessoa, Fernando (Antonio Nogueira)

Cage, John (Milton, Jr.) 1912- ..... **CLC 41**
See also CA 13-16R; CANR 9

Cain, G.
See Cabrera Infante, G(uillermo)

Cain, Guillermo
See Cabrera Infante, G(uillermo)

Cain, James M(allahan) 1892-1977 .... **CLC 3, 11, 28**
See also AITN 1; CA 17-20R; 73-76; CANR 8, 34; MTCW

Caine, Mark
See Raphael, Frederic (Michael)

Calderon de la Barca, Pedro 1600-1681 .... **DC 3**

Caldwell, Erskine (Preston) 1903-1987 .... **CLC 1, 8, 14, 50, 60**
See also AITN 1; CA 1-4R; 121; CAAS 1; CANR 2, 33; DLB 9, 86; MTCW

Caldwell, (Janet Miriam) Taylor (Holland) 1900-1985 .... **CLC 2, 28, 39**
See also CA 5-8R; 116; CANR 5

Calhoun, John Caldwell 1782-1850 .... **NCLC 15**
See also DLB 3

Calisher, Hortense 1911- .... **CLC 2, 4, 8, 38**
See also CA 1-4R; CANR 1, 22; DLB 2; MTCW

Callaghan, Morley Edward 1903-1990 .... **CLC 3, 14, 41, 65**
See also CA 9-12R; 132; CANR 33; DLB 68; MTCW

Calvino, Italo 1923-1985 .... **CLC 5, 8, 11, 22, 33, 39, 73; SSC 3**
See also CA 85-88; 116; CANR 23; MTCW

Cameron, Carey 1952- .... **CLC 59**
See also CA 135

Cameron, Peter 1959- .... **CLC 44**
See also CA 125

Campana, Dino 1885-1932 .... **TCLC 20**
See also CA 117; DLB 114

Campbell, John W(ood, Jr.) 1910-1971 .... **CLC 32**
See also CA 21-22; 29-32R; CANR 34; CAP 2; DLB 8; MTCW

Author Index

Christie
See Ichikawa, Kon

Christie, Agatha (Mary Clarissa) 1890-1976 ...... **CLC 1, 6, 8, 12, 39, 48**
See also AAYA 9; AITN 1, 2; CA 17-20R; 61-64; CANR 10, 37; CDBLB 1914-1945; DLB 13, 77; MTCW; SATA 36

Christie, (Ann) Philippa
See Pearce, Philippa
See also CA 5-8R; CANR 4

Christine de Pizan 1365(?)-1431(?) .... **LC 9**

Chubb, Elmer
See Masters, Edgar Lee

Chulkov, Mikhail Dmitrievich 1743-1792 .... **LC 2**

Churchill, Caryl 1938- .... **CLC 31, 55**
See also CA 102; CANR 22; DLB 13; MTCW

Churchill, Charles 1731-1764......... **LC 3**
See also DLB 109

Chute, Carolyn 1947- .... **CLC 39**
See also CA 123

Ciardi, John (Anthony) 1916-1986 .... **CLC 10, 40, 44**
See also CA 5-8R; 118; CAAS 2; CANR 5, 33; CLR 19; DLB 5; DLBY 86; MAICYA; MTCW; SATA 1, 46, 65

Cicero, Marcus Tullius 106B.C.-43B.C.............. **CMLC 3**

Cimino, Michael 1943- .... **CLC 16**
See also CA 105

Cioran, E(mil) M. 1911- .... **CLC 64**
See also CA 25-28R

Cisneros, Sandra 1954- .... **CLC 69**
See also AAYA 9; CA 131; DLB 122; HW

Clair, Rene .... **CLC 20**
See also Chomette, Rene Lucien

Clampitt, Amy 1920- .... **CLC 32**
See also CA 110; CANR 29; DLB 105

Clancy, Thomas L., Jr. 1947-
See Clancy, Tom
See also CA 125; 131; MTCW

Clancy, Tom .... **CLC 45**
See also Clancy, Thomas L., Jr.
See also AAYA 9; BEST 89:1, 90:1

Clare, John 1793-1864 .... **NCLC 9**
See also DLB 55, 96

Clarin
See Alas (y Urena), Leopoldo (Enrique Garcia)

Clark, (Robert) Brian 1932- .... **CLC 29**
See also CA 41-44R

Clark, Eleanor 1913- .... **CLC 5, 19**
See also CA 9-12R; CANR 41; DLB 6

Clark, J. P.
See Clark, John Pepper
See also DLB 117

Clark, John Pepper 1935- .... **CLC 38**
See also Clark, J. P.
See also BLC 1; BW; CA 65-68; CANR 16

Clark, M. R.
See Clark, Mavis Thorpe

Clark, Mavis Thorpe 1909- .... **CLC 12**
See also CA 57-60; CANR 8, 37; CLR 30; MAICYA; SAAS 5; SATA 8, 74

Clark, Walter Van Tilburg 1909-1971 .... **CLC 28**
See also CA 9-12R; 33-36R; DLB 9; SATA 8

Clarke, Arthur C(harles) 1917- ...... **CLC 1, 4, 13, 18, 35; SSC 3**
See also AAYA 4; CA 1-4R; CANR 2, 28; MAICYA; MTCW; SATA 13, 70

Clarke, Austin 1896-1974......... **CLC 6, 9**
See also CA 29-32; 49-52; CAP 2; DLB 10, 20

Clarke, Austin C(hesterfield) 1934- .... **CLC 8, 53**
See also BLC 1; BW; CA 25-28R; CAAS 16; CANR 14, 32; DLB 53, 125

Clarke, Gillian 1937- .... **CLC 61**
See also CA 106; DLB 40

Clarke, Marcus (Andrew Hislop) 1846-1881 .... **NCLC 19**

Clarke, Shirley 1925- .... **CLC 16**

Clash, The .... **CLC 30**
See also Headon, (Nicky) Topper; Jones, Mick; Simonon, Paul; Strummer, Joe

Claudel, Paul (Louis Charles Marie) 1868-1955 .... **TCLC 2, 10**
See also CA 104

Clavell, James (duMaresq) 1925- .... **CLC 6, 25**
See also CA 25-28R; CANR 26; MTCW

Cleaver, (Leroy) Eldridge 1935- .... **CLC 30**
See also BLC 1; BW; CA 21-24R; CANR 16

Cleese, John (Marwood) 1939- ..... **CLC 21**
See also Monty Python
See also CA 112; 116; CANR 35; MTCW

Cleishbotham, Jebediah
See Scott, Walter

Cleland, John 1710-1789 .... **LC 2**
See also DLB 39

Clemens, Samuel Langhorne 1835-1910
See Twain, Mark
See also CA 104; 135; CDALB 1865-1917; DA; DLB 11, 12, 23, 64, 74; MAICYA; YABC 2

Cleophil
See Congreve, William

Clerihew, E.
See Bentley, E(dmund) C(lerihew)

Clerk, N. W.
See Lewis, C(live) S(taples)

Cliff, Jimmy .... **CLC 21**
See also Chambers, James

Clifton, (Thelma) Lucille 1936- .... **CLC 19, 66**
See also BLC 1; BW; CA 49-52; CANR 2, 24; CLR 5; DLB 5, 41; MAICYA; MTCW; SATA 20, 69

Clinton, Dirk
See Silverberg, Robert

Clough, Arthur Hugh 1819-1861.. **NCLC 27**
See also DLB 32

Clutha, Janet Paterson Frame 1924-
See Frame, Janet
See also CA 1-4R; CANR 2, 36; MTCW

Clyne, Terence
See Blatty, William Peter

Cobalt, Martin
See Mayne, William (James Carter)

Coburn, D(onald) L(ee) 1938- ...... **CLC 10**
See also CA 89-92

Cocteau, Jean (Maurice Eugene Clement) 1889-1963 .... **CLC 1, 8, 15, 16, 43**
See also CA 25-28; CANR 40; CAP 2; DA; DLB 65; MTCW; WLC

Codrescu, Andrei 1946- .... **CLC 46**
See also CA 33-36R; CANR 13, 34

Coe, Max
See Bourne, Randolph S(illiman)

Coe, Tucker
See Westlake, Donald E(dwin)

Coetzee, J(ohn) M(ichael) 1940- .... **CLC 23, 33, 66**
See also CA 77-80; CANR 41; MTCW

Cohen, Arthur A(llen) 1928-1986 .... **CLC 7, 31**
See also CA 1-4R; 120; CANR 1, 17; DLB 28

Cohen, Leonard (Norman) 1934- .... **CLC 3, 38**
See also CA 21-24R; CANR 14; DLB 53; MTCW

Cohen, Matt 1942- .... **CLC 19**
See also CA 61-64; CANR 40; DLB 53

Cohen-Solal, Annie 19(?)- .... **CLC 50**

Colegate, Isabel 1931- .... **CLC 36**
See also CA 17-20R; CANR 8, 22; DLB 14; MTCW

Coleman, Emmett
See Reed, Ishmael

Coleridge, Samuel Taylor 1772-1834 .... **NCLC 9**
See also CDBLB 1789-1832; DA; DLB 93, 107; WLC

Coleridge, Sara 1802-1852....... **NCLC 31**

Coles, Don 1928- .... **CLC 46**
See also CA 115; CANR 38

Colette, (Sidonie-Gabrielle) 1873-1954 ...... **TCLC 1, 5, 16; SSC 10**
See also CA 104; 131; DLB 65; MTCW

Collett, (Jacobine) Camilla (Wergeland) 1813-1895 .... **NCLC 22**

Collier, Christopher 1930- .... **CLC 30**
See also CA 33-36R; CANR 13, 33; MAICYA; SATA 16, 70

Collier, James L(incoln) 1928- ..... **CLC 30**
See also CA 9-12R; CANR 4, 33; MAICYA; SATA 8, 70

Collier, Jeremy 1650-1726........... **LC 6**

Collins, Hunt
See Hunter, Evan

Collins, Linda 1931- .... **CLC 44**
See also CA 125

Collins, (William) Wilkie 1824-1889 .... **NCLC 1, 18**
See also CDBLB 1832-1890; DLB 18, 70

Craig, A. A.
See Anderson, Poul (William)

Craik, Dinah Maria (Mulock) 1826-1887 .... **NCLC 38**
See also DLB 35; MAICYA; SATA 34

Cram, Ralph Adams 1863-1942.... **TCLC 45**

Crane, (Harold) Hart 1899-1932 .... **TCLC 2, 5; PC 3**
See also CA 104; 127; CDALB 1917-1929; DA; DLB 4, 48; MTCW; WLC

Crane, R(onald) S(almon) 1886-1967 .... **CLC 27**
See also CA 85-88; DLB 63

Crane, Stephen (Townley) 1871-1900 ..... **TCLC 11, 17, 32; SSC 7**
See also CA 109; 140; CDALB 1865-1917; DA; DLB 12, 54, 78; WLC; YABC 2

Crase, Douglas 1944- .... **CLC 58**
See also CA 106

Craven, Margaret 1901-1980....... **CLC 17**
See also CA 103

Crawford, F(rancis) Marion 1854-1909 .... **TCLC 10**
See also CA 107; DLB 71

Crawford, Isabella Valancy 1850-1887 .... **NCLC 12**
See also DLB 92

Crayon, Geoffrey
See Irving, Washington

Creasey, John 1908-1973.......... **CLC 11**
See also CA 5-8R; 41-44R; CANR 8; DLB 77; MTCW

Crebillon, Claude Prosper Jolyot de (fils) 1707-1777 .... **LC 1**

Credo
See Creasey, John

Creeley, Robert (White) 1926- .... **CLC 1, 2, 4, 8, 11, 15, 36**
See also CA 1-4R; CAAS 10; CANR 23; DLB 5, 16; MTCW

Crews, Harry (Eugene) 1935- .... **CLC 6, 23, 49**
See also AITN 1; CA 25-28R; CANR 20; DLB 6; MTCW

Crichton, (John) Michael 1942- .... **CLC 2, 6, 54**
See also AAYA 10; AITN 2; CA 25-28R; CANR 13, 40; DLBY 81; MTCW; SATA 9

Crispin, Edmund .... **CLC 22**
See also Montgomery, (Robert) Bruce
See also DLB 87

Cristofer, Michael 1945(?)- .... **CLC 28**
See also CA 110; DLB 7

Croce, Benedetto 1866-1952 ...... **TCLC 37**
See also CA 120

Crockett, David 1786-1836 .... **NCLC 8**
See also DLB 3, 11

Crockett, Davy
See Crockett, David

Croker, John Wilson 1780-1857 .. **NCLC 10**
See also DLB 110

Crommelynck, Fernand 1885-1970 .. **CLC 75**
See also CA 89-92

Cronin, A(rchibald) J(oseph) 1896-1981 .... **CLC 32**
See also CA 1-4R; 102; CANR 5; SATA 25, 47

Cross, Amanda
See Heilbrun, Carolyn G(old)

Crothers, Rachel 1878(?)-1958..... **TCLC 19**
See also CA 113; DLB 7

Croves, Hal
See Traven, B.

Crowfield, Christopher
See Stowe, Harriet (Elizabeth) Beecher

Crowley, Aleister................. **TCLC 7**
See also Crowley, Edward Alexander

Crowley, Edward Alexander 1875-1947
See Crowley, Aleister
See also CA 104

Crowley, John 1942-.............. **CLC 57**
See also CA 61-64; DLBY 82; SATA 65

Crud
See Crumb, R(obert)

Crumarums
See Crumb, R(obert)

Crumb, R(obert) 1943-............ **CLC 17**
See also CA 106

Crumbum
See Crumb, R(obert)

Crumski
See Crumb, R(obert)

Crum the Bum
See Crumb, R(obert)

Crunk
See Crumb, R(obert)

Crustt
See Crumb, R(obert)

Cryer, Gretchen (Kiger) 1935-...... **CLC 21**
See also CA 114; 123

Csath, Geza 1887-1919........... **TCLC 13**
See also CA 111

Cudlip, David 1933- .... **CLC 34**

Cullen, Countee 1903-1946 ..... **TCLC 4, 37**
See also BLC 1; BW; CA 108; 124; CDALB 1917-1929; DA; DLB 4, 48, 51; MTCW; SATA 18

Cum, R.
See Crumb, R(obert)

Cummings, Bruce F(rederick) 1889-1919
See Barbellion, W. N. P.
See also CA 123

Cummings, E(dward) E(stlin) 1894-1962 ..... **CLC 1, 3, 8, 12, 15, 68; PC 5**
See also CA 73-76; CANR 31; CDALB 1929-1941; DA; DLB 4, 48; MTCW; WLC 2

Cunha, Euclides (Rodrigues Pimenta) da 1866-1909 .... **TCLC 24**
See also CA 123

Cunningham, E. V.
See Fast, Howard (Melvin)

Cunningham, J(ames) V(incent) 1911-1985 .... **CLC 3, 31**
See also CA 1-4R; 115; CANR 1; DLB 5

Cunningham, Julia (Woolfolk) 1916- .... **CLC 12**
See also CA 9-12R; CANR 4, 19, 36; MAICYA; SAAS 2; SATA 1, 26

Cunningham, Michael 1952- .... **CLC 34**
See also CA 136

Cunninghame Graham, R(obert) B(ontine) 1852-1936 .... **TCLC 19**
See also Graham, R(obert) B(ontine) Cunninghame
See also CA 119; DLB 98

Currie, Ellen 19(?)-............... **CLC 44**

Curtin, Philip
See Lowndes, Marie Adelaide (Belloc)

Curtis, Price
See Ellison, Harlan

Cutrate, Joe
See Spiegelman, Art

Czaczkes, Shmuel Yosef
See Agnon, S(hmuel) Y(osef Halevi)

D. P.
See Wells, H(erbert) G(eorge)

Dabrowska, Maria (Szumska) 1889-1965 .... **CLC 15**
See also CA 106

Dabydeen, David 1955- .... **CLC 34**
See also BW; CA 125

Dacey, Philip 1939- .... **CLC 51**
See also CA 37-40R; CAAS 17; CANR 14, 32; DLB 105

Dagerman, Stig (Halvard) 1923-1954 .... **TCLC 17**
See also CA 117

Dahl, Roald 1916-1990........ **CLC 1, 6, 18**
See also CA 1-4R; 133; CANR 6, 32, 37; CLR 1, 7; MAICYA; MTCW; SATA 1, 26, 73; SATA-Obit 65

Dahlberg, Edward 1900-1977... **CLC 1, 7, 14**
See also CA 9-12R; 69-72; CANR 31; DLB 48; MTCW

Dale, Colin...................... **TCLC 18**
See also Lawrence, T(homas) E(dward)

Dale, George E.
See Asimov, Isaac

Daly, Elizabeth 1878-1967......... **CLC 52**
See also CA 23-24; 25-28R; CAP 2

Daly, Maureen 1921-............. **CLC 17**
See also AAYA 5; CANR 37; MAICYA; SAAS 1; SATA 2

Daniels, Brett
See Adler, Renata

Dannay, Frederic 1905-1982 .... **CLC 11**
See also Queen, Ellery
See also CA 1-4R; 107; CANR 1, 39; MTCW

D'Annunzio, Gabriele 1863-1938 .... **TCLC 6, 40**
See also CA 104

d'Antibes, Germain
See Simenon, Georges (Jacques Christian)

Danvers, Dennis 1947-............ **CLC 70**

Danziger, Paula 1944- .... **CLC 21**
See also AAYA 4; CA 112; 115; CANR 37; CLR 20; MAICYA; SATA 30, 36, 63

Dario, Ruben .... **TCLC 4**
See also Sarmiento, Felix Ruben Garcia

Darley, George 1795-1846 .... **NCLC 2**
See also DLB 96

Daryush, Elizabeth 1887-1977 .... **CLC 6, 19**
See also CA 49-52; CANR 3; DLB 20

Daudet, (Louis Marie) Alphonse
1840-1897 .... **NCLC 1**
See also DLB 123

Daumal, Rene 1908-1944 .... **TCLC 14**
See also CA 114

Davenport, Guy (Mattison, Jr.)
1927- .... **CLC 6, 14, 38**
See also CA 33-36R; CANR 23; DLB 130

Davidson, Avram 1923-
See Queen, Ellery
See also CA 101; CANR 26; DLB 8

Davidson, Donald (Grady)
1893-1968 .... **CLC 2, 13, 19**
See also CA 5-8R; 25-28R; CANR 4; DLB 45

Davidson, Hugh
See Hamilton, Edmond

Davidson, John 1857-1909 .... **TCLC 24**
See also CA 118; DLB 19

Davidson, Sara 1943- .... **CLC 9**
See also CA 81-84

Davie, Donald (Alfred)
1922- .... **CLC 5, 8, 10, 31**
See also CA 1-4R; CAAS 3; CANR 1; DLB 27; MTCW

Davies, Ray(mond Douglas) 1944- .. **CLC 21**
See also CA 116

Davies, Rhys 1903-1978 .... **CLC 23**
See also CA 9-12R; 81-84; CANR 4

Davies, (William) Robertson
1913- .... **CLC 2, 7, 13, 25, 42, 75**
See also BEST 89:2; CA 33-36R; CANR 17; DA; DLB 68; MTCW; WLC

Davies, W(illiam) H(enry)
1871-1940 .... **TCLC 5**
See also CA 104; DLB 19

Davies, Walter C.
See Kornbluth, C(yril) M.

Davis, Angela (Yvonne) 1944- ...... **CLC 77**
See also BW; CA 57-60; CANR 10

Davis, B. Lynch
See Bioy Casares, Adolfo; Borges, Jorge Luis

Davis, Gordon
See Hunt, E(verette) Howard, Jr.

Davis, Harold Lenoir 1896-1960 .... **CLC 49**
See also CA 89-92; DLB 9

Davis, Rebecca (Blaine) Harding
1831-1910 .... **TCLC 6**
See also CA 104; DLB 74

Davis, Richard Harding
1864-1916 .... **TCLC 24**
See also CA 114; DLB 12, 23, 78, 79

Davison, Frank Dalby 1893-1970 ... **CLC 15**
See also CA 116

Davison, Lawrence H.
See Lawrence, D(avid) H(erbert Richards)

Davison, Peter 1928- .... **CLC 28**
See also CA 9-12R; CAAS 4; CANR 3; DLB 5

Davys, Mary 1674-1732 .... **LC 1**
See also DLB 39

Dawson, Fielding 1930- .... **CLC 6**
See also CA 85-88; DLB 130

Dawson, Peter
See Faust, Frederick (Schiller)

Day, Clarence (Shepard, Jr.)
1874-1935 .... **TCLC 25**
See also CA 108; DLB 11

Day, Thomas 1748-1789 .... **LC 1**
See also DLB 39; YABC 1

Day Lewis, C(ecil)
1904-1972 .... **CLC 1, 6, 10**
See also Blake, Nicholas
See also CA 13-16; 33-36R; CANR 34; CAP 1; DLB 15, 20; MTCW

Dazai, Osamu .... **TCLC 11**
See also Tsushima, Shuji

de Andrade, Carlos Drummond
See Drummond de Andrade, Carlos

Deane, Norman
See Creasey, John

de Beauvoir, Simone (Lucie Ernestine Marie Bertrand)
See Beauvoir, Simone (Lucie Ernestine Marie Bertrand) de

de Brissac, Malcolm
See Dickinson, Peter (Malcolm)

de Chardin, Pierre Teilhard
See Teilhard de Chardin, (Marie Joseph) Pierre

Dee, John 1527-1608 .... **LC 20**

Deer, Sandra 1940- .... **CLC 45**

De Ferrari, Gabriella .... **CLC 65**

Defoe, Daniel 1660(?)-1731 .... **LC 1**
See also CDBLB 1660-1789; DA; DLB 39, 95, 101; MAICYA; SATA 22; WLC

de Gourmont, Remy
See Gourmont, Remy de

de Hartog, Jan 1914- .... **CLC 19**
See also CA 1-4R; CANR 1

de Hostos, E. M.
See Hostos (y Bonilla), Eugenio Maria de

de Hostos, Eugenio M.
See Hostos (y Bonilla), Eugenio Maria de

Deighton, Len .... **CLC 4, 7, 22, 46**
See also Deighton, Leonard Cyril
See also AAYA 6; BEST 89:2; CDBLB 1960 to Present; DLB 87

Deighton, Leonard Cyril 1929-
See Deighton, Len
See also CA 9-12R; CANR 19, 33; MTCW

Dekker, Thomas 1572(?)-1632 .... **LC 22**
See also CDBLB Before 1660; DLB 62

de la Mare, Walter (John)
1873-1956 .... **TCLC 4**
See also CA 110; 137; CDBLB 1914-1945; CLR 23; DA; DLB 19; MAICYA; SATA 16; WLC

Delaney, Franey
See O'Hara, John (Henry)

Delaney, Shelagh 1939- .... **CLC 29**
See also CA 17-20R; CANR 30; CDBLB 1960 to Present; DLB 13; MTCW

Delany, Mary (Granville Pendarves)
1700-1788 .... **LC 12**

Delany, Samuel R(ay, Jr.)
1942- .... **CLC 8, 14, 38**
See also BLC 1; BW; CA 81-84; CANR 27; DLB 8, 33; MTCW

Delaporte, Theophile
See Green, Julian (Hartridge)

De La Ramee, (Marie) Louise 1839-1908
See Ouida
See also SATA 20

de la Roche, Mazo 1879-1961 ...... **CLC 14**
See also CA 85-88; CANR 30; DLB 68; SATA 64

Delbanco, Nicholas (Franklin)
1942- .... **CLC 6, 13**
See also CA 17-20R; CAAS 2; CANR 29; DLB 6

del Castillo, Michel 1933- .... **CLC 38**
See also CA 109

Deledda, Grazia (Cosima)
1875(?)-1936 .... **TCLC 23**
See also CA 123

Delibes, Miguel .... **CLC 8, 18**
See also Delibes Setien, Miguel

Delibes Setien, Miguel 1920-
See Delibes, Miguel
See also CA 45-48; CANR 1, 32; HW; MTCW

DeLillo, Don
1936- ..... **CLC 8, 10, 13, 27, 39, 54, 76**
See also BEST 89:1; CA 81-84; CANR 21; DLB 6; MTCW

de Lisser, H. G.
See De Lisser, Herbert George
See also DLB 117

De Lisser, Herbert George
1878-1944 .... **TCLC 12**
See also de Lisser, H. G.
See also CA 109

Deloria, Vine (Victor), Jr. 1933- .... **CLC 21**
See also CA 53-56; CANR 5, 20; MTCW; SATA 21

Del Vecchio, John M(ichael)
1947- .... **CLC 29**
See also CA 110; DLBD 9

de Man, Paul (Adolph Michel)
1919-1983 .... **CLC 55**
See also CA 128; 111; DLB 67; MTCW

De Marinis, Rick 1934- .... **CLC 54**
See also CA 57-60; CANR 9, 25

Demby, William 1922- .... **CLC 53**
See also BLC 1; BW; CA 81-84; DLB 33

Demijohn, Thom
See Disch, Thomas M(ichael)

de Montherlant, Henry (Milon)
See Montherlant, Henry (Milon) de

de Natale, Francine
See Malzberg, Barry N(athaniel)

Denby, Edwin (Orr) 1903-1983 ..... **CLC 48**
See also CA 138; 110

Dunsany, Lord .... **TCLC 2**
See also Dunsany, Edward John Moreton Drax Plunkett
See also DLB 77

du Perry, Jean
See Simenon, Georges (Jacques Christian)

Durang, Christopher (Ferdinand) 1949- .... **CLC 27, 38**
See also CA 105

Duras, Marguerite 1914- ...... **CLC 3, 6, 11, 20, 34, 40, 68**
See also CA 25-28R; DLB 83; MTCW

Durban, (Rosa) Pam 1947- .... **CLC 39**
See also CA 123

Durcan, Paul 1944- .... **CLC 43, 70**
See also CA 134

Durrell, Lawrence (George) 1912-1990 .... **CLC 1, 4, 6, 8, 13, 27, 41**
See also CA 9-12R; 132; CANR 40; CDBLB 1945-1960; DLB 15, 27; DLBY 90; MTCW

Durrenmatt, Friedrich .... **CLC 1, 4, 8, 11, 15, 43**
See also Duerrenmatt, Friedrich
See also DLB 69, 124

Dutt, Toru 1856-1877........... **NCLC 29**

Dwight, Timothy 1752-1817...... **NCLC 13**
See also DLB 37

Dworkin, Andrea 1946- .... **CLC 43**
See also CA 77-80; CANR 16, 39; MTCW

Dylan, Bob 1941- ...... **CLC 3, 4, 6, 12, 77**
See also CA 41-44R; DLB 16

Eagleton, Terence (Francis) 1943-
See Eagleton, Terry
See also CA 57-60; CANR 7, 23; MTCW

Eagleton, Terry .... **CLC 63**
See also Eagleton, Terence (Francis)

Early, Jack
See Scoppettone, Sandra

East, Michael
See West, Morris L(anglo)

Eastaway, Edward
See Thomas, (Philip) Edward

Eastlake, William (Derry) 1917-..... **CLC 8**
See also CA 5-8R; CAAS 1; CANR 5; DLB 6

Eberhart, Richard (Ghormley) 1904- .... **CLC 3, 11, 19, 56**
See also CA 1-4R; CANR 2; CDALB 1941-1968; DLB 48; MTCW

Eberstadt, Fernanda 1960- .... **CLC 39**
See also CA 136

Echegaray (y Eizaguirre), Jose (Maria Waldo) 1832-1916 .... **TCLC 4**
See also CA 104; CANR 32; HW; MTCW

Echeverria, (Jose) Esteban (Antonino) 1805-1851 .... **NCLC 18**

Echo
See Proust, (Valentin-Louis-George-Eugene-)Marcel

Eckert, Allan W. 1931- .... **CLC 17**
See also CA 13-16R; CANR 14; SATA 27, 29

Eckhart, Meister 1260(?)-1328(?) .. **CMLC 9**
See also DLB 115

Eckmar, F. R.
See de Hartog, Jan

Eco, Umberto 1932- .... **CLC 28, 60**
See also BEST 90:1; CA 77-80; CANR 12, 33; MTCW

Eddison, E(ric) R(ucker) 1882-1945 .... **TCLC 15**
See also CA 109

Edel, (Joseph) Leon 1907- ...... **CLC 29, 34**
See also CA 1-4R; CANR 1, 22; DLB 103

Eden, Emily 1797-1869 .... **NCLC 10**

Edgar, David 1948- .... **CLC 42**
See also CA 57-60; CANR 12; DLB 13; MTCW

Edgerton, Clyde (Carlyle) 1944- .... **CLC 39**
See also CA 118; 134

Edgeworth, Maria 1767-1849...... **NCLC 1**
See also DLB 116; SATA 21

Edmonds, Paul
See Kuttner, Henry

Edmonds, Walter D(umaux) 1903- .. **CLC 35**
See also CA 5-8R; CANR 2; DLB 9; MAICYA; SAAS 4; SATA 1, 27

Edmondson, Wallace
See Ellison, Harlan

Edson, Russell .... **CLC 13**
See also CA 33-36R

Edwards, G(erald) B(asil) 1899-1976 .... **CLC 25**
See also CA 110

Edwards, Gus 1939- .... **CLC 43**
See also CA 108

Edwards, Jonathan 1703-1758........ **LC 7**
See also DA; DLB 24

Efron, Marina Ivanovna Tsvetaeva
See Tsvetaeva (Efron), Marina (Ivanovna)

Ehle, John (Marsden, Jr.) 1925- .... **CLC 27**
See also CA 9-12R

Ehrenbourg, Ilya (Grigoryevich)
See Ehrenburg, Ilya (Grigoryevich)

Ehrenburg, Ilya (Grigoryevich) 1891-1967 .... **CLC 18, 34, 62**
See also CA 102; 25-28R

Ehrenburg, Ilyo (Grigoryevich)
See Ehrenburg, Ilya (Grigoryevich)

Eich, Guenter 1907-1972 .... **CLC 15**
See also CA 111; 93-96; DLB 69, 124

Eichendorff, Joseph Freiherr von 1788-1857 .... **NCLC 8**
See also DLB 90

Eigner, Larry .... **CLC 9**
See also Eigner, Laurence (Joel)
See also DLB 5

Eigner, Laurence (Joel) 1927-
See Eigner, Larry
See also CA 9-12R; CANR 6

Eiseley, Loren Corey 1907-1977 ..... **CLC 7**
See also AAYA 5; CA 1-4R; 73-76; CANR 6

Eisenstadt, Jill 1963- .... **CLC 50**
See also CA 140

Eisner, Simon
See Kornbluth, C(yril) M.

Ekeloef, (Bengt) Gunnar 1907-1968 .... **CLC 27**
See also Ekelof, (Bengt) Gunnar
See also CA 123; 25-28R

Ekelof, (Bengt) Gunnar .... **CLC 27**
See also Ekeloef, (Bengt) Gunnar

Ekwensi, C. O. D.
See Ekwensi, Cyprian (Odiatu Duaka)

Ekwensi, Cyprian (Odiatu Duaka) 1921- .... **CLC 4**
See also BLC 1; BW; CA 29-32R; CANR 18; DLB 117; MTCW; SATA 66

Elaine .... **TCLC 18**
See also Leverson, Ada

El Crummo
See Crumb, R(obert)

Elia
See Lamb, Charles

Eliade, Mircea 1907-1986 .... **CLC 19**
See also CA 65-68; 119; CANR 30; MTCW

Eliot, A. D.
See Jewett, (Theodora) Sarah Orne

Eliot, Alice
See Jewett, (Theodora) Sarah Orne

Eliot, Dan
See Silverberg, Robert

Eliot, George 1819-1880.... **NCLC 4, 13, 23**
See also CDBLB 1832-1890; DA; DLB 21, 35, 55; WLC

Eliot, John 1604-1690 .... **LC 5**
See also DLB 24

Eliot, T(homas) S(tearns) 1888-1965 .... **CLC 1, 2, 3, 6, 9, 10, 13, 15, 24, 34, 41, 55, 57; PC 5**
See also CA 5-8R; 25-28R; CANR 41; CDALB 1929-1941; DA; DLB 7, 10, 45, 63; DLBY 88; MTCW; WLC 2

Elizabeth 1866-1941 .... **TCLC 41**

Elkin, Stanley L(awrence) 1930- ... **CLC 4, 6, 9, 14, 27, 51; SSC 12**
See also CA 9-12R; CANR 8; DLB 2, 28; DLBY 80; MTCW

Elledge, Scott .... **CLC 34**

Elliott, Don
See Silverberg, Robert

Elliott, George P(aul) 1918-1980..... **CLC 2**
See also CA 1-4R; 97-100; CANR 2

Elliott, Janice 1931- .... **CLC 47**
See also CA 13-16R; CANR 8, 29; DLB 14

Elliott, Sumner Locke 1917-1991 ... **CLC 38**
See also CA 5-8R; 134; CANR 2, 21

Elliott, William
See Bradbury, Ray (Douglas)

Ellis, A. E. .... **CLC 7**

Ellis, Alice Thomas .... **CLC 40**
See also Haycraft, Anna

Ellis, Bret Easton 1964- .... **CLC 39, 71**
See also AAYA 2; CA 118; 123

Ellis, (Henry) Havelock 1859-1939 .... **TCLC 14**
See also CA 109

Frost, Frederick
See Faust, Frederick (Schiller)

Frost, Robert (Lee) 1874-1963 ... **CLC 1, 3, 4, 9, 10, 13, 15, 26, 34, 44; PC 1**
See also CA 89-92; CANR 33; CDALB 1917-1929; DA; DLB 54; DLBD 7; MTCW; SATA 14; WLC

Froy, Herald
See Waterhouse, Keith (Spencer)

Fry, Christopher 1907-....... **CLC 2, 10, 14**
See also CA 17-20R; CANR 9, 30; DLB 13; MTCW; SATA 66

Frye, (Herman) Northrop 1912-1991 .... **CLC 24, 70**
See also CA 5-8R; 133; CANR 8, 37; DLB 67, 68; MTCW

Fuchs, Daniel 1909- .... **CLC 8, 22**
See also CA 81-84; CAAS 5; CANR 40; DLB 9, 26, 28

Fuchs, Daniel 1934- .... **CLC 34**
See also CA 37-40R; CANR 14

Fuentes, Carlos 1928 ...... **CLC 3, 8, 10, 13, 22, 41, 60**
See also AAYA 4; AITN 2; CA 69-72; CANR 10, 32; DA; DLB 113; HW; MTCW; WLC

Fuentes, Gregorio Lopez y
See Lopez y Fuentes, Gregorio

Fugard, (Harold) Athol 1932- .... **CLC 5, 9, 14, 25, 40; DC 3**
See also CA 85-88; CANR 32; MTCW

Fugard, Sheila 1932- .... **CLC 48**
See also CA 125

Fuller, Charles (H., Jr.) 1939- .... **CLC 25; DC 1**
See also BLC 2; BW; CA 108; 112; DLB 38; MTCW

Fuller, John (Leopold) 1937- .... **CLC 62**
See also CA 21-24R; CANR 9; DLB 40

Fuller, Margaret .... **NCLC 5**
See also Ossoli, Sarah Margaret (Fuller marchesa d')

Fuller, Roy (Broadbent) 1912-1991 .... **CLC 4, 28**
See also CA 5-8R; 135; CAAS 10; DLB 15, 20

Fulton, Alice 1952-............... **CLC 52**
See also CA 116

Furphy, Joseph 1843-1912........ **TCLC 25**

Fussell, Paul 1924-............... **CLC 74**
See also BEST 90:1; CA 17-20R; CANR 8, 21, 35; MTCW

Futabatei, Shimei 1864-1909...... **TCLC 44**

Futrelle, Jacques 1875-1912 ...... **TCLC 19**
See also CA 113

G. B. S.
See Shaw, George Bernard

Gaboriau, Emile 1835-1873 ...... **NCLC 14**

Gadda, Carlo Emilio 1893-1973 .... **CLC 11**
See also CA 89-92

Gaddis, William 1922- .... **CLC 1, 3, 6, 8, 10, 19, 43**
See also CA 17-20R; CANR 21; DLB 2; MTCW

Gaines, Ernest J(ames) 1933- .... **CLC 3, 11, 18**
See also AITN 1; BLC 2; BW; CA 9-12R; CANR 6, 24; CDALB 1968-1988; DLB 2, 33; DLBY 80; MTCW

Gaitskill, Mary 1954-............ **CLC 69**
See also CA 128

Galdos, Benito Perez
See Perez Galdos, Benito

Gale, Zona 1874-1938 .... **TCLC 7**
See also CA 105; DLB 9, 78

Galeano, Eduardo (Hughes) 1940-... **CLC 72**
See also CA 29-32R; CANR 13, 32; HW

Galiano, Juan Valera y Alcala
See Valera y Alcala-Galiano, Juan

Gallagher, Tess 1943-.......... **CLC 18, 63**
See also CA 106; DLB 120

Gallant, Mavis 1922- .... **CLC 7, 18, 38; SSC 5**
See also CA 69-72; CANR 29; DLB 53; MTCW

Gallant, Roy A(rthur) 1924- .... **CLC 17**
See also CA 5-8R; CANR 4, 29; CLR 30; MAICYA; SATA 4, 68

Gallico, Paul (William) 1897-1976 ... **CLC 2**
See also AITN 1; CA 5-8R; 69-72; CANR 23; DLB 9; MAICYA; SATA 13

Gallup, Ralph
See Whitemore, Hugh (John)

Galsworthy, John 1867-1933 .... **TCLC 1, 45**
See also CA 104; CDBLB 1890-1914; DA; DLB 10, 34, 98; WLC 2

Galt, John 1779-1839............ **NCLC 1**
See also DLB 99, 116

Galvin, James 1951-.............. **CLC 38**
See also CA 108; CANR 26

Gamboa, Federico 1864-1939...... **TCLC 36**

Gann, Ernest Kellogg 1910-1991.... **CLC 23**
See also AITN 1; CA 1-4R; 136; CANR 1

Garcia, Christina 1959- .... **CLC 76**

Garcia Lorca, Federico 1898-1936 .. **TCLC 1, 7, 49; DC 2; PC 3**
See also CA 104; 131; DA; DLB 108; HW; MTCW; WLC

Garcia Marquez, Gabriel (Jose) 1928- ... **CLC 2, 3, 8, 10, 15, 27, 47, 55; SSC 8**
See also Marquez, Gabriel (Jose) Garcia
See also AAYA 3; BEST 89:1, 90:4; CA 33-36R; CANR 10, 28; DA; DLB 113; HW; MTCW; WLC

Gard, Janice
See Latham, Jean Lee

Gard, Roger Martin du
See Martin du Gard, Roger

Gardam, Jane 1928-.............. **CLC 43**
See also CA 49-52; CANR 2, 18, 33; CLR 12; DLB 14; MAICYA; MTCW; SAAS 9; SATA 28, 39

Gardner, Herb.................... **CLC 44**

Gardner, John (Champlin), Jr. 1933-1982 .... **CLC 2, 3, 5, 7, 8, 10, 18, 28, 34; SSC 7**
See also AITN 1; CA 65-68; 107; CANR 33; DLB 2; DLBY 82; MTCW; SATA 31, 40

Gardner, John (Edmund) 1926-..... **CLC 30**
See also CA 103; CANR 15; MTCW

Gardner, Noel
See Kuttner, Henry

Gardons, S. S.
See Snodgrass, William D(e Witt)

Garfield, Leon 1921-.............. **CLC 12**
See also AAYA 8; CA 17-20R; CANR 38, 41; CLR 21; MAICYA; SATA 1, 32

Garland, (Hannibal) Hamlin 1860-1940 .... **TCLC 3**
See also CA 104; DLB 12, 71, 78

Garneau, (Hector de) Saint-Denys 1912-1943 .... **TCLC 13**
See also CA 111; DLB 88

Garner, Alan 1934-............... **CLC 17**
See also CA 73-76; CANR 15; CLR 20; MAICYA; MTCW; SATA 18, 69

Garner, Hugh 1913-1979 .... **CLC 13**
See also CA 69-72; CANR 31; DLB 68

Garnett, David 1892-1981 .... **CLC 3**
See also CA 5-8R; 103; CANR 17; DLB 34

Garos, Stephanie
See Katz, Steve

Garrett, George (Palmer) 1929- .... **CLC 3, 11, 51**
See also CA 1-4R; CAAS 5; CANR 1; DLB 2, 5, 130; DLBY 83

Garrick, David 1717-1779 .... **LC 15**
See also DLB 84

Garrigue, Jean 1914-1972 .... **CLC 2, 8**
See also CA 5-8R; 37-40R; CANR 20

Garrison, Frederick
See Sinclair, Upton (Beall)

Garth, Will
See Hamilton, Edmond; Kuttner, Henry

Garvey, Marcus (Moziah, Jr.) 1887-1940 .... **TCLC 41**
See also BLC 2; BW; CA 120; 124

Gary, Romain .... **CLC 25**
See also Kacew, Romain
See also DLB 83

Gascar, Pierre .... **CLC 11**
See also Fournier, Pierre

Gascoyne, David (Emery) 1916- .... **CLC 45**
See also CA 65-68; CANR 10, 28; DLB 20; MTCW

Gaskell, Elizabeth Cleghorn 1810-1865 .... **NCLC 5**
See also CDBLB 1832-1890; DLB 21

Gass, William H(oward) 1924- ... **CLC 1, 2, 8, 11, 15, 39; SSC 12**
See also CA 17-20R; CANR 30; DLB 2; MTCW

Gasset, Jose Ortega y
See Ortega y Gasset, Jose

Gautier, Theophile 1811-1872 ..... **NCLC 1**
See also DLB 119

Gawsworth, John
See Bates, H(erbert) E(rnest)

Gaye, Marvin (Penze) 1939-1984 . . . **CLC 26**
See also CA 112

Gebler, Carlo (Ernest) 1954- . . . . **CLC 39**
See also CA 119; 133

Gee, Maggie (Mary) 1948- . . . . **CLC 57**
See also CA 130

Gee, Maurice (Gough) 1931- . . . . **CLC 29**
See also CA 97-100; SATA 46

Gelbart, Larry (Simon) 1923- . . . **CLC 21, 61**
See also CA 73-76

Gelber, Jack 1932- . . . . **CLC 1, 6, 14**
See also CA 1-4R; CANR 2; DLB 7

Gellhorn, Martha Ellis 1908- . . . **CLC 14, 60**
See also CA 77-80; DLBY 82

Genet, Jean
1910-1986 . . . **CLC 1, 2, 5, 10, 14, 44, 46**
See also CA 13-16R; CANR 18; DLB 72; DLBY 86; MTCW

Gent, Peter 1942- . . . . **CLC 29**
See also AITN 1; CA 89-92; DLBY 82

George, Jean Craighead 1919- . . . . . . **CLC 35**
See also AAYA 8; CA 5-8R; CANR 25; CLR 1; DLB 52; MAICYA; SATA 2, 68

George, Stefan (Anton)
1868-1933 . . . . **TCLC 2, 14**
See also CA 104

Georges, Georges Martin
See Simenon, Georges (Jacques Christian)

Gerhardi, William Alexander
See Gerhardie, William Alexander

Gerhardie, William Alexander
1895-1977 . . . . **CLC 5**
See also CA 25-28R; 73-76; CANR 18; DLB 36

Gerstler, Amy 1956- . . . . **CLC 70**

Gertler, T. . . . . **CLC 34**
See also CA 116; 121

Ghalib 1797-1869 . . . . **NCLC 39**

Ghelderode, Michel de
1898-1962 . . . . **CLC 6, 11**
See also CA 85-88; CANR 40

Ghiselin, Brewster 1903- . . . . **CLC 23**
See also CA 13-16R; CAAS 10; CANR 13

Ghose, Zulfikar 1935- . . . . **CLC 42**
See also CA 65-68

Ghosh, Amitav 1956- . . . . **CLC 44**

Giacosa, Giuseppe 1847-1906 . . . . . . **TCLC 7**
See also CA 104

Gibb, Lee
See Waterhouse, Keith (Spencer)

Gibbon, Lewis Grassic . . . . **TCLC 4**
See also Mitchell, James Leslie

Gibbons, Kaye 1960- . . . . **CLC 50**

Gibran, Kahlil 1883-1931 . . . . **TCLC 1, 9**
See also CA 104

Gibson, William 1914- . . . . **CLC 23**
See also CA 9-12R; CANR 9; DA; DLB 7; SATA 66

Gibson, William (Ford) 1948- . . . **CLC 39, 63**
See also CA 126; 133

Gide, Andre (Paul Guillaume)
1869-1951 . . . . **TCLC 5, 12, 36**
See also CA 104; 124; DA; DLB 65; MTCW; WLC

Gifford, Barry (Colby) 1946- . . . . **CLC 34**
See also CA 65-68; CANR 9, 30, 40

Gilbert, W(illiam) S(chwenck)
1836-1911 . . . . **TCLC 3**
See also CA 104; SATA 36

Gilbreth, Frank B., Jr. 1911- . . . . **CLC 17**
See also CA 9-12R; SATA 2

Gilchrist, Ellen 1935- . . . . **CLC 34, 48**
See also CA 113; 116; CANR 41; DLB 130; MTCW

Giles, Molly 1942- . . . . **CLC 39**
See also CA 126

Gill, Patrick
See Creasey, John

Gilliam, Terry (Vance) 1940- . . . . **CLC 21**
See also Monty Python
See also CA 108; 113; CANR 35

Gillian, Jerry
See Gilliam, Terry (Vance)

Gilliatt, Penelope (Ann Douglass)
1932- . . . . **CLC 2, 10, 13, 53**
See also AITN 2; CA 13-16R; DLB 14

Gilman, Charlotte (Anna) Perkins (Stetson)
1860-1935 . . . . **TCLC 9, 37**
See also CA 106

Gilmour, David 1944- . . . . **CLC 35**
See also Pink Floyd
See also CA 138

Gilpin, William 1724-1804 . . . . **NCLC 30**

Gilray, J. D.
See Mencken, H(enry) L(ouis)

Gilroy, Frank D(aniel) 1925- . . . . **CLC 2**
See also CA 81-84; CANR 32; DLB 7

Ginsberg, Allen
1926- . . . . . **CLC 1, 2, 3, 4, 6, 13, 36, 69; PC 4**
See also AITN 1; CA 1-4R; CANR 2, 41; CDALB 1941-1968; DA; DLB 5, 16; MTCW; WLC 3

Ginzburg, Natalia
1916-1991 . . . . **CLC 5, 11, 54, 70**
See also CA 85-88; 135; CANR 33; MTCW

Giono, Jean 1895-1970 . . . . **CLC 4, 11**
See also CA 45-48; 29-32R; CANR 2, 35; DLB 72; MTCW

Giovanni, Nikki 1943- . . . . . **CLC 2, 4, 19, 64**
See also AITN 1; BLC 2; BW; CA 29-32R; CAAS 6; CANR 18, 41; CLR 6; DA; DLB 5, 41; MAICYA; MTCW; SATA 24

Giovene, Andrea 1904- . . . . **CLC 7**
See also CA 85-88

Gippius, Zinaida (Nikolayevna) 1869-1945
See Hippius, Zinaida
See also CA 106

Giraudoux, (Hippolyte) Jean
1882-1944 . . . . **TCLC 2, 7**
See also CA 104; DLB 65

Gironella, Jose Maria 1917- . . . . **CLC 11**
See also CA 101

Gissing, George (Robert)
1857-1903 . . . . **TCLC 3, 24, 47**
See also CA 105; DLB 18

Giurlani, Aldo
See Palazzeschi, Aldo

Gladkov, Fyodor (Vasilyevich)
1883-1958 . . . . **TCLC 27**

Glanville, Brian (Lester) 1931- . . . . . . **CLC 6**
See also CA 5-8R; CAAS 9; CANR 3; DLB 15; SATA 42

Glasgow, Ellen (Anderson Gholson)
1873(?)-1945 . . . . **TCLC 2, 7**
See also CA 104; DLB 9, 12

Glassco, John 1909-1981 . . . . **CLC 9**
See also CA 13-16R; 102; CANR 15; DLB 68

Glasscock, Amnesia
See Steinbeck, John (Ernst)

Glasser, Ronald J. 1940(?)- . . . . **CLC 37**

Glassman, Joyce
See Johnson, Joyce

Glendinning, Victoria 1937- . . . . **CLC 50**
See also CA 120; 127

Glissant, Edouard 1928- . . . . **CLC 10, 68**

Gloag, Julian 1930- . . . . **CLC 40**
See also AITN 1; CA 65-68; CANR 10

Gluck, Louise (Elisabeth)
1943- . . . . **CLC 7, 22, 44**
See also Glueck, Louise
See also CA 33-36R; CANR 40; DLB 5

Glueck, Louise . . . . **CLC 7, 22**
See also Gluck, Louise (Elisabeth)
See also DLB 5

Gobineau, Joseph Arthur (Comte) de
1816-1882 . . . . **NCLC 17**
See also DLB 123

Godard, Jean-Luc 1930- . . . . **CLC 20**
See also CA 93-96

Godden, (Margaret) Rumer 1907- . . . **CLC 53**
See also AAYA 6; CA 5-8R; CANR 4, 27, 36; CLR 20; MAICYA; SAAS 12; SATA 3, 36

Godoy Alcayaga, Lucila 1889-1957
See Mistral, Gabriela
See also CA 104; 131; HW; MTCW

Godwin, Gail (Kathleen)
1937- . . . . **CLC 5, 8, 22, 31, 69**
See also CA 29-32R; CANR 15; DLB 6; MTCW

Godwin, William 1756-1836 . . . . . . **NCLC 14**
See also CDBLB 1789-1832; DLB 39, 104

Goethe, Johann Wolfgang von
1749-1832 . . . . **NCLC 4, 22, 34; PC 5**
See also DA; DLB 94; WLC 3

Gogarty, Oliver St. John
1878-1957 . . . . **TCLC 15**
See also CA 109; DLB 15, 19

Gogol, Nikolai (Vasilyevich)
1809-1852 . . . . . **NCLC 5, 15, 31; DC 1; SSC 4**
See also DA; WLC

Gold, Herbert 1924- . . . . **CLC 4, 7, 14, 42**
See also CA 9-12R; CANR 17; DLB 2; DLBY 81

Goldbarth, Albert 1948- .... **CLC 5, 38**
See also CA 53-56; CANR 6, 40; DLB 120

Goldberg, Anatol 1910-1982 .... **CLC 34**
See also CA 131; 117

Goldemberg, Isaac 1945- .... **CLC 52**
See also CA 69-72; CAAS 12; CANR 11, 32; HW

Golden Silver
See Storm, Hyemeyohsts

Golding, William (Gerald)
1911- ..... **CLC 1, 2, 3, 8, 10, 17, 27, 58**
See also AAYA 5; CA 5-8R; CANR 13, 33; CDBLB 1945-1960; DA; DLB 15, 100; MTCW; WLC

Goldman, Emma 1869-1940 .... **TCLC 13**
See also CA 110

Goldman, Francisco 1955- .... **CLC 76**

Goldman, William (W.) 1931- .... **CLC 1, 48**
See also CA 9-12R; CANR 29; DLB 44

Goldmann, Lucien 1913-1970 ...... **CLC 24**
See also CA 25-28; CAP 2

Goldoni, Carlo 1707-1793 .... **LC 4**

Goldsberry, Steven 1949- .... **CLC 34**
See also CA 131

Goldsmith, Oliver 1728-1774 .... **LC 2**
See also CDBLB 1660-1789; DA; DLB 39, 89, 104, 109; SATA 26; WLC

Goldsmith, Peter
See Priestley, J(ohn) B(oynton)

Gombrowicz, Witold
1904-1969 .... **CLC 4, 7, 11, 49**
See also CA 19-20; 25-28R; CAP 2

Gomez de la Serna, Ramon
1888-1963 .... **CLC 9**
See also CA 116; HW

Goncharov, Ivan Alexandrovich
1812-1891 .... **NCLC 1**

Goncourt, Edmond (Louis Antoine Huot) de
1822-1896 .... **NCLC 7**
See also DLB 123

Goncourt, Jules (Alfred Huot) de
1830-1870 .... **NCLC 7**
See also DLB 123

Gontier, Fernande 19(?)- .... **CLC 50**

Goodman, Paul 1911-1972 .... **CLC 1, 2, 4, 7**
See also CA 19-20; 37-40R; CANR 34; CAP 2; DLB 130; MTCW

Gordimer, Nadine
1923- .... **CLC 3, 5, 7, 10, 18, 33, 51, 70**
See also CA 5-8R; CANR 3, 28; DA; MTCW

Gordon, Adam Lindsay
1833-1870 .... **NCLC 21**

Gordon, Caroline
1895-1981 .... **CLC 6, 13, 29**
See also CA 11-12; 103; CANR 36; CAP 1; DLB 4, 9, 102; DLBY 81; MTCW

Gordon, Charles William 1860-1937
See Connor, Ralph
See also CA 109

Gordon, Mary (Catherine)
1949- .... **CLC 13, 22**
See also CA 102; DLB 6; DLBY 81; MTCW

Gordon, Sol 1923- .... **CLC 26**
See also CA 53-56; CANR 4; SATA 11

Gordone, Charles 1925- .... **CLC 1, 4**
See also BW; CA 93-96; DLB 7; MTCW

Gorenko, Anna Andreevna
See Akhmatova, Anna

Gorky, Maxim .... **TCLC 8**
See also Peshkov, Alexei Maximovich
See also WLC

Goryan, Sirak
See Saroyan, William

Gosse, Edmund (William)
1849-1928 .... **TCLC 28**
See also CA 117; DLB 57

Gotlieb, Phyllis Fay (Bloom)
1926- .... **CLC 18**
See also CA 13-16R; CANR 7; DLB 88

Gottesman, S. D.
See Kornbluth, C(yril) M.; Pohl, Frederik

Gottfried von Strassburg
fl. c. 1210- .... **CMLC 10**

Gottschalk, Laura Riding
See Jackson, Laura (Riding)

Gould, Lois .... **CLC 4, 10**
See also CA 77-80; CANR 29; MTCW

Gourmont, Remy de 1858-1915 .... **TCLC 17**
See also CA 109

Govier, Katherine 1948- .... **CLC 51**
See also CA 101; CANR 18, 40

Goyen, (Charles) William
1915-1983 .... **CLC 5, 8, 14, 40**
See also AITN 2; CA 5-8R; 110; CANR 6; DLB 2; DLBY 83

Goytisolo, Juan 1931- .... **CLC 5, 10, 23**
See also CA 85-88; CANR 32; HW; MTCW

Gozzi, (Conte) Carlo 1720-1806 .. **NCLC 23**

Grabbe, Christian Dietrich
1801-1836 .... **NCLC 2**

Grace, Patricia 1937- .... **CLC 56**

Gracian y Morales, Baltasar
1601-1658 .... **LC 15**

Gracq, Julien .... **CLC 11, 48**
See also Poirier, Louis
See also DLB 83

Grade, Chaim 1910-1982 .... **CLC 10**
See also CA 93-96; 107

Graduate of Oxford, A
See Ruskin, John

Graham, John
See Phillips, David Graham

Graham, Jorie 1951- .... **CLC 48**
See also CA 111; DLB 120

Graham, R(obert) B(ontine) Cunninghame
See Cunninghame Graham, R(obert) B(ontine)
See also DLB 98

Graham, Robert
See Haldeman, Joe (William)

Graham, Tom
See Lewis, (Harry) Sinclair

Graham, W(illiam) S(ydney)
1918-1986 .... **CLC 29**
See also CA 73-76; 118; DLB 20

Graham, Winston (Mawdsley)
1910- .... **CLC 23**
See also CA 49-52; CANR 2, 22; DLB 77

Grant, Skeeter
See Spiegelman, Art

Granville-Barker, Harley
1877-1946 .... **TCLC 2**
See also Barker, Harley Granville
See also CA 104

Grass, Guenter (Wilhelm)
1927- .. **CLC 1, 2, 4, 6, 11, 15, 22, 32, 49**
See also CA 13-16R; CANR 20; DA; DLB 75, 124; MTCW; WLC

Gratton, Thomas
See Hulme, T(homas) E(rnest)

Grau, Shirley Ann 1929- .... **CLC 4, 9**
See also CA 89-92; CANR 22; DLB 2; MTCW

Gravel, Fern
See Hall, James Norman

Graver, Elizabeth 1964- .... **CLC 70**
See also CA 135

Graves, Richard Perceval 1945- .... **CLC 44**
See also CA 65-68; CANR 9, 26

Graves, Robert (von Ranke)
1895-1985 ..... **CLC 1, 2, 6, 11, 39, 44, 45; PC 6**
See also CA 5-8R; 117; CANR 5, 36; CDBLB 1914-1945; DLB 20, 100; DLBY 85; MTCW; SATA 45

Gray, Alasdair (James) 1934- ...... **CLC 41**
See also CA 126; MTCW

Gray, Amlin 1946- .... **CLC 29**
See also CA 138

Gray, Francine du Plessix 1930- .... **CLC 22**
See also BEST 90:3; CA 61-64; CAAS 2; CANR 11, 33; MTCW

Gray, John (Henry) 1866-1934 .... **TCLC 19**
See also CA 119

Gray, Simon (James Holliday)
1936- .... **CLC 9, 14, 36**
See also AITN 1; CA 21-24R; CAAS 3; CANR 32; DLB 13; MTCW

Gray, Spalding 1941- .... **CLC 49**
See also CA 128

Gray, Thomas 1716-1771 .... **LC 4; PC 2**
See also CDBLB 1660-1789; DA; DLB 109; WLC

Grayson, David
See Baker, Ray Stannard

Grayson, Richard (A.) 1951- .... **CLC 38**
See also CA 85-88; CANR 14, 31

Greeley, Andrew M(oran) 1928- .... **CLC 28**
See also CA 5-8R; CAAS 7; CANR 7; MTCW

Green, Brian
See Card, Orson Scott

Green, Hannah .... **CLC 3**
See also CA 73-76

Green, Hannah
See Greenberg, Joanne (Goldenberg)

Green, Henry .... **CLC 2, 13**
See also Yorke, Henry Vincent
See also DLB 15

Author Index

Green, Julian (Hartridge) 1900- .... **CLC 3, 11, 77**
See also CA 21-24R; CANR 33; DLB 4, 72; MTCW

Green, Julien 1900-
See Green, Julian (Hartridge)

Green, Paul (Eliot) 1894-1981...... **CLC 25**
See also AITN 1; CA 5-8R; 103; CANR 3; DLB 7, 9; DLBY 81

Greenberg, Ivan 1908-1973
See Rahv, Philip
See also CA 85-88

Greenberg, Joanne (Goldenberg) 1932- .... **CLC 7, 30**
See also CA 5-8R; CANR 14, 32; SATA 25

Greenberg, Richard 1959(?)- .... **CLC 57**
See also CA 138

Greene, Bette 1934- .... **CLC 30**
See also AAYA 7; CA 53-56; CANR 4; CLR 2; MAICYA; SAAS 16; SATA 8

Greene, Gael .... **CLC 8**
See also CA 13-16R; CANR 10

Greene, Graham (Henry) 1904-1991 ... **CLC 1, 3, 6, 9, 14, 18, 27, 37, 70, 72**
See also AITN 2; CA 13-16R; 133; CANR 35; CDBLB 1945-1960; DA; DLB 13, 15, 77, 100; DLBY 91; MTCW; SATA 20; WLC

Greer, Richard
See Silverberg, Robert

Greer, Richard
See Silverberg, Robert

Gregor, Arthur 1923- .... **CLC 9**
See also CA 25-28R; CAAS 10; CANR 11; SATA 36

Gregor, Lee
See Pohl, Frederik

Gregory, Isabella Augusta (Persse) 1852-1932 .... **TCLC 1**
See also CA 104; DLB 10

Gregory, J. Dennis
See Williams, John A(lfred)

Grendon, Stephen
See Derleth, August (William)

Grenville, Kate 1950- .... **CLC 61**
See also CA 118

Grenville, Pelham
See Wodehouse, P(elham) G(renville)

Greve, Felix Paul (Berthold Friedrich) 1879-1948
See Grove, Frederick Philip
See also CA 104

Grey, Zane 1872-1939 .... **TCLC 6**
See also CA 104; 132; DLB 9; MTCW

Grieg, (Johan) Nordahl (Brun) 1902-1943 .... **TCLC 10**
See also CA 107

Grieve, C(hristopher) M(urray) 1892-1978 .... **CLC 11, 19**
See also MacDiarmid, Hugh
See also CA 5-8R; 85-88; CANR 33; MTCW

Griffin, Gerald 1803-1840 .... **NCLC 7**

Griffin, John Howard 1920-1980.... **CLC 68**
See also AITN 1; CA 1-4R; 101; CANR 2

Griffin, Peter .... **CLC 39**

Griffiths, Trevor 1935- .... **CLC 13, 52**
See also CA 97-100; DLB 13

Grigson, Geoffrey (Edward Harvey) 1905-1985 .... **CLC 7, 39**
See also CA 25-28R; 118; CANR 20, 33; DLB 27; MTCW

Grillparzer, Franz 1791-1872...... **NCLC 1**

Grimble, Reverend Charles James
See Eliot, T(homas) S(tearns)

Grimke, Charlotte L(ottie) Forten 1837(?)-1914
See Forten, Charlotte L.
See also BW; CA 117; 124

Grimm, Jacob Ludwig Karl 1785-1863 .... **NCLC 3**
See also DLB 90; MAICYA; SATA 22

Grimm, Wilhelm Karl 1786-1859 .. **NCLC 3**
See also DLB 90; MAICYA; SATA 22

Grimmelshausen, Johann Jakob Christoffel von 1621-1676 .... **LC 6**

Grindel, Eugene 1895-1952
See Eluard, Paul
See also CA 104

Grossman, David .... **CLC 67**
See also CA 138

Grossman, Vasily (Semenovich) 1905-1964 .... **CLC 41**
See also CA 124; 130; MTCW

Grove, Frederick Philip .... **TCLC 4**
See also Greve, Felix Paul (Berthold Friedrich)
See also DLB 92

Grubb
See Crumb, R(obert)

Grumbach, Doris (Isaac) 1918- .... **CLC 13, 22, 64**
See also CA 5-8R; CAAS 2; CANR 9

Grundtvig, Nicolai Frederik Severin 1783-1872 .... **NCLC 1**

Grunge
See Crumb, R(obert)

Grunwald, Lisa 1959- .... **CLC 44**
See also CA 120

Guare, John 1938- .... **CLC 8, 14, 29, 67**
See also CA 73-76; CANR 21; DLB 7; MTCW

Gudjonsson, Halldor Kiljan 1902-
See Laxness, Halldor
See also CA 103

Guenter, Erich
See Eich, Guenter

Guest, Barbara 1920- .... **CLC 34**
See also CA 25-28R; CANR 11; DLB 5

Guest, Judith (Ann) 1936- .... **CLC 8, 30**
See also AAYA 7; CA 77-80; CANR 15; MTCW

Guild, Nicholas M. 1944- .... **CLC 33**
See also CA 93-96

Guillemin, Jacques
See Sartre, Jean-Paul

Guillen, Jorge 1893-1984 .... **CLC 11**
See also CA 89-92; 112; DLB 108; HW

Guillen (y Batista), Nicolas (Cristobal) 1902-1989 .... **CLC 48**
See also BLC 2; BW; CA 116; 125; 129; HW

Guillevic, (Eugene) 1907- .... **CLC 33**
See also CA 93-96

Guillois
See Desnos, Robert

Guiney, Louise Imogen 1861-1920 .... **TCLC 41**
See also DLB 54

Guiraldes, Ricardo (Guillermo) 1886-1927 .... **TCLC 39**
See also CA 131; HW; MTCW

Gunn, Bill .... **CLC 5**
See also Gunn, William Harrison
See also DLB 38

Gunn, Thom(son William) 1929- .... **CLC 3, 6, 18, 32**
See also CA 17-20R; CANR 9, 33; CDBLB 1960 to Present; DLB 27; MTCW

Gunn, William Harrison 1934(?)-1989
See Gunn, Bill
See also AITN 1; BW; CA 13-16R; 128; CANR 12, 25

Gunnars, Kristjana 1948- .... **CLC 69**
See also CA 113; DLB 60

Gurganus, Allan 1947- .... **CLC 70**
See also BEST 90:1; CA 135

Gurney, A(lbert) R(amsdell), Jr. 1930- .... **CLC 32, 50, 54**
See also CA 77-80; CANR 32

Gurney, Ivor (Bertie) 1890-1937 ... **TCLC 33**

Gurney, Peter
See Gurney, A(lbert) R(amsdell), Jr.

Gustafson, Ralph (Barker) 1909-.... **CLC 36**
See also CA 21-24R; CANR 8; DLB 88

Gut, Gom
See Simenon, Georges (Jacques Christian)

Guthrie, A(lfred) B(ertram), Jr. 1901-1991 .... **CLC 23**
See also CA 57-60; 134; CANR 24; DLB 6; SATA 62; SATA-Obit 67

Guthrie, Isobel
See Grieve, C(hristopher) M(urray)

Guthrie, Woodrow Wilson 1912-1967
See Guthrie, Woody
See also CA 113; 93-96

Guthrie, Woody .... **CLC 35**
See also Guthrie, Woodrow Wilson

Guy, Rosa (Cuthbert) 1928- .... **CLC 26**
See also AAYA 4; BW; CA 17-20R; CANR 14, 34; CLR 13; DLB 33; MAICYA; SATA 14, 62

Gwendolyn
See Bennett, (Enoch) Arnold

H. D. .... **CLC 3, 8, 14, 31, 34, 73; PC 5**
See also Doolittle, Hilda

Haavikko, Paavo Juhani 1931- .... **CLC 18, 34**
See also CA 106

Holland, Isabelle 1920- .... **CLC 21**
See also CA 21-24R; CANR 10, 25; MAICYA; SATA 8, 70

Holland, Marcus
See Caldwell, (Janet Miriam) Taylor (Holland)

Hollander, John 1929- ...... **CLC 2, 5, 8, 14**
See also CA 1-4R; CANR 1; DLB 5; SATA 13

Hollander, Paul
See Silverberg, Robert

Holleran, Andrew 1943(?)- .... **CLC 38**

Hollinghurst, Alan 1954- .... **CLC 55**
See also CA 114

Hollis, Jim
See Summers, Hollis (Spurgeon, Jr.)

Holmes, John
See Souster, (Holmes) Raymond

Holmes, John Clellon 1926-1988.... **CLC 56**
See also CA 9-12R; 125; CANR 4; DLB 16

Holmes, Oliver Wendell
1809-1894 .... **NCLC 14**
See also CDALB 1640-1865; DLB 1; SATA 34

Holmes, Raymond
See Souster, (Holmes) Raymond

Holt, Victoria
See Hibbert, Eleanor Alice Burford

Holub, Miroslav 1923- .... **CLC 4**
See also CA 21-24R; CANR 10

Homer c. 8th cent. B.C.- .... **CMLC 1**
See also DA

Honig, Edwin 1919- .... **CLC 33**
See also CA 5-8R; CAAS 8; CANR 4; DLB 5

Hood, Hugh (John Blagdon)
1928- .... **CLC 15, 28**
See also CA 49-52; CAAS 17; CANR 1, 33; DLB 53

Hood, Thomas 1799-1845........ **NCLC 16**
See also DLB 96

Hooker, (Peter) Jeremy 1941-...... **CLC 43**
See also CA 77-80; CANR 22; DLB 40

Hope, A(lec) D(erwent) 1907- .... **CLC 3, 51**
See also CA 21-24R; CANR 33; MTCW

Hope, Brian
See Creasey, John

Hope, Christopher (David Tully)
1944- .... **CLC 52**
See also CA 106; SATA 62

Hopkins, Gerard Manley
1844-1889 .... **NCLC 17**
See also CDBLB 1890-1914; DA; DLB 35, 57; WLC

Hopkins, John (Richard) 1931- ...... **CLC 4**
See also CA 85-88

Hopkins, Pauline Elizabeth
1859-1930 .... **TCLC 28**
See also BLC 2; DLB 50

Hopley-Woolrich, Cornell George 1903-1968
See Woolrich, Cornell
See also CA 13-14; CAP 1

Horatio
See Proust, (Valentin-Louis-George-Eugene-)Marcel

Horgan, Paul 1903- .... **CLC 9, 53**
See also CA 13-16R; CANR 9, 35; DLB 102; DLBY 85; MTCW; SATA 13

Horn, Peter
See Kuttner, Henry

Hornem, Horace Esq.
See Byron, George Gordon (Noel)

Horovitz, Israel 1939- .... **CLC 56**
See also CA 33-36R; DLB 7

Horvath, Odon von
See Horvath, Oedoen von
See also DLB 85, 124

Horvath, Oedoen von 1901-1938... **TCLC 45**
See also Horvath, Odon von
See also CA 118

Horwitz, Julius 1920-1986......... **CLC 14**
See also CA 9-12R; 119; CANR 12

Hospital, Janette Turner 1942- ..... **CLC 42**
See also CA 108

Hostos, E. M. de
See Hostos (y Bonilla), Eugenio Maria de

Hostos, Eugenio M. de
See Hostos (y Bonilla), Eugenio Maria de

Hostos, Eugenio Maria
See Hostos (y Bonilla), Eugenio Maria de

Hostos (y Bonilla), Eugenio Maria de
1839-1903 .... **TCLC 24**
See also CA 123; 131; HW

Houdini
See Lovecraft, H(oward) P(hillips)

Hougan, Carolyn 19(?)- .... **CLC 34**
See also CA 139

Household, Geoffrey (Edward West)
1900-1988 .... **CLC 11**
See also CA 77-80; 126; DLB 87; SATA 14, 59

Housman, A(lfred) E(dward)
1859-1936 .... **TCLC 1, 10; PC 2**
See also CA 104; 125; DA; DLB 19; MTCW

Housman, Laurence 1865-1959 ..... **TCLC 7**
See also CA 106; DLB 10; SATA 25

Howard, Elizabeth Jane 1923- ... **CLC 7, 29**
See also CA 5-8R; CANR 8

Howard, Maureen 1930- ..... **CLC 5, 14, 46**
See also CA 53-56; CANR 31; DLBY 83; MTCW

Howard, Richard 1929- ...... **CLC 7, 10, 47**
See also AITN 1; CA 85-88; CANR 25; DLB 5

Howard, Robert Ervin 1906-1936... **TCLC 8**
See also CA 105

Howard, Warren F.
See Pohl, Frederik

Howe, Fanny 1940- .... **CLC 47**
See also CA 117; SATA 52

Howe, Julia Ward 1819-1910 ..... **TCLC 21**
See also CA 117; DLB 1

Howe, Susan 1937-............... **CLC 72**
See also DLB 120

Howe, Tina 1937-................ **CLC 48**
See also CA 109

Howell, James 1594(?)-1666 .... **LC 13**

Howells, W. D.
See Howells, William Dean

Howells, William D.
See Howells, William Dean

Howells, William Dean
1837-1920 .... **TCLC 41, 7, 17**
See also CA 104; 134; CDALB 1865-1917; DLB 12, 64, 74, 79

Howes, Barbara 1914- .... **CLC 15**
See also CA 9-12R; CAAS 3; SATA 5

Hrabal, Bohumil 1914-......... **CLC 13, 67**
See also CA 106; CAAS 12

Hsun, Lu .... **TCLC 3**
See also Shu-Jen, Chou

Hubbard, L(afayette) Ron(ald)
1911-1986 .... **CLC 43**
See also CA 77-80; 118; CANR 22

Huch, Ricarda (Octavia)
1864-1947 .... **TCLC 13**
See also CA 111; DLB 66

Huddle, David 1942- .... **CLC 49**
See also CA 57-60; DLB 130

Hudson, Jeffrey
See Crichton, (John) Michael

Hudson, W(illiam) H(enry)
1841-1922 .... **TCLC 29**
See also CA 115; DLB 98; SATA 35

Hueffer, Ford Madox
See Ford, Ford Madox

Hughart, Barry .... **CLC 39**
See also CA 137

Hughes, Colin
See Creasey, John

Hughes, David (John) 1930- .... **CLC 48**
See also CA 116; 129; DLB 14

Hughes, (James) Langston
1902-1967 .... **CLC 1, 5, 10, 15, 35, 44; DC 3; PC 1; SSC 6**
See also BLC 2; BW; CA 1-4R; 25-28R; CANR 1, 34; CDALB 1929-1941; CLR 17; DA; DLB 4, 7, 48, 51, 86; MAICYA; MTCW; SATA 4, 33; WLC

Hughes, Richard (Arthur Warren)
1900-1976 .... **CLC 1, 11**
See also CA 5-8R; 65-68; CANR 4; DLB 15; MTCW; SATA 8, 25

Hughes, Ted 1930- ..... **CLC 2, 4, 9, 14, 37**
See also CA 1-4R; CANR 1, 33; CLR 3; DLB 40; MAICYA; MTCW; SATA 27, 49

Hugo, Richard F(ranklin)
1923-1982 .... **CLC 6, 18, 32**
See also CA 49-52; 108; CANR 3; DLB 5

Hugo, Victor (Marie)
1802-1885 .... **NCLC 3, 10, 21**
See also DA; DLB 119; SATA 47; WLC

Huidobro, Vicente
See Huidobro Fernandez, Vicente Garcia

Huidobro Fernandez, Vicente Garcia
1893-1948 .... **TCLC 31**
See also CA 131; HW

Hulme, Keri 1947- .... **CLC 39**
See also CA 125

Hulme, T(homas) E(rnest)
1883-1917 .... **TCLC 21**
See also CA 117; DLB 19

Hume, David 1711-1776............ **LC 7**
See also DLB 104

Humphrey, William 1924-......... **CLC 45**
See also CA 77-80; DLB 6

Humphreys, Emyr Owen 1919-..... **CLC 47**
See also CA 5-8R; CANR 3, 24; DLB 15

Humphreys, Josephine 1945-.... **CLC 34, 57**
See also CA 121; 127

Hungerford, Pixie
See Brinsmead, H(esba) F(ay)

Hunt, E(verette) Howard, Jr.
1918- .... **CLC 3**
See also AITN 1; CA 45-48; CANR 2

Hunt, Kyle
See Creasey, John

Hunt, (James Henry) Leigh
1784-1859 .... **NCLC 1**

Hunt, Marsha 1946-.............. **CLC 70**

Hunter, E. Waldo
See Sturgeon, Theodore (Hamilton)

Hunter, Evan 1926- .... **CLC 11, 31**
See also CA 5-8R; CANR 5, 38; DLBY 82; MTCW; SATA 25

Hunter, Kristin (Eggleston) 1931-... **CLC 35**
See also AITN 1; BW; CA 13-16R; CANR 13; CLR 3; DLB 33; MAICYA; SAAS 10; SATA 12

Hunter, Mollie 1922-............. **CLC 21**
See also McIlwraith, Maureen Mollie Hunter
See also CANR 37; CLR 25; MAICYA; SAAS 7; SATA 54

Hunter, Robert (?)-1734............ **LC 7**

Hurston, Zora Neale
1903-1960 .... **CLC 7, 30, 61; SSC 4**
See also BLC 2; BW; CA 85-88; DA; DLB 51, 86; MTCW

Huston, John (Marcellus)
1906-1987 .... **CLC 20**
See also CA 73-76; 123; CANR 34; DLB 26

Hustvedt, Siri 1955-............. **CLC 76**
See also CA 137

Hutten, Ulrich von 1488-1523....... **LC 16**

Huxley, Aldous (Leonard)
1894-1963 .. **CLC 1, 3, 4, 5, 8, 11, 18, 35**
See also CA 85-88; CDBLB 1914-1945; DA; DLB 36, 100; MTCW; SATA 63; WLC

Huysmans, Charles Marie Georges
1848-1907
See Huysmans, Joris-Karl
See also CA 104

Huysmans, Joris-Karl............. **TCLC 7**
See also Huysmans, Charles Marie Georges
See also DLB 123

Hwang, David Henry 1957-........ **CLC 55**
See also CA 127; 132

Hyde, Anthony 1946-............. **CLC 42**
See also CA 136

Hyde, Margaret O(ldroyd) 1917- ... **CLC 21**
See also CA 1-4R; CANR 1, 36; CLR 23; MAICYA; SAAS 8; SATA 1, 42

Hynes, James 1956(?)-............ **CLC 65**

Ian, Janis 1951- .... **CLC 21**
See also CA 105

Ibanez, Vicente Blasco
See Blasco Ibanez, Vicente

Ibarguengoitia, Jorge 1928-1983.... **CLC 37**
See also CA 124; 113; HW

Ibsen, Henrik (Johan)
1828-1906 ..... **TCLC 2, 8, 16, 37; DC 2**
See also CA 104; DA; WLC

Ibuse Masuji 1898-............... **CLC 22**
See also CA 127

Ichikawa, Kon 1915-............. **CLC 20**
See also CA 121

Idle, Eric 1943-................. **CLC 21**
See also Monty Python
See also CA 116; CANR 35

Ignatow, David 1914-...... **CLC 4, 7, 14, 40**
See also CA 9-12R; CAAS 3; CANR 31; DLB 5

Ihimaera, Witi 1944- .... **CLC 46**
See also CA 77-80

Ilf, Ilya........................ **TCLC 21**
See also Fainzilberg, Ilya Arnoldovich

Immermann, Karl (Lebrecht)
1796-1840 .... **NCLC 4**

Inclan, Ramon (Maria) del Valle
See Valle-Inclan, Ramon (Maria) del

Infante, G(uillermo) Cabrera
See Cabrera Infante, G(uillermo)

Ingalls, Rachel (Holmes) 1940-..... **CLC 42**
See also CA 123; 127

Ingamells, Rex 1913-1955 .... **TCLC 35**

Inge, William Motter
1913-1973 .... **CLC 1, 8, 19**
See also CA 9-12R; CDALB 1941-1968; DLB 7; MTCW

Ingelow, Jean 1820-1897 .... **NCLC 39**
See also DLB 35; SATA 33

Ingram, Willis J.
See Harris, Mark

Innaurato, Albert (F.) 1948(?)- .. **CLC 21, 60**
See also CA 115; 122

Innes, Michael
See Stewart, J(ohn) I(nnes) M(ackintosh)

Ionesco, Eugene
1912- .... **CLC 1, 4, 6, 9, 11, 15, 41**
See also CA 9-12R; DA; MTCW; SATA 7; WLC

Iqbal, Muhammad 1873-1938 ..... **TCLC 28**

Ireland, Patrick
See O'Doherty, Brian

Irland, David
See Green, Julian (Hartridge)

Iron, Ralph
See Schreiner, Olive (Emilie Albertina)

Irving, John (Winslow)
1942- .... **CLC 13, 23, 38**
See also AAYA 8; BEST 89:3; CA 25-28R; CANR 28; DLB 6; DLBY 82; MTCW

Irving, Washington
1783-1859 .... **NCLC 2, 19; SSC 2**
See also CDALB 1640-1865; DA; DLB 3, 11, 30, 59, 73, 74; WLC; YABC 2

Irwin, P. K.
See Page, P(atricia) K(athleen)

Isaacs, Susan 1943- .... **CLC 32**
See also BEST 89:1; CA 89-92; CANR 20, 41; MTCW

Isherwood, Christopher (William Bradshaw)
1904-1986 .... **CLC 1, 9, 11, 14, 44**
See also CA 13-16R; 117; CANR 35; DLB 15; DLBY 86; MTCW

Ishiguro, Kazuo 1954- ...... **CLC 27, 56, 59**
See also BEST 90:2; CA 120; MTCW

Ishikawa Takuboku
1886(?)-1912 .... **TCLC 15**
See also CA 113

Iskander, Fazil 1929-............. **CLC 47**
See also CA 102

Ivan IV 1530-1584 .... **LC 17**

Ivanov, Vyacheslav Ivanovich
1866-1949 .... **TCLC 33**
See also CA 122

Ivask, Ivar Vidrik 1927-1992....... **CLC 14**
See also CA 37-40R; 139; CANR 24

Jackson, Daniel
See Wingrove, David (John)

Jackson, Jesse 1908-1983 .... **CLC 12**
See also BW; CA 25-28R; 109; CANR 27; CLR 28; MAICYA; SATA 2, 29, 48

Jackson, Laura (Riding) 1901-1991 .. **CLC 7**
See also Riding, Laura
See also CA 65-68; 135; CANR 28; DLB 48

Jackson, Sam
See Trumbo, Dalton

Jackson, Sara
See Wingrove, David (John)

Jackson, Shirley
1919-1965 .... **CLC 11, 60; SSC 9**
See also AAYA 9; CA 1-4R; 25-28R; CANR 4; CDALB 1941-1968; DA; DLB 6; SATA 2; WLC

Jacob, (Cyprien-)Max 1876-1944 ... **TCLC 6**
See also CA 104

Jacobs, Jim 1942-................ **CLC 12**
See also CA 97-100

Jacobs, W(illiam) W(ymark)
1863-1943 .... **TCLC 22**
See also CA 121

Jacobsen, Jens Peter 1847-1885 .. **NCLC 34**

Jacobsen, Josephine 1908-......... **CLC 48**
See also CA 33-36R; CANR 23

Jacobson, Dan 1929- .... **CLC 4, 14**
See also CA 1-4R; CANR 2, 25; DLB 14; MTCW

Jacqueline
See Carpentier (y Valmont), Alejo

Jagger, Mick 1944-............... **CLC 17**

Jakes, John (William) 1932- .... **CLC 29**
See also BEST 89:4; CA 57-60; CANR 10; DLBY 83; MTCW; SATA 62

James, Andrew
See Kirkup, James

James, C(yril) L(ionel) R(obert) 1901-1989 .... **CLC 33**
See also BW; CA 117; 125; 128; DLB 125; MTCW

James, Daniel (Lewis) 1911-1988
See Santiago, Danny
See also CA 125

James, Dynely
See Mayne, William (James Carter)

James, Henry 1843-1916 ..... **TCLC 2, 11, 24, 40, 47; SSC 8**
See also CA 104; 132; CDALB 1865-1917; DA; DLB 12, 71, 74; MTCW; WLC

James, Montague (Rhodes) 1862-1936 .... **TCLC 6**
See also CA 104

James, P. D. .... **CLC 18, 46**
See also White, Phyllis Dorothy James
See also BEST 90:2; CDBLB 1960 to Present; DLB 87

James, Philip
See Moorcock, Michael (John)

James, William 1842-1910 ..... **TCLC 15, 32**
See also CA 109

James I 1394-1437 .... **LC 20**

Jami, Nur al-Din 'Abd al-Rahman 1414-1492 .... **LC 9**

Jandl, Ernst 1925- .... **CLC 34**

Janowitz, Tama 1957- .... **CLC 43**
See also CA 106

Jarrell, Randall 1914-1965 .... **CLC 1, 2, 6, 9, 13, 49**
See also CA 5-8R; 25-28R; CABS 2; CANR 6, 34; CDALB 1941-1968; CLR 6; DLB 48, 52; MAICYA; MTCW; SATA 7

Jarry, Alfred 1873-1907........ **TCLC 2, 14**
See also CA 104

Jarvis, E. K.
See Bloch, Robert (Albert); Ellison, Harlan; Silverberg, Robert

Jeake, Samuel, Jr.
See Aiken, Conrad (Potter)

Jean Paul 1763-1825 .... **NCLC 7**

Jeffers, (John) Robinson 1887-1962 .... **CLC 2, 3, 11, 15, 54**
See also CA 85-88; CANR 35; CDALB 1917-1929; DA; DLB 45; MTCW; WLC

Jefferson, Janet
See Mencken, H(enry) L(ouis)

Jefferson, Thomas 1743-1826 .... **NCLC 11**
See also CDALB 1640-1865; DLB 31

Jeffrey, Francis 1773-1850....... **NCLC 33**
See also DLB 107

Jelakowitch, Ivan
See Heijermans, Herman

Jellicoe, (Patricia) Ann 1927-...... **CLC 27**
See also CA 85-88; DLB 13

Jen, Gish .... **CLC 70**
See also Jen, Lillian

Jen, Lillian 1956(?)-
See Jen, Gish
See also CA 135

Jenkins, (John) Robin 1912-....... **CLC 52**
See also CA 1-4R; CANR 1; DLB 14

Jennings, Elizabeth (Joan) 1926- .... **CLC 5, 14**
See also CA 61-64; CAAS 5; CANR 8, 39; DLB 27; MTCW; SATA 66

Jennings, Waylon 1937-........... **CLC 21**

Jensen, Johannes V. 1873-1950.... **TCLC 41**

Jensen, Laura (Linnea) 1948- ...... **CLC 37**
See also CA 103

Jerome, Jerome K(lapka) 1859-1927 .... **TCLC 23**
See also CA 119; DLB 10, 34

Jerrold, Douglas William 1803-1857 .... **NCLC 2**

Jewett, (Theodora) Sarah Orne 1849-1909 .... **TCLC 1, 22; SSC 6**
See also CA 108; 127; DLB 12, 74; SATA 15

Jewsbury, Geraldine (Endsor) 1812-1880 .... **NCLC 22**
See also DLB 21

Jhabvala, Ruth Prawer 1927- .... **CLC 4, 8, 29**
See also CA 1-4R; CANR 2, 29; MTCW

Jiles, Paulette 1943-........... **CLC 13, 58**
See also CA 101

Jimenez (Mantecon), Juan Ramon 1881-1958 .... **TCLC 4**
See also CA 104; 131; HW; MTCW

Jimenez, Ramon
See Jimenez (Mantecon), Juan Ramon

Jimenez Mantecon, Juan
See Jimenez (Mantecon), Juan Ramon

Joel, Billy .... **CLC 26**
See also Joel, William Martin

Joel, William Martin 1949-
See Joel, Billy
See also CA 108

John of the Cross, St. 1542-1591 .... **LC 18**

Johnson, B(ryan) S(tanley William) 1933-1973 .... **CLC 6, 9**
See also CA 9-12R; 53-56; CANR 9; DLB 14, 40

Johnson, Charles (Richard) 1948- .... **CLC 7, 51, 65**
See also BLC 2; BW; CA 116; DLB 33

Johnson, Denis 1949-............. **CLC 52**
See also CA 117; 121; DLB 120

Johnson, Diane (Lain) 1934- .... **CLC 5, 13, 48**
See also CA 41-44R; CANR 17, 40; DLBY 80; MTCW

Johnson, Eyvind (Olof Verner) 1900-1976 .... **CLC 14**
See also CA 73-76; 69-72; CANR 34

Johnson, J. R.
See James, C(yril) L(ionel) R(obert)

Johnson, James Weldon 1871-1938 .... **TCLC 3, 19**
See also BLC 2; BW; CA 104; 125; CDALB 1917-1929; DLB 51; MTCW; SATA 31

Johnson, Joyce 1935-............. **CLC 58**
See also CA 125; 129

Johnson, Lionel (Pigot) 1867-1902 .... **TCLC 19**
See also CA 117; DLB 19

Johnson, Mel
See Malzberg, Barry N(athaniel)

Johnson, Pamela Hansford 1912-1981 .... **CLC 1, 7, 27**
See also CA 1-4R; 104; CANR 2, 28; DLB 15; MTCW

Johnson, Samuel 1709-1784......... **LC 15**
See also CDBLB 1660-1789; DA; DLB 39, 95, 104; WLC

Johnson, Uwe 1934-1984 .... **CLC 5, 10, 15, 40**
See also CA 1-4R; 112; CANR 1, 39; DLB 75; MTCW

Johnston, George (Benson) 1913- ... **CLC 51**
See also CA 1-4R; CANR 5, 20; DLB 88

Johnston, Jennifer 1930-........... **CLC 7**
See also CA 85-88; DLB 14

Jolley, (Monica) Elizabeth 1923- ... **CLC 46**
See also CA 127; CAAS 13

Jones, Arthur Llewellyn 1863-1947
See Machen, Arthur
See also CA 104

Jones, D(ouglas) G(ordon) 1929-.... **CLC 10**
See also CA 29-32R; CANR 13; DLB 53

Jones, David (Michael) 1895-1974 .... **CLC 2, 4, 7, 13, 42**
See also CA 9-12R; 53-56; CANR 28; CDBLB 1945-1960; DLB 20, 100; MTCW

Jones, David Robert 1947-
See Bowie, David
See also CA 103

Jones, Diana Wynne 1934- .... **CLC 26**
See also CA 49-52; CANR 4, 26; CLR 23; MAICYA; SAAS 7; SATA 9, 70

Jones, Edward P. 1951-........... **CLC 76**

Jones, Gayl 1949-............... **CLC 6, 9**
See also BLC 2; BW; CA 77-80; CANR 27; DLB 33; MTCW

Jones, James 1921-1977.... **CLC 1, 3, 10, 39**
See also AITN 1, 2; CA 1-4R; 69-72; CANR 6; DLB 2; MTCW

Jones, John J.
See Lovecraft, H(oward) P(hillips)

Jones, LeRoi .... **CLC 1, 2, 3, 5, 10, 14**
See also Baraka, Amiri

Jones, Louis B. .... **CLC 65**

Jones, Madison (Percy, Jr.) 1925- ... **CLC 4**
See also CA 13-16R; CAAS 11; CANR 7

Jones, Mervyn 1922-.......... **CLC 10, 52**
See also CA 45-48; CAAS 5; CANR 1; MTCW

Jones, Mick 1956(?)-............. **CLC 30**
See also Clash, The

Jones, Nettie (Pearl) 1941- .... **CLC 34**
See also CA 137

Jones, Preston 1936-1979 .... **CLC 10**
See also CA 73-76; 89-92; DLB 7

Jones, Robert F(rancis) 1934-....... **CLC 7**
See also CA 49-52; CANR 2

Jones, Rod 1953- . . . . **CLC 50**
See also CA 128

Jones, Terence Graham Parry 1942- . . . . **CLC 21**
See also Jones, Terry; Monty Python
See also CA 112; 116; CANR 35; SATA 51

Jones, Terry
See Jones, Terence Graham Parry
See also SATA 67

Jong, Erica 1942- . . . . **CLC 4, 6, 8, 18**
See also AITN 1; BEST 90:2; CA 73-76; CANR 26; DLB 2, 5, 28; MTCW

Jonson, Ben(jamin) 1572(?)-1637. . . . . . **LC 6**
See also CDBLB Before 1660; DA; DLB 62, 121; WLC

Jordan, June 1936- . . . . **CLC 5, 11, 23**
See also AAYA 2; BW; CA 33-36R; CANR 25; CLR 10; DLB 38; MAICYA; MTCW; SATA 4

Jordan, Pat(rick M.) 1941- . . . . **CLC 37**
See also CA 33-36R

Jorgensen, Ivar
See Ellison, Harlan

Jorgenson, Ivar
See Silverberg, Robert

Josipovici, Gabriel 1940- . . . . **CLC 6, 43**
See also CA 37-40R; CAAS 8; DLB 14

Joubert, Joseph 1754-1824 . . . . **NCLC 9**

Jouve, Pierre Jean 1887-1976 . . . . . . **CLC 47**
See also CA 65-68

Joyce, James (Augustine Aloysius) 1882-1941 . . . . **TCLC 3, 8, 16, 35; SSC 3**
See also CA 104; 126; CDBLB 1914-1945; DA; DLB 10, 19, 36; MTCW; WLC

Jozsef, Attila 1905-1937. . . . . **TCLC 22**
See also CA 116

Juana Ines de la Cruz 1651(?)-1695 . . . **LC 5**

Judd, Cyril
See Kornbluth, C(yril) M.; Pohl, Frederik

Julian of Norwich 1342(?)-1416(?) . . . . **LC 6**

Just, Ward (Swift) 1935- . . . . **CLC 4, 27**
See also CA 25-28R; CANR 32

Justice, Donald (Rodney) 1925- . . **CLC 6, 19**
See also CA 5-8R; CANR 26; DLBY 83

Juvenal c. 55-c. 127 . . . . **CMLC 8**

Juvenis
See Bourne, Randolph S(illiman)

Kacew, Romain 1914-1980
See Gary, Romain
See also CA 108; 102

Kadare, Ismail 1936- . . . . **CLC 52**

Kadohata, Cynthia. . . . . **CLC 59**
See also CA 140

Kafka, Franz 1883-1924 . . . . . . **TCLC 2, 6, 13, 29, 47; SSC 5**
See also CA 105; 126; DA; DLB 81; MTCW; WLC

Kahn, Roger 1927- . . . . **CLC 30**
See also CA 25-28R; SATA 37

Kain, Saul
See Sassoon, Siegfried (Lorraine)

Kaiser, Georg 1878-1945 . . . . **TCLC 9**
See also CA 106; DLB 124

Kaletski, Alexander 1946- . . . . **CLC 39**
See also CA 118

Kalidasa fl. c. 400- . . . . **CMLC 9**

Kallman, Chester (Simon) 1921-1975 . . . . **CLC 2**
See also CA 45-48; 53-56; CANR 3

Kaminsky, Melvin 1926-
See Brooks, Mel
See also CA 65-68; CANR 16

Kaminsky, Stuart M(elvin) 1934- . . . **CLC 59**
See also CA 73-76; CANR 29

Kane, Paul
See Simon, Paul

Kane, Wilson
See Bloch, Robert (Albert)

Kanin, Garson 1912- . . . . **CLC 22**
See also AITN 1; CA 5-8R; CANR 7; DLB 7

Kaniuk, Yoram 1930- . . . . **CLC 19**
See also CA 134

Kant, Immanuel 1724-1804 . . . . . . **NCLC 27**
See also DLB 94

Kantor, MacKinlay 1904-1977 . . . . . . **CLC 7**
See also CA 61-64; 73-76; DLB 9, 102

Kaplan, David Michael 1946- . . . . . . **CLC 50**

Kaplan, James 1951- . . . . **CLC 59**
See also CA 135

Karageorge, Michael
See Anderson, Poul (William)

Karamzin, Nikolai Mikhailovich 1766-1826 . . . . **NCLC 3**

Karapanou, Margarita 1946- . . . . **CLC 13**
See also CA 101

Karinthy, Frigyes 1887-1938 . . . . . . **TCLC 47**

Karl, Frederick R(obert) 1927- . . . . . **CLC 34**
See also CA 5-8R; CANR 3

Kastel, Warren
See Silverberg, Robert

Kataev, Evgeny Petrovich 1903-1942
See Petrov, Evgeny
See also CA 120

Kataphusin
See Ruskin, John

Katz, Steve 1935- . . . . **CLC 47**
See also CA 25-28R; CAAS 14; CANR 12; DLBY 83

Kauffman, Janet 1945- . . . . **CLC 42**
See also CA 117; DLBY 86

Kaufman, Bob (Garnell) 1925-1986 . . . . **CLC 49**
See also BW; CA 41-44R; 118; CANR 22; DLB 16, 41

Kaufman, George S. 1889-1961 . . . . . **CLC 38**
See also CA 108; 93-96; DLB 7

Kaufman, Sue . . . . **CLC 3, 8**
See also Barondess, Sue K(aufman)

Kavafis, Konstantinos Petrou 1863-1933
See Cavafy, C(onstantine) P(eter)
See also CA 104

Kavan, Anna 1901-1968 . . . . **CLC 5, 13**
See also CA 5-8R; CANR 6; MTCW

Kavanagh, Dan
See Barnes, Julian

Kavanagh, Patrick (Joseph) 1904-1967 . . . . **CLC 22**
See also CA 123; 25-28R; DLB 15, 20; MTCW

Kawabata, Yasunari 1899-1972 . . . . **CLC 2, 5, 9, 18**
See also CA 93-96; 33-36R

Kaye, M(ary) M(argaret) 1909- . . . . . **CLC 28**
See also CA 89-92; CANR 24; MTCW; SATA 62

Kaye, Mollie
See Kaye, M(ary) M(argaret)

Kaye-Smith, Sheila 1887-1956. . . . . **TCLC 20**
See also CA 118; DLB 36

Kaymor, Patrice Maguilene
See Senghor, Leopold Sedar

Kazan, Elia 1909- . . . . **CLC 6, 16, 63**
See also CA 21-24R; CANR 32

Kazantzakis, Nikos 1883(?)-1957 . . . . **TCLC 2, 5, 33**
See also CA 105; 132; MTCW

Kazin, Alfred 1915- . . . . **CLC 34, 38**
See also CA 1-4R; CAAS 7; CANR 1; DLB 67

Keane, Mary Nesta (Skrine) 1904-
See Keane, Molly
See also CA 108; 114

Keane, Molly . . . . **CLC 31**
See also Keane, Mary Nesta (Skrine)

Keates, Jonathan 19(?)- . . . . **CLC 34**

Keaton, Buster 1895-1966 . . . . **CLC 20**

Keats, John 1795-1821 . . . . . . **NCLC 8; PC 1**
See also CDBLB 1789-1832; DA; DLB 96, 110; WLC

Keene, Donald 1922- . . . . **CLC 34**
See also CA 1-4R; CANR 5

Keillor, Garrison . . . . **CLC 40**
See also Keillor, Gary (Edward)
See also AAYA 2; BEST 89:3; DLBY 87; SATA 58

Keillor, Gary (Edward) 1942-
See Keillor, Garrison
See also CA 111; 117; CANR 36; MTCW

Keith, Michael
See Hubbard, L(afayette) Ron(ald)

Kell, Joseph
See Wilson, John (Anthony) Burgess

Keller, Gottfried 1819-1890 . . . . **NCLC 2**
See also DLB 129

Kellerman, Jonathan 1949- . . . . **CLC 44**
See also BEST 90:1; CA 106; CANR 29

Kelley, William Melvin 1937- . . . . . . **CLC 22**
See also BW; CA 77-80; CANR 27; DLB 33

Kellogg, Marjorie 1922- . . . . **CLC 2**
See also CA 81-84

Kellow, Kathleen
See Hibbert, Eleanor Alice Burford

Kelly, M(ilton) T(erry) 1947- . . . . **CLC 55**
See also CA 97-100; CANR 19

Kelman, James 1946- . . . . **CLC 58**

Knox, Calvin M.
See Silverberg, Robert

Knye, Cassandra
See Disch, Thomas M(ichael)

Koch, C(hristopher) J(ohn) 1932- . . . **CLC 42**
See also CA 127

Koch, Christopher
See Koch, C(hristopher) J(ohn)

Koch, Kenneth 1925- . . . . **CLC 5, 8, 44**
See also CA 1-4R; CANR 6, 36; DLB 5; SATA 65

Kochanowski, Jan 1530-1584. . . . . **LC 10**

Kock, Charles Paul de
1794-1871 . . . . **NCLC 16**

Koda Shigeyuki 1867-1947
See Rohan, Koda
See also CA 121

Koestler, Arthur
1905-1983 . . . . **CLC 1, 3, 6, 8, 15, 33**
See also CA 1-4R; 109; CANR 1, 33; CDBLB 1945-1960; DLBY 83; MTCW

Kohout, Pavel 1928- . . . . **CLC 13**
See also CA 45-48; CANR 3

Koizumi, Yakumo
See Hearn, (Patricio) Lafcadio (Tessima Carlos)

Kolmar, Gertrud 1894-1943. . . . . . . **TCLC 40**

Konrad, George
See Konrad, Gyoergy

Konrad, Gyoergy 1933- . . . . . . **CLC 4, 10, 73**
See also CA 85-88

Konwicki, Tadeusz 1926- . . . . . **CLC 8, 28, 54**
See also CA 101; CAAS 9; CANR 39; MTCW

Kopit, Arthur (Lee) 1937- . . . . **CLC 1, 18, 33**
See also AITN 1; CA 81-84; CABS 3; DLB 7; MTCW

Kops, Bernard 1926-. . . . . **CLC 4**
See also CA 5-8R; DLB 13

Kornbluth, C(yril) M. 1923-1958. . . . **TCLC 8**
See also CA 105; DLB 8

Korolenko, V. G.
See Korolenko, Vladimir Galaktionovich

Korolenko, Vladimir
See Korolenko, Vladimir Galaktionovich

Korolenko, Vladimir G.
See Korolenko, Vladimir Galaktionovich

Korolenko, Vladimir Galaktionovich
1853-1921 . . . . **TCLC 22**
See also CA 121

Kosinski, Jerzy (Nikodem)
1933-1991 . . . **CLC 1, 2, 3, 6, 10, 15, 53, 70**
See also CA 17-20R; 134; CANR 9; DLB 2; DLBY 82; MTCW

Kostelanetz, Richard (Cory) 1940- . . **CLC 28**
See also CA 13-16R; CAAS 8; CANR 38

Kostrowitzki, Wilhelm Apollinaris de
1880-1918
See Apollinaire, Guillaume
See also CA 104

Kotlowitz, Robert 1924-. . . . . **CLC 4**
See also CA 33-36R; CANR 36

Kotzebue, August (Friedrich Ferdinand) von
1761-1819 . . . . **NCLC 25**
See also DLB 94

Kotzwinkle, William 1938- . . . **CLC 5, 14, 35**
See also CA 45-48; CANR 3; CLR 6; MAICYA; SATA 24, 70

Kozol, Jonathan 1936- . . . . **CLC 17**
See also CA 61-64; CANR 16

Kozoll, Michael 1940(?)- . . . . **CLC 35**

Kramer, Kathryn 19(?)- . . . . **CLC 34**

Kramer, Larry 1935- . . . . **CLC 42**
See also CA 124; 126

Krasicki, Ignacy 1735-1801 . . . . **NCLC 8**

Krasinski, Zygmunt 1812-1859 . . . . **NCLC 4**

Kraus, Karl 1874-1936 . . . . **TCLC 5**
See also CA 104; DLB 118

Kreve (Mickevicius), Vincas
1882-1954 . . . . **TCLC 27**

Kristeva, Julia 1941- . . . . **CLC 77**

Kristofferson, Kris 1936- . . . . **CLC 26**
See also CA 104

Krizanc, John 1956- . . . . **CLC 57**

Krleza, Miroslav 1893-1981. . . . . **CLC 8**
See also CA 97-100; 105

Kroetsch, Robert 1927- . . . . . . **CLC 5, 23, 57**
See also CA 17-20R; CANR 8, 38; DLB 53; MTCW

Kroetz, Franz
See Kroetz, Franz Xaver

Kroetz, Franz Xaver 1946- . . . . **CLC 41**
See also CA 130

Kroker, Arthur 1945- . . . . **CLC 77**

Kropotkin, Peter (Aleksieevich)
1842-1921 . . . . **TCLC 36**
See also CA 119

Krotkov, Yuri 1917- . . . . **CLC 19**
See also CA 102

Krumb
See Crumb, R(obert)

Krumgold, Joseph (Quincy)
1908-1980 . . . . **CLC 12**
See also CA 9-12R; 101; CANR 7; MAICYA; SATA 1, 23, 48

Krumwitz
See Crumb, R(obert)

Krutch, Joseph Wood 1893-1970. . . . **CLC 24**
See also CA 1-4R; 25-28R; CANR 4; DLB 63

Krutzch, Gus
See Eliot, T(homas) S(tearns)

Krylov, Ivan Andreevich
1768(?)-1844 . . . . **NCLC 1**

Kubin, Alfred 1877-1959 . . . . **TCLC 23**
See also CA 112; DLB 81

Kubrick, Stanley 1928-. . . . . **CLC 16**
See also CA 81-84; CANR 33; DLB 26

Kumin, Maxine (Winokur)
1925- . . . . **CLC 5, 13, 28**
See also AITN 2; CA 1-4R; CAAS 8; CANR 1, 21; DLB 5; MTCW; SATA 12

Kundera, Milan
1929- . . . . **CLC 4, 9, 19, 32, 68**
See also AAYA 2; CA 85-88; CANR 19; MTCW

Kunitz, Stanley (Jasspon)
1905- . . . . **CLC 6, 11, 14**
See also CA 41-44R; CANR 26; DLB 48; MTCW

Kunze, Reiner 1933-. . . . . **CLC 10**
See also CA 93-96; DLB 75

Kuprin, Aleksandr Ivanovich
1870-1938 . . . . **TCLC 5**
See also CA 104

Kureishi, Hanif 1954(?)-. . . . . **CLC 64**
See also CA 139

Kurosawa, Akira 1910-. . . . . **CLC 16**
See also CA 101

Kuttner, Henry 1915-1958. . . . . **TCLC 10**
See also CA 107; DLB 8

Kuzma, Greg 1944-. . . . . **CLC 7**
See also CA 33-36R

Kuzmin, Mikhail 1872(?)-1936 . . . . **TCLC 40**

Kyd, Thomas 1558-1594. . . . . . . **LC 22; DC 3**
See also DLB 62

Kyprianos, Iossif
See Samarakis, Antonis

La Bruyere, Jean de 1645-1696. . . . . . **LC 17**

Lacan, Jacques (Marie Emile)
1901-1981 . . . . **CLC 75**
See also CA 121; 104

Laclos, Pierre Ambroise Francois Choderlos de 1741-1803 . . . . **NCLC 4**

Lacolere, Francois
See Aragon, Louis

La Colere, Francois
See Aragon, Louis

La Deshabilleuse
See Simenon, Georges (Jacques Christian)

Lady Gregory
See Gregory, Isabella Augusta (Persse)

Lady of Quality, A
See Bagnold, Enid

La Fayette, Marie (Madelaine Pioche de la Vergne Comtes 1634-1693. . . . . . . **LC 2**

Lafayette, Rene
See Hubbard, L(afayette) Ron(ald)

Laforgue, Jules 1860-1887. . . . . **NCLC 5**

Lagerkvist, Paer (Fabian)
1891-1974 . . . . **CLC 7, 10, 13, 54**
See also Lagerkvist, Par
See also CA 85-88; 49-52; MTCW

Lagerkvist, Par
See Lagerkvist, Paer (Fabian)
See also SSC 12

Lagerloef, Selma (Ottiliana Lovisa)
1858-1940 . . . . **TCLC 4, 36**
See also Lagerlof, Selma (Ottiliana Lovisa)
See also CA 108; CLR 7; SATA 15

Lagerlof, Selma (Ottiliana Lovisa)
See Lagerloef, Selma (Ottiliana Lovisa)
See also CLR 7; SATA 15

Le Clezio, J(ean) M(arie) G(ustave) 1940- . . . . **CLC 31**
See also CA 116; 128; DLB 83

Leconte de Lisle, Charles-Marie-Rene 1818-1894 . . . . **NCLC 29**

Le Coq, Monsieur
See Simenon, Georges (Jacques Christian)

Leduc, Violette 1907-1972 . . . . **CLC 22**
See also CA 13-14; 33-36R; CAP 1

Ledwidge, Francis 1887(?)-1917 . . . **TCLC 23**
See also CA 123; DLB 20

Lee, Andrea 1953- . . . . **CLC 36**
See also BLC 2; BW; CA 125

Lee, Andrew
See Auchincloss, Louis (Stanton)

Lee, Don L. . . . . **CLC 2**
See also Madhubuti, Haki R.

Lee, George W(ashington) 1894-1976 . . . . **CLC 52**
See also BLC 2; BW; CA 125; DLB 51

Lee, (Nelle) Harper 1926- . . . . . . **CLC 12, 60**
See also CA 13-16R; CDALB 1941-1968; DA; DLB 6; MTCW; SATA 11; WLC

Lee, Julian
See Latham, Jean Lee

Lee, Lawrence 1903- . . . . **CLC 34**
See also CA 25-28R

Lee, Manfred B(ennington) 1905-1971 . . . . **CLC 11**
See also Queen, Ellery
See also CA 1-4R; 29-32R; CANR 2

Lee, Stan 1922- . . . . **CLC 17**
See also AAYA 5; CA 108; 111

Lee, Tanith 1947- . . . . **CLC 46**
See also CA 37-40R; SATA 8

Lee, Vernon . . . . **TCLC 5**
See also Paget, Violet
See also DLB 57

Lee, William
See Burroughs, William S(eward)

Lee, Willy
See Burroughs, William S(eward)

Lee-Hamilton, Eugene (Jacob) 1845-1907 . . . . **TCLC 22**
See also CA 117

Leet, Judith 1935- . . . . **CLC 11**

Le Fanu, Joseph Sheridan 1814-1873 . . . . **NCLC 9**
See also DLB 21, 70

Leffland, Ella 1931- . . . . **CLC 19**
See also CA 29-32R; CANR 35; DLBY 84; SATA 65

Leger, (Marie-Rene) Alexis Saint-Leger 1887-1975 . . . . **CLC 11**
See also Perse, St.-John
See also CA 13-16R; 61-64; MTCW

Leger, Saintleger
See Leger, (Marie-Rene) Alexis Saint-Leger

Le Guin, Ursula K(roeber) 1929- . . . . **CLC 8, 13, 22, 45, 71; SSC 12**
See also AAYA 9; AITN 1; CA 21-24R; CANR 9, 32; CDALB 1968-1988; CLR 3, 28; DLB 8, 52; MAICYA; MTCW; SATA 4, 52

Lehmann, Rosamond (Nina) 1901-1990 . . . . **CLC 5**
See also CA 77-80; 131; CANR 8; DLB 15

Leiber, Fritz (Reuter, Jr.) 1910-1992 . . . . **CLC 25**
See also CA 45-48; 139; CANR 2, 40; DLB 8; MTCW; SATA 45; SATA-Obit 73

Leimbach, Martha 1963-
See Leimbach, Marti
See also CA 130

Leimbach, Marti . . . . **CLC 65**
See also Leimbach, Martha

Leino, Eino . . . . **TCLC 24**
See also Loennbohm, Armas Eino Leopold

Leiris, Michel (Julien) 1901-1990 . . . **CLC 61**
See also CA 119; 128; 132

Leithauser, Brad 1953- . . . . **CLC 27**
See also CA 107; CANR 27; DLB 120

Lelchuk, Alan 1938- . . . . **CLC 5**
See also CA 45-48; CANR 1

Lem, Stanislaw 1921- . . . . **CLC 8, 15, 40**
See also CA 105; CAAS 1; CANR 32; MTCW

Lemann, Nancy 1956- . . . . **CLC 39**
See also CA 118; 136

Lemonnier, (Antoine Louis) Camille 1844-1913 . . . . **TCLC 22**
See also CA 121

Lenau, Nikolaus 1802-1850 . . . . . . **NCLC 16**

L'Engle, Madeleine (Camp Franklin) 1918- . . . . **CLC 12**
See also AAYA 1; AITN 2; CA 1-4R; CANR 3, 21, 39; CLR 1, 14; DLB 52; MAICYA; MTCW; SAAS 15; SATA 1, 27

Lengyel, Jozsef 1896-1975 . . . . **CLC 7**
See also CA 85-88; 57-60

Lennon, John (Ono) 1940-1980 . . . . **CLC 12, 35**
See also CA 102

Lennox, Charlotte Ramsay 1729(?)-1804 . . . . **NCLC 23**
See also DLB 39

Lentricchia, Frank (Jr.) 1940- . . . . . . **CLC 34**
See also CA 25-28R; CANR 19

Lenz, Siegfried 1926- . . . . **CLC 27**
See also CA 89-92; DLB 75

Leonard, Elmore (John, Jr.) 1925- . . . . **CLC 28, 34, 71**
See also AITN 1; BEST 89:1, 90:4; CA 81-84; CANR 12, 28; MTCW

Leonard, Hugh
See Byrne, John Keyes
See also DLB 13

Leopardi, (Conte) Giacomo (Talegardo Francesco di Sales Save 1798-1837 . . . . **NCLC 22**

Le Reveler
See Artaud, Antonin

Lerman, Eleanor 1952- . . . . **CLC 9**
See also CA 85-88

Lerman, Rhoda 1936- . . . . **CLC 56**
See also CA 49-52

Lermontov, Mikhail Yuryevich 1814-1841 . . . . **NCLC 5**

Leroux, Gaston 1868-1927 . . . . **TCLC 25**
See also CA 108; 136; SATA 65

Lesage, Alain-Rene 1668-1747 . . . . **LC 2**

Leskov, Nikolai (Semyonovich) 1831-1895 . . . . **NCLC 25**

Lessing, Doris (May) 1919- . . . . **CLC 1, 2, 3, 6, 10, 15, 22, 40; SSC 6**
See also CA 9-12R; CAAS 14; CANR 33; CDBLB 1960 to Present; DA; DLB 15; DLBY 85; MTCW

Lessing, Gotthold Ephraim 1729-1781 . . . . **LC 8**
See also DLB 97

Lester, Richard 1932- . . . . **CLC 20**

Lever, Charles (James) 1806-1872 . . . . **NCLC 23**
See also DLB 21

Leverson, Ada 1865(?)-1936(?) . . . . **TCLC 18**
See also Elaine
See also CA 117

Levertov, Denise 1923- . . . . . . **CLC 1, 2, 3, 5, 8, 15, 28, 66**
See also CA 1-4R; CANR 3, 29; DLB 5; MTCW

Levi, Jonathan . . . . **CLC 76**

Levi, Peter (Chad Tigar) 1931- . . . . . **CLC 41**
See also CA 5-8R; CANR 34; DLB 40

Levi, Primo 1919-1987 . . . . **CLC 37, 50; SSC 12**
See also CA 13-16R; 122; CANR 12, 33; MTCW

Levin, Ira 1929- . . . . **CLC 3, 6**
See also CA 21-24R; CANR 17; MTCW; SATA 66

Levin, Meyer 1905-1981 . . . . **CLC 7**
See also AITN 1; CA 9-12R; 104; CANR 15; DLB 9, 28; DLBY 81; SATA 21, 27

Levine, Norman 1924- . . . . **CLC 54**
See also CA 73-76; CANR 14; DLB 88

Levine, Philip 1928- . . **CLC 2, 4, 5, 9, 14, 33**
See also CA 9-12R; CANR 9, 37; DLB 5

Levinson, Deirdre 1931- . . . . **CLC 49**
See also CA 73-76

Levi-Strauss, Claude 1908- . . . . **CLC 38**
See also CA 1-4R; CANR 6, 32; MTCW

Levitin, Sonia (Wolff) 1934- . . . . **CLC 17**
See also CA 29-32R; CANR 14, 32; MAICYA; SAAS 2; SATA 4, 68

Levon, O. U.
See Kesey, Ken (Elton)

Lewes, George Henry 1817-1878 . . . . **NCLC 25**
See also DLB 55

Lewis, Alun 1915-1944 . . . . **TCLC 3**
See also CA 104; DLB 20

Lewis, C. Day
See Day Lewis, C(ecil)

Lewis, C(live) S(taples) 1898-1963 . . . . **CLC 1, 3, 6, 14, 27**
See also AAYA 3; CA 81-84; CANR 33; CDBLB 1945-1960; CLR 3, 27; DA; DLB 15, 100; MAICYA; MTCW; SATA 13; WLC

Lewis, Janet 1899- . . . . **CLC 41**
See also Winters, Janet Lewis
See also CA 9-12R; CANR 29; CAP 1; DLBY 87

Lewis, Matthew Gregory 1775-1818 . . . . **NCLC 11**
See also DLB 39

Lewis, (Harry) Sinclair 1885-1951 . . . . **TCLC 4, 13, 23, 39**
See also CA 104; 133; CDALB 1917-1929; DA; DLB 9, 102; DLBD 1; MTCW; WLC

Lewis, (Percy) Wyndham 1884(?)-1957 . . . . **TCLC 2, 9**
See also CA 104; DLB 15

Lewisohn, Ludwig 1883-1955. . . . . . **TCLC 19**
See also CA 107; DLB 4, 9, 28, 102

Lezama Lima, Jose 1910-1976 . . . **CLC 4, 10**
See also CA 77-80; DLB 113; HW

L'Heureux, John (Clarke) 1934- . . . . **CLC 52**
See also CA 13-16R; CANR 23

Liddell, C. H.
See Kuttner, Henry

Lie, Jonas (Lauritz Idemil) 1833-1908(?) . . . . **TCLC 5**
See also CA 115

Lieber, Joel 1937-1971. . . . . **CLC 6**
See also CA 73-76; 29-32R

Lieber, Stanley Martin
See Lee, Stan

Lieberman, Laurence (James) 1935- . . . . **CLC 4, 36**
See also CA 17-20R; CANR 8, 36

Lieksman, Anders
See Haavikko, Paavo Juhani

Li Fei-kan 1904- . . . . **CLC 18**
See also CA 105

Lifton, Robert Jay 1926- . . . . **CLC 67**
See also CA 17-20R; CANR 27; SATA 66

Lightfoot, Gordon 1938- . . . . **CLC 26**
See also CA 109

Ligotti, Thomas 1953- . . . . **CLC 44**
See also CA 123

Liliencron, (Friedrich Adolf Axel) Detlev von 1844-1909 . . . . **TCLC 18**
See also CA 117

Lima, Jose Lezama
See Lezama Lima, Jose

Lima Barreto, Afonso Henrique de 1881-1922 . . . . **TCLC 23**
See also CA 117

Limonov, Eduard. . . . . **CLC 67**

Lin, Frank
See Atherton, Gertrude (Franklin Horn)

Lincoln, Abraham 1809-1865. . . . . **NCLC 18**

Lind, Jakov . . . . **CLC 1, 2, 4, 27**
See also Landwirth, Heinz
See also CAAS 4

Lindsay, David 1878-1945 . . . . **TCLC 15**
See also CA 113

Lindsay, (Nicholas) Vachel 1879-1931 . . . . **TCLC 17**
See also CA 114; 135; CDALB 1865-1917; DA; DLB 54; SATA 40; WLC

Linke-Poot
See Doeblin, Alfred

Linney, Romulus 1930- . . . . **CLC 51**
See also CA 1-4R; CANR 40

Li Po 701-763 . . . . **CMLC 2**

Lipsius, Justus 1547-1606 . . . . **LC 16**

Lipsyte, Robert (Michael) 1938- . . . . **CLC 21**
See also AAYA 7; CA 17-20R; CANR 8; CLR 23; DA; MAICYA; SATA 5, 68

Lish, Gordon (Jay) 1934- . . . . **CLC 45**
See also CA 113; 117; DLB 130

Lispector, Clarice 1925-1977 . . . . **CLC 43**
See also CA 139; 116; DLB 113

Littell, Robert 1935(?)- . . . . **CLC 42**
See also CA 109; 112

Littlewit, Humphrey Gent.
See Lovecraft, H(oward) P(hillips)

Litwos
See Sienkiewicz, Henryk (Adam Alexander Pius)

Liu E 1857-1909 . . . . **TCLC 15**
See also CA 115

Lively, Penelope (Margaret) 1933- . . . . **CLC 32, 50**
See also CA 41-44R; CANR 29; CLR 7; DLB 14; MAICYA; MTCW; SATA 7, 60

Livesay, Dorothy (Kathleen) 1909- . . . . **CLC 4, 15**
See also AITN 2; CA 25-28R; CAAS 8; CANR 36; DLB 68; MTCW

Livy c. 59B.C.-c. 17 . . . . **CMLC 11**

Lizardi, Jose Joaquin Fernandez de 1776-1827 . . . . **NCLC 30**

Llewellyn, Richard . . . . **CLC 7**
See also Llewellyn Lloyd, Richard Dafydd Vivian
See also DLB 15

Llewellyn Lloyd, Richard Dafydd Vivian 1906-1983
See Llewellyn, Richard
See also CA 53-56; 111; CANR 7; SATA 11, 37

Llosa, (Jorge) Mario (Pedro) Vargas
See Vargas Llosa, (Jorge) Mario (Pedro)

Lloyd Webber, Andrew 1948-
See Webber, Andrew Lloyd
See also AAYA 1; CA 116; SATA 56

Locke, Alain (Le Roy) 1886-1954 . . . . **TCLC 43**
See also BW; CA 106; 124; DLB 51

Locke, John 1632-1704 . . . . **LC 7**
See also DLB 101

Locke-Elliott, Sumner
See Elliott, Sumner Locke

Lockhart, John Gibson 1794-1854 . . . . **NCLC 6**
See also DLB 110, 116

Lodge, David (John) 1935- . . . . **CLC 36**
See also BEST 90:1; CA 17-20R; CANR 19; DLB 14; MTCW

Loennbohm, Armas Eino Leopold 1878-1926
See Leino, Eino
See also CA 123

Loewinsohn, Ron(ald William) 1937- . . . . **CLC 52**
See also CA 25-28R

Logan, Jake
See Smith, Martin Cruz

Logan, John (Burton) 1923-1987. . . . . **CLC 5**
See also CA 77-80; 124; DLB 5

Lo Kuan-chung 1330(?)-1400(?). . . . . . **LC 12**

Lombard, Nap
See Johnson, Pamela Hansford

London, Jack. . . . . **TCLC 9, 15, 39; SSC 4**
See also London, John Griffith
See also AITN 2; CDALB 1865-1917; DLB 8, 12, 78; SATA 18; WLC

London, John Griffith 1876-1916
See London, Jack
See also CA 110; 119; DA; MAICYA; MTCW

Long, Emmett
See Leonard, Elmore (John, Jr.)

Longbaugh, Harry
See Goldman, William (W.)

Longfellow, Henry Wadsworth 1807-1882 . . . . **NCLC 2**
See also CDALB 1640-1865; DA; DLB 1, 59; SATA 19

Longley, Michael 1939- . . . . **CLC 29**
See also CA 102; DLB 40

Longus fl. c. 2nd cent. - . . . . **CMLC 7**

Longway, A. Hugh
See Lang, Andrew

Lopate, Phillip 1943- . . . . **CLC 29**
See also CA 97-100; DLBY 80

Lopez Portillo (y Pacheco), Jose 1920- . . . . **CLC 46**
See also CA 129; HW

Lopez y Fuentes, Gregorio 1897(?)-1966 . . . . **CLC 32**
See also CA 131; HW

Lorca, Federico Garcia
See Garcia Lorca, Federico

Lord, Bette Bao 1938- . . . . **CLC 23**
See also BEST 90:3; CA 107; CANR 41; SATA 58

Lord Auch
See Bataille, Georges

Lord Byron
See Byron, George Gordon (Noel)

Lord Dunsany . . . . **TCLC 2**
See also Dunsany, Edward John Moreton Drax Plunkett

Lorde, Audre (Geraldine) 1934- . . . . **CLC 18, 71**
See also BLC 2; BW; CA 25-28R; CANR 16, 26; DLB 41; MTCW

Lord Jeffrey
See Jeffrey, Francis

Marks, J
See Highwater, Jamake (Mamake)

Marks-Highwater, J
See Highwater, Jamake (Mamake)

Markson, David M(errill) 1927- .... **CLC 67**
See also CA 49-52; CANR 1

Marley, Bob .... **CLC 17**
See also Marley, Robert Nesta

Marley, Robert Nesta 1945-1981
See Marley, Bob
See also CA 107; 103

Marlowe, Christopher
1564-1593 .... **LC 22; DC 1**
See also CDBLB Before 1660; DA; DLB 62; WLC

Marmontel, Jean-Francois
1723-1799 .... **LC 2**

Marquand, John P(hillips)
1893-1960 .... **CLC 2, 10**
See also CA 85-88; DLB 9, 102

Marquez, Gabriel (Jose) Garcia ...... **CLC 68**
See also Garcia Marquez, Gabriel (Jose)

Marquis, Don(ald Robert Perry)
1878-1937 .... **TCLC 7**
See also CA 104; DLB 11, 25

Marric, J. J.
See Creasey, John

Marrow, Bernard
See Moore, Brian

Marryat, Frederick 1792-1848 .... **NCLC 3**
See also DLB 21

Marsden, James
See Creasey, John

Marsh, (Edith) Ngaio
1899-1982 .... **CLC 7, 53**
See also CA 9-12R; CANR 6; DLB 77; MTCW

Marshall, Garry 1934- .... **CLC 17**
See also AAYA 3; CA 111; SATA 60

Marshall, Paule 1929- .. **CLC 27, 72; SSC 3**
See also BLC 3; BW; CA 77-80; CANR 25; DLB 33; MTCW

Marsten, Richard
See Hunter, Evan

Martha, Henry
See Harris, Mark

Martin, Ken
See Hubbard, L(afayette) Ron(ald)

Martin, Richard
See Creasey, John

Martin, Steve 1945- .... **CLC 30**
See also CA 97-100; CANR 30; MTCW

Martin, Webber
See Silverberg, Robert

Martin du Gard, Roger
1881-1958 .... **TCLC 24**
See also CA 118; DLB 65

Martineau, Harriet 1802-1876.... **NCLC 26**
See also DLB 21, 55; YABC 2

Martines, Julia
See O'Faolain, Julia

Martinez, Jacinto Benavente y
See Benavente (y Martinez), Jacinto

Martinez Ruiz, Jose 1873-1967
See Azorin; Ruiz, Jose Martinez
See also CA 93-96; HW

Martinez Sierra, Gregorio
1881-1947 .... **TCLC 6**
See also CA 115

Martinez Sierra, Maria (de la O'LeJarraga)
1874-1974 .... **TCLC 6**
See also CA 115

Martinsen, Martin
See Follett, Ken(neth Martin)

Martinson, Harry (Edmund)
1904-1978 .... **CLC 14**
See also CA 77-80; CANR 34

Marut, Ret
See Traven, B.

Marut, Robert
See Traven, B.

Marvell, Andrew 1621-1678.......... **LC 4**
See also CDBLB 1660-1789; DA; DLB 131; WLC

Marx, Karl (Heinrich)
1818-1883 .... **NCLC 17**
See also DLB 129

Masaoka Shiki .... **TCLC 18**
See also Masaoka Tsunenori

Masaoka Tsunenori 1867-1902
See Masaoka Shiki
See also CA 117

Masefield, John (Edward)
1878-1967 .... **CLC 11, 47**
See also CA 19-20; 25-28R; CANR 33; CAP 2; CDBLB 1890-1914; DLB 10; MTCW; SATA 19

Maso, Carole 19(?)- .... **CLC 44**

Mason, Bobbie Ann
1940- .... **CLC 28, 43; SSC 4**
See also AAYA 5; CA 53-56; CANR 11, 31; DLBY 87; MTCW

Mason, Ernst
See Pohl, Frederik

Mason, Lee W.
See Malzberg, Barry N(athaniel)

Mason, Nick 1945- .... **CLC 35**
See also Pink Floyd

Mason, Tally
See Derleth, August (William)

Mass, William
See Gibson, William

Masters, Edgar Lee
1868-1950 .... **TCLC 2, 25; PC 1**
See also CA 104; 133; CDALB 1865-1917; DA; DLB 54; MTCW

Masters, Hilary 1928- .... **CLC 48**
See also CA 25-28R; CANR 13

Mastrosimone, William 19(?)- ...... **CLC 36**

Mathe, Albert
See Camus, Albert

Matheson, Richard Burton 1926- ... **CLC 37**
See also CA 97-100; DLB 8, 44

Mathews, Harry 1930- .... **CLC 6, 52**
See also CA 21-24R; CAAS 6; CANR 18, 40

Mathias, Roland (Glyn) 1915- ...... **CLC 45**
See also CA 97-100; CANR 19, 41; DLB 27

Matsuo Basho 1644-1694............ **PC 3**

Mattheson, Rodney
See Creasey, John

Matthews, Greg 1949- .... **CLC 45**
See also CA 135

Matthews, William 1942- .... **CLC 40**
See also CA 29-32R; CANR 12; DLB 5

Matthias, John (Edward) 1941- ...... **CLC 9**
See also CA 33-36R

Matthiessen, Peter
1927- .... **CLC 5, 7, 11, 32, 64**
See also AAYA 6; BEST 90:4; CA 9-12R; CANR 21; DLB 6; MTCW; SATA 27

Maturin, Charles Robert
1780(?)-1824 .... **NCLC 6**

Matute (Ausejo), Ana Maria
1925- .... **CLC 11**
See also CA 89-92; MTCW

Maugham, W. S.
See Maugham, W(illiam) Somerset

Maugham, W(illiam) Somerset
1874-1965 .... **CLC 1, 11, 15, 67; SSC 8**
See also CA 5-8R; 25-28R; CANR 40; CDBLB 1914-1945; DA; DLB 10, 36, 77, 100; MTCW; SATA 54; WLC

Maugham, William Somerset
See Maugham, W(illiam) Somerset

Maupassant, (Henri Rene Albert) Guy de
1850-1893 .... **NCLC 1; SSC 1**
See also DA; DLB 123; WLC

Maurhut, Richard
See Traven, B.

Mauriac, Claude 1914- .... **CLC 9**
See also CA 89-92; DLB 83

Mauriac, Francois (Charles)
1885-1970 .... **CLC 4, 9, 56**
See also CA 25-28; CAP 2; DLB 65; MTCW

Mavor, Osborne Henry 1888-1951
See Bridie, James
See also CA 104

Maxwell, William (Keepers, Jr.)
1908- .... **CLC 19**
See also CA 93-96; DLBY 80

May, Elaine 1932- .... **CLC 16**
See also CA 124; DLB 44

Mayakovski, Vladimir (Vladimirovich)
1893-1930 .... **TCLC 4, 18**
See also CA 104

Mayhew, Henry 1812-1887 ...... **NCLC 31**
See also DLB 18, 55

Maynard, Joyce 1953- .... **CLC 23**
See also CA 111; 129

Mayne, William (James Carter)
1928- .... **CLC 12**
See also CA 9-12R; CANR 37; CLR 25; MAICYA; SAAS 11; SATA 6, 68

Mayo, Jim
See L'Amour, Louis (Dearborn)

Maysles, Albert 1926- .... **CLC 16**
See also CA 29-32R

Maysles, David 1932- .... **CLC 16**

Merimee, Prosper
1803-1870 .... **NCLC 6; SSC 7**
See also DLB 119

Merkin, Daphne 1954- .... **CLC 44**
See also CA 123

Merlin, Arthur
See Blish, James (Benjamin)

Merrill, James (Ingram)
1926- .... **CLC 2, 3, 6, 8, 13, 18, 34**
See also CA 13-16R; CANR 10; DLB 5; DLBY 85; MTCW

Merriman, Alex
See Silverberg, Robert

Merritt, E. B.
See Waddington, Miriam

Merton, Thomas
1915-1968 .... **CLC 1, 3, 11, 34**
See also CA 5-8R; 25-28R; CANR 22; DLB 48; DLBY 81; MTCW

Merwin, W(illiam) S(tanley)
1927- ...... **CLC 1, 2, 3, 5, 8, 13, 18, 45**
See also CA 13-16R; CANR 15; DLB 5; MTCW

Metcalf, John 1938- .... **CLC 37**
See also CA 113; DLB 60

Metcalf, Suzanne
See Baum, L(yman) Frank

Mew, Charlotte (Mary)
1870-1928 .... **TCLC 8**
See also CA 105; DLB 19

Mewshaw, Michael 1943- .... **CLC 9**
See also CA 53-56; CANR 7; DLBY 80

Meyer, June
See Jordan, June

Meyer, Lynn
See Slavitt, David R(ytman)

Meyer-Meyrink, Gustav 1868-1932
See Meyrink, Gustav
See also CA 117

Meyers, Jeffrey 1939- .... **CLC 39**
See also CA 73-76; DLB 111

Meynell, Alice (Christina Gertrude Thompson)
1847-1922 .... **TCLC 6**
See also CA 104; DLB 19, 98

Meyrink, Gustav .... **TCLC 21**
See also Meyer-Meyrink, Gustav
See also DLB 81

Michaels, Leonard 1933- .... **CLC 6, 25**
See also CA 61-64; CANR 21; DLB 130; MTCW

Michaux, Henri 1899-1984 ...... **CLC 8, 19**
See also CA 85-88; 114

Michelangelo 1475-1564 .... **LC 12**

Michelet, Jules 1798-1874 .... **NCLC 31**

Michener, James A(lbert)
1907(?)- .... **CLC 1, 5, 11, 29, 60**
See also AITN 1; BEST 90:1; CA 5-8R; CANR 21; DLB 6; MTCW

Mickiewicz, Adam 1798-1855 ..... **NCLC 3**

Middleton, Christopher 1926- ...... **CLC 13**
See also CA 13-16R; CANR 29; DLB 40

Middleton, Stanley 1919- .... **CLC 7, 38**
See also CA 25-28R; CANR 21; DLB 14

Migueis, Jose Rodrigues 1901- ..... **CLC 10**

Mikszath, Kalman 1847-1910 ..... **TCLC 31**

Miles, Josephine
1911-1985 .... **CLC 1, 2, 14, 34, 39**
See also CA 1-4R; 116; CANR 2; DLB 48

Militant
See Sandburg, Carl (August)

Mill, John Stuart 1806-1873 ..... **NCLC 11**
See also CDBLB 1832-1890; DLB 55

Millar, Kenneth 1915-1983 .... **CLC 14**
See also Macdonald, Ross
See also CA 9-12R; 110; CANR 16; DLB 2; DLBD 6; DLBY 83; MTCW

Millay, E. Vincent
See Millay, Edna St. Vincent

Millay, Edna St. Vincent
1892-1950 .... **TCLC 4, 49; PC 6**
See also CA 104; 130; CDALB 1917-1929; DA; DLB 45; MTCW

Miller, Arthur
1915- ...... **CLC 1, 2, 6, 10, 15, 26, 47; DC 1**
See also AITN 1; CA 1-4R; CABS 3; CANR 2, 30; CDALB 1941-1968; DA; DLB 7; MTCW; WLC

Miller, Henry (Valentine)
1891-1980 .... **CLC 1, 2, 4, 9, 14, 43**
See also CA 9-12R; 97-100; CANR 33; CDALB 1929-1941; DA; DLB 4, 9; DLBY 80; MTCW; WLC

Miller, Jason 1939(?)- .... **CLC 2**
See also AITN 1; CA 73-76; DLB 7

Miller, Sue 19(?)- .... **CLC 44**
See also BEST 90:3; CA 139

Miller, Walter M(ichael, Jr.)
1923- .... **CLC 4, 30**
See also CA 85-88; DLB 8

Millett, Kate 1934- .... **CLC 67**
See also AITN 1; CA 73-76; CANR 32; MTCW

Millhauser, Steven 1943- .... **CLC 21, 54**
See also CA 110; 111; DLB 2

Millin, Sarah Gertrude 1889-1968 .. **CLC 49**
See also CA 102; 93-96

Milne, A(lan) A(lexander)
1882-1956 .... **TCLC 6**
See also CA 104; 133; CLR 1, 26; DLB 10, 77, 100; MAICYA; MTCW; YABC 1

Milner, Ron(ald) 1938- .... **CLC 56**
See also AITN 1; BLC 3; BW; CA 73-76; CANR 24; DLB 38; MTCW

Milosz, Czeslaw
1911- .... **CLC 5, 11, 22, 31, 56**
See also CA 81-84; CANR 23; MTCW

Milton, John 1608-1674 .... **LC 9**
See also CDBLB 1660-1789; DA; DLB 131; WLC

Minehaha, Cornelius
See Wedekind, (Benjamin) Frank(lin)

Miner, Valerie 1947- .... **CLC 40**
See also CA 97-100

Minimo, Duca
See D'Annunzio, Gabriele

Minot, Susan 1956- .... **CLC 44**
See also CA 134

Minus, Ed 1938- .... **CLC 39**

Miranda, Javier
See Bioy Casares, Adolfo

Miro (Ferrer), Gabriel (Francisco Victor)
1879-1930 .... **TCLC 5**
See also CA 104

Mishima, Yukio
.... **CLC 2, 4, 6, 9, 27; DC 1; SSC 4**
See also Hiraoka, Kimitake

Mistral, Gabriela .... **TCLC 2**
See also Godoy Alcayaga, Lucila

Mistry, Rohinton 1952- .... **CLC 71**

Mitchell, Clyde
See Ellison, Harlan; Silverberg, Robert

Mitchell, James Leslie 1901-1935
See Gibbon, Lewis Grassic
See also CA 104; DLB 15

Mitchell, Joni 1943- .... **CLC 12**
See also CA 112

Mitchell, Margaret (Munnerlyn)
1900-1949 .... **TCLC 11**
See also CA 109; 125; DLB 9; MTCW

Mitchell, Peggy
See Mitchell, Margaret (Munnerlyn)

Mitchell, S(ilas) Weir 1829-1914 .. **TCLC 36**

Mitchell, W(illiam) O(rmond)
1914- .... **CLC 25**
See also CA 77-80; CANR 15; DLB 88

Mitford, Mary Russell 1787-1855 .. **NCLC 4**
See also DLB 110, 116

Mitford, Nancy 1904-1973 .... **CLC 44**
See also CA 9-12R

Miyamoto, Yuriko 1899-1951 ..... **TCLC 37**

Mo, Timothy (Peter) 1950(?)- ...... **CLC 46**
See also CA 117; MTCW

Modarressi, Taghi (M.) 1931- ...... **CLC 44**
See also CA 121; 134

Modiano, Patrick (Jean) 1945- ..... **CLC 18**
See also CA 85-88; CANR 17, 40; DLB 83

Moerck, Paal
See Roelvaag, O(le) E(dvart)

Mofolo, Thomas (Mokopu)
1875(?)-1948 .... **TCLC 22**
See also BLC 3; CA 121

Mohr, Nicholasa 1935- .... **CLC 12**
See also AAYA 8; CA 49-52; CANR 1, 32; CLR 22; HW; SAAS 8; SATA 8

Mojtabai, A(nn) G(race)
1938- .... **CLC 5, 9, 15, 29**
See also CA 85-88

Moliere 1622-1673 .... **LC 10**
See also DA; WLC

Molin, Charles
See Mayne, William (James Carter)

Molnar, Ferenc 1878-1952 .... **TCLC 20**
See also CA 109

Momaday, N(avarre) Scott
1934- .... **CLC 2, 19**
See also CA 25-28R; CANR 14, 34; DA; MTCW; SATA 30, 48

Monroe, Harriet 1860-1936 .... **TCLC 12**
See also CA 109; DLB 54, 91

Monroe, Lyle
See Heinlein, Robert A(nson)

Montagu, Elizabeth 1917- . . . . NCLC 7
See also CA 9-12R

Montagu, Mary (Pierrepont) Wortley 1689-1762 . . . . LC 9
See also DLB 95, 101

Montagu, W. H.
See Coleridge, Samuel Taylor

Montague, John (Patrick) 1929- . . . . CLC 13, 46
See also CA 9-12R; CANR 9; DLB 40; MTCW

Montaigne, Michel (Eyquem) de 1533-1592 . . . . LC 8
See also DA; WLC

Montale, Eugenio 1896-1981 . . . CLC 7, 9, 18
See also CA 17-20R; 104; CANR 30; DLB 114; MTCW

Montesquieu, Charles-Louis de Secondat 1689-1755 . . . . LC 7

Montgomery, (Robert) Bruce 1921-1978
See Crispin, Edmund
See also CA 104

Montgomery, Marion H., Jr. 1925- . . CLC 7
See also AITN 1; CA 1-4R; CANR 3; DLB 6

Montgomery, Max
See Davenport, Guy (Mattison, Jr.)

Montherlant, Henry (Milon) de 1896-1972 . . . . CLC 8, 19
See also CA 85-88; 37-40R; DLB 72; MTCW

Monty Python . . . . CLC 21
See also Chapman, Graham; Cleese, John (Marwood); Gilliam, Terry (Vance); Idle, Eric; Jones, Terence Graham Parry; Palin, Michael (Edward)
See also AAYA 7

Moodie, Susanna (Strickland) 1803-1885 . . . . NCLC 14
See also DLB 99

Mooney, Edward 1951- . . . . CLC 25
See also CA 130

Mooney, Ted
See Mooney, Edward

Moorcock, Michael (John) 1939- . . . . CLC 5, 27, 58
See also CA 45-48; CAAS 5; CANR 2, 17, 38; DLB 14; MTCW

Moore, Brian 1921- . . . . CLC 1, 3, 5, 7, 8, 19, 32
See also CA 1-4R; CANR 1, 25; MTCW

Moore, Edward
See Muir, Edwin

Moore, George Augustus 1852-1933 . . . . TCLC 7
See also CA 104; DLB 10, 18, 57

Moore, Lorrie . . . . CLC 39, 45, 68
See also Moore, Marie Lorena

Moore, Marianne (Craig) 1887-1972 . . . CLC 1, 2, 4, 8, 10, 13, 19, 47; PC 4
See also CA 1-4R; 33-36R; CANR 3; CDALB 1929-1941; DA; DLB 45; DLBD 7; MTCW; SATA 20

Moore, Marie Lorena 1957-
See Moore, Lorrie
See also CA 116; CANR 39

Moore, Thomas 1779-1852 . . . . NCLC 6
See also DLB 96

Morand, Paul 1888-1976 . . . . CLC 41
See also CA 69-72; DLB 65

Morante, Elsa 1918-1985 . . . . CLC 8, 47
See also CA 85-88; 117; CANR 35; MTCW

Moravia, Alberto . . . . CLC 2, 7, 11, 27, 46
See also Pincherle, Alberto

More, Hannah 1745-1833 . . . . NCLC 27
See also DLB 107, 109, 116

More, Henry 1614-1687 . . . . LC 9
See also DLB 126

More, Sir Thomas 1478-1535 . . . . LC 10

Moreas, Jean . . . . TCLC 18
See also Papadiamantopoulos, Johannes

Morgan, Berry 1919- . . . . CLC 6
See also CA 49-52; DLB 6

Morgan, Claire
See Highsmith, (Mary) Patricia

Morgan, Edwin (George) 1920- . . . . . CLC 31
See also CA 5-8R; CANR 3; DLB 27

Morgan, (George) Frederick 1922- . . . . CLC 23
See also CA 17-20R; CANR 21

Morgan, Harriet
See Mencken, H(enry) L(ouis)

Morgan, Jane
See Cooper, James Fenimore

Morgan, Janet 1945- . . . . CLC 39
See also CA 65-68

Morgan, Lady 1776(?)-1859 . . . . . . NCLC 29
See also DLB 116

Morgan, Robin 1941- . . . . CLC 2
See also CA 69-72; CANR 29; MTCW

Morgan, Scott
See Kuttner, Henry

Morgan, Seth 1949(?)-1990 . . . . CLC 65
See also CA 132

Morgenstern, Christian 1871-1914 . . . . TCLC 8
See also CA 105

Morgenstern, S.
See Goldman, William (W.)

Moricz, Zsigmond 1879-1942 . . . . . TCLC 33

Morike, Eduard (Friedrich) 1804-1875 . . . . NCLC 10

Mori Ogai . . . . TCLC 14
See also Mori Rintaro

Mori Rintaro 1862-1922
See Mori Ogai
See also CA 110

Moritz, Karl Philipp 1756-1793 . . . . . . LC 2
See also DLB 94

Morland, Peter Henry
See Faust, Frederick (Schiller)

Morren, Theophil
See Hofmannsthal, Hugo von

Morris, Bill 1952- . . . . CLC 76

Morris, Julian
See West, Morris L(anglo)

Morris, Steveland Judkins 1950(?)-
See Wonder, Stevie
See also CA 111

Morris, William 1834-1896 . . . . NCLC 4
See also CDBLB 1832-1890; DLB 18, 35, 57

Morris, Wright 1910- . . . CLC 1, 3, 7, 18, 37
See also CA 9-12R; CANR 21; DLB 2; DLBY 81; MTCW

Morrison, Chloe Anthony Wofford
See Morrison, Toni

Morrison, James Douglas 1943-1971
See Morrison, Jim
See also CA 73-76; CANR 40

Morrison, Jim . . . . CLC 17
See also Morrison, James Douglas

Morrison, Toni 1931- . . . . . CLC 4, 10, 22, 55
See also AAYA 1; BLC 3; BW; CA 29-32R; CANR 27; CDALB 1968-1988; DA; DLB 6, 33; DLBY 81; MTCW; SATA 57

Morrison, Van 1945- . . . . CLC 21
See also CA 116

Mortimer, John (Clifford) 1923- . . . . CLC 28, 43
See also CA 13-16R; CANR 21; CDBLB 1960 to Present; DLB 13; MTCW

Mortimer, Penelope (Ruth) 1918- . . . . CLC 5
See also CA 57-60

Morton, Anthony
See Creasey, John

Mosher, Howard Frank . . . . CLC 62
See also CA 139

Mosley, Nicholas 1923- . . . . CLC 43, 70
See also CA 69-72; CANR 41; DLB 14

Moss, Howard 1922-1987 . . . . CLC 7, 14, 45, 50
See also CA 1-4R; 123; CANR 1; DLB 5

Mossgiel, Rab
See Burns, Robert

Motion, Andrew 1952- . . . . CLC 47
See also DLB 40

Motley, Willard (Francis) 1912-1965 . . . . CLC 18
See also BW; CA 117; 106; DLB 76

Mott, Michael (Charles Alston) 1930- . . . . CLC 15, 34
See also CA 5-8R; CAAS 7; CANR 7, 29

Mowat, Farley (McGill) 1921- . . . . . CLC 26
See also AAYA 1; CA 1-4R; CANR 4, 24; CLR 20; DLB 68; MAICYA; MTCW; SATA 3, 55

Moyers, Bill 1934- . . . . CLC 74
See also AITN 2; CA 61-64; CANR 31

Mphahlele, Es'kia
See Mphahlele, Ezekiel
See also DLB 125

Mphahlele, Ezekiel 1919- . . . . CLC 25
See also Mphahlele, Es'kia
See also BLC 3; BW; CA 81-84; CANR 26

Mqhayi, S(amuel) E(dward) K(rune Loliwe) 1875-1945 . . . . TCLC 25
See also BLC 3

Mr. Martin
See Burroughs, William S(eward)

Mrozek, Slawomir 1930- . . . . **CLC 3, 13**
See also CA 13-16R; CAAS 10; CANR 29; MTCW

Mrs. Belloc-Lowndes
See Lowndes, Marie Adelaide (Belloc)

Mtwa, Percy (?)- . . . . **CLC 47**

Mueller, Lisel 1924- . . . . **CLC 13, 51**
See also CA 93-96; DLB 105

Muir, Edwin 1887-1959 . . . . **TCLC 2**
See also CA 104; DLB 20, 100

Muir, John 1838-1914 . . . . **TCLC 28**

Mujica Lainez, Manuel
1910-1984 . . . . **CLC 31**
See also Lainez, Manuel Mujica
See also CA 81-84; 112; CANR 32; HW

Mukherjee, Bharati 1940- . . . . **CLC 53**
See also BEST 89:2; CA 107; DLB 60; MTCW

Muldoon, Paul 1951- . . . . **CLC 32, 72**
See also CA 113; 129; DLB 40

Mulisch, Harry 1927- . . . . **CLC 42**
See also CA 9-12R; CANR 6, 26

Mull, Martin 1943- . . . . **CLC 17**
See also CA 105

Mulock, Dinah Maria
See Craik, Dinah Maria (Mulock)

Munford, Robert 1737(?)-1783 . . . . **LC 5**
See also DLB 31

Mungo, Raymond 1946- . . . . **CLC 72**
See also CA 49-52; CANR 2

Munro, Alice
1931- . . . . **CLC 6, 10, 19, 50; SSC 3**
See also AITN 2; CA 33-36R; CANR 33; DLB 53; MTCW; SATA 29

Munro, H(ector) H(ugh) 1870-1916
See Saki
See also CA 104; 130; CDBLB 1890-1914; DA; DLB 34; MTCW; WLC

Murasaki, Lady . . . . **CMLC 1**

Murdoch, (Jean) Iris
1919- . . . . . . **CLC 1, 2, 3, 4, 6, 8, 11, 15, 22, 31, 51**
See also CA 13-16R; CANR 8; CDBLB 1960 to Present; DLB 14; MTCW

Murphy, Richard 1927- . . . . **CLC 41**
See also CA 29-32R; DLB 40

Murphy, Sylvia 1937- . . . . **CLC 34**
See also CA 121

Murphy, Thomas (Bernard) 1935- . . . **CLC 51**
See also CA 101

Murray, Albert L. 1916- . . . . **CLC 73**
See also BW; CA 49-52; CANR 26; DLB 38

Murray, Les(lie) A(llan) 1938- . . . . . **CLC 40**
See also CA 21-24R; CANR 11, 27

Murry, J. Middleton
See Murry, John Middleton

Murry, John Middleton
1889-1957 . . . . **TCLC 16**
See also CA 118

Musgrave, Susan 1951- . . . . **CLC 13, 54**
See also CA 69-72

Musil, Robert (Edler von)
1880-1942 . . . . **TCLC 12**
See also CA 109; DLB 81, 124

Musset, (Louis Charles) Alfred de
1810-1857 . . . . **NCLC 7**

My Brother's Brother
See Chekhov, Anton (Pavlovich)

Myers, Walter Dean 1937- . . . . **CLC 35**
See also AAYA 4; BLC 3; BW; CA 33-36R; CANR 20; CLR 4, 16; DLB 33; MAICYA; SAAS 2; SATA 27, 41, 70, 71

Myers, Walter M.
See Myers, Walter Dean

Myles, Symon
See Follett, Ken(neth Martin)

Nabokov, Vladimir (Vladimirovich)
1899-1977 . . . . **CLC 1, 2, 3, 6, 8, 11, 15, 23, 44, 46, 64; SSC 11**
See also CA 5-8R; 69-72; CANR 20; CDALB 1941-1968; DA; DLB 2; DLBD 3; DLBY 80, 91; MTCW; WLC

Nagy, Laszlo 1925-1978 . . . . **CLC 7**
See also CA 129; 112

Naipaul, Shiva(dhar Srinivasa)
1945-1985 . . . . **CLC 32, 39**
See also CA 110; 112; 116; CANR 33; DLBY 85; MTCW

Naipaul, V(idiadhar) S(urajprasad)
1932- . . . . **CLC 4, 7, 9, 13, 18, 37**
See also CA 1-4R; CANR 1, 33; CDBLB 1960 to Present; DLB 125; DLBY 85; MTCW

Nakos, Lilika 1899(?)- . . . . **CLC 29**

Narayan, R(asipuram) K(rishnaswami)
1906- . . . . **CLC 7, 28, 47**
See also CA 81-84; CANR 33; MTCW; SATA 62

Nash, (Frediric) Ogden 1902-1971 . . **CLC 23**
See also CA 13-14; 29-32R; CANR 34; CAP 1; DLB 11; MAICYA; MTCW; SATA 2, 46

Nathan, Daniel
See Dannay, Frederic

Nathan, George Jean 1882-1958 . . . **TCLC 18**
See also Hatteras, Owen
See also CA 114

Natsume, Kinnosuke 1867-1916
See Natsume, Soseki
See also CA 104

Natsume, Soseki . . . . **TCLC 2, 10**
See also Natsume, Kinnosuke

Natti, (Mary) Lee 1919-
See Kingman, Lee
See also CA 5-8R; CANR 2

Naylor, Gloria 1950- . . . . **CLC 28, 52**
See also AAYA 6; BLC 3; BW; CA 107; CANR 27; DA; MTCW

Neihardt, John Gneisenau
1881-1973 . . . . **CLC 32**
See also CA 13-14; CAP 1; DLB 9, 54

Nekrasov, Nikolai Alekseevich
1821-1878 . . . . **NCLC 11**

Nelligan, Emile 1879-1941 . . . . **TCLC 14**
See also CA 114; DLB 92

Nelson, Willie 1933- . . . . **CLC 17**
See also CA 107

Nemerov, Howard (Stanley)
1920-1991 . . . . **CLC 2, 6, 9, 36**
See also CA 1-4R; 134; CABS 2; CANR 1, 27; DLB 6; DLBY 83; MTCW

Neruda, Pablo
1904-1973 . . . . **CLC 1, 2, 5, 7, 9, 28, 62; PC 4**
See also CA 19-20; 45-48; CAP 2; DA; HW; MTCW; WLC

Nerval, Gerard de 1808-1855 . . . . . . **NCLC 1**

Nervo, (Jose) Amado (Ruiz de)
1870-1919 . . . . **TCLC 11**
See also CA 109; 131; HW

Nessi, Pio Baroja y
See Baroja (y Nessi), Pio

Neufeld, John (Arthur) 1938- . . . . . . **CLC 17**
See also CA 25-28R; CANR 11, 37; MAICYA; SAAS 3; SATA 6

Neville, Emily Cheney 1919- . . . . **CLC 12**
See also CA 5-8R; CANR 3, 37; MAICYA; SAAS 2; SATA 1

Newbound, Bernard Slade 1930-
See Slade, Bernard
See also CA 81-84

Newby, P(ercy) H(oward)
1918- . . . . **CLC 2, 13**
See also CA 5-8R; CANR 32; DLB 15; MTCW

Newlove, Donald 1928- . . . . **CLC 6**
See also CA 29-32R; CANR 25

Newlove, John (Herbert) 1938- . . . . . **CLC 14**
See also CA 21-24R; CANR 9, 25

Newman, Charles 1938- . . . . **CLC 2, 8**
See also CA 21-24R

Newman, Edwin (Harold) 1919- . . . . **CLC 14**
See also AITN 1; CA 69-72; CANR 5

Newman, John Henry
1801-1890 . . . . **NCLC 38**
See also DLB 18, 32, 55

Newton, Suzanne 1936- . . . . **CLC 35**
See also CA 41-44R; CANR 14; SATA 5

Nexo, Martin Andersen
1869-1954 . . . . **TCLC 43**

Nezval, Vitezslav 1900-1958 . . . . . . **TCLC 44**
See also CA 123

Ngema, Mbongeni 1955- . . . . **CLC 57**

Ngugi, James T(hiong'o) . . . . **CLC 3, 7, 13**
See also Ngugi wa Thiong'o

Ngugi wa Thiong'o 1938- . . . . **CLC 36**
See also Ngugi, James T(hiong'o)
See also BLC 3; BW; CA 81-84; CANR 27; MTCW

Nichol, B(arrie) P(hillip)
1944-1988 . . . . **CLC 18**
See also CA 53-56; DLB 53; SATA 66

Nichols, John (Treadwell) 1940- . . . . **CLC 38**
See also CA 9-12R; CAAS 2; CANR 6; DLBY 82

Nichols, Peter (Richard)
1927- . . . . **CLC 5, 36, 65**
See also CA 104; CANR 33; DLB 13; MTCW

Author Index

O Hehir, Diana 1922- . . . . **CLC 41**
See also CA 93-96

Okigbo, Christopher (Ifenayichukwu) 1932-1967 . . . . **CLC 25**
See also BLC 3; BW; CA 77-80; DLB 125; MTCW

Olds, Sharon 1942- . . . . **CLC 32, 39**
See also CA 101; CANR 18, 41; DLB 120

Oldstyle, Jonathan
See Irving, Washington

Olesha, Yuri (Karlovich) 1899-1960 . . . . **CLC 8**
See also CA 85-88

Oliphant, Margaret (Oliphant Wilson) 1828-1897 . . . . **NCLC 11**
See also DLB 18

Oliver, Mary 1935- . . . . **CLC 19, 34**
See also CA 21-24R; CANR 9; DLB 5

Olivier, Laurence (Kerr) 1907-1989 . . . . **CLC 20**
See also CA 111; 129

Olsen, Tillie 1913- . . . . . **CLC 4, 13; SSC 11**
See also CA 1-4R; CANR 1; DA; DLB 28; DLBY 80; MTCW

Olson, Charles (John) 1910-1970 . . . . . **CLC 1, 2, 5, 6, 9, 11, 29**
See also CA 13-16; 25-28R; CABS 2; CANR 35; CAP 1; DLB 5, 16; MTCW

Olson, Toby 1937- . . . . **CLC 28**
See also CA 65-68; CANR 9, 31

Olyesha, Yuri
See Olesha, Yuri (Karlovich)

Ondaatje, Michael 1943- . . . . **CLC 14, 29, 51, 76**
See also CA 77-80; DLB 60

Oneal, Elizabeth 1934-
See Oneal, Zibby
See also CA 106; CANR 28; MAICYA; SATA 30

Oneal, Zibby . . . . **CLC 30**
See also Oneal, Elizabeth
See also AAYA 5; CLR 13

O'Neill, Eugene (Gladstone) 1888-1953 . . . . **TCLC 1, 6, 27, 49**
See also AITN 1; CA 110; 132; CDALB 1929-1941; DA; DLB 7; MTCW; WLC

Onetti, Juan Carlos 1909- . . . . **CLC 7, 10**
See also CA 85-88; CANR 32; DLB 113; HW; MTCW

O Nuallain, Brian 1911-1966
See O'Brien, Flann
See also CA 21-22; 25-28R; CAP 2

Oppen, George 1908-1984 . . . . **CLC 7, 13, 34**
See also CA 13-16R; 113; CANR 8; DLB 5

Oppenheim, E(dward) Phillips 1866-1946 . . . . **TCLC 45**
See also CA 111; DLB 70

Orlovitz, Gil 1918-1973 . . . . **CLC 22**
See also CA 77-80; 45-48; DLB 2, 5

Orris
See Ingelow, Jean

Ortega y Gasset, Jose 1883-1955 . . . **TCLC 9**
See also CA 106; 130; HW; MTCW

Ortiz, Simon J(oseph) 1941- . . . . **CLC 45**
See also CA 134; DLB 120

Orton, Joe . . . . **CLC 4, 13, 43; DC 3**
See also Orton, John Kingsley
See also CDBLB 1960 to Present; DLB 13

Orton, John Kingsley 1933-1967
See Orton, Joe
See also CA 85-88; CANR 35; MTCW

Orwell, George . . . . **TCLC 2, 6, 15, 31**
See also Blair, Eric (Arthur)
See also CDBLB 1945-1960; DLB 15, 98; WLC

Osborne, David
See Silverberg, Robert

Osborne, George
See Silverberg, Robert

Osborne, John (James) 1929- . . . . **CLC 1, 2, 5, 11, 45**
See also CA 13-16R; CANR 21; CDBLB 1945-1960; DA; DLB 13; MTCW; WLC

Osborne, Lawrence 1958- . . . . **CLC 50**

Oshima, Nagisa 1932- . . . . **CLC 20**
See also CA 116; 121

Oskison, John M(ilton) 1874-1947 . . . . **TCLC 35**

Ossoli, Sarah Margaret (Fuller marchesa d') 1810-1850
See Fuller, Margaret
See also SATA 25

Ostrovsky, Alexander 1823-1886 . . . . **NCLC 30**

Otero, Blas de 1916- . . . . **CLC 11**
See also CA 89-92

Otto, Whitney 1955- . . . . **CLC 70**
See also CA 140

Ouida . . . . **TCLC 43**
See also De La Ramee, (Marie) Louise
See also DLB 18

Ousmane, Sembene 1923- . . . . **CLC 66**
See also BLC 3; BW; CA 117; 125; MTCW

Ovid 43B.C.-18th cent. (?) . . . **CMLC 7; PC 2**

Owen, Hugh
See Faust, Frederick (Schiller)

Owen, Wilfred 1893-1918 . . . . . . **TCLC 5, 27**
See also CA 104; CDBLB 1914-1945; DA; DLB 20; WLC

Owens, Rochelle 1936- . . . . **CLC 8**
See also CA 17-20R; CAAS 2; CANR 39

Oz, Amos 1939- . . . **CLC 5, 8, 11, 27, 33, 54**
See also CA 53-56; CANR 27; MTCW

Ozick, Cynthia 1928- . . . . . . **CLC 3, 7, 28, 62**
See also BEST 90:1; CA 17-20R; CANR 23; DLB 28; DLBY 82; MTCW

Ozu, Yasujiro 1903-1963 . . . . **CLC 16**
See also CA 112

Pacheco, C.
See Pessoa, Fernando (Antonio Nogueira)

Pa Chin
See Li Fei-kan

Pack, Robert 1929- . . . . **CLC 13**
See also CA 1-4R; CANR 3; DLB 5

Padgett, Lewis
See Kuttner, Henry

Padilla (Lorenzo), Heberto 1932- . . . **CLC 38**
See also AITN 1; CA 123; 131; HW

Page, Jimmy 1944- . . . . **CLC 12**

Page, Louise 1955- . . . . **CLC 40**
See also CA 140

Page, P(atricia) K(athleen) 1916- . . . . **CLC 7, 18**
See also CA 53-56; CANR 4, 22; DLB 68; MTCW

Paget, Violet 1856-1935
See Lee, Vernon
See also CA 104

Paget-Lowe, Henry
See Lovecraft, H(oward) P(hillips)

Paglia, Camille (Anna) 1947- . . . . **CLC 68**
See also CA 140

Pakenham, Antonia
See Fraser, Antonia (Pakenham)

Palamas, Kostes 1859-1943 . . . . **TCLC 5**
See also CA 105

Palazzeschi, Aldo 1885-1974 . . . . **CLC 11**
See also CA 89-92; 53-56; DLB 114

Paley, Grace 1922- . . . . **CLC 4, 6, 37; SSC 8**
See also CA 25-28R; CANR 13; DLB 28; MTCW

Palin, Michael (Edward) 1943- . . . . . **CLC 21**
See also Monty Python
See also CA 107; CANR 35; SATA 67

Palliser, Charles 1947- . . . . **CLC 65**
See also CA 136

Palma, Ricardo 1833-1919 . . . . **TCLC 29**

Pancake, Breece Dexter 1952-1979
See Pancake, Breece D'J
See also CA 123; 109

Pancake, Breece D'J . . . . **CLC 29**
See also Pancake, Breece Dexter
See also DLB 130

Panko, Rudy
See Gogol, Nikolai (Vasilyevich)

Papadiamantis, Alexandros 1851-1911 . . . . **TCLC 29**

Papadiamantopoulos, Johannes 1856-1910
See Moreas, Jean
See also CA 117

Papini, Giovanni 1881-1956 . . . . **TCLC 22**
See also CA 121

Paracelsus 1493-1541 . . . . **LC 14**

Parasol, Peter
See Stevens, Wallace

Parfenie, Maria
See Codrescu, Andrei

Parini, Jay (Lee) 1948- . . . . **CLC 54**
See also CA 97-100; CAAS 16; CANR 32

Park, Jordan
See Kornbluth, C(yril) M.; Pohl, Frederik

Parker, Bert
See Ellison, Harlan

Parker, Dorothy (Rothschild) 1893-1967 . . . . **CLC 15, 68; SSC 2**
See also CA 19-20; 25-28R; CAP 2; DLB 11, 45, 86; MTCW

Powell, Anthony (Dymoke)
1905- . . . . **CLC 1, 3, 7, 9, 10, 31**
See also CA 1-4R; CANR 1, 32; CDBLB 1945-1960; DLB 15; MTCW

Powell, Dawn 1897-1965 . . . . **CLC 66**
See also CA 5-8R

Powell, Padgett 1952-. . . . . **CLC 34**
See also CA 126

Powers, J(ames) F(arl)
1917- . . . . **CLC 1, 4, 8, 57; SSC 4**
See also CA 1-4R; CANR 2; DLB 130; MTCW

Powers, John J(ames) 1945-
See Powers, John R.
See also CA 69-72

Powers, John R. . . . . **CLC 66**
See also Powers, John J(ames)

Pownall, David 1938-. . . . . **CLC 10**
See also CA 89-92; DLB 14

Powys, John Cowper
1872-1963 . . . . **CLC 7, 9, 15, 46**
See also CA 85-88; DLB 15; MTCW

Powys, T(heodore) F(rancis)
1875-1953 . . . . **TCLC 9**
See also CA 106; DLB 36

Prager, Emily 1952-. . . . . **CLC 56**

Pratt, Edwin John 1883-1964 . . . . . . **CLC 19**
See also CA 93-96; DLB 92

Premchand . . . . **TCLC 21**
See also Srivastava, Dhanpat Rai

Preussler, Otfried 1923-. . . . . **CLC 17**
See also CA 77-80; SATA 24

Prevert, Jacques (Henri Marie)
1900-1977 . . . . **CLC 15**
See also CA 77-80; 69-72; CANR 29; MTCW; SATA 30

Prevost, Abbe (Antoine Francois)
1697-1763 . . . . **LC 1**

Price, (Edward) Reynolds
1933- . . . . **CLC 3, 6, 13, 43, 50, 63**
See also CA 1-4R; CANR 1, 37; DLB 2

Price, Richard 1949- . . . . **CLC 6, 12**
See also CA 49-52; CANR 3; DLBY 81

Prichard, Katharine Susannah
1883-1969 . . . . **CLC 46**
See also CA 11-12; CANR 33; CAP 1; MTCW; SATA 66

Priestley, J(ohn) B(oynton)
1894-1984 . . . . **CLC 2, 5, 9, 34**
See also CA 9-12R; 113; CANR 33; CDBLB 1914-1945; DLB 10, 34, 77, 100; DLBY 84; MTCW

Prince 1958(?)- . . . . **CLC 35**

Prince, F(rank) T(empleton) 1912- . . **CLC 22**
See also CA 101; DLB 20

Prince Kropotkin
See Kropotkin, Peter (Aleksieevich)

Prior, Matthew 1664-1721. . . . . **LC 4**
See also DLB 95

Pritchard, William H(arrison)
1932- . . . . **CLC 34**
See also CA 65-68; CANR 23; DLB 111

Pritchett, V(ictor) S(awdon)
1900- . . . . **CLC 5, 13, 15, 41**
See also CA 61-64; CANR 31; DLB 15; MTCW

Private 19022
See Manning, Frederic

Probst, Mark 1925- . . . . **CLC 59**
See also CA 130

Prokosch, Frederic 1908-1989. . . . **CLC 4, 48**
See also CA 73-76; 128; DLB 48

Prophet, The
See Dreiser, Theodore (Herman Albert)

Prose, Francine 1947-. . . . . **CLC 45**
See also CA 109; 112

Proudhon
See Cunha, Euclides (Rodrigues Pimenta) da

Proust, (Valentin-Louis-George-Eugene-)Marcel
1871-1922 . . . . **TCLC 7, 13, 33**
See also CA 104; 120; DA; DLB 65; MTCW; WLC

Prowler, Harley
See Masters, Edgar Lee

Prus, Boleslaw . . . . **TCLC 48**
See also Glowacki, Aleksander

Pryor, Richard (Franklin Lenox Thomas)
1940- . . . . **CLC 26**
See also CA 122

Przybyszewski, Stanislaw
1868-1927 . . . . **TCLC 36**
See also DLB 66

Pteleon
See Grieve, C(hristopher) M(urray)

Puckett, Lute
See Masters, Edgar Lee

Puig, Manuel
1932-1990 . . . . **CLC 3, 5, 10, 28, 65**
See also CA 45-48; CANR 2, 32; DLB 113; HW; MTCW

Purdy, A(lfred) W(ellington)
1918- . . . . **CLC 3, 6, 14, 50**
See also Purdy, Al
See also CA 81-84

Purdy, Al
See Purdy, A(lfred) W(ellington)
See also CAAS 17; DLB 88

Purdy, James (Amos)
1923- . . . . **CLC 2, 4, 10, 28, 52**
See also CA 33-36R; CAAS 1; CANR 19; DLB 2; MTCW

Pure, Simon
See Swinnerton, Frank Arthur

Pushkin, Alexander (Sergeyevich)
1799-1837 . . . . **NCLC 3, 27**
See also DA; SATA 61; WLC

P'u Sung-ling 1640-1715 . . . . **LC 3**

Putnam, Arthur Lee
See Alger, Horatio, Jr.

Puzo, Mario 1920- . . . . **CLC 1, 2, 6, 36**
See also CA 65-68; CANR 4; DLB 6; MTCW

Pym, Barbara (Mary Crampton)
1913-1980 . . . . **CLC 13, 19, 37**
See also CA 13-14; 97-100; CANR 13, 34; CAP 1; DLB 14; DLBY 87; MTCW

Pynchon, Thomas (Ruggles, Jr.)
1937- . . **CLC 2, 3, 6, 9, 11, 18, 33, 62, 72**
See also BEST 90:2; CA 17-20R; CANR 22; DA; DLB 2; MTCW; WLC

Qian Zhongshu
See Ch'ien Chung-shu

Qroll
See Dagerman, Stig (Halvard)

Quarrington, Paul (Lewis) 1953-. . . . **CLC 65**
See also CA 129

Quasimodo, Salvatore 1901-1968 . . . **CLC 10**
See also CA 13-16; 25-28R; CAP 1; DLB 114; MTCW

Queen, Ellery . . . . **CLC 3, 11**
See also Dannay, Frederic; Davidson, Avram; Lee, Manfred B(ennington); Sturgeon, Theodore (Hamilton); Vance, John Holbrook

Queen, Ellery, Jr.
See Dannay, Frederic; Lee, Manfred B(ennington)

Queneau, Raymond
1903-1976 . . . . **CLC 2, 5, 10, 42**
See also CA 77-80; 69-72; CANR 32; DLB 72; MTCW

Quin, Ann (Marie) 1936-1973 . . . . **CLC 6**
See also CA 9-12R; 45-48; DLB 14

Quinn, Martin
See Smith, Martin Cruz

Quinn, Simon
See Smith, Martin Cruz

Quiroga, Horacio (Sylvestre)
1878-1937 . . . . **TCLC 20**
See also CA 117; 131; HW; MTCW

Quoirez, Francoise 1935-. . . . . **CLC 9**
See also Sagan, Francoise
See also CA 49-52; CANR 6, 39; MTCW

Raabe, Wilhelm 1831-1910 . . . . **TCLC 45**
See also DLB 129

Rabe, David (William) 1940-. . . **CLC 4, 8, 33**
See also CA 85-88; CABS 3; DLB 7

Rabelais, Francois 1483-1553 . . . . **LC 5**
See also DA; WLC

Rabinovitch, Sholem 1859-1916
See Aleichem, Sholom
See also CA 104

Radcliffe, Ann (Ward) 1764-1823 . . **NCLC 6**
See also DLB 39

Radiguet, Raymond 1903-1923 . . . . **TCLC 29**
See also DLB 65

Radnoti, Miklos 1909-1944 . . . . **TCLC 16**
See also CA 118

Rado, James 1939- . . . . **CLC 17**
See also CA 105

Radvanyi, Netty 1900-1983
See Seghers, Anna
See also CA 85-88; 110

Raeburn, John (Hay) 1941-. . . . . **CLC 34**
See also CA 57-60

Ragni, Gerome 1942-1991 . . . . **CLC 17**
See also CA 105; 134

Rahv, Philip . . . . **CLC 24**
See also Greenberg, Ivan

Raine, Craig 1944- . . . . **CLC 32**
See also CA 108; CANR 29; DLB 40

Raine, Kathleen (Jessie) 1908- . . . **CLC 7, 45**
See also CA 85-88; DLB 20; MTCW

Rainis, Janis 1865-1929 . . . . **TCLC 29**

Rakosi, Carl . . . . **CLC 47**
See also Rawley, Callman
See also CAAS 5

Raleigh, Richard
See Lovecraft, H(oward) P(hillips)

Rallentando, H. P.
See Sayers, Dorothy L(eigh)

Ramal, Walter
See de la Mare, Walter (John)

Ramon, Juan
See Jimenez (Mantecon), Juan Ramon

Ramos, Graciliano 1892-1953 . . . . . **TCLC 32**

Rampersad, Arnold 1941- . . . . **CLC 44**
See also CA 127; 133; DLB 111

Rampling, Anne
See Rice, Anne

Ramuz, Charles-Ferdinand
1878-1947 . . . . **TCLC 33**

Rand, Ayn 1905-1982 . . . . **CLC 3, 30, 44**
See also AAYA 10; CA 13-16R; 105; CANR 27; DA; MTCW; WLC

Randall, Dudley (Felker) 1914- . . . . . . **CLC 1**
See also BLC 3; BW; CA 25-28R; CANR 23; DLB 41

Randall, Robert
See Silverberg, Robert

Ranger, Ken
See Creasey, John

Ransom, John Crowe
1888-1974 . . . . **CLC 2, 4, 5, 11, 24**
See also CA 5-8R; 49-52; CANR 6, 34; DLB 45, 63; MTCW

Rao, Raja 1909- . . . . **CLC 25, 56**
See also CA 73-76; MTCW

Raphael, Frederic (Michael)
1931- . . . . **CLC 2, 14**
See also CA 1-4R; CANR 1; DLB 14

Ratcliffe, James P.
See Mencken, H(enry) L(ouis)

Rathbone, Julian 1935- . . . . **CLC 41**
See also CA 101; CANR 34

Rattigan, Terence (Mervyn)
1911-1977 . . . . **CLC 7**
See also CA 85-88; 73-76; CDBLB 1945-1960; DLB 13; MTCW

Ratushinskaya, Irina 1954- . . . . **CLC 54**
See also CA 129

Raven, Simon (Arthur Noel)
1927- . . . . **CLC 14**
See also CA 81-84

Rawley, Callman 1903-
See Rakosi, Carl
See also CA 21-24R; CANR 12, 32

Rawlings, Marjorie Kinnan
1896-1953 . . . . **TCLC 4**
See also CA 104; 137; DLB 9, 22, 102; MAICYA; YABC 1

Ray, Satyajit 1921-1992 . . . . **CLC 16, 76**
See also CA 114; 137

Read, Herbert Edward 1893-1968 . . . . **CLC 4**
See also CA 85-88; 25-28R; DLB 20

Read, Piers Paul 1941- . . . . . . **CLC 4, 10, 25**
See also CA 21-24R; CANR 38; DLB 14; SATA 21

Reade, Charles 1814-1884 . . . . **NCLC 2**
See also DLB 21

Reade, Hamish
See Gray, Simon (James Holliday)

Reading, Peter 1946- . . . . **CLC 47**
See also CA 103; DLB 40

Reaney, James 1926- . . . . **CLC 13**
See also CA 41-44R; CAAS 15; DLB 68; SATA 43

Rebreanu, Liviu 1885-1944 . . . . **TCLC 28**

Rechy, John (Francisco)
1934- . . . . **CLC 1, 7, 14, 18**
See also CA 5-8R; CAAS 4; CANR 6, 32; DLB 122; DLBY 82; HW

Redcam, Tom 1870-1933 . . . . **TCLC 25**

Reddin, Keith . . . . **CLC 67**

Redgrove, Peter (William)
1932- . . . . **CLC 6, 41**
See also CA 1-4R; CANR 3, 39; DLB 40

Redmon, Anne . . . . **CLC 22**
See also Nightingale, Anne Redmon
See also DLBY 86

Reed, Eliot
See Ambler, Eric

Reed, Ishmael
1938- . . . . **CLC 2, 3, 5, 6, 13, 32, 60**
See also BLC 3; BW; CA 21-24R; CANR 25; DLB 2, 5, 33; DLBD 8; MTCW

Reed, John (Silas) 1887-1920 . . . . . . **TCLC 9**
See also CA 106

Reed, Lou . . . . **CLC 21**
See also Firbank, Louis

Reeve, Clara 1729-1807 . . . . **NCLC 19**
See also DLB 39

Reid, Christopher (John) 1949- . . . . . **CLC 33**
See also CA 140; DLB 40

Reid, Desmond
See Moorcock, Michael (John)

Reid Banks, Lynne 1929-
See Banks, Lynne Reid
See also CA 1-4R; CANR 6, 22, 38; CLR 24; MAICYA; SATA 22

Reilly, William K.
See Creasey, John

Reiner, Max
See Caldwell, (Janet Miriam) Taylor (Holland)

Reis, Ricardo
See Pessoa, Fernando (Antonio Nogueira)

Remarque, Erich Maria
1898-1970 . . . . **CLC 21**
See also CA 77-80; 29-32R; DA; DLB 56; MTCW

Remizov, A.
See Remizov, Aleksei (Mikhailovich)

Remizov, A. M.
See Remizov, Aleksei (Mikhailovich)

Remizov, Aleksei (Mikhailovich)
1877-1957 . . . . **TCLC 27**
See also CA 125; 133

Renan, Joseph Ernest
1823-1892 . . . . **NCLC 26**

Renard, Jules 1864-1910 . . . . **TCLC 17**
See also CA 117

Renault, Mary . . . . **CLC 3, 11, 17**
See also Challans, Mary
See also DLBY 83

Rendell, Ruth (Barbara) 1930- . . **CLC 28, 48**
See also Vine, Barbara
See also CA 109; CANR 32; DLB 87; MTCW

Renoir, Jean 1894-1979 . . . . **CLC 20**
See also CA 129; 85-88

Resnais, Alain 1922- . . . . **CLC 16**

Reverdy, Pierre 1889-1960 . . . . **CLC 53**
See also CA 97-100; 89-92

Rexroth, Kenneth
1905-1982 . . . . . . **CLC 1, 2, 6, 11, 22, 49**
See also CA 5-8R; 107; CANR 14, 34; CDALB 1941-1968; DLB 16, 48; DLBY 82; MTCW

Reyes, Alfonso 1889-1959 . . . . **TCLC 33**
See also CA 131; HW

Reyes y Basoalto, Ricardo Eliecer Neftali
See Neruda, Pablo

Reymont, Wladyslaw (Stanislaw)
1868(?)-1925 . . . . **TCLC 5**
See also CA 104

Reynolds, Jonathan 1942- . . . . **CLC 6, 38**
See also CA 65-68; CANR 28

Reynolds, Joshua 1723-1792 . . . . **LC 15**
See also DLB 104

Reynolds, Michael Shane 1937- . . . . **CLC 44**
See also CA 65-68; CANR 9

Reznikoff, Charles 1894-1976 . . . . **CLC 9**
See also CA 33-36; 61-64; CAP 2; DLB 28, 45

Rezzori (d'Arezzo), Gregor von
1914- . . . . **CLC 25**
See also CA 122; 136

Rhine, Richard
See Silverstein, Alvin

R'hoone
See Balzac, Honore de

Rhys, Jean
1890(?)-1979 . . . . **CLC 2, 4, 6, 14, 19, 51**
See also CA 25-28R; 85-88; CANR 35; CDBLB 1945-1960; DLB 36, 117; MTCW

Ribeiro, Darcy 1922- . . . . **CLC 34**
See also CA 33-36R

Ribeiro, Joao Ubaldo (Osorio Pimentel)
1941- . . . . **CLC 10, 67**
See also CA 81-84

Ribman, Ronald (Burt) 1932- . . . . **CLC 7**
See also CA 21-24R

Ricci, Nino 1959- . . . . **CLC 70**
See also CA 137

Rice, Anne 1941- . . . . **CLC 41**
See also AAYA 9; BEST 89:2; CA 65-68; CANR 12, 36

Romains, Jules 1885-1972 .... CLC 7
See also CA 85-88; CANR 34; DLB 65; MTCW

Romero, Jose Ruben 1890-1952 ... TCLC 14
See also CA 114; 131; HW

Ronsard, Pierre de 1524-1585 .... LC 6

Rooke, Leon 1934- .... CLC 25, 34
See also CA 25-28R; CANR 23

Roper, William 1498-1578 .... LC 10

Roquelaure, A. N.
See Rice, Anne

Rosa, Joao Guimaraes 1908-1967 ... CLC 23
See also CA 89-92; DLB 113

Rosen, Richard (Dean) 1949-....... CLC 39
See also CA 77-80

Rosenberg, Isaac 1890-1918....... TCLC 12
See also CA 107; DLB 20

Rosenblatt, Joe .... CLC 15
See also Rosenblatt, Joseph

Rosenblatt, Joseph 1933-
See Rosenblatt, Joe
See also CA 89-92

Rosenfeld, Samuel 1896-1963
See Tzara, Tristan
See also CA 89-92

Rosenthal, M(acha) L(ouis) 1917-... CLC 28
See also CA 1-4R; CAAS 6; CANR 4; DLB 5; SATA 59

Ross, Barnaby
See Dannay, Frederic

Ross, Bernard L.
See Follett, Ken(neth Martin)

Ross, J. H.
See Lawrence, T(homas) E(dward)

Ross, (James) Sinclair 1908-....... CLC 13
See also CA 73-76; DLB 88

Rossetti, Christina (Georgina)
1830-1894 .... NCLC 2
See also DA; DLB 35; MAICYA; SATA 20; WLC

Rossetti, Dante Gabriel
1828-1882 .... NCLC 4
See also CDBLB 1832-1890; DA; DLB 35; WLC

Rossner, Judith (Perelman)
1935- .... CLC 6, 9, 29
See also AITN 2; BEST 90:3; CA 17-20R; CANR 18; DLB 6; MTCW

Rostand, Edmond (Eugene Alexis)
1868-1918 .... TCLC 6, 37
See also CA 104; 126; DA; MTCW

Roth, Henry 1906- .... CLC 2, 6, 11
See also CA 11-12; CANR 38; CAP 1; DLB 28; MTCW

Roth, Joseph 1894-1939.......... TCLC 33
See also DLB 85

Roth, Philip (Milton)
1933- ...... CLC 1, 2, 3, 4, 6, 9, 15, 22, 31, 47, 66
See also BEST 90:3; CA 1-4R; CANR 1, 22, 36; CDALB 1968-1988; DA; DLB 2, 28; DLBY 82; MTCW; WLC

Rothenberg, Jerome 1931-....... CLC 6, 57
See also CA 45-48; CANR 1; DLB 5

Roumain, Jacques (Jean Baptiste)
1907-1944 .... TCLC 19
See also BLC 3; BW; CA 117; 125

Rourke, Constance (Mayfield)
1885-1941 .... TCLC 12
See also CA 107; YABC 1

Rousseau, Jean-Baptiste 1671-1741 ... LC 9

Rousseau, Jean-Jacques 1712-1778... LC 14
See also DA; WLC

Roussel, Raymond 1877-1933 ..... TCLC 20
See also CA 117

Rovit, Earl (Herbert) 1927-......... CLC 7
See also CA 5-8R; CANR 12

Rowe, Nicholas 1674-1718........... LC 8
See also DLB 84

Rowley, Ames Dorrance
See Lovecraft, H(oward) P(hillips)

Rowson, Susanna Haswell
1762(?)-1824 .... NCLC 5
See also DLB 37

Roy, Gabrielle 1909-1983....... CLC 10, 14
See also CA 53-56; 110; CANR 5; DLB 68; MTCW

Rozewicz, Tadeusz 1921-........ CLC 9, 23
See also CA 108; CANR 36; MTCW

Ruark, Gibbons 1941- .... CLC 3
See also CA 33-36R; CANR 14, 31; DLB 120

Rubens, Bernice (Ruth) 1923-... CLC 19, 31
See also CA 25-28R; CANR 33; DLB 14; MTCW

Rudkin, (James) David 1936- ...... CLC 14
See also CA 89-92; DLB 13

Rudnik, Raphael 1933-............. CLC 7
See also CA 29-32R

Ruffian, M.
See Hasek, Jaroslav (Matej Frantisek)

Ruiz, Jose Martinez .... CLC 11
See also Martinez Ruiz, Jose

Rukeyser, Muriel
1913-1980 .... CLC 6, 10, 15, 27
See also CA 5-8R; 93-96; CANR 26; DLB 48; MTCW; SATA 22

Rule, Jane (Vance) 1931-.......... CLC 27
See also CA 25-28R; CANR 12; DLB 60

Rulfo, Juan 1918-1986............. CLC 8
See also CA 85-88; 118; CANR 26; DLB 113; HW; MTCW

Runyon, (Alfred) Damon
1884(?)-1946 .... TCLC 10
See also CA 107; DLB 11, 86

Rush, Norman 1933-.............. CLC 44
See also CA 121; 126

Rushdie, (Ahmed) Salman
1947- .... CLC 23, 31, 55
See also BEST 89:3; CA 108; 111; CANR 33; MTCW

Rushforth, Peter (Scott) 1945- ..... CLC 19
See also CA 101

Ruskin, John 1819-1900.......... TCLC 20
See also CA 114; 129; CDBLB 1832-1890; DLB 55; SATA 24

Russ, Joanna 1937-............... CLC 15
See also CA 25-28R; CANR 11, 31; DLB 8; MTCW

Russell, George William 1867-1935
See A. E.
See also CA 104; CDBLB 1890-1914

Russell, (Henry) Ken(neth Alfred)
1927- .... CLC 16
See also CA 105

Russell, Willy 1947-.............. CLC 60

Rutherford, Mark .... TCLC 25
See also White, William Hale
See also DLB 18

Ruyslinck, Ward
See Belser, Reimond Karel Maria de

Ryan, Cornelius (John) 1920-1974 ... CLC 7
See also CA 69-72; 53-56; CANR 38

Ryan, Michael 1946- .... CLC 65
See also CA 49-52; DLBY 82

Rybakov, Anatoli (Naumovich)
1911- .... CLC 23, 53
See also CA 126; 135

Ryder, Jonathan
See Ludlum, Robert

Ryga, George 1932-1987 .... CLC 14
See also CA 101; 124; DLB 60

S. S.
See Sassoon, Siegfried (Lorraine)

Saba, Umberto 1883-1957 .... TCLC 33
See also DLB 114

Sabatini, Rafael 1875-1950 .... TCLC 47

Sabato, Ernesto (R.) 1911-..... CLC 10, 23
See also CA 97-100; CANR 32; HW; MTCW

Sacastru, Martin
See Bioy Casares, Adolfo

Sacher-Masoch, Leopold von
1836(?)-1895 .... NCLC 31

Sachs, Marilyn (Stickle) 1927- ..... CLC 35
See also AAYA 2; CA 17-20R; CANR 13; CLR 2; MAICYA; SAAS 2; SATA 3, 68

Sachs, Nelly 1891-1970 .... CLC 14
See also CA 17-18; 25-28R; CAP 2

Sackler, Howard (Oliver)
1929-1982 .... CLC 14
See also CA 61-64; 108; CANR 30; DLB 7

Sacks, Oliver (Wolf) 1933- .... CLC 67
See also CA 53-56; CANR 28; MTCW

Sade, Donatien Alphonse Francois Comte
1740-1814 .... NCLC 3

Sadoff, Ira 1945-.................. CLC 9
See also CA 53-56; CANR 5, 21; DLB 120

Saetone
See Camus, Albert

Safire, William 1929-............. CLC 10
See also CA 17-20R; CANR 31

Sagan, Carl (Edward) 1934-........ CLC 30
See also AAYA 2; CA 25-28R; CANR 11, 36; MTCW; SATA 58

Sagan, Francoise .... CLC 3, 6, 9, 17, 36
See also Quoirez, Francoise
See also DLB 83

Sahgal, Nayantara (Pandit) 1927- . . . **CLC 41**
See also CA 9-12R; CANR 11

Saint, H(arry) F. 1941- . . . . **CLC 50**
See also CA 127

St. Aubin de Teran, Lisa 1953-
See Teran, Lisa St. Aubin de
See also CA 118; 126

Sainte-Beuve, Charles Augustin
1804-1869 . . . . **NCLC 5**

Saint-Exupery, Antoine (Jean Baptiste Marie Roger) de 1900-1944 . . . . **TCLC 2**
See also CA 108; 132; CLR 10; DLB 72; MAICYA; MTCW; SATA 20; WLC

St. John, David
See Hunt, E(verette) Howard, Jr.

Saint-John Perse
See Leger, (Marie-Rene) Alexis Saint-Leger

Saintsbury, George (Edward Bateman)
1845-1933 . . . . **TCLC 31**
See also DLB 57

Sait Faik . . . . **TCLC 23**
See also Abasiyanik, Sait Faik

Saki . . . . **TCLC 3; SSC 12**
See also Munro, H(ector) H(ugh)

Salama, Hannu 1936- . . . . **CLC 18**

Salamanca, J(ack) R(ichard)
1922- . . . . **CLC 4, 15**
See also CA 25-28R

Sale, J. Kirkpatrick
See Sale, Kirkpatrick

Sale, Kirkpatrick 1937- . . . . **CLC 68**
See also CA 13-16R; CANR 10

Salinas (y Serrano), Pedro
1891(?)-1951 . . . . **TCLC 17**
See also CA 117

Salinger, J(erome) D(avid)
1919- . . . . **CLC 1, 3, 8, 12, 55, 56; SSC 2**
See also AAYA 2; CA 5-8R; CANR 39; CDALB 1941-1968; CLR 18; DA; DLB 2, 102; MAICYA; MTCW; SATA 67; WLC

Salisbury, John
See Caute, David

Salter, James 1925- . . . . **CLC 7, 52, 59**
See also CA 73-76; DLB 130

Saltus, Edgar (Everton)
1855-1921 . . . . **TCLC 8**
See also CA 105

Saltykov, Mikhail Evgrafovich
1826-1889 . . . . **NCLC 16**

Samarakis, Antonis 1919- . . . . **CLC 5**
See also CA 25-28R; CAAS 16; CANR 36

Sanchez, Florencio 1875-1910 . . . . . **TCLC 37**
See also HW

Sanchez, Luis Rafael 1936- . . . . **CLC 23**
See also CA 128; HW

Sanchez, Sonia 1934- . . . . **CLC 5**
See also BLC 3; BW; CA 33-36R; CANR 24; CLR 18; DLB 41; DLBD 8; MAICYA; MTCW; SATA 22

Sand, George 1804-1876 . . . . **NCLC 2**
See also DA; DLB 119; WLC

Sandburg, Carl (August)
1878-1967 . . . **CLC 1, 4, 10, 15, 35; PC 2**
See also CA 5-8R; 25-28R; CANR 35; CDALB 1865-1917; DA; DLB 17, 54; MAICYA; MTCW; SATA 8; WLC

Sandburg, Charles
See Sandburg, Carl (August)

Sandburg, Charles A.
See Sandburg, Carl (August)

Sanders, (James) Ed(ward) 1939- . . . **CLC 53**
See also CA 13-16R; CANR 13; DLB 16

Sanders, Lawrence 1920- . . . . **CLC 41**
See also BEST 89:4; CA 81-84; CANR 33; MTCW

Sanders, Noah
See Blount, Roy (Alton), Jr.

Sanders, Winston P.
See Anderson, Poul (William)

Sandoz, Mari(e Susette)
1896-1966 . . . . **CLC 28**
See also CA 1-4R; 25-28R; CANR 17; DLB 9; MTCW; SATA 5

Saner, Reg(inald Anthony) 1931- . . . . **CLC 9**
See also CA 65-68

Sannazaro, Jacopo 1456(?)-1530 . . . . . . **LC 8**

Sansom, William 1912-1976 . . . . **CLC 2, 6**
See also CA 5-8R; 65-68; MTCW

Santayana, George 1863-1952 . . . . . **TCLC 40**
See also CA 115; DLB 54, 71

Santiago, Danny . . . . **CLC 33**
See also James, Daniel (Lewis); James, Daniel (Lewis)
See also DLB 122

Santmyer, Helen Hooven
1895-1986 . . . . **CLC 33**
See also CA 1-4R; 118; CANR 15, 33; DLBY 84; MTCW

Santos, Bienvenido N(uqui) 1911- . . . **CLC 22**
See also CA 101; CANR 19

Sapper . . . . **TCLC 44**
See also McNeile, Herman Cyril

Sappho fl. 6th cent. B.C.- . . . . **CMLC 3; PC 5**

Sarduy, Severo 1937- . . . . **CLC 6**
See also CA 89-92; DLB 113; HW

Sargeson, Frank 1903-1982 . . . . **CLC 31**
See also CA 25-28R; 106; CANR 38

Sarmiento, Felix Ruben Garcia 1867-1916
See Dario, Ruben
See also CA 104

Saroyan, William
1908-1981 . . . . . **CLC 1, 8, 10, 29, 34, 56**
See also CA 5-8R; 103; CANR 30; DA; DLB 7, 9, 86; DLBY 81; MTCW; SATA 23, 24; WLC

Sarraute, Nathalie
1900- . . . . **CLC 1, 2, 4, 8, 10, 31**
See also CA 9-12R; CANR 23; DLB 83; MTCW

Sarton, (Eleanor) May
1912- . . . . **CLC 4, 14, 49**
See also CA 1-4R; CANR 1, 34; DLB 48; DLBY 81; MTCW; SATA 36

Sartre, Jean-Paul
1905-1980 . . . **CLC 1, 4, 7, 9, 13, 18, 24, 44, 50, 52; DC 3**
See also CA 9-12R; 97-100; CANR 21; DA; DLB 72; MTCW; WLC

Sassoon, Siegfried (Lorraine)
1886-1967 . . . . **CLC 36**
See also CA 104; 25-28R; CANR 36; DLB 20; MTCW

Satterfield, Charles
See Pohl, Frederik

Saul, John (W. III) 1942- . . . . **CLC 46**
See also AAYA 10; BEST 90:4; CA 81-84; CANR 16, 40

Saunders, Caleb
See Heinlein, Robert A(nson)

Saura (Atares), Carlos 1932- . . . . **CLC 20**
See also CA 114; 131; HW

Sauser-Hall, Frederic 1887-1961 . . . . **CLC 18**
See also CA 102; 93-96; CANR 36; MTCW

Saussure, Ferdinand de
1857-1913 . . . . **TCLC 49**

Savage, Catharine
See Brosman, Catharine Savage

Savage, Thomas 1915- . . . . **CLC 40**
See also CA 126; 132; CAAS 15

Savan, Glenn . . . . **CLC 50**

Saven, Glenn 19(?)- . . . . **CLC 50**

Sayers, Dorothy L(eigh)
1893-1957 . . . . **TCLC 2, 15**
See also CA 104; 119; CDBLB 1914-1945; DLB 10, 36, 77, 100; MTCW

Sayers, Valerie 1952- . . . . **CLC 50**
See also CA 134

Sayles, John (Thomas)
1950- . . . . **CLC 7, 10, 14**
See also CA 57-60; CANR 41; DLB 44

Scammell, Michael . . . . **CLC 34**

Scannell, Vernon 1922- . . . . **CLC 49**
See also CA 5-8R; CANR 8, 24; DLB 27; SATA 59

Scarlett, Susan
See Streatfeild, (Mary) Noel

Schaeffer, Susan Fromberg
1941- . . . . **CLC 6, 11, 22**
See also CA 49-52; CANR 18; DLB 28; MTCW; SATA 22

Schary, Jill
See Robinson, Jill

Schell, Jonathan 1943- . . . . **CLC 35**
See also CA 73-76; CANR 12

Schelling, Friedrich Wilhelm Joseph von
1775-1854 . . . . **NCLC 30**
See also DLB 90

Scherer, Jean-Marie Maurice 1920-
See Rohmer, Eric
See also CA 110

Schevill, James (Erwin) 1920- . . . . **CLC 7**
See also CA 5-8R; CAAS 12

Schiller, Friedrich 1759-1805 . . . . **NCLC 39**
See also DLB 94

Schisgal, Murray (Joseph) 1926- . . . . . **CLC 6**
See also CA 21-24R

Stead, Christina (Ellen) 1902-1983 . . . . **CLC 2, 5, 8, 32**
See also CA 13-16R; 109; CANR 33, 40; MTCW

Stead, William Thomas 1849-1912 . . . . **TCLC 48**

Steele, Richard 1672-1729 . . . . **LC 18**
See also CDBLB 1660-1789; DLB 84, 101

Steele, Timothy (Reid) 1948- . . . . **CLC 45**
See also CA 93-96; CANR 16; DLB 120

Steffens, (Joseph) Lincoln 1866-1936 . . . . **TCLC 20**
See also CA 117

Stegner, Wallace (Earle) 1909- . . . **CLC 9, 49**
See also AITN 1; BEST 90:3; CA 1-4R; CAAS 9; CANR 1, 21; DLB 9; MTCW

Stein, Gertrude 1874-1946 . . . . **TCLC 1, 6, 28, 48**
See also CA 104; 132; CDALB 1917-1929; DA; DLB 4, 54, 86; MTCW; WLC

Steinbeck, John (Ernst) 1902-1968 . . . . . **CLC 1, 5, 9, 13, 21, 34, 45, 75; SSC 11**
See also CA 1-4R; 25-28R; CANR 1, 35; CDALB 1929-1941; DA; DLB 7, 9; DLBD 2; MTCW; SATA 9; WLC

Steinem, Gloria 1934- . . . . **CLC 63**
See also CA 53-56; CANR 28; MTCW

Steiner, George 1929- . . . . **CLC 24**
See also CA 73-76; CANR 31; DLB 67; MTCW; SATA 62

Steiner, Rudolf 1861-1925 . . . . **TCLC 13**
See also CA 107

Stendhal 1783-1842 . . . . **NCLC 23**
See also DA; DLB 119; WLC

Stephen, Leslie 1832-1904 . . . . **TCLC 23**
See also CA 123; DLB 57

Stephen, Sir Leslie
See Stephen, Leslie

Stephen, Virginia
See Woolf, (Adeline) Virginia

Stephens, James 1882(?)-1950 . . . . . . **TCLC 4**
See also CA 104; DLB 19

Stephens, Reed
See Donaldson, Stephen R.

Steptoe, Lydia
See Barnes, Djuna

Sterchi, Beat 1949- . . . . **CLC 65**

Sterling, Brett
See Bradbury, Ray (Douglas); Hamilton, Edmond

Sterling, Bruce 1954- . . . . **CLC 72**
See also CA 119

Sterling, George 1869-1926 . . . . **TCLC 20**
See also CA 117; DLB 54

Stern, Gerald 1925- . . . . **CLC 40**
See also CA 81-84; CANR 28; DLB 105

Stern, Richard (Gustave) 1928- . . . **CLC 4, 39**
See also CA 1-4R; CANR 1, 25; DLBY 87

Sternberg, Josef von 1894-1969 . . . . . **CLC 20**
See also CA 81-84

Sterne, Laurence 1713-1768 . . . . **LC 2**
See also CDBLB 1660-1789; DA; DLB 39; WLC

Sternheim, (William Adolf) Carl 1878-1942 . . . . **TCLC 8**
See also CA 105; DLB 56, 118

Stevens, Mark 1951- . . . . **CLC 34**
See also CA 122

Stevens, Wallace 1879-1955 . . . . **TCLC 3, 12, 45; PC 6**
See also CA 104; 124; CDALB 1929-1941; DA; DLB 54; MTCW; WLC

Stevenson, Anne (Katharine) 1933- . . . . **CLC 7, 33**
See also CA 17-20R; CAAS 9; CANR 9, 33; DLB 40; MTCW

Stevenson, Robert Louis (Balfour) 1850-1894 . . . . **NCLC 5, 14; SSC 11**
See also CDBLB 1890-1914; CLR 10, 11; DA; DLB 18, 57; MAICYA; WLC; YABC 2

Stewart, J(ohn) I(nnes) M(ackintosh) 1906- . . . . **CLC 7, 14, 32**
See also CA 85-88; CAAS 3; MTCW

Stewart, Mary (Florence Elinor) 1916- . . . . **CLC 7, 35**
See also CA 1-4R; CANR 1; SATA 12

Stewart, Mary Rainbow
See Stewart, Mary (Florence Elinor)

Still, James 1906- . . . . **CLC 49**
See also CA 65-68; CAAS 17; CANR 10, 26; DLB 9; SATA 29

Sting
See Sumner, Gordon Matthew

Stirling, Arthur
See Sinclair, Upton (Beall)

Stitt, Milan 1941- . . . . **CLC 29**
See also CA 69-72

Stockton, Francis Richard 1834-1902
See Stockton, Frank R.
See also CA 108; 137; MAICYA; SATA 44

Stockton, Frank R. . . . . **TCLC 47**
See also Stockton, Francis Richard
See also DLB 42, 74; SATA 32

Stoddard, Charles
See Kuttner, Henry

Stoker, Abraham 1847-1912
See Stoker, Bram
See also CA 105; DA; SATA 29

Stoker, Bram . . . . **TCLC 8**
See also Stoker, Abraham
See also CDBLB 1890-1914; DLB 36, 70; WLC

Stolz, Mary (Slattery) 1920- . . . . **CLC 12**
See also AAYA 8; AITN 1; CA 5-8R; CANR 13, 41; MAICYA; SAAS 3; SATA 10, 70, 71

Stone, Irving 1903-1989 . . . . **CLC 7**
See also AITN 1; CA 1-4R; 129; CAAS 3; CANR 1, 23; MTCW; SATA 3; SATA-Obit 64

Stone, Oliver 1946- . . . . **CLC 73**
See also CA 110

Stone, Robert (Anthony) 1937- . . . . **CLC 5, 23, 42**
See also CA 85-88; CANR 23; MTCW

Stone, Zachary
See Follett, Ken(neth Martin)

Stoppard, Tom 1937- . . . **CLC 1, 3, 4, 5, 8, 15, 29, 34, 63**
See also CA 81-84; CANR 39; CDBLB 1960 to Present; DA; DLB 13; DLBY 85; MTCW; WLC

Storey, David (Malcolm) 1933- . . . . **CLC 2, 4, 5, 8**
See also CA 81-84; CANR 36; DLB 13, 14; MTCW

Storm, Hyemeyohsts 1935- . . . . **CLC 3**
See also CA 81-84

Storm, (Hans) Theodor (Woldsen) 1817-1888 . . . . **NCLC 1**

Storni, Alfonsina 1892-1938 . . . . **TCLC 5**
See also CA 104; 131; HW

Stout, Rex (Todhunter) 1886-1975 . . . **CLC 3**
See also AITN 2; CA 61-64

Stow, (Julian) Randolph 1935- . . **CLC 23, 48**
See also CA 13-16R; CANR 33; MTCW

Stowe, Harriet (Elizabeth) Beecher 1811-1896 . . . . **NCLC 3**
See also CDALB 1865-1917; DA; DLB 1, 12, 42, 74; MAICYA; WLC; YABC 1

Strachey, (Giles) Lytton 1880-1932 . . . . **TCLC 12**
See also CA 110; DLBD 10

Strand, Mark 1934- . . . . . . **CLC 6, 18, 41, 71**
See also CA 21-24R; CANR 40; DLB 5; SATA 41

Straub, Peter (Francis) 1943- . . . . . . **CLC 28**
See also BEST 89:1; CA 85-88; CANR 28; DLBY 84; MTCW

Strauss, Botho 1944- . . . . **CLC 22**
See also DLB 124

Streatfeild, (Mary) Noel 1895(?)-1986 . . . . **CLC 21**
See also CA 81-84; 120; CANR 31; CLR 17; MAICYA; SATA 20, 48

Stribling, T(homas) S(igismund) 1881-1965 . . . . **CLC 23**
See also CA 107; DLB 9

Strindberg, (Johan) August 1849-1912 . . . . **TCLC 1, 8, 21, 47**
See also CA 104; 135; DA; WLC

Stringer, Arthur 1874-1950 . . . . **TCLC 37**
See also DLB 92

Stringer, David
See Roberts, Keith (John Kingston)

Strugatskii, Arkadii (Natanovich) 1925-1991 . . . . **CLC 27**
See also CA 106; 135

Strugatskii, Boris (Natanovich) 1933- . . . . **CLC 27**
See also CA 106

Strummer, Joe 1953(?)- . . . . **CLC 30**
See also Clash, The

Stuart, Don A.
See Campbell, John W(ood, Jr.)

Stuart, Ian
See MacLean, Alistair (Stuart)

Stuart, Jesse (Hilton) 1906-1984 . . . . **CLC 1, 8, 11, 14, 34**
See also CA 5-8R; 112; CANR 31; DLB 9, 48, 102; DLBY 84; SATA 2, 36

Taylor, Peter (Hillsman)
1917- ..... **CLC 1, 4, 18, 37, 44, 50, 71; SSC 10**
See also CA 13-16R; CANR 9; DLBY 81; MTCW

Taylor, Robert Lewis 1912- .... **CLC 14**
See also CA 1-4R; CANR 3; SATA 10

Tchekhov, Anton
See Chekhov, Anton (Pavlovich)

Teasdale, Sara 1884-1933 .... **TCLC 4**
See also CA 104; DLB 45; SATA 32

Tegner, Esaias 1782-1846 .... **NCLC 2**

Teilhard de Chardin, (Marie Joseph) Pierre
1881-1955 .... **TCLC 9**
See also CA 105

Temple, Ann
See Mortimer, Penelope (Ruth)

Tennant, Emma (Christina)
1937- .... **CLC 13, 52**
See also CA 65-68; CAAS 9; CANR 10, 38; DLB 14

Tenneshaw, S. M.
See Silverberg, Robert

Tennyson, Alfred
1809-1892 .... **NCLC 30; PC 6**
See also CDBLB 1832-1890; DA; DLB 32; WLC

Teran, Lisa St. Aubin de .... **CLC 36**
See also St. Aubin de Teran, Lisa

Teresa de Jesus, St. 1515-1582 ...... **LC 18**

Terkel, Louis 1912-
See Terkel, Studs
See also CA 57-60; CANR 18; MTCW

Terkel, Studs .... **CLC 38**
See also Terkel, Louis
See also AITN 1

Terry, C. V.
See Slaughter, Frank G(ill)

Terry, Megan 1932- .... **CLC 19**
See also CA 77-80; CABS 3; DLB 7

Tertz, Abram
See Sinyavsky, Andrei (Donatevich)

Tesich, Steve 1943(?)- .... **CLC 40, 69**
See also CA 105; DLBY 83

Teternikov, Fyodor Kuzmich 1863-1927
See Sologub, Fyodor
See also CA 104

Tevis, Walter 1928-1984 .... **CLC 42**
See also CA 113

Tey, Josephine .... **TCLC 14**
See also Mackintosh, Elizabeth
See also DLB 77

Thackeray, William Makepeace
1811-1863 .... **NCLC 5, 14, 22**
See also CDBLB 1832-1890; DA; DLB 21, 55; SATA 23; WLC

Thakura, Ravindranatha
See Tagore, Rabindranath

Tharoor, Shashi 1956- .... **CLC 70**

Thelwell, Michael Miles 1939- ..... **CLC 22**
See also CA 101

Theobald, Lewis, Jr.
See Lovecraft, H(oward) P(hillips)

The Prophet
See Dreiser, Theodore (Herman Albert)

Theroux, Alexander (Louis)
1939- .... **CLC 2, 25**
See also CA 85-88; CANR 20

Theroux, Paul (Edward)
1941- .... **CLC 5, 8, 11, 15, 28, 46**
See also BEST 89:4; CA 33-36R; CANR 20; DLB 2; MTCW; SATA 44

Thesen, Sharon 1946- .... **CLC 56**

Thevenin, Denis
See Duhamel, Georges

Thibault, Jacques Anatole Francois
1844-1924
See France, Anatole
See also CA 106; 127; MTCW

Thiele, Colin (Milton) 1920- .... **CLC 17**
See also CA 29-32R; CANR 12, 28; CLR 27; MAICYA; SAAS 2; SATA 14, 72

Thomas, Audrey (Callahan)
1935- .... **CLC 7, 13, 37**
See also AITN 2; CA 21-24R; CANR 36; DLB 60; MTCW

Thomas, D(onald) M(ichael)
1935- .... **CLC 13, 22, 31**
See also CA 61-64; CAAS 11; CANR 17; CDBLB 1960 to Present; DLB 40; MTCW

Thomas, Dylan (Marlais)
1914-1953 .... **TCLC 1, 8, 45; PC 2; SSC 3**
See also CA 104; 120; CDBLB 1945-1960; DA; DLB 13, 20; MTCW; SATA 60; WLC

Thomas, (Philip) Edward
1878-1917 .... **TCLC 10**
See also CA 106; DLB 19

Thomas, Joyce Carol 1938- .... **CLC 35**
See also BW; CA 113; 116; CLR 19; DLB 33; MAICYA; MTCW; SAAS 7; SATA 40

Thomas, Lewis 1913- .... **CLC 35**
See also CA 85-88; CANR 38; MTCW

Thomas, Paul
See Mann, (Paul) Thomas

Thomas, Piri 1928- .... **CLC 17**
See also CA 73-76; HW

Thomas, R(onald) S(tuart)
1913- .... **CLC 6, 13, 48**
See also CA 89-92; CAAS 4; CANR 30; CDBLB 1960 to Present; DLB 27; MTCW

Thomas, Ross (Elmore) 1926- ...... **CLC 39**
See also CA 33-36R; CANR 22

Thompson, Francis Clegg
See Mencken, H(enry) L(ouis)

Thompson, Francis Joseph
1859-1907 .... **TCLC 4**
See also CA 104; CDBLB 1890-1914; DLB 19

Thompson, Hunter S(tockton)
1939- .... **CLC 9, 17, 40**
See also BEST 89:1; CA 17-20R; CANR 23; MTCW

Thompson, Jim 1906-1977(?) .... **CLC 69**

Thompson, Judith .... **CLC 39**

Thomson, James 1700-1748 .... **LC 16**

Thomson, James 1834-1882 ...... **NCLC 18**

Thoreau, Henry David
1817-1862 .... **NCLC 7, 21**
See also CDALB 1640-1865; DA; DLB 1; WLC

Thornton, Hall
See Silverberg, Robert

Thurber, James (Grover)
1894-1961 .... **CLC 5, 11, 25; SSC 1**
See also CA 73-76; CANR 17, 39; CDALB 1929-1941; DA; DLB 4, 11, 22, 102; MAICYA; MTCW; SATA 13

Thurman, Wallace (Henry)
1902-1934 .... **TCLC 6**
See also BLC 3; BW; CA 104; 124; DLB 51

Ticheburn, Cheviot
See Ainsworth, William Harrison

Tieck, (Johann) Ludwig
1773-1853 .... **NCLC 5**
See also DLB 90

Tiger, Derry
See Ellison, Harlan

Tilghman, Christopher 1948(?)- ..... **CLC 65**

Tillinghast, Richard (Williford)
1940- .... **CLC 29**
See also CA 29-32R; CANR 26

Timrod, Henry 1828-1867 .... **NCLC 25**
See also DLB 3

Tindall, Gillian 1938- .... **CLC 7**
See also CA 21-24R; CANR 11

Tiptree, James, Jr. .... **CLC 48, 50**
See also Sheldon, Alice Hastings Bradley
See also DLB 8

Titmarsh, Michael Angelo
See Thackeray, William Makepeace

Tocqueville, Alexis (Charles Henri Maurice Clerel Comte) 1805-1859 ..... **NCLC 7**

Tolkien, J(ohn) R(onald) R(euel)
1892-1973 .... **CLC 1, 2, 3, 8, 12, 38**
See also AAYA 10; AITN 1; CA 17-18; 45-48; CANR 36; CAP 2; CDBLB 1914-1945; DA; DLB 15; MAICYA; MTCW; SATA 2, 24, 32; WLC

Toller, Ernst 1893-1939 .... **TCLC 10**
See also CA 107; DLB 124

Tolson, M. B.
See Tolson, Melvin B(eaunorus)

Tolson, Melvin B(eaunorus)
1898(?)-1966 .... **CLC 36**
See also BLC 3; BW; CA 124; 89-92; DLB 48, 76

Tolstoi, Aleksei Nikolaevich
See Tolstoy, Alexey Nikolaevich

Tolstoy, Alexey Nikolaevich
1882-1945 .... **TCLC 18**
See also CA 107

Tolstoy, Count Leo
See Tolstoy, Leo (Nikolaevich)

West, Morris L(anglo) 1916- . . . . . **CLC 6, 33**
See also CA 5-8R; CANR 24; MTCW

West, Nathanael
1903-1940 . . . . **TCLC 1, 14, 44**
See also CA 104; 125; CDALB 1929-1941; DLB 4, 9, 28; MTCW

West, Paul 1930- . . . . **CLC 7, 14**
See also CA 13-16R; CAAS 7; CANR 22; DLB 14

West, Rebecca 1892-1983 . . **CLC 7, 9, 31, 50**
See also CA 5-8R; 109; CANR 19; DLB 36; DLBY 83; MTCW

Westall, Robert (Atkinson) 1929- . . . **CLC 17**
See also CA 69-72; CANR 18; CLR 13; MAICYA; SAAS 2; SATA 23, 69

Westlake, Donald E(dwin)
1933- . . . . **CLC 7, 33**
See also CA 17-20R; CAAS 13; CANR 16

Westmacott, Mary
See Christie, Agatha (Mary Clarissa)

Weston, Allen
See Norton, Andre

Wetcheek, J. L.
See Feuchtwanger, Lion

Wetering, Janwillem van de
See van de Wetering, Janwillem

Wetherell, Elizabeth
See Warner, Susan (Bogert)

Whalen, Philip 1923- . . . . **CLC 6, 29**
See also CA 9-12R; CANR 5, 39; DLB 16

Wharton, Edith (Newbold Jones)
1862-1937 . . . . **TCLC 3, 9, 27; SSC 6**
See also CA 104; 132; CDALB 1865-1917; DA; DLB 4, 9, 12, 78; MTCW; WLC

Wharton, James
See Mencken, H(enry) L(ouis)

Wharton, William (a pseudonym)
. . . . **CLC 18, 37**
See also CA 93-96; DLBY 80

Wheatley (Peters), Phillis
1754(?)-1784 . . . . **LC 3; PC 3**
See also BLC 3; CDALB 1640-1865; DA; DLB 31, 50; WLC

Wheelock, John Hall 1886-1978 . . . . **CLC 14**
See also CA 13-16R; 77-80; CANR 14; DLB 45

White, E(lwyn) B(rooks)
1899-1985 . . . . **CLC 10, 34, 39**
See also AITN 2; CA 13-16R; 116; CANR 16, 37; CLR 1, 21; DLB 11, 22; MAICYA; MTCW; SATA 2, 29, 44

White, Edmund (Valentine III)
1940- . . . . **CLC 27**
See also AAYA 7; CA 45-48; CANR 3, 19, 36; MTCW

White, Patrick (Victor Martindale)
1912-1990 . . **CLC 3, 4, 5, 7, 9, 18, 65, 69**
See also CA 81-84; 132; MTCW

White, Phyllis Dorothy James 1920-
See James, P. D.
See also CA 21-24R; CANR 17; MTCW

White, T(erence) H(anbury)
1906-1964 . . . . **CLC 30**
See also CA 73-76; CANR 37; MAICYA; SATA 12

White, Terence de Vere 1912- . . . . . . **CLC 49**
See also CA 49-52; CANR 3

White, Walter F(rancis)
1893-1955 . . . . **TCLC 15**
See also White, Walter
See also CA 115; 124; DLB 51

White, William Hale 1831-1913
See Rutherford, Mark
See also CA 121

Whitehead, E(dward) A(nthony)
1933- . . . . **CLC 5**
See also CA 65-68

Whitemore, Hugh (John) 1936- . . . . . **CLC 37**
See also CA 132

Whitman, Sarah Helen (Power)
1803-1878 . . . . **NCLC 19**
See also DLB 1

Whitman, Walt(er)
1819-1892 . . . . **NCLC 4, 31; PC 3**
See also CDALB 1640-1865; DA; DLB 3, 64; SATA 20; WLC

Whitney, Phyllis A(yame) 1903- . . . . **CLC 42**
See also AITN 2; BEST 90:3; CA 1-4R; CANR 3, 25, 38; MAICYA; SATA 1, 30

Whittemore, (Edward) Reed (Jr.)
1919- . . . . **CLC 4**
See also CA 9-12R; CAAS 8; CANR 4; DLB 5

Whittier, John Greenleaf
1807-1892 . . . . **NCLC 8**
See also CDALB 1640-1865; DLB 1

Whittlebot, Hernia
See Coward, Noel (Peirce)

Wicker, Thomas Grey 1926-
See Wicker, Tom
See also CA 65-68; CANR 21

Wicker, Tom . . . . **CLC 7**
See also Wicker, Thomas Grey

Wideman, John Edgar
1941- . . . . **CLC 5, 34, 36, 67**
See also BLC 3; BW; CA 85-88; CANR 14; DLB 33

Wiebe, Rudy (H.) 1934- . . . . . . **CLC 6, 11, 14**
See also CA 37-40R; DLB 60

Wieland, Christoph Martin
1733-1813 . . . . **NCLC 17**
See also DLB 97

Wieners, John 1934- . . . . **CLC 7**
See also CA 13-16R; DLB 16

Wiesel, Elie(zer) 1928- . . . . . **CLC 3, 5, 11, 37**
See also AAYA 7; AITN 1; CA 5-8R; CAAS 4; CANR 8, 40; DA; DLB 83; DLBY 87; MTCW; SATA 56

Wiggins, Marianne 1947- . . . . **CLC 57**
See also BEST 89:3; CA 130

Wight, James Alfred 1916-
See Herriot, James
See also CA 77-80; SATA 44, 55

Wilbur, Richard (Purdy)
1921- . . . . **CLC 3, 6, 9, 14, 53**
See also CA 1-4R; CABS 2; CANR 2, 29; DA; DLB 5; MTCW; SATA 9

Wild, Peter 1940- . . . . **CLC 14**
See also CA 37-40R; DLB 5

Wilde, Oscar (Fingal O'Flahertie Wills)
1854(?)-1900 . . . . **TCLC 1, 8, 23, 41; SSC 11**
See also CA 104; 119; CDBLB 1890-1914; DA; DLB 10, 19, 34, 57; SATA 24; WLC

Wilder, Billy . . . . **CLC 20**
See also Wilder, Samuel
See also DLB 26

Wilder, Samuel 1906-
See Wilder, Billy
See also CA 89-92

Wilder, Thornton (Niven)
1897-1975 . . . . . **CLC 1, 5, 6, 10, 15, 35; DC 1**
See also AITN 2; CA 13-16R; 61-64; CANR 40; DA; DLB 4, 7, 9; MTCW; WLC

Wilding, Michael 1942- . . . . **CLC 73**
See also CA 104; CANR 24

Wiley, Richard 1944- . . . . **CLC 44**
See also CA 121; 129

Wilhelm, Kate . . . . **CLC 7**
See also Wilhelm, Katie Gertrude
See also CAAS 5; DLB 8

Wilhelm, Katie Gertrude 1928-
See Wilhelm, Kate
See also CA 37-40R; CANR 17, 36; MTCW

Wilkins, Mary
See Freeman, Mary Eleanor Wilkins

Willard, Nancy 1936- . . . . **CLC 7, 37**
See also CA 89-92; CANR 10, 39; CLR 5; DLB 5, 52; MAICYA; MTCW; SATA 30, 37, 71

Williams, C(harles) K(enneth)
1936- . . . . **CLC 33, 56**
See also CA 37-40R; DLB 5

Williams, Charles
See Collier, James L(incoln)

Williams, Charles (Walter Stansby)
1886-1945 . . . . **TCLC 1, 11**
See also CA 104; DLB 100

Williams, (George) Emlyn
1905-1987 . . . . **CLC 15**
See also CA 104; 123; CANR 36; DLB 10, 77; MTCW

Williams, Hugo 1942- . . . . **CLC 42**
See also CA 17-20R; DLB 40

Williams, J. Walker
See Wodehouse, P(elham) G(renville)

Williams, John A(lfred) 1925- . . . . **CLC 5, 13**
See also BLC 3; BW; CA 53-56; CAAS 3; CANR 6, 26; DLB 2, 33

Williams, Jonathan (Chamberlain)
1929- . . . . **CLC 13**
See also CA 9-12R; CAAS 12; CANR 8; DLB 5

Williams, Joy 1944- . . . . **CLC 31**
See also CA 41-44R; CANR 22

Williams, Norman 1952- . . . . **CLC 39**
See also CA 118

Literary Criticism Series Cumulative Topic Index

This index lists all topic entries in the Gale Literary Criticism Series *Contemporary Literary Criticism, Literature Criticism from 1400 to 1800, Nineteenth-Century Literature Criticism,* and *Twentieth-Century Literary Criticism.*

NCLC Cumulative Nationality Index

ISBN 0-8103-7979-1
90000
9 780810 379794